CRIME, CRIMINALITY AND CRIMINAL JUSTICE

CRIME, CRIMINALITY AND CRIMINAL JUSTICE

SECOND EDITION

ROB WHITE
SANTINA PERRONE

OXFORD

OXFORD
UNIVERSITY PRESS

Oxford University Press is a department of the University of Oxford.
It furthers the University's objective of excellence in research, scholarship, and education by
publishing worldwide. Oxford is a registered trademark of Oxford University Press in the UK
and in certain other countries.

Published in Australia by
Oxford University Press
253 Normanby Road, South Melbourne, Victoria 3205, Australia

National Library of Australia Cataloguing-in-Publication data

White, R. D. (Robert Douglas), 1956 author.
Crime, criminality and criminal justice / Rob White, Santina Perrone.

2nd edition

ISBN 9780195520125 (paperback)

Includes index.
Crime–Australia.
Criminology–Australia.
Criminal justice, Administration of–Australia.
Perrone, Santina, author.

364.994

Edited by Amanda Morgan
Cover and text design by Kim Ferguson
Typeset by diacriTech, India
Proofread by Pete Cruttenden
Indexed by Karen Gillen
Printed by Markono Print Media Pte Ltd

CONTENTS

LIST OF FIGURES

LIST OF TABLES

LIST OF ACRONYMS

ABS	Australian Bureau of Statistics
ACCC	Australian Competition and Consumer Commission
ACOSS	Australian Council of Social Services
ACT	Australian Capital Territory
ACWAP	Australasian Council of Women and Policing
ADR	Alternative Dispute Resolution
AFP	Australian Federal Police
AHRC	Australian Human Rights Commission (formerly HREOC)
AIC	Australian Institute of Criminology
AIFS	Australian Institute of Family Studies
AIHW	Australian Institute of Health and Welfare
ALRC	Australian Law Reform Commission
AOD	Alcohol and Other Drugs
ASOC	Australian Standard Offence Classification
AYAC	Australian Youth Affairs Coalition
BAT	British American Tobacco
BOCSAR	New South Wales Bureau of Crime Statistics and Research
BWS	Battered Woman Syndrome
CASA	Centre Against Sexual Assault
CAT	Convention Against Torture and other Cruel, Inhuman or Degrading Treatment or Punishment
CBO	Community Based Order
CCC	Crime and Corruption Commission (Queensland)
CCO	Community Correctional Order
CCTV	Closed-Circuit Television
CDPP	Commonwealth Director of Public Prosecutions
CIB	Criminal Investigation Branch
CIT	Cash in Transit
CLC	Community Legal Centre
CPA	Communist Party of Australia
CPTED	Crime Prevention Through Environmental Design

CRC/CROC	(United Nations) Convention on the Rights of the Child
DPP	Director of Public Prosecutions
EFTPOS	Electronic Funds Transfer at Point of Sale
ERA	Excellence in Research for Australia
GBB	Good Behaviour Bond
GLAD	Gay Men and Lesbians Against Discrimination
GLM	Good Lives Model
GMO	Genetically Modified Organisms
HAD	Homosexual Advance Defence
HREOC	Human Rights and Equal Opportunity Commission
ICC	International Criminal Court
ICCPR	International Covenant on Civil and Political Rights
ICVS	International Crime Victimisation Survey
IMF	International Monetary Fund
IOM	Integrated Offender Management
IRS (USA)	Internal Review Service
ISO	Intensive Supervision Order
JR	Justice Reinvestment
LER	Low Economic Resource
LPP	Local Priority Policing
MSN	Microsoft Network
MVT	Motor Vehicle Theft
NCJSF	National Criminal Justice Statistical Framework
NCRS	National Crime Recording Standard
NESB	Non English Speaking Background
NISATSIC	National Inquiry into the Separation of Aboriginal and Torres Strait Islander Children
NMVTRC	National Motor Vehicle Theft Reduction Council
NSA	National Security Agency
NSW	New South Wales
NT	Northern Territory
OCSAR	Office of Crime Statistics and Research (South Australia)
OECD	Organisation for Economic Co-operation and Development

OHS	Occupational Health and Safety
PACCOA	Parole and Community Corrections Officers Association of Australia
PDO	Periodic Detention Order
PSO	Protective Services Officer
QLD	Queensland
RNR	Risk Need Responsivity Model
S&M	Sadism and Masochism/Sadomasochism
SA	South Australia
SMS	Short Message Service
SNS	Social Networking Services
TAS	Tasmania
UDHR	Universal Declaration of Human Rights
UEWI	Unlawful Entry With Intent
UN	United Nations
UNEP	United Nations Environment Program
VCCAV	Victorian Communities Council Against Violence
VIC	Victoria
VIS	Victim Impact Statement
WA	Western Australia
YRAP	Youth Restorative Action Project
YSAS	Youth Support and Advocacy Service

ACKNOWLEDGMENTS

The authors and the publisher wish to thank the following copyright holders for reproduction of their material.

Australian Institute of Criminology for all figures and tables (AIC); Australian Institute of Health and Welfare for extract from (2014b) *Youth justice legislation*, http://www.aihw.gov.au/youth-justice/legislation/ and (AIHW) (2012a) Juvenile Justice in Australia 2010–11, Juvenile Justice Series No.10, AIHW, Canberra. (CC-BY 3.0); Commonwealth Copyright for extract from Johnston, E. (1991) *Report of the Royal Commission into Aboriginal Deaths in Custody* (5 vols), Australian Government Publishing Service, Canberra. (CC-BY 3.0); Federation Press, Sydney for extracts from T. Anthony & C. Cunneen (eds), *The Critical Criminology Companion*, Federation Press, Sydney, 2008; High Court of Australia for extract from *Green v The Queen Criminal Law Review Division* 1998; Parliament of Victoria for extract from Law Reform Committee (2013) *Inquiry into Sexting: Report of the Law Reform Committee for the Inquiry into Sexting, Parliamentary Paper No. 230*, Parliament of Victoria, Melbourne. Reproduced by permission of the Speaker of the Legislative Assembly of Victoria; State of New South Wales (NSW Parliament) for extract from *Section 23 (2) of the New South Wales Crimes Act*; Taylor & Francis Books (UK) for Barry, M. (2006) *Youth Offending in Transition: The Search for Social Recognition*, London: Routledge and Cohen, S. (1972) *Folk Devils and Moral Panics: The Creation of the Mods and Rockers*, MacGibbon & Kee, London and Ward, T. & Maruna, S. (2007) *Rehabilitation: Beyond the Risk Paradigm*, Routledge, London and White, R. (2008b) *Crimes against Nature: Environmental Criminology and Ecological Justice*, Willan Publishing, Devon and Zehr, H. & Mika, H. (1998) 'Fundamental Concepts of Restorative Justice', *Contemporary Justice Review*, 1(1), 47–56.

Every effort has been made to trace the original source of copyright material contained in this book. The publisher will be pleased to hear from copyright holders to rectify any errors or omissions.

CRIME AND CRIMINALITY

INTRODUCTION: UNDERSTANDING CRIMINAL JUSTICE

CRIME
Acts that
are legally
prohibited by
the state and
deemed to be
deserving of
punishment
and control.

HARM
Physical or
other kinds of
injury, distress
or damage
to humans,
environments
and non-
human animals
resulting
from acts or
omissions that
are either legal
or illegal.

Crime and victimisation are important issues of concern to the public and policy-makers alike. Part 1 of this book is about **crime** and victimisation in Australian society. It describes and analyses various kinds of crime-related **harm**, most of which are deemed to be 'criminal' in the eyes of the law. In doing so, it traces the general profile, patterns and trends of various crimes—from traditional street crimes, such as property crime and crimes against the person, to crimes of the powerful, including white-collar crime and state crime to transnational crime, including war crimes, environmental crime and cyber-crime— and explores their social dynamics and consequences. An important theme of Part 1 is the critical influence of social difference in determining who commits which kinds of crime against whom, and how this influences the responses of the state and members of society to both the perpetrator and those impacted by their crimes.

The following chapters commence with a survey of criminologicial theories or explanations of crime, and an examination of the main categories of crime. The emphasis in this part of the book is on tracing the social construction of crime, the prevalence of various types of criminal or antisocial behaviour, the profile of those who engage in this behaviour and the contours of social harm associated with these acts. The historical evolution of theorising about and responding to victims of crime is also explored, with an emphasis on underscoring the process of social construction of victimhood.

The question of how we define crime, and how we define the perpetrators and victims of crime, is inextricably bound up with social processes. Crime and victimisation are not socially neutral concepts, nor is society's conceptualisation and response to these phenomena static. For example, men are more likely than women to engage in violent crimes; working-class people are more likely than middle-class people to be prosecuted for offending behaviour, especially in regard to street offences, with the notable exception of sexual assault; and sexual assault is overwhelmingly perpetrated by men against women, who are disproportionately the victims of such crime. In other words, social divisions—based upon aspects of identity such as class, gender, ethnicity, Indigenous status, age, disability and religion—have major influences on who does what to whom and why, as well as how the criminal justice system responds. Inequalities and social differences, and the intersection between these aspects of identity, must be taken into account if we are to understand fully the social nature of crime and its control in Australian society (Bartels 2012a).

Moreover, categories of state-sanctioned crime and recognition of their corollary, victims, change with the passage of time, through the criminalisation and decriminalisation process. This section recognises and explores the influence of social opinion on the conceptualisation of, and state response to, crime and deviance. Instrumental to understanding the social construction of crime is an examination of the media, and its influence on social perceptions of and response to crime.

DEFINING CRIME

'Crime' is not a straightforward concept. How crime is defined and viewed varies according to how we answer the question 'what is crime?' There are in fact many diverse conceptions of crime, each reflecting a different scientific and ideological viewpoint. Hagan (1987), for example, identifies seven different approaches to the definition of crime, ranging from a 'legal-consensus' definition to a 'human rights' definition. For present purposes, we can summarise broad differences in definition as follows:

- *Formal legal* definition: regards crime as that activity defined by the state; that is, if an act is proscribed by the criminal law, and is subject to state sanction in the form of a specific penalty, then it is a crime.

- *Social harm* conception: considers crime to involve both criminal offences (e.g. assault) and civil offences (e.g. negligence), given that each type of action or inaction brings with it some type of harm. According to this perspective, all acts resulting in harm should attract some sort of penalty.

- *Cross-cultural universal norms* perspective: states that crime is ubiquitous; in essence, it does not vary across cultures. Thus, murder is murder regardless of the society in which it is committed, and we can therefore postulate conduct norms that cut across diverse cultural backgrounds.

- *Labelling* approach: argues that crime only exists when there has been a social response to a particular activity that labels that activity as criminal. If there is no label, there is, in effect, no crime.

- *Human rights* approach: regards crime as having occurred whenever a human right has been violated, regardless of the legality or otherwise of the action. Such a conception expands the definition of crime to include oppressive practices such as racism, sexism and class-based exploitation.

- *Human diversity* approach: defines crime in terms of the manner in which deviance represents a normal response to oppressive or unequal circumstances. A major focus here is on power relations, and the attempts by dominant groups to restrict human diversity of experience, language and culture (e.g. the interventions of the British Empire in reordering indigenous peoples' ways of life).

From a strictly legal perspective, the answer to 'what is crime?' is an unproblematic given; it is simply what the law says it is (see White et al. 2012). In this view, the state has a central place in marking out the boundaries of right and wrong by defining what is criminal and what is not. For an act to be criminal it must be legally prohibited by the state and sanctions must apply. A failure to act, where the law imposes a duty to do so (referred to as an omission), is also illegal and punishable by law. According to this perspective, the state thus has the ultimate power to shape the reality of crime and how society responds to that reality. This is the bottom line when it comes to how most criminal justice institutions operate, regardless of how the above-mentioned perspectives might also shape official reactions to behaviour that could be seen as harmful but not legally criminal. One of the key limitations of this definition of crime, however, is that it provides a narrow conception of harm. Furthermore, it often disregards the issue of state-sponsored actions that may themselves be sources of considerable harm, but which are not criminalised by that self-same state (Maier-Katkin et al. 2009; see also Chapters 12 and 13).

Most sociologists and criminologists adopt a much wider definition of crime that encompasses notions of 'harm' and 'deviance', which are not necessarily acknowledged as criminal by the state. For some theorists, the key emphasis is on a human rights approach to harm, which introduces the concept of universal rights—inalienable rights that all governments should guarantee to all persons, given that a failure to do so negatively impacts human prospects and wellbeing—and the equitable distribution of such. Such rights may include security rights (the prevention of basic physical and psychological harms from genocide, torture, murder, rape etc.), as well as economic rights (the right to private property), political rights (the right to vote public officials into office) and autonomy rights (freedom of speech, assembly and press) (see, for example, Loader & Sparks 2010; Murphy & Whitty 2013; Schwendinger & Schwendinger 1975; Talbott 2010, 2005). In many cases, harmful actions, such as price fixing, tax evasion or preventable workplace 'accidents', are ignored or downplayed by agencies of criminal justice, even though they cause great social harm, including death. For others, the emphasis is less on defining certain acts as bad or good than on examining the social processes by which an act comes to be seen as a crime. According to this perspective, the law is not an external, objective truth that is applied consistently; the concern is therefore to explore the group interactions and institutional procedures that make certain people and certain actions more liable to be labelled criminal than others (see, for example, Muncie 1996; Rubington & Weinberg 1978).

From a historical and cross-cultural perspective, we find that legal definitions of crime are transitory and relative. 'Crime' varies greatly depending upon the historical period, and the social and cultural context within which it operates. In medieval Europe, for example, when the Christian Church was the arbiter of what was deemed to be right and wrong, key crimes included heresy (i.e. going against Church doctrine and beliefs) and usury (charging interest on money lent to another person). With the advent of secular systems of law, crime began to be defined less in religious terms and more in respect to property rights (e.g. theft) and acts against the state (e.g. treason). Comparative analysis shows us that what is considered a crime in some countries is not regarded criminal in others and that, within any given country, an act may be defined into (criminalised) or out of existence (decriminalised) over time. Some examples of this national and temporal variability in legislated crime include (Asal et al. 2012; Bartunek 2014; Bibby & Harrison 2014; Conway-Smith 2013; Corderoy 2013; Dow 2013; Grenfell & Hewitt 2012; Hagan 2012; Nossiter 2014; O'Malley 2013a; Powell 2010; Rankin 2011; *The Age* 2013a; Titterington et al. 2013):

- Bigamy is considered illegal in Australia, whereas in many traditional Islamic countries, polygamous relations, whereby men are permitted to have up to four wives at the same time, are permitted.

- While permissible in Australia, some countries, including the Netherlands, France and Belgium, have recently moved to outlaw the wearing of traditional Islamic dress, including the burqua.

- Euthanasia—the right to die, either by physician-assisted suicide, active euthanasia (doctor administering a lethal injection) or peaceful deliverance (suicide via self-administered intervention)—is illegal in Australia but permitted in some form in Belgium (minimum age of 12), Sweden, Luxembourg and the Netherlands.

- The physical punishment of children (smacking) is prohibited in 33 countries, including Germany, New Zealand, South Sudan and Venezuela, but is considered legal in Australia, the United States, Canada and Britain.

- The use of drugs, such as alcohol or cannabis, is subject to widely varying rules and sanctions across countries. For example, after years of prohibition across the United States, two states (Washington and Colorado) have recently legislated to legalise marijuana, and 20 other states have approved the use of marijuana for medical purposes. New Zealand has legalised all psychoactive substances (e.g. synthetic cannabis) that contain ingredients that meet safety standards.

- Female genital mutilation (surgical cutting of the genitalia to ensure virtue by controlling sexual desire), which is illegal in Australia, is considered a traditional rite of passage into womanhood in many Muslim nations, including Somalia and The Gambia.

- Same-sex marriage has been legalised in 16 countries, including the United States (some states), Britain, New Zealand, Canada and Iceland, but remains illegal in Australia.

- Homosexuality and sodomy, decriminalised in Australia some years ago, remain illegal in approximately 70 countries, primarily Muslim (38 of the 54), attracting severe penalties such as life imprisonment (e.g. Uganda) and corporal and capital punishment (e.g. Nigeria).

- Transgender status has recently been recognised by the High Court of Australia, paving the way for representations of 'sex' to move beyond the normative gender binary of male and female currently reflected in the law and legal documents.

- Abortion laws have been liberalised to varying degrees in Australia from 1998 and in most other countries, while abortion remains totally illegal in seven countries in Latin America and Europe.

- Laws have been introduced in Australia to criminalise violation of privacy in public by use of emerging information and communication technologies (e.g. 'upskirting' and 'downblousing') and the unauthorised distribution of sexual imagery (e.g. sexting).

- At the international or global level, there continue to be disputes and negotiations over how to define war crimes, terrorism and environmental crimes, and the acceptability of practices such as state-sanctioned torture.

- Conflicts between states may stem, in part, from disagreements over what is considered a crime (e.g. bulldozing residential buildings in an occupied territory, such as Gaza) or simply national security (e.g. the military occupation of Iraq as a forward defence against terrorist attacks on Coalition allies).

We could also consider the question 'what is crime?' from the perspective of mass media portrayals (see Chapter 2). The popular image of crime is unquestionably that of street crime, involving assaults, murder, theft and sexual assault, largely committed by strangers. These images are bolstered by advertising that explicitly uses the fear of crime as a means to sell security devices and promote private policing as the answer to the presumed problem. The media emphasis tends to be on certain types of predatory crime, and such crime tends to be sensationalised. Moreover, much emphasis is given to the distinctiveness of criminals (e.g. features such as skin or hair colour), and the appropriateness of victim behaviour (e.g. how they were dressed or how much alcohol they had consumed); hence, criminality and victimhood are frequently based on stereotype and caricature. In the main, complex crimes and crimes of the powerful tend not to be dealt with in either mainstream or fictional accounts of crime.

Finally, if we ask the question, 'what is crime?' from a commonsense and everyday perspective, we might find that it operates as a loose notion based upon morality. Most people break the law at some stage in their lives, but common crimes (e.g. use of 'soft' illegal drugs) do not always translate into the offenders being perceived or responded to as criminals by members of society at large. Crime is frowned upon, but certain types of crime are nevertheless more likely to be regarded as socially acceptable despite such behaviours being legally proscribed (e.g. minor or victimless crimes such as speeding, fare evasion, vagrancy and prostitution). Of course, there are no universal moral truths; perceptions of moral appropriateness reflect the sociological composition and values of any given society. Furthermore, morality and the law are not always congruent. Some actions considered lawful (e.g. the sale and distribution of non-violent and non-child-related pornography, prostitution and abortion) may be wholly or partially legal, but still be considered immoral, especially by those with strong religious beliefs. It is for this reason that law and, by extension, the definition of crime, is seen by some as less of an expression of morality and more of an expression of power (Cotterrel 2011). In the end it is the state that assigns a criminal status to individuals, regardless of general public opinion or sentiment. The second part of this book explores how, over time, public opinion and shifting conceptions on morality can influence changes in the criminal law and thus a shift in what is considered a criminal, health or moral problem.

CRIME AND CRIMINAL LAW

The criminal law identifies those behaviours deemed by lawmakers to be deserving of punishment and control. Which acts are considered wrongful reflects a historical process; over time various acts are prohibited (or, conversely, legalised) into the future because of the legal precedents set by the past.

This can make law reform slow and difficult, as demonstrated by the prolonged processes of recasting the concept of spousal conjugal rights to intercourse as a criminal offence in the case of spousal rape (Larcombe & Heath 2012). Under the law of coverture, women were seen to be fused into the legal identity of men upon marriage. In such a (fictional) legal unity, there could be no concept of rape and, furthermore, it was assumed that women granted consent to sexual relations upon entering the marriage contract. It took a concerted struggle before harm within the marriage contract was socially and legally acknowledged. It was not until 1993 that the United Nations High Commissioner for Human Rights published the Declaration on the Elimination of Violence against Women, which established marital rape as a human rights violation. To this day, some UN member states only criminalise rape in marriage where the individuals are legally separated, and non-member states vary widely in their conceptualisation of non-consensual marital intercourse (UNICEF 2008).

Which acts are considered harmful is also a political process, in which the contemporary tenor of law-and-order politics sets the parameters and tone of legislation relating to crime and crime control (see further Chapters 23 and 24). To put it differently, criminal laws are a human product, but cannot be reduced to human behaviour. They are social constructions forged in historical and social circumstances that put their unique stamp upon what and who is considered to be harmful enough to be criminalised at any point in time (Matthews 2009). Clearly, not all harmful acts (interpersonal or social) are criminalised. This alone makes it clear that decisions about the criminal law are contested rather than technical. The overall aim of criminal law is to prevent certain kinds of behaviour regarded as harmful or potentially harmful, and to do so through a rational system of adjudication and punishment. The challenge for lawmakers is to choose which harms to criminalise and which to deal with through other types of social regulation (e.g. civil proceedings).

The key purposes of criminal law are encapsulated in three broad objectives (Findlay et al. 2005):

- *moral wrongness:* the criminal law is a vital instrument in deterring immoral behaviour
- *individual autonomy:* the criminal law should only be used against behaviour that injures the rights and interests of other people ('harms to others' approach)
- *community welfare:* the principal purpose of criminal law is to protect the physical wellbeing of members of a community.

Importantly, the different reasons or purposes of criminal law are frequently in conflict with each other, and these contradictory rationales, in turn, reflect specific ideological or philosophical differences. For instance, conservative versions of New Right thinking about law and order see the upholding of certain moral standards as a crucial aspect of criminal law. Libertarian perspectives within the broad New Right framework, however, see such legislation as an encroachment upon individual rights and liberty. While the first perspective favours criminalisation of activity deemed to be immoral, the second seeks to keep out of the criminal court those activities freely chosen by individuals, which appear to do no real harm to others around them (see Chapter 24; White et al. 2012).

THE ACT AND THE INTENT

In most cases, according to criminal law, two elements must be present to constitute a crime—the act and the intent:

> All crimes comprise some form of prohibited conduct which may be an act or (in rare cases) an omission. This conduct element denotes the external or physical component of a crime. Another element found in

many (but not all) crimes is the mental state of the person at the time when the prohibited conduct was performed. This may take several forms such as intention, recklessness or knowledge in relation to the prohibited conduct ... However, there are many crimes, known as offences of strict liability and of absolute liability, which do not require any such awareness at all. (Findlay et al. 2005: 20)

Conduct elements of a crime refer to the accused's conduct (**actus reus**); that is, 'guilty act'. This refers to the physical aspect of committing a crime. The prohibited conduct must have been performed voluntarily (e.g. not being forced to do it, or not doing it while sleepwalking). The mental element of a crime refers to a determination that the accused's conduct was accompanied by a prescribed state of mind (**mens rea**); that is, 'guilty mind'. This reflects the idea that people ought to be judged by their free choice of action.

In some instances, the law will ignore the subjective approach (which focuses on the mental element) in favour of arguments based on the community welfare grounds of *public interest* (particularly if future crime is to be prevented or reduced). This is particularly the case, for example, in regards to environmental law.

The issue of legal personhood is wrapped around the notion that all adults have the necessary mental capacity to make judgments and take responsibility for their actions. Exceptions to this mental responsibility element of crime have to be proven in court, as in the case of those who can show that they were insane (within certain defined legal prescriptions) at the time when the prohibited behaviour took place—this is known as the M'Naghten Rules (see Finnane 2012 for a review of its historical application in Australia). The age of criminal responsibility in Australia across all states and territories is 10—an age below which a child is deemed by law to be incapable of committing a criminal offence. Furthermore, between the ages of 10 and 14, children are presumed incapable of wrongdoing under legislation or common law (this is known as the legal doctrine of *doli incapax*), and this presumption must be rebutted before criminal proceedings can be brought against them (i.e. the prosecution must prove beyond a reasonable doubt that the child knew that the act was wrong 'as distinct from an act of mere naughtiness or childish mischief' (Lord Lowry in *C (A minor) in v DPP* [1955] 2WLR 383; see also Richards 2011; Schetzer 2000; Urbas 2000).

The issue of criminal responsibility can, however, be problematic. This is especially true in relation to corporations, where the concept of *mens rea* is difficult to apply. Notwithstanding, the concept of corporate criminal responsibility has been successfully established, to varying degrees, in many jurisdictions, including Australia, the United Kingdom and the United States (see, for example, Perrone 2000; Taylor & Mackenzie 2013; Woodley 2013), albeit to limited practical effect in the specific area of criminal law.

THE CRIMINALISATION PROCESS

Assessment of the conduct and mental elements of crime provide some inkling into the social dynamics that underpin criminality. What is deemed to be *criminal* and who is defined as an *offender* involves a social process in which officials of the state formally intervene and designate certain acts and certain actors as warranting a criminal label. Until an act, or actor, has been processed in particular ways by the state, there is no 'crime' as such. This is regardless of the actual behaviour that takes place. In other words, crime does not 'exist' until there has been an official reaction to the event.

To become a criminal is to be labelled so by the criminal justice system. To understand this, we have to shift the focus away from the discussion of varying definitions of crime (including arguments regarding different types of social harm and whether to criminalise these) to an analysis of the ways in

ACTUS REUS
A Latin term meaning 'guilty act'. An element of criminal responsibility comprising the physical components of a crime. These may be wrongful acts, omissions or a state of affairs that constitute a violation of the law.

MENS REA
A Latin term meaning 'guilty mind'. An element of criminal responsibility comprising the mental components of a crime. The focus is on criminal intent; that is, a person's awareness that their actions were wilful and wrongful.

which something or someone becomes institutionally recognised as being criminal. In this account, the emphasis is on the factors that determine the social status of an event or person.

What is important, for present purposes, is that how criminal justice officials (especially the police) intervene in any given situation has a direct impact on whether any particular event, or any particular individual, will be officially criminalised. *The criminalisation process* is contingent upon how discretion is used throughout the criminal justice system. Our attention is thus drawn to the role of the criminal justice institutions in constituting crime, rather than to the actual act or conduct itself.

To illustrate this point, it is useful to consider how the process of becoming a young offender involves a number of steps and pathways into, or diversions from, the criminal justice system, such as (Australian Bureau of Statistics (ABS) 2014a):

- A young person enters into the criminal justice system as a result of someone reporting an event to the authorities, or the police observing a young person in the act of doing something illegal or antisocial.

- The police officer intervenes and an investigation is undertaken, which involves questioning of the young person. A crime may be deemed to have been committed but, in the case of a minor offence, the investigating officer may exercise their discretion, simply deciding to move the young offender along with or without issuing an unofficial caution.

- Depending on the nature of the behaviour observed or reported, and the attitude and cooperation demonstrated by the young person, the police officer may decide to proceed further against the alleged offender. The young person is taken to the police station, and the crime and victim(s) (if applicable and identifiable) are recorded by police. At this stage, the officer may decide to pursue non-court action against the young person. Where this involves a formal caution, the young person's parent(s) or where unavailable, an independent third person, are called into the station for a tripartite discussion about the incident (police, young person and their parents).

- Alternatively, the young person may be charged but diverted from court via the option of doing police-assigned community work (as is possible in South Australia) or, more likely, participation in a juvenile conference (or equivalent). In the latter case, the young person will be required to meet with any victims, as well as others affected by the offence, in order to work out some kind of reparation for the harm caused.

- If the incident is more serious, the police officer may decide to formally proceed against him or her via court action. Once formally charged with an offence, the young person will generally be issued with a summons, which outlines the date the person is required to attend court and the reasons why.

- If the incident or alleged offence is very serious, then the young person may be required to apply for bail. This enables the defendant to remain out of custody awaiting trial, on the basis of a monetary guarantee and/or pledge to present before the court at the required time.

- In some instances, the option of bail will not be offered or an application for such will be declined, and the young person will be placed in detention on remand (i.e. in secure custody awaiting trial).

- If the young person proceeds to court (usually a children's court, which has special rules and procedures to take into account the special needs and circumstances of children), his or her guilt or innocence is legally determined.

- If found guilty of an offence, the judge or magistrate can impose a variety of sanctions (alternative penalties or dispositions), which range from simply issuing a warning to imposing a fine or placing the young person on some kind of community-based behavioural order (which restricts his or her activity, or demands that he or she attend special training or drug and alcohol sessions), through to incarcerating a young person in a youth detention centre.

This story of a young person's progress through the criminal justice system will vary greatly in practice, depending upon a wide range of factors, including:

- whether the incident was deemed a crime and, if so, the degree of seriousness involved
- how visible the crime was
- whether there were any victims involved and, if so, the nature and extent of the harm occasioned
- who reported the incident, and whether they were taken seriously by the police
- whether the police have the resources to deal with the particular kind of crime reported or observed, and whether it was serious enough, in the light of existing resources, to elicit a response
- the nature and strength of the evidence available to police
- the characteristics, attitude and behaviour of the young person
- if and how well the police know the young person, and his or her family and friends
- the statutory options available for processing the young person in the particular jurisdiction, such as police cautioning schemes or juvenile conferencing options
- the influence of official reports by social workers and other professionals on how best to deal with the young person
- the 'acting' skills of the young person in court and in the police station
- the attitude of the magistrate or judge, in relation to the offence at issue and the appearance and demeanour of the young person in court
- the quality of legal representation
- the previous criminal record of the young person.

As indicated in the scenario outlined above, for any crime to be officially recognised and recorded as a crime, the gatekeepers of the system—the police—have to make initial assessments regarding the nature of the offence, the status of the reporter, the status of the offender and the status of the victim. When the assessment concludes that the event is considered worth proceeding with officially, then it will be considered worthy of recording officially. The crime then becomes a 'fact'.

CONCLUSION

Generally speaking, there tends to be broad consensus that certain types of activities are harmful and represent significant enough wrongdoing to warrant state sanction, notwithstanding that there may be a degree of uncertainty regarding the moral quality of the wrongdoing in particular instances. These include, for example, crimes involving death (murder and manslaughter), crimes involving bodily injury (e.g. physical assaults and sexual assaults) and a number of property offences (e.g. robbery, theft and damaging property). More contentious is how best to deal with social harms relating to things such as occupational health and public safety offences (e.g. physical injury in the workplace, and injury resulting from the consumption of or exposure to hazardous goods), offences against public order (e.g. rioting or offensive language) and environmental offences (e.g. pollution, or toxic and hazardous waste). Particularly volatile areas of dispute are those dealing with 'paternalistic' offences (e.g. gambling, prostitution, pornography or obscene literature), as these tend to highlight major philosophical differences regarding the place and role of the criminal law in society.

The intention of Part 1 of this book is to disentangle the varying forms and types of social harm and, in so doing, provide an analysis both of their substantive content and the reasons underlying their incorporation into, or exclusion from, mainstream processes of criminalisation. Before doing so, however, it is useful to explore further the concept of the various sociological and criminological theories postulating explanations for why crime occurs and how criminality generally is perceived.

In reviewing the broad spectrum of theories on crime, it is imperative that appropriate account be taken of their historical, philosophical and political positioning. The discipline of criminology has evolved over time to provide a conceptual framework for systematic and critical analysis of crime theorising and societal responses to crime. Chapter 1 provides an overview of criminology and its current state, and briefly outlines criminological data and research methods.

DOING CRIMINOLOGY

CHAPTER OVERVIEW

INTRODUCTION

This chapter provides an introduction to the discipline and study of criminology, including a broad overview of criminological research data and methodologies. The intention is to situate various strands of criminology within their particular social and intellectual contexts, and to outline some of the key research approaches associated with the field. To 'do criminology', it is important to begin with an appreciation of the changing status of criminology as a professional practice, and acknowledge the key tensions and intellectual challenges associated with conducting contemporary work in this field. This chapter examines a number of these issues.

Criminology is an interdisciplinary field within the behavioural sciences, drawing its theoretical frameworks and research tools from a wide range of professional disciplines and institutions, including law, sociology, chemistry, social anthropology, journalism and media studies, social psychology, medicine, psychiatry, cultural studies, political science and economics. Despite the heterogeneity of its intellectual roots, criminology is, broadly speaking, the study of crime as behaviour and is concerned with three main interrelated areas of inquiry, directed at the individual and societal level:

- why and how societies define crime and harm in a particular way, the implications of this understanding for the nature and extent of crime within a society, and the impact on the lives of people within those societies, including offenders and victims (this can incorporate the sociology of law and the study of victimology)
- theories of crime causation, sometimes referred to as *criminogenesis*, that attempt to explain why certain people offend and certain crimes are committed
- the study of social responses to crime, which examines the operation and activities of the formal institutions of criminal justice, such as the police, courts and corrections that are engaged in crime control and prevention.

What criminologists do within each of these areas—and the conclusions they draw—is shaped by their view of, and relationship to, criminology as an intellectual project which, in turn, is largely shaped by the discipline within which the theorist is situated and its historical and cultural context.

On the one hand, many people adopt what could be called a vocational, administrative or professional approach to criminology. In this view, the role of criminology is tied to improving the immediate practices of the criminal justice system and to solving crime problems in the community.

CRIMINOGENESIS
The origins or causes of crime; situations or factors tending to produce or promote crime or criminality.

Generally, this approach is directed at improving some aspect of the criminal justice system at some level: a program, an institution or a strategy. Often, it is linked to attempts to solve a particular social problem or address a specific administrative difficulty within the bounded world of the existing system.

In contrast to this uncritical approach to examining and improving the existing criminal justice system, the oppositional paradigm is a strand of criminology that emphasises a critical or analytical approach. This paradigm adopts an externalist perspective, suggesting that one must stand back from 'objective' reality and question the very construction of that reality—the social context of policy decisions and the fundamental raison d'être of the law; that is, the social, political and economic processes through which laws are created and enforced. This approach delves into the deeper philosophical issues of the day; for example, why do we continue to use institutions such as prisons when they unquestioningly do not work to prevent offending or reoffending? The objective of this kind of questioning is not to suggest improvements to the existing criminal justice system, but to query its actual validity and viability. As such, it might well advocate the abolition of prisons in their present shape and form.

There are often strong links between these two approaches: the administrative and the critical. The broader variability in criminological perspectives in general is due, in part, to the nature of the relationship between the administrative vocational orientation (with a practical focus on what can be done here and now to improve the existing system) and its critical counterpart (with a focus on why things ought to be done in one way or another).

SOCIAL CONTEXT OF CRIMINOLOGY

CRIMINOLOGY
The systematic study of crime, criminality and criminal justice systems, focusing on the definitions and causes of crime, the process of criminalisation, crime prevention, systems of social control, and the treatment, rehabilitation and punishment of offenders.

Within **criminology**, there are various perspectives on the nature of the state, of society, and of crime and crime control. The kind of work criminologists do reflects particular ideological and political dispositions on the part of the people doing it. Broadly speaking, the work that criminologists perform can be classified according to a conservative, liberal or radical political orientation. Each of these ideologies preference a certain set of assumptions, research methods and analysis, and validity criteria (see White et al. 2012).

But what criminologists do is not only a matter of personal predilection for a particular 'theory' or political framework as shaped by their particular worldview (Walsh & Ellis 2004). It is also very much bound up with the conditions under which intellectual labour in general is undertaken; that is, the sites and conditions of knowledge production, which are 'spaces of conflict and competition' (Bourdieu & Wacquant 1992: 17). Intellectual histories of criminology (and sociology) reveal the institutional base of particular disciplines or fields, and the manner in which they constitute authority and objectivity, and therefore shape the general character of academic work (Hebenton & Jou 2008). Thus, for example, writers such as Gouldner (1970) and C Wright Mills (1959) have commented on how social research in the United States was of direct service to the military, the corporate sector, state bureaucrats and social workers, and that, accordingly, sociology's dominant ideological character in the 1950s through to the 1970s tended to be predominantly conservative. Analysis of British (Cohen 1981) and Australian (Carson & O'Malley 1989) criminology likewise views the foundations of the field as being constructed first and foremost as a service discipline for state agencies, especially given the importance of the state's crime control apparatus as a key site or institutional domain for much criminological work.

Conversely, the emergence of critical and reflective criminologies that challenged correctionalism and the generally conservative nature of 'mainstream' criminology were associated with the political struggles of the 1970s (see Box 1.1). This emergence stemmed from action around such issues as prison abolition, police misconduct, Indigenous rights, racism and women's liberation (see, for example, Brown & Hogg 1992; Sim et al. 1987). Furthermore, at least part of the explanation for a 'radical tinge' within the Australian criminological field over the past 25 years or so has been the establishment of criminology as a discipline within the tertiary education sector (Pratt & Priestly 1999). The development of academic criminology as a bona fide program of study and research within universities opened the door to progressive, critical work. But such work also has had to contend with the need to break the shackles of a 'markedly empiricist and pragmatic sociology' (Carson & O'Malley 1989: 351), as well as the pressures to conform to the *conservative hegemony* underpinning criminology's institutional development.

The increasingly significant place of criminology within academia has provided some space for development of the critical potential of the field. This is evident in the relatively recent establishment of an annual Critical Criminology Conference, and the active participation of critical criminologists in the more mainstream conferences of the Australian and New Zealand Society of Criminology. As well, recent publications demonstrate the continuing relevance and attractions of critical criminology (see, especially, Anthony & Cunneen 2008), some of which are featured throughout this book. However, the conditions underpinning why and how criminology is currently flourishing within academia will inevitably have some impact on what criminologists, critical or otherwise, actually do.

BOX 1.1 CLASS ANALYSIS AND CRIMINOLOGY

Where does class and class analysis fit within the relatively short history of Australian criminology? To answer this we have to appreciate the difference between critical criminology in the 1970s and early 1980s, and criminology in the twenty-first century. For example, the work of left-wing criminologists in the 'radical era' was largely informed by two key influences. First, many critical criminologists were directly engaged with, and had practical ties to, reformist groups such as prisoner action groups, feminist collectives and Indigenous rights activists (see Brown 2002a). Secondly, many likewise were members of, or fellow travellers with, militant socialist organisations, including the Communist Party of Australia (CPA), the Socialist Workers Party and the International Socialists, right through to the Socialist Left of the Labor Party. Importantly, *socialism* was not simply a slogan; it was often and usually linked to education in the basic concepts and principles of Marxism. This involved reading the works of Marx, Lenin, Gramsci, Mao, Trotsky and others directly, and discussing the relevance and significance of revolutionary leaders, movements and events for understanding and acting within the Australian context.

DECLINE OF THE LEFT
By the late 1980s and into the 1990s, intellectual life took on a different character in academia. The demise of the CPA and its publication *Tribune*, which was once a staple diet for the Left on campus (regardless of a person's specific party affiliation), left a huge hole in radical politics and radical education. In its heyday, the CPA had over 30,000 active members, trained and educated militants in the fight for a new society. Socialist parties of the Left, such as the CPA, were important in socialising a whole generation of activists into using the concepts of class analysis, and learning the lessons of revolutionaries throughout history and across the globe. It also exposed them to the possibilities and pitfalls of the new social movements that were also emerging at the time.

The fall of the Berlin Wall and the demise of the Soviet Union in 1989, however, presented further difficulties for socialist politics. The association of Marxism with Stalinism, and the failure of Soviet-style communism, reinforced the discrediting of Marxism and its proposed alternatives to capitalism. This process was intensely ideological, as evidenced in popular proclamations at the time that neo-liberal capitalism constituted the 'end of history'.

POSTMODERNISM

The diminished presence and influence of the Left radical parties and party factions was reinforced by the intellectual attractions of *postmodernism* in academic circles. Regardless of the specific contributions and distractions of postmodernism, it nevertheless served to both reflect and fuel a nihilistic and pessimistic political mode on campuses across the country. Class analysis soon virtually disappeared as a way in which to frame the world. This was a transition that demanded delivery of criticism but seemingly little commitment to activism. One consequence of these transitions is that relatively few of the younger (and early career) criminologists today have actually read original socialist texts—such as the *Communist Manifesto* (Marx & Engels 1848), *German Ideology* (Marx & Engels 1932), *The 18th Brumaire* (Marx 1852), *State and Revolution* (Lenin 1917), *Imperialism: The Highest Stage of Capitalism* (Lenin 1917), *Prison Notebooks* (Gramsci 1929–35), *What Is To Be Done* (Lenin 1905) and *Capital and Theories of Surplus Value* (Marx 1863)—and certainly not in the context of activist politics. Meanwhile, mainstream social science floundered around the class question, sometimes by dismissing it altogether and sometimes by privileging individualism as a key concept over and above class (and thus conflating the politics of **neo-liberalism** with its material and collective manifestations). At any rate, very few in academia today learn 'class' in the same way that it was learned in the past. It is not that class has gone away (although there have been changes in actual class relations), but that basic understandings of class and class analysis have been altered. In its stead, there developed approaches that more often than not were antagonistic to Marxist class analysis, or that wished to sever any meaningful connection with the class politics of socialism.

NEO-LIBERALISM
A political philosophy that supports the enhancement of the private sector in modern society through economic liberalist measures, including freeing up trade, opening markets, privatisation and deregulation.

COMMERCIALISATION OF ACADEMIC CRIMINOLOGY

The ways in which criminologists perform their work is both bounded by, and always posed in relation to, the major changes occurring in the society at large. Thus, for instance, recent years have seen the commercialisation of Australian academic criminology as part of a general process related to the ascendancy of neo-liberal ideas and institutions (Israel 2000; see also Kayrooz et al. 2001). For example, in terms of research, there have been notable changes in the nature of funding, toward greater reliance on and competition for, contract research for both private and public sector bodies. The dominance of government funding has been observed by Walters (2003) to produce a 'market-led criminology' that focuses on risk management, privatisation and cost-effectiveness.

In terms of teaching, it has been pointed out that there has been a substantial shift in meeting the needs of the private sector for certain types of workers. To take law as one example, 'An entire generation of new contract lawyers is required to effect the privatisation of public goods and the facilitation of global market activity, as well as to resolve intellectual property dilemmas arising from new technologies' (Thornton 2000: 271). In both teaching and research, therefore, there have been pressures to make criminology (and law) more 'relevant' to 'market forces'. To facilitate this approach, the management of Australian universities has generally shifted from collegial to corporate structures (see Israel 2000; Thornton 2000).

The commercialisation of academia has a number of implications for curriculum and teaching. For example, in discussing the problems of treating a law degree as commodity, Thornton (2000: 271) observes that:

> 'Law schools are encouraged to mass produce service-oriented professionals by offering technocratic, skills-based courses which satisfy the admitting authorities but accord scant regard to the university's traditional raison d'être of dispassionate inquiry. The result is that there is a danger of returning legal education to the "'trade school" mentality of the past'. Similar pressures and processes are apparent in relation to criminology as a field, and the social sciences generally. (Kayrooz et al. 2001)

Commercialism poses a number of dilemmas. Among those problem areas identified by Israel (2000) are: legal and ethical problems (e.g. potential conflicts of interest); management of information (including intellectual property rights and suppressing academic exchange in order to secure market advantage); and changes in research direction through pressures from funding bodies and government departments (especially the prioritisation of empirical data collection and technical discussions about process over theoretical critique and reflexive evaluation, which have a longer-term political reform agenda) (see also Burawoy 2009; Walters 2003; Young 2011, 2004). Other researchers have pointed to the channelling of academic work into 'safe, well-defined' rather than speculative areas of research, and the redirection of teaching efforts into areas tangential to academic expertise (Kayrooz et al. 2001).

CHANGES IN WORKING CONDITIONS

Accompanying the pressures to 'go commercial', there are also changes happening in workplace relations, whether within academic institutions, in government departments or in government-funded institutes. Specifically, most criminologists now work under some kind of performance management regime, where the key word is 'productivity', as defined in terms of grants, industry links and demonstrable publishing record (refereed publications). This generally translates into greater workload intensity, as expectations and time spent on grant applications and project management rises.

Changes in the conditions underpinning research and teaching are being accompanied by emergent shifts in the organisation of the labour force within criminology. This has a number of dimensions, including: the construction of 'precarious employment' at the bottom, comprised of individuals who are basically dependent upon non-recurrent research grants; the interpenetration of university and government-based criminologies, such as state-originated consultancy work (see O'Malley 1996); and evaluation research that focuses predominantly on cost–benefit analysis. Increasingly, intellectual work is being constructed at a system level, first and foremost as entrepreneurial activity. This involves varying kinds of division of labour within the criminological enterprise, collaboration and partnerships across sectors, and the escalation of money-making and institutional fiscal objectives in determining project 'worth'. Individual professional status is, in effect, being evaluated, from the point of view of occupational advancement and institutional job security, by the number and total funding of grants one receives (regardless of source or purpose). Power and kudos now attach to successful grant and consultancy outcomes, and this is propelling academics to apply for grants and consultancies as a matter of course (O'Malley 1996). In some ways, these pressures within academia are heightened for criminologists, given the broader shifts in criminal justice, which have seen extensive marketisation of things such as prisons, policing, security services and crime prevention.

CONCERNS ABOUT CAREERISM

External pressures by government departments and funding bodies, as well as commercial firms, for particular kinds of research and particular kinds of skilled workers, have obvious implications for how academic criminologists construe and carry out their tasks. In recent years, there has been a marked expansion in student numbers generally, and in the demand for criminology graduates in particular. This has been driven both by changes in the occupational structures of criminal justice and law enforcement agencies (e.g. the growing importance of academic credentials vis-à-vis promotion structures within police services), and by greater propensity of government agencies to commission and allocate research and evaluation based on specifically 'criminological' expertise. As Presdee and Walters (1998: 163) point out, however, what the state deems 'good research' and a 'good researcher' is bounded by certain ideological parameters: 'there will always be demands by the state for "operational" research whilst discarding "critical" research as unscientific'. The precise skills and knowledge required by criminal justice officials and agencies tend to reflect administrative and careerist concerns rather than those associated with critique and acknowledgment of the political processes underpinning the production of new knowledge.

The market has always in some way shaped the substantive nature of research. It has also played a major role in how academic criminology has augmented the labour power of students for their future jobs within the state and corporate sectors. This does not mean that academic criminology is inherently 'conservative' or 'uncritical', or 'vocationally oriented'. But many students do look to courses to enhance their labour market opportunities (not surprisingly, given the structural problem of unemployment), and research is frequently tied to specific industry-defined 'problems' that require investigation and resolution (a process enhanced by university efforts to increase their funding base).

All of these issues have implications for how crime is defined, how we constitute the targets of crime control, the role of criminal justice workers and the broad systemic responses to perceived issues of concern. Where do matters pertaining to social injustice and social inequality fit into this scenario, and how do we ensure that they are and continue to be worthy of serious consideration?

DOING CRIMINOLOGICAL WORK

Given the broad trends and issues outlined above, it is critical to question how these commercial changes are affecting criminological theory, research and practice. It would be erroneous to posit a direct causal relationship between the social context of criminological work (e.g. pressures to do administrative rather than critical criminology) and the actual work undertaken. To do so would imply that criminologists always do what they are told, or what is immediately relevant and 'practical', as deemed by the relevant funding or institutional body. As with social life generally, there are layers of complexity, ambiguity and flexibility associated with the commercialisation and intensification of intellectual labour that need to be teased out. Not least to consider is the self-conscious reflection by criminologists about what they are doing, and why.

ISSUES OF INDEPENDENCE OF THOUGHT

Shifts in modes of governance accompanying the turn of the century, particularly those associated with globalisation, modernity and neo-liberalism, have given rise to concerns regarding independence of criminological thought, especially for strands of critical inquiry that challenge the production of knowledge (Garland & Sparks 2000; Walters 2003). There are certainly difficulties in attempting to engage in theoretical or critical criminological work in a context that does not reward such work. If we examine the 'core curriculum' of teaching and research today, we find that very often what is valued is what will generate funds, and this is largely influenced by the agendas of state instrumentalities and corporate bodies. In practice, this usually means the use of professional expertise in a restricted, technocratic manner and/or in ways that will best serve the client, whether corporate or state. Theoretical work or work that is explicitly concerned with issues of 'social justice' tend to be considered 'asset strippers' (see Thornton 2000) in that they cost money (salaries) but bring few financial resources back into the enterprise or institution.

The material realities of intellectual production are such that 'what counts' is always bounded by considerations of power and purpose: different knowledge claims have differing degrees of legitimacy and institutional support. We cannot afford to downplay the social processes of knowledge production and, in particular, the struggles over meaning and the uses to which knowledge are put. For example, as Israel (2000) indicates, there are a number of examples within Australian criminology where 'integrity' has led to either loss of contract, censorship or exclusion from the 'expert' commercial or state market. The same problems arise with respect to evaluation research; namely, issues of co-optation and/or exclusion based upon the perceived 'independence' of the evaluator.

In addition, instances of direct industry, government and university interference in academic work may be relatively rare (i.e. as far as we know: this is an issue worthy of further research in its own right), but they nevertheless do constitute a major concern (see Kayrooz et al. 2001). A classic, extreme example of this within criminology is the attempt by the South Australian Attorney-General's Department to suppress two papers presented at the 1996 Australian and New Zealand Sociology of Criminology conference held in New Zealand: 'never before had a government department, let alone a foreign government, threatened legal action against presenters, the Society itself (including its members) and the host university' (Presdee & Walters 1998). As discussed by Presdee and Walters (1998), the response to their evaluation of crime prevention in South Australia took the form of various acts of government intimidation, including use of both formal and informal sanctions. Situating the response within a Foucauldian frame of analysis, the authors argue that the conflict was ultimately over what counts as knowledge or truth. At the heart of the issue was how power is exerted, both directly and indirectly, to control or regulate the production of knowledge.

The 'policing of knowledge' (see Presdee & Walters 1998) occurs in various ways, as does the 'silencing' process. This includes the practice of data gatekeeping by state institutions; that is, the denial of requests by researchers to access quantitative data and records not publicly available, often on economic rationalist grounds (see, for example, Carlton & Segrave 2011). More generally, the status of knowledge claims (and persons making those claims) very much depends on where a person is positioned institutionally within the criminal justice field or university sector, and the kinds of work (specifically) we are talking about. Knowledge production is not a socially neutral process, as Snider (2000: 193) observes:

> The knowledge claims of sociology and criminology, when they legitimate increased repression and control over traditional (lower class) criminals, are not only heard, they are embraced and celebrated. Only when they legitimate tightened social control over hegemonic groups are they 'obviously' inadequate.

The definitions of what are deemed to be 'important' crimes and the preferred crime responses are part and parcel of a larger political process involving many different players and diverse ideological cross-currents. Scraton (2000) makes the point that critical criminologists are free to research, to write and to teach, but only at the periphery not at the core. This is because the 'mainstream' is inherently and integrally linked to the status quo (propping up existing institutions and ways of doing things). It is 'mainstream' precisely because it is embedded in the dominant relations of power and knowledge. This mainstreaming of criminological inquiry is evident in the positioning of state authorities as themselves the producers of criminological data and research. State control of the development, implementation and consumption of knowledge enables it to refocus inquiry towards the administration of people, things and events in a way that lends support to existing or intended public policy directions, and draws critical attention away from their impacts and effects. Ultimately, many warn that this development poses challenges for the conduct and legitimacy of criminological research that is rigorous, provocative and socially relevant (Goldson 2010; Haggerty 2004; Walters 2003).

THE SCIENTIFICATION AND POLITICISATION OF CRIME

To illustrate the embededness of power in the construction and maintenance of criminological knowledge, one can note the continuing scientification and dichotomous process of politicisation and depoliticisation of crime control in the public realm globally (Edwards & Sheptycki 2009; Nelken 1994; Sheptycki 2004; Stenson & Sullivan 2001). The politicisation of crime is manifest in law-and-order campaigns designed for maximum cross-class electoral appeal, where the central concern is to get tough on crime (meaning 'working-class crime'), primarily through enacting more repressive laws and/or harsher punishment (see Chapters 20 and 21). A modicum of social peace (read social control) is necessary to the maintenance of political legitimacy in times of intense change and institutional transformation, and to ensure the 'normal' operation of the market. The depoliticisation of crime relates to how crimes of the powerful are ignored or downplayed; social, structural and systemic reasons for inequality are rarely explicitly discussed or addressed; and 'solutions' are conceptualised in technical rather than social terms (e.g. more police, more programs and better targeting of resources).

The politicisation of crime in contemporary criminology is often supported by partisan appeals to social scientific truths as the basis for public policy; that is, claims as to 'what works' based on notions of objective and rational investigation by 'experts' in the field in question (Downes & Morgan 2007). Of course, no science is value-neutral, since it develops in a social context (Hebenton & Jou 2008). In the context of electorally driven ideological competition over law and order, this scientification of criminology can result in the manipulation of scientific research to support established or proposed public policies (see, for example, Hope 2004; Maguire 2004; Young 2011).

Criminologists have an important role to play in regards to public debates, and in respect to how and where to turn the criminological gaze. How crime and social harm are socially constructed has major implications for how institutional responses are framed. Criminologists are aware of this, and take this into account as they reflect upon their practice. Some agree with and support government agendas, some attempt to subvert these agendas and some attempt to shift government agendas through their professional practice. Whether or not one agrees with the perspective of particular researchers, it is naïve to presume that they do not engage in reflective criminology or know the historical and theoretical literature pertaining to their field of expertise.

The degree to which criminologists continue to exert influence over the public debate has, however, been brought into question in recent years, with some claiming a seeming inverse relationship between the expansion of the discipline, both in terms of student numbers and the proliferation of academic research, and its policy relevance (Garland & Sparks 2000; Matthews 2009; Radzinowicz 1999). Curie (2007), for example, posits that considerable knowledge exists with respect to crime causation and what works in preventing crime and violence. Yet, despite broad consensus regarding the failure of incarceration to stem crime, criminologists have been unable to reverse the societal drive towards increasingly punitive and repressive policies.

STRUCTURAL AND INSTITUTIONAL TENSIONS

Behind the self-conscious rationalisation of what criminologists do, there lies a series of structural and institutional tensions. For example, one can distinguish between what criminologists may say they are doing (e.g. crime prevention as community empowerment) and what they actually, if inadvertently, may be doing (e.g. reinforcing a technical, apolitical approach). Interpretation of what criminologists do is also guided by how a funding agency responds at a program, project or political level. Systematic and evidenced-based study may lead to certain preferred pathways and recommendations, but there is no guarantee that criminological 'science' will ultimately be accepted by government ministers or be used to inform government policy, especially in the face of populist media pressures to 'get tough on crime' (see Chapter 2).

Conscious reflection on criminological practice is crucial to criminologists becoming more than 'information gatherers for government' (Presdee & Walters 1998: 165) or purveyors of the 'powerful commonsense, which brackets out any recognition of crime as an ideological artefact of the legal definitions of the state, the criminal law and its knowledge producing processes' (Brown & Hogg 1992: 113). What makes intellectual labour in criminology 'intellectual' hinges on how criminologists respond to the conditions and authority structures of their work. Writing in a different but relevant context, Connell (1983: 250) makes the point that:

> Intellectual work is not necessarily radical, but it must always be subversive of authority in its own domain. There is nothing exotic about this, it is implicit in the very notion of intellectual *work*. If the answers to problems are settled by received authority, there is literally no intellectual work to be done.

Elsewhere Connell (1983: 239) also observes:

> The more immediately active power is in an intellectual labour process, and the more dominant interests shape the criteria of intellectual work and evaluate the products, then the more likely the product is to be composed of lies.

The institutional context of intellectual labour has no small part in influencing the extent to which 'subversion of authority' and 'not telling lies' features in everyday criminological work. So, too, it shapes the manner in which intellectual work is put to bureaucratic and ideological uses, regardless of the intent or awareness of the social scientist (see Mills 1959; Young 2011). There will always be tensions between what criminologists want to do, and what others will do with the product of their labour. The question of professional and personal integrity is inevitably bound up with how criminologists negotiate the pressures and limits imposed upon them within the labour processes of intellectual work (the specific resources available) and by forces external to their immediate work environment (e.g. media, government bureaucrats and politicians).

Criminology in Australia may have developed in conservative directions in response to the critical and theoretical potentials within criminology (Carson & O'Malley 1989), but that development has been neither uniform nor totally conservative in nature. As Finnane (1998) points out, a key 'founding father' of the field, Sir John Barry, held a range of views, some conservative and some progressive.

Barry's commitment to reform in some areas, it is argued, would have placed him at the radical end of the political spectrum. Who produces knowledge, who controls it and the uses to which it is put are all sites of contestation involving complicated institutional pressures and many different kinds of choices on the part of the intellectual. Criminological work is full of paradoxes and contradictions (see Cohen 1985). Thus, our understanding of 'crime' and responses to 'crime' ought to be informed by a sense of the incomplete: of gains as well as losses, continual struggles over meaning and truth, hegemony as a process not an outcome, contradictions that generate new and unusual resistances, and individual initiatives and mass actions. It also implies the use of many different types of methods in the carrying out of criminological work.

CRIMINOLOGICAL RESEARCH

Central to the production and evaluation of criminological theory is criminological research. What criminologists do as researchers and evaluators involves the use of various methods to investigate, document, analyse and interpret phenomenon. Like crime theorising, approaches to criminological research vary in accordance with political persuasion and **epistemological** orientation; that is, understandings of knowledge and the acquisition of knowledge.

TYPES OF DATA COLLECTION

Data collection is the process of gathering and collating information on variables of interest to a particular investigation (e.g. individuals, communities, strategies, programs, policies and agencies) systematically and in accordance with established methods. It is necessary to collect data in order to investigate research questions, test **hypotheses**, analyse behaviours and meanings, and evaluate outcomes. As summarised in Box 1.2, there are many different types of information that might be collected, and many different methods of accessing these data. Determination of preference for defining data is influenced by many ideological and practical considerations. Prior to commencing a research project, it is imperative to carefully consider the source of the information available, the nature of the data sought, and the purposes to which it will be put. A formal data-collection protocol is necessary

EPISTEMOLOGY
A branch of philosophy focused on the nature, scope and acquisition of knowledge.

HYPOTHESES
Proposed explanations for a phenomenon that requires testing and evaluation to establish merit.

BOX 1.2   TYPES AND METHODS OF DATA COLLECTION

- *Document analysis:* agency files and reports, maps, correspondence, budgets
- *Media representations:* newspaper editorials, articles and letters, cartoons, magazines, films, radio transcripts, social media content
- *Official statistical records:* police statistics, Australian Bureau of Statistics (ABS) data, hospital emergency department data, local council data
- *Internet and computer records:* digital footprints, computer data, memory stick and hard drive data
- *Record-keeping:* referral records, diaries, daily contact sheets, attendance records, crime/prison records
- *Literature reviews:* journal articles, government reports, community research
- *Surveys:* questionnaires, telephone surveys, suggestion boxes

- *Group discussions:* invited respondents, public meetings, teleconferences, public submissions
- *Focus groups:* specific sample groups, briefing and debriefing sessions
- *Life histories:* selective in-depth discussions, story-telling
- *Unobtrusive research:* closed circuit camera surveillance, undercover surveillance, archival information, graffiti, review of digital footprints
- *Peer research:* friendship and family networks
- *Ethnography (data collection in natural settings):* field notes, diaries, personal documents, interviews (structured, semi-structured or unstructured), observation, participant observation, surveys, questionnaires, oral histories

Source: adapted from White (2006a)

---

to ensure that data collected is appropriate, accurate and consistent—a fundamental precondition for maintaining research integrity.

There are three types of data: quantitative, qualitative and interpretive (see, for example, Bevir & Kedar 2008; Jupp et al. 2011; Silverman 2011; Thorne et al. 2013; White & Coventry 2000).

QUANTITATIVE DATA

Quantitative data is concerned with *counting* and *measurement*. It is any data that is presented in mathematical form. Within the field of criminology, quantitative research refers to the empirical investigation of social phenomena, such as events and behaviours, via the use of statistics, numerics, mathematical modelling or other mathematical techniques. The process of measurement enables observations between two or more variables investigated (e.g. offender characteristics and the distribution of crime in society) to be expressed mathematically, with a view to establishing causation or association.

When undertaking quantitative research, the researcher generally commences with a hypothesis or set of narrow questions that reflect a conceptual framework (belief held about the phenomenon under investigation). Sample numerical data is then collected from sources relevant to the area of investigation. The individual pieces of information collected are then aggregated and analysed using statistical methods in an effort to test the hypothesis or answer the research questions and determine the generalisability (reproducibility) of findings. Crime statistics are useful in that they provide a standardised measure of the level of criminal activity. Common numerical expressions of observed behaviour in criminology include:

- *Number:* a simple numerical count that establishes the frequency of a phenomenon (e.g. the number of people that have actually been charged by police with a criminal offence).
- *Rate:* converts a frequency into a specific ratio (e.g. the number of people in Australian prisons expressed as a proportion of the total Australian population). Rates are usually expressed in relation to units of time (fluctuations in the rate of offences per week or month or year), and are usually scaled to control for population size (e.g. prisoners per 100,000 population).
  Rates can be differentiated into:
  - *Prevalence:* proportion of the population that has committed a crime at a specific point in time (point prevalence) during a given period; say, over the past 12 months (period prevalence) or at some point in their life (life time prevalence).

QUANTITATIVE DATA
Data that has numerical significance; that is, it can be counted and measured on a numerical scale. This data is used to investigate broad statistical inferences, associations and correlations through the use of scientific methods.

- *Incidence*: the proportion of new offenders identified in a population over a given period (month, year etc.) usually expressed as a rate per head of population). Note: whereas prevalence counts all offenders, incidence will count only first-time offenders.
- *Trend*: broad changes in rates (upward or downward movement) over specified time periods (for instance, overall, crime levels or rates have been consistently falling in many Western nations over the past 20 years).

Not all empirical data is analytical, in the sense of testing for causal hypotheses; empirical data that does not directly test causation is described as empirical but descriptive. Quantitative methodologies may involve the use of formal pre-set questionnaires and surveys (e.g. asking people specific questions or propositions that have a limited number of optional answers: yes/no or agree/disagree to some extent, as measured on a Likert scale), as well as drawing upon formal records (e.g. the use of official police statistics). Due to its concern with ascertaining the empirical meaning of observable phenomenon and establishing generalisable conclusions, the quantitative method lends itself to large-scale studies that often deal with large volumes of numerical data, sometimes at a national level. Data that pertains to a cross-section of a study population (a sample of offenders officially processed), rather than the entire population (all offenders officially processed) is referred to as a one-dimensional data set; the ability to draw conclusions on causality from cross-sectional data is bounded.

QUALITATIVE DATA

QUALITATIVE DATA
Data concerned with understanding and describing meaning and experience rather than drawing statistical inferences.

Qualitative data is concerned with describing and *understanding* human behaviour and perceptions, and the reasons governing that behaviour. It is about gaining information on decision-making—how and why people make the decisions that they do, and their perceptions, attitudes and views on particular issues. It provides for more in-depth appreciation of how people make sense of their lives, and emphasises *their* meanings, motivations and emotions.

Qualitative researchers draw on a wide range of methodologies for gathering information, but typically rely on a combination of:

- *description:* based upon field notes and reflexive journal entries generated through participant or non-participant observation
- *interviews:* structured, semi-structured or non-structured discussions with research participants (individually or in groups, in person or over the phone) based around certain core questions or themes
- *document analysis:* also referred to as textual or content analysis, it involves a review and analysis of the content of recorded human communications as expressed in books, digital records, laws, official records, diaries etc.

The objective of qualitative research is to gain information that will enable the researcher to better appreciate the social contexts and social processes that inform people's actions: how people feel about themselves, their neighbourhoods and their issues of concern. Rather than investigating a specific proposition, qualitative research often generates hypotheses from the analysis of the data collected. Conventionally, qualitative methods produce information in relation to particular cases studies and do not seek to generalise conclusions. Observations are expressed as propositions only; that is, informed assertions. As such, qualitative method tends to be oriented toward small-scale research, involving interactions with small, focused samples and in local contexts.

For the purposes of interpreting and reporting findings, qualitative researchers organise data into categories or patterns of behaviour based on coding. Coding is an interpretive research technique that enables information derived qualitatively (generally from some form of interviewing) to be analysed and presented in statistical form. For example, of the 50 people interviewed, 25 thought that the youth skateboard ramp was a good idea; 95 per cent of these were male and most (80%) lived within the local area. Statistical analysis is, however, generally confined to simple frequencies, tabulations and cross-tabulations that do not lead to statistical correlations or tests.

INTERPRETIVE DATA

Interpretive data is basically concerned with *critical analysis*. It is intended to ground knowledge and be a form of reflection on the social meaning of official documents, existing statistical collections, policy statements, media reports and citizen attitudes. As a starting point, interpretive research regards the social world as a construct that is subjectively experienced rather than an objective collection of external 'facts', and views human action as meaningful and historically and culturally contingent (Nelken 1994). The role of research is therefore to provide interpretive understanding to the subjective meaning attributed to social phenomenon. In this view, social science and the subjects it studies are located within particular linguistic, historical and values standpoints. This contrasts strongly with the drive to identify generalisable laws independent of cultural–historical specificity.

INTERPRETIVE DATA
Data collection concerned with critical analysis, and intended to be a form of reflection on the social meaning of human action.

Accordingly, this form of research is concerned with identification and/or application to the material under review, of the perspectives that underlie key issues. It is an attempt to expose the assumptions, discourses and ideological propositions embodied in particular policies, programs and strategies. The 'data' collected is, in effect, the *meanings* assigned to particular forms and types of information, and the theories that are implicit in the language used and concepts employed in documentation of an issue or trend. Interpretive data seeks to unpack these meanings and situate them contextually.

The contribution of this form of data collection, therefore, is to provide critical appraisal of taken-for-granted assumptions, and thus to open the door for alternative explanations, programs for action or suggestions for reform. Although there is a degree of overlap between qualitative and interpretive research, specifically in the common use of descriptive data, interpretive research adopts a distinctive approach to research design, as well as the analysis and assessment of data (see, for example, Bevir & Kedar 2008).

RESEARCH METHODS

Closely linked to the different types of data collection and sources of data are discrete research methods. There are a number of different methods generally used in criminology. These go by a variety of names (e.g. experimental, survey, naturalistic, ethnographic and legalistic) and generally serve to provide different kinds of information about the social world. For present purposes, three broad methods will be discussed (see Table 1.1). Importantly, while each method tends to be identified with certain types of data collection (e.g. reliance on questionnaires or use of interviews) and certain sorts of conceptual concerns (e.g. 'cause and effect', 'meaning and process' or 'context and decision-making'), they may in fact use a wide variety of specific data-collection techniques.

TABLE 1.1 METHODS OF RESEARCH

METHOD	RATIONALE	MAIN TYPE OF DATA COLLECTION	LIMITATIONS
Experimental	Establish cause and effect: e.g. use of pre- and post-intervention surveys	Quantitative: e.g. large-scale surveys; use of official statistics; use of control and research groups	Constant change in study area: e.g. people moving in and out; high study participant attrition rates; inability to control for all extraneous variables impacting outcomes
Naturalistic	Examine meaning and processes: e.g. descriptions and perceptions of people	Qualitative: e.g. in-depth interviews; observations	Restrictions or biases in sample selection: e.g. participation refusals or difficulty interpreting answers; cannot be replicated, verified or generalised
Contextual	Uncover contexts and decision-making processes: e.g. conditions under which a program is introduced	Documentary: e.g. meeting records; briefing papers; official files	Inadequate or incomplete records: e.g. inability to gain a sense of informal processes and interactions

Source: adapted from White & Coventry (2000)

EXPERIMENTAL AND QUASI-EXPERIMENTAL METHODS (PRE- AND POST-INTERVENTION SURVEYS)

This is a form of research that seeks to establish evidence of causation between two or more variables empirically; that is, it investigates the *cause and effect* of interventions on a test population and, on the strength of a statistical relationship, extrapolates the findings more broadly (Imai et al. 2013). This type of empirical research method primarily involves intervening in the lives of subjects for the purposes of determining an outcome. Establishing causation between the intervention and the outcome involves a process in which pre-test measurements are taken of a target group or area before the experimental intervention (a particular treatment program, strategy or project) is implemented. The purpose of pre-testing is to observe the relationship between the variables being tested; that is, to establish the relationship between the *independent variable/s* (which will be subject to manipulation by the researcher) and the *subject/s* response (known as the *dependent variable* because its presence or intensity will vary in accordance with manipulation of the independent variable). This is followed by post-test measurements after the intervention has had time to take effect. Pre-test and post-test measurements are also taken of a matched 'control' group or area where no intervention has occurred. The assumption here is that observed differences between the *experimental* group or area, and the *control* group or area, can be attributed to the intervention. Milgram's 'authority obedience' study is a classical social psychology experiment, the findings of which are still fiercely debated today (see Box 1.3).

BOX 1.3   MILGRAM'S AUTHORITY OBEDIENCE EXPERIMENT

In July 1961 Stanley Milgram, a Yale University psychologist, devised an experiment to test the preparedness of study participants to obey an authority figure when issued with instructions to commit acts that conflicted with their personal conscience. The experiment, which was conducted only 18 months after the Holocaust, and in the midst of the trial of Nazi war criminal Adolf Eichmann, was intended to answer popular questions of the time, including: 'What sort of people, slavishly doing what they are told, would send millions of fellow humans into gas chambers?' and 'Is it possible that Eichmann and his millions of accomplices in the Holocaust were simply following orders?' (Shea 2013).

To test the power of authority, Milgram recruited hundreds of Americans to determine how far they would go in punishing a fellow human being. Research participants were deceived into think-ing that they were acting out the role of a teacher in a stimulus–response experiment designed to test memory recall under laboratory conditions. On instruction from the experimenter (posing as an authority figure in a lab coat), the teacher was required to administer electric shocks of increasing intensity to a learner (an actor pretending to be a volunteer) each time they failed to accurately recall a learning exercise. Unbeknown to the test subjects, the 'shock machine' they utilised did not actually generate a shock. The teacher and learner were physically separated into different rooms and therefore unable to communicate with one another.

In one variant of the experiment, the person being shocked, who had disclosed they had a heart condition, started banging on the door, shouting out more and more desperately as the voltage level increased, and then fell silent. At this point some test subjects indicated a desire to stop the experiment and check on the learner, while others began questioning the purpose of the experiment. The majority (62%), however, elected to continue to the final massive 450 volt shock following assurance that they would not be held responsible for any consequences.

The findings of the experiment led Milgram (1973: 76) to conclude that:

> [O]rdinary people simply doing their jobs, and without any particular hostility on their part, can become agents in a terrible destructive process. Moreover, even when the destructive effects of their work become patently clear, and they are asked to carry out actions incompatible with fundamental stand-ards of morality, relatively few people have the resources needed to resist authority.

In essence, the experiment's findings suggested that the drive to obey authority—and thereby avoid social isolation—is a far more powerful force that one's own views of morality.

It is important to note that this study is not without its critics (Shea 2013); some claim that the experimental standards are not consistent with those of twenty-first-century research, and the study is unethical both with respect to the deceit of and impact on test subjects. While such an experiment cannot be replicated today, due to the application of stringent ethical standards to research, it has attracted much attention in the light of the use of state-sanctioned torture on captives in the war on terror and, in particular, the treatment of prisoners at Guantanamo Bay and Abu Ghraib (see Chapter 12).

True experimental designs involve the random assignment of test subjects to groups (or conditions within a group). These sorts of studies are said to have high levels of *validity* (measurement accuracy) and *reliability* (ability to achieve a repeatable outcome if the study is repeated). Experimental studies that do not involve the use of random control groups are referred to as *quasi experimental*; they are considered adequate but less rigorous than experimental designs (Deaton 2009). In relatively recent years, new techniques have been developed to assess the efficacy of experimental studies, notably meta-analysis. This involves the calculation of 'effect sizes' (the magnitude of the difference in outcome for treatment and control groups) for each study reviewed. Conclusions are then drawn across the groups of studies (Lipsey & Wilson 2001).

The major concern of this research methodology is with group comparisons using quantitative data, including large-scale surveys, as well as official statistical records (e.g. crime and victimisation rates in a specific locale before and after a crime prevention initiative). A major difficulty with this method is that while measured differences can be controlled statistically, it is extremely difficult to have full control over the numerous unmeasured variables that may impact outcomes, such as the conditions in which the tests are being conducted. People are dynamic, areas are dynamic and change is a constant feature of human and urban life. Some of the practical problems associated with this research method include (see, for example, Deaton 2009; Imai et al. 2013):

- understanding that changes that occur in the area between the pre-test and post-test measures may confound the results (e.g. new housing developments or a change in police numbers or police strategies)
- ensuring that respondents are representative of the target population (which itself may change over time), and the ability exists to compare groups over time (because of changing demographics in an area; for example, an influx of older or younger people)
- distinguishing between the impacts of the intervention and naturally occurring fluctuations in social phenomena over time (e.g. burglary rates declining because of improved economic prosperity or an ageing offender population)
- using different measurement methods in the pre-test and post-test phases (e.g. changes in how the police record offences or how a crime is defined)
- recognising that experiments provide a black box view of causality; that is, they are able to identify average causal effects, but are unable to explain the mechanism by which the observed changes come about.

Aside from pragmatic difficulties associated with ensuring integrity in the conduct of research using experimental designs, there are concerns that experimental research approaches decontextualise the human experience by approaching humans as entities independent of the historical, cultural and economic context within which they exist. In doing so, they have a tendency to lend tacit support to the prevailing social order.

NATURALISTIC METHODS (DESCRIPTIONS AND PERCEPTIONS OF PEOPLE)

This method of research, of which one variant is ethnography, usually emphasises actors speaking for themselves, in natural environments, and as they normally do (Fraser 2013; Goodwin & Goodwin 2013; Jackson 2005; Shover 2012). It is a means of gaining information about people's perceptions, meanings and interpretations through observing behaviour (with subjects conscious of the researcher and their purpose) or asking them directly about specific features of their lived experience; that is, their everyday reality, and how norms, values, rules and justice practices impact their daily routines and behaviour. The emphasis is on *meaning and process*. It is based upon the gathering of qualitative data through in-depth interviews and through observation (field narratives, video footage etc.), and often involves narrative or discourse analysis. Naturalistic observation differs from structured observation because it involves observing behaviour as it naturally unfolds without any attempt at intervention by the researcher.

One of the advantages of this type of research is that by directly observing subjects ('deviant' or 'criminal' populations) in a natural setting, there is a greater likelihood that the researcher is witnessing true behaviour as opposed to behaviour that may have been unduly impacted by artificial environments and contexts, such as within a laboratory or within a focus group involving individuals not actually part of the subject's social structure. This method also permits researchers to observe the behaviours of society's most marginalised and disenfranchised populations (e.g. the homeless, street present injecting drug users, sex workers and prisoners), whose life conditions cannot be manipulated in a laboratory due to ethical concerns (e.g. artificial confinement of subjects). This method is also useful in supporting claims of external validity. It is one thing to claim generalisability of the findings of an experimental study to a larger population, but another to be able to claim confidently observance of those findings among subjects in their natural environment.

A major difficulty with this method is, however, its resource intensiveness; that is, the range and number of sources of information that are to be used and the time required to gain the subjects' trust and acceptance, and to gather and analyse large volumes of data. This is partly a question of having adequate resources to undertake such intensive research. It is also a matter of determining who to talk with, and why. Some other problems associated with this method include:

- restrictions or biases in the selection of people who are to be interviewed because of lack of resources, interpreters and trained interviewers (the nature and type of sample)
- refusal to be interviewed by those most negatively affected by, or who have the most critical views of, a particular program or project (self-exclusion tends to skew the findings in a positive direction)
- differing interpretations of what was 'observed' and what 'caused' the observed behaviour in a local area because of varying assumptions, philosophies and values held by participants, including researchers and evaluators (issues of consistency, reliability and preferencing one truth over another) and the inability to control for extraneous variables
- difficulties in interpreting the findings, insofar as the accounts given by participants are, in turn, subject to reinterpretation and repackaging in written form by the researcher (reflexive selection of what is or is not important in any specific account)
- where obtrusive observation is involved, difficulty in ascertaining whether the researcher's presence has negatively impacted on observed behaviour (e.g. subjects behaving in a way that conforms with what they anticipate the researcher is expecting to see)
- that studies cannot be replicated, verified or generalised due to the protected nature of participant identities (usually via the use of pseudonyms), and the changing nature of research sites (buildings being demolished) and participants' lives (moving away from their environment and into prison or another geographic area).

CONTEXTUAL ANALYSIS (CONDITIONS UNDER WHICH A PROGRAM IS INTRODUCED)

This type of research method has multiple meanings but essentially contends that no observed action has intrinsic meaning outside of context; context establishes the frame for analysing and interpreting observed phenomena (Christensen 2010; Goffman 1974). The principles of context analysis can be applied in a range of situations; for example, to explain the role of group context on the actions and attitudes of individuals (see, for example, Bursik & Grasmick 1996; Iverson 1991). It is also commonly associated with evaluation of a program, project or strategy that has been underway for some time. With respect to use of the term within a program evaluation context, this method of research is oriented toward *process evaluation* (assessing the processes involved in program operation and delivery), but is also useful in examining an initiative retrospectively or 'after the fact' (to determine the extent to which an intervention is serving those for whom it is intended). The main concerns of the research would typically include: examining how an initiative was implemented; whether implementation went as planned; and the ways in which the context within which the initiative was implemented facilitated or undermined the impact of the initiative.

The major areas of concern targeted by this method include: who was involved; the structure and decision-making processes of an initiative; the nature and extent of community and interagency involvement; and the extent of implementation. The emphasis is on 'context and decision-making'. It is based upon the gathering of documentary evidence (e.g. project plans, funding contracts, meeting records and newsletters) and interviews with planners, key stakeholders, participants and (for comparative purposes) non-participants.

A major difficulty with this method is that it may not be possible to observe or to document all significant aspects of the implementation process, or to gain a considered opinion about an initiative from a representative sample of participants. Some of the other problems with this research method include:

- difficulties in gaining a full picture of the informal as well as the formal ways in which people interact, which has a major bearing on implementation processes (issues of personality and shared interests)
- differing interpretations among participants as to the meaning of concepts such as 'interagency cooperation' or 'community consultation' (which requires sensitivity to the multiple meanings of key terms)
- an emphasis on 'context', which may imply that the lessons learned from the evaluation are largely unique to the project and may not be transferable to other local areas (thus limiting project replicability; that is, applicability to other target groups, projects and regions)
- the political sensitivity of information gathered about implementation, which may result in efforts to censor the findings or to criticise the evaluator (protecting one's own turf or sectoral interests).

The problems and difficulties associated with each of the research methods outlined above are not insurmountable. In many cases they simply require the researcher to be conscious of the limitations of the method used, and acknowledge these in the research findings. More generally, it is a truism that the best way to overcome many of the biases and intrinsic limitations of various research methodologies is to consider the use of two or more methods in undertaking a research project (known as 'triangulation'). Triangulation is particularly useful for enhancing the validity and therefore credibility of qualitative data. It ensures that observed variances in results are reflective of a naturally occurring behaviour and not a methodological artefact (Anderson et al. 2011).

In short, research methods are not mutually exclusive; it is possible, and indeed desirable, to use a mixed-methods approach and a variety of data-collection techniques in undertaking criminological research. To some extent, the kinds of methods and techniques to be used stem from the research questions themselves. The 'how' of research is thus inseparable from the 'why' of research.

MEASURING CRIME AS AN EXAMPLE OF CRIMINOLOGICAL RESEARCH

The ways in which crime is measured are intertwined both with how crime is defined (and what is deemed to be serious and harmful) and how it is responded to by institutions of criminal justice (through specific campaigns, programs and interventions). To take one example of the complexities of crime measurement, the sources of criminal law vary around the country, because there is no single body of criminal law governing the whole of Australia. Each state and territory has its own set of criminal laws, and there is also federal criminal law. From jurisdiction to jurisdiction, major differences can thus exist in relation to things such as offence definitions, their range of seriousness, legal definitions of permissible defences and prescribed punishments (see Chapter 19).

From the point of view of analysis, social scientists also have their differences when it comes to crime and crime statistics (see Jupp et al. 2011; Nettler 1984). Three broad strands within criminology that deal with measurement issues can be identified (White et al. 2012; see also Chapter 6):

- The *realist approach* adopts the view that crime exists 'out there' in society and that the **'dark figure' of crime** (crimes that are undetected and/or unreported) needs to be uncovered and recorded. As there are limitations to the gathering of official statistics (e.g. reliance solely on police records of reported offences), the role of criminology is to supplement official statistics (those generated by the police, courts and prison authorities) through a range of informal or alternative measures. The emphasis is on the problem of omission: to uncover the true or real extent of crime utilising supplementary data-gathering methods, such as victim surveys, self-report surveys, test situations and hidden cameras.

- The *institutionalist approach* adopts the view that crime is a 'social process', and it rejects the notion that we can unproblematically gain a sense of the real extent of crime by improving our measuring devices and techniques. This approach concentrates instead on the manner in which official institutions of crime control actually process suspects and thus define certain individuals and certain types of behaviour as being 'criminal'. The emphasis is on the problem of bias: to show how some people and events are designated criminal status by the criminal justice system, while others are not.

- The *critical realist approach* argues that crime measurement can be characterised as having elements of both 'social process' and a grounded 'reality'. The task of measurement, from this perspective, is to uncover the processes whereby the crimes against the most vulnerable and least powerful sections of the population have been ignored or under-represented. The emphasis is on the problem of victimisation: to demonstrate empirically how certain groups are especially vulnerable to crime and to the fear of crime, and conceptually to criticise the agencies of crime control for their lack of action in protecting these groups.

There are, then, debates within criminology over how and what to measure and, often, these debates reflect basic divisions within the field regarding the definition of crime itself.

'DARK FIGURE' OF CRIME
A criminological term used to describe criminal acts and omissions that are not detected and/or reported to the police and therefore are not captured in officially recorded crime statistics.

SOURCES OF CRIME STATISTICS

Notwithstanding these debates, it is nevertheless a truism that most criminologists still rely upon some type of crime statistics in order to interpret or make sense of crime (however defined). Likewise, researchers and policy-makers frequently refer to official sources of data in their work. Even with limitations, official crime data provides a valuable measure of overall communal wellbeing and some indication of broad crime patterns.

Statistical information is collected by police services (including the Australian Federal Police), courts (lower and superior courts), correctional services (including community corrections), crime prevention units and regulatory agencies (e.g. the Australian Competition and Consumer Commission (ACCC)). Some key sources of official crime data in Australia include:

- police offence information systems
- police records on apprehensions and juvenile cautioning

- court criminal case management systems
- correctional services, including community correctional services
- juvenile conferencing teams
- fine enforcement registers or systems
- family incident reports or equivalent.

Published statistical information comes in a variety of forms and is available from a diverse range of agencies. Some of the better-known agencies include:

- Australian Institute of Criminology (AIC)
- Australian Bureau of Statistics (ABS) National Centre for Crime and Justice Statistics
- Sentencing Advisory Council (Victoria)
- New South Wales Bureau of Crime Statistics and Research (BOCSAR)
- Crime Research Centre (University of Western Australia)
- Office of Crime Statistics and Research (South Australia) (OCSAR)
- Australian Institute of Health and Welfare (AIHW)
- Australian Institute of Family Studies (AIFS)
- Crime and Corruption Commission (Queensland).

Information about victims, crimes and criminal justice issues is also available from sources such as centres against sexual assault (CASAs), the Australian Human Rights Commission (AHRC), hospital accident and emergency departments, and State and Commonwealth Ombudsman offices.

COMPARING CRIME STATISTICS

Official data is particularly useful as a means of examining trends and patterns associated with crime and victimisation. There are, however, a number of technical problems in trying to compare crime statistics across different jurisdictions and over time. Through the National Criminal Justice Statistical Framework (NCJSF), the ABS National Centre for Crime and Justice Statistics attempts to build connections across the main sectors of the criminal justice system nationally. For example, it has developed the Australian Standard Offence Classification (ASOC) as a means of providing a uniform national statistical framework for classifying offences for use by justice agencies, agencies with an interest in crime and justice issues, and other persons. Although defined differently according to local state laws, distinct crimes nevertheless can be grouped in such a way as to make comparisons between states possible; for example, homicide and related offences are coded under headings such as 'murder', 'attempted murder', 'manslaughter' and 'driving causing death'. Each specific type of offence is assigned an appropriate code. It should be noted that coding and, indeed, recording practices change over time, leading to an artificial increase or decrease in recorded crime levels.

As indicated by the range of crimes, offences, harms and victims discussed elsewhere in this book, the particular offences chosen for attention by the ABS and other criminal justice agencies tend to reflect a fairly narrow and conventional range of socially harmful behaviour. Even so, the ABS also notes that its statistics may be different from those published by police services in individual states and territories, because of different definitions of offences and counting rules (ABS 2014b). In response to this situation, a National Crime Recording Standard (NCRS) has been developed to address the lack of a consistent standard in initial police recording processes. The NCRS comprises a uniform set of business rules and requirements developed in collaboration with police agencies across Australia to guide the recording and counting of criminal incidents for statistical purposes.

Another issue that further complicates statistical comparison relates to the fact that a criminal incident may involve a number of offenders, victims, offences and/or multiple counts of a single offence type. Accordingly, *counting rules* have been established to record and measure different aspects of the criminal event.

For example, individuals may have more than one arrest, conviction or prison reception during the recording period, so counting only individuals would substantially undercount the number of offenders dealt with by the criminal justice system. Similarly, counting only charges, convictions or prison receptions would not show the number of distinct persons actually involved in crime, and in fact would overcount the number of offenders. Likewise, counting only the most serious offence for which an offender is convicted results in an underestimation of the volume of crime actually committed in any given jurisdiction. The NCJSF is designed to deal with these kinds of issues in a coherent manner that allows for standardised methods of collecting and compiling criminal justice data across the country.

For these reasons, considerable care must be taken in interpreting comparative statistical data and trend analyses (see Box 1.4). This is especially the case when comparing cross-national statistics. For instance, there are great variations in the nature of record-keeping, definitions of juveniles and adults and specific types of crimes, and data-processing techniques across jurisdictions. Some countries record all arrests and court appearances; others only record convictions. This is important because, in many

BOX 1.4   INTERPRETING STATISTICAL TRENDS

Several years of statistics should be examined in order to gauge *trends*, rather than year-to-year fluctuations, as sometimes exceptional events occur in a given year; for example, homicide figures are quite static, but one singular event involving multiple deaths (e.g. the murder of seven people in the Hoddle Street massacre in Melbourne in 1987 and the Port Arthur massacre in Tasmania in 1986, which resulted in 35 deaths) can skew the figures in any given year.

Trends should normally be expressed in *rates* rather than absolute figures in order to obtain a more accurate measure of changes in crime, such as number of crime incidents per 100,000 people or number of car thefts per 100,000 vehicles.

We need to ensure that *like is being compared with like*, since changes can occur in the way in which statistics are compiled over time; for example, variance in counting rules, legal definitions and changes.

Weatherburn (2011: 7) cautions against non-critical interpretation of changes in police recorded rates of crime or data derived from this information. Specifically, he suggests that the golden rule be applied; namely, 'we do not observe a change in crime; we infer a change in crime'. Inference should be based on answers to the following questions:

1   Has the recorded rate of some offence changed?
2   Is the change attributable to chance or seasonal variation?
3   Does it involve an offence that victims report to police or an offence that is normally only recorded when police discover it?
4   Is there any reason to believe police have changed in their willingness to record crime or in the way they record it?
5   Is the trend consistent with other relevant data (e.g. accident or emergency data, self-reported offending data or crime victim survey data)?

jurisdictions today, there is a major emphasis on pre-court diversion programs and court-ordered diversion programs, which will affect the officially recorded number of convictions. A lower conviction rate, therefore, is not necessarily a reflection on declining crime in society, or that the number of people coming into contact with the criminal justice system is likewise reducing. Another area of concern is the nature of the offences that may come to court notice, and that may result in a conviction. In some jurisdictions, this may include such things as failure to pay a train fare. In others, there may be a more rigid distinction between minor or trivial offences that may be proceeded against without involvement of the court, and more serious criminal justice matters that do end up in court.

SOCIAL FACTORS AFFECTING CRIME STATISTICS

A number of social factors can also affect the production of crime statistics (Weatherburn 2011). These include:

- the use of extra police in responding to specific offences, which will result in an apparent increase in that offence (e.g. traffic offences)
- public willingness to report crime; there is, for example, a perennial under-reporting of some crimes, such as sexual assault and threatened assault
- the influence of media attention on public perceptions about levels of crime, which can increase the attention directed by law enforcement agencies to certain crimes, resulting in increased arrest rates for those crimes (e.g. possession of knives or guns, and bikie-related crime)
- the influence that media attention on certain forms of crime, such as domestic violence, can have on public reporting of that crime
- the effects of public recognition of a social harm on levels of professional intervention to address that harm, as has occurred in relation to the mandatory reporting of child abuse generally and child sex abuse specifically
- the over-representation of working-class crime in criminal statutes and the under-representation of corporate crime
- amendments to the criminal law, such as the introduction in New South Wales of the *Summary Offences Act* (1988), which witnessed a 293 per cent increase in reports of offensive behaviour in the six-month period following its introduction
- the way harmful events are classified and officially responded to, such as whether preventable workplace death is processed as a homicide or a regulatory offence
- seasonal variations in crime, such as the annual rise in non-domestic assaults in January—a period where more people are out in public taking advantage of the warm weather
- changing opportunities for crime (e.g. through the advent of digital technology, ATMs and credit cards)
- the effect of political pressure on the way in which crime is reported (e.g. recent publicity encouraging the reporting of suspicious activities that might threaten national security).

In addition to these social influences on crime reporting and recording, funnel theory contends that changes in legal justice processes exert determinative influence on crime statistics (Moulton 2013). This theory applies the metaphor of the funnel to the criminal justice system, and proposes that the system selectively regulates the routing of persons through its process streams (police, courts and corrections). Changes in inputs, throughputs and outputs of the criminal justice system are thus seen to be reflective of changes in the funnel, rather than tangible changes in offending behaviour in society. Flows through a funnel are determined by its size, which is constrained by its resource base; thus, there is a limit to the number of crimes that can be processed by the system. Changes in legal process can result in flow constriction (e.g. the increasing complexity of law, which has resulted in case finalisation delays in the courts, or changes in legislation that introduce new crimes or keep offenders in prison for longer periods) or can speed up the flow (e.g. greater processing efficiency following a reduction in police patrols, which results in a reduction in detected crime, or changes to community correctional practices, which divert more offenders away from imprisonment). A change in crime rates unable to be explained by funnel theory is therefore said to be the only scenario where claims of actual changes in criminal behaviour in society are likely to be legitimate.

In order to gauge the nature and frequency of many different types of social harm, it is imperative that social scientists utilise a wide variety of research methods and techniques (see Jupp et al. 2011). A critical perspective that acknowledges the limitations of official statistics needs to be matched by the development of systematic and alternative forms of data collection, such as self-report data. This involves surveying a specific population of interest (e.g. homeless people, young people or white-collar workers) and asking them to disclose whether they have committed one or more crimes over a given period. As self-reported offences may not necessarily have been detected and/or recorded by police, this data offers an insight into the dark figure of crime.

Crime victim surveys are similar, in that they ask a defined population to disclose whether they have been the victim of certain crimes over a defined period and, if so, whether they reported their victimisation to police. An annual crime victim survey is conducted by the ABS nationally (see Chapter 6). They also administer a separate survey on personal safety (the Personal Safety Survey) as well as jurisdictionally specific surveys on crime victims. Used in isolation these methods are subject to limitations; for example, sampling bias (respondents may not be a true cross-representation of the studied population), recall bias (inflating or under-stating participation in criminal activity or experience of victimisation, due to faulty memory) and desirability bias (active manipulation of the truth in an effort to inflate criminal activity, with a view to impressing the researcher or downplaying the true extent of activities for fear of reprisals, such as criminal prosecution). Studies have demonstrated, however, that providing participants with anonymity and confidentiality, and structuring interviews to minimise bias, can result in reliable and valid data.

While each of these alternative approaches is one-dimensional—focused on the characteristics of either offenders or victims only—when used as supplementary tools to official crime statistics, they enable a more robust picture of crime and offending in society, and a more informed consideration of crime trends over time.

ISSUES FOR CONSIDERATION

DIVISIONS OF LABOUR IN ACADEMIA

One issue requiring close consideration is the nature of the labour process within academic work. For example, the proletarianisation of intellectual labour is manifest in the tendency toward the intensification of labour (increased volume of work), the tendency to increase and rigidify the division of labour (specialisation into teaching, research and administrative tasks at varying levels of responsibility) and the tendency toward routinisation of high-level tasks (expert intervention and codification of existing tasks). In practical terms, this translates for some intellectual workers into the reduction of autonomy (immediate control over the labour process), the deindividualisation of skills and qualifications (fragmentation of tasks) and the downgrading of status (income levels in relation to volume of work performed). How these processes are manifested across the academic labour market needs to be further investigated.

It needs to be acknowledged, as well, that there are 'winners and losers' in this reshaped intellectual climate, and this too will have an impact on the nature of the criminological field as a whole. Those who, for whatever reason (ideological, financial or career), play the funding game the right way will be institutionally privileged over time. There is the danger that the 'winners', by their actions (e.g. gatekeeping roles for funding agencies or journal editorial boards) or non-actions (e.g. ignoring the voices and contributions from 'the fringes'), will succeed in narrowing the scope of what is considered 'legitimate' or 'good' criminology. A conservative hegemony in criminology is contingent upon: what research gets commissioned; who gets published; whether evidenced-based research dominates to the exclusion of other types of research; which departments or researchers are invited to tender for consultancies and research; and the extent to which critical criminologists are marginalised institutionally, professionally and politically. How this manifests itself is an open-ended question, if history is any guide and as analysis of the plurality of scholarship within the key mainstream criminology journals testifies (Pratt & Priestley 1999).

THE STATE OF ACADEMIA: SILENCING THE DEBATE

To unpack the above discussion further, it is important to situate the intellectual challenges confronting independent thought in criminology within the wider academic environment (Aitkin 2013). In particular, multi-billion-dollar cuts to the higher education budget over the past few years, in conjunction with the demise of tenure and collective decision-making by schools and faculties, have created enormous uncertainty and fear. Freedom of expression for academics and engagement in vigorous debate on public policy (e.g. on the appropriateness of Australian involvement in the Vietnam war, communism, feminism and issues of race and women's rights), once considered core to academe, are under serious threat. Non-renewal of senior academic contracts on the basis of the discordance of their views with government policy positions (e.g. climate change, Indigenous affairs and immigration) is not uncommon.

Universities are now a major earner of export income for Australia—hence their 'rankings' are largely based on the generation of research income. The predominance of research activity over teaching has been cemented with establishment by the Commonwealth of the Excellence in Research for Australia (ERA) system. Run by the Australian Research Council, its role is to ensure accountability for research funding by assessing and ranking the contribution of academic staff to the production of knowledge in Australia against a set of metrics considered to be international benchmarks. Negative findings can spell disaster for academics and this inevitably influences the type of research academics choose to engage in. Only publications in the 'best' journals are recognised by the ERA, thereby establishing a hierarchy of research methodologies based on the intellectual persuasions of those journals (Aitkin 2013).

RESEARCH METHODS: BRIDGING THE 'DIVIDE'

There is no one research method that can provide all the answers in any particular research project. Yet, there is a longstanding division between quantitative criminology and qualitative criminology—a split that seems to pit different criminologists against each other. Specifically, there is an assumption within some circles that quantitative or empirical criminology is inherently conservative, while qualitative criminology is somehow always progressive and enlightening. The association of particular types of data collection and particular research methods with particular forms of intellectual work (e.g. positivist research on the dark figure of crime) can translate into critiques that are politically informed, rather than based on analysis of the evidence per se.

Conversely, other forms of research may be considered methodologically suspect if framed in terms of explicit social values (e.g. social justice), despite the acknowledged importance of the interplay between values, evidence and method in conducting and interpreting research. For example, Sherman and his colleagues (2006) employ a rigid hierarchy to rate the efficacy of research methodologies, with randomised control trials ranked as the best option, followed by quasi-experimental designs. All methodologies are ranked against the same scientific criteria regardless of context; that is, the object of inquiry or the research questions (Matthews 2009).

A major challenge for both criminological training and criminological research is to foster the notion of research collaboration in ways that will transcend this seeming divide. As Garland and Sparks (2000: 202) put it 'we can no longer "think" criminology in the institutional contexts and intellectual thought-styles in which it was previously located, especially if criminology is to remain strategically relevant from a public debate and social policy perspective'.

CONCLUSION

This chapter has provided an introduction to the politics and practices surrounding the 'doing' of criminology. Criminology is a type of intellectual labour. As such, it always occurs within a particular social context. This context, in turn, continually shapes the content and dynamics of criminological work, whether this is vocationally oriented or more critical in nature.

The second part of the chapter considered briefly different types of data collection and research methods commonly used in criminological research. Discussion of crime measurement illustrated the complexities of undertaking grounded research, and the ambiguities and limitations associated with analysis and interpretation of official statistics.

Chapter 2 examines in greater detail the role played by the media in shaping public perceptions of crime, the development of 'moral panics' and associated community discourse on crime control, and the institutional responses to crime in general and social deviance in particular.

DISCUSSION QUESTIONS

1   What is conservative criminology? What is critical criminology?

2   'The conditions under which researchers and criminologists work will necessarily influence the content of that work'. Discuss.

3   To whom should criminologists be accountable?

4   What is the relationship between social values and scientific research? Can there ever be such a thing as value-free criminology?

5   How relevant and influential is criminology in shaping public debate on and society's response to crime?

FURTHER READING

Ellis, L., Hartley, R.D. & Walsh, A. (2010) *Research methods in criminal justice and criminology: an interdisciplinary approach*, Rowman & Littlefield, Pennsylvania.

Israel, M. (2000) 'The commercialisation of university-based criminological research in Australia', *Australian and New Zealand Journal of Criminology*, 33(1): 1–20.

Jupp, V., Davies, P. & Francis, P. (eds) (2011) *Doing criminological research* (2nd edn), Sage, London.

Kayrooz, C., Kinnear, P. & Preston, P. (2001) *Academic freedom and commercialisation of Australian universities: perceptions and experiences of social scientists*, Discussion Paper No. 37, Australia Institute of Criminology, Canberra.

Weatherburn, D. (2011) 'Uses and abuses of crime statistics', *Crime and Justice Bulletin*, 153, Bureau of Crime Statistics and Research, Sydney.

CRIME AND THE MEDIA

2

CHAPTER OVERVIEW

- POPULAR IMAGES OF CRIME
- POPULAR IMAGES OF CRIME CONTROL
- CRIME WAVES AND MORAL PANICS
- FEAR OF CRIME AND DEVIANCY AMPLIFICATION
- ISSUES FOR CONSIDERATION
- CONCLUSION
- DISCUSSION QUESTIONS
- FURTHER READING

INTRODUCTION

As indicated in Chapter 1, how one thinks about crime is heavily influenced by what one knows about crime. The sources of knowledge include personal experience, academic textbooks and journal articles. They include word-of-mouth stories and family histories. They include legends and tales told down the ages. But most of all, today, our knowledge of crime is informed by media portrayals of harm.

This chapter provides an overview of how the media conveys ideas and images of crime, crime control and deviancy. The chapter begins with a brief description of common media images. It then considers some of the key concepts that underpin the media's substantive portrayals of crime—phenomena such as crime waves, moral panics and fear of crime—and the social consequences associated with these.

Exposure to popular images of crime presented in and through the mass media, including the increasingly influential internet, shapes how we come to 'know' crime and social harms. It also strongly influences the way many people think about related issues of crime control, including security, risk and vulnerability—issues that will be discussed in this chapter. The chapter concludes by raising a number of issues that continue to capture the imagination of criminologists and others about the effects and impacts of the mass media on societies and individuals.

POPULAR IMAGES OF CRIME

The electronic and print media have a significant influence on the general portrayal of crime in society; they are the principal generators of crime images that permeate popular consciousness (see Box 2.1). As such, the media have a tremendous impact on the conceptualisation of crime in society (see Bloustien & Israel 2003; Ericson et al. 1994; Grabosky & Wilson 1989; Jewkes 2004; Sarre 1994).

In both fictional and factual media programs and reportage, crime tends to be construed primarily as 'street crime'. Such crime is associated with personal terror and fear, with violence depicted as central. The sensationalisation of crime, in particular, has important implications for the **fear of crime** among certain sections of the population. This fear is heightened by the portrayal of crime as random in nature, with anyone and everyone a possible target for victimisation.

FEAR OF CRIME

Fear of crime is basically about emotions. The basis for such fears may be rational or irrational, depending upon specific types of evidence and specific types of harm.

BOX 2.1   COMMON MEDIA IMAGES OF OFFENDING

- Focus on street crime
- Implies a break down in 'law and order'
- The problem is seen as one of bad people and immoral acts
- Notion that crime and deviancy is getting worse
- A graphic emphasis on and portrayal of street violence
- Depiction of 'perverts' and bizarre behaviours as commonplace
- Use of social stereotypes, especially in regards to youth, the working class and ethnic minorities
- A key theme that the criminal or deviant is distinctive and identifiable

---

MORAL PANIC
A moral panic is generated when moral outrage is created by the media labelling certain groups or activities as deviant, and a threat to the social and moral order. The media convey a sensationalised image of crime and make unusual events usual events in our lives.

Furthermore, crime is often related to morality, and specifically to the decline of that morality. What is 'wrong' is plain for all to see and the 'criminal' is distinctive, and identifiably different from everyone else in society. Overall, the message conveyed by the media is that there is a continuing 'law-and-order' problem in society, and that things are constantly getting worse. Against this tide of disorder and lawlessness, the police and other crime fighters are generally portrayed as 'superheroes', who are infallible and who use violence legitimately in order to counter the violence of the streets.

The media play a central role in shaping our impressions of crime and crime control, as well as generating the impetus for legal changes and reinforcing particular types of policing strategies (see Box 2.2). For example, the **moral panics** (see Cohen 1973a,b) generated by the media on problems such as 'king hits' have lead to changes in the law (e.g. the introduction of one-punch laws) and the adoption of certain police methods (e.g. increased and aggressive street presence in particular locales). It has been demonstrated that the interests of the police and the media are entwined; they have a symbiotic relationship, in that the media rely upon the police for much of their information, and the police, in turn, use the media to portray and legitimise certain images relating to their work.

BOX 2.2   COMMON MEDIA IMAGES OF CRIME CONTROL

- A focus on successful apprehension
- Emphasis on the techniques of crime fighting, such as crime scene investigation
- The crime-fighter presented as hero
- Police violence seen as ordinary and/or good practice
- Confronting crime outside of legal procedure is appropriate if it works
- Major silences when it comes to police brutality, racism and corruption
- The theme that deviancy can and should be combated through any means necessary
- Police can break the law to enforce the law

The media thus convey a sensationalised image of crime, and a protective view of police and policing practices—and they create the impression that atypical criminal events are commonplace. As Grabosky and Wilson (1989: 11) comment: 'The most common types of crime according to official statistics, crimes against property, receive relatively little media attention. By contrast, crimes of violence, which are numerically uncommon, are accorded much greater coverage.'

In particular, there is a skewed focus on 'street crime' and bizarre events. Meanwhile, the destruction of the environment, domestic violence, white-collar crimes and occupational health and safety crimes (issues that are covered in subsequent chapters) tend not to receive the same kind of coverage or treatment by the mainstream media outlets.

POPULAR IMAGES OF CRIME CONTROL

With regard to crime control, the usual implication is that once a crime has been brought to the attention of the authorities, investigation will generally lead to detection and capture of the offender. This is very different from the reality of much police work, with a significant proportion of street crimes not proceeding to the prosecution stage. In fictional accounts of crime fighting, the police are usually endowed with special qualities or features (e.g. supernatural abilities, big guns and martial arts skills), and violence is central and always justified because of the nature of the 'criminals' at hand. The nature of actual policing is again misconstrued, with the mundane aspects—interviewing, reviewing file material, research, traffic regulation and so on—generally absent.

Another facet of fictional accounts is that the police are not accountable to anyone; they can even step outside the bounds of the law, because we all know they are on 'our' side. Thus, the police are always honest and incorruptible, even though evidence in real life shows that corruption of the police is a constant challenge. Notable examples include the Fitzgerald inquiry into police in Queensland (Fitzgerald 1989), and the Wood (1997) inquiry in New South Wales, which revealed widespread and systematic corruption.

Most of us probably know very little about the police and what they actually do. The overall perception of police work tends to be shaped predominantly by the media. There is almost no escaping the daily diet of crime and police stories (both fictional and 'factual'), since they are widely circulated through a variety of media—television and radio news broadcasts, 'cop' shows, infotainment programs, movies, the daily tabloids, magazine articles and talkback commentaries. Although varied, media representations tend to produce a somewhat skewed picture of both crime and policing.

MEDIA PRESENTATIONS OF POLICING

Since crime and policing are inextricably intertwined, portrayals of the crime problem almost inevitably will be associated with images of how best to engage in crime control. Although media portrayals of the police vary considerably, fictional images of police work give us some insight into the stereotypical roles and styles of policing (Cunneen & White 1995; Findlay 2004a). How these images and stereotypes relate to the real world of police work will be considered in Part 2 (see Chapters 16 and 17). Indeed, a major role of criminology is to separate out the myths and the simplistic representations of policing from the realities and the complexities of actual policing. Common media stereotypes include (Cunneen & White 1995):

- *The rogue cop:* the officer who uses unconventional methods to catch the 'bad guys'. Although the rogue cop employs violent techniques that overstep legal boundaries, this departure from formality is portrayed as acceptable, since society is being protected from predatory crime.
- *The boy scout:* 'the mountie always gets his man' type who, in contrast to the rogue cop, always does things by the book, and is honest and incorruptible. This is a wholesome type of officer, who smiles, speaks nicely to everyone and treats them fairly throughout the investigatory process.

- *The crazy cop:* this character is a bit twisted but is essentially okay. The craziness here is viewed as a special sort, necessary to handle the serious situations being faced, such as drug busts, espionage and anti-terrorist raids.
- *The superhero:* this character is endowed with distinctive special qualities. These may be physical, such as superhuman strength or expertise in martial arts, or they may be technological, such as reliance upon extraordinary weapons or advanced computer systems.
- *The sleuth:* the officer who uses brains rather than brawn in order to outwit the criminal mind, and who generally is more sophisticated and educated than your average street cop.

While in detective novels women have always been well represented at crime scenes in a variety of roles—whether they be investigative or prosecutorial—as police officers on television they are usually assigned peripheral roles. However, there are many recent programs that do incorporate active female characters in a wide variety of policing capacities (e.g. *Prime Suspect, Crime Scene Investigation, Law & Order* and *Homeland*). The issue is therefore less about the omission of women from certain aspects of police work and more about the types of problems they encounter (e.g. sexist responses from male officers). Furthermore, media portrayals may overstate the extent of women's involvement in senior management or criminal investigation positions, relative to their actual position in the police hierarchy (see, for example, Chapter 16).

Despite the vast array of police images, the idea essentially conveyed by most fictional accounts is that policing is largely a masculine occupation that is intrinsically violent. The fictional presentation of crime control tends to reinforce the stereotype that police work is mainly consumed with investigation, detection and capture of criminals. By downplaying the mundane, less visible aspects of daily police work, or ignoring them altogether, media portrayals of policing create and/or perpetuate a misconstrued perception of police as predominantly crime fighters.

CRIME WAVES AND MORAL PANICS

Deviancy as such is not always presented in the media as a bad thing. One only has to consider the weekly TV guide and the variety of shows that depict unusual events, people and places to know that being 'different' is not necessarily a problem. From portrayal of witches and vampires to individuals with strange personal habits (e.g. hyper-cleanliness), extraordinary attributes do not always equate to 'criminal'. Indeed, we can ask whether specific forms of deviancy are presented as:

- a problem
- negative
- a social problem
- due primarily to the unique features of an individual
- something to be worried about
- something requiring some kind of state or societal response.

To this list we can also add the question: is the 'deviant' always 'good' or 'bad', or is this left somewhat ambiguous sometimes in relation to the 'true' character of those deemed to be different?

For the purposes of crime drama, then, deviancy is not always criminal; it alludes to variation from a presumed 'norm' or 'standard' of behaviour, activity, appearance or capability. In some cases the deviancy itself is presented as a virtue, especially when it can assist in solving crimes and pursuing just causes (e.g. programs such as *The Mentalist*).

The portrayal of certain people or acts as bad or evil very much depends upon social context and the social content of media representations. In fiction, crimes of violence are frequently the staple diet of books, movies and TV shows. The spectacular, the disturbing and the visceral are highlighted in great (and gross) detail. Such crimes repulse us and yet attract our attention as well. Tales of the dark side of human nature have long fascinated people.

In non-fiction media, sensationalistic accounts of crime likewise predominate. More than this, however, crime tends to be framed in two major ways—through **crime waves** and moral panics. To understand why and how this is the case we need to consider the rationale or purpose of the media generally.

The media is essentially a profit-driven mechanism, the main objective of which is to sell its products by capturing as wide a share of the market as possible. Media content is therefore consciously selected and packaged in a manner designed to attract attention. Ericson et al. (1991: 345) argue that 'news outlets do not mirror reality but construct it in terms of their own criteria and resources'. Accordingly, the media paints a sensationalised portrait of crime; as mentioned above, it is presented as individualised, random, bizarre and violent (Daly 1995). Relatively common crimes, such as minor property theft, and some forms of white-collar crime such as work-related death and environmental destruction, receive little media attention, while extraordinary events, such as homicide (especially mass murder), attract disproportionate coverage (Perrone 2000, 1999; Warr 1991). The media also tends to 'frame' particular groups and individuals through specific sorts of typification (see Box 2.3).

CRIME WAVE
The way in which increased reporting of particular types of crime (especially street crimes such as assault, rape or homicide) increase public awareness of this crime. There need not have been an actual increase in the crime for a crime wave to occur; the increase exists only in public perception.

BOX 2.3   MEDIA TYPIFICATIONS OF YOUNG PEOPLE

The construction of a commonsense, consensual view of society is 'achieved' through continual processes of typification. Through these processes, what is 'normal' and what is 'deviant' become naturalised as everyday perceptions of the nature of social reality. By highlighting what is 'abnormal' or 'deviant', the media both passes judgment on what is seen as 'bad' behaviour and implicitly reaffirms the presumed status quo (White 1990: 106–7). In effect, the media 'selects events that are **atypical**, presents them in a **stereotypical** fashion, and contrasts them against a backcloth of normality which is **over-typical**' (Lea & Young 1984: 64). This is illustrated in media depictions of young people (White 1990):

- The 'ideal' young person:
  - Commercial advertising: healthy, wealthy and fun-loving; freedom, mobility, affluence
  - The 'exceptional' young person: achievements gained through exceptional talent or by serious hard work.
- Young people as a 'threat':
  - Challenging convention: lack of respect for authority, consumption of drugs and alcohol, alternative dress, hair or music
  - Juvenile offenders: vandals, hoons, larrikins, youth gangs.
- Young people as 'victims':
  - Problems of youth: youth suicide, homelessness, unemployment; objects of adult pity
  - Middle-class youth: controlled by drugs or alcohol.
- Young people as 'parasites':
  - Do nothing: lazy, lacking incentive, wasting their time, hanging around
  - Taking everything: reliant upon adults, on welfare, on hand-outs, leeching off others.

Analysis of how young people are presented in the media reveals a picture in which white, middle-class 'kids' are considered 'good', and minority or Indigenous and working-class young people are 'bad'. When the so-called 'good' young people are implicated in crime, this is seen as something that stems from events beyond their conscious control (e.g. unscrupulous drug dealers). When 'bad' young people are arrested for a crime, this is seen to be entirely their own fault and to reflect their essential evilness (e.g. they indulge in drugs by choice). The class, gender and ethnic inequalities in the way the media portrays young people and crime warrants ongoing analysis and critique.

CRIME WAVE REPORTING

The selectivity of media representations of crime is also manifest in the construction of 'crime waves'. By choosing to focus upon certain events, customarily serious street crimes, the media is able to influence public perceptions of crime trends; that is, by increasing social awareness of a certain type of crime, the impression is given that there is widespread commission of that crime. In a comprehensive analysis of media news content, however, Ericson et al. (1991) found that 90 per cent of crime stories were presented in the absence of substantiating evidence.

It is important, therefore, to separate the images and realities of crime in society. The media shape our perceptions of crime, and in the process they define crime in particular ways. A 'crime wave' refers to the way in which increased reporting of particular types of crime (usually street crimes, such as assault, rape, drug offences or homicide) increases the public awareness of this crime. Significantly, there need not have been an actual increase in the crime for a crime wave to occur. The increase exists only in public perception.

It needs to be reiterated that there need not be a connection between an increase in specific crimes and a crime wave. To take an example, we can consider the case of 'home invasion'. There is already some ambiguity with this term insofar as a run-of-the-mill home burglary can sometimes be conflated with a home invasion. In media parlance, however, home invasion is often tied to the bashing of elderly people in their own home. Extensive media coverage of several events, even if these are separated time-wise by weeks, months or even years, can convey the message that there is an increase in such crimes. The home invasion crime wave is thus an artefact of how the crime is reported, not necessarily a reflection of actual criminal trends.

A crime wave 'works' from the point of view of media sales partly because of the sensational nature of whichever crime the media focus on—whether this be drunken louts in public spaces, dangerous driving hoons in the local neighbourhood, home invasions or violent youth gangs. Graphic depictions of people and events, and the emphasis on stranger-danger, bolster the sense of imminent harm for members of the general public. The crime in question is presented as being ubiquitous—being everywhere and affecting everyone.

Another reason crime wave reporting can touch a public nerve is that such reporting tends to implicitly be based upon specific notions of risk and vulnerability. For example, while elderly people are the least likely to suffer assaults or more serious crimes (i.e. the risk is low), when they do they are most vulnerable to serious physical and psychological consequences (i.e. the harm is great). In other words, the impact is greater for them than others who may be victimised in a similar way. Fear of consequences, where the consequences are grave, can outweigh rational consideration of the odds of being harmed in this way. Conversely, some of those most likely to experience victimisation, such as young men being assaulted (see Chapter 6), are rarely considered victims in the same way, as it is presumed that they are more capable of withstanding such attacks. The risk is higher, but the harms are assumed to be less important than in the case of other groups in society (see Green 2007).

Whether the media actually shapes public perceptions of crime, or whether they are merely reflecting and reinforcing these perceptions, is a debatable issue (see, for example, Chan 1995). Nonetheless, the impact of media crime representations on law making and law enforcement cannot be ignored. The sensationalism surrounding crime waves can result in public moral panics and a heightened fear of crime (see, for example, Cohen 1972; Jewkes 2008; Pearson 1983; White 1990; Windshuttle 1978). These can, in turn, impact upon the political process insofar as governments often attempt to respond to public perceptions of crime by adopting innovative or tougher law-and-order initiatives. Media (mis)representation of singular events may also unintentionally create or fuel racist, sexist and other stereotypes, and thereby promote social divisiveness (see Chan 1995; Morgan & Poynting 2011; Poynting et al. 2004).

CONSEQUENCES OF CRIME WAVES

Crime waves thus can and do have real consequences, regardless of factual basis; for example, extensive media coverage of child abuse has led to changes in the law, such as the introduction of mandatory reporting of suspected incidents. Similarly, the fear generated by press coverage of assaults on elderly people or young women has periodically led to calls for more police, tougher sentences and greater police power. Saturation coverage of specific events, such as the mass slaying of dozens of people at Port Arthur in Tasmania in the late 1990s, can be seized upon to quickly tap into public opinion and change laws (in this instance, gun laws). The potential crime wave can be as frightening as the actual one-off event.

Given the close relationship between the police and the media, major questions can be asked as to who benefits from the selective reporting of specific crimes, especially around government budget time. There has been the suggestion, for example, that police unions, in particular, are not reticent to feed stories to the media as a means to garner pay rises, increased numbers and greater powers for their members (White & Richards 1992). The relatively recent advent of police media units also ensures a close symbiotic relationship between journalists and the police—a classic example of 'we'll feed you the stories, if you deal with crime stories in ways that are generally advantageous to us'.

MORAL PANIC

The notion of 'crime wave' is closely linked but separate from the concept of 'moral panic'. This refers to a concept first developed by Cohen (1972) in his study of the Mods and Rockers in England. This study showed how moral outrage was created by the media in the way they demonised certain groups (in this case, spectacular youth subcultures) as being deviant and a threat to the social and moral order. As Cohen (1972: 9) explains:

> Societies appear to be subject, every now and then, to periods of moral panic. A condition, episode, person or group of persons emerges to become defined as a threat to societal values and interests; its nature is presented in a stylised and stereotypical fashion by the mass media; the moral barricades are manned by editors, bishops, politicians and other right-thinking people; socially accredited experts pronounce their diagnoses and solutions; ways of coping are evolved or (more often) resorted to; the condition then

disappears, submerges or deteriorates and becomes more visible. Sometimes the object of the panic is quite novel and at other times it is something which has been in existence long enough, but suddenly appears in the limelight. Sometimes the panic passes over and is forgotten, except in folklore and collective memory; at other times it has more serious and long-lasting repercussions and might produce such changes as those in legal and social policy or even in the way society conceives itself.

The moral panic is inherently media-driven, but incorporates a wide variety of stakeholders and opinion makers. Inevitably, they involve societal condemnation of specific activities, whether it is the presumed link between satanic rituals and rock music, or mass shootings and the availability of guns. Ordinary events or persons can be represented as extraordinary occurrences and as threats to those around them. The moral panic serves to clarify (from particular points of view) the moral boundaries of the society in which they occur, ostensibly creating consensus and mutual concern (see Jewkes 2008).

A recent Australian book, *Outrageous! Moral panics in Australia* (Poynting & Morgan 2007) provides a series of case studies that identify specific turning points of intensified moral indignation around particular marginalised groups of people whose actions were seen as deviant. In particular, work is presented that considers such topics as riots, young car drivers, rock and roll music, youth subcultures and drug use, racialised portrayals of particular ethnic minority communities, gang rapes, and disease and sexuality. The book demonstrates how the media constructs certain groups and practices as being 'dangerous', 'deviant' and 'destructive', and how this is intertwined with social responses that call forth repressive measures and collective revulsion.

Moral panics are characterised by a series of interconnecting elements (see Box 2.4). They embody notions of **deviance** and a public awareness that there is a social problem that must be addressed. They demand collective action on the part of the public, and thus the mobilisation of concerned people to address and change specific social conditions (Goode & Ben-Yehuda 1994). As Becker (1963) observed many years ago, the social construction of 'outsiders'—the 'Other' in present-day academic discourse—is achieved through the concerted action of 'moral entrepreneurs', prominent individuals who take the lead in forging a social consensus that a problem exists and that it must be dealt with in a certain way.

DEVIANCE
Behaviour that breaks a rule within a social group and is viewed with disapproval and negatively labelled by the group. Deviance implies deviation from some presumed norm, and the transgression marks the person as an outsider to the mainstream.

BOX 2.4   KEY ELEMENTS OF A MORAL PANIC

- concern (e.g. heightened level of concern over certain kinds of behaviour)
- hostility (e.g. increased level of hostility toward group, now seen as 'enemy' of respectable society, and who are seen as responsible for the threat)
- consensus (e.g. substantial or widespread agreement among a given group [e.g. elites] or community and/or society-wide)
- disproportionality (e.g. degree of public concern over the behaviour itself, the problem it poses, or condition it creates is far greater than is true for comparable, even more damaging, actions—'objective molehills have been made into subjective mountains')
- volatility (e.g. they erupt suddenly and nearly as suddenly subside; they tend to be local and time-delimited)

Source: Goode & Ben-Yehuda (1994)

'FOLK DEVILS' AND ETHNICITY

Moral panic does not have to be discrete or one-off, nor are specific events necessarily separated from each other in mass media discourse. Indeed, as Poynting et al. (2004) convincingly argue, the persistence of any particular group being seen as a 'folk devil' (i.e. an object of hostility that focuses the moral and social anxieties embedded in a moment of panic) stems from the ways in which discourses are assembled over time. For instance, they point to the manner in which the 'Arab Other' has been socially constructed in the media in New South Wales. This has involved an ongoing cycle of moral panic, the elements of which have included ideological constructs of 'crime-prone Arab immigrants, violent Muslim terrorists, Middle-Eastern queue-jumping refugees with no respect for civilised rules, and Muslims who are seen as failing to integrate' (Poynting et al. 2004: 49). Both moral panic and the construction of folk devils are complicated social processes that operate over time and in ways that reinforce certain key messages and stereotypes.

Congregations of ethnically identifiable young people have frequently been publicly associated with images that are negative, dangerous and threatening (Asquith 2008; see also Chapter 7). The media have tended to emphasise the 'racial' background of youth groups, and their presumed criminality, to the extent that identification with a particular ethnic group becomes equated with 'gang membership'. The extra visibility of young ethnic minority people feeds the media's moral panics over gangs, as well as bolstering a racial stereotyping based upon physical appearance (White 2013a).

Research demonstrates, however, that crime is more of a socio-economic issue than a cultural one (Collins et al. 2000). There is in fact very little reliable evidence that shows that 'ethnic crime' as such is a problem. Instead, its roots appear to lie in factors such as inequality rather than ethnic background (see Chapter 7).What is a problem, however, is the 'racialised' reporting of crime in which the media uses ethnic identifiers in relation to some groups, but not others (e.g. Anglo-Celtic Australians). Moreover, the 'explanations' for such 'ethnic crime' tend to pathologise the group, as if there was something intrinsically bad about being, for example, Lebanese or, more generally, Middle Eastern. These distorted images also suggest that the origins of the criminality stem from outside Australia and are related to immigration policies and 'foreign' ideas and cultures, rather than the social and economic inequalities within this country.

This racialisation has a major impact upon public perceptions of the people and the issues portrayed, as well as on the response of state agencies such as the police. Such images and representations circulate at the global level and reinforce 'folk devil' reputation in the same moment as representing fundamental shifts in the nature of moral panic (see Box 2.5).

In the light of these trends, it is argued that globalisation can often accentuate nationalism and xenophobia. It does this through regimes of surveillance and the blurring of boundaries between policing and counter-terrorism; through authorities turning a blind eye to racist vilification and violence—a form of 'permission to hate'; and in struggles over the symbolic presence of Islam in Western cities (e.g. banning the building of mosques, minarets, Muslim schools and prayer rooms, and challenging the right of Muslim women to wear the veil—hijab, jilbab, niqab and burqa).

In a similar vein, the dominant construction of Aboriginality within the media is largely negative and tends to be associated with stereotypes such as the long-grasser, juvenile joyrider, petty thief and drunk (Jakubowicz & Goodhall 1994; Sercombe 1995; Trigger 1995). In their analysis of the images of Indigenous people in the media, Jakubowicz et al. (1994) argue that positive images tend to be limited to rural and remote locations, where their traditional way of life is romanticised. In contrast, images of Indigenous people in urban settings are presented in the context of criminality and disorder.

BOX 2.5   GLOBAL MORAL PANIC AND ISLAMOPHOBIA

In the global 'West', the racialised 'Muslim Other' has become the pre-eminent 'folk devil' of our time. Morgan and Poynting (2012) argue that this is a global process, involves popular demonology and is oriented toward the containment of communities of deviance associated with this demonisation. The nature of moral panic has been transformed in three key ways:

- First, from 'self-limiting, temporary and spasmodic' to there being connection between discrete moral panics insofar as the process of producing 'folk devils' is ongoing and cumulative. In other words, there is a 'global stock' upon which each 'splutter of rage' draws, engendering cycle after cycle of panic, of a variety of scope and localities.
- Second, from 'local or national panic' to the presentation of the threat to 'our civilisation' as transnational. That is, contemporary Islamophobia is grounded in popular anxieties around transnationalism, in which there operates a global cultural space in which this alternative transnational imagined community is nourished.
- Third, whereas the 'old' media were the key players in moral panic, nowadays the media have passed through epochal changes involving temporal as well as spatial compression. For instance, the media today is global and virtually instantaneous, plus there is new social media and the advent of 'citizen journalists' who contribute to the process of producing or challenging contemporary panics and folk devils.

Source: Morgan & Poynting (2012)

Whatever the setting or the subtext, the images are largely marginal to mainstream Australian culture so that Indigenous people are presented to the Anglo-Celtic gaze as separate and 'other'; as not belonging to ordinary, modern life.

These stereotyped images do little to promote understanding of the wide and varied experience of Indigenous people.

The social consequences of moral panics include such things as ostracising and penalising particular groups in society on the basis of their presumed immoral and threatening behaviour and presence (e.g. particular migrant or ethnic minority youth). It can involve passing of legislation and stepped-up police efforts to prevent or prohibit certain types of activity (e.g. certain types of drug use). It may involve the violation of human rights under the rubric of the greater good (e.g. ill treatment of asylum seekers). The persistence of moral panic and crime wave discourses in the media also feeds a more generalised fear of crime, a phenomenon that likewise shapes how people interact and relate to one another.

FEAR OF CRIME AND DEVIANCY AMPLIFICATION

The fear of crime is today a powerful tool in shaping public opinion (e.g. influencing perceptions of behaviour and everyday activities), driving government policy (e.g. usually toward more punitive criminal justice responses), producing commercial rewards (e.g. through the sale of security devices) and more generally making all of us feel ill at ease in our homes, neighbourhoods, streets and even workplaces. The media obviously has a major role to play in this process, both through fictional portrayals of crime and harm, and news and current affairs programs and articles that focus on dramatic instances of violence and mayhem.

What distinguishes 'fear of crime' from the 'moral panic' is that the former has come to be a central part of social life (see Box 2.6), which the latter feeds into. To put it differently, while one can select and identify particular moral panics (although these are ever-present and continuously overlap), the present era has been characterised as being engulfed by a generalised sense of risk and uncertainty—a background radiation of popular anxiety (Poynting & Morgan 2007). Constant media attention given to threats, risks, harms and danger reinforce this overwhelming sense of unease and anxiousness. This, in turn, creates a series of specific and general feedback loops.

BOX 2.6   CONTEXTUALISING THE FEAR OF CRIME

Fear of crime is profitable for those who have something to sell. For the media organisations, that 'something' is fear itself, since this is a major generator of interest, and hence income. Stories aimed at mobilising deep-seated anxieties in the public are hard to ignore. And people will pay to find out about those apparent and alleged threats and risks which, while frightening to know, are nonetheless seemingly present in their lives.

In the book *Inventing fear of crime*, Lee (2007) explores why and how fear of crime has come to feature so prominently in contemporary political and social life. He argues that a whole industry has arisen around the concept in ways that are self-serving for criminologists (e.g. research grants for surveys of crime victims) and politicians alike (e.g. tapping into emotional reservoirs that enhance election campaigns). Importantly, Lee (2007) describes the making of 'fearing subjects', which are formed in the context of major social structural changes associated with neo-liberalism. In a nutshell, wider political, economic and ideological changes have produced active subjects whose fear of crime becomes their own responsibility to govern. The transformation in state governance away from direct responsibility for citizen welfare and safety thus translates into the so-called 'responsibilised citizen'. In this kind of citizenship, it is up to each individual to seek their own market solutions to their fear of crime problem and the avoidance of risky situations (e.g. by purchasing deadlocks and security doors or by becoming part of a gated community).

Analysis of the fear of crime has been usefully organised around themes of power relations and the relationship between fear and power (see, for example, Lee & Farrall 2009). Specifically, study has been directed at analysis of the power to define fear of crime in particular ways to particular political ends (e.g. skewing crime statistics such that a tough law and order agenda is favoured by the public). Other work has examined the power of fear of crime to operate as a form of social exclusion (e.g. certain ethnic minority men who experience being feared may exclude themselves from some arenas of public space such as bars and city streets). The power of fear of crime discourses has also been looked at insofar as these discourses help to construct everyday geographies and subjectivities (e.g. feelings of anxiety and feelings of where we feel safe from victimisation).

Source: Lee (2007)

DEVIANCY AMPLIFICATION

Various studies have pointed to the ways in which the media portray certain types of youth subcultures, which in turn lead to a form of **deviancy amplification** (Cohen 1973a,b; Collins et al. 2000; Young 1971). That is, the sort of public labelling pertaining to some groups of young people actually generates further 'deviant' behaviour in the labelled group. More generally, the link is made between the actual cultural, social and economic experiences of working-class young people, and the manner in which the state—particularly the police—intervenes in their lives, both coercively (shown by arrest rates) and ideologically (e.g. through the promulgation of 'moral panics' over young people's behaviour and attitudes).

Consider for the moment the impact of media reporting on graffiti (White 1990). This issue has attracted much scrutiny and sensational treatment by the mass media over the years. Whether pitched at the level of crime wave (i.e. increasing incidents of graffiti) or moral panic (i.e. increasing dangerousness of graffiti gangs), the periodic highlighting of graffiti as a social wrong can generate police action at those times. The combination of action by authority figures and media targeting has other social consequences as well.

For instance, constant or intense media attention can both affirm a 'graffiti gang' identity, and help to amplify this identification for the young people involved. Persistent media stories on graffiti can thus reinforce the notoriety of such activity. One result of this is the burgeoning of graffiti groups, which thrive on the media attention given to their work. Media coverage itself may thus actually contribute to the bonding of individuals around a central activity that simultaneously acts as a key to subcultural identification.

Looked at from a cultural criminology perspective (see Chapter 5), the buzz or kick from doing graffiti can be enhanced by the media. In a similar vein, performing 'stupid' or 'insane' physical stunts that are then conveyed to millions via YouTube ensures the repetition of these same stunts, regardless of how many young people get hurt or injured in the process. Everyone, it seems, wants to be a 'jackass'. Reputations can be made (or lost) through the medium of the internet and other forms of mass communication.

Pushing things to the extreme is in part a social response to the tendency toward sanitised public spaces (e.g. enclosed shopping centres and malls) and a heavy fixation with safety and security. Thus, 'fear appears to be a condition of the risk society, not specifically fear of crime, but fear of harm in general. As a result, many people will be afraid who are not necessarily part of those social groups generally thought to be more vulnerable to harm, but they will perceive themselves, their homes, and their families as being under threat' (Green 2007: 111). The media is instrumental in fostering this 'fear of harm in general'. Paradoxically, the media is also instrumental in allowing significant communication space to those who push the boundaries of what is deemed safe and reasonable. While social boundaries are determined through such processes, what lies beyond the conventional then becomes attractive to many who are bored or unchallenged by the promise of private security.

Specific feedback loops can be conceptualised in terms of processes of deviancy amplification. At a more general level, the fear of crime also has widespread implications for policy and governmental decision-making. Here the 'feedback' is less about social constructions of deviancy and crime than issues pertaining to social control and criminal justice policy. Fear of crime is basically about emotions. The basis for such fears may be rational or irrational, depending upon specific types of evidence and specific types of harm. However, the key point is that such feelings propel people to act, to think and to behave in particular ways.

The affective dimensions of social life thus play an important part in shaping human behaviour and institutional practices. Highly volatile criminal cases can draw forth disproportionate reactions from the public and judiciary alike. The so-called 'ethnic gang rape' is especially susceptible to this kind of treatment (see, for example, Dagistanli 2007; Warner 2004). Playing the race card within media discourse can also be used to entrench themes of racial violence (and judicial leniency), as in the case of the moral climate surrounding the introduction of 'get tough' legislation in Western Australia (Hinds 2005).

Political support for tougher sentences and harsher law and order regimes largely depends upon a cultural context in which popular punitiveness is ingrained rather than challenged. A universalised fear of crime provides the ground upon which emotive responses to complex social problems can predominate over and above those offered on the basis of criminological evidence or alternative political ideologies. Under such circumstances, the affective will beat out the rational every time.

ISSUES FOR CONSIDERATION

MEDIA IMPACT ON LEGISLATION

Media tabloidisation and highlighting of lethal street violence, particularly in areas such as Kings Cross in Sydney, saw public calls for the term 'king hit' to be replaced by 'coward punch' and put pressure on the New South Wales Government to act quickly, symbolically and forcefully in response to cases such as those of Thomas Kelly and Daniel Christie (two men who died after being 'king hit' in the Cross). One-punch laws were subsequently introduced in January 2014, which added two new offences to the *Crimes Act 1900* (NSW):

- assault causing death
- an aggravated version of that offence where the offender is intoxicated at the time of committing the offence.

Maximum penalty: imprisonment for 20 years.

Aggravated maximum: imprisonment for 25 years.

These changes largely ignored the recommendations of law reform commissions in Australia (especially Western Australia and Queensland) that had expressly recommended against their introduction (Quilter 2014). Commentators have criticised this particular Act on the basis of technical difficulties in the Act itself (e.g. defining 'intoxication'), as well as the lack of a definitional or operational gap requiring such law reform (Quilter 2014: 101). Media frenzies such as this basically lead politicians to enact bad law. As Garland (2001: 112) puts it, responses tend to be 'urgent and impassioned, built around shocking but atypical cases, and more concerned to accord with political ideology and popular perception than with expert knowledge or the proven capabilities of institutions'. In this instance, the increase in media reporting on the topic of 'pubs and violence' since 2003 has not been matched by figures from the NSW Bureau of Crime Statistics and Research, which show that, if anything, there has been a marked decline in non-domestic assault incidents recorded by NSW Police in Kings Cross over the past five years (BOCSAR 2014). Bad law is thus founded upon bad news that actually distorts overall trends.

PORTRAYAL OF POLICE AND 'VILLAINS'

Different images of police and policing connote different styles and approaches to policing. The dominant portrayal of police at any point in time reflects social context and social change. For example, early media portrayals of the police in Britain featured narratives in which the police were close to the community, and community policing was the accepted style of policing (see Jewkes 2008). By contrast, one need only think of the arrival of 'Dirty Harry' (a Clint Eastwood character) in the 1970s and the emphasis on violence and guns as the means to resolve conflict and deal with offenders. With so many different crime and cop shows on television, from a wide diversity of national locations (e.g. the United States, Canada, Germany, Australia, New Zealand and Britain), it would be of interest to study the specific types of images that define what contemporary policing is or ought to be like, and to compare these cross-nationally and over time.

The popular appeal of recent programs such as the *Underbelly* series also needs to be explained. Do viewers relate to and empathise with the villains and, if so, why is this the case? At least in some instances, the sex, drugs, violence and excitement of criminality—at least as portrayed on screen—could well be seen as attractive rather than dissuading people from a 'life of crime'. On the other hand, how do such shows feed into phenomena such as crime waves, moral panics and fear of crime? The media may present distorted views of crime and crime control, but the social impact or ramifications of such distortions are certain to be complex and multi-directional.

This discussion raises some of the most perennial and perplexing questions about the mass media:

- On the one hand, it is universally acknowledged that what the electronic and print media convey has an impact on how people think generally about issues such as crime, terrorism, violence and so on. Otherwise, for example, why would advertisers, politicians and public relations firms spend so much money on and in an industry that had no or little social influence? The notions of moral panic and fear of crime are entirely premised upon the media having widespread effects on public attitudes and behaviour.

- On the other hand, big questions remain as to the particular effect of the media on specific individuals and groups of people. What evidence is there to support or deny particular 'media effects' in concrete cases? To what extent are images promulgated by the mass media a major cause of or contributory factor in criminal, harmful or deviant behaviour? For example, do movies about gangs create gang-like responses among groups of teenagers? Does hate crime stem from social reactions to the extensive use of stereotypes and vilification of certain groups by the media? How do action movies, war video games and DVDs that feature horror and terror themes (and, we might add, the nightly news) sensitise or desensitise viewers to real-world suffering and atrocities?

- Moreover, it is not only attitudes and beliefs that may be conveyed and that may be influential. Crime fiction, both print and visual, often provides detailed information about how particular crimes are committed (and solved). Knowledge and techniques are important components of the processes that underpin harm and victimisation. The 'how to' can be just as important as the 'why' when it comes to engagement in specific acts that do harm. Crime, too, is learned behaviour, and the mass media can be a significant if not entirely reliable teacher.

- Finally, what evidence is there that the mass media can have prosocial effects on the public? Concerted publicity campaigns, usually paid for by government, on domestic violence, for example, are justified on the grounds that they are meant to contribute to a general cultural change in regards to such violence. How effective are such campaigns, and what is the basis for the effectiveness? For instance, drink driving campaigns (e.g. 'if you drink and drive you're a bloody idiot') may be necessary but not sufficient to curb driving while under the influence of alcohol. The success of such campaigns may lie in the fact that they are multi-pronged and, as such, involve such things as mandatory sentencing for drunk drivers and extensive breath-testing on the part of the police.

CONCLUSION

This chapter has provided a brief overview of key concepts and trends associated with crime and the media in Australia. The mass media are dominated by privately owned, commercially oriented businesses. The fortunes of the industry are dominated by the revenue to be gained by sensationalist accounts of crime. Newspapers, television programs, fiction and factual material, internet sites and so on heavily depend upon discourses that stress the deviant and the unusual. More often than not, this translates into a fixation on crime and the promulgation of the fear of crime.

The 'silences' in media portrayals are as socially significant as what actually appears. Instances of social injustice, abuse of authority, state crime and harms perpetrated by the powerful feature less than the mundane crimes of the working class and the spectacular crimes of the ethnic minority. The 'success' stories of innovative justice likewise rarely feature in the overall media treatment of crime and criminal justice (Graham & White 2014). Moreover, when the reality of crime—as measured and evaluated through the lens of criminological research and institutional reporting—is considered carefully, the images of crime and crime control presented in the media are shown to be highly suspect. That this is indeed the case is demonstrated in the chapters to follow.

DISCUSSION QUESTIONS

1 What are the media, and why are they so powerful?

2 Consider the main crime-related programs on TV over the past week. What are the predominant images of 'crime' and the 'criminal' that they present'?

3 Are crime waves real or do they only have real consequences?

4 What is the relationship between moral panics and the fear of crime, and how does each affect everyday life?

5 We may say that we do not believe everything we see or hear in the media—but how then do we distinguish between what is 'truth' and what the media says is happening?

FURTHER READING

Dagistanli, S. (2007) '"Like a pack of wild animals": moral panics around "ethnic" gang rape in Sydney', in S. Poynting & G. Morgan (eds) *Outrageous! Moral panics in Australia*, ACYS Publishing, Hobart.

Jewkes, Y. (2008) *Media & Crime*, Sage, London.

Lee, M. & Farrall, S. (eds) (2009) *Fear of crime: critical voices in an age of anxiety*, Routledge-Cavendish, Oxon.

Morgan, G. & Poynting, S. (2012) 'Introduction: the transnational folk devil', in Morgan & Poynting (eds) *Global Islamophobia: Muslims and moral panic in the west*, Ashgate, Farnham.

Quilter, J. (2014) 'One-punch laws, mandatory minimums and "alcohol-fuelled" as an aggravating factor: implications for NSW criminal law', *International Journal of Crime, Justice and Social Democracy*, 3(1): 81–106.

3

TRADITIONAL CRIMINOLOGICAL THEORY

CHAPTER OVERVIEW

- GAINING PERSPECTIVE
- POSITIVISM AND INDIVIDUAL CRIMINAL BEHAVIOUR
- LIBERTARIAN AND TRADITIONAL CONSERVATIVE THEORIES
- ISSUES FOR CONSIDERATION
- CONCLUSION
- DISCUSSION QUESTIONS
- FURTHER READING

INTRODUCTION

The study of crime is essentially the study of society; how we define and view crime is itself shaped by our conceptions of what kind of society we live in, and what sort of society we would like to see. The study of crime is also a study of behaviour; its explanations and causes. Theories of *criminogenesis* (causes of crime) emphasise many different reasons for committing criminal offences or engaging in deviant behaviour. Some theories challenge how we define 'crime' and 'delinquency', arguing that there is no essential definition or reality of crime. The focus of the many different theories varies considerably. Some concentrate on examining the criminal act; some the offender. Others see crime as a social process; still others look at it in terms of power relations.

The manner in which the causes are represented has major implications for strategies of crime prevention and crime control. Again, depending upon the theory adopted, the solution may be seen in terms of punishment, treatment or rehabilitation of offenders; restitution involving victims and offenders; or major structural change requiring transformations in the nature of basic social institutions. Specific theories, therefore, arise from specific ways of viewing crime, the role of criminal justice institutions and the appropriate strategies for grappling with criminal and deviant behaviour.

This chapter is the first of three that provide a brief examination of prominent criminological perspectives on crime (for elaboration, see White et al. 2012). Two of the most important foundational perspectives—the classical and positivist conceptions of crime, criminal behaviour and crime control—are the present focus. While each of these theoretical approaches tends to centre on the individual, when considered together, it is clear that they provide diametrically opposed views as to where the offender fits within the broader criminological explanation. The chapter concludes with a discussion of New Right variations on the themes expressed in both classical and positivist perspectives.

CRIMINO-LOGICAL THEORY The frameworks within which the main explanations for criminal behaviour or criminality are located. Perspectives include the individual; the situational; and the structural.

GAINING PERSPECTIVE

Criminological theory can be presented in abstract fashion as discrete perspectives or approaches. Each approach or paradigm attempts to understand a particular phenomenon by asking certain types of questions, using certain concepts and constructing a certain type of framework of analysis and explanation. In practice, it is rare to find government departments or academic criminologists relying exclusively on any one criminological framework or approach. Often, wide-ranging ideas and concepts are combined in different ways in the course of developing policy, or in the study of a specific empirical problem.

For the sake of presentation, it is nevertheless useful to present 'ideal types' of the various theoretical strands within criminology. The use of ideal types provides a means by which we can clarify main ideas and identify important differences between the broad approaches adopted in the field. An ideal type does not exist in the real world. Rather, the intention is to abstract from concrete situations the key elements or components of a particular theory or social institution, and possibly to exaggerate these elements in order to highlight the general tendency or themes of the particular perspective (see Freund 1969). An **ideal type** is an analytical tool, not a moral statement of what ought to be. It refers to a process of picking up different aspects of social phenomena and combining them into a typical model or example. For instance, an ideal bureaucracy would include impartial and impersonal merit and promotion structures, set rules and regulations, and a hierarchical chain of command. We know, however, that people who work in bureaucracies are not always promoted on the basis of qualifications; nor is decision-making always rational. By constructing a model of a typical bureaucracy we are able to compare how different organisations actually are structured and how they in fact work in the real world.

Criminological theories tend to locate their main explanation for criminal behaviour or criminality at the *individual*, the *situational* and the *structural* levels (see Box 3.1). Some researchers find the causes of crime in looking at the personal characteristics and background of individual offenders. Others examine aspects of situations within which the individual has been placed, the types of interactions that person has with other people, and how these contacts influence that person's behaviour. Finally, there are those who look to the nature of society as a whole for their explanation. A conservative perspective, for example, may see crime as ultimately stemming from the lack of moral values and inadequate discipline in a society. Liberal and more radical analyses point to issues relating to inequality and social divisions. The vantage point from which one examines crime—from a focus on personal characteristics through to societal institutions—shapes the ways in which one thinks about and acts upon criminal justice matters.

IDEAL TYPE
An ideal type is an analytical tool, rather than a moral statement of what ought to be. It comprises a process of choosing different aspects of social phenomena and combining them into a typical model or example.

BOX 3.1   MAIN FOCUS OF TRADITIONAL THEORIES

FOCUS ON INDIVIDUAL FACTORS

The focus here is on the personal or individual characteristics of the offender or victim. This type of study considers, for example, the influence of intelligence, mental illness, substance abuse or motivation on the nature of crime causation or victimisation. This level of analysis tends to look to biological, psychological or biosocial factors that are said to have an important determining role in why certain individuals engage in criminal activity. The key concern is with explaining crime or deviant behaviour in terms of the choices or characteristics of the individual. Typical explanations for offending include:
- *people choose to commit crime*
- *biological reasons*, such as different levels of intelligence, lead poisoning or abnormal chromosomes

- *psychological reasons*, such as aggression or lack of self-control
- *biosocial reasons*, such as abusive or dysfunctional childhoods or a lack of love and inhibited self-control through exposure to screen violence
- *pathological conditions*, such as mental illness.

FOCUS ON SITUATIONAL FACTORS

The site of analysis here is the immediate situation or circumstances within which criminal activity or deviant behaviour occurs. Attention is directed to the specific ecological or environmental factors and opportunities available for the commission of certain types of offences as well as the sociology of deviance; that is, how individuals define their life situation and how the behaviour of individuals is variously labelled by the criminal justice system and other members of society. A key concern is the nature of the interaction between different players within the system, the effect of local environmental factors on the nature of this interaction, and the influence of group behaviour on social activity. Typical explanations for offending include:

- *inadequate socialisation*, such as a lack of education in distinguishing between 'right' and 'wrong'
- the result of *negative labelling*, such as the stigma of being called a 'delinquent' or 'deviant'
- *poor school performance*, including a low level of attainment or alienation from learning institutions
- *poor parenting*, including lack of supervision, neglect or maltreatment
- *homelessness*, as characterised by a lack of stable and safe shelter
- *neighbourhood-scale mechanisms*, including social and demographic risks (e.g. racial heterogeneity), high levels of social disorganisation, low institutional resources and poor collective efficacy
- *peer group, subcultural influences and social learning*, including participation in deviant or criminal social networks or youth gangs, viewing violent media images and playing violent video games.

FOCUS ON SOCIAL STRUCTURAL FACTORS

This approach tends to look at crime in terms of broader social relationships—and the major social institutions—of the society as a whole. The analysis makes reference to the relationship between classes, sexes, socio-economic status (employed versus unemployed), different ethnic and racial groups, and various other social divisions in society. It also investigates the operation of specific social institutions, such as education, the family, work and the legal system, in constructing and responding to crime and deviant behaviour. Typical explanations for offending include:

- *colonialism and social disempowerment*, such as denial of culture
- *racism and discrimination*, such as negative biases in the system
- *poverty, inequality and social marginalisation* including social exclusion and a lack of means to attain desired ends
- *unemployment*, such as a lack of opportunities for paid work.

Within criminology there is a natural diversity of viewpoints, as different writers and researchers see the world through very different analytical spectacles. The objectives and methods of analysis used in criminology thus reflect certain underlying ideas and concerns of the writer. In reading criminological material then, it is important to examine the assumptions of the writers, the key concepts they use and the methods and arguments employed to support their theories, in order to identify their conceptions of society and of human nature, and the kinds of reforms or institutions that they ultimately support. It is also important to identify the silences in a particular theory or tradition; that is, the questions not being asked, and why. Finally, it is crucial to consider the social relevance of the theory or perspective. What does it tell us about our society and the direction our society is or ought to be taking? For students of criminology to develop an informed view of key issues, it is important to understand that, fundamentally, the study of crime involves identifying and analysing the values and opinions of various criminologists.

CLASSICAL THEORY AND INDIVIDUAL CHOICE

The advent of criminological thinking can be traced back to the middle of the eighteenth century, when social philosophers began turning their minds to systematic consideration of concepts such as crime and law. This thinking gave birth to the classical school of thought, which has at its core a utilitarian philosophy of crime and punishment. According to **classical theory**, human beings are considered equally capable of reason, and hence are deemed responsible for their actions. All individuals are considered to have free will, which enables them to act in their own best interests. However, in recognition of the possibility of predation from others, individuals agree to forgo some of their freedoms in exchange for protection by the state.

The law then is a natural expression of legitimate political authority; a reflection of the consensual relationship between the state and individual members of a society. Since individuals are viewed as having equal power to reason and support a rational system of justice, any laws and rules developed under such a system are seen to be reasonable and binding for all (known as the *social contract*). Thus, rule is by consensus, which in turn is rationally established. As such, an individual who engages in crime either acts irrationally or knowingly makes a bad choice. The purpose of punishment within the law is therefore to deter individuals from impinging upon and violating others' rights and interests, thereby affirming the legitimacy of the social contract.

The two leading figures in the development of classical criminology were Cesare Beccaria and Jeremy Bentham (see White et al. 2012).

CESARE BECCARIA

In 1764 Cesare Beccaria, an Italian enlightenment philosopher, wrote *On crimes and punishment*, a profound critique of the existing systems of law and criminal justice (Beccaria 1764). His treatise was an indictment on the arbitrary and inconsistent nature of judicial decision-making characteristic of the *anciens regimes* (monarchic and aristocratic rule) across Europe, which included the practice of conviction without trial and the personal granting of mercy. It also condemned the unduly harsh and barbaric forms of punishment dispensed by the courts of the day, which included extensive use of the death penalty and the routine use of torture. Beccaria argued that these practices, primarily aimed at exacting retribution, were irrational and therefore ineffective as a basis for crime control (Paternoster 2010).

According to Beccaria, the basis for all social action should be the utilitarian concept of the greatest happiness for the greater number in society. Translated into the criminal justice sphere, this meant that crime should be considered an injury to society as a whole rather than just the injured parties. The purpose of punishment should therefore not simply be oriented towards social revenge or retribution, but should also ensure the greatest good for society; that is, it should be oriented towards deterring individuals and others from committing crime, rather than wreaking vengeance. Essentially, prevention of crime was considered more important than the punishment itself.

CLASSICAL THEORY
Classical theory locates the source of criminality within the rational, reasoning individual, and sees it as a matter of choice and intent on the part of the offender. The classical school of criminology emphasises choice, responsibility and intent.

Humans were seen as essentially rational and motivated by self-interest. For punishment to work as a deterrent, it needed to be rationally applied. Beccaria proposed a set of principles to make the exercise of authority more rational. These principles were premised on the notion that as self-interested and rational creatures, a more rational system of justice would actually be more effective at deterring crime.

To this end, Beccaria proposed a series of legal reforms, including:

- codification and publication of the law—clearly written and communicated laws and punishments, which assisted in educating people to exercise their choices in an informed manner
- abolition of draconian and arbitrary punishments and restraints on judicial power—humane but sufficiently severe punishment (severe enough to offset the perceived rewards of crime) applied in a systematic manner rather than on the individual whim of the judiciary
- administration of punishment in a swift and certain manner—for example, through the establishment of a professionalised police and judicial system
- proportionality of punishment—punishment that fit the crime; that is, punishment commensurate with the harm caused to society, with least harmful acts punished least severely and those causing greatest harm punished most severely.

JEREMY BENTHAM

UTILITA-RIANISM
A principle central to classical theory, which is grounded in normative ethics. This principle holds that a normative course of action is the one that results in maximum utility, typically defined as maximising happiness and minimising suffering.

The classical view of criminology was further developed in the writings of Bentham, a British philosopher and social reformer (1789). In particular, Bentham provided a more robust intellectual foundation for Beccaria's deterrence-based model of human behaviour, positioning human beings and society within a normative framework of **utilitarianism**. Bentham argued that all behaviour is hedonistic, reducible to the universal twin goals of seeking pleasure and avoiding pain, which operate through the principle of utility. Actions that result in pleasure bring utility, while those that produce pain result in disutility. Individual happiness is thus maximised when the sum total of activity brings greater pleasure than pain. The inclination to offend is thus based on rational choice; a conscious decision that the offending action will bring, on balance, greater pleasure than pain. Importantly, Bentham recognised that the pleasures and pains that inform assessment of utility, and therefore determine behaviour, are subjective (those understood by the individual) and not necessarily those that exist objectively (Paternoster 2010).

For Bentham, the criminal law provides a framework of social interaction; it is a social contract between individuals and the state, based upon a rational exchange of rights and obligations, which delimits the boundaries within which individuals can pursue their own conceptions of wellbeing. Given that human beings exercise free will and have equal capacity to reason, enforcement of the criminal law should be based on making adherence the most rational thing to do, in the light of the fact that violation would almost certainly mean the experience of negative sanctions. Thus, punishment should offer more pain than transgression of the law is worth.

RESPONSIBILITY FOR ONE'S ACTIONS

Classicism locates the source of criminality within the rational, reasoning individual, and sees it as a matter of choice and intent on the part of the offender. Related to this is the notion that, in order for individuals to make rationally informed choices, they should be made familiar with the law and its punishments. Punishment is intended to deter individuals from making the wrong choices with regard to both their immediate and future activities, through the threat of possible pain (penalty). Since individuals are free moral agents, and act rationally and deliberately to maximise their self-interests, they must be held responsible for their actions.

Classical criminal policy focuses primarily on the criminal act, and suggests equal punishments for equal crimes. The emphasis is on equal treatment because of the presumption of equal rationality and the necessity for equality in legal proceedings. The punishment should be commensurate with the severity of the crime. It is assumed that, through punishment, the offending individual will come to see obeying the law as the most rational of choices. For the sake of equality, it is thought that penalties should be fixed prior to sentencing, and be administered on the basis of the actual offence that has been committed, rather than on the basis of any prior offences committed or speculation regarding the offender's possible future offending.

The classical school of criminology emphasises human agency; that is, choice, free will, intent and therefore responsibility. This is a voluntaristic conception of crime, which locates the reasons for crime within the individual social actor. It stresses equality before the law, and equality in people's capacity to reason and make choices. Crime is seen as a violation of the legal consensus, which itself is seen to reflect the social contract. It is regarded as imperative that the law be codified, neutral and impartial, and punishment should be intended to deter individuals according to the pleasure–pain principles. The main emphasis of classical criminology is on the criminal act, and the equal and systematic application of laws in relation to this act (see Box 3.2). In essence, as evident in Chapters 19 and 23, the classical school of thought forms the cornerstone of contemporary criminal justice systems in Australia.

BOX 3.2   KEY IDEAS OF THE CLASSICAL PERSPECTIVE

- Humans are *rational, hedonistic* and *utilitarian*; they calculate pleasure and pain.
- Humans *exercise agency*; they make choices on the basis of *free will*.
- Individuals *choose* to commit crime out of *self-interest*; they are *responsible* for their actions.
- The law represents a *social contract* between individuals and the state; crime is an act that breaches the social contract.
- *Punishment* is an appropriate response to crime and serves the purpose of *deterrence*.
- In punishing the offender, the law should focus on the *act* and what has been done *not* on past or future behaviour.
- To maximise its deterrent capabilities, punishment should be *proportional* and applied *uniformly*, *swiftly* and *with certainty*.

THE 'JUST DESERTS' APPROACH

Today, classical thinking is evident in legal doctrine that emphasises conscious intent or choice (e.g. the notion of *mens rea*—the guilty mind) in both sentencing principles (e.g. the idea of culpability or responsibility) and the structure of punishment (e.g. gradation of penalties according to seriousness of offence).

Philosophically, the classical perspective sees its modern counterpart in the 'just deserts' approach to sentencing. In this perspective, four basic principles are proposed (see Pettit & Braithwaite 1993; see also Chapter 23):

1   No one other than a person found to be guilty of a crime must be punished for it.
2   Anyone found to be guilty of a crime must be punished for that crime.

3   Punishment must not be more than of a degree commensurate with, or proportional to, the nature or gravity of the offence and culpability of the criminal.

4   Punishment must not be less than of a degree commensurate with, or proportional to, the nature or gravity of the offence and culpability of the criminal.

Such principles seek to focus on the offence, not the offender; to deter the offender from reoffending according to the pleasure–pain principle; and to ensure that justice is served by dispensing equal punishment for similar crimes. 'Just deserts' philosophy eschews individual discretion and rehabilitation as aims of the justice system. Justice must be done (i.e. proportional punishment must be meted out) and must be seen to be done (i.e. there should be no exceptions).

THE PROBLEM OF INDIVIDUAL DIFFERENCES

The main problem of classical theory and its variants, such as rational choice theory, is that they tend to ignore individual differences between criminal actors. They assume that everyone is a rational actor capable of exercising free choice. Behavioural economists challenge the concept of perfect rationality, arguing that individuals make decisions on the basis of bounded rationality, drawing on imperfect knowledge and generally employing rules of thumb or judgmental heuristics that are shaped by their culture, learned behaviour, normative expectations, emotional state, risk sensitivities and immediate environment (Clark & Cornish 1985; Jacobs & Wright 2010). Moreover, they ignore the existence of 'irrational' offenders—young people, those with a mental illness or disorder or intellectual disability and those affected by drugs or alcohol—who do not have the same rational capacities as others and are thus singled out within the law as possessing diminished responsibility for their actions (Davey 2014; Ritchie 2011). It is noteworthy that these offenders comprise the majority of the prison population (see Chapter 25). Recognition of diminished responsibility is particularly evident within the juvenile justice area; for example, in legal doctrine pertaining to the age of criminal responsibility and *doli incapax*, both of which relate to competency and responsibility. A key tension within the classical tradition is whether to emphasise full criminal responsibility on the part of juveniles, or whether to acknowledge different capacities depending upon age.

More generally, classicism has been criticised for assuming equality of choice for all, ignoring the impact of social context (e.g. environmental factors and social interactions with peers and agents of the criminal justice system) on individual decision-making. While modern-day rational choice theories have, to varying degrees, sought to address this deficiency in their analyses (for an overview of the economic models of crime literature see, for example, Van Der Weele 2012), other detractors point to a more critical flaw in the rational choice theory; namely, the failure to account for the impact of fundamental structural divisions and inequalities (e.g. poverty, racism and sexism) on individual decision-making (see, for example, Young 2011, 1981).

For very different reasons, locating crime causation within the individual—by way of their supposed exercise of free will or choice—has also been criticised by another school of criminology; namely, the positivists.

POSITIVISM AND INDIVIDUAL CRIMINAL BEHAVIOUR

While classicism had established a philosophical theory of crime causation and crime control, the establishment of criminology as a distinct professional discipline appears to have been founded instead on the positivist school of thought (Paternoster 2010). In contrast to classical thinking, which portrayed human behaviour as the product of rational free will, the hallmark of **positivism** is the notion that human behaviour is *determined*; that is, it is shaped by complex internal and external factors, such as physiology, personality and social upbringing, which reside outside of the individual's control. Positivism further asserts that pathological differences exist between offenders and while criminal pathology affects a minority of people, these individual differences must be acknowledged and classified or measured in some way. Thus, positivists concentrate on the offender—as opposed to the criminal act—and on identifying and correcting the characteristics that predispose him or her to criminal behaviour. Since offenders are not necessarily responsible for their criminality, administration of punishment is considered an inappropriate response to offending behaviour. The focus should instead be on *rehabilitating* the offender through the administration of appropriately tailored treatment; that is, treatment that meets the needs of the individual.

This perspective is clearly steeped in the scientific study of crime and its causes, with the practitioner's role cast in an analytical and remedial mould; that is, to identify deterministic factors particular to an offender, and then to treat the offender or correct the problem in some way. This type of reasoning places a lot of power in the hands of the 'expert', whose job it is to diagnose, classify and ultimately prescribe treatment for the individual. A central idea of positivism is that when a person is sentenced, he or she is sentenced to receive help. The idea is thus to treat the criminal, not the crime.

When it comes to the operation of the criminal justice system, the positivist concept of treatment or rehabilitation differs from the classicist emphasis on punishment. For example, positivism translates into an argument in favour of tailored sentences, which in the extreme form may translate to indeterminate sentences if there is little or no likelihood that the offender can be 'cured'; the criminal act is downplayed in favour of concentration on the offender. Since each offender is an individual, unique from all other offenders, treatment must be individualised. The length of sentence in custody therefore depends upon the diagnosis and classification (degree of severity of offender condition/issues, degree of dangerousness and degree of reoffending risk), rather than simply the circumstances and seriousness of the criminal act that was committed. This reflects a preoccupation less with civil rights and notions of justice and more with ensuring sentencing reflects the personal characteristics of offenders (Seba 2013).

Positivism is an overarching perspective, and within this general orientation are located a variety of different explanations for crime and criminal behaviour (see White et al. 2012). Although positivism embraces a diverse range of ideas, techniques and concepts specific to particular scientific disciplines, a central proposition is that a *moral consensus* exists in society in relation to what constitutes 'deviant' and 'normal' behaviour.

Positivist approaches that see behavioural problems in terms of individual pathology or deficiency can be categorised into three main strands:

- those that focus on biological factors
- those that concentrate on psychological factors
- those that present biosocial explanations for crime.

BIOLOGICAL POSITIVISM

There are two broad strands within the *biological explanatory framework*. One argues that, in essence, the offender is 'born' criminal. Criminality and criminal behaviour are thus seen as primarily attributable to inherited predispositions. The other similarly argues that biological factors are crucial in determining

POSITIVISM
The hallmark of positivism is that behaviour is determined, in the sense that individual behaviour is shaped by factors outside the individual's control. Positivism further asserts that individual differences exist between offenders, and these in turn can be acknowledged and classified.

behaviour, but sees these as stemming from the environment rather than simply being inherited. In this framework, criminals are 'made' as a result of exposure to environmental factors that affect their biological functioning (see Anderson 2007; Fishbein 1990; Walby & Carrier 2010). The most famous contributor to the first strand of biological positivism was Cesare Lombroso.

CESARE LOMBROSO

PHRENOLOGY
A seventeenth-century pseudoscience that amalgamated primitive neuroanatomy and moral philosophy. Phrenologists believed that human personality and character was determined by skull size. Although discredited, phrenology influenced the development of nineteenth-century psychiatry and modern neuroscience.

Cesare Lombroso, a nineteenth-century Italian sociologist, is regarded by some as the founder of criminology. Influenced largely by the natural sciences, and in particular Charles Darwin's theory of evolution, and the earlier studies of **phrenology** (see, for example, Ward & Durrant 2011), Lombroso eschewed the established classicist notion that all individuals naturally possessed the motivation to commit crime and acted out of free will. He argued instead that crime was inherited; that offenders were 'born criminal' and were thus driven to commit crime because of their innate biological nature. This school of thought, known as anthropological criminology, introduced a scientific approach to the study of crime and criminals.

Lombroso's general theory (1876) postulated that criminals are distinguishable from law-abiding citizens by multiple physiological traits or anatomical anomalies, such as a sloping forehead, unusually sized ears, abnormal dentition (protruding teeth), facial and/or cranial asymmetry, supernumerary fingers and toes, excessively long arms and other physical stigmata (including tattoos); these physical attributes were said to represent degeneracy. Essentially, criminals were considered to be biologically inferior—atavistic (primitive) throwbacks to an earlier evolutionary form of subhuman that rendered them closer to a primate than a human being—and their immorality or criminality was visible to all in the constitution of their bodies. Different categories of criminals, such as thieves, rapists and murderers, were said to be distinguishable by specific characteristics.

Lombroso later modified his views, recognising that for some categories of offender, such as the 'criminaloid' (occasional offender), criminals by passion, moral imbeciles and criminal epileptics, predisposing organic factors played a diminished role relative to precipitating factors such as the environment, opportunity and poverty. Notwithstanding, the element of biological determinism remained within his theorising. For example, in accounting for female delinquency and criminality, Lombroso argued that due to the inherently passive nature of the female sex, the female offender was in fact a genetic anomaly—biologically closer to a man than a woman.

In focusing on the criminal rather than the crime, Lombroso sought to shift the legal focus from personal, moral responsibility that was characteristic of classicist enlightenment, to the level of danger or threat to society that an individual actually posed. Lombroso thus advocated that punishment should be proportional to the dangerousness of the criminal rather than the seriousness of the crime committed. While this idea was not fully accepted by lawmakers, it did influence the development of security measures for offenders considered to be the mentally incompetent and dangerous.

OTHER BIOLOGICAL THEORIES AND STUDIES

Although Lombroso's research methods were clinical and descriptively detailed, they could not be regarded as scientifically rigorous since they failed to include control groups. Despite the questionable nature of his methods and empirical findings, biological determinism remained influential, predominantly throughout Europe, into the early twentieth century. For example, Charles Goring (1913) in his examination of 3,000 English convicts, failed to corroborate Lombroso's findings regarding the link between physiological traits and criminality, but he did conclude that criminals were shorter, lighter and endowed with less intelligence than non-criminals. Like Lombroso, Goring's approach lacked scientific rigour, with intelligence levels determined not through validated testing tools but, rather, on the basis of his subjective judgment.

In the United States, William Sheldon (1940) linked criminality to body somatotypes (body build and shape). Based on body measurements and ratios derived from photographs of nude figures, Sheldon proposed a typology of physique that he considered genetic and therefore not subject to fluctuations in weight. The three categories of somatotypes identified were said to be associated with human temperament: endomorphic (soft and round—associated with being relaxed, sociable and fond of eating); mesomorphic (muscular and strong—associated with being energetic, courageous and assertive); and ectomorphic (thin and fragile—associated with being brainy, artistic and introverted). He concluded that mesomorphic body types were most likely to engage in criminal activity.

Scientific developments in the study of genetics in the twentieth century have also led to theories postulating a link between criminality, chromosomes and our genetic makeup. For example, proponents of the 'double male or supermale' syndrome argue that those inheriting XYY syndrome (a genetic condition involving the presence of an additional Y chromosome in a male) are more likely to demonstrate lower intelligence, developmental delays, negative temperamental traits and behavioural patterns that put them at risk of engaging in criminal activity (see Fishbein 1990; Pyeritz et al. 1977).

ENVIRONMENTAL FACTORS

The other strand of positivist criminology situated within the biological explanatory framework similarly argues that biological factors are crucial in determining behaviour, but that these may stem from complex interactions between genes and the environment rather than simply being inherited. In this framework, criminals are 'made' as a result of exposure to environmental factors that affect their biological functioning (see Anderson 2007; Fishbein 1990). For example, much work has been done on how consistent and excessive consumption of psychopharmacological inducements—such as cocaine, alcohol, PCP and amphetamines—influence behaviour, with suggestions that these kinds of external factors propel or facilitate those under their influence to commit crimes (see Fishbein 1990). Most recently, Raine (2013), concentrating on the impact of environmental damage to the frontal lobe of the brain, has claimed that a mother who smokes during pregnancy is twice as likely to give birth to a child who will become a violent offender. Likewise, he claims that babies born with foetal alcohol syndrome are at a 50 per cent greater risk of offending later in life.

Advocates of environmental biological positivism have, in recent years, turned to advancements in neuroscience (the study of the brain and nervous system) and, in particular, the use of magnetic resonance imaging in support of their claims. There is now a body of evidence that purports to demonstrate a biological basis for alcohol and other forms of addiction previously attributed to human weakness or moral deviance. In this view, addiction (a condition affecting many people caught up in the criminal justice system) is a chronic disease that materially alters the neural pathways (interconnections) in the brain. Increasing damage to the pathways results in increasingly lesser capacity on the part of the individual to stop engaging in the addictive behaviour, whether it is gambling or alcohol and drug dependency (see, for example, Short 2013b). In a similar vein, brain imaging studies have been used to support the theory that heavy exposure to violent screen material 'hard wires' growing brains, increasing aggression and reckless behaviour, and reducing empathy. Images of violence are said to be stored in the brain in much the same way as trauma is stored by those experiencing Post Traumatic Stress Disorder (Browne 2013).

Others point to the possible connection between the increasing use of sugar and chemical additives (colourings and preservatives) in food and drinks, biochemical changes in the body and consequent rising levels of conditions such as Attention Deficit Hyperactivity Disorder (ADHD), delinquency and criminal behaviour (Schauss 1980). In a similar vein, some researchers seeking to explain longer-term fluctuations in crime trends claim a link between exposure to lead emissions/contaminants, lower IQ levels in children and rising crime levels some 20 years post exposure (see, for example, Corderoy 2013; Needleman et al. 2002; Nevin 2007).

The suggestion of an environmental basis for the biological determinants of crime suggests the possibility of a biological intervention or 'correction' to prevent criminal behaviour occurring. This corrective might take the form of removing the source of the problem (e.g. removing lead from one's living environment or banning alcohol sales) or regulating the biochemical and physiological operations of the body through appropriate treatment (e.g. drugs that restore hormonal equilibrium or ensure a regular heart rate).

PSYCHOLOGICAL POSITIVISM

As with biological positivism, psychological positivism looks to external or internal factors that propel some people into committing crime and over which they have little direct control. The focus of investigation is, however, on *psychological mechanisms* underlying crime, such as mental illness (including moral insanity—thought to be a form of genetically inherited degeneracy that manifests in immoral behaviour) or personality or maladaptive behavioural traits that result in defective and disordered reasoning (e.g. lack of empathy, excessive risk-taking, egocentricity and impulsivity). Essentially, this school of thought contends that the thinking processes of criminals are different from those of non-criminals; that errors and distortions in thinking negatively impact internal regulatory processes of self-control and make some people behave in an immoral, delinquent or criminal fashion (Schirmann 2013).

This strain of positivism emerged from within the medico-legal professions, developed through the work of doctors and psychiatrists in the criminal justice system itself (prisons and institutions for the criminally insane), who noticed significant differences between offenders and identified a range of offenders who did not seem entirely responsible for their actions. It is not surprising then that the focus is on pathology; its appropriate scientific diagnosis, classification and treatment to fix the illness or condition of each offender.

Psychological approaches include those that focus on 'personality types' (see Farrington 1996a) and present typologies of abnormalities in the psychological structure of individuals (e.g. 'over-aggressive' or 'highly strung'). Such approaches often see the formation of particular personality types as linked to certain biological predispositions as well as developmental experiences. One variant of this approach, the psychoanalytic, draws its intellectual roots from Freud's work on the study of the human psyche and, in particular, the conscious and unconscious mind. According to this approach, criminality is viewed as unconsciously motivated, shaped by experience and processes beyond those consciously apparent to the subject, such as unresolved events or problems in early childhood (see Gibbons 1977). For example, Yochelson and Samenow (1976), doctors working in a prison psychiatric hospital in the United States, conducted a longitudinal study of inmates designed to understand the makeup of their 'criminal personality' through the use of psychoanalysis. Of the 255 males studied, 52 'errors' in thinking patterns were identified that, while not unique to criminals, purportedly distinguished a criminal personality from a non-criminal personality. These errors in thinking included: restlessness and dissatisfaction; pursuit of excitement; habitual anger; a lack of empathy; feeling no obligation to anyone; and poor decision making. A number of these 'errors' fit with a diagnosis of Antisocial Personality Disorder.

The psychiatric theory of deviant behaviour is based on the assumption that certain childhood experiences have an effect that transcends all other social and cultural experiences (Clinard 1974). Such explanations adopt a medical model, in which deviancy or criminality is seen to reside within the maladjusted individual. All human beings are seen as having inherited universal needs, such as the need for emotional security. It is thought that if such needs are unmet during childhood, then particular personality patterns form in later life, resulting especially in those personality types associated with deviant or criminal behaviour. Family experiences and early patterns of socialisation that negatively affected development are thus seen as determining later behaviour. The development of antisocial or criminal behaviours are viewed as an individual's means of dealing with particular personal traits such as aggressiveness, emotional insecurity or feelings of inadequacy generated by unmet needs in childhood. Glueck and Glueck (1950), for example, in their longitudinal study of 500 juvenile delinquents and 500 matched non-delinquents in Boston, United States, attributed badly behaved children and delinquent children to 'broken homes' characterised by absentee or uncaring parents who demonstrated little affection.

BIOSOCIAL POSITIVISM

More sophisticated biological and psychological accounts of criminality, often based on studies of identical and fraternal twins, accept that human behaviour is subject to a combination of biological and environmental influences (Pilcher 2013). These are referred to as *biosocial approaches*, which characteristically view behaviour as the product of a complex interplay between nature (biology) and nurture (socio-environmental factors), rather than assuming an either–or position. Proponents of this perspective argue that human beings have a 'conditional free will'; that is, individual choice within a set, yet to some degree changeable range of possibilities (Fishbein 1990).

Eysenck (1984), for example, put forward the argument that behaviour can be explained as resulting from a combination of biological and environmental influences. His study analysed crime in terms of two broad processes of development:

- the differential ability to be conditioned, wherein genetic inheritance affects one's ability to be conditioned; that is, the sensitivity of the autonomic nervous system inherited by individuals determines whether each individual is an extrovert or an introvert, and thus how well each is able to be conditioned in society
- the differential quality of conditioning, whereby family conditioning makes use of a range of techniques, some of which are more efficacious than others. The way in which a child is reared, therefore, has an impact on the child's subsequent behaviour.

More contemporary versions of biosocial criminology have attempted to extend gene-environment research by exploring the respective influences of genetics, neighbourhood context (neighbourhood level indicators of disadvantage) and exposure to violent crime on individual propensity for violence (Barnes & Jacobs 2012).

In summary, the biosocial argument posits that a combination of biological potentials, set through inheritance and interacting with environmental potentials shaped by socialisation practices and other environmental factors, determine the overall propensity to commit crime. Human behaviour thus contains a biological and a social element (see, for example, Moffitt 1996; Raine 2013).

WHY DO PEOPLE *NOT* OFFEND?

According to Hirschi (1969) and, later, Gottfredson and Hirschi (1990), the basic question criminologists need to answer is not 'Why do some people offend?', but 'Why do most people *not* offend?' These theorists argue that individuals learn not to offend through the development of self-control. By extension, those who do offend lack self-control. Gottfredson and Hirschi see self-control as a single psychological construct or personal attribute. This single construct is made up of several elements; namely:

- impulsivity, or an inability to defer gratification
- lack of perseverance
- preference for risky behaviour
- preference for physical, as opposed to mental, activity
- self-centredness
- low threshold for frustration.

Gottfredson and Hirschi argue that effective child-rearing is critical to the development of self-control, a focus that draws inspiration from the early work of Glueck and Glueck (1950). Poor child-rearing practices, such as lack of supervision (particularly by the mother) and poor attachment to the father, lead to low self-control and higher rates of criminal offending. The theory also asserts that opportunity for offending is important, but only when combined with low social control. Adequately socialised individuals would, therefore, not succumb to criminal opportunity. Prevention can therefore only be effected through early intervention efforts at the developmental stage to address identified deficiencies in child-rearing practices.

In contemporary examples of positivist research, this perspective is remarkable in that it attempts to combine both positivist and classical elements (see Box 3.3).

BOX 3.3   CONTROL THEORY: COMBINING POSITIVISM AND CLASSICISM

Control theory, as formulated by Hirschi (1969), is premised upon the idea that it is an individual's bond to society that makes the difference in terms of whether or not the person abides by society's general rules and values. From this perspective, all people are inherently antisocial, and thus all people would commit crime if they so dared. It is the nature of the bond that children have with their society that ultimately determines their behaviour (Empey 1982; Nettler 1984). It is the combination of attachment, commitment, involvement and belief that shapes the life world of young people, and that essentially dictates whether or not they will take advantage of conventional means and goals of social advancement, or whether they will pursue illegal pathways to self-gratification.

It is up to society, and its agents, to step in and ensure that its younger members are imbued with the right bonds. In other words, there is a high degree of intervention necessary if children and young people are to be guided the right way, and if they are to follow paths that uphold social values, but that ultimately go against their essential antisocial nature. Without adequate socialisation—a strong social control presence of some kind—criminal behaviour would be common.

In related work, Gottfredson and Hirschi (1990) argue that the central issue in explaining crime is that of self-control; that is, people differ in the extent to which they are restrained from criminal acts (see also Wilson & Herrnstein 1985). This, in turn, is linked to the question of social bonding, and especially the problem of ineffective child-rearing. The theory incorporates elements of other theories and perspectives: classical theory, in its acceptance of the idea that people are basically self-seeking; biosocial positivism, in its focus on the importance of proper 'conditioning' or training of the young; and sociological perspectives, which look to the nature of the family as a key variable in the development of self-control.

The theory does not analyse specific social divisions (e.g. class, gender and ethnicity), but rests upon a conception of human nature that sees all people as essentially driven by the same kinds of 'universal tendency to enhance their own pleasure'. Given this, the crucial issue is then one of how best to socialise all people to conform to society's values and to engage in conventional law-abiding behaviour.

In policy terms, the answer to crime lies in redressing the defective social training that characterises offenders who have in some way 'lost control'. In other words, the emphasis from a practitioner's perspective will be to reattach young people to some kind of family, recommit them to long-range conventional goals, involve them in school and other constructive activities, and have them acquire beliefs in the morality of law (Empey 1982: 269).

Importantly, the control perspective is premised upon the idea that 'deviancy' stems from lack of self-control (which, in turn, is related to intrinsic human tendencies to engage in antisocial behaviour, because they are naturally self-seeking and self-interested), and that this is fundamentally a matter related to the processes of socialisation.

In summary, the positivist perspective in criminology emphasises the role of external and internal determinants of crime and criminality. People, it is argued, do not choose to engage in deviant or criminal behaviour; they are ostensibly locked into such behaviour by a wide range of biological and/or psychological influences beyond their immediate control. The positivist position stresses 'individual differences' among people, and therefore the necessity of pinpointing the main factor or factors that have given rise to individual criminality. Pinpointing of such factors is done through testing, diagnosis, classification and treatment, all of which centre upon individual traits and needs as perceived by the 'expert professional'. Biology is not necessarily fate; appropriate diagnosis and early intervention to address identified deficiencies and risks can prevent the development of criminal behaviour or reduce the risk of reoffending.

Taken to its logical conclusion, positivist perspectives, which tend to the medicalisation of criminal behaviour, call for a rethink of the classical model of proportional and uniform punishment. They suggest that material differences in moral responsibility or culpability for criminal behaviour warrant more individualised responses; those responses should be more appropriatly directed towards the provision of tailored treatment to rehabilitate the offender and eliminate societal risk, rather than deterrence or retribution (see Box 3.4).

THE PROBLEM WITH INDIVIDUALLY FOCUSED POSITIVIST CRIMINOLOGY

The earliest biological explanations of crime tended to be fairly pessimistic about positive action to prevent or deal with crime, since crime was regarded as resulting from something essential to the nature of the individual. Individuals were regarded as having been born with certain biological attributes that could not be changed and which locked some into a life of crime and antisocial behaviour. Despite professing to invoke a scientific basis for the study of crime causation, early studies under the positivist rubric lacked methodological rigour. Findings were based on small sample sizes, selection and sampling biases were rife (especially gender biases), and the lack of control groups (non-offenders with whom to

---

BOX 3.4   KEY IDEAS OF POSITIVIST APPROACHES

- The focus is on *characteristics* of the offender.
- Crime is *caused by a pathology* or *other deficiency* residing within or external to the individual.
- The offender is *determined and/or predisposed* to certain types of behaviour.
- There is a *moral consensus* in relation to what constitutes *'deviant' and 'normal' behaviour*.
- The response to crime is *individualised treatment*, based upon diagnosis of the individual condition or problem.
- Crime prevention equates to *early intervention*.
- Criminal justice is based upon a *'scientific' approach*, involving measurement, evaluation and treatment.

---

test hypotheses) meant that conclusions drawn lacked statistical power and could not be validated nor generalised beyond the immediate study group.

Moreover, contrary to the presumed neutrality of 'scientific' research, racist and sexist value-laden assumptions were often built into the study of biological differences, intelligence and social behaviour. These assumptions invariably led to conclusions that intelligence, poverty, social deviance (homosexuality, substance abuse, prostitution etc.) and crime were attributable to characteristics such as race and gender, rather than being the product of social or criminal justice processes (see, for example, Herrnstein & Murray 1994). At the core of this thinking is a presumption that race and gender and their human characteristics (ethnic and gender mores, beliefs and behaviours) are the product of biology and therefore inheritable.

Despite the lack of sound evidence for such claims, biological theories of crime and moral degeneracy were used by the Nazis to justify the practice of **eugenics** (including forced sterilisation and medical experimentation) and ultimately the extermination of millions of people—Jews, Roma, the mentally ill, blind, deaf, developmentally disabled, promiscuous women and homosexuals—by attributing to them inherent criminality or inferiority. Such action was justified on the grounds of moral superiority; the only way to preserve a genetically superior master race (the physical and cognitive elite) was to eliminate contamination from the genetically abnormal and therefore inferior (Rafter 2008).

As the discipline evolved, more contemporary versions of positivist criminology incorporated environmental and sociological factors into their theorising on crime and crime prevention. These approaches no longer regarded the human condition as permanent, arguing that appropriate intervention by those well placed can 'fix' the specific problems that predispose each individual to crime. One problem with individually focused positivism is that it puts an inordinate amount of power into the hands of a few 'experts', who may argue for ever greater levels of intervention in the lives of citizens generally and, as history has demonstrated, especially the lives of the poor and minority groups (Cullen 2011). For example, it can be argued that in order to deal adequately with the 'predisposition' to crime (based upon biological or psychological indicators), intervention should ideally take place before the crime or deviant act is actually committed. How early are we to intervene to 'change' someone? Who is going to do this? Should we 'treat' people when in fact no crime or law-breaking has occurred if crime predispositions are identified? Further questions can be asked regarding the 'norms' and 'values' against which we are to measure people's behaviour and the social impact of attempting to mould each individual into passive conformity against an ideal model of acceptable behaviour.

EUGENICS
A social philosophy advocating the improvement of the genetic quality of the human race via scientific means; that is, controlled human reproduction to promote breeding of individuals with desired heritable traits and reduce breeding of individuals with undesirable heritable traits.

LIBERTARIAN AND TRADITIONAL CONSERVATIVE THEORIES

It is useful to briefly review New Right variations on the themes expressed in classical and positivist perspectives.

LIBERTARIAN APPROACH

The right-wing *libertarian perspective* is a modern version of the classical approach. It is based upon a moral philosophy of egoism (selfishness), in which the only constraint on behaviour is the duty not to initiate force over others. The notion of a competitive ethos pervades this perspective. This is usually tied to the idea of rights to private property as being the first virtue of the legal and criminal justice system. Accordingly, crime is defined in terms of the infringement of private property, including infringements of one's physical self. Since this perspective conceives of human nature as being possessive and individualistic—and conceives of crime mainly in terms of private property—the role of the state is seen as being restricted to those instances where other people actually come to harm through one's social actions (see Tame 1991). So-called 'victimless crimes' are therefore considered in need of decriminalisation, insofar as they do not directly affect those beyond oneself. In other words, 'anything goes' in this perspective: people should have complete liberty to do as they will, as long as they do not infringe illegally upon the property of others.

From the point of view of rational choice theory, we need to assume that most 'criminals' are rational agents who can be deterred from committing additional crimes by an increase in the punishment they might expect to receive (Buchanan & Hartley 1992). According to the advocates of this approach, the most economically efficient way to manage the crime problem is to privatise institutions such as prisons, and to increase the probability of detection and conviction of offenders. The broad philosophical orientation of rational choice theory is also closely related to the adoption of prevention techniques directed primarily at reducing opportunities for crime (see Felson 1994), rather than at the structural reasons for offending behaviour or the **criminalisation** process itself.

TRADITIONAL CONSERVATIVE APPROACH

The *traditional conservative perspective* takes a broader view than that of the right-wing libertarian regarding what constitutes a crime. The conservative view of crime includes not only activity that endangers property or the person, but also includes morality. Hence, attacks on certain traditional values and people's respect for authority generally may be linked to criminality. From this point of view, crime is not only a matter of free choice: it is also linked to certain intrinsic aspects of humanity. In particular, people are seen as possessing certain 'natural urges' that go against the more civilised or divine purposes of society. Whether it be a concept of 'original sin' or a secular theory of human nature that sees people in a negative light, the idea is that all people are somehow inherently evil or flawed. In order to constrain these urges, it is felt necessary to establish a strong order based upon personal sacrifice, self-discipline and submission to authority (Tame 1991). In this respect, the traditional conservative mirrors some of the concerns of the positivist approach, insofar as certain attributes are 'given': they are not a matter of individual choice (see also Box 3.3). Order must take precedence over all else, including justice. Crime is said to be caused by the unwillingness of people to accept discipline, by the undermining of traditional loyalties such as to the (patriarchal) family and by the pursuit of immediate individual gratification without appropriate hard work.

CRIMINA-LISATION
The process by which certain acts or particular people or groups are defined as criminal. What is deemed to be 'criminal' and who is defined as an 'offender' involves a social process, by which officials of the state formally intervene and designate certain acts and certain actors as warranting a criminal label. Until an act, or actor, has been processed in particular ways by the state, there is no 'crime' as such.

According to this approach, punishment is an essential part of deterrence, not only because it establishes personal responsibility for one's actions, but also because punishment has an important symbolic impact on society as a whole. That is, punishment is seen in terms of its effect on the establishment of moral solidarity through stigmatisation. Strong emphasis is placed upon the importance of morality in the maintenance of social authority: thus, someone who does something deemed to be wrong or harmful must be punished swiftly and appropriately in order to set the moral standard. Unlike the libertarian perspective, the conservative point of view often favours increased state intervention in everyday social life, because it is felt that only strong coercive measures will ultimately keep people in line and teach them the discipline they require to live as members of a civilised community.

The overriding message of these theories is that there is a need to 'get tough on criminals', hold them responsible for their actions and punish wrongdoers in a consistent manner so they get their 'just deserts'. People make choices and, according to these theories, they must pay for these choices. In essence, the argument is that 'if you do the crime, then you must do the time'. However, particularly in the traditional conservative worldview, there are certain traits that intrinsically incline humans towards antisocial, deviant or evil behaviour.

ISSUES FOR CONSIDERATION

THE FOCUS ON INDIVIDUALISM

The focus on the individual is a hallmark of the approaches discussed in this chapter. However, as indicated in Box 3.1, there are varying levels of analysis that can and should be taken into account in explaining crime and deviant behaviour. Nevertheless, the fact is that, regardless of social background or social circumstance, certain individuals are more prone to commit crime than others. This may be attributable to a tendency to make the wrong choices. It may be the consequence of being under the influence of alcohol or another type of drug. It may be a result of not really knowing right from wrong because of inadequate parenting. How to solve the conundrum of 'voluntarism' versus 'determininism' is partly a question of individual biography. Yet, as the next two chapters illustrate, each individual also resides within certain social contexts and milieux that simultaneously shape his or her choices and opportunities.

EMERGENCE OF NEUROCRIMINOLOGY

NEUROCRI-MINOLOGY
A form of biological positivism that concentrates on studying the (psychopathic) brains of criminals. The objective is to use scientific techniques to identify those with genetic and neurological predispositions for violent behaviour and engineer a treatment or prevention strategy.

Biologically oriented crime theorising lost favour in the mid-twentieth century, following extreme manifestations of its application, most notably the Holocaust. Indeed, for many years any approach that even hinted at the legitimacy of considering biological factors in theorising on crime was viewed extremely cautiously (Wright & Cullen 2012). Biosocial variants of positivist criminology that have adopted a more sophisticated appreciation of the interplay between nature and nurture have, however, re-emerged in the twenty-first century and have been influential in the field of developmental crime prevention (Rocque et al. 2012; see also Chapter 28). While some of the remedies for violent criminals proposed by these variants (including sedatives and other forms of drug therapy, nutritional programs, family-centred parenting programs, pre-school programs and other early interventions) appear relatively benign, though not necessarily exempt from concerns posed earlier, other approaches including those proposed by some proponents of **neurocriminogy** raise serious ethical questions.

For example, in his recent controversial book, Raine (2013) visualises a futuristic world in which neuroscience will enable prediction of violent propensities early in life. When this point is reached, he advocates the utility of compulsory brain imaging tests for all young males (based on the fact males are statistically far more likely to commit murder than females) to determine their likelihood of yielding to violent behaviour. As a crime prevention measure, he proposes that those identified with a neuroanatomical psychopathic brain be removed from mainstream society and relocated to some form of highly regulated holding facility for the detention of dangerous individuals (not necessarily a prison), either indefinitely or until some 'cure' can be engineered. He also opens the door to more radical biological interventions as appropriate, such as brain surgery and chemical castration.

This approach raises significant ethical and civil rights concerns, such as: what are or should be the rights of parents and children with respect to early intervention efforts to identify criminality? How do these rights sit against those of potential victims? Should people be licensed to parent? From an extreme prevention point of view, it raises the spectre of, and ethical dilemmas associated with, designer humans (babies whose gender, personality and physical characteristics have been chosen by parents aided by emerging reproductive technologies) (McMahon 2013) and extension of the use of coerced sterilisation (a practice currently allowed under Australian law for children with disabilities, subject to approval by the Family Court or guardianship board) (Nelson 2013).

THE CHALLENGE FOR SENTENCING

As neuroscience evolves, it is posing new challenges for the legal profession and for criminal sentencing, spawning a new branch of law known as neurolaw. In particular, it raises critical questions regarding personal moral and legal responsibility and, therefore, blameworthiness. If individuals have little or no control over their behaviour, then to what degree should they be punished, and what is the most appropriate form and intention of that punishment?

Indeed, many of the policies proposed by classical and New Right theories are problematic from the point of view of assumed objectives of punishment, such as deterrence. In particular, the capacity of harsh, or even proportional, punishment to deter individuals from reoffending has been the subject of long debate. There is substantial evidence that imprisonment, in particular, is counterproductive and serves only to exacerbate rates of offending, rather than deterring offenders (see Ritchie 2011; see also Chapter 25). Prison (and the 'big stick' in general) is both ineffective and expensive. In a similar vein, the use of indeterminate sentences, ostensibly designed to treat the problems underpinning offender actions, have proven to be unjust and unproductive from the point of view of preventing future criminal behaviour.

The debate concerning the need for harsher penalties, as advocated by traditional conservatives, has negative consequences in and of itself. For example, it engenders a fear of crime that is out of all proportion to the realistic possibility of victimisation. The problem of how to deal with the fear of crime—independent of how to deal with crime per se—is an urgent issue today, since it has a number of potentially negative social consequences (see Chapter 2).

Crime itself tends to be defined narrowly in the perspectives described in this chapter. For the majority of these theorists, the major concern is with street crime. Crimes of the powerful and crimes of the state are hardly mentioned. Where they are mentioned, the state is seen as able to deal adequately with the problem, since there is no conception that the state itself may favour the powerful over the powerless.

Despite these criticisms and questions, there are elements that are of importance to contemporary criminological debate. It is clear that criminological theories (at least at the present time) need to take account of the individual to be seen as legitimate. This clearly contains a number of elements. For example, while New Right perspectives assert issues of individual responsibility, they also highlight individual rights and, in particular, the right to feel safe and secure. The rights of victims, which have been ignored by the majority of criminologists, also are brought to the fore within these perspectives. Victims' rights and needs can no longer be ignored within criminological theory (see Chapter 6). Further, as indicated by the popularity of some New Right perspectives, theories need to go beyond a view of human activity as purely rational or formally logical. Values, emotions and ideas evident in the debate about crime clearly point to the need for criminological theory to understand both the political and cultural role crime plays in societies.

CONCLUSION

The theories discussed in this chapter locate crime within individual attributes, whether in regards to 'rationality' or 'pathology', or a combination of the two. The 'remedy' in each case is to deal with the individual directly: either to coerce the individual back into rational decision-making or to cure the individual of a predisposing tendency to commit deviant acts. In the end, the objective is to reintegrate the offender into the consensus. This can be achieved through the threat and experience of punishment and/or by the intervention of expert assistance to resocialise and rehabilitate the individual.

Chapters 4 and 5 provide a further elaboration of many of the concerns expressed by the positivist perspective in particular. That is, while classical and New Right theories tend to emphasise individual responsibility and choice in human behaviour, the bulk of contemporary criminological theorising tends to look to factors beyond the individual's control as crucial in explaining social deviance. In so doing, they take into account issues pertaining to social opportunity, power and interests, how people make sense of their social worlds, and alternative views of social harm.

DISCUSSION QUESTIONS

1   What is criminological 'theory'?
2   'Crime is a personal responsibility.' Discuss.
3   Are we masters of our own fate? Why or why not is this the case?
4   'Biology counts, but it is not the only determinant of social behaviour.' Discuss, with examples.
5   If crime is related to individual attributes (e.g. personal choices or biological propensities), under what specific circumstances should the liberty of individuals ever be curtailed?

FURTHER READING

Gottfredson, M. & Hirschi, T. (1990) *A General theory of crime*, Stanford University Press, Stanford.

Paternoster, R. (2010) 'How much do we really know about criminal deterrence?', *The Journal of Criminal Law & Criminology*, 100(3): 765–823.

Rafter, N. (2008) 'Criminology's darkest hour: biocriminology in Nazi Germany', *Australian and New Zealand Journal of Criminology*, 41(2): 287–306.

Wright, J.P. & Cullen, F.T. (2012) 'The future of biosocial criminology: beyond scholars' professional ideology', *Journal of Contemporary Criminal Justice*, 28(3): 237–53.

Young, J. (1981) 'Thinking seriously about crime: some models of criminology', in M. Fitzgerald, G. McLennon & J. Pawson (eds), *Crime and society: readings in history and theory*, Routledge & Kegan Paul and the Open University, London.

4 MAINSTREAM PERSPECTIVES

CHAPTER OVERVIEW

- SOCIOLOGICAL THEORIES
- LABELLING PERSPECTIVES
- MULTIFACTORIAL EXPLANATIONS
- REPUBLICAN THEORY
- ISSUES FOR CONSIDERATION
- CONCLUSION
- DISCUSSION QUESTIONS
- FURTHER READING

INTRODUCTION

This chapter discusses sociological theories and perspectives that see the causes of crime as stemming from social factors. The chapter deals with conceptions of deviancy that focus on the social structures, processes and practices that determine or shape both individual and group behaviour (e.g. job and educational opportunities, and neighbourhood dynamics), and the subjective meanings that people bring to their actions and the actions of others (especially values, norms and cultures). The dynamics of a society and processes of social interaction are seen to provide the essential context within which crime and criminality is socially constructed.

Although representing a significant departure from traditional theorising on crime, the theories discussed below are considered 'mainstream' in two senses. First, they are among the most widely recognised and utilised approaches in the field of criminology. Whether modern variations of strain theory, applications of labelling perspectives, multifactorial explanations of social causes or hybrid theories that meld elements of the various sociological theories (as in republican theory), these are the key perspectives informing how we think about and respond to crime today. Second, they are mainstream insofar as they can be, and are incorporated into existing systems of criminal justice. They observe processes of social construction and imply change in certain practices, but they do not seek to transform the justice system in its entirety.

SOCIOLOGICAL THEORIES

Rather than reduce deviant or criminal behaviour solely to the individual level, *sociological perspectives* argue that in order to understand the nature and occurrence of crime, we need to look at macro-level factors and, specifically, social structure and conditions that mould and shape norms, values, culture and behaviour. Individual action is thus attributable to social causes, and crime can be seen as a manifestation of social pathology; that is, a 'social fact'. According to this perspective, sociologists and criminologists are both concerned with connecting wider situational factors (immediate socio-economic opportunities and avenues for learning of norms, values and subcultural attributes) and social structural factors (e.g. poverty, employment and educational levels and patterns) with criminal activity.

Crime is seen as essentially a social phenomenon that cannot be reduced to personal psychology or individual biology. Since the 'criminal' or 'delinquent' is considered a product of a specific kind of social order, the impulse to commit crime is seen as 'normal' and is socially induced. Moreover, sociological perspectives argue that in order to understand behaviour, it is necessary to acknowledge that different societies give rise to different social structures and different kinds of behaviour.

ÉMILE DURKHEIM: COLLECTIVE CONSCIOUSNESS AND ANOMIE

Émile Durkheim, a French sociologist, primarily studied what he referred to as 'social facts' (as opposed to scientific facts): phenomena that have an existence independent of the actions of individuals, but which exert coercive influence over them (Durkheim 2004). These facts comprise formal laws and regulations as well as informal rules, including, for example, religious rituals and family norms. According to Durkheim (1997), society is essentially comprised of a series of social facts. Humans are conceived of as inherently egoistic but society is disciplined and held together by the **collective consciousness**: common beliefs, ideas and values that together establish society's moral foundations. The collective consciousness both shapes and is shaped by the interactions of individuals within a society; without it, society is incapable of surviving, for it serves as a unifying force. It is from the collective conscious that the state derives its authority.

Durkheim believed that societies vary in their ability to impose social regulation, and that the values of a society vary in their ability to achieved a desired social integration. He noted two important social pathologies that could disrupt social interaction and, ultimately, lead to social disintegration; namely, **anomie** and forced division of labour. Anomie is a condition of society (not of the individual), usually prompted by rapid change, where the norms and values of a society are in flux or even partially destroyed. It describes a situation of social deregulation in which shared beliefs and values are broken down, and where moral guides to and constraints on behaviour have weakened (Durkheim 1951; see also Brown 1979). As applied to issues of crime, a distinction is drawn between anomie and egoism, both of which revolve around social norms (see Taylor et al. 1973):

- **anomie**: refers to a lack of social regulation in which the unrestricted appetites of the individual conscience are no longer held in check ('anything goes'); that is, a state of normlessness where appropriate norms are not in place to inhibit deviant behaviour
- **egoism**: refers to a normative phenomenon in which a value has been placed on the unrestricted pursuit of individual desires ('greed is good'); that is, the presence of norms that actively encourage the development of unregulated aspirations, and thus encourage and sustain deviant behaviour.

Rules of conduct are clearly important in establishing social solidarity, but Durkheim also recognised that rules alone are insufficient, for they themselves can be the source of problems. Such is the case in situations of *forced labour*: a strictly regulated and unhealthy or pathological division of labour that does not reflect the actual distribution of aptitude, capacities and desires in society. Essentially, people are forced to take positions and perform roles they do not choose and/or for which they are unsuited. The consequent desire to change the system by those left unhappy with the distribution of labour can destabilise social solidarity.

Durkheim's conception of crime differs from conventional ideas. Crime is considered an act that offends the social consciousness. Furthermore, it is inextricably tied up with the fundamental conditions of all social life and serves a social function: it provides an outlet for the release of social tensions and, in some circumstances, can pave the way for social changes. Using this conceptual framework, a social scientist is able then to examine the nature of a society in order to determine whether deviancy can be

COLLECTIVE CONSCIOUS-NESS
Shared ideas, beliefs and values that establish society's moral foundations and which operate as a unifying force within society.

ANOMIE
A lack of social regulation in which the unrestricted appetites of the individual conscience are no longer held in check ('anything goes').

EGOISM
A normative phenomenon in which a value has been placed on the unrestricted pursuit of individual desires ('greed is good').

explained in terms of individual pathology in a healthy society (one in which values are well established by a collective consciousness that regulates behaviour), or whether it is linked to an inappropriately socialised individual in a pathological society (values are not well established, have been destroyed or work against the aims of integration and regulation).

SOCIAL STRAINS

Consistent with Durkheim's conceptions of the collective consciousness and anomie, the underlying theme of many sociological theories is that crime is a result of social disjuncture or *social strains* within a society. The strains or sources of tension are thought to be generated by the society itself: they do not reside within the individual (e.g. as in the case of a person feeling strained or pressured by circumstance). The cause of crime is seen as being located in social structures and/or social values that in some way are unfair or socially pathological. To deal with crime therefore requires strategies and policies that are pitched at institutional reform, rather than solely at changing or modifying the individual in some way.

By and large, sociological theories see crime as a natural violation of the social consensus. It is a phenomenon linked to strains created by *structural opportunities* and *cultural processes*. Decisions are made by people in the context of whether they have the means or opportunities to achieve their goals relative to other people in society, and whether, through social circumstance, they associate with others who share their ideas and cultural understandings regarding acceptable and unacceptable behaviour. The key social conflict in this perspective is that arising from a disjuncture between social means and cultural ends. *Deviant behaviour* is viewed as a meaningful attempt to solve problems faced by groups of individuals who are located in particular disadvantaged positions within the social structure (see Box 4.1).

BOX 4.1   KEY IDEAS OF SOCIOLOGICAL THEORIES

- Crime is a violation of the social consensus; it is a *natural* and *meaningful response* to *social strains*.
- Crime is *socially induced*; it is caused by *social strains* associated with structural opportunities and cultural processes:
  (a) Crime and structural opportunities
    - Crime is the product of *social disorganisation*.
    - There are links between *urban environments and crime*.
    - Issues of *migration and settlement* processes may contribute to crime.
    - Issues *of economic deprivation* may contribute to crime.
    - *Strain theory* regards crime as the product of a disjuncture between 'culturally defined goals' and 'institutionalised means'.
    - *Individual responses* to the *means–ends* equation *vary*, and these responses differentiate law-abiding from maladaptive and unlawful behaviour.
  (b) Crime and cultural processes
    - *Differential association* regards crime as a cultural phenomenon, in the sense that it is learned behaviour.
    - The emphasis is on *group contexts* and *group formations*.
    - Subcultural theories examine the concept of *blocked opportunities* and *group dynamics*.

- There is a concern with *collective behaviour* and diverse lived experiences.
- There is a concern with *class differences* in *cultural goals*, and accentuation of 'subterranean values'.
- Individual *conscious choice is limited* and largely determined by the social options available to them.
- Crime can be prevented via *institutional reform*, such as urban planning and social intervention to expand educational and employment opportunities, and to foster healthy peer associations.
- The *criminal justice system* is essentially *neutral*—it responds to violations of the social consensus impartially and for the purpose of upholding values and norms in society.

SOCIAL DISORGANISATION

There are several different strands of thought among sociological theories of crime that focus on societal strain. Some of these draw attention to opportunity structures relating to education and paid work; others concentrate on peer networks and the learning of particular norms and values. One of the earliest formulations of *strain theory* is that which proposes a link between crime and social disorganisation. Also known as a *social ecology perspective*, this approach, advanced by the Chicago school of sociology in the 1920s and 1930s, attempts to link the nature and extent of crime with specific social processes; namely, the structural conditions of urban life at the neighbourhood level of analysis.

Shaw and McKay (1942), for example, identified high rates of juvenile offending to be endemic in areas characterised by social disorganisation. These neighbourhoods were typically plagued with economic deprivation and poverty, and demonstrated a tendency to ethnic heterogeneity and high rates of residential mobility. Situating their observations within the economic and political context of the time (a period of mass migration to the United States), Shaw and McKay examined the patterns and impacts of successive waves of immigrants to Chicago. They observed fairly consistent patterns of movement into inner-city neighbourhoods of the urban spatial grid, followed by gradual movement to outer areas. This process of concentrated urban settlement and transition was seen to produce tensions and chaos in neighbourhoods, making social cohesion and, therefore, social order, difficult to maintain.

Against this backdrop, Shaw and McKay examined the life histories of juvenile offenders, coming to the conclusion that juvenile offending is intimately linked to the transitional processes of social change and family disruption; a natural social process of settling in experienced by new immigrants. Specifically, the communities within which they resided were in a constant state of flux and were seen to exhibit a high degree of social disorganisation. The new immigrants were rarely integrated into the wider social, economic and political systems. Questions of language, education, work skills and social networks all came into play in shaping the life affairs of individuals and immigrant communities. In these communities, customary social norms that produced networks of trust, civic participation and informal social control (which customarily produce conforming behaviour and a willingness to intervene on others' behalf) were often weakened or in apparent conflict with the norms of the new society, thus increasing the vulnerability of these communities to higher crime rates. Shaw and McKay concluded that delinquency was not attributable to causes at the individual level, but rather constituted a normal response to abnormal conditions (i.e. unhealthy neighbourhood ecological conditions).

While Shaw and McKay's observations were initially confined to issues of social disorganisation and transient immigrant populations, their subsequent theorising on crime causation acknowledged a broader association between poverty, unemployment, diminished opportunities and crime.

Essentially, they contended that even where mainstream goals had been internalised by a population, structural disadvantage (especially prevalent in times of widespread economic deprivation, such as occurred in an economic depression) could deny people the opportunity to achieve those goals, thus engendering crime.

OPPORTUNITY THEORY

While social disorganisation theory provided a reasonable explanation for street crime at the neighbourhood level, its generalisability appeared limited, especially in times of economic prosperity. Specifically, it could not account for the growing incidence of crime in economically prosperous times. *Opportunity theories*, which emphasise the importance of analysing social values and social structures in examining crime causation, offer a solution to this dilemma. According to Merton (1957), for example, individuals in a society are institutionally socialised into a broader system of cultural values. Malintegration occurs where there is a disproportionate balance or disjuncture between the culturally defined goals of a society and the institutionalised means whereby these goals can be achieved. He argued that all individuals share the same cultural goal (in this case, the 'American Dream' of financial success, fame and status), but that they have different opportunities to achieve success through the established institutionalised means (e.g. employment and education). That is, in a society where emphasis has been placed upon certain valued goals, but the universal provision of appropriate means to attain these goals has been neglected, malintegration is inevitable. Like Durkheim, Merton also made reference to the term 'anomie' in explaining crime, but used it to describe the dichotomy between mainstream society's expectations of its citizens and what they were able to actually achieve given their level of social opportunity. Where social structures of opportunity in society are unequally distributed, the majority of citizens will be prevented from realising the dream and some of these may resort to maladaptive (deviant or destructive) or illegal behaviours.

In the context of the pursuit of universal cultural aspirations, individuals are regarded as having the capacity to make meaningful choices on how to negotiate their future pathway, but their choices are bounded by their location within the social structure. One can choose whether to accept or reject culturally defined goals, and whether to accept or reject the institutional means of attaining these goals. For example, within mainstream criminology, the importance of youth employment opportunities is stressed time and again as being a crucial variable in the conditions that give rise to varying forms of youth criminality. The issue of the lack of individual opportunity for economic and social advancement is particularly pertinent in a period of generalised high unemployment. From the point of view of policy, the opportunity approach places great emphasis on enhancing and developing more opportunities for young people in the labour market so as to reduce incentives to commit crime. The key point of this perspective is that, ultimately, the source of 'strain' or conflict is not seen to reside within the individual, but within the structure of society and its institutions. It is thus the tensions existing between cultural goals and available means that provide the impetus for different types of individual adaptation (see Box 4.2).

LEARNING THEORIES OF DEVIANCE: DIFFERENTIAL ASSOCIATION

Following on from social disorganisation and opportunity theories, sociologists began exploring the impact of culture on people's perceptions of acceptable and unacceptable behaviour, in particular, on how individual learning processes are manifested in youth subcultures. Sutherland and Cressy (1974)

BOX 4.2 INDIVIDUAL ADAPTATIONS TO THE GOALS AND MEANS OF SOCIETY

- *Conformism:* This category comprises the majority of people, who are said to accept the culturally defined goals and the institutionally defined (law-abiding) means of attaining them (paid work).
- *Innovation:* These individuals may subscribe to the culturally defined goals (of success), but they do not have the institutionalised means of achieving them legitimately (e.g. money to pay for education). The result is that they resort to 'innovative' means to achieve their goals, some of which include criminal activity (e.g. committing theft or fraud).
- *Ritualism:* Individuals acknowledge the culturally defined goals, but they also recognise that they cannot attain them. Nevertheless, they decide to pursue the institutionalised means. To put it differently, these people simply go through the motions (e.g. attending school), even though they cannot achieve the goals of success set for them by society.
- *Retreatism:* Individuals choose to reject both the mainstream goals and the socially approved means of achieving them. Instead, they adopt a retreatist position, in which they opt out of the existing cultural and institutional framework (e.g. by consuming or abusing drugs or alcohol).
- *Rebellion:* The cultural goals are no longer seen as relevant, so they are replaced with something else. These individuals are not retreating into oblivion, but instead are creating their own goals and their own means of achieving these (e.g. countercultural activity).

Source: adapted from Merton (1957)

---

argue, for example, that crime is essentially cultural in nature, in the sense that it is learnt behaviour. Crime is not simply determined by biological factors or youthful experiences of lack of economic opportunity. They came to this conclusion based on observed patterns of recurring high crime rates in certain geographical regions which, once established, appeared to be sustained by successive generations of inhabitants. As a means of explaining this generational transmission of delinquent values, Sutherland and Cressy developed a theory of **differential association** over a period of many years. This theory seeks to explain how (not why) criminal behaviour is learnt in interactions between people. What is differentially associated is the behaviour, in that some individuals will associate with the holders of criminal norms, while others will not.

The theory draws on concepts of cultural transmission and construction. According to this perspective, the 'self' is regarded as a social construct, subject to construction and reconstruction through the process of interaction and communication with others. Thus, people learn to define themselves, their situations and their conduct in relation to the law, and this learning takes place within specific group contexts; that is, members of intimate personal groups that hold similar beliefs. Importantly, one learns not just the techniques of crime, but also assimilates the cultural and psychological attitudes positive to commission of crime; that is, its motivations, drives, values and rationalisations. The association of certain classes of conduct, either legal or illegal, is derived from the group's approval or disapproval. Clearly, individuals are exposed to both law-abiding citizens and those that hold anti-law-abiding attitudes. These opposing ideas create 'cultural conflict'. Merely associating with pro-criminal groups does not necessarily result in criminal behaviour. Instead, differential association proposes that an individual will commit to a criminal path when, on balance, the attitudes,

DIFFERENTIAL ASSOCIATION
A theory that seeks to explain how criminal behaviour is learnt in interactions between people. This theory argues that people learn to define a situation and their conduct in relation to the law, and that this learning takes place within specific group contexts.

associations and patterns favourable to law-breaking exceed those unfavourable to law-abiding. This tendency will be reinforced through early and frequent exposure in life to strong pro-criminal attitudes held by those of high social standing within the person's social milieu.

If we are to intervene in young people's lives to stop them from offending, then according to this theory, we must attempt to change the way in which certain groups define their immediate situations and their relationship to law-abiding or law-breaking behaviour (see Box 4.3).

COLLECTIVE BEHAVIOUR: YOUTH SUBCULTURES

The idea that decisions to engage in deviant or criminal behaviour are collective in nature has been the subject of inquiry for those who look to youth **subcultures** as the source of the problem. Various writers have argued, for instance, that societal economic strains are reflected in specific class subcultures that emphasise working-class ways of doing things, and working-class concepts of the social world. Cohen (1955), for example, focused on delinquency among working-class young people in American slum areas, suggesting that gang subculture developed as a working-class response to the conflict with cultural norms of the middle class and the perceived lack of economic and social opportunity. Each subcultural formation adopted distinctive norms and values considered favourable to the geographic area in which it formed, such as 'toughness' and disrespect for authority. In this way, subcultures served as an alternative source of the self-esteem denied their members by conventional society.

Cloward and Ohlin (1960), by contrast, argue that all social classes aspire to the same basic cultural goals (wealth, success and security), but the working class is at a disadvantage in achieving these desired ends.

SUBCULTURES
Small cultural groups that have fragmented from the mainstream and have formed alternative values and meanings about life.

BOX 4.3   KEY ELEMENTS OF DIFFERENTIAL ASSOCIATION

1 Criminal behaviour is learned.
2 Criminal behaviour is learned in interaction with other persons in a process of communication.
3 The principal part of the learning of criminal behaviour occurs within intimate personal groups.
4 When criminal behaviour is learned, the learning includes: (a) techniques of committing the crime; and (b) the specific direction of motives, drives, rationalisations and attitudes (e.g. stealing a car and justifying the theft).
5 The specific direction of motives and drives is learned from definitions of the legal codes as favourable or unfavourable.
6 A person becomes delinquent because of an excess of definitions favourable to violation of law over definitions unfavourable to violation of law.
7 Differential associations may vary in frequency, duration, priority and intensity.
8 The process of learning criminal behaviour by association with criminal and anti-criminal patterns involves all the mechanisms that are involved in any other learning.
9 While criminal behaviour is an expression of general needs and values, it is not explained by those general needs and values, because non-criminal behaviour is an expression of the same needs and values (e.g. adrenalin rushes from illegal and from legal activities).

Source: Sutherland & Cressy (1974)

Frustrated with the perceived lack of justice presented by blocked or absent opportunities to pursue their goals, some working-class young people may be tempted to pursue alternative, illegitimate opportunity structures and practices that provide more lucrative economic benefits.

Whether it is conflict between middle-class values and working-class values, or the adoption of illegitimate opportunity structures specifically related to one's class background, delinquency and crime are seen to be collective phenomena. Related to this type of analysis is the contemporary literature on youth gangs, again with an emphasis on the group nature of youth offending and antisocial behaviour (see van Gemert et al. 2008; Hagedorn 2007; Short & Hughes 2006).

Matza (1964) and, later, Downes (1966) have argued that working-class boys neither reject nor invert the dominant culturally prescribed values of society. Rather, youth subcultures often simply accentuate particular 'subterranean values' that are a part of normal society (e.g. adventure, fun and risks that provide a challenge and produce an adrenalin rush) but sometimes take them too far. In the face of restricted access to opportunity, the response of young people is to resort to a form of 'manufactured excitement' of their own, which is sometimes achieved through illegal means (Matza 1964) such as high speed, illegal racing or climbing without safety equipment. From a sociological perspective, the answer to crime being learned behaviour that takes place in a subcultural context is to dismantle delinquent subcultures and replace them with something more positive (see also the discussion of cultural criminology in Chapter 5).

THE PROBLEM OF UNIVERSAL CULTURE AND VALUES

In summary, sociological theories examine the nature of social constraints as they relate to behaviour; that is, the disjuncture between aspirations and opportunities, and between dominant values and subcultures. These kinds of disjuncture produce friction, frustration and strain, which result in criminal behaviour. In emphasising the importance of social values and macro social structures in the production of crime, sociological theories signal a major shift away from attempts to locate the causes of crime (particularly youth crime) within the individual. It is claimed that crime is not a matter of disturbed people acting out their personal pathologies; rather, crime is a case of normal people coping with abnormal or unequal circumstances created by social structures and processes. The policy options informed by sociological theories include enhancing structural and cultural opportunities in order to overcome the disparity between ends and means, and encouraging the development of 'healthy' peer networks and relationships. On a preventative level, this translates into the provision of training, and educational, vocational and rehabilitation programs.

Mainstream sociological theories continue to influence contemporary theorising on crime but they are subject to a number of notable limitations. Most evidently, with the exception of Sutherland (1949), the focus of strain-based perspectives tends to be on theorising working-class crime, particularly acquisitive street crime and, to a lesser extent, various forms of expressive antisocial behaviour (subcultural theorists). In doing so, they largely support the picture of crime painted by official statistics: that crimes are overwhelmingly committed by the less powerful and less socially mobile in society.

This acceptance of crime as given naturally flows from the adoption of a consensus approach to theorising crime causation. The various perspectives reviewed thus far start with the proposition of a universal set of values in society that all its members embrace and common goals that all strive to achieve. Not surprisingly, given genesis of many of these theories in the United States, societal goals are conceptualised in terms of the *'American Dream'* that is, a desire to acquire material possessions and the associated fame and social status that accompanies upward mobility. Social marginality and inequality, and the motivations for crime this engenders, are thus generally expressed in purely economic terms. Many theorists have questioned the generalisability of these cultural presuppositions; that is, the relevance of Western concepts of values and social participation to other political, social and cultural settings. For example, Willis et al. (1999) highlight the irrelevance of relative deprivation and economic frustration as drivers of crime in Islamic societies, due to religious belief in fatalistic predetermination: people are poor because God deems that they be.

The concept of a general consensus in society not only denies the possibility of value pluralism both within and across societies, but tends also to affirm traditional gender stereotypes. The assumption built into these theories is that economic strains arising from structural impediments to success are largely experienced by males, since societal expectations of financial success apply to them as traditional breadwinners; hence, the almost exclusive preoccupation with male offending. This patriarchal view of society fails to acknowledge the lack of choice regarding participation in the workforce faced by women of the era. Nor do these theories adequately account for female crime and deviance. While male offending is considered a normal, functional response to blocked opportunities, on the rare occasion in which mention of female participation in crime is made, it is done so in the context of signifying weakness. Alternatively, as is the case with some differential association and subcultural theories, female offenders are characterised as incidental, serving as 'helpmates' or 'facilitators' of their male counterparts (Cloward & Ohlin 1960; Cohen 1955). These theories are also generally silent on issues of race. Social disorganisation theory does draw inferences on the association between immigration, social disorganisation and crime, but even so the issue of race is considered only in the context of broader observations on social class.

Finally, by starting with a consensual values proposition (i.e. the existence of 'core values'), these theories fail to question the legitimacy of the state or acknowledge the role it plays in the creation of structural inequalities (e.g. poverty, racism and sexism) and the consequent marginalisation and criminalisation of certain classes of people. As suggested by non-orthodox theories of crime (see Chapter 5), the state has the ultimate power to control the means of production, to define crime and to apply the criminal label; these activities are neither neutral nor impartial. The process and effects of attributing a criminal label to someone in society is the main focus of enquiry of labelling perspectives, which are reviewed next.

LABELLING PERSPECTIVES

LABELLING
A labelling approach to the definition of crime argues that crime only really exists when there has been a social response to a particular activity that labels that activity as criminal. If there is no label, there is in effect no crime.

Labelling theories are closely associated with the *interactionist theories*, which argue that the social world is actively made by human beings in their everyday interactions (see Berger & Luckmann 1971). Most prominent in the 1960s and 1970s, such perspectives challenge the notion that the world and crime are objectively given, arguing instead that crime should be viewed as a social process; that is, human beings do not simply respond passively to external stimuli: they possess choice, they are creative and they bring to bear their own meanings upon situations. The meanings that people attach to situations and the manner in which they define situations, in turn, have an impact on behaviour. Labelling perspectives therefore focus on subjectivity, seeing our perceptions of ourselves—both positive and negative—as arrived at through a process of interactions with others and through negotiating the multiple possible definitions of a situation or event.

The broad interactionist perspective focuses on how people typify one another (i.e. see each other as a particular type of person, such as 'mentally ill' or 'young offender'), how people relate to one another on the basis of these typifications and the consequences of these social processes (Rubington & Weinberg 1978: 1). Application of labelling concepts to the study of crime can be traced back to the work of Tannenbaum (1938), who argued that offenders are fundamentally no different from non-offenders in regards to the impulse to first commit crime, but that dramatisation of the offending act, followed by social interaction in the form of the 'tagging' or labelling of the offender, starts a demonisation process that accounts for the development of subsequent offending.

From this perspective, deviance or criminality is not something that is objectively given; it is subjectively problematic (Plummer 1979). The labelling perspective therefore attempts to provide a **processual account** of deviancy and criminality. Essentially, it argues that deviancy itself can be the result of the interactive process between individual juveniles and the criminal justice system; that, for example, police intervention can actually produce deviancy. In early versions of labelling theories, it was asserted that deviancy is not an inherent property of behaviour, but something that is conferred upon the individual by society. In other words, deviance is created by social reaction. According to Becker (1963: 9):

> [T]he impact of social reaction on certain types of behaviour or on particular categories of people is crucial to explaining the criminalisation process. In short, social groups create deviance by making the rules whose infraction constitutes deviance, and by applying those rules to particular people and labelling them as outsiders. From this point of view, deviance is not a quality of the act the person commits, but rather a consequence of the application by others of rules and sanctions to an 'offender'. The deviant is one to whom the label has successfully been applied; deviant behaviour is behaviour that people so label.

The argument here is that we need to look at the impact of the application of certain labels (e.g. 'bad', 'criminal' and 'delinquent') in fostering deviant behaviour. Public labelling, it is argued, may affect individuals' self-identity and transform them so that they see themselves in the light of the label. The process of labelling is tied up with the idea of the self-fulfilling prophecy. That is, if you tell someone that they are 'bad' or 'stupid' or 'crazy' sufficiently often, that person may start to believe the label and to act out the stereotypical behaviour associated with it, thereby further reinforcing the label.

A further aspect of the public labelling process is that *stigmatisation* may occur. This involves the application of a negative label that becomes the 'master' (or dominant) definition of the person to whom it is applied. Regardless of current behaviour or past experiences, a person may become known to the wider community mainly or solely in terms of the label applied to him or her. A negative label, such as 'criminal' or 'delinquent', can colour the perceptions of people with whom the individual interacts and influence how the community in general treats that person (Goffman 1963). Where such stigma exists, a situation may arise where the 'deviant' begins to live up to the dictates of the label and to change his or her identity and behaviour accordingly (see Box 4.4).

PRIMARY DEVIATION AND SECONDARY DEVIATION

In order to describe the process of labelling, Lemert (1969) distinguished between **primary deviation** and **secondary deviation**. His concern was to explain how individuals come to be committed to the delinquent label, and to a delinquent career.

* *Primary deviation*: Most people at some stage in their development engage in activities regarded as deviant. They do so for a wide variety of social, cultural and psychological reasons. However, the important thing at this stage is that when people engage in deviant activity they do not fundamentally change their self-concept. That is, the individual's psyche does not undergo a symbolic re-orientation or transformation. There is no change in identity, and deviance is seen as nothing more than a passing event with no long-term behavioural effects.

PROCESSUAL ACCOUNT
A processual account of crime involves the study of the processes of creating crime and deviancy rather than discrete acts themselves or their aetiology.

PRIMARY DEVIATION
Primary deviation occurs when an individual engages, at some stage in their early development, in activities regarded as deviant, usually for a variety of social, cultural and psychological reasons.

SECONDARY DEVIATION
Secondary deviation is said to occur when, because of the social reaction to primary deviation, a person experiences a fundamental reorientation of his or her self-concept, and thus his or her behaviour.

BOX 4.4   CRIME AS SOCIAL PROCESS

- A deviant act occurs (deviation from societal or legal norms).
- A public label is applied (by courts, teachers, parents and counsellors).
- Stigmatisation occurs (a blot on your record; a stain on your character).
- In response to this stigmatisation, a new identity is formulated (as a means of defence, or coping with negative social reaction to oneself).
- The construction of a new identity is formed in accordance with the label bestowed upon the individual (living up to the content of the label).
- A commitment is formed to the roles and behaviour of the attached label (learning the behaviour and norms of the role identified in the label).
- Longer-term pursuit of a deviant career occurs as dictated by the labelling process (becoming a 'criminal' or 'delinquent').

- *Secondary deviation*: The main focus of labelling theory is with secondary deviation. This occurs when the individual engages in primary deviation, and then there is some kind of official reaction to that behaviour. For example, an individual is apprehended by the police for truanting from school. The individual may begin to employ a deviant behaviour or role based upon this new status, which has been conferred upon him or her by state officials, as a means of defence or adjustment to the overt and covert problems created by the public social reaction to their original behaviour. Secondary deviation is said to occur when, because of the social reaction to the primary deviation, the person experiences a fundamental re-orientation of their self-concept, and thus their behaviour and social interactions.

These ideas are also encapsulated in the notion of crime as social process (see Box 4.4).

JUVENILE CRIME AND LABELLING

Labelling theories in criminology have had their greatest impact in the specific area of juvenile justice. This is not surprising, given the general view that young people and children are more impressionable than older people, and therefore more likely to respond to any labelling that might occur. It is argued that if a young person comes to court and is labelled as an offender, this process of public labelling and stigmatisation creates a new identity for the young person and, as a consequence, that individual will become committed to the roles and behaviour of the 'delinquent'.

Whether they are good or bad, negative or positive, constructive or destructive, labels, it is argued, do affect and have consequences for subsequent behaviour. Matza (1964) investigated the question of 'delinquency' on the basis of the proposition that crime itself is ubiquitous; that is, most people at some stage engage in some form of criminal, deviant or antisocial behaviour. In studying youth subcultures and delinquents, a 'naturalistic' approach was adopted, one that was committed to providing an account describing youth experiences from the point of view of young people. This not only enabled the researcher to reconsider the question of values and to challenge the idea that only working-class young people experience strain, but also enabled the researcher to explore the motivational accounts provided by the actors themselves as to why they engage in certain types of activity. Sykes and Matza (1957) and Matza (1964) described the ways in which young people use certain **techniques of neutralisation** (an extension of Sutherland's differential association theory) as a way of denying the moral bind of law (e.g. 'they started it' or 'no one got hurt'). The techniques broadly include the following:

- *Denial of responsibility:* the offence is not consciously willed; the offender was a victim of circumstance or was forced into a situation beyond their control.
- *Denial of injury:* the offender's actions are justifiable since they did not cause harm or damage.
- *Denial of the victim:* the victim is deserving of the actions of the offender.
- *Condemnation of the condemners:* those condemning the offender's actions are motivated by spite, or are blame shifting; they therefore have no moral authority to condemn.
- *The appeal to higher loyalties:* the offence served a greater good (customarily those of a subgroup to which the offender belongs) and therefore the consequences are justified; for example, the offence was committed to protect a friend.

Furthermore, Matza argued that the actions of the juvenile justice system, and especially youth perceptions of the competence of officials and the application of sanctions, affect the 'will to crime' of young people, and form part of the ways in which they neutralise their moral restraint. In studying young people, Matza found that juveniles eagerly explore all aspects of social life. He found that in this process they tend to drift between the two poles of conventional and unconventional behaviour (including crime), without being fully committed to either. In the end, most juveniles drift towards conventional lifestyles and behaviour as their permanent pattern of experience. However, Matza found that if, during the teenage years of drift, there is official intervention and social reaction to specific kinds of unconventional behaviour, it may precipitate the movement of the juvenile into a permanent state of delinquency.

The central policy concern of the labelling approach, therefore, is to find ways in which to prevent the criminalisation and marginalisation of a young person so that they do not become a career criminal or long-term deviant. If we accept the proposition that contact with the criminal justice system—police, courts or detention centres—serves to sustain deviant careers by stigmatising the offender and impacting their subsequent life opportunities and relationships (for studies providing empirical support for these claims, see Fader 2011; Gatti et al. 2009; Lopes et al. 2012; McGrath 2010), then the solution is posed in terms of diversion. From a labelling perspective, individuals should be diverted away from the formal processes of the justice system in order to escape any possible negative consequences arising from the formal public labelling process. In this way, future commitment to a deviant career can be averted. For those young people within the system, deinstitutionalisation (i.e. the removal of youth from institutions) and their placement in the community are advocated in order to minimise negative labelling.

LABELLING—A LIMITED THEORY?

In summary, labelling theory concentrates its attention on the social reaction to crime; that is, the process of social control. The approach sees crime and deviance as socially constructed categories (rather than objective phenomena) that are maintained, perpetuated or amplified by the labelling process. The process of social reaction defines not only acts, but also people. Criminality is thus something that is conferred upon some individuals, and on some types of behaviour, by social control agents who have the power to do so, and who have sufficient authority and credibility to make the label stick (i.e. cause the label to be internalised so that it shapes personal identity and action).

Importantly, this perspective draws attention to the ironic nature of social control, in that efforts to control crime and deviancy are frequently counterproductive, producing self-fulfilling, criminogenic

TECHNIQUES OF NEUTRALI- SATION
A term used to describe the ways in which young people use certain techniques to neutralise or deny the moral bind of law; for example, 'they started it' or 'no one got hurt'.

effects (adoption of the criminal label, leading to career offending). The implications of labelling perspectives for juvenile justice are that we should do what we can to minimise the harmful effects of labelling and stigmatisation. This can be achieved through a wide variety of diversionary practices that attempt to keep young people from entering too far into the official criminal justice system (see Box 4.5).

Like other sociological theories discussed earlier in this chapter, labelling perspectives refocused attention away from human and environmental pathologies, and aberrant behaviour, towards the social construction of deviance. Individuals commit deviant or criminal acts not because of *who* they are but because of *what* they become following the application of a stigmatic label that criminalises them and adversely impacts their self-perception and subsequent interactions with others.

While offering useful insights into the powerful and negative effects of social control, the labelling approach has been criticised on a number of fronts (Taylor et al. 1975). One of the most enduring criticisms is that it does not offer any explanation of the motivations or circumstances underlying the primary deviance; that is, the original behaviour that instigated the labelling process. While this is a valid criticism, its proponents argue that the labelling approach never set out to achieve that objective; it is not a theory per se, but rather a perspective and, as such, it offers insight into one—albeit important—aspect of the crime causation puzzle (Plummer 1979). They argue that since most young people engage in criminal or deviant activity at some point in their developmental trajectory, and in only few instances does primary deviance escalate to secondary deviance, that it is appropriate to focus on the mechanisms that effect the latter.

Notwithstanding the plausibility of such claims, there is a tendency to depict recipients of a criminal or deviant label as overly passive. While labelling perspectives acknowledge that in not all situations will the label attach—even in contexts where repeated labelling has taken place—it is not entirely clear what gives the recipient the capacity or will to reject the label and why this is not the case for all people. Conversely, the perspective is silent on why some individuals assume a deviant identity that manifests all the features of secondary deviance without ever having been publicly labelled.

BOX 4.5   KEY IDEAS OF THE LABELLING PERSPECTIVE

- Humans exercise choice but their *self-identity is shaped* through a process of *interaction* with other people and with social institutions.
- Crime is a subjective phenomenon but is *defined by the state* through a process of action and reaction; *criminality is conferred* by those with the power to label.
- Focus on *social responses* to crime and deviance rather than questions of aetiology; labelling as a form of *social control.*
- Labelling and its negative effects (stigmatisation) can lead to *deviancy amplification.*
- The criminal justice system is *not neutral and impartial* in its application of criminal and deviant labels.
- Punishment should be a measure of last resort; *diversion* from the formal justice system is preferred.
- Crime can be prevented through *decriminalisation*, *judicious use of formal responses* (radical non-intervention, minimal intervention and deinstitutionalisation) and measures that seek to *reconfigure an offender's self-image.*

Another criticism is that much of the focus of labelling perspectives is on a limited range of minor infractions committed by delinquents, with common forms of property crime, serious street crimes and crimes of the powerful omitted from the discussion. There is almost universal agreement around the harmfulness and criminality of acts such as rape and murder, so is it appropriate to focus only on societal reactions with respect to such crimes when they are the offender's primary offence? Relatedly, while the labelling approach serves to humanise the individual by removing moral judgment associated with their actions, there is no mention of the value in officially responding to offending behaviour as a means of acknowledging the 'lived reality' of crime for its victims—a reality that can be quite traumatic and sometimes life-changing.

Finally, while labelling perspectives introduce the important concept of power in defining and responding to crime, analysis of its operation is concentrated at the individual and organisational levels of social control only; for example, the power of individual police officers to officially proceed with an offender, and the power of the courts to divert individuals away from or further into the criminal justice system. Absent from consideration is a structurally based critique of power that acknowledges the inherently exploitative and stigmatic nature of political and socio-economic frameworks, such as capitalism. Consideration of the structural nature of power would, for instance, highlight the way in which labelling of Indigenous people in Australia is bound up with broader issues of colonialism: specifically, the historical nature of the relationship between Aboriginal people and the police, and the way in which the act of going through the justice system and being labelled is viewed by some as an important rite of passage (Hudson 2013; Ogilvie & Van Zyl 2001; see also Chapter 7).

MULTIFACTORIAL EXPLANATIONS

Most theories of crime causation at some stage refer to issues of *free will* and *determination*; that is, most writers on criminal offending tend to speak about crime as entirely or mainly a matter of personal choice (thereby stressing the responsibility of the person for their actions), or as something largely determined or shaped by forces outside of the person's conscious control (thereby stressing the need for treatment or social reform of some kind).

There are myriad reasons why any particular individual may engage in crime, although broad social patterns in offending behaviour are apparent. As demonstrated in this and the previous chapter, theories and studies of criminal offending point to a wide range of causal factors. These include *individual factors* (ranging from personal choice, to psychological damage arising from an abusive childhood, to mental illness); *situational factors* (including poor school performance, homelessness and deviant peer cultures); and *social structural factors* (relating, for instance, to inadequate moral education and socialisation, racism and social inequality). Therefore, a multiplicity of specific factors help to explain crime.

KEY RISK FACTORS OF YOUTH OFFENDING

In a review of empirical research on the predictors and correlates of offending, Farrington (1996b) provides a systematic outline of the key *risk factors* associated with youthful offending. Among the many factors cited are:

- *prenatal and perinatal factors:* for example, early childbearing; substance use during pregnancy; low birth weight

- *hyperactivity and impulsivity:* for example, hyperactivity–impulsivity attention deficit; lack of inhibition
- *intelligence and attainment:* for example, low nonverbal intelligence and abstract reasoning; cognitive and neuropsychological deficit
- *parental supervision, discipline and attitude:* for example, erratic or harsh parental discipline; rejecting parental attitudes; violent behaviour
- *broken homes:* for example, maternal and paternal deprivation; parental conflict
- *parental criminality:* for example, convicted parent(s); poor supervision
- *large family size:* related to parental inattention and overcrowding
- *socio-economic deprivation:* for example, low family income; poor housing
- *peer influences:* for example, male group behaviour; delinquent friends
- *school influences:* for example, use of praise and punishment; classroom management
- *community influences:* for example, high residential mobility; neighbourhood disorganisation; physical deterioration; overcrowding; type of housing
- *situational influences:* for example, specific opportunities; benefits outweighing expected costs; seeking excitement.

It is the combination of these factors, and their association with certain categories of young people, that explains variations in the propensity for criminal behaviour and/or criminalisation among young people. As Farrington (1996b) observes in explaining the development of offending, a major problem is that most risk factors tend to coincide and be interrelated. For example, adolescents living in physically deteriorated and socially disorganised neighbourhoods disproportionately tend also to come from families with poor parental supervision and erratic parental discipline, and tend also to have high impulsivity and low intelligence. The concentration and co-occurrence of these kinds of adversities make it difficult to establish their independent, interactive and sequential influences on offending and antisocial behaviour.

Australian reviews and commentaries likewise identify a wide range of interacting and interrelated factors—pertaining to the individual, peer groups, family, school and community—as integral to any explanation of youth offending (see Developmental Crime Prevention Consortium 1999; Toumbourou 1999). The notion that there are multiple factors that influence behaviour, and multiple stages or points of transition that represent especially important moments in a person's life, provides for a complex model of criminal behaviour (see Box 4.6).

Developmental perspectives on behaviour provide an avenue for revitalisation of labelling concepts. Specifically, they offer a possible solution to a core criticism of labelling approaches discussed above: the failure to elucidate the intervening mechanism between attribution of a deviant label and consequent behavioural adjustment in keeping with the label. Developmental approaches suggest a number of social dynamics through which myriad causal mechanisms operate over the life course, and researchers have adopted this approach to explain the detrimental impacts of formal labelling on life chance processes (see, for example, Lopes et al. 2012; Sampson & Laub 1993; see also Chapter 27).

MULTIDIMENSIONAL APPROACH

Social development is influenced by a wide range of factors, most of which are outside the conscious control of the individual. Identification of 'risk' and 'protective' factors is essential in explaining why children and young people act the way they do, and how they cope or interact with their environments. Such analysis must also consider the impact of cultural factors and personal resiliency on life trajectories,

| BOX 4.6 | KEY IDEAS OF MULTIFACTORIAL ANALYSIS |

MULTIPLE FACTORS AT MULTIPLE LEVELS

- *Risk factors*: these include factors that increase the likelihood of an offence occurring or being repeated. These factors might include the characteristics of an individual (e.g. a child's impulsivity), the family (a parent's harsh discipline or weak supervision), the social group (peers that encourage or tolerate the occurrence of crime) and the community (a community that is disorganised and offers few alternatives to crime as a source of money or activity).
- *Protective factors*: these include factors that reduce the impact of an unavoidable negative event, help individuals avoid or resist temptations to break the law, reduce the chances that people will start on a path likely to lead to breaches of the law and promote an alternative pathway. Again, these factors might include responding to the needs of the individual (through active promotion of self-esteem), enhancing family relationships (through advice and information), fostering positive social group activity (through sport) and community building (facilities and social structures that support involvement and attachment).

MULTIPLE LIFE PHASES AND TRANSITION POINTS

- *Pathways*: developmental perspectives view life as a progression through various stages and transition junctures. These include, for example, the movement of a child from the family as the prime setting for their activity, through early education, primary school, high school and adolescence, and adult life. Positive experiences in each setting and transition point will foster prosocial behaviour.
- *Vulnerabilities*: at each life stage or transition point there is the risk of possible negative experiences that may put individuals on an at-risk pathway. These might include, for example, experience of failure in schooling, alienation, becoming involved with an antisocial peer group and unemployment. This perspective recognises that, while behaviour can be changed more easily in the young than in the old, later transition points are also sensitive times, and it is important to structure intervention to diminish the risk of movement into harmful paths at these times as well.

Source: adapted from Developmental Crime Prevention Consortium (1999)

---

as well as socio-structural variables. Empirical study has ascertained that there are numerous and diverse factors that have varying degrees of impact on any individual's life experiences and life course. While certain factors have a persistent effect on life chances (e.g. poverty and dysfunctional family life), ongoing research is needed to determine the *ever-changing* and *ever-expanding* 'risk' factors affecting child development, and to positively identify relevant 'protective' factors in any given situation.

The hallmark of multifactorial approaches is that they usually stress the need for *multidimensional and holistic ways of working* at the local community level. They also acknowledge the crucial role of community members, including children and young people themselves, in the social development process. In other words, the theoretical framework gives rise to concern to address social problems using multipronged methods and involving a wide number of agencies. Many causes require many tactics and strategies operating across a number of fronts.

REPUBLICAN THEORY

Another theoretical perspective that brings together a wide range of concepts and ideas is *republican theory*. This theory attempts to combine elements of strain theory and labelling perspectives (among other theoretical approaches) through a series of practical institutional measures, including *reintegrative shaming*.

REPUBLICAN LIBERTY

DOMINION
Within criminological theory, 'dominion' refers to republican notions of liberty. Dominion is a form of freedom or positive liberty protected by the law and culture of a community. Crime occurs when the dominion status of an individual is diminished or destroyed.

The core concept of this theory is the notion of *republican liberty* or *republican* **dominion**. This refers to a form of *negative liberty*, whereby non-interference in our lives by other people (including state officials) is protected by law and general community norms. According to the authors of republican theory, Braithwaite & Pettit (1990), the prime goal of any society should be to maximise the enjoyment of dominion (personal liberty).

In this framework, crime is seen as the denial of personal dominion at three different levels.

- A negative challenge to the *dominion status of the victim*. A threat to, or disregard for, the dominion of an individual is an attack on the status of that individual as someone who holds a protected dominion status in society. If someone commits a crime against an individual, then the criminal act asserts the vulnerability of the victim to the will of the criminal, nullifying the protected status of the victim.

- If successful, the criminal attempt not only disregards the victim's dominion, but also directly *undermines*, *diminishes* and perhaps even *destroys the victim's dominion*. For example, kidnapping or murdering someone will destroy that person's dominion, while stealing a person's property will diminish his or her dominion by undermining certain exercises of dominion that person might otherwise have pursued (e.g. it diminishes the liberty to use that property).

- Every crime also represents communal evil; it does an *evil to the community as a whole*. A crime not only affects the dominion status of the individual victim, but also endangers the community's dominion generally. This is because the fear of crime, or lack of action taken to assist the victim, can have the impact of reducing the liberty of those who fear possible victimisation of themselves.

EQUILIBRIUM MODEL

If every act of crime represents damage to dominion, then the system's task is to promote dominion by rectifying or remedying the damage caused by the crime. What should the courts do in response to the convicted offender, for example?

Theoretically, in sentencing the convicted offender, the courts need to consider certain elements. First, the offender must recognise the personal liberty of the victim in order to restore the victim's status. In order to do this, the offender must withdraw the implicit claim that the victim did not enjoy the dominion that was challenged by the crime. Second, in order to restore the victim's former dominion—which may not only have been disregarded, but also may have been diminished or destroyed—there must be some form of recompense for the damage done to the individual's personal dominion. And, third, there must be a general reassurance given to the community in general of a kind that may undo the negative impact of crime on their enjoyment of dominion.

The republican theory thus assumes an *equilibrium model* of criminal justice, because it seeks to restore the dominion status of the victim by reintegrating the victim back into society so that he or she can once again exercise personal dominion. Abstractly, the recognition of dominion of the victim by the offender requires a mix of measures, both symbolic and substantive.

COMMUNITARIANISM

From a republican point of view, the causes of crime lie in a combination of social and psychological factors. Part of the problem is the lack of a self-sanctioning conscience. This is where an individual has not learned adequately the interpretation and acceptance of societal norms as being right and just. One of the results of a punitive and stigmatising system is that it propels people into associating with other similarly ostracised individuals (e.g. in a criminal subculture) who individually and collectively do not develop this conscience.

The lack of adequate and appropriate social connections is expressed in the concept of *communitarianism*. This describes interdependency at a societal level, involving relationships of loyalty, trust and concern. Interdependency is itself reflected in a person's relationship to school, work, marriage and stable residence. The issue of social opportunity is important insofar as it affects the interdependencies and, eventually, the moral development of an individual.

The response to crime in a specific sense is to utilise the least restrictive measures possible, and to undo the wrong that has been committed. The republican theory of criminal justice is intended to deal with the victim so he or she can once again exercise public dominion, and the community can be reassured. The focus is on maximising personal dominion for the victim. However, there is also the assumption that the offender should be reintegrated, so that his or her dominion also can be reinstated. The theory seeks a minimalist response on the part of the state to the offender. A reintegrative equilibrium needs to be established where the victim, the community and the offender are considered.

REINTEGRATIVE SHAMING: BRAITHWAITE

The republican response to crime therefore bases itself on the concept of *reintegrative shaming* (see Braithwaite 1989). This involves a process in which the offender is shamed for the action, but is not 'cast out' as a person. It describes a process whereby the offender is publicly rebuked for the harm caused, but is then forgiven and reintegrated into the mainstream of society. As part of the reintegrative shaming process, the victim is directly involved in proceedings, and can be compensated in some way for the harm done. In arguing this line, Braithwaite looks to labelling theory in order to highlight how his theory moves away from the undesirable effects of shaming.

In discussing labelling theory, the stigmatising and self-fulfilling effects on an individual of being termed 'bad' through the criminalisation process were highlighted. There is a need, however, to distinguish between stigmatisation, which increases the risks of reoffending by the shamed actor, and reintegrative shaming. In terms of the preferred second approach, disapproval is extended while a relationship of respect is sustained with the offender. Stigmatisation is disrespectful: it is seen as a humiliating form of shaming, where the offender is branded an evil person and is cast out permanently. Reintegrative shaming, by contrast, seeks to shame the evil deed but sees the offender in a respectable light. The shaming is finite, and the offender is given the opportunity to re-enter society by way of recognising the wrongdoing, apologising and repenting. In this way, shame is seen as useful as a means of combating crime as long as it is not applied in a stigmatising fashion.

From a crime prevention perspective, steps should be taken to promote valued norms (which, in turn, become the basis for the formation of a self-sanctioning conscience) and to foster greater communitarianism by enhancing educational, work and social opportunities. The criminal justice system ought to incorporate a broad range of informal and more formal institutional arrangements, such as conferences of the offender and victims, and be oriented towards the least intrusive kind of intervention possible (see, for example, Murphy & Helmer 2013; Kim & Gerber 2012).

Republican theory provides for a whole range of variables that are associated with crime, at the level of both the individual (interdependency) and society (communitarianism). The theory thus provides a description of 'background' characteristics of the 'typical offender' (e.g. young, unemployed, male and transient), although it does not really explore how these factors interact with the given environment that leads to offending.

ISSUES FOR CONSIDERATION

CRIME AND SOCIETY

The profiles of young offenders tend to look basically the same. Young men typically aged 12–16 years at first offence and 15–17 years when in first contact with police (Richards 2009), with low income, low educational achievement, no employment and a weak attachment to parents, and who move frequently, are the most likely to wind up in juvenile detention centres (see Braithwaite 1989; Cunneen & White 2011). While researchers continue to identify a range of risk factors (e.g. drug abuse) and protective factors (e.g. family cohesion) that influence whether an individual engages in criminal or antisocial behaviour (Catalano & Hawkins 1996), it is the wider structural context of youth experience that shapes the overall life chances and life experiences of young people (White & Wyn 2013; Wyn & White 1997).

To say that the wider structural context is such a strong determinant of youth behaviour and opportunity is to assert that youth offending occurs within certain specific political, economic and social contexts. Rather than treating phenomena such as 'socio-economic disadvantage' and 'unemployment' as specific causal factors, among many others, it is necessary to view such phenomena as consequences of wider structural transformations in society. To address youth crime, for instance, therefore requires an analytical shift from simple multifactorial analyses to consideration of broader social processes that give rise to and exacerbate particular risk factors. In practice, why certain young people commit particular crimes is only answerable by consideration of their personal life history, their immediate life circumstances and their position in the wider social structure. For example, the decision to commit vandalism may incorporate elements of an abusive childhood, difficulties at school, unemployment and bad experiences with authority figures, or it could be as simple as 'having a good time'.

CRIME AND THE INDIVIDUAL

While it is important to think about general theories on crime and crime causation, it is also insightful to consider the specific reasons why young people commit particular crimes, and how these might relate to general theories of crime. Take property offences, for example: a 1996 New South Wales study involving interviews with juvenile theft offenders in detention centres found that the main reasons given for shoplifting were to obtain clothes or money for clothes, and to obtain food or money for food (Freeman 1996). The majority of young offenders also said they committed break-and-enter offences in order to obtain money, with about half of these young people wanting to use the money to buy drugs and/or alcohol. Almost half of the offenders convicted for stealing a motor vehicle said that they had committed the offence because of the want or need of transport. Similarly, a study in Victoria of teenagers in low-income neighbourhoods found that 80 per cent of young people in the study viewed illegal activity as an important means whereby people their age could supplement an inadequate income (White et al. 1997). Drug dealing and shoplifting were considered the main ways to get money and, in either case, the reason for the activity was primarily financial.

ROLE OF ALCOHOL AND DRUGS

These examples illustrate that certain types of crimes (e.g. property crime and drug dealing) are very much related to particular groups of offenders (low income or unemployed) for very specific ends (obtaining money or having transport). This is important insofar as it indicates that it is crucial to consider the social context of crime in any genuine attempt to bring together the individual, situational and structural elements of crime. Taking into account social context, we can also better understand the place and role of alcohol and other drugs in the lives of some young people. Studies have shown, for example, that substance use—particularly the use of marijuana and alcohol—is strongly associated with young-offender status (Howard & Zibert 1990; Putnins 2001). Higher rates of tobacco, alcohol and cannabis use have also been observed in those young people who, for whatever reason, are out of school but not in full-time employment (Lynskey & Hall 1998; Tressider et al. 1997). Drug use (and abuse) has been associated with a lack of positive things to do, boredom, lack of employment and educational opportunities, and a general sense of pessimism that things are not going to get any better. Furthermore, many offenders report using substances at the time of their offence, with alcohol the substance most often associated with the act of offending (Putnins 2001: 14).

What young people think about their circumstances, how they think about themselves, and how others view them all have major repercussions for the ways in which they relate to issues of crime and society. Invariably, as well, the social position of young people also brings them into regular contact with agents of the criminal justice system. More theoretical and empirical work is needed to explore the lived experiences of youth crime: motivations, emotions, sensate experiences and meanings associated with human behaviour. How young people perceive and emotionally respond to the world around them is central to this task.

THE ENDURING LESSONS OF LABELLING

Plummer (2011) has recently argued that despite being a generational narrative (a world perspective of its time), labelling perspectives have left a set of important and abiding concerns for criminologists to consider; namely, the importance of societal reactions to, and labelling of, crime and offenders. The endurance of these lessons can be seen in the development of new lines of sociological inquiry focused on societal reactions that are informed by labelling perspectives, including:

- the role played by the media in the demonisation and stigmatisation of particular crimes and offenders—activities that can generate public hysteria and moral panic (see Chapter 2).
- the symbiotic relationship of the media and the public and the rise of penal populism—increasingly harsh public attitudes to sex offenders, youth crime, antisocial behaviour and recidivists

(see Chapters 24 and 25) that have led to more punitive justice responses such as the introduction of sex-offender registers and antisocial behaviour laws. These measures raise concerns regarding the long-term effects of stigma.

- the creation of social exclusion by the state—the way in which societies 'essentialise' and 'demonise' the others (see Chapter 8), casting deviants outside the conventional order through the creation of 'hyperghettos, of territorial stigmatisation', for example, or via confinement in prisons or detention centres.

- the expansion of control cultures—the exponential encroachment of state control on individuals' personal lives through the medicalisation of deviance (see Chapters 3 and 25), the privatisation and bureaucratisation of control agencies (see Chapter 17) and the increasing application of technology in effecting community-based sanctions (see Chapter 26). These developments have all been accused of expanding, strengthening and deepening the net of social control and thereby amplifying deviance, which are traditional concerns of labelling proponents.

CONCLUSION

The development of official responses to crime, especially in the context of juvenile offending, has been heavily influenced by the theories and perspectives outlined in this chapter. The 'special conditions' that have characterised the ways in which young people have been processed within the criminal justice system are in no small part a result of the influence of ideas relating to social structure and social processes, and their impact on youth behaviour (see Chapter 21). The responses of the system to young people are by no means uniform or consistent, and the multiplicity of programs and institutions in part reflects the many different ideas about the causes of juvenile offending. The emphasis on group work and outreach work in some programs, for example, is related to the notion of peer-group influence and subcultural values, and how these shape a young person's attitudes towards criminal or deviant behaviour. Provision of training and educational programs is clearly linked with concerns to overcome blocked opportunities and encourage positive developmental outlets for young people. The decriminalisation of some juvenile offences, ongoing concerns to divert young people from the formal court system and the development of alternatives to detention represent systemic responses to issues raised by labelling perspectives.

The application by criminologists of the ideas summarised in this chapter tends to manifest in the form of multifactorial explanations of youth crime. However, in doing this, criminologists generally refrain from presenting a hierarchy of causes. The result is that immediate causes are cited (e.g. unemployment, labelling and poor schooling) and reformist measures are advocated (e.g. training schemes or alternative schools), but rarely are substantial changes to the social structure as a whole demanded. For those who wish to see major social change occurring, the questions of power and of social interests are of paramount importance. Where multiple factors are at the foreground of analysis, the tendency is to respond to the phenomenon of crime through emphasis on developing specific projects and programs. More radical perspectives, which are the subject of the following chapter, view such proposals as very limited unless they are linked directly to a wider politics of social change. Chapter 5 reviews those perspectives that challenge criminological orthodoxies.

DISCUSSION QUESTIONS

1 What makes an explanation of crime 'sociological' rather than 'classical' or 'positivist'?

2 'You are who you hang around with; you do what your peers do.' Discuss in regards to crime and criminal activity.

3 In what ways can labels be resisted? In what ways can they be used in a positive way?

4 What is republican liberty, and why is it central to republican concepts of criminal justice?

5 'Multifactoral analysis provides descriptive theory of specific causal agents, but it tends to ignore underlying structural causes of crime.' Discuss.

FURTHER READING

Becker, H. (1963) *Outsiders: studies in the sociology of deviance*, Free Press, New York.

Braithwaite, J. (1989) *Crime, shame and reintegration*, Cambridge University Press, Cambridge.

Merton, R. (1957) *Social theory and social structure*, Free Press, New York.

Plummer, K. (1979) 'Misunderstanding labelling perspectives', in D. Downes & P. Rock (eds), *Deviant interpretations*, Martin Robertson, Oxford.

Sykes, G. & Matza, D. (1957) 'Techniques of neutralization: a theory of delinquency', *American Sociological Review*, 22: 664–70.

5 CHALLENGES TO CRIMINOLOGICAL ORTHODOXIES

CHAPTER OVERVIEW

- RADICAL PERSPECTIVES
- CRITICAL CRIMINOLOGY
- STRUCTURALIST CRIMINOLOGY
- PEACEMAKING CRIMINOLOGY AND RESTORATIVE JUSTICE
- CULTURAL CRIMINOLOGY
- GREEN CRIMINOLOGY
- ISSUES FOR CONSIDERATION
- CONCLUSION
- DISCUSSION QUESTIONS
- FURTHER READING

INTRODUCTION

This chapter presents brief overviews of selected strands within criminological theory that in some way represent challenges to the orthodoxies of classical, positivist and mainstream sociological perspectives examined in preceding chapters. The challenges are of a theoretical nature, particularly when it comes to how 'harm' is conceptualised and understood within specific approaches. The challenges are also often of a political nature, in that they invite adherents to question the basic foundations of the contemporary criminal justice system and its core assumptions.

The chapter begins by reviewing long-established Marxist and feminist perspectives, which were instrumental in shifting the lens of theorising on crime and social control to a macro social context, but which are now situated on the margins of contemporary criminology. This is followed by short summaries of several perspectives that are rapidly making their mark in the field, including structural criminology, peacemaking criminology, restorative justice, cultural criminology and green criminology. As much as anything, the chapter indicates the vibrancy and self-critique that is essential to exploration of criminological theory, now and into the future.

RADICAL PERSPECTIVES

This chapter commences with a review of the foundational radical perspectives—Marxist and feminist approaches—that emerged in the middle of the twentieth century. To this point, theories on crime causation and social control had been based on a consensual view of social order: all citizens embraced a core set of values and norms, and crime was considered a transgression of the social consensus. Within this societal framework, social control served a functional purpose: to maintain equilibrium.

Restoration of societal order following a crime was hence regarded an underlying objective of, and fundamental justification for, punishment.

Labelling perspectives represented a significant challenge to this established orthodoxy by questioning the unproblematic conceptualisation of crime as fact. The creation of crime and criminality, it was argued, was instead an active social process, with certain groups in society more vulnerable to application of the labels 'criminal' and 'deviant'. This paradigm shift from consensus was further accentuated by Marxist and feminist perspectives, which adopted a conflict-based view of society that revolved around analysis of structural power and power relations.

According to this view, individuals are defined not so much by personal attributes or by reference to universalising statements regarding 'choice' and 'determinism', but by their position and opportunities in society, as dictated by class divisions and unequal gender relations. To understand crime and social control, therefore, we need to examine the actions of the powerful in defining and enforcing a particular kind of social order, and the activities of the less powerful in the context of a repressive social structure within which they have fewer resources and less decision-making power than others. Within this framework, Marxist and feminist concepts of social control are firmly aligned with repressive responses to deviant behaviour and repressive power relations more generally. These perspectives focus on exposing the disjuncture between the state's theoretical intent (the law's stated objectives), its practical form and effects (how and to whom laws are applied in practice) and the underlying motivations for and consequences of this disparity (Lucken 2013; see also Chapter 22).

MARXIST PERSPECTIVES

A key characteristic of **Marxist** conceptions of crime and criminality is their focus on the way in which institutionalised power (social, economic and political) is organised and exercised in society. As the name suggests, these perspectives draw on Marxist theory of human behaviour and institutional arrangements to explain crime, although it should be noted that there is no Marxist theory of deviance per se. According to Marx and Engels (1848; see also, for example, Bute 1981), human activity in a capitalist society is defined in economic terms: the sale of human labour in exchange for purchasing power. The output of human labour (goods and services) is controlled by the ruling class (increasingly, national and transnational corporations); most individuals in society are therefore wage earners whose capital largely lies in their ability to keep working. The relationship of people to property created under capitalism is said to be characterised by a history of class struggle over the means of production.

Within this framework of social relations, Marxism sees the state as variously linked to the specific interests of the capitalist ruling class—the powerful few who own the means of production—and the activities of the state reflect the interests of capital in general. These activities, in the shape of laws and regulation, foster the accumulation of capital, maintain the legitimacy of unequal social relations and control the actions of those who threaten private property relations and the public order. In other words, the state in a capitalist society is a capitalist state. As such, the general tendency of state institutions (e.g. the police, the judiciary, prisons and community programs) is to concentrate on specific kinds of behaviour (usually associated with working-class crime) as being 'deviant' and 'harmful'. Other kinds of destructive or exploitative behaviour that result in greater social and economic harm, and which are usually associated with crimes of the powerful (e.g. white-collar crime and human rights violations), are deemed to be less worthy of state criminalisation and/or intervention (see, for example, Simon 2012; see also Chapters 12 and 13).

MARXIST PERSPECTIVES Marxist perspectives focus on individuals' relative position within the economic structure of a society, as defined by their relationship to the means of production. The state, as a legal and political superstructure, sets the conditions of economic relations, thereby defining the social consciousness, which includes concepts of crime.

From a Marxist viewpoint, how issues are constructed and how crime and criminality are defined and responded to, relate directly to the individual's position in the class structure (see White 2008a; White & van der Velden 1995). If social power is concentrated in the hands of those who own the means of production, they will influence and generally dictate what behaviour is and is not defined as criminal. The concern of the Marxist criminological approach is to highlight the inequalities of a class-divided society (e.g. wealth versus subsistence or poverty; business profits versus low wages and exploitative working conditions) and the impact these have on the criminalisation process (Spitzer 1975).

The powerful are seen as designing the laws in their own collective interest, while having greater capacity to defend themselves individually if they do break and bend existing rules and regulations. The less powerful in society are seen as propelled to commit crime through economic need (subsistence-related crimes such as shoplifting, welfare fraud and workplace theft) and socio-cultural alienation (e.g. graffiti, vandalism, assault, public nuisance and disorder offences). They are also the main targets of law enforcement and wider criminal justice agencies, as reflected in statistics that show an over-representation of the unemployed, poor and marginalised in prisons, police lock-ups and criminal courts, mainly for economic or socio-cultural crimes (see Chapters 7 and 25). By contrast, there are relatively few prosecutions of corporations annually, despite the fact that their crimes can occasion large-scale financial loss, permanent disability and even loss of life. On the rare occasions when such prosecutions do occur, they are generally considered civil or regulatory transgressions rather than acts worthy of prosecution under the criminal law (see Chapters 12 and 22). Essentially, then, the capitalist system 'degrades people while upgrading property and wealth' (Bute 1981: 109).

Radical perspectives refute state definitions of crime which, far from being the embodiment of societal consensus, are considered to be reflective of and designed to specifically protect capital interests, and to foist a certain form of law and order (middle-class standards of propriety and public order) on the working class. They argue instead for a human rights and social injury based conception of crime, comprising violations of such things as human dignity, physical and material needs and necessities, and the right to self-determination (Bute 1981).

By providing a structural perspective on social institutions, social processes and social outcomes, Marxist approaches argue that revolutionary or profound transformation of capitalist society is required if 'crime' is to be addressed in a socially just manner; namely, emancipation of social relations (Chambliss 1975). This includes measures designed to: collectivise ownership over the means of production; abolish iniquities in the distribution of societal resources; democratise institutional power (e.g. participatory involvement of citizens in, and election to, decision-making positions within the criminal justice system); strengthen public accountability of state apparatus (police, courts and correctional facilities); and reform the law to ensure it adequately reflects working-class interests and upholds human rights.

FEMINIST PERSPECTIVES

FEMINIST PERSPECTIVES
Feminist perspectives provide a gendered critique of structural relations within society. Society is regarded as fundamentally androcentric (centred on men). Crime (committed against women and by women) is attributable to social oppression and economic dependency.

In common with Marxist approaches to criminology, **feminist perspectives** are concerned with fundamental power differentials in society that lead to the inequitable distribution of economic and social resources, and produce disparities in the opportunities available to different groups in society for social advancement and institutional influence. Feminists, however, provide a gendered critique of societal relations; that is, they focus on the fundamental divisions and power inequalities between men and women. Specifically, they contend that women's structural disadvantage and men's structural domination are entrenched features of patriarchy. In an androcentric society (one that is focused on men), sexual inequality and disempowerment of women are inevitably embodied in the law and the operations of the criminal justice system.

The feminist approach, which rose to prominence in the 1970s, was closely associated with second-wave feminism, a radical phase of social movement that altered social and political consciousness by highlighting the structural oppression of women, and the general abuses and 'hidden' levels of violence directed towards them (Heidensohn 2012). It draws attention to the fundamental distinction between sex (a biological classification of male/female based on genitalia) and gender (a social construct of masculine/feminine based on learned culture of typical and 'appropriate' male and female traits, dress, roles and behaviours) in discussing differences between men and women. This distinction is seen to be at the nub of explanations of male and female offending and victimisation.

Feminism challenged criminology in at least two ways. First, there was the relative neglect within criminology itself of issues relating to female crime and women as victims of crime. Second, the theories and studies that did exist tended to reinforce certain stereotypes and conservative portrayals of the 'proper' place of women in society. Feminist writers sought to rectify these matters through critiques: not only of the criminal justice system, but also of the dominant sexist assumptions underpinning mainstream criminological theories of crime (Naffine 1987; Smart 1989, 1976; see also Chapter 8). Feminist theorists pointed out, for example, that while women are generally under-represented in the criminal justice statistics as both offenders and victims, the neglect of women in criminological inquiry was also partly the result of the overwhelming predominance of males in the criminology discipline and the criminal justice system. In terms of research and theory, and at the level of the practitioner (judges, barristers, solicitors, prison officers and police), the system has traditionally been composed mainly of men who have largely pursued male areas of interest.

As a consequence of this male structural domination, the law and the exercise of legal power reflect a male (white) construction of reality (e.g. the interpretation of the legal concept of the 'reasonable man') that disqualifies women's knowledge and experience (Easteal et al. 2012; Smart 1989). Even though there have been periodic challenges to the overt sexist practices of the law and law enforcement by some male legal practitioners, this has not changed the overall orientation of the system towards women; that is, its systematic bias. As discussed in Chapter 22, while the law purports to be neutral and impartial, its gendered nature and differential application to women and men in practice, can produce substantive injustices.

Contrary to traditional criminological theorising, feminist perspectives place the nature of female offending and victimisation into a wider social, economic and political context, rather than one that reduces female experience to biological or psychological determinants, or ignores the female experience altogether. Critical to this contextualisation is an understanding of the manner in which the criminalisation process itself is seen to be heavily laden with sexist assumptions that reinforce **phallogocentrism** and reproduce structural inequalities of gender in society (Gelsthorpe & Morris 1990; Smart 1989). This is thought to occur with respect to both the construction of offending behaviour and the portrayal of victims. The central proposition of much feminist analysis is that women are treated differently in and by the criminal justice system, because of the persistence of traditional gender stereotypes and biases regarding 'appropriate' and 'feminine' behaviour for women (and men).

PHALLO-GENTROCISM
The privileging of males in the construction of social meaning.

In the case of victimisation, for example, feminist analysis pays much attention to the ways in which certain crimes against women have historically been considered 'private matters' outside the realms of the criminal law and therefore essentially not criminal (e.g. domestic violence) or have been subject to trivialisation (e.g. rape trials involving sex workers) and double standards of morality (e.g. assessments of 'real' rape and victim worthiness based on traditional gender stereotypes of appropriate roles and behaviour) (Easteal et al. 2012).

Similarly, in the case of criminalisation, feminist analysis unveils the manner in which institutions of social control police women's bodies and behaviours in ways that reinforced the *objectification and commodification* of women; that is, the notion of women as only wives, mothers, sexual property (owned by a male partner), nurturers and domestic workers, rather than as complete individuals in their own right. For instance, the justice system has historically construed certain categories of offending as sex-specific, despite the fact that they are perpetrated by both males and females. Examples of the gendered application of law include prosecution of prostitution, shoplifting and infanticide—offences for which women are over-represented in official criminal statistics—and the historical construction of female delinquency in relation to immorality and promiscuity (Alder 1985; Belknap 2010; Caputo & King 2011; Chesney-Lind & Sheldon 1992; Cunneen & White 2011; Reeve 2013).

Feminist perspectives argue that the causes of offences committed against and by women are inextricably linked to conditions of *social oppression* and *economic dependence*. Many argue, for example, that men's violence against women is not a product of biological urges (as in the case of rape) or the actions of 'bad' or 'mad' men momentarily provoked into losing their temper (in the case of domestic abuse), but rather is an expression of patriarchal culture; an acting out of masculine power and entitlement through coercive control, designed to maintain women's subordinate status (Fisher 2012; Kaukinen et al. 2013). It is a reflection of the institutionalised objectification of women perpetuated in advertising and pornography that depicts women as passive and vulnerable sex aids to be taken violently (Kahlor & Eastin 2011; Reist 2013; Short 2013a). Relatedly, female crimes are largely regarded as a response to persistent patterns of abuse (e.g. murdering a partner after years of domestic violence, or crimes associated with drug or alcohol dependency—substances used to cope with early childhood abuse and trauma) and their economic marginalisation, which makes them dependent on men and/or the welfare apparatus of the state (e.g. acquisitive crimes such as welfare fraud, shoplifting and prostitution) (see, for example, Brennan et al. 2012; Cain & Howe 2008).

Since the crucial issue is that of relative social power and access to community resources, feminist perspectives advocate radical changes to the existing operation of the criminal justice system and, indeed, to institutional power relations in society as a whole. The vision is one of empowerment of women through greater political, economic and social equality. Specific measures to achieve this goal include: affirmative action programs to increase women's workforce participation in meaningful ways and at all levels (including recruitment into criminal justice agencies such as the police force and the judiciary); anti-sexist training for agents of social control (including police and the judiciary); provision of gender-specific legal, criminal justice, victim and welfare services and support systems; and legal reform.

CRITICAL CRIMINOLOGY

CRITICAL CRIMINOLOGY
Critical criminology builds upon the basic concepts and strategic concerns of the Marxist and feminist perspectives, generally from the point of view of a broadly anti-capitalist position. Critical criminology is basically concerned with structures of power: how power is conceptualised and exercised.

Critical criminology represents a further development of the broad radical strands within criminology. In particular, it builds upon the basic concepts and strategic concerns of the Marxist and feminist perspectives; namely, to challenge and broaden traditional criminological inquiry by focusing attention on the institutional forces (social, political and economic) that both give rise to crime and shape the nature and focus of crime control efforts. Generally speaking, it does so from the point of view of a broadly anti-capitalist position, which incorporates the ideas of creating a social and natural environment that is not associated with heterosexist, racist and destructive practices of production and consumption. What distinguishes critical criminology per se is its concern with structures of power, and how these invariably reflect and promote a particular worldview of social order and its maintenance. These power structures are seen to be institutionalised in particular ways, and to reflect social interests that oppress specific categories of people. Essentially, critical criminology concerns itself with the *critique of domination* (Shroyer 1973; see also Michalowski 2010). How power is conceptualised, however, marks out one of the main differences of approach within critical criminology.

Critical criminologists concur that power is central to all systems of state control. They also agree that the present operation of the criminal justice system is unfair and biased, and advantages certain groups or classes above others. The primary task of the critical criminologist is to expose the nature of the underlying power relations that shape how different groups are treated in, and by, the criminal justice system. As articulated by Michalowski (2010: 4): 'Wherever power operates behind a scrim of ideology, law, and rhetoric that obscures its existence, the not-so-simple act of revealing its presence is an unavoidable critique of the domination that power makes possible'. In many cases, the task is also conceived in terms of seeking to initiate action and develop strategies that will transform the present social order, including the criminal justice system.

The focal point of critique within this perspective is the process by which power is mobilised within the broad sphere of criminal justice. For present purposes, two general trends are identified within the critical criminological literature (see Table 5.1). The *structuralist approach* tends to focus on power as something that is ingrained in social structures, and that manifests itself in the form of the actions of institutions and the activities of sectional interest groups (see Michalowski 2010; Scraton & Chadwick 1991). The *postmodern approach*, on the other hand, sees power in terms of language, and the ways in which knowledge production shapes human experience while simultaneously engendering conflict over meaning (see Arrigo & Bernard 1997; Easteal et al. 2012; Lea 1998). The differences between these approaches are seen by some writers to be so great as to warrant treatment as distinct models of social inquiry (Arrigo & Bernard 1997; Russell 1997). Others do not necessarily share this

TABLE 5.1 KEY IDEAS OF STRUCTURALIST AND POSTMODERN CRIMINOLOGY

STRUCTURALIST	POSTMODERN
Deals with issues of class, gender, race and ethnicity	Deals with continuous struggle over linguistic production
Focuses both on crimes of the powerful and crimes of the less powerful	Focuses on conflicts over 'reality' as expressed in and through language
Key concepts include marginalisation, criminalisation and racialisation	Key concepts include discourse and discursive subject positions
Response is based on notions of social empowerment, redistribution of social resources and participatory democracy	Response is based on notions of replacement discourses, conflicts over discursive frames and pluralism

view, or are less definitive about the break between the two perspectives (Einstadter & Henry 1995; Henry & Milovanovic 1994).

STRUCTURALIST CRIMINOLOGY

**STRUCTUR-
ALIST
CRIMINOLOGY**
Structuralist
criminology is
concerned with
the exercise
of power
that leads to
oppression and
domination
both in terms
of structural
relations
in society
(economic,
cultural and
political) and in
terms of social
control systems
and practices.

For **structuralist criminology**, 'crime' is defined in terms of oppression and domination. Some groups are particularly vulnerable to oppression both in terms of structural relations in society (economic, cultural and political) and in terms of social control systems and practices (policing and punishment) that operate to embed and reproduce oppressive structural relations. Members of the working class (especially its more powerless sections, including the 'underclass'), women (especially those who are poor, sole parents and socially isolated), ethnic minority groups (especially those from non-English-speaking backgrounds, the newly arrived and refugees) and Indigenous people (especially those worst affected by long-term colonisation processes and institutional disadvantage) are those most likely to suffer from the weight of oppressive structural relations, and social control practices based upon class division, sexism and racism.

The focus of analysis for structuralist criminology is both the crimes of the powerful (including crimes of the state) and the crimes of the less powerful. In examining the crimes of the powerful, attention is directed to issues related to (Michalowski 2010):

- *Ideology:* especially the nature of law-and-order politics fuelled by mass media generated public fear of street crime. This focus on individual-level crime and harm occurs to the benefit of those engaged in elite and organisational deviance, which continues to be considered outside the frame of 'real crime'. Concomitantly, it occurs at the expense of recognition of the victimisation suffered by the masses at the hands of those engaged in the pursuit of domination. For example, ideological justification of the invasion of Iraq on the grounds that it engaged in a war crime of aggression served to normalise actions such as aerial bombings of civilians and state torture of suspected terrorists.
- *Political economy:* the impact of privatisation and globalised capitalist projects (state and corporate), including dispossessing people of their land, livelihood and culture, and destruction of the environment, in the pursuit of economic progress and profit; for example, the recent acquisition by Cargill (a US corporation) of 130,000 acres of land in Columbia for a variety of commercial purposes including agricultural farming, mining and construction (Magdoff 2013).
- *The state:* managerial rather than democratic modes of rule, whereby functional power in the form of national decision-making is stripped from the people and vested in the hands of the economic elite (corporate entrepreneurs and their lobbyists) and technical specialists (scientists, engineers etc.), thus enabling policy to be shaped by the vested interest of capital. Gonzales (2012), for example, exposes the power of economic elites in the United States to advocate successfully for the introduction of nuclear energy while opposing support for alternatives, such as solar energy, that cannot be dominated by a small number of corporations or indeed any one nation.

The structural context of crime vis-à-vis capitalist development and institutional pressures is viewed as central to any explanation of crimes of the powerful.

The crimes of the less powerful are examined from the point of view of the specific experiences of particular sections of the population. Different forms of criminality are thus linked to specific layers of the working class, particular categories of women and men, certain ethnic minority groups and Indigenous people in a variety of rural and urban settings. There is a twofold emphasis: on the specificity of crime and criminal involvement (specific groups and specific kinds of activity); and on the generalist features that unite the disparate groups (shared economic, social and political circumstances).

Crime is seen to be associated with broad processes of political economy that affect the powerful and the less powerful in quite different ways. For the powerful, there are pressures associated with the securing and maintenance of state power, and specific sectional interests in the global context of international trade and transnational corporate monopolisation. For the less powerful, the cause of crime is seen to lie in the interplay between marginalisation (separation from mainstream institutions) and criminalisation (intervention and labelling by state authorities). Of particular note is the increasing racialisation of crime, in which certain communities are targeted for media and police attention in the 'war against crime' or the 'war against terror' and 'public disorder' (see Chapter 8).

For structuralist criminology, a response to crime must be built upon a strategy of social empowerment. This means involving people directly in decisions about their future through direct participatory democracy. It also requires a redistribution of social resources to communities on the basis of social need and equity.

POSTMODERN APPROACH

By contrast with structuralist critical criminology, which concerns itself with forms of authority, power and injustice related to capitalism, postmodern critical approaches situate crime within historical and cultural contexts, and examine power in relation to the ability to create meaning. The starting point for a *postmodern* (or *social constructionist*) *approach* to critical criminology is the idea that language structures thought. Language is seen as the crucial intervening variable between social relationships and institutions, and all methods of knowing the social world (Arrigo & Bernard 1997). Crime is thus defined in terms of linguistic production (language and discourse), and relationships of power that shape the nature of this production. The social world is effectively limited to, and constituted by, the collective reality of language. In other words, there is no necessary logical connection between the use of language and what it purports to describe: there are no 'objective truths', only different ways of speaking about and describing social reality. Since meaning itself is inherently unstable, exploration of social reality can only be centred on local manifestations rather than broader generalisations.

Those who control the means of expression are seen to hold the key to controlling and exercising power over others. Simultaneously, however, it is acknowledged that where there is power (in any social relationship), there is also resistance to this power. Language and meaning are contested, and there is always a dynamic tension between dominant social voices and those that are silenced or expelled by the dominant modes of expression.

The key to social transformation, therefore, lies in analysing the languages that construct social relationships in a particular way, to the advantage of some and to the disadvantage of others. Exposing the discourses (modes of speech, knowledge and categorisation of the social world) of everyday life opens the door to other expressions of reality that have been submerged by the dominant or hegemonic discourse. The main method of the social constructionist is that of discourse analysis, which examines how meaning and sense are constructed in everyday language. This involves a process of deconstruction of meaning to reveal the hidden and suppressed meanings embodied in certain social relationships.

An important part of this *deconstruction of meaning* is to examine the discursive subject positions that inform the way in which people speak and think. For example, in the field of criminal justice there are a number of activities and social roles or positions. These include, for instance, offending (the offender), lawyering (the lawyer), policing (the police officer) and judging (the judge or magistrate). It is argued by postmodern writers that the people (subjects) who assume these positions speak, think, feel and know through the language that is embodied in these structures. Thus, the person who assumes the discursive subject position of police officer, who engages thereby in 'policing', does so in a manner that reflects and embodies what it is to 'be a police officer' (rather than, say, a husband, mother, lover or football player). Insofar as this is the case, then these subjects can be described as being decentred, in the sense of not being entirely in control of their own thoughts. They act and think like a 'police officer' from the moment that they assume or take on the policing discursive subject position.

THE LANGUAGING OF REALITY

The pivotal question for the social constructionist is how the dominant linguistic regime (legal jargon and categories) in the criminal justice system dismisses particular languages (e.g. the emotional experiences of rape victims) that express a different view and experience of the social world. The *languaging of reality* is demonstrated in the legitimacy found in the acceptance of certain discursive subject positions (the judge as credible and rational), but not others (the victim as not credible or rational). It is argued that: 'By dismissing these oppositional languages, certain versions of how to think, act, feel and be are indirectly de-valued' (Arrigo & Bernard 1997: 44). The task, therefore, is to expose the different ways in which criminal justice is languaged, and to offer a voice to those who have been silenced by the dominant discourses of the law. The key question is 'whose "languaged" (and therefore social) interests are valued and devalued in the prevailing (or alternative) definitions of crime' (Arrigo & Bernard 1997: 48; see also Easteal et al. 2012).

In another sense, the 'cause' of crime is seen to lie in linguistic domination itself. That is, the linguistic domination varyingly 'criminalises' that speech, thought and behaviour that resists, delegitimises or opposes the potency of the discourse in effect. For some, the solution to this dilemma is to develop replacement discourses that will neutralise the power of the dominant languages that regulate and discipline the lives of alienated collectivities (especially ethnic minority people, Indigenous people, women and gay men and lesbians). The emphasis, therefore, is on social inclusiveness, diverse modes of communication and a pluralistic culture. To undercut the dominance of the hegemonic discourses, and to acknowledge the specificity of different 'voices', the main focus for action (if any) is at the local level, and through decentralised means of social control and interaction. For other writers, however, any attempt to establish a replacement discourse is itself a form of linguistic imposition (Lea 1998; Morrison 1994). For these people, we can deconstruct meaning, but the construction of alternative discursive frames is simply not on the agenda (to do so implies new conflicts revolving around knowledge, power and resistance).

In summary, critical criminology is part of an important tradition of struggle and political conflict to win or defend social and human rights within a class-divided, sexist and racist social structure. The structuralist and postmodernist strands of critical criminology share this oppositional stance to what they see as an unjust society. One of the hallmarks of critical criminology is its association with direct interventions in various law-and-order and criminal justice debates. Indeed, more than this, one of the main contributions of this strand of criminological activity has been to raise for public discussion a series of important social issues. Much of this type of research, scholarship and commentary has been informed by a concern to publicise existing injustices, and potential abuses, of criminal justice institutions (Anthony & Cunneen 2008; Carrington & Hogg 2002; Schissel & Brooks 2002).

PEACEMAKING CRIMINOLOGY AND RESTORATIVE JUSTICE

What unifies the many different approaches within the critical criminology perspective is a deep concern with issues of oppression and injustice. These are seen to stem from structural inequalities in resource allocation and decision-making power. Accordingly, institutional reform is not seen as an end in itself, but as part of a profound transition towards a more equal, fairer society. To take a specific example, a call for the abolition of prisons (or at the least a radical reduction in the prison population) may reflect the position that those who end up in prison are the most vulnerable sections of the population (in terms of income, employment and educational background) and, hence, are unfairly criminalised and further penalised for their predicament. But to abolish prisons is not enough. Until the conditions that give rise to the creation of 'surplus populations', and ethnic and racially based social divisions are confronted, piecemeal institutional reform will not be sufficient to forestall suffering and pain in the future.

Abolitionism argues that the criminal justice system fails both morally and in terms of its stated objectives. It advocates against a state that inflicts pain under the guise of reducing criminal activity. Accordingly, there is a call for the abolition of prisons, the abolishment of capital punishment and action to be taken against slavery, racism, sexism and classism. The essential philosophy of abolitionism is that punishment and repression never solve problems. In this regard, it effectively captures the essential character of peacemaking criminology, a theoretical perspective that has emerged relatively recently.

PEACEMAKING CRIMINOLOGY

In **peacemaking criminology** it is argued that any criminal justice system that operates within a framework of retributive justice fails at every level. The criminal justice system represents a state-sanctioned means of inflicting pain under the guise of reducing criminal activity and, yet, the imposition of punishment and repression never solves—and never will solve—social problems. Founded by Pepinsky and Quinney (1991), the basic philosophy of this approach is that we cannot solve violence or human suffering with more violence and more human suffering (negative forms of peace). Instead, it is argued that humanistic and restorative principles need to be adopted at the level of dealing with the offender, and in dealing with wider social conflicts as well (see also Barash 1991; Wozniak et al. 2008). Peacemaking is 'a criminology that seeks to end suffering and thereby eliminate crime' (Quinney 1991: 11). The emphasis is on a positive peace and the promotion of social justice based on transformative strategies that are themselves premised upon participatory forms of conflict resolution; that is, strategies that promote harmonious interaction without criminalising and victimising (Pepinsky 1991).

Drawing upon various peacemaking traditions—such as religious, humanistic and feminist approaches to understanding and responding to violence—peacemaking criminology criticises models of interaction based upon the idea of winners and losers. Rather, and in contrast, the approach speaks about openness, trust and cooperation (Moyer 2001). In many cases, it is argued that, literally, peace

PEACEMAKING CRIMINOLOGY
Drawing upon various peacemaking traditions, peacemaking criminology criticises models of interaction based upon the idea of winners and losers. It promotes instead mediation, conflict resolution and reconciliation as preferred responses to wrongdoing, violence and human suffering.

begins at home; that is, it is important that each individual lives his or her everyday life based upon love, forgiveness, kindness and hope (see, for example, Quinney 1991). These principles and concepts are also pertinent to developing a critique of a society that is class-divided, racist and sexist, and that predominantly operates on the basis of power, domination, exploitation and control over others.

Not surprisingly, peacemaking criminology tends to stress mediation, conflict resolution and reconciliation as preferred methods with which to deal with human suffering and wrongdoing. Non-violent ways of thought and action are essential to the peacekeeping conception of restorative justice. The intent is to understand how and where people make peace (Pepinsky 1991) in order to supplant existing criminal justice models that are based upon militaristic notions of the 'war' on crime.

Though various models of peacemaking have been developed based on the foundational philosophical principles outlined by Pepinsky and Quinney (1991) (for an outline of these, see Wozniak 2009), one of the key challenges of peacemaking criminology has been to translate a philosophy of 'being nice' into the practical realities of actual conflicts and instances in which social harm is occurring. To put it differently, how does one move beyond expressing the sentiments of compassion and empathy, reconciliation and reintegration, to addressing concretely the real sites of conflict? Part of the answer to this is provided in work by McEvoy (2003). Based upon grounded interventions with paramilitary groups in Northern Ireland, McEvoy argues that a 'new' peacemaking criminology might include:

- an explicit focus on jurisdictions where actual political or ethnic conflicts are occurring
- a recognition of the idea that political engagement is necessary and that conflict transformation should be based upon the objective of trying to make a difference
- a substantive engagement with human rights discourses, particularly as a counterweight to those sorts of moral relativism that can impede practical intervention
- a reframing of the evaluation of 'what works' into a political rather than a technical exercise, thereby acknowledging the profound transformations in individuals, groups and communities that would be the result of peacemaking criminology.

Similarly, a recent review by Braithwaite et al. (2010) of peacemaking efforts in Bougainville, Papua New Guinea after decades of civil war, identifies three key elements that facilitated movement from conflict to peace:

- 'top-down' architecture, which included government and other organisations such as the Australian mining industry, interested in exploiting the mineral resources and the local labour
- 'bottom-up' development, which involved members of local tribes in conflict with one another
- 'middle-out' links between the two, comprising women's movements, youth church organisations and leaders within those groups that were ultimately the key to the peacemaking process.

While the top-down and bottom-up approaches 'operated in symbiotic fashion, each making space for, and reinforcing, the other' (Braithwaite et al. 2010: 1), real change only occurred as a result of credible commitment to implementation of a top-down architecture and a bottom-up reconciliation, with a middle-out group of networkers connecting the two and serving as the catalyst for change. Adaptability, interdependence, resource recycling and sustainability were considered critical in achieving peace agreements. Key lessons learned from comparing the Bougainville experience with that of other conflict zones include (Braithwaite et al. 2010: 103–31):

- Local ownership is paramount to peacebuilding.
- International influence is important in terms of supporting peace-building efforts but should not be used to control.

- Both men and women should participate in leadership roles.
- In drawing up a constitutional design for a conflict area, it is important to include incremental steps of agreement.
- Aid is more effective when provided in the years following the first few years of peace; dividends should be created and earned by the locals.
- A community-based justice system is needed to support effective policing during and after the conflict.
- It is imperative that the military not be involved in the problem.
- Peacekeepers' experiences during the process strengthen character.

Essentially, these learnings convey a notion of positive peace that emphasises the importance of working incrementally towards political and economic arrangements that are minimally exploitative, achieved through non-violent measures, arrived at through a process of inclusion and reconciliation involving all relevant stakeholders, and which seeks to ultimately solve the less overt oppression generated by structural violence.

An important observation of peacemaking criminology generally is that very often war and the war on crime are interlinked, and share many of the same attributes and institutional dynamics. Philosophically, and increasingly at a practical level of intervention, peacemaking criminologists wish to challenge violence, repression and humiliation as preferred modes of conflict resolution, whether this be at the level of individuals, groups, families, communities or nation-states. Conversely, drawing upon human rights discourses and restorative justice activities such as community mediation, and by stressing the positive value of non-violent alternatives and the vital need to address the material reasons for social differences, peacemaking criminology aims to transform social settings in more profound ways than traditional criminal justice approaches.

RESTORATIVE JUSTICE

In some versions, this impetus for system transformation is likewise the objective of restorative justice. In general, the aim of *restorative justice* is to develop policies whereby the offender makes reparations for wrongdoing and, in doing so, restores the victim's and the general population's faith in society. Conceptually, restorative justice sees crime as fundamentally a violation of people and interpersonal relationships, and the point of action is to seek to heal and put right the wrongs (Zehr 1990). The justice process, in this framework, is seen to belong rightly to the community, rather than exclusively to the state (see Box 5.1). It is this sense of community as central that Morrison and Vaandering (2012: 138) contend sets restorative justice apart from other paradigms of justice; it is distinct from other forms of discipline in that it 'uniquely emphasises social engagement over social control'. Restoration is made possible under this framework of justice by the uncoupling of punishment as a necessary component of achieving retribution from responses to criminal wrongdoing (Foley 2013). It allows for emphasis to be placed on reparation of harm to victims, addressing the offender's needs and competencies and sending offenders a message of disapproval about the impact of the crime (Bazemore 1997).

There are various specific models of restorative justice, ranging from circle sentencing, family group conferencing and reparative probation, through to victim–offender mediation (see Chapter 27). Each model has different key objectives—from promoting citizen involvement to ensuring victims' needs are met—and these shape the manner in which restorative justice is institutionalised in practice. For some types of juvenile conferencing, for instance, the theoretical model informing the practice is that of republican theory (see Chapter 4), with an emphasis on reintegrative shaming and repairing harm in the framework of restoring dominion. Generally speaking, however, programs or models that seek to

---

BOX 5.1   PRINCIPLES OF RESTORATIVE JUSTICE

Restorative justice can be usefully summarised as being based upon three interrelated propositions (Zehr & Mika 1998):

- *Crime is fundamentally a violation of people and interpersonal relationships*: the key issue is that victims and the community have been harmed and are in need of restoration. Victims, offenders and the affected communities are seen as the key stakeholders in justice and, as such, ought to be directly involved in the justice process.
- *Violations create obligations and liabilities*: it is felt that the offenders are obliged to make things right as much as possible for the harms and liabilities their violations have caused. However, it is also argued that the community's obligations are to victims and offenders, and for the general welfare of its members. Obligations are thus both individual and collective in nature.
- *Restorative justice seeks to heal and put right the wrong*: the starting point for justice is the need of victims for information, validation, vindication, restitution, testimony, safety and support. The process of justice ought to maximise the opportunities for exchange of information, participation, dialogue and mutual consent between victim and offender, and the justice process ought to belong to the community. The offenders' needs and competencies also are to be addressed. In the end, justice needs to be mindful of the outcomes, intended and unintended, of its responses to crime and victimisation.

Source: Zehr & Mika (1998)

---

respond to wrongdoing in a reparative manner incorporate the following features, referred to by Roche (2003) as 'restorative value prescriptions':

- *participation:* involvement to varying degrees, of all parties linked to the wrongdoing—'victim', 'offender' and 'community'—in a restorative encounter that attempts to produce a consensual response to the harm caused by the offending (as opposed to the passive role played by these parties in traditional justice)
- *personalism:* recognition of the personal and interpersonal harms caused by offending, by focusing on the impact of the offending on the victim, the offender, their family and the wider community (as opposed to the state, which is the focus of traditional justice)
- *reparation:* identification and reparation of the harm (physical, material and emotional) caused by the wrongdoing (as opposed to repairing normative harm, which is the focus of punishment in traditional justice)
- *reintegration:* promotion of opportunities to assist the offender to rebuild ties with their community that have been damaged as a consequence of their wrongdoing, with an eye to preventing reoffending (as opposed to purely punishment and rehabilitation as core goals of traditional justice).

Under the restorative justice umbrella, there are differences between those who see restorative justice as, essentially, a form of diversion from the formal criminal justice system, and those who view it as a potential alternative to that system, and thus as something that could supplant the existing system (see Bazemore & Walgrave 1999). Whatever the specific differences, it appears that the central thread underlying restorative justice is the spirit within which 'justice' is undertaken—the intent and outcomes of the process are meant to be primarily oriented towards repairing harm that has been caused by a crime, and this means working to heal victims, offenders and communities that have been directly injured by the crime (Bazemore & Walgrave 1999; Roche 2003; Zehr & Mika 1998).

CULTURAL CRIMINOLOGY

Cultural criminology places crime and its control within a cultural context; that is, it views crime and social control as creative constructions or cultural products that carry particular meaning rather than objective or natural phenomena; that meaning is determined by those with the power to do so. Cultural criminologists challenge the assumption underlying much of orthodox criminology: that crime and deviance is attributable to a lack of culture. By privileging the empirical phenomenon, irrespective of whether it is meaningful, traditional criminology overlooks or discounts the culture that is produced by all collective human activity. Cultural criminology seeks to 'bring back identity action and vocabularies of motives into discussions about transgressions' (Landry 2013: 5). As such, it sets out to reinterpret criminal behaviour as a technique for resolving certain psychic and emotional conflicts created by the contradictions and idiosyncrasies of modern life.

Although relatively new (emerging in the mid-1990s), its main tenets draw heavily from the sociological schools of criminological thought (especially interactionist and subcultural strands), as well as critical criminology. What cultural criminology introduces, however, is a reflection on crime and criminalisation that is informed by the peculiarities and exactitudes of late modern socio-cultural environments (e.g. consumer culture and aspirational culture). As an approach, cultural criminology is clearly interdisciplinary, representing a 'phenomenology of transgression' fused with a sociological analysis of late modern culture. It draws attention to both structure and agency, and the intersection of culture and criminalisation. Specifically, it is premised on the idea that we are seeing the incremental criminalisation of everyday life, and that this, in turn, is generating varying kinds of cultural response (Hayward & Young 2004). The thematic focus is on the excitement, pleasures and opportunities for engaging in deviance, including, for example (Presdee 2000):

- the spectacle of violence—popular movies, car crashes and catastrophes
- sexual activities, such as sadomasochism
- rap and rave
- street performance and carrying of weapons
- hate crime and racist violence.

THE EMOTIONS OF CRIME

Emotions and the study of emotions are an important part of cultural criminological work. For example, in the context of late modernity, the contradictory practices and processes of Western market forces and consumer culture are said to have polarised further the division between the 'haves' and 'have nots', heightened consumer expectations and dissatisfaction, and produced new forms of desire and emotional states that are often destructive (Hayward 2004; Martin 2009). The work of Katz (1988) provides a useful framework for elucidating the changing emotional responses (feelings and desires) engendered by Western consumerism. In exploring the relationship between crime and the emotional states of offenders, Katz (1988) turned his attention to the seductions of crime and the compulsions felt by people engaging in various types of criminal projects. Crime, in emotional terms, is exciting and exhilarating. It represents a transcendence of the mundane; an opportunity to creatively explore emotional worlds beyond that of 'normal' rational behaviour. Part of the thrill of crime is seen to lie precisely in the risk that one will be shamed if caught. Thus, being successful in activities such as shoplifting or joyriding is not only about 'getting away with it' but also about avoiding the shame people would feel if they did get caught. These risks thus constitute an important part of the excitement of the

CULTURAL CRIMINOLOGY
Cultural criminology refers to a body of scholarship that views crime and social control agencies as cultural products. A main focus is on the emotions of crime; the varied emotional dynamics and experiential attractions (pleasures, excitement and control) that constitute an essential element of much crime and antisocial behaviour.

deviant experience. If an arrest does occur, this is seen by Katz as a kind of 'metaphysical shock', in that it implies that persistence in the activity would now signal a commitment to a deviant identity. This, in turn, would undermine the emotional impact of knowingly being deviant, particularly since such thrill-seeking deviance is seldom tied to the notion of criminal identity or criminal career.

For Katz (1988) it is important to examine the lived experiences of criminality; to consider the emotional and interpretive qualities of crime. Emotions such as humiliation, arrogance, ridicule, pleasure and excitement are often central to why we act as we do. Indeed, the study of the emotions of crime is capturing greater interest within criminology, particularly since criminal behaviour is deeply and ambiguously emotional (see Box 5.2). It is argued that different states of emotional arousal, from fear and anger through to pleasure and excitement, have major bearings on individual and group behaviour, and for the policies and practices of criminal justice institutions (see De Haan & Loader 2002). Locating activity within an emotional universe is a feature characteristic of cultural criminology.

Cultural criminology refers to a body of scholarship that tends to focus on the pleasures, excitement and opportunities for psychic resolution involved in certain modes of criminality (Ferrell & Sanders 1995; Ferrell et al. 2004, 2008; Hayward 2002). The focus, therefore, tends to be on the varied emotional dynamics and experiential attractions that constitute an essential element of much crime and antisocial behaviour. As mentioned, Presdee (2000) writes about the dynamics of the spectacle of violence in popular movies, sexual activities such as sadomasochism, and the attractions of rap and rave. Ferrell (1997) describes the liberating feelings and sense of power and resistance associated with writing graffiti. A common theme in much of this work is that deviance offers the perpetrator a means of 'self-transcendence': a way of overcoming the conventionality and mundanity of everyday life (Hayward 2002).

BOX 5.2   EMOTIONS AND CRIME

- *States of emotional arousal*: pleasure, fear, anger, sadness, disgust, remorse, resentment, shame and guilt are intimately implicated in numerous fields of criminological inquiry.
- *Emotions of crime*: criminal behaviour is deeply and ambiguously filled with emotions of various kinds, including those of guilt and shame:
  - there is a need to study affective dimensions of criminal behaviour
  - there is a need to study the feelings of offenders, victims and community members, and how these are represented as well as dealt with within the institutions of criminal justice (e.g. courtroom practices).
- *Emotions of punishment and social control*: these include moral ambiguity of public reactions to crime, and the interplay of emotions, as with the fear of crime and impassioned demands for order:
  - on the one hand, there is populist punitiveness and heightened emotions but, on the other, there are also attempts to remove emotions from formal criminal justice through sentencing guidelines and intelligence-led policing
  - there is the integration of emotions such as 'shame' directly in the processes of criminal justice (as in some forms of juvenile conferencing)
  - the issues relate to which emotions are being mobilised, by whom and for which purposes.

The contribution of cultural criminology to the understanding of youth violence, for example, is that violence is not only a rational or strategic means to an end for poor, dispossessed, marginalised and disadvantaged youth; it can be exciting and thrilling as well. Thus, there is increasing evidence that some types of violence stem from the efforts of young people themselves to engineer situations and events with the intended aim of increasing the likelihood of violence occurring (Jackson-Jacobs 2004; Schinkel 2004). From this perspective, the gang provides a forum or ready-made opportunity structure within which to engage in what is felt to be exhilarating activity. Fighting is fun; and gangs provide an avenue to increase the thrill factor beyond the norm. Violence can thus be seen as attractive and desirable in its own right, as well as being linked to instrumental purposes (e.g. defending male honour and defending oneself). Such violence thus achieves a number of rational, emotional, psychological and social purposes simultaneously (White 2013a; White & Mason 2006).

More sophisticated accounts also make the link between the loss of ontological security (a sense of place and belonging) at an individual level, which makes people feel at risk in an unstable world, and achieving a sense of 'controlled sense of loss of control', by engaging in risky practices that push one's physical boundaries in situations regarded by most as uncontrollable (see Hayward 2002). Consider car surfing, for example. This involves a person standing on top of a speeding car and putting him/herself at considerable personal risk in so doing. So why do it? The emotional answer is that it is fun and exciting; the analytical answer is that it represents a choice to engage in a controlled sense of loss of control. According to cultural criminologists, as everyday life becomes more routinised, sanitised and criminalised (e.g. increasing controls on the use of public space) and traditional avenues of stimulation and expression disappear, so too there will be greater propensity among people to transgress the boundaries of what is deemed to be acceptable behaviour. While much of the literature on edgework (pushing the limits) is centred on extreme sports dominated by men such as base jumping and skydiving, some theorists have explored edgework in the context of the embodied nature of anorexia (Gailey 2009), the management of emotions (Lois 2005) and occupational risk-taking in the stock market (Wexler 2010).

From a conceptual point of view, cultural criminology and the sociology of emotions have at their heart the basic argument that causal explanations of criminality that stress the importance of structural, environmental, genetic or rational choice factors, over and above the emotional and interpretative qualities of crime, are often guilty of stripping away and repressing key individual emotions such as humiliation, arrogance, ridicule, cynicism and, importantly, pleasure and excitement; emotions that, in many cases, are central to the criminal event. Activities relating to the street cultures of youth, such as vandalism, drugs, cruising, peer-group violence and vandalism, are therefore seen as ways of exerting control and providing avenues of expression when traditional avenues of youthful stimulation and endeavour have long since evaporated. They are meaningful emotionally as much as anything else.

GREEN CRIMINOLOGY

Another area of recent interest is that of green or environmental criminology (see Beirne & South 2007; White & Heckenberg 2014). Much of this work has been directed at exposing different instances of substantive social and environmental injustice. It has also involved critique of the actions of nation-states and transnational capital for fostering particular types of harm, and for failing to address adequately or regulate harmful activity. Drawing upon a wide range of ideas and empirical materials, criminology that deals with environmental harm has ventured across a range of areas of concern.

For example, it has documented the existence of lawbreaking with respect to pollution, disposal of toxic waste and misuse of environmental resources (Pearce & Tombs 1998). Other work has emphasised the dynamic links between distribution of environmental risk (particularly as these affect poor and minority populations) and the claims of non-human nature to ecological justice (Bullard 1994). It has also considered the specific place of animals in relation to issues of 'rights' and human–non-human relationships on a shared planet (Benton 1998). In general, and given the pressing nature of various environmental issues, many criminologists are now seeing environmental crime and environmental victimisation as areas for concerted analytical and practical attention; as areas of work that require much more conceptual development and empirical attention (see Chapter 14).

At the centre of green criminology is the notion of environmental *harm*. Specific types of harm include illegal transport and dumping of toxic waste; the transportation of hazardous materials, such as ozone-depleting substances and the illegal traffic in real or purported radioactive or nuclear substances; the proliferation of e-waste generated by the disposal of tens of thousands of computers and other equipment; the unsafe disposal of old ships and aeroplanes; the illegal trade in flora and fauna; and illegal fishing and logging. However, within green criminology, harm is being re-conceptualised in more expansive ways than is generally the case within mainstream criminology. Certainly the question of legal versus illegal is by no means the central issue (see Box 5.3).

Broadly speaking, green criminology is concerned with the study of environmental harm, environmental laws and environmental regulation by criminologists. The barriers to, and prospects of, a more ecologically balanced world are interwoven with powerful social interests and the contestation of what matters when it comes to change and transformation. Differences in the conceptualisations of environmental harm reflect, to some degree, differences in social position and lived experience (e.g. issues of class, gender, indigeneity, ethnicity and age). They are also mired in quite radically different paradigmatic understandings of 'nature' and 'human interests' (a variety of values and assumptions of eco-philosophy). From the point of view of green criminology, environmental harm is intrinsically contestable, both at the level of definition and in terms of visions of what is required for desired social and ecological change.

BOX 5.3   THREE APPROACHES TO CONCEPTUALISING ENVIRONMENTAL HARM

CONVENTIONAL CRIMINOLOGY

This is based on legal conceptions of harm, as informed by laws, rules and international conventions. The key issue is one of legality, and the division of activities into legal and illegal categories:

- *illegal taking of flora and fauna:* including illegal, unregulated and unreported fishing, illegal logging and trade in timber and illegal trade in wildlife
- *pollution offences:* from fly tipping (illegal dumping) through to air, water and land pollution associated with industry
- *transportation of banned substances:* illegal transport of radioactive materials and the illegal transfer of hazardous waste.

ECOLOGICAL PERSPECTIVES

Conceptions of harm are tied to ecological wellbeing and holistic understandings of the interrelationship between species and environments. The key issue is that of sustainability, and the division of social practices into benign and destructive from the point of view of ecological sustainability, specifically:

- *the problem of climate change:* in which the concern is to investigate those activities that contribute to increases of carbon dioxide and methane levels in the atmosphere and, hence, global warming, such as the replacement of forests with cropland
- *the problem of waste and pollution:* in which the concern is with those activities that defile the environment, leading to things such as the diminishment of clean water
- *the problem of biodiversity:* in which the concern is to stem the tide of species extinction and the overall reduction in species through application of certain forms of human production, including the replacement of forests with agricultural land.

GREEN CRIMINOLOGY

Justice conceptions are based upon notions of human, ecological and animal rights and egalitarian concerns. The key issue is weighing up of different kinds of harm and violation of rights within the context of an eco-justice framework:

- *environment rights and environmental justice:* in which environmental rights are seen as an extension of human or social rights so as to enhance the quality of human life, now and into the future
- *ecological citizenship and ecological justice:* in which ecological citizenship acknowledges that human beings are merely one component of complex eco-systems that should be preserved for their own sake via the notion of the rights of the environment
- *animal rights and species justice:* in which environmental harm is constructed in relation to the place of non-human animals within environments and their intrinsic right to not suffer abuse, whether this be one-on-one harm, institutionalised harm or harm arising from human actions that affect climates and environments on a global scale.

Source: White (2008b)

ISSUES FOR CONSIDERATION

NEED TO ANALYSE THE NATURE OF POWER

Some approaches to criminology tend to have a simple view of the nature of power; that is, there is a notion that some people have power (the powerful) and others do not (the powerless); there is no serious attempt to analyse the nature of power. This criticism has sometimes been directed at Marxist, feminists, structuralist and allied types of approaches. While acknowledging the need for further analysis of, and sensitivity to, the dynamics of power at a micro as well as macro level, most critical criminology nonetheless maintains that social power is best understood as being concentrated in particular directions. It is seen to have substantially different effects according to different groups' resources and capacities, and this, in turn, is related to the institutionalised nature of inequality.

That the core concerns of these perspectives continue to resonate today is without dispute when one considers the propensity of poverty to be concentrated, thereby giving rise to opportunity capture and unequal political and economic representation. A recent report released by Oxfam International (Fuentes-Nieva & Galasso 2014) found, for example, that:

- Almost half of the world's wealth is now owned by just 1 per cent of the population, and amounts to $110 trillion; this represents sixty-five times the total wealth of the bottom half of the world's population.
- The bottom half of the world's population owns the same as the richest eighty-five people in the world.
- Seven out of ten people live in countries where economic inequality has increased in the past 30 years.
- Between 1980 and 2012, the richest 1 per cent increased their share of income in twenty-four out of twenty-six countries while the bottom became poorer.

Furthermore, despite concerted efforts, women in Australia (and, indeed, worldwide) continue to experience extraordinary levels of economic inequality and widespread violence. For example:

- Australian women's workforce participation continues to lag at 65 per cent compared to 79.7 per cent for males. Moreover, women still only earn approximately 83.5 cents for every dollar earned by their male counterparts (Summers 2013).
- Just under a third of Australian women have experienced physical assault, and nearly one in five has been subject to sexual assault. Intimate partner violence is the leading cause of preventable injury, illness and death, with approximately one woman killed each week in Australia by a partner or former partner. Levels of violence and sexual assault are even higher amongst Indigenous women; while representing just 2 per cent of Australia's population, Indigenous women account for 15 per cent of national homicide victims (Abrahams et al. 2014; VicHealth 2006).
- Worldwide, rape in marriage is still not considered a crime in some countries (e.g. India); customs that devalue women persist (e.g. foeticide and dowry); one in four women is sexually assaulted while pregnant; and approximately 10 million children are forced into under-age marriage (Bryce 2013; Dhillon 2014; Hague & Sardinha 2010; Short 2013c).

Why and how institutionalised inequality and overtly sexist practices exist therefore deserves continued scrutiny. Given the critique of 'capitalism' that lies at the base of much of the radical, critical, peacemaking, cultural and green criminologies, these perspectives need to be able to spell out in more precise terms the nature of capitalism in the light of processes of internationalisation and globalisation, and how its institutions (e.g. transnational corporations and nation-states) have an impact on the crime debate. For example, it is not always clear whether critical criminology is arguing that the basis of all crime is ultimately economic or, rather, that the capitalist system merely exacerbates conflict and tension that exist independently from the economic relations inherent within capitalism. In either case, there is a need to examine the precise way in which capitalism acts to exacerbate tension, and both produce and define crime.

POSTMODERNIST APPROACH TO POWER

Postmodern criminologists do not conceptualise power in the same way as those who adopt a more structural perspective. Their view tends to draw upon the work of Foucault (1980), who points to the decentralisation of power within modern society; that is, it is not held solely by the state or in one particular class or group of people. Rather, the argument is that power is dispersed through-out society. Furthermore, power is not necessarily seen as always negative, but as a generalised feature of social life. Thus, power, when used to oppress, creates resistance, and this in itself is a source of power. According to Foucault, power can be associated with pleasure as well as repression. It can also flow in more than one direction simultaneously.

Foucault's ideas have been highly influential, but at times they have been oversimplified or distorted in some postmodernist work. For example, postmodern criminology emphasises that language always constitutes, and is constituted by, the relationship between knowledge, power and resistance, and this leads to some logical dilemmas. For instance, it has been pointed out that: 'If all discourses and definitions are power effects involving repression, then power is ubiquitous. It is everywhere and therefore nowhere' (Lea 1998: 173). If power, and resistance, are always present, then by what criteria are we to discern whether or not any particular social relationship is 'oppressive' or 'liberating'? Here the notion of a power differential becomes central to conceptual analysis. Major problems arise if crucial qualitative distinctions are not made regarding the relative power differences between different individuals and groups.

Another difficulty with the postmodernist approach is that deconstruction as a method of analysis can lead to infinite regress (Lea 1998). That is, if there is no 'objective' world, and there really is no reality outside the dynamics of language, then all knowledge is indeterminate and relative. There is no endpoint to the deconstruction process. This can be extremely confusing as words are further defined and interrogated in relation to other words, and the language of analysis becomes ever more complex and obscure. It can also preclude the necessity or capability to act on the understandings we currently have, since these are always changing and are always subject to further deconstruction. Furthermore, if there is no intrinsic foundation to 'facts' about the social world (because these are socially constructed through language), then what criteria can be invoked to determine whose 'voices' should be heard and which groups to support in our work? If the key criterion is that of looking to those voices that have been 'silenced' by the dominant languages of the law, then it raises the prospect of not only enabling oppressed minorities (e.g. ethnic minority groups) to resist better, but also extreme right-wing nationalist or white supremacist groups (e.g. neo-Nazis; see Lea 1998). This can only happen, however, if there is no normative basis to the work of the postmodern criminologist. But implicit in a values framework is the idea of some kind of meta-narrative regarding what is deemed to be 'good' and 'right'.

THE NEED FOR PRACTICAL APPLICATIONS

By way of contrast, some of the new directions in criminology described above have been criticised for providing little more than a utopian vision of society generated by intellectuals in their ivory towers and, ultimately, for failing to provide an accessible and adequate empirical and theoretical understanding of crime and crime control (Balfour 2006; Grewcock 2012; Van Swaaningen 1999). For example, McEvoy (2003) is highly conscious of the fact that too often the tendency in peacemaking criminology is to stimulate interest in the perspective but to pay much less attention to practical application. The perspective is pitched at a level of abstraction and philosophical reflection that offers a different way of framing and thinking about crime and criminality, but as an emerging form of criminological theory it has some way to go in providing more specific, grounded analyses of relevant issues and trends. Moreover, big questions remain with respect to analysis of different types of violence; namely, whether and under what conditions violence can be seen as liberating or repressive, the legitimacy or otherwise of violence that enables the state or community to wield authority and to enforce collective decisions, and the moral basis upon which to condemn (or support) those who utilise violence to achieve social goals. Resolution of these practical and conceptual issues is most likely through specific case studies and strategic interventions, as illustrated, for example, by McEvoy (2003) in relation to conflict in Northern Ireland, Braithwaite et al. (2010) in relation to conflict in Papua New Guinea, and Beitzel and Castle (2013) in relation to conflict in Northern Uganda.

CONCLUSION

The criminological perspectives offered in this chapter largely deal with issues of power and conflict resolution. Close consideration of the approaches forces us to confront issues concerning the social interests in which the state acts (and, frequently, how it acts in opposition to the less powerful, and against species and environmental rights and welfare). They also pose major philosophical questions about what it is to be human (and, as such, our experiences as emotional beings), our relationships with nature (specifically, how the human–environment nexus is conceived) and the place of violence in the constitution of our everyday lives as well as criminal justice systems (and how to overcome the entrenched nature of such).

The perspectives also create awareness of the potential long-term conflict that can be produced by states that prioritise the interests of one group of society over and above the interests of other groups. In doing so, they give advance warning of the likely social impact of the dismantling of the welfare state, the 'racialisation' of public order policing, the social exclusion of people from basic citizenship rights and the degradation of the environment on a planetary scale. The result of such trends may be personalised in the form of high suicide rates (affecting the individual), and collective in the form of riots and general social unrest (affecting whole communities). There is a lot at stake.

While the focus to this point has been on theorising the causes of crime and justice responses, the following chapter turns to exploration of victimology within criminology; that is, the nature, patterns, consequences and justice system responses to harms occasioned by crime. As is the case with theorising crime causation, the study of victims within victimology is a deeply contested affair.

DISCUSSION QUESTIONS

1 What are the main criminological orthodoxies being challenged in this chapter?
2 Why are Marxism and feminism considered foundational perspectives for the critical and radical perspectives that followed?
3 'Cultural criminology shares many elements with strain theory and labelling perspectives.' Discuss.
4 What is being restored in 'restorative justice'?
5 Why is green criminology gaining in importance in the twenty-first century?

FURTHER READING

Anthony, T. & Cunneen, C. (eds) (2008) *The critical criminology companion*, Federation Press, Sydney.

Arrigo, B. & Bernard, T. (1997). 'Postmodern criminology in relation to radical and conflict criminology', *Critical Criminology*, 8(2): 39–60.

Ferrell, J., Hayward, K. & Young, J. (2008) *Cultural criminology: an invitation*, Sage, Los Angeles.

Landry, D. (2013) 'Are we human? Edgework in defiance of the mundane and measurable', *Critical Criminology*, 21(1): 1–14.

Simon, D.R. (2012) *Elite deviance* (10th edn), Pearson, New York.

6 VICTIMS AND VICTIMOLOGY

CHAPTER OVERVIEW

- WHO IS A VICTIM?
- STATISTICAL ACCOUNTS OF VICTIMISATION
- THE PAINS AND CONTEXT OF VICTIMISATION
- VICTIM PARTICIPATION
- INSTITUTIONALISING VICTIM PARTICIPATION
- VICTIMS AND VICTIMOLOGY
- ISSUES FOR CONSIDERATION
- CONCLUSION
- DISCUSSION QUESTIONS
- FURTHER READING

INTRODUCTION

VICTIMOLOGY
Victimology is the study of victimisation, including societal conceptualisation of 'victim', victimisation profiles and risk distribution for various categories of crime, the relationship between victims and offenders, and interactions between victims and the criminal justice system.

Although victimisation dates back to the evolution of humanity itself, the systematic study of victims is relatively new. The term **victimology** was coined in 1947 by Benjamin Mendelsohn, an Israeli lawyer, and subsequently became drawn into the discipline of criminology by German criminologist Hans Von Hentig (1948). Since its inception, victimology has grown from a relatively nebulous set of concepts and interests to become a key area of concern within criminology (Jaishankar 2008).

The aim of this chapter is to consider critical concepts and issues within victimology, including discussion of the label 'victim', and how victimisation is socially and statistically constructed. The chapter begins by discussing the prevalence of, and risk distribution for, different kinds of victimisation in Australia, as well as the nature of the relationship between victims and offenders. This is followed by a review of societal responses to victimisation, with an emphasis on victim needs and support services. An important part of this discussion is the changing nature of victim interactions with, and participation within, the criminal justice system, including consideration of victim compensation and victim impact statements.

The chapter also presents an overview of the main strands within victimology so as to illustrate the complex ways in which a 'victim' is conceptualised in the criminological research. Reference will be made here to issues relating to the social processes underpinning the 'making of victims', and the manner in which the status of victim itself carries certain connotations and policy implications.

WHO IS A VICTIM?

According to the United Nations General Assembly:

> 'Victims' means persons who, individually or collectively, have suffered harm, including physical or mental injury, emotional suffering, economic loss or substantial impairment of their fundamental rights, through acts or omissions that are in violation of criminal laws operative within Member States, including those

laws proscribing criminal abuse of power (Declaration of Basic Principles of Justice for Victims of Crime and Abuse of Power 1985).

Victims can be divided into two categories (see Cook et al. 1999):

- **primary victims**: those who are the immediate victims of and directly impacted by, a crime
- **secondary victims**: those other than the direct victim who may also suffer harms and trauma, such as those who are witnesses to a crime, family members, friends, neighbours and whole communities.

The extent and seriousness of the issue of **victimisation** is clear when one considers that, according to official crime statistics, between 800,000 and 1.4 million crimes are recorded in Australia each year (ABS 2014a; AIC 2013a; Rollings 2008). While the vast majority of these offences are crimes against property, significant numbers of Australians are affected by crimes against the person. In 2012, for instance, for every 100,000 Australians, there were 1.1 murders, 0.7 attempted murders, 0.2 manslaughters, 2.8 kidnappings/abductions and 80 sexual assaults recorded. This data does not enumerate unique persons or organisations, and therefore cannot produce a total number of victims. Moreover, since these figures report on primary victims (individuals, households, organisations and motor vehicles) only, they exclude the friends and family of the victim, and the community in general, who also suffer as a result of the crime (ABS 2013a).

As confronting as these figures are, they grossly under-represent the true extent of victimisation in Australia since they only capture a select range of personal and household offences (some examples of excluded crimes are non-sexual assault, criminal damage, arson, fraud and driving causing death). Furthermore, they exclude data inconsistent with National Crime Recording Standards (e.g. assault data from Queensland, Victoria and Tasmania), unreported crimes, many forms of white-collar crime, state crime and environmental crime. Based on a wider range of offence categories and factoring in a multiplier effect for crimes commonly unreported, Rollings (2008) estimated that just under 12 million crimes were committed in Australia in 2006. Notwithstanding the data limitations associated with each of the data presented, considered in aggregate it indicates a significant and wide-ranging experience of victimisation in Australia. As will become evident shortly, victimisation affects people both directly (in regards to actual harm) and indirectly (in regards to fear of crime). In either case, it exerts major influences on how individuals, groups and communities carry out the day-to-day routines of living.

STATISTICAL ACCOUNTS OF VICTIMISATION

There is no single source of data that provides a comprehensive picture of crime victimisation in Australia. Rather, there are multiple sources of data relating to different aspects of victimisation. The Australian Bureau of Statistics (ABS) produces two major types of national data collection on crime victimisation. The first of these is the Recorded Crime—Victims Australia data set (ABS 2013a), which is a composite of administrative records on reported and/or recorded crime derived from state and territory police agencies. The second is direct reports from members of the public about their experiences of crime, as collected regularly in household surveys across Australia, notably the Crime Victimisation Australia survey (ABS 2014b) and the Personal Safety Australia survey (ABS 2013b). A specific sub-set of information on the experience of victimisation by Indigenous and Torres Strait Islander people is also available in the form of the National Aboriginal and Torres Strait Islander Social Survey data set (ABS 2009a), but this information is collected infrequently.

VICTIMS
Persons who, individually or collectively, have suffered harm, including physical or mental injury, emotional suffering, economic loss or substantial impairment of their fundamental rights.

PRIMARY VICTIMS
Those who are subject to and feel the direct impacts of a crime.

SECONDARY VICTIMS
Individuals other than primary victims who are witnesses to or impacted by a crime, including family members, friends, neighbours, bystanders and whole communities, who may also suffer tangible losses and/or intangible harms, including trauma, as a result of a crime.

VICTIMS AS RECORDED BY POLICE

VICTIMISATION
The process by
which a person
learns to be
a victim, and/
or the ways in
which authority
figures
determine who
is or who is
not 'worthy' of
being deemed
a victim, and/or
the processes
that surround
becoming a
victim.

For the purposes of crime measurement and statistical analysis, the ABS has defined 'victim' in different ways, depending upon the offence category (ABS 2013a: see explanatory notes):

- For murder and attempted murder, manslaughter and driving causing death, assault, sexual assault and kidnapping/abduction, the victim is an individual person.
- For robbery, the victim may be either an individual person or an organisation. Where the robbery involves an organisation or business, the element of property ownership is the key to determining the number and type of robbery victims. If the robbery only involves property belonging to an organisation, then one victim (i.e. the organisation) is counted, regardless of the number of employees from which the property is taken. However, if robbery of an organisation also involves personal property in an employee's custody, then both the organisation and employee(s) are counted as victims.
- For blackmail/extortion, the victim may be either an individual person or an organisation.
- For unlawful entry with intent (UEWI), the victim is the place or the premises that is defined as a single connected property that is owned, rented or occupied by the same person or group of people.
- For motor vehicle theft (MVT), the victim is the motor vehicle.
- For other theft, comprising theft of motor vehicle parts or contents theft from a person (excluding by force), theft from retail premises, theft (except motor vehicles) and illegal use of property (except motor vehicles), the victim is either an individual person or an organisation.

In snapshot, crime statistics collected by state and territory police services across Australia reveal the following types and patterns of victimisation for the year 2012 (see ABS 2013a):

- The offence categories with the largest number of victims recorded by Australian police were: other theft (n = 500,552), unlawful entry with intent (n = 214,222) and motor vehicle theft (n = 58,574). By way of contrast, there were only 457 instances of homicide and related offences, and 440 cases of blackmail/extortion. Property offences have consistently accounted for the vast bulk of the major crimes (96%). Of these offences, the most commonly recorded is 'other theft', which includes crimes such as pickpocketing, bag snatching and shoplifting.
- The overall number of victims increased by 1.2 per cent between 2011 and 2012. Those offence categories recording an increase included MVT (6%), murder (4.5%—note this is off a low base of 244 total murders in 2011), armed robbery (4%), sexual assault (3%) and UEWI other (1%). By contrast, total robberies continued to trend downwards, dropping 4 per cent during 2012, following a 7 per cent drop in 2011.

VICTIMISATION RATES

To interpret the significance of these statistical changes requires consideration of a broader time frame than a year-to-year comparison, since changes in the number of annually recorded crime victims fail to account for increases in the population over time. As a result, increases in crime counts may reflect an increase in the general population in the period under review rather than a genuine increase in the actual likelihood of a person becoming a victim of crime (AIC 2013a). By adjusting for population changes, crime victimisation rates provide a more accurate picture of changes over time.

Looking at crime rates in Australia from 1996 (AIC 2013a, 2014a), it is significant that, for example, in 1996 the rate of robbery victimisation exceeded that of sexual assault (89 as opposed to 79 per 100,000 population). This changed in 2004, when the sexual assault victimisation rate increased to 95 per 100,000 while robbery declined to 82 per 100,000. Since then, the rate of robbery victimisation has consistently remained below the rate of sexual assault victimisation. In 2012, there were 58 victims of robbery per 100,000 population, compared with 80 victims of sexual assault per 100,000 population. It is also noteworthy that despite increasing in number in 2012, the victimisation rate of MVT has decreased by 64 per cent since 2000 to 258 per 100,000 population in 2012. Similarly, in 2012 UEWI victimisation occurred at a rate of 944 per 100,000 population; an overall decrease of 59 per cent since its peak in 2000, when the rate was 2,281 per 100,000 population.

Between 1995 and 2010 (the last year for which national assault records were available), assault was the most commonly experienced personal crime, accounting for the vast majority of recorded violent crimes against the person (which includes homicide, assault, sexual assault and robbery). During this period, the assault victimisation rate increased by 44 per cent from 563 to 810 per 100,000 population between 1995 and 2002, and then declined by 34 per cent to 753 in 2012. Murder, attempted murder and manslaughter victimisation rates have tended to remain fairly stable over this period, all consistently recording rates below 2 per 100,000 population.

VICTIM CHARACTERISTICS

Victim characteristics, such as sex, age and Indigenous/Torres Strait Islander status, vary according to the nature of the offence category. Based on 2012 recorded crime data (ABS 2013a), males were more likely than females to be victims of robbery (71%), blackmail/extortion (71%), murder (67%) and attempted murder (71%). They were also more likely to be victims of assault in states and territories for which data was available (between 58% in the Australian Capital Territory and 52% in South Australia), although females outnumbered assault victims in the Northern Territory and Western Australia (63% and 52%, respectively). By contrast, females were more likely than males to be victims of sexual assault (83%) and kidnapping/abduction (57%).

During 2012, persons aged 24 years or less comprised the majority of recorded victims of sexual assault (72%), with almost half of all sexual assaults perpetrated against those aged between 10 and 19 years (48%). Females aged 15–19 recorded the highest victimisation rate for sexual assault, at a rate of more than four times the overall female rate of victimisation for sexual assault. Those aged less than 25 years also comprised the majority of kidnapping/abduction victims (66%). In contrast, 77 per cent of all victims of murder were aged over 25, with the largest categories of victims aged between 25 and 34 years (25%) and over 55 years (21%). Robbery victims also tended to be older, with 45 per cent aged between 20 and 34 years. Across all selected states and territories (excluding Victoria, Tasmania and Queensland) the highest proportion of victims of assault (25%) were aged between 25 and 34 years in 2012; however, the victimisation rate for assault was highest in the 15–24 year age group for both sexes. The rate was higher for females, who were victimised at a rate of 1,116.5 per 100,000 population compared with 1,055 per 100,000 for males. Males were victimised at a higher rate than females in all other age categories.

Aboriginal and Torres Strait Islander status data for victims of assault was available in 2012 for New South Wales, South Australia and the Northern Territory (ABS 2013a). The data demonstrates that 66 per cent of assault victims in the Northern Territory identified as Aboriginal or Torres Strait Islander, compared to 11 per cent in South Australia and 7 per cent in New South Wales. In all selected states and territories, female Aboriginal and Torres Strait Islander people experienced a greater incidence of assault than their male counterparts. In particular, in the Northern Territory, 81 per cent of female assault victims identified as Aboriginal and Torres Strait Islander, compared to 41 per cent of males. Overall, Aboriginal and Torres Strait Islander people experienced assault victimisation at a much higher rate than non-Indigenous people (more than six times the rate in South Australia, more than five times the rate in the Northern Territory and almost four times the rate in New South Wales).

Overall, Indigenous people are almost twice as likely as non-Indigenous people to be the victim of physical or threatened violence, and Indigenous women are 31 times more likely to be admitted to hospital for assault-related injuries compared with non-Indigenous women. Additionally, the rate of homicide for Indigenous people is 8.5 times higher than for non-Indigenous people (Steering Committee for the Review of Government Service Provision 2011).

RELATIONSHIP TO OFFENDER

Between 2008 and 2010, 73 per cent of victims of murder knew their offender, whether a friend/acquaintance (37%) or family member (36%). The latter, referred to as domestic homicides, was comprised largely of homicide between intimate partners (66%). Contrary to popular belief (see Chapter 2), only 13 per cent of homicides across Australia could be classified as stranger homicides; that is, occurring between two parties that had no prior relationship (AIC 2013b; see also Chapter 10). With regards to assault, 64 per cent of all perpetrators were known to the victim in 2012 (data based on New South Wales, South Australia, the Northern Territory and the Australian Capital Territory only), while 28 per cent could be classed stranger assaults (ABS 2013a).

Equal proportions of victims were assaulted by 'known other' (33%) and family (32%) members in selected states and territories. Females were victimised by family members at a much higher rate than males (193 per 100,000 population, compared with 75 per 100,000). Conversely, males were assaulted by strangers at over three times the rate experienced by females (190 per 100,000 population, compared with 57 per 100,000).

A noteworthy observation in relation to ethnicity is that Indigenous and Torres Strait Islander women are more likely to be assaulted or sexually assaulted by someone known to them as compared to non-Indigenous women. This is especially the case in the Northern Territory, where 66 per cent of women were sexually assaulted by assailants known to them, as compared to 49 per cent of non-Indigenous and Torres Strait Islander women. In the case of homicide, a larger proportion of homicides against Indigenous people are committed by intimate partners (61%) as compared with non-Indigenous homicides (24%) (Steering Committee for the Review of Government Service Provision 2011).

LOCATION OF VICTIMISATION

The location of crime again varies according to offence category (ABS 2013a), with obvious connections observed in 2012 between certain offences, such as other theft offences (which includes shoplifting) and certain types of locations, such as retail locations (34%). Most sexual assaults take place in a residential location (64%), as do most homicides (62%), UEWI (71%) and MVT (45%). Robbery and kidnapping tend to occur in a community setting such as on a street or footpath (39% each). Community locations also featured predominantly in cases of assault involving male victims in most states and territories for which data was available (56% in the Northern Territory, 54% in the Australian Capital Territory and

42% in South Australia). However, in New South Wales and Western Australia, the largest proportion of assaults involving male victims transpired at a residential location (39% and 42%, respectively). Similarly, aside from the Northern Territory, in which assaults against females was slightly more likely to take place at a community location (40% compared to 37% in a residential location), the most common location where assaults against women occurred was at a residential location (66% in Victoria, 64% in South Australia, 67% in Western Australia and 55% in the Australian Capital Territory).

VICTIMS AS RECORDED BY VICTIM SURVEY

Not all victims of crime will report their victimisation, and hence official statistics are highly likely to understate the true extent of victimisation, especially for certain categories of crime, such as sexual assault. Household surveys therefore serve to supplement the officially recorded statistics and provide a more robust understanding of the nature and patterns of victimisation across Australia. In order to gauge trends in victimisation, the ABS undertakes periodic household surveys that involve individuals self-reporting their experiences of crime as well as reporting their perception of problems in their neighbourhoods, and their feelings of safety (ABS 2014b). The surveys involve persons aged 15 years or older and, in the specific case of sexual assault, persons aged over 18 years. The crime and safety surveys concentrate on those categories of more serious crime that affect the largest number of people: household crime (including break-in, attempted break-in MVT, theft of property from a motor vehicle, malicious property damage and other theft) and personal crime (including physical and sexual assault, threatened assault [face-to-face and non face-to-face] and robbery). Key findings of the 2012–13 study include:

- *Household crime:* it was estimated that of the 8.9 million households in Australia at the time of the survey, at least 6.3 per cent of households (n = 555,900) were victims of at least one incident of malicious property damage; 3.1 per cent of households (n = 276,200) were victims of at least one theft from a motor vehicle; 2.8 per cent of households (n = 248,800) were victims of at least one other type of theft; 2.7 per cent of households (n = 239,700) were victims of at least one break-in to their home, garage or shed, with a further 1.9 per cent (n = 171,000) experiencing at least one attempted break-in; and 0.6 per cent of households (n = 57,200) experienced at least one MVT. Victimisation rates for household crimes were invariably lower in 2012–13 across all offence categories compared to 2008–09 when the last survey was conducted. The most significant declines were recorded for malicious property damage (6.3% compared to 11.1% in 2008–09), MVT (0.6% compared with 1.1% in 2008–09) and attempted break-in (1.9% compared with 3.1% in 2008–09).

- *Personal crime:* it was reported that of the 18.4 million persons aged 15 years and over in Australia at the time of survey, 3.1 per cent (n = 576,800) were victims of at least one threatened assault, including face-to-face and non face-to-face threatened assault; 2.7 per cent (n = 498,000) were victims of at least one physical assault; 0.4 per cent (n = 65,700) were victims of at least one robbery; and 0.2 per cent (n = 40,700) were victims of at least one sexual assault (people aged 18 years and over only). Like household crime rates, victimisation rates for some personal crimes were also lower in 2012–13 compared to 2008-09. Specifically, declines were recorded for face-to-face threatened assault (2.8% compared with 3.9% in 2008–09), robbery (0.4% compared with 0.6% in 2008–09) and physical assault (2.7% compared with 3.1% in 2008–09).

Household and personal crimes varied greatly across states and territories. For example, the lowest levels of total household victimisation were experienced in Queensland (15.2%), followed by New South Wales (15.6%) and South Australia (16.1%), whereas the highest were experienced in the Northern Territory (28.7%), closely followed by Western Australia (27.5%). The Northern Territory also had the highest level of personal victimisation in the country, with an estimated 9.6 per cent of persons aged 15 years and over experiencing at least one of the selected personal crimes, compared with a rate of 5.5 per cent in New South Wales and 6.2 per cent in Victoria. In particular, the rate of physical assault (4.6 per 100,000 people) and sexual assault (0.4 per 100,000) in the Northern Territory exceeded the national averages (2.8 per 100,000 and 0.2 per 100,000, respectively) by 56–100 per cent (note that sexual assault figures have a very high rate of relative standard error).

VICTIM CHARACTERISTICS, RELATIONSHIP TO OFFENDER AND LOCATION OF VICTIMISATION

As with officially recorded offences, victim characteristics—such as sex, age and relationship to offender—vary according to the nature of the offence category. Males were more likely than females to be victims of robbery (82%), threatened assault (76%) and assault (82.5%). Younger persons aged between 15–19 years and 20–24 years were especially vulnerable to physical assault, recording victimisation rates of 5.1 per cent and 5.0 per cent, respectively. This compares to rates of 3.3 per cent for persons aged 35–44 years and 2.2 per cent for persons aged 45–54 years. Those aged 55–64 years and 65+ were the least likely to experience a physical assault (1.3% and 0.5%, respectively). By contrast, females were more likely than males to be victims of sexual assault (65%), with prevalence rates for those aged 18–19 and 20–24 much higher than for those in all other age categories (0.7% and 0.6%, respectively, compared to the national rate of 0.2%).

With regards to the relationship between the offender and victim, in the case of physical assault, the offender was known to the overwhelming majority of female victims (76.5%), and most victims overall (58.1%). The offender was most likely to be a family member (11.9%), especially in the case of female victims (18.3%) and the offence was most likely to take place in the victim's home (29.9%), particularly in the case of female victims (47.8%). The victim's home (or the home of another) was also the most likely location for the most recent incident of MVT experienced by households (47%; followed by in the street or other open land at 38%) and theft from a motor vehicle (61%; followed by in the street or other open land at 12%).

While this survey of statistical data on patterns of victimisation provides an indication of how people are victimised for different kinds of offences, it is important to bear in mind that the data is not definitive. For instance, data on sexual assault might usefully be bolstered by interviews with staff at women's refuges and centres dealing with sexual assault, as well as perusal of hospital emergency room records. A range of data sources and empirical studies are required to gauge fully the 'dark figure' of crime, especially in cases involving interpersonal violence among family members.

There is also a growing recognition of the extent to which small businesses are victims of crime. The Small Business Crime Safety survey conducted by the AIC across Australia in 2002 found that for every 100 businesses surveyed, 62 incidents of burglary occurred, with liquor outlets being particularly vulnerable. Just under half of the businesses surveyed had experienced at least one incident of crime. The study also found that just as a small number of offenders are responsible for a disproportionate number of crimes, a small number of businesses are also repeatedly targeted and account for a large proportion of all crimes measured in the survey (Taylor & Mayhew 2002).

THE PAINS AND CONTEXT OF VICTIMISATION

Statistical analysis, such as that undertaken above, can be useful in highlighting general patterns of victimisation across the community. It is also useful for identifying the specific social circumstances and contexts associated with victimisation, allowing for social differences to be acknowledged across different dimensions of the victimisation process. Undertaking granulated analysis across the spectrum of national victimisation is critically important in informing general and targeted crime prevention efforts (see Chapter 28), and identifying areas for further research and investigation. The critical importance of evidence-based efforts to prevent or minimise victimisation becomes clear when one considers the extent and the nature of the harms and 'pains' associated with victimisation.

THE PAINS OF VICTIMISATION

The pains of victimisation are manifold and substantial and are experienced at numerous levels— individual, household, organisational and societal (see, for example, Rollings 2008; Webber 2010). Quantification of harm and appreciation of its effects on communities is, however, complicated by a number of issues. Victimisation commonly produces tangible or monetised costs; that is, visible costs that have a market price, including, for example, physical harms and financial costs associated with replacing stolen goods, repairing damaged property, treating injuries sustained (e.g. medical expenses and lost income) and safeguarding against future victimisation through the adoption of defensive home ownership practices (e.g. costs associated with installing security alarms and locks).

These direct costs are borne materially by individuals, households and organisations. But the harms arising from crime do not stop at the point of commission; they reverberate far beyond the immediate victim. For example, aside from monetary losses accruing to an individual who has been assaulted (and, where relevant, family members), financial harms may also be experienced at the organisational level in the form of lost production, sick leave and paid family violence leave expenses borne by the victim's employer (Schneiders 2012). Beyond that, still, the community ultimately feels the weight of individual level harms in the form of: increased healthcare costs; increased insurance premiums; lower gross domestic product and export income due to withdrawal of victims from productive life; increased costs of goods and services; and increased taxes and the redirection of scarce community resources away from welfare and social justice areas and into the criminal justice system (police, courts and correctional services), crime-prevention programs and victim services and compensation.

The largest aspect of the costs of crime are, however, intangible; that is, 'quality of life' costs that change victims' perceptions and behaviour, and impact their social wellbeing. Unlike tangible or monetised costs, intangible costs are not always visible, are difficult to quantify since there is no easily measured and objective market price, and often have widespread and long-lasting effects (physical, emotional and psychological) on individuals, groups and communities (see, for example, Cook et al. 1999; Rollings 2008). Intangible costs are most commonly associated with crimes against the person, especially violent crimes such as assault and sexual assault. Depending on the nature of the crime and the type of harm, victims may suffer from post-crime trauma and depression (including feelings of guilt, blame and unworthiness; a crisis of self-esteem or self-worth; a loss of identity; and difficulty imagining a life free from pain, fear and suffering) (Kunst & Wilsem 2012; Laxminarayan 2012; Rogers 2010), they may be fearful for their lives and they may change their behaviour by restricting their social activities (e.g. avoiding places perceived to be dangerous or going out at night—especially walking through parks or waiting at isolated or unattended public transport stations) and friendship networks.

Victims may be so incapacitated through physical injuries or psychological and emotional wounds that they decide to move away from a neighbourhood or home. It has been suggested, for example, that domestic violence is responsible for significant levels of female homelessness (Murray 2011; Homelessness Taskforce 2008).

As per tangible harms, 'quality of life' harms also produce collateral damage in the form of secondary victimisation. This is self-evident in the case of the primary victim's family or those witnesses to a crime, but less so with respect to the victim's local community, which may, for example, suffer the adverse consequences of a loss of capital investment in high crime areas (lower house prices and lower community infrastructure and amenities). The community—and, indeed, society more broadly—may also suffer indirectly, through fear of crime caused by a disjuncture in perceived and actual crime victimisation risks (Davis & Dossetor 2010; Hipp 2013). Ultimately, this fear can adversely impact freedom and enjoyment of movement, and lead to gated communities (see Chapter 28).

The impacts of crime vary depending upon such factors as the nature of the person, the type of harm, the social networks of the victim and the community context (ABS 2012a). In some cases, the pain is not 'realised' until well after the event, particularly in the case of those indirectly impacted by crime. For example, a considerable body of evidence now exists in relation to the negative consequences of childhood and adolescent exposure to violence in the home and community, including developmental delays, physiological changes to the brain disrupting emotional control centres and impairing cognitive function, substance abuse, eating disorders, reduced educational and employment outcomes, teenage pregnancy, mental health problems, reduced adult socio-economic status, chronic disease, suicide attempts and engagement in criminal activity, including abusive and violent behaviours (see, for example, Covey et al. 2013; Stark 2013).

Despite the difficulties of enumeration, it is clear that from an economic point of view alone, the impact of crime on the Australian public (tangible and intangible) is considerable, estimated to be in the order of approximately $36 billion annually, which represents 4.1 per cent of the nation's gross domestic product (Rollings 2008). Astounding as this figure appears, it is highly likely to be a conservative estimate. It has been estimated by KPMG (Forsyth 2013), for example, that in 2013 violence against women alone cost the Australian economy $14.7 billion. Furthermore, Access Economics (2004) estimates that by 2021–22, violence against women will cost Australian employers $4.5 billion.

DISTRIBUTIONS OF RISK AND IMPACT

While crime and its consequences can have both immediate and widespread impact, it is important to acknowledge that the risks and pains of victimisation are not equally distributed in society. An important issue for consideration then is the way in which the incidence of crime and its consequences, as well as the fear of crime, are differentially distributed among social groups.

VICTIMISATION AND VULNERABILITY

One way of analysing the distribution of victimisation risk and impact is to consider the concept of 'inherent vulnerability'; that is, the essential features of victimisation that render some people and locations more prone to victimisation or fear of victimisation than others due to personal attributes (Rock 2007; Walklate 2011). A significant distinction here is between groups that are at 'high risk' of crime and groups that have a 'high impact' of crime.

It has been observed, for example, that one of the crucial factors affecting risk of crime, fear of crime and geographical mobility in urban areas is gender (Davis & Dossetor 2010; Drakulich & Rose 2013; Painter 1992; Yavuz & Welch 2010). For instance, although males are more at risk of violence in public places than women (who are generally at greater risk within the home), studies demonstrate that women tend to experience greater levels of fear associated with personal safety in public than men. This heightened sensitivity to environmental risk and the potential consequences of crime has been attributed to their sense of a greater physical and social vulnerability to victimisation, especially sexual harassment, rape and sexual assault. Although men are generally physically stronger and tend to possess a masculine presence and identity (confident and fearless), recent research does point to broader application of vulnerability, with men reporting diminished feelings of control and fear when in unfamiliar locations or unpredictable situations, and feelings of fear for the safety of female partners; feelings customarily not expressed due to socialisation norms that discourage displays of emotion (Drakulich & Rose 2013; Yavuz & Welch 2010).

Similarly, as already established through the earlier review of both recorded crime statistics and survey victimisation data, and other research across the globe (Green 2007), older people are significantly less likely to be victims of assault than other demographic groups such as younger people, particularly those under the age of 25 years. They are therefore statistically not at 'high risk' of physical victimisation. However, if subjected to assault, the physical impact is likely to be greater than in the case of a younger victim, due to the older person's relative frailty. The nature of the impact plays an important role in how victims perceive and fear the possibilities of crime victimisation.

GEOGRAPHIES OF VICTIMISATION

A second way of considering risk distribution is to examine the patterning of victimisation as structured by such things as demographic profile (age, ethnicity and socio-economic status), lifestyle and mobility patterns, and neighbourhood characteristics, such as social disorganisation or concentrated pockets of disadvantage and social deprivation (see, for example, Green 2007; Vilalta 2011). Various theoretical models have been applied to the study of victimisation patterning, the most influential of which has been the routine activities framework developed by Cohen and Felson (1979), which focuses on the environments in which individuals carry out their daily activities and interactions, and the risks for victimisation these introduce (for a detailed review, see Chapter 25). For example, the risk of violent victimisation is said to be positively associated with the frequency with which individuals attend venues licensed to sell alcohol (Brennan et al. 2010; Kershaw et al. 2008). In relation to the risk of residential burglary, research has consistently identified patterns of spatial clustering in which burglaries tend to be concentrated. Furthermore, within those clusters, particular types of dwellings appear to be consistently targeted (Johnson 2010).

Spatial and temporal analysis of who gets victimised, where, by whom and why, provides important insight into the social dynamics and power structures of the society as a whole (Wilkinson 2009). For example, women are more likely to be subjected to specific kinds of harassment and harm depending upon the time of day, the nature of public or private space they occupy and the company they are in. In fact, research in the United Kingdom suggests that women experience higher levels and a wider spectrum of crime than men (Painter 1992), and that this is directly related to the organisation of physical environments and spaces, and the nature of women's interactions within these spaces.

REPEAT VICTIMISATION

**REPEAT
VICTIMISATION**
Victimisation
that occurs
when a crime
is committed
in the same
location or is
perpetrated
against the
same individual
on more than
one occasion.

Crime occurs neither uniformly nor randomly across the population, nor does it happen the same way in every location. It tends to be concentrated on particular people and found in particular places. The recurrence of crime is known as **repeat victimisation**. This is where certain people or places are victimised more than once. It is a phenomenon common to many crimes, including, for example, domestic or family violence, incest and paedophilia, burglary and wilful entry with intent, hate crimes and bank robberies. Repeat victimisation of personal crimes can be especially traumatising, and have profound, long-lasting and cumulative negative effects (Scott-Storey 2011).

At first glance, the full implications of repeat victimisation are not self-evident. Australian Bureau of Statistics' victimisation data (2014b), for example, indicates that the majority of households that experienced crime in 2012–13 were involved in only a single incident. These proportions ranged from 96 per cent that experienced a MVT, to 79 per cent that experienced an attempted break-in. Notwithstanding, significant proportions of households experienced repeat victimisation in the case of attempted break-in (22%), malicious damage (21%), other theft (20%), completed break-in (18%) and theft from a motor vehicle (15%).

Overall, the majority of people over the age of 15 years also experienced just one incident of personal crime over the same timeframe. For example, 81 per cent of households who experienced a break-in experienced only one incident and 76 per cent of those that experienced robbery did so on only one occasion. Levels of repeat victimisation, where identified, were, however, much higher than for household crimes. For example, it is estimated that over 50 per cent of individuals that experienced physical assault in 2012–13 did so on more than one occasion (21% on two occasions and 30% on three or more occasions). An even greater proportion of survey respondents (68%) reported repeat episodes of threatened violence (18% on two occasions and 47% on three or more occasions). Just under a quarter of respondents experiencing robbery (24%) also reported multiple incidents of victimisation (11% on two occasions and 9% on three or more occasions) (ABS 2014b).

When examined in the context of relative proportions (crime as opposed to victims), however, it becomes apparent that repeat victimisations account for a disproportionately large amount of crime. While the annual prevalence rate of repeat victimisation is low (2.4 per cent of households and 1.4 per cent of persons aged 15 and over), these households or individuals account for more than half the incidents of crime occurring during the year. In the case of property crimes, half the incidents occur in just over one-quarter of all households, with 10 per cent of all victimised households experiencing three or more incidents. Together, these accounted for 25 per cent of all incidents (ABS 2014b). In the case of violent crime, two-thirds of the incidents are experienced by 41 per cent of victims (Mukherjee & Carcach 1998). Moreover, it is clear that repeat violent victimisation is differentially distributed within the community. For example, in 2012–13, 36 per cent of women who were victims of physical assault reported three or more incidents, in comparison to 27 per cent of men (ABS 2014b). In Australia and, indeed, worldwide, repeat physical violence is perpetrated against women largely by known perpetrators, especially husbands or intimate partners; this pattern holds true regardless of race, class, religion or cultural background (Garcia-Moreno & Watts 2011).

Attempts to explain repeat victimisation often centre on the contribution of the victim to increasing their risk exposure, especially in the context of sexual assault. However, ecological models caution against simplistic interpretations, suggesting instead that victimisation can only be understood in the broader context of the microsystems (social interactions in immediate environments such as the family and peer groups), eco-systems (larger social system in which microsystems are embedded) and macrosystems (cultural norms) operating within society (Aosved & Long 2006; Bronfenbrenner 1977). In applying the ecological approach to sexual assault specifically, Grauerhotz's study of sexual revictimisation (2000) concluded that revictimisation is determined by multiple factors related to: personal history (e.g. the victim's prior experience of traumatic sexualisation); the relationship in which revictimisation occurs (e.g. in the context of a domestic or familiar situation where the ability to resist unwanted sexual advances is reduced); the community (e.g. a lack of family support—such as commonly occurs within families in the context of child sexual abuse); and the larger culture (e.g. blaming victim attitudes and practices that protect male perpetrators of violence) (see also Kahlor & Eastin 2011; Meyer & Post 2006).

DOUBLE VICTIMISATION

Within victimology, the concept of **double victimisation** or secondary victimisation is an important one. This refers to the ways in which the state response to victimisation and, in particular, the legal processes that the victim endures, compounds the primary victimisation, adding further burdens and serving as a 'vehicle for the damage to be inflicted again' (Rogers 2010: 30; see also Laxminarayan 2012). For instance, rape victims can be described as doubly victimised or re-traumatised because of the disempowering and stigmatic nature of courtroom processes. Not only is the victim story ignored, but it is also reframed, effectively putting the victim 'on trial' through suggestions that they invited or provoked the incident in some way, and therefore calling into question or minimising the nature of the harms experienced (Easteal et al. 2012; see also Chapter 22).

The forensic process of interrogation—an integral feature of adversarial justice—essentially forces victims to relive the original trauma. While court proceedings ostensibly demand truth, serving to pass judgment on the guilt or innocence of an accused, in the mind of the victim the verdict is in part an assessment of their credibility; a legal sanctioning of their image as 'good' or 'bad'. Therefore, as suggested by Rogers (2010: 33), 'the pain of a loss of identity and the death of an image of oneself following assault can readily be exacerbated by the demand for truth and certainty that takes place in a courtroom'. In the case of a 'not guilty' verdict there is, furthermore, a complete denial of the harms experienced by the victim; in essence, a public stripping away of the very title 'victim'.

Sex workers can also be seen as doubly victimised in the sense that they are sexually exploited by men and victimised by the courts, which operate with a double standard that criminalises them but not their male clients (Brown et al. 2001; Graycar & Morgan 1990; Scutt 1990).

REPORTING OF VICTIMISATION

How individuals and households respond to victimisation varies with the nature of the offence and the victim's view of the incident. This is reflected in large differences in rates of reporting to police in 2012–13 for offences across both household and personal categories of crime (ABS 2014b):

* 93 per cent for household victims of motor vehicle theft (the highest rate of reporting across all selected crime categories)
* 78 per cent for household victims of break-in (compared to only 43% for attempted break-in)
* 55 per cent for household victims of theft from a motor vehicle
* 50 per cent for victims of robbery
* 50 per cent for victims of assault

DOUBLE VICTIMISATION
The way in which the state's response to victimisation can add further burdens to the victim; for instance, rape victims may be doubly victimised because of the way in which courtroom processes put women 'on trial' by suggesting they invited the incident in some way.

- 37 per cent for victims of face-to-face threatened assault (compared to only 25% for victims of non face-to-face threatened assault)
- 34 per cent for victims of sexual assault (note that a standard error of 25%–50% applies, so consider with caution).

It is noteworthy that property crimes (especially motor vehicle theft and break-ins) are reported at much higher rates than crimes against the person. This is likely to reflect the evidence of loss requirements associated with claims on insurance policies. Also reported at higher rates are completed as opposed to attempted crimes. The lowest rate of reporting was for sexual assault, with only one in three being officially reported. While the high standard of error (refer above) diminishes confidence in the accuracy of this figure, research in Australia and internationally substantiates the view that the majority of sexual assault offences are not reported, especially those involving intimate partners (Berg et al. 2013; Catalano et al. 2009; Johnson et al. 2008; Kelly et al. 2005; Temkin & Krahé 2008; Willis 2011). The reasons for not reporting crime are varied, including (Family and Community Development Committee 2013; Roberto et. al. 2013):

- feeling of shame and humiliation (not wanting others to know) and/or the view that the incident is a personal matter to be taken care of by the victim themself (in cases of assault involving a known offender, especially an intimate partner or where reporting a crime would cast aspersions on masculinity; this is especially prevalent among rural populations)
- feelings of guilt and self-blame for the victimisation
- fear that claims of victimisation will not be believed (prevalent among marginalised or vulnerable groups, including the homeless and those with disabilities) or that they will be deemed 'unworthy' victims
- a perception that the offence is not life-threatening or serious enough to warrant taking official action
- fear of the consequences of taking official action, such as further abuse, lack of independent financial resources to make major lifestyle changes (e.g. leaving an abusive partner), and re-traumatisation by the justice system
- active discouragement by those in a position of trust and authority (as has occurred in the case of the widespread silencing of sexual abuse victimisation by organisations such as churches and community welfare organisations) or the perpetrator
- concerns with self-incrimination where the victim was involved in unlawful behaviour at the time of victimisation or is known to police
- distrust of authorities (especially among Indigenous Australians and certain ethnic minorities) or a perception that there is nothing the police can do (especially in cases of household victimisation).

VICTIM PARTICIPATION

Until recently, victims have not had a very prominent place in the criminal justice system. This has not always been the case. Before the emergence of formal law and courts, for example, the extent of retribution for harms suffered, and the administering of this retribution, was basically in the hands of the direct victims and their families (see Chapter 22).

With the emergence of formalised, codified law, the state claimed 'ownership of conflict', taking on the role of victim (Englebrecht 2011; McShane & Williams 1992). Notions such as the 'King's peace' reinforced the centrality and coercive power of state authority. No longer was the direct victim the key protagonist; increasingly, it was the state that defined harm, and had sole legal responsibility for dealing with infringements of the wellbeing of its citizens. Legal definitions of harm did not necessarily fit with victims' perceptions of the harm they had suffered. There was, in essence, a modification in the victim's role—from an individual who directly seeks compensation for harms experienced, to one that provides support for the state prosecutor's case. In this reoriented role, the actual harm experienced by the victim is largely ignored, and the primary focus is directed towards the offender. Real harm was thus subordinated to theoretical concepts of legal harm and the victim became the forgotten party in criminal justice processes.

The net result of these developments is that concepts of 'harm' and 'victim' are wrapped around legal, rather than social, conceptions. It was the state, not the individual, that pursued the case and the victim basically had no right to participate in processes such as the investigation of the case, the laying of charges, bail, plea bargaining, prosecution, sentencing or parole. The victim, by and large, became the forgotten and excluded element in the whole process of criminal justice.

In the past 50 years, however, victim dissatisfaction with the criminal justice system—especially relating to the ability of the law to represent the experiences of victims, the lack of participatory opportunities for victims, and the failure by courts and perpetrators to acknowledge the true extent of the harm experienced—has fuelled a concerted push around the notions of victim participation and victim rights (Booth 2002; Mastrocinque 2010; McEvoy & McConnachie 2012; Waller 2011). In the 1970s, for example, the impetus for such a push came from a number of quarters:

- The Women's liberation movement was concerned with the victimisation of women, highlighting the need to discuss and analyse issues such as rape, domestic violence and indecent assault. Campaigns were mounted that advocated the notion that the personal is political, and that crimes against women needed a strong societal response; effectively a shift from private to public suffering.

- The rise of non-government grassroots victim support and assistance groups was an important development in the politicisation of victimhood. This victims' movement saw victims of crime and their friends and families forming associations with each other, such as the Victims of Crime Assistance League (VOCAL) and Centres Against Sexual Assault (CASAs), to agitate for the provision of welfare services and procedural rights for victims. These groups often entered into the victim debate with very different political agendas (including conservative calls for harsher, more punitive measures for offenders), but were united in raising issues and perspectives from a victim's point of view.

- Academia itself began to draw attention to the prevalence of victimhood, its consequences and policy implications concerning the conditions, needs and rights of victims. A new discipline—*victimology*—emerged, which cut across many other disciplines, such as forensic psychology, medicine, law, social science, social work and criminology. Specific theoretical perspectives in the 1980s, such as left realism and New Right criminology, also highlighted the plight of victims.

- At the international level, victimisation became an issue in relation to human rights. For instance, groups such as Amnesty International defined and redefined how we view victims. Here the main concern was with the oppressive role of the state. Victimisation was expanded to include not only torture and capital punishment but also forced migration. The United Nations 1985 Charter of Victims' Rights affirmed further the notion of securing recognition of victims' rights as a universal good, without prejudicing the rights of the accused.

- The impetus for change also came from governments themselves to a certain extent. Initially, such moves were more symbolic than substantial, such as the issue of compensating victims of crime. In recent years, however, there have been dramatic shifts in policy and service provision that have been designed to encourage direct victim participation in the criminal justice process.

VICTIM ASSISTANCE: PROGRAMS AND PROCEDURES

The services available to victims vary greatly, as do the service providers. Box 6.1 outlines the variety of needs of victims: needs that have obvious implications for the kinds of services ultimately required by victims.

Over time, a range of initiatives has developed worldwide to improve the standing of victims, especially with regards to criminal justice processes across all stages (pre-trial, trial and sentencing). These vary in nature, depending upon the state and country of jurisdiction, but are generally designed to improve procedural justice (respectful treatment and fairness during the court process so as to

---

BOX 6.1   NEEDS OF VICTIMS OF CRIME

- *Support:* This includes from family and friends, as well as from victim support agencies (e.g. Centres against Sexual Assault) and other support groups (e.g. Compassionate Friends and Broken Rites).
- *Information and knowledge:* This includes on services available; on the progress of the police investigation; on the role of the Office of Public Prosecutions and likely timeframes for prosecution; on court process and explanations of legal requirements; on the role the victim plays in court; and on possible outcomes and sentences.
- *Choices:* accurate information that allows victims to make their own choices. Service providers have noted the importance of victims being able to regain some control over their lives. Being able to make their own decisions empowers the victim. This has implications with regard to, for example, voluntary or compulsory participation in preparing victim impact statements.
- *To have their say:* it is important for victims to be able to have their say, to tell their story (completely) and to be heard. One way to achieve this is through victim impact statements, but this is not the only possible avenue for this to occur (e.g. victim–offender mediation and victim impact panels within prisons).
- *Immediate help and advice:* the sooner the victim receives positive support and advice, the easier the recovery will be. This is where government-funded Victims of Crime Services can be particularly useful and important.
- *Follow-up by police and the criminal justice system:* victims need to be kept informed at all stages of the police investigation and prosecution, and to be told of decisions affecting them as they happen and not to find out by accident or in court.
- *A coordinated system of services:* streamlined and easy to access so that victims can quickly gain knowledge of how the system works and what is available; and that has a broadly restorative focus, so that all agencies work together to restore the victim as quickly as possible to the way they were before the crime or to deal better with the consequences of the crime.
- *Sensitivity and understanding:* This includes by family and friends, police, medical practitioners, service providers, prosecutors, the judiciary and particularly the media.

Source: adapted from Cook et al. (1999: 40–1)

avoid re-victimisation, and the ability to directly participate in proceedings and affect the outcome), informational justice (receipt of adequate information about procedures), interpersonal justice (respectful treatment by parties to the legal proceedings) and ability to cope (measures that assist in dealing with the effects of victimisation) (Laxminarayan 2013; Laxminarayan et al. 2013). They include (see Cook et al. 1999; Kirchengast 2009; McShane & Williams 1992; Victorian Community Council Against Violence 1994; Webster 2011):

- *Victim notification:* victims are kept informed of the developments of the case and the hearing date, as well as court decisions relating to offender sentencing and re-entry into the community post release.
- *Victim impact statements (VISs):* these are written statements made by victims and/or their families and introduced to the court at the sentencing stage, which are designed to elucidate the victim's feelings on the harms caused by the offending. VISs are subdivided into those that are formally structured and formatted, and others that are unstructured and open-ended. In some cases, there is facility for victims to present their experiences verbally in court. There are major differences, as well, with regard to whether VISs are or ought to be compulsory or voluntary. In the United States, for example, VISs are optional in some states; however, in others they are mandatory. In Australia, where VISs are used, they are voluntary. South Australia was the first jurisdiction in the world to allow a victim to make an actual recommendation as to sentence and to include a 'social impact statement', known as a 'community impact statement'.
- *Court orientation:* victims are introduced to the court system so that they are able to identify the main players and feel comfortable with the court layout.
- *Transportation:* services are provided to victims to enable them to travel to and from the court.
- *Escorting:* this is a support service or 'handholding' exercise, so that the victim is not left alone in the court and has someone to refer to throughout the proceedings.
- *Compensation:* some forms of physical and emotional injury may be compensated via state agencies such as a crimes compensation tribunal. Alternatively, victims may receive compensation either through civil proceedings (e.g. under the law of torts) or criminal proceedings, where a court orders that compensation be paid.
- *Victim–offender mediation:* these are programs aimed at involving the victim in direct contact with the offender so that the offender can see for him or herself the harm caused, and so that victims and offenders can jointly be involved in attempts to resolve the harm that has been perpetrated.
- *General support services:* these include counselling services, youth and women's refuges and alcohol and drug services. These are meant to centre on the immediate and long-term needs of the victim.

A general survey of victim-oriented services and forms of participation may generate a list of involvements as described above. However, in practice, it is important to distinguish the different aims and objectives of the array of programs, and to acknowledge the 'punishment' rationale that still tends to predominate in the area of victim support. Taking into account the ways in which victim needs can be formally recognised and victim participation takes place, it can be said that the main orientations of victim support programs and procedures are:

- *A focus on prosecution processes:* this is centred on the court case itself and the offender. Thus, the use of VISs is to assign penalty, and to assist in the prosecution of offenders. It is not necessarily victim-centred per se, even though the victim may possibly gain some sense of satisfaction by preparing a VIS and being more actively involved in the court case.

- *A focus on conflict resolution processes:* this involves some form of mediation and *restorative justice.* The intention here is to restore dominion or personal liberty, both for the offender and the victim. Rather than focusing exclusively on the prosecution process, such processes promote more active victim participation, and attempt to make good the harm in a way that shames the deed, but not the offender.
- *A focus on reparation and/or compensation:* this is so that offenders are made aware of the consequences of their activities, and the victim(s) gains some type of financial recompense for harms suffered. The victim may be actively involved in determination of levels and nature of compensation. However, how payments are organised and administered is largely a matter for the courts and/or state compensation agencies to determine.
- *A focus on provision of support services:* this refers to areas such as counselling, funding of safe and secure refuges and the provision of information to victims so that they are better able to understand their victimisation in a wider context. Central to this orientation is the idea of meeting victim needs directly, rather than dealing with the offender.

The first three of these areas are the most dynamic in terms of recent developments in the area of victim participation. The provision of resources to meet victim needs remains under-funded and largely under-resourced. In part, this can be explained by the fact that as we move toward victim support, we move further away from the criminal justice system and the main objects of that system.

INSTITUTIONALISING VICTIM PARTICIPATION

While victim participation is generally now seen as an important component in the criminal justice process, there are nonetheless a number of practical difficulties that have emerged as victims have been brought back into the process and given a voice. The primary challenge relates to the framing of victim rights as capable of being met only at the expense of recognition of, or constraints upon, offender rights (Henderson 1985). To illustrate these we can examine issues relating to the granting of victim participatory rights, in the form of VISs, in relation to offender re-entry into society.

The United Nations Declaration on Victims' Rights has prompted the favouring of VISs by governments around the world. This preference, however, needs to be placed into the context of both law-and-order politics (and the implications this has for the symbolic value of VISs) and the practical difficulties in making such statements work for, and to the benefit of, victims. These are interrelated points, insofar as the retributive flavour of much current use of VISs in effect may represent a shift away from the rights of the victim in lieu of an emphasis on getting tougher on the offender.

To assess the issues surrounding VISs, we can examine the arguments in favour of and against the use of such statements (see Booth 2012; De Mesmaecker 2012; Erez et al. 1994; Rosebury 2011).

ARGUMENTS IN FAVOUR OF VICTIM IMPACT STATEMENTS

- *System consequences:* these include recognition of the victim's status as a party to the proceedings, and dignity; increased victim cooperation, which is important insofar as the prosecution and court system depends upon this cooperation, particularly in relation to the provision of testimony to support the prosecution case; and enhanced system efficiency, in that there is better reflection of the community's response to crime, which may in turn increase proportionality and accuracy in sentencing.

- *Victim needs:* these include increasing the victim's satisfaction with justice; psychological healing and restoration; reducing feelings of helplessness and lack of control; and providing a measure that can symbolise the importance of the victim in the criminal justice process.
- *Sentencing goals:* these include enhancing retribution by measuring the extent of harm; increasing the deterrent effect by increasing prosecutorial efficiency; providing insight into the need for incapacitation if the victim has knowledge of the defendant's potential for future criminal activity; promoting rehabilitation as the offender confronts the reality of the harm he or she has caused the victim; and increased emphasis on restitution as a sentencing objective through the recasting of the crime as an act against the victim.

ARGUMENTS AGAINST VICTIM IMPACT STATEMENTS

- *System consequences:* these include challenges to procedural fairness and the undermining of the court's insulation from unacceptable public pressure; the fact that actual harm is already taken into account in the gradations and sentencing dispositions of the criminal law, and that VISs may result in a substitution of the victim's subjective (and highly emotional) approach to consideration of the crime (based on personal experience of harm) for an objective one as practised by the courts (based on logical generalisations across a number of cases); the possibility that sentencing disparity may result, depending upon the nature of the VISs (such that like cases are not treated alike) and whether the victim is forgiving or vindictive; potential delays and longer trials; and that VISs may have limited relevance in jurisdictions that employ a determinate sentencing scheme for certain types of offences (i.e. fixed penalties for selected offences).
- *Victim needs:* these include issues pertaining to the victim's health and welfare (e.g. it may be a traumatic process to relive the crime); that victims may be subject to unpleasant 'cooling out' and cross-examination, which may produce further 'victimisation' of the victim; the possibility of creating unrealisable expectations in victims regarding the purpose of participation, especially with regards to court outcomes; and that the requirements of a VIS (e.g. type of information sought, and manner in which it is constructed) may create difficulties for some victims (e.g. those with literacy issues).
- *Legal and human rights:* these include concerns that the rights gained by victims may be rights lost to the defendant; how the use of VISs may constitute a systemic push away from enlightened and progressive responses to crime in favour of populist and punitive measures that signal a reversion to retributive, repressive and vengeful punishment; and issues relating to instances of unfounded or excessive allegations of victims.

ASSESSING THE USE OF VICTIM IMPACT STATEMENTS

To assess the practical implications of the use of VISs, it is necessary to examine closely the form in which VISs are being administered, the likely outcomes of their widespread use and the underlying philosophical basis upon which they rest. Further to this, however, we should realise how the notion of 'victim' itself is socially constructed (e.g. domestic violence definitions have generally been expanded to include psychological harm), and how the decisions made by judges and magistrates incorporate certain concepts of 'victimisation' and 'victimhood', which may be reinforced and/or ignored in the process of considering VISs. For instance, it has been argued by the CASA in Victoria that the use of VISs may perpetuate hierarchies of disadvantage within the sentencing process (e.g. based on distinctions between 'good' or 'deserving' women, and 'bad' or 'undeserving' women), and that they may shift the focus from the offender to the victim, and from the crime to the consequences. It is argued that such a shift undermines examination of the central issue of the case: the culpability of the offender (McCarthy 1993).

In assessing the effectiveness of VISs, it is important to recognise that victims are not uniform and therefore their expectations, and assessment of the usefulness, of VISs will vary widely (Laxminarayan 2012; Lens et al. 2013). Research indicates that VISs are not commonly used by victims (Roberts & Manikis 2012), largely because of a lack of awareness of victim rights. Studies that examine the effectiveness of VISs, as perceived by those who use them, commonly point to a disjuncture between purpose and outcome. Specifically, victim satisfaction with VISs is almost invariably connected to expectations of impact on sentence, and therefore a sense of dissatisfaction arises when these expectations are (frequently) not realised. In such situations, victims tend to regard participation via the avenue offered by the VIS to be merely a symbolic gesture rather than a substantive measure (see Englebrecht 2011; Erez 1994; Webster 2011). Ashworth (2010) points to the dangers of allowing victims input into sentencing where the main objective is not restorative but instead purely punitive, and the ongoing tension between service rights (the right for a victim to participate in justice processes) and procedural rights (the rights of the offender to a fair and objective process of judgment).

A second issue relating to the victim–offender relationship is concerned with offender release from prison. For many victims of violence, the thought of living in the same community as the person who caused them such terrible harm and deep psychological trauma is frightening. The need to respond to these concerns has recently been acknowledged in research literature and government policy. In particular, the main concern is with ensuring victim safety and personal security while addressing the need for offender reintegration into the community. In New South Wales, as in many other states, victims have two kinds of rights in relation to the issue of impending release (Garkawe 2002: 261):

- *The right to information:* victims have the right to be kept informed of the offender's impending release or escape from custody, or of any change in security classification that results in the offender being eligible for unescorted absence from custody. This right has implications for system management, but does not present any civil liberty concerns as such in relation to the inmate.
- *The right to participation:* victims have the right to make submissions with respect to decisions on whether 'serious offenders', such as registered sex offenders, are eligible for unescorted leave of absence. This right can have an impact on prisoner rights, in that victim submissions may influence the relevant authority (e.g. parole board or prison officials) to disallow, defer or place more stringent conditions on any external leave granted to the prisoner.

ASSESSING THE IMPLEMENTATION OF VICTIM RIGHTS

Given the impact that the exercise of different rights may have, it is essential to explore the rationale behind how such rights ought to be implemented in practice. Garkawe (2002) discusses the specific contexts within which different rights ought to be exercised. Most commentators acknowledge that the 'right to information' concerning criminal justice decision-making processes and outcomes is desirable and should be encouraged. However, the use of the 'right to participate' does require certain qualifications. For example, the right of victims to present a submission to a parole hearing needs to be based upon the requirement that any evidence so presented must be legally relevant to the decision-making task at hand (e.g. documented threats or negative behaviour directed towards the victim on the part of the prisoner) and factually verifiable.

Somewhat more contentiously, there is a range of subjective matters of concern to victims that also needs to be evaluated. Victims may be fearful of the offender, perceive them to be untrustworthy or may not have forgiven their actions. This raises the question of how or if the criminal justice system ought to respond to the emotional reactions of victims. Garkawe (2002: 271) suggests that the victim's views may be of some relevance in a small minority of cases where the conditions of parole (or day release) are being determined. In other words, conditions relating to contact with victims or members of the victim's family, and place of residence or movement, might be subject to special conditions imposed as a result of victim submissions.

The official position of the Parole and Community Corrections Officers Association of Australia (PACCOA) is that notification of victims is important and needs to be formally recognised (2003). However, it is also acknowledged that any notification system has to balance several competing interests. In general, PACCOA does not support the concept of issuing release notifications to communities, only to primary victims or their personal representatives (or statutory authorities where there is perceived risk to any individual in the community). PACCOA believes that victim services and probation or community corrections share the responsibility of both protecting their clients and assisting them to deal with the fear and mistrust that each may hold for the other.

Garkawe (2002) points out that information about things such as prisoners' places of detention, where prisoners will reside after being released, and details of their treatment or participation in prison programs may breach prisoners' privacy and may be used by some victims or their families to harass prisoners or their families. In the light of this, it is suggested that the privacy rights of prisoners should prevail in the absence of genuine concerns regarding the victims' security. From a victim perspective, the interest in what happens to offenders is immediately relevant. It is thus important that victims' needs be fully considered when assessing offender risk. This involves knowing as much as possible about the circumstances of the victimisation, including the personal relationship between the victim and offender.

In each of the areas briefly examined, it is clear that there are a number of practical problems associated with victim participation. Nevertheless, the place of the victim within the criminal justice system, while problematic, is now assured. What is less certain is the precise role of the victim, and how he or she will benefit from developments across the various areas of involvement.

VICTIMS AND VICTIMOLOGY

The criminological study of victims and victimisation not only centres on crime and safety statistics, the dynamics of victim events and geography, and the impacts and fears of victims over time, but also includes causative theories on victimisation and the interplay between victim and offender. As summarised in Box 6.2 (over the page), there are three main approaches to the study of victims: positivist, left-realist and critical victimology (see Mawby & Walklate 1994; Walklate 2012, 2007, 1990).

While the diverse approaches to victimology, taken together, provide us with a more precise sense of the level of victimisation in the community, more needs to be said about the victimisation process as a whole. For example, too often victimisation is seen in terms of a snapshot in time, as simply an 'event'. Analysis of the processual aspects of victimisation suggests a more complex and ambiguous process.

BOX 6.2   APPROACHES TO VICTIMOLOGY

POSITIVIST VICTIMOLOGY

This approach is informed by the idea that crime, and victims, exist in an 'objective' sense, so victimisation can be measured simply by observation and/or scientific methods. The main method of investigation adopted is the *victimisation survey*. The main orientations and findings of positivist criminology include:

- victim status determined by criminal law or self-evident (visible suffering) and does not extend to offenders
- an identification of factors relating to the potential risk of victimisation (e.g. examination of people, situations and places that are associated with the risk of crime and a focus on the regular patterning of victimisation among the poor, young males and ethnic minority groups)
- investigation that tends to concentrate on interpersonal crimes of violence and certain types of property crimes, rather than crimes of the powerful (business corporations), including crimes of the state (e.g. police brutality and war crimes) and crimes occurring in the home (e.g. domestic violence and elder abuse)
- a tendency to regard victims themselves as being implicated in their own victimisation (victim precipitation is said to occur, for instance, where a young woman is hitchhiking; she is said to have willingly gone into an at-risk situation).

LEFT-REALIST VICTIMOLOGY

This approach is primarily concerned with the *gaps* in mainstream victim surveys, and with *documenting* particular types of victimisation. The major contributions and propositions of left-realist victimology include:

- presumption that the law determines who counts as a victim
- placing crime victims at the centre of the research gaze in a manner that, methodologically, will provide better and more precise information about the nature and processes of victimisation (e.g. undertake geographically focused local surveys that generally involve interviews and in-depth discussion about the issues)
- undertaking victim research in a way that provides an adequate representation of women, ethnic minority groups, young people and the poor
- attempting to broaden the scope of questions asked about crime by tapping into issues such as the private sphere of child abuse, as well as corporate crime, environmental crime and health and safety regulations at work.

CRITICAL VICTIMOLOGY

This perspective looks at victimisation as a *social process*. In particular, it examines how victims are created by the operation of institutions and particular forms of interaction. Victimhood is contingent upon who is doing the labelling, and on the manner in which official labels are conferred. The main orientations of this perspective include:

- consideration of the victim neither as objective nor self-evident; this cannot be determined by criminal law definitions alone

- a concern with how the label comes into being, who applies the label and under what circumstances (e.g. gay and lesbian bashings, and the denial of victim status when the police choose not to respond)
- a concern to uncover the power relations that underpin how institutions confer victim status, and ignore or silence other kinds of actual social harm by protecting the perpetrator
- a broader conceptualisation of crime, focusing on human rights abuses (e.g. victims of state brutality, such as civilian victims of war; victims of institutional state actors, such as offenders; and victims of structural oppression, including women, racial minorities and the poor)
- an interest in moving beyond simple descriptive categories, such as 'victim' and 'offender', to view human behaviour in the light of situational and structural contexts (e.g. who suffers from so-called victimless crimes such as prostitution and drug-taking).

VICTIM STATUS

Victimisation involves a process of symbolic interactionism whereby the label 'victim' is bestowed upon certain individuals, demarcating them from non-victims. Over time, recipients of the label learn to wear the status; that is, victimhood becomes intrinsic to the self. How the construction of victim identities occurs, and under what circumstances, has a major bearing on how victim status is socially constructed, and the personal and social significance attached to the label (Dunn 2012; Holstein & Miller 1990; Walklate 2011). For example, victims are generally portrayed as passive, rather than active, which denies human agency; that is, the notion that humans make their own world, if not always under the circumstances of their choosing.

The application of *victim status* tends to be loaded with negative connotations, such as weakness, passivity, powerlessness and other such terms, especially when applied to female victims of crime. This process of labelling can have a disempowering effect. For instance, it has been argued that, traditionally, women were trained to be potential rape victims from an early age: they were taught to cry, plead and look for a male protector, but never to fight and win (Brownmiller 1976). For others, the experience of victimisation and fear of victimisation is so ingrained it is simply a 'part of life'—so normalised as to render the label 'victim' meaningless (Jordan 2008). In response, feminists prefer the use of the term 'survivors' of rape and/or incest, rather than victims. It is argued that imposing a strong, positive label on those subjected to harm will enhance their resilience and ability to regain control and power over their lives. This new terminology is forward focused, implying that the status of victim is not fixed, but can be changed.

In a similar vein, it has been argued that certain conceptions of the 'ideal victim', derived from socially constructed hierarchies of victimisation, are a culturally ingrained part of male-dominated society (Christie 1986). This builds into certain definitions of crime notions of who really is a true or worthy victim. For example, rape victims tend to be judged against a stereotype of the *innocent*, virginal or chaste woman attacked by a stranger. This means that when certain women (e.g. sex workers, trafficked women, the homeless or those addicted to drugs or alcohol) attempt to utilise the law and law enforcement agencies in response to interpersonal crime, they may be denied full victim status and/or not be treated seriously by police or judges. Similarly, how a rape victim reacts to an assault (e.g. struggle or not struggle), her personal sexual history (e.g. active or not, a history of few or multiple sexual partners), her behaviour and demeanour (inebriated or sober, dressed conservatively or provocatively) and her marital status (e.g. single or partnered) all tend to have implications regarding her worthiness to claim and 'achieve' victim status (McCarthy 1993).

Analysis of the politics and disempowering aspects of *victimhood* can also be applied to groups such as Indigenous people, who are frequently referred to as victims (of colonialism, poverty and racism). Again, this can imply passive acceptance of circumstance. What of the notion of active struggle? Until recently, most non-Aboriginal writers treated Aboriginal history in generally and often exclusively negative terms, ignoring the strength and courage that exemplifies active struggle against repression and genocide. In fact, the Aboriginal experience is a heterogeneous one, marked by achievements and disasters, but fundamentally by the active participation of Indigenous people in fighting against enforced victimisation (Palmer & Collard 1993).

One of the issues here is the way in which victim status is universalised, so that, for example, all Aboriginal people are seen as being the same. This master status is fictitious, because it cannot apply equally to all in the same way. The diversity of experience from group to group, and from region to region, makes it difficult to ascribe to a whole people a uniform experience. Certainly when it comes to issues surrounding victim status, and the connotations of passivity and helplessness, such a view does more damage than good. It reflects a patronising attitude that contributes to the making of victims, rather than acceptance of rights, dignity and respect.

VICTIMISATION AS A PROCESS
BHOPAL UNION CARBIDE PLANT EXPLOSION

If victimisation is to be considered in a more dynamic way, it must be viewed as a process (see Box 6.3). For example, in considering the Bhopal Union Carbide plant explosion in India, at one level this event was tragic and produced numerous victims. But when the incident is examined more closely, the process of victimisation clearly continued well beyond the immediate incident (see Walklate 1990). On the fifth anniversary of the explosion, for instance, over 200 environmental groups met to discuss the continuing ecological impact of the explosion, and to acknowledge that deaths were still continuing as a consequence of the explosion. The incident, and the response to the victimisation, reverberated worldwide. This is indicated in the way in which people in the United States who had Union Carbide factories in their neighbourhoods demonstrated their concerns over the prospect of a similar occurrence, and their action led to changes in legislation and a closer monitoring of the process.

CHILD ABUSE

Another example of victimisation as a social process is that of child abuse (Walklate 1990; see also Egger 1994; Harding 1994). Several decades ago this was a 'hidden' problem, concealed by a persistent wall of denial. However, social momentum built up, and ignorance and a historical reluctance to 'interfere' in the private domain of the family and home were eventually overcome. Child abuse was finally acknowledged as a real problem, much public anger was vented over its occurrence and the campaign momentum was to translate into numerous changes in legislation and in law enforcement practices. For example, reporting of child abuse was introduced in some Australian states and territories in the 1970s and is mandated in all Australian jurisdictions, albeit with legislative inconsistencies. There are differences of emphasis in degree of harm required, such as the requirement to report sexual abuse only (Western Australia), sexual and physical abuse (Victoria and the Australian Capital Territory) or all forms of child abuse and neglect (all other jurisdictions). There are also difference in

---

BOX 6.3   VICTIMISATION AND ITS AFTERMATH

In the book *Torture, truth and justice: the case of Timor-Leste*, Stanley (2008a) explores the devastating impact and legacy of torture for victims, their families and communities. In this and other work (Stanley 2008b), the point is made that torture is commonly used towards marginalised and vulnerable groups within society, and its use is in fact becoming more widespread in recent years. It is a compelling tool for states and other powerful actors, but what gets left unsaid is that, while it may have short-term value for perpetrators (although this 'value', too, is highly questionable), the consequences for victims are long lasting and wide-ranging. Victims can emerge from their experiences with an array of medical complaints that require treatment, as well as suffering numerous psychological effects. The list of harms is long.

These various physical, emotional and psychological conditions, in turn, have a severe impact on the ability of individuals to move forward from the status of 'victim' to that of 'survivor'. Stanley argues that it is essential for criminologists to study and analyse torture as a social and criminological phenomenon. This research and practical focus needs to incorporate what victims themselves have to say about their experiences—as in the case of Timor-Leste, particularly in the lead-up to independence—and to include critical assessment of how the needs and feelings of victims are dealt with from the point of view of justice for torture victims. Torture victims are victims. Why and how this is the case needs to be interrogated. So, too, does the social response to such victimisation. These issues also demand concepts that acknowledge the state as perpetrator of crime and creator of victims (see Chapters 12 and 13).

---

the state of mind provisions that activates a reporting duty, with some jurisdictions requiring belief of harm/abuse on reasonable grounds (the Australian Capital Territory, Victoria, Western Australia and the Northern Territory), and others suspicion on reasonable grounds (New South Wales, South Australia and the Commonwealth) or knowledge or reasonable suspicion (Queensland). There are also differences in the range of occupations mandated to notify authorities of abuse or suspected abuse (from a limited range, to an extensive list, to every adult; occupations most commonly required to report are professions in frequent contact with children in the course of their work, such as teachers, doctors, nurses and police).

In 2011–12, there were 252,962 notifications involving 173,502 children, which represents a rate of 34 per 1000 Australian children. Just under half of these notifications (46%) were investigated, resulting in 48,420 substantiations relating to 37,781 children—a rate of 7.4 per 1,000 children in Australia (AIHW 2013d). An important dimension to the discussions of forms of victimisation such as child abuse is that of time. Such abuse can occur over a number of years, but the manifestation of pain and trauma may not occur instantly, emerging later in a person's life. This may be so for at least two reasons. In some cases, people will block out of their mind particularly stressful and painful incidents. As they get older, or if they receive counselling, they may begin to remember what their mind had put to rest. In other cases, it might be that people have always remembered, but were afraid to publicly speak about or tell anyone about their ordeals. For example, many of the boys brought to Australia as 'orphans' (in many cases they were not) at the end of the World War II were to suffer abuse in their new institutional settings. Following media publicity of their experiences, the boys, now grown men, are finally admitting their experiences of abuse. Similarly, in the recent *Betrayal of Trust* Victorian joint parliamentary inquiry, many grown men and women (one aged 87) revealed for the very first time childhood abuse at the hands of trusted figures in organisations of high standing, such as the Catholic and Anglican Churches and the Salvation Army, some 70-plus years after the abuse took place (Family and Community Development Committee 2013).

It is important to view victimology as a process, or we may frighten and disempower people at a community level. As noted in Chapter 2, this fear can generate moral panics that emphasise crime control rather than causation. Furthermore, a processual account can also appreciate better the dilemmas of victimisation. For instance, everyday approaches to victimisation tend to fix on exclusive categories of 'victim' and 'offender', failing to recognise the duality of the victim–offender status in many instances. For example, the woman who beats her child may also be suffering abuse. Similarly, members of the 'underclass' layers in society who engage in criminal activities are, also arguably, its most vulnerable victims. Ultimately, we need to question what it is about our social system that makes victims, and offenders (see, for example, Chapter 7).

ISSUES FOR CONSIDERATION

TOWARDS A HOLISTIC VICTIM STRATEGY

It has been commented that an integrated victim assistance strategy must be built upon an inter-related series of guiding principles. Such a strategy would, ideally, fulfil a number of objectives at the same time, such as encouraging victims to report crime through to universal supports that assist in fostering and expediting the victim's recovery (Victorian Community Council Against Violence 1994: 153). One of the issues arising from acknowledgment of these areas of need, and of basic guiding principles, is how to generate the political will to both fund and adopt a holistic victim strategy. In other words, the temptation in a world of hard-core 'law and order' politics is to make victim participation equivalent to offender-centred sanctioning processes (e.g. via use of victim impact statements and the like). The real challenge is to devise victim assistance in such a way that it becomes truly victim-centred, and meets the needs of the victim rather than simply those of vengeance.

If we are to take the needs and rights of victims seriously, it is clear that more resources and financial commitments are required across a span of relevant areas, from crisis support to crime prevention (see Grant et al. 2002). It is also clear that resourcing of competing priorities (crime prevention versus victim support) needs to be informed by the evidence rather than concerns with popular appeal. For example, in 2013 the Victorian Government allocated $270 million towards the establishment of a scheme designed to place Protective Services Officers at every rail station while cutting $25 million from the community health budget, which includes funding for domestic violence programs. To put these funding priorities into context, it is important to consider that only one in every 30 crimes committed against the person occurs at public transport locations, while a third of all women are physically abused or sexually assaulted in their lifetime—most by intimate partners in their own home (*The Age* 2013; VicHealth 2006).

EFFECTS OF CRIME AND RECOGNITION OF HARM

A second broad issue for further consideration could be that of the study of the consequences and nature of crime, and the fear of crime, on specific groups and society more generally. Here, con-cern can centre on issues such as the distinction between 'high risk' and 'high impact' of crime, and how victimisation is distributed in these terms. Furthermore, much more can be said about the social construction of crime within victimology itself. In particular, continuing prominence is given to 'street crime' and interpersonal crime over and above that of crimes of the powerful or the state. How these emphases might in turn reinforce the fear of crime, and serve to legitimate or delegitimate (silence) suffering, is an issue of policy and political relevance (Snell & Tombs 2011; Walklate 2012). Even in the context of visible harm, the nature of the construction of victimhood is highly fluid. This is clear when one considers that it was only in July 2002 that victims of terrorist attacks sustained outside Australia were eligible for compensation under a national compensation scheme. Prior to that, only victims living in South Australia were eligible for compensation (*The Age* 2013b).

VICTIM–OFFENDER CATEGORISATION

The nature of victim–offender categorisation also needs further critical scrutiny. For example, on the one hand, the dichotomy between victim and offender can obfuscate the fact that very often the same person can be both simultaneously (e.g. battered women who kill their abusing partners). It can also obfuscate the overlap between offending and victimisation, overstating the visibility and vulnerability of one group (the victim) while understating that of the other (the offender). Research tells us that repeat offenders often start off as victims themselves, especially in the case of violence and sexual abuse. Offenders in general are also much more susceptible to violent victimisation, rendered vulnerable because of the risky lifestyle they adopt—either through choice or necessity (Fagan & Mazerolle 2011; Jennings et al. 2012; Muftic et al. 2012; Shaffer & Ruback 2002).

On the other hand, the image of the stereotypical victim (i.e. middle class and respectable) shares attributes with the white-collar offender (i.e. middle class and respectable), to the extent that when crimes of the powerful come before the legal system they are handled most often outside of the criminal arena, simply as civil cases (McShane & Williams 1992) or, at the least, fail to generate the same kind of criminal sanction as drawn by those engaged in street crime. For example, despite the harmful consequences and apparent scale of the problem, workplace bullying is not actually illegal. There is no statutory scheme in Australia that proscribes bullying. Victoria did introduce *Brodie's Law* in June 2011, following the suicide of Brodie Panlock after experiencing relentless bullying in her workplace. The law makes serious bullying a crime punishable by up to 10 years in jail. However, it is not an anti-bullying law per se; rather, it extends the application of the stalking provisions in the *Crimes Act 1958* (Vic) to include behaviour that involves serious bullying. As such, it has no application in the majority of workplace bullying cases, which instead are dealt with as either workers' compensation matters or as breaches of health and safety legislation.

It is often the case that there is a perceived competition for community service funding, especially between victim and offender services, and this likewise can impinge upon how 'rights' issues are dealt with politically and administratively (see Anderson 1995). Three categories of victim rights have been identified (see Garkawe 2002; Karmen 1996):

- *those gained only at the expense of offenders:* for example, where a victim's consent or willingness to participate can influence the rights of prisoners, as in the case of a parole process that negatively values applications in which some kind of restorative victim program has not taken place
- *those gained only at the expense of the state:* that is, the criminal justice system and associated human services; for example, the right to certain information and notification, as well as services and support workers
- *those gained at the expense of both offenders and the state:* for example, the right to have input into system decision-making processes, such as bail or parole.

USE OF VICTIM IMPACT STATEMENTS

As noted above, the use of VISs in proceedings within court has engendered considerable debate in recent times (see Erez & Rogers 1999; Herman & Wasserman 2001; Seymour 2001). Many of the arguments revolve around the use of the VIS as an objective rational account of the harm done by the offender to the victim, or their emphasis on the harm and fear felt by the victim. Traditionally, the courts have held that the subjective accounts of the harm and suffering by the victim should not be the only consideration when passing sentence (Erez & Rogers 1999).

The use of VISs in the parole process poses additional potential problems. For instance, there is the possibility that their use will pass sentence on the offender for a second time, in effect extending the period of imprisonment beyond the period envisioned by the sentencing court. This would constitute a form of double jeopardy for the inmate. However, in practice, it would appear that, for example, as in the Tasmanian case (see Black 2003), the potential contribution of victims to parole board decisions does not relate so much to whether parole is granted, but the sort of conditions imposed on a parole order.

A potentially more important issue in the debate about victim impact statements is that their use may create classes of victims. This may well affect the parole selection criteria and parole conditions for inmates (see John Howard Society of Alberta 1997). If this were so, some prisoners would be disadvantaged in applying for parole, depending on the social status, educational level and ability to articulate the consequences of the offence on the victim's life, since victims vary greatly in their skills to express the harm done (John Howard Society of Alberta 1997). More generally, Black (2003: 5) points to a range of procedural issues that also require further attention: 'What should be done with new allegations against an offender? How should inflammatory or prejudicial material be dealt with and how should the veracity of victim submissions be determined? Should an offender have a right of rebuttal? These questions have serious ramifications, particularly if victim submissions are influential in parole decision-making.' Similar kinds of questions can be raised in relation to victim input into day release and other types of release from prison.

TRANSITIONAL JUSTICE PRACTICE
Various judicial and non-judicial practices adopted by countries around the world, including international prosecutions, truth commissions, reparations programs and various kinds of institutional reforms, that are designed to redress the legacies of massive human rights abuses, such as war crimes and genocide.

RESTORATIVE JUSTICE

While victim rights discourses have traditionally been framed in zero-sum terms (capable of being met only at the expense of offender rights), more progressive variants of victim-centred criminology recognise the need to also consider the offender's fate, leading to the rise in popularity of restorative justice as a nodal point of victim–offender relations. The restorative justice movement has a number of different dimensions that demand consideration in the context of balancing victim–offender rights. Specifically, while it is often suggested that victims are broadly satisfied with engagement in things such as juvenile conferencing processes, questions remain as to whether such processes could address the substantive needs of victims adequately in all cases (e.g. in the case of rape, incest and sexual assault; see, for example, deCastella et al. 2011; Tomazin 2013). The role of reconciliation in addressing victim concerns—and particularly the need for 'justice'—is not only pertinent to instances of individual criminal harm, but also is highly relevant in **transitional justice practice** in regards to cases of widespread, systemic social harms (as with apartheid under the former South African regime or crimes of war, such as the systematic abduction of children to use as sex slaves and soldiers in Northern Uganda) and to the phenomenon of genocide (as in, for example, Rwanda). In other words, what are the limitations, as well as the strengths, of restorative justice approaches as applied to various kinds of social harm? (See, for example, Ame & Alidu 2010; Beitzel & Castle 2013; McEvoy & McConnachie 2012.)

CONCLUSION

Recent years have seen much greater public and academic attention directed at 'the victim' in relation to the criminal justice system. This chapter has provided an outline of the major theoretical, philosophical and practical considerations relevant to the study of victimology. The social construction of victimhood and the implications of the labelling of individuals in society as 'victims' was explored, as were various aspects of the extension of victim participation within the criminal justice system, especially in regard to prosecution, compensation and victim–offender mediation. It is clear that not only do victims need recognition within the context of existing criminal justice institutions, but also that much greater effort should be placed upon providing them with appropriate support services and avenues for constructive engagement in criminal justice matters.

From the point of view of 'victimology', as a specific area of academic and government research, there is a range of issues that warrant ongoing discussion and debate. One of the most important of these is the guiding rationale behind any sort of victim-centred intervention at the policy level. In addition, there is concern to not individualise victimisation (e.g. by focusing on precipitative factors in crime) or to simply provide descriptions of which social groups are victimised more than others (e.g. charting out conventional victim patterns). Rather, it is important to see victimisation as a dynamic social process, and one that also involves the institutions of the state as perpetrator of crime. Critical to a more holistic consideration of victimhood is an appreciation of the victim/offender duality and the structural and institutional inequalities that underlie much criminality and criminalisation, which is the topic of consideration in Chapter 7.

DISCUSSION QUESTIONS

1   What factors influence the distribution of victimisation risk and fear of crime?

2   What are the dilemmas faced by the criminal justice system in balancing the rights of victims with those of offenders?

3   How does left-realist victimology differ from critical victimology?

4   What are the advantages of a processual understanding of victimisation?

5   Why is it important to consider torture victims within the broader fields of victimology and criminology?

FURTHER READING

Cook, B., David, F. & Grant, A. (1999) 'Victims' needs, victims' rights: policies and programs for victims of crime in Australia', *Australian Institute of Criminology Research and Public Policy* Series No. 19, Australian Institute of Criminology, Canberra.

Moriarty, L. (ed.) (2003) *Controversies in victimology*, Anderson Publishing Company, Cincinnati.

Rosebury, B. (2011) 'The political logic of victim impact statements', *Criminal Justice Ethics*, 30(1): 39–67.

Walklate, S (2007) (ed.) *Handbook of victims and victimology*, Willan Publishing, Devon.

Waller, I. (2011) *Rights for victims of crime: rebalancing justice*, Rowman & Littlefield, Plymouth.

7 CRIME AND SOCIAL INEQUALITY

CHAPTER OVERVIEW

- THINKING ABOUT INEQUALITY
- COMMUNITY RESOURCES, CRIME AND CRIMINALITY
- INTERSECTIONS: MIGRATION, ETHNICITY AND CRIME
- INTERSECTIONS: INDIGENOUS PEOPLE, COLONIALISM AND CRIMINALITY
- ISSUES FOR CONSIDERATION
- CONCLUSION
- DISCUSSION QUESTIONS
- FURTHER READING

INTRODUCTION

As intimated in the previous chapter, crime and its impacts are not equally patterned or distributed in society. As will be revealed in this and following chapters, neither is the administration of criminal justice. For instance, prisons tend to be overwhelmingly filled with poor and disadvantaged people, not the better off and the wealthy. Similar social and economic disparities are reflected in the types of crime people engage in and why, as well as the profile of those most likely to be victimised by particular types of crime. For example, white-collar crime is by definition about crimes of the powerful, which tend to affect poor and wealthy alike, while most street crime is heavily skewed along class lines; it is generally committed by working class and less privileged individuals and tends to be intraclass (committed against individuals within the same class; generally the most vulnerable in society).

Contrasts of poverty and wealth are at the core of both criminality (which refers to the characteristics of criminals who undertake specific types of crimes) and criminal justice (which refers to the network of institutions and programs intended to prevent or respond to crime). Social inequality fundamentally determines who does what when it comes to crime, and who ends where when it comes to social reactions to crime.

The aim of this chapter is to explore briefly some of the key axes of inequality, and to link these to specific sorts of criminality and criminalisation. The focus is on those at the bottom end of the social hierarchy, rather than those who wield the most power, can marshal the most assets and exercise the most financial clout. The latter group, those in positions of extensive socio-economic power, will be dealt with in greater depth in the discussion of crimes of the powerful and transnational crimes (see Chapters 12 and 13).

The chapter begins with a discussion of various inequalities and the notion of intersections; that is, how different inequalities relate to each other in complex and variable ways and how this web of inequality contributes to an overall profile of social and economic disadvantage. It then outlines the strong relationship between low socio-economic status, engagement in certain types of criminal behaviour and contact with the institutions of criminal justice. It concludes with short vignettes of how inequalities of class, gender, ethnicity, race and age are manifested in the criminal justice arena.

THINKING ABOUT INEQUALITY

Social difference is constructed through a variety of institutional and social practices. In some cases, social difference is clearly linked to social inequality, and reflects major differences in the material lived reality of diverse social groups. In others, it is less a matter of inequality than that of acknowledged and 'acceptable' difference (e.g. the presence of different forms of Christianity, Islam or Judaism, or of the many other different religions, being part of the cultural and communal fabric of a particular society).

However, the heterogeneity of a population is also reflected in processes that reinforce and reproduce particular (and often negative) stereotypes, material differences and social inequalities. One consequence of this is that the location of different categories and groups of people in the social structure has major implications for their wellbeing, social opportunities and life prospects. Such social differentiation is institutionally and ideologically legitimated and contested across a range of social domains. Empirically, there is often an intersection of diverse social structural positions. This is reflected analytically in attempts to map these intersections according to notions such as **class**, gender and **ethnicity**. Indeed, a range of social inequalities can be so identified:

* *inequalities associated with class relations and economic processes:* for example, disparities in income and wealth; labour market opportunities and unemployment; and poverty and homelessness
* *inequalities associated with gender relations and social constructions of sexuality:* for example, differential treatment of women and men in paid work settings, education and the public sphere; negative social sanctions against gays and lesbians; and separate roles in domestic labour
* *inequalities associated with ethnic and cultural relations and racist ideologies and practices:* for example, differential access to economic, social and political resources and decision-making, depending upon ethnic and cultural background; and persistent denial of human rights
* *inequalities associated with community relations and state political structures:* for example, difficulties in access to decision-making at local, state and federal government levels; and employment of differential methods of access to the provision and delivery of important services (e.g. child care, education, sport and recreation), according to factors such as geography and disability
* *inequalities associated with age:* for example, disparities in access to economic, social and political resources and decision-making because of arbitrary and inconsistent legal rules and administrative procedures (in areas such as welfare provision, voting rights, and wages and employment conditions).

VARIETIES OF INEQUALITY AND SOCIAL EXCLUSION

These inequalities cut across each other and intersect in many different ways. For example, where one lives and the circumstances surrounding family life have obvious and major impacts upon life chances and social opportunities. Growing up in the bush or in the city, in the outback or in the metropolitan centre, shapes who we are and greatly influences what we end up doing, in part because of access or lack of access to resources, education, institutional supports and social networks. These life differences extend well beyond geographical location to characterise entire subsections of the community. Indigenous women, for example, occupy a differential socio-economic position in Australian society from non-Indigenous women. Yet, as women, both suffer from the oppressive nature of male-dominated institutions and certain types of male violence (e.g. rape and assault), albeit the incidence and severity of violence perpetrated against Indigenous women is disproportionately high (Mouzos & Makkai 2004; Steering Committee for the Review of Government Service Provision 2011).

CLASS
A concept fundamental to understanding how people access societal resources, whether these are economic, social, cultural or political. It refers to specific relationships of people to the means of production in a society; that is, the ownership and control of production.

ETHNICITY
Cultural attributes within social groups that form the basis of a shared sense of identity both within the group itself and by those outside it. Commonalities may include: physical appearance, religious allegiance, language, custom, attachment to an ancestral homeland or some combination of these.

Significant variance exists in the levels of inequality within community subgroupings, themselves generally considered disadvantaged, and these differences may be the product of variable socio-economic conditions experienced over time. For example, migrants who immigrate during periods of economic recession have very different settlement experiences from those who do so during periods of economic growth and expanding industries, yet each may be initially considered an 'outsider' to their new host country. Likewise, inner-city, wealthy young people may have affluent lifestyles, unlike their poorer counterparts in the suburbs, yet both groups, belonging as they do to the master category of young people, may be denied the respect, worth and appreciation they deserve for who they are now, rather than who they might be in the future; that is, respectable adults with a capacity to contribute productively to societal wealth and wellbeing.

There are many different types of social exclusion and social marginalisation. However, some are more profound than others. Some are difficult to 'grow out of', and some are intrinsic to the inequalities besetting society as a whole. For some, the only meaningful way out of the impasse is social transformation. For others, inequality is transient in nature, albeit still involving certain penalties of position (e.g. being 'young' and unable to exercise adequate social agency).

While there are various intersections between inequalities relating to class, gender, ethnicity, **race** and age, it is nevertheless important to bear in mind the specific nature of each as well. For instance, class inequality can be explained in terms of exploitation and the appropriation of surplus in any society (resulting from concentrations of private property in a capitalist society), while **colonialism** provides the best description of inequalities pertaining to Indigenous peoples (physical and cultural dispossession). Racism, sexism and ageism all label social structures and social attitudes that demean, devalue and delimit the other.

Different social inequalities have their own origins, their own histories and their own theoretical bases. Yet, in practice, there is frequently a merging of interests, experiences and exclusions. This is not a neutral or ad hoc process. Rather, it tends to congeal around the question of resources and the capacities of different groups and individuals to marshal resources for their own benefit. The hegemonic or dominant form of social distribution in Australian society—as a class-divided society—is based upon the class allocation of resources. This, too, cannot be ignored.

FIVE TYPES OF CAPITAL

It has long been recognised that different types of capital are produced and reproduced in the family. The work of Bourdieu (1990, 1986), in particular, is centred on the idea that throughout their lives individuals accrue, in varying ways and to different extents, social, cultural, economic and symbolic capital that, although distinct, can be transformed into each other under particular conditions. More contemporary considerations of capital also include reference to political capital. Social resources can thus be conceptualised in terms of five types of 'capital' (see Barry 2006; Castiglione et al. 2008; Dupont 2006):

- **social capital**: valued interpersonal relationships and connections both within and across social structures (including peer groups and networks), which generate aggregate resources (e.g. action and cooperation); a distinction can be made here between bonding capital (capital derived from associations and groups sharing common norms and values) and bridging capital (capital derived from connections across dissimilar groups and networks)
- *economic capital:* the financial resources (including inheritance, income and assets) or the means to acquire financial resources (e.g. a bank loan) to secure not only the necessities but also the luxuries of everyday living

RACE
Not a biological given but a social construct, based upon perceived differences between groups on the basis of factors such as physical features, cultural background, language, religion and country of origin.

COLONIALISM
The process by which Indigenous people have been dispossessed of their lands and culture by the invading culture. Colonialism has had a severe impact on Indigenous cultures and ways of life, as have its continuing effects of discriminatory policies and practices on Indigenous life chances within mainstream social institutions.

- *cultural capital:* legitimate competence or status that comes from institutional knowledge of one's cultural identity, in the form of art, education and language, which can be transmitted from one individual to another
- *political capital:* the capacity to exert influence over, or to exploit political processes, in order to secure desired objectives and outcomes
- *symbolic capital:* an overarching resource that brings prestige and honour gained from the collective, legitimate and recognised culmination of the other four forms of capital (social, economic, cultural and political). It is, in effect, a symbol of recognition and distinction received from a group.

Social inequality describes the variation in, and distributions of, these capitals among the population as a whole. Depending upon the nature of the community or group in question, the importance of certain types of capital diminishes or grows in importance. The concept of *multiple oppressions* refers to overlapping sites of identity and experience that reflect a matrix of relations involving different sites of power and domination (see Pettman 1992). There are, then, multiple layers of inequality, which are interwoven and interactive, and these involve variable access to different types of capital. Since access to capital significantly moderates structural disadvantage, lack of access to capital serves to aggravate disadvantage and increase the potential for negative life outcomes, including involvement in crime. To understand the structural sources of disadvantage in society, however, requires consideration of macro-level variables, including the important element of class.

THE IMPORTANCE OF CLASS ANALYSIS

The multiple differences that inform social experience—class, ethnicity, gender, race and age—call for a 'both/and' conceptual stance when it comes to understanding and interpreting social inequality. For instance, depending upon context, an individual or group can be an oppressor (e.g. part of the colonial ruling class), a member of an oppressed group (a woman) or both (a white colonial ruling-class woman).

Fundamentally, however, class analysis is important—indeed, central—to questions of crime and social inequality. This is not to denigrate or belittle the consciousness of complexity in contemporary social analysis, especially in the light of 30 or more years of theorising *intersections* (the acknowledgment that there are complex relations between gender, class, race and ethnicity, among other features of social life). However, too often the mode of intersection analysis itself ends up striving to achieve an equality of concepts, rather than reflecting the hegemony of class in social life. We live in a capitalist society. This is the determining aspect of our lives from the point of view of production, consumption and community. It is this that structures the basic material resources that underpin what we do, when we do it, with whom we do it, and how we do it. Class as a lived relation predominantly *shapes* as well as interacts with other key facets of our social being.

Other social divisions in society (based upon gender, race, ethnicity, disability or age) are not class-based divisions per se. The nature of these divisions is nevertheless shaped by the structural relations of class in particular ways. In other words, inequality and discrimination are, in part, sustained by practices and decisions based upon class interests. For example, contemporary discussions of women's oppression, and discrimination relating to Indigenous peoples and ethnic minorities, have to address the different class resources within each of these communities and social categories. Social divisions that reflect unequal gender, ethnic and race relations are thus themselves intersected by significant class cleavages (Bangura 2011).

As indicated in the discussion in Chapter 5, while 'race' or 'gender' oppression cannot be reduced to explanations that subsume this oppression simply under 'class exploitation', it needs to be acknowledged that the class structuring of gender, ethnicity and race at the level of lived experiences is central to

SOCIAL CAPITAL
Reciprocal relations between people that include valued relations with significant others, generated through relationships, which in turn bring resources from networks and group membership (e.g. peer groups).

an understanding of economic and social inequality. To put it differently, the different dimensions of sexism and racism are inextricably intertwined with the development and extension of capitalism on a world scale. The economic, ideological and political relations of oppression are thus inseparable from the context of capitalism within which they exist (see Connell 2007; Cunneen 1985; Williams 1989). Ultimately, capitalism is essentially hostile to the promotion of human rights and personal empowerment, and to alternative social arrangements and philosophies that can result in a more inclusive society.

COMMUNITY RESOURCES, CRIME AND CRIMINALITY

The problem of class is perhaps best illustrated by considering the ways in which resources tend to be distributed in a class-based society such as Australia. Under capitalist regimes, community resources are distributed via the market, the state and informal community or family networks.

THE LABOUR MARKET

It is the structure and dynamics of the labour market that determine the kinds of jobs that are available, where the jobs are located, who is most likely to work in them and what kind of pay and conditions attach to them. For example, the social construction of a 'teenage labour market', often associated with fast food outlets, ensures that young workers are paid less than their older counterparts for work that nevertheless brings substantial profit to the company (see White 1997). Issues of low wages, part-time work opportunities and poor working conditions affect the amount of income available to teenagers. In the first quarter of 2014, for example, just under a third (30%) of young people aged 15–17 years who were employed, worked part-time hours (less than 35 hours per week) (ABS 2014c). In a similar vein, segregated and unequal labour markets for women, relative to men, also translate into lower rates of pay based upon the gender divide, ultimately culminating in the popularly recognised phenomenon of the *glass ceiling* (a figurative barrier to upward promotion for female employees within corporate career structures). In the first quarter of 2014, over half (54%) of employed women were working part-time hours compared with just a fifth of all men (20%) (ABS 2013c).

These trends reflect wider changes in the labour market, with full-time job opportunities available (especially for young people) declining since the 1970s. Additionally, there has been substantial growth in industries offering part-time employment, such as retail and hospitality services, which generally offer lower rates of pay (ABS 2014d). In August 2011, three-quarters of young people aged 15–19 years had a relatively low individual weekly income of $299 or less, compared to 26 per cent of all Australians, 37 per cent of Indigenous Australians and 30 per cent of Australian females (Steering Committee for the Review of Government Service Provision 2014).

Where one resides also has a major impact on job chances and job choices, as analysis of neighbourhoods and social inequality bears out (see, for example, Brotherhood of St Laurence 2014; Phillips et al. 2013; Vinson 2004). Some rural areas and certain public housing 'ghettos' are especially prone to systematic disadvantage and widespread exclusion from full-time employment markets.

FAMILY RESOURCES

In material terms, people's standard of living is determined largely by their access to economic resources and the opportunities for consumption this provides. In addition to labour market participation, the family is also a source of financial and other types of social support. Family resources need to be considered in aggregate terms; that is, levels of regular income, as well as accumulated wealth in the form of bank balances, shares, superannuation and property holdings (ABS 2012b). Overall family resources are, however, contingent upon both the prior class status and resources of a family, and how families respond to changing circumstances. Upper- and middle-class families typically have the resources to shield members from economic hardship; working-class families, on the other hand, 'do it hard' when it comes to making ends meet and satisfying basic human needs (Jamrozik 2009). Certain changes can have a devastating effect on family life and wellbeing:

> The total sum of material resources available to any household is determined not only by income generation (number of members of household engaged in what kinds of paid work, for example), but also by housing costs relative to income, family size, inheritance, and sole-parent status. What can change the financial status of a person is transitions associated with the labour market (gaining or losing a job), the state welfare apparatus (gaining or losing a pension or other benefit), marriage (divorce or death or a partner, or marrying into money), and family resources (assets available in relation to number of potential recipients). A change in circumstance for the parent will inevitably affect the family situation of a child. (White & Wyn 2013: 131)

Differences in family resources translate into differences in local services, access to transport, leisure activities, job opportunities, neighbourhood security and policing, schools and housing options. In 2009–10, almost one in four Australians (23% or 4.9 million people) lived in households located within the lowest two quintiles of both disposable household income and household net worth (low wealth or economic resources) (ABS 2012b). Low economic household resources had a clear impact on standards of living, as demonstrated by Box 7.1.

Here, too, the issue of differential disadvantage is patently obvious when one considers the spatial clustering of low socio-economic households in Australia. Approximately 1 in 10 Australians live in the most disadvantaged 10 per cent of neighbourhoods. The proportion is even higher for Indigenous Australians, with over a third (37%), or 1 in 3, living in the poorest 10 per cent of neighbourhoods (ABS 2013d; see also Phillips et al. 2013).

BOX 7.1   HOUSEHOLD CHARACTERISTICS OF LOW ECONOMIC RESOURCE HOUSEHOLDS 2009–10*

- Average weekly disposable household income for people in low economic resource (LER) households was $465, which represented less than half (45%) of that of people in other households ($1033).
- Average weekly LER household expenditure on goods and services (including rent) was 57 per cent ($500) of the average expenditure of other households ($872).
- Housing, food and transport accounted for 57 per cent of total LER household expenditure on goods and services, compared to only 45 per cent for all other households.
- Expenditure by people in LER households on recreation was considerably lower ($50) than for people in other households ($108).
- Less than one-fifth of LER households (17%) reported being able to save money most weeks, compared with almost half (46%) of other households.
- Just under a quarter (24%) of LER households spent more money than they received most weeks—twice the rate of other households (12%), indicating a degree of dependence on limited assets or credit to meet weekly expenses.

- Almost a third (31%) of LER households were unable to pay a utility bill on time in the past 12 months (compared to 8% for other households); 20 per cent had sought financial help from friends or family (compared with 5% of other households); and 10 per cent sought assistance from welfare or community organisations (compared with 1% of other households).
- Just under half (43%) of LER households indicated they would not be able to raise $2000 in a week in an emergency, compared to only 7 per cent of other households. A range of other financial stress indicators were more prevalent among LER households: 10 per cent had gone without meals in the past 12 months due to cash flow problems, and 8 per cent had resorted to pawning or selling possessions. By contrast, only 1 per cent of other households had resorted to either of these lengths.

Note all income figures are equivalised; that is adjusted to facilitate comparison of income levels between households of differing size and composition. This reflects the requirement of larger households for a higher level of income to achieve the same standard of living as smaller households.

Source: Australian Bureau of Statistics (2012b)

STATE RESOURCES

The third source of the allocation of community resources is that of the state. The state does this routinely in the form of corporate and middle-class welfare (e.g. tax breaks and tax cuts) and social welfare for the poor (e.g. pensions and unemployment relief). However, the latter is stigmatic and typically is structured around notions of 'deserving' and 'undeserving' (as determined by means testing and activity tests). Moreover, social welfare support and payments are pitched at the lowest level possible (below the poverty line) so as to serve as a disincentive to reliance upon such payments. Increasingly, social welfare (as opposed to corporate and middle-class welfare) has been constructed not as a social justice entitlement, but essentially as an individual responsibility, with the state intervening as a last resort, and only then under strict conditions (Hall 2014; Jamrozik 2009; Mann 2009). It is also far easier than ever to be excluded from state benefits on the basis of rules, regulations and procedures that make breaching likely, especially for the most vulnerable of recipients.

The institutionalisation of marginalisation is reflected in the punitive and miserly structure of welfare allocations and the clear connection between welfare dependence and poverty. For example, in 2010, 37 per cent of those on social security payments lived below the poverty line, including 52 per cent of Newstart allowance recipients, 45 per cent of those on a parenting payment and 42 per cent on a disability support pension. Of all Australians living below the poverty line, 62 per cent drew their main income from social security benefits (Australian Council of Social Service 2012). Changes in 2013 that saw single parents (of whom 90% are women) moved onto the Newstart allowance (linked to the Consumer Price Index, which is typically lower than average weekly earnings), resulting in loss of weekly income of $60–$110, are likely to shunt the poor even deeper into poverty (Passant 2013).

As indicated by Figure 7.1, the institutionalisation of marginalisation is also reflected in the frequent movement across the spheres of institutional control; for example, from welfare to criminal justice. This is particularly so in relation to 'state wards', the vast majority of whom end up in the deepest and harshest parts of the criminal justice system: the prison.

FIGURE 7.1   ADULT POLICE DETAINEES, BY SOURCE OF INCOME (NON-CRIME GENERATED) IN PAST 30 DAYS, 2011 (PERCENTAGE)

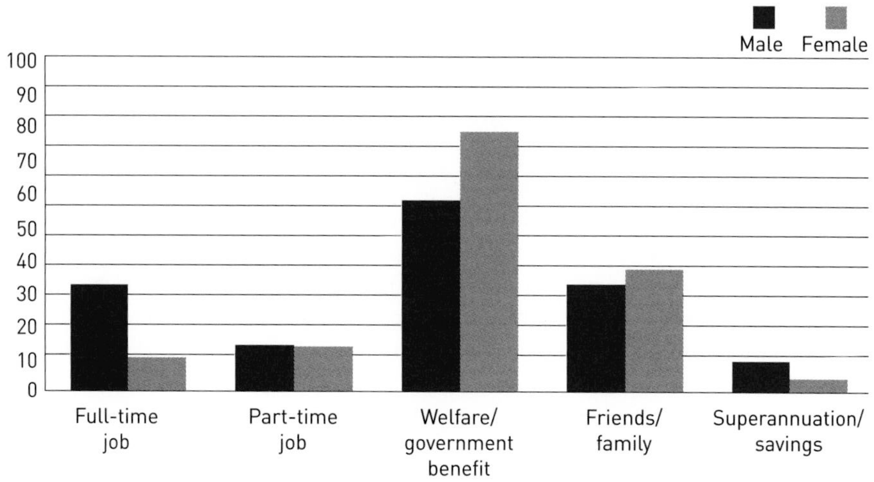

Source: AIC (2013a: 87)

UNEMPLOYMENT

The phenomenon of unemployment is the biggest single factor in the transformation of the relationship between the market, the state and informal exchanges, insofar as it is the labour market that most determines individual, family and community capacities, and wellbeing in a wage-based economy. In 2011–12, for example, a person in a family with the reference person (the person with the highest ranked employment position) in full-time employment had only a 3 per cent poverty rate. The rate of poverty increases sharply to 17 per cent where the reference person is in part-time employment, and a staggering 70 per cent for a family with the reference person unemployed (Phillips et al. 2013).

Overall, young people are the most likely to experience high rates of unemployment in Australia. In March 2014, for example, the national unemployment rate was 5.8 per cent, whereas the rate of unemployment for those aged 15–19 years was 16.9 per cent (ABS 2014c). Aboriginal and Torres Strait Islander young people experience even higher rates of unemployment, with 30.5 per cent of those aged 15–19 years unemployed in 2011 (ABS 2014d).

With few exceptions, losing one's job equals reduced capital in its different forms, and therefore reduced social and economic mobility, as well as reduced citizenship. As illustrated in Figure 7.1, criminal justice statistics also reveal a strong relationship between a lack of legitimate or substantial sources of income and criminalisation. In 2011, over three-quarters (78%) of female and over half (57%) of male police detainees reported welfare/government benefits as their main source of non-crime generated income.

While these figures are not disaggregated on the basis of Indigenous status, earlier work by Weatherburn and colleagues (1996) clearly identified a strong relationship between unemployment, financial stress and crime, as well as increased risk of being charged and imprisoned, among a sample of Indigenous respondents to a National Aboriginal and Torres Strait Islander Social Survey.

MARGINALISATION AND CRIME

More generally, social disadvantage and marginalisation, characterised by long-term unemployment, poverty, social exclusion and declining opportunities, continue to directly affect the physical and psychological wellbeing of people in many communities. Such social problems are entrenched at a spatial level, and are increasingly concentrated in specific locations within our cities (Phillips et al. 2013). The persistent concentration of accumulated disadvantage and inequality in particular geographical pockets is sometimes referred to as a process of ghettoisation. The social costs of marginality are inevitably translated into the economic costs of crime.

The social costs of marginality are also transformed into behaviour that is officially defined as 'antisocial' and 'dangerous'. All of this is bound to have an impact on the self-image of marginalised people and their efforts at self-defence in a hostile environment. The pooling of social resources and the construction of identities that are valued by others (if only one's peers) finds expression in a range of cultural forms, including various youth subcultures, 'gang' formations and criminal networks (Cunneen & White 2007; Hagedorn 2007).

The concentration of disadvantage in particular individuals and in particular communities is at the root of most street crime (see Table 7.1). It is the structurally unequal and socially disadvantaged position of people that provides the context for certain types of criminality and the commission of certain types of crimes. To put it differently, typical patterns of crime are linked with specific classes and particular motivational factors. Certain behaviours emerge out of very specific class circumstances, and are subject to particular limits and pressures associated with class location (see Reiman 1998; White & van der Velden 1995). Class situation is thus a prime influence in type of criminality.

TABLE 7.1 CRIMES OF THE LESS POWERFUL

WORKING-CLASS CRIMINALITY

- linked to relative powerlessness and social exclusion from decision-making
- tends to be interpersonal in nature and relatively limited in scope in terms of the extent of harm wrought

TYPES OF CRIMES	EXAMPLES
Economic	Street crime; workplace theft; low-level fraud; breach of welfare regulations; prostitution; drug dealing
Socio-cultural	Vandalism; graffiti; assault; rape; murder; resistance via strikes and demonstrations; public order offences; workplace sabotage; gang fights

MOTIVATIONS	EXAMPLES
Subsistence	Gaining illegal income to meet basic income needs; attempting to supplement low wages and income relative to subsistence levels
Alienation	Separation from mainstream social institutions such as education and work; a structural and economic sense of powerlessness
Exhilaration	Gaining worth, value and excitement by transgressing the ordinary rules and norms of bourgeois society

CRIMINALISATION	EXAMPLES
Limited means to effect crime	Reliance on limited resources, including the body, to carry out the crime
State intervention	Key target for state surveillance, detection, investigation and intervention; few resources to challenge charges and protect interests within the law and courts
Sentencing	Harms codified in criminal law; certain crimes subject to harsher sentencing regimes via mandatory sentencing

Source: White (2008a)

DISADVANTAGE AND SPECIFIC PATTERNS OF CRIME

There is indeed a strong and recurring link between the socio-economic status of individuals (and communities) and the incidence of criminal offending. Offenders who are deepest within the criminal justice system, especially in prisons, disproportionately come from disadvantaged situations and backgrounds featuring low socio-economic status, and highly volatile and dysfunctional family relationships. This is a cross-national and cross-jurisdictional phenomenon, as evidenced in a wide variety of reports, research studies and discussion papers dealing with socio-economic status and offending patterns. Some relevant examples of this literature include:

- Australia (Vinson 2004)
- New Zealand (Papps & Winkelmann 2000)
- United States (Michalowski & Carlson 1999)
- Canada (Kitchen 2006)
- Scotland (Scottish Government 2005)
- England (Whitworth 2012a)
- England and Wales (Office of the Deputy Prime Minister 2002)
- Finland (Aaltonen et al. 2011)
- France (Fougere et al. 2006)
- Spain (Buonanno & Montolio 2008).

While the specific conditions and influences that mark the relationship between socio-economic hardship and crime vary (depending upon factors such as local neighbourhood social cohesion, state interventions to address mass unemployment and the nature of law enforcement), overall there is a strong positive correlation. This holds for cross-country comparisons as well as nation-specific analysis (Fajnzylber et al. 2002).

Socio-economic status has a number of interrelated dimensions that in conjunction create the conditions for disadvantage and offending behaviour. Poverty, social inequality, unemployment and poor housing, among other debilitating factors (e.g. child abuse and neglect), are strongly linked to greater propensity to commit certain types of crimes and engage in particular sorts of antisocial behaviour (see Baldry et al. 2002; Karmen 2000; White 2008a). The literature in this area demonstrates that disadvantaged background is disproportionately linked to:

- offending behaviour
- engagement in antisocial conduct
- heightened perceptions of threats to safety and increased fear of crime
- greater incidence of victimisation.

For example, there is strong evidence for a positive relationship between long-term unemployment and criminal activity (Aaltonen et al. 2011; Chapman et al. 2002), and where communities are embroiled in high levels of unemployment, social disorganisation is likely to be highly prominent (Wilson 1996).

Hagan (1996) reviewed the literature on the relationship between class and crime in the United States. He found that class is linked to crime, but emphasised that the link was an indirect one, and was mediated through other factors, such as family relationships and community structures. In a similar vein, work by Weatherburn and Lind (2001) in Australia found that the crucial variable in explaining youth crime was parental neglect. However, this variable only had critical effect in the context of wider economic and social stresses at the neighbourhood level, such as unemployment. The roles of parenting and delinquent peers are presented as intermediary factors in the relationship between economic stress and youthful criminality.

Long-term unemployment appears to increase the likelihood of involvement in crime because of its association with reduced labour market chances (Chapman et al. 2002). The longer a person is unemployed, the more difficulty they have in finding stable work. Consequently, illegal means of earning a livelihood become more attractive. This is exacerbated by a subjective sense of reduced opportunity in the formal economy. Poor expectations of finding legitimate work enhance a willingness to turn to crime (Chapman et al. 2002). Conversely, involvement in education increases expectations of return to the labour force and therefore diminishes the relative attractiveness of criminal activity.

The argument that inequality causes crime is often expressed, but is difficult to prove empirically because both crime and inequality are very general concepts. Gaining insight into the relationship requires more specific identification of the factors involved. For example, the relationship is supported by research on homicide, which consistently shows a link between higher rates of homicide and higher rates of economic inequality (Elgar & Aitkin 2010; Kapuscinski et al. 1998; Void et al. 2002). As well, it is hard not to locate the high levels of violence, crime and imprisonment among some Indigenous communities within the context of their location as an **underclass** within Australian society, with little hope for the future and serious problems of ill-health and social deprivation (see Blagg 2008a; Weatherburn 2006).

The processes accompanying the relationship between disadvantaged socio-economic status and the incidence of offending indicate the following trends:

- *The homogenisation of offenders:* this results as they pass through the gatekeepers and filters of the criminal justice system, such that the most disadvantaged (who essentially share the same social characteristics) are those who occupy the most places within prison.
- *The multidirectional influence of factors:* for example, unemployment and cumulative disadvantage is associated with crime, and crime is associated with unemployment and cumulative disadvantage, and the reciprocal and exacerbating influence of such factors on each other.

Theoretical explanations for the link between socio-economic status and the incidence of offending point to:

- *structural factors:* for example, the overall state of the economy, levels of unemployment generally, welfare provision (range and ease of qualification for) and healthcare provisions, and how the dynamics of the labour market are reflected in the 'warehousing' capacities of the prison
- *situational factors:* relating to the personal characteristics of offenders relative to their opportunities in the competition for jobs, and how marginalisation and the attractions of the criminal economy contribute to offending
- *factors relating to social disorganisation:* as manifest at family and community levels; for example, when the intergenerational effects of the unemployment–criminality nexus translate into reduced levels of knowledge about ordinary work, and the concentration of similarly placed people in particular geographical areas.

UNDERCLASS
People who are not working, whose source of income lies permanently outside the capital–wage relationship, and whose economic conditions are normally at or below relative subsistence level. While linked to the working class, the underclass is separated from it structurally and behaviourally.

TABLE 7.2 CRIMES OF CHRONIC DISADVANTAGE

UNDERCLASS CRIMINALITY
• linked to relative powerlessness and social exclusion from mainstream institutions • tends to be interpersonal in nature and relatively limited in scope, but also includes professional crime

TYPES OF CRIMES	EXAMPLES
Economic	Drug dealing; protection rackets; robbery; prostitution; black market
Socio-cultural	Vandalism; assault; rape; murder; collective fighting
MOTIVATIONS	**EXAMPLES**
Subsistence	Gaining illegal income to meet basic income needs; reliance upon the informal economy, welfare and charity; exclusion from formal labour market
Socialisation	Intergenerational reproduction of unemployment, poverty and illegal means of subsistence; sense of territoriality; wealth generation as part of professional or organised crime
Resistance	Protection and celebration of ethnic and racial identity
CRIMINALISATION	**EXAMPLES**
Limited means to effect crime	Reliance on limited resources to carry out the crime, but may be organised into criminal collectives
State intervention	Periodic target for state surveillance, detection, investigation and intervention; some limited capacity to protect interests through use of bribes and threats
Sentencing	Harms codified in criminal law; certain crimes subject to harsher sentencing regimes via mandatory sentencing; street credibility may be linked to the experience of imprisonment

Source: White (2008a)

DEPRIVED FAMILIES

Persistent and intergenerational disadvantage sometimes manifests itself in the form of 'criminal families'. Indeed, a network of 'professional' offenders and lifestyle offending is part of the characteristic features of an underclass (see Table 7.2). The so-called 'underclass' includes, for example:

• those people living substantively or exclusively by means of illegal or criminal activities (e.g. theft, drug dealing and gambling)

- those who 'work' at subsistence wages for those living off the proceeds of their actions and those of others (e.g. extortion, prostitution and gang protection rackets)
- those living off subsistence welfare (both government and non-government)
- those significantly dependent on subsistence-level non-waged income generation in the black or underground economy (e.g. busking, hawking and begging)
- dependants of the above (White & Wyn 2013).

Importantly, researchers have discovered that a key characteristic of the time-varying (persistent) and intergenerational effects of disadvantage is spatial location—both present neighbourhood location and consecutive generational neighbourhood location. Essentially, the poorest sections of society are not only situated in the poorest neighbourhoods, but have been so situated for consecutive generations (Sharkey 2013, 2008; Wodtke et al. 2011).

SURVIVAL MEASURES

In essence, deprived individuals, families and communities will organise their own means and forms of subsistence and enjoyment. They will especially do so under circumstances in which they are excluded from desirable residential areas and separated from opportunities to find paid work. Moreover, even if work is there to be had, illegality may be far more rewarding, secure and satisfying as a source of income than the insecurities and exploitations of precarious employment in the formal sectors of the economy.

In the case of working-class and underclass criminality, the generating force for much of this crime is subsistence or to supplement one's income relative to subsistence levels. With regard to underclass criminality specifically, crime has more of a survival component and plays a greater part in basic economic subsistence. The extreme marginalisation and disconnection experienced by members of the underclass translates into a greater dependency upon alternative survival measures—often including 'serious' crime linked to a 'criminal career' and the 'criminal economy'.

Over time this may change. For example, the initial motivating factor may have been survival, but this commonly escalates into the commission of very serious crime that nets large amounts of money. The need motivator is thus overtaken by the greed factor, or the ongoing quest for legitimacy and respect based on level of earnings. Working-class economic crime is more supplementary in character, and includes such things as stealing from job sites, avoiding tax through payment by cash in hand and low-level social security fraud.

Within the context of institutional definitions of crime, there are substantively different patterns and experiences of criminality associated with different class circumstances (see, for example, Chapter 12). Particular forms of criminality, however, may be *class specific* (linked solely to one particular class), *class related* (predominantly linked to one particular class) or *cross-class* (universal) in nature. Nevertheless, in general, there are major differences in the motivations behind working-class criminality (e.g. theft of money for purposes of immediate consumption) and capitalist criminality (e.g. theft of money linked to start-up capital for investment). Moreover, the alienations experienced by members of the working class resurface in antisocial behaviour and crimes of violence that often reflect the economic and social tensions associated with class situation, including poor conflict negotiation skills.

As discussed earlier, however, social inequality is not one-dimensional. In order to illustrate the intersections between differing types of social difference and inequality, the next two sections will consider issues pertaining to immigration and colonialism.

INTERSECTIONS: MIGRATION, ETHNICITY AND CRIME

As indicated in Chapter 2, one of the crime stereotypes frequently perpetuated by the media is that of the 'racial threat' (Blalock 1967). Referred to by Chiricos et al. (2004) as the 'racial typification of crime', this emphasis on the presumed intersection between migration, ethnicity and crime has led to the stigmatisation of entire communities of visibly different ethnic minorities. They are commonly portrayed as dangerous, ethnically synonymous with particular crimes (e.g. the Muslim terrorist, the Lebanese rapist or the Vietnamese drug dealer), politically volatile, culturally incompatible and therefore threatening to the social status quo; that is, the dominant white, Anglo-Saxon, Christian majority. As detailed in Chapter 8, this process of 'othering' has very real consequences in terms of group alienation, marginalisation and criminalisation.

Studies that have specifically examined the issue of migration and crime in Australia have drawn conclusions that challenge the crime–ethnicity stereotype. They have generally found that, overall, the incidence of crime among migrants is significantly lower than among the general population, as measured by representation in criminal justice statistics (conviction rates and prisoner populations) (see Eastel 1994; Hazlehurst 1987; Hazlehurst & Kerley 1989; Yeager 1996). Offences committed by migrants are mostly minor in nature, but do involve crimes against the person and drug-related offences. Interestingly, the longer the period of residence in the adopted country, the closer offending rates of migrants parallel those of the general population.

In recent years, however, this pattern appears to be changing in some jurisdictions, if country of origin is accepted as an indicator of ethnicity. Crime data suggests a trend in some jurisdictions in Australia in which greater numbers of **ethnic minority** people are being sent to prison (refer to Figure 7.2). As at 30 June 2013, almost one in every five Australian prisoners (19%) was born in a country other than Australia. The largest percentage of overseas-born prisoners were those born in New Zealand (3% or 883 prisoners), followed by Vietnam (2% or 735 prisoners) and the United Kingdom (2% or 537 prisoners).

ETHNIC MINORITY Australians whose cultural background is neither Anglo-Australian nor Indigenous.

FIGURE 7.2   IMPRISONMENT RATE, SELECTED COUNTRY OF BIRTH, 2013[a]

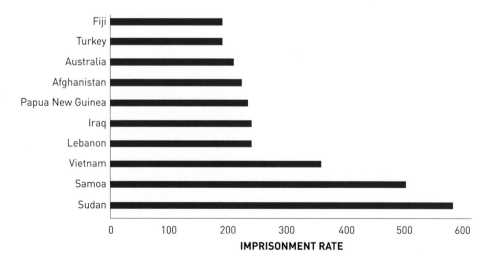

Source: Australian Bureau of Statistics (2013e)

[a]Rate per 100,000 of relevant population

While absolute numbers of overseas prisoners are not large relative to the total number of inmates in the system, previous research has found marked variance in crime rates by immigrant group (see, for example, Francis et al. 2006; Freilich & Howard 2002; Mukherjee 1999). In order to obtain a more accurate representation of the relationship between immigration and crime, it is therefore necessary to examine imprisonment rates by country of birth. Doing so reveals rates of imprisonment that are significantly higher in some overseas-born communities relative to the Australian-born population (131 per 100,000 adult Australian population). Sudanese-born prisoners had the highest imprisonment rate (582 prisoners per 100,000 adult population born in Sudan; a rate almost 4.5 times that of Australian-born prisoners), followed by Samoan-born prisoners (501 prisoners per 100,000 adult population born in Samoa; a rate almost four times that of Australian-born prisoners). Overall, the number (n = 5,795) of overseas born prisoners is large enough to warrant official concern about how best to manage and design facilities and programs for specific groups.

TRENDS OVER TIME

The most comprehensive analysis of ethnicity and crime in Australia was carried out by Mukherjee (1999), using police data from Victoria and data from the National Prison Census. Acknowledging the limitations of data collection and statistical analysis in this area, Mukherjee (1999) looked at crime statistics in relation to country of origin of alleged offenders across the broad offence categories of violent, property, drug and other. The data from Victoria showed that, in 1993–94, the vast bulk of alleged offenders were born in Australia (99,511), followed by those born in the United Kingdom (2,968), New Zealand (2,297) and Vietnam (2,220). Numerically, therefore, the key offending group was comprised mainly of Australian-born people. However, the size of the population of migrant groups varied substantially, so that, for example, there were a disproportionate number of alleged offenders born in New Zealand, Lebanon, Vietnam, Turkey and Cambodia relative to each community's population size. To put this over-representation into perspective, however, one needs to compare absolute numbers as well as rates per 100,000 population. Thus, almost 100,000 alleged offenders were Australian-born, compared with just over 2,000 Vietnamese-born.

In comparing Victorian data from 1993–94 with data from 1996–97, Mukherjee (1999) noted that the proportion of alleged offenders who were Australian born actually grew from 75 per cent to 77 per cent. Substantial increases in the number of alleged offenders were observed in relation to those people born in Hungary, Fiji, Vietnam, Poland and Romania. Substantial decreases were observed for groups born in Ireland, Sri Lanka, the United Kingdom and New Zealand. In both data sets, a majority of alleged offenders from all birthplace groups were processed for property offences.

In some respects, Mukherjee's (1999) broad observations hold true today. As indicated, prison populations overwhelmingly comprise people born in Australia, and this profile has remained unchanged over at least the past 15 years. For example, over the past five years, the proportion of Australian-born prisoners has varied minimally, comprising between 79 per cent and 81 per cent of the total prison population. Also remaining consistent over this period is the observation that New Zealand, Vietnam and the United Kingdom are the top three countries of origin for non Australian-born prisoners (countries with long-established populations in Australia), and represent the most common source countries of migration to Australia annually. The proportion of total prisoners in Australia drawn from these countries has also remained steady at 3 per cent for New Zealand, 2–3 per cent for Vietnam and 2 per cent for the United Kingdom. What does change frequently, however, is the rate of imprisonment by immigrant group. For example, as indicated earlier, Sudanese-born prisoners were over-represented relative to the total number of Sudanese-born people in Australia in 2013 (ABS 2013e). In 2011 and 2012, Nigerian-born prisoners had the highest rate of imprisonment (1,014 and 1,079 per 100,000 adult population born in Nigeria, respectively) followed by Indonesians (653 per 100,000 adult population born in Indonesia both years) (ABS 2011a, 2012c). In 2009 and 2010, however, Tongan-born prisoners had the highest rate of imprisonment (635 and 531 per 100,000 adult population born in Tonga, respectively) (ABS 2009b, 2010).

One of the possible explanations put forward for the changing profile of immigration, ethnicity and crime over time posits that recent arrival immigrant groups will generally be those most over-represented in crime statistics in relative terms (Francis et al. 2006). This is said to be due to a number of factors including: the social fluidity and non-coping that accompanies transition to a new country; the familiar pattern of settlement for new arrivals into geographical locations characterised by disadvantage and high crime; and the high proportion of young people amongst new arrivals—a risk factor for engagement in crime generally. Francis et al. (2006), however, suggest that higher rates of crime among new arrivals reverse dramatically in the years following settlement and with the take-up of citizenship (seen as a commitment to the adopted country).

Patterns of incarceration in Australia appear to provide some support for this proposition, with disproportionately high rates of imprisonment witnessed among the Sudanese- and Nigerian-born population over the past four years. It is pertinent to note that over the past 10 years, for example, the Sudanese-born population represented one of the fastest-growing immigrant populations in Australia, increasing by 9.2 per cent over the period. Similarly, from 2006, the Nigerian population, which in absolute terms is quite small, grew by over 50 per cent (ABS 2013f).

SELF-REPORT STUDIES

The evidence that levels of crime among ethnic minority groups in Australia has increased in recent years needs to also be assessed in the light of self-report studies. For example, Junger-Tas (1994: 179) found a 'striking disparity in delinquency self-reports of ethnic minorities and their over-representation in police statistics'. Such differences suggest a degree of bias in the criminal justice system. Although this may take a number of forms, there is evidence that problems associated with police–ethnic minority youth relations are a contributory factor, with selected groups of teenagers more likely to be arrested, charged and convicted of offences than others (see Cunneen & White 2011; see also Chapters 8 and 17). The increased frequency of involvement with the criminal justice system, particularly in relation to drug offences and use of violence, means that the heightened media attention on ethnic minority young people does bear some relation to what is occurring at a grassroots level.

MARGINALISATION OF ETHNIC MINORITY YOUNG PEOPLE

To understand what is happening, it is necessary to consider the structural changes that have had an impact on ethnic minority young people in recent years. Analysis of social indicators, such as employment and levels of education, suggests that many of these young people are being marginalised economically and socially from the mainstream institutions of school and work (White & Wyn 2013). In many of the working-class areas where ethnic minority youth live, the manufacturing industry has collapsed or declined, affecting the livelihoods of their parents and their own employment prospects (ABS 2014d). It is telling in this context that just over a quarter of adults living in Australian households below the 50 per cent poverty line were born in a non-English-speaking country (ACOSS 2012).

The bleak outlook young people face in relation to employment prospects is exacerbated by factors such as inadequate schooling facilities and resources. Not only are young people consequently marginalised in terms of their ability to consume, but also in terms of lifestyle choice. The commercialisation of leisure and recreation means that ethnic minority young people may even be excluded from these public areas, as they lack the means to pay if they want to play, and zero tolerance approaches to policing public space means that they are more likely to come under the gaze of the law (Martin 2009; Poynting 1999; see also Chapters 8 and 17). This suggests that the difficulties experienced by young ethnic minority people are inextricably linked to their class situation (see Collins et al. 2000; White & Perrone 1997).

THE IMAGE OF ETHNIC YOUTH GROUPS

A key problem with ethnic minority youth groups is that prejudicial stereotyping in the media often leads to the differential policing of the whole population group. This not only violates the ideals of treating all citizens and residents with the same respect and rights, but also can inadvertently lead to further law-breaking behaviour (e.g. carrying weapons to protect oneself from racist violence). The negative images of ethnic minority people therefore not only stigmatise the community as a whole, but, to some degree, also create a self-fulfilling prophecy, generating the very conditions they purport to fear.

For example, the notion of ethnic youth gangs has featured prominently in media reports of youth activities and youth violence since the late 1990s (Collins & Reid 1999; Mills & Keddie 2010; White 2013a). Much of the public consternation regarding so-called ethnic youth gangs relates directly to the use of public space by ethnic minority young people. The presence of large groups of young people on the street, or young people dressed in particular ways or with particular group affiliations, appears to have fostered the idea that Australia, too, has a gang problem similar to that found in countries such as the United States. This not only misconstrues the nature of 'gangs' in the United States (see Klein et al. 2001), which are far more diverse and complex than media images imply, but it also misrepresents the dynamics of youth group formation. There is a substantial difference between specific criminal organisations, which are usually not age-specific and are expressly concerned with criminal activity (e.g. criminal bikie gangs), and youth groups, which tend to be loose affiliations of age-based peers, and in which illegal activity is incidental to group membership and formation (see Perrone & White 2000).

In the specific case of ethnic youth gangs, the activities and perceptions by and of ethnic minority youth present a special case. The extra visibility of young, ethnic minority people (relative to the Anglo norm) feeds the moral panic over 'youth gangs'. Whole communities of young people can be affected, regardless of the fact that most young people are neither systematic lawbreakers nor particularly violent individuals. The result is an inordinate level of public and police suspicion and hostility being directed towards people from certain ethnic minority backgrounds.

A Sydney study has pointed out that the groups that exhibit the highest rates of imprisonment—including the Lebanese, Vietnamese and Turkish—also have the highest unemployment rates (Collins et al. 2000; Collins 2005). This association suggests that problems connected with social exclusion are likely to be central to any explanation of youth offending involving particularly disadvantaged groups. Collins and colleagues (2000) also identified social marginalisation as a critical factor behind ethno-specific peer association and the consequent perception of widespread involvement in 'youth gangs' among Lebanese youth. There was a high level of intracultural association between young Lebanese people, so that their friends were primarily drawn from the same ethnic group. The main purpose of these groups was not to engage in criminal behaviour, but to defend themselves against experiences of racism and exclusion from the cultural mainstream.

Collins and colleagues' (2000: 143) analysis of violence and aggression between ethnic groups suggests it has more to do with questions of gaining legitimate status and displays of masculinity than with inter-ethnic conflicts. Their experience of institutional racism and economic marginalisation leads them to form associations that offer them a sense of identity, community, solidarity and protection. Group membership also provides them with what Collins and colleagues describe as a 'valorisation of respect in the face of marginalisation' (Collins et al. 2000: 150). Within the group, values of loyalty and toughness prevail in the face of real and perceived outside threats. In some cases the collective assertion may also take the form of contempt for 'Aussies' (as the dominant social group), as well as wariness of other ethnic minority groups, even though they are also struggling to garner respect and reputation in a hostile environment.

The effect of this is to create a negative dynamic in which the experiences of structural exclusion are reinforced by the young people's collective response to it. Institutionalised racism (restricted life chances and the dominance of monocultural norms), economic marginalisation (unemployment and poverty) and reliance upon particular notions of masculinity (reliance on physical and symbolic markers of toughness) place these young people in a particularly vulnerable and volatile social situation. Their response is the assertion of their identity and collective social power via membership of street groups and engagement in fighting. While this is a response to the experience of racism, disrespect to 'manhood' and perceived threats from outsiders, it paradoxically both reinforces their subordinate, 'outsider' position while fuelling further negative social reaction.

In a political environment in which race politics is a predominant feature, the spectre of ethnic criminality is effectively bolstered by the actions of ethnic minority youth themselves, as they struggle to negotiate their masculinities, ethnicities and class situations. In this way, the activities of ethnic minority youth are open to distortion and sensationalism in ways that portray them as 'racist', 'unAustralian' and socially divisive (see White 2013a; White & Perrone 2001). A clear example is the sensationalised media reporting of the trial of a number of Muslim young people over gang rape charges in Sydney between 2000 and 2004, which was brought into sharp focus following the 11 September 2001 terrorist attacks in the United States. From that point onwards, Muslim immigrants in particular began to be viewed as political threats to national security, the public perception of criminality became culturalised (seen as something inherent to a person's ethnicity or cultural background) and Australia witnessed a gradual retreat from multiculturalism (Humphrey 2007; Mills & Keddie 2010; Poynting & Mason 2008; Poynting et al. 2004; see also Chapter 8). The lasting legacy of this racialisation of crime and violence remains evident today, with the target of media attention in Melbourne recently turning to African-background young people (especially the Sudanese community), their alleged involvement in gangs (described as 'tribe mentality') and general propensity to violence (Nunn 2010).

INTERSECTIONS: INDIGENOUS PEOPLE, COLONIALISM AND CRIMINALITY

The relationship between Indigenous people and the criminal justice system can only be understood within the context of their dispossession from their lands and culture and the suppression of resistance to the structures of colonial domination (Douglas & Finnane 2012; McKenna 2012; Reynolds 2006).

Indigenous people have been subject to over two centuries of colonial rule, a process that has had a devastating impact on Indigenous culture, economic activities and family life. A concise summary of the consequences of European invasion and continuing subjugation is provided in the report of the Royal Commission into Aboriginal Deaths in Custody:

> Colonial takeover denied Aboriginal people the right to live by their own rules, to decide on their own policies. They were denied the freedom to run their own economic and family life. They were also denied the right to own land, to earn a secure living as farmers, merchants, or in the labour market at their own discretion, to earn a family wage, to receive welfare benefits, to live where they pleased. Under various policies their private, reproductive lives were under scrutiny by government and missionary officials. They could not necessarily marry the person they chose, fraternize with people of their choice, speak to people of a certain colour skin, live in a particular street or on a particular reserve. They could not decide how many people they shared their house with. They were not eligible for old age pensions, for workers' compensation, for maternity allowances or for child endowment. Even when legislation on such matters changed in the 1940s and 1950s, it was often the manager of the mission or reserve rather than the individual who was paid this money. They could not run their own bank accounts. Anyone who objected could end up exiled hundreds of kilometres away or imprisoned for an unknown time. After release, they could be again banished from their families. The law extended its arm into the bedroom and into the post-natal ward. Children were taken from mothers after birth, others were taken once they reached the age of three or four years. Many Aboriginal families were thus denied the right to nurture, to rear and educate, to love their own children, to see them grow up. They lost these children, and the children became lost themselves. Who were they? Often children had been taught to detest everything Aboriginal, and this could extend to themselves once they realized their skin was not white (Johnston 1991).

To understand the contemporary criminality and imprisonment of Indigenous people demands recognition that 'white Australia has a black history'. As part of this recognition, there is also a need to acknowledge the resilience and capacities of people who have survived, despite the genocidal policies of successive governments.

The experiences of Indigenous peoples have been fundamentally shaped by colonialist processes, and yet their experiences are variable because of the diverse social worlds that they inhabit and the distinctiveness of several cultural and language groups within the artefact of colonial classification of 'Aboriginal' (Morgan 2012; White & Wyn 2013). There is great variability in Indigenous communities, and the Indigenous population as a whole is heterogeneous across many different dimensions. What unites the many is the shared experiences of injustice, inequality and oppression at the hands of a colonial state, an experience that continues to the present day (see Morrissey 2006).

As at the last Census (2011), there were an estimated 669,881 Aboriginal and Torres Strait Islander people—the Indigenous peoples of Australia—in Australia, comprising approximately 3 per cent of the total Australian population. Almost a third of all Indigenous people resided in the Northern Territory (29.8%), with the proportion in other jurisdictions ranging from 4.7 per cent in Tasmania to 0.9 per cent in Victoria. The Indigenous population is relatively young compared to the non-Indigenous population. In 2011, 36 per cent of Indigenous peoples were under 15 years of age, compared to 21.6 per cent of non-Indigenous people (ABS 2014e). In terms of cultural identification, almost two-thirds (62%) of Indigenous people aged 15 years and over identified with a clan, tribal or language group (AIHW 2011b). Furthermore, while the majority of Indigenous Australians (82.8%) spoke only English at home, 9 per cent spoke an Indigenous language in addition to English (16.3% in the Northern Territory) and 1.8 per cent did not speak English well or at all (up to 12.1% in the Northern Territory) (Steering Committee for the Review of Government Service Provision 2014).

THE IMPACT OF COLONISATION

Since the initial British invasion of 1788, the Indigenous peoples of Australia have been subjected to myriad interventions, exclusions and social controls. This is not simply a historical legacy; it is part of the fabric of everyday life for many Indigenous peoples today. Colonialism has had a severe impact on Indigenous cultures and ways of life, as have the continuing effects of discriminatory policies and practices on Indigenous life chances within mainstream social institutions. The dislocations and social marginalisation associated with colonialism have had particular ramifications for Indigenous young people. It is worth noting that, historically, young Indigenous women were particularly prone to policies that were intended to separate them from their families and communities, and that constituted a form of cultural and physical genocide under the United Nations Genocide Convention 1948 (see Goodall 1990; Haebich 2011). Today, it has been argued that, rather than breaking up of communities on the basis of a welfare or protectionist rationale, the same thing is occurring through systematic 'criminalisation' of young Indigenous people, although the main target now is young men (NISATSIC 1997; Cunneen 1994).

The negative impact of constant state intervention into the families and communities of Indigenous peoples cannot be overestimated. The Stolen Generations Inquiry estimated that between one in ten and one in three Aboriginal children, depending on the period and location, were removed from their families between 1910 and 1970; most Indigenous families have thus been affected by this phenomenon (NISATSIC 1997: 37). The nature of state intervention—whether for welfare or criminalisation purposes—has had a profound effect on Indigenous ways of life, their relationship to authority figures such as the police, and their experiences of Indigenous people as they grow up in a (post) colonial context (Haebich 2011).

OVER-REPRESENTATION IN THE CRIMINAL JUSTICE SYSTEM

There is a close relationship between social marginalisation (incorporating racial discrimination and economic and social exclusion) and criminalisation (which constitutes one type of state response to marginalisation). Extensive research has been undertaken in recent years on the over-representation of Indigenous peoples in the criminal justice system; research that has provided considerable evidence of seemingly intractable over-representation in most jurisdictions, and particularly at the most punitive end of the system: in detention centres (Beresford & Omaji 1996; Cunneen et al. 2013; Cunneen & White 2011; Johnston 1991; NISATSIC 1997).

For example, a recent report found that Aboriginal and Torres Strait Islander (Indigenous) young people were highly over-represented among those subject to juvenile justice supervision (AIHW 2012a):

- Although only around 5 per cent of Australians aged 10–17 years are Aboriginal and Torres Strait Islanders, almost two-fifths (39 per cent or 7,265) of those under juvenile justice supervision on an average day in 2010–11 were Indigenous young people. This is a rate of 23 per 1,000 Indigenous young people, compared with just 1.5 non-Indigenous young people per 1,000. Indigenous young people were therefore fifteen times as likely to be under supervision than their non-Indigenous counterparts on any given day. This over-representation of Indigenous young people was observed in all states and territories with available data (Western Australia and the Northern Territory did not provide data), ranging from three times in Tasmania to more than eighteen times in New South Wales.
- On an average day in 2010–11, over a third (37%) of those in community-based supervision and nearly half (48%) of those in detention were Indigenous young people aged 10–17 years. For example, of the 1,045 young people in detention on an average day, 455 (44%) were Indigenous

males, compared with 495 (47%) non-Indigenous males; and fifty-five (5.3%) were Indigenous females compared with thirty (2.9%) non-Indigenous females. Indigenous young people were fourteen times as likely as non-Indigenous young people to be under community-based supervision on an average day and almost twenty-four times as likely to be in detention.

- Indigenous young people under supervision were also more likely to be younger than non-Indigenous young people. Approximately one-quarter (24%) of Indigenous young people under supervision on an average day were aged 10–14, compared with 14 per cent of non-indigenous young people. Additionally, an Indigenous person aged 12 was forty times as likely to be under supervision as their non-Indigenous counterpart, but only ten times as likely if aged 17. Indigenous young people were also more likely to have entered supervision for the first time at a younger age. In 2010–11, just over a third (35%) of Indigenous young people had first entered supervision when they were aged 10–13, compared with just one-eighth (15%) of non-Indigenous young people.
- Indigenous young people also had longer and deeper supervision histories; they were less likely to be new entrants to supervision than non-Indigenous young people (27% compared to 35%) and much more likely to have experienced detention at some point in their supervision history than non-Indigenous young people (67% compared with 54%).

These patterns of criminal justice intervention continue an historical trend that criminologists have noted for quite some time (Blagg 2008a; Cunneen 2001; Cunneen & White 2011). Today, Australia has the dubious reputation of incarcerating Indigenous people at an extraordinarily high rate (as at June 2013, 1,977 Aboriginal and Torres Strait Islander prisoners per 100,000 adult Aboriginal and Torres Strait Islander population, or around fifteen times greater than the non-Indigenous population); a rate higher than virtually any other country in the world (ABS 2013e).

There are two principal explanations for this phenomenon. First, it is a straightforward reflection of their higher level of involvement in crime compared with the general population. Second, it results from racial discrimination within the criminal justice system and the broader society. The history of colonialism and the policing of Indigenous young people and the broader Indigenous community has, in essence, been one of selective intolerance. The two explanations are not contradictory and may interact in a process of mutual reinforcement (see Blagg 2008a; Cunneen 2001; Wundersitz 2010).

There certainly appears to be a relationship between poverty, disadvantage, unemployment and crime rates, although the exact nature of that relationship is complex. As well, young Indigenous people often come from families under stress (in many cases associated with the impact of the Stolen Generations), another factor associated with involvement in crime and which has also been implicated in rising rates of child maltreatment among Aboriginal children (Guthridge et al. 2012). For example, an Aboriginal child in Victoria is ten times more likely to come into contact with child protection than non-Indigenous children (Perkins 2014). In 2011, 16 per cent of Indigenous people aged over 15 years were unemployed as compared to 5.2 per cent for the Australian population as a whole. This figure, however, belies the true extent of unemployment in the Indigenous community. When one considers relative rather than absolute figures (rate of Indigenous unemployment per 100,000 Indigenous people in Australia), just under half (46.2%) of all Indigenous Australians aged 15–64 were unemployed in 2011. In Australia, Indigenous people are between two and three times as likely to be unemployed at the time of their reception into prison compared with non-Indigenous people (Biles 1992; Walker & McDonald 1995). Poverty and alcoholism are also implicated in the relatively high number of justice procedures offences (which includes offences such as non-payment of fines) and public order offences (e.g. public drunkenness) among Indigenous people (see Chapter 11). Clearly then, structural factors of gender, class and race, and the effects of two centuries of cultural dislocation and oppression are deeply implicated in the level of crime within the Indigenous population (Cunneen 2001; Cunneen & Kerley 1995; Cunneen et al. 2013; Wundersitz 2010).

ISSUES FOR CONSIDERATION

CRIME AND ITS INTERSECTIONS

We know that there is a strong correlation between poverty and crime, yet not all poor people engage in criminal activity; nor are all 'criminals' necessarily drawn from backgrounds of poverty and marginalisation. Poverty may be conceptualised as the field of resources and relationships that may predispose some people to be criminal or delinquent compared to others, but it cannot predict which people will deviate and for what reasons. Social inequality is the structural framework within which different types of criminality are formed and manifest, depending upon class-based resources that inhibit and/or facilitate crime commission. Social disadvantage expresses one pole of the determining predispositions toward certain types of criminality (e.g. street crime). Social privilege represents another pole, which points to very different types of crime and criminality.

The question of intersections is incredibly complex, and can be empirically difficult to capture given this complexity. Not surprisingly, there is always a tension between the universal and the specific when it comes to any particular social class or social category. For example, women can be seen as a non-homogeneous group when we consider the great differences in experience, perspective and needs among diverse groups of women. Yet, women are also linked via dominant cultural expectations and roles in relation to things such as womanhood, sexuality and mothering. Similarly, there may be the impression of homogeneity within racial groups, such as Indigenous people, because of the imposing structures of the colonial state. Yet, there is also great ethnic variation, differences in class situation, ties to particular country and specific histories of repression and resistance. Social inequality that involves phenomena such as racism, sexism, colonialism and so on is never experienced quite the same way by different groups and individuals. Groups are not homogenous, despite the fact that they may share common histories and experiences. It is important, therefore, to undertake a more granular analysis; one that examines community context and the balance of risk and protective factors in the lives of individuals within high risk communities, in order to make sense of why some individuals and communities have higher crime involvement than others (in relation to Indigenous communities see, for example, Ferrante 2013; Homel et al. 1999; McCausland & Vivian 2010).

It is also important to describe and take into account how different groups and social categories relate to each other in different contexts. For example, people of colour may share in the marginalisations associated with social disadvantage, prejudice and discrimination. But a colonial history is different from a migrant history, a history of slavery is different from a history of dispossession, and a history of white forced adoption and institutionalisation is different from a black history of forced separation (on the latter, see Cuthbert & Quartly 2012). How specific groups relate to each other over time is also part of the historical construction of society as a changing living entity. As the migrant morphs into the established Australian, what is to be his or her relationship to the first peoples of this continent? People change, but do peoples change and, if so, how and under what circumstances? These are questions of history that go to the heart of the dynamics of social inequality and social transformation.

Other related issues for exploration here might include: the relationship between rurality, masculinity and violence; intergenerational transmission of trauma and social disadvantage and, possibly, crime; and comparative criminology, which might examine how countries such as those comprising Scandinavia, which promote equality of opportunity through the adoption of universalistic and egalitarian policies in the fields of education, health and social security, compare in this regard to other countries (see Pratt 2010a,b).

CONCLUSION

This chapter has provided insight into how disadvantage, as one manifestation of social inequality, is linked to patterning and distribution of certain types of criminality. As later chapters will demonstrate, the other side of the inequality coin involves crimes of the powerful (including dominant classes and powerful states), crimes that are qualitatively different from those committed by members of the working classes and underclasses of late capitalism. Class division and class struggle underpin much contemporary criminality as measured by traditional criminal justice efforts and records. Issues of poverty, unemployment and disadvantage are never far from the surface when discussing street crime and crimes associated with the professional underclass of criminals.

Social inequality is complex, however. It is for this reason that crime, as it pertains to specific population groups, needs to be put into its appropriate historical and social context. Issues of racism and resettlement, for example, have shaped how certain migrant groups have become part of the Australian social mosaic in ways that lend themselves both to engagement in crime (through lack of resources) and to specific types of crime, such as drug dealing (because of language and cultural ties to sources in the country of origin). Similarly, the ongoing realities of colonialism in the lives of Indigenous Australians have a continuing and demonstrable influence on the involvement of Indigenous people with criminal justice. Issues of social justice are likewise at the forefront of any discussion of Indigenous offending and victimisation.

Chapter 8 explores in further detail the concept of social difference. In particular, it explores the process by which difference (manifest in a variety of ways) is recast as deviance and therefore worthy of criminal justice attention.

DISCUSSION QUESTIONS

1   What is 'class', and why does it matter?

2   What social factors seem most influential in shaping patterns of crime? Why do these factors persist over time?

3   Why can it be argued that when it comes to relationships between Indigenous Australians and the criminal justice system, the line between victim and offender is blurred? In what ways does an understanding of the history of colonialism in Australia help to explain the current relationship between Indigenous Australians and the criminal justice system?

4   Identify some of the ways in which geographical region, inequality and crime intersect.

5   What factors might account for the increased representation of ethnic minority groups in the criminal justice system?

FURTHER READING

Douglas, H. & Finnane, M. (2012) *Indigenous crime and settler law: white sovereignty after empire*, Macmillan, Basingstoke, Palgrave.

National Inquiry into the Separation of Aboriginal and Torres Strait Islander Children from their Families (Australia) (NASATSIC) (1997) *Bringing them home: report of the national inquiry into the separation of Aboriginal and Torres Strait Islander children from their families*, Commissioner: Ronald Wilson, Human Rights and Equal Opportunities Commission, Sydney.

Poynting, S., Noble, G., Tabar, P. & Collins, J. (2004) *Bin Laden in the suburbs: criminalising the Arab other*, Sydney Institute of Criminology Series, Sydney.

White, R. (2008) 'Class analysis and the crime problem', in T. Anthony & C. Cunneen (eds), *The critical criminology companion*, Federation Press, Sydney.

Wundersitz, J. (2010) 'Indigenous perpetrators of violence: prevalence and risk factors for offending', *Research and Public Policy Series*, No. 105, Australian Institute of Criminology, Canberra.

8

CRIME AND SOCIAL DIFFERENCE

CHAPTER OVERVIEW

- TRANSFORMING DIFFERENCE INTO DEVIANCE: ETHNIC MINORITY GROUPS IN WESTERN SYDNEY
- SOCIAL DIFFERENCE AND SUBORDINATE STATUS: GENDER-PATTERNED CRIME
- SOCIAL DIFFERENCE AND FEARED STATUS: DISCOURSES SURROUNDING DISABILITY
- STATUS OFFENCES AND SOCIAL DIFFERENCE: JUVENILE CRIME
- SEXUALITY AND SOCIAL DIFFERENCE
- ISSUES FOR CONSIDERATION
- CONCLUSION
- DISCUSSION QUESTIONS
- FURTHER READING

INTRODUCTION

This chapter continues the discussion of crime and difference, but examines more closely issues pertaining to social difference. A key organising theme of the chapter is that of social status, and how this influences the manner in which different groups in society are treated in and by the law, including the criminal law. In this regard, the emphasis is on constructions of certain categories of people as being deviant, based upon visible markers such as appearance, behaviour, age, sex or particular expressions of their unique forms of humanity.

The chapter begins by considering how social difference, itself not necessarily problematic, may be transformed into social deviance: there are certain social processes that bring to the surface differences between and among people in ways that stigmatise and separate them from the mainstream. These processes apply to particular ethnic minority groups. They are also relevant to people with disabilities and those with mental illness.

The question of subordinate status is central to the discussions in this chapter. It is for this reason that we discuss the unequal positioning of women within society and how women have historically been portrayed in relation to issues such as crime and criminality. Our concern is less with the actual incidence of crime among women (although this is briefly examined) than with the discourses surrounding female deviancy, many of which reinforce the subordinate or lower status of women via the lens of (biological and social) difference.

This is followed by discussion of physical and mental differences and how these are socially constructed and linked into matters of criminal justice. The chapter also considers status offences; that is, offences that entirely revolve around the social status of a particular population group rather than the question of harm or criminality per se. The chapter concludes with an examination of sexuality, law and criminalisation, for even the most intimate acts are subject to discourses and interventions that separate out the 'wrong' and the 'right', the 'harmful' and the 'harmless'.

TRANSFORMING DIFFERENCE INTO DEVIANCE: ETHNIC MINORITY GROUPS IN WESTERN SYDNEY

Mainstream social institutions tend to present and deal with particular groups in society in ways that tend to treat their defining social characteristics as liabilities. These 'liabilities' may, in turn, be associated with criminal tendencies or the propensity to engage in activities that are deemed to be socially unacceptable. Insofar as this is the case, we might well ask the question: what are the key social characteristics of those who are presented as 'deviant' or whom we are supposed to 'fear'? What is it about certain people—their appearance, capacities, competencies or (lack of) conformities—that make them suspect in the public eye? How and why is it that certain groups are singled out as being social problems?

One way to answer these questions is to chart those who historically and/or in the contemporary period have been seen as 'deviant', perhaps criminally inclined and certainly likely to break legal norms. A short list might include, for example:

- people with mental illness
- people of colour ('black people')
- gay men and lesbians
- people with intellectual and physical disabilities
- young people from the 'wrong side of the tracks', especially the unemployed
- ethnic minority groups
- those who attempt suicide
- street beggars
- people who abuse drugs and alcohol
- members of unorthodox religious groups, usually labelled as 'cults'.

What makes any particular group a 'threat' or 'deviant' or someone to be 'feared' tends to relate to stereotypes and images that mobilise and reinforce the perception that such groups are dangerous and predisposed towards criminality; that they pose a threat of violence and social and moral harm to the 'Australian' way of life, and 'family values'. Difference is construed as threatening if 'differences' from the 'norm' are seen to challenge what are deemed by the powerful and the mainstream to be ordinary ways of doing things and behaving (Blalock 1967; Spitzer 1975) (see Box 8.1).

BOX 8.1   ETHNIC MINORITY GROUPS IN WESTERN SYDNEY

Consider the example of ethnic minority youth in the western suburbs of Sydney. Young people in the western suburbs of Sydney, particularly areas such as Bankstown and Lakemba, have featured prominently in media reports and academic study in recent years. From the point of view of the media and politicians, young Muslim men—of 'Middle Eastern appearance'—have become the bête noir of sensationalised reportage and political intolerance (see Poynting et al. 2004). The public discourse has vilified Lebanese (Australian) young men in particular (see Poynting & Morgan 2007) as members of 'rape gangs' or 'terrorists'. This has been occurring for a number of years (dating at least back to the time of the first Gulf War in the early 1990s), but intensified following the 11 September jihadist terrorist attacks in the United States (and other global acts of terror involving Muslim perpetrators, such as the Bali bombings in 2002, the London bombings in 2006 and the Glasgow airport attack in 2007) and a series of well-publicised rape trials involving Lebanese-background young Muslim men between 2000 and 2003 (Humphrey 2007; Kabir 2011). Indeed, for many years, state elections in New South Wales have not only been largely based upon law-and-order issues, but have also featured racialist discourses that vilify particular ethnic minorities. The Muslim and the Arab, in particular, have become the contemporary societal scapegoat, the alleged source of the state's crime problems and social ills and, in recent years, the potential threat to national security.

THE OTHERING PROCESS

This process of differentiating and distancing certain minority groups from the respectable, trustworthy and law-abiding majority is referred to as 'othering'. The campaign to 'other' the Muslim—to render them incompatible with Australian culture—and the consequent rise of *Islamophobia*, has been reinforced by specific events in which individual members of the community have committed violent crimes. A social process over a number of years has transformed social difference into **social deviance** (see Figure 8.1). One consequence of this is that, even though most of the young men in a commuity were born in Australia or have been here since they were little children, they are treated as *outsiders*. Already subject to economic disadvantage and social marginalisation, a generation of young people has grown up in a social atmosphere hostile to their culture, to their community, to their religion and to their very presence. This has not been a linear process, but has involved complex transactions that over time have fed back into the overall transformation of social relationships. The direction of change, however, has tended toward the social construction of the 'Arab Other' (see Morgan & Poynting 2011; Poynting & Mason 2008; Poynting et al. 2004).

The outcome of this *othering process* has been captured in sustained academic study of these young people and their neighbourhoods. For example, Collins et al. (2000) observe that for many young people, the way to overcome marginalisation and alienation is to find other ways to affirm their social presence—to form or join a gang. From this vantage point, gang membership is significant, not because of presumed criminality but because it provides a means to valorise their lives and empower them in the face of outside hostility, disrespect, racism and vilification; it is a form of defensive posturing. This is consistent with Black's (1983) theory of crime as a form of social control, which contends that many offences are actually expressions of grievance; a form of 'self-help' that fulfils the desire for justice by those unwilling or unable to pursue such through traditional avenues (law enforcement).

The process of transformation from 'difference' to 'deviance', and the violence associated with this transformation, which has implications for all of the young people concerned, is also illustrated in recent events in Sydney, in particular the Cronulla riots in 2005 (see Collins 2007; Collins & Reid 2009; Noble 2009; Poynting 2007). Lebanese/Muslim-background Australians featured prominently, initially as targets and then later as protagonists, in the beach riots of December 2005. As highlighted by Mason (2011b), despite the riots involving thousands of Australian-background young people engaged in acts of intimidation, abuse and violence directed towards individuals of 'Middle Eastern' appearance, attention focused on the retaliatory attack undertaken the following day by individuals characterised by police as being of Lebanese/Muslim/Middle Eastern background, with their behaviour described by social commentators as 'un-Australian', reflective of 'tribal mentality' and evidence of the failure of ethnic integration into Australian society (Mills & Keddie 2010). Tellingly, the then Prime Minister, John Howard, and other prominent social commentators refused to characterise the original violence as racist behaviour, despite the fact that many protestors appealed to national identity by carrying

SOCIAL DEVIANCE
The way in which some groups in society are presented and responded to by mainstream social institutions, which tend to treat their defining social characteristics as liabilities associated with criminal tendencies or the propensity to engage in activities that are deemed to be socially unacceptable.

Australian flags, chanted racist slogans and waved defamatory placards directed at people of Middle Eastern background (Bliuc et at. 2012). One has only to consider the widely circulated SMS text message that instigated the original violence, to appreciate the clearly racist motivation—the reclaiming of Australia from immigrants:

> This Sunday every F—ing Aussie in the shire, get down to North Cronulla to help support Leb and Wog bashing day... Bring your mates down and let's show them this is our beach and they're never welcomed back... let's kill these boys (cited in Collins & Reid 2009).

FIGURE 8.1   DYNAMICS OF DEVIANCY

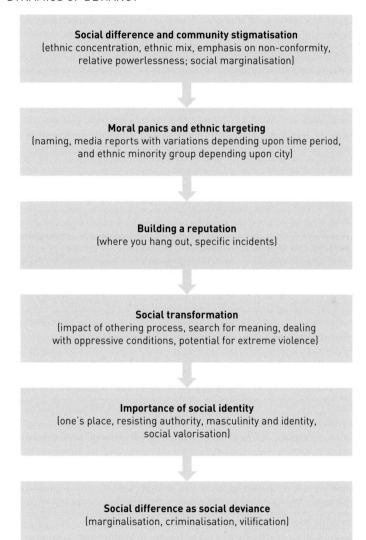

Social difference and community stigmatisation
(ethnic concentration, ethnic mix, emphasis on non-conformity, relative powerlessness; social marginalisation)

Moral panics and ethnic targeting
(naming, media reports with variations depending upon time period, and ethnic minority group depending upon city)

Building a reputation
(where you hang out, specific incidents)

Social transformation
(impact of othering process, search for meaning, dealing with oppressive conditions, potential for extreme violence)

Importance of social identity
(one's place, resisting authority, masculinity and identity, social valorisation)

Social difference as social deviance
(marginalisation, criminalisation, vilification)

Source: White (2008c: 144)

One commonality that exists between the diverse groups identified as a 'social problem' is that very often they are subject to negative differential treatment on the basis of who they are (their ethnicity, their culture and their religious beliefs), not what they do. Furthermore, they tend to be a numerical minority vis-à-vis the wider population, and to be marginalised in various ways from mainstream economic, social and cultural life. As well, the media frequently presents particular groups in narrow stereotypical ways that reinforce their status as subordinate, feared or of lesser status than the presumed social mainstream. For example, since 11 September, the media has been accused of inflaming tensions between Muslim and other Australians by relentlessly linking Islam, religious fundamentalism, extremism and terrorism in sensationalised and unbalanced ways. This media-practised extremism not only damages entire communities, but some community leaders also fear that it can in fact prove to be a self-fulfilling prophecy: radicalising peaceful Muslims repulsed by the pervasive and humiliating media negativity and criminalisation of their culture (Tahiri & Grossman 2013).

Those construed as outsiders, misfits and deviants who stand outside convention are also sometimes implicated in particular forms of criminality in the popular media. This is often the case, for example, in movie portrayals of homicide that tie mental illness to serious violent crime. Memorable screen psychopaths include the characters of Norman Bates in *Psycho*, Mick Taylor in *Wolf Creek*, Jack Torrance in *The Shining* and Michael Myers in *Halloween* (Stephens 2013).

The processes of social inclusion and social exclusion are not forged only at the level of broad societal resources and structural disadvantage. Nor are they just constituted through ideological and political processes of separation and differentiation. Exclusion and inclusion are made in the crucible of the everyday, in the mundane activities and relationships of people as they negotiate their daily lives. Social difference is a lived reality.

SOCIAL DIFFERENCE AND SUBORDINATE STATUS: GENDER-PATTERNED CRIME

A **subordinate status** can have major implications for how the dynamics of deviancy and crime are played out in practice. Historically, the position of women within male-dominated or patriarchal societies has meant that female criminality has tended to be portrayed and understood in very sex-specific ways. To understand why this has been the case, it is necessary to consider the ways in which the social construction of **gender** shapes both the incidence of law breaking and the consequent response of the criminal justice system. Discourses of masculinity and femininity, relationships between and within genders, and the intersection of gender with class and ethnicity are just some of the ways gender shapes patterns of crime.

Until the 1970s, gender-patterned crime was taken for granted. Men's involvement in crime, and women's exclusion from it, was more or less accepted without question. In the past 30 years, feminist research on women and crime has rendered problematic the normality of male crime. By challenging positivist criminology's acceptance of crime as straightforward and unproblematic, feminists have opened up a rich seam of knowledge (see Belknap 2010; White et al. 2012). Today, the issue of gender is a central theme in the study of crime.

Feminist contributions to the study of crime emerging in the 1960s, include:
* the development of feminist theories of crime that place issues of gender at the centre of the analysis, and offer non-sexist explanations of women's involvement in crime; for example, the 'pathways'

SUBORDINATE STATUS
The unequal positioning of a particular group in society; for example, the historical position of women within male-dominated or patriarchal societies has meant that female criminality has tended to be portrayed and understood in very sex-specific ways.

GENDER
Gender refers to the distinction between masculine and feminine. It is a social construct not a biological given. The social construction of gender shapes both the incidence of law breaking and the response of the criminal justice system.

perspective highlights histories of traumas and victimisations as significant risk factors for women's offending

- removal of the silence around crimes against women, such as domestic violence, sexual assault and homicide
- demands for law reform in areas such as prostitution, women's imprisonment, rape and domestic violence
- emphasis on the broad range and diversity of female offending, and analyses of how gender shapes women's involvement in specific types of crime, such as prostitution and gangs
- challenging of traditional gender-role portrayals and the normative conceptualisation of maleness/masculinity and femaleness/femininity in historical theorising on crime
- analysis of the treatment of women by the criminal justice system, including recognition of the essentialist and stereotyped notions of the 'good virtuous woman', that have shaped the criminal justice system's treatment of female offenders and victims and, especially, their incarceration on the grounds of immorality (e.g. disorderly conduct, intoxication, prostitution and having consensual sex outside marriage—an offence for which men were never incarcerated)
- analysis of the link between poverty, ethnicity and women's involvement in crime (as opposed to biological, psychological and/or sexual characteristics) and the criminalisation of survival behaviours such as prostitution.

By the 1980s, feminist insights into the role of gender in shaping women's relationship with the criminal justice system led to studies that explored men as gendered subjects. Since then, the concept of masculinity has emerged as key in explaining men's involvement in crime (see Messerschmidt 1997, 1986; Polk 1994b). The concern of this chapter, however, is not with feminist criminology per se (instead, see Belknap 2007; Naffine 1997, 1987; White et al. 2012) or with the later studies of masculinity. Rather, the focus is on how non-feminist understandings of social differences, based upon gender, have had an impact upon public and criminological interpretations of female criminality.

Before the advent of feminism and feminist criminology, there was actually very little dedicated research on female offenders. On the rare occasions when female criminality was studied (by men), essentialist, male-generated, sexist stereotypes about them prevailed (e.g. Cesare Lombroso's physically degenerate female and Sigmund Freud's 'anatomy as destiny'). Women were assumed to be 'naturally' passive and non-criminal, while men were 'naturally' aggressive and active. Male engagement in crime was understood as a logical extension of their normal behaviour, in that, for example, so-called natural male aggression provides the grounding for criminally violent behaviour in some men. From this perspective, when women broke the law, they were doubly deviant, also violating cultural norms and expectations about what it is to be a woman (Belknap 2010; Carlen & Worrall 2004). Their crimes were portrayed as an aberration best explained as the result of inadequate socialisation and maladjustment. One of the few early studies on female crime, for example, was a book by W I Thomas, tellingly called *The unadjusted girl* (1923).

Statistically speaking, we know that historically, and today, women commit fewer crimes than men. For example, in 2012–13, the ratio of male to female offenders was almost four to one (ABS 2014a). We also know that men disproportionately commit the more serious crimes, such as homicide (6.5 per 100,000 population in 2011–12 compared to 1.1 per 100,000 population for females) and acts intended to cause injury (547 per 100,000 population compared to 141 per 100,000 for females) (ABS 2014a). The few areas where women's crime does exceed that of men's are shoplifting, prostitution, 'promiscuity' and offences related to childcare (e.g. leaving a child unattended) (AIC 2013a;

Gelb 2010; Smart 1976; Spooner & Butt 2013). Among juveniles, girls are much more likely to be the subject of care and protection orders compared to boys, especially those in detention (Alder 1997; Marien 2012; Vecchiato et al. 2011).

This data suggests that where women do predominate as offenders, it is in areas that relate to their female-gendered role. The crimes relate to their sexuality (prostitution and promiscuity), to their domestic role (shoplifting and social security offences) and to their roles as primary child-rearers (crimes against children and infants, including infanticide, illegal abortion and neglect). In regard to **status offences** (offences based upon age prohibitions for certain types of behaviour), young women have predominated in areas such as promiscuity, ungovernability and running away from home.

In *The criminality of women*, Otto Pollack (1961) argued that criminal statistics disguise the true extent of female crime. Again, this argument was based upon an essentialist or biological reductionist account of gender and crime. According to Pollack (1961), the real rate of female crime is hidden by a number of factors:

- Women possess a 'natural cunning and deceitfulness' that gives them the capacity to disguise their crimes. This derives from their passive role in sexual intercourse, and their ability to fake orgasm: something a man cannot do.
- Women's menstruation is symbolic of their deviance/offending.
- It is easy for women to disguise their crimes, because most take place in the privacy of the home or other domestic settings. Women's criminal acts are therefore less visible than traditional male crimes, such as burglary, and consequently they are less easily exposed. Their victims are likely to be vulnerable social groups, such as children and the elderly, who are unable to draw attention to their victimisation.
- Women often instigate criminal acts by persuading or inspiring men to carry out the deed, but are rarely themselves perpetrators.
- When women do come to the attention of law-enforcement agencies, they are treated more leniently than men. Pollack's **chivalry thesis** suggests that male law enforcers are reluctant to charge women who violate the law, and even more reluctant to imprison them. This aversion to implementing the law is based on the assumptions that women are not 'really' criminal, that they are supposedly unable to cope with the stress of social retribution and, because of their status as nurturers, the incarceration of women would cause innocent children to suffer.

In contrast to Pollack's assumptions and assertions, statistical analyses of the relationship between gender and sentencing, for example, have found that differences in sentencing are attributable to factors other than gender, including offence type, prior convictions and other legally relevant variables (Douglas 1987; Grabosky & Rizzo 1983). With regard to juvenile offending, Carrington (1993) has argued that both girls and boys who appear before the children's courts on welfare matters are likely to receive harsher dispositions than those who appear on criminal matters.

More recently, Gelb's (2010) review of a small sample of matched female and male offenders (n = 166) sentenced in Victoria for armed robbery found differential sentencing outcomes (shorter terms of imprisonment) favourable to women over men, even after controlling for factors relevant to sentencing (seriousness of offence, prior offending, plea type and weapon use). This finding held true for three categories of offender: young first offenders, adult first offenders and adult recidivist offenders. The scale of the sentencing difference in these groups was observed to be substantial, with average terms for men approximately twice as long as those for women. The reasons for this disparity, however, often revolved around issues pertaining to psychological disorder, prior victimisation experiences,

STATUS OFFENCES
Offences that apply only to young people; the assumption is that until they reach a suitable age (as determined by legislators and courts), young people should be subject to particular types of social controls.

CHIVALRY THESIS
The theory that one of the reasons for the apparently low female crime rate is that traditional male attitudes to women make male law enforcers reluctant to apply the full weight of the law.

drug abuse and primary childcare responsibilities. Similar findings for a variety of offences (including white-collar crime) have been observed elsewhere in Australia (Jeffries & Bond 2010; Lawrence & Homel 1992; Naylor 1992), the United Kingdom (Hedderman & Gelsthorpe 1992) and the United States (Daly & Bordt 1995; Van Slyke & Bales 2013).

The sentencing experience does not appear to be uniform for all women across Australian jurisdictions. Bond and Jeffries (2010), for instance, found that Indigenous women are less likely to be sentenced to a term of imprisonment than non-Indigenous women in Western Australian higher courts. Similar to Gelb (2010), factors attributable to sentencing disparity between Indigenous and non-Indigenous women appear not to be related to paternalistic attitudes as such, but rather to judicial areas of focal concern, including mental health, familial trauma and substance abuse, as well as the perceived social cost to children and the community associated with incarceration (see further Jeffries & Bond 2013). By contrast, they found that Indigenous women were more likely to be sentenced to a term of imprisonment in Queensland lower courts than their non-Indigenous counterparts, even after controlling for relevant sentencing factors (Bond & Jeffries 2011).

Thus, gender, specifically and on its own, appears to have limited explanatory value without contextualising the sentencing process. However, as pointed out in Chapter 10, while this is the case for most crimes, there are cases when gender is of central importance. For instance, the law of provocation has meant that many men who killed their partners in certain circumstances received a more lenient disposition than women who killed their partners in self-defence, often after years of domestic abuse (see Chapter 22).

MORAL PANIC ABOUT WOMEN'S CRIME

Nonetheless, the specificity of social difference—the idea that girls and women have a special nature that sets them apart from both men, and criminal behaviour generally—continues to underpin contemporary discussions of gender and criminality. This is evident, for example, in the public concern over female violence. Women's apparent increase in offending, it is argued, is due to a rise in serious assaults including homicide. There is some evidence that general trends in female offending have in fact been influenced by feminist critiques of the use of welfare complaints (e.g. those of 'uncontrollable' or 'exposed to moral danger') against girls and women, and that one consequence of agitation around these questions has been the movement of women from welfare to criminalisation (see Carrington 2006). Be this as it may, periodic moral panics (see Chapter 2) place much attention on the question, 'Are women committing more aggressive and violent crimes today than in the past?'

There has been limited broad-scale research into this matter to date; however, justice statistics do support the notion that far greater proportions of female offenders are being processed for violent offences in Australia and elsewhere (Gelb 2010). For example, over the 14-year period from 1996–97 to 2009–10, there was a 49 per cent increase in the rate of female assault offending in Australia (AIC 2012). Since that time, however, the rate of female offending for the category of acts intended to cause injury has decreased by approximately 8 per cent to a rate of 141 per 100,000 population in 2012–13 (as compared to 547 per 100,000 for men) (ABS 2014a; see also Gelb 2003; Ross & Forster 2000). There is also evidence to suggest that Indigenous women are disproportionately processed for acts intended to cause injury. This over-representation is clear when one examines the profile of women prisoners. In 2013, acts intended to cause injury were the most serious offence recorded for one in every three (34.1%) Aboriginal women prisoners, as compared to under one in ten (9.1%) non-Indigenous women prisoners (ABS 2012c). Aboriginal women accounted for 65 per cent of all acts intended to cause injury committed by imprisoned women; a level of over-representation that has increased over time (Bartels 2012a, 2010; Stubbs 2011).

Both qualitative and quantitative studies indicate that explanations for increasing female violence are inevitably linked to issues such as drugs, economic need, deviant partners and declining social opportunities (Kruttschnitt et al. 2008). Studies addressing Indigenous women's violence specifically have identified links with alcohol intoxication and domestic violence (see Stubbs 2011). With regards to the increasing proportion of women incarcerated for violent offences, some have suggested the 'Pandora effect'; essentially the corollary of the chivalry thesis, this approach postulates that increasing punitiveness towards women is an unintended, though inevitable consequence, of the feminist spotlighting of women's offending (see Heidensohn 2012). While the evidence suggests little change over time in the size of the gender gap between women and men when it comes to violent crime (and indeed crime overall), the specific character or context of the violence is important to consider. Changing circumstances in the wider society—in regards to family structures, economic opportunities, types of drug use, patterns of alcohol consumption and availability of weapons—have ramifications for the specific nature of female violence. Thus, 'While gendered social boundaries have insured that many of the features of women's violent offending have remained relatively stable, the conditions under which women negotiate these boundaries are not as enduring' (Kruttschnitt et al. 2008: 32).

Yet, the basis for the moral panic remains the same: crimes of violence seem to contradict the role, status and place of women in society. Insofar as the public concern is driven by these considerations, it reinforces the particular and subordinate position of women within the larger social structure. This is materially and culturally expressed in inequalities and oppressions across a range of social domains, such as contribution to community, financial resources, workplace inequality, restricted roles in legal and social institutions and experience of violence (see ALRC 1994b). Violence by women, therefore, to some extent is threatening to the status quo insofar as it is interpreted as indicating a major shift in gender roles. Female violence is problematic because it might be symptomatic of wider changes in the gendered social order that challenge existing structures of domination–subordination between the sexes.

TYPIFICATION
The process of defining situations in ways that allow for mutual communication, as well as defining what is 'normal' and 'abnormal'. How people typify one another (e.g. 'mentally ill'), and relate to one another on the basis of these typifications, has major social consequences.

SOCIAL DIFFERENCE AND FEARED STATUS: DISCOURSES SURROUNDING DISABILITY

Deviance or criminality is not something that is simply objectively given; it is subjectively problematic (Plummer 1979). For example, it can be argued that deviancy itself can be the result of the interactive process involving individuals and the criminal justice system. What makes people 'different' from each other is defined through social processes of **typification** and acknowledgment. Certain groups can come to be seen as a problem insofar as their actions or appearances seem to disturb the status quo in some fashion. This is especially the case when it comes to *disability* and *mental illness*, both of which involve social distancing from particular people precisely because of their perceived distance from mainstream social norms. Their social status is that of someone or something to be avoided or feared.

How we respond to other people in our social interactions depends upon how we *define the situation*. The symbolic nature of behaviour means that the first stage of any interaction is one of definition. When people share the same definitions, communication is likely to be straightforward and clear, enabling interpretation of the significance of the interaction itself. The basis of our interaction with other people is the use of *typifications*, which are drawn upon as part of our recipe knowledge that we use in order to make sense of the world (Berger & Luckmann 1971).

The first step in communication, therefore, is defining situations in a process of interaction. Sometimes situations are misinterpreted if we define them incorrectly. For example, an observer may draw upon a variety of explanations to interpret a scenario involving two men embracing and kissing each other: it could be a greeting (at an airport), a congratulatory gesture (on a sports ground) or a love affair (in a club or on the street). What is important in terms of our behaviour is not the circumstances (i.e. the objective elements of an observed situation, such as the setting and the players), but whether we have defined the situation in the same way; that is, whether we share the same definition or interpretation of a situation.

Typification is not only about defining situations in ways that allow for mutual communication. It also involves defining what is 'normal' and what is 'abnormal'. Social life is guided by norms or rules that may vary in accordance with specific cultural context, but nevertheless set out the recipe for what is to be considered 'natural' or 'usual' when it comes to formulating everyday perceptions of attitudes, behaviours and appearances. In essence, conformity is rewarded, through social inclusion, and non-conformity is sanctioned, through social exclusion. Sometimes the process of social exclusion extends to criminalisation of those who are deemed to be separate in some way from the mainstream. How people typify and label one another (e.g. 'mentally ill') and how people relate to one another on the basis of these typifications has major social consequences (Rubington & Weinberg 1978). For some, it can lead to social ostracism and even imprisonment.

Those groups that fall outside a generally accepted norm—relating, for example, to ability–disability, or mental health–mental illness—are more likely to suffer social stigma and social exclusion. One aspect of the perception of people with intellectual disabilities or mental illness, for instance, is that they always look or act differently from 'normal' people. In some cases, the public perception is that intellectual disability or mental illness is associated with things such as sexual deviancy or criminal behaviour. Often, the concept of 'dangerousness' is linked to people with mental illness or an intellectual disability. These kinds of public myths and misconceptions reinforce the status of such people as a group to be feared.

The social status of those who experience various kinds of disability, especially the more visible disabilities, is largely constructed through various kinds of discourse. How we 'language' disability thus has significant ramifications for how disability is viewed, and for societal responses to people with disabilities. This is illustrated in Box 8.2, which summarises several key discourses surrounding disability.

BOX 8.2 DEVIANCY AND DISCOURSES OF DISABILITY

MEDICAL DISCOURSE
- Focuses on the *physical and mental* characteristics of the person, rather than the notion of disability as a social construct
- *Individualises disability* and generates connotations of individualistic deficit
- *Depoliticises issues*, such as human rights and disability, since the problems are seen as technical in nature, relating to biomechanical and psychological processes.

- *Professionalises disability*, rendering it a matter for professional judgment
- *Excludes consumer viewpoints* by elevating the voice of professional expertise
- Reduces crime causality to *individualism*

CHARITY DISCOURSE

- Defines the needs of people with disabilities in *patronising* and *condescending* terms as in need of personal help, as objects of pity, as dependent and eternal children, and as low achievers by ideal standards
- Contains themes of *benevolence* and *humanitarianism* (rather than rights), for which the client is to be grateful
- Emphasises *'total institutions'*, which can involve placing individuals in disability-specific facilities where they can be cared for

LAY DISCOURSE

- *Medical* and *charitable* notions prevail
- *Blatantly discriminatory* ideas inform social practices, such as talking loudly on the presumption that people with disability need to be spoken to differently from other people, or that they cannot perform tasks in an ordinary workplace
- *'Aesthetic anxiety'*: an emphasis on deviations from 'normal' appearances
- Emphasis on the importance of *'body'*, *control* and *autonomy* in modern society

RIGHTS DISCOURSE

- Emphasises themes of *self-reliance*, independence and *consumer wants* (rather than needs)
- Focuses on key concepts such as *discrimination*, *exclusion* and *oppression*
- *Opposes typifications* and themes of dependence and 'help'
- Emphasises *control* and *choices*
- Strives for *equality of citizenship*

Source: adapted from Fulcher (1989)

INTELLECTUAL DISABILITY, MENTAL ILLNESS AND CRIMINOLOGY

Consideration of discourses and typifications is important because, if the dominant discourses serve to reinforce the deviancy of people with intellectual disability and mental illness, they also simultaneously smooth the path for the disproportionate representation of such people within criminal justice institutions. This is indeed the present situation; one that has been exacerbated by the deinstitutionalisation of people with mental illness and intellectual disability from the 1970s onwards. This deinstitutionalisation involved a shift from institutions such as separate psychiatric custodial hospitals to community care. However, in many instances there was little care or support in the community to which those with mental illness had been shifted (Rosenberg et al. 2009).

The Human Rights and Equal Opportunity Commission (HREOC) conducted a National Inquiry into the Human Rights of People with Mental Illness in 1993 (HREOC 1993). The report found that Australians affected by mental illness were especially disadvantaged, and that they suffered from widespread and systematic discrimination. Deinstitutionalisation had exacerbated the problems experienced by people with mental illness, because community-based agencies were chronically underfunded. The difficulties in finding adequate housing, employment and treatment have resulted in disproportionate numbers of people with mental illness being homeless, with many ending up being housed in the institutions of the criminal justice system. The inquiry also found an alarming lack of knowledge among many health, education, welfare and juvenile justice professionals about various psychiatric, behavioural and emotional problems that can affect children and young people. This has implications for both juvenile and adult corrections.

In 2013, the Australian Human Rights Commission (AHRC, formerly HREOC) revisited aspects of this inquiry in its national review of barriers to accessing justice for those with disabilities (AHRC 2014). It is a damning indictment that over a decade on, many of the findings of the 1993 review were reaffirmed. In particular, the AHRC found that across Australia, 45 per cent of people with disabilities live in poverty or near poverty—a situation that has deteriorated since the mid-1990s. Australians with disabilities now face decreased employment opportunities and educational outcomes. People with disabilities also experience a relatively high risk of incarceration and repeat contact with the criminal justice system. For example, one study cited in the report found that in 2012, over a third (38%) of prison entrants and almost a half of prison discharges (46%) reported having been informed by a health professional (doctor, psychiatrist, psychologist or nurse) that they have a mental health disorder or condition, including drug and alcohol abuse (AIHW 2013e).

This finding has been confirmed by other recent research, which has found even higher proportions of mental health over-representation among non-incarcerated criminal justice populations. For instance, Baksheev et al. (2011) found that three-quarters of detainees in police facilities in Melbourne met the criteria for mental disorder diagnosis (see also AIC 2009; Forsythe & Gaffney 2012). Moreover, the rates of mental illness among offender and prison populations are significantly higher than rates of mental illness in the wider community, estimated to be around 20 per cent (ABS 2008a), and have been consistently so for some time (see NSW Law Reform Commission 1996; Ogloff et al. 2007). There are also high levels of traumatic brain injury among prisoner populations, estimated to be between 25 and 50 per cent of adult prisoners (Lee 2013). Existing data reveals a very strong link between acquired brain injury and those people being arrested, interviewed, charged, convicted and imprisoned (see Langdon 2007; Schofield et al. 2006).

While it is possible that people with intellectual disabilities are more likely to commit certain types of offences, widespread ignorance about the nature of intellectual disability, mental illness and acquired brain injury among officials throughout the criminal justice system, coupled with popular misconceptions regarding these conditions, contribute to their over-representation. For example, people with intellectual disability can be arrested and drawn into the criminal justice system for public order offences stemming from the public display of signs and symptoms associated with their disability (perceived abnormal behaviour), rather than any deliberate harm to others (Lurigio 2013).

Importantly, the AHRC (2014) review refocuses our attention on the intersection between criminality and victimisation, finding that many offenders with disability have themselves been victims of violence that has not been adequately responded to, and which has contributed to a cycle of offending and reoffending. While societal prejudices of those with intellectual disabilities coalesce around the feared, violent offender, it is important to recognise that people with disabilities are far more likely to be the victims of crime (see also Hart et al. 2012). In particular, women and girls with disability experience significantly higher rates of violence more frequently and over longer periods by more perpetrators. It has been estimated that up to 90 per cent of Australian women with an intellectual disability have been the victim of sexual abuse, with more than two-thirds (68%) being victimised as children (before the age of 18 years) (VicHealth 2011).

STATUS OFFENCES AND SOCIAL DIFFERENCE: JUVENILE CRIME

'Juvenile', 'youth', 'young person' and 'delinquent': these terms are loaded with associations, many of which are negative. Think 'juvenile' and the word 'delinquency' is not far behind. Think 'young person' or 'youth' and words like 'out of control', 'underage drinking' and 'drugs' may come to mind. Other associations might be 'suicide', 'unemployment' and 'troubled'. To be young today is often to be designated to an inferior and unenviable position in society.

AGE MARKERS

Although words like 'juvenile' and 'youth' are used loosely to describe people whose age falls within a range somewhere between 8 and 24 years, in criminal law the term 'juvenile' has a specific meaning based on biological age (see Box 8.3). That is, childhood and adolescence is bounded by consideration of the idea that young people have varying stages of development and varying levels of understanding and susceptibility to risk (Kelly 2011). The vulnerability and developmental aspects of youth are legally protected through a range of criminal and civil legal measures designed to take into account their overall level of maturity (see Schetzer 2000; Western Australia Office of Youth Affairs 2000). These measures involve elements of prescription and compulsion (as with the imposition of compulsory schooling), and elements of proscription and prohibition (as with the banning of alcohol sales to people under a certain age; see Box 8.3).

As evident from Box 8.3, the law shapes the eligibility and responsibility of children and young people around distinct *age markers*. Variations will occur between jurisdictions, but there are similar key transitional ages across the states and territories. In some cases there may be variation in what a child or young person may or may not do, subject to permission being granted by the parent or guardian, a court or relevant government department.

BOX 8.3   KEY TRANSITION AGES FOR ACTIVITIES

- *Under 10:* no criminal responsibility; compulsory schooling
- *10 to 14*: criminal responsibility (but rebuttable presumption of *doli incapax*); compulsory schooling
- *15 to 18:* eligible to leave school; gain a driver's licence; take up full-time employment; engage in sexual activity (although different age provisions may apply for same-sex relationships); qualify for social security payments if various eligibility criteria are satisfied; and consent to medical and dental treatment
- *18 to 21:* able to drink and buy alcohol and cigarettes; live independently; rent a house; borrow money; open a bank account; marry; vote; and watch R-rated movies
- *21 to 25* adult rather than youth wages; movement towards full adult social security entitlements

A partial list of how the law positions young people includes the following:

- *Criminal law:* international instruments (e.g. the Convention on the Rights of the Child 1959, ratified in Australia in 1990) hold that criminal responsibility should not be fixed at too low an age, bearing in mind the facts of emotional and intellectual maturity. In the Australian context, this generally means 10 years of age as the minimum age of criminal responsibility, with the doctrine of *doli incapax* also applying to young people up to the age of 14 (a rebuttable presumption that children who have turned 10 and not yet reached the age of 14 are incapable of knowing that their criminal conduct was wrong).
- *Contracts and leases:* as a general rule, people under the age of 18 are not bound by contracts, leases, and other transactions unless they are for their benefit. Opening a bank account or borrowing money is possible at age 18, although the former is possible at any age as long as there is parental or guardian consent.
- *Driving:* gaining a driver's licence is generally possible at 16 years (a learner's permit) with a provisional licence available at 17 years.
- *Alcohol and cigarettes:* a young person under the age of 18 is not permitted to buy alcohol or cigarettes, or to possess or consume alcohol in a public place. Drinking alcohol at a private residence is not generally covered by law, with the exception of New South Wales, Queensland and Tasmania, which have laws controlling the secondary supply of alcohol to minors on private property (Australian Drug Foundation 2010).
- *Medical treatment:* generally at 14 years or over, young people can legally give consent to their own general medical or dental treatment.

STATUS OFFENCES

One implication of having such age-based parameters around permissible activity is that juveniles, in particular, are subject to additional legal control measures called *status offences*. These refer to those offences that only apply to young people, such as 'uncontrollability', 'incorrigibility', 'running away from home' and 'in need of care and protection'. The idea here is that, until they reach a suitable age (as determined by legislators and courts), young people should be subject to particular types of social controls, as they are in moral danger.

Underlying the distinctions between child, juvenile and adult are assumptions about the biological and psychological development of a 'normal' human being. Childhood is seen as an age of innocence in which physiological foundations for moral categories of 'right' and 'wrong' are believed to be absent or undeveloped, making the notion of *mens rea*—the intention to commit a wrongful act—inappropriate. A child that violates legal expressions of morality by, for example, killing a parent, or another child, is seen as in need of psychological help rather than punishment or moral correction. In some cases, where the behaviour has been exceptionally shocking, and especially when it has attracted widespread media coverage, there may be prolonged debate about how the law should be applied. For example, the murder of 2-year old James Bulger by two 10-year-old boys in England in 1993 generated huge public controversy over the appropriate application of *doli incapax*. The presumption of the inability to form criminal intent was successfully rebutted in this instance, and the accused were prosecuted as adults (*Good Weekend* 2013).

The notion of adolescence as a separate stage in the lifespan is a modern one. In his classic work *Centuries of childhood*, Aries (1973) points out that until about the middle of the nineteenth century, childhood was not regarded as an age of innocence, and children were unprotected from the often harsh realities of existence. Although there were class differences, in general, children wore the same clothes as adults and were expected to both work and play beside them. They worked down mines and in mills and went to taverns alongside adults. Nor did the law or the instruments of social control make any formal distinction between adults and children. Children as young as eight were hanged on the gallows, incarcerated in jails or transported (Morris & Giller 1987: 6; Seymour 1988: 8–9), although there were occasions when childhood was recognised as a mitigating factor (Platt, cited in Morris & Giller 1987: 8). It was only in the middle of the nineteenth century that the legal changes associated with the establishment of the modern system of juvenile justice were initiated (Cunneen & White 2011). Status offences were one outcome of this process of social differentiation.

As indicated above, when it comes to status offences, young women have historically been treated differently from young men because of the paternalistic role of the state in seeking to enforce dominant ideologies of femininity on young women (including their presumed disposition towards passivity and therefore vulnerability)—whether related to intoxication (Piper 2010), larrikinism (Bellanta 2010) or to sexualised behaviour (Alder 1997; Pasko 2010). Many young women come to the attention of the juvenile justice system not because they represent a threat to society but because they fail to conform to conventional standards of how a young woman should behave. Even in more sexually liberated times, where discourses on teen sexuality abound and there is a sexualised market of 'raunch culture' that actively targets pre-pubescent girls, young women who challenge traditional stereotypes about female sexuality, or who behave 'like a man' in engaging in adventurous behaviour (initiating sex and/ or engaging in casual sexual encounters), are far more likely to be seen as at risk, in danger and out of control today (Bishop 2013), and therefore in need of the 'protection' of the state (see Box 8.4).

The law has changed in Australia, and categories such as 'ungovernability' have been removed from the statutes. It has been suggested that these policy shifts, introduced in response to concerns regarding the sexuality and independence of young women, have produced unintended negative consequences. Specifically, young women who may previously have appeared before the courts on welfare or status offences now appear increasingly likely to enter the juvenile justice system under criminal charges (All Party Parliamentary Group on Women in the Penal System 2012; Carrington & Pereira 2009; Gelsthorpe & Worrall 2009). However, it remains the case that young men significantly outnumber young women within the juvenile justice system. In 2010–11, for instance, they were twice as likely as women to be proceeded against by police, more than three times as likely to be proven guilty in a Children's Court, four times as likely to be in community-based supervision, and five times as likely to be in detention. Young women, however, appear to be drawn into supervision at an earlier age than young men. In 2010–11, for example, young women aged 15–16 years experienced the highest rate of supervision, compared with 16–17 years for young men (AIHW 2012b).

Children and young people are not the only groups who have been subjected to status offences. For example, the historical banning of alcohol for Indigenous people in effect created an offence for those Indigenous people caught consuming it (Hudson 2011). Distinctions were made between who was eligible to drink alcohol (non-Indigenous Australians) and who could not (Indigenous Australians), purely on the basis of ascribed characteristics. It was membership of a group that determined whether a person had the right to engage in the activity. Drinking of alcohol in general was not seen as a social harm. Deviancy was thus attached to the person and his or her membership of a certain group, not the activity as such.

BOX 8.4   SEXTING, GENDER AND YOUNG PEOPLE

'Sexting' is a term that has entered community and legal parlance relatively recently. It is used to describe the transmission of material of a sexual or sexually explicit nature—such as suggestive or provocative photos or videos of people fully or partially naked—via electronic means, including text message, online social media, email and other such technology. Though electronic production, transmission and distribution of erotic images is not necessarily an offence per se, it can become so when the material depicts young people under the age of 18, in some cases amounting to child pornography offences under the *Crimes Act 1914*. This is the case, even if the young person involved self-produced and self-transmitted the material voluntarily (Salter et al. 2013). Although intended to protect minors from paedophiles, the child pornography provisions of the *Crimes Act 1914* have been used to prosecute minors who have unintentionally broken the law by sexting images of themselves or others and those who have unwittingly received such material (minors and adults); in some jurisdictions, the perpetrators have ended up on the Sex Offender Register, with lifelong repercussions. Ironically, the law of sexual consent is set two years lower than the definition of a 'child' under child pornography laws; hence, it is legal for two consenting young people to engage in sex at age 16, but illegal for 16-year olds to send sexually explicit images of themselves to their partner (Salter et al. 2013).

While the precise number of young people (aged 10–17) prosecuted for sexting-related offences in Australia is unknown for various reasons (Walker et al. 2011), they are thought to number in the hundreds. One report asserts that so many young people have been placed on the Victorian Sex Offender register that it has compromised the ability of police to monitor sex offenders who pose a real threat to children (Brady 2011a). Australian studies have revealed that the legal response to sexting poses a significant risk of criminalising young people, with an esti-mated 7–40 per cent of young people having sent or received a sexually explicit image (Salter et al. 2013; *The Age* 2013c). A study in the United States found that 39 per cent of teenagers had received sexually explicit images via text or email intended for another person (*The Age* 2013c).

As with young people's sexuality generally, much of the public commentary around sexting has revolved around the risks posed to young women (see also Chapter 15). This has included concern with the risk of abuse and exploitation (even when sexting is engaged in consensually), the life consequences of unauthorised distribution of their images, and the risk that technology poses for cultivation of a sexually promiscuous and sexually assertive generation of young wom-en—a discourse that does not extend equally to the sexting practices of young men (Brady 2011b). The discussion rarely acknowledges the possible usefulness of digital communication in assisting girls—generally marginalised by their age and gender expectations—to negotiate within consen-sual relationships by communicating their sexual desires at a distance (Hasinoff 2012).

SEXUALITY AND SOCIAL DIFFERENCE

In this final section we consider how sexuality, sexual practices and social difference are played out in ways that mean that certain types of activities are deemed deviant or criminal, while others are not. The discussion leaves aside the larger questions relating to treatment of sex as a commodity (and the break between sex and reproduction after the advent of the contraceptive pill), and the historical development of sexuality, as reflected in changing values and morality over the ages (including the social construction of homosexuality and its later legal acceptance as a legitimate mode of sexual being). Box 8.5 outlines the ways in which sexuality and desire have been configured in contemporary society across various dimensions.

BOX 8.5   SEXUALITY AND DESIRE

- *Desire* (biology, commodification and diverse constructions): such as erotica and pornography
- *Sex tied to bourgeois institutions* (Puritanism and gender roles): acceptable and unacceptable sex
- *Identification* (collective, group and subcultural social patterns): for example, sadomasochism (S & M) groups
- *Fluidity* (cross-cultural stages and acceptances of difference, impact of notions of risk on practices of desire): such as using or not using condoms
- *Repressions* (lies, violence and silences): for example, the unwillingness of people to tell the full truth in social surveys of sex

---

There are two interrelated questions we can ask about sexuality and desire. First, what varieties of sexuality are there? The answer to this includes reference to descriptions such as transexual, transvestite, bisexual, heterosexual, homosexual and queer. Second, what varieties of sexual *practice* are there? The answer might include references to S & M, procreation, gay sex, straight sex and group sex. It might go further to include such things as prostitution, cybersex, fidelity, celibacy, phone sex, and oral, anal, statutory and unprotected sex.

The importance of identifying varieties of *sexuality* and types of *sexual practice* is that it provides some indication of the wide range of human activities related to sex and sexuality generally. Sex is important because it is an 'ordinary' human practice; something that humans do, and like to do. Sex is, however, culturally and historically variable in terms of what kinds of acts are 'learned' in any particular culture, society or group, and what kinds of sex and sexuality are 'approved' in any particular social setting. In addition, sex itself may be linked to other activities, such as drugs and music. It is always both intimate *and* social at the same time.

THE LAW AND SEXUAL PRACTICE

All human practices are in some way or another subject to the legal gaze or the rule of social approval. In other words, one can identify what is 'legal' and 'illegal' when it comes to sexual practices in any given country. There is great variability in how the law treats different acts and behaviour in different societies; for example, homosexuality is banned in approximately 70 countries, primarily Muslim, and those found guilty of homosexual activity may be liable to severe punishments, including the death penalty (Conway-Smith 2013; Nossiter 2014). The law frames how sexuality is expressed, and the when, where, with whom and how sex takes place.

There are provisions in the law pertaining to, for example, adult–child sex, age of consent, multiple wives or husbands, public versus private acts, and paying money for sex. Traditionally, regulation of sexual practices has privileged a very narrow range of human sexual expression—that regarded as 'sanctified natural, safe, normal, healthy, mature, profitable, legal or politically correct' (Crofts et al. 2013). As Crofts et al. (2013: 53) indicates, in most centuries this has translated to heteronormative sex within coupled and monogamous relationships. Who and what gets criminalised is fluid, in the sense that public mores and values can shift and change over time. This may be a result of concerted campaigns to legalise certain types of sexual practice and/or social categories (as with homosexuality in the West). It may be a result of changing gender roles and conceptions of the individual as a sexual being (e.g. women being seen as autonomous rather than as under the authority of father or husband). Thus, rape in marriage becomes a criminal offence as women's position in society changes its status within marriage itself.

SADOMASOCHISTIC SEXUAL PRACTICES AND THE LAW

How we analyse sexual identity and sexual practice inevitably calls forth varying and conflicting opinions. Consider, for example, the phenomenon of *sadomasochistic sexual practices* (S & M), which involves deliberate pain and humiliation, albeit for the purposes of pleasure. From the point of view of cultural criminology (see Chapter 5), Presdee (2000: 88) makes the observation that 'forms of S & M practices no longer constitute a subculture but are becoming more and more a part of acceptable everyday life'. In evidence of this, Presdee (2000) cites a wide range of movies, books, magazines and even advertising that in some way deals with S & M themes and practices. Most familiar among these to mainstream society is the bestselling novel trilogy *50 Shades of Grey*, which features explicitly erotic scenes involving bondage/discipline, dominance/submission and sadism/masochism. He also notes the widespread popularity of body piercing (including tongue, nipple, penis and clitoral adornments) and its relationship to altered sensuality during sexual activity. For Presdee (2000) the key question relates to why something that seems to be so popular is at the same time routinely subjected to criminalisation (as in several highly publicised cases involving gay men in London). A central reason for this pertains to the use of physical violence as part of the sexual activity. Using the analogy of violent sports (e.g. ice hockey or, closer to home, Aussie rules football), Presdee points out that some types of consensual-based violence are already deemed to be acceptable in society—so why not S & M? In other words, how is legitimacy constructed and socially bestowed when it comes to different types of violence?

One answer to this question is found not simply among conservative lawmakers and traditionalist judges, but within the ranks of critical criminology. In particular, writing from within a radical feminist perspective, Jeffreys (1993) provides a trenchant critique of S & M that hinges upon the notion of 'consent'. Jeffreys (1993) argues that close analysis of actual practices, and careful consideration of how proponents of S & M justify their activities, demonstrates ambiguities at the core of the consent–coercion interface. While Presdee (2000) asserts that consensual S & M ought not to be criminalised, Jeffreys (1993) challenges whether 'consent' is really consent. For example, she points to the idea of *consensual nonconsensuality*—situations where consent is reconceptualised to mean that if you consent to be in an S & M situation, then you somehow automatically consent to let the other person(s) do whatever he or she wants to you (1993: 182). For Jeffreys (1993) this is highly problematic, not least because it seems to allow for incidents where a person who has given the presumed consent later considers that in fact he or she has been seriously assaulted. For Jeffreys (1993) the key issue is not one of criminalisation or decriminalisation; rather, it is about power and abuses of power, under the cover of a nominal 'consent'.

Similarly, Crabbe (cited in Short 2013c) points to the pervasiveness of increasingly misogynistic pornography and the manner in which it is normalising aggressive sex, including fellatio inducing gagging, heterosexual anal sex and double penetrations (where a woman is penetrated anally and vaginally simultaneously). She argues that widespread availability of such imagery to young people (including through mainstream avenues such as popular novels) is distorting their perceptions of sex and pleasurable human relations. Her concern is not to pass judgment on the rightness or wrongness of various sexual practices depicted in aggressive pornography, but rather with the negative consequences for consent among young women; that is, the growing perception among young people that the sexual practices conveyed in hard-core pornography are *the norm* and therefore consenting to engaging in such practices is the *expectation*. As Crabbe puts it (cited in Short 2013c: 16):

> Porn creates a sense of what is normal, what is expected, and that we ought to consent to ways of doing sex that are not just derived from the interaction between those individuals engaged in the experience, and what they would like to be doing. We are hearing many stories from young women about their partners initiating the signature sex acts from pornography and of the women struggling with both wanting to please their partners, wanting to be accommodating and generous in their sexuality, but not wanting to engage in those sex acts.

Essentially, Crabbe and Corlett (2010) argue that pornography is 'eroticising inequality'.

ISSUES FOR CONSIDERATION

WHO IS STUDIED, AND WHY?

There are a range of issues that emerge from analysis of subordinate, inferior and alternative statuses within mainstream society. Interestingly, in one sense 'social exclusion' (which is frequently associated with low social status) also occurs as an unintended consequence of the process of selecting the objects of study. Consider the following quotation:

> As a result of the fascination with 'nuts, sluts and perverts', and their identities and subcultures, little attention has been paid to the unethical, illegal, and destructive actions of powerful individuals, groups and institutions in our society. (Liazos 1994: 381)

Liazos (1994) asks why is it that sociologists and others tend to concentrate on the life circumstances and behaviours of the most vulnerable, less powerful groups in society, more or less to the exclusion of the powerful? In other words, we need to critically address the issue of why we tend to focus on certain categories of people, rather than others, for criminological analysis. The intellectual gaze itself thus has implications for who is studied and why. Further to this, we need to reiterate both the importance of studying the 'top end of town' (see Chapters 5 and 12), and the politics of how research funding and government agencies influence and shape the choices of who we study, and why and how we do so (see Chapter 1). For some social scientists, the key issue is basically one of rules and rule-breakers rather than deviance per se, an approach that suggests that power is central to the analysis (see Box 8.6).

BOX 8.6   DEVIANCE AS RULE-BREAKING

In their book *Deviance and social control: Who rules?*, Marshall and colleagues (2007) observe that deviance can be defined as behaviour that breaks a rule within a social group and is labelled with disapproval. The book looks at the bizarre and everyday behaviours that some sociologists have labelled deviance, including, for example, such characters as witches, anorexics and heroin users. It is pointed out that: 'If right and wrong, normality and deviance were matters of contest between the very powerful and the less powerful, then the contest was what should be studied rather than the behaviour per se' (Marshall et al. 2007: 8). Accordingly, Marshall and colleagues (2007) argue that the best sociological story about deviant behaviour is one that emphasises conflict over rules, and stresses the part played in these conflicts by professions, especially the human service professionals.

   Interestingly, the ways in which rules are interpreted by professionals such as criminologists have major ramifications for how the 'normal' and the 'pathological' are defined, and how those groups, which apparently transgress criminal boundaries more than others, are portrayed within the criminological tradition. Cunneen (1999a), for example, raises the question of the role of criminology in relation to Indigenous people in Australia, and how professional intervention, such as data collection on over-representation within the criminal justice system—but without sustained critique of colonialism—actually contributes to the further repression of Indigenous people (see also Chapter 13). In other words, if there is no challenge to the power relations that sustain certain rules and shape rule-breaking behaviour at a concrete level, then mainstream professionals are in effect gatekeepers of the very systems of deviancy that they study and within which they work.

THE DISTINCTION BETWEEN PERSON AND ACTION

Discussion of subordinated statuses needs to distinguish between people who are marked out on the basis of certain intrinsic qualities (e.g. intellectual and physical state or appearance, and sexuality and sexual preference) and who are treated differently (and unfairly) based upon 'who they are', and specific actions that may be objectively harmful (e.g. unsafe sexual practices, and street violence) and that warrant sanction of people for 'what they do'. The distinction between person and action is indeed crucial. Consider, for example, matters pertaining to sex and health. Anal sex is not exclusively homosexual sex: it is heterosexual practice as well. In regards to the transmission of HIV/AIDS, therefore, the crucial issue is not (homo)sexuality as such, but the question of protected or unprotected anal sex. Problems arise when we conflate certain sexual practices (e.g. anal sex) with deviancy, rather than the health and safety issue of HIV transmission through unsafe sexual practices (Jeffreys et al. 2010).

   The latter also implies certain legal responsibilities and 'duty of care' in sexual activity, insofar as knowingly engaging in unprotected sex as an HIV/AIDS carrier is not only deviant but criminal, regardless of sexual orientation. Furthermore, invocation of the criminal law can stigmatise an entire community, such as occurred in 2008 when a sex worker was charged and imprisoned in the Australian Capital Territory for providing sexual services while 'knowingly infected with HIV'. This occurred despite the fact that no evidence of unsafe practice was presented before the court. Victoria and the Australian Capital Territory are the only two jurisdictions in Australia that prohibit HIV-infected sex-workers from doing sex work. Victoria entrenches the stigmatisation of HIV-positive sex workers even further by allowing HIV-positive community members to hire such sex workers (Jeffreys et al. 2010).

Being young and being female intrinsically makes for a complicated life, especially when we consider issues of status and decision-making. This is as apparent in the case of risk and sex, as it is in other areas of social life. For example, many young women do not feel comfortable with supplying or having condoms on their person. A 'trade-off' is sometimes made between: (a) potential problems or risks associated with unprotected sex; and (b) potential problems or risks associated with insisting on protection and being known as or called a 'slut' because of preventive measures. In other words, 'responsibility' in sexual practice is closely tied to social constructions of different kinds of risk (see White & Wyn 2013). The choices and ambiguities surrounding risk are not only seen in regards to use of condoms. Risk is also constructed around the idea of consent, particularly in relation to how to draw the line between 'yes' and 'no' when it comes to sexual activity. Moreover, the influence of alcohol and the presence of so-called date rape drugs further puts at jeopardy notions of actual and presumed consent.

FRAMING ETHNICITY AND ETHNIC DEVIANCE

Like all deviance, the concept of 'ethnic deviance' is a matter of framing. The framing of ethnicity in society shapes the manner in which the creation of ethic deviance is understood. Ethnicity can be construed in multiple ways, but its invocation as a form of negative demarcation from the majority, a marking of deviance, often masks the root of societal conflict. Ethnic identity itself is fluid. While all persons in a society have attachments to a larger group identity (e.g. based on geographical boundaries, nationhood, race, religion or language), these identifications shift with time. However, they become more salient for individuals under periods of threat. When faced with attack, an individual's identity becomes more defined by their group attachment, which affords safety and trust. Stripping ethnic or cultural difference from a conflict allows recognition of the true source of the dispute—often at the core of 'ethnic' conflict are class conflicts initiated or aggravated by competition for scarce resources; that is, the socio-economic disadvantage of minority groups (Murer 2012). Unfortunately, political opportunism and media-generated racist stereotypes serve to disconnect minority ethnic young people from national identity and reinforce the safety of the 'ethnic' identity group (see Morgan & Poynting 2011). In such circumstances, the 'ethnic youth gang' likewise expresses multiple meanings—for those on the inside and those on the outside—and group violence founded in vilification as well as common heritage comes to dominate street interaction (White 2013a).

CONCLUSION

This chapter has provided a brief outline of how social difference, as translated into different kinds of social status, has an impact upon perceptions of, and responses to, particular population groups. In most of the cases under consideration, the quality of the group—ethnicity, gender, age, ability and sexuality—is intrinsic to the nature of the group in question; that is, people have certain attributes that are part and parcel of who they are, what they are born with and what makes them the person they are in contemporary society. How social difference is constructed has major implications for the legitimacy of certain groups and behaviours in any particular social situation. It also highlights the power relations that ultimately underpin who or what is seen as 'normal' or 'deviant' at any point in time.

When social difference is materially and symbolically translated into social deviance—say, in relation to particular population groups, such as ethnic minority groups or gay men and lesbian women—then not only moral reprobation but often criminalisation is not far behind. So, too, certain social practices whether tied to age, as in the case of juveniles, or diversity of sexual practices across the adult population may be branded 'bad' or 'good', depending upon the wider social climate, including via the judgments of courts and tribunals. The criminalisation of social difference, therefore, is not necessarily about objective harms—it is about defining the boundaries of what are 'acceptable' and 'unacceptable' behaviours, and social memberships, in Australian society.

Chapter 9 is one in a series that examines in some detail conventional street crimes, with a focus on crimes against property, including theft, robbery, vandalism and fraud.

DISCUSSION QUESTIONS

1 Which groups in Australian society have high social status, and which groups have lower social status? Why is this the case and why does it matter?

2 'Criminalisation is linked to social status.' Discuss.

3 'The problem is not one of ethnic youth crime or deviance but rather racism, and the problem is getting worse.' Discuss.

4 'People with disabilities require additional care, support and protection from the state—but often receive prison.' Discuss.

5 'Yesterday's deviance is today's difference.' Discuss with reference to sexual practice.

FURTHER READING

Australian Human Rights Commission (2014) *Equal before the law: towards disability justice strategies*, Australian Human Rights Commission, <http://www.humanrights.gov.au/equal-law-towards-disability-justice-strategies>.

Cunneen, C. & White, R. (2011) *Juvenile justice: youth and crime in Australia*, Oxford University Press, Melbourne.

Marshall, H., Douglas, K. & McDonnell, D. (2007) *Deviance and social control: who rules?*, Oxford University Press, Melbourne.

Presdee, M. (2000) *Cultural criminology and the carnival of crime*, Routledge, London.

Salter, M., Crofts, T. & Lee, M. (2013) 'Beyond criminalisation and responsibilisation: sexting, gender and young people', *Current Issues in Criminal Justice*, 24(3): 301–16.

9 CRIMES AGAINST PROPERTY

CHAPTER OVERVIEW

- PROPERTY AS A RELATIONSHIP
- SOCIAL DYNAMICS OF PROPERTY CRIME
- VANDALISM AND CRIMES AGAINST PROPERTY
- ISSUES FOR CONSIDERATION
- CONCLUSION
- DISCUSSION QUESTIONS
- FURTHER READING

INTRODUCTION

The preceding few chapters have focused on crimes of inequality and social difference—critical dimensions in any analysis of crime and criminality. This and Chapter 10 continue to unpack recorded offending in Australia with a view to analysing in greater detail the different major categories and sub-categories of offending. As with previous chapters, although statistical information is presented, it is not done so unproblematically; attention is drawn to the historical context within which select categories of crime have evolved, the way in which laws are differentially applied, and the institutionalised interests best served by the framing and administration of different laws.

Property crimes, the subject of this chapter, are unlawful acts generally perpetrated with the intention of gaining money and/or property, and usually do not involve the use of force or threat of force against a person. They form one of two major divisions of crime, the other being violent crimes or crimes against the person, which will be examined in Chapter 10. Property crimes not only refer to physical property, such as burglary of items from a home or office, but also to intellectual property, such as the theft of ideas and information (see Chapter 15). Typically, property crime includes unlawful entry with intent (also referred to as break and enter or burglary), motor vehicle theft and 'other theft', which includes offences such as pickpocketing, bag snatching, shoplifting and bicycle theft. This category of crime also includes damage to property, such as graffiti, vandalism and arson.

As this chapter illustrates, most official definitions of, and social responses to, property crime are oriented towards those categories of criminal activity dubbed 'street crime'; that is, activities that are fairly visible (often occurring in public places) and involving transparent methods of commission. This can be contrasted with property and other kinds of crimes perpetrated by corporations and the powerful, such as insider trading and copyright breaches, which are far less visible. As Chapter 12 demonstrates, while these crimes are more likely to involve theft on a grand scale, they rarely attract the same kind of publicity or concerted police attention directed at the more traditional forms of property crime.

This chapter begins by discussing the character of 'property' as a relationship between individuals, contrasting the ways property has been defined under feudalism and capitalism. The contemporary social dynamics of property crime are then examined. This is followed by brief descriptions of traditional property crimes but excludes discussion of cyber-crime as a modern form of property theft, since this is dealt with specifically in Chapter 15. We then examine vandalism and crimes against property as another variant on the theme of property crime.

PROPERTY AS A RELATIONSHIP

Laws relating to the protection of property are largely a modern phenomenon, and are closely tied to the evolution of capitalism as a political and economic system. Before the seventeenth century there were few goods to steal, and most wealth was held in the form of land. In Europe the class that owned the wealth (the land-owning aristocracy) also controlled the administration of justice and the formulation of law. Its members employed servants to protect them and their goods. Consequently, they had little interest in developing property laws, although groups lower down the social scale would have benefited from this, especially those in trade, manufacturing and farming.

The Industrial Revolution of the eighteenth and nineteenth centuries changed this by creating a new class of industrialists for whom legal protection of property was essential. Machinery production made portable goods available in large numbers, and expanded the opportunities for **theft**. A succession of laws designed to protect private ownership was gradually enacted (Hall 1952). The notion of individual ownership was extended to information and ideas, so that by the nineteenth century, knowledge and ideas (artistic and commercial creations of the mind) could be owned through, for example, **intellectual property** laws, which include copyrights, trademarks, patents, industrial design rights and trade secrets.

FEUDAL RIGHTS AND DUTIES

'Property' as a concept cannot be tied down to one particular meaning: the concept is very much bound up with social context, and its meaning has changed over time as society has changed (see MacPherson 1978). At one level, *property*, as such, simply refers to a relationship between humans. The content of this relationship is nonetheless variable depending upon circumstances. This is perhaps most evident in the transition from feudalism to capitalism in Europe.

In the feudal regimes of England in the fourteenth century, for example, property was directly tied to certain social status and social functions (see Fine 1984). Ownership was attached to the performance of definite social functions. Owners had neither absolute rights to use and abuse their property according to their will nor exclusive rights under all circumstances to bar others from use of their property. For example, serfs (peasants), who were essentially in a relationship of bondage to the Lord of the Manor (the person who owned the land they occupied and worked), had traditional rights to use common land held in the open field system for various purposes, such as grazing livestock and mowing meadows for hay. There were, therefore, certain paternalistic or social responsibility constraints on the rights pertaining to private property. For example, an obligation to meet the needs of the poor must predominate over the rights of ownership; feeding those who worked your land was a duty and obligation, even if it meant opening your lands to harvest and hunting by the peasantry.

According to *natural law*, there existed an obligatory collection of rights and duties. These implicated various classes in different ways. For instance, not only did property owners owe paternalistic duties to the poor, but the poor were subjected to all kinds of personal obligations to the propertied. These obligations expressed relations of personal dependence, servility and bondage.

THE CAPITALIST CONCEPT OF PROPERTY

The transition from feudalism to capitalism entailed changes in the mode of production generally (e.g. industrialisation, new applications of science and technology, and the creation of a new wealth class, the *bourgeoisie*) as well as significant social transformation; in particular, the emancipation of the peasantry

THEFT
The taking of another person's property with the intention of permanently depriving the owner of the property illegally and without permission; but without force, threat of force, use of coercive measures, deceit or having gained unlawful entry to any structure.

INTELLECTUAL PROPERTY
Property of the mind or intellect that is protected by legal safeguards, including copyright law, patents and trademarks, the aim of which is to ensure that the profits of creative work or intellectual effort are returned to the legal owners.

from their traditional ties and obligations to the landed gentry, and the release of the nobility from their traditional duty toward those who shared their lands. An important physical manifestation of this was the literal enclosure of land for commons for restricted usage by the owner. Within the context of the prevailing social responsibility framework, this redefinition of social relationships entailed the relocation of the obligations of the poor from individual property owners to the state, in order to avoid oppressive conditions arising for the poor because it reinforced their personal dependence, and for the rich because it imposed upon them arbitrary restrictions' (Fine 1984: 18).

Under feudalism, traditional obligations attached to property served to exclude the majority from new forms of property, including private property (in the case of peasants, who were excluded from substantive property ownership) and international trade (in the case of private businesses, which were confronted by state monopoly charters that excluded them from trade in certain overseas markets). The acquisition of property was therefore a major issue associated with the emergence of a new type of social order. Moreover, from the point of view of technical innovation and broader cultural development, the stagnant, narrow and backward character of economic relations based on personal obligation became a problem. A new sort of 'property' had to come into being if feudalism were to be superseded by capitalism. Indeed, the protection of private property, as defined within a bourgeois rights framework, came to be equated with the goal of universalised justice.

The notion of *private property*, in the new understanding of the concept, was closely linked to liberal ideas of *freedom*, *equality* and *consent*. It came to be identified with individual freedom (of mobility and of labour), private rights (of conscience and of religion) and the notion of equality, in that every property owner was seen to be equal to every other (in that exclusive access, the same rules of trespass and so on applied to all persons, regardless of social and economic standing). Property was no longer tied to obligation; its new foundation was that of self-interest and individual propriety considerations.

CHANGES IN MODES OF PRODUCTION

The shift from feudal property relations to bourgeois or capitalist property relations was fundamental to the wider transitions taking place (see Mandel 1982). These transitions included:

- *the separation of the producers from their means of production and subsistence:* especially the expulsion of peasants from their lands
- *the formation of a social class that monopolises these means of production:* the accumulation of capital in money form and the transformation of the means of production (mechanisation), thereby rendering them so expensive that only the owners of considerable money-capital could acquire them
- *the transformation of labour power into a commodity:* the appearance of a class that owns nothing but its labour power, which is obliged to sell to the owners of the means of production in order to subsist.

CHANGES IN LEGAL RELATIONS

Accompanying these transformations were a series of changes in legal relations, especially with regards to the nature of property relations (see Fine 1984). The most profound change was the movement away from the obligations of *duty* and *responsibility* to the concept of the exclusive power to alienate one's possessions in any manner one desired, without the bonds of custom or traditional responsibility. This shift in the legal and social status of property relations allowed for several interrelated phenomena:

- *the commodification of countryside:* the transformation of production (e.g. stock) into commodity production (e.g. wool), and the sale of privately owned goods (e.g. pheasants) on luxury markets, thereby resulting in the displacement of peasants from the land

- *the movement of labour:* the emancipation of peasants from traditional ties and obligations to the landed aristocracy, thereby freeing them as a workforce of 'free' labourers for the emergent capitalist class
- *the shift in the responsibility of the rich for the poor via customary obligation to the notion of state responsibility for social welfare:* thereby severing the connection between wealth (and wealth generation) and (privatised) social responsibility.

Under capitalism, the law became structurally oriented towards the protection of the property rights of owners of capital, whether private or state. *Capital* has its own specific meaning, and a distinction became drawn between property that is wealth-generating and property that is for direct use. Yet the law provides for a universal protection of bourgeois property rights, regardless of the specific character of the property in question. In this way, bourgeois legal relations became oppressive, in that they became based on individual legal subjects as property owners, and made no formal distinction between capitalist private property (which represents power over labour) and personal private property (which may be no more than labour power) (see Fine 1984; Hall & Scraton 1981).

In other words, the law 'protects the property of every individual irrespective of the economic and social function of that property; it thus protects both the ownership of private consumption goods and of capital goods' (Hunt 1976). This creates the illusion that factual situations are identical because they happen to be reflected in the same legal institution. The social consequence, however, is to reinforce the wealth and power of those with capital over and above the interests of those whose only real property is for their own immediate use (e.g. a house to live in) or for the purposes of subsistence (selling labour for a wage).

Under feudalism, the law tended to be construed in terms of natural law principles that justified the social place and status of the aristocracy (e.g. the notion of the 'divine right of kings and queens to rule'). Under capitalism, the privilege and power of the capitalist class rests upon its protection of capital in its many forms (e.g. money, land, rent or technology). Bourgeois conceptions of private property provide the legal and social cover for the maintenance and perpetuation of this class domination.

SOCIAL DYNAMICS OF PROPERTY CRIME

In societies such as Australia, where private property is at the heart of the economic system (i.e. class-based, capitalist societies), the majority of laws will reflect this fact (e.g. criminal law, corporations law, the *Trade Practices Act*, equity and trusts, and tax law), the efforts of law enforcement will be focused largely on defending property, and property crimes will inevitably constitute the largest category of crime recorded. It is important to note, however, that the measurement of such crimes tends to be biased towards certain types of property offences, especially those proscribed by the criminal law. For example, most recorded property crimes involve:

- no violence
- little or no contact with victims
- relatively small personal loss.

As outlined in Chapter 6, the willingness of victims to report property crime is contingent upon a number of factors, of which insurance status is especially important. For those with property insurance (e.g. house and/or contents, business, car or boat), the prospect of recovering most or all of the losses incurred as a result of a theft serves as a strong incentive to report the crime. However, a large proportion of property crime goes unreported each year because of a variety of factors, including being uninsured, being unaware that property has been stolen, a perception that the amount stolen is too trivial to report, and a lack of confidence that reporting the crime will result in recovery of the stolen goods.

REPORTED PROPERTY CRIMES

STREET CRIME
Highly visible crimes that occur in public spaces and usually involve little skill on the part of perpetrators.

BURGLARY
The unlawful entry of a dwelling, house or any other premises, such as a business, school or shop, with or without force, with the intent to steal; in some states, burglary is referred to in the statutes as 'break, enter and steal'.

SHOPLIFTING
The action of stealing merchandise from a shop or business establishment while pretending to be a customer.

Most definitions of property crime deal with **street crime** varieties that involve a direct and transparent gaining of property, rather than corporate crime and large-scale, organised theft, which is often more difficult to detect. Accordingly, statistics dealing with the official measurement of property crime tend to be based upon selected offence categories. These commonly include (ABS 2011a):

- *Unlawful entry with intent* (UEWI), commonly referred to as 'break and enter' or **burglary**: the unlawful entry of a dwelling (house, flat, unit, caravan, garage or residential shed) or any other premises (including, but not limited to, a business, bank, school, factory, shop or church), with or without force, with the intent to steal. Aside from break, enter and steal, and burglary, other forms of UEWI include unlawful entry to a structure with intent, ram raid (robbery of a shop where the front window is smashed with a vehicle to gain access), smash and grab (robbery of a shop involving smashing of a window and seizing of accessible goods with a quick getaway), and home invasion (burglary of a dwelling while the residents are at home but not involving an assault).

- *Motor vehicle theft*: the unlawful taking of a motor vehicle (car, motorcycle, campervan, truck, bus and plant/equipment vehicles, such as road graders or forklifts) without the consent of the owner/possessor, with the intention of depriving them temporarily or permanently of the use of the vehicle. This category excludes damage to or tampering/interfering with motor vehicles. The theft of motor vehicle parts or contents from a motor vehicle is covered in a separate category of *motor vehicle theft other*.

- *Other theft*: unlawfully taking or obtaining money, goods or services (other than a motor vehicle, or property from a motor vehicle) without force, threat of force, violence, coercion or deceit, with the intention of permanently depriving the owner/possessor of such. This category encompasses a wide range of offences, including but not restricted to theft from a person (pickpocketing, bag snatching not by force, bicycle theft, theft of livestock or animals, and theft of passports, cheques, credit cards and EFTPOS cards), theft from a residential premises (where entry was gained lawfully), theft from a retail premise/business (**shoplifting**, fuel drive-offs, and taking of goods not for sale, such as tools, equipment, furnishings and leaving a restaurant without paying), theft of intellectual property (copyrights, patents, computer software piracy etc.) and fare evasion.

- *Fraud, deception and related offences*: offences involving a dishonest act or omission undertaken for the purposes of deceiving to obtain a benefit. This category is quite extensive, incorporating acts as varied as identity fraud (assuming someone else's identify), cheque/credit/EFTPOS card fraud, income taxation fraud, social security fraud (federal), social welfare fraud (state) and fraud against insurance companies.

- *Damage to property*: the wilful and unlawful destruction, damage or defacement of private or public property (e.g. land, buildings, vehicles, equipment, money or animals) so as to render it imperfect or inoperative. This category includes graffiti, vandalism and arson.

RELATIVE IMPORTANCE OF PROPERTY CRIME

One of the most striking features of recorded data on crime is the overwhelming predominance of property crime. Despite the preponderance of media attention on violent crime, property crime victimisation, both in absolute and relative terms, occurs at much higher rates than violent crime (AIC 2013a; see also Chapter 6). However, when considering the extent of property crime, it is important to be aware of the trivial nature of many of the incidents. Although property crimes such as theft appear in annual police reports as 'serious crimes', these events usually involve no violence or direct contact with victims. For example, as indicated in Figure 9.1, shoplifting has been estimated to account for almost two-thirds (61.5%) of the eight major categories of traditional street crime recorded.

Most property crimes also involve relatively small personal loss. Based on the latest cost of crime figures for Australia (Rollings 2008), it can be observed, for example, that although property loss to shop theft in Australia was estimated to be $756 million in 2005, the median value of shop thefts reported to police across Australia was estimated at $110 million. Overall, shop theft accounted for just over 9 per cent of the total cost of crime in Australia (see Figure 9.1). This compared with the estimated average cost of $1700 per incident of assault (at a total cost of $1.4 billion), $2300 per incident of robbery, $7500 per incident of sexual assault and a staggering $1.9 million per incident of homicide. To put these figures into context, while violent crimes accounted for less than 10 per cent of traditional street crimes in Australia in 2005 (9.1%), they contribute just over a third (35%) of the total cost of crime (see Figure 9.1).

This is not to suggest that the costs of all property crime are trivial. Motor vehicle theft was estimated in 2005 to cost $7000 per vehicle, while burglary was estimated to cost just under $3000 per incident in 2005. The contribution to the total cost of crime was particularly disproportionate for burglary. As indicated in Figure 9.1, while burglary comprised just 6.8 per cent of traditional street crimes in Australia in 2005, it contributed just under a quarter of the total costs of crime (23.8% or $2.23 billion).

SHOPLIFTING

Stealing from retail stores, commonly referred to as shoplifting, is broadly defined as the 'theft of goods for sale, other than motor vehicles, by avoiding payment for those goods' (ABS 2011b: 56). Although, as noted above, the value of items shoplifted tends to be small, the sheer volume of shoplifting that is

FIGURE 9.1   VOLUME AND COSTS OF CRIME, EXCLUDING ARSON, FRAUD AND DRUGS (PERCENTAGE)

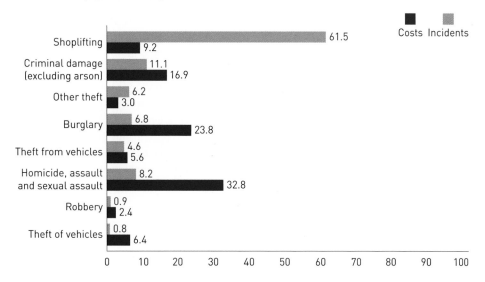

Source: Rollings (2008: xiii)

believed to occur, as well as its overall economic value, warrants close attention. While the actual volume of shoplifting is unknown due to significant levels of under-reporting, inaccurate retail stock systems and low levels of apprehension (Clarke & Petrossian 2012; Hayes et al. 2011), the Australian Retailers Association has estimated the annual cost of shoplifting to the retail industry to be approximately $5 billion (cited in Morgan et al. 2012). Common targets of retail theft in New South Wales between April 2008 and March 2011 were supermarkets (22%), department stores (19.7%) and shopping complexes (10.3%). The top three commonly stolen items were clothing (almost 20%), communications/home entertainment goods (16.5%) and alcohol (14.4%) (Mahomad 2011).

In 2009, it was estimated that the inventory shrinkage (loss to shoplifting, employee theft and administrative errors) rate of 22 retailers in Australia whose collective sales exceeded $23 billion in the 2008–09 financial year was 1.39 per cent of retail sales, which amounted to $2.16 billion (Centre for Retail Research 2009). Employee and customer theft accounted for 75 per cent of inventory shrinkage. These sorts of losses can seriously affect the financial viability of a business. This is particularly the case for small businesses, which lack the security measures available to larger stores and are therefore vulnerable to repeat victimisation, with financially crippling consequences. For instance, a survey of small businesses conducted in 1999 found that there were 674 incidents of shoplifting experienced per 100 businesses (Taylor & Mayhew 2002). A loss in sales of 2–3 per cent for these retailers can amount to a 25 per cent loss in profit (Nelson & Perrone 2000). The effects of shoplifting are not, however, merely confined to the immediate victim, for the costs of crime are generally passed on to consumers.

Interestingly, employees are responsible for a substantial proportion of stock losses suffered by retailers. Figures are not available for Australia, but the 1994 National Survey of Retail Crime and Security conducted in the United Kingdom found that staff theft accounted for 30 per cent of 'stock shrinkage (Nelson & Perrone 2000).

Studies into the motivation of shoplifters suggest multiple drivers (Caputo & King 2011; Klemke 1982; Krasnovsky & Lane 1998; Shtier 2011), which can broadly be categorised as either rational or non-rational. While rational offenders are motivated by economic gain (whether for subsistence or greed), the actions of non-rational offenders is said to be symptomatic of psychological and social stressors, including familial conflict or, in a small proportion of cases, kleptomania (a pathological compulsion to steal). In such instances, the act of shoplifting serves as an antidote to emotional trauma or grief or an outlet for social aggression (Shtier 2011). Often these motives are intertwined. For example, a high percentage of offenders are unemployed, which may be a source of psychological and social stress. For young shoplifters, the excitement itself is also a motivation (Klemke 1982). Situational opportunity is an important determinant, with self-service stores being particularly soft targets for casual shoplifters. In some respects, retail outlets contribute directly to the volume of shoplifting by having liberal return policies (no need to have a receipt) and displaying concealable, removable, available, valuable, enjoyable and disposable (CRAVED) merchandise in an enticing manner or a manner that facilitates theft (unsecured or located close to unprotected store exits). Indeed, shoplifting rates for various items provide a gauge of display appeal to retailers (Clarke & Petrossian 2012; Nelson & Perrone 2000).

BURGLARY

The term *burglary* is one of a number used to describe the unlawful entry or attempted entry of a structure (residential or otherwise) with the intention of stealing. Burglary is commonly referred to as 'stealing from dwelling' or 'break and enter' and appears in the Australian Bureau of Statistics recorded crime—victimisations data under the category of UEWI (unlawful entry with intent). The absence of the use or threat of force is what distinguishes burglaries from residential robberies. The prevalence of burglary in Australia is very high, with just over a quarter (27.2%) of all traditional street crime recorded in 2012 comprising burglaries (ABS 2013a). While burglary can occur in a variety of locations (e.g. private, retail, administrative/professional and community settings), almost three-quarters (n = 151,919 or 71%) of all burglaries occurred in a residential location in 2012, and this proportion has been generally consistent over the past 10 years (66–71%). Given the voluminous nature of residential burglaries, Grabosky (1995: 1) suggests that 'the odds are that most residents of Australia's urban areas will become the victim of a burglary at least once in their lives'. In terms of popular items stolen in burglaries, a recent New South Wales study (Fitzgerald & Poynton 2011) found that in 2010 cash was the item most often stolen in break-ins (31%), followed by laptop computers (26%), jewellery (22.6%), still cameras (15.3%) and mobile phones (14.6%).

Australia's burglary prevalence is also high by international standards. The most recent results of the International Crime Victimisation Survey (ICVS) in 2003–04, which reported data from thirty mostly developed countries, ranked Australia in fifth-highest position in terms of burglary prevalence (2.5%) against the international average of 1.8 per cent. Australia was equal with the United States, but recorded a lower prevalence rate than England and Wales (3.5%) and New Zealand (3.2%) (AIC 2008). Interestingly, while the prevalence rate declined significantly from 3.9 per cent in the 1999 ICVS, the same proportion of Australians surveyed (36%) considered it likely or very likely that their house would be burgled in the forthcoming year.

While burglaries are quite costly, the invasion of privacy and the lost sense of security can have a severe psychological impact on victims, as devastating as the loss or destruction of property itself. Burglary elevates home insurance premiums, accelerates neighbourhood decay and encourages withdrawal into private fortresses and the adoption of private security services (Taylor 1995). Burglary is also an issue for businesses. The burglary of shops, warehouses and offices causes stress, financial loss and practical problems to managers, employers and employees. The 1999 Crimes against Small Business Survey found that 27 per cent of small businesses had experienced a burglary in the preceding financial year (Taylor & Mayhew 2002). Most residential burglaries occur on weekdays in the daytime, between the hours of 6 am and 6 pm, when people are likely to be at work, dropping children off at school or out doing the shopping, and homes are vacant (Morgan et al. 2012). The reverse is true for businesses, with many occurring on weekends and in the evenings (Ratcliffe 2001). As suggested by Cromwell et al. (1991), burglary offences are largely the result of opportunistic exploitation of premises that are rendered temporarily vulnerable.

While residential burglary occurs across the socio-economic spectrum, as indicated in Chapter 6, burglary victimisation is not uniformly distributed across geographic regions, with the most vulnerable households situated in lower socio-economic, high crime-rate areas and subject to repeat victimisation (see also Erdogan et al. 2013; Fitzgerald & Poynton 2011; Grove 2011; Whitworth 2012b). Physical geography plays an important part in the distribution of burglaries for a variety of reasons. Burglars often select targets from locations they observe in their daily activity. This, together with the need to physically travel to and from their home to the crime site, means they tend to choose targets that are in close physical proximity to their homes and which offer known escape routes (Brantingham & Brantingham 1981; de Frances & Titus 1993). Ratcliffe (2001: 3), for example, found that in Canberra the average journey from the offender's home to residential targets was 5 kilometres, and that one-third of burglaries were committed by offenders who travelled less than 1500 metres from their home. The term *distance decay* has been used to describe the way in which the commission of crimes reduces with distance from the perpetrator's home (Rengert et al. 1999).

MOTOR VEHICLE THEFT

Motor vehicle theft is also regarded as a serious problem by law enforcement agencies, partly because of the high rate of theft—in 2013, 54,343 registered motor vehicles were stolen Australia wide, amounting to 149 cars per day or one theft every 10 minutes—and partly because of the financial cost to the community—estimated to be in the order of $626 million in 2012–13, exclusive of the significant criminal justice costs associated with investigation, prosecution and punishment of offenders (CARS 2014; National Motor Vehicle Theft Reduction Council [NMVTRC] 2013). Unlike burglary, which is for the most part committed in residential locations, the chance of a motor vehicle being stolen from a residential setting is only slightly higher (45%) than from a community location, such as a street, footpath or car park (39%) (ABS 2013a).

International research indicates that as with most street crime, motor vehicle theft is closely associated with socio-economic status (Copes 1999; Walsh & Taylor 2007). Research undertaken by CARS (2014), which is funded by the NMVTRC, confirms this proposition within the Australian context, finding that the most disadvantaged areas had a car theft rate of 6.38 per 1,000 vehicle registrations, which was 3.8 times higher than the least disadvantaged areas (1.68 per 1,000 vehicle registrations). Almost three in five (57%) cars stolen in the most disadvantaged areas had no immobiliser, compared to 41 per cent in the least disadvantaged areas. This is likely to reflect the generally newer nature of vehicles in the least disadvantaged areas.

One of the most remarkable features of motor vehicle thefts compared to other stolen property is the high rate of recovery, especially over the past 6 years. Vehicles that are recovered are classified as short-term thefts motivated by opportunistic purposes (e.g. joy riding, transportation or to perpetrate another crime). By contrast, vehicles that are not recovered are classified as profit-motivated thefts. These are thefts that lead to on-sell of the stolen vehicle, either as a whole or in separated parts (AIC 2013a). In 2011, 40,244 of the 55,386 motor vehicle thefts were classified as short term, which equates to a 71 per cent national recovery rate for stolen vehicles. This compares favourably with the United States, which recorded a 61 per cent recovery rate in 2008 (Roberts 2012). As indicated by Figure 9.2, the vehicle category with the greatest proportion of profit-motivated thefts in Australia was 'motorcycle'. Less than half of the 7,701 motorcycles stolen in 2010–11 were recovered (n = 3,258 or 42%).

Politicians are sensitive to community concerns that cars are stolen by young joyriders who pose a risk to both themselves and to others. In response to such concerns, there has been a concerted effort in recent years to establish a multipronged strategy to deal with motor vehicle theft, one that incorporates a range of situational techniques and social prevention approaches (see Chapter 28). This has seen a significant reduction in motor vehicle thefts, with the victimisation rate declining by 66 per cent since 2000 to 245 per 100,000 population in 2011. Victimisation rates did increase, however, in 2011 for the first time since 2000, and continued to increase in 2011–12. Overall, motor vehicle thefts have increased by 7 per cent since 2010 (ABS 2013a; AIC 2013a).

Car theft is attractive to marginalised young men because it offers them various rewards. It helps them establish their masculine identity, and also offers excitement as well as a means of transport, status and prestige among peers and passengers. The physical space inside the car has both a symbolic and practical dimension. The young occupants can escape the intrusion of adults, and they can travel where they want, when they want and with whom they want. They are free to create their own social world (White 1990). This analysis is supported by Salmelainen's (1995) study of young offenders in detention centres, who identified the need for transport (49.6%), and excitement, thrills and fun (24.1%) as the most frequently given reasons for motor vehicle theft.

FIGURE 9.2   SHORT-TERM AND PROFIT-MOTIVATED MOTOR VEHICLE THEFTS BY TYPE OF VEHICLE, 2010–11 (PERCENTAGE)

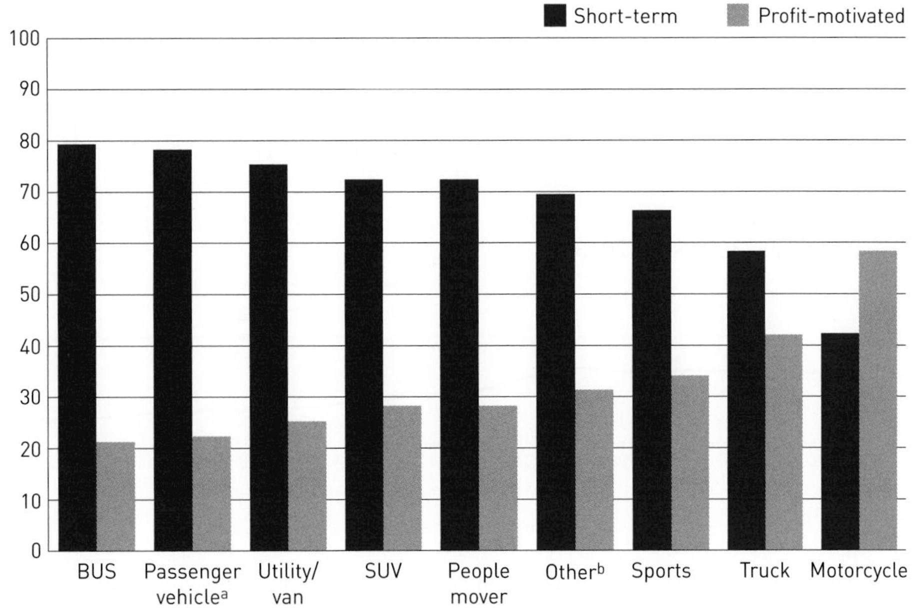

Source: AIC (2013a)

[a] Includes small, medium, large and unknown passenger vehicles

[b] Includes motor homes

DECLINE IN TRADITIONAL PROPERTY CRIME

Up until 2010, the overall trend in traditional property crime victimisation had been one of decline in Australia (see Figure 9.3). This decline was witnessed across the three major categories of unlawful entry with intent (burglary), motor vehicle theft and other theft (which contains a significant component of shoplifting). From 2010, however, victimisation rates began to increase across all categories, despite the fact that the actual volume of crime in some instances reduced substantially (e.g. there has been an 11 per cent decline in robbery incidents since 2009–10). The highest percentage increase over time was recorded against the category 'other theft', which increased by 5 per cent between 2010 and 2011. This was the greatest increase recorded for this category in nine years. Increases in UEWI and MVT victimisation were the first recorded since 2000.

It should be noted, however, that while the actual number of incidents rose markedly in some cases (e.g. there were 26,404 additional victims of other theft in 2011 compared to the previous year), the increases in victimisation rates were relatively small, with both UEWI (965 per 100,000 population in 2011) and MVT victimisation (245 per 100,000 population in 2011) increasing by approximately 1 per cent between 2010 and 2011, and other theft victimisation increasing by 4 per cent (2,155 per 100,000 population in 2011). Moreover, despite increasing since 2011, property crime victimisation rates have decreased dramatically since 2000. In particular, the rate of UEWI victimisation has decreased by 58 per cent and the rate of MVT victimisation has decreased by 66 per cent since 2000.

FIGURE 9.3   PROPERTY CRIMES, 1996–2011 (RATE PER 100,000 PERSONS)

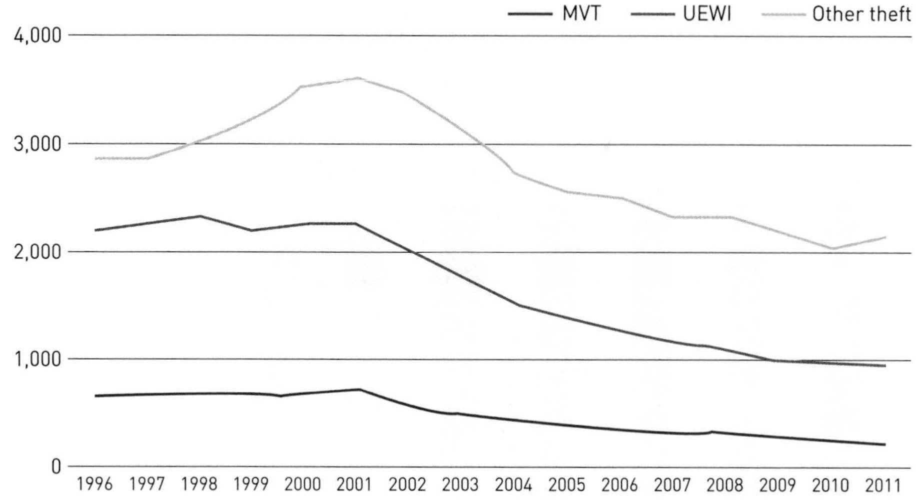

Source: AIC (2013a)

As noted earlier, the 'other theft' category contributes the largest proportion of all crime across the major categories of traditional property crime included in the national statistics. This is not surprising given the broad range of offences within its ambit, including pickpocketing, bag snatching, stealing (including shoplifting), theft from a motor vehicle, theft of motor vehicle parts, accessories or petrol, stealing of stock or domestic animals, and theft of non-motorised vehicles, boats, aircraft or bicycles.

Overall, property crimes occur across a wide variety of locations, as shown in Figure 9.4. This is not surprising given the expansive nature of crimes captured under the traditional property crime rubric. Almost one in three property crime victimisations (31%) occurred in a retail setting in 2011, rendering it the most frequent location for property crime. The next most common location for property crime was a residential dwelling (29%), followed by on-the-street/footpath (14%). Recreational (4%), other community (6%) and transport (6%) were the least likely locations for property crime victimisation.

OFFENDER CHARACTERISTICS

There is no 'typical' property crime offender as such. Property crime involves a wide range of crimes, many different motivations, and a high level of participation by a broad spectrum of the population (Tarling 1993). To some extent, property crime offending is ubiquitous, especially if we consider offences such as shop stealing, which are widespread and involve many different types of individuals across all ages. Nevertheless, conventional property crime tends to be associated with the following offender characteristics:

- young people
- men
- Australian-born population
- people living in areas of high social disadvantage

FIGURE 9.4   PROPERTY CRIME BY LOCATION, 2011 (PERCENTAGE)

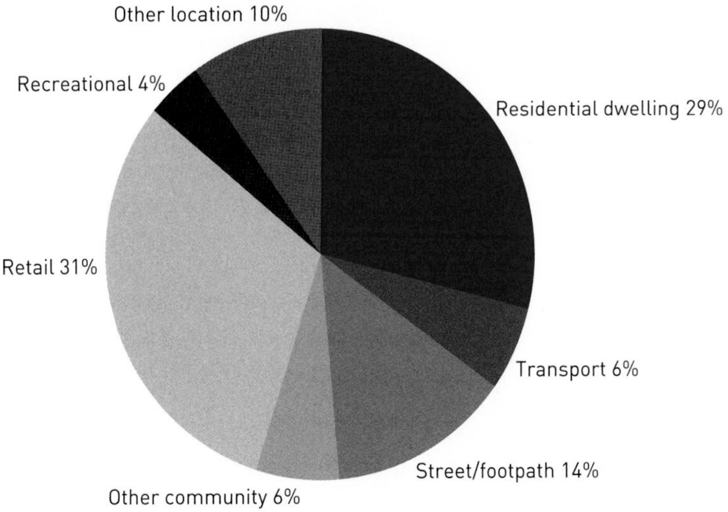

Source: AIC (2013a)

- increased frequency of offending during periods of high unemployment
- certain types of family background (especially those with a history of neglect and abuse)
- poor school performance and school exclusions (truancy and expulsion)
- drug use.

Youthfulness is a particularly striking feature of traditional property crime offending across all major categories (ABS 2014a), and the literature suggests this is a common profile across time and place (Rosevear 2012). For example, in 2012–13, just under half (48%) of all offenders processed for a UEWI were young people aged 19 years or younger, with just under a third (31%) aged 15–19. This represents an offender processing rate of 250.9 per 100,000 population in the 15–19 age bracket. Those aged 15–19 similarly comprised the majority of offenders apprehended for thefts (29% or a rate of 1,210 per 100,000). The recorded rate of offending has consistently been highest in the 15–19 year age group over the past five years. Overall, theft was the most common principal offence against which young people aged 15–19 were processed in 2012–13, comprising one in every five offences (22.2%) (ABS 2014a).

Maleness is the other striking feature of traditional property offending across all categories (ABS 2014a). For example, in 2012–13, 86 per cent of all offenders apprehended for UEWI were male. Males had an offending rate of 102 per 100,000 for this offence, compared to a rate of only 16.6 per cent per 100,000 for females. Likewise, males featured prominently in the theft category. In 2012–13, almost two in every three offenders (64%) processed for theft were male. This represents an offending rate of 393 per 100,000, compared to a rate of 216.3 per 100,000 for females. However, it is important to emphasise that theft was the most common principal offence for which female offenders were processed in 2012–13, comprising just over a quarter (25.5%) of all offences. Research suggests that a large proportion of this is related to shoplifting (Morgan et al. 2012).

PROPERTY CRIME AND SOCIAL DISADVANTAGE

Traditional theft is largely attributable to the existence of social inequality and social disadvantage. This is demonstrated by the fact that the majority of offenders charged, prosecuted and sanctioned for property crimes are working-class defendants, many of whom struggle to make ends meet financially. As discussed in Chapters 5 and 7, low socio-economic status is perhaps the most significant determining factor in cases of street crime, although this, too, is intertwined with other intersecting social causes, such as latent colonialism, in the case of Indigenous people.

A study of burglary conducted by Devery (1991) in Sydney, for example, found that the largest number of break-enter-and-steal offenders come from districts of low socio-economic status. In his analysis of the correlation between social disadvantage and involvement in property crime, Weatherburn (1996: 213) similarly argues that there is 'a strong relationship between the level of social disadvantage in an area and the proportion of its residents actively engaged in some form of property crime'. Neighbourhood-level dynamics, related to economic and social stress on parenting, also has an impact on offending rates (Weatherburn et al. 2001).

Who gets criminalised for property crime arises out of the process of detection, investigation, arrest and conviction, and this process is socially determined. For example, those with less experience (e.g. juvenile offenders) and those who operate in loosely organised groups (e.g. young people) may be more visible in their neighbourhood, and thus more likely to get caught or be spotted in a stolen vehicle (see Cunneen & White 2011). At the other end of the spectrum are those who tend to be arrested less frequently, such as career or professional criminals, who are more skilled and entrepreneurial and may be linked to organised groups (e.g. car theft rings) and who engage in property crime as a 'job'; that is, as a principal generator of income. Again, this reinforces the point that property crime offenders are a varied group, and that there is no 'typical' property criminal.

As previously canvassed in Chapter 6, unlike violent crime such as homicide, a large proportion of property crimes are perpetrated by a small number of repeat offenders. Hence, whereas homicide is usually a one-off incident, the same individual may be responsible for a disproportionate number of property crimes over a given period of time. It is therefore essential to distinguish between those people who participate in property crime and the frequency of their engagement in it. As indicated above, repeat offenders tend to come from disadvantaged social backgrounds. The specific motivations for burglary provide some indication of the class and social dynamics underpinning such crimes (see Box 9.1).

FRAUD AND DECEPTION-RELATED CRIME

Fraud and deception-related crime are also property offences but do not have the same visibility as the traditional street crimes canvassed thus far. The range of fraud and deception-related offences is quite broad, including credit card fraud, cheque fraud, social security fraud, forgery, counterfeiting, scams (e.g. lotteries, pyramid schemes, chain letters, fake notifications or offers from a bank or financial institution or established business, and requests to send bank or credit card details), identity fraud, fraudulent trade practices and many other deception offences (ABS 2012e, 2011a).

It is virtually impossible to estimate the total cost of fraud in Australia, but Rollings (2008) put the figure at $8.5 billion in 2005. Personal fraud alone is considered to have cost Australians $1.4 billion in 2010–11 (ABS 2012e) and, in recent years, has been recognised as a growing threat to personal and financial security, as well as the economy and global commerce. This threat emanates from both non-electronic methods of fraud, often committed through more traditional channels, such as in person,

BOX 9.1   OFFENDER PERSPECTIVES ON BURGLARY

A study of burglary in Tasmania included interviews with 60 imprisoned burglars on their experiences of doing burglary (Goodwin 2007). It found that, while 37 per cent of the respondents said they had a job in the six months before their imprisonment (which, conversely, means that 63% did not), most of these jobs were manual occupations, such as labouring, fruit picking and factory work. Goodwin (2007) found that the legitimate income of the majority of the offenders was quite low, with 62 per cent earning $200 or less from legal means (e.g. employment and social security). On the other hand, the majority (80%) of the offenders stated that they needed more than $200 per week to live on, and about a third of the sample said that they needed $1,000 per week or more. Expenditure included things such as food, rent, clothes, drugs and alcohol. Over half of the offenders had left school before completing grade 10. Most respondents were from socially disadvantaged neighbourhoods and had a history of low income.

There were thirty-three offenders who said they were committing crime on a daily or weekly basis in the six months before imprisonment. These offenders were asked how much money they were getting per week from crime. Twenty-one said they were receiving $1,000 a week or more, and ten of these offenders said they were obtaining $5,000 a week or more. Those who had committed ten or more burglaries in their lifetime (n = 49) were deemed to be 'experienced' burglars. The two most common motivations for committing a burglary were to obtain money (43%) and to obtain drugs (41%). Other reasons for committing burglary included to obtain alcohol, to relieve boredom, and for the rush or thrill it provided. The majority of the experienced burglars had burgled both houses and businesses, but more said that they preferred to burgle businesses rather than houses.

Nearly all of the offenders interviewed had used drugs in their lifetime, with most using substances such as marijuana, amphetamines and morphine in the six months prior to imprisonment. Interestingly, most of the offenders had committed their first crime before they started using drugs, yet a high proportion reported spending considerable amounts each week on drugs. There was also an observable link between burglaries and expenditure on drugs and alcohol and for partying generally.

Fewer than half of the experienced burglars said they usually planned their burglaries, and the methods of target selection described by most lacked sophistication.

Issues of intoxication and chaotic lifestyles go hand in hand with experiences of social deprivation, marginalisation and uneven employment opportunities.

Source: Goodwin (2007)

and electronic methods of fraud, perpetrated in digital and online environments. Indeed, the rapid expansion and availability of internet technology and the increase in electronic storage, transmission and sharing of information has increased people's vulnerability to electronic fraud in recent years (see Chapter 15).

Perhaps because of the difficulties associated with detection (much large-scale fraud involves professional thieves and organised crime syndicates, some on an international scale) and the humiliation associated with having fallen prey to scams and/or having lost substantially large sums of money, fraud is believed to be one of the most under-reported offences, with fewer than 50 per cent of incidents reported to police or other authorities (AIC 2013a). The one exception is fraud against the Commonwealth and, in particular, welfare fraud, which is far likelier to be detected (Prenzler 2011).

WELFARE FRAUD

Welfare fraud, also referred to as 'benefit fraud' or 'social security fraud' is the practice of fraudulently claiming Commonwealth benefits (e.g. the parenting payment, Newstart allowance [unemployment benefits], disability support pension or youth allowance [student]); that is, intentionally claiming a benefit when not entitled. Centrelink does not produce fraud estimates per se, reporting instead on payment 'errors' detected through compliance and eligibility reviews.

A study by Prenzler (2011) found that over the three-year period from 2006–07 to 2008–09, approximately 15.7 per cent (n = 1,972,833) of the 12,574,725 Centrelink reviews undertaken resulted in the cancellation or downward adjustment of benefits. Overall, $1.4 billion in overpayments was identified, with fraud accounting for over a quarter (26.2%) of invalid payments. With regards to the most common types of fraud, the single parenting payment and Newstart allowance featured as the top two among the fifteen most common benefit types, together accounting for 72 per cent of convictions and $33.5 million in debt in the 12-month period 2008–09.

On average, approximately 15.1 per cent of fraud investigations resulted in a prosecution referral to the Commonwealth Director of Public Prosecutions (CDPP). Almost two-thirds of referrals to the CDPP resulted in actual prosecution and 98.8 per cent of prosecutions resulted in conviction. It is noteworthy that while a number of offences against the Commonwealth can be referred to the CDPP, including internal corruption and fraud (incidents committed by employees or contractors of a government agency), 69 per cent of all defendants prosecuted by the CDPP in 2008–09 were referred by Centrelink (Prenzler 2011). That figure increased slightly to 70 per cent in 2010–11 (AIC 2013a). While the study did not provide an offender profile, other research by the ABS (2011d) indicates that, unlike UEWI and theft, where the median age of offending is 21, offenders are older in fraud cases, with a median age of 29 years.

Between 2001–02 and 2008–09, there was a 54.5 per cent increase in the number of Centrelink customers subjected to a compliance review. The prospects of detecting welfare fraud are therefore increasing significantly (Prenzler 2011). This increase has been enabled by a range of anti-fraud measures adopted in Australia and internationally, including data-matching capabilities between government agencies, enhanced identity verification checks, covert surveillance and video recording, and greater use of forensic accounting practices in fraud investigations. Many of these practices have been criticised for generating a 'punitive approach to welfare support' that relies excessively on prosecution and stigmatises welfare recipients (Bradbury 1988: 26). Moreover, there is a real possibility of criminalising welfare recipients who have inadvertently misrepresented their eligibility circumstances. Marston and Walsh (2008) argue that this is increasingly likely due to the casualisation of the labour force and the unstable circumstances of the working poor and unemployed—society's most marginalised and vulnerable (Marston & Walsh 2008).

VANDALISM AND CRIMES AGAINST PROPERTY

Property crime is not only about theft. It also incorporates concerns about damage to property and various kinds of vandalism. Vandalism involves the wilful and deliberate destruction or defacement of property. Although few vandals actually get caught (Geason & Wilson 1989), the evidence of such activity permeates the urban environment in the form of wall graffiti, broken windows and street lights, damage to playground equipment, smashed telephone boxes and carving on park benches.

The legal term given to vandalism is **criminal damage**. It refers to a wide range of offences against property where the objective is damage of the property rather than financial gain. Malicious damage to property is one of the most numerous offences recorded by the police. In 2012–13, over half a million households (n = 555,900) reported at least one incident of malicious property damage (ABS 2014b). Allowing for a 4.3 multiplier effect to account for unreported incidents (see Rolling 2008), it is estimated that in 2012–13 there were 2.4 million incidents of criminal damage. Although many incidents are relatively trivial, they are a source of concern to the community. In the 2009–10 Crime Victimisation survey, one in five respondents considered graffiti to be a social disorder issue in their local area, with a similar proportion also considering property damage to be a social disorder problem in their local area (ABS 2011c). Although comparatively minor per incident (approximately $1,250), the aggregate costs associated with this form of damage can be significant, totalling approximately $1.58 billion in 2005 (Rollings 2008). La Grange (1996), however, argues its costs are often overstated.

Research on the nature of vandalism indicates that it is distributed evenly among young people generally. La Grange (1996: 140) argues that while 'some vandals may be antisocial youths who deliberately seek ways to express themselves in costly rampages of destruction—as is believed by the public and portrayed by the media—many are ordinary youths who do their damage spontaneously and with little thought of its costs or consequences'. This is consistent with self-report data on juvenile offending, which suggests that such offending is more uniformly spread across the youth population than arrest figures may indicate (Cunneen & White 2007; Mukherjee 1997). On the other hand, Hollands (1995: 65) found that only 13 per cent of the young people interviewed in his study in Newcastle, England admitted to ever personally being involved in any kind of vandalism, with the vast majority of acts being petty in nature (e.g. stealing street signs or traffic cones). Perhaps the best way to interpret vandalism is to consider the varied meanings that attach to the phenomenon. These are summarised in Box 9.2.

GRAFFITI

The question of meaning is also important to consider in attempts to understand the nature of **graffiti**. Graffiti comes in many forms, from scribblings on public toilet walls to murals in the CBD. It can

CRIMINAL DAMAGE
A wide range of offences against property, including vandalism, where the objective is destruction, damage or defacement of the property rather than financial gain.

GRAFFITI
The unsolicited, unauthorised and deliberate defacement of public or private property by writing, scratching, marking, spraying, stencilling or affixing of materials.

BOX 9.2   THE MEANINGS OF VANDALISM

- *Acquisitive vandalism:* damage is incidental and effected in the course of acquiring money or property such as stripping lead, removing street signs and looting coin boxes.
- *Tactical vandalism:* this is a conscious tactic used to advance some end other than acquiring money or property, such as through the use of slogans and graffiti of a political nature.
- *Vindictive vandalism:* this is a form of revenge against persons or institutions believed to be the source of personal grievance, such as school vandalism.
- *Play vandalism:* this is motivated by curiosity and the spirit of competition and skill. The fact that property may be destroyed is often minor or incidental, as in the case of skateboarding.
- *Malicious vandalism:* this is apparently mindless and wanton destruction related to subjective feelings such as boredom, despair, failure and frustration, depending upon context.

Source: adapted from Muncie (2009) and Cohen (1973a,b)

---

involve offensive words or phrases, creative self-expression or political protest. But whether written by pen, spray can or paint brush, it is always public and displayed on someone else's property. A study in New South Wales (Fitzgerald 2000: 1) found that most graffiti occurred at educational institutions (40.4%), followed by residential (15.5%) and transport locations (14.8%).

In terms of offender profile, a study of graffitists apprehended in Western Australia between 2003 and 2009 (Taylor et al. 2012), found that almost two-thirds (65.5%) were male, and while age of first offence ranged from 6–55 years, the mean age was 15 years. A small number (13.7%) of offenders were pre-teens at the time of their first graffiti offence and just over a fifth (21.9%) were adults at the time of their first graffiti offence. This confirms previous research that identifies graffiti writing as primarily an adolescent activity initiated between the ages of 6–17 years, with a peak offending age of 15. While just over a third (36.5%) only committed a single offence in the three-year period under review, the remaining majority were recidivist offenders, with almost a third (29%) offending in all three years. Again, this confirms the earlier findings relating to property offenders generally; that is, a small pool of offenders tends to be responsible for a large amount of crime.

Graffiti varies greatly in the message being conveyed and the style of its presentation (see, for example, Dovey et al. 2012; Ferrell 1996; Forrester 1993; United States Bureau of Justice Assistance 1998). Understanding how and why it occurs involves asking questions about its meaning in its various forms, and why specific types are produced. Such an analysis has important implications for crime-prevention strategies and for interpretation of the place of graffiti within youth culture generally (Iveson 2000; White 2001; see also Sutton et al. 2014).

Even a cursory review of different graffiti forms reveals the following types of graffiti work:

- *Political graffiti:* graffiti with an explicit political message of some kind. Mostly this form of graffiti originates from the grassroots, from individuals and groups who wish to challenge the legitimacy of the present political economic order or specific government policies. It might include anarchist graffiti (with the anarchist circle around an 'A'), socialist graffiti ('Down with the IMF and World Bank'), feminist graffiti ('Wimmin Take Back The Night') and national liberation graffiti ('Free East Timor'; 'English Out of Ireland'). It can be racist or homophobic. Political graffiti can also occasionally reflect the efforts of the powerful to claim legitimacy, in the form of top-down propaganda designed to look like grassroots activity. For example, when the United States invaded the small Caribbean island of Grenada in the 1980s, US troops allegedly spray painted 'Welcome' slogans in the main town centres.

- *Protest graffiti:* also political in nature, but targets the form and content of commercial signs. It includes the activities of the BUGAUP (Billboard Utilising Graffitists Against Unhealthy Promotions) organisation, as well as spontaneous actions of individual citizens against racist, sexist and violent billboards and advertising. This graffiti is designed to highlight the offensive nature of mainstream, commercial visual objects in our cityscapes and public spaces.

- *Graffiti art:* tends to be a well-organised, skilled activity that has a strong aesthetic dimension. It involves the crafting of 'pieces' in which artistic effort is the major consideration. It is informed by defined techniques, learning strategies, evaluation and group forums. It is a socially organised activity with subcultural elements of association, group deliberation, initiation processes and development of mastery of execution.

- *Tagger graffiti:* this form of graffiti is often, but need not be, linked to graffiti art. In some cases, it is seen to represent the first stages of a 'career' in graffiti art, in which novices begin by simply applying themselves to low-level 'tagging' of city sites. The emphasis is on being 'seen' in as many places as possible. It often takes the form of peculiar forms of writing, with distinctive signatures being developed to establish individual and/or group identity. The message is simply one of 'I'm here' and 'This, too, is my space'.

- *Gang graffiti:* not simply created to establish a presence, but also serves to claim territory. The intent is to communicate claims about gang identity and prowess, and to establish, often in a threatening manner, that this or that gang rules a particular neighbourhood. Whether a group of youth is in fact a gang as such is irrelevant. Middle-class suburbs may be targeted, even though the members of the group do not engage in criminal gang activity. The connotation of the graffiti is that particular territory is the preserve of certain young people.
- *Toilet and other public graffiti:* may contain a wide range of messages. It is intended to communicate certain points of view, to be part of a 'discussion', to 'gossip', to establish ascendancy of some writers over others or simply to have fun by stirring the pot. The precise character and content of the graffiti will tend to vary according to location (e.g. train stations, bus shelters or university student toilet blocks).

The location of graffiti provides insight into the circumstances of its production (see, for example, Carrington 1989). Where the graffiti is located can imply a wide variety of protagonists, messages and dynamics underpinning the graffiti production. There are differences between the toilet graffiti of males and females, the substantive content of train graffiti and the types of wall graffiti in particular urban sites. The physical place of graffiti implies different types of audiences (e.g. girls only) and different types of messages (e.g. emphasis on sexuality and social relationships).

Graffitists crave public recognition—to have people view their work—but the very public nature of the act of doing graffiti means that it is also risky. Accordingly, Ferrell and Weide (2010: 51) contend that 'each act of writing graffiti involves a deliberate decision, weighing visibility, location and risk'. Some locations are considered 'safe' places for graffiti production (e.g. toilets), while others are 'dangerous' in terms of the risks accompanying the production process (e.g. moving trains). This influences who does what type of graffiti and why. These factors can be linked to particular conceptions of social identity, such as male bravado stemming from certain notions of masculinity, which, in turn, may be associated with particular kinds of risk-taking behaviour on the part of young men.

Graffiti is meaningful activity: it is undertaken for a reason, including youthful rebellion against social normativity, the construction of sub-cultural identities, a manifestation of creativity and energy, and a form of communication between youth group members. How and why it takes places varies enormously (see, for example, Carrington 1989; Dovey et al. 2012; Farley & Sewell 1976; Ferrell 1996; McAuliffe 2013; Taylor 2013). Vandalism implies destruction, whereas graffiti is generally creative and intended not to destroy existing surfaces but, if anything, to preserve them—in order that there be spaces to comment, protest, demonstrate artistic skill or identify territory. Graffiti writing, in its many forms, is often seen as a fairly normal rather than exceptional aspect of everyday social life.

How vandalism (and graffiti) is defined, however, does have a bearing on general perceptions of graffiti. As a broad category, the notion of vandalism does little to illuminate the substantive and varied nature of graffiti work. Yet, from one point of view, graffiti can be seen as vandalism, insofar as it affects the preservation of property in a particular way; namely, its appearance. In this respect it can be said to be 'bad' insofar as it is perceived to deface existing surfaces in an unfavourable (and illegal) way. However, it can also be seen to be street art and therefore 'good' if, for example, it is associated with legal graffiti sites or with spray paint graffiti artists who are commissioned to decorate bus shelters. In Melbourne, for instance, the graffiti-covered laneways are considered a premier tourist attraction, featured in travel books and international tourism promotion, and the Lord Mayor, Robert Doyle, has even referred to one lane as a 'nursery' for young graffiti artists learning their trade (Gough & Arup 2013). The activity may be the same, but the social context is what determines whether it is deemed to be vandalism (Dovey et al. 2012; McAuliffe 2012; Young 2012).

ISSUES FOR CONSIDERATION

THE ELDERLY AND PROPERTY CRIME

As people and property change, so too will the nature of property crime. For instance, older people are more likely to be victims of financial abuse (e.g. fraud, deception and commercial exploitation) than of predatory crime (e.g. robbery, assault and homicide). Australia is presently experiencing the phenomenon of structural ageing. This concept refers to changing demographic patterns based upon the age composition of the population. Populations change in age composition as a result of four interrelated dynamics: births, deaths, immigration and emigration (Jackson 2001: 203). At the moment the trend in Australia is for the median age to be old; that is, for the population as a whole to be weighted towards the older rather than the younger end of the age spectrum. The country is experiencing structural ageing (the increasing proportion of the population to be found at older ages), as well as numerical ageing (the absolute growth in the number of senior citizens).

These trends carry with them greater opportunity for property crimes directed at the elderly, who are more likely to own their own home and hold more assets than younger generations. For example, as people get older they often convey the power of attorney to younger loved ones, especially adult children. However, both within families and in those instances involving trusted outsiders (e.g. lawyers or accountants), there is greater scope for the phenomenon of substitute decision-making processes. These basically involve the financial ripping-off of elderly people through illegal or illegitimate means, particularly in cases where elderly people suffer from dementia or other age-related illnesses that render them fragile or that impair their ordinary capacity for judgment. In 2013, Seniors Rights Victoria estimated that 40 per cent of all cases of elder abuse presenting to their organisation involved financial abuse (Petrie 2013). Will property crime against the elderly increase alongside the shifts in structural demographic patterns and, if so, how?

NEW TECHNOLOGIES AND THEFT

We can also anticipate new and more extensive kinds of theft associated with the development of new technologies for purchasing goods and services (e.g. internet and electronic commerce). Such technologies, which are getting ever more sophisticated and prevalent, are now relied upon for exchanging money for goods and services in traditional areas, including healthcare, accommodation services and retail, banking and investment services. The new world of communication technologies is the 'natural' world of young people, who have been described as digital natives (see White & Wyn 2013). That is, young people today have grown up with the technologies and are intimately familiar with them. Mobile phones, iPods, iPads, MP3s, DVDs, CDs, social media blogs and emails: the range of technologies and digital cultures that pertain to these technologies is growing rapidly. So, too, is the possibility for various kinds of property-related fraud and consumer rip-off. Downloading a certain call tune for your mobile phone may be very expensive. Answering a call may turn out to be a financial nightmare. Texting on the wrong telecommunications plan could well translate into huge debts. If not directly implicated in crime, the costs associated with the new technologies may well propel some into crime as a means to afford what the digital age has to offer.

NEW FORMS OF CRIME PREVENTION

Another issue relating to property crime has to do with the displacement effect of new forms of crime prevention and property protection (Schneider & Kitchen 2002). For example, the threat or risk of burglary can lead to architectural, urban planning, design and security measures that protect certain spaces (e.g. the gated neighbourhood, residences with full-time security guards, office buildings with guards, malls and shopping centres with strict rules of entry). One consequence of this may be that certain types of property crime may well be displaced to other areas that are less able to afford the crime prevention measures on offer commercially. In other words, crime will flow to those areas where reduced levels of effort, resources and money have been put into security. However, displacement may take different forms not simply related to place:

- *spatial or geographical displacement:* the same crime is committed in a different place; for example, in the following suburb
- *temporal displacement:* the same crime is committed against the same target at a different time; for example, in the evening instead of the day
- *tactical displacement:* the same crime is committed against the same target, but using a different modus operandi (i.e. different way or by different means); for example, ram raids instead of manually smashing a shop front
- *target displacement:* the same type of crime is committed, but a new target is selected in place of the original; for example, from burgling offices to burgling residences
- *type of crime displacement:* there is a change in the nature of criminal activities from the type of crime originally intended; for example, from break-and-enter to street mugging.

What some individuals or groups do to protect themselves against property crime will not only affect how and where property crime generally will occur, but also which types of crime will be committed.

A good example of tactical and target displacement in recent years relates to motor vehicle theft. Motor vehicle theft rates have dropped dramatically since 2001 (see Chapter 28), primarily due to the introduction of technological advances in vehicle security, including standard installation of electronic engine immobilisers, which require access to a vehicle's keys and transponder to steal the vehicle. As an innovative response to this impediment, the National Motor Vehicle Theft Reduction Council (NMVTRC) has noted a trend towards increased residential burglary as a means of accessing the keys that will enable a secure car to be stolen (NMVTRC 2013). In a recent NMVTRC study, a quarter of all cars stolen were taken as a result of a house burglary (Butt 2014). In essence, this amounts to double victimisation. Furthermore, it has been observed that thieves are increasingly targeting newer model vehicles (fewer than five years old), with 70 per cent of these thefts perpetrated with the use of stolen keys (Butt 2014). This targeted and tactical displacement would appear to be a consequence of the increased effort to commit crime, the idea being that if the effort is going to be increased, then the reward should be also. Finally, the NMVTRC has suggested that home burglaries committed with the intention of stealing vehicle keys have become more brazen, with offenders electing to enter occupied premises and resort to violence, or the threat of violence (NMVTRC 2013).

MORAL GEOGRAPHIES

McAuliffe (2012) reminds us that moral philosophy (otherwise known as ethics) has at its core a concern with differentiating between good and bad, right and wrong. The concept of moral geographies looks at the relationship between ethics and space; that is, the relationship between normative expectations of behaviour as geographically contextual, and consideration of appropriate and inappropriate use of space. It is an area of obvious relevance to the discussion of graffiti and the manner in which it is variously celebrated or criminalised. For instance, some street art has become popular with many members of the public, culminating in galleries specialising in street art and the listing of street art in the world's largest auction houses, including Bonhams and Sotheby's. However, while some street artists have met with commercial success, including the much-celebrated British artist Banksy, it is important to recognise that their works involve the same illegal activity as graffiti and, indeed, many famous street artists started off as illegal graffitists (Young 2012). Just as art is in the eye of the beholder (and so, too, it seems the law), notions of 'property' are similarly contested. As research by Young (2012: 311–12) concludes, graffitists do not make decisions on placement of their art based on 'the supposed ownership of a wall or fence', but rather based on the norms of graffiti culture, which 'respect the hierarchy of writers or artists'. Moreover, while the law considers graffiti 'property damage', many graffitists would consider urban spaces as 'conglomerations of surfaces' that offer different opportunities for visibility of their works. Essentially, society's anxiety over the imagery projected by illegal graffiti (as depicting social decline) has meant that people engaged in such activity are criminalised despite the same work being actively promoted in sanctioned spaces (e.g. in Melbourne's laneways).

CONCLUSION

This chapter has provided discussion of various crimes against property: both property theft and vandalism of property. Underpinning contemporary notions of property crime are very specific conceptions of 'private property', notions that reinforce the right of individuals to exclusive use of their possessions, generally without community obligations or duties. In a society in which private rather than communal property dominates, it is not unexpected that the most extensive categories and prosecutions of crime will be property crime.

The discussions in this chapter also reinforce the point that most of this kind of crime is committed by people at the lower end of the socio-economic scale; that is, crimes such as burglary, welfare fraud and motor vehicle theft tend to be committed by individuals and groups who already suffer from some kind of social disadvantage. Such disadvantages are compounded by personal drug and alcohol use, and the combination of factors that makes individuals live life on the edge. Crimes against property are not, however, the exclusive preserve of the poor, the vulnerable, the substance addicted and the unemployed. As discussed in later chapters, the powerful likewise commit property crimes of great magnitude, and corruption (another form of 'property' crime) is linked to crimes of the state. In either case, the main victims or losers are those who can least afford to have their money and possessions taken or ruined.

Chapter 10 continues to spotlight 'street crime', but focuses on crimes against the person; that is, street violence and violent crimes.

DISCUSSION QUESTIONS

1   What are the key differences between feudal and capitalist notions of property?
2   What are the most common forms of property crime, and in what ways do they affect the ordinary person?

3   What explanations can you suggest for the observed decline in traditional property crimes?

4   'Welfare fraud is largely a crime of poverty.' Discuss.

5   'Graffiti is both a celebration of urban freedom and a blight on the landscape.' Discuss.

FURTHER READING

Fine, B. (1984) *Democracy and the rule of law: liberal ideals and Marxist critiques*, Pluto, London.

Goodwin, V. (2007) *Burglary in Tasmania: the offender's perspective*, Briefing Paper, no 4, Tasmanian Institute of Law Enforcement Studies, University of Tasmania, Hobart.

Marston, G. & Walsh, T. (2008) 'A case of misrepresentation: social security fraud and the criminal justice system in Australia' *Griffith Law Review*, 17(1): 285–300.

Nelson, D. & Perrone, S. (2000) 'Understanding and controlling retail theft', *Trends and Issues in Crime and Criminal Justice*, no 152, Australian Institute of Criminology, Canberra.

Young, A. (2012) 'Criminal images: the affective judgement of graffiti and street art', *Crime, Media, Culture*, 8(3): 297–314.

10 CRIMES AGAINST THE PERSON

CHAPTER OVERVIEW

- STREET VIOLENCE AND VIOLENT CRIME
- HETEROSEXISM AND HOMICIDE
- ISSUES FOR CONSIDERATION
- CONCLUSION
- DISCUSSION QUESTIONS
- FURTHER READING

INTRODUCTION

As indicated in the previous chapter, property offences represent the bulk of all recorded crime in Australia. Notwithstanding, the most widely feared criminal offences are those associated with violence, such as murder, rape, assault, and robbery. Readily sensationalised by the media, these types of activities are frequently presented as a potential threat to all and as increasing. The threat of danger from unpredictable strangers is a common theme in media reports and fictional programs (see Chapter 2). So, too, is the notion that everyone is a target for such violence. Within the context of 'stranger danger', it is also acknowledged that women are more prone to be victims of sexual assault and men more likely to suffer from unprovoked violence on the street. Indeed, for most people, fear of physical or emotional harm is greater than concern about material loss (Indermaur 1996; Tulloch et al. 1998; Weatherburn et al. 1996).

Criminal violence of these kinds is not the only lethal or serious form of violence. As a later chapter will demonstrate, violence is also linked to state interventions, allowing phenomena such as torture and extrajudicial killing (see Chapter 13). Nevertheless, when the public thinks of criminal offences, the assumption is that the most serious of these relate to violent street crime. Moreover, public perceptions of the level of violent crime are greatly disproportionate to the actual prevalence of such crimes in the community (Davis & Dossetor 2010). Accordingly, this chapter considers the nature of violent crime, and the social dynamics linked both to its occurrence and official responses to it.

A major theme of the chapter is to expose how the seriousness of, and explanations for, crimes such as homicide are socially constructed and how this framing of harm is subject to variability. For example, women who kill men, and men who kill gay men, are issues that can be interpreted sociologically through the lens of heterosexism. Heterosexism refers to the domination of a particular kind of gender order, one that assumes binary categories of sexuality (e.g. gay or straight) and privileges one over the other (straight over gay). What this lens shows us is that certain types of actions associated with certain types of social situations give rise to social and legal definitions of harm that are highly contestable. The reproduction of a particular gender order is implicated in how courts have defined and responded to certain types of homicide.

STREET VIOLENCE AND VIOLENT CRIME

As far as the criminal justice system is concerned, 'violent crime' refers to the following crimes against the person (ABS 2011b):

- *Homicide and related offences:* the unlawful killing, attempted killing or conspiracy to kill another person (includes murder and manslaughter).
- *Acts intended to cause injury:* acts of force, injury or violence (excluding homicide and related offences) or threat of such (in the form of face-to-face direct confrontation, and where there is reason to believe that the attempts or threats can be immediately enacted), which are intended to cause injury but not kill another person and where there is no sexual or acquisitive element (includes common **assault**, serious assault either resulting in injury or not resulting in injury, stalking, drink/food spiking and setting mantraps).
- *Sexual assault:* physical and intended physical contact of a sexual nature directed toward another person who has not consented, or has consented as a result of intimidation or deception, or whose consent is proscribed (e.g. incest, rape and intended or attempted rape). Sexual assault is considered 'aggravated sexual assault' when it involves actual sexual intercourse, the infliction of injury, possession or use of a weapon, sexual assault against a child, or when penetration occurs in the company of other offenders.
- *Kidnapping, abduction and false imprisonment:* the unlawful taking away or confinement of a person against their will, or the will of their parent, guardian or custodian, or attempted threat of abduction (including for the purposes of ransom or gain, sexual intent or intention to marry).
- *Robbery:* the unlawful taking of the property of another (with the intention to permanently deprive them of it) by the use, and/or threatened use, of immediate force or violence. Robbery is considered aggravated when it involves the infliction of injury or violence, the use of a weapon, or is committed in the company of other offenders. Though this category of crime clearly involves an element of property crime, it is categorised as a violent crime, given the use of force or threat of force renders it a more serious offence (AIC 2014a).
- *Blackmail and extortion:* unlawful demand for money, property or some form of benefit from, or intended to cause impairment to another person, under threat of continued violence should the demand not be met. Blackmail or extortion may involve the use and/or threatened use of immediate force or violence but, importantly, must involve the threat of future violence if demands are not met.

As Weatherburn (2011: 1) observes, it is important to acknowledge that, like all acts or omissions punishable by law, acts coming under definitions of violence constitute a continuum from less serious or harmful (e.g. pushing someone in the chest) to the more serious (e.g. assaulting someone so severely that they are hospitalised or even killed), and that what is defined as *violent crime* varies over time and from place to place. Moreover, a careful appraisal of violence must include the violence perpetrated by powerful institutions, such as transnational corporations and nation-states (see Chapters 12 and 13). These harms are contentious from the point of view of the definition of criminality, and of denial of harm, precisely because of the power relationships they embody and the interests involved. For present purposes, our concern is mainly with street violence, and later with particular kinds of homicide.

VIOLENT CRIME

Traditionally, most police and court attention has been concentrated on violence associated with street crime and, more recently, within domestic settings. Assault is by far the most frequently experienced

HOMICIDE
Unlawful interpersonal assaults and other acts directed against another person that occur outside the context of warfare, and prove fatal (includes murder and manslaughter).

ASSAULT
The direct infliction of force, injury or violence upon a person, including attempts or threats, providing the attempts or threats are in the form of face-to-face direct confrontation and there is reason to believe that the attempts or threats can be immediately enacted.

ROBBERY
The unlawful taking of property, with intent to permanently deprive the owner of the property, from the immediate possession of a person or an organisation, or control, custody or care of a person, accompanied by the use and/or threatened use of immediate force or violence.

form of violent victimisation in Australia, and has been consistently so over time (see Figure 10.1; see also Chapter 6). Due to discrepancies in the recording of assault data across jurisdictions, the ABS ceased reporting aggregated assault data some time ago. Although such information is available from Australian states and territories, changes in the ABS requirements for data collection in 2011 have meant that assault victimisation data from Queensland, Victoria and Tasmania no longer meet the criteria for inclusion in national statistics. Consequently, the national picture for assault is incomplete. Bearing this caveat in mind, it can be ascertained that an aggregate 116,103 assaults were officially recorded across the remaining jurisdictions (New South Wales, South Australia, Western Australia, the Northern Territory and the Australian Capital Territory) in 2012, representing a victimisation rate of 968 per 100,000 population across those jurisdictions. This compares to victimisation rates (across Australia) of 80 per 100,000 population for sexual assault, 58 per 100,000 for robbery, 2.8 per 100,000 for kidnapping/abduction and 2.8 per 100,000 for murder (ABS 2013a).

Violent acts are overwhelmingly crimes committed by males. In 2012–13 (ABS 2014a), males comprised 75 per cent of all offenders processed for acts intended to cause injury as a principal offence, 85 per cent of all offenders processed for murder and 95 per cent of all offenders processed for sexual assault. Furthermore, while violent crimes are perpetrated by offenders across all age categories, crime patterns indicate that offending rates are highest among the young, especially the 15–19 age group. For example:

- the rate of offending for acts intended to cause injury was 738 per 100,000 population in the 15–19 age group and this ratio diminished with each subsequent age group (examples include 720 per 100,000 for 20–24-year olds, 510 per 100,000 for 35–39-year olds and 91 per 100,000 for 55–59-year olds)
- the rate of offending for robbery/extortion was 84.7 per 100,000 among 15–19-year olds, compared to the next highest rate of 42 per 100,000 for 20–24-year olds
- the rate of offending for sexual assault was 60 per 100,000 for 15–19-year olds compared to the next highest rate of 40 for 20–24-year olds.

The exception to this pattern is homicide, where the highest rate of offending is within the 20–24 year age category, at 8.6 per 100,000 compared to 6.1 per 100,000 15–19-year olds. Overall, however, the median ages for violent acts against the person are significantly higher than those for property crime. In particular, the median ages for UEWI and theft were 20 and 21 respectively in 2012–13, compared with median ages of 29 for acts intended to cause injury and abduction/harassment, 31 for homicide and 33 for sexual assault. Robbery was the exception, recording a median age of 20 but, as indicated earlier, this crime involves an acquisitive element and therefore straddles the property/person divide.

With regard to victimisation, males are assaulted at higher rates than females for all age categories except the 15–24-year age group (AIC 2013a) and, overall, only 28 per cent of victims were assaulted by strangers in 2012 (ABS 2013a). Context is, however, essential in understanding the experience of violent victimisation by different sub-populations in Australia. When recorded victimisation data is disaggregated by sex, it becomes apparent that assault, like homicide, can be divided into two major categories: men who assault men in a public setting, and men who assault women in their home. Women were almost twice as likely as men to be assaulted in their home in 2012 (64% compared to 38% of men) and to be victimised by a family member (49% compared to 17% of men) (ABS 2013a). By contrast, males are assaulted by strangers at over twice the rate experienced by females (193 per 100,000 population compared to 75 per 100,000 for females in 2011) (AIC 2013a).

Sexual assault victimisation shares many of the same general characteristics as assault. Most obviously, contrary to popular misconception, sexual assault is predominantly perpetrated in residential settings (64%) and by known assailants (81% in 2011) as opposed to strangers (ABS 2013a). However, in stark contrast to the broader category of assault, females are victimised at significantly higher rates (133 per 100,000 population in 2011) than males (26 per 100,000 population) across all age categories. Females in the age bracket of 15–19 years recorded the highest victimisation rate for sexual assault—a rate greater than four times the overall female rate of victimisation for sexual assault.

As canvassed in Chapter 6, Indigenous Australians and, in particular Indigenous women, are over-represented as both victims and offenders of violent victimisation relative to population share. In general, Indigenous people experience violence at rates typically 2–5 times the rate experienced by non-Indigenous people, and rates of violent victimisation are even higher in some remote communities (Bryant & Willis 2008; Wundersitz 2010). It has been observed that levels of recorded violence are generally higher in regional and remote locations, increasing in inverse proportion to the size and remoteness of the location (Carrington et al. 2010; Memmott 2010).

Again, robbery proves the exception to the general profile of violent victimisation. Only 9.6 per cent of all robberies were perpetrated in residential locations in 2012, with the majority (50%) committed in community settings and over a quarter (29%) taking place in retail locations (ABS 2013a). Overall, males experience higher rates of robbery victimisation than females across the age spectrum, especially in the 15–19 and 20–24 year age categories. Almost two-thirds of all robberies were unarmed, but of those incidents perpetrated with the assistance of a weapon, knives were the weapon of choice in just under half (47%), followed by firearms (17.5%). Similar to theft, robbery can be experienced by business operators, with the issue of cash in transit (CIT) armed robbery attracting attention in Australia in recent years. This involves the perpetration of an armed robbery against an armoured or non-armoured vehicle transporting valuables such as cash, securities, jewellery, bullion and other such currency (Smith & Louis 2010). Between 2000 and 2008, 61 CIT armed robberies were recorded by the larger cash in transit companies across Australia. The vast majority of these were perpetrated by male offenders and while age of offender details were scant, the average age appears to be higher (20–29 years) than for other property offenders (see Chapter 9) and many violent offenders. Moreover, while most robberies occur at night or in the early hours of the morning, CIT armed robberies mainly occur between 6 am and 11.59 am (56%).

TRENDS OVER TIME

Official records provide quite a lot of information about how often, when and where serious crimes such as homicide, assault and robbery take place. They also tell us a great deal about the victims and perpetrators of violent crime. As indicated in Figure 10.1, some crimes—especially homicide—seldom change in terms of number of incidents per year. Homicide rates are virtually static, in the sense that there is little real variation from year to year. Though the rate per 100,000 people fluctuates yearly (due to the relatively small number of victims) it has never exceeded two per 100,000 over the past 16 years, and the overall trend has been slightly downward over the course of the past two decades (AIC 2013a; Bricknell 2008). Similarly, the rate of kidnapping/abduction victimisation has never been higher than four per 100,000 population over the same timeframe, peaking at four per 100,000 in 1999 before decreasing to 2.3 per 100,000 in 2012 (ABS 2013a).

Other crimes, such as assault and sexual assault, are more likely to fluctuate, and to increase or decrease according to reporting trends and fluctuations. The rate of recorded assault rose significantly across Australia between 1995 and 2006. For the reasons outlined earlier, national rates are no longer able to be monitored systematically. Sexual assault peaked in 2001 and, since then, has fluctuated annually but stabilised in the past few years. Robbery seemed to peak in 2001 and has since then generally declined, although armed robberies increased by 4 per cent in 2012. However, recent analysis of violent crime in Australia points out that increases in recorded assault, especially sexual assault, may be an artefact of increased reporting of assault, as much as indicating actual increases (Bricknell 2008). For example, greater awareness and public understanding of child protection issues could be correlated with the large increase in recorded assault and sexual assault among males and females under the age of 14 years. Similarly, the introduction of specialist police intervention in the area of domestic violence, such as Safe at Home in Tasmania and the establishment of family violence units in Victoria (over thirty operating across the state) may be linked to both an increased reporting of domestic violence incidents, and increased prosecutions related to this form of violence (Kleinman 2014).

FIGURE 10.1   VIOLENT CRIMES, 1996–2011 (RATE PER 100,000 PERSONS)

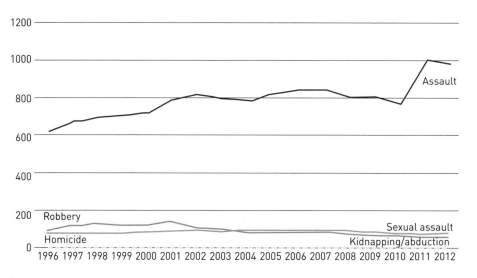

Note: Homicide and kidnapping/abduction occur at rates of less than five per 100,000 each and are difficult to distinguish on this chart. Assault figures exclude Queensland, Victoria and Tasmania for 2011 and 2012; therefore, rates for those years are based on aggregate population of relevant jurisdictions; changes in assault figures should be interpreted cautiously.

Source: AIC (2013a); ABS (2014b)

HOW SOCIETY VIEWS STREET CRIME: 1880S LARRIKINS AND TODAY'S GANGS

Establishing the actual prevalence of violent crime is thus not simply a matter of reflecting its general occurrence within the community, but is intertwined with the nature of contemporary law enforcement procedures as well as existing reporting formats and communication strategies. The other thing to realise about violent crime is that the visibility and extent of such crimes is frequently attached to specific types of group formation and public events. Moral panic (see Chapter 2) helps to frame how citizens and residents perceive violent crime, especially in public spaces. Analysis of moral panics and violence alerts us to the fact that concerns about street crime and, in particular, fear over 'youth gangs' are in fact perennial (Collins et al. 2000; Poynting et al. 2001; White 2013a).

For instance, children and youth of the working classes in the nineteenth century were implicated in a succession of moral panics relating to their activities and presence on the street. From the mid-1800s onwards, most major cities in the Western world witnessed the emergence of, and panics over, groups of young people on the street. Variously branded—from street Arabs in London, to hoodlums in San Francisco, to larrikins in Melbourne—the banded-together large groups of young men were essentially linked to urbanisation and industrialisation.

It was in Sydney and Melbourne in the 1880s that the Australian youth group formations known as the *larrikins* were most prominent and visible, although these groups were also of concern in places such as Brisbane (Finch 1993; Finnane 1994a; Maunders 1984; Murray 1973). The larrikins tended to have a distinctive form of dress, featuring hard black hats, bell bottomed trousers, high heeled and pointy boots, colourful scarves and collarless shirts, although the descriptions of men and women tended to be highly exaggerated in media reports of the day (Murray 1973). By the 1880s, many of the larrikins (and their female partners, the *larrikinesses* or *donahs*) were organising into *pushes*; that is, gangs. These pushes sometimes had initiation ceremonies, and some appeared to be highly structured (Murray 1973).

Extensive negative media treatment of larrikins and larrikinism, from the 1880s to the turn of the century, saw concerted attempts to curtail their activities. According to Murray (1973: 78), the term 'larrikin' was to gain an official status in the records of crime in 1883. In relation to an assault and robbery, the description of the wanted youths stated that they are of 'larrikin appearance'. Once established, the term then morphed into a new kind of fixed status: the larrikin (see also Finnane 1994a; Grabosky 1977).

As the history of *hooliganism* tells us, such behaviour is far from unique to larrikins or to this particular period in time (Pearson 1983). But the association between larrikins, larrikinism and specific types of offences allows for an even greater sense of targeting and labelling. It actively facilitates and justifies official interventions that are highly distinctive, discrete and discriminatory.

A century later, it is the so-called ethnic youth gangs and, in particular, Middle Eastern gangs of Sydney that are featured in moral panics about street-present youth (Mills & Keddie 2010; Poynting et al. 2004; Poynting & Mason 2008; White 2013a). Like the push larrikins, these youth likewise take it to the streets. It is here where they, too, are most visible. They, too, are notable for their appearance. And they, too, have managed to create their own category of offence, for which they are named: those pertaining to 'Middle Eastern appearance'. This time, however, the Lebanese youth is considered a 'foreigner' as well as an 'outsider'. This is so, even though history tells us that, like the street Arab and the larrikin, contemporary youth are products of their own time, neighbourhoods and circumstances. They are 'made in Australia' (White 2013a, 2008a).

TYPES OF PUBLIC VIOLENCE

Public violence associated with groups takes many different forms, ranging from gangs through to gatecrashing and other forms of crowd 'disorder'. Consider, for example, the following examples of public group violence:

YOUTH GANGS

Although studies of gang development, composition and organisational infrastructure reveal that they do not arise out of malicious intentions, but rather form out of a complex tapestry of subcultural, ideological and economic motivations that mainly revolve around security and survival

(Lynch & Krzycki 1998), *youth gangs* are almost by definition implicated in violence. While, periodically, gang members may amass in numbers, using SMS and phone technologies, their engagement in street fights include organised battles as well as spur-of-the-moment conflicts. Contemporary Australian gang research emphasises the fluid nature of youth group formation, while acknowledging the centrality of violence to gang membership compared to those young people who do not identify as a gang member (White 2006b; White 2013a; White & Mason 2006). While sometimes involving large numbers of people, gang violence tends to be highly targeted in terms of protagonists. It is rarely random, and it occurs on a frequent basis. It is not 'surprising', but is central to the very idea of gang-related behaviour.

RIOTS

Riots describe a situation in which large numbers of people seem to spontaneously engage in frenzied unlawful, antisocial and violent behaviour that is highly emotional, and sometimes undirected, but often involves protest against alleged police violence (Barkan 2013; McDonald 2012). Recent race riots in the Australian setting have seen hundreds of people take to the streets, generally directing their anger at property such as cars, and to authority figures such as the police. The trigger for riots on Palm Island, and the Sydney suburb of Redfern in 2004, was the death of young Indigenous people apparently in relation to some kind of police intervention (see Cunneen 2007). In the western suburbs of Sydney, in Macquarie Fields, things came to a head after a car chase led to the death of two young local men (see Lee 2005). Longstanding resentments within marginalised communities can suddenly come to the fore when circumstances change quickly. As analysis of the Bathurst Motorcycle Race riots in the 1980s shows us, the actions of the police themselves can serve as a catalyst for riotous behaviour (Cunneen et al. 1989). In these particular cases, the riots were purposeful, in that they had specific meaning for the participants, and reflected longstanding antagonisms that found their expression in anti-authority resistance. In other words, there is a social history to each of these events. Much the same can be said about the Cronulla riots of 2005, which were based upon an ostensible concern to 'defend' the beach against 'Outsiders' (see Chapters 7 and 8).

MOBS

Mobs, on the other hand, have a slightly different social dynamic (Barkan 2013). While mob violence is superficially similar to riots, it also exhibits distinctive features. Here, the key variable is 'the crowd', and the transformation of the crowd, interacting under intensely emotional sentiments, into a mob. Consider, for example, the following: a group of school students gather in the Queen Street Mall in Brisbane (2004), and shortly thereafter a brawl breaks out involving dozens of young people; at Skyworks in Perth, unchecked alcohol consumption leads to the rapid acceleration of extensive street fighting and random assaults (2004) (see, for example, Knowles 2004; Morfesse & Gregory 2004). In these instances, there need not be any 'purpose' or 'intent' to the violence. It happened spontaneously, and grew out of the crowd dynamics.

GATECRASHERS
Uninvited individuals or groups of individuals that attend a private event.

GATECRASHERS

Gatecrashers likewise can be involved in events that are sparked largely by immediate crowd dynamics rather than intent to harm (see Box 10.1). Recent years in Australia have seen a litany of reports about how gatecrashers have destroyed property and threatened people at private birthday parties and the like (ABC 2014a; Silverman 2011; Thompson & Doherty 2012; Toohey 2003). From Adelaide to Sydney,

Melbourne to Perth, the presence of hundreds of gatecrashers at some parties has been facilitated by new communication technologies, such as SMS and Facebook, and the search by some for venues that do not rely upon security guards and bouncers to keep order. Not all gatecrashed parties end in violence. Again, this largely depends upon the atmosphere of the event, the composition of the group, the quantity of alcohol consumed and how order is maintained by hosts.

Two kinds of violence have been noted. The first involves fights between partygoers (between different groups of gatecrashers, or between the host group and the 'invading' group). The second involves fights against the police, where the 'battle with the cops' can become the objective of the gatecrashing participants (see Toohey 2003). If police–gatecrasher conflicts occur over time, a pattern of ritual confrontation may develop in which the purpose of taking over the street is less about gatecrashing than setting up the confrontation to come.

BOX 10.1   GATECRASHING AS A SOCIAL PHENOMENON

- *What:* gatecrashers are those people who attend a private party without an invitation
- *When:* usually weekends, at someone's special occasion, such as an eighteenth or twenty-first birthday party or a wedding
- *Who:* young people between 14 and 25 years of age; active participation of private school students; all classes and ethnic backgrounds
- *Why:* the demise of school dances and reliance on private parties; availability and costs of the night-time economy for teenagers under 18; the thrill of getting past security and/or the anticipation of something 'happening' that is different; the promise of excitement and stimulation
- *How:* large numbers of people (up to several hundred) congregating together; heavy alcohol use; often late arrival (after closing time of pub, club or bottle shop); internet and SMS texting as sources of information; sometimes congregation outside premises
- *What:* may add to excitement of the party; may be associated with violence (conflict is linked around refused entry or being asked to leave); may involve weapons and at times serious injury or death; may involve police baiting

Source: Sutton et al. (2008)

The presence of a large number of people in one place—the formation of crowds—can shape group behaviour, depending upon the purpose of the crowd formation. In some crowd situations, mob-like behaviour may emerge, insofar as being in a crowd seems to offer the opportunity to 'lose one's mind', and thereby to lose the normal social controls that guide decent human interaction. *Mob mentality* describes the situation in which the crowd dictates general behaviour over and beyond the individual.

Although gatecrashers can be dealt with by way of existing laws, including trespassing, and assault and criminal damage charges (where violence or property damage is involved), South Australia has legislated specific gatecrashing laws—*Summary Offences (Gatecrashers at Parties) Amendment Act 2007* (SA). Breaches of this legislation attract a maximum penalty of 12 months' jail or a fine of up to $5,000 for refusal to leave immediately when asked to do so by an authorised person. In 2014, Queensland also enacted amendments to the *Police Powers and Responsibilities Act 2000* (Qld), which gives police additional powers to deal with out-of-control parties. These are defined as 'a gathering of at least 12 people with at least three engaging in out of-control conduct [which] includes things like trespassing, damaging property, disorderly conduct, fighting, doing obscene acts, making unreasonable noise, throwing objects to harm people' (Queensland Police 2014: 1). Under the law, gatecrashers who cause or contribute to an event becoming out-of-control can be fined a maximum of $12,100 or be imprisoned for up to 12 months. Party/event organisers can also be prosecuted.

VIOLENCE AND DRINKING PATTERNS

Much of the literature indicates that aside from the demographic variables canvassed already (being young and male), social environment plays a significant role in acts of violence. A major shaping effect on social environments and the nature of interpersonal relations within these is that of alcohol and other forms of drug use (AOD), such as 'ice' (see Chapter 11). The ABS annual Crime Victimisation survey (ABS 2014b), which reports on the experience of victimisation (reported and unreported) across a representative sample of Australians, found that of the estimated 449,000 physical assaults disclosed by participants in 2012–13, AOD was considered a contributory factor in 83 per cent of cases. Overall, males comprised an estimated 67 per cent of victims of AOD-related physical assault. There is also a clear association between age and the involvement of AOD as a contributory factor in physical assault. Specifically, the younger the victim age category, the higher the proportion of AOD-related assault, with 21 per cent of victims of AOD-related physical assault aged between 18 and 24 years of age.

Research has found a strong and positive association between frequency of patronage at licensed premises and the likelihood of violent victimisation (Brennan et al. 2010; Kershaw et al. 2008). Certain categories of licensed premises are more frequently associated with increased likelihood of the risk of alcohol-related harm compared to others, with many male-on-male assaults occurring in close proximity to hotels, pubs and nightclubs (as opposed to clubs and restaurants). The propensity for assaultive violence also tends to cluster in areas with spatially dense distributions of alcohol outlets (Grubesic & Alex-Pridemore 2011). Moreover, within and across the types of licensed venues, the potential for alcohol-related violence is increased by high-risk exhibit features, such as the continued serving of intoxicated persons and the offering of discounted drinks between certain hours; and environmental factors, such as uncleanliness, uncomfortable settings, poorly designed seating and bar access, and poor ventilation (see Briscoe & Donnelly 2001; Graham & Homel 2008).

Violence around licensed premises is also associated with frustrations arising from queuing outside clubs, pubs and nightclubs, and associated patron perceptions of discriminatory and/or unnecessarily delayed processes of entry. The proliferation of vertical drinking establishments has also been linked to increased levels of alcohol-related harms. These consist of establishments in which patrons are forced to stand while drinking and have nowhere to place their glasses. This is associated with an increased pace of drinking and consequential social harms (Nicholas 2008). In general, a small number of problematic licensed premises are associated with a disproportionate amount of violence, with hotels and nightclubs being most problematic. Hotels with extended or 24-hour trading record a greater number of assaults compared to those with trading standard hours (Briscoe & Donnelly 2003, 2001).

At a population level, more drinking tends to lead to more violence, and less drinking to less. However, at the aggregate level, it has been noted that there are clear variations between different drinking cultures in the fraction of violence attributable to drinking. For example, the proportion of alcohol-related violence is higher in Nordic and eastern European countries than in Mediterranean countries in Europe (Felson et al. 2011; Room & Rossow 2001). Broad cultural contexts thus have a significant influence on how one drinks, and the association between drinking and violence generally.

This is also relevant to how men in groups drink, an issue explored in depth by Tomsen (1997a,b). The social context of collective drinking means that antisocial behaviour is a built-in feature of a top night out for young men: 'Rowdy acts of misbehaviour, like pushing, arguing, swearing, loudness and obscenity, are all valued for being part of a continuum of social rule-breaking which heightens the pleasurable experience of drinking as time out' (Tomsen 1997b: 29). Thus the question of masculinity, a central feature of most violence in Australian society, also features in discussions of drinking patterns as well.

AOD has also been implicated in the case of intimate partner violence, both physical and sexual (Devries et al. 2013; Wundersitz 2010), as well as homicide. In their review of homicides committed in Australia between 2008–09 and 2009–10, Chan and Payne (2013) concluded that alcohol consumption—by either the victim or the offender—preceded nearly half of all homicide incidents (47%). Alcohol consumption by the victim was more frequent in the case of acquaintance homicides (46%) than those involving strangers (18%) or domestic homicides (26%). By contrast, offender consumption of alcohol was slightly more prevalent among acquaintance homicides (43%) than domestic homicides (36%).

TYPES OF HOMICIDE

Homicide is unlawfully causing the death of another person. A broader definition, provided by Daly and Wilson (1988: 14), is that it refers to 'those interpersonal assaults and other acts directed against another person (e.g. poisonings) that occur outside the context of warfare, and that prove fatal'. Australian law recognises that the death of a person at the hands of another may take a variety of forms. It may be deliberate and planned, thus constituting *culpable homicide*, or it may be the unintentional consequence of a lawful act, such as the administration of a drug by a suitably qualified person, which accidentally and non-negligently results in the death of the patient. This form of homicide is termed *excusable homicide*. *Justifiable homicide*, which is also exempt from prosecution, covers homicides that occur as the result of the legal demands placed on an individual, such as the police shooting of an armed suspect. While culpable homicides meet the full force of the law, excusable and justifiable homicides do not.

Culpable homicides are divided into **murder** and **manslaughter**. Murder is the intentional killing of another by a person who is sane and who is old enough to be legally responsible for the act, a killing that results from reckless indifference to life (where there was an intention to cause grievous bodily harm in the knowledge that death or grievous bodily harm is probable), or a killing without intention occurring in the course of committing a crime (felony murder). Manslaughter covers a range of culpable homicides that satisfy the elements of murder but where there are mitigating circumstances. There are two main forms of manslaughter (ABS 2011b; Polk & Warren 1996):

- *voluntary manslaughter*—the unlawful killing of another person while deprived of the power of self-control by virtue of significant **provocation** or excessive self-defence, intoxication or a mental abnormality or defect that amounts to diminished culpability (e.g. post-natal depression; see De Bortoli et al. 2013)
- *involuntary manslaughter*—the unlawful killing of another person that does not include any malice or intent to kill, but rather results from some other negligent (criminal, gross or culpable) act or omission (e.g. the omission of an action to care for a dependent, such as an infirm, elderly person or a child, or an industrial death under grossly negligent circumstances) or unlawful or dangerous act (e.g. assault, reckless driving or driving under the influence).

It is important to note that for the purposes of national data collection, the AIC, which runs the National Homicide Monitoring Program, excludes driving-related fatalities from its definition of homicide, with the exception of those immediately following a criminal event, such as a robbery or

MURDER
The intentional killing of another by a person who is sane, and old enough to be legally responsible for the act, or a killing resulting from reckless indifference to life or the unintentional taking of a life in the course of committing a crime (felony murder).

MANSLAUGHTER
Culpable homicide that satisfies the element of murder but involves mitigating circumstances; for example, as a result of provocation or excessive self-defence (voluntary manslaughter), or as a result of negligent acts or omissions, or unlawful or dangerous acts (involuntary manslaughter).

PROVOCATION
A legal defence in cases of homicide where the behaviour of the victim precipitated his or her death by causing the offender to suddenly and temporarily lose self-control; if this is accepted as a mitigating circumstance, the charge of murder is commuted to manslaughter.

a motor vehicle theft. By contrast, the ABS includes all cases of driving causing the unlawful death of another person as a result of culpable, reckless or negligent driving. Published data on national homicide figures will therefore differ, depending on the source.

Perpetrators of homicide in Australia are overwhelmingly male, comprising between 91 per cent (2008–09) and 82 per cent (2006–07) of offenders historically. The female rate of offending has remained fairly stable since 2008–09 at 0.4 per 100,000 population, whereas male offending rates have declined from a peak of 3.8 per 100,000 in 1992–93 to 2.5 per 100,000 between 2008–09 and 2009–10 (Chan & Payne 2013: 24–5). Female offenders have historically been older than male offenders, peaking at between 35 and 39 years, and with a median age of 38 years, whereas the age profile of male offenders has historically been younger, with a median age of 29. Between 2008–09 and 2009–10, 59 per cent of all homicides were committed by offenders aged less than 35 as compared with 41 per cent of females. In general, violence rises steeply towards the end of the male offender's teenage years, peaks in the early to mid-twenties, and then falls rapidly (Chan & Payne 2013: 26; James & Carcach 1998: 27). Consistent with historical trends, Indigenous Australians were over-represented as homicide offenders between 2008–09 and 2009–10, with an offending rate five times higher (7.1 per 100,000 population) than non-Indigenous offenders (1.3 per 100,000 population). This over-representation was more pronounced for males (almost six times higher than the rate of non-Indigenous males) than females (almost three times higher than non-Indigenous females) (Chan & Payne 2013).

Most victims of homicide are also male (68%), and have been so historically, although almost a third are female, and females are over-represented as victims of intimate partner homicide (61% or three in five). Males are more likely to be the victims of a friend or acquaintance (86%). Indigenous Australians were also over-represented as victims, with a rate almost four times that of non-Indigenous Australians. This over-representation is even more marked for Indigenous women, who had a victimisation rate of 3.5 per 100,000 population between 2008–09 and 2009–10, compared to 0.7 per 100,000 for non-Indigenous women (Chan & Payne 2013).

Between 2008–09 and 2009–10, almost three-quarters of all homicides occurred between people who knew one another (see Box 10.2). Over a third of all homicides occurred between friends or acquaintances (37%); with an almost equal proportion (36%) occurring in domestic contexts—of these, two-thirds (66%) occurred between intimates. Only 13 per cent of all homicides occurred between strangers, which is a slight decrease on the historical trend (Mouzos 2002: 12–13). When strangers are killed, the perpetrator is almost invariably male. In a ten-year analysis of patterns of homicide by females, only 8 per cent occurred between strangers (Mouzos 2002: 31). Although they attract the greatest public attention, multiple homicides in public settings and serial murders are relatively rare in Australia.

BOX 10.2   HOMICIDE: OFFENDER–VICTIM RELATIONSHIPS 2008–09 TO 2009–10

- *Domestic homicide:* an incident involving the death of a family member or other person within a domestic relationship—comprises 36 per cent of homicide victims across the following sub-categories:
  - intimates partner homicide: where the victim and offender are in a current or former intimate relationship, including spouses and ex-spouses, de factos and former de factos, current or former boyfriends or girlfriends, extramarital lovers and partners or former

partners (including same-sex relationships)—comprises 66 per cent of all domestic homicides

- filicide: parental killing (including custodial and non-custodial parents or step parents) of a son or daughter (includes infanticide, which involves the killing of a child less than 1 year old)—comprises 12 per cent of all domestic homicides
- parricide: the killing of a custodial or non-custodial parent, or step-parent by a child—comprises 11 per cent of all domestic homicides
- siblicide: the killing of one sibling by another—comprises 2 per cent of all domestic homicides
- other family relationships: the killing of an individual by someone related to them but not otherwise classified above (such as a grandparent, aunt/uncle or cousin)—comprises 9 per cent of all domestic homicides

- Acquaintance *homicide:* an incident involving a victim and perpetrator known to, but not residing with each other, including friends, neighbours, sex rivals, gang members and business relationships—comprises 37 per cent of homicide victims
- *Stranger homicide:* where the victim is 'relatively unknown' to the offender (unknown or known for less than 24 hours)—comprises 13 per cent of homicide victims
- *Unclassified (relationship unknown):* this category comprises nearly 8 per cent of homicide victims

Source: Chan & Payne (2013)

HETEROSEXISM AND HOMICIDE

Heterosexism is a defining feature of who kills whom, and how; that is, most homicide is committed by males; the 'public' victims of homicide are generally men; and the 'private' victims are generally women. This socially structured pattern reflects the dominance of heterosexism as a particular mode of sexual identification and practice. From honour killings of wives and daughters to violence perpetrated to defend male honour in public places (see Polk 1994b), homicide tends to reflect certain notions of masculinity and use of male violence. As demonstrated in the next two sections (and in Box 10.3), heterosexism is also reflected in how the law and legal authorities deal with issues such as women who kill, and men who kill gay men.

HATE CRIME

Homicide that goes against the general pattern, in that it involves people who do not generally know each other, usually involves particular circumstances. For example, **hate crime**, sometimes described as bias crime or prejudice-related crime, is violence, bigotry and hostility that is directed at vulnerable individuals or groups on the basis of their actual or perceived sexuality, disability or membership of a racial, ethnic or religious minority group. Often, the motive behind the violence is the intimidation of the group as a whole (Cunneen et al. 1997; Garland 2011). According to Perry (2009), hate crime is intended to emphasise the 'othering' of those visibly different, and both reflects and reinforces existing hegemonic power structures and hierarchies of domination and subordination. Violence includes assault, homicide, vilification, harassment and attacks on property, including firebombing and graffiti. In Australia, most hate crimes have been directed against minority groups, including

HETEROSEXISM
The domination of a particular kind of gender order—one that assumes binary categories of sexuality (such as gay or straight) and that privileges one over the other (straight over gay). It is linked to the practices of hegemonic masculinity that assert the dominance of males over females.

HATE CRIME
Violence that is directed at individuals or groups on the basis of their actual or perceived sexuality, disability or membership of a racial, ethnic or religious minority group.

BOX 10.3   VIOLENCE AND HETEROSEXISM

'Sexual desire has important links to human unconscious drives and to the differences between male and female bodies, but all human sexuality is a highly variable and culturally divergent matter. Recognising this is the first challenge of understanding sexual prejudice and related violence' (Tomsen 2009: 1). In the book *Violence, prejudice and sexuality*, Tomen (2009) acknowledges that sexual desire is very diverse, and is shaped by culture and changes over time. However, popular (and some expert) opinion that reproduces the belief that one's sexuality is preordained and closed ('We are born straight or gay' as universal categories) means that sexual prejudice can appear as natural, with devastating social consequences.

In particular, Tomsen (2009) demonstrates how this binary model of sexuality has very serious ramifications, especially in regards to violence directed against sexual minorities, including 'homosexual' men. In explaining such violence, there is a need to unpack how sexuality is socially packaged and incorporated into hegemonic notions of masculinity, and recognise how heterosexism is inherently based upon social exclusion through the construction of normality versus deviancy. The subordination of sexual minorities is not only evident in the violence generally directed against them, but is also evident in how mainstream institutions, such as courts of law, respond to and interpret such violence, including the selective defence of such violence. For Tomsen (2009), violence against sexual minorities is less about pathology ('homophobia') than about the ways in which perpetrators police and punish sexual deviance, and enforce conventional gender identity.

---

gay men and lesbian women, disabled communities, Indigenous Australians and migrants from non-English-speaking backgrounds (NESB), especially the Jewish, Muslim, Asian and Indian communities (Mason 2012, 2011a).

The pattern of hate crime is quite distinct from other forms of violence, including the usual pattern of homicide discussed earlier:

- Unlike most violence, which occurs between people who have some form of relationship with one another, hate crime often involves the targeting of people who are strangers to the assailant and have had no engagement of any kind with them. It is the perception that the victim belongs to a particular group that leads to the violence, rather than their individual characteristics or behaviour (Chakraborti & Garland 2012; Garland 2011; HREOC 1991a). At the same time, hate crimes also include attacks on individuals who are known to perpetrators, but the motive for their attack is not tied up with *who they are individually*, but rather *what they represent*—their perceived membership of a particular hated group (Tomsen 2001: 3). In either scenario, the intention is to send a threatening, symbolic message not only to the immediate victim, but also to the wider group or community to which they belong (Garland 2011).

- Hate crimes, particularly homicide, are characterised by the use of excessive force and brutality. Victims may be taunted and tortured before being murdered; frenzied stabbing is common, injuries may have sexual overtones and sexual organs may be mutilated and dismembered (see Dunn 2012; Martin 1996; Mouzos & Thompson 2000: 2). Not surprisingly, the perpetrators of hate crimes often work in groups. Victims of hate-crime homicides are often older than most homicide victims, while perpetrators are often younger and often unemployed (Mouzos & Thompson 2000: 3).

As a specific example of hate crime, key features of gay-related homicide are presented in Box 10.4. In the ten years between 1989 and 1999, some thirty-seven men were identified as being victims of hate-related homicide in New South Wales alone (Mouzos & Thompson 2000: 2), although the real figure is probably higher, estimated by Thompson at around eighty since the late 1970s (cited in Feneley 2013). As indicated in Box 10.4, the killings are distinctive in a number of ways.

Homicide therefore has more than one face: it can involve familiars and intimates, and in some instances is expressly about dealing with strangers who have been identified as 'others' or 'outsiders'. Who kills whom and why, and the responses of the system to killing, offer further insights into the nature and dynamics of homicide in a heterosexist society.

BOX 10.4   FEATURES OF GAY-RELATED HOMICIDE

- Incidents are highly likely to involve multiple offenders, and highly unlikely to involve multiple victims.
- The victim is most likely to be killed in the privacy of their own home.
- The victim is more likely to be older than the offender.
- The victim is more likely to be brutally beaten to death (with hands or feet or some blunt instrument), or repeatedly stabbed to death with a knife or some other sharp instrument.
- The victim is more likely to be killed by a stranger.
- The offender is more likely to be aged between 15 and 17 years, and on average is five years younger than the offender of a non-gay-hate homicide.
- Victims and offenders are more likely to be 'white'.
- Victims are more likely to be in the workforce than are their killers.

Source: Mouzos & Thompson (2000)

WOMEN WHO KILL MEN

It is clear from official statistics that women represent a small percentage of violent offenders and that when they resort to lethal violence, the most likely victim is an intimate partner. Furthermore, there is often a history of violence between the victim and the offender in homicide cases involving intimate partners. For example, between mid-1996 and mid-1999, there was documented evidence of prior domestic violence in 30 per cent of intimate-partner homicides, and in 80 per cent of these cases, the victim was female. Research undertaken in New South Wales showed that in 70 per cent of the cases where women killed their husbands, there was evidence of previous domestic violence, and in half of these, the woman claimed that she was acting in response to an immediate threat (Brown et al. 2001: 497; see also Morgan 2002).

The law's response to women who kill has been problematic in a number of different ways, particularly in instances where domestic violence is evident. The legal rules that traditionally gave shape to the doctrine of self-defence (a complete defence to homicide), for example, were designed (or interpreted) by the courts to tailor the defence to a factual paradigm involving a one-off confrontational encounter between two strangers (typically men) of roughly equal size and strength (see Brown et al. 2001; Scutt 1990). The idea of provocation reflected assumptions regarding established patterns of male interpersonal conflict and, in particular, the acceptability of male violent responses to alleged breaches of personal honour (Capper & Crooks 2010). This paradigm is inappropriate in the context of domestic violence and where the offender is a woman. In other words, the core concepts underpinning self-defence fail to take into account the actual experiences of women. Instead they emphasise (Toole 2012; VLRC 2004):

- *imminence of attack* (an immediate response to the original threat) versus the reality of the threat of violence that is real but not imminent, resulting in pre-emptive defensive attacks and the consequent arming of victims before attack, or of killing during a lull in violence in the course of a battering incident
- *proportionality* (of violence involved between the parties) versus experience of seriousness of attack that necessitates a more severe response due to disparities in physical strength and previous experience in physical combat
- *serious harm* versus foreknowledge of the violence to come based upon experience of past beatings
- *duty to retreat* versus lack of access to effective peaceful mechanisms for retreat or avoidance.

Lack of appreciation by the courts of women's defensive behaviour within its surrounding circumstances was compounded by the fact that the courts frequently minimised the deceased's violence towards the accused; and by appeal to 'standards of reasonableness' based upon the hypothetical reasonable man.

BATTERED WOMAN SYNDROME

One result of the persistent criticisms of the courts' failure to take into account gender-specific experience has been the emergence of, and increasing reliance upon, the *battered woman syndrome* (BWS) discourse in court (see Morgan 2012). This describes a psychological condition in which the cumulative effect of surviving domestic violence for the women concerned may be a particular state of mind characterised by features such as 'learned helplessness' and 'chronic fear'. These features mean that a woman is psychologically unable to escape a violent relationship, or particular incidents of violence, even when the opportunity is ostensibly open for her to do so. However, the BWS has been criticised on a number of grounds, such as an overemphasis on the psychology of the defendant, and consequent underemphasis on the context in which the offence took place, reinforcing the notion that the accused's behaviour was not objectively reasonable, but only to be evaluated in the light of a particular psychological state; and placing attention on the pathology of the defendant in ways that diminish the pathology of the offender or situation (Scutt 1995).

In legal terms, the danger of the BWS, in practice, is that rather than transforming self-defence (and the gender biases in the law pertaining to this), it may be used more frequently in support of those defences that stress emotional response (provocation) or mental instability (diminished responsibility), both of which may serve to reinforce particular gender stereotypes and locate the problem within individual psyches (rather than as a social problem). To put it differently, legal applications of the BWS tend not to focus directly on what it was about the circumstances of domestic violence that could produce a criminal response in reasonable women, but rather on the transient psychological state occurring in otherwise normal women as a result of surviving such abuse (Scutt 1995).

Close analysis of homicide (against women, and by women), and the defences used by men or women who kill, indicate that there have historically been strong gender biases running throughout the law (see Chapter 22). Recent changes in legal rules and court interpretation have in essence been generated by concerted campaigns undertaken by feminist activists, both within the legal system and outside of it, on issues such as female homicide in cases associated with domestic violence, but the legal response has been divergent across Australian jurisdictions (Fitz-Gibbon & Stubbs 2012; Sheehy et al. 2012a).

As recent rethinking about the BWS approach indicates, for every step forward in defending against criminal charges in such cases, success has tended to be partial and to raise even more questions. For example, a recent study by Sheehy et al. (2012b) of homicide prosecutions of battered women in Australia between 2000 and 2010 found that of the 67 cases finalised, only two resulted in a murder conviction and one of these was the result of a guilty plea. This implies that over the past decade, there has been increasing recognition of the context of domestic violence in assessing the criminal culpability of battered women defendants. However, while battered women are now seldom convicted of murder in Australia, there has been a normalisation of manslaughter convictions obtained on the basis of guilty pleas (58% of cases) rather than successful reliance on defences such as defensive homicide or self-defence, which may have resulted in non-conviction or a reduced sentence. Notwithstanding the tendency towards guilty pleas, there is growing recognition in Australian courts—especially in Victoria and New South Wales—that some women have limited options but to resort to lethal force in order to defend themselves against the dangerous nature of the intimate partner violence to which they are subjected. Just short of one in five women (19%) Australia-wide successfully pursued a plea of self-defence, thereby avoiding conviction. In Victoria and New South Wales, the success rate was even higher, with courts acquitting a quarter of all those pursing a self-defence plea, mainly on the grounds that their lethal actions constituted reasonable defensive measures.

There is also evidence to suggest that the law of defensive homicide in Victoria (a partial defence to homicide), which was established in 2005 as a 'safety net' for women who kill an intimate partner under circumstances of prolonged exposure to domestic violence, is operating contrary to original intent. Specifically, it is being successfully exploited by male offenders who kill other males and intimate female partners, resulting in the paradox that 'defensive homicide has the potential to both unfairly advantage and unfairly disadvantage an abused woman' (Toole 2012: 67; see also Fitz-Gibbon & Pickering 2012; Fitz-Gibbon & Stubbs 2012; Flynn & Fitz-Gibbon 2011; and Chapter 22).

MEN WHO KILL GAY MEN

Biases in criminal law pertaining to homicide are apparent in other areas as well. In this instance, the concern is once again with the adequacy or legitimacy of defence—albeit from the point of view of inappropriate means to gain acquittal or lower potential penalty.

The context for this discussion is recent social research and legal investigation regarding the circumstances surrounding gay hate-related homicide (see especially Tomsen & Crofts 2012; Tomsen 2009). In other words, the concern here is with men who kill other men who the perpetrators *identify* as being gay.

A *gay prejudice-related homicide* or *gay hate-related homicide* is a lethal act of violence where the victim may have been gay or perceived to be gay and the offender's actions were motivated to some significant degree by prejudice or homophobia. To appreciate how juries and courts have responded to instances of gay hate-homicide, it is useful to briefly review the defences available to and drawn upon by accused persons.

SELF-DEFENCE VERSUS PROVOCATION

It is important to distinguish between *self-defence* and *provocation* under the law (see Criminal Law Review Division 1998). The *law of self-defence* acknowledges that a person has a basic right to repel an unlawful attack. Self-defence has two components: first, that an honest belief be held on the part of the accused in relation to the need to use force (must honestly believe a threat); and second, that the accused's response is reasonable in the circumstances.

A finding that a person acted in self-defence entitles that person to be acquitted of the offence charged. Self-defence is a complete defence to all crimes of violence, including murder. The accused bears the onus of pointing to some evidence that may anchor the defence. Once the accused has done so, the onus is on the prosecution to disprove the defence beyond reasonable doubt. The objective issue is whether there were reasonable grounds for the belief of the accused.

The *defence of provocation* does not offer outright acquittal. Rather, it leads to a conviction for *manslaughter* (rather than murder). As with self-defence, the onus is on the accused to present evidence in support of the defence, and the defence must be disproved by the prosecution beyond reasonable doubt.

The key feature of provocation is captured in section 23 of the New South Wales *Crimes Act 1900*:

23. (2) ...an act or omission causing death is an act done or omitted under provocation where:

the act or omission is the result of loss of self-control on the part of the accused that was induced by any conduct of the deceased (including grossly insulting words or gestures) towards or affecting the accused; and

that conduct of the deceased was such as could have induced an ordinary person in the position of the accused to have so far lost self-control as to have formed an intent to kill, or to inflict grievous bodily harm upon, the deceased, whether the conduct of the deceased occurred immediately before the act or omission causing death or at any previous time.

The *subjective element* in this case refers to an assessment of the gravity of the conduct alleged to have provoked the accused by reference to relevant characteristics such as age, sex, race, ethnicity, physical features, personal attributes, personal relationships or past history; that is, assessment of specific features of the individual. The *objective element* refers to assessment of whether provocation of that gravity would cause an 'ordinary person' to lose self-control. In other words, the accused lost self-control in response to provocative conduct, in circumstances where an ordinary person could have been induced to lose self-control and act as the accused did.

The dilemma is that the law requires a juror to make a judgment about the response that could be evinced from an ordinary person. Thus, if a juror were to find that ordinary persons are homophobic, then that juror, no matter how fair-minded and free of homophobia he or she may be, would be obliged to take that perceived homophobia into account in determining whether or not the defence of provocation had succeeded or failed (Criminal Law Review Division 1998).

HOMOSEXUAL ADVANCE DEFENCE AND THE 'ORDINARY PERSON'

In New South Wales, a number of persons charged with murder, and who asserted at trial that they had killed in response to an unwanted, non-violent homosexual advance by the deceased, have either been acquitted outright (by way of the defence of self-defence) or found not guilty of murder but guilty of manslaughter (by way of the partial defence of provocation) (see Tomsen & Crofts 2012).

The *homosexual advance defence* (HAD), also referred to as the gay panic defence, is not in itself a legally recognised defence. It is a term used to describe cases in which an accused person alleges that he acted either in self-defence or under provocation in response to a homosexual advance made by another person (Sewell 2001). There are several difficulties with such a defence. First, in HAD cases the deceased is often the only person present during the killing, and so no contradictory version of events will be available. Second, in HAD cases a jury may equate a homosexual advance with a predatory, homosexual attack, with no distinction being drawn between an offensive, but innocuous, remark or action, and a real sexual assault involving physical force, which calls for the use of self-defence. Third, acceptance of HAD reinforces hostility to homosexuals, and reinforces particular conceptions about the protection of 'male honour' and 'masculinity'. In other words, it is about sexual identity and 'masculine social respect' rather than immediate danger posed by a sexual advance by a gay man (Tomsen & Crofts 2012: 427).

The attitude of judges toward issues of homosexuality influences how they perceive the 'ordinary person' and how they would expect them to behave. Contrast the following statements made by two different judges in the controversial High Court case of *Green v The Queen* [1997] (HCA 50; (1997) 191 CLR 334; (1997) 148 ALR 659; (1997) 72 ALJR 19), which involved the stabbing of a 22-year-old male with a pair of scissors by his 36-year-old male friend following an unwanted sexual advance:

Brennan CJ:

> Some ordinary men would feel great revulsion at the homosexual advances being persisted with under the circumstances and could be induced to so far lose their self control as to form the intention to and inflict grievous bodily harm. They would regard it as a serious and gross violation of their body and their person.

Kirby J:

> The 'ordinary person' in Australian society today is not so homophobic as to respond to a non-violent sexual advance by a homosexual person as to form an intent to kill or to inflict grievous bodily harm. He or she might, depending on the circumstances, be embarrassed; treat it at first as a bad joke; be hurt; insulted. He or she might react with the strong language of protest; might use such physical force as was necessary to effect an escape; and where absolutely necessary assault the persistent perpetrator to secure escape. But the notion that the ordinary 22 year old male (the age of the accused) in Australia today would so lose his self-control as to form an intent to kill or grievously to injure the deceased because of a non-violent sexual advance by an homosexual person is unconvincing.

As contended by Sewell (2001: 48, 58) 'the successful use of HAD provides evidence that the objective tests for provocation and self-defence are applied with a liberal dose of homophobia'. It reflects a heterocentric view of society; that is, one that privileges heterosexual views of appropriate sexuality and casts the homosexual into the role of the 'deviant' and 'morally abhorrent' other. Dwyer (2011a: 421) goes further, arguing that the homosexual panic defence conveys a message that it is acceptable to kill a gay person on the basis of a 'sexual miscommunication'. While some states have now moved to ban the HAD defence entirely (Tasmania, Victoria and Western Australia) and the temtories (the Australian Capital Territory and the Northern Territory) have amended provocation provisions to mitigate the more problematic aspects of the HAD defence, some jurisdictions (Queensland and New South Wales) still permit use of provocation on the basis of a HAD defence (Tomsen & Crofts 2012).

How the laws of self-defence and the partial defence of provocation are interpreted and used in our courts will have a major bearing on broad community perceptions, attitudes and practices. The 'ordinary person' is constructed in and through the law, as well as through popular culture and mainstream socialisation agencies such as schools. Analysis of homicide, and defences pertaining to homicide, must therefore include reference both to social context as well as legal rules and principles. Sociolegal research is an important avenue by which to do this.

ISSUES FOR CONSIDERATION

PERCEPTIONS OF VIOLENCE

As with every other social phenomenon, the way we perceive and respond to violence is intimately connected with relationships of domination and subordination. Public perceptions of violence do not occur in a social vacuum, but are shaped by institutions such as the media and the criminal justice system. These tend to focus on street crimes as the primary threat to social order, and point to young, working-class males as the problem. This perspective fails to acknowledge the extent to which street crime is only one of many forms of violence. White-collar crime, state crime and domestic violence are 'hidden' forms of violence that arguably cause more social harm, yet have only become public issues in relatively recent years (see Chapters 12 and 13).

CULTURE AND CRIME

The notion that there exists a 'violence gene' has rekindled interest in the idea that violence is linked to biological predispositions (Beaver et al. 2010). Despite evidence that violent behaviour has a biological and psychological component, the actual manifestation of violent behaviour is nevertheless most powerfully shaped by culture (see Ferrell et al. 2008; Mitchell & Vanya 2009; Morley & Hall 2003). This has numerous dimensions to it. Attitudes towards violence within the community, the social construction of masculinity and patriarchal power structures, the legal system and its implementation and the availability of weapons are just some of the ways in which cultural factors are integral to the expression of violence (see, for example, Kaukinen et al. 2013; McPhedran et al. 2010). Yet, discussion of a genetic factor, especially when linked to particular population groups (such as Maori), tends to both undermine cultural explanations while at the same time blaming particular groups for social processes outside of their historical control (such as colonialism). If violence is inherent to certain people, then violence prevention is basically about controlling those people: a phenomenon that parallels the colonial experience generally. In particular, it has been suggested that violent behaviour by Indigenous men in Australia towards family members is driven by the need to compensate for the sense of powerlessness experienced relative to the dominate mainstream society; these emotional issues are traceable to the experience of colonisation, disconnection from the land and economic marginalisation (see Day et al. 2012).

Trends in levels of violence need to be understood as arising out of the complex interplay of social, political and economic forces that occurs within nations at any point in time (Indermaur 1996; Roth 1994). Largely, these are played out at a level outside the control of individuals. They include changes in factors such as the demographic distribution of the population, the availability of weapons or drugs, police resources, cultural sensitivities towards violence and levels of inequality. These forces do not all operate in the same direction. For example, a decline in the number of young males will normally be associated with a decline in levels of crime and violence (Rosevear 2012), but if job availability for this group is in decline, then this is likely to be associated with higher levels of some types of violence (see Aaltonen et al. 2012). The complexity of these forces necessitates a measured response to claims that violence is increasing, and a resistance to explanations that simply attempt to pathologise particular social groups.

GENDER AND VIOLENT CRIME

A major issue today is whether society as a whole is becoming more violent, and within this over-arching trend, whether women specifically are becoming more violent proportionately to what has traditionally been the case. A number of studies have found that the proportion of female prisoners who have been apprehended and sentenced for a violent crime has increased internationally (Shepherd et al. 2012), and that in Australia at least most of this is accounted for by a rise in the number of females imprisoned for robbery. ABS data reveals that the number of women imprisoned for robbery has indeed increased—from 6.9 per cent in 1995 to 11.9 per cent in 2002. In contrast, the number of women sentenced for non-violent crimes, including deception offences and break and enter, has declined (Gelb 2003). No such changes have occurred in the type of offences for which males have been imprisoned, with both violent and non-violent offences having remained fairly stable.

A similar trend was found in Fitzgerald's study of court data in New South Wales for the period 1994–98 (Fitzgerald 1999). While the number of women appearing before the Higher Courts declined by 31.5 per cent, from 355 persons to 243, the number of women appearing for robbery rose from twenty-six individuals to forty-six individuals. Fitzgerald (1999) argues that this may have contributed to the rise in female imprisonment from eighty-seven (24.5%) to 117 (48.1%) over the same period. Like Gelb, Fitzgerald concludes that the change in the nature of female offences is one of the reasons for the growth in female imprisonment. Similar patterns of female processing for robberies has been observed in Victoria, with a 16 per cent increase noted in 2008, while young male robberies declined over the same period (see Shepherd et al. 2012).

Since that time however, the proportion of female offenders imprisoned for robbery offences has decreased substantially, with only 6.2 per cent of all female prisoners processed for robbery as a principal offence across Australia in 2013 (ABS 2013e). As discussed previously (see Chapter 8), evidence in fact suggests little change over time in the size of the gender gap between women and men when it comes to violent crime, although the specific character or context of the violence is important to consider (Kruttschnitt et al. 2008).

MALES AS VICTIMS OF CRIME

Conversely, the high levels of under-reporting of violence (especially men who are the victims of homophobic violence) disguise the extent to which males, as well as females, are victims of violence. The same factors that influence men's involvement in violence also prevent them from identifying themselves as victims. For different reasons, the victimisation of men and women has been a hidden social issue. While feminism has lifted the veil on female victims of domestic violence and sexual assault, the extent to which males are also victims of males remains an issue that is worthy of much greater attention, especially in relation to sexual assault.

CHANGING NATURE OF CRIMES AGAINST THE PERSON

Just as the nature of property crime has changed, so too has the nature and definition of crimes against the person in the modern era, with new laws emerging in areas such as drink spiking, rock throwing, road rage and one-punch drunken assaults (see ABC 2014b; Carey & Dowling 2013; Loughnan 2010). For example, one illustration of how what is defined as criminal is socially constructed and historically specific is recent and growing concern over cyber-bullying and related activities associated with computer technology (see Box 10.5).

BOX 10.5   CYBER-VICTIMISATION

CYBER-VICTIMISATION
Crimes against the person relating to the use and misuse of computer technologies, such as identity theft, cyber harassment and online sexual exploitation of children.

A growing form of crime against the person relates to the use and misuse of computer technologies (Roberts 2008). The kinds of harms perpetrated through computers include such things as:

- *identity theft:* the online misappropriation of identity tokens (such as email addresses, web pages and the combination of username and password used to access systems), typically for financial gain
- *online sexual exploitation of children:* including pornographic child sex imagery; the sexual grooming and solicitation of children by paedophiles; and children accessing unsuitable material online
- *cyber harassment:* a type of cyber-victimisation; cyber-bullying conducted online, which may include threats, insults and teasing; cyber-stalking entailing the use of emails and instant messages; through to attempts to access confidential information and computer monitoring.

Roberts (2008) describes the specific harms of cyber-victimisation and the nature of the victimisation associated with each of these sorts of activities, and calls for further research into their impact and developing appropriate responses.

Computers and other communication technologies (e.g. mobile phones and social networking sites) can be used to facilitate activities that degrade and humiliate others. They can also be used to prepare a pathway for the actual physical and sexual abuse of victims. Much of the violence here is of an intentional nature, and of a sort that is simultaneously intimate and public.

Source: Roberts (2008)

CONCLUSION

This chapter has explored the issue of crimes against the person by examining issues such as street violence and homicide. Conventional analysis of such crimes tends to focus on the characteristics of events and individuals (as victims and as offenders), and thus to frame the issues in terms of specific situational factors. An underlying theme of this chapter is that the nature of violence is in fact inseparable from the kind of society within which it emerges. Whether it is public violence on the streets or specific kinds of homicide, all violence is in some way socially constructed and stems from particular social contexts.

A key question in regards to contemporary manifestations of violence is how violence generally has become normalised in Australian society; that is, images, threats and actual incidents of violence are evident throughout the mainstream institutions, including the media, the family, schools, sports fields and workplaces. Violence is not unusual to most people; it is an active ingredient in their lives as spectators, observers, watchers, participants and victims. Given the prevalence of violence as a social phenomenon, and especially via the spectacle (witness most Hollywood movies today), the issue is less one of explaining why there is violence than one of explaining why there is not more of it.

As this chapter has tried to indicate, violence is rarely socially neutral. That is, the perpetrators tend to be male, and the targets of violence are very often from vulnerable and socially distanced groups. Certain types of violence are deemed to be legitimate and indeed celebrated (as with a clean hit on the sports field or a military campaign that goes well). Other forms are subject to public censure (as with men bashing women in public). Others still, like intimate partner violence, largely remain the preserve of the private domain.

Why different types of violence call forth different responses also points to the sociological significance of culture in framing violence generally.

Despite the contentious framing of violence by the criminal justice system in some contexts, crimes involving violence, especially at the street level, generally involves some degree of legally proscribed behaviour. Chapter 11 moves into murkier territory, with an examination of crimes against convention and the contested nature of 'deviant' behaviour.

DISCUSSION QUESTIONS

1   Is violence simply part of the human condition?

2   Why do men commit more violence than women?

3   Are women and girls getting more violent? If so, how do we explain this? If not, why not?

4   'Playing professional football and engaging in pub fights are part and parcel of the same culture.' Discuss.

5   'Heterosexism permeates Australian society.' Discuss, providing examples.

FURTHER READING

Bricknell, S. (2008) 'Trends in violent crime', *Trends and Issues in Crimes and Criminal Justice*, no. 359, Australian Institute of Criminology, Canberra.

Chan, A. & Payne, J (2013) 'Homicide in Australia: 2008–09 to 2009–10. National Homicide Monitoring Program Annual Report', *AIC Monitoring Report*, No. 21, Australian Institute of Criminology, Canberra.

Polk, K. (1994) *When men kill: scenarios of masculine violence*, Cambridge University Press, Cambridge.

Sheehy, E., Stubbs, J. & Tolmie, J. (2012) 'Defences to homicide for battered women: a comparative analysis of laws in Australia, Canada and New Zealand', *Sydney Law Review*, 34(3): 467–92.

Tomsen, S. & Crofts, T. (2012) 'Social and cultural meanings of legal responses to homicide among men: masculine honour, sexual advances and accidents', *Australian & New Zealand Journal of Criminology*, 45(3): 423–37.

11 CRIMES AGAINST CONVENTION

CHAPTER OVERVIEW
- DEVIANCY AND CONFORMITY
- DRUGS AND ALCOHOL
- PUBLIC ORDER OFFENCES
- ANIMAL ABUSE
- ISSUES FOR CONSIDERATION
- CONCLUSION
- DISCUSSION QUESTIONS
- FURTHER READING

INTRODUCTION

This chapter deals with issues of criminality in relation to the notion of convention. Our concern is less with the question of illegality per se than with the contested nature of the perceived intersection between illegality, deviance and morality. As will become apparent, perceptions of 'conventional' and 'unconventional' behaviour are very much based upon variable conceptions of 'harm' and 'victimisation', as well as contextual factors such as the public or private nature of the behaviour engaged in and the status of the individual or group engaging in the behaviour. A key concern will be to explore how and why certain types of activities are seen as deviant and yet, in some cases, strangely attractive at the same time. For other activities, the interest is not so much the push–pull factors that attract or repel vis-à-vis that particular activity, but why such activities have garnered attention as matters deserving of public attention and reprobation at particular points in time.

The kinds of activities described in this chapter include those commonly engaged in by many across socio-demographic divides, to varying degrees and for varying periods of time. They are familiar, but nonetheless socially problematic from the point of view of perceptions of deviancy and harmfulness (and, in some cases, actual harms). They include drug and alcohol use, and low-level public order offences such as swearing, public drunkenness and prostitution.

The chapter also considers relatively newly defined forms of deviancy, in particular relating to animal abuse. This area is contentious precisely because of the ambiguities surrounding what is acceptable and unacceptable behaviour toward particular creatures, involving different kinds of harm. Creating new conventions is, in part, about criminalisation of what has gone unchallenged before. While in some cases there appears to be a clear victim (e.g. the mistreatment of domestic animals like dogs or cats) and thus criminal sanctions may be applied in a straightforward way, in other instances systematic abuse of animals is largely ignored by the law (e.g. in relation to what happens within piggeries and cage hen coops). As with many of the activities described in this chapter (and indeed throughout the book), the question of 'when is a crime a crime?' boils down to a matter of when and where we establish social boundaries and who does so, and how these are, in turn, enforced in relation to particular kinds of transgression.

DEVIANCY AND CONFORMITY

A fundamental aspect of crime and deviancy is that what is deemed criminal is not immutable; it varies greatly from society to society, and over the course of human history (see Chapter 1). Not all rules and rule-breaking activities connote criminality as such. Social transgression is not necessarily subject to criminal sanction, although public disapproval does provide a rough indicator of perceptions of level of harm. Moreover, some activities call forth reactions that are at times ambivalent, and that may be the source of divided opinion rather than consensus.

There is a longstanding sociological truism that crime is functionally important in any society, insofar as it sets out the boundaries of acceptable and unacceptable behaviour (Inverarity et al. 1983). In this sense, then, it is deviance that establishes conformity. Each is implicated in the other, and one cannot exist except in relation to its opposite. Hence:

> [t]o classify crime among the phenomena of normal sociology is not to say merely that it is an inevitable, although regrettable phenomenon, due to the incorrigible wickedness of men [sic]; it is to affirm that it is a factor in public health, an integral part of all healthy societies'. (Durkheim 1962: 11)

As Durkheim also observed, even in the society of saints there would be some concept of 'crime' ('sin', 'transgression' or 'wrong'), as this demarcates the 'good' from the 'bad', the 'acceptable' from the 'unacceptable'. Not kneeling for long enough, mumbling one's prayer or overeating at the dinner table, the activities of a saint are subject to various kinds of scrutiny that have some bearing on how others see him or her, and the standards of behaviour deemed acceptable.

SOCIAL BOUNDARIES AND LEGAL BOUNDARIES

Central to this conception of deviancy, therefore, is the notion of social boundaries. Without deviancy, and without punishment, there would be no real demarcation as to what is *acceptable behaviour* or *unacceptable behaviour* in any given society or situation. *Deviancy* (or transgression) is thus essential to any society insofar as the rules and norms of any society are forged in a consensus regarding what is *not* allowable. Yet even within a presumed consensus about deviancy and conformity, there is generally scope for personal initiative and expression of diversity; for example, the suit as a standard and acceptable form of business dress allows for wearing an extraordinary choice in ties.

A distinction also needs to be made here between social acceptability and legal acceptability (which impacts both individual rights and privileges). There is a difference, for example, between:

- deviancy that refers to legally acceptable behaviour (e.g. using a mobile phone in a public place) that is regarded as socially unacceptable (e.g. speaking loudly into your mobile phone in a restaurant)
- behaviour that is illegal and socially unacceptable (e.g. stealing a mobile phone from someone)
- behaviour that is generally illegal (e.g. graffiti or marijuana) but considered legal and socially acceptable in particular contexts (e.g. graffiti in designated Melbourne CBD laneways or the use of medical marijuana)
- behaviour that is illegal but attracts variable opinion regarding social acceptability (e.g. fare evasion or tax evasion).

Both concepts of permissibility (formal legal norms and informal social norms) are important in any consideration of behavioural conventions and changes in these over time. Central to Foucault's work on power, knowledge and social control (1980) is the process by which social ideas or norms become historically elevated to assume a natural and inevitable status. For example, abortion and homosexuality at various times and across various countries have been deemed both legally prohibited and socially unacceptable. Both activities remain criminalised to various degrees cross-nationally, with acts of homosexuality punishable by corporal means, including death in some countries (Conway-Smith 2013; Nossiter 2014). However, public opinion has shifted considerably in Australia and most Western nations and, in the process, there have been major changes in legal rules and social norms (Asal et al. 2012; Rankin 2011).

Current debates over euthanasia likewise illustrate how conventions may be challenged politically as well as through individual acts (Bartunek 2014; Martin 2013; Medew 2014; Titterington et al. 2013). As Asal et al. (2012) highlight, a wide array of variables impact public perception of and legal responses to various behaviours, including: economic and democratic conditions (degree of modernisation and political opportunity structures open to minority groups); the influence of religiosity; the impact of globalisation; and the nature of the legal framework in effect and its regard to the role of the nation-state in protecting civil rights and liberties, as well as human rights more broadly.

The tension between what is acceptable and what is unacceptable is also frequently not a question of *what* is being engaged in, but *how* and *where*. As discussed below, such is the case, for example, with drug use, and in particular the consumption of alcohol. Illicit drugs are generally banned by law (the exceptions usually being for therapeutic purposes), and their use is highly restricted and subject to the threat of criminal sanctions. The consumption of alcohol, however, is legal within certain defined limits. These limits relate to factors such as age of the person, drinking and driving, levels of intoxication and place of consumption (home, pub or club versus in a park or on the street).

Moreover, *good behaviour* and *good taste* (and, correspondingly, *bad behaviour* and *bad taste*) are themselves socially determined by the powerful in any particular society. Those with power, wealth and status establish formal and informal standards of dress, activity, appearance and consumption, against which all else is evaluated and judged (see Bourdieu 1986). How others who are not powerful respond to this hierarchy of standard-setting and boundary maintenance is nevertheless fluid, and involves degrees of resistance as well as conformity. As discussed shortly, the use of 'bad language' in public provides a case in point.

DEVIANCY AS A DRIVER OF SOCIAL INNOVATION

Pushing the boundaries, challenging existing norms and values, and transgressing the ordinary rules of social interaction are the characteristics of the deviant. But, when enough people engage in the same activities to a great enough extent, deviancy itself can become integral to wider processes of social change. Consider, for example, the case of skateboarding. What was once considered unusual, offensive, dangerous and deviant has undergone dramatic transformations in the past twenty years or so. Young people were engaging in a form of activity that, because of their enthusiasm and high participation rate, has become part of the surrounding environment, accompanied by the expansion of commercial opportunities and the routinisation of what were once seen as extraordinary activities (White & Wyn 2013). The proliferation of skate parks, the development of youth services that incorporate skateboarding, the incorporation of small-wheeled vehicles into official road rules, and a general prominence in television and movie features all confirm the present-day legitimacy of what once was seen as deviant. Deviancy can thus be a driver of social innovation; it is not only the focus for social control and the reinforcement of traditional and conventional modes of activity.

Analysis of deviancy and crime tells us much about the nature of society generally. How deviance is classified and dealt with by authority figures is basically a social structural question, one that reveals how institutions work, how people collectively behave and how power is mobilised. In addition to social structural matters pertaining to the construction of deviancy and conformity at any point in time, there are also issues relating to the meaning of the activity for the participants. Indeed, one of the features of this chapter is to study how certain activities (e.g. drug use or swearing) have certain meanings and express certain values for those engaging in them. The meaningfulness of deviancy is a crucial aspect in discerning how and why certain activities persist, even in the face of general social pressures and state actions to prevent or stop them.

VICTIMLESS CRIME

Differentiating behaviour worthy of both legal condemnation and punishment, and universal social reprobation from that simply considered deviant but not criminal, often centres on ideological arguments regarding the perceived seriousness of the behaviour in question, which can range from the trivial though annoying through to the extremely serious. The issue of seriousness is commonly tied up with consideration of consequences or harms—for both individuals immediately impacted and society more broadly. A core consideration here is that of victimisation and, in particular, debate regarding whether the deviant activity involves a discernible victim whose rights are clearly violated or threatened, or whether it is a *victimless crime*.

First introduced by Schur (1965), the concept of victimless crime, also known as 'morality-based crime' or 'public-order offences' (Clement & Barbrey 2008), refers to acts not universally condemned as criminal but which are also considered sufficiently taboo, annoying or socially undesirable as to warrant some form of state intervention (Koster et al. 2009; Stylianou 2010). By contrast with violent crimes such as homicide and sexual assault, which are outlawed on the basis that they are *mala in se* (wrong per se) so-called victimless crime (e.g. prostitution, abortion, drug use and homosexuality) is considered *mala prohibita* (wrong by virtue of prohibition). Not surprisingly, while the state response to *mala in se* offences is generally uncontested, considerable ambiguity and debate surround the appropriate social responses to victimless crime. These debates stem from ideological differences regarding conceptualisation of harmfulness and moral wrongfulness. Debates variously draw upon the following normative models to justify or challenge the limiting of individual liberty (Stylianou 2010):

- *Libertarianism* (harm to others) adopts the principle that restrictions on individual freedom to pursue pleasure can only ever be justified where such pursuit is at the expense of the rights of others; legal intervention is thus for the purposes of controlling behaviour that violates others' rights in a *harmful* rather than merely *bothersome* way.
- *Paternalism* (harm to self) adopts the libertarianism principle, but extends the ambit of protection further to include harm to self as well as harm to others; intervention in victimless crime is thus justifiable where limiting individual freedom protects against *self-harm*.
- *Moralism* (harmless wrongdoing) endorses the principles of both libertarianism (social control to protect others) and paternalism (social control to protect actors), but also supports the exercise of social control where actions are inconsistent with ethical principles, including activities that are intrinsically wrong and thereby transgress normative ethical boundaries or moral authorities (nature, religion and society or tradition). Behaviour here is assessed within a frame of binary opposites—*right* versus *wrong*, *negative* versus *positive*—that is not reliant on consequentialist arguments (tangible harms).

Application of the three normative models outlined above to the issue of prostitution serves to illustrate the level of contest surrounding activities drawn into the ambit of victimless crime. From a libertarian perspective, it could be argued that prostitution involves a willing exchange between consenting individuals of a desired activity, product or service proscribed by law. Furthermore, sex work takes many forms, and for some it is the end product of choice exercised among a number of employment alternatives; it is pleasurable, skilful and rewarding work (McGrow 2013). Since the activity occurs without victim, criminalising or otherwise controlling such activity is unwarranted in the absence of direct harm and complaint. Full decriminalisation of prostitution, it is argued, would provide sex workers with formalised labour rights, protection of human rights, and a legal requirement for the protection of health and safety (ABC 2013b). While this argument has gained traction in relation to other consensual adult sexual relations, such as homosexuality and same-sex partnering, which are no longer deemed harmful in a criminal law sense, significant debate continues to circle the legitimacy of prostitution. Stigma continues to attach to certain forms of prostitution, with street-present sex work considered especially deviant.

A paternalistic approach to social control, on the other hand, might regard sex workers as themselves victims of society, forced into prostitution through the denial of 'legitimate' employment opportunities, commoditised and subject to degrading, abusive and exploitative treatment (see Reeve 2013). This approach, which regards sex workers as victims essentially in need of rescue, forms the basis of the Swedish legal framework, which has elected to criminalise the buyer of sex worker services rather than the provider (Levy & Jakobsson 2014; McGrow 2013; Niemi 2010).

Finally, proponents of the moralism perspective would argue that prostitution is intrinsically wrong: that it is immoral, 'unnatural', socially undesirable or unacceptable since it threatens the social and moral order. This argument is essentially about status, morality and value judgment, rather than about objective evidence of harm per se.

Other kinds of activity, such as abortion, are even more contentious since there continues to be vigorous debate over whether a victim exists. Some activities, such as smoking, have the capacity to affect the health of others (e.g. the children of parents who smoke or members of the general public) who passively inhale smoke, thereby becoming unwitting victims since they have little control over their exposure. Recognition of the harms of passive smoking and the rights of non-smokers to a smoke-free environment has prompted the gradual prohibition of smoking in certain contexts. For example, legislation banning smoking in cars when minors aged 16–18 years are present are in effect in almost all Australian jurisdictions, commencing with South Australia in 2007. Similarly, from 2000 there has been a push to ban smoking in some outdoor public areas, including playgrounds and al fresco dining areas. Drug use of many different kinds is frequently discussed as a victimless crime, although who is harmed and how is part of a perennial debate.

DRUGS AND ALCOHOL

At one level, there is nothing new about human beings using drugs. Most cultures in history have some kind of relationship with psychoactive substances of some kind that alter consciousness in some way, whether through drinking wine or beer, smoking hashish, drinking kava or snorting special powders. In most cases, there are rules and rituals that guide who, when, where and why substances may be ingested, and how to behave once this has occurred, and these vary according to purpose, including social, spiritual, medical, artistic and simple pleasure-seeking (Caita-Zufferey 2013). It has been estimated that, globally, 210 million people use illicit drugs annually (Australian Crime Commission 2011), with over 250 substances in existence and over seventy new substances identified in 2012 (European Monitoring Centre for Drugs and Drug Addiction &

Europol 2013). In Australia, specifically, the 2010 National Drug Strategy Household Survey (AIHW 2011b) identified the top three drugs used by Australians aged 14 years and over as cannabis (10.3%), ecstasy (3.0%) and amphetamines/methamphetamines (2.5%). In terms of lifetime use, the survey found that over a third of interviewees (35.4%) had tried marijuana/cannabis, one in ten (10.3%) had tried ecstasy and just short of one in ten had tried cocaine and methamphetamines (7.3% and 7%, respectively).

In general, then, drug use is a 'natural' part of life, historically and in contemporary times. However, drug use is never a simple affair. There are conventions, regulations and laws that dictate which drugs are legitimate, and shape the patterns of private and public use of drugs. Our concern, therefore, is not to judge whether drug-taking is good or bad, but to consider how drug use fits into the everyday life patterns of society and to consider the historical evolution of drug use and its regulation in the context of the progressive redrawing of boundaries between social policy and criminal justice.

LEGITIMACY AND NON-LEGITIMACY

The use of psychoactive drugs of various kinds has both a legitimate and non-legitimate character. There are some drugs, such as alcohol, that are legal, and some drugs, such as marijuana and heroin, that are largely illegal. However, even with legal drugs there are social and legal guidelines regarding consumption. Binge drinking, for example, is not seen as socially acceptable according to mainstream definitions of appropriate behaviour, yet there is the perception that it is becoming increasingly acceptable behaviour among young people these days, both men and women; part of an intoxication culture that values hedonistic drinking as a pleasure-state within the experience economy (Fry 2011; Harrison et al. 2011). An age of responsibility (usually 18 years) legally demarcates when a person is eligible to publicly buy or drink alcohol. Similarly, if one is intoxicated in a public place, this is seen to be problematic, especially if it is associated with social harm of some kind (e.g. fighting or urinating in public). Becoming intoxicated at home and in private seldom calls forth a major public reaction.

What to drink, when, how, and how much are subjects for deliberation, not simply left to random chance. Important shifts in attitudes and thinking about drinking among the younger population have been highlighted in recent research. For example, drinking heavily has been associated with the notion of 'calculated hedonism'; that is, a calculated and planned, rational hedonism in which young people plan to 'let loose' (Brain 2000; Roche et al. 2008). Related to this is the idea of a 'culture of intoxication', a culture that is informed by a tradition of 'weekday restraint and weekend excess' (Measham 2006: 258). A significant part of the criminalisation of drug use stems from drug abuse, not simply access to a prohibited substance. When this occurs in public, it gets noticed.

Which substances are deemed legal and which illegal is determined by specific social and historical processes. For example, alcohol was temporarily outlawed in the United States during the **Prohibition** era in the 1920s and early 1930s. It is similarly banned today in a number of countries, including some parts of India, and Muslim-majority countries such as Saudi Arabia. The reasons alcohol consumption may be prohibited range from concerns relating to social welfare and public order to religious proscriptions on the use of such drugs (e.g. the temperance movement in North America and Australia was largely headed by Christian activists, while some Muslim countries ban alcohol use outright).

A history of drug laws in Australia shows that, very often, which drugs are considered to be 'bad' and which to be 'good' is decided politically rather than as the result of a neutral, technical or scientific exercise. Manderson (1993) provides a detailed history of Australian drug laws. An important part of Manderson's argument is that moral panics over drug use (e.g. relating to opium, heroin and cannabis)

PROHIBITION STRATEGIES
Programs for controlling drug use that focus on banning the availability of illegal substances.

tend to be associated with racism and powerful international pressures rather than genuine concerns about the welfare of users.

THE USE OF OPIUM

For most of the nineteenth century, psychoactive substances, now prohibited, were subject to free market enterprise. Opium, for example, was considered a medicinal substance; a tonic with euphoric or oblivion-inducing properties recognised as a legitimate option for alleviating the pain of medical ailments. Accordingly, it was freely available from village stores and corner shops (Shiner 2013). Over time, increasingly stringent moral injunctions were progressively introduced over supply (e.g. morphine and opium could only be supplied through pharmacists) and possession (e.g. morphine and cocaine could be obtained on prescription, as a legitimate medical treatment for addiction), ultimately culminating in prohibition. The fusion of morality and medicine was justified on paternalistic and public health (medical/pharmacological) grounds; namely, changes in manufacturing processes and the introduction of hypodermic injection raised concerns about purity of substance and hygienic administration, as well as enhancing drug potency and the likelihood of negative physiological and psychological effects, including addiction and overdose (Shiner 2013). Since addicts were conceived of as suffering from 'pathologically impaired moral faculty' (Mold 2008: 7), state interventionism was warranted to rehabilitate and 'correct' not only those already affected by drug addiction, but also to protect the broader community from its evil powers of addiction.

Shiner (2013) suggests that such arguments masked the powerful interests underlying the introduction of drug prohibition and its eventual criminalisation. In particular, prohibition served the interests of the industrial classes, which required a ready, able and disciplined work force to further the capitalist economy. Moral crusaders thus focused attention on the association between drug use and the lower classes, the subversive nature of drug taking and the need to reform manners and control behaviours that challenged social order. The emergence of laws intended to control antisocial behaviours among the lower order coincided with an emerging welfare state, illustrating not only a core tension within state regulation, but also the forging of a path from social policy regulation to criminalisation. This process of criminalisation has, over time, crystallised less around notions of risk rather than immorality (Caita-Zufferey 2013), fuelled by periodic moral panics over unregulated behaviour seen to threaten the very fabric of society (David et al. 2011).

Closer examination of the historical banning of opium in places like Australia and the United States also reveals racist motivations. The proponents of a 'White Australia' led particularly vicious and racist campaigns against Chinese residents and workers throughout the 1880s. As part of these anti-Chinese crusades, opium use was especially targeted and vilified. Yet, for the Chinese, opium was an important part of everyday life:

> The Chinese did not drink their opium, or take it in tablet form or subcutaneously as White Australians did; although occasionally chewed, it was the most invariable custom of the Chinese to smoke it, especially prepared in pipes, often in 'dens' fitted out for the purpose. Smoking was at once a private and absorbing reverie and a social activity. For the Chinese, opium functioned as a recreational drug, like alcohol or tobacco. Like any such drug, therefore, there were occasional users, regular users, abusers and addicts; there were houses in which the smoking of an opium pipe was regarded as a social courtesy, and others in which it was a serious business. Opium was, in short, as entrenched in the social life of the Chinese as ethyl alcohol is in that of Anglo-Australians. (Manderson 1993: 20)

While a personage such as Sherlock Holmes (fictional though he was) might have been portrayed as an occasional needle-user of similar drugs, the Chinese style of drug use was closely linked to their very presence in the country. The prohibition of opium smoking was, in effect, another form of discrimination against the Chinese, alongside other inequitable government measures, such as the levying of special taxes and exclusion from welfare provisions.

DRUG USE AND THE CRIMINAL JUSTICE SYSTEM

There is a strong connection between drug use, drug abuse and the institutions of criminal justice. Initially, this is because the law makes certain drugs illegal, and also because certain types of behaviour—often associated with substance misuse—are criminalised by the law. There is social harm related to drug use where the issue is criminalisation arising from substance abuse, such as intoxication and alcohol-related violence. There is also crime related to illegal drug use where the issue is criminalisation arising from the substance use itself (e.g. taking a banned substance such as ecstasy). In either case, the connection between drugs and crime is generally construed around some notion of harm. Garland (2001) identifies the cognitive shift in the notion of harm from one of harm *to* users as opposed to harm *by* users as key to the transformation of drug policy from one of *harm minimisation* to one of *penal* welfarism. The latter sees drug users as culpable, dangerous and deserving of punishment and tight control because of the harm they inflict on society, whereas the former regards users as socially deprived and in need of support. Other kinds of harm, such as contracting hepatitis C or HIV in conjunction with certain types of drug use, such as use of needles, is also of concern to the criminal justice system, especially in regards to the prisoner population, and requires consideration of pragmatic harm reduction approaches (see Chapters 25 and 28).

Much criminological work has been done in relation to **illicit drug offences**, which generally include: possession; sale, dealing or trafficking; importing or exporting; and manufacture or cultivation of drugs. Two broad categories of offenders are identified—consumers and providers—and criminal justice responses tend to differ in relation to each category.

What is perhaps less acknowledged in much media discussion of drugs and crime is the nature and extent of criminal offences and regulatory breaches relating to the use of *legal* or *licit drugs*. Various transgressions are possible:

- age-related laws and licensing arrangements of pubs and clubs
- age-related and place-based smoking laws
- drinking and driving laws
- alcohol bans and community laws
- prescription drug misuse.

Here the categories of offender tend to be demarcated by 'status' (as in the case of underage drinkers, or those who drink in communities that have been designated as 'dry' or in alcohol-free areas such as some streets or parks), and by 'behaviour' (as in the case of inappropriate social activities while taking a substance, whether alcoholic or non-alcoholic). Consider the case of driving and alcohol use. While it is legal to drink alcohol if one is of legal age, it is not legal to drink alcohol over a prescribed quantity and then drive a car. In other words, alcohol use is invariably regulated in relation to other kinds of activities in which we might engage. There are also strong links between certain legal drugs, such as cigarettes, and public health campaigns warning of the dangers of this activity. While cigarette smoking remains legal for adults despite the overwhelming medical evidence as to its harmfulness, the past two decades have witnessed a dramatic increase in the volume of regulatory activity relating to smoking. Whereas it was previously acceptable to smoke cigarettes in movie theatres, restaurants,

ILLICIT DRUG OFFENCES
Offences that include the possession, sale, dealing or trafficking, importing or exporting, manufacture or cultivation of drugs or other substances prohibited under legislation (e.g. cannabis or heroin).

public foyers and even university classrooms, smoking legislation designed to mitigate the prospect and consequences of passive smoking has severely restricted the physical boundaries within which such activity is considered permissible. For example, most workplaces, restaurants, public transport and taxis have now been declared smoke-free areas. In essence, the law is seeking to protect simultaneously the rights of smokers and non-smoking members of the public.

When it comes to illicit drugs, there are two key issues of analytical and practical concern from the standpoint of the criminal justice system, which considers the activity in strictly legal terms. The first has to do with the relationship between involvement in drugs and engagement in criminal and antisocial behaviour. We know, for example, that illicit drug use is high among police detainees, with the number testing positive to methamphetamine (known as ice), cocaine, cannabis and heroin ranging between 45 per cent and 80 per cent across Australia between 2006 and 2011 (AIC 2013a). Furthermore, almost half of all police detainees attributed their offending to alcohol or other drugs (Payne & Gaffney 2012). We also know that it is high among young offenders (Howard & Zibert 1990; Putnins 2001) and offenders more generally. In 2012–13, for example, illicit drug offences were recorded as the principal offence for almost one in five offenders formally processed by police across Australia. The rate of illicit drug offending was 51.3 per 100,000 population, surpassed only by the rate of offending for acts intended to cause injury (546.8 per 100,000 population), although some level of drug use is likely to be involved in the latter (ABS 2014a).

While drug use is certainly associated with offending behaviour, the exact nature of the relationship is unclear. Public perceptions are that illicit drug use leads to acquisitive types of crime because of the need to fund an expensive drug habit. There is certainly significant research evidence to support this perceived association, demonstrating that engagement in property crime for income-generation purposes is strongly related to drug-use type, frequency, dependence and expenditure levels (see Bradford & Payne 2012; Kinner et al. 2009 Payne & Gaffney 2012; Sweeney & Payne 2011). But it is important to recognise that this is not the only possible relationship. It could be that the physiological effects of drugs such as alcohol or marijuana reduce inhibitions and so increase risk-taking behaviour, especially violence (Payne & Gaffney 2012). Alternatively, the causal relationship may be in the opposite direction, with demographic and social factors contributing to engagement in crime, which in turn leads to increased substance use because, for example, people engaged in crime take drugs and encourage newcomers to do the same. Or perhaps it is just that those who take drugs and those who engage in crime have a number of characteristics in common (e.g. a history of abuse, neglect and violence), and they are not causally related (see YSAS 2013; AIC 2005).

A second and crucial issue for criminal justice officials such as the police is that the effects drugs, both legal (e.g. alcohol) and illegal (e.g. 'ice', which is a high-quality methamphetamine), have in reducing inhibitions, increasing susceptibility to paranoia, and heightening levels of agitation and irritability, and therefore increasing risk-taking behaviour, especially violence. Such behaviours include verbal abuse, creating a public disturbance, stealing or damaging property, and physical abuse. While the evidence on the link between amphetamine use and violence remains inconclusive (Gately et al. 2012; Torok et al. 2012), there appears to be a significant body of evidence linking alcohol and violence, especially in the case of young people (Lindsay 2012; AIHW 2011b). The recently formed (2008) National Alliance Against Alcohol Related Violence, for instance, estimates that one in five people are affected by alcohol violence alone. Research into the link between alcohol consumption in licensed premises, aggression and street violence (Graham et al. 2011; Mazerolle et al. 2012; Rowe et al. 2010) identifies a wide range of venue precinct features, as well as management and alcohol-serving practices that contribute to the problem (see Box 11.1).

BOX 11.1   AGGRESSION IN AND AROUND LICENSED PREMISES

The book, *Raising the bar: preventing aggression in and around bars, pubs and clubs* (Graham & Homel 2008), provides a sustained analysis of how and why aggression, violence and injury occur in and around public drinking establishments. It provides a situational analysis of many different factors that, together, influence drinking patterns and patterns of violence.

Not all drinking establishments are the same, and the differences between them are significant. For example, Graham and Homel (2008) show why drinking establishments are high risk for aggression, why some establishments are riskier than others, the effectiveness of existing interventions and policies, and the importance of better regulatory models for achieving safer drinking establishments.

Issues such as letting patrons get highly intoxicated, how shoddy bar environments encourage shoddy behaviour, the ways in which bouncers who act as guards or enforcers can provoke situations, and the importance of community action around drinking establishments and public violence are among the concerns of the book. The authors argue that, to grapple with this particular kind of alcohol-related violence, there is a need to adopt a multi-pronged approach, one that targets, among a number of other key factors, the type and extent of alcohol consumption. It is argued that, in essence, rather than adopting a punitive and individualistic approach (that targets particular patrons and licensees), lawmakers should find solutions that are framed within a public health perspective, so that the social problem of alcohol-related violence can be properly addressed as a public problem warranting consistent and long-term intervention.

Source: Graham & Homel (2008)

ALCOHOL CONSUMPTION AND SOCIAL DISORDER

Alcohol use represents a special case when it comes to legal issues and criminal offences. Although a licit drug, there are a number of negative health and social effects that tend to accompany excessive alcohol consumption. In Australia approximately 1,676 deaths and 48,910 hospitalisations are attributable to alcohol intoxication annually (Rowe et al. 2012). Aboriginal Australians in particular bear a disproportionate burden of alcohol-related disease (Calabria et al. 2010). As canvassed earlier, alcohol is also associated with the commission of a range of offences, from making too much noise through to serious assaults. Indeed, the most recent findings of the Drug Use Monitoring in Australia Program (DUMA) report a greater proportion of drug-using police detainees attributing their offending to alcohol use (41%) compared to illicit drug use (32%) (Payne & Gaffney 2012). In 2010, the total cost to society of alcohol-related issues was estimated to be over $14 billion—a fifth of which was attributable to criminal justice costs (Manning et al. 2013). Moreover, research indicates that up to 70 per cent of public disorder offences are alcohol related (cited in Rowe et al. 2012).

Research has examined the different types of drinkers and the probability of committing disorder offences depending upon patterns of drinking. How much, and the way in which one consumes alcohol is directly related to the probability of committing disorder offences across a number of dimensions: drink driving; verbal abuse; creating a public disturbance; stealing property; damaging property; and physical abuse (Makkai 1998). Moreover, as indicated in Table 11.1, the frequency of engaging in social disorder increases according to the propensity to drink heavily, binge drink and drink in harmful ways.

TABLE 11.1 ALCOHOL CONSUMPTION AND PROPENSITY FOR ALCOHOL-RELATED DISORDER

PROPENSITY FOR DISORDER	NON-DRINKER %	MODERATE %	HEAVY %	BINGE %	HARMFUL OR HAZARDOUS %
None	94	86	63	45	57
Single	2	6	13	12	7
Repeat	1	4	9	9	12
Multiple repeat	2	3	10	17	14
Chronic	2	2	5	17	10

Source: 1993 and 1995 NDS National Household Surveys, pooled file weighted sample, cited in Makkai (1998: 6)

COMORBIDITY AND DRUGS

COMORBIDITY
Overlapping problems such as homelessness, abuse, family difficulties, mental illness and deteriorating physical health. Commonly used to refer to the combination of drug and alcohol abuse with a medically defined mental illness.

Another significant problem is that of **comorbidity** among drug-dependent individuals presenting to the criminal justice system. For instance, psychiatric wellbeing is intertwined with drug use, and these in turn are linked to struggles with accommodation and income, homelessness, abuse, family difficulties and deteriorating physical health (AIC 2008, 2005). Furthermore, the issues arising from the drugs–crime nexus are often compounded in the face of poly-drug use, which is prevalent among offenders with complex drug dependencies, typically comprising those most deeply implicated in the criminal justice system (Sweeney & Payne 2011). The extent and nature of drug use is profoundly affected by social patterns, with the most public and harmful uses associated with low socio-economic background and those with few social resources.

In contrast, it is entirely possible for some individuals to take drugs (even hard-core drugs) and not need to engage in criminal activity, because of their superior socio-economic resources, which enable them to access the substances without visibility, and fund their purchases through legal means, thereby maintaining productive social functionality. They also have readier access to health and medical services as needed. Hollywood celebrities who consume drugs are rarely deemed dangerous or threatening, but rather as victims and vulnerable. Their behaviour may be classified as deviant, but this deviance is seen to go with the lifestyle (rich celebrity) or the industry (fashion or acting). And when a celebrity dies from a drug-related overdose, be it Amy Winehouse, Michael Jackson, Heath Ledger or *Glee* star Cory Monteith, the title of 'junkie' never enters the post-mortem discussion (Middendorp 2013). Similar arguments apply to medical professionals who have ready access to illicit drugs and whose abuse is both facilitated and cloaked by their position of respectability (Medew 2013a). Treatment and rehabilitation are expensive, but affordable to such drug users. In contrast, those with limited financial resources are ironically commonly provided access to rehabilitative options only once drawn into the criminal justice system (Shiner 2013).

DRUG CULTURE

It is thus important to locate drug use within the context of specific sorts of drug culture. For instance, the high profile given to illegal drugs in the mass media has been accompanied by moral panics over drug use among teenagers. Headlines about deaths linked to the taking of ecstasy and lurid details about deaths due to heroin overdoses, and the detrimental physical and mental health of users generally, have further reinforced public concern over how best to tackle the 'war on drugs'. However, as a proportion of all crimes committed by juveniles formally processed by the criminal justice system, drug offences are not especially significant. In 2012–13, for example, only 12 per cent of all young offenders were processed for illicit drug offences as a primary offence (ABS 2014a; see also Cunneen & White 2011). Furthermore, most prosecutions for drug offences are for minor offences, except where this is linked to alcohol-related and other drug-related violence. There are also significant age-related differences in drug use. At a younger age, people tend to experiment with individual drugs, including alcohol; as they get older, into their late teens and early twenties, there is a greater tendency to start mixing different kinds of drugs.

Drug use connected to youth dance cultures (particularly ecstasy) continues to generate controversy. However, this, too, requires closer scrutiny if we are to understand the influence of specific drug cultures on drug-taking practices. For example, the use of drugs in association with rave parties has changed and evolved over time. When the rave scene commenced, raving was an informal, self-generated, subcultural leisure activity. Those in the 'scene' were also in the 'know' when it came to appropriate and safe drug use. Entrants into the culture were socialised into this kind of drug use. The drugs may have been illegal, but the drug taking was done under internally regulated guidelines. Over time, however, rave parties became more commercialised and increasingly found a home in clubs. Rave culture was radically altered, as was the clientele who attended the rave parties (Chan 1999). In this scenario, many new young people were introduced to raving, but without the subcultural training in suitable drug-use precautions. This diminution in informal mechanisms of drug regulation has resulted in a concomitant increase in the likelihood of drug-related problems occurring (especially overdosing), particularly among first-time and naïve drug takers.

Recent discussions about the nature of teenage drug use also point to the 'normalisation' of young people's drug use—its movement away from the periphery of youth subculture and incorporation into conventional youth lifestyles and identities. In the light of documented significant increases in the prevalence and frequency of teenage drug use in recent decades, in places such as England and Western Europe, as well as Australia, young people are viewing and using drugs, including cannabis, ecstasy and meth/amphetamines, very differently today, from how they once did (see Blackman 2010; Duff 2003; Gatto 1999; Parker et al. 1998; Parker 2005; Olsen 2009). Whereas particular drugs were considered exotic, and drug use was typically associated with 'deviancy' and law-breaking behaviour, contemporary youth now regard it as a normal and uncontroversial aspect of the young person's life experience. Duff (2003) suggests that many drug users, far from being pathological, mentally ill or irresponsible, as depicted in the popular media, are 'well-adjusted, responsible and outgoing'. Their use of drugs is a deliberate and strategic recreational activity. For many, rave dance parties and ecstasy use represent a conscious connection between particular pleasure, excitement and enjoyment pursuits and the drug that best suits the occasion. The consumption of different substances is used strategically to express one's allegiances to particular youth cultures and scenes, and thus to reinforce a particular social identity (see Duff 2003).

Further analysis of youth drug use refines this understanding. Shildrick (2002: 36), for example, argues that 'a concept of "differentiated normalization", which allows for the ways in which different types of drugs and different types of drug use may be normalised for different groups of young people, may be a more appropriate tool for understanding contemporary youthful drug use' than perspectives that see normalisation in more generalist terms. Green and Moore (2013) find support for this approach in their recent work on the process by which young people situated within a crystal methamphetamine smoking network negotiate their identities within a broader context of the mainstreaming of other illicit drugs within the leisure landscape. The most common identity management technique against stigma among the group was appeal to the value of autonomy, control and responsible drug use linked to recreational practices.

LEGALITY, ILLEGALITY AND SOCIAL HARM

How drugs are classified as legal or illegal is closely related to political processes as well as changing moral values. For many years the term 'drugs' was closely associated with the idea of illegal substances, but today there are many legal drugs used by the community that are just as harmful, including cigarettes, alcohol, some synthetic cannabinoids (see Barratt et al. 2013; Callinan 2014) and prescription drugs. From this perspective, then, drug use is part of everyday behaviour rather than limited to specific, deviant groups.

This is not to suggest that drug use is not associated with social harm. Collins and Lapsley (2008), for instance, estimated that of the $56.1 billion economic cost associated with licit and illicit drug use in 2004–05, tobacco accounted for the majority (56%), followed by alcohol (27%), illicit drugs (15%), and alcohol and illicit drugs combined (2%). The problem is not simply one of production, supply and consumption of prohibited substances, nor simply a matter of economic cost. A major issue is the effect of psychoactive drugs on people's behaviour in ways that make them a danger to others.

Although the relationship between drug use and antisocial behaviour is not direct, it is clear that it is closely associated with damaging effects, from violence outside pubs and clubs to domestic violence (see Chapter 10) and dangerous driving. Nor is the harm limited to victims, since many drugs, including those available legally, also have serious health consequences for users. For instance, in 2010, most drug overdoses worldwide involved prescription, opioid-based analgesics such as oxycodone, hydrocodone and methadone (cited in Australian Crime Commission 2013). Within Australia, there is great concern about drugs such as 'ice', with its use linked to devastating short- and long-term physical and psychological effects, including the development of psychosis that manifests in unpredictable violence (including homicide and rape) and deaths linked to acute toxicity (Baker & McKenzie 2013; Hagan 2013; Medew 2013b).

There is consequently great concern to prevent its use whatsoever. Overall, alcohol remains the most common form of drug addiction for 46 per cent of those seeking treatment for addictions in Australia in 2011–12 (AIHW 2013c). For these reasons, any consideration of drug use necessarily crosses the boundaries between criminal justice, health, and welfare and education. Responding to drug use and abuse therefore requires both sensitivity to social context and an appreciation of adopting holistic and multifaceted approaches that best manage drug use and minimise harm, rather than banning drug use altogether.

PUBLIC ORDER OFFENCES

Public order offences are offences relating to personal behaviour and demeanour that involve, or may result in, breaches of public order or decency, or which indicate criminal intent, or that are otherwise controlled or proscribed on moral or ethical grounds (ABS 2011b). Also variously described as 'street offences', 'police offences' and 'summary offences', public order offences include: offensive, indecent or obscene behaviour (e.g. offensive language, racial vilification or incitement of hatred, blasphemy, begging, vagrancy, public drunkenness, busking without a permit or coarse gesticulation); disorderly conduct (e.g. trespass on private or public land, riot and affray, criminal intent [associating with known criminals or behaving in a manner or possessing tools, clothing or other material that suggest an intent to commit a criminal offence], desecration of graves and hoaxes causing public nuisance); and regulated public order offences (including betting and gambling offences, consumption of alcohol or cigarettes in regulated spaces, prostitution, offences against public order or sexual standards). These offences do not generally involve a specific victim(s), although behaviours (e.g. offensive language and offensive behaviour) may be directed at a single victim.

Public order offences cover a wide ambit of activities and it is therefore not surprising that in 2012–13, almost one in five (19%) apprehended offenders officially processed by police had a public order offence listed as their principal offence (ABS 2014a).

There are three main features to public order offences (Brown et al. 2001: 942):

- the *centrality of the police* (and police discretion) in initiating and prosecuting such charges
- the regulation of behaviour *in public places* (the policing of 'public order' and public spaces)
- the processing of most charges *summarily, in the lower courts* (or, in some cases, via on-the-spot fines).

It is useful to bear these elements in mind when specific types of offence are being considered. There are major issues surrounding who gets targeted under public order offence provisions, and what the punishment process entails. Consider, for example, the case of the 'dancing man of Hobart' (see Box 11.2). The point of this story is that there seem to be fewer and fewer places for eccentric characters like the dancing man to express themselves legitimately. Aggressive and coercive crime prevention can, in fact, rob the social environment of interesting and exotic people, as well as breed resentment at both the uniformity of community spaces and how such spaces are regulated. Conformity may well be enforced, but at what social cost?

PUBLIC ORDER OFFENCES
Offences involving personal conduct that breaches or may lead to a breach of public order and decency, or that is indicative of criminal intent, or that is otherwise regulated or prohibited on moral or ethical grounds.

JUVENILE OFFENCES IN PUBLIC PLACES

The vast majority of public order offences are dealt with by magistrates' courts; in 2012–13, for example, magistrates' courts dealt with 94 per cent of all public order offences (ABS 2014f). In legal terms and in relation to criminal law, such offences are seen to be relatively trivial and less serious in nature. Nevertheless, although victimisation may not be especially traumatic, victim surveys suggest that public order offences are potentially more powerful and widespread sources of fear in the community, affecting perceptions of safety as well as levels of crime and disorder (see ABS 2011a). Typically, dangerous or noisy driving, people being insulted, louts, youth gangs, illegal drugs and public drunkenness are identified by respondents as social disorder problems.

Many public order types of offences—and, correspondingly, many state responses to public disorders of various kinds—revolve around the activities of young people (those under the age of 25 years). The specific features of juvenile offending itself shape the media perceptions of youth criminality and police

---

BOX 11.2   THE DANCING MAN OF HOBART

The 'Dancing Man' died in Melbourne in May 2003. His death sparked spontaneous outpourings of grief, love and sadness in Hobart, his place of residence and his dancing stage for a number of years. Most people did not know his name (Anthony James Day); they only saw him dancing: in the main city mall, at civic events, in all manner of public spaces.

He left Hobart shortly after being fined for failing to obey the direction of a police officer to 'move on', and died soon after.

Tributes were written in the mall in chalk. Alas, the chalk memorial was washed away by local council workers that same night. The next day, undeterred, friends, acquaintances and complete strangers gathered to celebrate his life by dancing in the mall.

Such are the contradictions and ambiguities of street life. Nuisance laws are used to sweep people off the streets. We grieve at the loss of vitality and creativity when the music stops. Yet the streets are kept clean—whether appropriate or not, whether we like it or not.

Source: Sutton et al. (2008: 138)

---

interventions in juvenile justice. For example, the following aspects of juvenile offending relate directly to how young people use public space (see Cunneen & White 2011, 1995):

- Young people tend to hang around in groups, and youth crime tends to be committed in groups.
- The public congregation of young people makes them particularly visible, and thus youth crime tends to be more readily apparent and detectable.
- Young people tend to commit crime in their own neighbourhoods, where there is greater likelihood that they will be recognised and identified by observers.
- The social dynamics of the offence means it is often public, gregarious and attention seeking.
- Youth crime is often episodic, unplanned and opportunistic, and related to the use of public space in areas such as shopping centres and public transport, where there is more surveillance.

The above characteristics in part reflect the nature of the restrictions on spatial mobility (e.g. transport costs, restrictions on access to user-pay entertainment, and increasing limitations on and surveillance of the use of semi-public spaces that have a capital accumulation imperative, such as shopping centres and malls) and social mobility (geographical isolation, labour market exclusion, poverty etc.) disproportionately suffered by young people (McAuliffe 2013; Rose 2000). The consequent public visibility and group behaviour of young people makes them more prone to arrest for certain types of crimes than their adult counterparts. In 2012–13, young people aged 10–24 years comprised the majority (54%) of offenders officially processed by police for public order offences (ABS 2014a). The highest rate of offending was recorded among those aged 15–19 (1,206 per 100,000 population), with the rate of offending steadily declining for each subsequent age category, reaching a low for those aged 65+ (11 per 100,000 population).

Simultaneously, non-criminal behaviour and less serious offending by young people are also subject to routine scrutiny by authority figures and other adults. Again, this is mainly because of the visibility of young people in public spaces, which is enhanced by the fact that they generally hang around in groups (White 1990). Further to this, large congregations of young people may be disruptive to the flow of pedestrian traffic, and may be accompanied by the making of noise, which may be disturbing to some bystanders and shopkeepers. The adoption of particular unconventional youth cultural 'styles' can mark some teenagers out from the crowd and bring them to the notice of other users of public space. The very presence of young people, much less what they are actually doing, can therefore be perceived as unsettling and problematic.

POLICE REACTIONS TO 'BAD BEHAVIOUR'

Perceptions of 'bad behaviour' and 'bad people' are important to consider when it comes to how and why police carry out their duties in relation to specific groups. Leaving aside for the moment the ongoing climate of distrust and disrespect characterising many local police–youth relations, it is significant that the justification for particular kinds of police action is provided by the apparent attitudes of the general public. This type of regulatory environment thus reflects particular concerns with, and conceptions of, acceptable and unacceptable behaviour in public places on the part of authority figures and other users of these spaces.

Perceptions of a 'problem' require some form of police 'solution'. Public consternation and media attention given to street behaviour (usually focusing on antisocial activity, youth gangs, public drunkenness, drug use, visible minorities and Indigenous people) have been reflected in discussions of *zero tolerance policing* and new public order legislation expressly targeting particular groups and types of social behaviour. The use of offensive language and offensive behaviour offences is thus generally highly targeted, and socially patterned (White 2002). Some groups of people are charged more than others, and this is reflected in the overall distributions of charges. This is especially the case in regards to Indigenous people (see Chapter 17).

OFFENSIVE LANGUAGE AND INDIGENOUS PEOPLE

When we consider broad public perceptions of civility, which often hinge upon the use of certain words, it is important to note that although offensive language laws exist throughout Australia, they do not necessarily criminalise swearing. Different thresholds exist across jurisdictions in terms of punishable language, and what is considered profane, indecent, offensive or obscene is largely contextual (Leaver 2011). Due to the ambiguities of offensive language laws, police are afforded a significant degree of discretionary power in terms of determining offence, especially in Victoria, where they are able to issue on-the-spot infringement notices for suspected offences against the *Summary Offences Act 1966*, as opposed to having the matter heard before a magistrate (Leaver 2011). Patterns of police intervention in dealing with 'offensive language' reveal a dilemma for young Indigenous people. They are being penalised for behaviour that in their cultural universe may be part of routine, everyday communication. It may not be defined or experienced by them as 'swearing'. For many young people, it is a normal and ingrained part of how they converse with their family and with each other. However, as pointed out in an Aboriginal submission to the Royal Commission into Deaths in Custody, what constitutes 'swearing' in some communities is that which is specifically forbidden by Aboriginal law; that is, swearing to certain kinds of 'poison relations': in-laws, or a sister swearing in front of a brother (Johnston 1991: 352).

Work that has investigated the nature, style and dynamics of swearing, specifically within Indigenous communities, has found that its cultural meaning is highly contextual and variable (Langton 1988). For example, there is no sanction on children swearing at or in front of their mothers in some communities, and there is no public sanction on swearing by women (contrast this with traditional conventions in Western society). To some extent, this is culturally specific, and reflects as much as anything the fact that English is not native to Aboriginal people and its use and patterns have developed in particular ways over time.

Significantly, swearing may be an integral part of 'making everybody happy', in that it is part of good-natured banter in the context of formally defined joking relationships. It can also be used aggressively, in order to precipitate a fight within a community or to exercise resistance against the dominant forces outside of it. The specific nature of swearing will differ according to the particular individuals and communities in question. Indigenous people are heterogeneous in composition. There are differences within the varying communities, and between individuals, in terms of political and spiritual beliefs, regional and family ties, traditional and contemporary lifestyles, class, and occupational position and social identity. How people swear is shaped by situational factors in particular social settings. The dynamics of swearing in relation to the police, in particular, can only be fully comprehended in the light of the historical relationship and ongoing conflicts between the police and Indigenous people (see Cunneen 2001; also Chapter 17).

While all crime is socially patterned, analysis of laws relating to public order throws into particularly sharp relief the issues of power and control that underlie all criminal justice issues. This may be because the social harm caused by behaviour such as swearing in public is generally perceived to be relatively small compared with more serious offences such as assault or burglary. Consequently, the subjective nature of the application of the law—that is, whose behaviour is defined as 'offensive'—is more visible.

PUBLIC DRUNKENNESS: CRIMINALISING HOMELESSNESS

Like offensive language, patterns of intervention in the case of public drunkenness reveal differential vulnerabilities to identification and criminal processing. The situation of homeless individuals is a case in point, especially in the context of changes to Victoria's *Summary Offences Act 1966*, which extend the application of infringement notices to public drunkenness (Adams 2012); Victoria and Queensland are the only states where it is illegal to be publicly drunk. Introduced under the guise of granting police greater powers to combat violence and antisocial behaviour, the laws have been extensively applied, with 23,503infringements issued in an 18-month period between 2009 and 2011. Of these, 91 per cent were issued against persons drunk in a public place, defined as including public highways, roads and streets, bridges, footpaths, alleyways, parks, gardens and other recreational locations, railway stations or platforms or carriages, wharves, piers and jetties (Adams 2012).

Adams (2012) highlights the discriminatory nature of enforcement of these laws, especially in the case of alcohol-dependent homeless individuals. Unable to drink within the privacy of their own home and unable to afford to drink in licensed establishments, homeless people have no option but to conduct their lives (which includes drinking) publicly. The high visibility of homeless people makes them vulnerable to targeting and to the discriminatory application of laws that criminalise otherwise legal behaviour when conducted within the private domain; discrimination that is based on their housing status rather than their behaviour per se. For those struggling with chronic alcohol dependence, engaging in conspicuous public drinking to excess creates a high-risk situation for criminalisation in a situation where the threat of an infringement provides no disincentive.

Indigenous rates of homelessness are high, especially in the Northern Territory (Goddard et al. 2012). When this is considered alongside the preference for Indigenous Australians (and other socio-economically disadvantaged and minority groups) to drink in public due to the strong sense of connection with the land and because of the unwelcoming feel of, and restrictive behaviour permitted within, licensed venues (Pennay & Room 2012), their vulnerability to processing for public order offences becomes clear.

Like many public order offences, the policing of public drunkenness raises interesting juxtapositions on the use of public space (its accessibility, entry controls, sanctioned behaviour and conduct rules) related to social class (Pennay & Room 2012). It is notable, for instance, that street drinking bans have proliferated across Australian urban centres at the same time that public drinking on the street has become increasingly legitimated in the form of continental style drinking; that is, the serving of alcohol on footpaths, often in the context of dining. As Pennay and Room (2012: 92) contend:

> the advent of footpath trading poses in stark terms the contrasting treatment of drinkers, often of different social classes—the street drinkers on one side of the street are outside the law, whereas those on the other side, within the pub's or restaurant's permitted use of public space, are within the law.

ANIMAL ABUSE

A new area of criminalisation that involves the construction of new conventions of behaviour relates to animal abuse. Beirne (2009) observes that rarely have animals been understood in criminology other than in terms of their legal status as the property of human masters. Laws against poaching—of deer, pheasants, rabbits and partridges—in England were designed not to protect animals, but the rights of the rich and powerful to do with these creatures as they willed at their exclusive command. In short, the law sought to protect one's property, not to protect the animal as such. Discussion of animal abuse is important insofar as it highlights how conventional ways of treating some animals becomes problematic, while raising questions over why some creatures are valued by humans and yet others are not. Crimes against convention, when it comes to animals, are about more than just dealing with instances of cruelty to animal companions such as dogs and cats. Closer scrutiny of the issues raises important questions about where the lines of convention in fact ought to be drawn and the appropriate nature of the relationship between human and non-human animals (Hughes & Lawson 2011; White 2013b).

Historically, it is true that laws have been enacted to forbid cruel and improper treatment of certain animals, but criminologists seldom considered animal suffering as the explicit focus of study. Moreover, in practice, law enforcement was at best haphazard, and the 'crime' did not rate highly in public consciousness or concern.

Phenomena such as arranging dog fights for entertainment and sports betting have, however, in recent years drawn much public condemnation in places such as the United States. The rise of both anti-cruelty movements (e.g. the Royal Society for the Prevention of Cruelty to Animals (RSPCA)) and animal rights movements (e.g. People for the Ethical Treatment of Animals (PETA)) has been instrumental in raising awareness of animal abuse issues, and in the development of alternative ways of thinking about such abuses (Hughes & Lawson 2011).

What counts as animal 'abuse' varies enormously within and between cultures and societies, however. Is locking up chickens in small coops a form of abuse? What counts as 'animal' abuse likewise varies depending upon the type and status of the animal one is referring to. Do fish have the capacity for conscious awareness, fear and pain? If they do, is fishing therefore a form of abuse? There are many questions that can be asked regarding which animals 'deserve' moral concern, protection and freedom from abuse, and how abuse itself is to be defined in legal and social terms (see, for example, Bastian et al. 2012; Cottee 2012; Moore 2013; Sunstein & Nussbaum 2006). To answer these questions, we need to appreciate why it is that human societies simultaneously respect and protect certain creatures (especially animal companions such as dogs, cats and birds, or animals scientifically 'closer' to us, such as primates), while allowing and even condoning the utterly dreadful treatment of others (as in the case of factory farming of battery hens to produce eggs or use of gestation stalls in intensive pig farming) (see Beirne 2004).

Legislation can cover a broad range of acts against animals, such as protection from cruelty, abandonment and poisoning, and ensuring that animals are provided with necessary sustenance and shelter. Nevertheless, there are major ambiguities in terms of how laws are framed and how they are translated into practice. For instance, the use of animals in laboratory testing may involve systematic mutilation and lead to the radical altering of eco-systems, as has occurred with the use of the Xenopus frog for pregnancy testing (Moore 2013); yet, this type of action is legally allowed as long as the animals are provided 'humane care and treatment' generally (see Beirne 2009).

Beirne (2009) asserts that the politics of selectivity is always at the heart of any given criminalisation process, and this pertains to animal abuse as well. He asks the questions: 'Which species are positively valued? Which are deemed worthy of legal protection? Which species are excluded from the circle of moral consideration?' The answer to these questions leads us to consider some of the debates and differences within the movements supportive of animal protection (Beirne & South 2007; Benton 1998).

SPECIESISM AND ANIMAL ABUSE

SPECIESISM
The practice of discriminating against non-human animals because they are perceived as inferior to the human species, similar to the way sexism and racism involve prejudice and discrimination against women and people of colour.

In general terms, concepts such as human-centred **speciesism** may be invoked. Coined by Ryder (1975), this term refers to the practice of discriminating against the suffering of non-human animals because they are perceived as inferior to the human species, in much the same way that sexism and racism involve prejudice and discrimination against women and people of colour (see also Munro 2004d; Singer 2002). Animal rights supporters argue that there are two kinds of animals—human and non-human—and that both have rights and interests as sentient, suffering beings affected by physical pain and torture; they question, however, the ethical relationship between animal species, asserting that the dominant ideology of speciesism enables humans to exploit non-human animals as commodities to be eaten, displayed, hunted and dissected for their benefit. Specific animal issues therefore include:

- animals as research objects
- animals as food
- animals as trophies
- animals as display (zoos).

Investigation of harm involving non-human animals generally starts from the premise that the central issue is harm to animals, and that humans are implicated in this process in varying ways and to varying degrees. Within mainstream criminology, the progressive thesis, for example, inquires into how young people who abuse animals progress to other types of criminal acts, such as harm against humans, including murder (Ascione 2001; Dadds et al. 2002; Panahi 2013). Animal cruelty is linked to antisocial behaviour generally. Thus, one feeds the other. Breaking one convention (that involves cruelty to non-human animals) is symptomatic of the breaking of others (that involve harms against other humans). The former, however, is prefigured in other social practices that value animals for human-centric purposes first and foremost—such as duck hunting, jumps horse racing and use as laboratory specimens—and that, in so doing, disregard the normal conventions of humaneness and care.

Other research has argued that systematic abuse of animals via factory farms (the commoditisation of animals in the process of industrial livestock production) ought to be considered at the same time as specific instances of harm to particular animals (Beirne 2004). Indeed, recent criminological commentary on the social impact of working in abattoirs suggests that those whose job it is to inflict suffering upon and ultimately kill animals on a daily basis are probably disproportionately more likely to be less empathetic towards their fellow humans (see Beirne 2004; MacNair 2002). In other words, where cruelty is in a sense built into the job (e.g. working in a slaughterhouse), the ramifications are that the job itself perverts the ordinary sensibilities of workers and takes them psychologically and socially in an unhealthy and negative direction. As contended by McLeod-Kilmurray (2012: 72), they become:

> mere cogs in the economic wheel of the industrialized food system almost as much as the nonhuman animals have. In order to fully participate in this system they need to divorce themselves from feelings such as empathy and community. They must also replace care about fellow humans and future generations as well as concern for nonhuman creatures, with short-term, narrowly defined economic benefits.

WELFARE APPROACH VERSUS RIGHTS-BASED APPROACH

Traditional theorising about animals, within an animal concern paradigm, can be largely characterised as lying on a scale ranging from a welfarist approach at one end of the scale, to a rights-based or ecological justice approach (interspecies justice) at the other end. The focus of the welfarist approach is the humane treatment of animals (Ibrahim 2006; Lusk & Norwood 2012; McLeod-Kilmurray 2012). This model advocates the protection of animals through increased welfare-based interventions, but not the prohibition of animal exploitation, including their commoditisation for industrial food production. The model is focused on improvements to the treatment of animals, but does not challenge the embedded exploitation of animals that is a consequence of their social and legal status (Ibrahim 2006). Implicit in this model of thought is the assumption that animals may still be exploited for their flesh, fur and skin, provided that their suffering is not 'unnecessary' or, as often put, the animals are treated humanely.

Closely associated with this perspective is the notion of protection of endangered species, and efforts to maintain the sustainability of animals in certain industries. For example, the poaching of abalone or lobster is prohibited insofar as it impinges upon the property rights of licensed fishers and taxation powers of the state, while simultaneously depleting species numbers (McMullan & Perrier 2002; Tailby & Gant 2002). Legislation that prohibits the illegal trade of wildlife, particularly endangered wildlife, is meant to protect species from criminal exploitation, although why and how species become endangered is less frequently addressed (e.g. degradation of habitats generally or destruction of local ecology through, for instance, clear-fell forestry). Intervention is mainly pitched at the species level, with efforts being put into conserving and maintaining viable numbers of particular species. Contemporary zoos sometimes justify their practices on the basis of this kind of conservation ethos. For example, Copenhagen zoo recently killed an18-month old giraffe by bolt gun and later euthanised four lions from the same family (to avoid inbreeding), sparking community outrage when it was revealed that the animals were healthy (Dell'Amore 2014).

At the other end of the spectrum is the rights-based approach, which looks for sites of oppression in the intersection between human and non-human animal. In its extreme form, this approach contends that animals have rights to live free from human interference. This approach argues for the abolition of animal exploitation through legal and non-legal change, and for the legal recognition of animal rights. Central to this approach is changing the legal character of animals from property to legal, rights-bearing entities (see Svard 2008; Wise 2004, 2001). The intention is to prevent the exploitation of non-human animals, both in regards to their products (e.g. milk, eggs and wool) and their lives (as in the case of animals killed for food). Any type of poisoning, trapping or hunting is seen as wrong, even where justified in terms of certain species impinging upon others (e.g. attempts to eradicate foxes in Tasmania).

In essence, the extension of human moral rights and concerns to non-human animals sees veganism set as the baseline for politics, with the moral rights of each individual animal asserted (Svard 2008).

In addressing the issue of animal abuse, Beirne (2009) argues that if the violation of animals' rights is to be taken seriously, then we need to examine why some harms to animals are defined as criminal, others as abusive but not criminal, and still others as neither criminal nor abusive. In pointing this out, Beirne (2009) emphasises that exploring these questions necessarily leads to a more inclusive concept of harm. It also means that much more empirical work needs to be done to see how laws are actually put into practice, where specific human interests fit into the picture and how the social control of animal abuse ought to be carried out at an institutional level (see White 2013b).

ISSUES FOR CONSIDERATION

'TOLERATING' DEVIANCY

Does analysis of social deviancy mean that we have to accept or be 'tolerant' of everything associated with a particular group? In other words, what ought to be the role of the criminologist in the study of particular groups, especially those that in some way or another challenge or break normal social conventions? As Cohen (1973b: xxvii) observed in relation to the study of youth subcultures: 'Those same values of racism, sexism, chauvinism, compulsive masculinity and anti-intellectualism, the slightest traces of which are condemned in bourgeois culture, are treated with a deferential care, an exaggerated contextualization, when they appear in the subculture.' One has to be careful about being too respectful and too understanding of practices that may in fact be very damaging and antisocial in nature. For example, rock throwing may be fun in some circumstances, but it can also kill people in others (Loughnan 2010). The latter is not defensible as an amusement, although its occurrence does demand analytical understanding and interpretation.

It is also essential to drill down to the specific nature of the activities in question. For example, there are qualitative differences between racist graffiti and graffiti art, and each occupies a different cultural universe. Much the same can be said for different patterns of drug use and alcohol consumption. The problem may not be 'graffiti in general' or 'drugs in general'. Rather, as detailed and fine-grained analysis may show, important differences exist in the specific nature of particular practices, and these differences have implications vis-à-vis social harm and community safety.

As this chapter demonstrates, it is also important to gain an understanding of the various meanings attached to specific acts, whether drug use, swearing or our relationship to animals. How we express meaning and how certain acts become meaningful is very important to how deviancy and conformism are construed by participants in any particular activity.

NEW FORMS OF VICTIMLESS CRIME

A review of victimless or morality-based crimes serves to underscore crime as a social phenomenon—this extends to processes of law making, legal transgression and societal responses to law breaking. Law evolves and is subject to modification and repeal in accordance with changing societal standards, cultural values and mores pertaining to appropriate behaviour. However, it is important to note the tensions and political influences underlying the enactment and enforcement of morality based laws, which do not always reflect societal consensus regarding acceptable societal behaviour—hence why that deemed acceptable in one jurisdiction is considered unacceptable in another. As Clement and Barbrey (2008) remind us, it is important to question *whose* morals serve as a template for legislated morals and *which social order* is in need of protection. The recent advent of sexting laws (see Chapters 10 and 15) serves as a pertinent example of an addition to the victimless crime stable. The law, as it presently stands, fails to differentiate between the consensual electronic exchange of self-photographed nude body images between a creator and recipient (both mainly teenagers), and child pornography (Jaishankar 2009).

THE WAR ON DRUGS

A series of reports by the Global Commission on Drug Policy (2013, 2012, 2011) are a damning indictment on the global war on drugs, citing widespread consequences for individuals and society alike. The Commission concludes that the burgeoning criminalisation and vast expenditure on aggressive and repressive drug policies, directed at manufacturers, traffickers and consumers of illicit drugs, has failed to curb demand, supply and consumption. Not only have such policies criminalised, marginalised and stigmatised those who use illicit drugs but do no harm to others, but they have also fuelled misconceptions about drug markets, drug use and drug dependence; have generated violence; and have had a detrimental impact on public health, driving HIV/AIDS and hepatitis C pandemics among injecting drug users (see also Green 2013). The Commission recommends a reallocation of limited resources away from law enforcement activities that punish drug users towards public health and prevention activities (see also Mostyn et al. 2012). In Australia alone, state, territory and federal governments collectively spent $1.7 billion on drug policy in 2009–10, of which $36 million was spent on harm-reduction strategies, $361 million on treatment services and $1.1 billion on law enforcement (Ritter et al. 2013).

A transformation in the framing of drug policy is evident in the United States, with the progressive decriminalisation of possession of marijuana and endorsement of its use for medical purposes (O'Brien 2013). Likewise, New Zealand's new synthetic drug law, the *Psychoactive Substances Act 2013*, establishes a regulatory process to potentially approve synthetic drugs on the basis of demonstrated safety.

CONCLUSION

The aim of this chapter has been to examine the dynamics and nature of behaviours that are generally deemed to be unacceptable to the mainstream. Crimes against convention simultaneously challenge the status quo and yet reinforce the key values and conventions of that status quo. The duality between deviancy and normalcy is never fully achieved. Rather, the conventional and the unconventional form part of a circle of meaning that shifts and changes constantly. For those engaged in the unconventional, the activity has meaning and is meaningful. For those concerned with upholding conventions, the question of boundaries is of utmost importance.

The more one investigates what are deemed to be unconventional or confrontational activities, however, the more one appreciates how mundane they often appear to be. They may be wrong and they may be harmful in some instances, but they are generally quite understandable from the point of view of others who share similar social spaces. By talking about these activities, and talking with those who engage in them, we are better able to appreciate their complexities—and their attractions.

It is also important to consider how such activities are often conducted without considered thought about consequences. Particularly, but not exclusively, for young people, activity such as being loud and boisterous in public spaces, using drugs for recreational purposes and so on may not be considered either deviant or unusual. So, too, the consequences arising from engagement in these sorts of activities may not be considered, or at the best considered abstractly rather than in terms of personal possibilities, likelihoods and responsibilities. Acts can thus be intentional at one level, but their consequences can be unintentional, unanticipated and unexpected. Such is the ambiguity of skirting the edges of convention.

Finally, the discussion of animal abuse highlights the dearth of attention to this issue within mainstream criminology (and criminology textbooks). It also brings home once again the importance of viewing the conventional and the unconventional as constantly shifting phenomena, applicable to many different kinds of human activity. Crimes against convention are socially constructed and socially created. This applies to the most ordinary and mundane aspects of everyday life.

Over the preceding few chapters our focus has been largely on street crime. Chapter 12 shifts into a consideration of crimes of the powerful, including those perpetrated by the state.

DISCUSSION QUESTIONS

1   Why can it be argued that drug use is an everyday activity?

2   Should drug use be regarded as a social problem?

3   Why does the policing of Indigenous Australians in public spaces reflect both political conflict and cultural difference?

4   'Analysis of deviancy tells us much about the nature of society generally.' Discuss four activities regarded deviant only a few years ago that are now regarded as everyday social activities.

5   'Killing animals for human consumption is murder.' Discuss.

FURTHER READING

Beirne, P. (2009) *Confronting animal abuse: law, criminology, and human–animal relationships*, Rowman & Littlefield, Lanham.

Global Commission on Drug Policy (2011) *War on drugs*, United Nations, <http://issuu.com/gcdp/docs/global_commission_report_english/1?e=0>.

Roche, A., Bywood, P., Borlagdan, J., Lunnay, B., Freeman, T., Lawton, L., Toveli, A. & Nicholas, R. (2008) *Young people and alcohol: the role of cultural influences*, DrinkWise Australia Ltd., Melbourne.

Schur, E. (1965) *Crimes without victims: deviant behavior and public policy*, Prentice-Hall, Englewood Cliffs.

Svard, P.-A. (2008) 'Protecting the animals? An abolitionist critique of animal welfarism and green ideology', in R. Sollund, *Global harms: ecological crime and speciesism*, Nova Science Publishers.

CRIMES OF THE POWERFUL   12

CHAPTER OVERVIEW

- WHITE-COLLAR AND CORPORATE CRIME
- CLASS AND CRIMES OF THE POWERFUL
- MEASURING CRIMES OF THE POWERFUL
- STATE CRIME
- ISSUES FOR CONSIDERATION
- CONCLUSION
- DISCUSSION QUESTIONS
- FURTHER READING

INTRODUCTION

As preceding chapters have revealed, the problem of crime is generally framed by the problem of disadvantage: most official criminal statistics and the work of most criminal justice agencies are oriented toward working-class or street crime. Indeed, public images and media representations of crime tend to emphasise precisely those sorts of crimes and antisocial behaviours associated with marginalised and vulnerable populations (see Chapters 2 and 7). It is poor people who are the most likely to engage with the criminal justice system, and it is poor people's crimes, and preoccupation with the aetiology and prevention of street crime, that remain the central focus of most criminological theory and practice.

This chapter shifts the criminological gaze from crimes of the less powerful, to crimes of the powerful committed by individuals and institutions. The focus is on white-collar, corporate and state crime. Public debate about 'law and order' continues to focus on traditional rather than white-collar crimes. This is partly explained by the ability of the wealthy and the powerful to neutralise and normalise their activities, so that their crimes are not recognised as 'real' crimes, but are instead seen as acceptable, even necessary, to conducting business or running the state (or, indeed, of doing both simultaneously).

WHITE-COLLAR AND CORPORATE CRIME

The association between crime and poverty, which consumed much of traditional criminological thinking, was first challenged by Edward Sutherland (1940), who coined the phrase **white-collar crime** in a speech to the American sociology society in 1939, conceptualising it as 'a crime committed by a person of respectability and high social status in the course of his [sic] occupation' (1949: 9). In shining the spotlight on the business sector, Sutherland made the point that crime in the 'suites' (hidden crime committed by organisations) is just as real and damaging as crime in the streets (visible crimes committed by individuals and 'gangs').

In many ways, white-collar crime is more serious than conventional crime because of its widespread nature and insidious effects—a reflection of the poorly regulated nature of corporate activities. The financial harms perpetrated are often staggering, involving losses far higher than the amounts of

WHITE-COLLAR CRIME
Broadly, crime committed by a person of respectability and high social status in the course of his or her occupation. However, the term is sometimes used to describe all crimes committed by non-manual workers in the course of their occupation.

money stolen during conventional crimes associated with the working class. Moreover, crimes committed in the course of doing business threaten individual, organisational and societal economic viability and, in the context of globalisation and the new opportunities for transnational corporate crime, have the potential to undermine domestic and global confidence in the legitimacy of our corporate and political leaders and institutions (McGee & Byingon 2009). In some circumstances such crimes can also have profound and adverse human impacts, resulting in preventable morbidity and premature mortality.

DEFINITIONS OF WHITE-COLLAR CRIME

The phrase *white-collar crime* is an umbrella term used variably to describe a plethora of crimes committed by business and government professionals in the course of their occupation. It generally refers to financially motivated, nonviolent crimes such as fraud, bribery, embezzlement, insider trading, Ponzi schemes, forgery and money laundering. While in common parlance today, the concept of white-collar crime is not without contest and controversy. Debates revolve around the appropriate characterisation of crimes of the powerful (criminal activity versus deviance, unethical practice or a mere fact of doing business), the range of activities to be drawn into the ambit of the white-collar crime label (property crimes versus social harms) and the range of offenders to whom the label should apply (organisations or individuals; elite or subordinate organisations; and senior executives, middle managers, or employees of low status). As illustrated below, these debates cannot be divorced from appropriate consideration of crime motivation, its relationship to organisational culture and the centrality of power.

Definitional arguments relating to white-collar crime are important for a number of analytical and political reasons. Consider, for example, the following perspective:

> White-collar crime, although technically classified under property crime, needs to be distinguished because of its considerable impact on society. White-collar crimes originally covered acts committed by business people and professionals, but today includes theft by employees, corruption, cheating on taxes, social security fraud, medi-fraud (billing by physicians for services not performed), as well as stock market swindles, consumer fraud, and price-fixing. It also includes various crimes committed with the aid of, or against, telecommunications systems and computers. (Mukherjee & Graycar 1997: 10)

This definition is too restrictive in one sense, yet paradoxically too expansive in another. First, it is premised upon legal formalism; that is, a strictly legal definition of crime requiring evidence of violation of law (Michalowski 2010). As such, it ignores a key thrust of white-collar crime analysis: its insistence upon going beyond official criminal definitions to recognition of broader social harms. Second, it disregards the centrality of class and social status in the construction of this crime category. The whole point of its emergence as a discrete category of crime was to focus greater attention on crimes of the powerful as distinct from crimes of the less powerful (see Rosoff et al. 1998). This definition blurs the boundaries between conventional crime and white-collar crime by situating petty crimes committed by blue-collar (manual) workers (e.g. cheating by tradespeople), shop assistants (e.g. fiddling cash registers) and non-managerial office workers (e.g. pilfering from employers), which involve no physical contact with victims and money or goods of little value, alongside the large-scale crimes of the rich and powerful, from bottom-of-the-harbour tax schemes, through to overservicing by professionals, such as doctors and dentists.

Each of these crimes has the hallmarks of white-collar crime (Benson & Simpson 2009; Kelley 1976), in that they involve property or economic crime resulting in financial losses, and are characterised by deceit, concealment and violation of some degree of trust. They also all involve intentional acts perpetrated largely without physical force or violence or the threat of such. However, the issue of power, and specifically abuse or exploitation of power, fundamentally differentiates these activities. A core feature of crimes of the powerful is that they are possible only by virtue of the offender's employment status and the level of trust (and therefore access to crime opportunities) afforded them by their organisational standing and respectability. For example, transnational money laundering facilitated by banks involves the participation of senior bank officers with considerable authority and operational knowledge.

Use of such wide, yet paradoxically narrow definitions of white-collar crime can undercut the intent of Sutherland's original contribution to the study of power. Alternatively, we might consider the perspective of Snider (2000), who analyses the process by which the penning of law redefines essentially criminal acts of the powerful as non-criminal, and non-problematic breaches of regulation. In considering white-collar and **corporate crime**—in this case, including both financial crimes (e.g. antitrust and insider trading) and social crimes (e.g. health and safety law violations, which are still oriented towards maximising corporate profit but put lives and quality of lives at risk), as well as offences against the environment—Snider argues that:

> Because its survival as an object of study is contingent on the passage and enforcement of 'command and control' legislation, corporate crime can 'disappear' through decriminalization (the repeal of criminal law), through deregulation (the repeal of all state law, criminal, civil and administrative) and through downsizing (the destruction of the state's enforcement capability). (Snider 2000: 172)

What Snider (2000), and Sutherland (1940) before her, focuses our attention on is the manner in which structural and ideological conflicts underpin differential assessment and treatment of analogous crimes committed by persons of respectability and high social standing, and 'street' offenders; and how socially injurious activity, even when engaged in by recidivists, is permitted to flourish in the face of permissive governmental attitudes and the favoured, non-punitive and non-socially stigmatic mechanisms of control (regulatory legislation rather than application of the criminal law). The issue here, then, is the legal recasting of the concept of white-collar crime away from questions of power (i.e. the social status of the offender) and towards matters of form (e.g. 'paper' crime, which is classless, in that it involves welfare fraud as well as corporate fraud). How crime and social harm is socially constructed has major implications for the framing of institutional responses.

This approach to consideration of white-collar crime opens the door to ideological debate on whether the definition should extend to activities that are not necessarily criminal, but which nonetheless cause great social, economic and environmental harm. In part, this broader conceptualisation recognises that criminality is defined by the powerful, and so their actions may escape the label of 'criminal', regardless of the harms caused.

The argument that criminologists should only concern themselves with acts that break the criminal law has been widely contested. Opponents of this position argue instead that it is essential for criminologists to challenge conventional social norms about what is and is not a crime. Clinard and Yeager (1980) argue that drawing attention to the different moral judgments that are applied to the activities of the rich, compared with those of the poor, is a central aspect of the criminologist's role in

CORPORATE CRIME
The illegal activities of businesses against members of the public, the environment, creditors, investors or corporate competitors; it includes crimes committed by corporate officials for their corporation, as well as the offences of the corporation itself.

questioning everyday assumptions about why some acts are defined as criminal and subject to close scrutiny by law enforcement agents, while others are ignored or treated much more lightly.

A TYPOLOGY OF WHITE-COLLAR CRIME: CORPORATE VERSUS INDIVIDUAL CRIME

The criticism that white-collar crime is too broad or narrow a category has led to the emergence of a number of other terms to differentiate specific types of illegalities within this broad umbrella concept:

- *Organisational illegalities* are 'individual or collective illegalities committed by corporate executives that are perceived as helping to achieve, or are congruent with, the organisational goals set by the dominant coalition within an organisation', such as price-fixing and insider trading (Slapper & Tombs 1999: 14).

OCCUPATIONAL CRIME
Criminal acts committed by employees in the course of their work, for personal gain.

- *Occupational crime* refers to criminal acts committed by employees (individuals or small groups) in the course of their work for personal interest—primarily financial gain (e.g. embezzlement, theft of merchandise and manipulation of sales) (Bookman 2008; Peltier-Rivest 2012). The term *employee crime* is also sometimes used. However, in the context of white-collar crime, it is perhaps more appropriate to distinguish between crimes committed by persons of respectability and high social status (e.g. managers and professionals with decision-making power and authority who fraudulently overcharge clients for personal gain) and those committed by ordinary workers (those not in key decision-making or high-status positions, who commit low-level theft).

ENTREPRE-NEURIAL CRIME
Punishable acts committed by individuals in positions of control within corporations, for personal benefit, by exploiting the resources and power deriving from the corporate form.

- *Entrepreneurial crime* refers to 'punishable acts [that] are committed by individuals in controlling positions within corporations, using the resources and power deriving from the corporate form as a vehicle to achieve ends which benefit the entrepreneur personally', such as fraud (Halstead 1992: 1).

- *Corporate crime* refers to the illegal and/or corrupt activities of businesses (the corporation as a whole) against members of the public (consumers and local communities), democratic processes, creditors (banks, financial institutions, companies and individuals), investors (including stockholders), corporate competitors, other countries (especially developing countries) and the environment (Clinard 1990; Robson 2010; Wilson 1987). It includes crimes committed by corporate officials that benefit their corporation, such as bribery of public officials to secure contracts, as well as the offences of the corporation itself, such as deceptive advertising, marketing and sale of unsafe products, dangerous working conditions, environmental pollution and bribery of officials who regulate corporate activities.

As reflected in the above taxonomy, many scholars draw a distinction between crimes based on motivation: those that benefit the corporation (organisational illegalities and corporate crime) and those that benefit the individual working within an organisation (employee crime and occupational crime). Nonetheless, although this distinction is useful, the motivational line between the two can blur. Some corporate crimes, such as price-fixing or insider trading, may benefit both the organisation directly and the individual indirectly, through such perks as bonuses, promotions and stock-option offers. Conversely, some corporate crimes, such as occupational health and safety transgressions, may benefit the corporation exclusively (in the form of cost savings). The intersection of different types of conduct is presented in Figure 12.1, which identifies various dimensions of corporate criminal conduct. Questions of harm, benefit and perpetrator can usefully be disentangled using this kind of typology.

FIGURE 12.1   TYPOLOGY OF CORPORATE CRIMINAL CONDUCT

	Corporate crime committed by a corporation itself	Corporate crime committed by the agents or controllers of a corporation
Corporate crime committed for the benefit of a corporation	**Type A** Corporate crime by a corporation for its own benefit	**Type B** Corporate crime by the agents or controllers of a corporation for the benefit of that corporation
Corporate crime committed against the interests of a corporation	**Type C** Corporate crime against a corporation but for the benefit of another corporation	**Type D** Corporate crime against a corporation but for the benefit of its agents or controllers

Source: Tomasic (1994)

CLASS AND CRIMES OF THE POWERFUL

If the starting point for analysing white-collar crime is the essential neutrality of acts sanctioned by statute, then conduct is considered in abstract rather than by reference to the character of the perpetrator. This approach, however, ignores the very differentiating feature of white-collar crime that sets it apart from conventional legal transgressions; namely, the class characteristics and backgrounds of its perpetrators. White-collar offenders are largely distinguished by social class or high socio-economic standing; a privilege traceable to class inequality.

As a structural relation, class reflects the different positions and capacity of people to marshal economic and political resources, as dictated by their relationship to the means of production (White & van der Velden 1995). In a society such as Australia, the ruling or dominant class is the capitalist class; that is, the owners of capitalist enterprises and those who manage the capital accumulation process on their behalf. It is the dominant class economically, but the smallest numerically. Not surprisingly, criminality in this instance aids the accumulation process from a business point of view and/or augments one's personal wealth. The typology of corporate criminal conduct captures this dynamic to some extent, but it does not explain it fully.

Accumulative and augmentative forms of criminality are closely linked aspects of class position. *Accumulative criminality* refers to corporate or organisational crime, as a direct link and natural flow-on of the capital accumulation process (i.e. profit enhancement and cost minimisation).

Augmentative criminality refers to the closely connected but distinct personal wealth-enhancement component in the criminality process, which flows from one's access to and advantage gained from an ownership and control position in the capital accumulation process. In the case of owners of capital, the personal augmentation of wealth through criminality may be the basis for accumulating capital, or for hiding accumulated capital. In the case of managers of capital, accumulative criminality (as a necessary feature of corporate business success or to stave off failure) may be the basis for expanded personal wealth (e.g. bonuses) or a calculated necessity in job retention.

PETIT BOURGEOIS CRIMINALITY

Other types of white-collar crime are linked to the social standing of those who occupy a more ambivalent but nevertheless generally privileged class position. For instance, as a class, the middle class or petit bourgeoisie (defined as including new middle layers of employment) is made up of small-scale owners of capital (e.g. family farmers, small landlords and small business owners), self-employed professionals (e.g. doctors and lawyers) and middle management levels of capitalist enterprises and various apparatus of the state. The petit bourgeoisie forms an intermediate layer poised between the capitalist and the working class proper. It constitutes a relatively privileged class grouping compared with the working class, but does not hold decisive social or economic power. The petit bourgeoisie has an ambiguous character, and a location between capital and wage labour. Criminality within this class grouping frequently consists of both accumulative and augmentative forms of criminality.

In the case of the petit bourgeois criminality, however, while generally incorporating features indicative of capitalist criminality, its diversity of circumstances is reflective of its position in the class structure. As such, petit bourgeois criminality would, in some sectors or circumstances, shade to that resembling the subsistence-level criminality of the working class or underclass (i.e. poor farmers, struggling small shopkeepers and independent tradespeople), while others would reflect the criminality of the capitalist sectors, albeit on a reduced scale (i.e. doctors, lawyers, engineers, real estate agents and small to medium businesses). With the latter, for example, one might think of fraud and overservicing in relation to Medicare and the Pharmaceutical Benefits Scheme on the part of some doctors.

WHAT EXPLAINS WHITE-COLLAR CRIME?

Compared with the amount of theorising that has occurred in relation to crimes committed by young working-class males, there have been relatively few attempts to explain corporate crime. One critical observation, however, is that the existence and extent of white-collar and corporate crime challenges any simplistic explanation of crime in terms of poverty, diminished opportunities or psychological pathology. Broadly speaking, corporate crime (as opposed to occupational crime) is typically explained in terms of structural features and sources (e.g. the demands of business competition and the opportunism inherent in business transactions), cultural processes (e.g. the normalisation of illegal behaviour) and the operation of the institutions of criminal justice (e.g. the low likelihood of activity being criminalised, transgressions being identified, and illegality being prosecuted and punished severely).

In terms of structural features, corporate survival—and survival of individuals within them, especially managers—depends on the accumulation and, indeed, maximisation of profit; that is, the maintenance of economic advantage. Where the capacity to make profits is blocked by environmental factors, such as government regulations or the price structure of competitors, companies will face considerable pressure (via the threat of penalties for not meeting organisational profit goals) to use illegal or unethical means to overcome the blockage. Perverse corporate incentive structures—together with opportunities for illegal behaviour, weak law enforcement and an ideological blurring between 'entrepreneuralism' and illegal behaviour—create conditions that lead to engagement in illegal acts (Lippke 2011; Rothe 2010). Those who examine the culture and dynamics of corporations from a critical perspective argue that the corporate form itself is inherently criminogenic, and the capitalist market (a political process in itself) creates conditions conducive to corporate crime. Crime is therefore a rational response to a rational objective (Box 1983; see also Bakan 2004; Glasbeek 2004; Tillman 2009).

In terms of cultural processes, Sutherland (1949) contended that lawlessness within corporations is not only endemic, but perpetuated through the process of differential opportunity to commit crime as well as the differential social organisation of employees favourable to crime. Organisations are said to impart to their agents not only the rationalisations for pro-criminal behaviour, but also the techniques of wrongdoing that facilitate illegal maximisation of profit-making opportunities while cloaked under a veil of secrecy and outward respectability. Sutherland drew on differential opportunity theory to explain the motivations—exploitation of the market for the purposes of profit maximisation—of some of the world's most successful and well-known corporations (e.g. Coca Cola Amitil, Alcoa and the Ford Motor Company) for engaging in abuses of power during World War II. These activities, including 'squeezing American government, consumers and workers, limiting materials, limiting production, inferior production, trading with the enemy, favouring the enemy, and providing scientific information' could essentially be described as war crimes (Galliher & Guess 2009: 173).

Applying Sutherland's theories to more contemporary practices, Mackenzie (2011), for instance, points to the psychological routines, practices and habits of high-end antiquities dealers that permit trade in artefacts (including fossils, objects of art and other items of historical significance) with dubious or no provenance (documented history of ownership). He describes this high-end group of affluent people as a pivotal link in the profitable transaction chain that generates a demand for looted objects by trading on a culture of risk-shifting; a culture premised on the notion that 'risks [are] things smart people shifted rather than controlled and accepted' (Braithwaite 2009: 440). Moreover, they are described as a secretive cohort, able to maintain public visibility through their shopfronts on prominent streets, while their inner workings are veiled and 'off limits for inspection for reasons of customer confidentiality, inter-dealer competition and apparent general preference for privacy over openness' (Mackenzie 2011: 137). This is contrasted with the meagre socio-economic circumstances of those actually undertaking the looting of cultural artefacts and the disadvantaged and vulnerable position they occupy at the lowest rung of the global trading chain—stripped of social respectability, easily identifiable and most likely to be prosecuted.

The bottom line is that corporations commit or enable the commission of an enormous number of offences, they reoffend regularly and such wrongdoing is not exceptional behaviour but the norm. Some industries, however, are more likely to engage in corporate crime than others. The pharmaceutical, motor vehicle, dot-com, telecommunications, energy trading and oil industries have been identified as particularly prone to corporate crime (Carson 1982; Sutherland 1949; Tillman 2009). Furthermore, large corporations have a disproportionate number of violations compared with small ones (Braithwaite 1984; Clinard & Yeager 1980), although smaller firms are often pressured by competitive and cost considerations to operate with less regard to regulations than bigger firms (Haines 1997).

MEASURING CRIMES OF THE POWERFUL

For a variety of reasons, it is very difficult to identify and measure the extent of crimes of the powerful, such as white-collar and corporate crime, and the harms generated by such activity. Part of the problem lies with determining which crimes specifically should be included in any compilation of such harms. For example, typical crimes might include:

- crimes against consumers, such as fraud, which includes consumer scams (ACCC 2012; Bartels 2012a; Steffensmeier et al. 2013) and marketing of defective and unsafe products (e.g. thalidomide, which caused infant mortality and birth defects in the thousands worldwide)
- environmental crime, the impact of which transects national borders (Gilbert & Russell 2002; Levi & Horlick-Jones 2013; see also Chapter 14)
- insider trading and fraudulent derivative trading practices (e.g. artificial stock inflation processes, which contributed to the global financial crisis in 2008–09) (Calabresi 2012; Tillman 2009)
- religious fraud, as when supposed spiritual leaders exploit the vulnerabilities of people in order to appropriate money and assets for their own use and to fund luxurious lifestyles (Rosoff et al. 1998)
- crime committed by or with the complicity of banking, financial, insurance and pension fund industries (including crimes of globalisation that violate international human rights conventions) (Rothe 2010)
- crimes by government (Chambliss et al. 2010), including grand corruption and state terrorism; that is, the bombing of civilian populations under the guise of war (Kramer 2010; Lasslett 2012)
- corruption of public officials to secure some form of advantage (e.g. Enron) (Kramer 2013; Otusanya 2012)
- medical crime, from prescription of medication without legitimate medical purpose to healthcare fraud (e.g. Medicare fraud) involving submission of claims for services never provided (Canadian Medical Association 2013) and falsification or suppression of research findings (Davis & Abraham 2013)
- computer and cyber-crime (Baglione et al. 2010; Brightman 2009; see also Chapter 19)
- illicit deals in cultural objects, such as archaeological and anthropological artefacts (Hannaford 2013; Mackenzie 2011), and art fraud (Alder et al. 2011).

Each of these crimes is typically characterised by difficulties in identification and reporting of wrongdoing by victims. Price-fixing, for example, is often achieved without the knowledge of consumers beyond that of higher prices. Even in the case of more transparent wrongdoing, such as consumer fraud resulting in discernible financial losses, the outward legitimacy of the fraudulent activity means that exposure is often not immediate, and when the wrongdoing finally comes to light, individuals are too embarrassed to reveal the exploitation of naivety involved, and therefore elect not to report the crime. Thus, while the national scam exposure rate in Australia was estimated to be 36 per cent between 2007 and 2010–11, and the victimisation rate 3 per cent (ABS 2012e), it must be borne in mind that only a very small proportion of consumer fraud scams are reported to police (ACCC 2012; Smith & Akerman 2008).

Similar issues apply in the case of exposure to products that were marketed for many years as safe, but are now recognised as producing long-term health risks and death (e.g. products containing asbestos, and cigarettes). The extended latency period for development of ill effects (e.g. a mean of 37 years for mesothelioma associated with exposure to asbestos) means that those suffering do not realise they have been victimised for many years. When the physical manifestations finally appear, aetiological uncertainties (the inability to definitively attribute morbidity or mortality to product exposure or consumption) often result in non-recognition and non-classification of the incident as a crime.

The complex issue of causality and attribution of responsibility is particularly evident in large-scale corporate disasters, such as the recent Fukushima Daiichi nuclear incident. Ostensibly triggered by a natural incident—a tsunami that followed an earthquake—the widespread environmental and human consequences that followed may have been avoided or mitigated through appropriate organisational safety processes and regulatory oversight (see Levi & Horlick-Jones 2013).

A significant impediment to community understanding of the magnitude of the white-collar crime problem is the great contrast in attention directed by official agencies towards generating and maintaining databases on 'street crime' and that devoted to 'suite crime'. Official statistical compilations of recorded crime offences and offenders concentrate almost exclusively on street offences, and do not provide information on social background (e.g. occupational status and income) and crime context (whether the crime was committed at work and/or facilitated by occupational opportunities), which would allow for a more nuanced assessment of crime type. Since white-collar and corporate crimes (e.g. art fraud and consumer scams as opposed to other categories of individually perpetuated fraud) are not recorded as discrete entities, it is unclear as to the proportion of all officially recorded crimes that might be classified as crimes of the powerful.

ANALYSING THE EXTENT AND CHARACTERISTICS OF CORPORATE CRIME

Attempts to analyse the extent of corporate crime draw on various data to provide direct and indirect indications of criminality. For instance, in one of the landmark studies, Sutherland (1949) calculated how often seventy of the largest corporations in the United States had been found to be violating legal and administrative codes in areas including trade practices, advertising, labour practices and copyright in the period from 1890, when the oldest of the companies investigated was first established, to the late 1940s. Sutherland found that the figure varied from one to fifty and that, on average, the companies had been found to have fourteen violations each, with the aggregate number of violations totalling 980. Sutherland acknowledged that this figure was certainly an underestimate, since the study had not attempted to include all the subsidiaries of the companies, and the analysis was limited to criminal offences only. Even so, on average, each corporation had been found guilty on four occasions. Sutherland observed that: 'In many states persons with four convictions are defined by statute to be "habitual criminals"' (Sutherland 1949: 25). If mandatory sentencing provisions applied to corporate crime in the way they can apply to conventional crimes, such organisations would be closed down.

More recently, Steffensmeier et al. (2013) developed a database of eighty-three cases of detected corporate fraud in the United States involving 436 defendants. These cases were the subject of major indictments initiated by the Corporate Fraud Task Force between 2002 and 2009, following the Enron and WorldCom scandals. The bulk of these major twenty-first-century crimes (69%) were found to have been committed for the purposes of gaining business advantage for the corporation, as opposed to self-profit (31%). While corporations varied in size, approximately a third employed 500 or fewer workers; a third were classified as moderately sized, comprising between 501 and 5,000 employees, and a third were considered large organisations with more than 5,000 employees. Approximately 13 per cent were classified as *Fortune 500* corporations (highest grossing revenue corporations). Most commonly represented industries included: scientific/technical/management services (23%); finance/

insurance/real estate and healthcare (23%); wholesale and retail trade; entertainment, accommodation and utilities (21%); manufacturing and construction (19%); and information (14%).

Offenders were overwhelmingly male (over 90%; for similar gender findings in Norway see Arnulf & Gottshalk 2013), characteristically older (on average in the mid-40s) than street offenders (on average in the mid-20s) and most commonly occupied positions of considerable authority within the organisation, as either high-ranking executives (44%) or upper-level officials (25%). The majority of individuals indicted played ringleader (37%) or major roles (32%) in the commission of the offences. Notable differences were identified in the small female sample. Specifically, no case of solo-executed fraud was committed by a women, nor did any of the cases involve all-female conspirators; most played minor roles in schemes (often sharing the role with spouses/lovers) and derived no personal financial benefit from their involvement. Most were reluctant rather than proactive participants, and the pathway to involvement was either through a romantic or close personal relationship with a main conspirator, or via occupation of a gateway position within the organisation (e.g. accounting or compliance officer) of strategic utility to commission of the crime (Steffensmeier et al. 2013).

No comparable, large-scale study of corporate crime has been conducted in Australia. Moreover, the ability to estimate accurately the extent of corporate crime is hampered by the fragmentary legislative, investigative and regulatory/prosecutorial framework that governs such activity. While there is no single source of data that captures the true extent of corporate crime, in recent years data on offenders prosecuted in Australian courts has included a sub-category of organisational offender. Examination of this data reveals that in 2012–13, corporate offenders comprised a miniscule proportion (n = 4,819 or 0.9%) of all offenders prosecuted in Australian criminal courts—superior and inferior (n = 559,112) (ABS 2014f)—and the vast majority were prosecuted in inferior courts (99.9%). The largest offence category for which organisational offenders were prosecuted was that of traffic and vehicle regulatory offences (58%), followed by miscellaneous offences (21%) and offences against justice (16%). For reasons outlined below, official criminal statistics cannot be relied on to provide an accurate indication of the true nature and extent of crimes of the powerful, neither in Australia nor in any other jurisdiction.

CRIMINAL LAW, INDIVIDUALISM AND CORPORATE CRIME

A fundamental difficulty in determining the extent of crimes of the powerful, and holding perpetrators to account, is the historically individualistic and partisan nature of criminal law. Contrary to the legal formalist position, which regards law as a set of neutral, factual rules and principles, critical criminology regards laws as a product of social, political and economic forces that reflect the interests of the ruling, capitalist class (Michalowski 2010; see also Chapters 5 and 22). Legal formalism directs collective attention (legal, media and public) to the private affairs of individual persons acting consciously to inflict harm on other individuals and/or property.

Glasbeek (2004, 2003) identifies several interrelated legal fictions relating to corporations that have served to foster and sustain systemic corporate wrongdoing. These include the ideas that: (a) the registered corporation is deemed to be a separate legal person, acting in its own right; (b) because the corporation needs others to think and act, it cannot be guilty of a criminal offence; and (c) corporate wrongdoing pays, because the structured criminogenic nature of the corporation is almost always avoided in cases where real people are actually prosecuted (see also Clough & Mulhern 2002; Ricketts & Avolio 2009–10).

Reduced to artificial legal abstractions devoid of mental and moral capacity, corporations have historically been rendered incapable of possessing the evil intent (*mens rea*) required of inherently human crimes that result in socially injurious harms. As such, many types of social harm perpetrated by corporations and/or corporate actors have not been incorporated into the criminal law or, if incorporated, are not vigorously pursued if to do so would undermine capitalist interests. Crimes of the powerful are intrinsically linked to the operation of the capitalist system as a whole. Such harms are inseparable from who has power, how they exercise this power and who ultimately benefits from the actions of the powerful.

> The problem ... in trying to tackle corporate crime is that virtually every act of the corporate sector is deemed, in some way or another, to be 'good for the country'. This ideology of corporate virtue, and the benefits of business for the common good, is promulgated through extensive corporate advertising campaigns, capitalist blackmail (vis-à-vis location of industry and firms) and aggressive lobbying. Anything which impedes business is deemed to be unreasonable, faulty, bad for the economy, not the rightful domain of the state, to undermine private property rights, and so on. In other words, the prevailing view promulgated by government and business is that, with few exceptions, the 'market' is the best referee when it comes to preventing or stopping harm and potential harm. Powerful business interests (which, among other things, provide big financial contributions to mainstream political parties) demand a 'light touch' when it comes to surveillance of, and intervention in, their activities. The state should not, therefore, play a major role in regulation of corporate activities beyond that of assisting in the maintenance of a general climate within which business will flourish. (White 2008b: 38)

Furthermore, the potential stigmatisation of 'respectable' members of the business community and the state means that one has to tread carefully before making accusations of impropriety or criminal wrongdoing. This is despite the fact that crimes of the capitalist class, which include white-collar crime and corporate crime, have significant material effects in terms of injury and death, in addition to the commonly understood financial losses (see Box 12.1).

BOX 12.1   LIFTING THE CORPORATE VEIL: THE CASE OF THE FORD MOTOR COMPANY

In 1978, the Ford Motor Company was prosecuted in the United States for three counts of reckless homicide following the deaths of three teenagers in Indiana. The young victims sustained fatal burns when the Ford Pinto in which they were travelling burst into flames subsequent to its involvement in a low velocity, rear-end collision.

At trial, evidence presented by way of internal company memoranda revealed that in the early stages of production, top executives within Ford became aware of an inherent design defect in the Pinto's circuit system, which constituted a lethal hazard. Due to the unsafe positioning of the tank between the bumper bar and the differential housing, if rear-ended, the Pinto's fuel tank was highly susceptible to movement, rupture and subsequent explosion, regardless of the speed of travel.

Notwithstanding that knowledge, a cognisant decision was made to continue manufacturing and marketing the vehicle without modification, on the basis that corrective operation was time-prohibitive and breached the vehicle's price, weight and expediency targets.

The cost—benefit analysis commissioned by Ford predicted that it would be cheaper for the company to absorb the costs of litigation and compensation of injured parties, or the surviving families of those killed due to the identified defect ((under)estimated to be $49.9 million), than it would be to recall and repair the production model at an estimated cost of $11 per vehicle or approximately

$137.5 million in total. Hence, for the sake of profit maximisation (a corporate imperative): 'the Ford Motor Company sold cars (for seven years) in which it knew hundreds of people would needlessly burn to death' (Dowie 1977: 32). An appraisal by Dowie (1977) puts the ensuing loss of life at between 500 and 900, and the number of permanently or temporarily disfigured and disabled as inestimable.

Capitalist economic theory, with its monetisation of all values (including that of life and well-being) assumes an equivalence between the value of, and risks faced by, capital and labour. Though consistent with economic imperatives, the thought of actuaries being paid to dispassionately reduce human life to dollars and cents calculations, and corporate executives compromising safety as a consequence of reconciling estimated human value with the budgetary bottom line, appears ethically unpalatable. However, despite the evidence of amoral premeditation in the decision to compromise public safety, Ford was acquitted of all charges.

Source: Perrone (2000)

Since white-collar crimes are usually directed in the first instance against other capitalists (e.g. anti-competitive practices) or against the rules governing the marketplace (e.g. insider trading), they have rarely been perceived by the general public as being of special interest to them personally. Moreover, corporate offenders do not commonly resonate with the public since they do not fit the societal stereotype of the street offender—the thief, murderer or rapist—perpetuated by the mass media.

Cullen et al. (2009) contend that until the 1960s and 1970s, when civil rights movements fostered concern for equality of justice, and media reports began to bring to light corporate malfeasance and the harms caused, the public was largely ignorant of corporate wrongdoing and certainly did not consider it tantamount to crime. Over time, what commenced as public obliviousness then circumscribed concern for corporate harms, has transformed into mistrust of big business and a call for just punishment of corrupt business leaders (Cullen et al. 2009; Holfretzer et al. 2008). This is especially evident in the growing public recognition that preventable workplace injury and deaths are, in some instances (e.g. where they involve wanton disregard for human life or gross negligence), tantamount to corporate criminal liability. Despite a hardening of public sentiment towards corporations and their human agents, political elites have generally been slow to enact legal measures commensurate with harms caused; corporate wrongdoing is almost invariably treated as an infraction of administrative or regulatory law (e.g. consumer laws and environmental protection laws) rather than conventional criminal laws.

Even in cases of unsafe workplace practices resulting in the death of employees or members of the public, organisations and corporate executives (on rare occasions) are more commonly prosecuted for breaches of health and safety Acts. These are generally construed by the media and regulatory authorities as accidents or mistakes rather than assault, manslaughter or murder (see, for example, Machin & Mayr 2012). Thus, those harmed are effectively denied the status of 'victim' (Snell & Tombs 2011). While a handful of successfully prosecuted corporate manslaughter or industrial homicide cases have been reported in the United States, the United Kingdom and Australia in relatively recent times, treatment of corporate transgressions via traditional homicide laws remains the exception rather than the rule (see, for example, Perrone 2000; Taylor & Mackenzie 2013; Woodley 2013). Moreover, prosecutions of corporate actors (particularly female offenders) and entities attract much more lenient penalties overall than those levelled at conventional crimes, even where they result in loss of human life (Perrone 2000; Van Slyke & Bales 2013; Woodley 2012).

In accounting for the light-handed legal response to white-collar crime, it is important to recognise that, aside from differential legal formulations of what are essentially comparable behaviours, based solely on offender status, corporate and white-collar offenders have access to superior legal resources than the average street offender. The financial advantage enjoyed by large corporations means that they are able to: hire expensive lawyers to mount powerful challenges to the laying of charges against them and/or their executives; vigorously contest the basis of matters brought before the courts; and draw on 'good character' stereotypes of individuals and organisations to neutralise responsibility and harm (Stadler & Benson 2012; Vieraitis et al. 2012), or to mitigate penalty if a finding of guilt is handed down (Perrone 2000).

An indication of this disparity is evidenced in official data pertaining to the adjudication of criminal matters in Australian courts. While defendants brought before Australian courts (superior and inferior) generally plead guilty (see Chapter 23), the vast majority of organisational defendants (60%) elected to contest charges (compared to 29.5% of non-organisational offenders) in 2012–13. It is also telling that 26.5 per cent of criminal charges laid against organisations were withdrawn by the prosecution prior to legal adjudication, compared to only 7.8 per cent in the case of non-organisational offenders.

The kinds of crimes associated with the powerful, and their underlying motivations, are outlined in Table 12.1.

TABLE 12.1 CRIMES OF THE POWERFUL

CAPITALIST CRIMINALITY	
• directly linked to ownership and control in the capital accumulation process • because the power is structural, the impact is generally diffuse and wide-ranging	
TYPICAL CRIMES	**EXAMPLES**
Economic	Breaches of corporate law; environmental degradation; inadequate adherence to industrial health and safety provisions; pollution; violation of labour laws; fraud; embezzlement
State	Police brutality; government corruption; bribery; violation of civil and human rights; misuse of public funds
MOTIVATIONS	**EXAMPLES**
Maximising profit	Structural imperative to minimise costs and maximise economic returns in a competitive capitalist market environment
Augmenting wealth	Attempts to bolster one's own personal position in the economic and social hierarchy
Social control	Violation of privacy and of human rights justified in the name of national interest, and whatever legal, coercive and propaganda means are necessary will be used to ensure public order, quell dissent and further private economic interests

(Continued)

TABLE 12.1 CRIMES OF THE POWERFUL (*Continued*)

CRIMINALISATION	EXAMPLES
Shaping definitions	Capacity to influence what is defined as harmful, and the definitions of certain acts as being civil or criminal harms
Protecting interests	Capacity to mobilise best legal assistance and intricate knowledge of the law
Sentencing	Use of stereotypes and criminal histories to mitigate against harsh punishments because of the nature of the offence (not seen as serious) and offenders (upstanding citizens)

Source: White (2008b)

THE TREND TOWARDS SELF-REGULATION

Another observation that speaks to the ability of the powerful to successfully deflect legal attention from interfering in their interests is the major shift over the past decade or so away from use of state coercion (in virtually any circumstance) in dealing with corporate wrongdoing, and specific instances of social and environmental harm. Instead, the preferred method of corporate regulation has been varying forms of *self-regulation*, and an emphasis on the use of gentle state persuasion, rather than government command (Perrone 2000). This contributes to the 'naturalness' of corporate crime: the way in which social harms, economic exploitation and environmental destruction are built into the fabric of everyday, ordinary life as a 'normal' feature of how we produce and consume. This is compounded by the fact that much of what occurs does so in a fully 'legal' way (regardless of actual harm). Moreover, where external controls (materially and ideologically) on profit maximisation are weakened, then we can reasonably expect to see an increased incidence in illegal corporate activity and, more generally, greater propensity for social harm regardless of legal definition.

TYPES OF RESISTANCE TO STUDYING CORPORATE CRIME

To address corporate criminality, then, requires a political understanding of class power and a rejection of formally legal criteria in assessing criminality and harm. This implies conflict over definitions of behaviour and activity (being good or bad, harmful or not so harmful, offensive or inoffensive), legitimacy of knowledge claims (media portrayals and expert opinion), and the role and use of state instruments and citizen participation in putting limits on corporate activity (via regulations and public access to commercial information).

For the criminologist, the study of corporate crime is fraught with difficulties; for example, the difficulty posed by the 'status shield' created around the social background and social standing of perpetrators (e.g. many corporate crooks are simultaneously big donors to charity), as well as corporate and state fortifications that facilitate denial of wrongdoing and resistance to exposure (mobilisation of vast resources and recourse to legal instruments). Trying to uncover crimes of the powerful can bring the wrath of the powerful down upon those who challenge their capacity to perform various wrongs. Sometimes this can involve law suits. In extreme circumstances, it can lead to death (Lasslett 2012).

Resistance to data-collection may go hand in hand with denial of harm on the part of the powerful. When it comes to more traditional academic research, the availability of data is complicated by many things, some of which are inherently political. For example, if logging is a prime source of government revenue in some regions or countries, then investigation that potentially threatens certain logging practices, or links environmental harm to the logging industry, may be stymied.

Research may also be seen as 'dangerous' to vested interests if corruption of officials is widespread. Research into environmental harm, for example, may well provoke negative reactions on the part of powerful interest groups. In some cases, as with Ken Saro-Wiwa, the outspoken critic of the Nigerian Government and the oil-exploring companies in his country, the penalty for mobilising against these interests was arrest and execution (see Saro-Wiwa 1995). Less authoritarian methods are also used to silence critics, dampen resistance and minimise public outcry. This can take the form of governments banning the publication of criminal statistics that threaten to tarnish the reputation of a country (see Van Dijk 2008). It is also apparent in the efforts of private companies to protect their interests through the use of strategic lawsuits against public participation (commonly referred to as SLAPPs), one effect of which is to curtail the free flow of information (see White 2005).

COSTS OF CORPORATE CRIME

The complexities and nuances of the crimes of the powerful thus demand even greater than usual investigatory sophistication and a steadfastly critical theoretical orientation if they are to be fully appreciated and unravelled (see Tombs & Whyte 2004). Powerful social interests not only perpetuate great harms, but they also obscure and mask the nature of the harm production. They are also best placed to resist the criminalisation process generally.

As well as problems with the way the law has been formulated, the difficulties and expense of mounting a case and prosecuting corporate criminals also explains why they are less likely than traditional criminals to face the law (Clough & Mulhern 2002). Prosecuting authorities often face extreme difficulties in locating and analysing the necessary documents to prove an event has occurred. It is not just that files can be shredded or deleted, and computers 'lost' (see Box 12.2; see also Shapiro 1990: 354), but also the sheer volume of material for investigation presents an enormous problem. The complex structure of companies is also a challenge to any investigation, especially when they belong to a global network (e.g. efforts to address gross exploitation of workers and international labour rights

---

BOX 12.2   ROLAH MCCABE VERSUS BRITISH AMERICAN TOBACCO

In 2002, Rolah McCabe became the first Australian, and indeed, person outside of the United States, to successfully sue a tobacco company (British American Tobacco (BAT)) for the negligent manufacture and marketing of cigarettes, and was awarded $700,000 in damages by the Supreme Court of Victoria. A smoker for many years, Rolah developed terminal lung cancer, which was attributable to her cigarette consumption.

In handing down his determination, Justice Eames found that BAT Australia Services had subverted the legal process of discovery by systematically destroying thousands of damaging internal company documents. These documents demonstrated knowledge on the part of BAT and its worldwide companies of the addictive properties of nicotine and the relationship between smoking and disease, as well as evidence of knowing employment of 'nicotine' technology to render cigarettes more addictive, and outlined product marketing strategies directed at all age groups.

While the decision was successfully appealed by BAT two months after Rolah's death, the legal matter was finally closed in 2011 (a decade after action commenced), after BAT reached a confidential financial settlement with the McCabe family.

Source: Birnbauer (2003); Hawthorne (2011); Liberman (2002)

abuses must contend with elaborate manufacturing, supply and distribution chains behind major brands such as Nike and Adidas; see Conner & Haines 2013). It is often unclear in which jurisdiction a crime took place, and prosecutors must frequently negotiate with the criminal justice systems of other nations and jurisdictions. This problem is one of the main impediments to the documentation and control of corporate crime today (Fisse & Braithwaite 1993).

It is for the aforementioned reasons that the true extent of corporate crime remains unknown. Notwithstanding the persistence of the cloak of invisibility that surrounds much corporate crime, as intimated earlier, while corporate crime is often perceived as a 'victimless' crime, the reality is quite different; its costs are enormous and certainly outweigh the costs of traditional crime (see Friedrichs 1996; Rothe & Friedrichs 2015; Shover & Wright 2001). There are obvious financial impacts for individuals. For example, it has been estimated that consumer fraud alone costs Australians close to $1 billion annually (ABS 2008b). There are also enormous indirect costs borne by society as a whole in the form of higher product and service costs, and reduced quality of care. In the United States, for example, Steffensmeier et al. (2013) identified false charges to Medicare of more than $4.8 billion between 2008 and 2011 (based on detected offences). But the circle of financial harm does not stop at its point of origin—it ripples far beyond national borders. Some economists and sociologists have, for example, concluded that a complex web of fraudulent and corrupt corporate practices (e.g. over-inflating of stocks, predatory lending and fraudulent underwriting practices), as well as an enabling market environment (e.g. poor corporate financial regulation and supervision, unsustainable monetary policy and over-inflated housing markets), were primarily responsible for the onset and severity of some of the largest stock market crashes, economic recessions and great depressions experienced in the United States.

As evidenced by the global financial crisis of 2007–08, these events reverberate internationally, stripping millions of dollars from national economies (through declines in consumption, business investment and trade) and adversely impacting the livelihoods, standards of living and psychological states of millions of people. One estimate places the losses to the United States economy alone at between $6 trillion and $14 trillion (equivalent to $50,000 to $120,000 for each household) (Atkinson et al. 2013) and another estimates total global losses at approximately $15 trillion (Yoon 2012). There are also serious attendant social costs as a result of the violation of community standards, and the creation of an atmosphere of cynicism and mistrust towards business and government in the community (Levi & Horlick-Jones 2013; Rosoff et al. 1998).

Aside from the financial consequences, corporate crime—from inadequate testing of products to the failure to acknowledge or release medical research results, to poor industrial safety standards and the release of toxic chemicals into the waterways—has very real and widespread physical impacts on both individuals and the environment. And the legacy of harms wrought by corporate wrongdoing (whether depicted as crimes or regulatory transgressions) are evidenced for many years after the initial event (Gilbert & Russell 2002). For example, while two workers were killed at the Fukushima plant in 2011 (most likely from the earthquake), the death toll in the aftermath of the nuclear disaster is likely to be extensive. Approximately 300 workers were exposed to radiation, which in future years may lead to serious illness and death. Furthermore, the leaking of radioactive waste into the broader environment has been estimated conservatively to give rise to up to 1,000 cancer-related deaths in the future (Levi & Horlick-Jones 2013). The future cost in terms of illness and disease, as well as the loss of non-human life (flora and fauna) due to polluted waterways, soil and air is inestimable. Moreover, the problem is far from over, with 200,000–330,000 tonnes of radioactive waste still sitting in makeshift tanks, vulnerable to leakages and with no method for safe disposal (Humber 2013; Tabuchi 2013).

In Australia, though asbestos has not been used in building materials since the 1980s and was officially banned across Australia in 2003, Safe Work Australia (2014b) estimates that in excess of 660 new cases of mesothelioma are diagnosed each year, with the mesothelioma-related death rate increasing annually from 416 in 1997 to 606 in 2011. A further 125 deaths in 2011 were related to asbestosis (also attributable to asbestos) and 1,394 asbestos-related hospitalisations were recorded between 1998–99 and 2009–10. Woodley (2013) places the death toll from mesothelioma in the United Kingdom at 2,347 in 2010, with as many as 4,000 further deaths related to chronic obstructive pulmonary disease, attributable to past exposure to fumes, chemicals and dusts in the workplace. As Segelov (2012) points out, while the first wave of victims were workers employed in the asbestos mines and the second wave comprised factory workers and tradespeople (e.g. dock workers, builders, plumbers, electricians and carpenters) who contracted asbestos disease through industrial exposure 'that is, working directly with asbestos products', the third and current wave consists of 'bystanders'—women who washed the clothes of those working with asbestos and everyday home renovators inadvertently exposed (see also Schmidt 2013).

STATE CRIME

Broadly speaking, **state crime** or state-organised crime refers to crimes involving the state acting against its own citizens, or against the citizens of another state as part of interstate conflict. Definitions of state crime are varied. This is mainly because descriptions of state crime cannot rely upon strict legal definitions, insofar as such definitions derive from the state itself. In other words, who does the defining and what is defined as a crime are intrinsically linked to issues of legitimacy and to the scope of analysis.

It has been suggested that there should be a deviance-based definition of state crime, one that involves some degree of subjectivity. Green and Ward (2000: 101; see also Green & Ward 2004), for example, argue that state crime should be defined as 'state organisational deviance involving the violation of human rights'. To determine whether a state has committed a crime requires the involvement of citizens as witness (or audience) in cases of acts or omissions that violate human rights.

Alternatively, Kauzlarich and colleagues (2003) argue that a holistic account and definition of state crime would include the following key elements:

- generates harm to individuals, groups and property
- is a product of action or inaction on behalf of the state or state agencies
- is where the action or inaction is related directly to an assigned or implied trust or duty
- is committed or omitted by a governmental agency, organisation or representative
- is done in the self-interest of (a) the state itself or (b) the elite groups controlling the state.

Michalowski and Kramer (2006) refer to 'state-corporate crime' to describe the intersection of state and corporate crime; that is, the commission of crime through cooperative venture between the state, transnational corporations and international financial institutions (e.g. the International Monetary Fund and the World Bank). The harms resulting from state-corporate crime (including facilitation of human rights violations, war and genocide) have a characteristically transnational dimension, occurring as they do within a global context, and have been referred to as 'crimes of globalisation'

STATE CRIME
Crimes involving the state acting against its own citizens, or against the citizens of another state as part of interstate conflict.

(Friedrichs 2007; Rothe 2010; Rothe & Friedrichs 2015). Tombs (2012: 170) teases out the symbiotic relationship between the state and corporations that permits the 'systematic and routine production of crimes and harms'; essentially the capitalist state is committed to the accumulation of profit over and above 'social values' and therefore prioritises and supports practices that promote such.

The existence of state crime points to a fundamental paradox—the state as both the official and primary guardian against criminal victimisation and one of the principal perpetrators of large-scale social crime and social harm (Friedrichs 2009–10). Attempts to explore and explain state crime in recent years have stressed the importance of processual accounts of state action and inaction in the face of ongoing major crimes, such as the genocide in Darfur and post-war violence in Guatemala (see Friedrichs 2009–10; Manz 2008). For the purposes of identification and taxonomy (categorisation or grouping) of the many different types of state crime, Kauzlarich and colleagues (2003) have developed what they call a 'complicity continuum of state crime' (see Table 12.2). The point of this model is to explicate differences in state behaviour according to the extent to which harm is the result of deliberate action. At one end of the continuum, state crimes such as genocide result from the conscious goal-directed activity of the state, while, at the other end, they result from a failure to act against preventable harm, such as the acceptance of inequality and the associated social problems that result from this.

TABLE 12.2 A COMPLICITY CONTINUUM OF STATE CRIME

OMISSION IMPLICIT	OMISSION EXPLICIT	COMMISSION IMPLICIT	COMMISSION EXPLICIT
• Inequality • Extraction of surplus value • Avoidable human suffering • Archetype: social stratification and inequality	• Bureaucratic failure • Regulatory dysfunction • Archetype: crash of Valujet 592	• Funding unethical experiments • Funding corporate destruction of cultures and communities • Archetype: US human radiation experiments	• Genocide • Nuclear weapons threats • War • Imperialism • Archetype: the Holocaust

Source: Kauzlarich et al. (2003)

CRIMES BY THE STATE

A summary of the kinds of crime typically described as *crimes by the state* is presented in Table 12.3 (for elaboration, see Rosoff et al. 1998). These crimes might be defined as harms that are deliberate, and involve conscious intervention by the state to achieve certain military or national security ends, or national interests. In the course of ostensibly protecting or promoting the 'national interest', the state engages in conduct that violates human rights and the rights of other sovereign nations.

USE OF GUINEA PIGS

The use of human guinea pigs encompasses a number of dimensions. It generally refers to governments' gross invasion of personal bodily integrity. This may take the form of enforced sterilisation of developmentally disabled citizens, or it could involve the testing of new drugs on an unsuspecting

TABLE 12.3 CRIMES BY THE STATE

CRIME	EXAMPLE	STATE JUSTIFICATION
Use of human guinea pigs	Sterilisation of developmentally disabled citizens	• Such actions are wrong, but understandable in the pursuit of public policy • Protection by the nation-state of particular sectoral interests requires the violation of human rights and citizenship entitlements • Some people may have to suffer in order that the majority enjoy the benefits of the whole
	Military germ or radiation warfare tests	
Violation of sovereignty	Bribery of government officials to obtain business contracts overseas	
	Illegal participation in the overthrow of other sovereign regimes	
Abuse of power	Internment of 'ethnic minority' citizens in times of war or terrorism	
	Dissemination of false or misleading information by state agencies	

Source: White & Habibis (2005)

population by government authorities. Alternatively, it could relate to the conscious withholding of treatment or drugs from certain population groups, in order to gauge the nature and effect of particular diseases, viruses or illness.

A notable aspect of the use of human guinea pigs is that it usually applies to people who are socially vulnerable or who are located within a particular institution that demands obedience of a particular type. In the first instance, subjects might include infants, pregnant women, terminally ill patients, poor people and people with disabilities. In the second case, the targets are usually soldiers and prisoners. Issues of what kinds of injections and other treatments soldiers are ordered to receive (on pain of being returned home in disgrace) surfaced in both the recent Gulf Wars involving Iraq. The American Civil Liberties Union estimates that approximately 10 per cent of the United States prison population participates in medical and drug experiments (see Rosoff et al. 1998). Given that over two million United States residents are currently under some kind of custody order (representing almost half of the world's prisoners), this translates into a potentially huge number of people who could be affected (Walmsley 2013).

VIOLATION OF SOVEREIGNTY

Another form of crime by the state is the violation of sovereignty. This includes bribery on the part of governments seeking business contracts for overseas markets. More dramatically, violation of sovereignty can involve varying degrees of interference in the affairs of another country. For example, the United States government, often via the Central Intelligence Agency (the CIA), has a long history of participation in attempts to overthrow foreign governments (Rosoff et al. 1998). Conversely, some regimes are maintained in power primarily, and sometimes solely, for the purposes of the military assistance to be derived, such as the United States' support of the Shah of Iran in the 1970s. In other cases, concerns for regional stability and economic interests translate to active or passive government support in the suppression of independence movements in other countries. Lasslett (2010), for example, provides a detailed account of the Australian Government's role in the Bougainville conflict in Papua New Guinea in the 1990s. The net result is that the citizens of the other country are deprived of basic human and civil rights.

The abuse of power by states involves crimes against humanity, such as state-sanctioned torture (including waterboarding and extraordinary acts of rendition evidenced at Abu Ghraib during the Bush administration) (see Carter 2012; Miller 2011), targeted killings, including use of drones for such purposes (May 2013), and the forced internment of ethnic minority citizens in times of war or in times of widespread concern about threats such as terrorism. During World War II, for example, ethnic Japanese people were imprisoned in Canada and the United States, while in Australia the main targets were ethnic Italians. Such internments represent gross violations of human rights, and are based solely upon ethnic characteristics rather than assessment of actual attitudes, experiences, contributions and community relationships. Such practices, albeit on a much smaller scale, still occur today, particularly in relation to police and state authorities' treatment of people of 'Middle Eastern' appearance. *Ethnic profiling* refers to state intervention on the basis of presumed ethnic background. Such profiling is based upon stereotypes, such as the assumption that all Muslims act in a certain way and are antagonistic to the West, and involve taking pre-emptive action, such as controlling whole ethnic groups to stop possible future offending. It does not matter that no crime has been committed, or that the vast majority of citizens (regardless of specific ethnic background) uphold the country's laws.

GATHERING AND DISSEMINATION OF INFORMATION

Another key aspect of state abuse of power relates to the gathering and dissemination of information. It is well known that state security services, such as the Australian Security Intelligence Organisation (ASIO) in Australia, or the Federal Bureau of Investigation (FBI) in the United States, have kept secret dossiers on citizens, and periodically used this (sometimes inaccurate) information to block job opportunities on the part of unsuspecting citizens. The true extent of United States government spying programs post 11 September was dramatically exposed by former United States National Security Agency (NSA) contractor, Edward Snowden, in 2013. In a series of leaks, Snowden lifted the lid on mass surveillance by the NSA of civilian phone and internet communications, as well as covert infiltration into the telecommunications activities of civilians, governments and heads of state outside the United States, including its allies (see, for example, Gallagher 2013); activities later confirmed by President Obama (see, for example, O'Malley 2013b). Such activity is by no means confined to the United States, with Snowden revealing a 'five-eyes' alliance comprising the United States, Britain, Australia, Canada and New Zealand (Dorling 2013). Indeed, Australia was recently embroiled in a phone-tapping controversy involving surveillance by our intelligence agencies of the Indonesian President, his family and inner circle (Alcorn 2013).

The main issues here relate to the kind of information that is collected, about whom, why and to what purpose. From the point of view of natural justice, it is problematic that some people are targeted for surveillance and intervention when no crime has been committed. Political dissent is not the same as subversion. Such actions raise the critical question of who is to guard the guardians, to ensure that agency power is not abused for personal or political purposes.

The way information is fed to the public by state agencies and politicians has a major bearing on the ebbs and flows of the democratic process. The United States, British and Australian intelligence organisations and, more generally, national leaders, were criticised for 'sexing up' claims about weapons of mass destruction in the months preceding the invasion of Iraq in 2003. In Australia in 2001, persistent claims by government officials that asylum seekers threw their children overboard when approached by Australian naval personnel was used to vilify refugees, and provide a political platform for the government to win the next federal election. In both of these examples, information and images were manipulated to the advantage of sectoral interests within government.

These violations of human rights are justified by the state in a number of ways. One of the most common, especially post 11 September, is that they are in the 'national interest', especially in relation to 'national security' (i.e. counter-intelligence, counter-terrorism, and protection of troops and allies), and that, while some people may have to suffer, the net result will be for the benefit of the majority. This type of ideological smokescreen is used frequently as a means to justify the unjustifiable: the systemic and intensive violation of human rights and democratic processes (Goderis & Versteeg 2012). Those who expose such violations are often accused of being disloyal, treasonous and ignorant of the 'real threat'. In such ways, a form of 'prescriptive patriotism' may be enforced as a means of stifling alternative viewpoints (O'Leary & Platt 2001).

CRIMES WITHIN THE STATE

Crimes within the state refer to harms that result from the action or inaction on the part of state agencies or officers situated within the inner sanctum of government or the power networks of its instrumentalities, acting in the course of their employment. Again, this type of crime has a number of different dimensions and aspects (see Table 12.4).

TABLE 12.4 CRIMES WITHIN THE STATE

CRIME	EXAMPLE	STATE JUSTIFICATION
Corruption	Misuse of public office for private purposes	Breaches of civil, criminal, and administrative law are wrong, but the problem is not the system but rogue individuals and organisational malfunctions. They need to be responded to by the state apparatus because they represent an attack on the rule of law and the status of the state as ultimate moral exemplar. When the state breaks the law, the legitimacy of the whole legal order is threatened.
	Illicit gain, usually through bribes, to promote certain outside agendas or direct government money to particular contractors	

(Continued)

TABLE 12.4 CRIMES WITHIN THE STATE (*Continued*)

CRIME	EXAMPLE	STATE JUSTIFICATION
Financial advantage	'Jobs for the boys'	
	Ignoring code violations in building, forestry and fishing industries	
Inadequate regulation	Failing to regulate the safety of imported medical devices	
	Lack of response to environmental pollution and/or harms	
Covering up	Perjury	
	Systematic denial of harms caused by state agencies	

Source: White & Habibis (2005)

CORRUPTION AND GRAFT

Corruption and doing things to one's financial advantage are typical criminal activities associated with crimes within the state. A member of the Australian Senate who uses the work phone account or travel account solely for personal purposes, or for the use of family members, is misusing their public office. Similarly, a politician who hires his or her lover as part of the office staff, without an open employment hiring process, is hardly doing the right thing by the electorate. Non-competitive allocation of jobs to family members and friends (nepotism) violates democratic procedures for allocating goods, services and opportunities. Diversion of political donations into a politician's own pocket is another form of corruption. If funds are stored in brown paper bags in the politician's office, then it is unlikely they will be accounted for using conventional audit methods.

One of the most common forms of corruption is when state bureaucrats or political leaders direct government money to favoured contractors in return for a kickback of some kind.

The reward may be financial, or the gaining of influence or support of existing business and friendship networks. State personnel may gain a financial advantage by overlooking code violations in an industry in which they have an interest, such as financial markets or direct ownership of businesses in the building, fishing, forestry or real estate industries. The term **graft** refers to those instances in which state officials make deals with businesses in return for money or favours. The Leighton scandal provides a recent example of this conduct, with $40 million in kickbacks allegedly paid by Leighton Holdings to corrupt Iraqi officials to secure a lucrative construction tender worth $750 million (McKenzie & Baker 2013a) in 2010. Internal company documents suggest widespread misconduct across Leighton Holdings' international operations, with corruption and bribery allegedly rife in Asian and Middle Eastern operations (McKenzie & Baker 2013b).

GRAFT
Those instances in which state officials make deals with businesses in return for money or favours.

Rosoff and colleagues (1998: 295) argue that 'graft has always been the "common cold" of American politics'. Much of this graft occurs at the local government level. To date, little research on graft has been done in Australia, although there is no suggestion that the nation is immune from this activity.

CRIMES OF OMISSION AND COMMISSION

The failure of governments to do their job adequately can also be seen as a form of crime that involves both omission as well as commission (see Table 12.2). Grabosky (1989b) presents a series of case studies that outline ways in which government institutions in Australia have failed to provide adequate regulation of harmful products and activities, and thus failed a wide range of citizens. In recent times, for example, a starch-based anaesthetic drip blamed for at least 20,000 deaths worldwide, and banned in the United States, Europe, Britain, Canada and Italy, is still permitted in Australia, despite Australian scientists leading the scientific research that exposed its risks (Barlass 2013).

Governments have also been criticised for allowing illegal telephone-tapping, fostering the abuse of prisoners, falsely accusing families and whole communities of social security fraud, failing to take responsibility in cases of obvious water pollution, and purposefully allowing nuclear testing in the knowledge of the radiation hazard to local populations, especially Indigenous Australians. Grabosky (1989) writes about gross waste and inefficiency in the expenditure of public funds as an area requiring further regulation, and greater scrutiny of government action in cases such as dealing with environmental pollution or other kinds of environmental harm.

COVERING UP ABUSES AND CRIME

Another problem related to inadequate regulation is the covering up of abuses and crimes by government officials. If something is exposed as a problem or as wrong, it threatens government and state officials with a loss of power domestically and geopolitically. The response, in some cases, is to engage in perjury; that is, to lie or pervert the course of justice, for example, by shredding records. Other responses are to deny any wrongdoing has occurred (including drawing upon 'experts' to refute the evidence) or to hide behind secrecy provisions.

For example, serious harms were caused by the British government as a result of nuclear testing at Maralinga in South Australia. The nuclear fallout threatened the health of personnel at the site and damaged local Indigenous people, as well as their culture and environment. However, information about the tests was classified as top secret, and it was decades before the full extent of the safety issues came to light and the inadequacy of information provision by the British to the Australian government was revealed (Grabosky 1989). More recently, evidence has come to light of the instrumental role played by health providers (medical doctors and mental health personnel) in turning a blind eye to and concealing medical evidence of physical and psychological torture, and ill-treatment of detainees (including torture) at the United States Naval Station Guantanamo Bay, Cuba (Iacopino & Xenakis 2011). Doctors employed in hospitals, as well as other health professionals and government officials across the globe, have also been implicated in (and in some cases prosecuted for) facilitating or concealing the illegal removal and transplant of human organs and the trafficking of human beings for such purposes. In some cases, transplantation of illegally sourced organs has been subsidised by the public health system (Ambagtsheer et al. 2013).

UNDERSTANDING STATE CRIME

Attempts to explain state crime range from situational and organisational factors to arguments that it is caused by structural factors endemic to the political and economic system. The argument that state crime is caused by organisational factors assumes that the 'normal' state and legal system is morally exemplary, but from time to time state agencies, and the individuals working within them, become corrupt or act inappropriately due to pressures arising out of a particular set of circumstances. From this perspective, state crime is the result of organisational pathology that can be identified and corrected.

Grabosky (1989) identifies the following organisational weaknesses that can lead to state crime:

- weak arrangements for external oversight
- powerlessness of prospective victims
- poor leadership by senior management
- inadequate direction by senior management
- inadequate supervision by middle management
- rapid organisational expansion
- strong goal orientation.

In this view, the reasons behind inadequate regulation or persistent abuse of people by state officials lie in weak institutions of external oversight. If prisoners, for example, are being abused, then we need to ask what the police, ombudsman, prison visitor or prison inspector is doing to rectify the situation.

Issues of corruption, lack of regulation and protecting one's back often reflect organisational features, and the activities of particular individuals and groups within the state system. However, they fail to explain state-sanctioned activity that systematically violates the most fundamental human rights, including the right to life (see Chapter 13). In contrast, structural explanations argue that the state can, and often does, support fundamentally unjust, abusive, unequal and immoral social relations and practices. From this perspective, 'normal' state activity can encompass active engagement in systematic social injury or harm. Such an argument rests on the assumption that the state is a site of political struggle and is dominated by powerful groups who will use it as a tool of oppression if they feel their interests are under threat.

ISSUES FOR CONSIDERATION

CORPORATE CRIME—HIDDEN DIMENSIONS

Corporate criminality is characterised by its invisibility as much as by its ubiquitous nature. It is nowhere, yet everywhere. There are a number of reasons for this. For instance, many corporate crimes are not publicly observable in the same way as many traditional crimes, such as assault or offensive behaviour. They may involve conversations behind closed doors, transactions in cyber-space and offshore accounting practices. Another aspect of corporate crime is that such harm may be defined as a regulatory infraction (e.g. failure to exercise due care when it comes to occupa-tional health and safety) rather than a crime (e.g. industrial homicide).

There also may be a gap between victim and offender, in terms of both time and place, and this can impede consciousness of the wrongdoing. For example, in the case of assault or burglary, the victim knows immediately or within a short time that a crime has occurred. In contrast, the link between exposure to a chemical and the birth of a child with a physical disability may take years to discover, and long-drawn-out legal processes to prove culpability on the part of the corporate perpetrator.

HUMAN RIGHTS VIOLATIONS AND THE STATE

Ward and Green (2000) describe a process whereby states may be involved in either a 'virtuous' spiral or a 'vicious' spiral in relation to gross violations of human rights. Each spiral makes reference to the dynamic ways in which norms about the institutionalisation of human rights are reinforced or abandoned, depending upon the particular political context. The virtuous spiral, for example, may involve a process whereby 'human rights violations are labelled as deviant by domestic, and later by transnational civil society in a mutually reinforcing process and, as a result, human rights norms are gradually adopted as criteria of the state's legitimacy. Human rights violations become illegitimate, in the process, because they are successfully labelled as state crimes' (Ward & Green 2000: 86). Such an analytical approach provides insight into how and why particular nation-states change their practices over time, either away from human rights violations or toward more intense ones. It also provides a guide to how nation-states do what they do to avoid being labelled human rights violators.

Violations of human rights are justified by states in a number of ways. One of the most common is that they are in the 'national interest' (e.g. use of torture in the global war on terror), and that, while some people may have to suffer, the net result will be for the benefit of the majority. This type of ideological smokescreen is used frequently as a means to justify what is wrong: the systemic and intensive violation of human rights and democratic processes.

CULTURE OF DENIAL

Furthermore, one of the problems in dealing with and discussing state crime is that it is not only governments and perpetrators who deny its existence, but citizens also 'turn a blind eye and a deaf ear' (Cohen 1993; Thomas 2011). Cohen (2001) provides a sustained analysis of how it is that, contrary to UN Conventions and everyday moral standards, governments deny their responsibility for acts such as genocide, torture and massacres—and how so often ordinary people allow this denial to occur (see also Chapter 13). Appeals to national loyalties, ethnic identifications and simply following orders are only some of a wide range of explanations put forward to justify the unjustifiable.

For example, consider the issue of the Gulf War(s), and how each individual relates to the rightness or wrongness of his or her country's involvement (or non-involvement). This entails a political and moral value judgment, one that is heavily influenced by personal factors, social contexts, flow of information and analytical interpretations. Yet, whether in favour of the war(s) or opposed to it, to remonstrate against the use of certain destructive weapons—such as those using depleted uranium (see White 2008b)—adds an interesting layer of complexity and responsibility. For those in support of a nation-state's military action, there is pressure to conform to the war effort and to be 'loyal' to the cause (relatively uncritical of things related to this cause). For those opposed, the main game is the antiwar movement, and issues such as depleted uranium weapons may be mobilised towards this end (the issue is used for instrumental purposes). Not only does one's political and ideological perspective colour how events are interpreted, but it also shapes how an individual's interpretation of events is interpreted and evaluated by those around them. This also can make discussion of depleted uranium weapons intensely complicated, as who is denying what varies depending on vantage point. At a minimum, it requires space for dialogue and reflection.

THE ABSENCE OF MORAL PANIC

The absence of moral outrage in relation to state crime is paralleled in relation to crimes of the powerful more broadly. David et al. (2011: 218) point to the differential social reaction to street crimes and corporate crime. For example, the global financial crisis triggered by the legally and morally questionable practices of bankers (mortgage brokers and elite financial executives) led to the 'transfer of private sector "bad" debt into public sector "sovereign debt"', resulting in economic slowdown worldwide and consequent loss of millions of jobs. Yet, despite jeopardising the national and international financial system, bankers did not become the modern-day elite folk devils; they were not the focus of moral panic.

As Critchter (2011: 261) contends, 'Above all, white-collar crime is perhaps not seen as threatening the moral order of society and white-collar criminals are too powerful to be cast as villains'. For Critcher (2011: 217) moral panics must be analysed within the broader context of societal power relations. Specifically, the scapegoating of 'outsiders and underdogs' (e.g. gang members and members of ethnic minority groups), and the regulation of their behaviour is a means of reinforcing and perpetuating hegemonic authority. White-collar criminals are too firmly entrenched within that hegemonic power structure to be driven out by the media or the state.

CONCLUSION

Crimes of the powerful do not occur in a social vacuum. A critical question for contemporary criminology is to what extent and in what ways criminology itself sustains different sorts of corporate and state crime, as well as how best it might contribute to addressing it (see Tombs & Whyte 2004). For example, silence on the part of criminology is, in itself, a form of response. This chapter has exposed the class-based patterns of white-collar and corporate criminality, and the types of crimes associated with those who wield economic and political power in society. For these crimes to become 'known' beyond a small circle of committed researchers (most of whom do not receive specific funding to investigate the crimes in question) is itself a question that goes to the heart of the politics of doing criminology.

How powerful groups and nation-states cover up illegal and criminal acts, how they deny wrongdoing and how they absolve themselves of responsibility for harming others are important topics for research and investigation. So, too, the 'culture of denial' pertaining to these kinds of crimes and associated harms has implications for the role and activities of criminology. Superficially, it raises issues as to whether criminologists are to be handmaidens of the state, or critics and agents of change. More profoundly, it warrants close attention from the point of view of personal security. Investigation of the crimes of the powerful, including crimes committed by organised criminal syndicates such as the Mafia, places the researcher at some risk. The powerful, by nature, do not like to have their activities scrutinised or exposed, and a wide array of legal and other instruments may be mobilised to silence the voices of criticism and dissent. A criminology that addresses the crimes of the powerful is a criminology that is prepared to put itself on the line for the greater good.

Chapter 13 explores in greater detail crimes committed on a transnational and global scale. Here, too, the themes of elite power (including the overriding power of the state) feature prominently.

DISCUSSION QUESTIONS

1   In what ways does the existence of corporate crime challenge conventional explanations of crime?

2   Why do you think that some sectors of industry seem especially prone to corporate crime?

3   How do you explain the fact that corporate criminals rarely face prosecution?

4   Describe two state crimes that have involved acts of omission rather than commission.

5   How relevant is the study of state crime to political actions undertaken by the contemporary Australian state?

FURTHER READING

Chambliss, W., Michalowski, R. & Krammer, R. (2010) (eds) *State crime in the global age*, Willan Publishing, Uffculme.

Cohen, S. (2001) *States of denial: knowing about atrocities and suffering*, Polity, Cambridge.

Rothe, D. & Friedrichs, D. (2015) *Crimes of Globalization*, Routledge, London.

Shover, N. & Wright, J. (eds) (2001) *Crimes of privilege: readings in white-collar crime*, Oxford University Press, New York.

Woodley, M. (2013) 'Bargaining over corporate manslaughter—what price a life?', *Journal of Criminal Law*, 77: (1) 33–40.

13 TRANSNATIONAL CRIMES AND GLOBAL CRIMINOLOGY

CHAPTER OVERVIEW

- STUDYING TRANSNATIONAL CRIME
- STATE-SPONSORED VIOLENCE
- STATES IN DENIAL
- TERRORISM
- TRANSNATIONAL ENVIRONMENTAL HARM AND ECO-GLOBAL CRIMINOLOGY
- ISSUES FOR CONSIDERATION
- CONCLUSION
- DISCUSSION QUESTIONS
- FURTHER READING

INTRODUCTION

ECO-GLOBAL CRIMINOLOGY
A criminological approach informed by ecological considerations and a critical analysis that is worldwide in its scale and perspective. It is based upon eco-justice conceptions of harm, which include consideration of transgressions against environments, non-human species and humans.

As indicated in Chapter 12, crimes of the powerful have increasingly assumed a transnational or global dimension. The subject of 'transnational crime' is, like crime generally, contentious from the point of view of definition and analytical focus. Mainstream concerns of criminal justice, as reflected in police agencies such as Interpol and the new international academic criminology, tend to view transnational crime in fairly conventional and restrictive definitional terms (Madsen 2009; Natarajan 2011; Van Dijk 2008).

Specifically, the concern is with those activities officially criminalised and thus considered transgressions of the law. Typically, the interest here includes such activities as:
- drugs trafficking
- money laundering and the black or underground economy
- terrorism
- organised crime
- corruption and business activity
- the development of internet-based criminal activity
- human trafficking.

The chapter begins with a discussion of 'methodology' in the larger sense of the word. That is, if we are to research crime and harm as a global phenomenon, then how is this to be achieved? There are important issues here with regard to perspective, scope of analysis and the ethics of doing such research. This is followed by discussion of issues pertaining to state-sponsored violence, terrorism and transnational environmental crimes.

STUDYING TRANSNATIONAL CRIME

Those writing within a critical criminology tradition tend to raise issues regarding both the notion of crime (preferring often to use terms such as 'harm' or 'human rights' as the appropriate yardstick) and the scope of analysis (which tends to go beyond conventional criminal categories) (see, for example,

Larsen & Smandych 2008; McCulloch & Pickering 2012). For instance, Aas (2007) situates analysis within the context of globalisation, and sees issues of crime as inherently contestable. Issues that are of concern include many of those identified in conventional criminology, but they also include:

- exploitation of workers and barriers to global movements of people
- global cities as sites for social exclusion and widespread social inequality
- migration and the emphasis on cultural essentialism as manifest in things such as nationalism, xenophobia, racism and fundamentalism
- the transformation from the more inclusive welfare-oriented state to the contemporary security state, featuring high levels of incarceration
- the need for a global frame that might benefit the rights of globally marginalised populations.

As this chapter demonstrates, there is a need to be open to new forms of analysis dealing with new types of transnational harm (for instance, **eco-global criminology**, which focuses on environmental issues), as well as offering critical scrutiny of contemporary issues such as terrorism. Moreover, as illustrated in this chapter, the role of the state has to be scrutinised, for specific nation-states can be a major perpetrator of crimes that ought to warrant universal condemnation (especially in regards to the use of torture).

Transnational crime refers to those criminal acts or transactions that span national borders and thereby violate the laws of more than one country (Natarajan 2011: xxv). According to McDonald (1997), an offence is transnational in nature if it is committed:

1   in more than one state
2   in one state but a substantial part of its preparation, planning, direction or control takes place in another state
3   in one state but involves an organised criminal group that engages in criminal activities in more than one state
4   in one state but has substantial effects in another state.

'International crime' refers to those harms that are recognised as crimes that threaten the peace, security and wellbeing of the world and are of concern to the international community. A number of these are identified in the Rome Statute, a United Nations instrument that covers core crimes such as **genocide**, war crimes, crimes against humanity and crimes of aggression. Such crimes (if they reach the prosecution stage) are tried by domestic courts within nation-states or, in some circumstances, by the International Criminal Court. Numerous agreements exist between nation-states regarding the treatment of acts that call forth the prosecution and punishment of individuals who perpetrate these acts. Table 13.1 provides a list of acts that are criminalised under various international conventions and agreements.

CONCEPTUAL DIFFICULTIES

There are interesting complexities in undertaking the study of international or transnational crime. Consider for example, Madsen's (2009: 8–9) discussion of transnational organised crime. These three distinct areas of concern—transnational crime, international law and organised crime—overlap in varying ways:

- There are crimes that are transnational and a violation of international law, yet not part of organised crime. An example of this is parental dispute over custody of a child, when one parent takes a child from one country to another without consent of the other parent.

TRANS-NATIONAL CRIME
Crime that is global in scope and reflects broad socio-economic processes and trends associated with globalisation. It includes, for example, illegal trade in wildlife, the international transfer of toxic waste, terrorism, illegal arms trade and people trafficking.

GENOCIDE
What distinguishes genocide from other forms of group violence is not so much the degree of violence but the fact that the action is designed to destroy another group. Genocide can occur without physical killing, it can occur with mixed motives and it can occur without the complete destruction of the group.

TABLE 13.1 'INTERNATIONAL CRIMES'

A PROTECTION OF PEACE
1 Aggression

B HUMANITARIAN PROTECTION DURING ARMED CONFLICTS
2 War crimes
3 Unlawful use of weapons
4 Mercenarism

C PROTECTION OF FUNDAMENTAL HUMAN RIGHTS
5 Genocide
6 Crimes against humanity
7 Apartheid
8 Slavery and related crimes
9 Torture
10 Unlawful human experimentation

D PROTECTION AGAINST TERROR-VIOLENCE
11 Piracy
12 Aircraft hijacking and sabotage of aircrafts
13 Force against internationally protected persons
14 Taking of civilian hostages
15 Attacks upon commercial vessels

E PROTECTION OF SOCIAL INTERESTS
16 Drug offences
17 International traffic in obscene publications

F PROTECTION OF THE ENVIRONMENT
19 Environmental protection
20 Theft of nuclear materials

G PROTECTION OF COMMUNICATIONS
22 Interference with submarine cables

H PROTECTION OF ECONOMIC INTERESTS
23 Falsification and counterfeiting
24 Bribery of foreign public officials

Source: Natarajan (2011: xxvii)

- There are organised crimes that violate international law, but which do not cross borders. An example of this is slave trading within a country, which involves organised syndicates.
- There are crimes that are organised and transnational, but do not violate international law. An example of this is the smuggling of genuine but non-taxed tobacco product from one country to another.
- There are crimes that are transnational, organised and a violation of international law. An example of this would be international drug-trafficking.

The notion of transnational crime thus evokes at least two different conceptual concerns. First, the crime must involve the movement of people, objects or decisions *across borders*. Secondly, the harm must be *recognised internationally* as a crime.

There are limitations with each of these considerations. For example, genocide is universally acknowledged as an evil, even if there are disputes in practice as to whether genocide is in fact occurring; (witness the debates over Sudan and how to interpret the tremendous loss of life in its southern regions due to systematic military interventions by various parties), and regardless of whether it simply occurs within the confines of a particular country's borders. Moreover, transnational harms may happen (e.g. disposal and congregation of plastic waste in the ocean, or the migration of toxic substances from producer countries to formerly pristine wilderness areas, thereby affecting humans and animals in the latter even though they have no connection whatsoever with the former), but these may not be considered 'crimes' in international law. In other words, the study of transnational harm or crime always involves contested definitions (restrictive or expansive, depending upon the place of formal legality in the definition) and complexities related to scale (since it may manifest in specific local or regional contexts, as well as across regions).

THREE APPROACHES TO TRANSNATIONAL CRIME

Consideration of scale and focus are implicit in the framing of research into transnational environmental harm. There are at least three different ways in which transnational research can be approached (White 2009a):

1 *Global*: refers to transnational harms, processes and agencies (*universal* effects, processes and agencies across the globe)
2 *Comparative*: refers to differences between nation-states, including 'failed states' (*particular* differences between nation-states and regions)
3 *Historical*: refers to epochal differences in modes of production and global trends (*systemic* differences over time, within and between different types of social formation).

The first approach focuses on globalisation as a far-reaching process where harm can be traced in its movements across the world and documented in many different locales (Smandych & Larsen 2008). The second approach has a comparative focus, with a concern to study particular countries and regions, including failed states, in relation to each other (Gros 2008). The nature of similarities and differences is fundamental to this kind of study. The third approach is based upon historical appreciation of social change and social differences (Cornforth 1976; Wright Mills 1959). It views trends and issues in terms of major epochs, such as the transitions from feudalism to capitalism, or the shift from competitive capitalism to global monopoly capitalism.

The researching of transnational **environmental crime** provides a useful illustration of how these approaches might be used and combined. After all, environmental harm crosses borders to incorporate all nation-states on planet Earth, as evident in ozone depletion and global warming.

ENVIRON-MENTAL CRIME
Unauthorised acts or omissions in relation to the environment that violate the law, and are therefore subject to criminal prosecution and criminal sanctions; more broadly, those activities that may be legal and 'legitimate', but which nevertheless have a negative impact on people and environments.

Comparative analysis shows us where some of the 'weak links' are (especially failed states, states at war and civil unrest) and thus hot spots for particularly worrisome environmental problems (e.g. dumping of toxic waste). Historical studies can alert us to the ways in which 'growth states' churn up natural resources, but also how ecological consciousness can grow out of affluence and a growing middle class. A global awareness of environmental harm may direct our concern not only to particular nation-states and regional issues, but also to non-state environments, such as the open seas of our oceans, that require our attention as well.

The specific name given to any particular approach may vary, as illustrated in Table 13.2, which provides a summary of recent titles given to various approaches to the study of transnational crime.

TABLE 13.2 STUDYING TRANSNATIONAL CRIME

TITLE	SUBSTANTIVE AREA OF STUDY
Comparative criminology	The nature of the crime problem in countries around the world
Transnational criminology	Cross-border forms of crime such as drug trafficking, arms trafficking, human trafficking and money laundering
International criminology	Crime that is specifically recognised widely across the world
Global criminology	Globalisation and its harmful consequences, such as structural adjustment policies of the World Bank
Supranational criminology	An encompassing study of international crimes that includes terrorism, war crimes, state crime and violations of human rights

Source: adapted from Friedrichs (2007)

ASSESSING SOURCES OF KNOWLEDGE

Studying transnational harm is not only a matter of choosing one's focus (e.g. global, comparative or historical) or substantive subject (e.g. terrorism, torture or environmental harm), however. There are also epistemological issues at stake. Consider, for example, the recent work by Connell on 'Southern theory' (2007). Connell queries whose knowledge, whose perspectives and whose ideas come to dominate our understandings of the social world. To some extent, this can be appraised by asking a series of key questions:

- Where does the claim of universality (e.g. about globalisation) actually stem from? How is universality linked to metropole/periphery relations?
- Whose literature is actually read and acknowledged? Whose voices are heard?
- Whose ideas are excluded from discussions of social theory? Whose perspectives are not addressed?
- What is erased in metropolitan accounts of the global—what space is presumed to be cleared or empty (e.g. especially those of Indigenous peoples)? What happened to colonisation and imperialism in the globalisation narrative?

Similar questions have been asked in regards to mainstream criminology. That is, commentators have tried to understand and explain why the knowledge that is most valued in global criminological circles is that primarily produced in and by the metropole of the United States, the United Kingdom and Europe (Aas 2007; Marshall 2008).

The *hegemony of the centre* influences the criminological project, whether this is in regards to terrorism or to environmental harm. For example, there are hegemonic accounts of how 'globalisation' is conceived and great selectivity in the manner by which authors are perceived to be authorities on the processes and effects of such. As Connell (2007) points out, rarely are authors, writers and researchers from the south (read, developing countries, Indigenous peoples, Islamic scholars and so on) consulted, read or acknowledged in the academic studies and research of the centre. This occurs even when the topic is their own country, and when the issues are of most pertinence and direct relevance to themselves and their people.

THE VARIETY OF GLOBAL HARMS AND RESEARCH APPROACHES

Thus, we are led to ask, from what vantage point are we going to assess the globe? Those who study are themselves physically grounded in the world—they live, work and play in specific places. They are embedded within particular intellectual fields and cultural contexts. To speak of the transnational, therefore, demands an appreciation that the 'transnational' is very often conceptually located within familiar scholarly universes. The development of a truly global criminology will require breaking the chains of parochialism, elitism and (implicitly) a colonialist mentality.

The bottom line for research into transnational harm is that, ultimately, we want to be able to better identify and deal with varying kinds of global harms. The complexity of the issues demands an approach that includes a wide number of sources and data types. That is, we want data that consists of quantitative (i.e. numerical counts) as well as qualitative (i.e. how people interpret and give meaning to the world around them) dimensions. Rather than being restricted by the limitations of the legal/illegal divide, we need to assert the prior importance of and urgency associated with notions of 'harm', especially if we are to deal adequately with state-sponsored violence (see the next section). This means assessing harm in many different contexts and guises, regardless of legal status and existing institutional legitimations.

The international nature of issues, trends, comparisons and networks is vital and ought to complement work done at the local, regional and national levels. Expanding the scope and vision of our work to include worldwide institutions, social processes and conduits of power (including resistance) is essential. The important thing is that research ought to take place on different scales (local through to global). Specific issues such as illegal logging or trade in endangered species demand specific types of research, and the development of responses that are specific to the nature of the problem. A case study approach may be appropriate for some types of investigation; others will require statistical comparisons and analyses. Whatever the specific methodology, we need to be conscious of the diversity of social situations and situated knowledge—related to class, race, ethnicity, gender and age—that will have a bearing on our knowledge about the environment. A socially inclusive research program acknowledges this, as well as the intersections of class exploitation, colonial oppression, racial injustice, gender inequality, age-based discrimination and environmental degradation.

STATE-SPONSORED VIOLENCE

STATE-SPONSORED VIOLENCE
A form of crime committed by the state that involves gross violation of human rights. This includes serious crimes against humanity and the systematic deprivation of rights through the use of repressive measures.

State-sponsored violence is a form of state crime that involves harms associated with gross violation of human rights and commission of serious criminal offences such as murder, rape, espionage, kidnapping and assault (see Table 13.3). These forms of state crime involve crimes against humanity and the systematic deprivation of rights through use of repressive measures (see Friedrichs 1996).

TABLE 13.3 STATE-SPONSORED VIOLENCE

TYPE OF VIOLENCE	EXAMPLES	STATE JUSTIFICATIONS
Genocide	'Ethnic cleansing' such as the Holocaust	• State action of this kind is wrong, but past atrocities cannot be dealt with by present governments. • Some actions can be justified by circumstantial necessities. • War and the war on terrorism dictates that human rights may have to be diminished in some cases.
	The Stolen Generation	
Torture	Special procedures that allow illegal confinement	
	Special laws and conditions that sanction torture	
Massacres	The justification of the killing of citizens with the concept of 'collateral damage'	
	The killing of prisoners or other vulnerable enemies	
Targeted state killing and group sanctions	Assassination of foreign opponents or enemies	
	Forced migration of people into settlement areas or camps	
State-sponsored terrorism	Support for groups that undertake acts of violence against selected targets	
	Support of religious-based communal violence	
Responses to dissent	Arrest and imprisonment of protesters	
	Banning of public assemblies and distribution of literature	

Source: White & Habibis (2005)

What is remarkable about this kind of state crime is that it is so widespread and yet has received so little attention from criminologists until relatively recently (Cohen 2001, 1993). Yet, the harm created through state action of this nature can far exceed that generated by conventional crime. State sanctioned genocide provides one of the most vivid examples of this.

GENOCIDE

The 1948 United Nations (UN) Convention on the Punishment and Prevention of Genocide defines genocide as a specific form of crime under international law, which applies in both war and peace. The UN convention contains two key elements—the definitions of protected groups and prohibited acts. It stipulates that 'genocide' means (Article 2):

> Any of the following acts committed with interest to destroy, in whole or in part, a national, ethnical, racial or religious group, as such:
>
> - killing members of the group;
> - causing serious bodily or mental harm to members of the group;
> - deliberately inflicting on the group conditions of life calculated to bring about its physical destruction in whole or in part;
> - imposing measures intended to prevent births within the group;
> - forcibly transferring children of the group to another group.

What is important to recognise about genocide is that while it often involves extreme forms of violence, in some cases it may not. The forced removal of children may not involve extreme, overt violence, but is still genocide (cultural genocide). In an extended discussion of genocide and the forced removal of Indigenous children from their families by colonialist governments, Cunneen (1999a: 131) observes: 'In summary, genocide can occur without physical killing, it can occur with mixed motives (some of which may be perceived to be beneficial), and it can occur without the complete destruction of the group.'

What distinguishes genocide from other forms of group violence is not so much the degree of violence but the fact that the action is consciously designed to destroy another group. How this is to be achieved will vary, and can involve a range of different measures—from massacres through to break-up of families and communities.

Examples of genocide include the massacre of hundreds of thousands of Armenians by Turkey in 1915, the Holocaust against the Jewish people in Europe perpetrated by the Nazi German state in the 1930s and 1940s, the episodes of 'ethnic cleansing' in Bosnia in the 1980s, mass killings in Rwanda in the 1990s and the current genocides in Syria and Iraq . Each of these instances of genocide involved conscious political choices and the engagement of state officials at some level of government. Contemporary analyses of genocide examine it as a form of social exclusion, ultimately linked to the elimination of the threatening 'other' (see Jamieson 1999).

TORTURE

Torture, likewise, is a state crime, if crime is understood in terms of a general world consensus against certain actions. According to the United Nations, the act of torture is an offence to human dignity and deserves to be condemned. In the Convention against Torture and other Cruel, Inhuman or Degrading Treatment or Punishment passed in 1984, 'torture' is defined as (Article 1):

> any act by which severe pain or suffering, whether physical or mental, is intentionally inflicted on a person for such purposes as obtaining from him [sic] or a third person information or a confession, punishing him for an act he or a third person has committed or is suspected of having committed, or intimidating or coercing him or a third person, or for any reason based on discrimination of any kind, when such pain or suffering is inflicted by or at the instigation of or with the consent or acquiescence of a public official or other person acting in an official capacity. It does not include pain or suffering arising only from, inherent in or incidental to lawful sanctions.

Not every country signs these types of Conventions, but nevertheless they do point to a world standard that says 'torture is wrong'. Yet, there are a number of countries that use torture or have recently (and routinely) used torture, and which persist in such conduct. In some cases, the use of torture is explicitly legitimated in law, as in the case of Israel, which until recently allowed it under certain specified circumstances. Other countries have used torture covertly, including the British army against the IRA in Northern Ireland. In 2004, the United States army was also accused of using torture against insurgents in Iraq, and under the policy of 'rendition' taking suspected terrorists into custody and transporting them to countries where they were tortured.

The use of special holding tanks and special procedures in dealing with alleged war criminals, illegal immigrants and terrorists opens the door to all kinds of human rights violations. Such is the case, for example, with regards to the American Government's action in penning prisoners up at Guantanamo Bay in Cuba, an action that the United States government deemed to be outside the jurisdiction of both domestic American law and the international community. The Australian Government's immigration policy locks up asylum seekers in remote and poorly resourced detention camps and has been criticised as, in essence, constituting a form of torture for many detainees, especially children (see Pickering & Lambert 2002; Weber 2002).

MASSACRES

Massacres occur both in peacetime and in war, and target a wide range of groups. The massacre of Indigenous peoples took place in select spots in Australia well into the twentieth century. In war, the main targets can include soldiers as well as civilians. For instance, in the first Gulf War in the early 1990s the victorious United States army deliberately killed retreating Iraqi conscripts. The use of cluster bombs, the planting of mines and the use of radioactive munitions in war have devastating and long-term consequences for combatants and non-combatants alike (see, for example, White 2008b).

The concept of 'collateral damage' reflects state acceptance that civilians will be killed in bombing raids and artillery barrages—no 'smart bomb' has yet been devised to kill only enemy soldiers. Liberation thus begets annihilation. In fact, reliance upon high technology, especially that which allows distance from the battlefront, opens the door for even greater killing of enemies and civilians.

COLLECTIVE PUNISHMENT

It is not uncommon for whole groups or populations to pay for the actions of a dictator or other individuals who may pose a threat to citizens or businesses of another country. This can occur during wartime conflicts, as indicated above. It can also occur when group sanctions are used as punishment for the actions of an individual. For example, bulldozing the house of a suicide bomber or razing a block of houses near a border crossing point penalises the innocent (who, in some cases, may not have even known about the activities of their housemate or family member). According to most legal conventions and criminal laws, only the guilty ought to be punished for a crime. When the state intervenes beyond this, critical questions can be asked concerning justice and human rights, quite apart from the distrust and resentment caused by group sanctions.

Another form of collective punishment is the forced migration of people into settlement camps and restricted areas. The emphasis here is on containment and denial of basic freedoms (of movement, of association, of speech etc.). Such was the lot of many Indigenous communities in colonial Australia (Johnston 1991). It is a process that has its contemporary counterparts in the world today, as in the case of refugee camps.

ASSASSINATION

Occasionally states do engage in more targeted and selective criminal acts (e.g. the assassination of Osama Bin Laden in 2011). The use of assassination to kill particular enemies is regularly practised against Palestinians by the Israeli government. Shortly after the events of 11 September 2001, there was talk in Washington about re-constituting a body within the US State Department that used to assassinate people in other countries (including numerous attempts to kill the former President of Cuba, Fidel Castro). What was interesting about this discussion was that in talking about re-constituting the unit, government officials were actually admitting to the existence within the United States government of an organisation that did illegally kill people.

DEATH PENALTY

The death penalty is also a form of state killing. Many nations have abolished the death penalty over the past 50 years, but there are notable exceptions. Each year, the United States, Russia and China collectively condemn thousands of people to die at the hands of the state. According to human rights organisations such as Amnesty International, this is a fundamental violation against humanity and cannot be justified on any grounds.

STATE TERRORISM AND FREEDOM FIGHTERS

The issue of state-sponsored terrorism presents one of the greatest challenges to human rights today. 'State-sponsored terrorism' refers to the support by states for groups that undertake acts of violence against its enemies. In some cases, the acts of violence are random in nature. The Taliban regime in Afghanistan hosted and supported terrorist organisations that embarked upon activities designed to kill and maim people in the most devastating and spectacular fashion.

But what do we mean by terrorist and terrorism, and how should these labels be applied? In what circumstances is the terrorist a 'freedom fighter' and the 'freedom fighter' a terrorist? Most of the anti-colonial and liberation struggles of the twentieth century involved movements whose members were branded terrorists and lawbreakers but who became legitimate political leaders after winning the struggle. Israeli leaders such as Golda Meir and Moshe Dayan engaged in terrorist acts in British-occupied Palestine. Nelson Mandela was accused of the same in apartheid South Africa. From this perspective, it seems that 'their' terrorism is terrorism, but 'our' terrorism is not something to be worried about. In the 1980s, the Sandinista government of Nicaragua took the United States to the World Court, where it was found guilty of illegal acts of war involving the mining of Nicaraguan territorial waters, but the United States refused to subject itself to this judgment (see also Dixon 1985).

State terrorism is not only about supporting groups that create terror, or engaging in actions that are lethal and illegal, in other countries. It also has an internal dimension, in the sense that some states may foster groups to enforce a particular type of order domestically, such as the notorious militias who terrorised opponents of Indonesian rule in East Timor prior to independence (see Stanley 2008a). Another example is the use of thuggery in Zimbabwe as a means to influence the electoral process in favour of the Mugabe regime. Alternatively, in some states, major communal violence has occurred. In some instances, the *inaction* of the state is the problem, as when it allows the 'right' ethnic or religious group to commit acts of violence. It is now known that in the months prior to the massacre of almost one million Tutsi people by the Hutu in Rwanda in 1994, both the United Nations and the French government were aware of what was taking place but did not intervene. Similarly, when Indonesia invaded East Timor in 1975, Western governments, including the United States and Australia, were aware that this violence was likely to occur but did nothing to prevent it.

STATE REPRESSION

'State repression' refers to the coercive control of individuals and groups who criticise the government. There are many forms of state repression, including:

- arrest and imprisonment
- banning of investigatory reporting
- banning of foreign critics
- the use of violence against demonstrators
- paramilitarisation of public order policing
- restrictive permit conditions
- withholding of permits to distribute political literature
- anti-terrorism laws that violate human rights and democratic principles.

The question of how states deal with dissent is increasingly central to the issue of state crime, including its definition and how best to respond to it.

STATES IN DENIAL

One of the key problems in dealing with and discussing state crime is that not only do governments and perpetrators deny its existence, but so too do citizens. Cohen (1993: 102) argues that: 'We have to remember (perhaps by inscribing this on our consciousness each morning) that state crimes are not just the unlicensed terror of totalitarian or fascist regimes, police states, dictatorships or military juntas.'

The point Cohen is making is that state crime is 'our' problem, too. Consider for a moment the issue of torture. The conflicts in the Middle East are well known worldwide. The terrorism experienced by the Israeli people at the hands of Palestinian suicide bombers parallels the terror of armed occupation experienced by the Palestinian people at the hands of the Israeli state. From an Israeli point of view, torture may be justified in some circumstances, such as when it is related to the seeking of information about, for example, a potential bomb attack. However, the UN Convention against Torture and other Cruel, Inhuman or Degrading Treatment or Punishment makes it clear that human rights are not negotiable:

Article 2

1. Each State Party shall take effective legislative, administrative, judicial or other measures to prevent acts of torture in a territory under its jurisdiction.
2. No exceptional circumstances whatsoever, whether a state of war or a threat of war, internal political instability or any other public emergency, may be invoked as a justification of torture.
3. An order from a superior officer or a public authority may not be invoked as a justification of torture.

In the important and ground-breaking book *States of denial: knowing about atrocities and suffering*, Cohen (2001) provides a sustained analysis of how it is that, contrary to UN Conventions and everyday moral standards, governments deny their responsibility for acts such as genocide, torture and massacres—and how, so often, ordinary people allow this denial to occur. Appeals to national loyalties, ethnic identifications, and simply following orders are only some of a wide range of explanations put forward to justify the unjustifiable.

Crelinsten (2003) has further developed the analytical framework introduced by Cohen to analyse the phenomenon of torture. He argues that torture is made possible, despite almost universal condemnation in legal codes, by the construction of a closed world that permits the use of torture against specific members of society, defined as enemies. In a complex analysis of the causes of torture, Crelinsten (2003: 296) explores the factors permitting torture by exploring domestic and international dimensions that impact upon perpetrators, victims and bystanders. He argues that torture is explained by the construction of a reality whose central feature is the creation of a powerful and dangerous enemy that threatens the social fabric:

> Laws are directed against this enemy, labels to describe this enemy are promulgated and disseminated via the mass media, people are divided into us and them, for us or against us. To imbue this purported enemy with sufficient substance, to render the presumed threat credible, the police or the military target groups most likely to be perceived by the general population as enemies, such as ethnic or religious minorities or political dissidents. If such groups happen to include violent insurgents or separatists at their radical fringe, so much the better, since the threat will be more easily depicted as real.

For torture to happen there needs to be some form of torture training. This usually includes 'techniques designed to supplant normal moral restraints about harming (innocent) others and to replace them with cognitive and ideological constructs that justify torture and victimisation and neutralise any factors that might lead to pangs of conscience or disobedience to authority' (Crelinsten 2003: 295). This type of analysis is also applied to how a torture-sustaining reality is maintained and institutionalised, how it can be dismantled or deconstructed, and how it can be prevented from forming in the first place. The analysis of the 'culture of denial' (Cohen 2001) is one of the important tasks for a criminology that wishes to unpack and expose the nature of state crime. Along the way there are bound to be uncomfortable moments. This is because criminologists themselves are implicated in this very culture (see Cunneen 1999).

TERRORISM

CONSTRUCTING THE 'OTHER'

As with any social phenomenon, and as indicated in the discussion of state terrorism, 'terrorism' is very complicated. It certainly has layers of complexity that need to be drawn out, but one of the key messages is that it is about constructing the 'other'. From the point of view of those who perpetrate acts of terrorism, it means seeing people as the 'other' in a particular way. From the point of view of governments that respond to terrorism, it means constructing the terrorist as the 'other', and one of the net results of that, unfortunately, may be to construct a whole category of people as the 'other'. Indeed, the backdrop of the present discussion is the events of 11 September 2001 in which 3,000 lives were lost in New York City and other lives lost in Washington DC. Since that time, a wide variety of theories that attempt to explain the nature of world terrorism have emerged. For example, there is the so-called 'clash of civilisations' idea, which says there is a fundamental difference between the Western world and the Muslim world. Accompanying such ideas, there has been an outpouring of racist sentiment directed at people of Arabic or Muslim backgrounds in Western nations (which amounts to Islamophobia) on a global scale (in regards to Australia see, for example, Morgan & Poynting 2012; HREOC 2004).

TYPES OF TERRORISM

A useful starting point is to acknowledge terrorism has been around for a long time and there are different forms and types of terrorism. The kind of definition used by official agencies such as the FBI in the United States is: 'The unlawful use of force or violence against persons or property to intimidate or coerce a Government, or the civilian population, or any segment thereof, in furtherance of political or social objectives' (Ronczkowski 2004: 18). Basically, terrorism is the calculated use of violence or the threat of violence to induce fear. The intent of this kind of terrorism is to coerce or intimidate governments or societies in the pursuit of goals that are generally political, religious or ideological.

Terrorism can be analysed in a range of different ways. For example, Ronczkowski (2004) identifies the following types of terrorism:
- political terrorism (e.g. directed at bringing about political or policy change)
- ecological terrorism (e.g. designed to halt clear-felling of old-growth forests)
- agricultural terrorism (e.g. use of chemicals to stop consumption of certain goods)
- narco terrorism (e.g. use of the drug trade to fund terrorism)
- biological terrorism (e.g. use of biological or chemical agents to injure, maim or cause death)
- cyber-terrorism (e.g. use of computer resources to disrupt service or destroy data).

The social profile of terrorists also has some bearing on the types of terrorism evident around the world today. For instance, there may be several different motivations for terrorist activity (see Ronczkowski 2004):
- right-wing (e.g. reactionary, ultra-conservative, fascist)
- left-wing (e.g. revolutionary, radical, environmentalist, anti-apartheid)
- fundamentalist (e.g. theological-based Christian, Muslim, Hindu)
- special interest (e.g. white supremacy)
- nationalistic (e.g. independence movements, anti-colonial)
- criminal (e.g. drug cartels).

The methods and targets are thus generally related to the express purposes of the terrorist group or organisation, and what they are specifically trying to achieve.

NATION-STATES AND TERRORISM

Why does terrorism happen? Why do people want to blow other people up, shoot and kill people, or rape people? A sociological response to this question requires an understanding of the process of 'othering'. Terrorism is about creating 'us' and 'them', and justifying actions on the basis of social difference. The 'othering' process is associated with dehumanising and devaluing people. Terrorism rests upon this social foundation.

The process of 'othering' goes in two directions. On the part of the terrorist, it is a denial of the humanness of the target. On the part of nation-states, it can involve denial of legitimate grievances and the consequences of prior historical events in favour of constructions of terrorists simply as 'bad' people.

The more one unpacks specific instances of religious, nationalist or political terrorism, the greater is the realisation that terrorism is often ultimately related to the actions of nation-states. One can consider, for example, genocide, ethnic cleansing and the Holocaust, and the impact on those people who have been subject to these kinds of activity. Would actions against perpetrators of such harms be considered terrorism if one were Armenian in Turkey in 1915, or Jewish in Nazi Germany, or Tutsi in Rwanda in the 1990s? State terrorism is related to the activities of nation-states and the machinations of nation-states on a world scale. Such terrorism can also generate resistance, which frequently is itself branded 'terrorism' in return.

Societies or states that marginalise populations or communities create the conditions for the emergence of the terrorist. This is the case in Palestine, as it was in Northern Ireland. In an analysis of suicide terrorism, Pape (2005) outlines a comprehensive study of global terrorism that includes every suicide terrorist attack from 1980 to 2003. He found that Islamic fundamentalism is not the primary driver of suicide terrorism. Rather, the major goal of every suicide terrorist campaign from Israel to Chechnya and Sri Lanka to Bali has been to compel modern democracies to withdraw military forces from territories that the terrorists view as their homeland. Thus, according to this analysis (Pape 2005), terrorism stems from social causes, regardless of the ideological and religious cover given to rationalising its use.

Terrorism is indeed a profoundly social activity in another sense as well. For the individual, it involves a social process that entails distancing oneself and being detached from the mainstream. The process of 'becoming a terrorist' is outlined in Figure 13.1.

TERRORISM AND CRIMINALITY

We conclude this brief discussion of terrorism as a global phenomenon by acknowledging the distinction between terrorism and other forms of criminality (see Ronczkowski 2004). Typically, a terrorist is distinguished from a street criminal by the fact that they are fighting for a political objective. They are motivated by ideology or religion. It is group focused. The terrorist is consumed with purpose: 'I am willing to die for my cause'. They are trained and motivated for the mission and they are on the attack. In contrast, the typical street criminal is engaged in crimes of opportunity, is uncommitted, is self-centred, pursues no real cause, is untrained (certainly in the art of murder and mayhem) and is escape-oriented. However, each activity is nevertheless subject to criminal sanctions—and murder, arson, vandalism and intimation are criminal acts in their own right.

FIGURE 13.1   BECOMING A TERRORIST

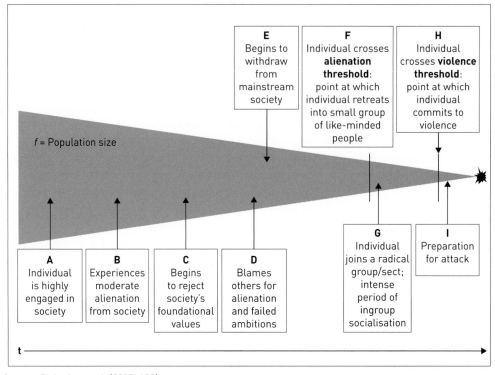

Source: Pickering et al. (2007: 108)

TRANSNATIONAL ENVIRONMENTAL HARM AND ECO-GLOBAL CRIMINOLOGY

Transnational environmental crime, as defined in conventional legal terms, refers to (White 2011):

- unauthorised acts or omissions that are *against the law* and therefore subject to criminal prosecution and criminal sanctions
- acts involving some kind of *cross-border transference* and an international or *global dimension*
- acts related to *pollution* (of air, water and land), *crimes against wildlife* (including illegal trade in ivory as well as live animals) and *illegal fishing* (abalone, whales, dolphins and lobster as well as fish).

These are the key focus of national and international laws relating to environmental matters, and are the main task areas for agencies such as Interpol. Some of the major international initiatives that formally specify certain activities as offences include (Forni 2010):

- Convention for Prevention of Maritime Pollution by Dumping Wastes and Other Matters (1972)
- Convention on International Trade of Endangered Species of Wildlife Fauna and Flora (CITES) (1975)
- International Tropical Timber Agreement (2011)

- Vienna Convention for the Protection of the Ozone Layer (1988)
- Montreal Protocol on Substances that Deplete the Ozone Layer (1989)
- Basel Convention on the Control of Transboundary Movements of Hazardous Wastes and their Disposal (1989)
- United Nations Framework Convention on Climate Change (1994)
- Kyoto Protocol (2005).

In technical legal terms, transnational environmental crime has been defined as follows:

> transnational environmental crime involves the trading and smuggling of plants, animals, resources and pollutants in violation of prohibition or regulation regimes established by multilateral environmental agreements and/or in contravention of domestic law. (Forni 2010: 34)

This definition embodies huge complexities of scale, scope and content. For example, the legal framework governing environmental matters in international law is defined by over 270 Multilateral Environmental Agreements and related instruments (Forni 2010: 34). The laws and rules guiding action on environmental crime vary greatly at the local, regional and national levels, and there are overarching conventions and laws that likewise have different legal purchase, depending upon how they are translated into action in each specific local jurisdiction. In part, differences in law-in-practice and conceptions of what is an environmental crime stem from the shifting nature of what is deemed harmful.

An 'eco-global criminology' refers to a criminological approach informed by ecological considerations and by a critical analysis that is worldwide in its scale and perspective (White 2011). It is based upon eco-justice conceptions of harm that include consideration of transgressions against environments, non-human species and humans (see Chapter 14). A concern with environmental crime inevitably leads the analytical gaze to acknowledge the fusion of the local and the global, and to ponder the ways in which many such transgressions transcend the normal boundaries of legality, jurisdiction, geography and social divide. This observation is important because so much environmental harm is intrinsically transnational in nature. Contemporary discussions of environmental crime, for example, deal with issues such as the illegal transport and dumping of toxic waste, the proliferation of electronic waste, transborder pollution that is either systematic (e.g. via location of factories) or related to accidents (e.g. chemical plant spills), the illegal trade in flora and fauna, and illegal fishing and logging. Whether conceptualised in conventional legal terms or based upon more encompassing ecologically based conceptions, the harm wrought is by nature mobile and easily subject to transference.

Moreover, the systemic causal chains that underpin much environmental harm are located at the level of the global political economy—within which the transnational corporation stands as the central social force—and this, too, is reflected in the pressing together of the local–global at a practical level. International systems of production, distribution and consumption generate, reinforce and reward diverse environmental harms and those who perpetrate them (White & Heckenberg 2014). These range from unsafe products to reliance upon genetically modified grains, the destruction of out-of-date ships and planes, through to the transportation and dumping of hazardous wastes. Dealing with transnational environmental crime requires a sense of scale, and of the essential interconnectedness of issues, events, people and places.

GEOGRAPHICAL CONTEXT

To fully appreciate the nature of global environmental crime and injustice, it is important to consider the physical location and scale of harm within particular geographical contexts. For eco-global criminology, this means plotting out the myriad types of harms, and recognising that some are common across the world, while others are specific to particular locations, regions and countries (see Table 13.4). The links between geographical scale and environmental harm can be spelled out through a simple mapping of environmental harms in different places around the world. In this way, layer after layer of harm, present and potential, can be determined by, on the one hand, investigating harmful ecological trends that involve degradation and destruction of environments (e.g. clear-felling of forests) and, on the other hand, considering existing documentation of specific types of environmental crime (e.g. illegal international trade in plants and animals). These crimes are interconnected and intertwined in various ways. What happens at the local level has consequences for those on the other side of the planet. What happens in any one place is thus intrinsically important to what happens worldwide.

The production of global environmental harm is partly determined through complex processes of transference (Heckenberg 2010) that frequently relocate certain types of harm and harmful activities to regions of least resistance. Harm can also be externalised from producers and consumers in ways that make it disappear (out of sight and outside the reach of adequate oversight). Producers may be unaware of or indifferent to the harms they cause to workers and consumers by what they produce. Consumers may be unaware or indifferent to the impact of what they consume; namely, the creation of harm elsewhere for humans and environments far removed from their everyday experience. The global trade in toxic waste (often under the cover of recycling), the illegal dumping of radioactive waste, carbon emission trading, and the shifting of dirty industries to developing countries constitute

TABLE 13.4 GEOGRAPHICAL SCALE AND ENVIRONMENTAL HARM

SCALE	EXAMPLE
The local	Lobster poaching in Nova Scotia, Canada
	Abalone theft in Tasmania, Australia
The national	Pollution related to pastoral industry in New Zealand
	Issues of drinking water in Palestine, Israel and Jordan
The regional	Logging in the forests of the Amazon
	Killing of elephants for their tusks in Africa
The global	Global warming and natural disasters
	Formation of huge plastic dumps in oceans
The transnational	Global trade in toxic waste
	Shifting of dirty industries to developing countries

Source: White (2011)

some of the worst aspects of the 'not in my backyard' syndrome. The result is a massive movement of environmentally harmful products, activities, processes and wastes to the most vulnerable places and most exploited peoples around the world.

The opportunities for certain types of crime are influenced by very specific local and regional factors (White & Heckenberg 2014). For example, the penetration and dominance of the Mafia in the waste-disposal industry in Italy provides a unique but devastating illustration of national difference (compared to countries where organised crime is not involved in this industry) that has an international impact (through dumping of toxic waste in international waters). In central and western Africa, the global bush meat trade is driven by several different factors, with dire consequences for apes, chimpanzees, gorillas and other primates especially, which are threatened with extinction. Local habitats for these animals are also being lost through logging and commercial developments. Not only are adult primates being killed for food and body parts, but orphaned primates are being sold on the exotic pet market, further contributing to the degradation of these species.

Specific places demand specific analysis, yet these are intrinsically linked to considerations that are universal in their relevance and application. For instance, transnational environmental harm is always located somewhere. That is, while risk and harm can be analysed in terms of movements and transference from one place to another, it is nonetheless imperative that threats to the environment be situated in specific regional and national contexts. This is important for several reasons. First, environmental threats originate in particular factories, farms, firms, industries and localities. Second, the political and policy context within which threats to the environment emerge is shaped by the nature of, and interplay between, local, national, regional and international laws and conventions. What happens at the local and regional level counts—whether we are referring to the Nordic countries or those of South Eastern Europe, Australasia or Latin America.

What happens at the local level is likewise implicated in decisions and processes that transcend the local, given the complex international ties and connections between businesses, governments, workers and activists. For example, Australian conservationists have linked up with their activist counterparts in Japan to influence the relationship between Japanese paper companies and a Tasmanian forestry company engaged in the clear-felling of old-growth forest. Protests have effectively been internationalised, although the destruction occurs in a specific place (White 2005). Business associations and cross-national environmental campaigns are illustrative of how closely connected we all are in an increasingly globalised world.

The challenge for eco-global criminology is to marshal ideas and evidence from many different sources and disciplines in order to identify where harms and risks are emerging as matters of possible social and political importance, and to develop pre-emptive strategies to begin to address potential problems before they create further harms and risks pertaining to humans, specific eco-systems and animals.

ISSUES FOR CONSIDERATION

TRANSNATIONAL RESEARCH

Engaging in research into transnational crime and harms involves a number of practical, scientific and political challenges (see, for example, Bayley 1999). Certain kinds of problems and difficulties are frequently encountered in pursuing cross-cultural crime and justice studies more generally.

Thus, for example, issues of parochialism and paternalism (see Aas 2007), and matters pertaining to the quality and limitations of comparative crime statistics (see Van Dijk 2008), are familiar to those engaged in the new global criminology, as well as to those interested specifically in analysis of transnational environmental harm.

Moving beyond one's own national borders to work with people in other locales and from other cultures is easier said than done. Gaining access to countries, regions and specific sites may be an issue, as is the expense associated with transnational study. Language differences and the subtleties of culture may intrude into the research process by causing delays and lead to misunderstandings about substantive issues. There are many practical as well as theoretical, economic and political issues associated with the study of transnational crime (White 2009a).

CHALLENGING THE ASSUMPTIONS

A number of assumptions are also frequently made about the nature and dynamics of transnational crimes such as terrorism and sex trafficking. For critical criminology, the challenge is to engage in research that allows the voices of many different parties to be heard, including those of the victims. Recent Australian work on sex trafficking, for example, provides an illustration not only of the importance of undertaking case studies across different national contexts, but also of challenging the dominant paradigm for understanding sex trafficking by listening carefully to what the women involved actually have to say about the issues (see Box 13.1).

BOX 13.1   CHALLENGING ASSUMPTIONS ABOUT SEX TRAFFICKING

The impact and consequences of viewing and responding to sex trafficking in narrow and restricted ways is explored in the book *Sex trafficking: international context and response* (Segrave et al. 2009). The book provides a critical examination of the international and national frameworks developed to respond to the issue of trafficking in persons, particularly the trafficking of women into sexual servitude (sex trafficking).

Drawing upon case studies in Australia, Serbia and Thailand, the research includes interviews with trafficking 'experts' that include policy-makers, police, immigration authorities, social workers, lawyers, United Nations agencies, and local and international non-government organisations. Of crucial importance, however, is the fact that the study draws upon the voices of women who have been trafficked. This is vital for, as the book demonstrates, the absence and silencing of trafficked women's diverse voices and experiences constitutes a major deficiency in discussions of the implementation and impact of anti-trafficking policies.

In particular, because the sex-trafficking agenda is dominated by particular understandings of the issues—which emphasise a 'search and rescue' approach to victimisation and justice considerations—the actual harms associated with forms of border enforcement that work to the detriment of the human rights of women from the global south largely remain unreported. In other words, the increased needs and desires for global mobility on the part of these women are overwhelmed by the discourses and inappropriate, and at times harmful, interventions of nation-states, which act so as to control rather than empower the lives of these women.

DENIAL OF STATE CRIME

State crime is rarely something that is affirmed by states; rather, it is precisely the locus of denial (Cohen 2001). Accordingly, information and data that may make denial more difficult is likely to be made scarce by the very agencies capable of producing them. Yet, on the other hand, regardless of humanitarian sentiment, passionate commitment and ideological predilection, those who claim that something is environmentally harmful (e.g. the use of depleted uranium in war weaponry) may do so with very little systematic evidence (see White 2008b). Responding to this situation ultimately means sifting through various types of evidence, listening to diverse voices of authority, and considering differing methods of investigation. For issues relating to environmental harm, there are serious practical challenges in relation to dealing with matters intrinsically multidisciplinary in nature, interconnected with other issues, highly politicised and global in scope.

In regards to state crime specifically, a major report on the forced separation of Aboriginal and Torres Strait Islander children from their families was released in 1997. The *Bringing them home* report provided a powerful and damning indictment of the actions of the Australian state over a long period. In response, the government of the day refused to acknowledge the problem. As Cunneen (1999: 136) has observed:

> In summary, the Australian Government has denied that genocide took place. Flowing from this is the denial of specific recommendations such as the need for an apology, the need for compensation, and the need for guarantees against repetition. In particular the requirement that action be taken against the contemporary removal of Indigenous children has been ignored.

Cunneen's work on this issue is relevant on two counts. First, it represents a sustained attempt to bring the government to account for actions that historically, and today, it has responsibility for. It is an attempt to break through the culture of denial relating to the state, Indigenous people and genocide. Secondly, it also represents a sharp rebuff to criminology and the role of criminology in genocide. Cunneen (1999: 137) asks the question: 'What did criminology do while the genocide was taking place?'

> Was criminology as a discipline merely accidentally involved in genocide or were the discursive foundations of criminology part of the same knowledges which legitimised the removal of Indigenous children? To what extent was criminology actually complicit in providing a scientific foundation for taking Indigenous children from their families and institutionalising them, and to what extent does it continue to do so today? In other words, we need to consider whether criminology had and has a stake in genocide.

State crime rarely occurs in a social vacuum. A critical question for contemporary criminology is to what extent and in what ways it sustains this sort of crime, as well as how best it might contribute to addressing it.

CONCLUSION

Discussion of transnational crime always opens the door for an interesting dilemma. On the one hand, part of the discussion of such crimes must include how nation-states themselves are implicated directly in certain types of criminal activity. On the other hand, to deal with international harms will require the cooperation of nation-states with each other, and with global agencies such as Interpol and the

United Nations. Individual nation-states can in fact be both 'perpetrator' and 'victim' when it comes to transnational crime.

Transnational crime is thus always political at one level. The role of the state is essential when considering what and who gets criminalised. For example, the disappearance of criminality and coercion in regard to environmental regulation (in favour of persuasion, self-regulation and cooperative strategies) shifts the locus of the problem from one of environmental and social harm to one of enhanced 'environmentally friendly' production. Such enhancements collectively degrade the global ecological commons.

On another front, the concentration of economic power at a global level, as manifest in the large transnational corporations, will obviously have an impact in the determination of what is deemed to be harmful or criminal, and what will not. It also means that, particularly in the case of business and environmental issues, the international character of capital and the trans-border nature of the harm make prosecution and regulation extremely difficult. This is the case even where national legal mechanisms have been put into place to minimise social and environmental harm and to protect specific environments. Not only do the powerful have greater scope to shape laws in their collective interest, but they also have greater capacity to defend themselves individually if they do break and bend the existing rules and regulations.

Eco-crime, which is clearly transnational in character and produces cross-national harms, is explored in greater detail in Chapter 14.

DISCUSSION QUESTIONS

1   What is the relationship today between the 'global' and the 'local'?
2   'What happens in India matters to the wellbeing of people in Australia'. Discuss.
3   Australia, as a nation-state, has been implicated in various kinds of state-sponsored violence. Provide examples.
4   Why would anyone decide to become a 'terrorist' and how can terrorism be prevented?
5   Should the study of international human rights be included within the field of criminology?

FURTHER READING

Aas, K. (2007) *Globalization & crime*, Sage, Los Angeles.

McCulloch, J. & Pickering, S. (eds) (2012) *Borders and crime: pre-crime, mobility and serious harm in an age of globalization*, Palgrave Macmillan, Basingstoke.

Natarajan, M. (ed.) (2011) *International crime and justice*, Cambridge University Press, Cambridge.

Segrave, M., Milivojevic, S. & Pickering, S. (2009) *Sex trafficking: international context and response*, Willan Publishing, Devon.

Van Dijk, J. (2008) *The world of crime: breaking the silence on problems of security, justice, and development across the world*, Sage, Los Angeles.

ECO-CRIME AND GREEN CRIMINOLOGY

14

CHAPTER OVERVIEW

- WHAT IS GREEN CRIMINOLOGY?
- ECO-CRIME
- CATEGORISING ENVIRONMENTAL HARM
- ENVIRONMENTAL VICTIMS
- RESPONDING TO ECO-CRIME
- ISSUES FOR CONSIDERATION
- CONCLUSION
- DISCUSSION QUESTIONS
- FURTHER READING

INTRODUCTION

This chapter builds on the previous chapter by providing a more detailed outline of how environmental crime can be understood and analysed. To speak of crimes against the environment or eco-crime (ecological crime) is to acknowledge some kind of specificity in the acts or omissions that makes them distinctly relevant to environmental considerations (Walters 2010). Yet, as with crime generally, there is much dispute over what is defined as environmentally harmful and what ends up legally proscribed as 'crime' per se (see Beirne & South, 2007; Brisman 2008; Situ & Emmons 2000; White 2008a).

The branch of criminology known as 'green criminology' generally adopts a stance toward the definitions and complexities of environmental harm that is critical and interpretive (see White & Heckenberg 2014). Not all things are as they seem, and part of the mandate of green criminology is to unpack the nature and dynamics of environmental crime by exploring the spatial and temporal dimensions of such crime. Above all, the concern is with who or what has been harmed, and how and why this takes place.

Green criminology as a field of sustained research and scholarship by its very nature incorporates many different perspectives and strategic emphases. This is because it deals with concerns across a wide range of environments (e.g. land, air and water) and issues (e.g. fishing, pollution and toxic waste). It involves conceptual analysis as well as practical intervention on many fronts, and includes multidisciplinary strategic assessment (e.g. economic, legal, social and ecological evaluations). It involves the undertaking of organisational analysis, as well as investigation of 'best practice' methods of monitoring, assessment, enforcement and education regarding environmental protection and regulation. Analysis of environmental crime also needs to be conscious of local, regional, national and global domains, and how activities in each of these overlap. It likewise requires cognisance of the direct and indirect, and immediate and long-term, impacts and consequences of environmentally sensitive social practices.

WHAT IS GREEN CRIMINOLOGY?

GREEN OR ENVIRONMENTAL CRIMINOLOGY
The study by criminologists of environmental harms, laws and regulations. Within green criminology, the three broad approaches to the conceptualisation of environmental harm are environmental justice, ecological justice and species justice.

Green criminology refers to the study by criminologists of environmental harms (that may incorporate wider definitions of crime than are provided by strictly legal definitions), environmental laws (including enforcement, prosecution and sentencing practices) and environmental regulation (systems of criminal, civil and administrative law designed to manage, protect and preserve specified environments and species, and to manage the negative consequences of particular industrial processes) (White 2011, 2008b).

In general, green criminology takes as its focus issues relating to the environment (in the widest possible sense) and harm (as defined in ecological as well as strictly legal terms). Much of this work has been directed at exposing different instances of substantive social and ecological injustice. It has also involved critique of the actions of nation-states and transnational companies for fostering particular types of harm, and for failing to adequately address or regulate harmful activity.

The key focus of green criminology is environmental crime, but green criminologists also study environmentally harmful activities not currently defined as crimes. Environmental crime is conceptualised in several different ways within the broad framework of green criminology. For some scholars, environmental crime is defined narrowly as that activity prohibited by law. For others, environmental harm is itself deemed a social and ecological crime, regardless of legal status—if harm is done to environments or animals, then from the point of view of the critical green criminologist, it is argued that such harms ought to be considered a 'crime'.

Scholars and researchers have been working on issues pertaining to environmental crime for many years, although without necessarily using the label 'green criminology' to describe their work. For instance, environmental harm and crime has been linked to the activities of corporations, and also to organised criminal syndicates in regards to the control and manipulation of waste disposal processes, and the production and distribution of toxic chemicals (Massari & Monzini 2004; Pearce & Tombs 1998; Ruggiero 1996).

Others have looked specifically at environmental crime, but generally within conventional frameworks. Here the focus has been on traditional illegal activities associated with the environment (e.g. illegal fishing), analysed within traditional criminological theoretical approaches. The key concepts and concerns of this work have been based upon legal concepts of environmental crime, existing legislative and regulatory measures around environmental crime, and the nature of official environmental law enforcement (Fyfe & Reeves 2009; Shelley & Crow 2009; Situ & Emmons 2000). Related to this, a conventional legal approach to the study of environmental crime sees it as a violation of criminal law and civil statutes; essentially, legal studies with environmental crime as the object of analysis (Bell & McGillivray 2008; Brickey 2008; Mehta 2009).

Questions pertaining specifically to environmental justice have also been of longstanding interest. The main thrust of this work has been to explore the empirical links between toxic environments and certain categories of people (inevitably the poor, the dispossessed and people of colour), and to actively struggle against the discrimination and racism that underpins such injustice. However, the key concepts and concerns of this work have emphasised issues relating to the distribution of environmental advantage and disadvantage, rather than crime per se (Bullard 2005; Pellow 2007).

The early pioneers of a distinctive 'green criminology' sought to provide a particular and self-conscious branding of the kind of work they engaged in. This occurred in the 1990s and was characterised by writing about the need for criminology to take environmental crimes seriously, and to do so in ways that would force criminology to rethink how it does what it does, and how to conceptualise the issues. Key concepts and concerns included the notion of green criminology itself, the idea that green criminology is a perspective not a theory, and the social and ecological importance of studying environmental crime and harm (Clifford 1998; South 1998; Lynch 1990).

Green criminology has emerged in the past twenty years as a distinctive area of research, scholarship and intervention. It is distinctive in the sense that it has directed much greater attention to environmental crime and harm than mainstream criminology. It has also heightened awareness of emergent issues, such as the problems arising from disposal of electronic waste (e-waste) and the social and ecological injustices linked to the corporate colonisation of nature (including bio-piracy and imposition of GMO crops in developing countries).

While the unifying link between and among green criminologists is the focus on environmental issues, important theoretical and political differences are nonetheless becoming more apparent over time. For example, some scholars argue that green criminology must necessarily be anti-capitalist and exhibit a broad radical orientation (Lynch & Stretesky 2003). Others construe the task as one of conservation and natural resource management, within the definitional limits of existing laws (Gibbs et al. 2010a; Herbig & Joubert 2006). Still others promote the idea that the direction of research should be global and ecological, and that new concepts need to be developed that will better capture the nature and dynamics of environmental harms in the twenty-first century (White 2011).

The hallmark of green criminology, regardless of diversity of opinion and the plurality of views, is that proponents argue for more attention to be directed to environmental and ecological issues. It is interesting in this respect that a number of prominent criminologists are now using their expertise from mainstream areas of criminology (e.g. situational crime prevention and general strain theory) to study specifically environmental issues such as illegal trade in elephant tusks, industrial pollution, and social problems arising from climate change (Agnew 2012; Lemieux & Clarke 2009; Mesko et al. 2010). Green criminology is not only expanding in its own right, but simultaneously there is also a greening of criminology more generally.

Environmental harm can be considered from the point of view of transgressions against humans, specific bio-spheres or environments, and non-human animals. Eco-justice can thus be theorised in terms of three broad concepts (White 2013b):

- *Environmental justice:* the main focus is on differences within the human population; social justice demands access to healthy and safe environments for all, and for future generations.
- *Ecological justice:* the main focus is on 'the environment' as such; to conserve and protect ecological wellbeing (e.g. the health of forests) is seen as intrinsically worthwhile.
- *Species justice:* the main focus is on ensuring the wellbeing of both species as a whole, such as whales or polar bears, and individual animals, which should be shielded from abuse, degradation and torture.

ECO-CRIME

Environmental crime or 'eco-crime' has become a major interest within criminology over the past decade, in part due to the depth and seriousness of global environmental harms (e.g. those associated with climate change), and in part due to the massive and widespread destruction of eco-systems and species in recent times. Contemporary discussions of transnational environmental crime, for example, engage a wide range of issues (Elliot 2007; Hayman & Brack 2002; White 2009b, 2008a). Among the topics under scrutiny are phenomena such as:

- illegal transport and dumping of toxic waste
- transportation of hazardous materials, such as ozone-depleting substances
- the illegal traffic in real or purported radioactive or nuclear substances
- proliferation of e-waste generated by the disposal of tens of thousands of computers and other equipment
- the safe disposal of old ships and aeroplanes
- local and transborder pollution, that is either systematic (via location of factories) or related to accidents (e.g. chemical plant spills)
- bio-piracy, in which Western companies usurp ownership and control over plants developed using 'traditional' methods, often involving indigenous peoples in the developing world
- illegal trade in flora and fauna
- illegal fishing and logging.

These particular crimes and harms can be categorised in diverse ways, as explored below.

Environmental crime frequently embodies a certain ambiguity. Eco-crime is not only located in models of risk (e.g. the precautionary principle) or evaluated in terms of actual harms (e.g. polluter pays), but is also judged in the context of cost–benefit analysis (e.g. license to trade or to pollute or to kill or capture). This goes to the heart of why environmental crime itself is consistently under-valued in law. It is the context that makes something allowable or, conversely, problematic.

The 'wrongdoing' studied within green criminology is initially informed by legal conceptions and constructions of harm. The nature and seriousness of harm—what makes something 'criminal' or not—is captured in the distinction between illegality (*malum prohibitum)* and serious harm (*malum in se)*. 'Illegality' refers to conduct that is prohibited by law but generally considered less serious than other types of social harms (homicide, for example). In many situations, harm to the environment is considered to be acceptable because it is an inherent consequence of industrial activities linked to significant economic benefits. Cutting down trees and pulling species out of the ocean are thus not intrinsically criminal or 'bad' activities from the point of view of the law. Within this framework, it is the illegal aspects of ordinary legitimate practices that are considered problematic. A key practical focus is developing the best tools and strategies possible to ensure compliance with licensing provisions and specific environmental regulations.

Other types of harms are referred to as conduct that is inherently wrong by nature, and is considered serious. The main issue here is to 'eradicate the problem' (usually framed in terms of banning of specific substances and/or activities). The intent of the law is the prevention and abolition of harmful practices, such as stopping certain types of polluting industries from destroying particular eco-systems and negatively affecting built environments of significance (e.g. the Taj Mahal in India).

Environmental crime is typically defined on a continuum ranging from strict legal definitions through to broader harm perspectives (see Bricknell 2010). For instance, the matter of legality does not prevent criminologists from critiquing certain types of ecologically harmful activities that happen to be legal, such as the clear-felling of forests. Specific types of environmental harms, as described in law, include illegal transport and dumping of toxic waste, the illegal transfer of hazardous materials such as ozone-depleting substances, the illegal traffic in radioactive or nuclear substances, the illegal trade in flora and fauna, and illegal fishing and logging. However, within green criminology there is a more expansive definition of environmental crime or harm that includes (White 2011):

- transgressions that are *harmful to humans, environments and non-human animals*, regardless of legality per se
- environmental-related harms facilitated by *the state*, as well as *corporations and other powerful actors*, insofar as these institutions have the capacity to shape official definitions of environmental crime in ways that allow or condone environmentally harmful practices.

Issues pertaining to state crime (the state as perpetrator of environmental harm) and transnational corporate crime (including the legitimacy granted to ecologically destructive acts and omissions on the part of large firms) demand attention in their own right. The label of 'environmental crime' tends to be applied to specific activities that are otherwise lawful or licensed (e.g. illegal cutting down of trees) but rarely if ever to environmental harms involving wide-scale regional environmental destruction, such as war-related degradation (e.g. deforestation due to use of Agent Orange) or to harms generated at a systems level (e.g. ever-expanding production and consumption of commodities that requires the systematic depletion of natural resources) (White 2013b).

With respect to the latter, harm can also be defined negatively, in terms of loss or diminishment. A key concept here is that of sustainability, where this refers to notions of ongoing ecological and environmental balance over time (Al-Damkhi et al. 2009; Merchant 2005). A loss of environmental resources or biological diversity can thus be construed as harmful if 'sustainability' is the yardstick by which harm is measured. The deliberate destruction or depletion of resources that significantly affect a region's economic or ecological stability would therefore be considered an environmental crime (Al-Damkhi et al. 2009: 121), as would those harms associated with the concept of **ecocide** (Higgins 2012).

Green criminology's broader conceptualisations of environmentally adverse activities are essential in evaluating systemic, as well as particularistic, environmental harms (Beirne & South 2007). For example, one can distinguish (and make the connection between) specific instances of harm arising from imperfect operational practices (e.g. pollution spills) and systemic harm created by normatively sanctioned forms of activity (e.g. clear-felling of Australian, Brazilian and Indonesian forests). The first is deemed to be 'criminal' or 'harmful' and thus subject to coercive social control. The second is not considered a criminal matter, although subject to regulation. The overall consequence is for global environmental problems to get worse, even in the midst of the proliferation of a greater range of regulatory mechanisms, agencies and laws.

Green criminology therefore provides an umbrella under which to theorise and critique both *illegal* environmental harms (i.e. environmental harms currently defined as unlawful and therefore punishable) and *legal* environmental harms (i.e. environmental harms currently condoned as lawful but which are nevertheless socially and ecologically harmful). How harm is conceptualised is thus partly shaped by how the legal–illegal divide is construed within specific research and analysis (White & Heckenberg 2014).

ECOCIDE
Ecocide describes the extensive damage, destruction to or loss of eco-systems of a given territory; where this occurs as a result of human agency, it is purported that a crime has occurred.

DIMENSIONS OF ECO-CRIME

There are a number of intersecting dimensions that need to be considered in any analysis of environmental harm (White 2013b). These include consideration of who the victim is (human or non-human); where the harm is manifest (global through to local levels); the main site in which the harm is apparent (built or natural environment); the scale of the harm (contained, dispersed or cumulative) and the timeframe within which harm can be analysed (immediate and delayed consequences). Many of the main features pertaining to environmental harm are inherently international in scope and substance, although they can be acutely local in terms of their impact.

Indeed, the categorisation of environmental harm is varied in that there are different ways in which environmental crimes have been conceptualised and classified. From the point of view of environmental law, for example, environmental harm encapsulates a wide range of concerns, some of which are subject to criminal sanctions but many of which are not (Boyd 2003). The kinds of issues canvassed under environmental law relate to laws and policies intended to protect water (e.g. pollution), air (e.g. ozone depletion), land (e.g. pesticide regulation) and biodiversity (e.g. endangered species). From the point of view of harm, writers have also incorporated under the environmental harm umbrella concerns relating to employee health (e.g. exposure to radioactivity) and pathological indoor environments (e.g. the home, hospitals and workplaces) (Curson & Clark 2004; Rosoff et al. 1998). Criminologists and others thus categorise environmental crimes in varying ways, and how they do so has implications for the way the subject is studied.

For instance, Carrabine et al. (2004) discuss environmental crimes in terms of primary and secondary crimes. 'Green crimes' are broadly defined as crimes against the environment. *Primary crimes* are those crimes that result directly from the destruction and degradation of the earth's resources, through human actions. *Secondary or symbiotic green crime* is that crime arising out of the flouting of rules that seek to regulate environmental disasters. The first set of crimes relates to the harm as being bad in itself; the second relates to breaches of law or regulation associated with environmental management and protection.

In recent years, researchers have studied a wide range of environmental harms associated with 'green', 'brown' and 'white' issues (White & Heckenberg 2014; White 2005).

'GREEN' TYPES OF ENVIRONMENTAL CRIME

Studying these types of crimes has been motivated by either a concern with species justice or an interest in conventional environmental crimes such as illegal fishing. For instance, work over the past decade has been carried out in respect to:

- deforestation and the devastation to plant, animal and human welfare and rights that has accompanied this process (Boekhout van Solinge 2010, 2008a,b; Green et al. 2007; Halsey 2005)
- the illegal theft and trade in reptiles in South Africa (Herbig 2010)
- fishing-related crimes, including the poaching of abalone and of lobster (McMullan & Perrier 2002; Tailby & Gant 2002)
- animal abuse that involves both systemic uses of animals, such as factory farming, and one-on-one abuse of animals (Beirne 2009; Sollund 2008)
- crime prevention and the illicit trade in endangered species involving many different kinds of animals (Schneider 2012, 2008; Wellsmith 2010)
- the illegal wildlife market in Africa, in particular the trade in elephant ivory (Lemieux & Clarke 2009) and the illegal wildlife trade in Russia and globally (South & Wyatt 2011; Wyatt 2013).

'BROWN' TYPES OF ENVIRONMENTAL CRIME

In regards to 'brown' issues, the main focus is on pollution and waste disposal. Relevant examples of such research include:

- the role of organised criminal syndicates in the dumping of waste, including toxic waste (Block 2002; Ruggiero 1996)
- inequalities associated with the location of disadvantaged and minority communities near toxic waste sites (Pellow 2007; Pinderhughes 1996; Saha & Mohai 2005)
- the use of medical and epidemiological evidence in demonstrating the nature and dynamics of toxic crimes (Lynch & Stretesky 2001)
- the global trade in electronic waste as a form of environmental crime that is of particular concern at the present time (Gibbs et al. 2010b; Interpol 2009)
- the social and cultural context within which local residents come to perceive what it is that pollutes their neighbourhoods and local rivers (Natali 2010)
- environmental racism linked to the social status of being poor or part of a minority group or indigenous community (Brook 2000; Bullard 1994)
- specific incidents where toxic materials have been dumped into developing countries by unscrupulous companies (White 2009c).

'WHITE' TYPES OF ENVIRONMENTAL CRIME

There are also a variety of 'white' types of environmental crime, which here refer to harms associated with the application of science and technology to the natural world. This is particularly the case with respect to analysis and critique of genetically modified organisms (GMOs):

- the abrogation of human rights and United Nations agreements in attempts to impose GMO crops on reluctant nation-states (Walters 2011, 2005, 2004)
- the implications of reliance upon GMO crops for biodiversity and the resilience of eco-systems to climate change (White 2011)
- the application of GMO technologies in relation to animals, which has been of critical concern among criminologists (White 2013a)
- the use of animals for medical testing and experimentation, which has been criticised as a form of speciesism (Sollund 2012; see also Chapter 11)
- the introduction and reliance upon toxic substances in the manufacture of objects such as children's toys, which are then distributed globally (Heckenberg 2013).

The range of substantive topic areas presently being investigated by green criminologists is growing and, increasingly, there is overlap across the diverse areas of interest and concern.

For some writers within green criminology, the first question to ask is, 'What harm is there in a particular activity?' rather than whether the activity is legal or not. Harm is at the centre of the analysis, and is generally conceptualised in regards to ecological and anti-speciesist considerations (Beirne & South 2007; White 2008a). Crime, as such, is less relevant as a category insofar as it tends to reflect narrow constructions of what is 'wrong' or 'bad' or 'harmful'. It also tends to be constructed in ways that reflect the interests of the most powerful in a particular social setting.

CATEGORISING ENVIRONMENTAL HARM

The range of substantive topic areas that green criminology is presently investigating is growing. So too, the complexities involved in studying environmental harm are being acknowledged. For example, environmental harms can be studied analytically according to four perspectives: focal considerations; geographical considerations; locational considerations; and temporal considerations. Figure 14.1 provides a summary of these.

FIGURE 14.1   KEY CONSIDERATIONS OF ENVIRONMENTAL HARM

Focal considerations:

[Identify issues pertaining to victims of harm]

Environmental justice	Ecological justice	Species justice
[humans]	[eco-systems]	[non-human animals]

Geographical considerations:

[Identify issues pertaining to each geographical level]

International	National	Regional/state	Local

Locational considerations:

[Identify issues pertaining to specific kinds of sites]

'Built' environment	'Natural' environment
[e.g. urban, rural, suburban]	[e.g. ocean, wilderness, desert]

Temporal considerations:

[Identify issues pertaining to changes over time]

Environmental effects	Environmental impact	Social impact
[short term/long term]	[manifest/latent]	[immediate/lasting]

Source: adapted from White (2013b, 2005)

Exploration of themes and issues within each of these areas can be used to uncover the diversity of perspectives, approaches and concepts to harm that are utilised in contemporary green criminology (see White 2005).

FOCAL CONSIDERATIONS

'Focal considerations' refers to concerns that centre on the key actors or players at the centre of investigation into environmental harm. In other words, the emphasis is on identifying issues pertaining to the victims of harm, including how to define who or what is an environmental 'victim' (Hall 2012, 2011; Williams 1996). Most green criminologists consider that the concept of 'harm' ought to encapsulate those activities that may be legal and 'legitimate' but which nevertheless negatively impact on people, environments and non-human animals (Beirne & South 2007; Lynch & Stretesky 2003). The emphasis placed upon either the human and/or the non-human, however, influences what to study and interpretation of the nature of environmental harm.

GEOGRAPHICAL CONSIDERATIONS

Varying types of environmental harm pertain to different geographical levels. Some issues are of a planetary scale (e.g. global warming), some are regional (e.g. oceans and fisheries), some are national in geographical location (e.g. droughts in particular African countries), while others still are local (e.g. specific oil spills). Similarly, laws tend to be formulated in particular geographically defined jurisdictions. The priority issues at any point in time will depend in part upon local contexts, and local environmental and criminogenic factors (e.g. rare species living in particular kinds of habitats). At the national level, different kinds of crimes and harms are linked to specific national contexts and particular geographical regions. For example, threats to biodiversity have been associated with illegal logging and deforestation in the Atlantic Forest of Brazil; illegal wildlife hunting and trade in Chiapas, Mexico; the commercial-scale illegal logging and shipment of illegal logs in Papua Province, Indonesia; and illegal fishing with dynamite and cyanide in Palawan, the Philippines (Akella & Cannon 2004).

LOCATIONAL CONSIDERATIONS

A distinction can be made between geographical area and 'place'. The latter refers to specific kinds of sites as described in the language of 'natural' and 'built' environment. The 'built' environment refers to significant sites of human habitation and residency. It includes urban and rural areas, and areas of cross-over between the two, consisting of major regional concentrations of people, and commuter suburbs and zones. The 'natural' environment consists of wilderness, oceans, rivers and deserts. These are sites in which human beings may be present, or through which they may traverse, but which are often seen as distinctive and 'separate' from human settlement per se; however, this needs to be qualified by acknowledging different ways in which humans interact with their environments, reflecting different cultural and material relationships to the land (see Langton 1998). Perceptions and consciousness of harm is partly linked to proximity of human habitation to the sources of harm themselves. A toxic spill in the middle of a major city, or contamination of its main harbour, is much more likely to capture public attention, and prompt government action, than something that happens in a remote wilderness area or on the high seas.

TEMPORAL CONSIDERATIONS

Another key issue for consideration relates to issues pertaining to changes over time. To some extent, such considerations are ingrained in contemporary environmental impact assessment in the guise of the 'precautionary principle' (Deville & Harding 1997; Harvey 1996). That is, what we do with and in the environment has consequences, some of which we cannot foresee. The short-term effects of environmental degradation include such things as the release of chlorofluorocarbons into the atmosphere, the long-term effect being the accumulation of greenhouse gases and ultimately climate warming. Environmental impacts begin with global warming as a manifest consequence of planetary change, and results in the latent consequences of changes in sea levels and changes in regional temperatures and precipitation (among other things). The social impact of environmental change is both immediate as in the case of respiratory problems or increased probability of disease outbreak, and long term (e.g. lower quality of life, alteration of physiological functioning).

The significance of conceptualising environmental issues in this way is that it demonstrates the link between environmental action (usually involving distinct types of community and environmental groups) and particular sites (e.g. urban centres, wilderness areas or seacoast regions). Some issues tend to resonate more with members of the public than others; other issues generally only emerge if an accident or disaster brings it to the fore.

ENVIRON-MENTAL VICTIMISATION
Specific forms of harm that are caused by acts (e.g. dumping of toxic waste) or omissions (e.g. failure to provide safe drinking water), leading to the presence or absence of environmental agents (e.g. poisons or nutrients) that are associated with human injury. Under certain circumstances, specific eco-systems and non-human animals can be considered victims too.

Temporal considerations also are relevant to analysis of discrimination relating to environmental harm. For example, environmental justice researchers deal with temporal issues by considering when and why poor or minority communities end up living near toxic waste facilities. A key question is whether the proximity between pollution and certain communities is the result of the placement of the facility in that community (direct discrimination), or whether the placement of the facility attracts these communities because housing values become depressed (indirect discrimination). By physically mapping out environmental harms over time, and in relation to population characteristics, it is possible to determine the kind of discrimination that is in fact at play (see, for example, Lynch et al. 2002; Stretesky & Hogan 1998). Did the pollution come to the people, or did the people come to live near the pollution? This is answerable through temporal analysis.

The detection and origins of some types of environmentally related harm may be unclear due to significant time-lags in manifestation of the harm. Here it is important to acknowledge the notion of cumulative effects. For example, this could refer to the way in which dioxins accumulate in fish flesh over time. It could also refer to the cumulative impact of multiple sources of pollution as in cases where there are a high number of factories in one area (e.g. places along the United States–Mexican border). Diseases linked to asbestos poisoning may surface many years after first exposure, and this, too, provides another example of long-term effects of environmental harm. Persistent use of pesticides in particular geographical areas may also have unforeseen consequences for local wildlife, including the development of new diseases among endemic animal species (as seems to have occurred in the case of the facial tumour disease now rampant among the Tasmanian devil population in Australia).

ENVIRONMENTAL VICTIMS

Environmental victimisation refers to specific forms of harm that are caused by acts or omissions leading to the presence or absence of environmental agents associated with human injury (Williams 1996). According to Williams (1996: 21), environmental victims are 'those of past, present, or future generations who are injured as a consequence of change to the chemical, physical, microbiological, or psychosocial environment, brought about by deliberate or reckless, individual or collective, human act or act of omission'. In response to a growing body of literature on non-human victims within green criminology and other disciples, this definition of 'victim' now needs to be extended to include animals, plants and eco-systems. In other words, the 'environment' itself should be counted as a possible victim of crime.

The majority of human victims of environmental degradation—stemming from industrial and commercial activities, global warming, loss of biodiversity and increased waste and pollution—are the poor and the dispossessed (see Bullard 2005; Shiva 2008). While all are threatened by global environmental disaster, there remain large social differences in the likelihood of exposure and subsequent resilience to injury, harm and suffering. For those who disproportionately bear the brunt of global patterns of environmental transformation, degradation and victimisation, significant questions arise as to who will compensate them for their often prolonged suffering, now and into the future.

When it comes to measuring the value of human life, some people count more than others and, in some circumstances, the health and wellbeing of certain people will be sacrificed on the altar of business profits and 'national' interests. This can be quantified in terms of United Nations figures on world poverty, disease, illnesses related to indoor and outdoor air pollution, life expectancy and other similar data sets. Victimisation is also measurable in terms of production processes worldwide, in which destruction of local environments is part and parcel of resource extraction and the recycling of commodities:

> The open burning, acid baths and toxic dumping pour pollution into the land, air and water and exposes the men, women and children of Asia's poorer peoples to poison. The health and economic costs of this trade are vast and, due to export, are not born [e] by the western consumers nor the waste brokers who benefit from the trade. (Basel Action Network and Silicon Valley Toxics Coalition 2002: 1)

In this example, the atrocity and suffering related to environmental harm is linked to a basic denial of human rights. This is not only evident in disparities in access to resources or in environmental living conditions; it is also found in the activities of regimes and companies that use violence against those who dare to threaten their economic and political interests. This has led some to argue that since environmental injustice and human rights are inextricably interwoven, the former should be recognised as a major component of the latter (Adeola 2000: 687).

This story is familiar the world over, including within developed countries. It is a story of lack of care for those who are culturally and socially constructed as 'other', and therefore denied societal compassion and the obligations of compensation. Denial of harm on the part of the advantaged and socially privileged is easier when stereotypes, denigrating images and self-interest are mobilised in order to ignore such harms. This has long been the substantive concern of environmental justice movements (see Bullard 2005; see also Hall 2013). Environmental injustice is accomplished precisely through the devaluing of those who suffer the consequences of environmental harms not of their own making but stemming from decisions made by someone else, in another part of the world, in the interests of those who will never share their environmental risks and harms.

As extensive work on specific incidents and patterns of victimisation demonstrate, some people are more likely to be disadvantaged by environmental problems than others. For instance, studies have identified disparities involving many different types of environmental hazards that especially adversely affect people of colour, ethnic minority groups and indigenous people in places such as Canada, Australia and the United States (Brook 2000; Bullard 1994; Langton 1998; Pinderhughes 1996; Rush 2002; Stretesky & Lynch 1999). In the context of discussions on differential environmental victimisation, it is also important to consider how particular substances (e.g. chemicals and heavy metals) differentially victimise by sex (e.g. different impacts for male and female in humans, and feminisation of marine species) and age (e.g. the developing foetus, the developing child, the infirm and the very elderly).

People from poor and non-English-speaking backgrounds living in Australia or the United States may also suffer disadvantages through their lack of participation in decision-making forums, as well as lack of information about potential hazards and risks. For example, methylmercury is a potent neurotoxin that can have serious health impacts, particularly for foetal growth. Apparently, a large proportion of canned tuna fish sold in the United States contains unsafe levels of methylmercury. Yet, the populations at risk of overconsumption—namely minorities and low-income groups—are most likely to be uniformed of the risks, and less likely to be aware of fish advisories and to change consumption habits (Pallo & Barken 2010).

In the specific area of environmental victimology, the literature to date has tended to focus on humans as victims rather than other species or particular environments (see, for example, Hall 2013; Jarrell & Ozymy 2012; Williams 1996). As our collective knowledge of global environmental harm increases, there is an appreciation that those humans who suffer environmental victimisation deserve even greater sustained analysis and strategic interventions than has previously been the case (see Hall 2013). This is not a straightforward task, and yet the complexity of the issue is further compounded when we include the non-human in addition to the human as victim.

NON-HUMAN ENVIRONMENTAL VICTIMS

The notion of environmental victim implies that someone or something is being harmed through the conscious or neglectful actions of another. From a green criminology perspective, environmental harm can be conceptualised in terms of justice, based upon notions of human, ecological and animal rights (White 2013b).

It is the social, economic and political characteristics of victim populations that make them vulnerable to victimisation in the first place (see Fattah 2010). This extends to the non-human as well as the human. Consider, for example, the choices made (by humans) about which species receive human protection and which do not (see Sollund 2012). Not all species are 'valued' in the same way (compare tigers with bees, and the campaigns to conserve both), and they too can be 'victims' (of policy or of introduced predators) but not always recognised as such (as in the case of the galaxias fish in Tasmania, for example). Indeed, the status and value of animals (of particular species and of individual animals) varies greatly according to circumstance, and depends upon larger ecological patterns and trends (see White 2013b). Likewise, appreciation of rivers, mountains and oceans is contingent upon how these are conceptualised in popular discourse and legal opinion (Stone 1972). Whether and how the non-human is viewed as victim is still a relatively new area of investigation within green criminology.

The notion of eco-justice signifies an active concern with both the human and the non-human. It incorporates the idea that animals and eco-systems can, under certain circumstances, be considered 'victims' too, as reflected in Table 14.1.

Acknowledgement of 'victim' status is crucial to understanding the ways in which environmental crime is being re-thought. For example, recent commentary and research on animal rights and animal welfare directs attention to the changing nature of 'animal law' and the ways in which animals as

TABLE 14.1 ECO-JUSTICE AND VICTIMS

ENVIRONMENT JUSTICE—THE VICTIM IS HUMANS

Environmental rights are seen as an extension of human or social rights so as to enhance the quality of human life, now and into the future.

ECOLOGICAL JUSTICE—THE VICTIM IS SPECIFIC ENVIRONMENTS

Human beings are merely one component of complex eco-systems that should be preserved for their own sake.

SPECIES JUSTICE—THE VICTIM IS ANIMALS AND PLANTS

Animals have an intrinsic right to not suffer abuse individually and collectively, and plants should not suffer degradation of habitat to the extent that it threatens biodiversity loss.

Source: Adapted from White (2013b)

property are being challenged by alternative conceptions of animals as 'persons' and/or as rights-holders in their own right (Beirne 2009; Sankoff & White 2009). Radical positions declare much of current practice and attitudes towards animals as fundamentally immoral and wrong, as a form of non-human oppression (see Svard 2008). From the point of view of species justice, each animal ought to be given the opportunity as far as possible to fulfil its potential as a sentient being.

If the non-human is to be acknowledged as a 'victim', then how will they be able to convey this to others? Clearly the 'voiceless' (such as trees, soil, rivers, bees, orchids and wombats) need a human translator to express the nature of the harms that they suffer. In practice, this basically means that there must be advocates who can speak on behalf of those who cannot articulate what is happening to them (see Besthorn 2013; Schlosberg 2007).

By listening carefully to the signs of nature, there is much to learn by bringing the non-human into the dialogue about ecological health and wellbeing.

In many countries the law allows for a modicum of protection for the non-human as well as the human. The definition of 'victim' is, however, evolving and expanding. For example, legal standing occasionally has been granted to human representatives of non-human entities, as with a river that was represented at a restorative justice conference in New Zealand by the Waikato River Enhancement Society (Preston 2011: 144, fn53). Thus 'surrogate victims' may be recognised as representing the community affected (including particular biotic groups and abiotic environs) for the purpose of court determinations.

Preston (2011: 143) describes how future generations *and* non-human biota may be considered victims in the context of environment court deliberations:

> Environmental harm may require remediation over generations and hence the burden and the cost of remediation is transferred to future generations. Remediation of contaminated land and restoration of habitat of species, populations and ecological communities are examples of intergenerational burdens passed from the present generation to future generations. Where intergenerational inequity is caused by the commission of an environmental offence, the victims include future generations...The biosphere and non-human biota have intrinsic value independent of their utilitarian or instrumental value for humans. When harmed by environmental crime, the biosphere and non-human biota are also victims. The harm is able to be assessed from an ecological perspective; it need not be anthropocentric.

RESPONDING TO ECO-CRIME

Within the spectrum of ideas and activities associated with green criminology are several analytical frameworks. This is represented and highlighted in the three approaches that together constitute an eco-justice perspective, with their varying focus on humans, eco-systems and animals (White 2013b). This is evident, for example, in debates over multiple land-use areas. This kind of dispute can involve those who argue that human interests should come first (from the perspective of environmental justice), or that specific ecological niches be protected (from the perspective of ecological justice), even if some animals have to be killed or removed from a specific geographical location. From the point of view of species justice, however, significant questions can be asked regarding the intrinsic rights of animals and the duty of humans to provide care and protection for non-human species.

Differences within green criminology also manifest when it comes to responding to environmental crime or harm. For many green criminologists the biggest threat to environmental rights, ecological justice and non-human animal wellbeing are system-level structures and pressures that commodify all aspects of social existence, that are based upon the exploitation of humans, non-human animals and natural resources, and that privilege the powerful over the interests of the vast majority. This view is not shared equally among green criminologists, however. In the end, how these questions are addressed has major implications for how responses to environmental harm will be framed.

From a critical green criminology viewpoint, environmental harm is related to exploitation of both environments and humans by those who control the means of production. Analysis of global capitalism provides answers to questions such as why it is that human societies simultaneously respect and protect certain creatures (especially animal companions such as dogs and cats) while allowing and even condoning the dreadful treatment of others (as in the case of factory farming of battery hens to produce eggs) (Beirne 2004; Torres 2007). It also allows us to better understand why it is that we strive to preserve some environments (via creation of national parks), while ensuring the devastation of particular eco-systems (e.g. clear-felling of old-growth forests).

Environmental harm takes place within the overarching context of a distinct global political economy. Most writers within the green criminology perspective concentrate on exposing specific types of criminal or harmful environmental actions or omissions. In doing so they have provided detailed descriptions and analyses of phenomena such as the illegal trade of animals, illegal logging, dumping of toxic waste, air pollution and threats to biodiversity. In many cases, the corpus of work identified within this field has highlighted issues pertaining to social inequality, speciesism, ecological and environmental injustice, and crimes of the powerful. What are less common, however, are examples of study that locate these harms, crimes, injustices and corrupt practices within the context of an explicit theoretical understanding of the state or economic relations, although sustained political economies of environmental harm are now starting to emerge (Stretesky & Lynch 2013; White 2013b).

There are several ways in which issues pertaining to environmental regulation, and the prevention of environmental harm, are framed (White 2008a). One approach is to chart existing environmental legislation and provide a sustained socio-legal analysis of specific breaches of law, the role of environmental law enforcement agencies, and the difficulties and opportunities of using criminal law against environmental offenders. Another approach places emphasis on social regulation as the key mechanism to prevent and curtail environmental harm, including attempts to reform existing systems of production and consumption through a constellation of measures and by bringing non-government and community groups directly into the regulatory process. A third approach presses the need for transnational activism, with an emphasis on fundamental social change. What counts is engagement in strategies that will challenge dominant authority structures and those modes of production that are linked to environmental degradation and destruction, negative transformations of nature, species decline and threats to biodiversity. Social movements are seen to be vital in dealing with instances of gross environmental harm.

By its very nature, the development of green criminology as a field of sustained research and scholarship will incorporate many different approaches and strategic emphases (White & Heckenberg 2014). For some, the point of academic concern and practical application will be to reform aspects of the present system. Critical analysis, in this context, will consist of thinking of ways to improve existing methods of environmental regulation and perhaps to seek better ways to define and legally entrench the notion of environmental crime. For others, the issues raised in this chapter are inextricably linked to the project of social transformation. From this perspective, analysis ought to focus on the strategic location and activities of transnational capital, as supported by hegemonic nation-states on a world scale, and it ought to deal with systemic hierarchical inequalities. Such analysis opens the door to identifying the strategic sites for resistance, contestation and struggle on the part of those fighting for social justice, ecological justice and animal rights.

ISSUES FOR CONSIDERATION

COMPETING INTERESTS

Much debate continues to occur over the alleged conflict between 'the environment' and 'the economy'. In practical terms, study of environmental harm cannot ignore the fact that pollution and waste, for example, are just the normal environmental costs of doing business. In a similar vein, many of the human activities involving 'nature' are themselves perfectly legal in certain circumstances, such as felling of trees, fishing and trading in animals (including live exports). Study of environmental harm, therefore, is intrinsically a study of the political economy of global systems of production, consumption and exchange. Without substantial changes in this overarching system, it is unclear how environmental harms can be diminished or eradicated.

Conflicts occur over which rights ought to take precedence in any given situation—human rights, rights of the environment or animal rights. Various social movements have emerged in defence of specific interests. For example, the environmental justice movement speaks out on behalf of human communities that have been forced to live close to toxic waste dumps and/or that are subject to environmental racism. Animal rights activists demand an end to cruelty to animals and, in some cases, the introduction of new rights that will counter 'speciesism' as a social phenomenon. Conservationists agitate to protect old-growth forests and to forestall continued exploitation of the world's tropical and temperate forests. Yet, frequently, action taken to sustain and cherish particular population groups, animals and eco-systems may impact negatively on others. Fencing off traditional lands in central Africa, for example, may satisfy conservation demands and those wishing to protect elephants, but simultaneously disadvantage and disempower local people who may have lived and worked in such areas for thousands of years.

FACILITATING HARM

Environmental harm is facilitated by the state, as well as corporations and other powerful actors. In many cases, it is embedded in national development policies and actively supported at a popular level. This has a number of important implications for officers and agencies engaged in environmental law enforcement and protection. For example, the budgets, resources and number of officers available for environmental regulation, including environmental law enforcement, are dictated by government priorities and corporate resistance. Not surprisingly, calls for self-regulation and deregulation—under the rubric of cutting the 'green tape'—can undermine efforts to ensure that environmental harm is addressed in ways that will make a substantial difference in the way things are done.

CONCLUSION

The kinds of harms and crimes studied within green criminology include illegal trade in endangered species, such as the trade in exotic birds or killing of elephants for their ivory tusks; illegal harvesting of 'natural resources', such as illegal fishing and logging; and illegal disposal of toxic substances and the resultant pollution of air, land and water. Wider definitions of environmental crime extend the scope of analysis to consider harms associated with legal activities such as the clear-felling of old-growth forests and the negative ecological consequences of new technologies such as use of genetically modified organisms in agriculture (e.g. reduction of biodiversity through extensive planting of GMO corn). More recent considerations include the criminological aspects of climate change, from the point of view of human contributions to global warming (e.g. carbon emissions from coal-fired power plants) and the criminality associated with the aftermath of natural disasters (e.g. incidents of theft and rape in the wake of Hurricane Katrina in New Orleans).

Green criminology has many different substantive contributions and theoretical dimensions. Debates will continue over how best to define concepts such as harm, crime and victim; over the moral calculus that weighs up human, eco-system and animals interests and rights; and over which interventions will achieve what kinds of intended and unintended outcomes. Dialogue around these issues will ensure lively and healthy deliberations over environmental matters now and into the future.

The next chapter continues to explore relatively new forms of criminological inquiry; namely, cyber-crime and new information technologies.

DISCUSSION QUESTIONS

1   Provide examples of the ways in which 'nature' is being transformed as a result of applications of new technologies (e.g. genetics research) or new approaches to resource use (e.g. mass production techniques).

2   What are some examples of 'brown', 'green' and 'white' environmental harms where you live?

3   'Climate change is a global example of ecocide'. Discuss.

4   What crimes are associated with threats to biodiversity? How should these crimes be addressed?

5   'Environmental harm can be conceptualised as involving acts and omissions that are both "legal" and "illegal"'. Discuss, using concrete examples.

FURTHER READING

Beirne, P. & South, N. (eds) (2007) *Issues in green criminology: confronting harms against environments, humanity and other animals*, Willan Publishing, Devon.

Hall, M. (2013) *Victims of environmental harm: rights, recognition and redress under national and international law*, Routledge, London.

South, N. & Brisman, A. (2013) (eds) *The Routledge international handbook of green criminology*, Routledge, London.

Walters, R., Westerhuis, D. & Wyatt, T. (eds) (2013) *Emerging issues in green criminology*, Palgrave Macmillan, Basingstoke.

White, R. & Heckenberg, D. (2014) *Green criminology: an introduction to the study of environmental harm*, Routledge, London.

15 CYBER-CRIME AND NEW INFORMATION TECHNOLOGIES

CHAPTER OVERVIEW
- CYBER-CRIME AND CYBER-SAFETY
- ELECTRONIC THEFT
- CYBER-BULLYING
- SEXTING
- HUMAN RIGHTS AND CYBER-SECURITY
- ISSUES FOR CONSIDERATION
- CONCLUSION
- DISCUSSION QUESTIONS
- FURTHER READING

INTRODUCTION

Digital information and communication technologies developed over the past decade have had a profound effect on social relationships in the contemporary era. Indeed, it has been observed that: 'In 2011, at least 2.3 billion people, the equivalent of approximately one third of the world's total population, had access to the internet' and that by 2017 it is estimated that 'the number of mobile broadband subscriptions will approach 70 per cent of the world's total population' (United Nations 2013: 6). Such technologies are already ingrained in the everyday life activities of most Australians. For example, many people use the internet for personal communication (email, blogging, Facebook, Twitter), as a medium for seeking information, and for shopping, banking and organising travel. They expect to use a wide range of digitally produced and mediated leisure and communication, including smartphones, iPods, iPads, MP3s and CDs, and enjoy television programs and films that are increasingly produced and distributed digitally (White & Wyn 2013). The computer and the mobile phone have ensured that present generations are plugged into extensive social networks and have access to a wide range of information and services online.

This chapter provides an exploration of the criminal dimensions of the new information technologies. The pervasive use of digital information technology has its dark side, and this is a key focus of criminological discussion and public debate (Grabosky 2007; Lee et al. 2013). Namely, the increase in the use of online technologies has been accompanied by a growth in *cyber-crimes*. Acts commonly included in notions of cyber-crime (United Nations 2013: 9) are:
- illegal access to a computer system
- illegal access, interception or acquisition of computer data
- illegal data transference or system interference
- production, distribution or possession of computer misuse tools
- breach of privacy or data protection measures
- computer-related fraud or forgery
- computer-related identity offences

- computer-related copyright and trademark offences
- computer-related acts causing personal harm
- computer-related acts involving racism or xenophobia
- computer-related production, distribution or possession of child pornography
- computer-related solicitation or 'grooming' of children
- computer-related acts in support of terrorism offences.

The purpose of this chapter is to provide a brief introduction to the problems associated with digital information technology. We use the word 'problems' because harmful activities involving these technologies are not always criminalised and, conversely, some activities are criminalised when perhaps they should not be. Issues of deviancy and criminality are dealt with in this chapter through discussion of cyber-crime and cyber-safety, electronic theft, cyber-bullying, sexting and matters pertaining to human rights and cyber-security.

CYBER-CRIME AND CYBER-SAFETY

This section explores the nature and dynamics of cyber-crime, and issues pertaining to cyber-safety. There is some overlap between these two topics, with each raising questions about the perils and pitfalls of new information technologies and phenomena such as the internet.

CYBER-CRIME

A variety of offences are associated with the use of information and communication technology. These offences are variously referred to as **cyber-crime**, e-crime, high-tech crime and computer crime. Three kinds of offences have been identified (Parliament of Australia Joint Committee 2004):

1   *An offence which is committed using the technology*: For example, conventional crime such as fraud committed by technological means, including identity fraud; grooming children in chat rooms by paedophiles that can end in actual contact with the child; and internet (bogus) banking, credit card fraud and money laundering.

2   *An offence which targets computers themselves, and seeks to destroy or alter stored information*: For example, denial of service attacks, where internet ports or the email of target computer systems are bombarded with data to prevent them from functioning (e.g. mass-mailing email systems); or attempts to disrupt a city's water supply by interfering with the computers which control it. This interference can be conducted through a number of means, including attacks by hackers, worms, viruses and trojans:

    - *Hackers*: people with sufficient technical ability to gain access to another person's computer or to a network through the use of stolen passwords, or interference technology, which provides access to networks and individual computers.
    - *Worm*: a self-replicating computer program that can delete files or send email documents.
    - *Virus*: a piece of program code that copies itself and then attaches to a 'host' computer's operating system. They can be destructive, altering files or erasing information from discs, or it can allow third parties to gain access to a person's computer without authorisation.
    - *Trojan*: a stand-alone program that must be transferred intentionally, such as through email. When opened it might alter or delete files on the machine, or access the user's email.

3   *An offence in which the computer is used as storage for information about an offence*: For example, a drug offence in which supply records are kept on computer.

CYBER-CRIME
Cyber-crime involves the use of information technology to commit a crime, the destruction or altering of stored information, and the use of computers to store information about an offence.

Within each of these offence categories a wide range of crimes can be committed, and a wide variety of actors may be involved in undertaking various cyber-crimes. As indicated in Box 15.1, there are insidious forms of crime-related activity embedded within the hidden reaches of the internet as well.

BOX 15.1   CONSTRUCTING THE 'CRYPTOMARKET'

Cryptomarkets are transforming the nature of crime, with both online and offline components. A 'cryptomarket' may be defined as:

> an online forum where goods and services are exchanged between parties who use digital encryption to conceal their identities. Because legal exchanges may be conducted in such a forum, it is not necessarily a site for the commission of cybercrime. However, the necessity or preference for users to conceal their identities points to a range of motivations, of which intention to commit crime is a significant one (other motivations may include political subversion or a commitment to privacy). (Martin 2013: 6)

Perhaps the best known or most notorious example of a cryptomarket is the illicit drugs website 'Silk Road'. Buyers and sellers use advanced digital encryption to log on to the site anonymously, where they then buy and sell all manner of legal, controlled and prohibited narcotics. The site is facilitated by a third-party administrator, who appropriates a percentage of each sale conducted, with the transactions completed using bitcoin, itself an encrypted e-currency. As Martin (2013) points out, this is certainly not the only such site to be found online. He identifies more than 100 different cryptomarkets offering a range of illicit goods and services including, but not limited to: stolen credit card information; forged identity documents; plagiarised university essays; hacking/cracking services; money laundering; child pornography; illegal firearms and ammunition; and even contract killings (Martin 2013: 6).

The proliferation of 'dark net' websites has major implications for existing traditional illicit goods distribution networks, for law enforcement agencies struggling to keep up with rapid technological changes and real-world events, and for criminological research concerned with issues of victimisation and criminal operations.

Other offences and offensive behaviours worth noting include:
- 'nuisance' emails and 'spam' (i.e. unsolicited commercial electronic messages)
- under-age access to material unsuitable for children
- illegal pornographic materials, such as that involving transmission of pornographic child sex imagery
- dissemination of hate or racist material online
- mishandling or ignoring of privacy provisions and illegitimate transfer of personal information
- cyber-bullying.

To these we can also add problems that have emerged with the expansion of new technologies such as Bluetooth and mobile phone texting. These range from their impact on the safe driving of cars to their use by street gangs to undertake illegal activity.

Victimisation surveys have revealed that the rate of individual cyber-crime victimisation is significantly higher than for 'conventional' forms of crime. For example:

> Victimisation rates for online credit card fraud, identity theft, responding to a 'phishing' attempt and experiencing unauthorised access to an e-mail account vary between 1 and 17 per cent of the online

population for 21 countries around the world, compared with typical burglary, robbery and car theft rates of under 5 per cent for these same countries. (United Nations 2013: 7)

CYBER-SAFETY

Public attention has not only been directed at computer offences, but also at the wider issue of **cyber-safety** (Parliament of Australia 2010). Concerns here relate to the nature, prevalence, implications and level of risk associated with cyber-safety threats, such as:

- online child abuse (cyber-bullying, cyber-stalking and sexual grooming)
- exposure to illegal and inappropriate content
- inappropriate social and health behaviours (e.g. technology addiction, online promotion of anorexia, drug use, underage drinking and smoking)
- identity theft
- breaches of privacy.

Concerns about cyber-safety acknowledge that digital communications can be used to cause harm. For instance, a study conducted by Wyn and Cuervo (2005) revealed sites that are aimed at people who have eating disorders (e.g. bulimia and anorexia), and that offer hints on how to hide their condition and how to lose more weight. Antisocial sites and negative uses of the internet are not uncommon and are frequently reported in the mainstream media. Being nasty is the pastime of some who 'troll' the internet for opportunities to upset, insult and bully others.

Wyn and Cuervo (2006) also note that the internet is used by hate groups to promote racism, discrimination and violence, to divulge their views, and to recruit new members. While, in the past, hate groups would recruit members, especially young people, through flyers, newsletters and small rallies, now the internet provides an easily accessible and direct way to gain recruits. Lee and Leets (2002) found that young people who spent more effort analysing and processing these messages were able to resist the narratives and found them racist and distasteful, while those who put less effort into analysing the messages received them more favourably. The research concluded that controlling the development of web pages by hate groups attracting young people to discrimination and violence is a major difficulty faced by government, parents and school authorities.

Cyber-racism generally involves aggressive, abusive and offensive behaviour toward members of other groups based on a belief that some races, religions and ethnic groups are inherently superior to others. The Australian Human Rights Commission (2011) has identified a number of different organisations to which people can report inappropriate material. In relation to internet websites, offensive material can be reported to the Australian Communication and Media Authority (ACMA), the Australian Human Rights Commission and to the police (federal, state and territory services). For YouTube, reports can be made through the Help & Safety Tool, while social networking sites such as Facebook, MySpace, Bebo and MSN generally have 'report abuse' links or equivalent. Generally speaking, while the potential harms are serious, the mechanisms for redress are customarily administrative and/or civil rather than criminal.

For some young people, the digital world offers a more attractive alternative space to their non-digital world, and they spend as much time as they can there. Some researchers have labelled this 'digital addiction', and it can take the form of excessive video game playing, accessing particular websites (e.g. pornographic sites and gambling sites) or becoming obsessed with chat rooms (Young 2004). The opportunity for exposure to illegal or harmful content is thus much greater for young people.

There are also cyber-safety issues related to the phenomenon of gatecrashing, such as when the location of parties is posted on Facebook and hundreds of strangers show up (see Chapter 10).

CYBER-SAFETY
Cyber-safety involves concerns about the nature and types of risks and threats associated with the use of information technology.

Concern has also been expressed about young people's use of social networking sites in relation to privacy; disclosure and breach of confidence; intellectual property rights, especially copyright infringement; defamation; and criminal laws, including harassment and offensive material (de Zwart et al. 2011). With regards to the latter, the issue of 'sexting' is especially relevant (see Chapter 8). Sexting is when someone sends inappropriate naked or sexual images or video footage of themselves or others by text message (see below; see also Chaper 8).

Investigation of the intergenerational dynamics shaping attitudes towards, and usage of, social networking services and cyber-safety have attempted to refocus attention on the ways in which young people themselves relate to new information technologies. These considerations are essential when it comes to crime prevention and harm-reduction strategies involving new information and communication technologies (see Sutton et al. 2013).

For example, conventional approaches to promoting cyber-safety among young people tend to focus on risk management, typically through educational and regulatory approaches. Most cyber-safety programs are delivered through the school setting, which is typically removed from other settings (e.g. the family and work) and social relationships (with peers, parents and other adults) in which young people regularly engage (Third et al. 2010: 9). Thinking about the issues in this way means that responses to cyber-safety need to acknowledge young people's expertise in technology and the use of the internet (Third et al. 2010). The emphasis, therefore, should be less upon risk management and regulation focused on young people, than on strategies that incorporate real-world experiences and knowledge acquisition.

Third et al. (2010: 24), for example, argue that the following principles should guide the development of cyber-safety education models:

- Development must be undertaken in partnership with young people and adults in order that cybersafety education can both be inclusive of young people's voices and expertise, and address adults' concerns and curiosities.
- Models for cybersafety education must acknowledge the technical and social expertise of young people by positioning them as experts.
- Models must be experiential—i.e. they must engage parents in learning about the social, technical and cultural dimensions of SNS.
- The ideal model will combine face-to-face with online delivery.
- Models will have scope to meet the specific technical skills needs of adults, as well as providing capacity for high level conversations about the socio-cultural dimensions of young people's technology use.
- Approaches need to be flexible and iterative so that they can keep pace with the emergence of new online and networked media technologies and practices.

Rather than being top-down in orientation and reflecting generational assumptions and fears, such principles begin with the idea that young people are more knowledgeable than previously assumed when it comes safety and security online.

ELECTRONIC THEFT

Although digital technology can be used to commit threatening and degrading types of crimes, such as cyber-stalking or internet pornography, most digital crime involves fraudulent access to property. As the use of computers and other digital technologies has grown, so have the ways in which people commit electronic theft, as indicated in Box 15.2 (see Grabosky et al. 2001).

BOX 15.2   ELECTRONIC THEFT AND CYBER-CRIME

- Internet payment systems:
  - issue of user authentication: manipulation of passwords and PINs
  - telemarketing fraud.
- Extortion:
  - payment in relation to a threat: to vandalise a website, to wipe out or overload computer systems, to encrypt data and make it inaccessible to the user.
- Fraud against government:
  - issues of access and authentication; theft of data and selling to third parties; unauthorised personal use of work equipment and services.
- Theft of services:
  - use of service without sufficient credit or subscription fraud (e.g. international mobile phone calls).
- Securities fraud:
  - investor risks; manipulation of company websites.
- Deceptive advertising:
  - illegal and objectionable material; misleading advertising practices.
- Misappropriation of intellectual property:
  - issues of copyright and pirated images/information/sound.
- Industrial espionage:
  - issues of security and vandalism; hacking.
- Theft of personal information:
  - misappropriate of personal information and issue of leaving commercial footprints.

Source: Grabosky et al. (2001)

One example of this kind of cyber-crime is that of copyright infringement. Intellectual properties are mental products that are protected by legal safeguards, including copyright law, patents and trademarks, the aim of which is to ensure that the profits of a creative work are returned to its legal owners. Information technology challenges the principle of 'ownership' of knowledge insofar as artistic creations such as music, films and multimedia combinations are easily copied, and disseminated more cheaply or even free. These developments are difficult to prevent and seriously threaten the viability of some industries. Between 2000 and 2003, for example, illegal downloading of music from internet sites cost the music industry an estimated 20 per cent of the $44 billion worldwide market, forcing partnerships and takeovers between music giants such as Sony and EMI (Dodd 2003).

Piracy and copyright theft is not confined to a small class of professional criminals. 'Piracy' activity—which encompasses such things as illegal music downloads and DVD copying—appears to be socially widespread, and undertaken on a regular basis by individuals who would otherwise consider themselves law-abiding citizens. The practice of using the internet to illegally copy software and pass it on to other people is therefore ubiquitous. According to the Australian Content Industry Group (2011), by 2016, eight million Australians will use the internet to regularly access online content illegally.

The public availability of electronic media for financial transactions has made buying and selling products (as well as the transfer of funds) quick and easy, but it has also made possible new types of fraud. Funds can be siphoned off in transit from one account to another, false accounts can be set up, sums of money altered and credit cards counterfeited. Email can be used to reach millions of potential victims at the tap of an electronic key. The Nigerian advance fee scam involved unsolicited emails being sent to individuals in Western countries with the request they assist in the transfer of a large sum of money that allegedly belonged to no one and needed to be transferred from a bank in Nigeria. Email recipients were told that in return for an advance fee they would receive a large commission. Investment scams use similar techniques and can provide convincing information about the potential value of their 'product', although in reality it may only exist in cyberspace. Another interesting type of 'true cyber-crime' is the theft of virtual property or virtual goods that people have purchased in cyber worlds such as Second Life (see Neal 2010; Wall 2007).

The costs of computer crime are virtually impossible to calculate accurately, but are certainly enormous. The Insurance Council of Australia estimates that cyber-crime costs companies worldwide around about $3 trillion each year, with around 67 per cent of computer users affected in some way. The areas of greatest impact are laptop theft, data or network sabotage, virus and trojan infection, computer fraud, denial of service attacks, and excessive network resource consumption through external scams (James & Murray 2003; Neal 2010).

According to the Internal Revenue Service of the United States, the top taxation scam for 2012 was identity theft, itself increasingly linked to manipulation of information online: 'The IRS is increasingly seeing identity thieves looking for ways to use a legitimate taxpayer's identity and personal information to file a tax return and claim a fraudulent refund' (IRS 2013: 1). Indeed, identity theft is a major concern for authorities in many jurisdictions, including Australia.

The Australian Competition and Consumer Commission (2013) provides a *Scam Watch* information sheet on identity theft. It alerts the reader to the different types of identity theft:

- Sending an email in reply to a request that appears to originate from your banking or financial institution or telecommunications provider. Known as phishing, these emails aim to deceive you into disclosing your personal and banking details to scammers. Most work by including special links in the email to take you to a combination of genuine and bogus websites.

- Phoney fraud alerts are similar to phishing scams where scanners trick you into handing over your personal details. A common fraud alert involves the scammer pretending to be from your bank informing you that your credit card or account has been cancelled because of suspicious criminal activity (various excuses are used). They will then deceive you into providing account details to 'confirm' your identity.

- Bogus job opportunities on job websites. The scammer may use or sell your personal information provided in the job applications.

- Card skimming is the illegal copying of information from the magnetic strip of a credit or ATM card. This can create a fake or 'cloned' card.

- Spyware is software that traces the activity on your computer. For instance, key-loggers record what keys you press on your keyboard. Scammers can use this information to steal online banking passwords or other personal information.

In discussing the nature and dynamics of this form of crime, Newman and McNally (2005) posit that there are three stages to identity theft:

Stage 1: *Acquisition* of the identity through theft, computer hacking, fraud, trickery, force, redirecting or intercepting mail, or even by legal means (e.g. purchase information on the internet).

Stage 2: *Use* of the identity for financial gain (the most common motivation) or to avoid arrest or otherwise hide one's identity from law enforcement or other authorities (e.g. bill collectors). Crimes may include account takeover, opening of new accounts, use of debit or credit card details, sale of personal information on the street or black market, acquisition ('breeding') of additional identity related documents such as driver's licence, passport, visas, health cards, etc., filing tax returns for large refunds or the commission of insurance fraud.

Stage 3: *Discovery*. While many misuses of credit cards are discovered quickly, the 'classic' identity theft involves a long time period prior to discovery, from 6 months to as long as several years. Evidence suggests that the time it takes to discover the theft is related to the amount of loss incurred by the victim.

Identity theft is perpetrated by a range of offenders. There are organised criminal groups involved, as well as individual hackers. Three types of organised identity crime groups have been identified (Smith 2013). They include traditional organised criminal groups that generate funds using identity crime such as software piracy, credit card fraud and card skimming (e.g. Japanese Yakuza, Asian triads and Eastern European gangs); organised groups with common objectives to perpetrate identity crime such as carding, underground malware markets and organised identity theft (e.g. Shadowcrew, Carderplanet, CardersMarket, Theft Services, DrinkOrDie, Rock-Phish, BotMaster and Mpack); and ideologically and politically motivated groups, such as terrorist groups who raise funds through identity crime for the financing of terrorism, fraud, money laundering and planned attacks (e.g. Imam Samudra (Bali) and Tariq Al-Daour (UK Al Qaeda cell)).

Using technology to counter high-tech crime is one of the keys to crime prevention in this area (Sutton et al. 2013). There are many everyday and basic examples of the application of technology to increase security and prevent risk, which are routine and familiar, and include the use of passwords to individuals' online accounts and the ability of parents to 'write in' preconfigured software in order to constrain their children's access to particular online sites. Firewalls and protective software are used by companies, organisations and individuals to protect their computers and network systems against hackers, viruses and spam (Neal 2010: 85). Opportunity reduction is the key to rendering efforts to commit such crimes high, with the rewards also reduced (see McNally and Newman 2008).

CYBER-BULLYING

The new information technologies have also opened up new opportunities for bullying and harassment. Ybarra and Mitchell (2004) argue that internet harassment is a significant public health issue for the harasser and the harassed alike. They comment that aggressors tend to be associated with poor parent–child relationships, substance use and delinquency. The traditional offline bully tends to be male, while online bullies are just as likely to be female as male, and are more likely to be high-school aged than middle-school aged (Years 9 and 10). More recently, attention has been drawn to the increased use of mobile phones to marginalise, bully and harass. An Australian study found that at least 30 per cent of the young people in Years 7–9 who were surveyed had experienced some kind of bullying or threats through their mobile phone (Australian Psychological Society 2004).

CYBER-BULLYING
Cyber-bullying refers to repeated and targeted harassment and bullying involving the use of information technologies such as the internet.

To put **cyber-bullying** into context, it can be observed that new information technologies are rapidly having an impact on people in ways unheard of only a few years ago (Collin et al. 2010; White & Wyn 2013). While digital information technologies may have had a significant effect on older people's lives, their impact on young people is even more profound. Moreover, young people increasingly produce as well as consume these media. Personal publishing and blogging are now commonplace, gradually shifting the balance from using the internet as a source of information to using it as a tool for communication.

One of the key aspects of new information technology use is social networking. Young people are enthusiastic users of Social Networking Services (SNS), with the majority engaging on a daily basis with SNS via a computer or mobile phone. Social Networking Services include services such as Facebook and YouTube, as well as Bebo.com, Twitter.com and Microsoft Network (MSN) (texting using a phone). It has been pointed out that:

- Australia's young people are 'the world's most prolific users of social media, and young people under 25 are the most active group when it comes to creating, updating and viewing social media' (Collin et al. 2010: 10).
- 90 per cent of 12–17-year olds and 97 per cent of 16–17-year olds use SNS.
- SNS is basically the number one online activity for 16–29-year olds. Their use has been enhanced and facilitated by the advent of mobile phones that access the internet.

Cyberspace, in its many dimensions, thus constitutes another form of community space. It is accessed by many, and for many it is a vital platform for communication and interaction. However, there are broad patterns surrounding who is or is not welcome to participate in social networking. West et al. (2009), for example, found that for US university students, parents are rarely reported to be Facebook friends and the general view is that they would not be welcomed. More generally, the students did not appear to conceive of there being two distinct realms, the public and the private; rather, the 'public' appeared to be the individual's private social world. Facebook is both a public and private community space, where one can be public to one's friends but private to one's parents (West et al. 2009).

Cyber-bullying likewise pertains to how private and public spaces are socially constituted in cyberspace. In simple terms, cyber-bullying has been described as a covert form of bullying that is carried out through the use of technology (AIC 2010a; Price & Dalgleish 2010). Covert bullying 'can be understood as any form of aggressive behaviour that is repeated, intended to cause harm, characterised by an imbalance of power and is hidden from, or unacknowledged by, adults. It can include the spreading of rumours or attempts at socially excluding others' (AIC 2010a). It is presented as a significant social problem for children and young people today.

Bullying has become a ubiquitous term to describe all manner of conflict between individuals and groups, with particular emphasis on bullying among adolescents. Definitions of bullying have changed over time to include indirect forms of bullying such as exclusion (Rigby 2003). This change also includes reference to the commonly held belief that bullying involves one individual bullying another individual. However, it is recognised that there is also a group basis to bullying (Rigby 2003). Thus, the definition of a bully has expanded from traditional perceptions of the bully as primarily individually based, to include the group as the source of bullying behaviour.

Situations arise whereby young people are members of a group that is more powerful than another group. Bullying may be motivated by a grievance or prejudice, rivalry, or simply to have fun at the expense of another. These acts of bullying are typically initiated and sustained by the connection with a group rather than driven by individual motives. The type of bullying undertaken and the motives for bullying are dependent upon the context within which it is occurs. Typically, schoolyard and cyber-bullying is where the normal rules of restraint do not apply. Bullying is not restricted to settling a gripe or asserting status in a one-off opportunistic situation but is the systematic, ongoing persecution of another over time (Rigby 2003).

As mentioned earlier, the specific context for what appears to be cyber-bullying requires careful appraisal. For instance, recent research into the patterns of text messaging among high school students in the United States provides an interesting interpretation of the content of such texting. It was pointed out that:

> As with emails, text messages can be forwarded to others, increasing the possibility of having private, damaging, or hostile information disseminated to multiple recipients. Additionally, text messages lack context and are thus subject to misinterpretation and misconstrued meanings, which can contribute to interpersonal conflict and damaged relationships whether intentional or not. (Allen 2012: 99)

Text messages can also involve aggression in the form of cyber-bullying, seen here as the wilful and repeated harm inflicted through the medium of electronic text.

Importantly, though, the prolific use of texting, combined with relatively high levels of hostile text messaging, manages to both routinise and increase the harms associated with cyber-bullying. This occurs because of the frequency of text messaging, and the opportunities that this provides for gossiping and the spreading of malicious rumours, all of which may contribute to conflict. This, in turn, can see the bullying proliferate online to include other third parties and associates.

Yet, for all this, the American study cited above (Allen 2012) found that students and staff members claimed that bullying did *not* occur in their school; rather, that 'drama' which involves gossiping and talking behind people's backs is very common:

> Drama involves situations where excessive time and attention may be devoted to the issue, where extraneous people become involved in the issue, or where overreaction and excessive emotionality may be intentionally prolonged by individuals, who are either intimately or peripherally involved with the situation. Drama often moves beyond the original individuals to include others who may have little stake in the original situation which sometimes adds to the intensity of the drama. (Allen 2012: 109)

However, students and staff conceded that texting contributes to conflict, and 'drama', and that either can lead to bullying.

There are also important links between what happens online, and what occurs offline. For example, a US study of current and former gang members in Fresno, Los Angeles and St Louis, Missouri found that 71 per cent of those interviewed reported using a social networking site (Decker & Pyrooz 2011). The two most prevalent activities were posting videos and watching gang-related videos. The next most prevalent activities were having a gang website and searching for gang-related information online. Less frequently cited were recruiting new members online and organising illegal activities online—although arranging a gang get-together can be usefully achieved via online communications. An important finding was that gang members said that, on the one hand, they had attacked someone on the street because of things that happened online and, on the other, that they had been both harassed or threatened online, and attacked on the street because of things that happened online.

Interestingly, recent work done on girls and violence indicates similar results. While cyber-bullying among girls has frequently been noted in the form of threatening text messages, name-calling and exclusion, less attention has been paid to other forms of violence production that is in some way linked to new communications technologies. Carrington (2013: 69), for instance, argues that there is 'a scarcity of research on how social networking can fan conflict in the parallel real worlds of young women, and how girls might engage in internet, Facebook and YouTube sites to promote, incite and normalise girls' violence'. In support of this as a substantial research question, Carrington (2013) points out that thousands of girls around the world use the internet to broadcast their physical fights with other girls—so much so, that there are consistently higher Google search results for girls' fights compared to boys' fights, except for boys fighting over girls.

There are a number of recognised challenges to SNS and other uses of the internet that simultaneously pose challenges for crime prevention (see Sutton et al. 2013). Crime prevention that misconstrues the positive benefits of new information technology, and the status and nous of young people as 'digital natives', will inevitably present as unwanted, coercive and ineffective. As with real-world community spaces, intervention involving the internet requires application of strategies that involve the active participation of the key users. Knowing what is actually going on, rather than assuming the worst, is a good place to start.

For example, some 'top tips for teens' to prevent cyber-bullying include advice such as educating oneself about what it is, safeguarding your passwords, not opening messages from people you do not know or from known bullies, logging out when finished with a computer or mobile phone, and restricting access of your online profile to trusted friends only (Jinduja & Patchin 2012). Parents are advised to know the sites that their children visit and their online activities, to ask for their passwords in case of emergency, and to encourage their children to tell them immediately if they, or someone they know, is being cyber-bullied (US Department of Health & Human Services 2013). Generally speaking, raising awareness of the issue is crucial to its prevention. Systematic review of cyber-bullying prevention strategies has identified a wide range of initiatives (Kraft & Wang 2009). Some of these include:

- no computer use in school and home for offender
- parent taking away offender's computer and mobile phone
- no access to social networking sites for the offender
- offender attending etiquette classes on weekends
- telling students in a class what to do if bullied online
- having clear rules for preventing cyber-bullying and enforcing penalties on cyber bullies
- having written policy on zero toleration about bullying, including online bullying
- ongoing cyber-bullying prevention programs in which students participate in activities to help raise their awareness about cyber-bullying and learn skills to prevent it.

Given the immersion in cyberspace by young people today, it is not that surprising that the threat of restricted internet and technology use is viewed as having an important deterrent effect on offenders. Clear rules with enforced penalties and ongoing prevention awareness programs form the backbone of crime prevention approaches relevant to this kind of behaviour (Kraft & Wang 2009).

SEXTING

Sexting is a term that is used in different ways but 'it generally concerns the digital recording of naked, semi-naked, sexually suggestive or explicit images and their distribution by email, mobile phone messaging or through the internet on social network sites, such as Facebook, MySpace and YouTube' (Lee et al. 2013: 36). It is a phenomenon that has become a social issue for a variety of reasons, not the least of which related to instances in which young people under the age of 18 have been prosecuted for criminal offences as a result of sexting (See Chapter 8).

There has been increasing production of sexting due to the availability of webcams, mobile phone cameras and video cameras. Simultaneously, there has been increasing distribution of such material due to texting, the internet, YouTube and Facebook. A recent dilemma in places such as Australia has been the conviction of teenage participants involved in sexting under the crime of 'child pornography'. This has led in some instances to young people being placed on mandatory sex offender registration lists—for behaviour that many young people regard as 'ordinary' and normal for the age-group in question.

From the point of view of criminological analysis, cyberspace offers new challenges, of which sexting is a part. However, to date, most attention has been on responding to the challenges rather than understanding them. Indeed, 'the intervention in this area so far has predominantly focused on reactively managing, rather than mapping out and understanding, risk around sexting' (Lee et al. 2013: 40). Recent investigations into sexting, however, are starting to unpack the complexities of sexting as a social phenomenon and the legal issues arising from it.

For example, the Parliament of Victoria Law Reform Committee (2013) has undertaken an extensive inquiry into sexting. The inquiry involved research from many different sources, and submissions from a range of agencies and authorities. The report of the inquiry acknowledges that the term sexting encompasses a wide range of practices, motivations and behaviours. It also points to the features of modern technology that can exacerbate its potential impact and harm, such as being able to send images anonymously, the speed with which images can be shared, and the difficulty in retrieving or destroying digital information once it has been created and shared. Stories of sextings that have 'gone viral' include images of young women spread among classmates via text messages through to posting of intimate photographs on social networking sites such as Facebook.

The practices of sexting are many and varied. They include a wide range of behaviours (Parliament of Victoria Law Reform Committee 2013: 19) that are as diverse as:

- a 15-year-old girl taking a topless photograph of herself and sending it via mobile phone to her 16-year-old boyfriend
- the boyfriend showing the photograph to his friends on the screen of his mobile phone
- romantic partners engaging in a webchat where they 'flash' one another
- a person posting a sexually explicit image on someone else's Facebook page
- a person recording a sexual assault using their mobile phone camera
- a person installing a hidden camera in a swimming pool changing room to record people getting changed
- a person sending an 11-year-old child explicitly-worded text messages as part of the 'grooming' of the child.

Given the range of behaviours available, most attention has been paid to peer-to-peer sexting by young people, and non-consensual sexting by young people and adults.

Peer-to-peer sexting can have elements of both consent and coercion. Depending upon the stages to which sexting has progressed, and the conditions under which it occurs, the (potential) victim(s) may not see or experience any harm. For some participants sexting is exciting and fun, a form of social transgression that is in its own way exhilarating (Lee et al. 2013). For others, it basically depends upon who is involved and how it is done. The stages of peer-to-peer sexting have been identified as: (1) requesting an image; (2) creating an image; (3) sharing an image with an intended recipient (consensually); and (4) sharing an image with other (non-consensually) (National Children's and Youth Law Centre, cited in Parliament of Victoria Law Reform Committee 2013: 22). There are possible harms associated with each stage of sexting—but, again, it is the social relationships and agency of the people involved that determines the nature of, or if there is a perception of, harm.

It has been argued that the dominant public discourse about sexting tends to ignore alternative narratives of sexting involving young people in favour of moralising based upon anxiety over paedophiles and child pornography. This reinforces a coercive and highly directive approach to the regulation of adolescent sexuality and risk taking that, in turn, generates its own unintended consequences. That is, it is suggested that 'the over-criminalisation of sexting by young people and attempts at its suppression have had unintended effects: they have incited sexting further into the public realm and legitimated the practice as an exciting, somewhat desirable activity for some young people' (Lee et al. 2013: 36). Reaction to sexting, therefore, can both ignore the pleasures and excitement associated with 'normal' risk-taking behaviour on the part of some young people, as well as amplify its appeal for others by over-criminalisation.

Non-consensual sexting has several different dimensions, but the bottom line is that it involves uses of intimate images that are disrespectful, inappropriate and/or exploitive. Well-known examples of this include surreptitious recording and transmission of sexual activity unbeknown to the female participant (as in the case of what occurred at the Royal Military College in Canberra), and the circulation of a nude photograph of a well-known female celebrity taken by an equally well-known AFL footballer (taken while she was in the shower, on his phone camera). Unauthorised recording and circulation of images, and sexually exploitive sexting, are among the particular harms arising from this kind of activity.

Importantly, it has been observed that the wider 'sexualisation of culture' in ways that are heterosexual and gendered means that, in practice, sexting is not a gender-neutral activity. Research suggests that 'more young women than young men send explicit images or texts, and more young women report sending sexting messages as a result of pressure from the opposite sex' (Parliament of Victoria Law Reform Committee 2013: 41). As many of the submissions to the Victorian inquiry illustrate, the 'victims' of non-consensual sexting are predominantly young women and social pressures by teen boys on girls and young women to send or post sexual images of themselves raise significant issues concerning the meaning of 'consensual' in the first place.

Nonetheless, specific harm is best assessed through examination of particular instances, and the conditions and circumstances underpinning the specific stages of sexting. As the committee also heard, young people may be aware of the risks but choose to participate in sexting anyway, since it was part of their social experience. Those who engaged in it often saw their behaviour as a normal and common practice among their peers, and that the wrong occurs when a sexting message is treated disrespectfully by someone within the peer group (see Parliament of Victoria Law Reform Committee 2013: 54). Accordingly, the committee recommended that educational and media campaigns directed toward sexting focus on the appropriateness of the behaviour of people who distribute intimate images or media without consent, rather than on the person who initially creates the intimate images or media. Moreover, a variety of criminal and civil law remedies have been suggested as well (see, for example, Box 15.3).

New communication technologies have engendered new ways in which to interact with one another. As the technologies evolve, so too will the diversity and type of criminal and harmful activity associated with them.

HUMAN RIGHTS AND CYBER-SECURITY

New technologies offer the promise of greater access to information for ordinary citizens. They also open the door to collation of more information about citizens. There are several issues pertaining to cyberspace and human rights that are worth brief consideration.

BOX 15.3   DEVELOPING A NON-CONSENSUAL SEXTING OFFENCE

Aware of the problems and limitations associated with the application of child pornography laws to sexting, the Parliament of Victoria Law Reform Committee (2013) suggests that a new sexting offence contain the following provisions:

Non-consensual sexting offence:

(1) A person commits an offence if they intentionally distribute, or threaten to distribute, an intimate image of another person or persons.

(2) It is a defence to a prosecution for an offence against subsection (1) to prove that either:

(a) The person or persons depicted in the image consented to the image being distributed by the accused in the manner in which it was distributed; or

(b) The person or persons depicted in the image consented, or may be reasonably presumed to have consented, to publication of the image.

Distribute means:

(a) To publish, exhibit, communicate, send, supply or transmit to any other person, whether to a particular person or not; and

(b) To make available for access to any other person, whether by a particular person or not.

Intimate image means a photograph or footage, whether in digital or another format, in which a person or persons are depicted:

(a) Engaged in sexual activity;

(b) In an indecent sexual manner or context; or

(c) In a state of partial or complete nudity.

Source: Parliament of Victoria Law Reform Committee (2013: 152)

Communications technology is used as a means of surveillance and repression, as well as creating platforms for unheralded sharing of formerly 'private' information. The internet lends itself to the possibility of systematic collection of information on individuals, something which is undertaken by a range of state, governmental and commercial bodies for a variety of purposes. These types of information collection have been described as 'data mining' or 'dataveillance' (Neal 2010: 87), and have recently been highlighted in the expose by former US intelligence analyst Edward Snowden that millions of everyday communications and data transfers worldwide are actively, routinely and systematically monitored by the United States government. As indicated in Chapter 12, such information appears to be equally monitored routinely by the Australian government.

Some forms of covert surveillance are seen to be legitimate, while others are not. For example, public police services (including international and regional networks such as Interpol and Europol) engage in monitoring and enforcement activities in relation to crimes such as online grooming and the threat of paedophiles, child pornography, fraudsters and terrorist groups. In some instances, police services will engage in their own version of identify 'fraud' as part of law enforcement efforts. For example, US federal law enforcement agents have been using social networking sites—including Facebook, LinkedIn, MySpace and Twitter—to search for evidence and witnesses in criminal cases and, in some instances, to track suspects (Nasaw 2010). This has included FBI agents creating fake personalities in order to befriend suspects and lure them into revealing clues or confessing, and to access private information and map social networks. Such tactics have been used, as well, in relation to internet chat rooms in order to lure pornography traffickers and suspected sex predators.

By contrast, a recent report by Reporters Without Borders (2013) highlights issues of state and corporate wrongdoing involving computer technology and information collection:

> 'My computer was arrested before I was.' This perceptive comment was made by a Syrian activist who had been arrested and tortured by the Assad regime. Caught by means of online surveillance, Karim Taymour told a Bloomberg journalist that, during interrogation, he was shown a stack of hundreds of pages of printouts of his Skype chats and files downloaded remotely from his computer hard drive. His torturers clearly knew as much as if they had been with him in his room, or more precisely, in his computer.

The 2013 *Enemies of the Internet* report of the Reporters without Borders group names five 'State Enemies of the Internet'; that is, five countries whose governments are involved in active, intrusive surveillance of news providers, resulting in grave violations of freedom of information and human rights. These are Syria, China, Iran, Bahrain and Vietnam. It also names five 'Corporate Enemies of the Internet'; that is, five private sector companies that are described as 'digital mercenaries' who provide two types of corporate products: equipment for large-scale monitoring of the entire internet, and spyware and other kinds of tools that permit targeted surveillance. The companies are Gamma, Trovicor, Hacking Team, Amesys and Blue Coat.

Meanwhile, there are also those who pursue information 'from the ground up' rather than the 'top down', and whose intentions may run counter to state and corporate interests. For instance, sociologists have identified three main groupings of 'hackers' (see Alleyne 2010):

1 Clandestine hacking:
    - ranges from mildly anti-establishment to the criminal and even 'cyber terrorist'
    - mainly directed against the state and corporate systems
    - virtual breaking and entering, intelligence gathering, technical attacks and repurposing
    - some in it for individualist gain and others for libertarian reasons.
2 Hacktivism:
    - hackers as political actors
    - various political aims and ends, including civil libertarians, anarchists and left-leaning advocates of particular causes
    - cyber-war tactics, including leaks, denial of service attacks, social media protest action and exposes on governments.
3 Open Hacking:
    - hacking as a subculture with different social norms
    - distaste for privatisation of information, and notion that the world is better off if it is open and free
    - interested in extending frontiers of democracy, sharing of information and better transparency.

Hacktivism fuses digital technology and political purpose (Jordan & Taylor 2004; Lindgren & Lundstrom 2011) for the purposes of bringing the world's attention to issues of freedom, open democracy, human rights violations and the need to protect the responsible global flow of information

(Fitri 2011). Its most famous web presence is 'Wikileaks', the most public and dramatic personage of whom is Julian Assange. Its mission is anti-censorship. According to its website:

> Wikileaks is a non-profit media organization dedicated to bringing important news and information to the public. We provide an innovative, secure and anonymous way for independent sources around the world to leak information to our journalists. We publish material of ethical, political and historical significance while keeping the identity of our sources anonymous, thus providing a universal way for the revealing of suppressed and censored injustices. (Wikileaks 2013)

Issues of national security and need for secrecy are juxtaposed with the need for open information and publication of the truth. However, when does freedom of speech threaten freedom? And when does suppression of freedom of speech threaten freedom? These are among the key dilemmas.

Political leaders find it easy to extol the virtues of allowing citizens unrestricted access to the internet and a belief in 'openness', as when US President Obama spoke with Chinese university students in Shanghai in 2009 (Lemon 2009). Yet, these same governments go on the offensive when their own governmental indiscretions and secret surveillance activities are revealed on the internet. US Vice President Joe Biden has referred to Julian Assange, for example, as a 'hi-tech terrorist'.

The consequences of leaking information and publishing confidential documents are far-reaching and personal. Bradley Manning was convicted of espionage in a military court for conveying thousands of confidential files to Wikileaks, Julian Assange ended up taking refuge in the Ecuadorean Embassy in London for fear of being extradited to the United States (from Sweden, where he was due to answer sex charges), since he was liable to be charged in the United States with serious criminal offences relating to the Wikileaks releases, and Edward Snowden, who likewise leaked sensitive US intelligence information, was granted political asylum in Russia to avoid political persecution by the United States. Meanwhile, the release of documents and videos on sites such as Wikileaks has revealed atrocities (e.g. the killing of civilians in Iraq by US troops in 2007), state corruption, war crimes and spying activities on the part of countries like the United States.

The internet and associated new communication technologies have also proven to be effective in popular resistance to state crimes and repressive regimes. This is nowhere more apparent than in regards to the Arab Spring. The young Arab generation called 'shabab' have been at the forefront of the revolutions in Egypt, Tunisia, Libya, Bahrain, Yemen and Syria. This generation is educated and under-employed, has high expectations, is media savvy, is consumer-oriented and has had to be highly entrepreneurial in the light of the job gap. YouTube, Facebook and Twitter have provided a platform for these people to connect with and speak to each other. As such, the new technologies have actively constituted, as well as reflected, youth culture in the Arab setting.

> The nature of the cyber realm—its openness, transparency, unruly dissenting voices, forums for free expression and immediate access to information uncensored by the state—stood in stark contrast to the authoritarian reality they were living in. It transformed the expectations and abilities of this Middle Eastern generation. The experience of connectivity and of solidarity convinced the *shabab* they could do something about their world, even in the face of government repression and the fear of reprisal. (Khalil 2011: 4)

For these young people, new information technologies have opened up possibilities in several different directions. For instance, when people witness a human rights violation, they can upload photos and videos to social networking sites and any other public websites as soon as possible by mobile phones, landlines, computers or any equipment that can connect and access the internet.

Social Networking Services have also been essential to mass mobilisations and spontaneous political actions.

In response to the kinds of transformative possibilities raised during the Arab Spring, other governments around the world have tried to curtail or ban the use of the social network services such as Twitter (banned in Turkey in 2014) and to break into the email accounts of human rights activists (as in China). The former regime in Egypt tried to disable social networking communication by cutting off internet and text messages, and the government in Iran has used SNS to track dissidents and arrest protesters. In some countries, the emphasis has been on the use of government-sanctioned Facebook sites to convey information rather than other sources. The use of the internet and responses of governments to its use, remains highly contentious in terms of cyber-privacy and cyber-security issues.

ISSUES FOR CONSIDERATION

NEW TECHNOLOGIES, NEW CRIME

Cyber-crime is a crime that has really come into its own in the twenty-first century insofar as new information technologies have provided new platforms and new opportunities for a wide variety of criminal activities. Some of these activities reflect traditional criminal offences, such as fraud. Others, however, stem from the nature of the new technologies themselves, as in the case of crimes committed in *Second Life*. As technologies develop and new technologies come into being, it can be anticipated that new forms of crime and deviance will also emerge. In this regard, perhaps science fiction will aid most when it comes to cyber-crime prevention, in that it provides insights into realities that are more quickly forthcoming than many of us can image today.

THE GLOBAL IMPACT

An important aspect of cyber-crime is that it is intrinsically global in nature. The internet and associated information technologies allow for rapid transfer and processing of massive amounts of data in a very short period of time. The collapse of time-space makes certain types of cyber-crime extremely difficult to prevent and prosecute. Moreover, the use of 'false identity' in the commission of offences also allows for relatively free movement of goods and services worldwide in ways that are largely undetectable at the time of commission. The advent of the 'dark net' further complicates law enforcement efforts.

Advanced technologies are inevitably put to a wide variety of social purposes, some of which are inherently bad or harmful, others of which reflect efforts to bypass normal channels and operations of the state. How nation-states regulate and respond to the uses of the internet is itself problematic, depending upon the politics surrounding issues such as privacy, data use and whole-scale surveillance systems. What is in the 'national interest' may not always coincide with either 'human rights' or 'citizen interests'. How these tensions are played out in practice will fundamentally shape and reflect relations of social power within any particular nation-state and, indeed, global political relations.

CONCLUSION

This chapter has provided a survey of contemporary and emerging issues pertaining to cyber-crime and new information technologies. These technologies present as a two-edged sword in that they offer both new opportunities for social interaction, commerce, recreation and communication, as well as enhanced threats to citizen rights and exposure to varied criminal and socially harmful activities.

Our concern in this part of the book has been to discuss the nature and dynamics of crime and social harm across a broad spectrum of activities. As this chapter demonstrates, detailed analysis of particular crimes is required in order to capture the complexities and paradoxes associated with specific forms of transgression. Old crimes persist and new crimes are emerging. Criminology has a vital role in identifying crime trends and explaining the nature and consequences of such harms.

Attention now turns to consideration of the responses by the criminal justice system to the crimes described in Part 1. The focus thus shifts from discussion of the 'problem of crime' to that of 'social control'. The intention of Part 2, therefore, is to provide a comprehensive review and critical assessment of how the institutions of criminal justice operate in theory and practice.

DISCUSSION QUESTIONS

1 'New information technologies have revolutionised how, why and when people engage with each other'. Discuss.

2 What is the difference between cyber-crime and cyber-deviance?

3 'Cyber-bullying is different/the same as bullying in person'. Discuss.

4 'Identity theft is the most common and damaging form of cyber-crime in terms of financial wellbeing and personal reputation'. Discuss.

5 'New information technologies can be used for "good" or for "evil" and how it is used partly depends upon how different parties interpret social and national interests'. Discuss in relation to state and private citizen uses of these technologies.

FURTHER READING

Jordan, T. & Taylor, P. (2004) *Hacktivism and cyberwars: rebels with a cause?*, Routledge, New York.

Lee, M., Crofts, T., Salter, M., Milivojevic, S., & McGovern, A. (2013) '"Let's get sexting": risk, power, sex and criminalisation in the moral domain', *International Journal for Crime and Justice*, 2(1): 35–49.

Parliament of Australia (2010) Joint Select Committee on Cyber-Safety, Parliament House, Canberra.

Parliament of Victoria, Law Reform Committee (2013) *Inquiry into Sexting: Report of the Law Reform Committee for the Inquiry into Sexting.* Parliamentary Paper No. 230, Parliament of Victoria, Melbourne.

Third, A., Richardson, I., Collin, P., Rahilly, K., & Bolzan, N. (2010) *Intergenerational attitudes towards social networking and cybersafety: a living lab*—Research Report, Cooperative Research Center for Young People, Technology and Wellbeing, Melbourne.

INSTITUTIONS OF CRIMINAL JUSTICE

INTRODUCTION

This section of the book is about crime and social control. It provides an introduction to the many different institutions of criminal justice, including state- and community-based agencies and bodies, that are directed in some way or another to preventing or limiting the harms associated with crime and offensive behaviour. In other words, the aim of Part 2 is to describe the ways in which society responds to crime in the Australian context.

The intention of this section is to provide a basic overview of the ways in which the state intervenes in the lives of offenders, victims and members of the wider community. Generally speaking, this intervention is informed by a 'crime control' logic, one that says that the purpose of criminal justice institutions is first and foremost that of controlling crime; in order to fulfil this task, the state wields enormous power.

THE STATE, VIOLENCE AND SOCIAL CONTROL

The vital importance of closely examining how the state responds to crime lies precisely in the fact that, ultimately, the law and criminal justice operate on the basis of violence. The actual use of violence and the threat of violence are the essential tools used by the state to ensure compliance with the law and deter citizens from engaging in antisocial behaviour. They are also central measures in the enforcement of public order, containing dissent and establishing a dominant moral and political regime or climate.

Violence perpetrated by the state is generally seen as 'legitimate'; that is, of all forms of violence in society, it is only that violence associated with particular state personnel (e.g. the police), for very specific purposes (e.g. law enforcement), that is seen to be acceptable and indispensable to the running of society. The direct coercion exercised by the state takes a number of different forms (e.g. police arrest procedures through to prison officer routines), as does the nature of the violence (e.g. forced restraint of offenders through to incarceration).

Given the magnitude, scope and possible misuses of state violence, it is not surprising that the legitimacy of state violence in particular cases must always be questioned. That is, it is essential to understand the context within which the state exercises its coercive powers, and to investigate the social consequences that accompany this kind of state intervention. In the end, the ways in which the state wields its powers are inseparable from the political and social framework of a society; that is, the state always represents particular social interests and a particular vision of the 'good' society.

The concept of social control can be interpreted and used in any number of different ways (see Cohen 1989). At its most general sociological level, it simply describes those social processes directed at or associated with the regulation of human behaviour. Pitched at this level of abstraction, the concept refers to the problem of *social order*: what it is that enables the broad patterns of a society to continue more or less in a uniform or non-conflictual way over time.

In its more specific senses, however, the notion of social control is usually evaluated in terms of specific social interests (e.g. based upon class, gender or ethnicity); particular institutional processes and personnel (e.g. criminal justice, education, health and welfare); and particular value judgments regarding the repressive or progressive aspects of social intervention (e.g. whose specific interests are being served and why). A sophisticated account of social control must in fact meld together a wide range of theoretical issues surrounding social structures and human agency, institutions and individuals in order to make sense of the structuring of social reality. It must also address a series of very concrete questions relating to who is doing the social control, why they are doing so and to what end are they doing so (see Cohen 1989).

Our concern in this book, however, is not to explore the concept of social control in all of its complexities and multiple uses. Rather, we wish to undertake a somewhat more modest and concrete project: an exploration of the more narrow terrain of state-organised reactions to crime and offending behaviour, with special attention being given to the formal institutions of criminal justice. As such, the book follows the more conventional trajectories of the basic criminological text. We simply want to describe and provide some initial critique and comments about the operation of the criminal justice system.

When speaking of the state institutions of social control, however, these must nevertheless be located within the wider social control analytical framework. And in this regard, it is essential to analyse and describe the functions of the state in general, insofar as fundamentally the social control of crime is reflective of the overall role of the state in society.

THE NATURE OF THE STATE

At a descriptive level, we can say that the state comprises a number of diverse and different components; for example, the legislative wing of the state comprises the elected representatives who sit in parliament. These elected representatives are supposed to set the policy agenda, make laws, and define crime and the means of responding to the infringement of laws.

The administrative wing of the state consists of the non-elected members of the bureaucracy, who can have a major influence on the drafting of legislation. Ostensibly, the bureaucracy is there merely to assist the politicians in the implementation of laws. In practice, they often exert significant influence on the structuring of the laws relating to areas such as social security, health, defence and justice.

The judicial wing of the state includes such things as the Magistrates, County and Supreme Courts, and the High Court of Australia, which arbitrates in constitutional matters. The many courts, tribunals and commissions have considerable power to influence the regulation of both private and public behaviour.

Ultimately, the agencies and institutions of the state rest upon a series of coercive public order agencies. These bodies include the police, prisons, defence forces and various surveillance organisations dealing with internal and external 'security'.

What complicates discussion of the state in Australia is that there are three tiers of government— the Commonwealth, state and local—all of which pass laws and issue sanctions of various kinds. There are a number of regulatory bodies or agencies that also have the power to make rules and regulations that affect various activities, such as the universities and the Australian Broadcasting Corporation.

It is apparent that, at a concrete level, the state is an expansive amalgam of various institutions incorporating both elected and non-elected people, and which is capable of generating many different sets of rules, regulations, laws and by-laws. Each facet of the state also operates ultimately through the threat of sanction, although the capacity to do so varies according to the body in question.

But whose state is it? Whose social interests are represented in the many activities of the state, and can we generalise about the basic functions performed by the state in fostering or maintaining a particular kind of social order? Here we can point to three broad perspectives on the nature of the state:

- A *conservative approach* argues that there is a consensus of values in society, and that individuals have a social contract with the state, such that the state defends our basic individual rights in return for the giving up of certain rights to the state. The state is viewed as neutral. It should play a minimal role in society generally, given that its main task is to protect individual rights and to ensure freedom from coercion. The state nevertheless has a role to play in upholding the core values and morals of a society, and in national defence (see Chapter 3).

- A *liberal* or *pluralist approach* argues that the state is not neutral, but reflects the diverse and competing interests that are evident in the community. The state and its institutions will respond to the pressures generated by different groups, and its main function is to resolve conflicts between the competing groups. The role of the state is to deal with social problems as they arise, and to ensure the smooth regulation of social competition and conflict. There is a developmental role for the state in terms of providing for the basic welfare and educational opportunities of its citizens (see Chapter 4).

- A *radical approach* sees the state as an agency of social power, which primarily serves the interests of the more powerful groups in society. The state is not neutral, and nor is it above the different sectional interest groups. In this framework, the state is seen to function in order to preserve, maintain and extend the powers of the dominant groups in society: to protect the interests of the powerful over and above those of the less powerful. The state operates to enhance the privileged position of certain classes and groups that already hold the balance of power in society (see Chapter 5).

These competing views of the state need to be acknowledged and borne in mind by any student of the criminal justice system. The use of violence and coercion by the state against offenders will be considered as justifiable in most instances; for example, by those who view it from a conservative perspective and who see the state as maintaining social order of a particular kind. A liberal perspective, on the other hand, would examine the patterns of state intervention and be concerned with limiting state power in those cases where such intervention does not take into account the interests of competing groups, unequal opportunities and pluralistic values within society. A radical perspective would argue that the state is fundamentally repressive, in that you cannot protect the rights of the less powerful in a society that is inherently unequal and fractured by deep social divisions, and that, therefore, the key challenges are how to contest state power and how best to protect human rights.

The legitimacy of state intervention is thus always a matter of some contention and debate. In part, it depends upon the ideological or philosophical position of the people involved, as indicated in the different perspectives on the state. However, it is also related to immediate practical questions. For example, is it right that we should in fact always obey the law? Is the law simply procedural justice (i.e. when the procedures are right, we then should accept the outcomes)? If we adopt a narrow view of law and legality, it is possible to legitimise the most vile atrocities and crimes against humanity, as in Nazi Germany and under the South African apartheid regime.

How can we, and should we, distinguish between 'the law' and 'justice'? What criteria should we use in making this distinction? In reviewing the mechanisms of social control exercised through the criminal justice system, we need to ask ourselves what is right and just, and what is not. To do so, however, means that we have to think through our basic morals, ethics and value frameworks.

In order to assess whether the mechanisms of the law and the operations of the criminal justice system are 'neutral' or 'biased', it is necessary to determine whose interests are reflected in our institutions. To do this means that we have to be sensitive to the major differences in life experiences and social opportunities of different sections of the population; for example, migrant women or Indigenous young people will have a different relationship to the dominant culture and mainstream society than a middle-class student attending an elite private school.

We also need to be aware of the things that unite members of a society, such as universal provision of human rights. It is our shared humanity that also links us together in demanding that certain antisocial or harmful activities be responded to by the state. How and under what conditions the state ought to intervene for the 'common good' is likewise a central question in any discussion of crime and social order.

THE INSTITUTIONS OF CRIME CONTROL

The formal institutions of crime control are part of a much broader system of social control in Australia. How we respond to crime involves a vast number of different agencies, institutions and specialist bodies. A rough indication of some of these is provided below.

CRIME PREVENTION

Schools, local government, health and community services, urban planners, community workers, police, Departments of Justice, Independent Commissions against Corruption, Crime and Corruption Commissions, crises lines.

DETECTION AND INVESTIGATION

Neighbourhood Watch, police, private security firms, Australian Crime Commission, media, Business Watch, Australian Securities and Investment Commission, Australian Taxation Office, Department of Social Security, Consumer Affairs organisations, Ombudsmen, Australian Customs Service, Australian Fisheries Management Authority, royal commissions.

LEGAL SERVICES

Community legal centres, Aboriginal Legal Services, private law firms, courts, Legal Aid, bail justices, Justices of the Peace.

TRIAL AND ADJUDICATION

Community Mediation Centres, Juvenile Conferences, courts, specialist courts, Children's Courts, police, Administrative Appeals Tribunal, Ombudsmen, Offices of Public Prosecution.

SENTENCING

Community Mediation Centres, courts, specialist courts, police, Offices of Public Prosecution.

PENALTY

Community Corrections, Prisoner Rights Groups, prisons, Probation Service, Parole Boards, Juvenile Justice.

POST-DETENTION

Ex-offender programs, Halfway Houses, Health and Community Services, Community Corrections.

VICTIMS

Centres Against Sexual Assault, Men Against Sexual Assault, Victims of Crime Assistance League, Broken Rites, Victim Support Services, police, Court Information Services.

Various agencies and institutions play a number of different roles in relation to criminal justice issues and practices, including both developmental and coercive roles (e.g. local government, health and community services). The above list is simply meant to provide an indication of the wide range of state and community, formal and informal, organisations and groups associated with criminal justice issues.

There are many, many ways in which crime, deviance and unlawful behaviour is dealt with in society. For example, there are informal ways of resolving disputes that often occur among feuding parties themselves; for example, by simply talking through the problem together. There are administrative ways of dealing with illegal activity, such as the use of fine payments for parking tickets. Civil laws are available to cover disputes between neighbours, industrial relations issues, sexual harassment and questions of liability that are not customarily dealt with by the criminal justice system. Government departments undertake activity and investigations that may have a bearing on criminal matters; for instance, the Taxation Department, the Department of Social Security, the police and Office of the Director of Public Prosecutions.

In general, however, a person who commits a criminal offence will be dealt with through the formal institutions of the police and courts. And if convicted and sentenced, they may spend time in a prison for the crime or, more likely, will be subjected to some kind of fine or community-based sanction.

PARADOXES AND CHALLENGES

The specific ways in which crime control is constructed and the different orientations of crime control reflect varying conceptions of the nature of crime and criminality (see Part 1). Moreover, how we view the causes of crime has direct implications for how we respond to it and how we attempt to control it (see White et al. 2012). One of the messages of Part 2 is that implicit within each institutional sphere are various, usually competing, approaches to crime control. This is apparent within both the formal institutions of criminal justice and the community-based institutions and agencies. Thus, an underlying concern of this part of the book is to expose the politics of social control as they pertain to the criminal justice area.

Depictions of offenders and criminal justice agencies are all too often based upon exaggeration, stereotype and conjecture (see Chapter 2). Politicians and the media have a tendency to back policies and actions that will keep certain people under control and under surveillance. Justice is seen essentially as a matter of personal responsibility, and the role of the state is to enforce a particular kind of order. Some people are affected by this more than others. The new punitiveness of the early twenty-first century is evident in the massive expansion in the use of imprisonment. Meanwhile, persistent calls are made to increase police powers and numbers, clamp down on outlaw bikie gangs, reduce violence in public places and restrict the movements of young people. Add to this the threats posed by terrorism and drugs, and there is a strong recipe for highly coercive forms of justice to be imposed.

Simultaneously and somewhat paradoxically, however, non-coercive alternatives are also being developed. The rise of therapeutic justice is associated with much greater community and judicial concern to deal with issues such as drug abuse, mental illness and other social ills in a problem-solving manner. Every jurisdiction in the country has in place some form of restorative justice program for juvenile offenders, an intervention that emphasises repairing harm rather than retribution. Indigenous people are developing their own mechanisms of crime control and criminal justice, with the advent of night patrols, Koori Courts and culturally sensitive alternatives to mainstream punishments. In the juvenile justice area, there has been a growth in the human rights perspective as a critical basis against which to evaluate policing practices, the operation of courts and youth conferences and the conditions under which young people are detained or sentenced to community work. Renewed criminological emphasis on crime prevention has likewise been used to challenge explicitly the coercive 'law and order' approaches.

Another area that is generating more critical attention is the relationship between the local and the global as it pertains specifically to criminal justice institutions. The international transference of ideas, methods, policies and exemplary practices is rapid and profound, thanks to the internet. Such transfers are having a burgeoning impact on how police do their work at the local level, how courts see their roles, how incarceration is transforming whole communities, and how crime in general is being responded to in societies such as Australia. Simultaneously, what happens here in this country—for example, the expansion and incorporation of conferencing into the mainstream of juvenile justice—is having an influence in other countries around the world. No country is immune from globalising processes that have direct and indirect consequences for how justice is carried out in practice. And each is, in its own unique way, a contributor to these processes.

We have tried in Part 2 to provide a broad survey and introduction to the major institutions of criminal justice and the issues specific to these. Our intention has been to provide a foundational overview of: the key players in criminal justice; the logic and operation of state agencies and social institutions in responding to (and creating) offensive behaviour; and the strengths and weaknesses of existing forms and methods of crime control and general theories and practices in criminal justice over time.

We have attempted to illustrate general processes of criminal justice with a number of empirical examples and references. However, the specific institutional forms, legislative frameworks, operational practices, and nature of community involvement vary greatly between the different state and territory, and federal, jurisdictions. The book thus offers a general guide to criminal justice, rather than a definitive or comprehensive overview of what is actually occurring in each separate jurisdiction.

It is our hope that, by combining baseline descriptions with substantive critiques of the institutions of criminal justice, the reader will be better able to appreciate the complexities, limitations and possibilities of the social control of crime in Australian society. An informed view of criminal justice is the best guarantee that the use of violence and coercion by the state will indeed reflect concerns with social justice.

16 POLICE ROLES AND TECHNIQUES

CHAPTER OVERVIEW

- ROLES AND TASK ORIENTATIONS
- PRIVATE POLICING
- POLICE ORGANISATIONAL STRUCTURES AND OPERATIONAL STRATEGIES
- ISSUES FOR CONSIDERATION
- CONCLUSION
- DISCUSSION QUESTIONS
- FURTHER READING

INTRODUCTION

One of the first points of contact with the criminal justice system for many people is the police. Due to their enormous discretionary powers the police are not only one of the most visible but also one of the most powerful agents of social control in society. Since police are able to exercise those discretionary powers in a manner that either directs offenders to, or diverts them away from, further penetration into the justice system, they are often described as the gatekeepers of the criminal justice system.

The aim of this chapter is to survey some of the basic features of police work in Australia. In particular, our concern is to review in broad terms the institutional framework of policing; that is, the roles, objectives and techniques of policing. The chapter begins by looking at the organisational structures of policing, with specific reference to the police occupational hierarchy, the mission or goals of policing, and the diverse task orientations of policing. This is followed by a discussion of different policing strategies.

A central concern of the chapter is to present in 'ideal typical' fashion two different models of policing: the so-called 'traditional' model and 'community policing' model. While neither of these models exists in pure form in the real world of policing, they do provide some indication of broad philosophical and operational differences in both perceptions and approaches to the doing of police work.

ROLES AND TASK ORIENTATIONS

By its very nature, policing is a complex activity that involves many different goals, tasks and personnel. One way to indicate the breadth of police activities is to briefly summarise the main objectives of the police, as contained in various 'mission' statements of police departments around the country. By and large, most police departments see their objectives in serving society in the following kinds of terms:
- ensuring that police services are based on community needs and satisfaction with service delivery
- minimising the level of crime and maximising the extent to which people feel secure from the effects of crime

- ensuring a level of public order that enables people to safely go about their lawful business
- encouraging greater involvement of citizens in policing, with a view to establishing a problem-solving partnership
- providing assistance to the public in circumstances of personal emergency
- promoting road safety and effective traffic management
- improving operational policing strategies, especially in the areas of public safety, and crime prevention and detection.

In practice, therefore, it appears that the public expects a great deal from our police and that they are consequently required to perform a wide variety of functions. Importantly, the police usually perform their roles simultaneously; that is, efforts to ensure public order are often intertwined with law enforcement, traffic management, and so on.

Police task orientations, although diverse, can be consolidated into five main areas: law enforcement; **order maintenance** and conflict resolution; crime prevention; provision of social services; and traffic management. These areas of police work are not, in practice, discrete. The intention of this section is simply to present a picture of the diverse activities engaged in by the police, while recognising that most police work cannot be neatly pigeon-holed into one or other 'task orientation' box.

LAW ENFORCEMENT

This essentially translates into crime fighting; that is, dealing with those who commit crimes. This involves activities such as detection, investigation, apprehension and prosecution of offenders. This function effectively comprises a minor proportion of police time. However, the overwhelming bulk of all detections, arrests and prosecutions are conducted by general duties uniformed officers. Furthermore, these activities usually arise out of their routine patrolling activities, and are often associated with other aspects of their duties, as listed below. Serious criminal cases are generally referred to specific departments, such as the Criminal Investigation Branch (CIB).

While **law enforcement** is an obvious function, police operate within a much broader framework and therefore are required to provide a range of other activities, some of which may be marginally related to **crime control**. Although largely ignored in both popular and fictional accounts of policing, these activities are central to policing and consume a large portion of police time.

ORDER MAINTENANCE AND CONFLICT RESOLUTION

Police have a role in restoring disruptive situations to normalcy, often without arresting individuals; that is, without recourse to the enforcement of the law per se. Activities to that end include public order surveillance, intervention, and monitoring of specific groups in particular locations, including: major public parades, sporting and other events (e.g. the Moomba parade, the Grand Prix and the Gay and Lesbian Mardi Gras); funerals (managing large congregations attending the services of dignitaries, heads of state, and rock or movie stars); strikes; marches; and football matches (particularly the AFL grand final). The role of police in these situations is to control and circumscribe public behaviour. Where crowds are deemed rowdy or unmanageable, the riot squad may be called upon.

Order maintenance is also often linked to the policing of 'domestic violence' and neighbourhood disputes. In order to maintain the peace, it may be necessary for the police to make arrests; hence, there is a natural overlap between 'law enforcement' and 'order maintenance' at a practical level.

ORDER MAINTENANCE
The restoration of disruptive situations to normalcy, often without arresting individuals. The role of police in these situations is to control and circumscribe public behaviour.

LAW ENFORCEMENT
Essentially crime fighting activities, such as detection, investigation, apprehension and prosecution of offenders.

CRIME CONTROL
The ways in which society responds to crime; in particular, how different institutions of criminal justice prevent or limit the harms associated with crime.

CRIME PREVENTION

This involves the creation and implementation of proactive programs and strategies designed to prevent crime and address the fear of crime. Examples of specific crime-prevention programs include Neighbourhood Watch and Business Watch, where information is provided to residents and/or business proprietors on how to secure their property and person against potential threat. Police involved in these programs often work closely with the community, local government, and agencies such as schools. More generally, a key aspect of crime prevention is the role of the police, often simply by their public presence, in deterring potential crime; that is, one of the central tasks of the police officer is to deter crime as part and parcel of their normal day-to-day activities.

PROVISION OF SOCIAL SERVICES

Because the police operate 24 hours a day, they may be required to offer a range of emergency services, from the simple (e.g. retrieving cats from trees) to the more serious, (e.g. coordination of air, land and sea search and rescue operations); these services are particularly vital under circumstances involving natural disasters, such as widespread flooding, bushfire, cyclone and drought. Police also are involved in the provision of: social welfare, psychiatric and other services (e.g. counselling abused women and children); mediating in domestic and other interpersonal tensions; dealing with unexpected childbirth; finding lost children; attending sudden deaths (e.g. motor vehicle accidents); dealing with potential suicides; and providing information to the public on a variety of matters both legal and general (e.g. providing street directions).

Such divergent expectations place an enormous strain on officers, and this raises questions regarding the training of officers and, indeed, their appropriate roles:

- First, have officers been trained to provide appropriate advice and responses to victims in crisis situations?
- Secondly, have they themselves been appropriately trained to deal emotionally with such situations?

TRAFFIC MANAGEMENT

Activities here are designed and implemented in an effort to ensure the smooth and safe flow of traffic. Included in this role are activities such as regulating traffic laws and driver habits; managing and enforcing drink driving campaigns (e.g. booze bus operations); handling licence allocation and suspensions; attending traffic accidents; participating in accident-prevention schemes (e.g. 'break the drive and stay alive'); and supervising evacuations from crisis areas.

As indicated in this outline of main task areas, the police clearly perform a wide variety of functions. Yet, despite the multifaceted nature of policing, within the public mind the 'crime fighter' image predominates; indeed, this also tends to be the view that police have of themselves (see Beyer 1993). In part, this is due to the essential fact that, whatever the specific task at hand, the police ultimately act on the basis of coercion. That is, whatever and however varied the roles and functions assigned to the police, their location in the social order is one that is premised upon the exercise of authority.

What do the police actually do with their time, especially given the many different tasks with which they may be engaged? A study in South Australia provides insight into the time that police put into different activities, across a range of possible alternatives (Dadds & Scheide 2000). The study found that police time can be roughly divided according to the following distributions:

- *community police services*—40 per cent (includes community patrols, police station services, community programs, information services and event management)

- *crime management*—32 per cent (includes targeting crimes against the person, crimes against property, illegal drug activity and other criminal activity)
- *traffic services*—13 per cent (includes traffic policing, and traffic crash investigation)
- *criminal justice support*—12 per cent (includes services to the criminal justice system, and custodial services)
- *emergency response management and coordination*—2 per cent
- *ministerial support services*—1 per cent.

Such information is useful in gaining a sense of the 'real world' of police work. It is also useful as a means of ensuring appropriate allocation of resources, establishing agency priorities, and broadening the measures used to determine or evaluate the performance of police services.

PRIVATE POLICING

Since the 1960s, private-sector policing has been a rapidly growing industry, with **private policing** agencies now employing more individuals than employed by the public police force (Prenzler et al. 2009; Sarre & Prenzler 2012). The economic rationale underpinning the move towards privatisation is clear: by removing the state monopoly on policing, competing organisations will absorb some of the financial responsibilities for the provision of a number of 'crime' services that traditional police, for various reasons, are unable to provide. There are concerns here, however, relating to the uneasy nature of the relationship between private- and public-sector police, the extensive powers held by some private police and their lack of training and industry accountability (see Fairchild 1994; Shearing 1992; Shearing & Stenning 1987).

The growth of private police over the past few decades has thus sparked considerable concern and debate among commentators and participants in the law-enforcement area. Private security services in Europe, North America and Australia far outstrip the public law-enforcement agencies when it comes to expenditure (annual spending for security) and number of personnel (see Bayley 1999a; Christie 1993; Prenzler & Sarre 1998). In Australia, for example, it was estimated that in 1998 the ratio of police to licensed security providers was one police officer to every 2.2 licensed security providers (Prenzler & Sarre 1998). Analysis of occupations pertaining to the security industry and the police show that in 2006 in Australia there were 52,768 personnel employed full-time in the security industry compared with 44,898 police. This constituted a major change from the previous decade, when full-time police outnumbered full-time security (Prenzler et al. 2009: 3). Several years later, it is estimated that there are around 100,000 people in Australia who operate some form of security function, and just under 60,000 operational police officers nationally (Sarre & Prenzler 2012: 31). Private police are engaged in a variety of tasks, as illustrated in box 16.1.

PRIVATE POLICING
Policing activities carried out by private agencies, usually in the areas of protecting property or personnel. Activities include security at train stations; in shopping malls, banks and office buildings; and in residential communities and quasi-government premises, such as dockyards and schools.

BOX 16.1   PRIVATE POLICING

- *Commercial interests:* security forces used in order to protect property, premises, employees and customers, including bouncers or doorkeepers (e.g. at bars or nightclubs, malls, banks, sports arenas, office buildings, factories and many government buildings)
- *Residential communities:* gated communities, privately protected apartments and condominium buildings

- *Interest communities:* banks, equities markets, contiguous businesses (e.g. private personnel to protect their operations, with security services provided for an annual fee)
- *Governments:* authorisation of quasi-governmental agencies to provide their own security (e.g. train stations, dockyards, school districts, computer information systems, 'bounty hunters' (United States))
- *Court security:* contracting 'in' of private court security and custodial services, prisoner transport and police 'lock up' management (e.g. Protective Security Officers (PSOs) used for in-court security)
- *Volunteerism:* use of unpaid citizens to provide crime-prevention information, patrol streets and assist police in emergencies (e.g. neighbourhood based groups such as Neighbourhood Watch, and vigilante groups)

A number of factors have been suggested to explain the rise and expansion of private policing in recent years. These include:

- an increase in the number and availability of goods that are easily stolen and easily converted to cash, such as tobacco, alcohol and drugs (both prescription and over the counter) (Indermaur 1995; Prenzler & Sarre 1998)
- the growth of the night-time economy and the accompanying need for security personnel such as bouncers (Tomkins 2005)
- the trend toward 'mass private property' in the form of shopping centres and the like (Shearing & Stenning 1987)
- the transnational character and ownership of private security as a lucrative business venture
- the seemingly less-effective work of public policing agencies when it comes to protection of property, securing information in the context of the newer communication technologies, and acting as personal body guards.

COMMUNITY POLICING
A style of policing that emphasises a conciliatory approach to police work. It seeks to move away from the authoritarian nature of traditional approaches, focusing instead on a co-participatory model that accepts that the community has a legitimate, active role to play in the policing process.

Importantly, private policing is intrinsically linked to user-pays market forces. Accordingly, 'while public police are expected to act in the public interest, private security is expected to act in the private interest of its clients' (Wilson et al. 1994: 285). Not surprisingly, these differences in objectives give rise to major questions regarding training, activities and accountability of each form of policing, as well as how each intersects and communicates with the other (see, for example, Bayley 1999a; Blagg & Wilkie 1995; Sarre & Prenzler 2012). Some of these issues are considered further in Chapter 17.

POLICE ORGANISATIONAL STRUCTURES AND OPERATIONAL STRATEGIES

Public policing activities are predominantly the responsibility of the police agencies of state and territory governments, with the Australian Federal Police (AFP) providing a **community policing** service in the Australian Capital Territory on behalf of the Australian Capital Territory Government. Funding for these services comes almost exclusively from state and territory government budgets, with some specific purpose grants provided by the Commonwealth. Police services represent the largest component of the justice system, accounting for approximately 71 per cent of total justice-related expenditure, while corrective services account for a further 23 per cent, and court administration the remaining 6 per cent (AIC 2013a).

The task orientations of the police incorporate a multitude of different roles and duties. However, as pointed out above, in practice the overall mission of the police tends to reflect a preoccupation with certain aspects of police work. This is generally reflected in the organisational structures of the police, often a complex web of departments that can include:

- *traffic and operations support* (e.g. traffic support and protective security)
- *crime* (e.g. state crime squads, forensic science centre and major fraud group)
- *operations* (e.g. general policing, community and cultural, and planning and research)
- *counter-terrorism coordination* (e.g. intelligence, major event planning and state emergency responses)
- *internal investigations* (e.g. internal security and internal investigations)
- *communications and information technology* (e.g. computer-aided dispatch, media and corporate communications)
- *training* (e.g. operational training and management supervision)
- *corporate resources* (e.g. supply and transport, legal services)
- *personnel* (e.g. employee relations and health services)
- *corporate policy, planning and review* (e.g. policy and projects, research and statistical services).

The allocation of personnel, resources and finances within a police department is the best indicator of the operational priorities of a department. If we are to investigate fully the performance of the police in relation to the task orientations listed earlier, then it is essential to do so in the light of the weight placed upon each, as reflected in the police organisational structure.

Another aspect of the police organisation is that of the personnel themselves, and how they are organised to carry out their roles. For example, Table 16.1 provides information on the hierarchy within policing in Australia, and the gender composition of the police services nationwide.

TABLE 16.1 COMPOSITION OF POLICE SERVICES AS AT 30 JUNE 2006—SWORN AND UNSWORN PERSONNEL BY RANK AND GENDER

RANK	MALE	FEMALE	TOTAL	% FEMALE
Senior Executive[1]	78	9	87	10
Superintendent	380	32	412	8
Inspector	1,364	111	1,475	8
Senior Sergeant	1,786	91	1,954	9
Sergeant[2]	7,678	992	8,683	11
Senior Constable	15,035	4,672	19,707	24
Constable[3]	9,343	4,495	13,838	33
Probationary Constable	616	222	838	27
Recruits	607	324	931	35
Cadets	51	32	39	39
Police Aides[4]	110	131	241	54

(Continued)

TABLE 16.1 COMPOSITION OF POLICE SERVICES AS AT 30 JUNE 2006—SWORN AND UNSWORN PERSONNEL BY RANK AND GENDER (*Continued*)

RANK	MALE	FEMALE	TOTAL	% FEMALE
ACPO/Spec. Constable[5]	77	31	108	29
Other[6]	140	26	166	16
Total Sworn Officers	36,285	10,701	46,986	23
Public Service Employee[7]	4,169	8,323	12,492	67
Other Personnel[8]	448	463	911	51
Total Personnel	41,886	20,031	61,917	32

[1] Includes Commissioner/Chief Commissioner, Deputy Commissioner, Assistant Commissioner and Commander. Includes Commanders in Victoria
[2] Includes Sergeant First Class in Western Australia, Sergeant (qualified and unqualified) in Tasmania and Brevet Sergeant in Northern Territory
[3] Includes Constable First Class in New South Wales and Western Australia, Confirmed Constables in Victoria, Constable (qualified and unqualified) in Tasmania, and Probationary Constable, Constable, Constable First Class and Senior Constable in Northern Territory and South Australia
[4] Includes Constables (not confirmed) in Victoria, Police Auxiliary in the Northern Territory, Aboriginal Police Liaison Officers in Western Australia, and Community Constables in South Australia
[5] Includes Aboriginal Community Police Officers (ACPO) in the Northern Territory
[6] Includes reservists and Protective Security Officers (PSO) in Victoria
[7] Includes civilian staff of the Northern Territory Police. New South Wales includes ministerial employees. Tasmania includes State Emergency Service officers and Forensic Science Service Tasmania (FSST) officers. Queensland includes temporary employees occupying public service positions
[8] South Australia includes staff paid weekly and other. NSW includes Transit Police. Western Australia includes wages staff.
Source: AIC (2010)

As indicated in Table 16.1, while females comprise just under a third (32.4%) of total personnel across Australia police services, their presence in the upper echelons of the hierarchy is noticeably thin, with women occupying just 10.5 per cent of senior positions (Sergeant to Senior Executive rank).

Most people involved directly in the delivery of police services are sworn police officers (employees recognised under each jurisdiction's Police Act). Sworn police officers exercise police powers such as:

* arrest
* summons
* caution
* detain
* fingerprint
* search.

In recent years there has been a trend towards civilianisation of police services, with some non-core activities undertaken by non-sworn officers or contracted to external providers (AIC 2008). For example, in Tasmania and Victoria, civilian personnel have a leading role in developing policies and programs in the area of crime prevention, while being located within the police service as such. Table 16.2 provides an indication of how Commonwealth-related policing is organised, according to sworn and unsworn status, by gender.

As conveyed by Table 16.2, female representation across selected Commonwealth law enforcement agencies remains low (36.6%), but varies considerably by agency and status. For instance, while women

TABLE 16.2 SELECTED COMMONWEALTH LAW-ENFORCEMENT AGENCY PERSONNEL AS AT 30 JUNE 2006[a]—BY GENDER

AGENCY	MALE	FEMALE	TOTAL
AFP[b]	1,955	1,217	3,172
Sworn	1,326	416	1,742
Unsworn	629	801	1,430
ACC	227	203	430
ACS	3,304	2,274	5,578
APS	1,254	193	1,447
CrimTrac	32	22	54
Total	6,772	3,909	10,681

[a] Includes full-time, part-time and casual staff
[b] Excludes ACT policing and APS personnel
AFP = Australian Federal Police
ACC = Australian Crime Commission
ACS = Australian Customs Service
APS = Australian Protective Service
Note: New South Wales had the largest police service across Australia (with some 14,634 sworn police officers and 3936 civilians), while the Australian Capital Territory had the smallest (620 and 195, respectively).
Source: AIC (2010)

represent 38.4 per cent of Australian Federal Police personnel, they comprise 40 per cent of Australian Customs Officers and over half (56%) of all unsworn officers.

In 2012–13, a total of 67,770 sworn police officers and civilians were employed by police services around Australia (Productivity Commission 2014). Although the number of police officers per 100,000 people varies across jurisdictions, on average, there were 268 operational police staff per 100,000 people in Australia in 2012–13.

GENDER AND POLICING

The specific tasks any particular police officer carries out depends largely upon where they are located in the broad organisational structure of a department (i.e. which area of operational or administrative activity), as well as where they are located within the occupational hierarchy (i.e. their rank). This has implications for the use of discretion, which is discussed in greater detail in Chapter 17. Likewise, the **gender ratio** (i.e. number of males relative to females) in policing has implications with regard to which decisions are made, at which level, by whom, and in which areas of police work. The nature of police culture is similarly intertwined with both organisational and gender issues.

In 2006, 23 per cent of sworn police officers (or 32 per cent of total police employees) were female and the trend has been toward the presence of more females and proportionately fewer males over the past few years (AIC 2010b). As indicated in Table 16.1, however, the proportion of women relative to men in the police services varies greatly according to their rank within the police hierarchy. The higher the rank, the fewer women there are, both in real numbers and in proportion to the overall gender composition of the police services. There are signs that this is changing and that women are

GENDER RATIO IN POLICING
The number of males relative to females in policing. The higher the rank, the fewer women there are, both in real numbers and in proportion to the overall gender composition of the police services.

moving up the ranks, but the progress is slow and uneven around the country (Prenzler & Fleming 2011).

There are a number of issues relevant to the processes of recruitment, retention and resignation of women within state police services. For instance, policing continues to be perceived to be a 'male' occupation in the eyes of many, and ideological opposition to women in policing has often been premised on the idea that policing is too physically demanding for women. It is interesting in this regard that a survey of police pre-entry physical tests demonstrated that discriminatory physical ability tests are still being used in most jurisdictions in Australasia, to the detriment of women (Sugden 2003). Moreover, such tests are also problematic because they are unable to predict the actual on-the-job performance of a police officer, and they do not reflect the changing nature of contemporary policing. By contrast, it was found that the elimination of pre-entry physical tests contributes to higher rates of recruitment and retention of women (Sugden 2003). These kinds of issues are frequently taken up by organisations such as the Australasian Council of Women and Policing (ACWAP) and conferences specifically oriented toward addressing issues of policing and gender.

For example, the Eighth ACAWP Conference, held in 2013, was an interactive forum that aimed to:

- examine and share models of policing from around the world with the potential to improve policing for women and children
- inform Australian policing of issues for women and policing globally
- provide a platform for meetings of women police and law-enforcement officers from around the globe
- provide an opportunity for academic debate and recommendations for further research into women and policing on a global scale
- develop and expand the global networks of women and policing.

The conference examined a broad range of issues, including:

- women in regions of conflict and women as peacekeepers
- international comparisons of women in policing and law enforcement around the globe
- investigating and prosecuting war crimes, including rape and genocide
- trafficking in women
- international networks for women in policing and law enforcement
- improving the status of women within policing and law enforcement
- all forms of violence against women, including domestic violence, sexual assault and female genital mutilation
- increasing diversity within policing and law-enforcement environments
- the roles of police and law-enforcement officers in protecting women's human rights
- best practice in policing for women.

Retaining women in policing is a matter of special mention. The kind of police work women engage in has some bearing on how long they stay and the contributions they make while serving as a police officer. For example, research in the United Kingdom found that female officers carved a niche for themselves in the specific areas of 'soft' policing initiatives such as community crime prevention. They did so in such a way as to reconfigure simultaneously existing components of police culture (especially those pertaining to the macho aspects of crime fighting) and to produce support for a more progressive model of policing (namely, community policing). Nonetheless, regardless of work role, women still tend to resign from policing at a higher rate than men (Prenzler & Fleming 2012). It has been suggested that this could be for 'family reasons'; yet research has found that there is considerable resistance to the idea of part-time work in policing, something which has been identified as a key mechanism to retain women in policing (Charlesworth & Robertson 2012).

HISTORICAL DEVELOPMENT OF POLICING

In order to understand the direction and organisation of police practices in contemporary Australia, it is essential to acknowledge the historical development of policing in this country (see Finnane 1994b, 1987). As James (1994a: 112–13) points out, factors such as Australia's penal colony origins, state responses to Aboriginal resistance to white settlement, and the role of police in industrial disputes helped to shape a particular public and occupational image of police.

One outcome that accompanied these developments was a quasi-military hierarchical command apparatus; another was the low social status ascribed to the police and their poor reputation. The historical development of policing in Australia is manifest in present-day debates over the broad nature and direction of policing (see, for example, McCulloch 2001a). This is particularly so with respect to the tensions between a modified military model of professionalism (or a paramilitary model) and a model of policing based upon working within a community framework (or a community policing model). In the end, analysis of the purposes of contemporary policing must take into account both the historical legacies and the debates over appropriate organisational frameworks.

MEASURING THE EFFECTIVENESS OF RESOURCES

The different task orientations of the police can subject them to contradictory demands, which may require quite different and, at times, opposing strategies of policing. Traditionally, strategies of policing have been developed with a view to improving basic crime-fighting measures, such as crime-reporting rates (i.e. number of crimes reported to the police) and crime clear-up rates (i.e. number of cases that involve direct police interventions in the processing of alleged offenders). In seeking to secure a greater portion of the public purse, arguments often hinge on the notion that there is a direct linear correlation between increased police numbers, powers or finances, and a decrease in crime.

The need to measure police effectiveness assumes added importance when one considers the extent of the financial burden generated by such techniques of social control. Available evidence on police effectiveness, however, suggests that the success of the police is fairly limited in terms of 'crime fighting' (Dixon 1998; Fyfe 1991; Grabosky 1989). In essence, substantial increases in staff, increased funding, more departmental bodies and enhanced powers have not substantially made much difference in the commission of crime. Thus, we should not overestimate the effects that improving police resources will have on crime rates.

In part, the limitations of traditional measures of policing (i.e. in relation to crime rates) stem from the fact that law-and-order responses to crime are generally reactionary in nature; as such, they generally fail to consider and address the fundamental causes of crime, most of which are beyond the ability of police alone to counter. In other words, crime is not simply an issue of law enforcement—we must also deal with the wider socio-economic forces underlying much of the crime problem. All these issues lead to problems in measuring the efficiency and competency of police, so perhaps a different measure of police effectiveness is needed, rather than simply relying upon statistical movements in the recorded rates of crime.

Furthermore, any questioning of the traditional measures of policing calls into question the main purposes and roles of the police, and introduces the idea that other facets of policing warrant greater attention than otherwise has been the case. For example, new measures of police activity (see Dadds & Scheide 2000) open the door to new types of evaluation of police performance, including various facets of community policing that do not hinge upon arrest rates or crime trends as such.

STYLES OF POLICING

The limitations associated with the traditional crime-fighting techniques of policing have been discussed at length by police and by criminologists in recent years. One consequence of these discussions has been renewed consideration of the basic objectives and styles of policing. For present purposes, we have distilled the essence of these discussions and debates into two general models of policing: the traditional policing model and the community policing model (see Table 16.3). These models do not exist in pure form in the real world; we use them here to highlight broad tendencies and philosophies. While the two models are presented here as discrete models that use opposing techniques, in practice the strategies and styles are not mutually exclusive. In fact, in the higher echelons of policing they are generally viewed as complementary strategies that address different aims, so that it is not uncommon to identify hybrid responses to the crime problem.

TABLE 16.3 MODELS OF POLICING

	TRADITIONAL POLICING	COMMUNITY POLICING
Primary roles and techniques	• Crime fighting • Reactionary (demand-led) techniques	• Peacekeeping • Pre-emptive (problem-solving) techniques
Measure of effectiveness	• Changes in crime rates and number of arrests	• Changes in police–community relations and peaceful restoration of order
View of prosecution	• A necessary and useful tool • Focus on crime control and ensuring offenders get their just deserts	• A measure of last resort reserved for the most serious cases • Focus on conflict resolution and diversionary and informal measures
Role of the community in policing	• Police are the experts; the community to play an auxiliary role	• Participatory decision making structures in which the community plays a partnership role
Relationship with other organisations	• Exclusionary and generally limited to other policing and regulatory agencies • Police behaviour should be reviewed internally	• Inclusive and involving multi-agency approaches and contacts • Police accountable, to some extent, directly to the communities which they serve
Relationship with the media	• To be used as a means of gaining increased resources and powers • Capitalises on the fear of crime	• To be used as an educational and promotional tool to inform the public about nature of certain crimes • A means to generate better community-level relations

Since one of the basic obligations of the police is to serve the community, these two models initially can be analysed in relation to the following dimensions of community–police relations (see Cunneen & White 1995):

- *policing in the community*—the extent to which police are present within a broad range of social institutions and settings, such as schools and at the neighbourhood level
- *policing of the community*—the particular task orientation(s) prioritised by police departments
- *policing by the community*—the degree to which the community (including the media and other governmental departments) participates in the policing process
- *policing for the community*—the degree to which particular community interests are represented and responded to by police.

The key issue in relation to the policing models is not whether the police are involved in and with the 'community' (however defined), but the character of police involvement, and the main goals or objectives of the policing task.

TRADITIONAL POLICING MODEL

Traditional policing is characteristically related to the paramilitary approach to crime control. This approach emphasises rapid response to an activity or behaviour after it has occurred (in this dimension it is sometimes described as reactive or demand-driven policing). It also includes crime-prevention strategies based upon armed-response capabilities as a deterrent to possible crime commission. Goals are expressed in terms of activities, not achievements or defined outcomes. No attempt is made to influence the environment; rather, the idea is to intervene in an environment and to respond to situations as they arise. In its reactive dimension, it focuses on individual incidents and the specific offender(s) and victim(s). In its crime-prevention dimension, it emphasises surveillance and the visible demonstration of coercive force (e.g. carrying of firearms).

Since this approach is police-centred, the public has mainly an auxiliary role to play in the effort to combat crime. Community–police consultative activities, unless organised and administered principally by the police, are viewed as interferences. Interactions with the community are based upon a client–server relationship, whereby the public is passively dependent upon the expertise of the police, assisting them by providing information (e.g. through the reporting of suspicious behaviour) and through cooperative assistance, as in investigatory enquiries.

In terms of responding to community interests, it is the more powerful groups in a community that have the greatest influence in setting the policing agenda and, alongside the police, that play a pivotal role in determining who is to be subject to surveillance. Traditional policing thus tends to reflect the interests and values of the dominant interest groups, as reflected in a preoccupation with protection of private property, a focus on 'street crime', and the regulation and control of dissident and disadvantaged minority groups.

In operational terms, emphasis is placed upon the professionalism of the police; it is argued that police themselves are the only people with the expertise required to deter criminals, to respond to specific events, and to investigate wrongdoing. An emphasis is placed on the techniques and the utility of coercive force in the fight against crime. The major orientation of such policing is with law enforcement and public order maintenance, with reliance on violence and the threat of violence as the main ways in which to deter and deal with crime.

In responding to crime, police seek to expand their powers, resources and personnel in the key operational areas linked to the crime-fighting function. Public reference is often made to crime statistics, particularly those that suggest an increase in crime rates. The media, in turn, frequently use these statistics in a manner that generates or reaffirms the public fear of certain types of crime, through, for instance, fostering the idea of 'crime waves' (see Chapter 2). Fear of crime, and the presence or suggestion of escalating crime rates, are then used by the police to justify calls for increased resources and/or powers, and the strengthening of other state social control apparatus, such as prisons. In many cases, the push for greater numbers and powers emanates from police unions, as well as political leaders (see, for example, Finnane 2000; White & Richards 1992).

Traditional policing also generally has a more insular orientation from the point of view of inter-agency endeavours with other government departments and/or community agencies. The preference is to leave policing to the police. At the institutional level, the ever-increasing complexity of modern-day law-breaking has prompted a strengthening of the commitment to inter-agency information sharing, but this is within a wider policing network—formerly involving, for example, bodies such as the National Crime Authority, the Australian Securities and Investments Commission, the Australian Security Intelligence Organisation and the Australian Bureau of Criminal Intelligence (Fairchild 1994; Hocking 1993)—but today also incorporating all relevant agencies engaged in the 'war against terrorism'.

A concern to keep police matters within police hands also extends to accountability processes. For instance, it is generally argued that existing internal review structures provide satisfactory checks on any alleged corruption or police mistreatment. It is felt that the police themselves, as professional crime fighters, are precisely those in society who have the expertise to investigate allegations involving fellow police officers.

Traditional policing incorporates many of the popular ideas about policing, including the importance of a strong 'blue line' separating society from the predations of deviants, criminals and those who would bring anarchy to the social order. The appeal and legitimacy of such policing is particularly reinforced in cases involving serious crimes such as homicide or rape, in dealing with 'professional criminals', and in instances of major public disorder such as riots. The events of 11 September 2001 in the United States, and subsequent wars in Afghanistan and Iraq, have also greatly strengthened the traditional methods and institutional power and authority of law-enforcement agencies.

COMMUNITY POLICING MODEL

By contrast, community policing is a style of policing that emphasises a more conciliatory, rather than coercive, approach to police work (see Putt 2010). As the name suggests, this is a style of policing that seeks to move away from the police-centred, authoritarian nature of traditional approaches, focusing instead on a co-participatory model of crime prevention that accepts that the community has a legitimate, active role to play in the policing process.

Although the precise nature of community policing is debatable (see Brogden 1999; Bryett et al. 1994), the various interpretations of this model hold in common a concern to directly include ordinary citizens in decision-making structures, so that operational strategies and techniques are conscious of 'community' interests, as well as 'police' interests (Beyer 1993; Fleming 2010). In practice, the involvement of the 'community' may range from the weakest possible kind of consultation through to full public control of police practices in some locations.

Some forms of community policing are basically reactive in nature, particularly in areas such as domestic violence and child abuse. In such instances, officers generally are specially trained and/or attached to special units (e.g. multicultural liaison units or domestic violence units) to better liaise with appropriate support and advocacy groups in the community. The emphasis is on improved interaction with the victims of particular kinds of crime, but attention also is directed at working with welfare, health and other agencies in campaigns and strategies designed to change the social environment within which certain crimes are committed.

More generally, however, the notion of 'community policing' is often associated with a problem-oriented approach to policing; one that uses proactive techniques. According to this approach, courses of action should be pre-planned and should be designed along preventative lines. Rather than dealing with the aftermath of a situation, police seek to intervene and influence the environment in which criminal activity or social disorder is likely to take place, in order to prevent its occurrence. This is achieved through a process that identifies recurring problems (e.g. through intelligence-gathering and prediction) and that devotes time and monetary resources towards the analysis of underlying causes of, and formulation of solutions to, criminal or antisocial behaviour. Rather than focusing on individual causes of crime, broader situational and structural levels of analysis are employed.

ACTIVITIES PROMOTING COMMUNITY POLICING

In terms of objectives, community policing does not focus exclusively on crime—it is a management approach primarily concerned with service provision and peace-keeping initiatives; that is, activities that seek to promote community welfare. Accordingly, efforts are made to establish a visible presence within the community in a variety of non-traditional roles. For example, in Victoria, off-duty police officers for many years ran Blue Light Discos. At a more formal level, there is the Police Schools Involvement Program. Under this program, police provide school children with relevant legal information on areas such as general road safety, and the rules and regulations governing bicycle riding (see Gronn et al. 2004; James 1994b). The appointment of Gay, Lesbian, Multicultural and Aboriginal Liaison Officers in many Australian jurisdictions, and overt police participation in cultural events involving minority groups (be these ethnic, Indigenous or sexuality based, such as the Mardi Gras) likewise serve as a public statement of police commitment to diverse sections of the community. Indeed, contemporary community policing is now often considered specifically in the context of vulnerable populations, whereby specific projects and programs are targeted at refugees, and groups defined by age, gender, sexuality or ethnicity (Bartkowiak-Theron & Asquith 2012; Bartkowiak-Theron & Crehan 2010).

This non-threatening police presence is intended to serve a dual function: it promotes the establishment of good trusting relationships with the local community, and it acts as a method of crime prevention. The emphasis is on peaceful resolution of conflict, with force to be used only as a last resort. In keeping with this non-confrontational approach, the media are viewed not as a tool for generating community fear, or reinforcing the crime-fighting dimensions of policing, but rather as an educative (e.g. drink-driving campaigns) and promotional tool. The concern is with presenting a less coercive image of policing, and on encouraging a form of community–police cooperation that has a broader preventative scope (e.g. working with groups of young people).

STYLES OF COMMUNITY POLICING

There are several different ways in which community policing might be construed, and alternative practices that could be adopted, depending upon the approach one chooses. Since the composition of the community is always changing, identification of community concerns requires constant dialogue with community representatives. This process demands analysis of the different social divisions and power distributions within the 'community'. The voices of specific constituencies that may not have been heard in the 'traditional policing' model (e.g. Indigenous people, ethnic minorities, women and young people) are listened to, albeit with varying degrees of practical response. This is partly reflected in the relatively recent attempts to change the face of policing so that it is more representative of the disparate social landscape, specifically by the recruitment of more women (see Prenzler 1995; Wilkinson & Froyland 1996) and people from a wider range of cultural backgrounds. There has also been greater attention directed towards the adoption of culturally sensitive training procedures.

In the more radical versions of community policing, crime-control issues are determined and implemented entirely by the local community itself (see, for example, Airo-Farulla 1992). For instance, there are many cases now across Australia where Aboriginal people are playing an increasing role in policing their own communities (see Willis 2010). This usually takes the form of Aboriginal Community Patrols, which are also known as Night Patrols, Street Patrols, Bare Foot Patrols or Mobile Assistance Patrols, depending on the region. In a review of the work of these patrols, Blagg and Valuri argue that:

> Community Patrols represent a distinct form of policing, as they fit neither in the public police nor private security. The public police act with the authority of the law and as its agents, while private security agencies tend to act as agents of business. Community Patrols, on the other hand, operate in the interests of a particular community or constituency. As such they represent a radically different alternative to both state and private paradigms of policing. (2004: 215)

PROBLEM-BASED POLICING

Where policing is not in the hands of the community itself, but is retained by the police, it has been argued that community policing must be weighted in the direction of the poor and disadvantaged (see Brogden 1999). The logic is that if 'quality of life' is at the core of the community policing philosophy, then those who are most vulnerable in society ought to have the most concerted protection and positive police action. Policing in this instance is meant to be based on social need, rather than being predominantly shaped by the political pull of the better-off classes and prosperous suburbs.

In responding to problem situations, diversionary or informal methods of crime control, such as police cautions and unofficial warnings, are favoured. In this sense, the community policing model moves away from the legalistic orientation of its traditional counterpart, functioning instead within a more flexible, problem-solving framework. To put it differently, the basic unit of police work is seen to be the problem, rather than a crime, a case, a call or an incident. Addressing problems means dealing with the conditions that create problems (AIC 2004b).

Furthermore, since there is an acknowledgment that solutions may not necessarily be provided by the police themselves, cooperative resolutions are sought through a multi-agency approach. Police are therefore prepared to liaise with other government and non-government agencies in their endeavours to both prevent and respond to crime. For example, in dealing with a case of domestic violence, rather than arresting and prosecuting an abusive partner, police act as mediators, referring them to a social worker, domestic violence centre, family counselling centre, Alcoholics Anonymous or some other relevant organisation.

Community policing represents a form of policing that shares many of the goals of traditional policing. However, it sees the fulfilment of the police mission in different terms. This can involve either a strategic concern in terms of how police broadly relate to 'the community' (e.g. as peacekeepers) or the use of specific tactics for specific types of crimes that rely upon a closer working relationship with specific community sectors (e.g. domestic violence). The appeal of this kind of approach lies in its apparent sensitivity to different sections of the community, such as young people or women; the emphasis on problem-solving approaches, which may be directed at the wider social causes of crime; and its potential for greater public accountability and public input into policing. It is also relevant in discussions of policing and terrorism (see Box 16.2).

FUSION BETWEEN POLICING MODELS

The ideas and practices associated with the 'traditional policing' and 'community policing' models have generated considerable debate within police departments, often with tensions emerging over what is perceived to be real, positive, effective policing: traditional authoritarian policing, which relies primarily upon the use of force, intervention and the muscled arm of the law; and the co-participatory community problem-oriented approach, which prefers peaceful resolution of conflicts and dialogue with the community. In some instances, there appears to be an informal ideological gulf between the two approaches, with traditional-style police accusing community-oriented members of being 'plastic cops' or 'wimps'. Indeed, there are deep divisions within political parties and the public at large in relation to what characteristics are seen to be indicative of a 'good cop'. This is partly due to the distortions and myths about policing conveyed by the mass media, some of which were discussed at the beginning of this chapter. In the end, however, most police departments and officers meld elements of both models into their operational strategies and daily practices to varying degrees, and with varying consistency.

BOX 16.2   COUNTER-TERRORISM AND COMMUNITY POLICING

A new area of police work that requires a careful rethink of the relationship between traditional policing and community policing is that of 'counter-terrorism'. McCulloch (2008: 215) argues that 'counter-terrorism policing shifts the risk from imagined victims "us" to imagined offenders "them". The integration of national security into law enforcement redraws and fortifies the imaginary border between the community to be protected and those they are to be protected from'. One consequence of this social process is the expansion of police powers across the board, ostensibly to deal with these new threats from the terrorist □other'. Be this as it may, as in most areas of police work, there are competing models regarding how best to deal with the specific threats posed by terrorism.

These approaches have been extensively reviewed and critiqued in a book by Pickering et al. (2008), *Counter-terrorism policing*. Pickering et al. argue that attempts to eradicate terrorism through force are ultimately counter-productive and can exacerbate the social conditions that give rise to terrorism. Instead, they favour a model that emphasises the development of layers of community trust, that involves dispersed forms of community–police interaction, and that includes diverse contributions to democratic policing.

Source: McCulloch (2008); Pickering et al. (2008)

A modern example of this fusion of traditional and community policing models is the introduction of intelligence-led policing techniques into the Australian context. This approach focuses primarily on the targeting of known offenders, and the management of crime and disorder through traditional policing measures (e.g. covert and overt surveillance). Attention is, however, focused on perceived crime 'hot spots'—areas exhibiting patterns of interconnected crime and incidents—through the application of criminal intelligence analysis. Key to the formulation and application of crime reduction and prevention strategies is the formulation of local partnerships (Ratcliffe 2003).

LOCAL PRIORITY POLICING

The introduction of Local Priority Policing (LPP) represents yet another example of the movement towards an integration of traditional and community-oriented policing styles. According to Victoria Police (2004), LPP is a both a philosophy and strategy that governs the manner in which policing services are managed and delivered to the Victorian community. A distinctive feature of LPP is the active role played by the local community in shaping police service priorities and in holding local police accountable for the quality and mix of services they provide to the local communities they serve. Local Priority Policing comprises the following principles:

* Local communities are encouraged to accept responsibility for their own safety and security.
* The community influences police service via a network of partnerships that inform the Victoria Police planning process.
* Local police are accountable and empowered to deliver police services to their community.
* The management of police resources is devolved to the appropriate local level, where the resources are deployed.
* Local safety and security issues are the prime focus of Victoria Police.
* The community's perception of safety and security is one measure of the effectiveness of police performance.
* Achieving an outcome of enhanced 'community safety' is the focus of police action.

INNOVATIONS IN POLICING

Innovations such as community policing, problem-oriented policing, third-party policing and intelligence-led policing have all resulted in police reassessing the effectiveness of traditional police practices such as rapid response to calls for service, patrolling and criminal investigation (see Bullock & Tilley 2009; Mazerolle & Ransley 2005; Ratcliffe 2008). While there is some overlap between these more recent approaches, there are also some key differences relating to the emphasis each places on partnerships with the community (see Table 16.4).

Broadly speaking, one can distinguish between 'bottom-up' approaches and 'top-down' approaches. Community policing, for example, provides an example of the former; intelligence-led policing, the latter. In either case, however, there are persistent criticisms that actual police practices do not match the theoretical orientation of the models in question, and that further reform of policy and practices is required (see Desmond & Valdez 2013; Mazerolle & Ransley 2005; Ratcliffe 2008; Sutton et al. 2014).

TABLE 16.4 INNOVATIONS IN POLICING AND THEIR ROLE IN CRIME PREVENTION

INNOVATION	DEFINITION	CRIME PREVENTION DIMENSIONS	ROLE OF PARTNERSHIPS
Community policing	An organisational strategy that leaves setting priorities and the means of achieving them largely to residents and the police who serve in their neighbourhoods (Skogan 2006)	Engagement and consultation with local communities to identify local crime problems	Regarded as central to community policing in which police and residents work together to identify and solve community problems
Problem-oriented policing	An approach to policing in which discrete pieces of police business (e.g. burglary, alcohol-related violence and car theft) are subject to analysis, with the aim being to identify the key causes of the problem so as to develop a more effective strategy for dealing with it (Goldstein 1990; Spelman & Eck 1987)	Adopts a problem analysis (SARA) and identifies crime hot spots through crime mapping and is place-based, with an emphasis on the adoption of situational crime prevention approaches	May involve partnerships with community groups or agencies, but can also simply involve a police-led response
Third-party policing	Police efforts to persuade or coerce organisations or non-offending persons (e.g. public housing agencies, property owners, parents, health and building inspectors, and business owners) to take some responsibility for preventing crime or reducing crime problems (Mazerolle & Ransley 2005)	Engagement with other organisations or individuals and use of a range of civil, regulatory and administrative laws aimed at creating or enhancing the crime-control capacities of third parties	Range from one-way approaches in which police coerce third parties to take action against crime to collaborative multi-agency approaches
Intelligence-led policing	A management philosophy/business model aimed at achieving crime reduction by disrupting offender activity (Ratcliffe 2008)	Combines crime analysis (e.g. data about the location of offences) with criminal intelligence (e.g. data about known offenders) and focuses police action on prolific offenders	Focus is on enhancing collaboration between different police units, through a top-down management approach so as to develop better crime intelligence

Source: Sutton et al. (2014: 203)

ISSUES FOR CONSIDERATION

RHETORIC VERSUS REALITY

Rather than concentrating upon rhetorical debates concerning the superiority of either a traditional or community-oriented approach to policing, it is far more instructive to examine where police departments themselves, and indeed governments, are committing their resources: are proactive or reactive programs being favoured, and what is the relationship between the two? Careful analysis is needed regarding when and how community policing is the favoured approach (e.g. is it the preferred style in relation to middle-class suburbs?), and when traditional, **paramilitary policing** is evident (e.g. is it the preferred style in relation to poor, working-class housing estates?). In other words, to gauge the nature of police work, it is essential to go beyond the mission statements of police services to analyse actual practices and actual community relationships.

PARAMILITARY POLICING
An approach to crime control that emphasises rapid response to activity after it has occurred. It also includes crime-prevention strategies based on armed-response capabilities as a deterrent to possible crime commission. The emphasis is on use of force and military-style engagement.

MULTI-SKILLING

Having noted the heterogeneous nature of police task expectations, it is possible to question the capacity of police to deliver a holistic service. Perhaps the multi-skilled nature of policing is unrealistic and we should instead be encouraging a more professionalised approach where task specialisation replaces general practice policing; for example, some officers would be solely concerned with the law enforcement aspects of policing, while others would be assigned a service provider role. But what would be the negative consequences of such a shift? Alternatively, if police officers are required to be multi-skilled across diverse areas of knowledge and practice, how can career pathways, promotional structures, and pre-service and in-service training and education best be structured to reflect this? What rewards are available for those who engage in increasingly sophisticated work-related tasks?

THE CHALLENGES OF PRIVATE POLICING

Significant questions remain with respect to the role and expansion of private policing relative to public policing in recent years. Key issues here relate to the training of private security providers, and how their performance can be monitored from the point of view of quality assurance, legal powers and overall relationship with members of the public (see Prenzler & Sarre 2012). The use of intelligence that has been privately gained for private benefit, the interaction between police and private police, and the relative career structures of public and private police also are matters of some interest. So, too, is the question: who is accountable to whom?

THE 'WAR ON TERRORISM': ASSESSING ITS IMPACT

Especially since the destruction of the twin towers in New York, nation-states around the world have been captivated by the threat of terrorist violence. One consequence of this is the emergence of a 'get tough' attitude toward potential suspects; an attitude that has the potential to reshape police attitudes towards street crime as well as their role in organised crime and counter-terrorism activities. The increasing links between government coercive agencies (e.g. federal police, state police, and national security and intelligence organisations) at all levels (including international cooperation via agencies such as Interpol) has implications with regard to police priorities, allocation of resources, and protection of basic human and citizenship rights. So, how has the 'war on terrorism' affected local, regional and national policing practices? (See generally Head 2002a; Head & Hoffman 2003; McCulloch 2008, 2003, 2002b; Michaelsen 2003.)

THE INTERNATIONALISATION OF POLICING

The world is a smaller place, due to advanced information technologies and communications systems. The phenomenon of globalisation, however it is defined in terms of specific features (i.e. economic trends, transfer of information, rise of transnational capital or formation of trading blocs), will inevitably have implications for police services. This is indicated in Box 16.3, which shows elements of the internationalisation of policing. For example, the adoption of certain policing strategies in New York City may be held up as 'best practice' for similar problems in Venezuela, Australia or the United Kingdom. This raises the issue of comparative police studies, and the importance of taking into account regional and local contexts, histories and approaches in discussions of 'what works' (see Andreas & Nadelmann 2006; Bayley 1999b; Brogden 1999; Pickering et al. 2008). How transferable are ideas and practices from one jurisdiction to another?

BOX 16.3 INTERNATIONALISATION OF POLICING

Study of transnational policing has noted a number of trends that signal greater movement toward global systems of law enforcement (Andreas & Nadelmann 2006). Key aspects include:

- negotiation of bilateral and multilateral law-enforcement agreements
- creation of bilateral and multilateral law-enforcement organisations, working groups and conferences
- inclusion of foreign police agents in training programs (and training of police from other countries in their own country)
- stationing of liaison officers in foreign countries
- role of transnational moral entrepreneurs who mobilise popular opinion and political support and lobby governments.

CONCLUSION

This chapter has reviewed a number of issues relating to policing, and included discussions on police roles, task orientations, organisational structures and personnel. Popular images of policing were touched upon (see also Chapter 2) and it can be noted that while the police actually engage in a wide range of activities, the public preoccupation with crime fighting persists. This view of policing is, however, not confined to the public domain. Many police themselves tend to concentrate on this aspect of their role, and the focus on coercive crime control has produced tensions regarding the ideal style of policing. Various dimensions of traditional policing and community policing were outlined, which indicate broad differences in philosophy and strategic direction. Although presented as competing models, the complementary nature of these approaches at a practical level is also apparent.

Chapter 17 continues the discussion of policing in Australia, with a specific focus on 'police culture' and on the targets of police activity. In particular, the chapter will explore in greater depth issues pertaining to the use and abuse of police power, and the nature of police discretion as a major feature of the practice of policing.

DISCUSSION QUESTIONS

1   The 'police' have only historically existed for less than two hundred years. Why do we need to have police and how should police be organised?

2   What skills do you think ought to be most valued when it comes to police work?

3   What are the key challenges relating to the expansion of the private police sector?

4   Should police officers undertake police work in their own communities or in other communities? Why?

5   'Counter-terrorism poses new dilemmas and challenges for police'. Discuss.

FURTHER READING

Andreas, P. & Nadelmann, E. (2006) *Policing the globe: criminalization and crime control in international relations*, Oxford University Press, New York.

Charlesworth, S. & Robertson, D. (2011) 'Policing, gender, and working time: an Australian case study', *Police Practice and Research: An International Journal*, 13(3): 241–53.

Mawby, R. (ed.) (1999) *Policing across the world: issues for the twenty-first century*, UCL Press, London.

Putt, J. (ed.) (2010) *Community policing in Australia*, Australian Institute of Criminology, Canberra.

Sarre, R. & Prenzler, T. (2012) 'Pluralised policing in Australia: answering the questions', *Australasian Policing*, 31–2.

DIFFERENT POLICING FOR DIFFERENT PEOPLE

17

CHAPTER OVERVIEW

- DIFFERENTIAL POLICING
- OVER-POLICING
- UNDER-POLICING
- POLICE CULTURE
- POLICE ACCOUNTABILITY
- ISSUES FOR CONSIDERATION
- CONCLUSION
- DISCUSSION QUESTIONS
- FURTHER READING

INTRODUCTION

As indicated in Chapter 16, deep divisions exist at a wider community level and within police circles regarding the appropriate objectives and styles of policing. The tensions over appropriate policing philosophy, operational practices and organisational structure stem in part from the conflicts generated by, or accompanying, day-to-day police work. This is most evident in the experiences of specific sections of the general population who may be concerned about 'over-policing' (e.g. Indigenous people and Arabic background people) and/or 'under-policing' (e.g. of racist or homophobic violence). Concerns have also been raised more generally regarding instances of police mistreatment of suspects or alleged offenders, and police corruption.

The aim of this chapter is to discuss the nature of police intervention as it pertains to particular communities and particular kinds of social harm. Particular attention is directed towards the issues of the over-policing and under-policing of marginalised and socially vulnerable sections of the population. In seeking to provide structural explanations for these kinds of policing practice, and other questionable aspects of police activity, the influence of a distinctive occupational culture—'police culture'—is explored. The various components of police culture are outlined, followed by a critical review of the applicability of the concept. The chapter concludes by briefly considering the issue of police accountability.

DIFFERENTIAL POLICING

The police have extraordinary powers to draw upon in their interventions. The very existence of these powers, and the social power which they embody, make their use a source of constant public concern. And the powers are there to be used. How they are used is dependent upon a range of factors, including the attitudes of the individual officer, departmental policies, the specific operational area of police work and the wider political environment. Ultimately, regardless of particular task orientation, the work of the police rests upon a foundation of socially legitimate coercive power.

While acknowledging the importance and potential benefits of discretionary decision-making, it is also vital that we consider the negative consequences of that extensive power; namely, infringements of the 'rule of law' and associated safeguards, such as due process, civil liberties and natural justice. A large body of evidence indicates that far from being applied neutrally and impartially, police discretion is regularly abused, and that abuse is discriminatory in nature (see, for example, Blagg & Wilkie 1995; Cunneen 2001; Dwyer 2011b; Fitzgerald 1989; Goldsmith & Lewis 2000; White 2009d; White & Alder 1994).

OVER-POLICING

OVER-POLICING
The practice whereby certain groups, such as young people, ethnic minorities (e.g. people of Arab background), Indigenous people and known criminals are subject to disproportionate policing; that is, they are regularly targeted by the police for surveillance and intervention.

One of the problematic consequences of selective law enforcement is the **over-policing** of large sections of the population. Particular groups tend to be targeted by police for surveillance and intervention, and this disproportionate attention is customarily viewed as undue harassment by the affected groups. This section examines some of the specific social targets of policing, the nature of the interaction between police and these groups, and the nature of the charges laid against these groups.

INDIGENOUS PEOPLE

Aboriginal and Torres Strait Islander people are particularly vulnerable to over-policing, as evidenced by their over-representation at all levels of the justice system: initial contact, arrest, conviction and imprisonment (Allas & James 1997; Bird 1992; Cunneen 2001; Cunneen et al. 2013; HREOC 1991a,b; Luke & Cunneen 1995; Ronalds et al. 1983; see also Chapter 7). Specific locales have had their own unique histories of police–community engagement. For example, the constant surveillance experienced by some Aboriginal communities was dramatically brought to public attention in the 1970s, following media reports on the policing of the Sydney suburb, Redfern, where there is a high concentration of Aboriginal people. Large numbers of police exerting enormous force constantly saturated this area, harassing, intimidating and arresting significant numbers of the Aboriginal population (Ronalds et al. 1983).

The identification of Aboriginal people with Redfern, and the continuing interest in establishing and maintaining a territorial affinity with the area has long been dogged by media and political controversy (Anderson 1993a,b). The negative discourses surrounding Redfern have included references to ghetto or slum conditions and, in particular, the status of the suburb as a breeding ground for crime and illegal drug use. Not surprisingly, these discourses of disfavour have also dovetailed with a particular kind of **differential policing** in the area. As documented by Cunneen (1990), there has been a history of complaints relating to police practices in Redfern. In particular, conflicts have centred on the numbers of police sent in on special operations, the discriminatory nature of policing practices, and the excessive use of force by police. Differential policing thus refers to a style of policing that negatively impacts those subject to police decisions based on particular sexual, racial and class dimensions and stereotypes.

DIFFERENTIAL POLICING
A style of policing that makes decisions based on sexual, racial and class dimensions, and in and of itself represents an abuse of police discretionary power.

The public presence, activities and interactions of Indigenous people on the streets have thus been fundamentally shaped by police–community relations, which have generally been very poor (see Beresford & Omaji 1996). Numerous studies and commentaries (Blagg 2008a; Bonney 1989; Broadhurst 1994; Cowlishaw 1988; Cunneen 2001; Cunneen & Robb 1987; Cunneen et al. 2013; Hall et al. 1994) have demonstrated the persistent 'racialised' nature of criminality in those regions with large Aboriginal populations. These communities experience high levels of police presence, and intensified, localised monitoring and surveillance.

INDIGENOUS YOUNG PEOPLE AND THE POLICE

Perhaps the most crucial factor in terms of criminal justice issues is that of the nature of policing as it pertains to Indigenous young people. Various studies have highlighted the often negative interaction between young Indigenous people and the police (Blagg & Wilkie 1995; Cunneen 1991, 2001; HREOC 1991a; Ogwang et al. 2006; White & Alder 1994). Many of the confrontations between Indigenous young people and the police take place in the public domains of the streets, parks, malls and shopping centres. The visibility and minority status of Indigenous people, their association in groups and the historical antagonisms between police and Indigenous communities (e.g. it has generally been the police who have taken children away from Indigenous families) contribute to ongoing tension and conflict between the parties.

High levels of contact with the criminal justice system, and disproportionately high numbers of young people in police custody and detention, mean that young Indigenous people are much more subject to heightened surveillance and possible intervention in public spaces. The regulation of Indigenous people's use of public space takes several different forms and is partly related to local political and law-enforcement circumstances. For instance, Cunneen and Robb (1987) examined the nature of 'law and order campaigns' in north-west New South Wales in the mid-1980s. They found that such campaigns were largely orchestrated by local power elites in the country towns, and that the key targets of the campaigns were Aboriginal people. The calls for more police and increased police powers were equated with clearing the streets of Indigenous people, who were presented as, in essence, the 'criminal problem'. Similar types of research, particularly into the media treatment of Indigenous young people, have likewise found that, invariably, they are represented almost exclusively in criminal terms (see Hil & Fisher 1994; Morris 1995; Sercombe 1995).

SUMMARY OFFENCES

This racialisation process has real material consequences when it comes to the actions of authority figures such as the police. Perceptions of a 'problem' require some form of police 'solution'. In many cases, intervention is premised upon use of legislation that allows police to charge Indigenous people with offensive behaviour and/or offensive language. For example, the *Summary Offences Act 1988* (NSW) (as amended) has a separate provision for 'offensive language'. This provision is actively used by police in dealing with public order matters. The problem with reliance upon such legislation, however, is that such provisions are 'inevitably vague and open-ended, with the characterisation of the behaviour left to the discretion of the police in the first instance, and subsequently to the discretion of magistrates' (Brown et al. 2001; Leaver 2011). Case law in this area has been uneven, with decisions about what constitutes 'offensive language' varying greatly, depending upon the predilections of the judge or magistrate, the specific circumstances and the parties involved (see Brown et al. 2001; see also Chapter 11). The consequences of this discretionary latitude is particularly pronounced in Victoria, where police are empowered to issue on-the-spot infringement notices for suspected offences against the *Summary Offences Act 1966*, as opposed to the customary process of having charges determined by a magistrate (Leaver 2011).

In examining the nature of offences for which Aboriginal people are routinely arrested and incarcerated, the pattern that clearly emerges is one of triviality. As was the case in Redfern, Aborigines are disproportionately arrested and incarcerated for minor public order offences such as hindering police, resisting arrest, abusive and/or vulgar language, public drunkenness, homelessness and other street behaviour deemed offensive (Adams 2012; Cunneen 1992a,b; Hall et al. 1994; Hogg 1991). Leicester (1995), for instance, reviewed all charges laid by police in Wiluna, Western Australia, for the period January to August 1994. The study found that of the 1071 charges laid during the specified period (99 per cent of which were directed towards Aboriginal people), 78 per cent (835) were 'street offences' and almost invariably were charges of disorderly conduct under the *Police Act 1892* (WA) or offences under the *Liquor Licensing Act 1988* (WA).

These charges are obviously the ones that offer the greatest potential for selective enforcement, given the public visibility of the behaviour in question and the consequent high probability of direct police intervention. Police have wide discretionary powers in relation to the enforcement of summary offences legislation, and the empirical evidence demonstrates the disadvantageous manner in which that discretion is applied to Indigenous people (e.g. customary use of arrest rather than summons).

The use of offensive language and offensive behaviour offences are generally highly targeted and socially patterned; that is, some groups of people are charged more than others, and this is reflected in overall distributions of charges. For example, a New South Wales study (Jochelson 1997) found that local government areas with high percentages of Indigenous people tended to have higher rates of court appearances for public order offences such as 'offensive behaviour' and 'offensive language'. There was an over-representation of Aboriginal people among the alleged offenders for offensive behaviour or offensive language in both those local government areas with high Indigenous populations and those with low proportions of Aboriginal people in their population. Data also shows that Indigenous people account for fifteen times as many offensive language offences as would be expected by their population in the community (cited in Heilpern 1999: 241).

Similarly, a Victorian study (Mackay & Munro 1996: 6) found that: 'Aborigines were 10.3 times more likely to be processed for "resist police", 11.8 times for "hinder police", 14.8 times for "indecent language" and 5.5 times for "offensive behaviour" in Victoria in 1993–94.' The use of local government ordinances in relation to public drinking, particularly as this affects Indigenous people, has also been questioned in the Victorian context (see Allas & James 1997). Furthermore, it appears to generally be the case that Indigenous young people brought before the courts are more likely to come from rural backgrounds (National Inquiry into Separation 1997).

DEATHS IN CUSTODY
Deaths of people who are in prison custody or police custody or detention that are caused or contributed to by traumatic injuries sustained, or by lack of proper care, while in custody or detention.

Offensive language is ultimately a matter of meaning, intent and context (see White 2002). What is particularly galling for many Indigenous people, young and old, is the way in which some police speak to them. Young people, for instance, report being called names, such as 'nigger', 'boong' and 'coon' by police (Beresford & Omaji 1996: 81). Cunneen (1991) examined language issues when interviewing young Indigenous detainees and found that police were often both racist and sexist in talking with the young people; for example, referring to young Indigenous women as 'black cunts'. Bad language and name-calling were also mentioned in submissions to the Royal Commission into Aboriginal **Deaths in Custody**: 'What's your fucking name?'; 'Where is fucking such and such...'; 'Aboriginal dog'; 'Fuck off inside'; 'You smell stinking' (Johnston 1991: 414–15).

For Indigenous young people in Australia, 'offensive language' provisions remain a key mechanism of social control on the part of the police. Interventions based upon such laws serve to reinforce popular images and perceptions of Indigenous deviancy through the actual criminalisation of specific individuals and groups. While official investigations and academic research into police–Indigenous relations have continually highlighted the problems—and hypocritical nature—of the use of offensive language charges,

BOX 17.1   A POLICING OFFENSIVE

In his book *Conflict, politics and crime: Aboriginal communities and the police*, Cunneen (2001) discusses the history of Indigenous–police contact, and the ongoing issues that have dogged this relationship from the very early days of colonialism. For example, the police have played an integral role in removing children from Indigenous families, in enforcing protectionist laws, in determining the allocation of welfare provision and in arresting Indigenous youth and adults of both sexes.

As with other studies, Cunneen (2001) observes that very often people charged with offensive language are also charged with other offences. This is known as the 'trifecta' and usually involves offensive language, resisting arrest and assaulting police (see also Jochelson 1997). In other words, not only are Indigenous people over-represented in offensive language charges, but they are also frequently charged with multiple offences. Very often these arise out of simple incidents, and are reflective of social processes relating to the nature of the contact in the first place.

Cunneen (2001) highlights several issues here. First, the offences are very often precipitated by the intervention of the police; that is, the police approach Indigenous people for some reason and then become the victim of the offences (Cunneen 2001: 97). Secondly, except for a notional 'community', the victim of the offence is almost invariably the police officer (Cunneen 2001: 29). Thirdly, the language in question has variable usages and meanings, and it is questionable whether the police would themselves be genuinely offended by it. As Jochelson (1997: 15) observes: 'In many of the cases involving Aboriginal people the legislation would appear to provide a trigger for detention for an Aboriginal person who has abusively challenged police authority rather than as a means of protecting members of the community at large from conduct which is patently offensive.'

very little has been done to either stem the tide of such charges or to monitor their use (Cunneen 2001). Meanwhile, greater media and political attention to 'law and order' issues, usually accompanied by calls for greater action to 'clean up the streets', means that offensive language laws will most likely be used more, rather than less, in the future, and applied to ever-widening social targets and situations.

ETHNIC MINORITY YOUNG PEOPLE

The relationship between young people and the police has generally been fraught with tension and conflict. This is not a new phenomenon. The systematic regulation of young people, particularly in public spaces, has been a key aspect of the maintenance of public order as conceived by authority figures for well over a hundred years (Finnane 1994a; Hogg & Golder 1987). There is an abundance of literature that points to the contemporary and ongoing problems between police and young people, including conflicts at the street level. Academic and community research has provided many insights into issues such as misuse of police powers, high levels of police intervention, the use of intimidation and violence in street policing, and generally poor relationships between young people and the police (Blagg & Wilkie 1995; White 2009d; White 2013a; White & Alder 1994; Youth Justice Coalition 1990). A significant feature of recent work in this area has been the prominent place of 'ethnic minority young people' in studies and debates over policing.

In general, a negative interaction between ethnic minority young people and the police breeds mistrust and disrespect (see Collins et al. 2001; White 2013a). A minority of people in any community is engaged in particularly antisocial behaviour and criminal activity. The problem in this case is that the prejudicial stereotyping often leads to the differential policing of the whole population group (Perrone & White 2000). This not only violates the ideals of treating all citizens and residents with the same respect and rights, but it can also lead to further law-breaking behaviour as young people react against what they feel to be unfair and unjust treatment. How young people relate to police is as much a question of how police respond to them as it is one of presumed criminality (see Box 17.2).

Research in Melbourne, Sydney and other capital cities around the country lends weight to claims of tensions in the relationship between police and young people from minority ethnic backgrounds (Collins et al. 2000; Poynting et al. 2004; White 2013b; White et al. 1999). These studies also highlight the currency of debates about appropriate styles of policing. Hostile experiences with police appeared to be common among the ethnic minority young people in these studies, although there were also marked differences in the policing experiences of different ethnic minority groups.

In a Melbourne study into ethnic youth gangs, for example, it was found that there were a number of distinctive ways in which police tended to relate to specific population groups (see White et al. 1999). While these particular features of police interaction are not unique to any specific group, some issues were of more concern to some groups than other issues. For example, most of the Pacific Islander young people complained of police harassment. In relation to the Turkish young men interviewed, a number reported being hassled, searched on the street, or threatened by the police. They did not think that this was fair. Several commented, as well, that the problem was not one of the police doing their job, and rightfully enforcing the law, but rather that of police not treating the young people with respect and dignity in the course of performing their legal duties. The Vietnamese young people also felt that the police unfairly targeted them, and that the nature of the contact was generally unpleasant. They spoke of racist policing, and of how young 'Asian' people tend to be key targets of unnecessary, and often racially offensive, police interventions.

BOX 17.2   POLICE AND VIETNAMESE YOUNG PEOPLE

In a study of Vietnamese youth and police relations in Melbourne, Lyons (1995: 170) identified a range of factors that influenced the relationship between the young people and authority figures. These included:

- unwarranted targeting and harassment of young people in public spaces
- high incidence of body search procedures used by police
- denial of young people's legal rights
- verbal, psychological and physical mistreatment by police
- non-reporting of police mistreatment through formal channels
- general lack of respect toward each other demonstrated in both subtle and overt means.
   Lyons (1995) also points out that ethnicity raised additional issues that complicated police–youth encounters. These included:
- police tendency to stereotype Indo-Chinese youth
- lack of command of the English language
- lack of knowledge of Australian law and legal rights, which influences the nature of contact
- police prejudice.

Source: Lyons (1995)

Recent research into the relationship between police and Vietnamese communities in Melbourne highlight a continuing problem of poor communication and a need for better understanding on both sides. It is observed that (Meredyth et al. 2010: 239):

> Police officers need to be able to understand when they should treat individual members of the public as citizens—and treat them the same—and when they need to give particular consideration to individuals as members of ethnically identified community groups, bearing in mind their historical density and current complexity.

On a positive note, the research itself is seen to contribute to the building of greater trust between two complex communities: Vietnamese-Australians and Victoria Police.

FACTORS IN DIFFERENTIAL POLICING

A number of factors play a part in the differential policing process. The level of contact young people have with the police, and their assessments of this contact, are shaped by things such as: the extent to which they are new arrivals as opposed to established groups; the degree to which they seek to preserve specific cultural and religious identity and practices that differ from the Anglo-Australian mainstream; their socio-economic status; and their level of visibility within the public streetscape (Collins et al. 2000; White & Perrone 2001; White et al. 1999).

The degree of assimilation into Anglo culture would appear to be a major determinant of police–ethnic youth relations; that is, how well established a newly arrived migrant group is, or how culturally distinctive a so-called established minority group is. For example, Vietnamese and Somalis are relatively recent arrivals on the Australian landscape and (as in the past with Italians, Greeks and other groups) they tend to be the new objects of Anglo right-wing fears and stereotyping, which may attract increased police attention. This in part explains why 95 per cent of Vietnamese young people interviewed in the Melbourne study had experienced police contact, with a majority of them assessing that contact as generally bad (White et al. 1999).

Meanwhile, Sydney researchers have observed that, especially in the light of the terror attacks on the Unites States on 11 September 2001, the 'Arab other' is fast becoming the pre-eminent 'folk devil' of our time (Morgan & Poynting 2011; Poynting & Mason 2008; Poynting et al. 2004). This is making worse what is, at times, a tense and conflictual relationship between Lebanese-Australian youth and police in the western suburbs of Sydney (see Collins et al. 2000). Work carried out by the Human Rights and Equal Opportunity Commission (HREOC 2004: 67) confirmed that a substantial number of consultation participants felt that Arab young men, in particular, were unfairly dealt with by the police. Going beyond unfair treatment, and alleged police harassment, there were also allegations of direct discriminatory conduct on the part of police: 'Of course Muslims and Arabs are targeted ... Guys get abused, they get called "terrorists" and "Bin-Ladens" by the police.' It is easy to see how, under these circumstances, police relations within certain communities would be less than convivial (see also White 2009d).

Discriminatory practices—whether based upon age, ethnicity or a combination of the two—cannot be tolerated at any level, and particularly at the hands of authority figures such as the police. How officials of the criminal justice system respond to and interact with members of the public is ultimately as indicative of the politics of 'race' as it is the politics of 'law and order'.

UNDER-POLICING

UNDER-POLICING
The practice whereby certain offences (e.g. racist or homophobic violence) are subject to less surveillance and intervention than otherwise ought to be the case.

So far we have concentrated on discretionary patterns that negatively impact certain groups of people in society, by targeting them for excessive official attention. It is also necessary, however, to examine the equally negative flipside of the discretionary problem; that is, the phenomenon of **under-policing**. Although, at a theoretical level, all citizens are afforded equal protection from harmful activity through the provision of public police services, in practice not all victimisation is viewed, nor responded to, equally by police. Under-policing refers to those instances where police persistently fail to respond to instances of violence perpetrated against certain (vulnerable) groups in society, thereby denying them official victim status.

DOMESTIC VIOLENCE

It is well established that women are most likely to encounter violence at the hands of male intimates, and since that violence is often perpetrated out of sight (in domestic locations), it is usually out of the public mind (White & Habibis 2005). Feminists consider the historical lack of official attention to domestic violence to be a product of patriarchal (i.e. male-dominated) social and institutional arrangements. They also identify police inaction as a significant contributor to this process (Scutt 1995; Stanko 1995).

Historically, police attitudes and responses to domestic violence have been guided by a 'hands off' philosophy, with this passivity justified on the grounds that domestic violence was a private affair. Despite the range of abuse suffered by women, including harassment, degradation, emotional humiliation, and physical and sexual assault and torture, the prevailing view was that domestic violence was a civil rather than criminal matter, and therefore criminal proceedings were rarely initiated by police (Hatty 1989; Scutt 1990). On those rare occasions in which an arrest did follow from police intervention, it was most likely to be in response to a disrespectful attitude towards the attending officer rather than the abuse suffered by the offender's partner (Buzawa & Buzawa 1993).

Police attitudes have substantially changed in recent years, with most jurisdictions now taking issues of violence against women much more seriously. Even so, questions remain about how police will make the shift from a persistent non-interventionist stance to an active role in policing domestic violence. Some jurisdictions, such as Tasmania, have legislated for, and emphasised in public policy, a strongly coercive approach to dealing with family violence matters. Under such circumstances, the police role is tied directly into concerted service provision in this area. How they will negotiate this role is subject to much question. Moreover, issues pertaining to family violence within Indigenous communities warrant their own particular sensitivities and methods of intervention (see especially Blagg 2008a; Kimm 2004). This is especially problematic for police, given their historical role as perpetrators of wrongdoing in relation to Indigenous people.

HOMOPHOBIC VIOLENCE

Consensual private homosexual activity was a criminal offence in most Australian jurisdictions until the 1980s. It is therefore not surprising that a mutually antipathetic and distrustful relationship has long existed between the police, and gay men and lesbians. Despite the decriminalisation of most consensual homosexual relations, gay men and lesbians continue to face high levels of public vilification, stigmatisation and violence (Feneley 2013; Mason 2002; Tomsen 2002, 2009).

A Victorian survey conducted by Gay Men and Lesbians against Discrimination (GLAD 1994) revealed that 70 per cent of gay men and women interviewed had experienced some form of verbal abuse, been threatened with violence, or been bashed or physically abused.

Even more startling were allegations by homosexual men (70%) and women (24%) that they had been subjected to harassment, entrapment and violent behaviour by police personnel. Complaints of mistreatment were not only confined to police actions but also made reference to police inaction. Some respondents claimed that police had either inappropriately responded to their reports of hate crime (abuse that is motivated by the victim's sexuality) or had failed to respond altogether (GLAD 1994). A smaller survey, conducted by the Australian Capital Territory Gay and Lesbian Police Liaison Network (1994), produced similar findings to the GLAD report, with many of the respondents perceiving the Australian Federal Police to be not only unsupportive but also homophobic.

In New South Wales, the level of violence experienced by gay men, in particular, has resulted in special initiatives to deal with hate crimes directed against people based upon their perceived sexuality. These initiatives have included the creation of a gay–lesbian client consultant located within the police force and the monitoring of male gay-hate homicides. More generally, the strong links between hate crime and broader social and cultural values has led to arguments that community education should be a central plank of any hate-crime prevention strategy (Golden et al. 1999: 270). Police, as well, ought to be recipients of such education.

RACIST VIOLENCE

Questions have also been raised in relation to the manner in which state authorities respond to another type of hate crime; that is, racial assaults. The National Inquiry into Racist Violence, initiated by the Human Rights and Equal Opportunity Commission (HREOC 1991) reported on the high susceptibility of people from non-English-speaking backgrounds to racist violence, because of the visibility of their differences from Anglo-Australian persons.

The irony of the situation is that while criminal violence and antisocial behaviour is often seen as part and parcel of the migrant presence on the street, there certainly is no corresponding moral panic about racist violence. This fuels another aspect of the contradictions faced by ethnic minority youth—when victimised, they are treated to systematic under-policing (White 1996a). An Australian Law Reform Commission (1992) report on multiculturalism revealed that the principal criticism levelled at police by non-English-speaking persons was a failure to take seriously, or respond to, reports of racist abuse (including physical attack). Police were generally perceived as rude, indifferent and racist. Similar claims were made over a decade later, this time by Arab and Muslim Australians. The Human Rights and Equal Opportunity Commission observes that there were instances when local police did not take reported race hate offences seriously, even when identifying information was provided, such as a car number plate. Unsurprisingly, this led to dissatisfaction with the police service generally (HREOC 2004: 163).

While there remain serious and persistent problems with the ways in which the police intervene, or fail to intervene, in cases involving domestic violence, homophobic violence and racist violence, it needs to be acknowledged that in recent years many police departments have attempted to rectify the situation in various ways. While most jurisdictions now have criminal sanctions against racial vilification (see McNamara 2002), the collection of statistics on race hate crimes, and concerted police action against race hate violence, remain matters of considerable weight. This is particularly so in the light of the negativity associated with 'ethnic crime' and negative stereotypes of Arabs and Muslims

BOX 17.3   ABUSES OF POLICE POWER

The systematic nature of differential policing in and of itself represents an abuse of police discretionary power, since decisions are based on sexual, racial and class dimensions. But abuse of police power takes other more specific forms as well:

- *Verbal abuse and intimidation:* verbal abuse can include racist taunts or comments (e.g. references to committing suicide), threatening language (e.g. threats of hanging) and gestures directed towards person by police.
- *Harassment*: this can include the unfettered use of 'name checks' (e.g. the asking of name and address), stopping young people, and questioning and detaining them without apparent good cause.
- *Abuse of procedural rights:* this includes things such as not advising of the accused's right to remain silent upon arrest, through to punishing those who challenge police authority (e.g. by speaking of their rights) by subjecting them to a wider range of charges than might normally be the case.
- *Misuse of physical violence:* this includes the use of unwarranted violence and excessive force against particular groups of people by police during arrest and interrogation, sometimes as a tool for coercing information or a confession, and sometimes to silence the critics of certain types of police (mis)conduct.

within the Australian social mosaic (Poynting et al. 2004; White & Habibis 2005). How and if police intervene in instances of race hate crime continue to be important questions.

POLICE CULTURE

There can be no doubt that police abuse of powers is real, that in some cases it is a routine aspect of everyday police practice, and that it is often directed towards the less powerful groups in society. How do we account for police misconduct of this nature? Likewise, how do we explain police corruption (i.e. the misuse of office for illegal gain)? Numerous scholarly investigations and government inquiries into police misconduct have discredited the 'bad apple theory', which sees corruption or mistreatment as basically an individual phenomenon (den Heyer & Beckley 2013; Prenzler 2011). Instead, such studies and reports have revealed that police corruption and abuse is not only widespread but also, to some extent, is an entrenched part of the world of policing (Chan 2008; Fitzgerald 1989; Lundman 1980; Manning 1989; Reiner 1992; Skolnik 1975; Skolnik & Fyfe 1993; Wood 1996).

What these inquiries suggest is that police behaviour cannot simply be individualised, since it is influenced by a range of institutional and occupational factors. Many of the core ideas that inform individual decisions are collectively shared. Generally, these ideas are not explicitly formulated in official documents, but are said to arise from the occupational culture or institutional values of policing, which shapes, sustains and legitimates certain behavioural patterns. One version of the nature of police culture is presented in Figure 17.1.

A useful review of this model of police culture is contained in the *Report of the commission of possible illegal activities and associated police misconduct* (Fitzgerald 1989). According to Fitzgerald,

FIGURE 17.1   POLICE CULTURE

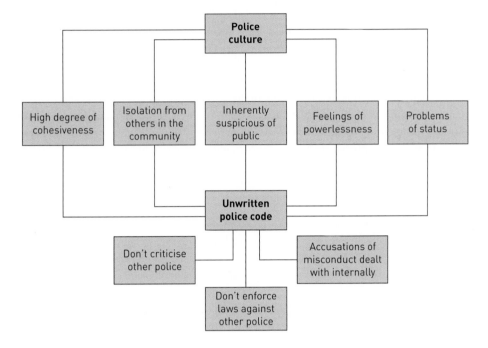

police culture comprises a number of components, which can be summarised under three broad themes (see also Reiner 1992; Skolnick 1975).

OPPORTUNITIES FOR POLICE MISCONDUCT

- *Attitudinal characteristics:* for example, police appear to be inherently suspicious of the public, basically viewing outsiders as dangerous and not to be trusted. Since police mainly interact with the public in confrontational situations, an 'us and them' mentality is created whereby there are perceived threats from the 'outside' to officers on the 'inside'.
- *Structural opportunities:* police work involves ambiguities. In many routine encounters, police face choices—to use law-enforcement options, to issue a warning, or to ignore the crime or antisocial behaviour altogether. This opens the door to the possibility of a number of abuses of power and misuses of police discretion.

SHIELDING POLICE MALPRACTICE

Any police misconduct or overstepping of the boundaries in the use of police powers is protected by the police code of silence, an unwritten set of rules that is upheld by appeals to police solidarity and loyalty to the force; for example, it is impermissible to criticise other police. Basically, police should not scrutinise each other's behaviour too critically. Criticism of this sort is viewed as particularly reprehensible if it is referred to outsiders.

ORGANISATIONAL FEATURES

How has this culture evolved and how is it reproduced? This is primarily a matter of recruitment practices, training regimes and socialisation into 'street cop culture' (e.g. on-the-job training is substantially carried out by older police, at least some of whom are imbued with the same old police culture).

Fitzgerald (1989) provides structural reasons for both the existence and continuance of police culture in its current form. It is thus the nature of the police work itself (e.g. recruitment, training and hierarchical relations), in combination with the negative aspects of police culture (e.g. the code of silence), that breeds corruption and misconduct. The existence of a culture built on the strict police code of silence and legal non-enforcement can lead to corruption and misconduct, such as the mistreatment of members of the public by the police.

CULTURE OF VIOLENCE

Since the Fitzgerald inquiry, there has been a proliferation of writing on the subject of police culture and its various dimensions. It has been cited as an explanation for many questionable police practices; for example, in the early 1990s with regard to the excessive use of force relied upon by the Victorian Police. In particular, concern was expressed then about the number of people either wounded or fatally injured as a consequence of police shootings. In Victoria, police wounded 47 citizens and shot dead a total of 30 people between 1984 and 1994; six of those killed had a psychiatric history. This level of police shootings exceeded that of all other states (Task Force Victor 1994). In theorising on the issue, it was suggested that Victorian police had laboured under a 'culture of violence'; that is, a tendency towards routine aggressive and open confrontation, which was likely to provoke violent reaction (Task Force Victor 1994).

COMPLEXITIES OF POLICE CULTURE

While acknowledging the conceptual value of police culture theories, some commentators have expressed reservations relating to its invocation as a causal explanation for police misbehaviour (James & Warren 1995; Shearing 1995; Shearing & Ericson 1991). In specific terms, from a methodological point of view, James (1994a) argues that many of the propositions about police culture, as put forward by Fitzgerald (1989) and others (see especially Skolnick 1975), do not bear up to sustained empirical investigation. For example, James points out that in a Victorian study it was found that, in fact, over 50 per cent of officers questioned said that their non-police friends mixed socially with their police friends, thus casting into doubt the idea that police are necessarily socially isolated as a group. It is further argued that 'diversities in operational practice and community contexts both within and between Australian police departments are such that a generalized perspective on police subculture is likely to be misleading' (James 1994a: 66).

The idea that police culture(s) is mutable and thus subject to change is especially highlighted in the work of Chan (2008, 1997, 1996). What authors such as Chan and James suggest is that police culture is a complex phenomenon, and that any generalisations regarding the basic elements of that culture, or the apparently fixed nature of police culture, need to be challenged both in terms of substantive empirical research and with regard to the development of strategies for positive reform.

James and Warren (1995) further highlight two of the major concerns surrounding discussions of police culture:

- Police culture is so generalised that cultural variations, both inter- and intra-departmentally, are ignored. Police departments are not uniform; they are set apart by divergent histories and structures, socio-political contexts and areas of specialisation. Since conventional formulations of police culture fail to reflect these divergences, they are unable to account for the discontinuities in police behaviour. The empirical evidence in fact suggests that police behaviour is variable and by no means always congruent with alleged rules. While police culture is almost invariably construed in unfavourable terms (i.e. the focus is on how it negatively impacts police in terms of generating impropriety), it can also have positive impacts in terms of generating propriety.

- Traditional theories of police culture are deficient in that they are founded upon tautological reasoning. Since they are unable to make reference to formal rules that govern behaviour, an inductive exercise is engaged in whereby observed behaviour is explained by reference to implicit rules that best explain that behaviour. Those rules are supposedly inculcated into recruits via a process of indoctrination so that they end up generating the very activity from which the rules were derived to begin with. As Shearing and Ericson (1991) argue, this approach is far too culturally deterministic in that it assumes police officers are 'cultural dopes' who unquestioningly abide by the internalised rules without actively participating in the construction of their active reality. This view of police culture completely fails to take account of the complex relationship between cultural values and actions. It is argued instead that police culture is contoured and moulded not by prescribed rules but by the stories and metaphors that are heard and retold within police circles. These stories are said to cultivate a framework of subjective meaning within which police can locate their choices of action or inaction (Shearing & Ericson 1991).

The twin ideas of cultural variability and non-deterministic cultural frameworks mean that any assessment of specific instances of police malpractice must be grounded in analysis of the situational factors that give rise to such cases. This requires moving beyond assumptions about 'police culture' in general, to sustained examination of local conditions, interactions between particular police officers, organisational contexts, political climate, training and recruitment programs, and composition of the service. It also implies that rather than being totally culturally determined in their actions, each police officer must accept some moral and ethical responsibility for the choices they make. And within large organisations such as police departments, there will be many different kinds of models of appropriate practice from which to choose—as indicated in our previous discussion of the different styles of policing.

In an important critique of the concept of police culture, Chan (1996) likewise argues that many existing definitions fail to account for internal differentiation and jurisdictional differences. Similarly, it is argued that such perspectives tend to imply officer passivity in the acculturation process. In addition to these criticisms of the prevailing use of the concept, Chan (1996) also points out two further problems: first, the idea of police culture is often insulated from the social, political, legal and organisational context of policing (e.g. instances where police corruption and misconduct exist with the tacit approval of the community); and, secondly, that an all-powerful, homogeneous and deterministic conception that police culture is insulated from the external environment leaves little scope for cultural change.

According to Chan (1996: 112), it is essential to rethink the concept of police culture. This requires the development of an alternative theoretical framework for understanding police culture; a framework that can account for 'the existence of multiple cultures, recognize the interpretive and creative aspects of culture, situate cultural practice in the political context of policing, and provide a theory of change' (see Chan 2008, 1997, 1996 for an extended presentation of this type of theorising about police culture).

POLICE ACCOUNTABILITY

Any discussion of police malpractice and police culture inevitably raises the question of to whom the police are to be held accountable. At one level, the answer is to be found in a political analysis of the social role of policing generally. For example, in seeking to account for contemporary policing practices, both in terms of operational focus (i.e. the targeting of some groups and the neglect of concerns affecting others) and with respect to the tactics and methods employed, one might consider the historical origins and continuing class role of the police.

POLICE AS ENFORCERS OF SOCIAL NORMS

Basically, police have been instrumental to the maintenance of the prevailing capitalist order, with an emphasis on protection of private property and public-order policing and, in particular, the social containment of certain communities; namely, the working class and minority groups (Farrell 1992; Finnane 1990; Scraton 1985). The use of police to regulate industrial confrontations in the interests of employers, for example, has long established them as partisan agents. In a similar vein, the enforcement of bourgeois morality and decency has also traditionally been achieved through the police, and has been directed towards the management of the 'dangerous' and 'disreputable' poor, who threatened the quality of life and economic advancement of the 'respectable' (Finnane 1994b; Scraton 1985).

The partisan nature of policing, and the historical preoccupation with dangerous classes and the regulation of public life, provides a useful backdrop for understanding the present over-policing of certain groups of people in public spaces, and the under-policing of private affairs. Political and occupational pressures dictate that the police be seen to be doing their duty to protect the public, and, in particular, defend those sections of the public that have direct economic interests in specific geographical and cultural localities. As well, the present state of (negative) relations between Indigenous people and police is also better understood in the context of the strategic role played by police in the colonisation process. Initially, as frontier forces, police oversaw and facilitated the process whereby Aboriginal people were marginalised and dispossessed of their land. Later, under the guise of protectors, or guardians, police became frontline agents for the genocidal 'welfare' system that resulted in wholesale intervention into the lives of Aboriginal and Torres Strait Islander families, clans and whole communities (Blagg 2008b; Cunneen 1994, 2001; Ronalds et al. 1983).

ACCOUNTABILITY

The issue of accountability, then, at this level can be considered in terms of the wider political, economic and social frameworks within which police carry out their tasks. To assess the nature of policing thus requires examination of the very structure of society, the nature and basis of its social divisions (e.g. class, gender, religion and ethnicity), and how and where policing fits in with respect to the dominant power relations within a society.

Generally speaking, however, most discussions of 'accountability' per se centre on how best to deal with or restrict specific abuses of police power (rather than broad policing patterns). At a formal level, one can point to several areas where the police are deemed to be held accountable. James (1994a: 13), for example, comments that there are senses in which police are at various stages accountable to the legislature, the executive and the judiciary: 'to the parliament or legislature for the enforcement of law; to the executive government for the carrying out of government policy; and to the judiciary for the ways in which police enforce the law and carry out policy'. However, in practical terms the actual content and methods of accountability vary greatly.

To understand the variability in how 'accountability' mechanisms operate in practice, we first have to acknowledge the difficulties with the concept itself. For example, accountability can mean everything from complete control over all aspects of operational activity through to simple review of broad policing policy. Likewise, notions of who is to do the accounting vary greatly—from perspectives that stress the role of the Police Minister (an elected parliamentary representative) to those who argue for a greater direct community role in overseeing police practices.

As it stands, there are a number of different institutional avenues for evaluation and assessment of police practices, including abuses of power and police corruption. Each of these has some relevance to the manner in which police carry out their duties. They include:

- internal investigation units within police departments (e.g. the Police Conduct Unit within Victoria Police)
- individual police performance indicators, which are used for promotional purposes (e.g. number of citizen complaints)
- judicial review of cases involving police impropriety
- ministerial and parliamentary review
- ombudsman or police complaints tribunals or authorities
- special inquiries such as royal commissions or task forces
- permanent oversight bodies such as criminal justice or anti-corruption commissions.

In most cases, the existing mechanisms of police accountability have been found wanting. This is so for a variety of reasons, including a lack of resources, lack of cooperation, failure to apply full judicial sanction, adoption of a limited reactive rather than proactive form of intervention, and political manipulation (see Biondo 2004; Freckelton & Selby 1988; Goldsmith & Lewis 2000; den Heyer & Beckley 2013; Prenzler 2011; Reiner 1985; Sarre 1989). Even where Police Standing Orders, legislation, and common law protections have been established to protect citizens from police abuse of power, the tendency is for these formal legal protections to be ignored or downplayed in many instances (see Warner 1994). It has furthermore been observed that internal affairs units within police services have been criticised for being too sympathetic to police accused of misconduct, and that police whistleblowers are often victimised, rather than protected, by their own organisations (Goldsmith 2001).

For adequate police accountability to occur, there is a need to develop an independent system of police oversight—one that incorporates elements such as clear definitions of police powers; suitable recruitment, training, and promotion processes; transparency of practices and procedures; an independent oversight body; and so on. The point is that the prevention of police corruption demands a whole-of-system reform if it is to be effective (Biondo 2004).

COMMUNITY POLICING

It has also been suggested that rather than attempting to institute a heavy-handed approach to police accountability, it is more desirable and feasible to link accountability with a particular approach to policing. As Sarre (1989: 111) comments: 'The essence of the argument is this: police abuses are less likely where the community as a whole will suffer as a result of them. Where the police see themselves as part of the community, it becomes clear that abuse of discretion will do as much harm to them as to those to whom the abuses are applied.'

Thus we come full circle once again to issues of policing style, and in particular the specific nature of 'community policing' as a practical method of police work (see Putt 2010). Furthermore, any consideration of 'community policing' must also fundamentally grapple with the wider political contexts and social roles of policing, as these have affected particular groups in the population.

Yet, critical appraisal of the concept and practices of community policing raises further issues in relation to accountability. For example, it has been argued that community policing is, or ought to be, by its very nature heavily reliant upon the use of discretion. As Brogden (1999: 180) comments:

> The decentralization required by community policing, and the resultant increased autonomy of the rank-and-file, may have three effects on the urban police institution. It may mean a loss in effective management control as a consequence of decentralization. Similarly, it may result in a loss of wider accountability and control. Finally, loss of external and internal supervision may lead to a breakdown of professional standards of behaviour by police officers.

And so the question remains: who is to police the police? And how is this to be accomplished?

PRIVATE POLICING

Such questions pertain not only to members of the police force but also to private police (Sarre & Prenzler 2012). For instance, recent years have seen a number of high-profile events and incidents in which private security guards have featured prominently. The death of popular cricketer David Hookes, after a confrontation with a bouncer outside a Melbourne pub in 2004, made national headlines. Analysis of violence associated with the night-time economy (specifically related to pubs, clubs and bars) has demonstrated the social impact of 'occupational masculinity'; masculinity related to performance of tasks within an occupation. In the case of private security, occupational masculinity is frequently based upon, and serves to heighten the incidence of, the use of violence (Tomkins 2005). In other words, the type of security provided (based upon aggressive physicality) may itself be a trigger to violence (generating resistance and aggressive responses on the part of patrons), rather than preventing it from occurring in the first place.

More generally, private policing has come under critical scrutiny for a variety of reasons in recent years. Problems that have been identified in various inquiries into the private security industry, for example, include:

- prosecutions of leading security companies for misrepresentations of patrol and alarm monitoring devices
- a pattern of serious assaults and failure to protect patrons on the part of crowd controllers in licensed premises
- corrupt relations between police and security officers trading in confidential information and preferential treatment for security repair firms
- an enormous waste of police resources responding to false alarms
- shoot-outs between armed robbers and cash-in-transit personnel involving death, injury and serious threats to public safety (Prenzler & Sarre 1998: 3).

Responses to these issues have generally pointed to the need for systematic training and accreditation of private police, legal and other forms of accountability mechanisms, and ongoing monitoring of the activities of personnel and firms within the private security industry. Part of the difficulty has been that whereas public police performance is evaluated in terms of crime rates and law enforcement, private police tend to be evaluated in terms of loss, risk and public disorder. That is, accountability is in the first instance to the employer, rather than to the public, and performance management is shaped by commercial criteria (see Stenning 2000). When speaking about 'accountability', therefore, one needs to always ask who is accountable to whom, and for what? The answer will inevitably make reference to multiple purposes, multiple obligations and multiple stakeholders.

ISSUES FOR CONSIDERATION

POLICING VULNERABLE COMMUNITIES

The manner in which police interact with persons with intellectual disabilities and mental illness is a matter of considerable and ongoing concern (see Box 17.4). This is especially so in light of estimates by Orygen Youth Health that one in four young people aged 15 to 24 is affected by mental health disorders (cited in Beaumont 2005). In the absence of adequate support services, numerous young people affected by mental health problems are increasingly coming to the attention of police. A Victorian study based on police surveys provided a conservative estimate of the level of police contact with this target group (Hearn 1993). Of those officers interviewed, 73.3 per cent reported having had contact with young people aged 13 to 21 who had mental health problems. Of that sub-sample, 37 per cent reported experiencing contact with the target group more than twice a month and 12.3 per cent more than twice a week. Once again, the manner in which police exercise their discretion has implications for this group of people. In responding to the public presence and behaviour of people with intellectual disabilities or mental illness, police may not have the training, knowledge or skills to adequately handle intervention situations. Studies have indicated that those with mental disabilities face an increased risk of arrest, especially if they are also homeless (see, for example, Robertson 1988; Teplin 1984).

BOX 17.4   VULNERABILITY AND POLICING

Contemporary policing is complex and multifaceted, and police services are being required to do more, often with fewer resources. A vital area of public concern relates to the interactions between police and vulnerable people, who include among others, young people, the elderly, people with disabilities, those from a culturally and linguistically diverse background, people with mental illness, Indigenous people, people with addictive behaviours, and sexually and gender diverse communities. The book *Policing vulnerability* (Bartkowiak-Theron & Asquith 2012) provides a consolidated treatment of issues surrounding policing and vulnerability.

The editors argue that the duty of care now demanded for their clients and users necessarily requires policing organisations to become:
- better informed about the diversity of their communities
- engaged with their communities in the development of policies and practices
- critically aware of shared human rights, and the ways these ethical stances and legal structures can lead to better practice outcomes for vulnerable people and populations, and all 'users' more generally (Bartkowiak-Theron & Asquith 2012: 14).

Importantly, the contributors to this book not only provide critical insight into the contexts and demands of modern policing, but also offer a series of theoretical models concerning diversity and policing, assess relevant policy in this area, and provide detailed analysis of policing practices, operations and procedures that have vulnerable populations as a focus. In other words, the book as a whole exposes current problems while providing practical suggestions for police organisations and frontline police officers in regards to their interaction with vulnerable people.

Source: Bartkowiak-Theron & Asquith (2012)

POLICING DISSIDENCE

Another area of recent controversy is that of the policing of political protests. Since the 1980s, Australia has followed overseas trends in the move towards a paramilitary style of public-order policing—involving mounted police charges, the use of dogs, pressure point tactics, capsicum spray gas, water cannons and plastic bullets (see Jefferson 1990; Waddington 1991). The forms of intervention (policies, tactics and weaponry) employed in the policing of the Bathurst Motorcycle Races, Austudy demonstrations, environmental rallies, school occupations, pickets and union marches over the past few decades have at various stages come under public scrutiny and have attracted considerable criticism (McCulloch & Clayton 1996). According to McCulloch (2002a, 2001b), excessive use of force by police is increasingly justified through the ideological lens of 'counter terrorism'. Insofar as police action is linked to attempts to deal with public events that can, at some level, be associated with 'dissident' groups, then state violence can be blamed on the victims of this violence. As with other measures designed to deal with public disorder, the objective seems to be one of 'cleaning the streets'—whether this is in relation to antisocial behaviour, criminal acts or political protest. How will this affect police–community relations, and what are the implications of this for police accountability?

The policing of public order represents special challenges for the police: *operationally* in terms of choice of tactics and strategies, and *politically* with regard to the social environment within which events take place. Such policing is highly visible, and has a high impact. Failure to prevent violence through police inaction, or escalating violence through police intervention, are constant dilemmas faced by police as they respond to specific kinds of events and situations. Evaluating public-order policing is partly a technical matter and partly depends upon what the mission and objectives of the policing are, and the social and political context within which it takes place. A lot always depends upon the relationship between *police* and *the policed*. Australian social scientific work on riots indicates that police action can sometimes be the spark that leads to riots among members of a particular community. This was the case, for example, with both Redfern in Sydney and Palm Island in Queensland, in which each riot was precipitated by the alleged killing of an Indigenous person by the police (Cunneen 2007).

The role of the police in *precipitating* riots thus is an important area of analysis and strategic thinking. Police activities in dealing with riotous behaviour can be analysed in terms of the dynamic interaction between the police and members of the public, an interaction that is seen to pre-empt and de-escalate potential disorder, or to lead to increased conflict. Here the key issue is how the policing methods themselves shape general outcomes within the context of a 'riot curve' (or 'disorder model') understanding of conflict (King & Waddington 2004). The assumptions about the policed, the techniques and style of intervention, and the operational strategies employed in dealing with riots all impact upon the course and consequences of riots. They are central to the management of public-order events, and reflect the fact that policing has moved well beyond simply reacting to social conflict.

The policing of demonstrations in recent years has been accompanied by critical examination of policing practices, including police violence and over-reaction, whether this be Melbourne (McCulloch 2001b), Seattle (Gillham & Marx 2000) or Genoa (della Porta & Reiter 2006). Three main interrelated strategic areas for protest control have been identified (della Porta & Reiter 2006):

- *coercive* strategies (e.g. use of weapons and physical force)
- *persuasive* strategies (e.g. discussion between police and protestors)
- *information* strategies (e.g. widespread information-gathering before, during and after a protest).

Years of experience with demonstrations, across many different national contexts, have been consolidated into forward planning and preventative work that draw upon coercive, persuasive and information strategies. Simultaneously, protest movements likewise have learned from experience how to maximise their political impact, even if this, at times, leads to conflict with police. Further issues of public-order policing relate to matters such as the influence of the wider political environment on specific event policing, the tensions between paramilitary styles and peacekeeping modes of operation, and the precipitation and amplification of violence due to the policing approach adopted. Good practice in public-order policing is hard to separate from political pressures to operate in particular ways. Whether it is policing of hooligans, anti-globalisation protests, environmental activists or rioters, the method of intervention has practical as well as symbolic purchase (see Sheptycki 2004).

POLICE TRAINING

It is important to investigate the specific nature of 'police culture' in particular localities and jurisdictions (e.g. country towns, and different states and territories). More generally, big questions remain as to how police department practices and cultures can be changed or modified in positive directions. At issue here is also the adequacy of pre-service and in-service training undertaken by the police. If we consider the multitude of tasks police officers are required to perform, and if we want to ensure that the rights of all persons are respected, it becomes apparent that police need to be multi-skilled and this requires specialist training on a variety of matters. How has the proliferation of 'police studies' courses within universities, and academically challenging programs within police academies, influenced the career structure, gender and ethnic composition, and core values of policing? What is the relationship between what is taught to the police, and how they engage in varying types of police work?

CONCLUSION

This chapter has surveyed a number of issues relating to police discretion and the manner in which police powers are exercised. It was established that far from being a neutral process, discretionary decision-making involves systematic procedural bias. Certain marginalised groups in society (e.g. Indigenous people and ethnic minority young people) tend to be targeted for high levels of police surveillance and intervention of a punitive type, while the activities of concern to other groups (e.g. domestic violence, homophobic violence and racist violence) are not dealt with adequately by the police.

In seeking to account for the systematic over- and under-policing of various groups in society, and specific abuses of police power, the concept of police culture was reviewed and critiqued. However, it was also acknowledged that police practices (both lawful and unlawful) should be viewed as an historical and social process; that is, as a product of the socio-political environment that shapes the role of police in society. These kinds of considerations must be borne in mind in any discussion of police accountability.

As gatekeepers to the criminal justice system, the police occupy a central position in the institutions of social control. Fundamentally, it is the police who provide the bridge between the wider community and the legal system. How the latter operates is the subject of the chapters to follow. This begins in Chapter 18, which considers issues pertaining specifically to the role of forensics, a matter of considerable relevance to policing and courts alike.

DISCUSSION QUESTIONS

1 'The police are meant to act in a fair and impartial manner at all times'. Discuss.

2 What are some of the reasons that over-policing occurs?

3 What are some of the reasons that under-policing occurs?

4 In what ways is police culture a good thing and an essential part of trying to work in a difficult occupation?

5 Who should police the police? Why and how should this be done?

FURTHER READING

Bartkowiak-Theron, I. & Asquith, N. (eds) (2012) *Policing vulnerability*, The Federation Press, Sydney.

den Heyer, G. & Beckley, A. (2013) 'Police independent oversight in Australia and New Zealand', *Police Practice and Research: An International Journal*, 14(2): 130–43.

Fitzgerald, G. (1989) *Report of the commission of possible illegal activities and associated police misconduct*, Queensland Government Printer, Brisbane.

Meredyth, D., McKernan, H. & Evans, R. (2010) 'Police and Vietnamese-Australian communities in multi-ethnic Melbourne', *Policing*, 4(3): 233–40.

White, R. (2009) 'Ethnic diversity and differential policing in Australia: the good, the bad and the ugly', *International Migration & Integration*, 10: 359–75.

FORENSIC STUDIES

18

CHAPTER OVERVIEW

- SCOPING THE FIELD
- FORENSIC APPLICATIONS
- UNDERTAKING CRIME SCENE EXAMINATION
- DNA PROFILING AND THE LIMITATIONS OF FORENSICS
- ISSUES FOR CONSIDERATION
- CONCLUSION
- DISCUSSION QUESTIONS
- FURTHER READING

INTRODUCTION

Police are in the frontline of investigating and prosecuting crime and, as we saw in the preceding two chapters, they do so in varying ways. An important component of both policing and prosecution is the use of **forensic evidence**. The term 'forensic' basically refers to the link between 'law' and 'science'. As this chapter reveals, this means that forensic studies is a broad area that encompasses many different strands of science, including the social sciences.

The chapter introduces the field of forensic studies. The first part outlines the key areas of work associated with forensics, and the types of interventions and expertise applied across various domains of the criminal justice system. The second part of the chapter explores specific issues pertaining to forensic studies. We begin by describing who does what from an occupational perspective, and briefly outlining specific areas of inquiry and expertise (e.g. forensic pathology, crime scene investigation and e-forensics). A distinction can be made between forensic studies (as a form of critical analysis of the field) and distinct forensic sciences (involving particular values, techniques and methodologies). This distinction is further explored in Box 18.1, which describes the rationale behind the inclusion of a chapter on forensics within a criminology textbook.

The philosophy of criminal justice (and of science) one holds will dictate the place and objectives of forensic interventions in any given situation. Notions of 'truth' will vary according to whether the evidence is required for prosecution purposes or scientific validity. 'Justice' may be achieved either with or in opposition to community input. Specific types of expertise will be relied upon more in some cases than in others, and yet great variability and differences of opinion also exist within particular expert communities. Forensics may have their greatest value in after-the-fact cases, as a reactive investigatory tool. However, the techniques and technologies of forensics can also be used in the prevention of social and environmental harms. The social purposes to which forensic science is put, and the social consequences of forensic intervention, are of significant concern to the forensic studies student.

FORENSIC EVIDENCE
Forensic evidence is the evidence presented in court that is based on specific areas of technical and vocational expertise.

BOX 18.1   FORENSIC STUDIES VS FORENSIC SCIENCE

There is no doubt that there is a vital place for critical analysis of forensics as an object of study. One need only think of the influence of the media, and their portrayal of forensics, on the police role, on criminal justice budgets, on how juries deliberate, on victims, on offenders, and on investigatory and scientific communities. Forensics is public, popular, pervasive and persuasive.

Forensic science refers to specific areas of technical and vocational expertise. Training in chemistry, ballistics, fingerprint analysis, DNA testing, computer forensics and so on can be highly specialised. So, too, crime scene investigation (including specific types of crime scene, such as arson and bushfire arson cases) demands the development of particular skills, capacities and expertise. Dealing with the human element of crime, which can draw upon the expertise of biology, bio-mechanics, psychology and social work, likewise is oriented toward hands-on or practical types of intervention.

Forensic studies refers to the study of forensics as a social phenomenon. The question here is less to do with 'how to' (e.g. laboratory science and crime-scene techniques) than with the overall implications of forensics for society as a whole. In this respect, the concern is to learn about how science and technology shape the work of the justice system. Thus, from the point of view of criminal justice education, it is forensic studies, rather than forensic science, that should be integrated into existing criminal justice programs. As Fradella et al. (2007: 271) observe: 'The goal of doing so is *not* to create forensic scientists; the goal is to provide students of the social sciences a meaningful understanding of the ever-increasing interplay between science and law as it affects the civil and criminal justice systems'.

The task of forensic studies, therefore, is not to train people in specific scientific disciplines or technical skill areas (this is more appropriately done within university and college courses specifically designed to teach chemistry, pharmacology, toxicology, psychology, social work, ballistics and so on). The main emphasis is on providing a generalist understanding of the field as a whole, including how developments across the field might feed into particular criminal justice processes (e.g. in combating environmental crimes—see below). The intent, as well, is to provide space for critical reflection on specific forensic practices (e.g. the expanded use of DNA testing— see below), and to inquire into the effectiveness or otherwise of forensics in regards to how the police, the courts and corrective services undertake their basic roles. A key element of this is how 'evidence' itself is socially constructed within legal and scientific discourses (e.g. in sex abuse cases—see below), and how different players within the criminal justice system conceptualise the nature of criminal investigation, criminal procedure, criminal evidence and courtroom practices.

FORENSIC SCIENCE
Specific areas of technical and vocational expertise, including training in chemistry, ballistics, fingerprint analysis, DNA testing and computer forensics. Crime scene investigation demands the development of particular skills, capacities and expertise.

FORENSIC STUDIES
The study of forensics as a social phenomenon. The question here is less to do with 'how to' than with the overall implications of forensics for society as a whole.

SCOPING THE FIELD

The field of forensics involves many different people doing many different kinds of things. Over the next few pages we shall explore the field by providing extensive lists of who does what. Those engaged in forensic interventions include state employees, such as those associated with the police, courts, hospitals, health and welfare agencies. They include specialist forensic departments, civilians as well as police, 'outside' experts such as private practitioners and university academics, and those who can establish their expertise in specific areas through credentials and/or applied experience.

To provide just one indication of what forensic practice might entail, let us consider employment positions in one well-known crime scene investigation location—Las Vegas (see Genge 2004).

EMPLOYMENT POSITIONS

The Las Vegas Metropolitan Police Department (LVMPD) serves as an interesting example. The various forensic positions employed there include:

- *Evidence custodian*: performs a variety of technical duties to ensure that *evidence* is properly processed, stored, protected and delivered, or to release and dispose of cleared property.
- Crime scene analyst I/II: responds to crime scenes, performing a wide variety of *investigative tasks* to document the crime, including on-scene photography, recovery of physical evidence and processing latent fingerprints.
- Criminalist I/II: performs various scientific analyses in a *laboratory setting* on physical evidence to deliver scientific consultation; to interpret and form conclusions from test results; to document such interpretations and conclusions in a variety of reports; and to testify as an expert at court proceedings.
- Document examiner: examines *documents* and document-related evidence within the environment of the scientific laboratory; interprets results; forms conclusions; and testifies at court as an expert witness.
- Firearms/tool mark examiner: performs scientific and laboratory analyses on *firearms and tool-mark evidence*; interprets test results and forms conclusions; prepares reports; and testifies in court as an expert witness.
- Forensic laboratory technician: provides technical support in a *forensic laboratory* and maintains evidence control; provides responsible staff assistance to professional laboratory staff; and completes a variety of laboratory tasks and procedures as assigned by the laboratory director.
- *Latent print examiner*: conducts *fingerprint* comparisons of latent prints and finger and palm print exemplar files; and performs various tasks relative to assigned areas of responsibility.
- Photo technician: provides *photographic support* to LVMPD and neighbouring police agencies; operates and maintains complex photographic equipment; and performs a variety of tasks relative to assigned areas of photography.

Other jobs that we might add to this list include:

- Serologists/DNA analyst: responsibilities include evidence relating to *biological fluids*; analysing blood, semen and saliva; analysing samples using short tandem repeat (STR) DNA technology; and interpreting test results.
- *Disaster victim identification*: logistics; tagging; temporary morgue; identification; repatriation; and liaising with local authorities and people.
- *Forensic major incident room*: coordination of people, skills, communications, documentation and expertise related to, for example, bombings, tsunamis, cyclones and war crimes.

SPECIFIC AREAS OF INQUIRY AND EXPERTISE

The history of forensic intervention begins essentially with the concern by key individuals to develop principles and techniques to identify and compare physical evidence (Saferstein 2007). The progression of forensic 'science' is marked by developments in areas such as:

- forensic serology (e.g. blood analysis)
- forensic toxicology (e.g. poisons)
- anthropometry (e.g. body measurements)
- fingerprints (e.g. identification techniques)

- blood grouping (e.g. identification purposes)
- comparison microscope (e.g. firearms examination)
- document examination (e.g. reading texts as evidence)
- microscopic analysis (e.g. techniques of analysis)
- crime laboratory (e.g. applying the scientific method)
- exchange principle for cross-transfer of materials (e.g. analysis of particles).

Today, forensic science encapsulates a wide variety of specific disciplines and substantive areas of investigation. A rough perusal of areas associated with forensic intervention includes, for example, the following categories (see James & Nordby 2003):

- *Forensic pathology*:
  - forensic pathologist (coroner/medical examiner)
  - classification of traumatic deaths
  - forensic toxicology (drugs, metal analysis)
  - forensic odontology (dental, bite-mark analysis)
  - forensic anthropology (physical human variability)
  - forensic taphonomy (animal, plant and human remains; in water environments; buried remains)
  - forensic entomology (study of insects).
- *Evaluation of the crime scene*:
  - crime scene investigation documentation
  - collection and preservation of physical evidence
  - recognition of bloodstain patterns.
- *Forensic science in the laboratory*:
  - linking the crime scene to a suspect
  - identification and characterisation of blood and bloodstains
  - identification of biological fluids and stains
  - techniques of DNA analysis
  - microanalysis and examination of trace evidence (e.g. glass, hair, fibres, paint, soils, gunshot residue)
  - fingerprints
  - forensic footwear evidence
  - forensic tyre impression and tyre-track evidence
  - firearm and tool-mark examinations
  - questioned documents (e.g. handwriting, photocopying)
  - analysis of controlled substances (e.g. botanical, chemical).
- *Forensic engineering*:
  - structural failures (e.g. building support, water damage, building collapse due to roof leakage or due to impact)
  - basic fire and explosion investigation (e.g. behaviour of fire)
  - vehicular accident reconstruction (e.g. energy, momentum).
- *Cyber-technology and forensic science*:
  - use of computers in forensic science (e.g. DNA, paint databases)
  - investigation of computer-related crime and forensic accounting.
- *Forensic application of the social sciences*:
  - forensic psychology (e.g. testing, deception syndromes)
  - forensic psychiatry (assessment)

- serial offenders (linking cases by **modus operandi** and signature)
- criminal personality **profiling** (e.g. death analyses, sexual assault investigations).
- *Forensic science and the law*:
    - forensic evidence and legal argument or lawyering skills
    - place of the jury
    - role of the judge.

This list continues to grow, and the work within specific areas of endeavour likewise continues to expand and become ever more sophisticated in terms of techniques, technologies and problem-solving approaches.

As will be considered shortly, the field of forensic intervention is large and is steadily expanding as new crimes and new techniques come to the fore. The sheer size of the field and its growth in recent years is posing a number of issues in relation to notions of expertise. Expertise can be conceptualised as entailing a number of components:

- vocational training
- generalist and/or advanced education
- credentials such as certificates or degrees
- experience as a practitioner
- specific training (chemistry) linked to forensics as a job (e.g. laboratory analyst).

There are a number of issues currently relevant to working within the field of forensics, which are briefly canvassed below.

JOBS AVAILABLE VERSUS SKILLS REQUIRED

There may be high job demand in certain areas, such as DNA testing, but few trained personnel to fill the jobs. This could be due to fact that the specialist training required means that potential employees have alternative discipline-specific vocational options (as chemists working in industry, for instance) that may be more attractive from the point of view of pay and conditions.

PROFESSIONAL TRAINING VERSUS EMPLOYMENT OPTIONS

A number of the tasks demanded of specific forensic interventions are highly skilled, yet permanent jobs for people with the requisite skills may not be available. Graduating with professional credentials may not be a guarantee of work in the area of forensics. Students may question the value of undertaking certain types of professional training if there is no return at the end.

TRAINING/EDUCATION PROVIDERS VERSUS CREDENTIALS AND STANDARDS

It may well be that there is a paucity of suitable training or education providers in particular areas, or that the quality of the training on offer is questionable. Particularly with the growth of interest in crime scene investigation and forensics generally, there is danger that sub-standard courses are being offered (see, for example, Fradella et al. 2007). Establishing and maintaining appropriate credentialling processes and standard-setting is crucial to ensuring a highly qualified workforce.

ON-THE-JOB TRAINING VERSUS TAFE/UNIVERSITY EDUCATION

A perennial issue when it comes to applied and vocationally oriented work is the extent to which the skills should be learned on the job or within purpose-specific educational institutions. In either case, the questions of accreditation and adequate supervision are important. Are there enough qualified

MODUS OPERANDI
Certain actions or procedures an offender engages in to commit a crime successfully. The modus operandi (MO) is a behaviour pattern that the offender learns as he or she gains experience in committing the offence.

PROFILING
The gathering of various kinds of information about a person or persons. Criminal profiling is an attempt to identify demographic variables, geographical location and behavioural patterns of an offender based on characteristics of previous offenders who have committed similar offences.

instructors in each locale to provide suitable training oversight and credible evaluation of student performance?

CIVILIAN ROLES VERSUS POLICE/SPECIALIST POLICE ROLES

For some types of forensic intervention, notably crime scene investigation, there is some dispute over whether the work should be reserved for sworn police officers or contracted out to trained civilian analysts. Moreover, the expertise of police, which has been developed over years of actual practice, may not be recognised by forensic science institutes and accreditation bodies. The balance between acknowledging practical experience and the need for further specialist education and training is a delicate one, demanding careful and honest scrutiny of skills and expertise.

The question of expertise and of who does what is compounded when one considers the vast range of activities that are linked to forensic intervention.

FORENSIC APPLICATIONS

For crimes, new and old, there are varying ways in which forensic interventions may be applied. This section provides a select few examples of relatively new areas of work within the Australian context.

IDENTIFICATION OF DIGITAL EVIDENCE

Changing crimes demand changing skills. For example, since the microchip revolution of the 1970s, computer crimes have increased, and include everything from identity fraud to money laundering to hacking to illegal pornography. Simultaneously, as information technology has developed so, too, has the need for police to enhance their investigation skills. Accordingly, the area of forensic computing has emerged out of the need to deal with criminal exploitation of digital technologies.

Computer crime is unique in that there are no physical boundaries as such, and much of what occurs does so in 'cyberspace' (see also Chapter 14). Six categories of web-based criminal activity have been identified (Britz 2009: 77):

1   *interference with lawful use of computers*: DOS attacks; viruses; worms; other malware; cyber-vandalism; cyber-terrorism; spam etc.
2   *theft of information and copyright infringement*: industrial espionage; identity theft; identity fraud etc.
3   *dissemination of contraband or offensive materials*: pornography; child pornography; online gaming; treasonous or racist material etc.
4   *threatening communications*: extortion; cyber-stalking; cyber-harassment etc.
5   *fraud*: auction fraud; credit card fraud; theft of services; stock manipulation etc.
6   *ancillary crimes*: money laundering; conspiracy etc.

Forensic computer science is still an emerging discipline, the role of which is to protect digital evidence from possible alterations, damage, data corruption or infection by design or carelessness (Britz 2009). Some of the sources of evidence of wrongdoing include:

• personal computers (hard drives, floppy discs, ZIP discs, CD-ROMs and DVDs)
• mobile telephones
• electronic organisers (digital diaries)
• smart cards.

It has been pointed out that problems in computer investigation include things such as inadequate resources, lack of communication and cooperation among agencies, and an over-reliance on automated programs and self-proclaimed experts (Britz 2009). Moreover, finding digital evidence can itself be very problematic. For instance, such evidence is volatile and susceptible to environmental factors (e.g. power surges or extreme temperatures), it is easily hidden, the sheer volume of evidence may make it difficult to perform an analysis on the scene and, in some cases, perpetrators build into their work self-destruct programs that have to be disarmed or circumvented if the investigator is to access the evidence (see Britz 2009).

Forensic computing involves the process of identifying, preserving, analysing and presenting digital evidence in a manner that is legally acceptable (McKemmish 1999). The identification of digital evidence requires knowing what evidence is present, where it is stored and how it is stored. This informs which processes can be employed to facilitate its recovery. The preservation of digital evidence depends upon examining electronically stored data in the least intrusive manner. This is especially important insofar as any alteration of data that is of evidentiary value, including measures linked to gaining access to the data, must be accounted for and justified. The analysis of digital evidence involves the extraction, processing and interpretation of the digital data (e.g. extracting data from a hard disc drive). The presentation of digital evidence involves the actual presentation in a court of law. This can involve responding to questions regarding the expertise and qualifications of the presenter, and the credibility of the processes used to produce the evidence being tendered.

Not all forensic work is about obtaining 'hard' evidence for the purposes of conviction. Forensics can also involve the development of models of behaviour as a means to both prevent crime and to develop profiles that can be used to assist in apprehending offenders once a crime has been committed.

CRIMINAL HOMICIDE AND OFFENDER BEHAVIOUR

Probably one of the most familiar forensic techniques—at least from the point of view of television and movie presentations of criminal psychology—is that of criminal profiling related to crime scene investigation. Bartol and Bartol (2005) describe three important features of offender behaviour at the scene of a crime:

1   *The modus operandi (MO):* this refers to certain actions or procedures an offender engages in to commit a crime successfully. The MO is a behaviour pattern that the offender learns as they gain experience in committing the offence.

2   The **signature or personation**: this is behaviour that goes beyond what is necessary to commit the crime. For example, the signature of a serial killer may involve certain items that are left or removed from the scene (a 'trophy' item) or other symbolic patterns (such as writing on a wall).

3   **Staging**: this refers to the intentional alteration of a crime scene prior to the arrival of the police, and is frequently done by someone who has an association or relationship with the victim. It can involve trying to alter the crime scene in order to divert suspicion, by wiping fingerprints from a weapon and putting it close to the body in such a way that the death looks like suicide, or re-dressing a victim after they have been sexually assaulted and then murdered.

'Profiling' is used to describe the gathering of various kinds of information about a person or persons. Criminal profiling 'is an attempt to identify demographic variables, geographical location, and behavioural patterns of an offender based on characteristics of previous offenders who have committed similar offences' (Bartol & Bartol 2005: 331). The success of profiling depends to some extent on the quality, extent and accessibility of records, so, not surprisingly, there has been a move in

SIGNATURE OR PERSONATION
Behaviour that goes beyond what is necessary to commit the crime. For example, the signature of a serial killer may involve certain items that are left or removed from the scene, or other symbolic patterns, such as writing on a wall.

STAGING
The intentional alteration of a crime scene before the arrival of the police, frequently done by someone with an association or relationship with the victim. It can involve trying to alter the crime scene in order to divert suspicion.

some jurisdictions toward computer-based models of offender profiles. However, close scrutiny of the accuracy, usefulness and success of professional profilers has so far indicated basic flaws and limitations in relation to specific crime-scene investigations. For instance, one flaw of modern profiling is 'the assumption that human behavior is consistent across a variety of different situations. The other flaw is the assumption that offense style or evidence gathered at the crime scene is directly related to specific personality characteristics' (Bartol & Bartol 2005: 333).

Nevertheless, criminal profiling has been shown to be particularly useful in serial sexual offences, such as serial rape cases and serial sexual homicides. More generally, profiling based upon existing criminal records at the very least provides an indication of the kind of person who might have committed the crime under investigation, even though it is unlikely to pinpoint the individual's exact identity. This type of generalist profile is used in dealing with various kinds of criminal activity.

BUSHFIRES AND FORENSIC PROFILING

The construction of offender profiles and arson typologies is, for example, an important part of preventing and responding to deliberately lit bushfires. Offender profiles include information such as 'race', age, gender, family relationships, level of social and interpersonal skills, intelligence and academic performance, personal stresses and motivations. Such profiles are based upon similarities in traits, behaviours and attributes among the offender population. An example of a bushfire arson typology is provided below (See Willis 2004):

1   *Bushfires lit to create excitement or relieve boredom:*
    - vandalism (fires are lit by individuals or groups)
    - stimulation (the fire-setter seeks the excitement and stimulation of seeing the arrival of fire crews, and possibly media)
    - activity (fires may be lit—by firefighters or others—in order to generate activity and relieve boredom from waiting for a naturally occurring fire to break out).
2   *Bushfires lit for recognition and attention:*
    - heroism (fires are lit to gain recognition, rewards and 'hero' status from reporting the fire and perhaps helping fight it)
    - pleading (fires are lit as a 'cry for help', for recognition and attention but to get help or assistance, rather than rewards or hero status).
3   *Bushfires lit for a specific purpose or gain:*
    - anger (fire is lit to secure revenge or as an expression of anger or protest)
    - pragmatic (fires are lit for purposes where other means of obtaining the objective are impractical or illegal, such as for land clearing)
    - material (fires are lit for material gain, such as by firefighters seeking overtime or other payments)
    - altruistic (the fire is lit to achieve an aim the fire-setter believes will benefit others, such as to gain funding for small rural fire services, or clear fuel loads to prevent a more serious fire in the future).
4   *Bushfires lit without a motive:*
    - psychiatric (fires are lit on the basis of psychological or psychiatric impulses derived from mental disabilities)
    - children (fires are lit as a form of play or experimentation).

5 *Bushfires lit with mixed motives*:
   - multiple (fires are lit on the basis of several motives arising at one time)
   - incidental (bushfires result from the spread of a fire that was lit with malicious intent, but without any expectation of a bushfire occurring).

Crimes such as bushfire arson do great damage to human lives and surrounding environments, including animals. In addition to psychological profiles and offender characteristics developed on the basis of existing criminal records, other technologies can be deployed as well to monitor bushland areas. Indeed, the use of forensic interventions in relation to broader environmental matters reveals a wide range of applications.

FORENSICS AND ENVIRONMENTAL CRIME

The use of science and technology as part of research into environmental harm (see Chapter 13) is becoming a vital part of work in this area. By drawing upon multiple scientific studies and knowledge-production techniques, composite socio-ecological accounts of harm can be compiled. Recent technical developments are listed below.

DNA TESTING

Illegal fishing and illegal logging can be tracked through the employment of DNA testing at the point of origin and at the point of final sale. Work done on abalone DNA, for example, demonstrates that particular species within particular geographical locations can be identified as having specific (and thus unique) types of DNA (Roffey et al. 2004; see also Ogden 2008). The use of phylogenetic DNA profiling as a tool for the investigation of poaching also offers a potential deterrent in that regular testing allows for the linking of abalone species and/or subspecies to a particular country of origin. This increases the chances of detection and thus may have relevance to crime prevention as such. The use of DNA testing to track the illegal possession and theft of animals and plants can thus serve to deter would-be offenders, if applied consistently, proactively and across national boundaries.

SATELLITE SURVEILLANCE

Illegal land clearance, including cutting down of protected trees, can be monitored through satellite technology. Compliance with or transgression of land-clearance restrictions, for example, can be subjected to satellite remote sensing in ways that are analogous to the use of closed circuit television (CCTV) in monitoring public places in cities. Interestingly, the criminalisation of land clearance, which primarily affects private landholders, was due in part to images of extensive rates of land clearance provided through satellite remote sensing studies. Use of such technologies also embed certain notions of 'value' and particular relations between nature and human beings, issues that warrant greater attention in any further development of this kind of technological application (Bartel 2005).

AUTOMATED VIDEO MONITORING

New software and digital hardware technologies, combined with use of Ethernet, the Internet Protocol, and wireless mesh-based networks, provide the opportunity for monitoring activity in almost any location in the world from any other location in the world (Hayes et al. 2008). Intelligent video monitoring embraces automation of much of the monitoring activity and the archival of only those incidents identified to be of interest (e.g. motion detection). Intelligent video analysis can facilitate the audits of large-scale, 24/7 monitoring operations, contributing to both deterrence and evidence-gathering in environmentally sensitive locations.

ENVIRONMENTAL FORENSICS

The contamination of land, water and air can be prevented by proactive testing of specific sites, movement routes and currents, by the establishment and collection of benchmark data, and by regular monitoring. To do this requires use of methods that might include chemical analysis, study of documentary records, use of aerial photographs, and application of trend techniques that track concentrations of chemical substances over space and/or time (Murphy & Morrison 2007). Bearing in mind that some contaminations, such as nuclear radiation, are not easily visible to human detection, both alternative methods of science and communal reflexivity over potential risks will be required (Macnaghten & Urry 1998).

A vast array of techniques and approaches to environmental forensics are now available (see United States Environmental Protection Agency 2001). For example, forensic sciences are now able to track the chemical signature of oil spills (Pasadakis et al. 2008) and to use sophisticated chemical and biological analyses to track such spills (as well as illegal disposal of waste) to their source (Mudge 2008). As well, the forensic sciences are now actively turning their attention toward climate change, with a view to contributing to monitoring efforts and identifying emerging environmental issues (Petrisor & Westerfield 2008).

FORENSICS WITHIN CRIMINAL JUSTICE SETTINGS

The doing of forensics within the context of the criminal justice system generally involves three distinct phases or areas of work. First, there is crime scene investigation. This may be followed by laboratory testing of the evidence gathered during the investigation phase. Lastly, there is the presentation of forensic evidence in court, a process that frequently involves expert testimony and interpretation. The forensic process has been described as including the following stages and considerations (Julian & Kelty 2012: 1):

* the detection and collection of traces at the crime scene—traces being remnants of activity and people (e.g. paint flecks, hair, fibres from clothing and weapon marks)
* the analysis of these traces at the laboratory
* the extent to which the mere existence (or non-existence) of traces and forensic results influence police investigations (Are they used to exonerate suspects early or, more typically, do they simply add weight to the prosecution's case?)
* how forensic science information is used by lawyers (Is it as valuable to the defence as it is to the prosecution?)
* how forensic evidence is presented in court (What is considered admissible? Who presents it? What criteria are applied to determine the scientific value of the evidence presented?)
* how juries understand forensic evidence and in what ways this influences their deliberations
* whether there is an over-reliance on forensic evidence in the courts and, most importantly, whether the reliance on forensic evidence improves the likelihood of justice for the accused.

It needs to be emphasised that the role and importance of forensics is basically threefold:

1   to *provide evidence* that links a perpetrator to a particular crime, and thus to enhance conviction
2   to *eliminate suspects* from the investigatory process (e.g. the white power is not heroin), and thereby ensure better targeting of time, money and resources

3   to *exonerate* those who have been wrongly convicted of a criminal offence (e.g. in rape or murder cases, there may be a mismatch of DNA between the alleged offender and the victim or crime scene). For present purposes, crime-scene investigation and the use of forensic evidence in court will be discussed in greater detail.

UNDERTAKING CRIME SCENE EXAMINATION

Recent Australian research into the forensic process has identified a number of issues pertaining to crime scene investigation (Julian et al. 2012). One issue relates to the purposes and roles to which forensics is put. For example, forensic science can have several roles in the criminal justice system (Roux et al. 2012), including both forensic investigation and forensic intelligence.

Forensic investigation refers to attempts to directly assist police investigators by studying traces in order to establish an activity and its criminal nature, and then to find the offender (e.g. in a major crime such as homicide, the goal is to assist in gathering and analysis of data and information, some of which may be used as evidence in determining who is responsible for the crime).

Forensic intelligence, on the other hand, is focused on making links and connections across different crime scenes and building up information on the mechanisms that underlie different forms of criminality (e.g. for volume crimes like burglary, the same shoe print may be found at multiple sites). What is collected at any one crime scene is thus valued beyond that particular crime scene insofar as it feeds into a broad crime analysis (the quantity of identifiable shoe prints actually shows a pattern of burglaries in particular neighbourhoods and types of residence). These patterns, in turn, can provide pointers to police and crime-prevention strategies that disrupt crime activities more generally (see Ratcliff 2008).

Other research has considered crime scene investigation as a particular kind of work. Here the concern has been to establish the qualities that go into making a 'good' investigator and how to recruit the best sort of people for this particular type of work (Kelty 2012a,b), and the processes and collaborative efforts that constitute 'good practice' at the crime scene (Kelty et al. 2012). Top performing crime scene investigators tend to demonstrate certain personal and professional qualities. The seven top attributes or skill sets of these investigators include (Kelty 2012a):

1   cognitive abilities (e.g. lateral thinking)
2   knowledge base (e.g. university degree, but not necessarily in sciences or forensic science)
3   experience (e.g. real-life and lived experiences)
4   work orientation (e.g. genuine dedication to the role)
5   communication skills (e.g. active listeners with good negotiation skills)
6   professional demeanour (e.g. not judgmental nor easily influenced by external factors or people)
7   approach to life (e.g. creative and innovative, at work and at home).

How and to what end crime scene investigation is carried out is thus profoundly affected by the personal qualities and critical skills of the personnel undertaking the work.

Similarly, to process a crime scene effectively and professionally will require collaboration involving many different players (Julian et al. 2012). Decisions made by first responders to a crime scene (e.g. police officers, emergency service workers or members of the public) will have major implications for the collection of data, information and evidence. So, too, the more serious the crime, the more likely it is there will be multi-organisational interactions (Kelty et al. 2012). The more personnel involved, the more likely it is they will be multidisciplinary (law enforcement, medicine, law, forensic science) and multi-organisational (health, justice, private legal/medical and police). A large part of forensics activity, therefore, involves negotiating with many different professionals and agencies in order to secure appropriate and just outcomes. Crime scene investigation and the collection and processing of forensic evidence are far more complex than many lay people imagine, especially if perceptions of crime scene investigation are primarily based upon television depictions.

THE USE OF FORENSIC EVIDENCE IN COURT

Considerable attention has also been given within Australia to issues surrounding the use of forensic evidence in courts (Cashman & Henning 2012; Edmond 2008; Edmond & San Roque 2012; Wheate 2010) and the degree to which juries understand DNA evidence (Goodman-Delahunty & Hewson 2010a,b; Goodman-Delahunty & Wakabayashi 2012). Our particular focus here will be on the use of forensic experts.

Generally speaking, most jurisdictions have a range of rules governing experts and their evidence (Pepper 2013). These are found in various Acts relating, for example, to evidence and to civil and criminal procedure. Typically, for an expert's opinion to be admitted into evidence on a particular issue, three requirements must be fulfilled:

1   The expert must have *specialised knowledge* that they are able to demonstrate to the court is based on the person's training, study or experience, and the evidence must be wholly or substantially based on that specialised knowledge.
2   The expert is required to *set out the assumptions* upon which the opinion is proffered.
3   The expert must also *set out all the reasoning* they have engaged in to arrive at their conclusion (see Pepper 2013).

Importantly, the expert witness's paramount duty is meant to be to the court and not to any party to the proceedings.

In the specific area of forensics, it has been argued that if the evidence is not good enough, it should not be used at all (Edmond 2012; Edmond & Roberts 2011). The key issue is one of reliability. Thus, as argued by Edmond (cited in Berkovic 2011), evidence relating to fingerprints, bite marks, voice recognition and interpretation of footage from CCTV should not be allowed into court unless it is shown to be robust.

Part of the problem seems to be the reception of judges to the so-called experts: 'In circumstances that would seem to create a pressing need for the exclusion of incriminating expert opinion evidence that is not demonstrably reliable, judges seem to be largely oblivious to problems with opinion evidence produced by the institutionalised forensic sciences' (Edmond & San Roque 2012: 53). This is not a problem unique to Australia, as is evident in the finding of a National Academy of Science report in the United States on forensic science:

> The report finds that the existing legal regime—including the rules governing the admissibility of forensic evidence, the applicable standards governing appellate review of trial court decisions, the limitations of the adversary process, and judges and lawyers who often lack the scientific expertise necessary to comprehend and evaluate forensic evidence—is inadequate to the task of curing the documented ills of the forensic science disciplines. (National Academy of Science 2009: 3–1)

The problem is not simply one of inaccuracy or skewed knowledge. Within the context of an adversarial system of criminal law, the difficulties revolve around the question of experts and bias. According to the NSW Law Reform Commission (2005), there are three varieties of 'adversarial bias':

1 *Deliberate partisanship:* 'an expert deliberately tailors evidence to support his or her client'.
2 *Unconscious partisanship:* 'the expert does not intentionally mislead the court, but is influenced by the situation to give evidence in a way that supports the client'.
3 *Selection bias:* 'litigants choose as their expert witnesses persons whose views are known to support their case'.

In order to counter such biases and to ensure greater reliability on the part of experts, a range of measures have been suggested to control expert evidence (Edmond 2012; Parliamentary Office of Science and Technology 2005; Victorian Law Reform Commission 2008). Some of these include:

* limiting the number of expert witnesses to be called
* appointing single joint experts (i.e. one expert appointed jointly by the parties, sometimes referred to as the 'parties' single joint expert') or court-appointed experts
* permitting experts to give evidence concurrently in a panel format (often referred to as 'concurrent evidence' or 'hot-tubbing'), or in a particular order
* introducing a code of conduct to be observed by experts
* formalising processes for instructing experts and presenting experts' reports
* requiring disclosure of fee arrangements
* imposing sanctions on experts for misconduct.

In the United States, two sorts of tests are used to decide whether a piece of evidence can be submitted to the court (see Parliamentary Office of Science and Technology 2005; Victorian Law Reform Commission 2008). In essence, these provide some measure by which to establish a reliability threshold.

The *Frye test* requires that techniques have gained general acceptance in the scientific community to which they belong.

The *Daubert test* considers four factors:

1 whether the technique can be and has been tested
2 whether it has been subjected to peer review/publication
3 what the known or potential error rate is
4 whether the evidence has widespread acceptance in the scientific community.

In the United Kingdom, efforts have been put into developing training programs for expert witnesses (through organisations such as the Academy of Experts, Council for the Registration of Forensic Practitioners, Expert Witness Institute, Forensic Science Society and the Society for Expert Witnesses). There has also been support for establishing a Forensics Sciences Advisory Council in the United Kingdom to oversee the regulation of the forensic science market and provide independent and impartial advice on forensic science (e.g. reliability and admissibility of evidence, evaluation of novel forensic techniques and technology, ensuring standardised procedures for carrying out certain tests, and an accreditation system) (Parliamentary Office of Science and Technology 2005). Proposals for the setting up of a suitable advisory panel in Australia have also been made (Edmond 2012).

The growth in the use of forensic evidence in Australian courts over the past three decades has heightened concern that sufficient safeguards be put into place to guarantee as far as possible accurate outcomes based upon robust expert opinion. Close scrutiny of the use of forensic evidence has uncovered numerous problems and difficulties (Edmond & San Roque 2012). Looking to the future, there are calls for institutionalisation of and commitment to excellence, first-class science, accuracy and transparency when it comes to forensic evidence (Kirby 2010). In particular, it is argued that attention needs to be paid to issues such as:

*   *avoiding human error* (e.g. the problem of contamination)
*   *avoiding fraudulent error* (e.g. 'giving of presents' at a crime scene such as a cigarette butt containing the DNA of a suspect)
*   *maintaining rigour of analysis* (e.g. introduction of stricter standards)
*   *upholding supervisory regulation* (e.g. provision of effective supervisory bodies)
*   *securing transparency* (e.g. availability of relevant evidence to all parties).

As with crime scene investigators and crime scene investigation, there is a need to professionalise many aspects of expert evidence, and to forge strong ongoing relationships across diverse organisational areas such as law, forensic science and medicine.

DNA PROFILING AND THE LIMITATIONS OF FORENSICS

The importance of a critical study of forensic science and its incorporation into criminal justice systems is highlighted when specific types of data collection and particular types of crimes are analysed in detail. The following discussion of DNA testing provides an example that both illustrates contemporary developments in the use of forensic techniques, and the problems that may arise with their deployment.

Probably the most visible and popular forensic method today is that of DNA testing. This allows the individualisation or near-individualisation of biological evidence, by sampling discrete individuals and matching their specific DNA signature to relevant investigatory sites.

In the United States, the labour-intensive demands and sophisticated technology requirements of DNA testing have affected the structure of the forensic laboratory as has no other technology in the past 50 years (e.g. through the construction of data banks, and in the form of a backlog of samples requiring DNA analysis). The first public sector use of such testing was in late 1988. Meanwhile in the United Kingdom, the National DNA Database held just under 2.9 million samples from individuals and 237,500 profiles from crime scenes as of March 2005. Recent years have seen a great increase in budgets, in the number of crimes detected using the database, and in the decreasing costs and speeding up of 'turn around' process to just five days (compared with almost a year in 1997). DNA testing was first used in 1985 (McCartney 2006a,b). In Australia, DNA testing was first used in criminal proceedings in 1989 and, currently, tests are performed by private companies and state forensic laboratories. The year 2000 saw the establishment of the CrimTrac agency, a national DNA database (see Easteal & Easteal 1990; Gans & Urbas 2002).

Overall, the trend has been toward greater expenditure and greater reliance upon DNA testing within criminal justice (see Williams & Johnson 2008). In some ways, it has come to be seen as the public image of 'justice', even though more training and labs are needed, and its central place within criminal justice has a number of implications for police.

The use of DNA has been associated with a range of emerging policy and procedural issues in criminal justice (McCartney 2006a; see also Briody 2004; Cashman & Henning 2012). Consider, for example, the following developments:

*   DNA testing may be used in the form of targeted intelligence screenings (a large number of samples from a specific geographical area as part of investigative technique). For example, a violent crime

in a particular local area may be responded to by a call for mass screenings of all people who live, work or travel to that area. This can generate tensions between police concerns to catch criminals, and citizen concerns to protect their human rights. Mass screenings can be accompanied by police intimidation of those who refuse to provide a sample, reluctance on the part of some individuals to participate, a sense that such strategies make the whole population prove its innocence, and that it may all be a giant waste of money, particularly if no culprit is found (McCartney 2006a,b).

- DNA databases can also be used as intelligence tools, not simply to support cases against suspects already identified (McCartney 2006a). This can occur in several different ways. For example, in a strictly criminal justice context, convicted offenders may be forced to provide DNA samples to the database. As the database grows, it can be used to further understand individual criminal careers over time, and more generally to undertake projections and planning based upon DNA profiling. DNA identikits and familial searching (e.g. taking samples from a sibling or parent) can be used as investigative tools stemming from, and directly linked to, existing criminal histories.

- A known risk of DNA databases, however, is that coincidental matches can and do occur, despite DNA evidence being seen as reliable (Edwards 2006). This is more likely to happen when the crime stain gives a mixed or partial profile, or when people with matching profiles come from certain ethnic communities or are closely related. The implication of DNA databases for Indigenous people are particularly worrisome from the point of view of DNA false positives, and potential long-term stigmatisation due to their contact with the criminal justice system from a very young age (see Gardiner 2005). The chances of finding coincidental matches increases when the size of the database increases, when the number of loci (i.e. regions of DNA) compared are small, and if there is a possibility that the person who committed the crime is a relative of someone already in the database. Edwards (2006: 98) points out that the inventor of DNA profiling, Sir Alex Jeffries, believes that fifteen loci should be compared to prevent coincidental matches—yet, the standard practice in Australia until recently was to only compare nine loci.

- On the other hand, DNA testing can also more positively be used for the purposes of identification of bodies. Both in regards to victims of tsunami (i.e. humanitarian purposes) and victims of repression (i.e. crimes against humanity), Australian police have been active worldwide in assisting governments and United Nations agencies (see, for example, Baines & Kelly 2005). The work may be gruesome, but it is essential. It allows for families to know where their loved ones have had their final rest and, in some cases, for the wheels of justice to turn in relation to certain horrific crimes.

- Conversely, DNA testing has also been used for the purposes of exposing wrongful convictions within the criminal justice system. For example, the Innocence Project was created in 1992 in the United States, and there is now an established Australian Innocence Network. The aims and objectives of this network are to prevent, expose, correct and educate the public on wrongful conviction and other types of injustice within the criminal justice system. The project is premised on the idea that, in some cases, DNA testing of evidence can prove a client's claims of innocence. Where biological evidence that can be subjected to DNA testing is not available, there still may be scope to assist clients—but it was the science behind DNA testing that revealed the extent of wrongful convictions in the first place.

- The use of DNA evidence involves forensic skills in the collection of evidence from the crime scene. In some instances, this can be used to circumvent public cooperation by relying upon scientific methods rather than social networks and community participation. However, where there is greater reliance on this one technique rather than traditional police detection methods (e.g. admissions, use of informants and witnesses), this may lead to abbreviated or skewed investigations. Police may adopt a 'lazy approach' on the misunderstanding that DNA testing is all they need to secure a conviction. This misconstrues the nature of what DNA can actually prove (McCartney 2006a,b).

- Offenders can also respond to DNA procedures in ways that sidestep its effectiveness within criminal justice forums. For example, offenders may adopt countermeasures to avoid leaving DNA evidence, such as wearing gloves or burning a stolen vehicle after use. Popular movies and television programs that feature a strong forensic investigation theme provide plenty of warning of its dangers to a potential offender. Insofar as this is the case, DNA testing alone is insufficient to guarantee detection and conviction.

- Defence lawyers may use 'science' to bamboozle jurors; for example, in rape cases, by casting doubt on the 'match' of the police DNA sample and their client's DNA because of the complexities of DNA testing itself. What matters is not whether the scientific proof is valid, but whether juries can be convinced that the science does not allow for a judgment 'beyond a reasonable doubt'. Alternatively, there have been murder cases in which the jury asked the judge why the coat (which was covered in blood) had not been tested for DNA, even though the defendant had already admitted to being at the murder scene. In this instance, the lack of 'science' was seen as problematic, even though the requirements of justice had been fulfilled (MacDowell 2005; see also Briody 2004, 2002).

While there is no doubt that DNA testing is transforming the work of police, lawyers and judges alike, it should not necessarily be seen as the central pivot of criminal justice work. Rather, with DNA only able to be used in addition to other evidence, it is essential to have police that can investigate crimes using more traditional methods, and to continue to command public cooperation as they do so (see also Chapter 16).

ISSUES FOR CONSIDERATION

ESTABLISHING AUTHORITATIVE EXPERTISE: THE CLASH OF THE 'EXPERTS'

Informed expert evidence is used regularly in courts, in probation hearings and in tribunals. For instance, the preparation of pre-sentence reports in relation to specific young offenders is part and parcel of the work of juvenile justice workers. The reports are meant to be professional and independent, and to reflect the expertise of the worker in making evaluative judgments about the behaviour and activities of particular clients. Testimony by psychologists, psychiatrists, ballistics experts, toxicologists, forensic social workers and so on are intended to provide the court (or other decision-making forums) with unbiased expert opinion and factual material, which can then provide a scientific and rational basis for decision-making.

A key issue within criminal justice when it comes to forensic evidence, however, is that of determining relevant and authoritative 'expertise'. For instance, the one incident (e.g. an assessment of a defendant's state of mind/being in a murder trial) may generate different opinions among those who ostensibly share the same kinds of clinical training and expertise (i.e. psychologists, social workers or psychiatrists may well disagree with the diagnosis and opinion of their colleagues). How, then, are we to decide which 'expert' is right and which is not?

In another case, this time involving an assessment of the factors related to rock-throwing off of a highway bridge, the same incident may involve different opinions by different types of experts.

For example, engineering expertise may be drawn upon to make comment on bridge structures, fencing options and risk analysis; and sociological expertise would address who and why certain people may engage in rock-throwing as a general phenomenon. What happens, however, when the findings of each expert, from quite different fields, are at cross-purposes, and thus lead to different conclusions regarding risk and dangerousness?

In either of the examples above, the role of the court and its officials is to sift through the expert testimony and, through cross-examination, determine which expert is 'right' or 'wrong', given the facts and context of the specific case. This raises the question, however, of the competence and expertise of juries and of judges to evaluate expert evidence, especially if they are unfamiliar with the science and expert opinion at hand.

THE PRIVILEGING OF EXPERT 'VOICES'

Another issue relates to the manner in which certain types of evidence, and certain voices, are privileged in court proceedings above others. According to constructivist or postmodern criminology (see Chapter 5), there are competing discourses within the criminal justice system, with certain styles and modes of interaction dominating. Translated into a forensics context, the question of what evidence is allowable, and how expertise is defined, has major implications for matters involving, for example, sexual abuse (see Box 18.2). Close analysis of courtroom procedures and legal processes allows for the exposure of what, in retrospect and in the light of detailed examination, seem to be blatant cases of injustice.

An important area for research relates further to the interplay between different discourses in the field of forensics. What is of interest is how different sorts of practitioners (e.g. doctors, psychologists, biologists, chemists, lawyers and police) view the purposes and outcomes of forensic investigation. Each group may frame the issues and select what they feel to be of importance quite differently, depending upon their training, background, occupational perspective and institutional setting. This may periodically lead to professional tensions and/or conflicts over procedures and policies. For example, there may be divides within the field based upon differing notions of 'evidence' versus 'science', or 'justice' versus establishing 'guilt'. How diverse practitioners construct their role (e.g. to catch criminals, to treat patients or to establish scientific validity), the meaning that they give to terms that are commonly associated with their work (e.g. 'evidence') and how different actors communicate across the occupational divide are all matters warranting investigation.

BOX 18.2   EXPERTISE AND CONTESTED EVIDENCE

In the book, *Court licensed abuse: patriarchal lore and the legal response to intrafamilial sexual abuse of children*, Taylor (2004) provides a detailed examination of how 'evidence' is constructed in and by the court in cases involving the sexual abuse of children. The study documents many cases where barristers challenge the veracity and admissibility of evidence by mothers and children.

It is argued, for example, that the admissibility and reliability of any evidence that is not tape-recorded, such as a social worker talking with the accused for instance, is questionable. The point is that many barristers in sex-offence cases will use at times absurd (but nonetheless effective) arguments where credible evidence is considered damaging to their client. Judges may collude in this process: 'Rather than looking for evidence that supports "truth-seeking", the judiciary often creates evidentiary rulings and practices that are "truth-defeating" (Taylor 2004: 47).

Furthermore, Taylor contends that research on sexual-offence proceedings, including cases involving very young children, shows significant levels of aggressive and derogatory cross-examination. What counts as 'evidence' and how 'expertise' is constructed in the legal process tends to reflect a professional and patriarchal discourse that actively limits justice for those who have already suffered profound attacks on their bodily integrity and human dignity. Who ends up being on trial is a question of major concern.

Source: Taylor (2004)

CONCLUSION

This chapter has provided a brief introduction to forensic studies. At the heart of most forensic interventions is the question of evidence. The admissibility, reliability and validity of evidence, and how different kinds of evidence are marshalled for uses in detection, prosecution, sentencing, probation and crime prevention, are at the core of many of the techniques and processes associated with forensics. For anyone with an interest in criminal justice, the vast array of scientific activity related to the field ought to be of considerable interest.

The interface between science and law, and the study of social processes and social consequences pertaining to how this link is manifest in specific kinds of practices, are among the essential concerns of forensic studies. A critical evaluation of forensic interventions—from use of DNA testing and policing, to novel applications of technology to forestall environmental crime—is important, in that forensic intervention is always at one and the same time a social process. It involves people with different skills, capacities, insights and worldviews engaging in activities that directly and indirectly impact upon individuals and communities. The application of the scientific method is never socially neutral.

Chapter 19 continues to explore criminal justice functions and personnel, focusing on the law, which frames criminal justice operations, and the legal profession critical to its administration.

DISCUSSION QUESTIONS

1   What does 'forensic' mean?

2   Describe how forensic work is usually portrayed in the media, and especially in popular television programs. To what extent do popular representations of forensic tasks and technologies reflect what actually happens in real life?

3   Why is it important to distinguish between forensic science and forensic studies?

4   'Forensic evidence can be a problem as well as a solution'. Discuss.

5   'New areas of criminalisation and social harm demand new techniques of forensic investigation'. Discuss and provide examples.

FURTHER READING

Britz, M. (2009) *Computer forensics and cyber crime: an introduction*, Prentice Hall, Upper Saddle River.

Genge, N. (2004) *The forensic casebook: the science of crime scene investigation*, Ebury Press, London.

James, S. & Nordby, J. (eds) (2003) *Forensic science: an introduction to scientific and investigative techniques*, CRC Press, Boca Raton.

McCartney, C. (2006) *Forensic identification and criminal justice: forensic science, justice and risk*, Willan, Devon.

Willis, M. (2004) *Bushfire arson: a review of the literature*. Research and Public Policy Series, No. 61, Australian Institute of Criminology, Canberra.

19 LAW AND THE LEGAL PROFESSION

CHAPTER OVERVIEW

- LIBERAL DEMOCRACY AND THE LAW
- THE CONCEPT OF LAW
- LEGAL SYSTEMS
- MAKING THE LAW
- KEY PLAYERS IN THE LEGAL SYSTEM
- ISSUES FOR CONSIDERATION
- CONCLUSION
- DISCUSSION QUESTIONS
- FURTHER READING

INTRODUCTION

The law is an important instrument of social control and criminal justice, shaping and regulating almost all facets of societal relationships, both human and corporate. As such, it is crucial to understand the fundamental precepts and institutions of the law, and how these impinge upon human behaviour and interaction. As this chapter indicates, there are many different dimensions to the legal system as a whole, including: operational mechanisms such as the courts, parliaments, statutory authorities, and court-related administrative tribunals; legal personnel, including judges, solicitors and barristers, and legal culture; and legal processes, such as committal proceedings and trial. The relationship between the different components of, and actors within, the legal system is an important feature of how citizens' 'rights' are meant to be protected and 'justice' provided for in the courtrooms of the nation.

The purpose of this chapter is to lay the groundwork for an understanding of the operational aspects of criminal justice as it is presently administered in the Australian context. The chapter provides an introduction to the concept of law, both international and domestic, and a descriptive overview of the contexts of different legal systems, the central institutions that formally underpin legal processes in Australia, the various branches and divisions of the law, the creation of laws by legislatures, and the key personnel within the legal system.

LIBERAL DEMOCRACY AND THE LAW

Law in liberal democracies is generally premised upon a series of key concerns. 'Liberalism', in this context, refers to a philosophical framework that privileges individual rights above all else (but within certain defined limits). The catchcry of the French revolution was 'Liberty, Equality and Fraternity'. It is these kinds of ideals that are integral to liberal ideology, although how they are interpreted varies greatly within liberal thought. 'Democracy', in this context, refers to a form of representative parliament that places political power into the hands of elected members who make the laws.

There are two crucial ideas that underlie the legal system in societies such as Australia. These are **universal suffrage** and the **rule of law**. Universal suffrage refers to the idea that every person in society should be able to have a vote in relation to the selection of his or her political leaders. Those who make the laws—the legislators and legislature—are thus supposedly in a position to reflect the 'will of the people' if they are voted into government on this principle.

The history of universal suffrage is one of struggle to gain the voting franchise. For example, the transition from feudalistic relations to a capitalist system involved a change from 'divine rule of monarchs' to rule by 'the people', and hence parliament replaced the monarchy. However, it was much later that members of the non-propertied classes, especially working-class men, won the right to vote, and later still before women were able to gain universal suffrage for themselves. It was not until 1968 that Indigenous people as a whole were formally granted the right to vote in Australia.

The rule of law basically means that all should be treated alike: without fear or favour; rich or poor; male or female; established Australian or migrant. The law is to apply universally to all classes of people. By extension, the state itself is bound by its own laws and principles of law.

Liberalism, as an ideology, underpins our legal system, in contrast, for example, with socialism or fascism. Some of the key principles of liberalism are (see Bottomley et al. 1991):

* *Liberty*: this is a variable concept, with ongoing debates within the tradition of liberalism itself. Negative liberalism desires freedom from state interference. Positive liberalism desires freedom of movement and choice, thereby requiring state intervention to protect one's autonomy.

* *Individualism*: a focus on the individual is another hallmark of liberalism. Priority is given to individuals and individual rights over the collective. Differences exist, however, with respect to the amount of liberty desired.

* *Equality*: again, there are differing conceptions of equality. Formal equality suggests that all persons have an equal chance to become unequal. Substantive equality suggests that everyone be provided with resources necessary to maximise their own creative energies.

* *Justice*: there are competing notions once again within the liberal tradition as to the meaning of this concept. Formal justice refers to the rules and procedures that establish a grounding for the achievement of justice. Substantive justice means not only following the rules and procedures but also that there is equality of outcomes.

* *Rights*: it is assumed that by virtue of being human, people have rights to life, liberty and property. Central to this is the idea that all things can be subject to ownership by the individual unless there are justifiable reasons why this should not be the case.

* *Rationality*: this refers to calculation. People are seen as essentially rational beings, who calculate choices and then make rational decisions. Likewise, as a society, the liberal view is that action should be taken in accordance with rules of logic and based on factual knowledge.

* ***Utilitarianism***: this refers to the idea of judging acts and institutions on the basis of the maximisation of the general welfare of society; that is, proposals should be evaluated in the light of the greater aggregate interest. In some cases, this may mean that the 'general good' will be seen to outweigh specific instances of inequality for some people.

The law, as informed by liberalism, is constitutionally based; that is, we have government through and by the laws. Our legal system is apparently built on a liberal conception of rights and justice, but is this really the case? Does it guarantee the things it sets out to do? These questions will be addressed over the next three chapters.

UNIVERSAL SUFFRAGE
The idea that every person in society should be able to have a vote in relation to the selection of their political leaders. Those who make the laws are thus supposedly in a position to reflect the 'will of the people'.

RULE OF LAW
The rule of law within which all people should be treated alike: without fear or favour; rich or poor; male or female; established Australian or migrant. The law is to apply universally to all classes of people.

UTILITAR-IANISM
Judging acts and institutions on the basis of the maximisation of the general welfare of society (i.e. proposals should be evaluated in the light of the greater aggregate interest).

THE CONCEPT OF LAW

In a pluralistic society, where diverse and potentially competing interests abound, the law represents, in theory, an instrument applied equally to all its citizens regardless of their strength or power, which enables the balanced coexistence of disparate pursuits (Roach Anleu 2002). The law, which comprises both legal rules and legal institutions, performs the following functions (Marantelli 1994; Terry & Giungni 2003):

- *Harmonises difference*: legal institutions create rules that resolve individual and group differences by establishing codes of conduct acceptable to the majority of community members, thereby reducing the likelihood of disputes arising.
- *Provides a framework for resolving conflicts as they arise*: legal rules provide legitimate avenues of redress, through prosecution and litigation, to deal with instances of legal transgression. As such, the law encourages adherence to the established boundaries of permissible conduct and reduces the possibility of individuals resorting to violent means to settle legal disputes that may nonetheless arise.
- *Provides protection and consistency*: as a general principle, legal rules confer rights and impose obligations that seek to protect those rights. These rights and obligations are of a reciprocal nature, so that for every right bestowed on an individual and/or corporation, there is a corresponding obligation imposed on another individual and/or corporation or all community members, and vice versa. For example, barring some exceptions, such as vilification or hate speech, individuals generally have a right to free speech and are under obligation not to impede another's freedom of speech. Theoretically, rights and obligations apply equally to all members of a community, thereby ensuring consistency of treatment.
- *Provides certainty and stability*: contracts can be entered into by individuals or corporations in the knowledge that the laws governing the contractual agreement are certain and stable, and that there are avenues of compensation available should a party to the contract breach the terms of agreement.
- *Facilitates the achievement of common community goals*: there is rarely, if ever, unanimous agreement on the goals to be pursued by a society. Legal rules encourage collective action for the advancement of common interests. For example, the imposition of water restrictions in times of drought serves to compel societal conservation of an increasingly scarce natural resource vital to the community as a whole.
- *Expresses community values*: the law enunciates values and principles embraced by the majority of community members, such as liberty, individualism and social justice. Theoretically, there is a separation between law and morality, so that while incest and bigamy are considered illegal in Australia, adultery is not. Arguably, however, some laws, including those governing abortion, prostitution, euthanasia and the use of some illicit drugs, reflect moral judgments (see Stylianou 2010; see also Chapter 11).
- *Provides for legal change*: legal institutions, including the Commonwealth and state legislatures and superior courts, have the power to effect changes to legal rules. The Commonwealth Parliament also has the capacity to change its own power, structure and procedures through amendments to the Constitution.

According to Weber (1957), the law is distinguishable from other mechanisms of regulation, such as morality and convention, in that conformity is compelled through probable threat of sanction and recognition by those subjected to regulation that the specialised agents of law enforcement, who are employed to uphold the law (themselves bound by the law), act with legitimacy.

LEGAL SYSTEMS

The 'law' is neither immutable nor the same everywhere. The principles and operation of legal systems vary considerably from jurisdiction to jurisdiction (i.e. from local and state contexts through to national and international contexts). In discussing what 'law' is, therefore, it is important to recognise differences and similarities, divergences and connections, between law as it is practised in different social and geographical environments.

LEGAL JURISDICTION
INTERNATIONAL LAW

The legal gaze can be cast widely to include a worldwide perspective. **International law** is that body of law pertaining to the global community (see Box 19.1). It deals with relations between countries, issues relating to human rights, and international conventions and covenants intended to shape how each national government deals with political, legal and social issues (Lester & Pannick 2004; O'Brien 2004). Examples of international law that have implications for legal judgment and institutional processes in Australia include the International Covenant on Civil and Political Rights (1966), the Universal Declaration of Human Rights (1949), the United Nations Refugee Convention (1951) and the Convention on the Rights of the Child (1990).

UNITED NATIONS

Closely associated with international law is the United Nations (UN), a body with almost universal representation from among the world's nation-states, developed principally to guarantee world peace after two world wars. The UN generally sits in New York (or, occasionally, Geneva) and makes decisions that are intended to influence and shape government policies and actions around the world. Insofar as the United Nations supposedly represents 'world opinion' on a wide range of matters, it is sometimes presented as being the ideal global law-enforcement body, capable of adjudicating international disputes.

There are problems with this concept, however, because it has no mechanisms, such as an international armed force (army or professional police force), with which it can legitimately enforce its decisions. Consequently, it has been powerless to prevent horrific human rights violations, such as the ethnic cleansings in Rwanda and the former Yugoslavia in the early 1990s, which culminated in large-scale civilian massacres, rape and torture (Melvern 2002; Reiff 1995). Although the United Nations Assembly has passed resolutions and conventions, it is often the case that they have not been enforced, monitored or regulated. In fact, some of these resolutions have been systematically vetoed, including Security Council resolutions on the restoration of peace in the Balkan region following the division of the former Yugoslavia (1991), resolutions calling upon Israel to cease settlement activities in East Jerusalem (1999) and the destruction of property in the Middle East (2001). If the United Nations is to be an effective law-enforcement body, then appropriate mechanisms must be put in place so that it can actually enforce any resolutions passed (Pajá 2002).

INTERNATIONAL LAW
That body of law pertaining to the global community. It deals with relations between countries, issues relating to human rights, and international conventions and covenants intended to shape how each national government deals with political, legal and social issues.

BOX 19.1   TRANSNATIONAL LEGAL ISSUES

The particular relevance of international law now and into the future becomes apparent when we consider the following transnational issues beyond the capacity of any individual nation to resolve (A-Khavari 2003; Evans 2002; Head 2002b; Humphrey 2003; Kneebone 2004; Krasner 2001):

- The current *international climate of anxiety*, which has been heightened by the increasing frequency of: terrorist attacks (e.g. '9/11' attacks against New York City and Washington in 2001; Bali bombings, 2002; the bombing of the Australian embassy in Indonesia, 2004); military disputes (e.g. Afghanistan war, 2001; Iraq war, 2003); and regional conflicts in Eastern Europe (e.g. Ukraine conflict, 2014), the Middle East (Islamist unrest in Egypt, 2013–present), Asia (Israeli–Palestinian conflict, late 1948–present) and Africa (Darfur, 2003) in recent years. Also relevant is the possibility of legal (rather than military) avenues for conflict resolution, as well as trial of those engaged in war crimes (e.g. the current United Nations investigation into atrocities allegedly committed by combatants in Bosnia and Herzegovina).

- The *mass population displacements* engendered by: war; political, religious, and/or cultural persecution and violence (e.g. the ethnic warfare in Rwanda and other African regions); and long-term political and economic crisis (e.g. drought and other natural disasters such as the Indian Ocean tsunami that devastated twelve nations in December 2004). The US-declared 'war on terrorism', combined with armed conflicts in a number of countries around the world, has seen the world's refugee population (those forcibly displaced as a consequence of persecution, conflict, violence and human rights violations) exceed 51 million for the first time post World War II (UNHCR 2014), thus posing significant transnational challenges for the management of the increasing flows of refugee and asylum seekers (see also Humphrey 2003).

- The *globalisation of world economic relationships since the mid-1980s*, including the role of transnational corporations (those that trade and operate beyond national boundaries) and 'supernational' entities, such as the European Union, which has tended to blur national and state boundaries. Globalisation has integrated world economies, resulting in the rapid transformation of worldwide labour markets and accompanying shifts in labour participation processes between nation-states with resulting benefits and challenges (IMF 2014, 2007). The increasingly mobile nature of capital and labour has necessitated the establishment of laws relating to international economic transactions, taking into account the legal ramifications of decisions made by bodies such as the International Monetary Fund (IMF) and the World Trade Organization, and treaties such as the North American Free Trade Act and the Free Trade Agreement between Australia and the United States.

- The *environmental crisis*, which cannot be dealt with solely at the local level (e.g. in the Rhine, which cuts across a variety of national boundaries, clean-up operations would require enormous consultation and cooperation between numerous countries) and which will demand overarching regulation of some kind (see White 2011).

A further limitation of this world body is that the main source of power lies not in the General Assembly (which has representation from all member countries) but in the Security Council (which comprises a dozen or so countries, of which five are permanent members). The permanent members of the Security Council (the early nuclear powers of the United States, Russia, China, Great Britain, and France) each have veto powers in their own right. This means that just one vote of dissent from a permanent member can ensure that a majority decision of the General Assembly will not be officially endorsed or actionable as a United Nations resolution (Pajá 2002).

INTERNATIONAL COURT OF JUSTICE

This court replaced the Permanent Court of International Justice in 1946, and is based at The Hague in the Netherlands. It seeks to settle conflicts between nation-states in accordance with international law. It is presided over by fifteen experienced judges from around the world, elected to nine-year terms of office by the United Nations General Assembly and Security Council. Again, this body faces the problem of enforcement.

For example, in the 1980s the United States was brought before the court by a small Latin American country, Nicaragua, which accused the United States of bombing its harbours and producing a manual encouraging assassination and state terrorism (see Dixon 1985). The court ruled in favour of Nicaragua, but the Unites States refused to acknowledge the court's jurisdiction in the matter. This shows that legal adjudication in such forums is inherently political. There are many 'success' stories as well; that is, instances where conflicts over laws between nation-states, or disputes over national boundaries, have been resolved by the international court.

INTERNATIONAL CRIMINAL COURT

The most recent addition to the international regulatory armoury is the establishment of the International Criminal Court (ICC) in July 2002 (Bellamy & Hanson 2002; Diba 2002; Pajá 2002). The ICC, also situated in The Hague, is a permanent, independent court of justice, dedicated to prosecuting perpetrators of the most universally heinous criminal acts committed against the international community (e.g. war crimes, genocide, crimes against humanity and crimes of aggression). While considered a significant international advancement, a fundamental shortcoming of the ICC is that its jurisdiction is consensual in nature, extending only to nation-states acknowledging that jurisdiction. Moreover, the ICC will not be compelled to assume jurisdiction over cases in which amnesty from prosecution has been granted.

NATIONAL SYSTEMS OF LAW

Australia is regarded as a **common law** country. 'Common law' refers to a type of legal system that has incorporated many of the values, principles, procedures and rules developed initially in England (for a history of Australian law and its relationship to English law, see Castles 1982). For example, a range of measures has been developed to safeguard the rights of the accused, such as the presumption that a person is innocent until proved guilty. In contrast, other legal systems are premised on the idea that one is guilty until proved innocent.

Common law, as a system operating in places such as Australia, New Zealand, England, the United States and English-speaking Canada, can be distinguished from **civil law**, which operates in such places as France and Quebec. It can also be distinguished from systems that are based primarily on Islamic law, Hindu law or Aboriginal law, each of which has different procedures and practices. Of course, even within each of these systems, variances are great. For instance, Australian common law differs considerably in application from the United States system of common law. So, too, the application of Islamic law in Libya is different from that in Saudi Arabia or Iran.

COMMON LAW
A type of legal system that has incorporated many of the values, principles, procedures and rules developed initially in England (e.g. measures developed to safeguard the rights of the accused, such as the presumption that a person is innocent until proved guilty).

CIVIL LAW
Civil law generally involves cases dealing with two (or more) parties. A party can bring a civil action against another party, whom it believes has wronged them. The two branches of civil law are the law of torts and the law of contracts.

The notion of common law is also used in another sense (Chisholm & Nettheim 2002). Here it refers to the fact that law is, for the most part, created by the courts (i.e. judge-made or case law). The main sources of law in Australia are:

LEGISLATION
Laws made
in state
and federal
parliaments,
and referred
to as 'Acts' or
'statutes'.

- *Legislation*: laws made in state and federal parliaments, and referred to as 'Acts' or 'statutes'.
- *Delegated legislation*: subordinate authorities, such as statutory authorities (e.g. universities) and local government councils, are delegated authority by parliament to make laws, regulations and by-laws within a certain prescribed range of matters beyond the control of state or federal governments.
- *Common law*: judge-made law based upon tradition (commonly accepted customs) and judicial precedent, which looks to previous decisions in similar cases as a measure of how to adjudicate in the present.

The relationship between common law and statute law is close, because some parliaments (e.g. Queensland, Western Australia, New South Wales, Tasmania and the Northern Territory) have periodically codified (by statutory means) the common law (i.e. they have set it into specific legislative frameworks), while the courts play a significant role in making law through interpreting parliamentary legislation (Urbas & Bronitt 2002).

The common law system is based on an adversarial approach, whereby opponents (adversaries) argue their case, usually through legal representatives, before an independent arbiter; namely, a judge or a magistrate and, in some instances, a jury. This is in contrast to the inquisitorial system of law commonly used in civil law European countries, where the judge does not simply look at the arguments but also enquires into the case, acting as an inquisitor (calling witnesses and questioning them), taking an active, proactive and sometimes investigative role.

There is a third sense in which 'common law' is used as well. Historically, there was a distinction in England between common law and the law of equity (see Chisholm & Nettheim 2002). Equity law referred to cases dealt with by the Lord Chancellor, and covered those issues that were perceived as not being dealt with equitably by the common law courts (e.g. property and trusts).

DIVISIONS OF THE LAW

There are two broad divisions of law within the common law system (Carvan 2002; Chisholm & Nettheim 2002; Meek 1999; Terry & Giungni 2003):

1 *Private law* broadly deals with laws relating to obligations, and with the relationship between individuals and/or corporations. Private law includes such areas as contracts, company law, family law, property law and torts.
2 *Public law* deals with relationships between the state and the individual citizen. Included in this category are administrative law (which allows individuals to have their dealings with public bodies such as the Department of Social Security (Commonwealth) monitored or reviewed by judicial officers), constitutional law and criminal law. In terms of criminal law, crimes committed against individuals are conceived of as crimes that violate the sovereignty of the state by breach of law.

Within the common law, there is also a distinction between criminal and civil legal proceedings. The criminal law deals with conduct regarded as offensive to the collective interests and/or morality of society—as opposed to the direct 'victim(s)'—and punishable by the state or Crown, on behalf of the community. Criminal offences are divided into:

- *Summary offences*: relatively minor offences, such as driving offences, being drunk and disorderly, and shoplifting, which are brought before the lower courts as hearings (or enquiries). Accused persons (defendants) pleading not guilty are often prosecuted by a police prosecutor and the defended hearing takes place before a magistrate, in the absence of a jury. If the defendant pleads guilty, the magistrate determines an appropriate sentence at a mention hearing.

- *Indictable offences*: cases of a more serious nature such as rape, assault, armed robbery and murder, which, if contested by the accused, are tried in superior courts by a judge and jury. These offences are sought to be proven by the state via a crown prosecutor, and the trial generally takes place in a higher court (intermediate or supreme courts). Aside from the Commonwealth, Australian Capital Territory, Tasmania and Victoria, indictable offences are further subdivided into felonies and misdemeanours.
- *'Hybrid offences'* (*also referred to as 'triable-either-way offences'*): offences, such as theft involving small amounts of money, carnal knowledge and car theft, that can be tried either summarily or by indictment. Hybrid offences initially appear before the lower courts, but if the offence falls within the jurisdiction of the Magistrates' Court and the magistrate is agreeable, the accused is then given the option of having the matter heard summarily or proceeding to a higher court on indictment.

In criminal cases, the accused is presumed innocent until they are proven guilty. The 'burden of proof', also referred to as the 'onus of proof', is borne by the prosecution, who must generally prove the defendant's guilt 'beyond all reasonable doubt'. Some offences, however, have a lower standard of proof (see Brown et al. 1996a).

The civil law generally involves cases dealing with two (or more) parties, be they people, corporations, the state or any combination thereof. One party, who believes their rights have been infringed, brings a civil action or suit against another party, whom they believe has wronged them, consequently resulting in injury or loss. There are two branches of civil law:

1 *Law of torts*: concerned with the preservation of duties and obligations shared between members of a community, and the protection of these rights from injury or harm. Wrongs suffered when these duties and obligations are infringed are known as 'torts', which can result from a range of acts and/ or omissions, including negligence, defamation, nuisance and trespass.

2 *Law of contracts*: concerned with preserving contractual obligations (duties), as stipulated in legally binding agreements entered into between parties. Legal contracts may involve agreements between parties (e.g. a vendor and purchaser, and neighbours) obliging the performance of an act(s) or cessation of an act(s). When a contract has been breached (agreed actions have not been completed, have been completed poorly, or have been completed in an untimely manner), the law seeks to ensure that the innocent party is adequately compensated.

In civil matters, it is not the state that initiates proceedings against the accused, but rather the plaintiff (the injured party). In contrast to criminal actions, where the objective is to punish the offender, in civil proceedings the plaintiff seeks a remedy for infringement of their rights (e.g. personal safety, or one's good name or reputation) from the defendant, who seeks to defend the action by denying liability. Remedies come in two forms: compensation for the injury or loss suffered, in the form of payment of damages; or an injunction, which is an authoritative warning prohibiting the defendant from continuing to engage in the injurious action(s), or committing threatened wrongful actions, or an order compelling a defendant to complete an agreed transaction or fulfil a contract (specific performance order). Aside from Victoria, civil cases in most Australian jurisdictions do not make use of a jury.

In civil proceedings, the burden of proof required to establish liability rests with the plaintiff, and the defendant does not enjoy the presumption of innocence. The standard of proof also differs from that generally prevailing in criminal jurisdictions. In order to bring a successful action against the defendant, the plaintiff must prove their case on the 'balance of probabilities' (a greater than 50 per cent probability), which is a lower threshold of proof than that required in criminal proceedings. The rationale for these key differences in the protections offered defendants in criminal and civil proceedings is that the defendant in civil matters does not face the potential risk of loss of liberty (through incarceration), only monetary loss, and hence rigorous safeguards are not required.

Importantly, an act may result in both criminal and civil proceedings (see Box 19.2). For instance, an assault occasioning injury may result in a criminal action designed to punish the offender for the assault, and a civil action aimed at recovering compensation for the injuries sustained. In such situations, the criminal action precedes the civil action and the outcome is deemed inadmissible evidence in any ensuing civil case. Increasingly, in the United States for example, women who have been raped (and who may experience a form of double victimisation due to the rigours and biases of criminal proceedings) are being encouraged to redress criminal offences through civil actions. By taking the latter course, the probabilities of success are greater (due to the lower standard of proof required—a preponderance of evidence rather than 'beyond all reasonable doubt' and the removal of some legal protections from the accused), and the women have the opportunity to be an equal player (rather than simply a passive victim relegated to witness status in a crime perpetrated against society) and achieve some form of justice (in the form of compensation) for their suffering (Graycar & Morgan 1999; McElroy 2004).

BOX 19.2   CRIMINAL AND CIVIL LAW CROSS-OVERS

One of the most celebrated landmark examples of the cross-over between criminal and civil law is the OJ Simpson case. Simpson, a national American football star, was accused of murdering his ex-wife, Nicole, and her friend, Ron Goldman, in June 1994. In October 1995, he was acquitted by a jury of all murder charges and cannot be retried in a criminal case (known as the 'double jeopardy' rule). The murder trial was, however, followed by a successful wrongful death civil suit initiated by the families of the victims, resulting in a superior court jury awarding punitive damages of at least US$8.5 million (A$11 million) and potentially a further US$25 million (A$33 million) against Simpson in 1997.

Source: Ayres & Gonzales (1997); Domestic Violence Benchbook (1995); Reed (1997); Reuters (1997); Stuart (1997);

MAKING THE LAW

Laws in society are made in two main places: parliament and the courts (Crawford & Opeskin 2004; Henderson 1988; Wilmott & Dowse 2002). Changes to the law have their origins in a wide variety of sources. They include, for example, lobby and pressure groups, media, trade unions, business organisations, and governmental pressure in the form of departmental requests. Law Reform Commissions (federal and state) are another source of legal change, although in some states they have been abolished. Legislative changes also can be initiated through various government agencies and departments. Deficiencies in existing legislation may be sought to be remedied in this fashion, or the law may be broadened or narrowed to take into account the actual implementation of laws at a practical level (Wilmott & Dowse 2002).

LEGISLATION

Parliament performs an essential function in Australia, in that the powers granted to the Commonwealth via the Constitution, including the power to make laws, are vested in the parliament. It is therefore the supreme law-making body. At a formal level, it is the elected members of parliament who are meant to play a large role in changing the law democratically, through canvassing community opinion on various issues and passing relevant legislation through the parliament (see Commonwealth of Australia 2012; Meek 1999). For all intents and purposes, however, it is the executive wing of government— in particular the cabinet, made up of key Ministers of the Crown, including the Prime Minister or Premier—that is the major decision-making body of government. It is here that the main outline of policy and law-making is mapped out and given first, and final, approval.

Once a legislative issue has been finalised via cabinet discussion and background briefing from the relevant department(s) within the public service, full public debate can ensue. Materials are forwarded to the Office of Parliamentary Counsel, so that the legal personnel can draft the proposed legislation. The draft legislation (a Bill) is then presented to the legislation committee of cabinet, to ensure conformity with cabinet's original approval, and then to the government committee, prior to final consideration by a full meeting of the government parties. It is after this exhaustive process that the Bill is initiated into parliament by a relevant minister giving notice of an intention to move or introduce the Bill. Upon introduction into the legislature, a Bill is subjected to three readings (this occurs in the lower house in cases where there are two houses of parliament):

- *First reading*: the draft legislation is literally read to parliament and circulated to members.
- *Second reading*: the broad principles and concepts of the proposed legislation are explained by the relevant minister and the Bill is debated.
- *Committee stage*: an all-in discussion occurs, whereby each clause of the Bill is read, debated and voted upon. Details of the Bill are tightened up and amended in light of previous discussions.
- *Adoption of the report of the committee*: a mere formality, whereby each house is asked to accept the report of the Committee of the Whole House.
- *Third reading*: the final opportunity for further debate and/or amendment prior to parliament voting on the Bill as a whole.

If the Bill is passed, the matter is subsequently transferred to the upper house (if there is one) where it undergoes a further three readings. If the Bill is again passed, it proceeds to the Governor-General (or, at the state level, the Governor), who assents to it. It thus becomes an Act of parliament, with a due date for proclamation. An Act of parliament does not actually become law until it has been officially proclaimed.

Delegated legislation, as mentioned above, refers to the transferring of power and authority to government instrumentalities (e.g. universities or local councils), so that they can create by-laws and rules of their own under specified guidelines.

Judge-made law and the protections of due process will be discussed in Chapter 20.

KEY PLAYERS IN THE LEGAL SYSTEM

The legal system is complex and covers a wide range of issues and social interactions. In addition to armies of secretaries, court reporters, photocopiers, bailiffs, transportation officers, social workers and volunteer information providers, there is a series of key legal positions within the administrative apparatus of criminal justice (see Chisholm & Nettheim 2002; Fitzroy Legal Service 2013; Meek 1999).

JUDGES

As indicated earlier, the role of the judge in contested matters is to act as an independent adjudicator, ensuring that the opposing parties follow correct evidentiary and procedural rules. At the conclusion of a trial or hearing, the judge addresses the jury, which involves summarising the central arguments raised by both parties and instructing and/or advising on the relevant principles of law to be applied. Once the jury arrives at a decision, the judge, formally referred to as 'Your Honour', pronounces sentence or, in the case of a civil matter, makes an order or awards damages.

Judges are appointed by the Governor-General in Council (federal), or Governor in Council (state), on advice from the government of the day (through its executive arm, the cabinet) in consultation with the president of the Bar Association and other eminent members of the legal profession. Although the Constitution does not specify the qualifications or background required for appointment to the judiciary, nor require an appointee to be qualified as a lawyer, those appointed as judges are mainly drawn from the mainstream of barristers of high professional standing. The rationale offered for the large salaries paid to judges is based on two assumptions:

1   If such persons were still in private practice, then they would be receiving very high incomes, based upon their extensive experience. Hence, in order to attract persons of the highest calibre to public positions, the remuneration must be comparatively favourable.

2   High salaries are said to prevent the possibility of bribery and corruption. Security of tenure until the statutory age of retirement (70 for federal judges, 65 for family law judges and those appointed to Fair Work Australia and variable (70–75) for state judges), protection from suit, and high income are meant to guarantee judicial neutrality, which is a fundamental principle of the 'rule of law' that guarantees all persons equality before the law (Spigelman 2001).

A QUESTION OF OBJECTIVITY

Although ostensibly selected on 'merit', judges have generally been drawn from a very narrow range of the population. By and large, the judiciary is homogenous in composition, dominated by male, white conservatives, the product of private school education, Anglo–Saxon in descent or origin, and part of 'the establishment' (ALRC 1994a; Davis & Williams 2003; Senate Standing Committee on Legal and Constitutional Affairs 1994). Given this profile, questions have been raised as to whether the social background of most judges causes them to judge 'ordinary' people coming before them according to that background, or whether they can judge individuals objectively. The composition of the legal profession (e.g. class background, religion, ethnicity, gender and nationality) undoubtedly has an impact on the decisions that are made. This has implications for the idea that the legal profession is neutral in the way in which it dispenses justice (see Chapter 20).

Further to this, and as intimated earlier, it is important to acknowledge that while the independence of the judiciary is a principle fundamental to the doctrine of separation of powers, in essence the appointment of judges is an intrinsically political process; it often hinges upon the connections different individuals have to elite networks existing within both the legal profession (chamber circles) and the government itself, making it especially difficult for women and those of ethnic minority background to achieve appointment on merit (McHugh 2004; Malleson 2002; Meek 1999). The practical manifestations of this process are clear, with Australia's High Court consisting entirely of male judges until the appointment of Mary Gaudron QC in 1987 (Davis & Williams 2003). Since its formation in 1903, there have only been four women justices appointed, three of these from 2005 to 2009.

TRAINING AND ASSISTANCE

Historically, an individual appointed as a judge was expected to have served a reasonable time in legal practice, and further formal, substantive training was not really provided. This convention assumed that having acquired professional and practical competency, knowledge, skills and experience of legal procedures through general practice, a judgeship could be taken on virtually immediately, without specific training (barring a short induction period). In relatively recent times, however, there has been a growing recognition of the importance of professional development and education for the judiciary, especially in light of their lengthy tenure and the increasing complexity of law.

Awareness that the administration of justice requires more than professional and practical competence has led to the establishment of various agencies in Australia dedicated to assisting judges in their duties and in the management of the courtroom process (Gleeson 2003; Spigelman 2001). For example, the Australian Institute of Judicial Administration, a research and education body established in 1986 and based in Victoria, offers a range of courses and services for judges, magistrates, tribunal members, court administrators, legal practitioners, academics and others with an interest in judicial administration, on diverse topics including sentencing, the conduct of civil and criminal trials, evidence procedures, culture and gender awareness, case management, court management, relationships between the judiciary and the executive, and family law. The Judicial Commission of New South Wales, also established in 1986, provides a more formal judicial training and continuing education program, organising conferences and seminars covering various subjects, including pre-bench training for newly appointed magistrates, as well as educational information, materials and a monthly journal. An equivalent body, the Judicial College of Victoria, was established in 2002.

Calls for the establishment of a body dedicated to the provision of systematic and uniform judicial education for the entire Australian judiciary (ALRC 2000) culminated in the creation of the National Judicial College in 2002. The college is principally concerned with the professional development of judicial officers (federal, state and territory), including orientation training for new judicial appointees and ongoing training for existing judicial officers. Interestingly, the annual budget allocated to the college in its first year of operation was $318,000, compared with the then $4.2 million annual budget of the Judicial Commission of New South Wales (Gleeson 2003).

Some commentators cite evidence of intrinsic sexism, non-legal biases, social disparities and general inequalities built into our system of justice (see, for example, Brown et al. 1996a,b; Easteal 2001; Graycar & Morgan 2002; Scutt 1990). Accordingly, they argue for the inclusion of more specific training or preparation on issues such as gender and cultural bias in judicial induction and professional development curricula. Various jurisdictions have responded to such calls by offering workshops that are intended to change existing judicial attitudes, and to give judges a better understanding of the lives and outlooks of people outside their immediate social experience. While there has been some resistance to the notion of judges undergoing additional training, particularly from within the judiciary itself (see Tedeschi 1994), some jurisdictions, such as Victoria, mandate post-admission continuing legal education (Victorian Department of Justice 2004a).

MAGISTRATES

The appointment of magistrates varies from state to state. In some states it used to be the case that magistrates were untrained and unpaid justices of the peace, drawn from the ranks of the public service. These individuals did not necessarily have any formal legal training. This situation has changed, and magistrates now possess legal training and legal backgrounds, although in some states unpaid bail justices can make minor decisions. In most jurisdictions, justices of the peace are now restricted to signing official documents, such as statutory declarations.

Magistrates, who are formally referred to as 'Your Worship' in court, tend to hear the less serious criminal and civil cases, and disputes relating to debts and tenancy questions. Magistrates also tend to be paid less than judges, enjoy lower status and presumably have less legal experience, both in terms of expertise and practice.

ATTORNEY-GENERAL

The position of Attorney-General is held by an elected member of parliament and minister of the Crown, who is the chief legal officer in a particular jurisdiction. In some states, the Attorney-General makes the final decision on whether to prosecute certain cases, or to determine whether contempt of court has occurred.

SOLICITOR-GENERAL

This is a non-political position, and is a principal adviser to the Attorney-General. It is held by a public servant whose duty it is to provide legal advice to the government.

DIRECTOR OF PUBLIC PROSECUTIONS

This is an employee of the state who performs the function of Crown lawyer. As a non-political public servant, the Director of Public Prosecutions (DPP) is meant to select cases for prosecution 'without fear or favour', and to organise the actual court action on the part of the Crown.

CROWN SOLICITORS

This is a broad general term. Crown solicitors include those employed by the DPP who, as Crown prosecutors, are responsible for representing the state with respect to indictable matters. Crown solicitors also include permanent public servants who act as advisers to the government, and parliamentary counsel, whose job it is to draft legislation in the appropriate legal form for presentation to parliament.

PRIVATE LEGAL PRACTITIONERS

Apart from the principal decision-makers and legal personnel employed by the state, there are also lawyers, most of whom are employed in private practice. Here we can make a number of distinctions, such as that between solicitors and barristers, although not every state divides the profession in this way. Historically, solicitors were associated with the Court of Chancery, the proctor was associated with the ecclesiastical courts (Christian religious courts) and attorneys were associated with common law courts (Chisholm & Nettheim 2002; Meek 1999).

SOLICITORS

Solicitors have ordinarily graduated from university with a law degree and spent time in a solicitor's office as an articled clerk or engaged in some alternative form of postgraduate practical legal training. They participate in many kinds of legal work, either on their own or in partnership with others, and sometimes in a firm. Although solicitors take part in some litigation practices at the lower court levels, the bulk of their work is spent dealing directly with clients, providing legal advice and drafting specialised legal paperwork, including wills, agreements, contracts and conveyancing documentation.

In complex criminal and civil matters proceeding to court, solicitors spend considerable time researching and preparing a brief (a collection of instructions) for barristers, containing a complete overview of the case, including the facts of the case, relevant documents and other materials (e.g. contracts and medical reports), witness details, and a summary of their likely evidence and anticipated crown and plaintiff arguments. Solicitors are usually members of the Law Society.

BARRISTERS

The term 'barrister' stems from the word 'narrator' (someone who tells a story). Consistent with the term's historical origins, barristers are considered experts at pleading a case in common law courts on behalf of their clients. Barristers are law graduates who, having spent time gaining experience in a law firm, fulfil the conditions to be 'admitted' to the Bar, which is the table from which a barrister argues a client's case in court. Aside from litigation, barristers also advise solicitors on questions of law and the settlement of court documents. The legal system has developed in such a way that solicitors are backroom persons, while barristers, who act on the information prepared by a solicitor, are in charge of the conduct of a trial in court. Barristers do not deal with clients directly, but instead do so indirectly through a solicitor. Barristers practise on their own, not in partnership nor through a firm. Generally, they share 'chambers' with other barristers. Instead of being members of the Law Society, barristers are members of the Bar Council, or Bar Association.

Barristers who have spent between 10 to 15 years practising in the profession can apply to take 'silk' (the term comes from their robes). If accepted, the title of Queen's Counsel (QC) (or Senior or Leading Counsel) has traditionally been conferred. In 2003, appointment of new QCs was suspended with many jurisdictions moving to abolish the title (e.g. in New South Wales, Queensland, the Australian Capital Territory and Victoria), and replacing it with the non-royalist 'Senior Counsel' (SC). A decade later, both Victoria and Queensland reintroduced the title and similar moves are currently being considered in NSW, Tasmania, Western Australia and New South Wales.

Appointments to senior counsel are made by the Governor, on the advice of the Attorney-General; as in the case of judicial appointments, this is clearly a highly political process. Since Queen's Counsel/Senior Counsel are recognised as respected senior members of the profession, when they appear in court their services are extremely expensive. This is the case because, until recently, they always had to be accompanied by a junior barrister. This practice of course raises questions about legal costs—if you want the best legal service representing you, then you must pay for the services of two individuals.

ISSUES FOR CONSIDERATION

'AUSTRALIAN' LAW

Not all 'law' in Australia is Australian law. This is especially the case when we consider the unique circumstances surrounding the relationship between Indigenous people and Australian legal institutions. A perennial and continuing dilemma for Indigenous peoples, and for Australian legislatures and courts, is how to grapple with the intersections of two laws: one historically grounded in the traditions of Indigenous people and that continues to have contemporary relevance in their lives, the other arising from the introduction of English and later Australian law into this part of the world. The importance of Indigenous law to Indigenous people is indicated in Box 19.3. The place of Aboriginal customary law is an issue that goes to the core of the colonial relations between the Australian state and Indigenous people. The acknowledgement, validation, interrelationships and dynamics of the two law systems warrant serious and critical scrutiny, as does legal reform that formally recognises Aboriginal customary law among Aboriginal people while retaining key elements of both Australian law and emergent international human rights law.

BOX 19.3   ABORIGINAL CUSTOMARY LAW

In the book *Restorative visions: crime, Aboriginality and the decolonisation of justice*, Harry Blagg provides a trenchant and powerful overview and critique of the intrusions of colonial power into Indigenous communities (Blagg 2008a). Here and elsewhere (Blagg 2008b: 137), it is emphasised that in many communities around the country:

- Aboriginal law still governs many aspects of daily life for many Aboriginal people, providing the maps of meaning that make communal life possible and predictable.
- Law provides an overarching framework of rules and obligations, forms of penalty and censure, codes of conduct, etiquette and address.
- It informs people about with whom they can associate and under what conditions, as well as their obligations and relationships to those around them.
- There is widespread support for greater recognition of Aboriginal law.

Indigenous forms of law, therefore, are still generally respected and practised by Indigenous people. As Blagg (2008b: 141) emphasises: 'The politics of liberation needs to be reconstructed to include the politics of tradition', building on traditional law and culture and the authority of elders. This can be achieved through widespread adoption of community justice mechanisms that include such things as Aboriginal courts, community patrols, family healing and Indigenous community programs.

Source: Blagg (2008a,b)

MANAGEMENT OF REFUGEE POPULATIONS

In a global climate preoccupied with stemming the terrorist threat, our international system of refugee protection, enshrined in the 1951 United Nations Refugee Convention, appears to be in crisis (Humphrey 2003). The quest to protect national borders against the threat of 'unauthorised entry' has witnessed the elevation of state interests over collective international responsibility for individual human rights, and a recasting and criminalisation of refugee and asylum seekers from humanitarian casualty to national sovereignty and security threat (often associated with terrorism).

Australia's management of refugee and asylum seekers, in particular, has generated considerable controversy in recent years (Head 2002a,b; Humphrey 2003; McCulloch 2004; Pickering 2005; White 2002). In 2001, the Australian Government introduced the *Border Protection (Validation and Enforcement Powers) Act* to deal with the refugee 'crisis' precipitated by the arrival of the MV *Tampa*, a Norwegian cargo ship carrying over four hundred asylum seekers (predominantly

Afghani, Iraqi and Iranian), rescued off Australia's coast when their vessel sank. These laws, premised on the principles of containment and repatriation, involve:

- a literal redrawing of Australia's territorial waters, through excising outlying islands (Cocos Islands, Ashmore Reef and Christmas Island), thereby making it more difficult for asylum seekers to enter Australia's official migration zone
- military interception of suspected 'people-smuggling' vessels approaching Australian waters
- dispatch of intercepted asylum seekers to detention centres on the Pacific islands of Nauru and Manus (the 'Pacific solution').

Since August 2012, people arriving in Australia by boat seeking asylum, and without a valid visa, are subjected to third country processing at an 'excised offshore place' (e.g. Christmas Island). Current government policy requires detention of anyone entering Australia without a valid visa. Australia is the only country worldwide to mandate the detention of asylum seekers through a policy of strict enforcement.

These laws clearly abrogate a number of traditional legal doctrines, including the 'rule of law' and international humanitarian laws and conventions. With respect to these issues, the award-winning book *Globalization and borders: death at the global frontier* (Weber & Pickering 2011) provides a powerful and moving account of border-related deaths in Australia. This work demonstrates how border deaths are hidden by state practices, and it raises even more questions about responsibility, accountability and morality in the treatment of 'illegalized travellers' (Weber & Pickering 2011).

NATURE OF THE LEGAL PROFESSION

Other issues of relevance to this chapter stem from the nature of the legal profession, which tends to be a very close-knit association that generally regulates and runs itself. In recent years, serious questions have been raised (see Duncanson 1991; Law Council of Australia 2004; van Caenegem 2003; Weisbrot 1990) regarding such issues as:

- *Curricula in law faculties*: the formulation of these curricula, their narrow and conservative nature, and their emphases on organisational and technical aspects of law tend to focus on the resolution of adversarial disputes rather than social aspects of legal education.
- *Admission process into the profession*: the criteria used to determine who becomes a lawyer, what hurdles need to be crossed, and who actually makes or should make decisions regarding entry into the profession. Also important to consider are issues pertaining to higher education costs and the related matters of affordability and equity.
- *Nature and costs of legal services*: the potential use of paralegal representation in courts and tribunals, as a means of reducing costs, and the transfer of more mundane legal work (e.g. property conveyancing) to non-lawyer specialists (see Chapter 22).
- *Language adopted by legal personnel*: the distancing of lawyers from their clients and people in general, and the implications this has for the administration of justice.

The relationship between the specific social meanings of criminal and civil law raises some important issues. For example, many victims of sexual assault look for the gravity of the offence to be demonstrated by conviction of the offender in the criminal courts. However, the processes of criminal justice (e.g. the traumatic process of giving evidence against defendants and being subject to personal scrutiny), and recent sentencing outcomes (e.g. in 2002–03 one in ten rapists convicted in Victoria received a wholly suspended sentence (Munro 2004d)), may deter some women from pursuing this option. While the civil law offers an alternative avenue for pursuing justice, important symbolic markers of social harm and social denunciation may be lost in those instances where women end up pursuing their cases via civil suits (e.g. see Barnett 1995).

CONCLUSION

This chapter has provided a broad overview of the Australian legal framework and apparatus. It began by describing key elements of liberalism and the law, and the international and national institutions of law. This was followed by a summary of the different divisions and branches of law, and the main ways in which the law is made in Australian society. The final part of the chapter detailed the main legal players within the criminal justice system and raised issues regarding the neutrality and impartiality of our legal representatives. Our concern in Chapter 20 is to examine more closely the nature of courts and court-related processes.

DISCUSSION QUESTIONS

1   What are some of the general purposes of law?

2   Why are international concerns becoming more central to the law at a national, regional and local level?

3   What are the key differences between criminal law and civil law?

4   Is it necessary that legal practitioners, including judges, have high social status in order that the law be respected and administered fairly?

5   'Indigenous law exists and it ought to be the foundation for the administration of justice among Indigenous people and Indigenous communities'. Discuss.

FURTHER READING

Blagg, H. (2008) *Restorative visions: crime, Aboriginality and the decolonisation of justice*, Hawkins Press, Sydney.

Commonwealth of Australia (2000), *Legislation handbook*, Department of the Prime Minister and Cabinet, Commonwealth of Australia, Canberra, <www.dpmc.gov.au/guidelines/docs/legislation_handbook.rtf>.

Fitzroy Legal Service (2013) *The law handbook*, Fitzroy Legal Service, Melbourne.

O'Brien, J. (2004) *International law*, Cavendish, London.

Weber, L. & Pickering, S. (2011) *Globalization and borders: death at the global frontier*, Palgrave Macmillan, Basingstoke.

COURTS AND COURT PROCESSES

CHAPTER OVERVIEW

- THE PROTECTIONS OF DUE PROCESS
- THE COURTS
- INTERPRETING THE LAW
- A QUESTION OF IMPARTIALITY
- ISSUES FOR CONSIDERATION
- CONCLUSION
- DISCUSSION QUESTIONS
- FURTHER READING

INTRODUCTION

The previous chapter described the legislative arm of lawmaking. Besides legislation, the other manner in which the law is made in practice is through judicial decision-making. That is, what judges do in the courts also constitutes a form of law making. The aim of this chapter is to provide a description of the system of law courts in Australia. We begin with a discussion of 'due process', and later will discuss the notion of 'judicial impartiality', since these are meant to be key aspects of a system intended to promote and protect legal equality and procedural fairness.

THE PROTECTIONS OF DUE PROCESS

At a formal criminal justice level, the protections and rights associated with a liberal form of legality (see Chapter 19) are in the first instance meant to be guaranteed by certain due process rights.

In this regard, a system of due process of law has developed as a formal means to guarantee the impartiality and neutrality of the tribunal. In Australia, due process of law is not guaranteed by the Constitution. Indeed, Australia is the sole major common-law country not possessing a Bill of Rights, Charter of Human Rights and Responsibilities, or other form of legislative mechanism that systematically enshrines the protection of our civil rights and liberties (Cowdery 2001; Victorian Department of Justice 2004a). Notwithstanding this fact, our well-established tradition of parliamentary democracy is regarded as adequately protecting the ingrained aspects of the traditions and conventions of 'common law'. Thus, concepts such as the accused being 'innocent until proven guilty', that all those providing testimony do so with full 'voluntary consent', that the officials of the Crown (e.g. the police) be 'publicly accountable' for their own behaviour and actions, and that there be 'unbiased judgment' in deciding cases are all fundamental principles underlying English and Australian legal institutions.

The fundamental role of due process and the upholding of the ideals of 'natural justice' is to ensure that no person be judged unheard—there must be a hearing and it must be fair. How do we guarantee that this will occur in a substantive way? In Australia, the key elements of due process are as follows (see Chisholm & Nettheim 2002; Fitzroy Legal Service 2013).

NOTICE MUST BE GIVEN

Persons must have sufficient knowledge, in advance, of the case to be answered. That is, the person must be informed as to why they are going to court (i.e. the charges), and they must be provided with sufficient time to prepare their defence.

PUBLICITY

Judicial proceedings are normally conducted in open court, since court proceedings are seen as public matters. The reason this occurs is to avoid 'inquisition' situations, where 'justice' is arrived at behind closed doors, with few public checks and balances upon judicial power. Under the principle of publicity, for justice to occur, justice must be seen to be done. There are, however, exceptions to this rule, and the court may either be cleared or testimony given 'in camera' (behind closed doors, with bans on publishing of the proceedings). For instance, this may happen on occasions where the public disrupts proceedings; where witnesses are afraid or embarrassed to give evidence in open court, such as in situations of sexual assault, child abuse or instances of intimidation; where evidence being heard is of a secret or security-related nature, such as Australian Security Intelligence Organisation information or police undercover work; and, in the case of proceedings involving children under the age of 17, where there are usually safeguards to protect the identity of both victims and young offenders from public exposure.

STANDARDS OF PROOF

These have developed over time. Historically, it has been the plaintiff and prosecution that bear the onus of proof. In civil cases, the plaintiff must prove their case on the balance of probabilities, while in criminal cases, the onus of proof lies with the prosecution, who must wholly prove their case beyond reasonable doubt.

EVIDENCE AND RULES GUIDING EVIDENCE

There are extensive rules that determine what is allowable as legal evidence. For example, confessions to police must be made voluntarily and persons must be warned beforehand of their rights. People must be informed that they are not obliged to say anything, and that anything they may say can be used against them in a court of law.

At the stage of determining the guilt or innocence of the accused, previous charges laid and the criminal history of that individual cannot wholly be used against them. However, at the sentencing stage, past records of offending behaviour or criminal convictions can be examined, and are influential in the determination of penalties to be imposed (see further Chapter 23).

Hearsay evidence, which crudely translated into non-legal parlance simply means 'gossip', is only admissible under certain conditions (e.g. much police testimony is in the form of hearsay evidence). Generally speaking, it is usually only direct, first-hand observations and accounts that are accepted as legitimate legal evidence. As part of the adversarial approach, each party is given the opportunity to tender evidence before the court (and jury) and to cross-examine the other side so as to raise objections or clarify matters.

IMPARTIALITY

Used in a specific procedural sense, impartiality fundamentally means that people are not allowed to be judges in their own cause. For instance, a judge who owns shares in BHP would not be permitted to preside over a matter coming before them that involved that company. In such circumstances, the judge would have to excuse or disqualify themselves, since they have a direct interest in the case. This principle applies also in situations where the accused is a friend or relative of the judge. It would be absurd, for example, for a judge to sit in judgment of their own daughter or son.

The ideal of impartiality is also reflected in the right of automatic challenge of potential jury members by the lawyers on each side of a case. This mechanism enables the prosecution and the defence to actively shape the composition of the jury, with the ideal result being some degree of impartiality.

TRIAL BY JURY

It is the role of the jury to decide the facts of the case in light of the way in which the judge has presented the law. People who sit on the jury are chosen from the electoral roll. Some individuals who receive notices to serve can apply for exemption. It is important to acknowledge that, in fact, a minority of cases actually involve juries (see Chapter 23).

Once attending members of the public arrive at the jury pool room, selection for particular cases occurs through a ballot. In order to actually sit on a jury, an individual needs to get beyond the lawyers' challenge stage. As indicated above, this is the point at which lawyers from either side have a number of opportunities to delete particular panel members from the larger body of potential jurors without having to provide specific reasons for doing so. In addition, lawyers may challenge jury selection in some instances due to such things as the relationship between the accused or victim and the potential juror (e.g. family member or co-worker).

In some states, a jury must arrive at a unanimous decision in order to convict the accused, this requirement being premised on the notion that the decision implies an absence of doubt (i.e. 'beyond a reasonable doubt'). However, in other states, juries can convict on the basis of a majority decision (usually there has to be agreement on the part of at least ten out of twelve jurors).

AVENUES FOR APPEAL

Disputes over convictions or sentences may be reviewed by the higher courts, on various grounds, via a variety of procedures. The existence of an appeal mechanism is designed to give the accused a further chance to either clear themselves of the charges, or to argue for a more lenient sentence due to mitigating circumstances. Such a mechanism has occasionally led to the release of unjustly imprisoned citizens, particularly if new evidence has been discovered at a later date.

There is also opportunity for appeal to the government, and the Governor in each state, for clemency in certain unusual instances. This may involve a 'pardon' or simply 'release' in situations that are highly contentious and that in some way infringe upon notions of 'natural justice' (e.g. Lindy Chamberlain).

LEGAL REPRESENTATION

This is a topic of some debate in Australia insofar as, while people are *entitled* to legal representation, they do not necessarily have a *right* to legal representation. Nevertheless, court decisions have reaffirmed the importance of adequate legal representations as a fundamental aspect of the provision of justice (see, for example, the discussion of the *Dietrich* case in Brown et al. 1996a).

Legal provision takes the form of private lawyers, state-provided court solicitors, legal aid lawyers, community legal centre legal staff, and lawyers with Aboriginal Legal Services (see also Chapter 22).

HABEAS CORPUS

This involves the issuing of a writ requiring a person to be brought before a judge or into court. It is designed especially to investigate the lawfulness of a person's detention, and to ensure against torture or coercion while in custody. This is an important principle insofar as it is meant to prevent people from 'disappearing' within the criminal justice system, or suffering undue or unjust hardship as a result of incarceration before trial. It is a fundamental human right.

THE COURTS

A key area of law-making is the courts themselves, through the establishment of precedent; that is, decisions made by judges, which subsequently become binding in the determination of future cases of a similar nature heard in courts of equal or lower standing in the same jurisdictional hierarchy. Decisions arrived at in superior courts in other jurisdictions, such as those in another Australian state or territory, or other common law country, are influential and may be used as precedent, but these determinations are *persuasive*, rather than *binding*.

Australia's court system is extensive and incorporates several tiers within both federal and state jurisdiction, as outlined in Figure 20.1 (see Crawford & Opeskin 2004; Fitzroy Legal Service 2013; Morris et al. 1992). State courts deal with the vast majority of offences and disputes arising in Australia. Federal courts customarily deal with matters falling beyond the jurisdiction of state laws, including constitutional matters.

Importantly, although Australia's criminal laws are closely modelled on the English common law tradition, there is no single body of laws governing Australia as a whole. Instead, our tradition of federalism has produced nine jurisdictions comprising the Commonwealth, two territories and six states, each of which is governed by its own distinct body of law (Urbas & Bronitt 2002). The operation of court systems within each of these jurisdictions is broadly comparable, though differences in operational procedure and legal authority are notable. One of the key features both across and within jurisdictions is the hierarchical structure of courts of law. Courts are arranged in a system of ascending importance, as determined by the seriousness of the matters with which they deal. In criminal matters, seriousness is determined by the nature of the alleged offence, while in civil contexts seriousness is determined in accordance with the level of monetary compensation being sought.

This hierarchical structure enables decisions made by lower courts to be reconsidered in higher courts where it is believed that an error of law has been made by a magistrate or judge in determining either a criminal or civil case. Courts of law that are able to hear cases on appeal are said to have appellate jurisdiction.

At the state and territory level, the court system has three tiers.

FIGURE 20.1   THE HIERARCHY OF COURTS IN AUSTRALIA

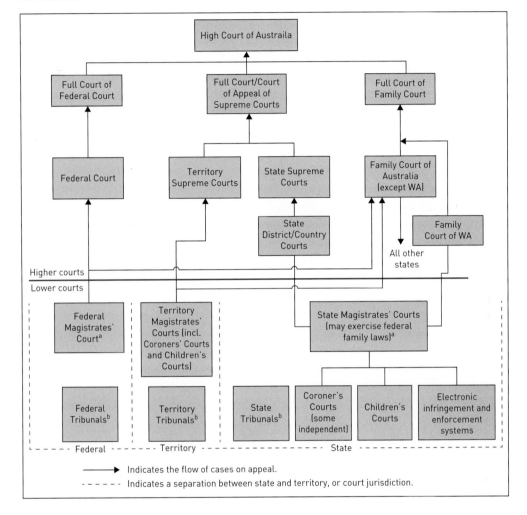

[a] In some jurisdictions, appeals from lower courts or district/county courts may go directly to the full court or court of appeal at the supreme/federal level; appeals from the Federal Magistrates' Court can also be heard by a single judge exercising the Federal/Family Courts' appellate jurisdiction.
[b] Appeals from federal, state and territory tribunals may go to any higher court in their jurisdiction.

Source: Steering Committee for the Review of Government Service Provision (2011)

INFERIOR COURTS

These are the lowest tier, and are presided over by a magistrate or, in some states, a justice of the peace. These courts have jurisdiction that enables them to deal with both criminal and civil matters of a relatively minor nature.

This level of courts—variously referred to as the Magistrates' Court, Court of Petty Sessions, Local Court and Court of Summary Jurisdiction—differs in name from state to state, and from offence to offence.

In Victoria, the Magistrates' Court has both civil and criminal jurisdiction (the former dealing with minor disputes relating to common law matters or state statutes, and the latter referring to summary offence matters such as property damage or minor road traffic accidents). In other states, criminal and civil jurisdiction is divided between two distinct courts. For example, in Western Australia, the Local Court has civil jurisdiction and the Court of Petty Sessions has criminal jurisdiction.

These courts, which are presided over by magistrates, enjoy a limited range of sentencing options and, generally, therefore, the penalties imposed at this level are relatively lenient. Magistrates' Courts also have a filtering function through their capacity to conduct preliminary hearings or committal proceedings with respect to indictable offences. The object of such proceedings is to determine whether there is a prima facie (at first sight) case to be answered; that is, whether the evidence is of sufficient weight to support a finding of guilt and, if so, to commit the accused to trial in a higher court. As the lowest rung in the Australian judicial hierarchy, inferior courts do not have appellate jurisdiction.

Over time, specialist courts (e.g. coroner's and children's) and problem-solving courts (Indigenous, drug, mental health and family violence) have been created as divisions of the traditional courts existing at this level to deal with specific types of offences and/or offenders regarded as requiring special attention (see Box 20.1).

An array of tribunals/commissions (e.g. Small Claims/Civil and Administrative Crimes Compensation, Workers' Compensation, Administrative Appeals, Residential Tenancy, Human Rights and

---

BOX 20.1 PROBLEM-SOLVING COURTS

Analysis of the work of problem-solving courts has identified several different types of speciality courts (Payne 2006: 3). Three distinct Australian court typologies have emerged:

Courts as case managers: characterised by significant changes in the way in which the judicial officer and the court operate

- primary function of the court is to work collaboratively with partner agencies in case management and program delivery for each offender
- court maintains significant and ongoing contact with the offender to enhance rehabilitation
- drug courts and mental impairment courts.

Courts as diversionary operators and case monitors: characterised by moderate changes to the adversarial nature of the courtroom while maintaining traditional judicial roles

- level of judicial monitoring is periodic and primarily for case determination
- a review process provides information for consideration in sentencing
- drug court diversion programs, family violence courts.

Courts as specialist adjudicators: primarily concerned with case processing and procedural justice for specific offender groups

- main objective is to seek criminal case determination that gives consideration to the information provided by experts and dedicated court advisors
- concerned with appropriate sentencing
- Indigenous courts and family violence intervention programs.

Source: Payne (2006)

Migrant Review) have also been established to deal with grievances between various parties, including individuals, organisations, the state and public decision-makers. These numerous bodies, which often dispense with the customary rules of evidence and formal procedure, include:

- *Coroner's courts*: have original jurisdiction to conduct inquests into the cause of unexplained deaths, deaths occurring in government institutions (e.g. a prison, remand centre or psychiatric hospital), and any fire occasioning property damage or destruction.
- *Children's courts*: deal with young people (generally under the age of 17 or 18 at commission of offence, depending on the state or territory) who commit summary or indictable offences, with the exception of homicide, in which case the court has the power to commit young offenders to trial in higher courts. A case may also be referred to a higher jurisdiction if the young person or their parent or guardian does not consent to the matter being heard in the children's court. Children's courts also hear petitions relating to placement of young persons in the care and protection of the state.
- *Indigenous courts*: developed under problem-solving approaches, using Indigenous justice practices to consistently address the underlying causes of offending behaviour by Indigenous people, who tend as a group to be over-represented at all levels of the criminal justice system . These courts, first convened in 1999 in South Australia and now also operating in New South Wales, Queensland and Victoria, are essentially sentencing courts, in that only offenders pleading guilty in inferior courts may be diverted to them. The ultimate aim of these courts is to ensure that the process of imposing penalty is culturally responsive to the needs of Indigenous offenders (see Blagg 2008a).
- *Drug courts*: initially emerged in Australia in New South Wales in 1999 as a response to the perceived failure of traditional court systems to effectively deal with drug-related offending (Freiberg 2003; Indermaur & Roberts 2003; Lawrence & Freeman 2002) and are now also operating in most states and territories (Wundersitz 2007). In a similar vein to other problem-solving courts (Dusmohamed & Burvill 2003; Freiberg 2001; King 2002; Kraszlan & West 2001), drug courts seek to enhance sentencing outcomes for drug-dependent offenders by diverting them away from traditional criminal justice processes (namely, imprisonment) and into court-ordered and supervised treatment and services.
- *Electronic courts*: permit regulatory or administrative offences, such as unpaid traffic infringement notices (speeding or parking fines), to be electronically registered as an order of the court without the need for a formal court hearing. Failure to comply with an order for payment may result in a warrant being issued to the sheriff for further enforcement action.
- *Small Claims Tribunals*: attend to claims from consumers against traders (whether involving sales, contracts or performance of work) involving small amounts of money (variously defined by state or territory). Tribunals and Commissions such as this (known as Civil and Administrative Tribunals in Victoria, New South Wales, the Australian Capital Territory and Queensland) are said to provide a less-expensive alternative to civil and administrative matters, and are presided over by referees rather than magistrates.
- *Crimes Compensation Tribunals*: determine applications for financial compensation from victims of criminal acts resulting in personal injury such as pain and suffering (whether physical or psychological) and/or loss of income.

Generally speaking, the inferior courts in Australia are the busiest in terms of number of cases determined. For example, of all the defendants finalised in Australian courts during 20012–13, 91.5 per cent were determined in Magistrates' Courts. This figure rises to 99.8 per cent if matters determined in the children's courts are excluded (ABS 2014f). Nonetheless, courts at this level do not carry the same prestige, legal weight, remuneration or resources of the higher courts. They also do not 'shape' the laws by creating precedent, and they involve a preponderance of guilty pleas (see Chapter 23).

INTERMEDIATE COURTS

These courts deal with cases of a more serious criminal and civil nature than the inferior courts, and are presided over by judges, who have extensive legal experience.

Courts at this level are referred to as District (New South Wales, Queensland and Western Australia), Local and District Criminal Courts (South Australia) or County Courts (Victoria), depending on the state (Tasmania and the territories do not have an intermediate tier of courts). The vast majority of all indictable criminal offences, such as assault, robbery, rape and culpable driving, are determined in these courts with the assistance of a jury, and proceedings tend to be formal. In recent years there have been moves to dispense with the jury system in civil cases at this level (Victorian Department of Justice 2004a). Intermediate courts are also able to hear appeals relating to conviction and/or sentence, as forwarded to them from inferior courts, if suitable ground for such an appeal exists.

SUPERIOR COURTS

These courts, also officiated by an experienced judge and involving a jury in contested matters, deal with the most serious criminal cases, including homicide and related offences (i.e. all are indictable cases) and the most important and complex civil disputes involving claims for an unlimited amount of compensation and/or damages. Known as Supreme Courts, as the name suggests they are the highest courts available at the state and territory level. In some instances, these courts are also able to take on federal jurisdiction to deal with offences committed under Commonwealth law, such as drug importation and fraud offences. They also act as key courts of criminal appeal from lower courts, each state and territory having established Courts of Criminal Appeal specifically for such purposes.

At the federal level, the court system has two tiers.

1   Inferior court:
   - *Federal Circuit Court of Australia or Federal Court* (previously known as the *Magistrates' Service or Federal Magistrates' Court of Australia*): a relatively new body, created by the Commonwealth in 1999 as an alternative to litigation in the Federal Court of Australia and the Family Court of Australia, and to alleviate the workload of those courts. It provides for less formal, cheaper, simpler and faster resolution of less-complex matters within its jurisdiction, such as family law and child support, administrative law bankruptcy, admiralty law, privacy and trade practices, copyright, human rights, industrial law and migration. At present, it does not have jurisdiction over criminal law, but may impose penalties for unlawful conduct under Commonwealth law, notably racial discrimination.

2   Superior courts:
   - *The High Court:* sits at the summit of the Australian court hierarchy and is the custodian of the Australian Constitution, which confers upon it original jurisdiction to settle legal conflicts involving matters covered by the Constitution, including disputes between state and Commonwealth governments, residents of different states, and actions against officers of the Commonwealth (e.g. review of administrative action taken in relation to asylum seekers claiming refugee status). Highly controversial cases of major national significance requiring

interpretation of the Constitution by the High Court have included, for example, the *Franklin Dam* case (1983) and the *Mabo* (1992) and *Wik* (1996) cases on native title to land. This court is also the highest Court of Appeal for both civil and criminal matters (though it has no power to consider new evidence in a criminal appeal), thereby setting the authoritative precedents that are binding on all lower courts throughout the land.

- *The Family Court:* deals with issues of divorce, settlement, custody, child support and the state of marriage. It sits in each state and territory.

- *The Federal Court:* deals with virtually all civil and some minor criminal matters arising under Australian federal law and that cut across state boundaries, including bankruptcy, telecommunications, native title, trade practices, copyright and extradition. It has appellate jurisdiction to determine appeal applications from the Federal Circuit Court and, in some instances, from state Supreme Courts exercising federal jurisdiction.

INTERPRETING THE LAW

The institutional processes associated with 'due process' are ostensibly designed to protect a citizen's legal rights. There are also rules that act as guidelines in regard to how judges interpret courtroom matters. At one level, the processes of law appear to be straightforward. Thus, there is the formal creation of the law by parliament, and the application of that law by the judiciary. However, the law is basically a matter of interpretation, since it is often up to the courts to determine the legal meaning of a particular law (Chisholm & Nettheim 2002; Fitzroy Legal Service 2013; Morris et al. 1992; Waldron 2005).

To assist judges in arriving at decisions in interpretational situations, the doctrine of precedent has evolved. This means that judges are bound by earlier decisions made by a court at a higher level. Case law is thus that form of adjudication that builds upon previous court decisions. Hence, although they may not necessarily be particularly (socially) conservative, each judge is to a certain extent constrained in their interpretational abilities, although part of the 'art' of judging is to be creative in providing justification for one's decisions. The conservative nature of the law is entrenched institutionally by the provision of an appeal process that allows for interpretation in higher courts to override that in the lower, and that makes reference to preceding cases as a means to rationalise contemporary decision-making.

Judges have a number of other interpretational aids, beyond that of the case law itself. These include:

- *Parliamentary aids:* there are definitional sections at the beginning of Acts of parliament, so that ambiguities are eliminated as far as possible.

- *Hansard:* this is an official record of what goes on in parliament, including documentation of parliamentary debates, so that what the politicians were actually saying about an Act and why it was introduced (its original intent) are available for review.

- *Interpretation Acts:* these set out the basic rules of the Acts. For example, the use of the words 'he' 'his', 'him' and so on, although clearly gender-specific in common use, have traditionally been deemed to be generic or 'universal' in meaning (i.e. to cover both sexes) in legal language.

In Australia, the legal system is based ostensibly on the principle of impartial justice being extended to all those coming before the law, and the provision of lawyers and judges to facilitate this.

A QUESTION OF IMPARTIALITY

It is useful at this point to pose questions regarding whether the legal system is indeed neutral and impartial. To do this we can initially consider the issue from the point of view of the legal processes themselves. Later on, we shall consider it from the perspective of the broad social function of law in a capitalist liberal democracy (see Chapter 22).

Part of the basis for claims of impartiality are built on the notion of precedent (judge-made law) as a guiding interpretational principle. The doctrine of precedent is meant to ensure that radical change or differential treatment of any kind is difficult to achieve. There are two elements of precedent (see Kirby 1996; Morris et al. 1992):

1   *Future judges are bound by precedent*: a decision made by a judge today can have an effect on a prospective basis. Judge-made law speaks to the integral role of the judge in both shaping future decisions and acknowledging the decisions that have gone before.

2   *Precedent operates in courts themselves*: courts are bound to accept the decisions of higher courts. The decisions of higher courts on interpretational matters are binding on lower courts. The hierarchy of courts ensures that precedent is set at the highest level possible within the legal system.

Hence, precedent dictates that a judge's decision today is guided by the decisions made previously and by the principles of the past. This principle is said to provide continuity in decision-making, so that decisions are made on strict legal criteria, and not on the basis of variable personal opinions.

Despite the various procedural and doctrinal safeguards, it is, however, possible to critique the notion of equality before the law in a number of ways. For example, in practice, due process rights are not always honoured. Not all persons are granted the right to remain silent, nor are individuals always presumed innocent (for examples of procedural injustice, see Brown et al. 2001). As indicated below and canvassed further in Chapter 21, there are a number of access to justice issues that indicate that, in fact, the law is not equal or equally applied.

The rule of law is premised upon the notion that, irrespective of position, wealth or influence, all individuals are treated alike in the eyes of the law. If that is to be so, then the issue of judges, and in particular judicial impartiality, is immediately pertinent. As mentioned earlier, impartiality in the judicial context includes such things as:

• *Judges preside over two parties seeking judgment:* in doing so, they put aside their own views, prejudices, and personal opinions and feelings to take on a strictly legal adjudication role. They are seen as a neutral umpire between two competing parties.

• *Political independence and neutrality:* under our system, the judge is by and large appointed for life and has a high income, and hence no political party or government should be able to influence or coerce that judge.

• *Judges are meant to play by legal rules:* they must follow precedents and the guiding principles of the law per se. If they do not do so, then institutionally there are mechanisms, such as the Courts of Appeal, designed to rein in any wandering from the prescribed legal route.

The above elements speak to an ideal picture of judicial impartiality. However, there are several factors to take into account if we are to assess how such 'impartiality' might work in practice. For example, government appoints judges. In itself this highly political process raises questions regarding impartiality and neutrality. Debate often occurs regarding appointments to the High Court of Australia, especially over whether a particular judge is 'liberal' or 'conservative' (politically, as well as in terms of legal thinking per se) and, more broadly, the degree to which judicial activism sits comfortably within the framework of legal precedent (Kirby 2007). Similarly, the appointment (or lack thereof) of women to senior judicial positions has long been a concern, and is often framed in terms of principles of meritocracy (i.e. promotion based on merit) and affirmative action (i.e. redressing an historical imbalance).

It is the state that defines the judiciary in terms of its functions, powers and goals, via funding or the creation of institutions themselves. A good example of this is seen in the situation when the government reorganises the institutions of the courts, as in the case of shifting the Arbitration Commission into the Industrial Court. The question of the independence of the judiciary from political interference becomes an issue when, in the course of a supposed organisational change, certain judges are neither reappointed nor reassigned within the legal system (Hamilton 1999; Kirby 2001).

The class and social background of the judiciary is also relevant, given the gender- and class-neutral image of the legal practitioner central to liberal legalism (Hunter & McKelvie 1999). How many judges and lawyers are women, Aboriginal or working-class people? The experience of being a woman, an Indigenous person or a worker, or a combination of these, will necessarily have some influence on how one views the world, and how one perceives what is 'just' under given circumstances. How can someone who is distant socially from the actual experiences of the majority of the population be in a position to judge adequately the actions of those self-same people?

A related question is the effect of the process of 'becoming a judge', regardless of class and social background. Here, we would need to investigate the processes of ideology formation and the acclimatisation process of judges as they move into elite circles and become part of the establishment in society. Socially, if a person spends most of their time with the wealthy and those of status in society, it can be expected that they may become acclimatised to a particularly narrow, and somewhat conservative, view of the social world.

Related to this, it can be suggested that a substantial part of law school training is itself a socialisation process; one that teaches people to distance themselves from the client and, at least indirectly, to imbue an elitist culture. Legal education also can foster a very restrictive conception of what the 'law' and legal work is about. One result of this may be a judicial attachment to 'legalism'; that is, to only see things in a narrow legalistic framework; one that may omit relevant social and historical facts.

ISSUES FOR CONSIDERATION

JUDICIAL AUTONOMY AND INDEPENDENCE

One issue of recent concern is how to best preserve the autonomy and independence of the judiciary from political interference. In the past, the restructuring of courts has been used as a pretext, in essence, to dismiss existing judges (Hamilton 1999; Kirby 2001; Marks 1994). In relatively recent times, a number of jurisdictions around Australia have appointed acting judges. Questions arise as to the ability of judges generally to provide 'neutral' and 'impartial' dispensations in the face of potential pressures and manoeuvrings of this kind (Conner 2004; Sackville 2005).

Alternatively, one might argue that the social background and socialisation of top legal personnel appear to engender a particular worldview and general philosophical uniformity among judges; one that is not socially neutral. Even where legal conventions and processes have not been subject to outside interference, therefore, the decisions made in court are seen to reflect the dominant power relations of society (Davis & Williams 2003; Finkelstein 2003).

THERAPEUTIC JURISPRU-DENCE
A philosophy that recognises the impact that laws, legal practices and procedures, and legal personnel (e.g. magistrates, judges and lawyers) can have on the psychological and emotional wellbeing of court participants. It argues for law reforms that centre on rehabilitating criminal tendencies, mitigating negative effects, and promoting positive behavioural change and the enhancement of individual wellbeing alongside justice principles, such as community protection.

THE EROSION OF DUE PROCESS

The protections of 'due process' have been severely challenged in recent years by the introduction of various kinds of counter-terrorism legislation, and by the practice of nation-states in bypassing the normal protections of liberal democratic law. In the first instance, countries such as the United States, Britain, Canada and Australia have passed laws that greatly increase the powers of the state to undertake surveillance and imprison citizens without the normal restraints of due process. This is allowed insofar as perceived threats to homeland security are invoked as a justification that overrides ordinary civil liberties and human rights.

In the second case, the practice of 'extraordinary rendition' allowed the United States to basically kidnap individuals from one country and transport them to others where torture is an 'accepted' practice. Generally speaking, the late twentieth century and early twenty-first century saw the resurgence in the use of torture by governments in many different parts of the world (Stanley 2008a,b). Celebrated instances of illegal imprisonment (e.g. holding of individuals without charge for long periods of time at Guantanamo Bay in Cuba by the US government) and the use of torture (e.g. by US officers in Abu Ghraib prison in Iraq) highlight the need for concerted action to stop acts that are still evident today, even though prohibited under international law.

THERAPEUTIC JURISPRUDENCE

Over the past decade, there has been a proliferation of courts informed by the concept of therapeutic jurisprudence. This is representative of a general system shift toward dealing with the causes of problems, rather than criminality per se. For example, the response of criminal justice institutions nationally to drug offending has generally been weighted toward a harm-minimisation model in recent years. This is evident in policies and programs relevant to police, courts and corrections. The broad areas include:

- police diversion
- court-based diversion programs
- drug courts
- compulsory drug treatment correctional centres.

The key concepts driving these initiatives are 'diversion' (not from the system, but to alternative programs within it) and 'therapeutic jurisprudence' (where the law itself functions as therapist to address underlying problems). The point of intervention is at least twofold (among other things): to provide for a reduction in or cessation of drug use; and to provide for a reduction in or cessation of drug or drug-related offending (see Wundersitz 2007). The question is, however, do the courts and, specifically, judges and magistrates, have the competency or expertise to make therapeutic decisions of this nature? Secondly, if insufficient resources are available to provide a full range of therapeutic alternatives to imprisonment, for everyone who needs them, then do such mechanisms thereby set up a two-tier system of justice, where available services in effect determine court outcomes? In other words, matters of equality, fairness and consequence are never far from the surface in discussions of court procedures and systems.

CONCLUSION

This chapter has discussed various aspects of due process and outlined the hierarchy of courts. It has also raised issues pertaining to judicial impartiality and the protection of rights. Chapter 21 further explores issues concerning the impartiality of the law and judicial processes by discussing issues relating specifically to access to justice and equality of outcomes (substantive justice).

DISCUSSION QUESTIONS

1   What is due process, and why is it so important? How is due process being eroded in practice?

2   Why do we have so many different types of courts in Australia?

3   Courts are in a hierarchy. What is the function or purpose of this hierarchy?

4   Justice is represented by a blindfolded woman holding scales. What does this represent when it comes to the process of judgment and how apt is this symbolism today?

5   Is the purpose of courts 'justice' or 'therapy', or both? Does it or can it have other purposes as well?

FURTHER READING

Fitzroy Legal Service (2013) *The law handbook*, Fitzroy Legal Service, Melbourne.

Kirby, M. Hon Jus (2006) 'Precedent—report on Australia', paper presented at the *International Academy of Comparative Law Conference*, 17 July 2006, Utrecht, The Netherlands.

Payne, J. (2006) 'Specialty courts: current issues and future prospects', *Trends & Issues in Crime and Criminal Justice*, No. 317, Australian Institute of Criminology, Canberra.

Sackville, R. Hon Jus (2005) 'Acting judges and judicial independence', paper presented at the *Judicial Conference of Australia*, 28 February 2005.

Stanley, E. (2008) 'Torture and terror', in T. Anthony & C. Cunneen (eds) *The critical criminology companion*, Hawkins Press, Sydney.

21 JUVENILE JUSTICE

CHAPTER OVERVIEW

- THE SOCIAL CONTEXT OF YOUTH OFFENDING
- THE CONTEXT OF JUVENILE JUSTICE
- JUVENILE JUSTICE SYSTEMS AND RESPONSES
- SOCIAL JUSTICE, CRIMINAL JUSTICE AND JUSTICE RE-INVESTMENT
- ISSUES FOR CONSIDERATION
- CONCLUSION
- DISCUSSION QUESTIONS
- FURTHER READING

INTRODUCTION

Most young people engage in rule-breaking behaviour at some time. Indeed, most people have at some stage, often in their younger years, broken the law or taken part in some type of antisocial behaviour. The kinds of things young people might do include drinking under age, crossing the street against the red light, riding a train or tram without a ticket, trying marijuana, making noise late at night, not going to class, and so on. Most of these activities are relatively harmless and trivial, and most young people are not criminals, nor will they continue to engage in unlawful activities—and certainly not serious ones—once they move into their post-teenage years.

Basically, a **young offender** is a person who has been officially designated as such by the criminal justice system. The designation 'young offender' rather than 'adult offender' indicates that the main division in this instance is one based upon age (usually applying to individuals under the age of 18). How different young people are dealt with at all stages of the juvenile justice system largely shapes who, in the end, is officially considered a 'young offender' (Cunneen & White 2011). Becoming a **young offender**, then, is not only about what a young person has done or about their age, but it is also very much influenced by how the system responds to the young person and what they have done.

This chapter provides a general introduction to the nature of youth offending and the operations of the juvenile justice system in response to this offending. The chapter describes which young people come to the attention of the criminal justice officials and why, and what happens to them once they enter into the juvenile justice system. The emphasis is on examining institutional responses to offending rather than the nature and dynamics of the offending itself (for this, see Cunneen & White 2011; see also Chapter 8).

YOUNG OFFENDER

A young offender is a person under the age of 18 who has been officially designated by the criminal justice system as having committed a crime.

THE SOCIAL CONTEXT OF YOUTH OFFENDING

Just as the young offender is socially constituted by the interventions of the criminal justice system, so too offending behaviour of a serious and persistent nature is forged in the context of specific kinds of social relationships and communal processes. For instance, the phenomenon of unemployment is the biggest single factor in the transformation of young people, their families and their communities.

In a wage-based economy, subsistence is largely contingent upon securing paid employment. If this is not available, then a number of social problems are often invoked, including and especially crime (see Wacquant 2008).

For young people in particular, the collapse of the full-time youth labour market has been devastating. The decline in manufacturing employment, use of new labour-saving technology, the movement and flight of capital away from inner cities and regional centres, changing workplace organisation based on casualised labour, massive retrenchments by private and public sector employing bodies, and competition from older (especially female) workers have all served to severely diminish the employment opportunities and conditions of young people in Western countries (see White & Wyn 2013; see also Chapter 8). Young people continue to face record unemployment levels in many countries, with rates in 2013 exceeding 60 per cent in Greece, 52 per cent in South Africa, 55 per cent in Spain and around 40 per cent in Italy and Portugal (OECD 2013). This is the context within which youth crime routinely occurs.

Why is it that the profiles of 'young offenders' tend to look basically the same throughout youth justice systems in 'advanced' industrialised countries? Those processed are predominantly young men, with an over-representation of minority ethnic groups, with low income, low educational achievement, poorly paid and/or casualised employment (if any) and strained familial relations; these are the standard defining characteristics of children and young people most frequently found in juvenile detention centres and custodial institutions, whether in Australia (AIHW 2014a, 2013; Cunneen & White 2011), England and Wales (Muncie 2013), Canada (Schissel 2002) or the United States (Krisberg 2005). The processes whereby identifiable groups of young people are criminalised tend to follow a distinctive social pattern. In effect, the criminal justice system has a series of filters that screen young people on the basis of both offence categories (serious/non-serious and first-time/repeat offending) and social characteristics (gender, ethnic status, cultural background, family circumstances, education, employment and income). It is the most disadvantaged and structurally vulnerable young people who tend to receive the most attention from justice officials at all points of the system.

Entrenched economic adversity has been accompanied by state attempts to intervene in the lives of marginalised groups, usually by coercive measures, which is itself a reflection of a broader shift in the role of the state from concerns with 'social welfare' to renewed emphasis on the 'repressive' (Goldson 2005; Wacquant 2008; White 1996c). The intrusiveness of the state is, in turn, biased toward some groups of young people more than others. This is indicated in the extreme over-representation of Indigenous young people in the criminal justice system in Australia (AIHW 2013e), New Zealand (Ministry of Justice and the Ministry of Social Development 2002) and Canada (Munch 2012). It is demonstrated in the massive over-representation of African Americans in jail, prison, or on probation or parole in the United States (Krisberg 2005), and the ways in which black young people are disproportionately negatively treated in England and Wales (see, for example, Goldson 2011). The history and dynamics of state intervention in particular communities varies considerably, but institutionalised racism has been, and will continue to be, extremely damaging to these groups.

To understand existing patterns of juvenile offending, we must appreciate the prime influence of local community conditions on youth behaviour and life experiences. The concentration of large numbers of unemployed young people in particular geographical locations increases the difficulties of gaining work for specific individuals (Hagedorn 2008; Wacquant 2008, 2012; Wilson 1996). Compounding this are limited educational opportunities. A recent Australian study found that 42 per cent of young people aged 17 to 24, and from the lowest socio-economic backgrounds, were neither in full-time employment or education (COAG Reform Council 2013: 65). Such demographic concentration simultaneously fosters the shared identification and physical congregation of unemployed young people with each other. It thus can act both to preclude these young people from attaining jobs, and to make them more visible in the public domain as an 'outsider' group.

In essence, the poor are being locked into areas characterised by concentrations of poverty, scarce employment prospects and overall declining economic fortunes. Poverty is being entrenched at a spatial level and this has major ramifications in terms of local community infrastructure. Poor people often live in areas with deteriorating housing, they suffer more profoundly any cutbacks in public amenities, and they are more likely to experience declining quality in their health, educational and welfare services. In addition, the neighbourhoods become heavily stigmatised as 'crime prone', thus giving rise to a policy of containment and attracting the more repressive interventions from state agencies.

The consequence of class inequality and transformations in the class structure that deepen this inequality is a sharpening of social tension and antagonism. A big issue for young people is that they are increasingly made to feel that they are 'outsiders'. This is confirmed daily in the form of exclusionary policies, and coercive security and policing measures, which are designed precisely to remove them from the public domain. For young people, this is often seen as unfair and unwarranted. It can certainly breed resentment and various forms of social resistance (see, for example, Ferrell et al. 2008; White & Wyn 2013).

THE PATTERNS OF YOUTH OFFENDING

While times are difficult for many young people, available evidence does not suggest a major crime upsurge. Most youth crime is relatively trivial in nature, and much of this activity takes place in public, and therefore highly visible, city spaces. Not surprisingly, research consistently shows that young people who become criminalised and enter the furthest into the criminal justice system tend to exhibit certain social characteristics (see Allard et al. 2013; Cunneen & White 2011). For example, a typical young offender profile would include the following characteristics:

- The peak age for offending is the late teenage years.
- Young men are far more likely to be charged with a criminal offence than young women, and are more likely to reoffend than young women.
- Increasingly, young offender populations now include greater proportions of ethnic minority youth from specific groups, although the bulk of young offenders are from Anglo-Australian backgrounds.
- Indigenous young people (male and female) are over-represented within the juvenile justice system nationally.
- Juveniles officially processed through the criminal justice system tend to come from low socio-economic backgrounds, with unemployment and poverty being prominent characteristics.
- Many young people who appear before children's courts do not live in nuclear two-parent families.
- Those young people most entrenched in the juvenile justice system are likely to have a history of drug and alcohol abuse.
- A disproportionate number of young offenders have intellectual disabilities or mental illness.

The general pattern of offending can be also be broken down in terms of extent and seriousness of offending. Typically, it is the case, for example, that a large proportion of juvenile offenders stop offending as they get older, and that a relatively small group of reoffenders account for a large number of court appearances (Allard et al. 2013; Cain 1996; Coumarelos 1994). Children and young people who offend can be categorised into three main groupings (see also Leober & Farrington 1998; McLaren 2000; Ministry of Justice and Ministry of Social Development 2002):

1 low-risk or minor offenders, who do not commit many offences and who generally 'grow out' of offending behaviour as part of the normal maturation process

2 medium-risk offenders, who commit a number of offences, some serious, mainly due to factors such as substance abuse and antisocial peers

3 high-risk offenders, who begin offending early (between 10 and 14 years of age), offend at high rates, often very seriously, and are likely to keep offending into adulthood.

The age at which offending first occurs, or at which criminalisation of the young person happens, has a major bearing on subsequent contact with the criminal justice system (see, for example, Allard et al. 2013; Harding & Maller 1997). The younger the person, the greater the likelihood of future reoffending. Again, different ages and different types of offending demand different kinds of responses.

These social characteristics must be taken into account in developing causal explanations for offending. They must also be accounted for when it comes to the development of general and youth-specific criminal justice services.

THE CONTEXT OF JUVENILE JUSTICE

The history of **juvenile justice** is the history of state intervention in the lives of working-class young people, ethnic minorities and Indigenous peoples (Bernard 1992; Blagg 2008a; Cunneen & White 2011; Cunneen et al. 2013; Pearson 1983). It is a history premised on attempts to deal with neglected children and delinquent youth; to control and manage sections of the population that do not fit notions of respectability; or to contain those who do not directly contribute to the economy via paid employment. To understand contemporary juvenile offending and juvenile justice requires some appreciation of the fact that it is the poor, the vulnerable, the dispossessed and the marginalised who are most likely to be the subject of intervention.

The key period in understanding the development of a separate system for dealing with juvenile offenders is the second half of the nineteenth century. This was an important period in the construction of other age-based differences involving young people, including restrictions on child labour and the introduction of compulsory schooling. The state began to intervene actively in the provision of 'welfare' for the children of the 'perishing classes'. In practice, these various measures were linked closely. For example, in the same year that the *Public Schools Act 1866* (NSW) was passed, the *Reformatory Schools Act* (for young people convicted of criminal offences) and the *Industrial Schools Act* and *Workhouse Act* (for vagrant children) were passed in the United Kingdom. In Australia, the first moves to identify and recognise the category of 'young offenders' occurred with the development of institutions for dealing with neglected and destitute children. The major legal change in Australia during this period was the modification of court procedures to allow for juveniles to be dealt with summarily (i.e. to have their less serious charges determined by a magistrate) (Seymour 1988: 3). More broadly, juvenile justice was an element in the expansion of state control and regulation that occurred during the latter part of the nineteenth and the early twentieth centuries.

The new juvenile courts that developed at the end of the nineteenth century were based on the notion of ***parens patriae***. The concept had originally referred to the protection of property rights of juveniles and others who were legally incompetent; however, it subsequently came to refer to the responsibility of the juvenile courts and the state to act in the best interests of the child.

JUVENILE JUSTICE
Juvenile justice refers to those laws, institutions and programs designed specifically with the needs and interests of young people under the age of 18 in mind.

PARENS PATRIAE
Parens patriae refers to the idea of the state acting in the role of parent on behalf of children and young people, in their best interests.

CHILDREN'S COURTS

In Australia, the major reason given for establishing children's courts was that they ensured that young people were tried separately from adults and were not subject to the harmful effects of contamination and stigma—particularly where the young person was before the court on neglect matters. Australian legislation establishing separate children's courts was introduced as follows:

* South Australia: *State Children Act 1895*
* New South Wales: *Neglected Children and Juvenile Offenders Act 1905*
* Victoria: *Children's Court Act 1906*
* Queensland: *Children's Court Act 1907*
* Western Australia: *State Children Act 1907*
* Tasmania: *Children's Charter 1918*.

The courts were to be parental and informal, with correction administered in a 'fatherly manner' (Seymour 1988: 70–1). Magistrates were to be specially selected, trained and qualified to deal with young people; probation officers were to play a special role in supervising young people and preparing background reports.

The legislation establishing children's courts in Australia gave jurisdiction to the courts over criminal matters (juvenile offending) and welfare matters (neglected children and young people). The children's courts also had exclusive jurisdiction, which meant that other, lower courts could not hear cases involving children. The legislation also stipulated that the children's court had to sit separately to the other courts, and that special magistrates had to be appointed. In practice, most magistrates were simply designated as children's magistrates, and only in the major cities did anything like special courts exist (Seymour 1988: 96).

With the increasing separation of children from adults in the judicial system, the provision of information to the court about the young person increased in importance. The development of probation was an important adjunct to the new children's courts. Charity workers provided special knowledge to the court about the young person (McCallum 2009: 121). The development of separate courts for young people led to a more systematic use of probation, and in various parts of Australia the children's court legislation allowed for juvenile offenders to be released on probation.

Today, the role of the children's court is to deal with young people in accordance with the special principles and procedures that have been developed as appropriate for this age group. However, the jurisdiction and status of the children's court varies between states and territories (see Sheehan & Borowski 2013). In some states, it is presided over by a magistrate and in others by a more senior judge. Most states have specialist children's courts operating in the cities. Outside these areas, the local magistrate can convene a children's court when necessary.

The children's courts have major jurisdiction over offences committed by young people. These include all *summary offences* (the less serious offences that are usually heard in a magistrate's court), although traffic offences are usually excluded from the children's court. The hearing in a children's court is summary; that is, before a magistrate and without a jury. The public is excluded from children's courts, and there are prohibitions on publishing the names of young people who go before the courts. For many *indictable offences* (the more serious offences, such as car theft and break and enter, which are usually heard before a judge and jury in a higher court), the young person can elect to have the matter dealt with by the children's court or in a higher court by a judge and jury. The court itself may decline jurisdiction and refer the case to a higher court. In some jurisdictions, if the young person has been charged jointly with an adult for an offence, the children's court can order that the matter be heard in an adult court. Finally, for *serious indictable offences* (e.g. homicide) where the offence might result in a sentence of life imprisonment and there is a prima facie case to answer, the young person will be committed to trial in the Supreme Court. Thus, while the children's court generally deals with offences committed by young people, there is a range of reasons for the matter to be heard in a different court.

THE AGE OF CRIMINAL RESPONSIBILITY

The age of criminal responsibility is an important requirement governing juvenile justice legislation. The age of criminal responsibility is 10 years old in all Australian states. The principle of *doli incapax* is also an important consideration affecting the attribution of criminal responsibility. As outlined in Chapter 1, *Doli incapax* means 'incapable of wrong'. It is a common law principle in Australia that a child younger than the age of 14 does not know their criminal conduct is wrong. They are presumed incapable of committing a crime because they lack the necessary criminal intention (*mens rea*). *Doli incapax* applies in all Australian states and territories. The presumption can be rebutted by the prosecution, who must demonstrate that the child knows the criminal act for which they have been charged is a wrongful act of some seriousness (rather than mere naughtiness or mischief). The principle has the effect of requiring police, prosecutors and magistrates to stop and assess the degree of responsibility appropriate for each child brought before the court.

In most states of Australia, young people cease to come under the jurisdiction of the children's court once they have reached 18 years of age:

> The upper age limit for treatment as a young person is 17 in all states and territories except Queensland, where the limit is 16. However, some young people aged 18 and older are involved in the youth justice system—for reasons which include the offence being committed when the young person was aged 17 or younger; the continuation of supervision once they turn 18; or their vulnerability or immaturity. Also, in Victoria, some young people aged 18–20 may be sentenced to detention in a youth facility (known as the 'dual track' sentencing system). (AIHW 2014a: 3)

The United Nations Convention on the Rights of the Child 1989 (CROC), to which Australia is a signatory, requires 18 to be the age at which young people become adults for the purposes of the application of the criminal law.

Formal Australian responses to youth offending are ostensibly based upon several important international approaches to youth justice. In particular, as indicated earlier, the United Nations' CROC is frequently cited as a significant guiding document when it comes to the principles underpinning juvenile justice and the conduct of decision-making processes.

The relationship between children and rights always hinges on the difference between 'being' and 'becoming'; that is, how best to protect young people's rights now (their immediate being) and their developmental potentials (their future becoming). Any discussion of juvenile justice must consider how 'youth' has been socially constructed according to age demarcations, as well as acknowledge that such demarcations are not inherently repressive, limiting or demeaning of children and youth. The vulnerability and developmental aspects of youth are legally protected through a range of criminal and civil legal measures designed to take into account their overall level of maturity. These measures involve elements of *prescription and compulsion* (as with the imposition of compulsory schooling), and elements of *proscription and prohibition* (as with the banning of alcohol sales to people under a certain age) (see Chapter 8).

In general, the crucial principle in dealing with young people (up to the age of 18) today is that of the 'best interests of the child'. This principle was established by the United Nations via the Convention of the Rights of the Child 1990, as one of the foundation principles underpinning all of the rights and freedoms of children. Article 3.1 of CROC states that: 'in all actions concerning children, whether undertaken by public or private social welfare institutions, courts of law, administrative authorities or legislative bodies, the best interests of the child shall be a primary consideration'.

Allied with this concept are other principles, such as (Cunneen & White 2011):

- the provision of conditions under which children can develop their full human potential, with human dignity, and the requirement that treatment be appropriate to the age of the child
- the capacity for children to participate and to express their views (if the child is capable of forming a view), including the right of the child to freedom of expression, thought, conscience and religion
- the recognition that children require special protection because of their special vulnerability and stage of maturation
- the recognition that in most circumstances the best interests of the child will be served by remaining with their family and their family being involved in their development.

The emphasis is on participation, and developmental opportunities, in an environment conducive to health and wellbeing generally. Such principles are reflected in specific juvenile justice legislation, along with more convention criminal justice concerns pertaining to accountability and traditional 'justice' matters (see Box 21.1).

BOX 21.1   JUVENILE JUSTICE LEGISLATION, AUSTRALIA

NEW SOUTH WALES

Amendments to Children (Detention Centres) Regulation 2005 (effective 2 March 2007)
Bail Act 1978
Children (Community Service Orders) Act 1987
Children (Criminal Proceedings) Act 1987
Children (Detention Centres) Act 1987
Children (Interstate Transfer of Offenders) Act 1988
Young Offender Act (Part 5 and Schedule 1) 1997

VICTORIA

Bail Act 1977
Children, Youth and Families Act 2005 (enacted in April 2007)
Crimes Act 1958
Sentencing Act 1991

QUEENSLAND

Bail Act 1980
Childrens Court Act 1992
Childrens Court Rules 1997

Criminal Code Act 1899
Criminal Law (Rehabilitation of Offenders) Act 1986
Young Offenders (Interstate Transfer) Act 1987
Youth Justice Act 1992
Youth Justice Regulation 2003

WESTERN AUSTRALIA
Bail Act 1982
Children's Court of Western Australia Act 1988
Court Security and Custodial Services Act 1999
Inspector of Custodial Services Act 2003
Sentence Administration Act 2003
Young Offenders Act 1994
Young Offenders Amendment Regulations 1995

SOUTH AUSTRALIA
Bail Act 1985
Criminal Law (Sentencing) Act 1988
Family and Community Services Act 1972
Young Offenders Act 1993
Youth Court Act 1993

TASMANIA
Bail Act 1994
Children, Young Persons and Their Families Act 1997
Police Offences Act 1935
Sentencing Act 1997
Youth Justice Act 1997

AUSTRALIAN CAPITAL TERRITORY
Bail Act 1992
Children and Young People Act 2008
Crimes (Restorative Justice) Act 2004
Crimes (Sentence Administration) Act 2005
Crimes (Sentencing) Act 2005

NORTHERN TERRITORY
Bail Act 1982
Youth Justice Act 2005
Youth Justice Regulations 2006
Source: AIHW (2014b)

Three other United Nations' agreements of importance to the administration of juvenile justice are:

- Standard Minimum Rules for the Administration of Juvenile Justice 1985 (also known as the Beijing Rules)
- Guidelines for the Prevention of Juvenile Delinquency 1990 (also known as the Riyadh Guidelines)
- Rules for the Protection of Juveniles Deprived of their Liberty 1990 (also known as the Havana Rules).

Together these international instruments have translated into 'diversion' as being a key principle of the juvenile justice systems in all jurisdictions in Australia (AIHW 2013b). At a policy level, for example, it has fostered the use of 'restorative justice', in the form of juvenile conferencing, as one method of diverting young people from the conventional sanctions of the criminal justice system (Cunneen & White 2011). Nonetheless, who gets diverted, and who does not, remains of substantial interest and concern.

JUVENILE JUSTICE SYSTEMS AND RESPONSES

In responding to youth crime and the images of youth deviance, many countries employ a combination of coercive measures (e.g. youth curfews, aggressive street policing and anti-gang interventions) and developmental measures (e.g. sports programs, parent classes and educational retention programs). While the specific approach to juvenile justice varies considerably from jurisdiction to jurisdiction (see Muncie 2013; Muncie & Goldson 2006), a common element is how 'the problem' is constructed and the specific characteristics of those young people held to be responsible for 'the problem'. As indicated earlier and as demonstrated in previous chapters, most justice systems deal predominantly with offenders from working-class backgrounds (including Indigenous and ethnic minority people), and thereby reflect the class biases in definitions of social harm and crime, as well as basing responses on these biases. At a social structural level, such processes confirm the role of 'crime' as the central problem (rather than poverty, unemployment or racism), neglecting or avoiding entirely the roles of class division and social inequality.

Comparative analyses of juvenile justice systems and processes indicate a number of global commonalities, as well as important national and regional differences in the perception and treatment of young people (Muncie 2004; Muncie & Goldson 2006). General trends include a winding back of welfare provision and greater focus on 'deeds' rather than 'needs', adulteration in some jurisdictions where young people are increasingly formally being treated as adults, and re-penalisation of many aspects of juvenile justice—including use of youth curfews, mandatory sentencing and zero-tolerance policing, as well as use of detention. Conversely, there has also been greater attention given to concepts and practices of restorative justice, and at least some acknowledgment of the importance of the Convention on the Rights of the Child in deliberations about juvenile justice. As Muncie (2005) emphasises, global processes of neo-liberalism are translated into a multiplicity of social forms with great variation, depending upon specific local contexts. How international trends are played out at the national and regional level is contingent upon a range of factors, not the least of which is local history and local sensibilities.

THE EMPHASIS ON RISK

Notwithstanding, there are two broad trends that are worthy of particular attention. In simple terms, these can be described as the emphasis on risk and risk aversion, and the emphasis on responsibilisation.

Prediction of risk has emerged as one of the most far-reaching changes in theory and practice in relation to juvenile justice (and justice systems more broadly) in places such as Australia, Britain, the United States and Canada. Indeed, the **concepts of risk** (risk factors, risk assessment, risk prediction and risk management) permeate juvenile justice systems (Cunneen & White 2006).

There are at least four different ways that the concept and measurement of risk is used in juvenile justice (Cunneen & White 2011):

1 in the context of *risk and protective factors* associated with offending behaviour
2 as an *assessment tool for access to programs* for young people under supervision or serving a custodial sentence
3 as a *classification tool* for young people in custody to determine their *security ratings*
4 as a *generic measure* for *activating legal intervention* (e.g. 'three-strikes' mandatory imprisonment).

When combined with government attempts to get tough on crime, especially when these efforts relate to juvenile offenders (e.g. moral panics about so called 'ethnic youth gangs'), the emphasis on risk can open the door to highly punitive and highly intrusive measures.

Closely linked to the concern with risk is the employment of actuarial methods of assessment, in which potential problems and problematic youth become the focus of government attention through *a priori* categorisation of young people based upon standardised risk assessment. The public activities of young people, particularly when it involves alcohol and illicit drugs, is likewise framed in the language of risk, both in regards to notions of risk-taking and persons being at risk because of their behaviour. This generally involves the charting up of specific risk and protective factors that are seen to influence how individuals negotiate particular transitions and pathways in their lives. Multi-factorial analysis of specific factors is statistically correlated with certain types of behaviour and certain types of people. The implication is that if certain factors are added together there will be a predictable certainty that deviancy (or pathology) will result (see, for example, Allard et al. 2013).

This kind of risk assessment is finding increasing favour in the juvenile justice field (Case 2007; MacDonald 2006; Muncie & Goldson 2006; Priday 2006). It is not only being used as a diagnostic tool (i.e. to pinpoint a person's specific needs and deficits), but also in a prognostic manner, to determine which young people are most likely to offend. Specific profiles of young people are constructed whereby all young people within a certain range of empirical indicators (e.g. age group, school record, type of family or previous criminal record) are dealt with according to the risk that they (presumably) pose now and into the future. It is a process of homogenisation wherein all people with certain similarities are to be treated similarly.

By their very nature, these kinds of risk assessment tools fail to capture the historical dynamics of societies. The tools reinterpret certain characteristics as representing the failings of individuals. This is because they are constructed on the basis of individualised data, rather than analysis of, for example, how state policy affects particular groups. The formation of specific kinds of groups and specific kinds of individuals, as the outcome of inequality, discrimination and the absence of opportunity, is basically lost in such analysis (Cunneen & White 2006). In its stead, it is the consequences of these processes that are central to who is or who is not deemed to be at risk.

For example, the combination of poverty, poor parenting, bad schooling and unemployment (as measured on pre-determined scales) might be said to equate to deviant behaviour (as defined in conventional criminal justice terms). Such calculations are then utilised to 'read back' into the life circumstances of certain individuals the probable trajectory that they will take. Interventions can then be organised even before the risk has actually been realised in practice.

The identification of 'at risk' youth typically involves three steps: the identification of specific indicators of the problem, the use of indicators to identify a target group, and the implementation of

CONCEPTS OF RISK
Concepts of risk underpin contemporary juvenile justice systems and intervention practices, and focus on matters pertaining to the causes and predictions of crime, and the assessment and management of young offenders.

an intervention to bring the target group into line with the mainstream. This popular policy process overlooks the ways in which institutions and policy processes contribute to social problems involving young people, and instead focuses on changing the young people themselves. The paradoxical element of this process is that the 'at risk' come to be stigmatised, adding to their sense of difference and marginality (White & Wyn 2013). Moreover, the phenomenon of 'false positives' means that individuals may suffer the negative consequences of unwanted and unneeded intervention solely due to their membership of a 'high risk' group, rather than due to their individual risk profile or actual behaviour (see Case 2007).

Ethnicity is an important component in this process. For example, being an Indigenous person is counted as a 'risk' factor in some assessment processes (Palmer 1999; Palmer & Collard 1993). When this occurs, one's heritage and community identity are degraded through their assessment as contributing factors to youth deviancy (Priday 2006). From the point of view of research into gangs, similar issues are apparent. Ethnicity and community ties are frequently construed as core elements of what goes into the making of a gang member (as evident in moral panics about 'ethnic youth gangs'). Strong ethnic identification can thus be considered a risk factor when it comes to group deviancy (see White 2013a).

This kind of totalising practice, one based upon statistical prediction, is matched by another totalising practice; namely, the assignment of the label 'deviant' to selected individuals. Such labelling confers a negative master status on the youths so labelled. This is achieved through the linking of key categorical descriptions in particular ways (e.g. Muslim, terrorist or gangs), a process that has been shown to play a vital part in the criminalisation of particular ethnic minority youth (Poynting et al. 2004). In other words, the justification for intervention is based upon employment of a social categorisation that precludes us thinking about the young person in any way except as deviant (even if expressed as 'at risk' rather than 'criminal' as such). This is essentially a question of social control.

When applied to specific youth groups, such as 'gangs', such risk analysis takes the form of *social profiling*. This involves constructing a matrix of variables and matching individuals to the variables described in the gang matrix. Such a process tends to be descriptive, and does little to provide a basis for understanding why and how specific groups of young people experience problems or fail to find meaning in their lives.

Moreover, while to some extent social characteristics and social background provide insight into probabilities of opportunity and life chances (based on historical experience and previous patterns), it is much more problematic to generalise from general trends down to individual experience. We know, for example, that there is a strong correlation between poverty and crime, yet all poor people do not become engaged in criminal activity; nor are all criminals necessarily from a poor background. Poverty may be conceptualised as the field of resources and relationships that may predispose some young people to be delinquent compared to others, but it cannot predict which young people will deviate and for what reasons (White & Wyn 2013). The same applies to gang membership and gang activities, as well as other forms of youth offending.

THE EMPHASIS ON RESPONSIBILITY

It is somewhat ironic that while risk is constructed in relation to the notion of *determinism* (one's social background, for example, determines the likelihood of engaging in juvenile crime), the other leading concept underpinning juvenile justice today puts the emphasis on *voluntarism* (the element of free will in human behaviour). A fundamental premise of *responsibilisation* is that responsibility for safety and wellbeing is no longer in the hands of the (welfare) state, but rather has been transferred back to communities, families and individuals (Muncie 2004). It is yet another aspect of *individuation*—the notion that it is up to the individual to make a life for themselves, to negotiate their own pathways through the economic and social structure, and to accept that life is basically a do-it-yourself kind of project.

In a criminal justice context, the notion of **responsibilisation** has several interrelated components (Muncie 2004), including:

- Communities should take primary responsibility for crime.
- When it comes to crime prevention, individuals should be held responsible for their own actions.
- Families, and in particular parents, have a responsibility to ensure that their children do not develop antisocial tendencies.

A fundamental premise of responsibilisation is that responsibility for safety and wellbeing is no longer the responsibility of the state, but is ultimately up to each individual. Those who commit crime ought to get their 'just deserts' since they are seen as the authors of their own fate.

In regards to juvenile justice, responsibilisation tends to be implicated in both how punitive justice and restorative justice approaches to punishment have been institutionalised in practice (Cunneen & White 2011). In general, there has been a significant shift in recent years away from a welfare or treatment perspective and towards a justice or retributive view of juvenile justice. Young offenders are seen to be responsible for their own actions, and so must suffer just deserts for any transgressions they have committed. With restorative justice, the emphasis is less on punishment per se than with repairing the harm. But even here, the emphasis tends to be on holding the young person accountable. The burden of responsibility basically falls on the individual to atone for or change their behaviour (Muncie 2004). In each case, the focus is the young offender.

The overarching focus of the juvenile justice system is coherent and consistent from the point of view of risk analysis and responsibilisation (but rather less so from the point of view of structural inequality and human rights). In other words, the point of intervention is less about the welfare and/ or rehabilitation of the young person than with making them accountable and ensuring a modicum of community safety. A hybrid system that combines punitive features with reparation philosophies makes sense only insofar as it reflects the profile of young offenders mentioned earlier. The serious and persistent offender is liable to be punished up to and including the use of detention. The low-risk offender is asked to make amends for their wrongdoing by repairing the harm and perhaps making an apology. Meanwhile, the potential offender is dealt with through deployment of risk-assessment technologies and ongoing surveillance in order to prevent future deviation.

SOCIAL JUSTICE, CRIMINAL JUSTICE AND JUSTICE REINVESTMENT

One way to assess the performance of juvenile justice systems is to consider the issue of **diversion**, regarded one of the key principles of juvenile justice. Assessment needs to take into account the types and level of diversion away from the system for young offenders. It also needs to consider the social characteristics of those who, regardless of general principles and policies, are nonetheless brought ever deeper into the system.

DIVERSION

The notion of diversion refers to several different things. Young people 'may be diverted from the youth justice system altogether (e.g. an informal warning by police); referred to services outside the system

RESPONSI-BILISATION
The shift in the burden of responsibility for crime and safety matters from the state to individuals, families and communities.

DIVERSION
The movement of young offenders away from the more formal and/ or harshest aspects of the criminal justice system in the light of their vulnerable social position, based on specific age-related needs and interests.

(e.g. drug and alcohol treatment); or diverted from continued contact with the system by police or courts (e.g. conferencing) '(AIHW 2014c: 2). Recent figures on the number and rate of young people under supervision in Australia (both in the community and in detention) show a significant fall in the number of young people under supervision in 2012–13. Yet, of those under supervision, young people aged 10–17 from the areas of lowest socio-economic status were more than five times as likely to be under supervision as those from the areas of highest socio-economic status (AIHW 2014a: 7).

Between 2008–09 and 2012–13, the level of Indigenous over-representation in supervision on an average day *increased* in all states and territories for which data were available, except in South Australia and Tasmania (AIHW 2014a: 1). Furthermore, in 2012–13, Indigenous young people were seventeen times as likely as non-Indigenous young people to have been under supervision; they were also, on average:

- younger (27% were aged 10–14, compared with 13%)
- more likely to complete multiple periods of supervision (22%, compared with 14%)
- spending longer, in total, under supervision during the year (195 days, on average, compared with 180) (AIHW 2014a: 1).

To put these figures into further perspective, the Indigenous youth population comprises less than 5 per cent of the total youth population in Australia, yet 49 per cent of all young men held in youth detention were Indigenous (i.e. almost half), and 54 per cent of all young women held in youth detention were Indigenous (i.e. more than half) (AIHW 2014c: 1). Indigenous young people under supervision were more likely than non-Indigenous young people to have lived in remote or very remote areas before entering supervision (10% compared with less than 1%), and also more likely to have lived in areas of lowest socio-economic status before entering supervision (44% compared with 35%) (AIHW 2014a: 15).

The notion of social justice is somewhat amorphous and can mean quite different things to different people. Nevertheless, key elements of the concept generally include (White 2013b):

- *dignity and respect* for the person, and protection of human rights
- *economic egalitarianism and social equality*, such that each person enjoys the same rights, opportunities and services as all other citizens
- *active engagement in social institutions*, and in decision-making that affects individuals and the groups or collectivities of which they are a part.

Social inequality is seen as a major hurdle in the attainment of social justice.

Since there are strong connections between community circumstances that give rise to street crime (e.g. economic marginalisation) and the community relations that sustain them (e.g. ethnic identification), community processes are also most likely to provide the best opportunities for their transformation.

Yet existing juvenile justice systems in Australia tend to exhibit a particular kind of bifurcation: 'soft' cases are dealt with leniently, developmentally and at the front end of system, while 'hard' cases are dealt with harshly, involve targeted populations, and shift particular young people toward the back end of the criminal justice system. This occurs in relation to juvenile conferencing as well. That is, 'restorative justice' measures are usually located at the front end of juvenile justice systems, as a form of diversion from going deeper into the criminal justice system, and reserved for first-time offenders and trivial offences. The system then filters out the 'hard' and the 'chronic'—Indigenous young offenders, those who most need assistance and those who could benefit from 'doing something' rather than having something 'done to them'—and places them in the harshest reaches of the system.

JUSTICE REINVESTMENT

Given that one consequence of this bifurcated system is extreme over-representation of the socially disadvantaged and, especially, of Indigenous young people, how then should juvenile justice systems address these issues? One response that is finding increasing favour is **justice reinvestment** (JR) (Schwartz 2010):

> Under this approach, a portion of the public funds that would have been spent on covering the costs of imprisonment are diverted to local communities that have a high concentration of offenders. The money is invested in community programs, services and activities that are aimed at addressing the underlying causes of crime in those communities. (Gooda 2010: 3)

Theoretically, 'The community has to be involved and committed to not only taking some ownership of the problem but also some ownership of the solutions ... Justice Reinvestment if done properly also provides offenders a form of accountability to their community ... Accountability to community is about making communities safer' (Gooda 2010: 5).

As is often the case in regards to the development and implementation of criminal justice policies, there is not just the one model of JR, nor do these find application in the same way in different jurisdictions due to unique and variable local characteristics (of offenders, of crimes and of communities) (see La Vigne et al. 2014):

- In one model, the idea is to redirect money from prisons to *communities* that feed directly into the prisons. Analysis is undertaken of the places from which detainees come, and how best to redirect funds back into those communities (see, for example, Allard et al. 2013; Australian Youth Affairs Coalition 2013; Gooda 2010).
  - However, by focusing the spotlight on these communities in this way (i.e. in a manner that portrays them as dysfunctional and deviant), the door is open for further stigmatisation of both community and individuals within them, and for coercive 'outside' intervention in these same communities.
  - Moreover, the JR focus on reinvestment as crime prevention and a decarceration strategy may obscure the broader social justice issues centring on employment, education and social inclusion that underpin much youth offending to begin with.
- In the second model, the idea is to redirect money from prisons to *individuals* needing drug rehabilitation and who are non-violent, or to tightened-up risks and needs assessments so that each person is carefully scrutinised, supervised and subject to sanctions that will improve the chances of keeping them out of prison (see AYAC 2001; La Vigne et al. 2014).
  - This would guarantee a modicum of success, but only insofar as it is based upon highly selective allocation of resources, usually to the 'less hard' cases and mostly directed at supporting or changing individuals, not to transforming the contexts within which their behaviour and activity is given impetus.

Each approach to justice reinvestment carries with it certain hopes and certain dangers. Each, as well, tends to deal with the symptoms of social disadvantage without addressing the structural causes underlying much juvenile offending. Moreover, in the context of tight government budgets, while the need for community development is growing rapidly (as the hard times hit), the resources for this are shrinking (due to government choice of priorities). Over-burdened services and practitioners can, at best, only hope to manage the social fallout of high levels of youth unemployment. Without dedicated job-creation strategies and efforts to improve overall educational outcomes, the success of justice reinvestment seems less than assured.

JUSTICE REIN-VESTMENT
Refers to the idea of taking funds and resources from criminal justice institutions such as prisons (which deal with the consequences of crime) and re-investing these in communities where imprisoned offenders originate and/or in individuals needing rehabilitation (addressing the source of the problem).

In the Australian context, however, justice reinvestment has had particular resonance in relation to the situation of Indigenous young people and their relationship to juvenile justice. In some instances, and in some communities, allocations of funding away from detention to community building 'makes sense' to local populations and communities that are already struggling to come to grips with severe disadvantage. Rather than a general panacea or response to gross (or 'hyper') incarceration, as in the United States (see La Vigne et al. 2014), JR is seen in Australia to be most relevant to select groups of young people. Overall detention rates and numbers are not high within this country; yet over-representation rates of Indigenous youth continue to be a national and international disgrace. In the light of this, JR approaches have garnered significant political support within Indigenous communities and advocacy bodies precisely because of the dire nature of the contemporary policies and practices affecting Indigenous youth across the country (see Cunneen et al. 2013; Gooda 2010).

ISSUES FOR CONSIDERATION

JUVENILE JUSTICE POLICY

Public policy is frequently driven by peculiar constructions of the problem rather than sustained and systematic evidence-based decision-making. This is as true in the area of juvenile justice as it is in other domains of criminal justice. Issues of major concern involving young people tend to centre on the use of alcohol, street violence, and a combination of the two. Much of the debate surrounding these issues occurs in the context of moral panic and citizen outrage (see Chapter 2). Closely linked to these is the issue of youth gangs. Yet, as careful analysis of the gang phenomenon reveals, all may not be what may at first glance appears to be the case (see Box 21.2). While violence stands out as a significant social problem, the solution does not lie in using 'big stick' tactics on the part of the state to deal with this. Rather, state intervention that focuses on job creation, educational opportunity and community building continue to be the most favoured policies by those who have studied street-level interactions and supposed deviant youth group formations.

BOX 21.2 YOUTH GANGS IN AUSTRALIA

In a recent monograph, White (2013a) provides the first-ever comprehensive and national study of youth gangs in Australia. Based upon research over a number of years, he argues that the main problem is not 'gangs' per se, but that of youth violence. Groups of young people, predominantly young men, are regularly engaged in harmful and at times lethal street violence. Frequently, this is stirred by alcohol and illicit drug use, within the cauldron of intense rivalries and group oppositions at the local community level.

Regardless of how transient their membership or their formation, youth 'gangs' always exist in relation to something else—a community, a locality, a cohort of students, an ethnic identification, class and gender dynamics, drugs availability or criminal organisations. Typically, gangs tend to form in working-class neighbourhoods where, economically, life is tough and opportunities are limited. Moreover, in many cases, gang membership is overlaid by ethnic identification and group experiences of racism and social put-downs.

Studying gangs is about studying the ways in which masculinity is constructed on the streets, and how social respect is gained and lost through physicality and violence. Respect is forged in the context of wider forces beyond one's control, such as structural unemployment, and must be won using the personal tools at hand; in this case, fists, knees, arms, head and, by extension of one's body, knives, guns and poles. It was found that youth gangs provide an outlet for young men to exercise their manhood in particular ways; to exhibit to the world around them their prowess and standing—as defined and celebrated within the street-oriented environment. Respect won on the street presents as an alternative to that of mainstream institutions and their markers of success. It is this alternative moral economy that makes the gang attractive, not just the exhilarations of collective action.

Source: White (2013a)

UNINTENDED CONSEQUENCES

Juvenile justice systems are designed in several different ways to be different from adult criminal justice systems. This is because young people are generally seen first and foremost in developmental terms—as 'becoming' rather than as 'being'. Constructing responses to juvenile offending in terms of 'risk' and 'responsibility', however, tends to undermine at least some of the assumptions regarding youth vulnerabilities. This is because the emphasis becomes that of young people as threats and/or as being liable for punishment on the basis of their individual actions. Again, it needs to be emphasised that such processes, in practice, tend to be oriented toward particular classes of young people, comprised mainly of those from disadvantaged backgrounds. Those with the most restricted structural opportunities are thus treated as among the most culpable when it comes to wrongdoing and what is deemed to be socially deviant behaviour.

CONCLUSION

Young offenders in Australia have long been considered different from adult offenders and, accordingly, have been dealt with institutionally as a distinct population group. This is reflected in the formation of specific children's courts, in the universal application of restorative justice measures (in the form of juvenile conferencing), in the different legal conventions that pertain specifically to youth (e.g. bans on media reporting of cases involving children and young people; and the doctrine of *doli incapax*) and in the provision of separate age-specific youth detention centres.

Yet, while age is seen to be a crucial factor in establishing policies, practices and institutions that are meant to acknowledge the vulnerabilities and developmental potentials of young people, issues of class, race, ethnicity and gender continue to entrench certain patterns of 'justice' within the overarching juvenile justice system. This is especially evident with regards to Indigenous young people, who persistently and disproportionately constitute the most imprisoned and least diverted group within juvenile justice. Appraisal of youth offending and of juvenile justice responses clearly demands appreciation of how social justice and criminal justice form an inextricable duality in which some suffer, or benefit, more than others.

The focus over the last few chapters has been on the legal framework governing the administration of justice in Australia. Chapter 22 turns attention to issues of 'justice' and, in particular, access to justice.

DISCUSSION QUESTIONS

1 What is a 'young person', as defined in criminal law and what is the significance of this categorisation?

2 In what ways are young people treated differently from adults by criminal justice institutions?

3 'Indigenous young people are different from other young people and deserve special treatment when it comes to criminal justice'. Discuss.

4 Juvenile conferencing has been introduced everywhere, and yet everywhere the same young people end up in the harshest end of the criminal justice system. So who benefits from restorative justice and why?

5 'Sometimes what young people need is a "short, sharp, shock"'. Discuss.

FURTHER READING

Australian Institute of Health and Welfare (2014) Youth justice, <http://www.aihw.gov.au/youth-justice>.

Cunneen, C. & White, R. (2011) *Juvenile justice: youth and crime in Australia*, Oxford University Press, Melbourne.

McKenzie, J. (2013) *Insights from the coalface: the value of justice reinvestment for young Australians*, Australian Youth Affairs Coalition, Sydney.

Sheehan, R. & Borowski, A. (eds) (2013) *Australia's children's courts today and tomorrow*, Springer, New York.

Schwartz, M. (2010) 'Building communities, not prisons: justice reinvestment and Indigenous over-imprisonment', *Australian Indigenous Law Review*, 14(1): 1–17.

ACCESS AND ALTERNATIVES TO JUSTICE

22

CHAPTER OVERVIEW

- ACCESS TO JUSTICE: CRITIQUES
- ALTERNATIVE DISPUTE RESOLUTION
- COMMUNITY LEGAL CENTRES AND PARALEGALS
- ISSUES FOR CONSIDERATION
- CONCLUSION
- DISCUSSION QUESTIONS
- FURTHER READING

INTRODUCTION

Our legal institutions subscribe to, or are premised upon, the idea that the legal system is both neutral and impartial, and that all persons are equal in the eyes of the law. However, once we delve into the mechanics of the system at the operational level, we discover that this fundamental premise is quite problematic. For instance, in the mid-1990s the Law Reform Commission of Australia undertook a study of biases against women in the legal system (ALRC 1994b). The study emerged in response to the apparent biases, disparities and general gender-based inequalities built into the system. More recently, the Productivity Commission (2014) released a draft report on Australia's system of civil dispute resolution, with a particular focus on cost factors constraining access to justice and equality before the law. Any findings of unequal treatment necessarily places doubt on the 'neutrality' of the legal and criminal justice systems. To understand how this might occur is one of the themes of this chapter.

To ask who uses the law, and who does not, is crucial to understanding the nature of Australian society as a whole, as well as the peculiar and specific place of law in reproducing the basic structures of this society. The overall purpose of the chapter is to introduce and explore the reasons why 'access to justice' is an issue of considerable public concern, although it must be said that (the lack of) government action often belies its importance. Why access to justice is ideologically significant, but practically inconsequential from the point of view of the state, is due to the central paradox of law in a socially unequal society:

- The legitimacy of the legal system rests upon the perception that notions of equality of treatment, fairness, due process and justice are, in fact, the core practical objectives of the present system, and that these are universal features of the legal system.
- Simultaneously, the operation of the legal system is intertwined with specific sectional interests (e.g. facilitation of business transactions, and fiscal and efficiency concerns of governments) such that the allocation of legal resources and the direction of legal work tends to favour those with the societal means to use the law for their own particularistic ends.

The instigation for public debate and government investigation of 'access to justice' is the perceived 'crisis of confidence' in the institutions fundamental to the rule of law in a democratic society. This chapter will explore why this 'crisis of confidence' is worthy of attention, and what the objectives and principles of a reform action plan might consist of.

ACCESS TO JUSTICE: CRITIQUES

It is important to consider the broad philosophical critiques of the existing legal system and liberal democratic notions of justice. For present purposes, we briefly consider the 'liberal', 'Marxist' and 'feminist' critiques, while acknowledging that there are also many other kinds of legal analysis and critique (see, for example, Davies 1994; Hampstead & Freeman 1985). This is followed by a detailed exposition of the problems and barriers impinging upon **access to justice** in the formal legal system.

ACCESS TO JUSTICE
A concept that refers to the ability of individuals and groups to use the law, including access to lawyers, and having their issues heard and dealt with adequately within the legal system, including the courts.

THEORETICAL AND PHILOSOPHICAL CRITIQUES
LIBERAL CRITIQUE

A liberal critique of the existing system of rights and justice is built on the gaps between theory and practice. In essence, this critique questions the presumed linear relationship between law and justice, arguing that the reality does not match up with the rhetoric. On the surface, the law itself is just, and there are both philosophical (the rule of law) and operational mechanisms (due process rights) in place that formally guarantee that liberal democratic ideals of equity, fairness and justice prevail. However, in practice, not everyone has equal access to these operational mechanisms, nor to the institutions that administer the law (i.e. courts, tribunals and other administrative agencies); legal outcomes are therefore inevitably unequal. Numerous substantial disparities are said to exist within our legal system itself, which tend to disproportionately disadvantage underprivileged groups in society, so that they have 'unmet legal needs' (Bottomley et al. 1991: 59).

MARXIST CRITIQUE

A Marxist critique of the legal system argues that the law and legal processes cannot be separated from the wider social, political and economic power relations in society, since it is these structural power bases that determine the activities of the state (Brickey & Comack 1986). The state (and by extension the law and legal institutions) is said to be organised and to function in a manner that advances the interests of the minority (the capitalist class) at the expense of the majority. According to Marxists, liberal principles of rights and justice primarily serve an ideological role, in that they mask and thereby legitimate profound social inequalities (Chambliss 1975; Collins 1982; Quinney 1975). As Hall and Scraton (1981: 468) put it:

> Law is not everywhere and anywhere the same. It is adapted in form and function to the social relations which it regulates ... The pursuit of 'legal equality' in a society based on the unequal division of wealth, property and power has meant that the law legitimates and legalises precisely those inequalities.

In legal terms, ideas of 'freedom' and 'equality' belie the substantive material differences between people. Each person stands equal in the eyes of the law, but not everyone enters into the legal world on equal footing. However, by divesting the individual of all social and economic characteristics (via the notion of the 'abstract legal subject', which implies equal treatment regardless of social circumstance), the law creates the illusion of equivalence in circumstance (see Fine 1984). In practice, the law operates to maintain a form of distributive justice that is clearly to the advantage of those who already have the larger share of social goods (e.g. through protection of private property, regardless of social function). As demonstrated by the example provided in Box 22.1, the law is also seen to favour those who have the economic and social resources to both define the nature of social harm and to defend themselves if prosecuted for criminal activity (e.g. hiring top legal defence teams; see Chapter 12).

From the point of view of a Marxist critique, the law is structurally bound to reflect the broad class interests of the capitalist class. It does so ideologically through promulgation of the notion of 'equality before the law', and it does so practically through use of technical, procedural and administrative means that subvert the political and social meaning of particular kinds of social harm. Fundamentally, the law is a site of class conflict and an arena for class struggle.

BOX 22.1   PROSECUTION OF WORK-RELATED DEATH

In recent years, numerous Australian states have advocated tough law-and-order policies for street criminals, especially those resulting in harms to the person. Consequently, individuals engaging in typical forms of criminal violence, such as homicide, are highly likely to be sought out, brought before the courts, convicted and sentenced to a sizeable term of imprisonment.

By contrast, as the justice system presently operates, rogue employers, including recidivists, have little to fear regarding the corresponding likelihood of facing criminal charges and/or severe penalties for egregious Occupational Health and Safety (OHS) violations resulting in death. In essence, the virtual non-employment of common law manslaughter provisions against employers has permitted them to evade being held even minimally accountable for grossly negligent behaviour culminating in death. While to date not a single employer has been incarcerated in Victoria over the death of an employee, it is interesting to contrast this situation with the conviction and incarceration of a number of employees in recent times for fatigue-related culpable driving causing death by negligence.

For example, in 1999 a jury convicted a truck driver, William Francis Saul, on charges of culpable driving and reckless conduct endangering life over a fatal accident in 1998 (Paxinos 1999). The incident, a head-on collision, was precipitated by the snapping of the vehicle's front axle spring, which caused the vehicle to veer into oncoming traffic when it failed to successfully negotiate a bend in the road. The driver was found to have knowingly driven a van with steering problems. What is disturbing in this case is that Saul claimed to have been informed by his employer, Grangeburn Meats (which went into liquidation some weeks after the incident), that the mechanical problems with the truck—which were obviously known to them—had been attended to. He furthermore alleged that after the incident he was directed by his employer to concoct a story alleging that the deceased driver had been on the wrong side of the road. The presiding County Court Judge, John Barnett, expressed appreciation that the prospect of losing his livelihood acted as a significant constraint on Saul's inclination to complain about the vehicle's condition. He also expressed alarm at the 'possibility of a conspiracy to pervert the course of justice' (cited in Paxinos 1999: 6) and the fact that Saul's employer, who permitted him to drive a truck that was 'fundamentally unsafe', had not been subjected to investigation. Nonetheless, Saul was sentenced to a four-year jail term.

Overall, the message conveyed by Victoria's prosecutorial record is that deaths at work occupy a privileged status in the eyes of the law. In failing to treat seriously cases of exceptional corporate negligence, our legal system is countenancing notions of social inequity and injustice.

Source: Perrone (2000)

FEMINIST CRITIQUES

Feminist critiques of the law cover a broad range of substantive areas. Some of these include: the historical subjugation of women through and by the law (e.g. women as mere chattels or property of men); the biases in legal access for women; the patriarchal nature of judicial decision-making and the composition of the bench; the struggles by women to be recognised as legal subjects in their own right; sex discrimination and affirmative action legislation; and the unequal applications of the law in specific areas such as torts, criminal law, labour law, and so on (see ALRC 1994b; Easteal 2001; Easteal et al. 2012; Graycar & Morgan 2002; Sachs 1976; Scutt 1990).

The basic premise of feminist critiques is that the law has been, and continues to be, closely linked to (indeed, an ingrained part of) the oppression of women and the maintenance of structures of male domination. The critiques are centrally concerned with issues of social power, the distribution of economic and social resources, and the differential position of different groups in society. Thus, for example, it is argued that laws relating to such areas as rape, prostitution, paid employment and marital status were traditionally drafted so as to perpetuate the dependency of women and to maintain certain myths regarding the 'proper' role of women in society. For example, law reformers and academics often argue that despite significant legislative amendment to sex laws over time, jurors' entrenched attitudes regarding the proper conduct of males and females continues to result in substantive injustices for victims of sexual assault. Thus, even in Victoria, which is regarded as possessing the most progressive sexual offences laws in Australia, it remained twice as difficult to secure a conviction for rape between 1997 and 1999 (when fewer than 25% of those charged with rape were convicted) than in the period from 1988 to 1989 (which saw 46% convicted) (Farrant 2001).

In analysis of the law, several different strands of feminist critique are evident (see, for example, Barnes 1999; Easteal 2001; Easteal et al. 2012; Naffine 1990). For example, some writers concentrate on revealing the legal biases in favour of men, and on the discriminatory and sexist nature of legislation (see Box 22.2), the composition of the legal fraternity, and so on. Others expose how the law encapsulates a 'male view of society'; one that ignores or devalues the priorities and experiences of women, such as human inter-dependence, human compassion and human need. Still others argue that the law should not be viewed as a monolithic entity—it is as complex and contradictory as the dominant social order it reflects. In essence, feminist critiques view the law as one of the key institutionalised ways in which male power is sustained and gender inequality maintained. To change the position of women (and men) in society calls for fundamental social transformation, including the law itself.

The criticisms offered by feminist analysis go beyond critique of the formal processes and outcomes of the legal process. They also include interrogation of the basic legal concepts that underpin the criminal law. For instance, the legal fiction of the **reasonable man** is a conception associated with the abstract legal person; but what characteristics is it premised on? If we deconstruct this legal principle, we find that the subject is male and middle-class, and reflects a male, middle-class masculinity (Naffine 1990). The subject is considered to be calculating and financially secure, to be self-interested and rational, in a middle-class masculine way. Women, and other groups in society (e.g. working-class men), who do not act according to this legal model of reasonableness are, therefore, considered unreasonable. Hence, presumably neutral legal principles, such as tests of 'reasonableness', reflect unequally in terms of actual experiences depending on one's sex, class and ethnicity (see Access to Justice Advisory Committee 1994; Crofts & Loughnan 2013; Naffine 1990; Toole 2012).

REASONABLE MAN
A legal principle that determines what an ordinary 'reasonable' person would do in particular circumstances, based on an abstract legal subject that tends to reflect a male, middle-class masculinity.

BOX 22.2   THE DEFENCE OF PROVOCATION: THE *RAMAGE* CASE

On 21 July 2003, millionaire businessman James Ramage punched his estranged wife, Julie, to the ground, strangled her to death, and then disposed of her body in remote bushland before confessing his crime to police. At trial the controversial defence of provocation was successfully drawn upon to argue that Ramage did not commit murder, but was instead guilty of the lesser charge of manslaughter. The defence argued that the killing was not a premeditated crime, but rather a loss of self-control provoked by Julie's 'cruel' verbal taunts about their sex life immediately prior to her death and her unwillingness to state clearly her long-term intentions regarding the future of their marriage. Rules of evidence pertaining to hearsay precluded Julie's family from expressing to the court their concerns regarding James' propensity to violence.

In October 2004, James Ramage was sentenced to 11 years' jail, with a minimum of 8 years for killing his wife Julie. Under Victorian law, murder carries a maximum penalty of life in jail, while the maximum penalty for manslaughter is 20 years' jail.

Outraged women's groups cite this case as further evidence of the law's anachronistic and prejudicial portrayal of women as men's chattels, able to be controlled through violent means in the face of relative legal impunity. A Victorian Law Reform Commission report (2003) indicates that provocation is one of the most frequently used homicide defences (used in approximately 25 per cent of cases) and overwhelmingly used by men (89 per cent), especially in the context of sexual intimacy and, specifically, the killing of women in circumstances of jealousy or control. In a sample of cases examined, in none of the cases in which a woman cited provocation as a defence to murder was she successful, whereas a third of men using this defence were convicted of manslaughter. At issue, then, is the injustice of a defence that is clearly gender biased. A subsequent Victorian Law Reform Commission Report (2004) urged that a new defence to murder, that of diminished responsibility, should be created to overcome the apparent biases of the provocation defence.

Following the conclusion of the trial, the Victorian Government introduced the law of defensive homicide (a partial defence to homicide). Although intended as a 'safety net' for women who kill an intimate partner under circumstances of prolonged exposure to domestic violence, evidence indicates that it is being successfully exploited by male offenders, especially in instances of intimate female partner homicide (Fitz-Gibbon & Pickering 2012; Fitz-Gibbon & Stubbs 2012; Flynn 2009; Flynn & Fitz-Gibbon 2011; Petrie 2013a; Toole 2012; see also Chapter 10).

Source: Crooks (2004); Gough (2004); Munro (2004a)

POSTMODERNISM

We conclude this section by simply noting that the broad philosophical frameworks outlined here—the liberal, the Marxist and the feminist—can and do use a number of empirical and conceptual methodologies. There is often overlap between the concerns raised within each perspective, and the substantive areas of legal analysis extend to a much wider variety of topics and issues than dealt with here (see Davies 1994; Rush et al. 1997). Furthermore, in some instances, such as 'postmodern' approaches, there may be a challenge to the orthodoxies of conventional social structural analysis (see Davies 1994; Thompson 1992).

Depending upon how it is defined, postmodernism may involve both a method of unpacking legal concepts and critically analysing the reality of the law, and a quite different philosophical stance with regard to how we come to know the world (see, for example, Arrigo & Bernard 1997; Easteal et al. 2012; Lea 1998; White et al. 2012). With regard to the latter, postmodernism raises questions regarding the capacity of any theory, through words or symbols, to represent social reality. It is argued, instead, that every statement about the world (i.e. 'discourse') always represents a particular kind of reality. By focusing on how the legal discourses shape reality, we are better able to identify and give voice to other understandings of the social world—such as those relating to Indigenous people, ethnic minority groups, women, and any others who have been marginalised in and by the law.

CRITIQUES BASED ON PRACTICE AND EXPERIENCE
ACCESSING THE COURTS

The issue of who is able to access the court system (civil, criminal and administrative) is a fundamentally important one as far as justice is concerned, for it shapes the evolution of legal argument and precedent, and hence affects future outcomes (Cranston 1992; Productivity Commission 2014; Senate Legal and Constitutional Affairs Reference Committee 2009). As Sarat (1986: 527) argues: 'The right to one's day in court, the right to be heard, the right to take part in procedures through which one's fate is determined all provide the basic substance of due process, which is, in turn, at the heart of our conceptions of fairness and justice.' A fundamental assumption here is that the traditional machinery of justice—courts and tribunals—can be relied upon to uphold the rights of disadvantaged individuals and groups in society and to deliver just outcomes (Law Society of New South Wales 1998).

Alleged criminal offenders of course have little option but to appear before the courts, since it is the state that brings the action against them. Consequently, victims of prosecuted crime, although not always satisfied with the outcome, at least have their wrongs acknowledged. When it comes to victims of civil wrongs, however, access to a public hearing is for various reasons (particularly financial ones) not always possible, especially in those cases where the plaintiff is an individual rather than a corporation. Unlike the criminal justice system, there is no civil justice 'system' per se. Instead, a range of alternative legal remedies are available to parties to a civil dispute that are unable to resolve their differences privately; these include federal, state and territory courts, statutory tribunals and a plethora of government and industry ombudsmen (Productivity Commission 2014).

Within the formal system of justice, individual plaintiffs at times constitute the largest category of civil litigants in the higher courts; however, this is partly attributable to the predominance of personal injury claims in the higher courts. While some of these personal injury suits are directed against individuals, many are the result of motor vehicle accidents, and it is therefore the third-party insurers that conduct the defence, often in the absence of assistance from those being supposedly sued (Cranston 1992). Many civil proceedings are of course debt or property recovery measures instituted against individuals by businesses or corporations. A significant proportion of these are undefended and many are determined by way of default judgment (Cranston 1992).

The nature of the litigation to which the courts are exposed serves to create biased outcomes (whether conscious or unconscious). If a court is continuously exposed to a certain type of litigant who customarily takes action against another type of litigant, then the first type of litigant is likely to be favoured as far as outcomes are concerned. If, through frequency of appearance, the courts are more exposed to the arguments forwarded by the first type of litigant, those arguments assume a persuasive quality.

LEGAL REPRESENTATION: ACCESSING LEGAL AID

INDIVIDUAL BARRIERS

The adversarial nature of the litigation process is based upon the concept of a battle in which the combatants are equally matched. In practice, the combatants are customarily represented by legal counsel. Whether protagonist or defendant, participants in the legal process face enormous financial costs, the bulk of which is absorbed by legal counsel (Access to Justice Advisory Committee 1994). For those with low incomes, the prospect of having to outlay vast amounts of money for legal representation, and additional costs in the event of an unfavourable outcome, acts as a significant deterrent against the pursuit or defence of one's rights.

One way of addressing this impediment to accessing the law is through the redistribution of resources. One of the traditional methods of extending court access to disadvantaged groups is through the provision of publicly funded legal aid services such as the Victorian Aboriginal Legal Service, Community Legal Centres and the Legal Aid Commission (see Noone & Tomsen 2006). As stated by the Chief Justice of the Supreme Court of South Australia in 1984:

> Once it is grasped that justice fails radically unless citizens, irrespective of means, have access to the professional assistance necessary to vindicate their legal rights, legal aid is seen to be as natural and as essential a component of legal justice as the judiciary, the court buildings and the court staff. (cited in Access to Justice Advisory Committee 1994: 226)

Despite the pivotal importance of legal assistance, the Legal Aid Commission has experienced enormous public funding cutbacks since the mid-1990s (Sackville 2003). Consequently, in an effort to ration available resources, the eligibility criteria for assistance have been tightened in the following ways (Productivity Commission 2014; Cook 2013; Cook & Lee 2013; Lee & Dow 2013; Bottomley et al. 1991):

- All applicants for legal aid must undergo a means test (which covers both income and assets), in order to prove that they are unable to afford legal services; that is, they must prove that they are poor. It is unreasonable to assume, however, that all individuals who are not 'poor' enough to qualify for legal assistance are sufficiently 'wealthy' to be able to afford independent legal representation. Preliminary estimates by the Productivity Commission (2014), for example, indicate that in some jurisdictions fewer than 10 per cent of households would likely qualify (based on current income and asset tests) for legal aid. Since legal aid is increasingly an option available only to those who are extremely impoverished, there is obviously a group of low- and middle- income earners in society who are doubly disadvantaged.
- The budgetary squeeze has meant that there has been a progressive curtailing of the scope of activities previously handled. Policy guidelines now direct the prioritising of indictable criminal matters in which the accused faces the prospect of imprisonment, a suspended sentence or other types of correctional orders. This process has been detrimental to young people, low-level criminal offenders, civil litigation, family law, community legal education, and law reform matters. Consequently, the legal system is customarily used as a forum for contesting criminal matters, rather than as a vehicle for social change or the pursuit of rights (e.g. tenants' rights and consumer rights).
- Men constitute the great proportion of all 'criminal' applicants for legal aid, while women constitute the principal applicants for family law matters. This situation is particularly problematic given that, in general, women are more financially dependent on others than men; they are less likely than men to be in paid employment, and those who do work earn on average a lower income than their male counterparts.

- The case also must undergo a merits test, which assesses whether the matter has a reasonable chance of success; that is, acquittal. Hence the spectrum of acceptable cases is narrowed even further.

Additionally, in June 1996 the Commonwealth ceased funding legal aid matters arising under state or territory laws. Not unexpectedly, this withdrawal of funding has exacerbated regional variations in the availability of legal aid, contributing further to the financial burden of community legal centres and other community organisations, and exacerbating the barriers to accessing justice for people living in regional, rural and remote areas, and migrants and refugees (Senate Standing Committee on Legal and Constitutional Affairs 2004; Law and Justice Foundation of New South Wales 2003).

The conditions outlined above suggest that many people are automatically excluded from seeking financial assistance and hence pursuing 'natural justice'. Evidence in relation to legal representation of defendants starkly highlights the ultimate outcome of such restrictive access criteria. In particular, the number of unrepresented applicants for divorce in our courts increased from a quarter in 1981 to just under three-quarters in 1999–2000. Similarly, approximately 35 per cent of applicants before the Family Court in matters involving interim application (child contact and residency hearings) are unrepresented (Crockett 2001). Some commentators have predicted that the stringent guidelines may leave innocent defendants with no option but to plead guilty if they are denied legal representation (Conroy 1996; Haberfield 1996).

It is interesting to note that, as decided in the case of *McInnis v The Queen* [1979] HCA 65; (1979) 143 CLR 575, legal representation has been seen as an entitlement, rather than a legal right. As Barwick CJ saw it: 'It is proper to observe that an accused does not have a right to be provided with counsel at public expense. He (sic) has, of course, a right to be represented by counsel at his own or someone else's expense. He has no absolute right to legal aid.' However, more recently, in the *Dietrich* case the defendant appealed to the High Court of Australia on the sole ground that his trial miscarried by virtue of the fact that he was not provided with legal representation. In a majority decision, the High Court quashed the conviction and made an order that there be a new trial (see Brown et al. 1996a: 273–92).

AGENCY BARRIERS

The Legal Aid Commission has not only experienced direct financial constraints but also has had to operate within the constraints imposed by the broader socio-political climate (Cook 2013; Cook & Lee 2013; Lee & Dow 2013; Access to Justice Advisory Committee 1994; ALRC 1994a). These have included the following types of factors and trends:

- The deteriorating economic situation, an increase in the volume of legislation and a concomitant escalation in law enforcement activities have meant that there has been an increase in the number of individuals requiring legal assistance.
- There has been an escalation in the costs associated with running these legal services, but despite this fact, legal aid funding has not increased in real terms. Consequently, many services are now no longer available.
- A combination of the above has meant that there has been an increase in the number of refusals for assistance.

FURTHER BARRIERS

Although thus far our discussion of impediments to justice has concentrated on issues relating to financial resources, Rawls (1971) suggests that individuals also can be denied access to other primary resources, both natural and social. Raz (1986), for instance, argues that in those situations where individuals are unable to exercise the options formally available to them, then personal autonomy is substantively denied. Personal autonomy can be restricted in the following ways (Access to Justice Advisory Committee 1994; ALRC 1994a):

- Non-English-speaking people, including some Indigenous people, encounter additional specific barriers through the lack of sufficient interpreters. It is obvious that access to justice is seriously impeded or denied in those instances where individuals experiencing contact with the legal system are unable to obtain adequate information about legal services, comprehend proceedings, or communicate with various legal personnel or organisations (Beston 2010; Rebetzke 2009; ALRC 1992). Suspects who are being interviewed in relation to criminal investigations, parties to litigation, and witnesses appearing in court should all be entitled to effective interpreting services.
- Some recently arrived immigrants also face cultural barriers, which psychologically constrain them from accessing the legal system (Ferrari & Costi 2012). This is especially the case for those originating from countries that operate under an oppressive legal system, where the police, judges and courts act as repressive agents.
- A lack of knowledge of either the law and its operations or the availability of services also impacts upon one's access to justice; these barriers are often based upon simple ignorance. Some individuals (whether they are immigrants or otherwise) may feel mystified or intimidated by what they perceive to be complex and unpredictable organisations and processes. Others, who lack legal knowledge, may simply see what has happened to them as unfortunate, rather than an infringement of their rights; hence, they may not recognise the basis for a claim of compensation.
- Geographical isolation presents another important barrier for those individuals living in rural communities (see Rice 2011; Giddings et al. 2001). For persons with disabilities, problems are also encountered in relation to accessing a variety of legal services. At the most basic level, this includes gaining physical access to courts.
- Almost a third of all Australian women have dependent children and they are usually the primary carers of those children (Australian Law Reform Commission 1994b; ABS 1993). For these women, the ability to access legal resources is adversely affected by significant time and energy costs. The operational hours of many legal services are prohibitive for many mothers, in that they function on a 9 am to 5 pm basis; their accessibility is therefore contingent upon the availability of childcare facilities. Additionally, the stresses experienced by women who encounter childcare problems may have a damaging effect on their capacity to instruct counsel or to deliver testimony.

These are some of the key barriers to legal access. They are readily acknowledged in liberal critiques of the existing legal system, and the main impetus for intervention is to remove or diminish these barriers in order to ensure 'justice for all'.

REDRESSING THE LACK OF ACCESS TO JUSTICE

In response to issues surrounding the lack of access to justice, various recommendations have been made that seek to redress this situation (see Box 22.3). According to the Access to Justice Advisory Committee, for example, the key objectives of an action plan to redress current difficulties ought to include (Access to Justice Advisory Committee 1994):

- *Equality of access to legal services*: 'All Australians, regardless of means, should have access to high quality legal services or effective dispute-resolution mechanisms necessary to protect their rights and interests. Equality of access to legal services requires that individuals who may not be able to afford legal services, but who have legitimate interests to protect, should have a range of opportunities available to them to bring (or defend) proceedings, without necessarily incurring liability for their own fees.' For example, legal aid, community legal centres, and the provision of pro bono legal services by lawyers (see further Productivity Commission 2014; Anderson & Renouf 2003; McLeay 2003; Ojelabi 2011a,b; Rice 2012;).

- *National equity*: 'All Australians, regardless of their place of residence, should enjoy, as nearly as possible, equal access to legal services and to legal services markets that function competitively. To the extent that there are variations in access among states or regions, they should have to be justified by reason of special, identifiable circumstances.' For example, uniformity is not necessarily a goal to be pursued in itself; people should not be denied access to legal services simply because of where they happen to live, such as rural and isolated areas of the country.

- *Equality before the law*: 'Australia's international obligations and domestic legislation reflect the principle that all Australians, regardless of race, ethnic origins, gender or disability, are entitled to equal opportunities in such fields as education, employment, use of community facilities and access to services.' For example, constitutional requirements, human rights, democratic rights and citizenship (Australian Human Rights Commission 2009).

How people in general perceive the legal system will have a major impact on their inclination to use legal services. Likewise, in addition to negative perceptions and how these influence behaviour, there are, as indicated, some real material problems in gaining access to justice. However, the tendency has been for governments to commit themselves in principle to system reform, but to be less forthcoming when it comes to policy development, allocation of resources or systemic changes to the legal status quo.

Addressing the problem of access to resources is a starting point, in that it helps to guarantee procedural equality. Nevertheless, a radical critique would argue that such reforms are piecemeal and that, ultimately, fundamental inequalities are ingrained in the justice system. These inequalities are, in turn, seen to reflect wider societal social disparities and power relations. The old adage 'a law for the rich and a law for the poor' basically sums up this position.

BOX 22.3   PRINCIPLES OF A REFORM ACTION PLAN

- Public institutions and organisations that enjoy special privileges conferred by legislation, such as law societies and Bar associations, must be accountable to the community (e.g. independent scrutiny, complaints procedures and information).
- The principle of accountability applies to the courts (as they themselves have recognised), but must be reconciled with the fundamental principle of the independence of the judiciary (e.g. justice must be seen to be done, public education and explanation of decisions).
- The law should be as clear and simple as possible (e.g. using plain language and the provision of interpreters).
- Legal institutions and lawyers should adopt a consumer-oriented approach to their work and responsibilities (e.g. public service professionalism and user-friendly services).
- Competition principles should apply to the legal services market, thereby bringing about a more flexible and efficient legal profession (e.g. varieties of legal work, and sources of legal information and advice).

Source: Access to Justice Advisory Committee (1994)

ALTERNATIVE DISPUTE RESOLUTION

Issues of legal costs and access to justice have given rise to various alternatives to the formal justice system. The purpose of this section is to describe **alternative dispute resolution** (ADR) methods and principles, and to explore the strengths and limitations of other alternative ways in which to obtain 'justice'. Some of the issues to consider in relation to the inaccessibility of the formal court system include:

- legal costs (e.g. costs of legal representation)
- psychological and social constraints (e.g. intimidation due to such things as the use of obscure legal jargon)
- the trauma of participation (e.g. children who have been abused, and victims of sexual crimes)
- lack of knowledge (e.g. seeing an event as 'unfortunate' rather than as an infringement on one's rights, such as to compensation)
- limited availability of services (e.g. hours of operation and geographical location)
- lack of court-related services (e.g. courtroom interpreters)
- inadequate or inappropriate legal advice and counselling (e.g. unwarranted pressures to plead guilty as part of court case management).

Criticisms of the formal system of justice, with its exorbitant costs and inbuilt intimidations, have produced a shift to informal systems of justice. Critics of the adversarial system claim that it is a win/lose situation; whether it be the criminal or civil law (King 2012; Gutman 2009; Wright 1991). They argue that it is a fault-based system, with little room for compromise. Associated with the adversarial system is also the professionalisation of conflict; barristers and solicitors take power away from the individual, so that the court process is a disempowering process (see Naffine 1990). The formal system also seems to produce an escalation in the conflict. The adversarial system has also been accused of lack of attention to concerns and needs of the victim. Furthermore, the adversarial system may restrain, but it does not resolve the conflict. Finally, the expense and conflicts associated with formal legal processes can be intimidating and disempowering. The answer, therefore, is to try to minimise reliance upon formal justice or to sidestep formal adjudication as much as possible.

The criticisms of the formal justice system have thus gone hand-in-hand with efforts to produce a different approach to dispute resolution, one that is located increasingly both inside and outside of the formal court system (King 2012; Gutman 2009; National Alternative Dispute Resolution Advisory Council 2000). Informal dispute-resolution mechanisms include basic 'self-help' strategies (e.g. do-it-yourself legal kits and advice on how to resolve neighbourhood disputes without use of legal experts). They also include a wide range of avenues that are structured within the system itself as ADR measures.

Informal and/or alternative dispute resolution mechanisms include:

- *Self-help*: where disputes are resolved directly by the parties involved. For example, instead of calling the police in response to a shopstealing incident, a shopkeeper may choose to deal with the offender himself or herself. Or an argument between neighbours regarding the previous night's noise may be resolved by simply talking about the disturbance among themselves.
- *Out-of-court settlements*: where disputes are resolved outside of the court as such, although the impetus may well be a calculation on the part of the disputing parties that it is cheaper to settle sooner, and through direct negotiation, rather than later and more formally via a judge or jury, given court costs and the potential costs of compensation arising from court-based decisions.

ALTERNATIVE DISPUTE RESOLUTION
A set of methods and strategies of dispute resolution that are less formal and less expensive than those provided by formal justice institutions, and which are in many cases directed at positive problem-solving and involve active citizen participation.

- *Dispute settlement centres*: where certain types of problems can be discussed with experienced practitioners and on a relatively informal basis, as with the case of Neighbourhood Mediation Centres.
- *Family mediation centres*: where issues pertaining to family law matters can be discussed in a non-threatening and constructive way in order to minimise disruption to family life.
- *Quasi-judicial bodies*: where specialised courts and tribunals are used in ways that are oriented toward problem-solving, and where legal procedures tend to be less formal. Examples include the Equal Opportunity Board, Civil and Administrative Tribunals, Crimes Compensation Tribunal, Administrative Appeals Tribunal and Transport Accident Commission.
- *Commonwealth and State Ombudsman*: where complaints against a state agency can be heard, investigated and attempted to be resolved, such that the agency should reconsider or change a decision, apologise to the complainant or, in some circumstances, pay compensation. A decision cannot be imposed upon either party as the main role of the Ombudsman is as mediator.
- *Industry ombudsman*: where complaints against a particular company or industry can be heard, such as the Telecommunications Industry Ombudsman or Banking Ombudsman. In some cases, such as the Banking Ombudsman Scheme, the decision is binding on the bank, but not the consumer.

What distinguishes these agencies, centres and institutions is that their operating procedures and rules are meant to be less formal, there are fewer delays in getting a case heard, and there is a large reduction in legal costs, since one need not be a lawyer to be an advocate. They thus serve as less formal mechanisms of conflict resolution, and operate outside of the usual courtroom type of legal framework.

The organisation and practices of various means to resolve disputes can be conceptualised in terms of different forms of decision-making, ranging from the more formal to the less formal, and with regard to different roles for the person leading the ADR session. For example, three different modes of ADR have been identified by the National Alternative Dispute Resolution Advisory Council (2000: 6):

- *facilitative ADR processes*: in which the third party provides assistance in the management of the process of dispute resolution, but generally has no advisory or determinative role (e.g. mediation, conciliation and facilitation)
- *advisory ADR processes*: in which the third party investigates the dispute and provides advice as to the facts of the dispute and, in some cases, advice regarding possible, probable and desirable outcomes, and how these can be achieved (e.g. investigation, expert appraisal, case appraisal and dispute counselling)
- *determinative ADR processes*: in which the third party investigating the dispute makes a determination that is potentially enforceable as to its resolution (e.g. adjudication, arbitration and expert determination).

Analysis of dispute-resolution methods raises the issue of what kinds of skills and qualities those conducting ADR sessions ought to possess (see, for instance, Charlton & Dewdney 2004; Ojelabi 2011a). In the United States, for example, a number of organisations have developed ethical standards for mediator conduct. These involve adhering to certain model standards of conduct, including elements such as impartiality and competence (see McGillis 1997). The issue of standards has also received considerable attention from Australian participants in ADR (see National Alternative Dispute Resolution Advisory Council 2000).

There is great diversity of dispute-resolution services and a proliferation of ADR methods across a wide range of areas. From neighbourhood conflicts to workplace problems, school-based disputes to victim–offender relationships, ADR types of processes are increasingly being applied and tested. The advantages of ADR methods include such things as: parties being able to choose the mode of dispute resolution that is most appropriate for their dispute; the focus on problem-solving; less expense and time; direct involvement of the parties themselves; and greater participant satisfaction.

LIMITATIONS OF ADR

Despite their advantages, ADR processes also have their limitations. Some of these include:

- An emphasis on 'neutrality' on the part of mediators and conciliators may not be appropriate in those instances where one party has been subjected to injury (e.g. discrimination) and is vulnerable relative to the other party (i.e. the need for an 'advocate' for the complainant.
- The concept of mediation or conciliation often implies movement on both sides, even though one side has been harmed.
- Agreements reached through mediation may not necessarily be enforceable.
- Imbalances in negotiation skills or in the power relationships between the parties may possibly lead to agreements that could be perceived as unfair (e.g. one party might be more articulate than the other).
- The skills and experience of mediators or arbitrators vary, which can lead to uneven or possibly unjust outcomes.

Acknowledgment of these kinds of issues are central to contemporary discussions about ADR standards in relation to both individual practitioners and ADR service providers, including government, community and commercial organisations (Sourdin 2012; Ojelabi 2011a,b; National Alternative Dispute Resolution Advisory Council 2000).

Criticism of alternative dispute resolution can also be linked to the theoretical critique of *informalisation* in general, which views it as a trend towards justice without law (see Arthur 2011; Baskin 1988; Ojelabi 2011a). While informalism has its strengths, some of the criticisms include:

- It implies an expansion of regulation; that is, the state is seen to intervene into more areas of life under the guise of less formal social control. Here we can ask who is funding the community-based organisations, who is setting them up, and whose interests are being represented? It is argued that informal dispute-resolution mechanisms have simply become institutions of social control located in the community and, increasingly, incorporated into the judicial system.
- The processes associated with informalisation are premised not on actually dealing with structures that generate conflict, but on neutralising conflict through appeals to mediation. This may have the effect of de-politicising social issues and portraying them as simply individual or personal problems. Accommodation is portrayed as the only possible resolution to the disputant's problems; this is basically depicting conflict as a bad thing that must be resolve at all costs, so that all interests are met. In reality, however, the parties are not evenly matched, and achieving justice may require an 'unequal' resolution of social conflicts.
- The use of informal measures may be tied to the commodification of justice, so that justice becomes something that involves norms related to the sale and buying of commodities. Mediation centres, for example, might simply produce manuals, kits and videos on legal issues, which in the end seek to professionalise and standardise mediation activity, and ultimately homogenise the conflict. The conflict is thus still construed as a private matter that is not open to public scrutiny. More generally, given the packaging of legal materials, one might ask how much actual community involvement and control there is in community mediation programs.

STRENGTHS AND WEAKNESSES OF ADR

Having noted these criticisms, it is nevertheless important to recognise that ADR involves a great many different models of practice, types of methods, institutional settings and strategic players. From the point of view of 'access to justice', many of these appear to offer greater scope for positive dispute resolution—especially for those who cannot afford legal services—than otherwise may be the case. There are, however, various strengths and weaknesses associated with both formal and informal types of justice (see Table 22.1).

TABLE 22.1 FORMAL AND INFORMAL JUSTICE: STRENGTHS AND WEAKNESSES

	FORMAL	INFORMAL
Strengths	• clearly defined roles • publicly defined powers • finite powers • consistency and predictability • adherence to due process • avenues of appeal • public nature	• proactive and reactive • less expensive • more accessible • fewer delays • promotes restorative solutions • conciliation • reintegration directly into community
Weaknesses	• financial costs • limited legal assistance • legalities and formal technicalities • alienation of client • adversarial conflict • effectiveness of dispositions • disempowering • long delays	• does not protect rights • inconsistent • personalises treatment • net widening • no appeal process • issues of accountability • harsher punishments • varying discretionary powers

COMMUNITY LEGAL CENTRES AND PARALEGALS

In recent years, concern also has been expressed that provision of legal services has taken place in an overly protected market, and that this has contributed to the high cost of legal services and inefficient service to consumers. Areas that have received attention have included the division between barristers and solicitors in some states, the reservation of legal work of lawyers, the entry requirements for lawyers, and lawyers' business structures—all of which in some way have been criticised from the point of view of diminishing competition (see Access to Justice Advisory Committee 1994).

Public provision of legal services is directly linked to both the cost of existing legal services and the inability of some people to afford these services. Lawyers' fees constitute a major cost for most people seeking access to the justice system. The prospect of an expensive bill for their lawyers' fees, and possibly another large bill for their opponent's lawyers in the event of losing a contested case, is enough to deter many people from pursuing or defending their legal rights.

In acknowledging this, governments have set up or funded alternative legal services of various kinds—the most prominent being 'legal aid'—in order to cater for the needs of those who otherwise could not afford legal assistance (Noone & Tomsen 2006; Chisholm & Nettheim 2002). The overall Australian pattern is that legal assistance (broadly defined as legal services for poor people) is provided:

- on an individual basis by private lawyers on a pro bono basis (free or at reduced rates)
- by public bodies, such as public solicitors and public defenders
- via Legal Aid Commissions
- through Community Legal Centres
- through specialist legal aid, such as the Victorian Aboriginal Legal Service that deals with issues including criminal law and land rights.

As we have previously discussed, however, there are a number of practical barriers that influence who can obtain legal aid as a specific form of institutionalised legal support (see also Lawry 2010). Whereas legal aid reflects 'official' concern about issues of access to justice and the evident need to provide services to poor people, the **Community Legal Centres** (CLCs) emerged from the 'grassroots' level up. The development of the centres was driven by political motivation to engage in wider social change (Noble 2012; Rice 2012). The development of the CLCs was not the same in each part of the country. For example, in Victoria and New South Wales the centres emerged as a result of the activities of law students and their awareness of the unmet legal needs of the poor. By contrast, in Western Australia such centres were established mainly through the efforts of welfare and youth workers, who sought to deal with the rights of welfare beneficiaries and issues of welfare law reform.

COMMUNITY LEGAL CENTRES Legal organisations informed by an ethos of addressing the unmet legal needs of the poor, disadvantaged and vulnerable, and using the law as a mechanism for substantive social reform.

CLCS: A RANGE OF SERVICES

Across Australia, CLCs were designed to challenge traditional legalistic methods of conflict resolution and courtroom practices (see Dunne 1985; Noble 2012; Noone & Tomsen 2006; Rice 2012). The centres have generally been driven by 'social justice' concerns, as well as ordinary legal service concerns; that is, rather than adoption of a narrow interpretation of 'justice' (usually meaning legal representation), the CLCs acknowledge that economics is just one barrier to justice and that structural changes are needed in society if we are to empower the disadvantaged and marginalised groups in the community. This translates into a range of services, including legal advice and referrals, caseloads, campaigning on broad law reform, and community education on welfare and other rights. Research has been carried out by various CLCs on issues such as police maltreatment of minority groups and the gender composition and 'masculine' nature of policing, prisoner rights and the privatisation of prisons. In the case of the Aboriginal Legal Service, considerable attention has been devoted to issues such as land rights, anti-discrimination matters, and input into the development of international conventions on Indigenous rights.

Community Legal Centres vary in terms of work orientation, office set-up, relationship with clients and level of engagement in social reform activities. In some places, great effort is made to resource individuals to struggle and assert their own rights. Most centres emphasise the importance of active community participation. Some provide easy-to-read law books, do-it-yourself legal kits and a variety of educational packages designed for the lay reader. The CLCs receive state funding, and this can create tensions and funding threats in cases where a CLC is critical of government policy or bodies such as the police (it is notable, for example, that funding to community legal centres was drastically cut by the Abbott Liberal Government in 2014, a consequence no doubt of the perception of the CLCs being overtly and overly 'political'). However, not all centres share the same political perspectives, and today many do not engage in social reform or structural change types of activities (Chesterman 1993). Nevertheless, a radical tradition of self-help and community action remains a hallmark of the movement as a whole; even though, as Noone and Tomsen (2006: 5–6) point out, legal aid policy as a whole is oriented toward the traditional legal services to individuals.

THE COMPETITION MODEL OF SERVICE DELIVERY

Over the past decade and a half there has been pressure on the CLCs to adopt a 'competition' model of service delivery (Glanville 1999). For community organisations generally, this has meant an increased focus on outputs in the form of service delivery (e.g. number of 'clients' served), a need to become more familiar with market mechanisms (e.g. user pays) and a need to develop skills in competing for available resources (e.g. different funding agencies).

An emphasis on market-oriented models of service provision has a number of implications with regard to how legal services might be conceptualised. For example, it has been argued that there are two competing models of public policy—one focused on 'citizenship', the other on 'consumerism'—and that adoption of one model or the other has major implications for the nature of legal service provision (see Sackville 2011; Glanville 1999). The emphasis in the first is on collective rights, universal availability, public provision and accountability. The emphasis in the second is individual rights, exchange relationships based upon money, market forces and 'rational choice'.

Contrary to the 'competition' model, it has been argued that CLCs should be funded and supported less on the basis of efficiency and consumer arguments than on the basis of social objectives and specifically a 'public interest test' (Glanville 1999: 155–6). The great strength of the CLCs lies in the fact that they have close links with their communities and this, in turn, is an important part of their accessibility and effectiveness. The danger of 'competition' funding and performance management models is that they could well undercut this relationship.

PARALEGALS

Consideration of the role of the CLCs begs the question of who, precisely, should be allowed to provide legal services. Should all legal work be in the hands of lawyers? Or, is it possible and desirable to allow other individuals to participate in legal-related areas? Such questions are central to discussion of the potential role of **paralegals**. Various committees and commentators have supported the idea of expanding the scope of paralegal practice. The kinds of work in which paralegals could engage includes such things as administration (e.g. management of legal offices), legal support (e.g. gathering evidence), advising (e.g. information about the law) and advocacy (e.g. before the Social Security Appeals Tribunal).

Community mediation centres and community legal centres have long supported the idea of greater use of semi-professional paralegals (see Regan 1990; Noone 1988). The movement has been supported both from the top down, arising out of the concern with costs of legal services, and from the bottom up, arising out of a concern with the achievement of justice.

In countries such as Canada, the United States and England, the use of paralegals is favoured, as they are perceived as far more accessible than lawyers (Noone 1988). This is because they draw upon commonsense skills, and they often have a vested interest in what is happening at the grassroots level. They speak in 'common' rather than 'legal' language and are less likely to distort the formal processes of institutions by engaging in hair-splitting activities such as arguing about definitions and technicalities.

In broad social terms, paralegals have also been able to provide a broad and flexible range of assistance beyond the conventional legal problem areas; that is, they provide assistance in areas customarily ignored by lawyers. Alongside politically committed lawyers, paralegals have been actively involved in

PARALEGAL
Someone who is not trained as a lawyer but who engages in legal-related work, for example researching the situation of residents affected by toxic environments, in order to assist communities on public interest matters and/or to provide basic legal advice.

traditionally 'non-conventional' justice areas, such as the environment, Indigenous populations and injured workers, and as advocates for the less powerful groups in the community. Crucially, they have links at the grassroots level, so that they are not merely implementing ADR mechanisms but also are oriented toward significant social change and public interest issues.

There are a number of issues, however, that must be closely considered in relation to the use of paralegals. Some of these include: ethical matters (e.g. relating to client confidentiality and disciplinary bodies for misconduct); quality control (e.g. is the service provided the same quality or better than that received from a legal practitioner?); training; supervision (e.g. access to an experienced solicitor); support (e.g. up-to-date legal information systems); cost-effectiveness; and career structures (Access to Justice Advisory Committee 1994). Many of these issues parallel those pertaining to ADR service providers and practitioners.

ISSUES FOR CONSIDERATION

GENDERED AID

Women receive a much smaller share of the legal aid dollar than men do. Why is this the case? One reason is that as lawyers and community organisations become aware of cuts to services and eligibility by Legal Aid Commissions, they become reluctant to refer people for assistance, as they are likely to be rejected under the more stringent guidelines. Another is that Legal Aid Commission policy guidelines tend to give priority to criminal matters. Most criminal defendants are men and most applicants for legal aid in criminal matters are men. Conversely, women are the majority of applicants in family law matters, and it is difficult to obtain legal aid in matters important to women, particularly family and civil law matters. In some places there are specialist women's legal services. These provide telephone advice services, regular 'divorce clinics', kits on divorce, assault and victims' compensation, direct service provision and community legal education. However, much more needs to be done in this area (see ALRC 1994b).

ALTERNATIVE DISPUTE RESOLUTION: ACCESS TO JUSTICE OR 'JUSTICE' WIDENING?

The formal justice system has attracted criticisms on a number of grounds: it is viewed as enormously expensive, overly adversarial in nature, disempowering and as customarily ignoring the rights of victims (Ojelabi 2012a,b; Access to Justice Advisory Committee 1994; ALRC 1994a). Such criticisms, which are broadly related to issues of disempowerment, have prompted the development of a whole range of ADR initiatives. In what sense can the very existence of these 'informal' mechanisms be seen as yet a further indictment of the 'formal' justice system?

Some general issues regarding ADR that require further consideration and critical evaluation revolve around the relationship between the 'formal' system and the ADR methods. For instance, has the proliferation of ADR agencies and methods been accompanied by a decreased use of the formal justice system, or does it represent a widening of 'justice' approaches into greater spheres of public life? Or, to put it differently, has the spread of ADR stimulated the growth in the number of disputes where a third-party professional becomes involved, and thereby removed citizens from solving their own problems?

Concern has been expressed that dispute-resolution techniques are becoming institutionalised as they become entrenched in the legal system. Many agencies and organisations have now created institutional 'gate-keeping' mechanisms that divert potential disputes to mediation or require mediation as an intermediary step in the larger legal process. For example, family law disputes now incorporate three stages of dispute resolution: a conference, a conciliation session and court adjudication. Does this institutionalisation mean that dispute resolution, in this particular setting, will be less flexible and more formal, and ultimately lead to greater costs for the parties involved?

Another issue of concern is the potential long-term effects of the institutionalisation of ADR in regards to bureaucratisation, large caseloads, funding pressures and the quality of case processing over time. Related to this is another interesting phenomenon. One result of the infusion of mediation into administrative and judicial procedures has been the perceived movement of lawyers into the practice of mediation, a move sometimes resented by non-lawyers, and a move that raises concerns about the 'legalisation' of what are intended to be alternative dispute-resolution processes (see Roberts 1994; National Alternative Dispute Resolution Advisory Council 2000).

CONCLUSION

In exploring the issue of access to justice, this chapter has demonstrated that, regardless of system rhetoric and legal safeguards, inequality exists, both in relation to legal treatment and social outcomes. In order to understand this discrepancy, it is necessary to acknowledge that the law does not exist independently; it cannot be considered in isolation from the socio-political context within which it operates.

Our concern in the next chapter is to go from general critique to consider the specific operation of the criminal justice system. In particular, the nature of adjudication and of sentencing will be examined.

DISCUSSION QUESTIONS

1   Why is access to justice such a problem from the point of view of 'equality' and the law?

2   What are the main barriers to justice in Australian society?

3   In what ways is informal justice better or worse than formal justice?

4   'In a truly just society, there would be no need for community legal centres and legal aid'. Discuss.

5   'Social inequality is embedded in the institutions of justice'. Discuss and provide examples.

FURTHER READING

Access to Justice Advisory Committee (1994) *Access to justice: an action plan*, Australian Government Publishing Service, Canberra.

Australian Law Reform Commission (1994) *Equality before the law: justice for women*, Report No. 69, part 1, Australian Government Publishing Service, Canberra.

King, M.S. (2012) 'Reflections on ADR, judging and non-adversarial justice: parallels and future developments', *Journal of Justice Administration*, 22: 76–84.

Productivity Commission (2014) *Access to justice arrangements: Productivity Commission draft report*. Commonwealth of Australia, Melbourne.

Sackville, R. (2011) 'Access to justice: towards an integrated approach', *The Judicial Review*, 10: 221–36.

JUDICIAL DECISIONS AND SENTENCING

23

CHAPTER OVERVIEW

- THE NATURE OF JUDICIAL DECISION-MAKING
- METHODS OF DETERMINING SENTENCES
- SENTENCING PENALTIES
- SENTENCING DEBATES AND REFORMS
- ISSUES FOR CONSIDERATION
- CONCLUSION
- DISCUSSION QUESTIONS
- FURTHER READING

INTRODUCTION

Equality before the law is said to be guaranteed through both philosophical rules (the rule of law) and operational procedures (due process rights). While formal justice is symbolically offered through the very existence of these rules and procedures, examined from the point of view of operational access and equity, a number of factors were identified in Chapter 22 as contributing to substantive injustice (inequality of outcomes), thereby bringing into question the impartiality of our justice system.

From the perspective of the general public, access to justice, and therefore confidence in our justice system, is very much influenced by the most visible image of justice in action—judicial decision-making or sentencing. The aim of this chapter is to examine more closely the administration of the law and, in particular, the nature of the decisions actually made in the courtroom: how decisions are made, how 'guilt' is determined and how sentencing takes place. Particular attention is paid to the underlying principles of sentencing and the range of disposition available to the court in dealing with convicted offenders. The chapter concludes with a review of recent sentencing debates and their impact on sentencing policies and practices.

SENTENCE
A penalty or penalties imposed by a court upon a defendant who is proven guilty of a criminal offence. The sentencing process constitutes the final act in the adjudication process and represents the symbolic principal act connected to the judicial function.

THE NATURE OF JUDICIAL DECISION-MAKING

The primary roles of the court are to determine the guilt or innocence of an accused person and, if a finding of guilt is arrived at, to determine **sentence**. How the court undertakes this decision-making process is, however, subject to ongoing evaluation, criticism and public concern.

The sociologist Max Weber (1954) describes the process of legal decision-making as formally rational, insofar as the organisational procedures and techniques employed in determining sentence are themselves intrinsically rational; that is, judged according to objective, abstract rules. According to Weber, the application of established rules and procedures in judicial decision-making, such as those governing the degree of flexibility or discretion exercised by the court, and the use of extra-legal sources (e.g. psychiatric, medical or welfare reports), ensures uniformity in dealing with like cases (see Inverarity et al. 1983). When examined alongside the objectives of sentencing, however, it is these very rules and procedures, and the tensions between them, that are the focus of many contemporary debates over judicial decision-making. Present discussions of the role of the court bring these methods into focus insofar as they pertain to matters such as the range of available sanctions, and the conditions under which those sanctions are applied (e.g. the degree of discretion able to be exercised by the judiciary).

DETERMINING GUILT

The media, academics and the judiciary itself often attack the 'discretionary' aspects of our legal system; that is, the active and creative ways in which judges deal with criminal matters on a case-by-case basis, especially when decisions handed down appear non-rational, inconsistent, or overly lenient or punitive (Mackenzie et al. 2012; Jones & Weatherburn 2010; Lovegrove 2008; Spigelman 2008; Davis 2007; Bagaric & Edney 2003; Finkelstein 2003). While variable treatment of convicted offenders is consistent with principles of social justice (i.e. individualised justice, which takes the complexity and circumstances of the offence and the offender into account, and tailors state intervention to ensure social needs are met and wellbeing is enhanced), it does not sit comfortably with principles of formal equality (ensuring equality of opportunity for individuals to become socially and economically unequal) and consistency (which is guided by sentencing patterns for particular offences).

Criticisms of sentencing discretion are often premised on the view that a more formal, rational and accountable system of justice is desirable. In order to minimise the opportunities for judicial discretion, there are often calls for the adoption of an administratively efficient and transparent basis for decision-making—one that introduces 'structured reasoning' based either on 'mandatory' procedures and rules or the adoption of guideline judgments or decision-making frameworks (see, for example, Hewton 2010; Lovegrove 2007; Roberts 2012). Decisions whether to prosecute, commit for trial, admit evidence, grant leave to appeal, allow **plea bargaining**, grant bail, use certain sentencing dispositions, and so on all involve the exercise of discretion by persons within the criminal justice system. However, the outcomes—at least when it comes to determining guilt—are remarkably similar.

ADVERSARIAL SYSTEM

Both historically and in modern times, media images of courts highlight the predominance of adversarial proceedings. The image is of the court as an arena of conflict, with the competitors (prosecution and defence) engaged in fierce verbal battles to win the contest. The reality of courtroom processes, however, stands in marked contrast to this highly dramatised, adversarial media imagery, with contested charges determined at trial a rare event. As indicated by Figures 23.1 and 23.2, defendants finalised in each type of court overwhelmingly are found 'proven guilty', with most pleading guilty as part of ordinary courtroom negotiation. For example, of the total number of defendants whose cases were subject to **finalisation** (adjudicated and non-adjudicated) in the higher courts in Australia during 2012–13 (n = 15,108), just over 78 per cent were proven guilty. This figure increases to 92 per cent when guilty verdicts are considered as a percentage of defendants subjected to **adjudicated finalisation** only (11,841). The production of guilty within magistrates' courts is even more pronounced, with 451,111 defendants proven guilty, which represents 88 per cent of all defendants finalised and a staggering 97 per cent of all defendants adjudicated. Of the total number of defendants adjudicated and proven guilty, the vast proportion (70 per cent) pleaded guilty, while the remainder were found guilty following a trial (ABS 2014f). Adjudication is thus by and large an uncontested affair.

PLEA BARGAINING
An agreement in a criminal case whereby the defendant is offered the opportunity to plead guilty by the prosecution, usually in exchange for a sentence discount (lesser charge or fewer charges) or a recommendation of a lighter maximum sentence, subject to court approval.

FINALISATION
Occurs when all charges against a person or organisation have been formally dealt with by the court.

ADJUDICATED FINALISATION
Occurs when all charges against a person or organisation have been finalised by way of a judgment or decision by the court. This involves the court making a determination regarding whether the defendant is guilty.

FIGURE 23.1   CRIMINAL CASES FINALISED IN MAGISTRATES' COURTS, 2012–13, BY
METHOD OF FINALISATION[a, b, c]

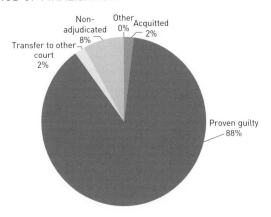

n = 514,897
[a] NSW refers to finalised appearances rather than defendants, resulting in possible overcounting. NSW
excludes defendants finalised by committal to a higher court
[b] includes guilty plea and guilty verdict
[c] includes defendants unfit to plead, defendants deceased, other adjudicated finalisations and cases finalised by unknown method

Source: Australian Bureau of Statistics (2014f)

FIGURE 23.2   CRIMINAL CASES FINALISED IN HIGHER COURTS, 2012–13, BY METHOD
OF FINALISATION[a, b]

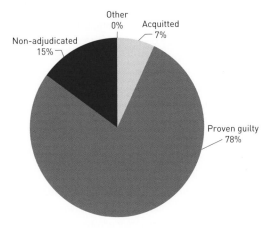

n = 15,108
[a] includes guilty plea and guilty verdict
[b] includes defendants deceased, transfers to other court levels and other non-adjudicated finalisations

Source: Australian Bureau of Statistics (2014f)

PLEA BARGAINING

In most cases people plead guilty because in one sense or another they actually are guilty. From a system perspective, however, such pleas also serve the interests of criminal justice agencies and the community generally because they expedite the process of adjudication (thereby alleviating the backlog of cases awaiting determination), reduce court costs and spare the victims of, and eyewitnesses to, crime the trauma of testifying and being subjected to cross-examination. As observed by Weatherburn and Nguyen da Huong (cited in Torre & Wraith 2013: 193), 'If everyone arrested were tried before a judge and jury ... the criminal justice system would either grind to a halt or become impossibly expensive to maintain'. One way of fostering guilty pleas at the earliest opportunity is through the practice of plea bargaining, also commonly referred to in Australia as 'negotiated pleas'.

Although a complex phenomenon that does not lend itself to simple definition, plea bargaining is essentially a process of informal discussion between prosecution (police and/or crown) and defence counsel and the accused, at any stage of the progress of a case through the courts (including post-trial in the case of a hung jury), regarding the agreed facts of a criminal case, the defendant's likely plea and the prospect of negotiating charge(s), subject to court approval. In most cases, plea bargaining involves efforts by the prosecutor—and in some jurisdictions the judiciary—to persuade an accused criminal to confess guilt to one or more charges. This may involve discussions around how best to deal with the **principal offence** (i.e. the most serious offence type). In exchange for waiving their right to trial, an accused may be offered a range of concessions from the prosecutor and the court, which generally results in the application of a more lenient sentencing disposition than would otherwise be imposed had a finding of guilt resulted from the process of contested adjudication (Flynn 2007; Fox 2002).

Theoretically, plea bargaining can involve the following forms of negotiation (Badgery-Parker 1995; Cowdery 2006; Gerber 2003; Legal Information Access Centre 2005):

- *Charge bargaining/charge agreement*: involves negotiation over the specific charges (type or number of counts) that will form part of the plea by the defendant (charges laid or proceeded with). The three options within this category include:
  - A defendant charged with multiple offences arising generally from one set of circumstances agrees to plead guilty to one or more of the charges in exchange for withdrawal of the balance of charges.
  - A defendant charged with a number of offences of varying degrees of severity agrees to plead guilty to the more serious offence on the grounds that the remaining charges are withdrawn.
  - A defendant agrees to plead guilty to a lesser charge(s) as substitution for a more serious charge within the same offence classification. For example, accepting a plea of manslaughter in return for dismissing charges for first-degree murder.
- *Sentence bargaining*: involves agreement to a plea of guilty for the stated charge(s) (rather than a reduced charge) in exchange for a lighter sentence. Unlike charge bargaining, sentence bargaining may involve some form of discussion with the judiciary regarding indication of sentence.

In practice, plea bargaining varies considerably Australia-wide and internationally, both in terms of the range of negotiations, the level of transparency involved in the negotiation process (i.e. whether the activity is formally facilitated or regulated) and the nature and extent of involvement of the courts (see, for example, Roach Anleu & Mack 2009). For example, in Victoria plea bargaining activities are largely a veiled affair, given the absence of a legislative base or formal guidelines regulating its conduct

PRINCIPAL OFFENCE
Where an individual or organisation is charged with multiple offences, the principal offence is the most serious offence type proven guilty or the most serious offence acquitted.

(Flynn 2011a). The acceptability of this lack of transparency has attracted considerable polarisation among the legal fraternity and public criticism regarding the legitimacy of plea bargaining activities (see also Box 23.1 and 23.2). By contrast, the legitimacy of plea bargaining is explicitly recognised in other jurisdictions. For instance, the practice has been codified in the United States (United States Federal Rules of Criminal Procedure 1966), and is regulated via prosecutorial guidelines in New South Wales (NSW Office of Public Prosecutions 2003) and the United Kingdom (United Kingdom Attorney General's Department 2009; see also Flynn 2011a). The formalisation of plea bargaining provides a mechanism for sanctioning discussions between the defendant (generally via defence counsel) and the prosecutor, and requires recording of all negotiations and disclosure of any agreement in open court or in camera for approval by the judge (the judiciary is essentially not bound to honour any agreement arrived at).

In contrast to the United States, where judges are, on request, directly involved in plea bargain negotiations with the defence and prosecution teams, and indeed approve the final plea, the Australian judiciary is discouraged from playing an active or overt role in plea negotiation. Critics argue that, in accordance with the rule of law and the doctrine of separation of powers, direct involvement in negotiations diminishes the position of 'judge' as impartial arbiter, transforming them instead into a central player in the adversarial process (Parthimos 1993).

Moreover, sentence bargaining, which is widely practised in the United States, does not occur explicitly within the Australian context. Indeed, judicial involvement in sentence discounting negotiations, especially those involving 'in camera' discussions (conducted in the judge's chambers) between a judge, and prosecution and defence teams on sentence indication (the likely sentence to be imposed by the judge), have been expressly condemned by the courts (Badgery-Parker 1995; Byrne 1988; Flynn 2007, 2011a; Langbein 1991; Mack & Anleu 1995) and victim rights advocates (Flynn 2011b). While Australian prosecutors cannot guarantee sentences in exchange for guilty pleas, they can agree to withhold some of the aggravating factors from the judge during sentencing submissions. Furthermore, they may agree not to appeal against sentence orders (Gerber 2003). It is nonetheless for the sentencing judge alone to decide what reductions on sentence (if any) to impose after a plea has been entered. As discussed below, however, in recognition of the utilitarian value of guilty pleas, it is a clear sentencing principle in Australian jurisdictions that the accused be given credit for a plea of guilty (Brown et al. 1996a; Field 2002) but the timing of a guilty pleas is a significant consideration (Tiedt 2010). By extension, sentencing leniency is an expected outcome of plea bargaining (Mack & Anleu 1995; McKenzie 2007).

ADVANTAGES OF PLEA BARGAINING

From a utilitarian standpoint, the attraction of plea bargaining is manifold. From the prosecution perspective, it guarantees a conviction (albeit for a lesser charge or crime), which is not a foregone conclusion in contested matters, despite the apparent strength of the evidence (e.g. the OJ Simpson trial; see Box 19.2). Furthermore, prosecutors are able to use plea bargaining to strengthen the case against a co-accused. A defendant may, for example, accept a plea bargain arrangement in exchange for providing damaging testimony against the second defendant. (Brown et al. 1996a; Siefman & Frieberg 2001)

The most compelling attraction is, however, administrative efficiency and the scale of the cost-saving potential afforded early guilty pleas. This is clearly illustrated through an examination of the statistics pertaining to duration of adjudication proceedings from initiation to finalisation. In 2010–11, under one-fifth (16%) of proceedings across adjudicated defendants in the higher courts were finalised in less than 13 weeks from the date of initiation, while 45 per cent were finalised in less than 26 weeks and almost a quarter (23%) in 52 weeks or more after initiation. Marked time differentials were, however, noted on the basis of the court processes undertaken to deal with the charges, which is primarily affected by the type of plea entered. Of those defendants that proceeded to trial and were found guilty by the court, half were finalised 52 weeks or more after initiation and 40 per cent of those acquitted were finalised in this same period. By comparison, just under one-fifth (18%) of defendants who pleaded guilty were finalised 52 weeks or more after initiation, while half were finalised in less than 26 weeks (AIC 2013a).

Although it is not possible to ascertain the proportion of guilty pleas induced through plea bargaining in Australia, the figure has been estimated at 50–85 per cent (Flynn 2007; Moles 2004). In examining the subset of cases committed for trial in New South Wales between 1998 and 2001, but negotiated as guilty pleas at the arraignment stage (n = 591 or 32%), Samuels (2002: 11) estimated that as much as $26 million of public monies can be saved each year in New South Wales alone. This led him to conclude that 'charge bargaining, as the primary means of facilitating the disposal of indictable offences by a plea of guilty rather than by trial, [is] essential to the administration of justice. Without it, the system could not cope'.

CRITICAL QUESTIONS ABOUT PLEA BARGAINING

According to critics, however, irrespective of specific form, critical questions regarding due process and 'justice' are called into question by the practice of plea bargaining. Most notably, it is regarded as a source of undue pressure on alleged offenders to confess guilty. This is due, in part, to a tendency to 'overcharge' alleged offenders; that is, laying several charges against a defendant to provide scope for plea negotiation (Samuels 2002). The pressure created by the negotiation process may:

- affect the defendant's ability to give voluntary consent to such processes
- provide inducement to admit to offences not in fact committed by the defendant, based on the apparent strength of the evidence and the prospect of conviction
- generally undermine the right to trial, the right to silence and the presumption of 'innocent until proven guilty' (Darbyshire 2000; Field 2002; Findlay et al. 1999; Roach Anleu & Mack 2009).

More generally, it has been argued that negotiations conducted in private not only contravene the concept of a transparent and publicly accountable judicial process (Flynn 2011a,b; Mack Anleu 1995), but also disadvantage defendants through a lack of judicial oversight. Though a judge may have misgivings about a matter over which they preside, they are only permitted to sentence a defendant on the facts presented before the court (Flynn 2007; MacKenzie 2007). Alternatively, it has been argued that prosecutorial guidelines on plea bargaining and 'sentence indication schemes' expose the inducements and bargains that relate to guilty pleas, and place them under judicial supervision, where the interests of the defendant can receive maximum protection (Findlay et al. 1999; Flynn, 2007 2011a; Sentencing Advisory Council 2007).

As noted above, the vast majority of individuals coming before the courts plead guilty, for whatever reasons. In instances where charges are contested, however, there is still a propensity toward the routine production of guilt in court. In part, this is due to the fact that police in court are viewed as the experts in crime. Moreover, police are experienced in courtroom work: they are repeat players. They know how the system works since they know how the courtroom drama is played out; hence, they know how to work the system to their own professional advantage. However, it must be also be acknowledged that many defendants are also repeat players (see Chapters 24 and 25).

BOX 23.1   'BARGAINED JUSTICE': THE CARL WILLIAMS CASE

On 28 February 2007, Carl Williams, a notorious underworld crime figure in Victoria, and convicted murderer and drug dealer, pleaded guilty to murdering rival gangland figures Jason Moran and Mark Mallia in 2003 and Lewis Moran in 2004. He also pleaded guilty to conspiracy to murder Mario Condello, a former lawyer and underworld figure murdered in 2006. The pleas, which stunned the public, were secured after seven months of plea bargaining negotiations between Williams' defence counsel and the Office of Public Prosecutions. These discussions were facilitated through the efforts of Purana Task Force investigators, who managed to persuade five of Williams' associates to submit evidence of his involvement in four murders.

As part of Williams' plea bargain, charges pertaining to the murder of a third Moran family member, Mark, and drug-trafficking activities, were withdrawn. Additionally, investigations into Williams' involvement in a further five murders were deemed concluded, though the basis upon which such determinations were arrived at were not disclosed. Media reports also speculated that as part of the deal to plead guilty, Williams had secured an undertaking that his parents' house would not be seized under proceeds of crime laws and that his father, George Williams, who suffers a serious heart condition, and who, at the time, was facing charges of trafficking amphetamines and dealing with the proceeds of crime, would be offered a suspended jail sentence.

In May 2007, Williams was sentenced to life imprisonment with a 35-year non-parole period (he was subsequently murdered in 2010 by fellow Barwon prison inmate, Matthew Charles Johnson). Flynn (2007) argues that the secrecy surrounding the plea bargaining process in Victoria, along with suppression orders prohibiting the release of information relating to Williams' previous finding of guilt in relation to a 2005 murder, led to public scepticism regarding the legitimacy of the Williams plea negotiations and fuelled perceptions that justice had been bargained, or traded away. Thus, while sentence bargaining is not practised within Victoria, the veiled nature of the Williams' plea negotiations made it difficult for the public to appreciate that the parole eligibility aspects of his sentence were granted in keeping with Victorian laws on sentencing reductions rather than as a result of the plea negotiations specifically.

It is noteworthy that George Williams was jailed in 2007 for four-and-a-half years with a minimum of 20 months, despite Carl Williams' plea deal allegedly securing his father sentencing concessions. In a subsequent appeal to have the sentence overturned, the defence urged the court to give more weight to the plea deal, which had spared the public millions of dollars. Defence counsel also revealed that at the time of the Williams deal, the prosecution had conceded that a three-year sentence—wholly suspended—was a tariff that would not be appealed against. In upholding the discretionary power afforded a judge to either accept or reject any deal that may have been struck as part of plea negotiations, the appeal ultimately failed and George Williams was released in 2009, after serving a 20-month sentence.

Sources: Flynn *(2007);* Herald-Sun *(2008);* Hughes & Robinson *(2007);* Hunt *(2008);* Munro & Butcher *(2007);* Wilkinson *(2007)*

BOX 23.2   THE HONEYMOON KILLER

On the fifth day of her honeymoon, Christina Thomas, a US citizen, died while scuba diving with her husband of 11 days, Gabe Watson, on Queensland's Great Barrier Reef. While initially considered a tragic accident, Gabe Watson, a certified rescue diver, was later charged with murder on the basis of his actions post discovering Christina was in trouble (e.g. choosing to ascend to seek help rather than attempting to bring Christina to the ocean surface) and aberrations in his account of events to police (offering sixteen alternative version of events).

The prosecution of this case shines a spotlight on the controversies surrounding the motivations and administration of plea bargaining in the Australian context. Gabe Watson was initially prosecuted in 2009, which resulted in a plea deal and the withdrawal of the charge of murder in exchange for a guilty plea to the less culpable charge of manslaughter by criminal negligence.

Initially, Watson was sentenced to four-and-a-half years' imprisonment, fully suspended after 12 months; however, the sentence was subsequently increased to 18 months. Following international outrage and the application of significant pressure from the Alabama Attorney General, the Queensland Attorney-General appealed the sentence on the grounds that it was manifestly inadequate. While the Queensland Court of Appeal upheld the sentence, the period of suspension was increased to 18 months, discounted for time already served. As one journalist reported at the time, 'The case ... sullied Australia's image. It sends all the wrong signals ... It sends the signal that you can kill and walk away and not face the kind of justice that you ought to' (Crawford 2009, cited in Flynn & Fitz-Gibbon 2010).

It is noteworthy that after Watson's release from prison in Australia, he faced a second prosecution initiated in Alabama in February 2012. The trial for capital murder by pecuniary gain was, however, terminated after six days and before the prosecution had even had an opportunity to present its case.

An examination of the case raises significant concerns regarding the degree to which prosecutorial resource constraints, and time pressures faced by the Queensland legal system, may have influenced the Director of Public Prosecutions to resolve the matter expeditiously (i.e. via plea bargaining), and raises serious questions regarding such motivations as a basis for exercise of prosecutorial discretion.

Source: Flynn & Fitz-Gibbon (2010)

An argument can be advanced that, due to the proliferation of guilty pleas, the process of guilt determination has progressively been removed from the courtroom arena, so that sentencing remains its predominant function.

THE JURY

The emphasis on the production of guilt within our criminal justice system is also apparent in public discussions on the role of the jury (Bronitt & Hogg 2003; Gleeson 2003; Findlay et al. 1999; Findlay & Duff 1988; O'Malley 1983). Since its evolution, the jury system has been heralded as a central pillar of democratic justice; an image largely popularised through media and screen depictions of the jury system in operation, none more so than the 1957 American classic drama, *12 Angry Men*. This is not to suggest that the value of the jury, as a key adjudicative mechanism, is undisputed. For example, concerns are often expressed in relation to the length and costliness of jury trials associated with the increasingly complex and technical evidence (including forensic evidence) required to be processed (French 2007; Goodman-Delahunty & Hewson 2010a,b; Goodman-Delahunty & Wakabayashi 2012; NSW Law Reform Commission 1986), the unrealistic expectations of forensic evidence (known as the CSI effect) (Hayes & Levett 2013; Holmgren & Fordham 2011; Wheate 2010; Wise 2010), their susceptibility to strong prejudices, which are anathema to their impartial role (Culhane et al. 2004; Fordham 2012; Taylor 2007) and, more recently, the threats to jury integrity posed by digital technology, which enables prejudicial information to be retrieved at a fingertip (Lowe 2011).

Aside from issues of operational efficiency, a fundamental and enduring concern relating to juries is that of composition and, in particular, the degree to which individuals who sit on juries are representative of society broadly, and those over whom they are called to pass judgment, specifically. In the context of a discussion on the routine production of guilt, it is pertinent to briefly examine the historical evolution of jury representation.

HISTORY OF THE JURY SYSTEM

While the modern-day jury is heralded as the bulwark of democratic participation in the administration of justice, historically it has effectively functioned as a representative of various sectional interests (Horan & Tait 2007; Quinault 2009). In the tenth century, juries were selected by the king, or his representative, from among the pool of neighbourhood witnesses to a dispute (i.e. those acquainted with the situation). Juries passed judgments that essentially served the interests of the Crown, on the basis of personal relevant knowledge, direct observations and community memory.

The twelfth century gave birth to the concept of the right to trial by one's 'peers', rather than the royal court, a concession begrudgingly granted by the monarchy to the aristocracy. Juries, comprised of noblemen, thus came to represent the interests of the hegemonic class (i.e. powerful barons or feudal lords). In the latter part of the Middle Ages, the new propertied classes began sharing power with the feudal lords and the jury composition changed accordingly. To qualify for jury participation in this period, a person had to meet three criteria: be local to the area in which the dispute arose, be of a propertied class (i.e. have significant property holdings) and possess knowledge of the subject matter in dispute. Essentially, then, the jury was likely to comprise neighbours of the same socio-economic background to the defendant who were familiar with at least one of the parties to the dispute and therefore the circumstances giving rise to the dispute.

The demise of medieval society and the associated growth of towns altered both the composition and role of the jury. The eighteenth and nineteenth centuries saw the gradual refashioning of the uniformity and familiarity of the jury such that by the twentieth century, jury members bore no relationship to the parties to the dispute and were called upon to determine the facts of a case on the basis of the evidence presented in court rather than any prior knowledge. Nonetheless, gender and property eligibility requirements continued to serve as barriers to effective cross-sectional community representation; jurors continued to be mainly men of some social standing.

WHICH GROUPS DO JURIES REPRESENT?

While juries have developed historically to be more inclusive and more demographically balanced (see, for example, Waugh 2008), in practice they still remain in many ways exclusive. It is, for example, argued that use of the electoral role to generate a jury pool is intrinsically biased in that it under-represents certain groups in society such as the homeless, the young and immigrant communities (McClintock 1997). As such, methods of jury selection continue to exclude diverse viewpoints and values and provide unequal opportunity for community participation. As illustrated in Table 23.1, the obstacles to broad community cross-representation are to be found in the extensive range of exemptions from jury service, jury vetting and the practice of peremptory challenges, and the ease with which potential jurors are able to self-excuse from jury participation (Horan & Tait 2007; NSW Law Reform Commission 2007a; Percy 2006; Queensland Law Reform Commission 2010).

JURIES AND INDIGENOUS PEOPLE

The issue of under-representation of certain sections of the community on the jury has important implications in terms of Indigenous people in particular, given their dramatic over-representation at all levels of the justice system (Briggs & Auty 2003; NSW Law Reform Commission 2007a; Weatherburn et al. 2006). This is especially evident in Western Australia, where a high proportion of people charged with offences are Aboriginal. Although the object of much justice system scrutiny, the opportunities for Aboriginal people to participate at the decision-making end of justice processes are remote. For a number of reasons, it is highly unlikely that Aboriginal people will be represented on a jury (for similar arguments on race in the United States, see McGuffee et al. 2007).

Two of the jury disqualification provisions appear to affect Indigenous people significantly; specifically, literacy rates are low among some sections of the Indigenous community and incarceration rates are high relative to the non-Indigenous community. Furthermore, many Aboriginal people live in remote locations, and because they follow traditional nomadic lifestyles with family tie and kinship obligations, cannot be called to serve on a jury, since they have no fixed address and therefore are unlikely to be listed in the electoral roll. Additionally, there is a requirement that, in order to be eligible for jury service, one must live within a specified kilometre radius of the regional centre where the courts are located; thus many people are excluded on the basis of geographical distance.

There are also customary prohibitions tied to customary Aboriginal laws, which circumscribe what an Aboriginal person is permitted to say (Bottomley et al. 1991). Finally, even if an Indigenous person is selected for jury duty, in some regional districts there is a strong possibility that they may know, or be related to, Indigenous defendants due to the extended concept of family relationships. Thus, there are doubts as to whether the jury is a true reflection of the composition of the population in general and Aboriginal people specifically.

Even in cases where a familial connection does not exist, Indigenous jurors may seek to be excused in cases involving Indigenous defendants on the grounds that they may lose standing within the community should they be associated with the conviction of another Indigenous community member (Clough et al. 2007).

Similarly, requirements for English proficiency and Australian citizenship limit the capacity of newly arrived migrant groups, refugees and culturally and linguistically diverse communities to be represented in the jury system. This is said to result in a jury mix that lacks ethnic and cultural heterogeneity, thereby curtailing social justice access and equity (Australian Law Reform Commission 1992; French 2007).

JURY MEMBERS: AMATEURS OR EXPERTS?

More generally, in relation to the role and nature of juries, we need to look at the logic of their operation. What kinds of decisions can or should they make, and what kinds of directions from the bench should

TABLE 23.1 JURY EXEMPTIONS AND EXCLUSIONS

NATURE OF EXCEPTION	EXAMPLES
Disqualification	• Australian residents who are non-citizens • Accused persons on bail for an indictable offence • Offenders convicted of an indictable offence and sentenced to a term of imprisonment (jurisdictions vary in relation to the type of offence, the length of the incarceration and the time that has lapsed since conviction/incarceration) • Convicted offenders subject to a continuing community-based order • Undischarged bankrupts
Ineligibility to serve	• Present or past (within the past 10 years in Victoria) legal practitioners and their staff, holders of judicial office, the Governor, police officers and others associated with the administration of justice/the courts (spousal exemptions for various professions also apply in some jurisdictions, such as SA and the NT) • Persons who are mentally ill, under guardianship or an administration order, or suffer from a physical (visual or aural impairment) or intellectual disability that renders them incapable of serving • Persons of advanced age (over 70 in SA and Qld only, although Queenslanders can opt in) • Persons unable to adequately understand or communicate in the English language (NT excludes those who cannot read, write and speak English; Qld excludes those unable to read and write English; NSW excludes those unable to read or understand English; Victoria and Tasmania excludes those who cannot communicate in, or understand English adequately; WA excludes those who lack understanding of English).
Right to be excused	• Those who suffer from ill/delicate health or incapacitation (e.g. pregnant women) • Those of advanced age (those aged 70 or over in NSW, and 65 in WA, Tas and the NT) • Those with long distances to travel (e.g. in Vic, more than 50 km if residing in Melbourne and more than 60 km if residing in a regional area; in NSW those residing 56 km from the court; in the NT a person who does not reside within the jury districts for Darwin or Alice Springs) • Persons practising certain professions (e.g. the clergy, dentists, pharmacists, medical profession, the self-employed and teachers) or involved in matters of special urgency or importance (e.g. ambulance officers and fire fighters) • Persons who have the care, custody and control of dependants, the sick, infirm or disabled (if alternative care is unavailable) and those unable to alter prior commitments / arrangements (e.g. a holiday or surgery)

Source: adapted from Horan & Tait (2007)

they receive (see, for example, Flynn & Henry 2012)? Critics tend to lean towards a preference for the professionalisation of the determination of guilt or innocence, so that such decisions are seen as technically rational in nature. This critique is based on the assumption that juries are technically incompetent; that is, largely incapable of understanding judicial instructions or summing-up of trial evidence. They are also said to be administratively irrational, in that the rationality of their decision-making is constrained by the lack of opportunity to question witnesses and counsel, and access relevant evidence and exhibits (Badgery-Parker 1995; Wood 2007a,b). If this is the case, the task of determining guilt should be removed from the hands of the amateurs and placed into the realm of the 'rational' experts.

Common law generally prohibits the interrogation of jurors for the purposes of ascertaining the nature and course of their deliberations, and justifications for their verdicts. This protection of the jury from disclosure has come to be known as the 'exclusionary rule' (Boniface 2008; Gumbert 2008; Kirby 1998; McClellan 2011). Consequently, such criticisms of the jury system are not readily subject to validation processes. Exemptions to this rule are granted, however, for research purposes. Existing research into jury decision-making processes (Findlay & Duff 1988; O'Malley 1983; Trimboli 2008; Warner et al. 2009; Warner et al. 2011) nonetheless casts allegations of jury irrationality into doubt (see Box 23.3). In particular, these studies reveal:

- The realities of jury decision-making are significantly different from media portrayals, which tend to focus almost exclusively on the more dramatic and controversial cases (e.g. the Rodney King and OJ Simpson cases in the United States and the Lindy Chamberlain case in Australia).
- There are high levels of juror understanding (completely, or substantially) of judges' instructions on the law and the summing-up of trial evidence.
- There are high levels of concordance between judge and jury assessments, in part due to the fact that the majority of jurors perceive the judge's summing-up to be the most significant help to a jury in reaching a verdict.
- Police claims that juries acquit too many defendants reflect their professional views of the desirability of a routine production of guilt, rather than a concern with the underlying principles of justice.

EROSION OF THE JURY SYSTEM

Notwithstanding this evidence, with the passage of time, debates over representativeness and rationality have been superseded by a questioning of the very survivability of the jury system in the face of its steady erosion within the civil justice system in a number of Australian jurisdictions. This erosion has been precipitated by the ascendancy of summary justice, which accompanied the expanded criminal jurisdiction of magistrates' courts in the interests of cost and efficiency. Essentially, through their ability to preside over 'either way offences' (i.e. matters that may be heard as either summary or indictable offences), lower courts are now permitted to determine a large range of criminal matters previously reserved for the higher courts, where trial by jury is an option available to the defendant (Findlay et al. 1999; Martin 2008; Weinberg 2008). In more recent times, a number of Australian jurisdictions have, moreover, legislated to provide for judge-alone trials in the case of indictable matters, although the proportion of defendants taking up this option remains low (O'Leary 2011).

BOX 23.3   JURY UNDERSTANDINGS AND PERCEPTIONS OF SENTENCING

A study by Warner et al. (2009; see also Warner et al. 2011) found that the opinion of jurors is a useful way in which to ascertain informed public opinion about sentencing. Public opinion is important both as a gauge of general confidence in the law, and as a significant force through which laws are changed or reformed. However, public opinion polls about sentencing tend to be based upon views that are uninformed and intuitive rather than the actual facts of the case, including a detailed knowledge of the offence and a sense of the offender as a real person.

The study, which commenced in 2007, is based on a sample of jurors involved in a jury trial adjudicated in a Tasmanian Supreme Court that had resulted in a guilty verdict. Once they had discharged their duties in delivering a verdict, study participants were required to remain in court to listen to sentencing submissions. Their views on sentencing were then sought to be ascertained over the following three stages:

1   Prior to the judge imposing sentence—nomination of a sentence considered appropriate to the given case, based on their knowledge of the facts alone.
2   Subsequent to the judge imposing sentence—expression of a view on the appropriateness of the sentence imposed by the judge, based on a package of materials prepared by the researchers. This included the judge's reasons for the sentence, as well as information on sentencing processes and relevant sentencing factors, current sentencing practices and crime patterns.
3   Subsequent to stages 1 and 2—based on interviews that further explored the juror's general views on sentencing matters, as well as their reactions to the particular case under review and the basis for their opinion on the sentence imposed.

The preliminary results of the study found that:
•   Given knowledge of a case, the opinions of jurors toward sentences is not as punitive as public opinion polls suggest. In aggregate, respondents were more likely to suggest a less severe disposition than that imposed by the judge. This is consistent with the findings of similar research (see, for example, Gelb 2008; Lovegrove 2007).
•   There is a dichotomy between jurors' views about sentencing in the abstract and jurors' views about the sentencing in particular cases in which they have been involved.
•   Jurors appear overwhelmingly satisfied with judges' sentencing decisions (90% rating them as very or fairly appropriate), but were least satisfied with the severity of sentence for sex and drug offences, indicating that pre-existing perceptions may be difficult to modify.
•   The more specific knowledge one has of a case, the more likely one's attitude to penalty will moderated away from harsher sentencing options.
•   Jury participation increases confidence in the criminal justice system.

Source: Warner et al. (2009)

IRRELEVANCE OF JURIES

The reality of modern adjudication therefore means that juries remain symbolically significant, but are substantively irrelevant in the vast majority of criminal cases. For example, in 2012–13, cases adjudicated in the magistrates' courts (n = 514,897) accounted for 94 per cent of adult criminal adjudication in Australia (n = 530,005) and 92 per cent of criminal matters adjudicated across all court levels (n = 561,554 across Magistrates', Higher and Children's courts) (ABS 2014f). Furthermore, while trial by jury is a fundamental entitlement of all accused persons brought before the higher courts, in 2007–08, around 81 per cent of all defendants waived that entitlement in favour of a guilty plea, thereby obviating the need for a jury (ABS 2009a). In effect, this means that the proportion of all criminal cases finalised by way of jury trial in Australia generally comprises less than 2 per cent.

As already established, public preoccupation rests with a comparative handful of cases determined in the higher courts, and, in particular, the exceptional cases involving jury trial. A review of court finalisations, however, reveals that when we speak of 'justice', we are, by and large, speaking of summary justice. Paradoxically, despite their overwhelming predominance in the adjudication arena (in terms of case volume), magistrates' courts are steeped in the 'ideology of triviality' (McBarnet 1981); that is, those matters presented before magistrates' courts are viewed as commonplace, inconsequential matters that are to be dealt with as expeditiously as possible. As non-adversarial proceedings tend to prevail through the prevalence of guilty pleas, juridical preoccupation turns almost exclusively to the determination of penalty. We are confronted with an image of 'machinery' justice, where judgments routinely roll off the conveyor belt, with minimal time for reflective consideration. The non-adversarial nature of the adjudication process is, in large part, a product of the cooperation demanded by summary justice, which is geared towards efficiently managing the enormous case load burdening the lower courts.

Case loads are especially pronounced in magistrates' courts on circuit in remote Aboriginal communities in Australia, also known as 'Bush Courts', with up to 100 cases heard per day (Siegel 2003). Time constraints imposed by such caseloads often lead to adverse justice outcomes for Aboriginal communities in the form of an overwhelming proportion of induced guilty pleas. Expressing concern over this situation, one magistrate presiding in the Katherine region of the Northern Territory commented: 'In four years in Katherine I didn't do very many hearings at all, so much did collapse into a plea at the end of the day, for which you could say "this isn't just, this is a sausage factory" (Siegel 2003: 8).

However guilt is ascertained—through voluntary admissions on the part of the accused, through pressures to plea bargain, through expert prosecution testimony or through the deliberations of a jury and trial process—the next task of the court is to assign a penalty of some kind. This is the major role of the contemporary court: to determine sentences.

METHODS OF DETERMINING SENTENCES

While sentencing is a core function of the courts, both the magistracy and judiciary have long acknowledged the difficulties of arriving at a disposition that appropriately balances the often competing interests of the state, victim and offender (see, for example, Ashworth et al. 1984; Cooke 1987;Fox 2006; Hampel 1990; Kirchengast 2010; Nicholson 2012; Spigelman 2008). The main concern of the following discussion is to convey the complexity of the sentencing task by outlining the interplay of divergent and often contradictory sentencing objectives, legal principles, decision-making criteria, and offender- and offence-specific factors that must be taken into consideration by the sentencer in discharging their discretionary powers.

SENTENCING AIMS

As will be explored in greater detail in Chapter 24, the range of sentencing aims and dispositions available to the courts, and the relative priorities afforded them throughout the centuries, reflect changes in the state's characterisation of and response to offences and offenders over time. The aims of sentencing, which are both symbolic and functional, are generally seen to include (NSW Law Reform Commission 2007b, 1996):

* denunciation and public reprobation
* retribution and 'just deserts'
* incapacitation and community protection
* rehabilitation and reform
* individual and general deterrence
* reparation and restitution.

As the principal symbolic statement of society's displeasure at the harm caused by the offender, the act of passing sentence satisfies the simple aim of formally denouncing the offence (signalling societal condemnation of such behaviour), and the often closely associated desire of imposing a measure of retribution for the resultant harm caused. Yet another aim of the courts is to ensure that serious offenders deemed a danger to society are incapacitated until such time as they cease to exhibit criminal propensities and therefore no longer constitute a threat to themselves or others; this sentencing objective serves to offer the community a degree of protection.

The notion of deterrence is also identified as a legitimate aim of sentencing. The sentence must be harsh enough to dissuade the offender from committing another crime in the future (specific deterrence). The punishment must also act to prevent other people who have been made aware of the offender's punishment from committing similar crimes (general deterrence). In other words, the sentence is meant to deter both the individual and any others from committing crime.

The courts are also concerned with rehabilitating and reforming offenders as a means of invoking contrition, and promoting the development of social and other skills that will assist in transitioning ex-prisoners back into the community. In a sense, this objective may also contribute to community protection by addressing the motivational incentives and other antecedents to reoffending. It should be noted that when dealing with young offenders (those chronologically or mentally under 18), sentencing is guided by the rehabilitative and welfare-oriented principles of the juvenile justice system rather than the punitive and retributivist principles of the adult court system (Barns 2011; Fox 2006; Freiberg et al. 1988; see also Chapter 21).

A final objective of the court, but one that is not necessarily a direct aim of sentencing per se, is that of restitution. The idea here is that some form of reparation and/or remuneration be made by the offender to the victim to compensate them for the harm(s) they have suffered as a result of the crime (e.g. financial payment or payback schemes).

These aims appear to be both competing and complementary, and hence careful consideration of the specific circumstances of offences and offenders is required by courts to ensure that the combination of objectives ultimately pursued produces 'just' outcomes. There are a number of common law principles fundamental to the maintenance of a just and equitable criminal justice system (Ashworth 2010; Australian Law Reform Commission 2006; Bagaric & Edney 2007; Freiberg & Krasnostein 2011; Hatzistergos 2010; von Hirsch & Fox 1994).

SENTENCING PRINCIPLES

PROPORTIONALITY

One interpretation of 'just' is encapsulated in the basic principle of sentencing law known as the proportionality principle. Grounded in a respect of offenders' basic human rights, this is the primary mechanism for ensuring fair outcomes. According to this axiom, sentences should always be reasonable, in that the severity of the sentence should be commensurate with the gravity of the harm occasioned, or the harm sought to be prevented, as determined in the light of the objective circumstances of the offence and the degree of offender culpability.

PARSIMONY

Recognising the inherent dignity and worth of offenders, the principle of parsimony functions as a restraint on the formidable power of the state; it precludes the imposition of a more severe disposition than that required to achieve the objective(s) of the sentence. While primarily concerned with public welfare, courts are mandated through this principle to also consider the offender's welfare and tend towards a merciful approach to sentencing. Cognisant of the devastating impacts that severe penalty can have on offenders and the community, imposition of the minimum, or least restrictive or coercive, option should be preferred over the maximum penalty, so long as the sentence fairly reflects the circumstances of the case. The courts thus work 'up' the table of penalties, rather than 'down'. Key questions are thus: why do we need to go to the next level? And could we achieve our aims by use of this lesser sentence? As discussed shortly, there are a number of mitigating and aggravating factors that a court takes into consideration in working through these questions.

CONSECUTIVE/ CUMULATIVE SENTENCE
A standard sentencing procedure where a person convicted of multiple offences receives a separate penalty for each crime, to be served consecutively.

TOTALITY

This principle applies to the sentencing of offenders convicted of multiple offences and/or the sentencing of offenders already serving a sentence. It acts to limit excess by ensuring that an offender receives an appropriate rather than a 'crushing' sentence overall. Once a number of sentences have been passed, each of which has been properly calculated in relation to the specific circumstances of the offence, and they have been made **consecutive** (also referred to as **cumulative**), the court is required to review the impact of the aggregate sentence and consider whether it is just and appropriate. Should the sum total of the individual sentences appear excessive, then appropriate adjustments can be made by restructuring the sentences (e.g. making some of the sentences **concurrent**) to reduce the head sentence (the overall sentence) or each of the individual sentences.

CONCURRENT SENTENCE
A deviation from standard sentencing procedure, whereby a person convicted of multiple offences is permitted to serve each sentence simultaneously.

CONSISTENCY

Sentencing inconsistency is regarded as one of the most significant contributors to the erosion of public confidence in the criminal justice system and the deterrent impact of punishment. Considered fundamental to maintaining a just and equitable criminal justice system, the principle of consistency in sentencing serves to ensure that like cases are treated alike, regardless of who passes sentence. Uniformity in sentencing is unrealistic, given the wide range of factors to be considered when sentencing an offender. However, this principle requires courts to adopt both similar approaches to sentencing (application of similar objectives and principles of sentencing as well as consideration of the same type of factors) and to arrive at similar outcomes (the nature and quantum of penalty) in dealing with like cases.

INDIVIDUALISED JUSTICE

This principle requires courts to consider and balance the full suite of facts, circumstances and relevant matters of a case in determining a just and appropriate sentence. To give full effect to this principle, judicial officers must possess broad sentencing discretion.

The broad range of dispositions available to magistrates and judges, combined with the considerable degree of discretion they are afforded (subject to appellate review and legislative restrictions) in selecting from among this range, facilitates both adherence to, and departure from, the principle of proportionality and consistency. These dispositions and a brief analysis of their application across Australia will be considered shortly.

First, however, it is necessary to consider some of the factors that assist courts in determining the seriousness of an offence and the appropriate sanction to impose upon an offender.

SENTENCING FACTORS

Defence and prosecution counsel will cite a number of factors relevant to sentencing during the plea process. This is an address by counsel to the court following a finding of guilt, which highlights the main factors relevant to sentencing from the point of view of both the defence and prosecution, and which ultimately seeks to influence the imposition of one form of penalty over another. Defence counsel will generally bring to the fore *mitigating factors* to argue the case for a more lenient disposition. By contrast, the prosecution will largely highlight the existence *of aggravating factors* in an effort to secure a harsher penalty. In determining sentence, the courts weigh the aggravating factors presented by counsel against the mitigating factors.

Table 23.2 lists a range of factors relevant to determining sentence. It is important to highlight that the factors listed are not mutually exclusive, nor is the inventory of factors by any means exhaustive. Indeed, given that the courts have not generally sought to prescribe the factors relevant to sentencing— the exception being the *Crimes (Sentencing Procedure) Amendment (General Sentencing Principles) Act* 2002 (NSW)—the list should be regarded as indicative only (Ashworth 2010; Bagaric 2000; NSW Law Reform Commission 2007b; Walker 1999; Warner 2003a). The Australian Law Reform Commission (2006: 6.35–6.149) has suggested structuring these factors into the following categories:

- factors relating to the offence
- factors relating to the conduct of the offender in connection with the offence
- factors relating to the conduct of the offender other than the specific conduct constituting the charged offence
- factors relating to the background and circumstances of the offender
- factors relating to the impact of the offence
- factors relating to the impact of conviction or sentence on the offender or the offender's family or dependants

TABLE 23.2 FACTORS RELEVANT TO SENTENCING

FACTS CONCERNING THE NATURE OF THE OFFENCE

- Offence gravity (summary or indictable; maximum or minimum penalty prescribed; self-defence; provocation)
- Involvement of identifiable victim (number involved; vulnerability due to age, mental or physical disability; level of harm/nature of impact; special status—e.g. police officer)
- Prevalence of the offence (rarity or frequency of; general deterrence; sentencing practices)
- Offence involving motivation of hatred or prejudice against a group (e.g. based on religion, racial or ethnic origin; language; sexual orientation)

FACTS CONCERNING THE NATURE OF THE OFFENDER

- Character of the offender (prior criminal history or absence thereof—not deemed relevant in all jurisdictions or for all offences (e.g. sexual offences in NSW))
- Age of the offender (youthfulness or old age as mitigating factors)
- culpability (mental state; intent; negligence; level of intelligence; presence of provocation)
- Cooperation with authorities ('discounting' based upon information provided about suspects, wanted offenders, or circumstances of crime; preparedness to turn state evidence)
- Remorse and plea (evidence of contrition; early guilty plea)
- Dangerousness (degree of risk posed to the community)
- Indigeneity (factors relevant to an offender's Aboriginality)

EFFECT OF OFFENCE AND PENALTY

- Hardship to the offender (injuries suffered by offender as a result of offence; ill effects of imprisonment on younger or older persons; impact on employment prospects)
- Hardship to others (offender's family and/or dependants)
- Rewards reaped by the offender (financial or other gain, such as reputation)

JUVENILES AND SPECIAL CONSIDERATIONS

- The young person's age is a mitigating factor in any penalty to be imposed
- A non-custodial order is better than detention in promoting the child's reintegration into the community
- Rehabilitation of the child is greatly assisted by the child's family and opportunities to engage in educational programs and employment
- A detention order should be imposed only as a last resort and for the shortest possible period

OTHER CONSIDERATIONS

- Method of committing offence (level of sophistication or planning involved; breach of trust)
- Degree of participation (sole perpetrator, key protagonist or ancillary player)
- Involvement of weapons (type and use of)
- Effect of mental disorder (diminished responsibility)
- Addictions (alcohol; drugs; gambling)
- Personal crisis (nervous breakdown; death in family)
- Trial delay (degree of negative impact on offender and their family)

Sources: adapted from Bagaric (2000); Fox (1994); Hopkins (2012); Warner (2010)

- factors relating to the promotion of sentencing purposes in the future
- factors relating to any detriment sanctioned by law to which the offender has been, or will be, subject as a result of the commission of the offence.

Many of the listed variables are self-explanatory, have already been described in previous chapters, or will be dealt with in Chapter 24, which examines in greater detail the philosophical and historical underpinnings of punishment. Hence, it is sufficient here to confine the discussion to aspects not canvassed thus far.

The most obvious basis for sentencing is the gravity or seriousness of the offence. In Australia, offence seriousness is codified in law via statutory offence classification and prescribed sentencing penalties. The more serious the offence, the harsher is the response or sentencing tariff; thus, at the extremes of the severity spectrum, murder receives a severe penalty while shoplifting is dealt with leniently. Of obvious regard in determining severity of offence is the level of violence (actual or threatened) involved, the presence or absence of a weapon, the number of victims and offenders involved, the visibility of the offence (whether it occurs in a private or public domain) and the impact of the crime on the victim(s); that is, the nature and degree of harm and/or damage sustained by the injured party or property (see Chapter 6).

An important process that takes place prior to sentencing an offender, and which is highly relevant to assessments of offence seriousness, is a determination of the precise nature of criminal responsibility and culpability. The legal notion of 'criminal responsibility' comprises constituent components: the idea that the accused has engaged in conduct (*actus reus*) prohibited by criminal law, and that they possess a mental state (*mens rea*) prohibited by criminal law. The former refers to acts, omissions or a state of affairs that constitutes a violation of the law. The latter refers to that element of criminal responsibility associated with the idea of fault, and is assessed in relation to concepts such as premeditation, negligence, recklessness, knowledge and intention. Criminal responsibility refers to the commission of a prohibited act accompanied by a mental element (e.g. to sexually assault someone, or to cause someone's death) (von Hirsch & Jareborg 2005).

The mental state of the offender is relevant not only from the point of view of criminal responsibility and 'fault' (e.g. insanity and diminished responsibility) but also from the point of view of 'defence' (e.g. self-defence, provocation and duress) (Stewart & Freiberg 2008). Did the person know the consequences of what they were doing? Was it an accident or the outcome of provocation? Was it due to negligence (failure to foresee and prevent a risk) or was the crime planned? The key issue here is the degree of blame or culpability that can be assigned to the offender. Someone with a mental disorder, for example, should be seen in quite a different way from a professional criminal who deliberately sets out to commit a crime for personal gain (Barns 2011; Finnane 2012; Wong 2013; Yannoulidis 2003).

Also of relevance in the determination of criminal responsibility is the issue of age. In all Australian jurisdictions, the statutory minimum age of criminal responsibility has now been raised to 10 years. Accordingly, persons under the age of 10 cannot be prosecuted for any crime by reason of action or omission, even murder. Under the common law principle of *doli incapax*, unless proven otherwise by the prosecution, a young person between the ages of 10 and 14 is considered incapable of committing a criminal act as they are considered not to have reached the 'age of discretion'; that is, they are cognitively immature (AIC 2005; Bradley 2003; Richards 2011).

Factors relating to the specific nature of the offender can also make a difference when it comes to the sentence imposed by a court; for example, someone with a prior criminal record and/ or someone who committed the offence while on a community-based order is generally treated differently from someone who has offended for the first time. The age of a person can also affect the type of response they receive from the court. Generally speaking, youthfulness is regarded as a mitigating consideration in sentencing, and the use of incarceration is viewed as a measure of last resort (see Cunneen & White 2011; see also Chapter 21). In other words, young people tend to receive different types of sentences from those imposed on adults and, in large part, the underlying rationale for this disparity in treatment is that the aim of sentencing should be rehabilitation rather than retribution.

The effect of the offence and the anticipated effect of the sentence on the offender and/or their family will also have some bearing on determination of penalty. The status of both the offender and victim are pertinent considerations here. For example, if the offender was an accountant who appropriated client funds, then their career as an accountant is over, and any additional penalty affecting future employability will exacerbate the impact of the offence for both the offender and their dependant(s). Likewise, if the victim were a member of the police force or an emergency services worker, or was very young, elderly or frail or otherwise incapacitated (e.g. in a wheelchair), the penalty might well be greater than would otherwise have been the case. Finally, offence motivation, such as a racial hatred, homophobia, religious hatred or other forms of prejudice against the group to which the offender perceives the victim to belong, serves to aggravate the seriousness of the crime.

A final set of factors that affect the sort of sentence one might receive include such things as the degree of cooperation with the authorities, and evidence of remorse for the crimes committed. A plea of guilty ordinarily leads to a reduction in the normal sentence on utilitarian grounds (administrative efficiency). The degree of 'discount' granted for a guilty plea is also influenced by a number of other factors, including the degree of contrition or remorse demonstrated by the offender (Howie 2008; Mackenzie 2007). Jurisdictions vary regarding the requirement to articulate the value of the discount provided to guilty pleas when passing sentence (Sentencing Advisory Council 2007). As discussed earlier, a plea of guilty also can be part of a formal or informal plea bargaining process. Interestingly, in recent times, there has been considerable debate within both judicial and academic circles regarding the impact that various forms of addiction such as drugs and gambling do, or should have, in mitigating sentence (Davis 2009; Marshall & Marshall 2003; Perrone et al. 2013; Sakurai & Smith 2003; Taylor 2004, 2002).

PRINCIPAL SENTENCE
Where a defendant is found guilty of multiple offences, the principal sentence relates to the most serious one based on the hierarchy of the Sentence Type Classification.

SENTENCING PENALTIES

Once a finding of guilt is announced, there are a number of sentencing options before the court (see Figures 23.3 and 23.4). These are allocated in the first instance on the basis of the principal sentence, which relates to the most serious sentencing option available for the offence in question. In Australia, there are two penalties that are no longer used; namely, capital punishment (the death penalty) and corporal punishment (punishment directed at the body and intended to cause bodily pain, such as caning). As explained in detail in Chapter 25, the broad range of sentencing options that are available can be generally grouped into three categories: reparation, supervision, and restricted movement or deprivation of liberty.

FIGURE 23.3   PRINCIPAL SENTENCE OF ADULT MALE DEFENDANTS FOUND GUILTY IN ANY COURT, 2010–11[a, b]

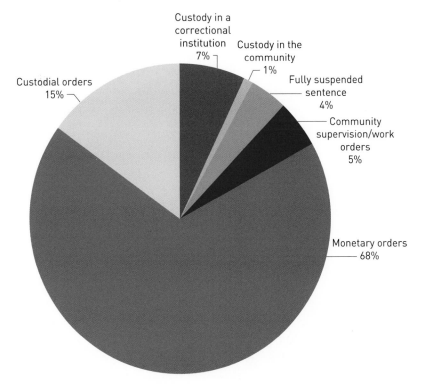

n = 368,120 (excludes defendants whose gender and/or type of custodial order handed down was unknown)
[a] includes magistrates' and higher courts
[b] includes intensive corrections orders, home detention and other orders restricting liberty though allowing living within the community

Source: AIC (2013)

UNSUPERVISED RELEASE

This form of action is essentially a decision to take no further action. The court may choose not to record a conviction, even though there has been a finding of guilt, as the conviction may itself be viewed as sufficient penalty or punishment in its own right. It may, for example, preclude the offender from participating in certain forms of civic or community life, or it may affect the person's chances of obtaining or retaining employment. The court may decide simply to admonish and discharge the offender; that is, publicly disapprove of the offender's behaviour and caution them not to repeat the harmful action again. Whether a conviction is recorded, the court may wish to adjourn or dismiss a case—in which case there is either no penalty attached to the behaviour or it is deferred under bond of good behaviour, where the offender undertakes not to reoffend.

FIGURE 23.4   PRINCIPAL SENTENCE OF ADULT FEMALE DEFENDANTS FOUND GUILTY IN ANY COURT, 2010–11[a, b]

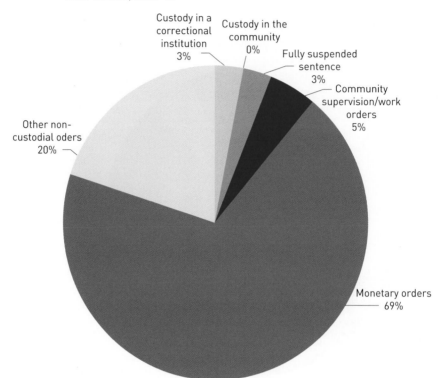

n = 103,888 (excludes defendants whose gender and/or type of custodial order handed down was unknown)
[a] includes magistrates' and higher courts
[b] includes intensive corrections orders, home detention and other orders restricting liberty though allowing living within the community

Source: AIC (2013)

FINANCIAL PENALTIES

If it is decided that the offender's behaviour warrants some penalty in addition to unsupervised release, a financial penalty may be imposed. The form of payment can range from a simple fine to the requirement to pay compensation to the victim for the injury or loss they have caused—although, strictly speaking, restitution and compensation orders are 'ancillary orders' rather than sentences of the court.

SUPERVISED RELEASE

The court may decide that the offender should be permitted to remain within the community, but that they should be subjected to some form of supervision. These community-based orders are very flexible sentences that permit the principles of punishment and rehabilitation to be given effect in the one sentence (see further Chapter 25). They generally require offenders to comply with certain core conditions (including reporting to the community correctional service at prescribed intervals) and/or to undertake certain activities (e.g. unpaid community work of some kind and/or attending treatment or counselling programs). In some states, a monetary sum (or bond) may also be fixed at the time of sentence, which the offender is liable to forfeit if the conditions of the 'recognisance' are breached.

These orders can be made either with or without conviction, and vary in relation to the intensity of the supervision (intensive correctional orders being the most onerous). Common to them all, however, is a requirement that the offender is expected to exhibit 'good behaviour'; that is, not to break the law or disturb the peace. If the conditions of the order are breached, they may be brought before the courts for re-sentencing. Before releasing an offender on an unsupervised order, the courts will normally request the preparation of a 'pre-sentence report' by a community correctional officer. This document provides guidance to the court on the offender's needs (especially as they relate to the factors underlying the offending behaviour) and the potential threat they pose to the community.

DEPRIVATION OF LIBERTY

The most extreme penalty is the deprivation of liberty—this means that the offender is physically restricted in where they can go, who they can see and what they can do. This is a drastic measure to take, and is generally used as a measure of last resort by the courts. Deprivation of liberty may be enforced either within or outside of formal correctional institutions and involve different degrees of monitoring. So, for instance, the offender may be confined to a term of continuous or periodic detention (where they attend prison on weekends, for example). They may be confined to their place of residence (home detention) or have an electronic tracking device fitted. These devices may be unconditional, in that they continuously track an individual's movements, or seek to restrict offenders from entering proscribed geographical areas or approaching particular individuals (e.g. potential victims or co-offenders) (see Black & Smith 2003; Gibbs & King 2003; Keay 2000; Queensland Corrective Services 2007).

Where an immediate term of incarceration is not imposed, but the court wishes to reserve the right to do so in the future, a suspended sentence may be handed down. Here, a sentence of imprisonment is suspended for a designated period, during which time certain conditions may be stipulated. Should the conditions be violated or further crimes committed, imprisonment may be imposed for all or part of the original sentence. As such, suspended sentences are often described as a 'sword of Damocles' poised over the head of the offender for the duration of the bond (Bartels 2009; Boyden 2005).

The type of penalty or disposition handed down by courts varies according to the sentencing criteria, guiding principles and sentencing factors outlined above. Figures 23.5 and 23.6 highlight the differences between the two adult court systems in terms of the penalty dispositions commonly levied.

Viewed comparatively, it is clear that while the majority of lower court cases do not involve heavier sentences, with magistrates preferring instead fines and non-custodial options, sanctions dispensed by the higher courts are at the harsher end of the severity scale, principally comprising custodial orders. Fines, which feature prominently in the lower courts, comprise one of the least used sentencing options within the higher courts. This disparity is, to some extent, reflective of the relative seriousness of the matters with which the respective jurisdictions predominantly deal, as well as the background of the offenders appearing before the respective courts.

FIGURE 23.5   PRINCIPAL SENTENCE OF ADULT DEFENDANTS FOUND GUILTY IN
MAGISTRATES' COURTS BY MOST SERIOUS OFFENCE, 2010–11

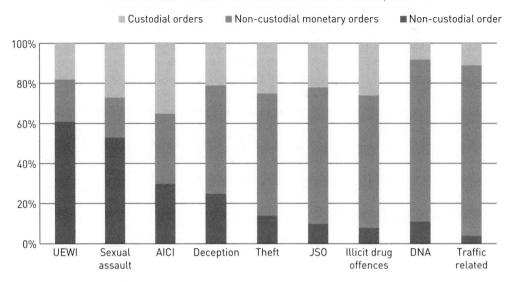

UEWI: unlawful entry with intent
AICI: acts intended to cause injury
JSO: offences against justice procedures, government security or government operations
DNA: dangerous or negligent acts endangering persons

Source: AIC (2013)

FIGURE 23.6   PRINCIPAL SENTENCE OF ADULT DEFENDANTS FOUND GUILTY IN
HIGHER COURTS BY MOST SERIOUS OFFENCE, 2010–11

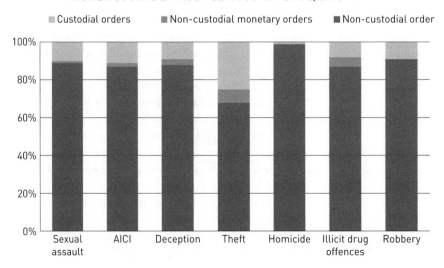

AICI: acts intended to cause injury

Source: AIC (2013)

SENTENCING DEBATES AND REFORMS

The courts' methods of determining guilt, and the sentences they impose, have profound consequences for the criminal justice system and for society generally. Sentencing practices and procedures have evolved over many years, and are subject to revision depending upon the political climate of the day.

'JUST DESERTS' VERSUS THERAPEUTIC JURISPRUDENCE

At a philosophical level, there has been considerable debate in recent years within legal and criminological circles regarding the purposes and nature of sentencing practices (Warner 2007). In particular, much of the discussion has revolved around differences between a 'just deserts' approach and a 'republican' approach. The 'just deserts' model emphasises consequentialist ends—such as retribution or general deterrence, and includes ideas such as punishment being proportional to the crime, the harm caused and the level of culpability, rather than any anticipated consequences accruing to the offender— determinant (or fixed) sentences, less judicial and administrative discretion, and an end to disparities in sentencing (see Ashworth & von Hirsch 1993; Edney 2005; Kirchengast 2010; Okimoto et al. 2009; von Hirsch 2003).

In contrast, the 'republican' approach to sentencing views the prime aim of sentencing as the restoration of dominion (or 'liberty') to the victim, the offender and the community. This perspective, which promotes non-adversarial forms of justice, refers to ideas such as reconciliation between victim and offender, recompense for the harm inflicted, and reassurance that the offence will not happen again by consideration of the specific attributes of the offender (see Braithwaite & Pettit 1990; Pettit & Braithwaite 1993; see also Chapter 4). This perspective has largely influenced restorative justice approaches to sentencing, which some commentators assert represents a return to pre-state societal practices, which used informal, participatory mechanisms of dispute resolution that sought to restore the parties and maintain community integrity (Weitekamp 1999).

In more recent times, the concept of therapeutic jurisprudence has emerged. This philosophy recognises the impact that laws, legal practices and procedures, and legal personnel (e.g. magistrates, judges and lawyers) can have on the psychological and emotional wellbeing of court participants. It argues for law reforms that centre on rehabilitating criminal tendencies, mitigating negative effects and promoting positive behavioural change and the enhancement of individual wellbeing alongside justice principles, such as community protection (Cannon 2008; Freiberg 2001; King 2008a,b). This perspective emphasises the importance of individual and collective self-determination—as opposed to coercion and paternalism—as well as ensuring procedural justice (listening to and respecting offenders) in decision-making and the promotion of positive behaviour (Cooper 1999; King & Guthrie 2008). It also advocates a new approach to the judicial sentencing role; one that draws on the discipline of transformational leadership and problem-solving judging (Daly 2006; King 2008a).

Opinion is thus divided regarding whether the emphasis within justice paradigms should be on 'retributive justice', 'restorative justice' or 'therapeutic justice'—and there are major policy and strategic differences that flow from how one views an ideal sentencing and/or criminal justice system. For instance, the republican approach has been highly influential in the development of restorative justice practices (e.g. family group conferences), sentencing circles and victim–offender mediation schemes (see Braithwaite 1989; King 2008a; Maxwell & Morris 1994; Morris & Maxwell 2003;

Winick & Wexler 2003). Likewise, therapeutic jurisprudence has manifested itself in Australia through the development of problem-oriented courts, such as drug courts, Indigenous courts, mental health courts, community courts and domestic violence courts, which seek to promote offender accountability and preparedness for, and participation in, rehabilitation (King Anthony 2008a,b, 2012).

INFLUENCE OF POPULIST PUNITIVENESS

Debates over sentencing are not, however, merely confined to academic and legal quarters. Since the 1960s, we have witnessed the increasing and powerful role played by 'the public' in not merely debating, but indeed shaping sentencing policy and practices. The transformation of public opinion into a driver for sentencing reform has largely accompanied the rising prominence of the victims' movement, and the subsequent growth in 'populist punitiveness'. Bottoms (1995: 40) uses this expression in reference to 'the notion of politicians tapping into, and using for their own purposes, what they believe to be the public's generally punitive stance' (see also Pratt 2002b; Sparks 2000; Tonry 1996). Hence, the public has taken its place alongside the state, the offender and the victim as a 'new axis of penal power' in the justice debate (Pratt 2002b: 81).

The ultimate expression of populist punitiveness is the mobilisation of law-and-order politics, often in the lead-up to an election, in an effort to appease the public's growing disillusionment with the ability of the justice system to deal effectively with offenders. Declining public confidence in the justice system generally, and the judiciary specifically, has been fuelled in no small part by media coverage of atypical sentences and exaggerated reports of an increasing crime threat, as well as the growing social anxieties experienced by the middle class (Buckingham 2004; Mackenzie 2006; Roberts & Indermaur 2007). For example, in 2001 and 2002, print and electronic media reports on a series of gang rapes in southwestern Sydney attacked the lenient sentences imposed on three young men of Lebanese background and the laxity of current immigration policies. Occurring at a time of existing community consternation over the arrival of 'boat people' and heightened public fear of the 'terrorist threat', such publicity served to situate the locus of the problem within the Arab and Muslim communities, and in particular 'ethnic youth gangs' (Poynting 2002; Warner 2004). The political response was an unequivocal condemnation of judicial practice and calls for increased penalties, resulting in the imposition of a 55-year jail term on one of a group of young Lebanese men subsequently involved in a series of aggravated sexual assaults.

More recently, public outrage at the 2013 rape and murder of Gillian Meagher, a 29-year-old Melbournian, by Adrian Ernest Bayley, who was on bail for an assault at the time and on parole for multiple rapes, led to sweeping changes to Victoria's parole system, including making breaching parole a criminal offence (*Bayley v The Queen* [2013] VSCA 295).

Public concerns over sentencing have focused, in particular, on a number of assumptions that generally have little or no basis in empirical reality, and/or fail to take into account the need to balance a number of sentencing objectives. These include perceptions that (Bagaric & Alexander 2012; Findlay 2004b; Freiberg & Gelb 2008; Morgan 2004; Ritchie 2012; Tomaino & Kapardis 2004; Walker & Hough 1988; Warner 2003a):

- The judiciary is out of touch with public opinion and has a propensity to being 'soft on crime'.
- Sentencing outcomes are inconsistent, and thus judicial discretion should be curtailed.
- Lenient sentences, especially when imposed for 'serious crimes', are evidence of inconsistent sentencing practices.

- Community safety is enhanced through the use of tougher sentences, especially the use of imprisonment.
- Crime is mostly violent and crime rates are increasing.
- There are significant discrepancies between the length of sentences imposed by courts and the period of detention actually served.
- Offenders are being released from prison 'too early', thus jeopardising community safety.

The debate over sentencing is thus taking place in the context of a push to increasingly punitive sentencing regimes and a growing 'culture of control' (Garland 2001; see also Cunneen et al. 2013). In responding to this pressure, the legislature has enacted a range of measures ostensibly designed to restore public confidence in the judiciary and introduce greater consistency and severity into sentencing practices. In practice, these moves ultimately serve to fetter judicial discretion by transferring some of the sentencing responsibility to parliament.

'TRUTH IN SENTENCING' LEGISLATION

Legislation of this type, which has been enacted by a number of Australian states, gives effect to the notion that penal practices should remain true to the intent of the sentence. In other words, a sentence of incarceration should be served in full. Accordingly, remissions, parole or pre-release measures—all of which affect the actual time spent by the offender in prison—are reduced or abolished. For example, the *Crimes (Sentencing Procedure) Amendment (Standard Minimum Sentencing) Act 2002* (NSW), enacted in February 2003, introduces standard non-parole periods for a list of 21 offences, including: murder (25 years for first degree and 15 years for second); a range of sexual offences, including rape in company or gang rape (15 years); and some forms of robbery (7 years). The court has the option not to impose the standard non-parole period, but must provide reasonable grounds for electing this course of action.

Similarly, the *Sentencing Legislation Amendment and Repeal Act 2003* (WA) and the *Sentence Administration Act 2003* (WA) have introduced a range of truth-in-sentencing-inspired changes, ostensibly designed to improve transparency of sentences and to ensure that offenders would be subject to state control for the entirety of their sentence rather than two-thirds of the time, as previously occurred under the automatic one-third remissions scheme. The laws also abolished sentences of imprisonment of 6 months or less and overhauled laws relating to parole and other forms of early release. The *Amendment and Repeal Act 2003* (WA) contained transitional arrangements that continued to guarantee that persons imprisoned after the commencement of the Act did not actually serve any longer terms in prison than they would have prior to 2003. In 2009, the general requirement to reduce the fixed-term of imprisonment by one-third was repealed, thereby granting sentencing judges full discretion to impose the maximum statutory penalty (ABC 2009).

INDEFINITE JAIL TERMS

Also referred to as indeterminate jail sentences, indefinite jail terms, as the term suggests, confine 'serious offenders' (defined as those committing certain homicide, rape, serious assault, kidnapping and armed robbery offences) to a term of imprisonment without establishing an end date. Indefinite jail terms are imposed on the grounds of preventative detention; that is, the community is protected from the potential commission of a criminal act by virtue of the incapacitation of a potential offender

(Lindsay 2009). Determination of an appropriate release date is left to the discretion of the state, and is premised on the offender no longer constituting a threat to the community. As such, prevention-based sentences transgress the proportionality principle of sentencing. Provisions of this nature exist in Victoria, Queensland, New South Wales, the Northern Territory, Western Australia, South Australia and Tasmania.

In Victoria, for example, the first indefinite sentence was imposed in 1995 on Kevin John Carr, a repeat sex offender who raped a 77-year-old woman at a train station in Melbourne in 1994, approximately one month after being released from prison. Carr had accumulated fifty-seven prior convictions over the course of 18 years, including five incidents of sexual assault/rape resulting in jail terms. In June 2009, County Court chief judge Michael Rozenes deemed Carr a continuing serious danger to the community and rejected an application to lift the indefinite jail sentence (Butcher 2009).

In recent times, indefinite sentencing, in the form of preventive detention legislation, has been introduced in Queensland (*Dangerous Prisoners (Sexual Offenders) Act 2003*), Victoria (*Serious Sex Offenders Monitoring Act 2005*) and Western Australia (*Dangerous Sexual Offenders Act 2006*) in response to growing community concerns about the unsupervised release of convicted sex offenders considered an ongoing risk to the community (Birgden 2007; Edgley 2007; Ronken & Johnstone 2008).

MANDATORY SENTENCING

Originating in the United States, these are legislated sentencing provisions that specify a range of penalties within a prescribed fixed maximum and minimum penalty. Customarily, the minimum penalty involves the imposition of a term of imprisonment for the commission of certain criminal offences. While in the United States mandated life terms of imprisonment for habitual reoffenders (those convicted of a third offence under three strikes laws) have primarily applied to serious violent offences (Hinds 2005), in Australia, they have generally applied to non-violent property offences.

Under mandatory sentencing regimes, judicial discretion is narrowed, in that factors may be taken into account but a sentence cannot be imposed below the specified statutory range (Sentencing Advisory Council 2008a). This often entails imposing a minimum punishment disproportionate to the severity of the offence. For example, before their repeal in October 2001 under intense international pressure, legislative amendments to the *Sentencing Act* 1995 (NT) introduced in 1997 made it mandatory (i.e. compulsory) for an adult first-time offender convicted of a designated range of property offences to receive a minimum term of imprisonment of 14 days, irrespective of the circumstances surrounding either the offence or the offender. Escalating mandatory minimum prison terms were also provided for offenders convicted of a second offence (90 days), and those convicted of a subsequent offence (1 year). Controversially, the same legislation (colloquially referred to as 'three strikes and you're out' legislation) also subjected juveniles to mandatory minimum terms of imprisonment: 28 days for juvenile repeat property offenders (aged 15 or 16) with escalating penalties for subsequent offences.

Similar sentencing provisions were introduced in Western Australia under 1996 amendments to the *Criminal Code* (WA). An offender (adult or juvenile) convicted of a third or subsequent home burglary must be sentenced to a minimum 12-month term of imprisonment or detention in a detention centre, which cannot be suspended. These mandatory provisions were later extended to violent and sexual offences, but their enactment originally targeted property offences, which led some commentators to suggest that they were populist responses that targeted one specific group in the community; namely, Indigenous Australians (Terblanche 2008).

Mandatory life sentences of imprisonment currently apply to all cases of murder in Queensland; New South Wales also has introduced mandatory life sentences for murder, but under a limited form (the court must be satisfied that the offence is so serious that community interests can only be met by the imposition of a mandatory life sentence). In June 2013, the New South Wales Government introduced the *Crimes Amendment (Murder of Police Officers) Act 2011*, which makes it mandatory for the court to impose a sentence of life imprisonment, without the possibility of parole, for the murder of a police officer under particular circumstances (e.g. if they were executed while conducting their duties).

GUIDELINE JUDGMENTS

This refers to a process whereby appellate courts (courts of criminal appeal) formulate general principles, rules and penalties for given offences, for the purpose of providing guidance to trial courts; that is, structuring sentencing discretion. Once promulgated, these judgments formally stipulate appropriate sentencing starting points for select offences, along with identifying aggravating and mitigating factors relevant to a departure from those guidelines. While the judgments are not prescriptive, sentencing judges must take them into account as an indicator and they are required to articulate, for each case at hand, their applicability or inapplicability (Spigelman 2008).

In New South Wales, for example, the Court of Criminal Appeal delivered the landmark decision of *R v Jurisic* in October 1998, in which it issued a formal sentencing guideline judgment for the offence of dangerous driving involving death. In doing so, Judge Spigelman made it quite clear that one of the specific objectives of the guideline judgments is to demonstrate the responsiveness of judges to public criticism of sentencing outcomes, thereby reinforcing public confidence in the integrity of the sentencing process (Spigelman 2008; Warner 2003b).

The court has subsequently considered sentencing guidelines in relation to the offences of break, enter and steal; commercial drug trafficking; armed robbery; dangerous driving; effect of a guilty plea on sentence; effect of an admission of guilt relating to other offences; and high range prescribed content of offences. While fairly well-established in overseas jurisdictions (see, for example, Roberts 2012), within Australia, guideline judgments remain highly controversial outside of New South Wales.

SENTENCING GRIDS

Sentencing grids or matrix legislation, also known as presumptive sentencing guidelines, are contained in, or based in, legislation. Originating in the United States in the 1970s, they involve the production of a two-dimensional graph with axes reflecting 'offence seriousness' and 'prior criminal record'. The penalty level to be selected is usually determined by reference to the sentencing range specified in the cell of the grid or matrix that concurs with the offender's offence and their recorded prior offending history. Other factors, such as aggravating and mitigating circumstances, may be included in the guidelines. Some departure from these guidelines is permitted, but a rationale for doing so is to be provided by the judiciary in the sentencing judgment. In essence, sentencing grids require judges and magistrates to carefully calibrate their sentences in accordance with a rigid mathematical formula, with very little scope for consideration of subjective, individual factors (Finn 1998).

SENTENCING ADVISORY COUNCILS

These independent statutory bodies were established in Victoria in 1994, New South Wales in 2003 and Tasmania in 2010 to provide sentencing support and educational services; that is, assist in the preparation of non-mandated guideline judgments and other matters, such as: the offences suitable for non-parole periods and their appropriate length; the preparation of research papers or reports; and provision of sentencing statistics, case summaries and sentencing practices. They are generally broadly based in terms of membership (including, for example, legal, law enforcement and correctional professionals, and a range of community member representatives such as special interest groups and victims of crime) and are required to consult with the community in the preparation of guideline judgments. In serving as a mechanism for gauging public opinion on matters of sentencing, these bodies seek to restore public confidence in the judicial process (Edwards 2012; Potas 2005).

PROBLEM-ORIENTED COURTS

It is important to highlight that not all recent sentencing reforms have involved efforts to rein in judicial discretion and impose tougher penalties. Indeed, the introduction of problem-oriented courts is an attempt to bring the objectives of offender rehabilitation and treatment back to the fore in sentencing determinations.

As discussed in the previous chapter, these are specialist courts, usually divisions of magistrates' courts, which have an offence or offender-specific jurisdiction, such as drug, Indigenous, juvenile, mental health and domestic violence (Dusmohamed & Burvill 2003; Freiberg 2003, 2005; Hands & Williams 2008; Harris 2004; Indermaur & Roberts 2003; Lawrence & Freeman 2002; Marchetti & Daly 2004). Suitable offenders (determined by criteria that vary from court to court) who plead guilty are diverted by magistrates to problem-oriented courts for sentencing purposes. Grounded in the principles and methods of therapeutic jurisprudence, these courts seek to integrate treatment services that are tailored to offence-specific needs (e.g. court mandated and supervised drug treatment, anger management therapy and counselling) with judicial case management, continuous judicial intervention, close monitoring of and immediate response to offender behaviour, and multi-agency involvement. The operation of these courts varies from jurisdiction to jurisdiction in terms of legislative foundation (e.g. the Victorian Koori Court is the only body to be established by legislation—*the Koori Court Act 2002*) and operational practices. However, they share the common feature of drawing together a team of professionals in an effort to achieve sentencing outcomes that enhance the wellbeing of offenders through appropriate treatment.

In the case of Indigenous courts, an additional objective is for sentencing to be culturally responsive to the needs of Indigenous offenders. A unique feature in this regard is the opportunity provided for direct community involvement (through Aboriginal elders and respected persons) in the sentencing process as a means of mediating the relationship between the magistrate and the Aboriginal defendant. The elder is required to demonstrate to the defendant the consequences of their actions for the victim and the Aboriginal community.

ISSUES FOR CONSIDERATION

THE EXERCISE OF JUDICIAL DISCRETION: COMPETING DEBATES

It is important to emphasise the commonly held judicial view that decision-making is not a science; that is, a purely logical exercise involving the mechanical application of set rules to arrive at a correct and consistent decision. The difficulties in applying this approach are to be found in the judicial balancing of a multiplicity of aggravating and mitigating factors relevant to both offence and offender, as well as weighing the various, often competing, objectives of sentencing. These difficulties in exercising judicial discretion have led some to propose that sentencing is in fact an art, implying that it is somehow an instinctive or intuitive skill (see Fox 2006; Hewton 2010). There remains considerable debate regarding preferred sentencing methodology to be employed.

The two competing methodologies are known as the **'two-stage'** or **'two-tier'** approach, and the 'instinctive synthesis' approach. The former refers to the establishment of a notional starting point for sentencing by considering the aspects of a case that more easily lend themselves to objective analysis (e.g. the gravity of the crime) and the allowable penalties within the relevant statutory range. This starting point is then adjusted once the more subjective, circumstantial aspects of a case are considered in the light of the individual circumstances of the offender (e.g. offender culpability) to arrive at a sentence. The alternative approach involves one step only—the consideration of all relevant factors simultaneously. Both approaches have attracted criticism: the two-stage approach for its calculation and rigidity, and the instinctive synthesis for lacking precision and transparency. The High Court has recently confirmed the legitimacy of both approaches (NSW Law Reform Commission 2007b; see also Lovegrove 2008 for an alternative model).

Clearly, the manner in which a sentencing court interprets and gives weight to the circumstances giving rise to a criminal offence is critical to the selection of an appropriate penalty. While criminological theory offers a broad range of perspectives and insights into crime causation and criminal behaviour that are seemingly relevant to the sentencing task, Edney (2006) underscores their conspicuous absence in the process of sentencing under Australian criminal law. Exploring this theme in relation to Indigenous offending, Edney (2005) argues that sentencing under Australian criminal law is generally confined to limited consideration of an individual's life course and does not give due consideration to intergenerational and historical forces that may underlie current offending behaviour. In particular, assessment of culpability fails to take account of social culpability; that is, such matters as historical dispossession and racial discrimination, as well as social and economic exclusion. In recent years, Indigenity has been recognised in some jurisdictions as relevant to mitigating sentence.

THE JURY: AN ANACHRONISM?

The composition and role of the jury continues to attract considerable debate in Australia and elsewhere. Some advocate the abolition of the jury and the conduct of criminal trials by judge alone on the grounds of systemic efficiency. Others recommend restricting their use to certain classes of offences at the upper range of seriousness. Others still recommend the adoption of a hybrid system such as that in existence in Scandinavian countries, comprising a judicial officer assisted by an expert and a limited number of community representatives (French 2007).

For those who favour retention of the jury system, the focus continues on ways to further enhance community representation. The United States has reformed its laws to now permit deaf

**TWO-TIER/
TWO-STAGE
APPROACH TO
SENTENCING**
The establishment of a notional starting point for sentencing by considering the aspects of a case that more easily lend themselves to objective analysis (e.g. the gravity of the crime) and the allowable penalties within the relevant statutory range. This starting point is then adjusted once the more subjective, circumstantial aspects of a case are considered in the light of the individual circumstances of offender (e.g. offender culpability) to arrive at a sentence.

persons to serve as jurors, with appropriate provisions being made for reasonable adjustments (e.g. provision of Auslan interpreters). In Australia, New South Wales has recently considered the eligibility of people who are profoundly deaf or those with significant hearing or sight impairment to serve as jurors (Napier & Spencer 2007; NSW Law Reform Commission 2006). In England and Wales, jury system disqualifications have been dramatically reformed so that ineligibility extends only to criminal charge and conviction, non-citizenship, mental disorder and age (under 18 or over 70) conditions.

SENTENCING DISCOUNTS FOR PLEADING GUILTY

The issue of discounting for guilty pleas is also worthy of consideration, especially in the light of law reforms such as mandatory sentencing and criminal case conferencing, which are said to reduce the incentive to plead guilty and may lead to a greater role for plea bargaining; that is, transference of decision-making from judges to the prosecution. In New South Wales, for example, tougher sentences that have sought to encourage early guilty pleas have led to a reduction in the discounts available to those pleading guilty from up to 35 per cent on sentence, to between 12.5 per cent and 25 per cent, depending on the timing of the plea (pre- or post-committal). Prescribing sentence discounts is said to interfere with judicial discretion and attacks the concept of individualised justice (Miralis 2008).

SENTENCING OPTIONS

With respect to sentencing options, it is noteworthy that use of fines has steadily declined over time, particularly in the higher courts. The reasons for this relate, in part, to the difficulties in recovering outstanding fines (up to an estimated 80% cent are never paid), principally because they fall beyond the financial capacities of most offenders. A radical proposal for resolving fine defaults is the suggestion that the repayment timelines for fines be adjusted in relation to the size of the offender's income and that the Australian Taxation Office be empowered to collect payments through automatic docking of pay or Centrelink payments, as now happens with PAYE income tax (Chapman et al. 2003). Social commentators have argued that the adoption of such a scheme, especially for public nuisance type offences, will do nothing to further the objectives of sentencing, and may indeed encourage fine defaulters to engage in more serious criminal activity in an effort to repay the fines (Walsh 2005).

CONCLUSION

This chapter has explored the nature of judicial decision-making and the work of the courts in determining guilt and penalty. The goals of sentencing vary considerably and the emphasis of the court will likewise vary depending upon the political, legal and social culture of any particular jurisdiction (Freiberg & Ross 1995). In recent years, for example, many Australian jurisdictions have seen greater emphasis on 'community protection' and 'retribution' as the priority purposes of sentences. This has translated at a practical level into a concern to impose longer and possibly harsher sentences on certain classes of offenders (e.g. serious and repeat offenders and sex offenders) and on certain categories of offence (e.g. home invasion and property crime).

The contemporary sentencing reforms outlined in this chapter clearly present specific challenges to many aspects of judicial decision-making. In particular, it is evident that the politics of law and order have been mobilised in ways that directly threaten the powers and ability of the courts to provide the kind of detailed weighing up of factors relevant to sentencing that has traditionally been required of the judiciary. Moreover, they compel the prioritisation of certain objectives of punishment (e.g. punitive and incapacitative aims) over those of others (e.g. rehabilitation), irrespective of the circumstances of the offender.

The method of determining sentence draws upon a wide range of criteria, and makes reference to the conditions surrounding the commission of the offence and to the attributes of the offender. Once the details of a case have been ascertained, it is up to the court to try to match the crime with an appropriate response. To do this, the court may use a wide range of dispositions, ranging from discharge through to imprisonment. As indicated through a review of recent sentencing reforms, however, judicial discretion has been significantly curtailed through a statutory appropriation of the sentencing responsibility. The consequent increasingly punitive sentences have real and material consequences, not only for the administration of justice but also in terms of outcomes for the most disadvantaged and vulnerable members of our community, especially Indigenous young people.

The most serious of the dispositions available to the court—imprisonment—will be examined in greater depth in Chapter 24. This is particularly pertinent to consider, given the propensity in recent years for governments and courts to impose prison terms as part of a sentence. There is a need for a just and consistent sentencing system. The question posed in Chapter 24 is where our ideas about sentencing—especially punishment—originate and how they have changed over the years.

DISCUSSION QUESTIONS

1   In recent years a number of issues have emerged with respect to judicial decision-making and sentencing. They include:

-   Should there be flexibility in sentencing, so that judges use their discretion to determine cases on the basis of the particular facts and features of each offence and offender? Or should the judiciary's freedom of choice be restricted, and judges be obliged to apply a uniform sentence on a mandatory basis? How do we make the law equal in application, but in a way that ultimately is fair and just given the specific circumstances of each case (Anthony 2012; Roberts 2012)?
-   If the law states that a person shall be sentenced to 5 years, should they serve the full 5 years in jail, or should they be eligible for remissions? What are the implications of abolishing remissions (automatic or for good behaviour), parole or early-release for prison life and inmate rehabilitation?
-   If an individual is charged with more than one offence, and convicted for more than one offence, should these sentences be served concurrently? Or should the sentences be served one after the other? This has major implications for the processing of cases (whether they involve guilty pleas or are contested), for the use of plea bargains (sentence reductions) and for the size of prison populations (Lovegrove 2004).
-   Should individuals be sentenced to a term that concludes at some fixed point in time, in accordance with the principles of proportionality and consistency (i.e. punishment to fit the crime and to be the same in all like cases)? Or should the sentence be open-ended, so that it is constantly under review, and fits the nature of the specific offender?

2   Should trial by jury be retained? If so:
    -   Should certain types of offences be excluded from jury consideration?
    -   Have Australian reforms to jury composition gone as far as they can? If not, what more can, and should, be done?

3   What role, if any, should criminological theory play in contemporary criminal justice administration (Edney 2006)?

4   Can greater and more creative use be made of the fine system to dispense justice?

5   What measures can be adopted to increase public confidence in the Australian courts and to moderate punitive attitudes?

FURTHER READING

Ashworth, A. (2010) *Sentencing and criminal justice* (5th edn.), Cambridge University Press, New York.

Flynn, A. (2011a) '"Fortunately we in Victoria are not in that UK situation": Australian and United Kingdom legal perspectives on plea bargaining reform', *Deakin Law Review*, 16(2): 361–404.

Hatzistergos, J. (2010) 'Reconciling the purposes and principles of criminal punishment', *Law Society Journal*, August: 78–90.

Hopkins, A. (2012) 'The relevance of Aboriginality in sentencing: "sentencing a person for who they are", *Australian Indigenous Law Journal*, 16(1): 30–52.

O'Leary, J. (2011) 'Twelve angry peers or one angry judge: an analysis of judge alone trials in Australia', *Criminal Law Journal*, 35: 154–69.

Roberts, J.V. (2012) 'Structured sentencing: Lessons from England and Wales for common law jurisdictions', *Punishment & Society*, 14(3): 267–88.

PUNISHMENT AND PENALTY

24

CHAPTER OVERVIEW

- AN HISTORICAL ACCOUNT OF PUNISHMENT
- AN INTERPRETIVE FRAMEWORK
- ISSUES FOR CONSIDERATION
- CONCLUSION
- DISCUSSION QUESTIONS
- FURTHER READING

INTRODUCTION

While Chapter 23 reviewed judicial decision-making processes and issues relating to sentencing, this chapter explores in greater detail one of the objectives of sentencing; that is, punishment. Punishment is undoubtedly a topic of perennial public interest, provoking intensely emotional and controversial debates regarding its aims, objectives, form and appropriate administration. Such debates are, of course, not new, for punishment has historically assumed a central importance in both political and moral spheres (Foucault 1991; Garland 1995; Matthews & Young 2003; Ulmer et al. 2008; Valier 2004).

Despite the conflictual nature of contemporary debates, there does appear to be some common ground—in the popular perception at least, punishment and imprisonment are often synonymous. Although the prison appears to be an intrinsic and permanent feature of our justice system (Tonry 2004), a historical review of punishment reveals that before the eighteenth century it was but one component (and by no means the most important one) in the punishment apparatus, and its purpose was vastly different from that ascribed to it today (Braithwaite 2001; Morris & Rothman 1998; Smart 1976).

The historical evolution of punishment, both conceptually and operationally, is briefly charted in this chapter and reviewed in the light of a number of seminal theoretical frameworks and explanatory paradigms (criminological, political and sociological). While each of these approaches and perspectives provides alternative interpretive justifications for, or critiques of, punishment, they commonly draw connections between the state, the legal system and society. More specifically, these accounts argue that the changing nature of punishment and its administration is best understood in terms of its relationship both as a reflection of, and contributor to, social function (e.g. control, power and domination) and cultural significance (societal 'mentalities' and 'sensibilities').

PUNISHMENT
The practice of imposing a penalty (physical pain, shame or restraint) onto an individual who has acted disobediently and/or defiantly by engaging in behaviour deemed legally and/or morally wrong in accordance with individual, communal, governmental, legal or religious principles.

AN HISTORICAL ACCOUNT OF PUNISHMENT

From the beginnings of human society, those who have caused harm to others have been subjected to **punishment**. However, the nature and administration of punishment (systems, mechanisms and techniques) have transformed dramatically over the past several thousand years. These developments have been intimately connected to changing conceptions of crime, which in turn have been shaped by prevailing political and institutional arrangements.

THE ADMINISTRATION OF PUNISHMENT
PERSONAL RETRIBUTION

SECULARISM
A principle espousing the separation of legal and governmental principles, practices and institutions from religion and/or religious doctrine.

In the early days of humankind (pre-dating the advent of the modern state and the consequent predominance of secular law or **secularism**), punishment was conceived of in terms of retribution; that is, it was guided by the old biblical adage 'an eye for an eye'. Punishment was localised, personalised and arbitrary, because it was mostly in the hands of the victim, who personally exacted vengeance for the wrong(s) or harm suffered.

Additionally, with the development of small groups and tribal forms between 200,000 and 25,000 years ago, harm was conceived in terms other than simply personal retribution (Ekstedt & Griffiths 1984). Individual harm was thus defined as group harm. This meant, in practice, that the victim's family, clan or tribe also had the right to administer punishment to the perpetrator, whether that punishment was participatory dialogue (designed to heal rather than hurt), recompense, banishment, injury, torture or even death.

It is important to emphasise the individualised and arbitrary nature of punishment at this stage: crime was defined in relation to the direct harm(s) against an individual's person or property (e.g. assault, theft and destruction of crops), and justice was meted out on the basis of local (predominantly kin-based) custom and the victim's tribal or clan elder's perceptions of appropriate vindication (Morris & Rothman 1998). It was argued that this direct involvement of the victim in the settlement of the dispute served to equalise the contestants, reducing inequalities generated by wealth, power and status (Braithwaite 2001; Peters 1995; Weitekamp 1999). Interestingly, this form of justice represents the precursor to modern restorative justice paradigms, which are examined in detail in Chapter 27.

ECCLESIASTICAL JUSTICE

In Europe, the first criminal codes appeared between 3500 and 400 BC and, increasingly, the state played a greater role in what had previously been seen as personal or group disputes. Thus, there was a shift away from personal or family-based retribution as outside agencies came to play an ever-greater role in processes of adjudication and punishment. This was particularly evident in the period from 400 BC to AD 500, when Roman law was established and, through military conquest, generalised across the domains of the Roman Empire.

ECCLESIAS-TICAL JUSTICE
The creation and administration of law and punishment on the basis of theological (religious) principles drawn from Christian teachings on personal morality.

In the medieval period in Europe (between AD 500 and 1450), religious and secular laws went hand in hand. Feudal justice, structured around a loosely organised state, was fused with **ecclesiastical justice**, structured around the Christian church. Crime in this period was defined not only in terms of personal harm but also increasingly in spiritual, moral and religious terms; it was viewed as a transgression or sin against both God and Christian society (Peters 1995). Closely associated with this rise to predominance of ecclesiastical influence was the transferral of part of the state's judicial decision-making power into the hands of religious leaders and prophets, who were thought to have spiritual authority in matters pertaining to the establishment of dogma and, by extension, definitions of crime. At this time there was no clear separation of church and state.

Vengeance was therefore now a matter for God, not simply to be left to individuals or their families. Consequently, the church acquired a new prominence as a separate judicial jurisdiction, assuming responsibility for immoral conduct within the community; this included matters not strictly criminal, such as blasphemy, adultery and divorce (Ingram 1990; Peters 1995). Although often acting in alliance with the state, and dispensing justice through the existing courts, those courts were dependent upon the ecclesiastical hierarchy, which possessed enormous interventionary and punitive powers (Spierenberg 1995). Not only was the church now viewed as a legitimate designer and perpetrator of punishment, but punishment was also no longer oriented solely toward retribution. It now assumed a disciplinary character and was oriented toward repentance, atonement and religious salvation; that is, correcting sinfulness (Peters 1995; Seiter 2005).

Failure to practise the correct religious rituals, or denunciation of religious beliefs, now resulted in ecclesiastical judgment and punishment, such as excommunication (public exclusion from the church and its sacraments). Perhaps the most vivid images of ecclesiastical justice are associated with the Inquisition's tribunals, which were established in the early years of the thirteenth century to deal specifically with the gravest of crimes—heterodoxy; that is, 'active dissent from ecclesiastical doctrine' (Peters 1995: 30).

Changes in conceptions of punishment are tied to changes in the laws themselves. However, we might note here that, even within the law, there can be competing views of punishment, and discernible changes in orientation over time. For example, within contemporary Christian religious circles, some fundamentalists swear by the scriptural severity of the Old Testament, with its theme of retribution; that is, 'an eye for an eye, a tooth for a tooth'. This approach promotes a visibly different conception of punishment from that of the New Testament, which is far more compassionate, asking individuals not to be judgmental, to act with forbearance, and to exercise community admonition and forgiveness; that is, to 'turn the other cheek' (Spierenberg 1995). There are similar disagreements and splits within contemporary Islamic interpretations of the Quran.

The feudal period (up to the mid-1700s) saw the state gradually monopolise criminal justice, but in a way that did not take over what had previously been the church's arena. The church and state expanded their legal powers and interventions together. Generally, offences were mainly defined as being those actions that were directed against the church, and those against the aristocracy or landowners. The rise of capitalism and, in particular, the advent of the Industrial Revolution, was to sever the connection between church and state, as the changing mode of production demanded a new type of legal and political apparatus (see Fine 1984). Notwithstanding, the relationship between religion, religious context and punishment (including the formulation of laws and actual sentencing practices) continues to endure to varying degrees in societies across the world today (see, for example, Ulmer et al. 2008).

SECULAR JUSTICE

With the development of the modern nation-state, large geographical areas were brought under direct political control, initially through monarchical and, later, parliamentary rule. This shift away from ecclesiastical predominance served to reinforce the state's public authority. The transfer of power from the church to the state was paralleled by a further transformation in conceptions of crime: it was now always constructed symbolically in terms of an offence against the state, and therefore society (Morris & Rothman 1998). Crime might affect individuals, but social order depended upon everyone being bound by the same rules and obligations. Hence the move away from personalised justice towards the 'territoriality' of law. This was achieved through the evolution of customs and laws, particularly building upon the codified secular criminal laws of ancient Rome (Peters 1995).

Punishment continued to be administered in terms of group and individual retribution, but secular rulers now assumed authority over the wrongdoer. Eventually, the state itself became the only agency that could legitimately punish offenders. The historical movement away from punishment under the aegis of the victim toward that of the law was justified on the grounds that it prevented blood feuds, which often spanned generations and proved socially debilitating (Morris & Rothman 1998). The consolidation and concentration of power in the hands of the nation-state meant that the church now had limited jurisdiction (e.g. over offences against religious doctrine) and limited means of dealing with breaches of church law (e.g. excommunication). By assuming command of punishment generally, the modern nation-state was able to exert considerable powers over the population, while protecting itself from the threat either of the church or of particular sections of the secular order (e.g. the barons).

THE NATURE OF PUNISHMENT

The history of punishment is a history of the development of social order, of the consequently different definitions of crime embraced, and of different groups or agencies in society that are seen to have the legitimate right to punish the wrongdoer. The history of punishment is also a story of different types of punishment. Here, a major distinction can be made between punishment directed at the body, and punishment directed at the mind of the offender.

PUNISHING THE BODY: CORPORAL AND CAPITAL PUNISHMENT

In the early days of the medieval period, punishment was principally physical in nature; designed to mirror the violence of the original crime onto the convict's body. Since it was for the most part a public affair, punishment conspicuously attacked bodily integrity (Foucault 1991; Spierenberg 1995). Depending upon the gravity of the offence, the courts had a wide range of punitive dispositions at their disposal, which Spierenberg (1995) divides into five categories of escalating severity and brutality:

- *flogging* (*whipping*): the most common form of corporal punishment
- *branding*: with red-hot irons or heated swords; this process inevitably resulted in a scar that permanently assigned the affected individual a criminal status
- *mutilation*: ranging from an incision in the cheek, to blinding, to the amputation of an ear (the most common form of mutilation), a thumb or an entire hand
- *merciful instant death*: including beheading, hanging (the gallows), garrotting (strangulation) and burying alive
- *prolonged death*: that is, death preceded by torture; forms of punishment in this category included the use of horses to rip the offender's limbs apart, the throwing of offenders to beasts, burning to death, breaking on the wheel (a process where the offender's bones are broken with an iron bar prior to being stabbed in the heart) and crucifixion. Though unquestionably gruesome, such extreme forms of punishment were exceptional, and reserved for those who had committed the most heinous offences.

In addition to these forms of punishment, European jurisdictions also customarily practised judicial torture as a means of 'assisting' the inquisitorial process. Confessions were sought and forcibly obtained through, among other things, forced drinking, the application of shin or thumb screws, use of the rack, and the hanging of weights to the toes of suspected offenders. Underlying many of these practices was an understanding of crime as evil, or as the manifestation of supernatural forces (Spierenberg 1995).

It is obvious that punishment was historically designed to subject offenders to pain, but it also exposed them to public humiliation and shaming, as demonstrated by images of people in stocks and pillories situated in market squares, and the use of banishment (the forced expulsion of an offender from their community and their relocation at a remote destination; physically isolating the offender from the community was also thought to protect society). The process of execution was particularly theatrical, often staged as a spectacle, complete with audience. The ceremonial nature of the execution ritual served to intensify the shaming process, for the condemned person was subjected to a number of publicly degrading acts both before and after the execution. For example, they were marched through the streets as part of an execution procession, with church bells heralding the event; and the corpses of selected offenders were displayed in public places (e.g. a gallows field), until they decomposed, as a means of public warning (Linebaugh 2003; Spierenberg 1995).

During this period, the law was considered an extension of the sovereign's body. Accordingly, crimes committed were considered a personal affront to the king himself rather than crimes against the public good, and punishment therefore served the purpose of exacting revenge upon the offender's body for the criminal injury suffered by the sovereign body. As the right to punish was directly vested in the authority of the sovereign during this time, public spectacle of torture, execution and humiliation ultimately served to ensure that society at large bore witness to the sovereign's vengeance, thereby publicly reaffirming the legitimacy and awe of sovereign rule and potentially discouraging the offender and/or onlookers from future crime (Foucault 1991).

PUNISHING THE MIND: DISCIPLINE AND THE ADVENT OF THE PRISON

Between the early seventeenth and mid-eighteenth centuries in Europe, society began to witness a gradual decline in the use of corporal and capital punishment, especially in the case of less serious offences. The preoccupation with barbarous inflictions on the body of the offender was steadily replaced with a concern to alter behaviour by focusing on the mind. In accounting for this change in judicial focus, the influence of public opinion cannot be underestimated. While the spectacle of torture and death was formerly a popular event among the lower classes, over time it became so routine and distasteful that it offended 'a new sensibility about pain and bodily integrity' (Morris & Rothman 1998: viii).

As punishment began to conflict too acutely with the community's moral sensibilities, it morphed into a source of conflict between the sovereign and the masses. The general population started identifying with the condemned, the offender's body often becoming a locus of compassion and respect. As the sovereign's right to punish was increasingly considered disproportionate, haphazard and unrestrained, juries began refusing to convict offenders (Lewis 1953). Moreover, executions became an occasion to vent expressions of public revulsion and to mock the law. For example, convicts were cheered, those placed on public display in stocks were liberated, and executions often resulted in public riots in support of the condemned (Foucault 1991; Spierenberg 1995).

Driven by reformist—as opposed to humanitarian—concerns with curbing the uneven distribution of power to punish and judge, the theatre of public torture gave way to more consistent, moderate and ubiquitous displays of punishment. The transformation to 'gentler' forms of punishment occurred in a graded, though relatively rapid fashion, notably with the advent of public chain gangs. Rather than repaying the wrongs of sovereign harm, punishment came to be conceived of as repayment for societal infractions, to be rectified via a regimen of forced work. The public display of chain gangs served to focus public attention on both the convict enactment of punishment and, ostensibly, to reflect on the crime (Foucault 1991).

The declining confidence in public punishment prompted a move in the early modern period towards administering punishment in seclusion; that is, away from the public eye. This transition from the public to the private was achieved through a variety of less spectacular punishments, such as fines, orders to keep the peace or banishment.

However, with the rise of a strong central state that strove for consistency in the administration of punishment, and the subsequent growth of disciplinary institutions and systems of micro-power (economic, social, political and military) in the eighteenth and nineteenth centuries, the use of penal bondage ultimately triumphed. Although incarceration took many forms (e.g. workhouses, transportation and imprisonment), in essence it served to reform offenders by depriving them of their liberty; that is, separating them involuntarily from the outside world through a process of physical confinement (Spierenberg 1995). As will be further explained shortly, penal institutions have undergone numerous transformations over time, both in form and purpose.

THE PURPOSES OF PUNISHMENT

Since the whole concept of punishment is morally problematic (Duff & Garland 1995), it requires justification. For example, why does the state have the right to punish its citizens? What should this punishment achieve? As we have demonstrated so far, punishment as a way of responding to crime has varied enormously over the years. This section expands on this theme of change by outlining how, in the process of change, punishment itself has been tied to various social purposes and rationalisations (see Table 24.1). In other words, we wish to review the core aims and justifications for punishment.

CONSEQUENTIALIST AIMS

Consequentialist theorists stress the instrumentalist, or utilitarian, objectives to be pursued through punishment. As a forward-looking perspective, state punishment of past offences, which necessarily involves some form of present pain, is never considered as good in and of itself. The administration of punishment and attendant pain is only ever warranted on the grounds that it produces positive future consequences or outcomes for society; it must either achieve socially desirable benefits or avert socially unwanted harms. These positive consequences are said to outweigh the pain associated with the act of punishment itself (Duff 1996; Feinberg 1991; Feinberg & Gross 1991; Rawls 1955).

DETERRENCE

One of the specific justifications for punishment most commonly advanced by consequentialist theorists is deterrence. This approach is also referred to as 'reductivism', since the objective is to reduce the level of future offending endured by society, through fear of consequences; namely, that engagement in 'negative' and disruptive behaviour will receive attention and punishment. The history of punishment demonstrates an overriding concern with achieving deterrence, which is generally subdivided into two constituent elements:

- *specific or individual deterrence:* punishment imposed retrospectively, which seeks to prevent the known offender from reoffending once sentenced
- *general or exemplary deterrence:* a prospective attempt to reduce the probability of lawbreaking in the wider community.

As potential offenders are considered to be rational decision-makers who assess the pros and cons of their intended action, it is argued that the likely deterrent effect of punishment can be calculated according to the additive and/or multiplicative effects of the following variables (see generally Stigler 1990):

- certainty and swiftness of punishment (and its necessary precursors: detection, prosecution and conviction)

TABLE 24.1 OBJECTIVES AND PRINCIPLES OF CRIMINAL PUNISHMENT

CONSEQUENTIALIST AIMS	EXPRESSIVE AIMS
Individual or general deterrence • Human nature viewed as voluntaristic, rationalistic and utilitarian • Emphasis on penalty or program as deterring future offending • Discourage individual offender from reoffending through punishment or reformation • Discourage others from offending prospectively through severity of punishment • Punishment may be proportional or non-proportional to the offence	**Denunciation and moral reprobation** • Punishment as symbolic response to harmful behaviour • Emphasis on expressing public disapproval of offender and/or offence • Punishment sets moral boundaries • Punishment reaffirms specific forms of authority and belief • Punishment maintains social cohesiveness
Reform and rehabilitation • Human nature viewed as deterministic, predisposed through biology, psychology and environment • Emphasis on correcting offender behaviour • Emphasis on 'therapeutic' programs focusing on reform, treatment and rehabilitation • Treatment to be tailored to the offender's needs • Environment supportive to positive changes in offender	**Retribution and 'just deserts'** • Emphasis on punishment as moral desert • Offenders are responsible for their actions and thus their punishments • Direct connection between crime and punishment • Emphasis on penalty based upon actual offending • Rehabilitative and/or deterrent aims of punishment viewed as unintended by-product
Incapacitation and community protection • Emphasis on protecting the community from the offender • Disproportionate punishment justified • Focus on offender behaviour and social harm not need • Concept of dangerousness, future risk of offending and social harm • Necessity of tailored control	

• type and severity of sanction
• communication and credibility of the threatened legal repercussions.

If we examine the underlying principles of deterrence theory, we can associate it clearly with public forms of punishment that pre-date imprisonment. Essentially, public displays of torture and execution were designed to manage the population at large through fear and threat. The public denunciation and punishment of offenders thus served as a symbolic means to an end, for in the process of delivering 'just deserts' the offender was sacrificed (made an example of to others) for the greater good of society. This approach to punishment as a ceremonial spectacle is particularly concerned with the broader deterrent effect of exemplary sanctions, regardless of whether these are proportional to the crime (Morris & Rothman 1998).

Since public executions and displays of corporal punishment were the most forceful, visible and enduring instruments of social control, the authorities enthusiastically used the occasion to advocate the supremacy and power of royal government; hence, the pomp and ceremony attached to the process (Spierenberg 1995). However, with the slow change in social sensitivity towards violation of the body, public displays of physical punishment were no longer considered a suitable means of harnessing state authority, or conveying moral lessons; hence, the necessity for alternative methods of punishment.

'HUMANITARIAN' JUSTICE: REHABILITATION AND REFORM

Following this period of concern with exemplary deterrence, attention was directed towards the promotion of specific deterrence and redemption. The primary mechanism for achieving these objectives was therapeutic intervention (e.g. drug treatment, counselling and/or therapy) tailored to the offender's offence-related needs. Historically, this change in direction away from cruel and unusual forms of punishment in modern criminal justice systems was explained in terms of the unfolding of historical **Enlightenment**, a period marked by social progression towards the attainment of humanitarian objectives such as rehabilitation and reformation (Bentham 1789). Mercy and benevolence correspondingly came to replace retribution and general deterrence as the guiding philosophy of punishment. Thus, although incarceration is nowadays associated with harsh punishment, when first conceived it represented a philanthropic alternative to the previously barbarous and draconian system of justice (Morris & Rothman 1998).

The litany of objectives attached to incarceration has increased over time, but its initial purposes were individualistic reformation, both of the mind and the soul (which were viewed as malleable entities), and redemption (Lewis 1953). Reforming the offender has been interpreted in a number of different ways. In the early years, it was tied to religious objectives; namely, the enforcement of morality and spiritual transformation. Prison labour, discipline and order was thus designed to correct people's moral habits and stimulate their spiritual instincts, rather than to punish their deeds (Spierenberg 1995). Heavily influenced by such reasoning, a regimented, quasi-military style of imprisonment was adopted throughout the 1830s. Prisoners were solitarily confined in small cells, and strict rules of silence were enforced. The rationale here was that solitude offered prisoners opportunities to reflect on their past sins, the prisoner's own conscience acting to inflict spiritual suffering, followed presumably by a process of healing (McGowen 1995). Prison conditions were made sufficiently unpleasant to deter prisoners from repeating the experience.

By the early 1900s, however, the idea of rehabilitation had taken root and prisons were consequently remodelled on the external world. The idea here was that prisoners should emerge from the experience of incarceration as 'better people'. They should be given the opportunity, through appropriate treatment, to rehabilitate and redeem themselves, and to ameliorate their behaviour (concede the wrongfulness of their action(s) and acquire a sense of civic duty) so that upon release they could reintegrate into society in a productive and law-abiding fashion. Isolation was therefore regarded as too artificial and was replaced with normalisation. Prisoners were given a degree of freedom of movement and permitted to interact in the exercise yard, and degrading labour practices were replaced with productive group work (O'Brien 1995).

INCAPACITATION AND COMMUNITY PROTECTION

Alongside the deterrent and rehabilitative rhetoric of punishment lies the concept of incapacitation. Generally considered a policy of last resort, this justification for punishment is premised on the notion that society is entitled to protection from individuals likely to offend in future. The focus here is not

ENLIGHTEN-MENT
An intellectual and philosophical movement away from the Middle Ages and its foundational principles. At the core of enlightenment thinking is the concept of rational, scientific discourse and judgment, and an emphasis on natural laws, individual rights and freedom for common people.

the needs of the offender, but rather their *future behaviour* and the consequent *social harm* caused or potentially caused. If imprisonment does not prevent future recidivism, it certainly reduces the present opportunities an offender has to engage in criminal and/or deviant behaviour, and for the period of detention, at least, diminishes the threat they pose to the general population.

Underlying the principle of community protection is the notion of *dangerousness*, and a concern to calculate the future risks to communal safety posed by offenders at liberty to engage in dangerous behaviour. But how does our system of criminal justice determine whether an offender is dangerous? Morris (1995) identifies three criteria against which dangerousness is assessed:

1 *Anamnestic prediction*: a person is perceived to be dangerous based on the seriousness and/or circumstances of the offence committed (what the offender has already done), and extrapolations from their past record of criminal activity, especially demonstrations of violent and dangerous tendencies, regarding future offending (what the offender is likely to do in the future).

2 *Actuarial prediction*: a person is perceived to be dangerous on the basis of how similar individuals in comparable circumstances to them have behaved in the past—it is deemed likely they will behave as others did.

3 *Clinical prediction*: a person is classified dangerous on the intuitive judgment of professionals who have access to the offender's social history and relevant psychological and medical records.

While the first category bases its predictions entirely upon actual behaviour, in the second, statistical prediction is based upon what other people with similar characteristics have done, and in the third on a professional or 'expert' analysis and prediction of dangerousness based upon an understanding of the offender as an individual (see also Bartholomew & Milte 1976; Farrington & Tarling 1983; Morris & Miller 1985).

Once identified, the dangerous offender is said to require tailored control. If we take this reasoning to its logical extreme, then 'selective incapacitation' or 'indeterminate sentencing' is deemed an appropriate response; that is, the offender should be imprisoned until they are judged fit for release back into the community. In this sense, behaviour displayed while in prison serves as a test—if a prisoner fails that test, they should remain confined. A concern for community security may thus be used as justification for detaining an offender (usually those classed 'serious recidivist offenders') for a longer period than their past offence(s) would otherwise warrant (Ashworth 2002; Morris & Rothman 1998; Vollard 2013; see also Chapter 23).

EXPRESSIVE AIMS OF PUNISHMENT

An alternative school of philosophical thought to the consequentialist stream is that oriented towards pursuing the expressive—symbolic and ideological—functions of punishment; namely, denunciation, condemnation and indeed moral reprobation of unlawful conduct (Feinberg 1991; von Hirsch 1993; see also Table 24.1). Rather than justifying punishment through reference to the pragmatic gains to be attained by society, non-consequentialist philosophies are grounded in backward-looking rationalisations. According to this school of thought, punishment is warranted by the mere fact that, in the past, a prohibited, socially repugnant and/or inherently 'wicked' act was committed. It is on the basis of their proven culpability that an offender is thought to merit state punishment, rather than on any future advantages to be gained through its infliction (Ashworth 1987; Curcio 1996; Feinberg 1991; Feinberg & Gross 1991).

In this sense, the state and law are not merely reactive but also take on a proactive, morally functionalist, or normative character. That is, they actively seek to set the symbolic parameters of socially acceptable behaviour through the public disapproval and stigmatisation of deeds that have assaulted our sensibilities (Glasbeek 1998; Hawkins 1969; von Hirsch & Ashworth 1992). Punishment is seen to resonate at a psychological and emotional level, in that the administration and rituals associated with punishment provide the focal point for the expression of deeply felt emotions. Public condemnation is, for example, said to exact a measure of vengeance or 'just deserts' for the harms wrought through wrongful conduct.

DENUNCIATION AND MORAL REPROBATION

Punishment is a social act; that is, it takes place in the context of, and with the active and passive participation of, communities of people. Fundamentally, punishment has a symbolic character, which is oriented toward drawing the lines of acceptable behaviour or conduct and, by corollary, denouncing activities deemed to be morally harmful or socially repugnant. Through public censure of an offender and/or their offensive behaviour, punishment functions to reaffirm the legitimacy of established rules demarcating 'right' and 'wrong' behaviour (Walker 1991). Furthermore, it functions to reaffirm certain forms of authority and belief. That is, the authority of any particular governing regime is in part based upon how punishment is organised and carried out in practice.

Denunciation and retribution have often been associated with one another, since severe punishments, while rationalised on the grounds of offence seriousness, simultaneously serve to symbolically reflect public indignation, a function referred to by Weatherburn (cited in Findlay et al. 1983: 133) as 'exclamatory'. As will be discussed shortly, however, a fundamental distinction between the two perspectives is that while the retributivist demands the act of punishment, the mere act of expressing disapproval in the process of pronouncing sentence satisfies denunciatory objectives.

RETRIBUTION AND 'JUST DESERTS'

The concept of retribution is imprecise, encompassing as it does a multitude of perspectives, some of which have already been touched upon (see, for example, Cottingham 1979; Curcio 1996; Davis 1986; Feinberg 1991; Gross 1991; Mackie 1991; Moore 1987; von Hirsch 1976; von Hirsch & Ashworth 1992). Perspectives on punishment that are imbued with moral terminology ('wrongdoing', 'morally fitting' and 'merits') and an emphasis on 'deserts' (punishment is just because wrongdoers deserve to be punished) are sometimes referred to as 'moralistic versions of retributivist theory'. By contrast, legalistic retributivism focuses on lawbreaking; that is, the imposition of a prescribed penalty in response to a legal transgression (legal guilt), irrespective of whether the offender incurs moral guilt (Feinberg 1991). Included among the approaches that have been banded under the retributivist banner are:

- *Repayment theory:* the act of punishment serves as a means by which the offender repays a debt, not just to the victim(s) of their crime but also to society generally.
- *Placation theory:* by punishing an offender, a wrathful God (who might otherwise remain angry) is appeased.
- *Annulment theory:* as long as an offender escapes punishment, the crime is permitted to remain in force and flourish. Punishment acts in a restorative capacity, to somehow cancel out or annul the evil intention embodied in the crime.

- *Satisfaction or vengeance theory:* punishment is seen to vindicate the retaliatory desire of the wronged individual (whether the immediate victim or others injured or insulted by the crime). An evil is acknowledged and repaid in kind; in so doing, the harm caused is avenged.
- *Denunciation theory:* punishment is justified on the grounds that it represents an emphatic expression of moral public outrage, and a formal admonition of the conduct in question.
- *Desert theory:* under this approach, it is a simple measure of justice that the offender be punished, and it is on the basis of the offender's moral culpability that they are deserving of punishment.
- *Penalty theory:* this follows on from desert theory, in that the appropriate measure of punishment is directly linked to the harm or suffering inflicted upon the victim, rather than the nature of the conduct itself.

Despite the diversity in form, retributivism is essentially predicated on a deontological view of punishment: the state has a right, indeed a positive duty, to inflict reciprocal punishment on the offender, solely on the grounds of their moral and/or legalistic desert. Any possible collateral consequences of punishment—whether rehabilitative and/or deterrent—are deemed irrelevant or supplementary at best (Moore 1987; Murphy, cited in Mackie 1991; see also Brownlee 1998). The act of punishment serves to restore equilibrium by counterbalancing the unfair advantage gained by the wrongdoer. Modern forms of retribution call for vengeance to be exacted in proportion to the seriousness of the offence committed and the degree of offender culpability. As canvassed earlier, the most extreme manifestation of retributive ideology is, of course, the application of capital punishment.

Table 24.1 outlines the main principles of punishment as discussed earlier. It is essential to acknowledge that the consequentialist and expressive schools of thought are polar extremes and that, in reality, justifications for punishment often draw upon a hybrid of the two. Such a marriage is problematic, since the principles often contradict one another both in theory and in practice. For example, a concentration on retribution and the administration of punishment per se can undercut the attempt to rehabilitate the offender. Similarly, if we express public disapproval in particular ways, this may serve to alienate offenders from their communities and thus hinder the process of reintegration once a sentence has been served.

AN INTERPRETIVE FRAMEWORK

CRIMINOLOGICAL PERSPECTIVES

In order to gain a broader sense of the changing nature of punishment and its justifications, it is useful to examine how social attitudes towards human nature and the source(s) of criminality have changed (or remained constant) over time. Most practical discussions of punishment have tended to revolve around two of the major perspectives or traditions in criminology: the classical and the positivist (see also Chapter 3; White et al. 2012).

THE CLASSICAL MODEL

The classical approach in criminology is broadly concerned with issues of *retribution, deterrence* and *justice*. This perspective, developed in the eighteenth century alongside structural changes such as capitalism that accompanied the Renaissance, is premised on the notion that human beings are equally rational, utilitarian and hedonistic agents who seek to maximise pleasure and minimise pain (Bentham 1789; Jevons 1879). The focus here is on voluntarism, or rational free will, which is construed as a moral issue. Crime is seen, therefore, not as a manifestation of supernatural forces, but rather the product of individuals either misusing their free will by consciously choosing (in a calculated way) to violate the law, or engaging in irrational behaviour through imprudent or improper use of reason. A neoclassical economic model of behaviour is advanced, in that the choice to engage in crime is posited to be the function of cost–benefit calculus: a perception that the potential net yield from legal non-compliance will offset the anticipated costs of legal punishment (see Akers 1990; Ellickson 1989; Kennedy 1983).

Having depicted the decision-making processes as rationally amoral, deterrence theory dictates that punishment offers more pain than transgression of the law is worth. An intrinsic justification for punishment is presented here: since offenders are regarded as entirely responsible for their actions, they deserve to be punished (Hovenkamp 1990; Moore 1987). In this sense, punishment fulfils a supposedly universal intuitive desire for retribution. In addition to advocating the concept of 'just deserts', classical theorists argue that punishment also serves a far more legitimate, utilitarian purpose, in that it should promote the greatest good for the majority in society (Beccaria 1767). In practical terms, this translates into a preventative focus: the law should seek to deter both the individual (offender) and others generally from engaging in legally offensive behaviour (which endangers societal wellbeing), through threat of inflicting pain. The idea of deterrence is likewise based on the conception that human beings are rational, hedonistic actors. Accordingly, punishment should offer more pain than transgression of the law is worth (von Hirsch 1976). Swiftness, severity and certainty of punishment are key to understanding the law's potential for controlling human behaviour.

This perspective acknowledges the consequentialist (or forward-looking) aspects of punishment (via the concept of deterrence). However, it also argues that, for ethical reasons, justice should take precedence over the potentially favourable consequences of indisputably harsh punishment. Hence, the claim that only guilty individuals are deserving of punishment and that punishment is justified only if it inflicts on the offender a measure of pain proportional to the offence actually committed. This approach therefore rejects draconian practices (e.g. the use of capital and corporal punishment) designed to 'make an example' of the guilty, even if these measures achieve positive consequences (e.g. general deterrence) (Duff & Garland 1995).

In this framework of rational justice, emphasis is placed upon equality of legal protections and legal treatment. In accordance with the rule of law, like cases are to be punished alike. Sentences should therefore be applied in a systematic, predictable and regular manner. In order for these principles to function effectively, punishment should be determined jurisprudentially; that is, it is a matter to be decided by the criminal courts, since they have traditionally represented the common man's rational view (Lewis 1953).

THE POSITIVIST TRADITION

In contrast to the classical school of thought, the positivist tradition is concerned with *therapeutic models* of behavioural correction: those that focus on *reform*, *treatment* and *rehabilitation*. This perspective rejects the notion that human beings are free moral agents, arguing instead that human behaviour is predisposed or determined by extraneous factors and forces beyond the individual's immediate, conscious control. These behavioural influences are variously interpreted as being biological, psychological, social or some composite of those variables (see Chapter 3; White et al. 2012). These features of development positively impel the individual toward crime.

According to this line of reasoning, crime is not a matter of individual choice but rather the product of individual pathological deficiency. Because offenders are 'diseased' or 'dysfunctional' in nature, they cannot be held fully accountable or responsible for their deviant actions. It therefore makes no sense to focus on punitive responses to offending behaviour; the justice system should instead be oriented towards providing appropriate treatment (Young 1981).

In advancing a treatment ideology, positivists eschew the classical premise of equal human capacities; instead they stress the individuality of, and differences between and among, offenders and non-offenders generally. Thus, while the classical approach speaks of punishment within a framework of equal rights and just deserts (the pain inflicted on an offender via the process of punishment should be roughly commensurate with the pain caused by the offender to their victim and the community), the positivist approach favours *individualised* treatment responses that are tailored to the offender's needs, personality and amenability to correction (O'Brien 1995). At an institutional level, this mentality has periodically translated into the imposition of indeterminate sentences; that is, the period of 'treatment' expires when the individual is deemed to be cured of their malaise. This encroachment on justice is likewise justified by reference to consequentialist arguments; that is, 'punishment' is justified not in relation to a past offence but rather is connected to the attainment of a future goal; namely, reform. Moreover, preventative detention (the selective detainment of offenders on the basis of predictions of future dangerousness) is instrumental in that it enhances community security, thereby increasing public confidence in the law (Duff & Garland 1995).

Historically, this approach followed the shift in the nineteenth century from religious dominance in legal matters to the rise of technical professionals, such as social workers, doctors, psychologists and psychiatrists who relied upon an empirical, scientific understanding of crime and criminality (Gilling 1997). These so-called experts sought to convert the penal system into an 'instrument of social engineering through which crime could be prevented' (Duff & Garland 1995: 8). In the move away from judge and jurist, decisions on quantum and type of sentence became a question not of legal and moral principle, but rather of scientific 'fact'. Application of this knowledge involves use of specialist rather than commonsense techniques, such as examination, diagnosis, classification and prognosis (Lewis 1953).

REHABILITATIVE DISILLUSIONMENT: BACK TO JUSTICE

The preceding discussion clearly demonstrates the parallels between theoretical analysis and institutional practice. In general, changes in the nature and justifications of punishment have broadly reflected a movement away from classical views towards positivist views. Further changes occurred in the period between the late 1960s and mid-1970s, partly because of the climate of growing disillusionment with the ability of rehabilitative models to achieve their stated objectives. As Martinson (1974: 25) put it: 'with a few isolated exceptions, the rehabilitative efforts that have been reported so far had no appreciable effect on recidivism'. That is, rehabilitation had not appeared to make much difference in the levels of reoffending behaviour.

In addition to the 'nothing works' critique (McGuire & Priestly 1992; Trotter 1995; Zimring 1983), reformative models increasingly came under attack from civil libertarians who expressed concerns regarding the abusive potential of the 'treatment' being administered. For example, while implemented under the guise of 'individualised treatment', the largely unchallenged 'mind-bending' strategies employed were considered overly intrusive, inhumane and unjust. In particular, criticisms were directed towards the arbitrary nature of individualised and indeterminate sentencing and the accompanying infringements of rights of due process (see generally MacKenzie 2013; Roche 1999). Furthermore, emergent prisoners' rights groups began to assert the importance of the offender's civil rights and integrity over state concerns for community protection and utilitarian punishment (Dawes & Grant 2002; Duff & Garland 1995).

Judicial strategies informed by concepts of 'dangerousness' were especially subjected to criticism, mainly on the basis of evidentiary problems. In addition to denying the offender's moral status, preventative detention was said to be based on inaccurate predictive techniques. When applied on a case-by-case basis, predictions of dangerousness were said to result in too many 'false positives'— with the result that individuals were inaccurately diagnosed as 'career criminals', and were likely to be detained unjustly and unfairly (Morris 1984; see also Vess 2011; von Hirsch 1985; von Hirsch & Ashworth 1992).

In the context of these criticisms, the classical model of justice experienced a renaissance in the latter part of the twentieth century. The 'back to justice' movement shifted the focus away from the offenders' mind and their needs to their responsibility, and hence their deeds, resulting in the repeal of indeterminate sentencing laws in some American states (von Hirsch 1985; von Hirsch & Ashworth 1992). More generally, it prompted *decarceration* and its constituent subsets, decriminalisation, diversion and deinstitutionalisation—a movement away from the use of incarceration as a preferred sanction for many offences and towards the use of community-based corrections (Cohen 1985; Sarre & Tomaino 2004). The 'back to justice' rhetoric underpinning the decarceration movement has had particular appeal in the area of juvenile justice, where a shift from so-called welfare models to justice models of criminal justice has been the subject of considerable public debate and academic attention (Cunneen & White 2011, 1995; Wing Lo et al. 2006).

Although the 'just deserts' model picked up steam in the 1970s and 1980s, the 1990s and the ensuing millennium have witnessed considerable debate regarding issues of public order, culminating in a revival of incapacitation as a justification for punishment. As Freiberg and Ross (1995: 138) surmise: 'harshness has replaced hope, retribution has replaced rehabilitation, and prevention has eroded proportionality'.

Moral panics, often fuelled by pre-election law-and-order bidding campaigns, have encouraged the system to step back from the notion of proportionality of punishment towards a concern for general deterrence and community safety, under the guise of detention and treatment (Brown 2002b; McCulloch 2004; Martin 2010). For instance, the *Community Protection Act 1991* (Vic.) was specifically legislated to keep a particular prisoner, Gary Ian David (aka Gary Webb), who had in the past suffered from an antisocial personality disorder, indeterminately detained beyond his original sentence on preventative grounds (Craze & Moyniban 1994). As discussed in Chapter 23, preventive detention laws have similarly been enacted in more recent times in response to community concerns about serious sex offenders.

Meanwhile, the idea of proportionality has been eroded where punishment guidelines have been put in place that offer much more draconian penalties than were hitherto provided for various types of offence. This is particularly so in cases of mandatory 'three strikes and you're out' sentencing legislation, and legislation targeting repeat and 'serious' juvenile offenders, such as that enacted in the early 1990s in the Northern Territory and Western Australia (Brown 2002b; Cunneen & White 1995; Martin 2010; Roche 1999; Tynan 2001).

POLITICAL PERSPECTIVES

Criminological theory has been influential in shaping the criminal justice system's view of crime and the purposes of punishment. However, criminological theory does not emerge in a vacuum. As with most theories that examine the exercise of state power (in this case the power to punish), criminology draws upon the knowledge generated by broader political theories of the state. These theories, in turn, offer competing ideological justifications for punishment, since they hold different views on social order, the state's legitimate role and boundaries, and the nature of the interactional relationship between the state and its citizens.

CONSERVATIVE THEORIES

Conservative theories of the state are based upon communitarian notions of collective conscience, or consensual values. It is argued that, for state institutions reflect the interests of the wider community, the state and its citizens cannot be considered in isolation from one another. Since the state is perceived to have an important role in the promotion of communal welfare, and the protection of community morals and values, a more interventionist system of justice is likely to be supported, whether that be of the punitive or rehabilitative type. The main justification for punishment offered here is that it *promotes a common good*, such as social defence and harmony (see Norris 1991).

LIBERAL THEORIES

Liberal theories of the state tend to highlight the plurality of community values and interests, rather than their commonality. Individual rights and freedoms are highly valued and thus fiercely guarded within this approach; hence, it is argued that the state's powers of intervention should be circumscribed. The state's role is to provide a secure framework within which individuals are permitted to pursue their own interests, however defined. According to this view then, punishment is justified on the grounds that it offers citizens *freedom of personal autonomy* (choice and movement) by protecting them against the threat of crime. State power is legitimate, however, only if it enhances rather than constrains individual freedom and privacy. The degree of punishment should thus not be overly intrusive, but should be restricted to that level necessary to secure its stated objectives (see Murphy 1995).

RADICAL THEORIES

A radical perspective of the state is premised on the notion of a conflictual social order characterised by opposing human interests and values. It is argued that these social divisions are generated and perpetuated by the economic structure; that is, the capitalist mode of production, which is built upon the inequitable relationship between owners of capital and those whose means and quality of life depend upon the sale of their labour. In a society based upon the relationship between capital and wage labour, many individuals are said to lack real autonomy, and the institutional exercise of social and political power is not seen as value-free or neutral. Instead, those who hold economic power in society create institutions that reflect their dominance, and this partiality is reflected in the discriminatory nature and operation of the justice system (Murphy 1995). It is claimed that crime is the structurally shaped outcome of social deprivation, alienation and competition, and that while it is not necessarily the socially deprived who commit the most crime, they tend disproportionately to bear the weight of criminalisation and punishment processes (Reiman 1979; White & van der Velden 1995). Punishment

---

BOX 24.1   PUNITIVENESS AND SOCIAL WELFARE

In a two-part article for the *British Journal of Criminology*, John Pratt explored the differences between countries with a punitive approach to criminal justice (featuring extensive use of imprisonment as a sanction), and those countries that are not punitive and that have accordingly relied much less on incarceration (Pratt 2008a,b; see also Pratt 2007). Pratt found that those countries that had well-developed social welfare services and a general societal ethic of 'community' were less likely to be punitive than those countries that had little in the way of a welfare net or that were reducing their commitments to universally provided healthcare, education, public transportation, housing provision and other relevant state-supported services and institutions.

The study found that there were major differences in punitiveness between countries, depending upon whether they adopted neo-liberal policies or state-guided interventions in matters of economy and social welfare. Furthermore, as countries moved from a well-established system of welfare provision toward a more individualistic market-driven model of welfare, the trend was towards adoption of more punitive forms of criminal justice than previously had been the case.

Pratt's work on the political economy and penal policy is preceded by that of Michael Cavadino and James Dinigan (2006). The authors engage in a comparative analysis of the political economies of, and penalties favoured by, twelve countries (the United States, England and Wales, Australia, New Zealand, South Africa, Germany, the Netherlands, France, Italy, Sweden, Finland and Japan), grouped into the four 'family groups' of nations: neo-liberal, conservative corporatist, social democratic corporatist and oriental corporatist.

The study concludes that divergence in penal policies and practices among these nations exist despite globalisation. This lack of homogeneity is seen to be strongly associated with differing forms of political economy. In particular, neo-liberal nations, archetypically the United States, are the most punitive. The highly individualistic social ethos espoused by these nations, and resultant social inequality, are said to reduce social cohesion, excluding and marginalising individuals, and indeed entire groups, thereby engendering anomie and alienation—conditions conducive to crime. As with Pratt's analysis, these findings support the proposition that countries with relatively high welfare spending relative to gross domestic product have relatively low imprisonment rates.

Source: Pratt (2008a,b)

---

is therefore said to be a *coercive tool* through which the economically powerful are able to regulate and contain those marginalised, unproductive members of society who are seen to threaten capitalist imperatives. Since society is built upon injustices, punishment of this nature cannot be morally justified.

SOCIOLOGICAL PERSPECTIVES

A third interpretive framework is that provided by sociological accounts of punishment. This approach argues that methods, justifications and ramifications of punishment, are neither obvious nor rationally self-evident (Garland 1995). To understand the various dimensions of punishment, it is therefore necessary to acknowledge its social foundations and purposes; that is, to accept that punishment is a microcosm of wider social processes (see Box 24.1). As Garland (1995: 20) puts it, punishment is 'a social artefact serving a variety of purposes and premised upon an ensemble of social forces'. What follows is a brief review of some of the main contributors to the sociology of punishment and their differing explanations regarding the nature of the relationship between punishment and society.

ÉMILE DURKHEIM: FUNCTIONALISM

According to Durkheim (1951; see also Sumner 1994), social solidarity is a necessary precondition for collective social existence. Punishment is regarded as intrinsic—indeed salutary—to social control, because it is functionally linked to the *maintenance and preservation of social solidarity*. Individuals are viewed as egoistic; that is, possessing insatiable desires. It is only through the evolution and preservation of cultural norms that restraints are placed on individual aspirations; that is, immoral, socially destructive individualism is subordinated to the wider social good (Watts 1996). When illegal activity is engaged in, society's equilibrium is disturbed, since the perpetrator has gained an unfair advantage over the majority of law-abiding citizens, who have continued to sacrifice some measure of personal desire; crime is therefore an attack on society as a whole. Punishment seeks to counterbalance the offender's illicit gains, thereby restoring the reciprocal order of social privileges and burdens (Ashworth 1987; Davis 1986). In the absence of normative regulation, a state of anomie (where society's norms have been rendered ambiguous or ineffective; in effect, a state of normlessness) prevails, the probable outcome of which is widespread illegality.

The regulatory process is hence important in sustaining the conditions conducive to cohesive and harmonious communal living, which in turn is an essential precondition to law-abidance. Laws rationally shape the collective conscience (a social framework of mutually accepted sentiments, beliefs, values and concerns) by establishing the boundaries of morally permissible pursuits and communicating the legitimate means of achieving those socially sanctioned goals (see Durkheim 1982; Garland 1995; Inverarity et al. 1983).

For Durkheim (2004: 71), crime itself is regarded as both normal and serving a critical integrative function in society and in the evolution of the moral consciousness. It 'implies not only that way to necessary change remains open, but that, in certain cases, it directly prepares for these changes. ... crime [can thus be] a useful prelude to reform'. Braithwaite (1992, 1989) expands upon this theme through his concept of the 'self-sanctioning conscience'. The idea here is that collectively shaming certain behaviour through the machinery of justice prompts a wider community internalisation of the wrongfulness, and shamefulness, of that behaviour. Our conscience acts responsively to ensure that the prospect of engaging in like conduct becomes morally abhorrent (consider, for example, the anti drink-driving campaigns over recent years).

For Durkheim, crime is in one sense a creation of punishment rather than an instigator of punishment. This is because punishment and the rituals of punishment have a broader role than simply responding to specific kinds of crime. The punitive process is a culturally reciprocal one in that it not only moulds collective sentiments but also serves as a symbolic expression and periodic reaffirmation of the collective conscience, or normative consensus (Garland 1995; Henham 1999). That is, it manifests and re-establishes moral boundaries by drawing attention to the negative consequences attached to undesirable behaviour. According to this viewpoint, the law and morality are indivisible and 'passion' underlies punishment; that is, sentiments regarding crime and punishment are deeply entrenched throughout the population (Garland 1995). Ultimately, punishment is the method by which societies reaffirm their core values and solidarity, particularly in the face of external threats to a community. In this sense, there is a political imperative to punish, for it serves to maintain control and authority.

MICHEL FOUCAULT: TECHNOLOGIES OF POWER

According to Foucault (1991), it is necessary to adopt an approach to the history of discipline and punishment that focuses on the *micro-processes of authority* and the *exercise of power*. He examined the processes of discipline—including the movement away from a focus on disciplining the body to disciplining the mind—and the evolution of the prison not as products of enlightened thinking, but rather in the light of changes to the technologies of power (economic, political and military).

Foucault endowed the history of incarceration with a special meaning. The prison became the representative institution of industrial society—the perfect realisation of the 'modern state'. To study the prison, therefore, was to improve understanding of the nature of bourgeois society (see Garland 1995; Morris & Rothman 1998). Prisons represent more than merely institutions designed to deprive liberty. They also represent a disciplinary tool—a place where useful social qualities can be instilled in a manner comparable to military units; that is, a system of living and working according to strict guidelines that reward achievement and punish non-conformity. Foucault draws our attention to the factory-like structures of prisons during the nineteenth and twentieth centuries, where prisoners were required to mass-produce goods on an assembly line. He argues that instilling in prisoners a strong work ethic and compelling them to make 'constructive' use of every waking minute equates to social training for a life of 'productivity' upon release.

Foucault also highlights the role of professionals in imposing control over their subjects (in this case, prisoners), as in the manner by which psychologists, medical staff and prison officers regulate and constantly control inmates. Constant classification, surveillance and enforced disciplinary training is designed to break the will of the offender and thereby convert them into a 'docile body' easily controlled by those in authority.

For Foucault, Jeremy Bentham's **Panopticon** epitomised the ultimate modern disciplinary institution, with its pervasive inclination to normalise through observation. Institutions constructed on this architectural model were specifically designed to convey the impression of an invisible omnipresence by keeping occupants in the dark regarding whether they were under surveillance. The consequent 'unequal gaze' afforded the authorities by continuous, anonymous surveillance was thought to prime occupants for the internalisation of disciplinary individuality.

Foucault argued that penal institutions and other hierarchical institutions, such as poor houses, schools, hospitals, mental institutions and factories, have evolved through society to resemble Bentham's Panopticon. The structural design is premised on the notion that individuals are less likely to contravene rules if they believe they are being monitored, even if they are not. As described by Bentham himself, the Panopticon represented 'a new mode of obtaining power of mind over mind, in a quantity hitherto without example' (Bentham 1995: 29).

According to Foucault (1991), penological failure has been a persistent and indeed a 'functional' characteristic of the modern prison ever since its inception—the prison system does not stem recidivism, nor does it effectively deter those in the wider community. Indeed, the system of disciplinary punishments operates effectively as a rational power–knowledge mechanism, which exists within wider strategies of domination and subjectification. In short, the prison system permits the powerful upper class to continue the subjugation of the lower classes. Converted into social outcasts through a continuous cycle of segregation, supervision and labelling, offenders—who are viewed by the powerful as the most volatile group in society (potential anti-heroes)—are rendered both politically and socially harmless. They become the scapegoats for society's crime problem, thus diverting public attention away from crime perpetrated by the powerful.

RUSCHE AND KIRCHHEIMER: THE POLITICAL ECONOMY OF PUNISHMENT

Positioning their theory of crime and social control within a Marxist framework, Rusche and Kirchheimer (2003) assert that changes in the modes of punishment throughout the ages are related to the different phases of major economic development and social structural change. Specifically, they argue the existence of a direct relationship between the use of imprisonment and labour market conditions, notably the rate of unemployment (see also Garland 1995; Howe 1994).

Rusche and Kirchheimer highlight the role of prisons and punishment in the class-based process of social and economic regulation. Prisons, it is argued, are tied to the dominant groups in society and their ability to wield power. Accordingly, crime rates are not a determinant of prison numbers. Instead, rates of incarceration and prison composition are determined by, and reflective of, the structure of class relations. Punishment is a necessary element in the *maintenance of class relations*. Hence, punishment reflects the vested interests of those who own the means of production and, in particular, the economic imperative to secure a ready supply of exploitable labour.

Prisons, it is contended, will fill with 'surplus populations' (i.e. the marginalised layers of the working class) in periods of high unemployment and this is related to the state of the economy rather than the state of crime per se. During periods marked by labour shortage, one method of assuring a ready supply of workers is through the enactment of laws that permit the ruling class to subjugate the lower classes. For example, England's vagrancy statutes, originally enacted in 1349, sought to compel all able-bodied people to work, through threat of imprisonment. Amendments to the statute in 1351 imposed a maximum wage and sought to restrict worker mobility by forbidding the working class from leaving their current employer in pursuit of more favourable working conditions (Chambliss 1994). During labour shortages, the use of corporal or capital punishment to deter crime is considered anathema, as it would result in the destruction or debilitation of a valuable resource. Accordingly, imprisonment becomes the preferred method of punishment for legal transgressions, as this enables the ruling class to exploit prison labour at a significantly reduced cost rather than paying the market value for that labour (see Box 24.2 below).

BOX 24.2   TRANSPORTATION AND AUSTRALIA'S CONVICT COLONY

Australia's history of penal colonisation provides a clear example of the political economy of punishment in practice. From the early seventeenth century, the English began transporting offenders to distant colonies, including Australia. From the First Fleet in 1787 to the final convict voyage in 1868, British convict ships had undertaken 829 voyages to Australia, depositing 168,000 unwilling emigrants from the British court system to penal institutions across Australia (Braithwaite 2001; Millett 2006).

Transportation in the Australian context was an experiment born of mutual convenience: the British sought an expedient, cheap and convenient solution to the warehousing of thousands of convicts considered the 'dangerous classes', following the refusal of American colonies to continue serving as repositories (Godfrey & Cox 2008). With the cessation of transportation to American in the 1770s, prison overcrowding in England had become a significant problem for the British government and the building of new penitentiaries considered too costly (Shaw 1977). Australian settlements, rich in natural resources but rendered developmentally backward as a consequence of chronic labour shortages, welcomed, at least initially, the augmentation of their labour force through receipt of the 'impure flood' of 'outcasts of society' (Calvert 1894: 17).

While considered 'hardened criminals' by the British, some historians regard the convicts as petty offenders, commonly the victims of economic hardship—often those displaced from the land through Britain's enclosure system (a process in which common land was converted into fully private ownership and use)—or political prisoners, including those attempting to form, or become a member of, a trade union. Murderers could be found among the convict body, but so too could individuals transported for minor first offences (e.g. stealing yards of lace or even a prayer book). In reality, the majority of men and women were transported for minor to mid-range property offences without violence (Braithwaite 2001; Coupe 2002; Hughes 2003; Old Bailey 2009).

Accounts of Australia's convict history depict penal systems as harsh and repressive, sustained through the administration of violent, capricious force (including regular floggings) and underscored by exploitative social relations enforced and maintained by high-ranking male gentry, nobility or military officials (Gilchrist 2007; Millett 2006). Founded, as it was, on 'legally degraded coerced labour' (Neal 1973: 507), Braithwaite (2001: 48) describes Australia's convict colony as a form of empire-building and the attendant transcontinental shifts of convict labour as the 'work of a hegemonic power' that uses penality as an 'instrument of imperial expansion'.

POST-MODERNISM
A late-twentieth-century cultural and intellectual movement founded on a radical reappraisal of the global, political, and social assumptions and innovations introduced by the modernist era. While disparate in their thinking, proponents of postmodernism share a fundamental distrust, or outright rejection (e.g. Michel Foucault and Julia Kristeva) of modern assumptions about culture, identity, history or language.

POST-STRUCTURALISM
A movement related to postmodernism, but influenced by existential phenomenology. Central to post-structuralism is a belief that depictions of the 'self' as separate and singular, and 'identity' as a stable 'self', are fictional constructs.

HOWE: PUNISHMENT, FEMINISM AND WOMEN

According to Howe (1994), the crucial issue is how control and discipline are extended over women, in both the public and the private spheres. Howe argues that histories of punishment almost without exception, completely *ignore the place of women*; they are essentially theories relating to the punishment of men. While a range of critical perspectives (Marxist, poststructuralist and feminist) has, over the past 25 years, challenged traditional conceptualisations of punishment and imprisonment in Western capitalist societies, they remain largely 'masculinist'.

Howe identifies a range of theoretical disjunctures in critical analyses of crime and punishment, including:

- the almost exclusively male focus of political economies of punishment and feminist accounts of the criminalisation of women
- the 'social histories' of the prison regime to which men and women were subjected and feminist histories of the incarceration of women
- the masculinist 'social' analysis of penality and feminist research on the punishment of women and theorisation of the disciplining of women's bodies
- research on oppressed groups of women (including women prisoners) and **postmodernist** and **post-structuralist** approaches, which regard the very category of 'woman' as deeply problematic.

Instead, it is argued that further feminist theoretical and empirical work is required to interpret punishment in general from within a more holistic perspective that examines the 'continuum of punishment'. In particular, a more social understanding of punishment (one that goes beyond equating 'the social' exclusively with male experience) must be informed by feminist research on women's imprisonment, and by post-structuralist studies of the disciplining of women's bodies. Thus, for example, analyses of the social control of women must take into account the ways in which punishment, discipline and power cross over institutional boundaries (e.g. family, welfare and prison), and how they impact on the female body within and without the prison walls.

The particular analytical spectacles that we wear have a major influence on what we see as the main issues and social relevance of punishment, and how society should engage in particular kinds of social control activity. The perspectives outlined here provide some indication of how different writers have tried to make sense of punishment and penalty by asking quite different types of questions in each case.

ISSUES FOR CONSIDERATION

PUNISHMENT—ETHICAL CONSIDERATIONS

Given the different perspectives on punishment in general, we need to consider whether modern approaches to punishment embody excessively punitive and unethical measures imposed under the pretext of 'correction' or 'treatment'.

One such approach, which periodically gains popular currency in Australia, is state-mandated 'chemical castration' to 'treat' sexual offenders as an alternative to incarceration or indeed surgical castration; that is, the intravenous administration of anti-androgen hormones, such as Depo-Provera, which are designed to reduce sexual desires (libido), fantasies and, ultimately, sexual activity (Meisenkothen 1999; Merkel 1993; Mosc 2003; Munro 2004c). It is interesting to note that, largely influenced by the eugenics movement, some American states in the early twentieth century enacted laws mandating castration as a punishment for a variety of societal infractions (e.g. rape, paedophilia and exhibitionism). Though such practices waned in popularity after World War II, new laws mandating chemical castration of sex offenders being released from prison into the community have been passed in at least nine US states, commencing with California in 1996 (mandatory for repeat sex offenders), closely followed by Florida, Georgia, Texas, Louisiana, Oregon, Iowa, Louisiana and Montana (for a detailed review, see Scott & Holmberg 2003). This enactment of castration statutes has prompted some commentators to argue that punishment has returned to the 'dark ages' (see, for example, Spalding 1998).

Aside from the moral objections to chemical castration, the effectiveness literature is indeterminate (of significant concern is the argument that drug therapies might control arousal and fantasy), but do not address the underlying psychological and environmental causes of men's sexual offending, including power play and aggression (McGilvray 2008).

Questions also need to be asked regarding the legitimate use of civil commitment proceedings to extend detention and supervision arrangements (either within the prison or a designated facility) after an offender's original sentence has expired (McSherry 2008; Vess 2009; Vollard 2013; Ward & Salmon 2011). The concept of post-sentence preventative detention has gained widespread currency in Australia in recent years, largely in response to the extensively publicised release of convicted child sex offenders into the community (Doyle & Ogloff 2009; see also Chapters 23 and 26).

Preventative detention is commonly justified on the grounds of 'community protection'. It is argued that individuals assessed as 'dangerous' are highly likely to reoffend, and therefore pose a continued risk to the community. Prolonged treatment of such individuals is therefore said to decrease the likelihood of further assaults once the offender is released and to protect society during the period of extended detention. The laws also serve to appease community standards, which demand harsher sentences for sexual offenders, especially those who harm children.

On the other hand, preventative detention laws raise a number of concerns, not the least of which relate to the abrogation of longstanding legal principles, including a presumption of innocence regarding future offences and the high probability of detaining individuals who are at no risk of future offending because risk assessment tools are unreliable. While the evidence indicates that past offending may be the best predictor of future behaviour, a significant number of inaccurate predictions, otherwise known as 'false positives', will inevitably be made (Bagaric & Edney 2003; Conte 2004; Hayes et al. 2009; McSherry 2004; Newbold 2004; Roche 1999; Scott & Holmberg 2003; Tonry 1996; von Hirsch & Ashworth 1992).

The evidence on the efficacy of selective incapacitation is variable. Moreover, most prisoners are ultimately permitted to re-enter the community. Thus, given the finite protection generally afforded the community through incapacitation, should the focus of punishment be on the offence or on the offender? Furthermore, what programs should be in place from the point of view of therapy, treatment, rehabilitation, the possibility of release, and so on (MacKenzie 2013; see also Chapters 25 and 26)?

CAPITAL PUNISHMENT

A number of countries routinely use torture, death and banishment as state-endorsed punishment, including China, Iran, Saudi Arabia, Pakistan and the United States. In 2013, executions worldwide increased by almost 15 per cent compared with 2012. Excluding China (which conducts the over-whelming majority of executions annually—numbering in the thousands), a minimum of 778 people were executed worldwide. Just three countries—Iran, Iraq and Saudi Arabia—account for almost 80 per cent of the confirmed executions conducted outside of China (Amnesty International 2014).

There have even been calls in the United States for executions to be televised (Giles 2001; Triotv 2004). Attempts to petition the courts for permission to televise executions, including an attempt by prominent US talk show host, Phil Donahue, to televise the execution of a convicted North Carolina murderer, have, to date, been unsuccessful (*Daily Miner* 2004). Proponents of this approach present a number of arguments, including the potentially enhanced deterrent value and the obligation of citizens to witness what is considered by many to be justifiable and 'civilised' policy in an increasingly violent society (Breyer 1994).

Officially, Australia has a longstanding opposition to capital punishment, and has reaffirmed this opposition by signing the Second Optional Protocol to the International Covenant on Civil and Political Rights, voting for the 2007 United Nations General Assembly resolution calling for a global moratorium on the death penalty. This strong stance has, however, been weakened in recent years in the wake of the publicity surrounding the executions of Australian citizens abroad (e.g. convicted drug trafficker Nguyen Tuong Van in 2005), Australians awaiting execution (e.g. members of the Bali nine) and the execution of non-nationals whose actions have harmed Australians on a large scale (e.g. the Bali bombers) (Kirby 2003; Longstaff 2003; Walton 2003). Australia appears now to pursue a two-stranded approach to executions: support for the execution of non-Australians and opposition to the killing of Australian citizens (*The Age* 2006).

CONCLUSION

This chapter has provided a brief review of the historical dimensions of punishment and has highlighted the relationship between conceptions of crime and of punishment. The aims and justifications of punishment have certainly changed over time, and also vary according to the perspective of the commentator. In speaking about the purpose(s) of punishment, it is important to distinguish between punishment as a concept and its association with a range of other concepts relating to imprisonment, which is a specific form of punishment.

A central question underpinning any discussion of punishment is who, in fact, gets punished? From this we can go on to ask, how are they punished, and why are they punished in this specific manner? These questions raise a number of issues relating to social division (e.g. differences based on class, ethnicity, race and gender), differential policing and punishment practices (e.g. depending on the social background of the offender) and, crucially, the nature of punishment generally as a means of social control in society.

Fundamentally, punishment is how societies and governments maintain social order. To this end, an evaluation of punishment becomes a critical element in evaluating the exercise of authority. In order to do this, we also need to explore actual instances and forms of punishment in order to determine who in fact is being subjected to whose order, what kind of control, and to what end. These are the concerns dealt with in Chapter 25, on the nature and experiences of imprisonment.

DISCUSSION QUESTIONS

1   Given the historical development of punishment in the west, do trends towards chemical castration for sex offenders and calls for the reinstatement of the death penalty in Australia signal a return to punitive justice rationales and draconian punishment practices of the past? If so, is this a desirable trend from the point of view of social cohesion, or does it represent the breakdown and fragmentation of societies in the face of economic, social, and political change on a global scale (Pratt 2002a)? Consider how responses to this question might differ according to the various sociological and criminological perspectives outlined in this chapter.

2   Should evidence of 'dangerousness' and 'risk' substantiate the invocation of preventative detention powers? If so, who should conduct such assessments? Furthermore, is such a policy morally justifiable, given the risk of misdiagnosing 'dangerousness' and the abrogation of human and other legal rights? Is incapacitation cost-effective?

3   How are we to assess and evaluate the different forms and types of punishments in society? That is, what criteria should we use to discern whether a particular punishment is 'good' or 'bad'? Further to this, given the different criminological, political, and sociological perspectives on punishment, is it possible to develop a 'general theory' of punishment capable of incorporating elements from each area into a unified perspective and, if so, is this approach desirable?

4   As highlighted in Chapter 2, media reportage of sentences, which theoretically serves both denunciatory and deterrent functions of punishment, is extremely skewed to the most egregious and sensational offences, and extreme penalties (those judged manifestly lenient or, in fewer instances, harsh). Accordingly, can denunciation continue to be advanced as an effective aim and tool of punishment? If so, how might media reporting of sentencing outcomes be improved in order to enhance the aims of denunciation and deterrence while also safeguarding human rights (see Rodrick 2011; Sarre 2011; Tomaino & Kapardis 2004)?

FURTHER READING

Foucault, M. (1991) *Discipline and punish: the birth of the prison*, Penguin, London.

Garland, D. (1995) *Punishment and modern society: a study in social theory*, Clarendon Press, Oxford.

Howe, A. (1994) *Punish and critique: towards a feminist analysis of penalty*, Routledge and Kegan Paul, London.

Morris, N. & Rothman, D. (eds) (1998) *The Oxford history of the prison: the practice of punishment in western society*, Oxford University Press, New York.

Sarre, R. (2011) 'We get the crime we deserve: exploring the disconnect in "law and order" politics', *James Cook University Law Review*: 144–61.

25 INCARCERATION AND PRISONISATION

CHAPTER OVERVIEW

- PRISONS, PRISONERS AND IMPRISONMENT
- PRISON OBJECTIVES AND POLICY CONTEXTS
- DANGEROUSNESS AND VIOLENCE
- ALTERNATIVES TO USE OF PRISONS
- ISSUES FOR CONSIDERATION
- CONCLUSION
- DISCUSSION QUESTIONS
- FURTHER READING

PRISONISATION
Changes a prisoner undergoes in prison (described as the 'pains of imprisonment'), which socialises them into the culture and social life of prison society. Also known as the 'convict code', this prison sub-culture generally involves a code of silence, distrust of and antagonism towards prison staff, and loyalty to other prisoners.

IMPRISONMENT
This involves physical confinement of a convicted offender to a penal institution (open or secure prison or jail) as a lawful punishment by the courts (a sentence of imprisonment).

INTRODUCTION

The previous chapter explored the theoretical and historical underpinnings of current understandings of punishment in society. The most extreme or harshest punishment in Australian society is that of incarceration or imprisonment. Putting someone into prison is also the most visible and enduring image of the social control of crime.

The prison occupies a central, symbolic role within the criminal justice system, and is meant to be a critical deterrent to further offending. The aim of this chapter is to examine the nature of the prison experience from several different angles. For example, the chapter begins by briefly surveying the extent of imprisonment in Australia, and the composition of the prison population. This is followed by a discussion of the concept of 'dangerousness', an idea that is often at the forefront of public debates over the use of prisons. The impact and effects of prison on offenders is then examined. Here the concern will be to outline the basic processes of **prisonisation**, or the culture of prison life, and to discern whether or not the prison experience lends itself to the prevention of crime either individually (in the case of specific inmates) or generally (with respect to other members of society).

The chapter concludes by touching upon recent areas of prison reform or change. These range from privatisation of prisons in the Australian context through to arguments in favour of prison abolition. The theme of this section is that of expansion versus contraction of the systems of incarceration, and the policy and theoretical directions that will influence prison developments into the future. The chapter concludes by identifying a wide range of issues that require further consideration and research.

PRISONS, PRISONERS AND IMPRISONMENT

The concept of **imprisonment** is not the same as that of **custody**. While the former describes lawful confinement to a penal institution under sentence of imprisonment, the latter describes the act of being lawfully confined to some form of institution for reasons other than serving a sentence of imprisonment. In determining total numbers of people in custody we have to be aware that there are six different types of custody in Australia.

These are:

- corrective services (prisons, prison farms, periodic detention centres, remand centres or community custody centres)
- police stations
- juvenile detention centres
- immigration detention centres
- military prisons or guard houses
- secure facilities in psychiatric hospitals.

The above categories relate to overlapping and interconnected systems of custody. For example, asylum seekers ('illegal immigrants') may be held in prison if other, more appropriate, facilities are not available; offenders in the defence forces may also be found in prison or police custody; and mentally ill offenders are not infrequently transferred between prisons and psychiatric hospitals according to their state of health and their manageability.

'Imprisonment' generally refers to instances where an offender has been officially sanctioned by the court and, as part of the court disposition, has been sentenced to a period of enforced detention. Custody, on the other hand, includes both instances of imprisonment and cases where movement of the individual is restricted prior to courtroom adjudication or departmental determination of legal status. For example, being taken into police custody can involve a person being held in a police lock-up for a set period of time without judicial involvement. To take another example, unsuccessful applications for bail are usually accompanied by the holding of an accused person in remand custody; that is, to await trial in a secure facility (rather than remand on bail). It is possible therefore to be held in custody in at least three different ways: in a police jail, in a remand centre or in a prison. Our concern in this chapter is with the last of these: the prison.

IMPRISONMENT RATES

The use of imprisonment is generally seen as a matter of last resort by the courts. In effect, it is meant to be designed for the most serious types of offences and most persistent of offenders. Yet, in 2013, more than 10 million people were held in prison throughout the world (Walmsley 2013). In Australia, the number of people in prison exceeded 30,000 for the first time (ABS 2014g) (see Box 25.1), of which just under a quarter (24%) were unsentenced. The actual rate of incarceration varies greatly from country to country, and from state to state (see Figure 25.1). For example, the most punitive nation-state in the world today is the United States, with an **imprisonment rate** at 716 prisoners per 100,000 people. After three decades of unabated growth in the American prison population, more than one in every 100 adults is now confined behind bars—a phenomenon referred to as 'mass incarceration'.

The total population in US custody, including prison and jail inmates, is over 2.2 million (Walmsley 2013). In 2007, the combined total of all probationers and parolees, prisoners and jail inmates in the United States was a staggering 7.3 million, which translates to one in thirty-one adults (or 3.2 per cent of all adult Americans) being under the control of the correctional system (Pew Center on the States 2009, 2008). Today, while America contributes 5 per cent of the world's population, it houses in excess of 20 per cent of the world's prisoners (Campbell 2013).

Countries such as the Russian Federation and China also have high rates of incarceration (475 and 121, respectively). The Chinese figures are artificially low since they exclude at least 650,000 prisoners who are in pre-trial detention or administrative detention. Despite this caveat, the total number of prisoners in the Russian Federation and China (681,600, and around 1.64 million [sentenced prisoners],

CUSTODY
This involves physically depriving a person of their liberty by confining them to some form of institution under lawful process or authority. In the case of a remand prisoner, this involves placement into custody while awaiting the outcome of legal proceedings.

IMPRISONMENT RATE
Provides an indication of the size of the prison population relative to the broader population. This may be expressed as the number of prisoners per 100,000 adults, or the number of prisoners per 100,000 people. Imprisonment rates allow for meaningful comparison to be drawn of prison populations across jurisdictions, since they control for differences in population size.

BOX 25.1 PENAL CULTURE AND HYPERINCARCERATION

In a recent book, Cunneen et al. (2013) provide a detailed examination of the re-valorisation of the prison in Australia since the 1970s. The conceptual underpinnings of *Penal culture and hyperincarceration* include the idea that there is a broad complex of law, policy and practice that frames the use of imprisonment, and that increases in imprisonment are not undifferentiated but very selective. For instance, increased imprisonment has been targeted at particular racialised groups, most dramatically evident in Indigenous over-representation figures, and at others marginalised within the wider society, such as people with mental health disorders and drug and alcohol addictions.

Analysis of penal culture needs to take into account that penality refers to the broad field of institutions, practices, discourses and social relations surrounding the ideas and practices of punishment. How we *think* and how we *feel* about offenders and their punishment is socially and historically constructed. For example, the removal of punishment from the public sphere (apparent in the shift from public displays of corporal and capital punishment to the use of closed institutions such as prisons) has resulted in a tempering of the empathetic response towards those who commit crime. 'Out of sight, out of mind' translates into scant public knowledge about the suffering that occurs within prison. Neo-liberal values and principles that emphasise personal responsibility (for welfare, education, employment and obeying laws) further reinforces the lack of compassion for offenders, while downplaying the need for structural responses to crime such as reducing unemployment rates or addressing the negative legacies of colonialism.

Penal culture is embedded in material practices, justified in intellectual systems, and experienced in ways that are specific both to the global age and to each particular national context. In Australia, it is costly to governments, to the vulnerable people who are the main targets of the hyperincarceration impulse, and to the social fabric. But, as sustained social and historical analysis demonstrates, it is also changeable.

Source: Cunneen et al. (2013)

---

respectively) is far lower than in the United States. By contrast, countries such as Finland, Ireland and Norway each recorded between 3,000 and 4,000 prisoners in 2013. Of thirty-seven of the world's major developed countries, Japan recorded the lowest rate of imprisonment in 2013, with fifty-one prisoners per 100,000 people. Over the same period, Australia ranked fourteenth, recording an imprisonment rate of 130 per 100,000 people (International Centre for Prison Studies 2013). However, it is important to note that although comparatively high, this is an underestimate since the rate used for Australia in the international comparison differs from the higher total rate of 170 per 100,000 reported by the Australian Bureau of Statistics, as cited below. It seems that the International Centre for Prison Studies may have reported the total non-Indigenous rate of imprisonment in Australian only.

The prison rate varies according to such factors as: the availability of alternative punishment or rehabilitation approaches (e.g. community-based corrections or work programs); local, regional and national 'law and order' politics, and the resultant contrasts in cultures of control (e.g. from the more punitive to those that stress reconciliation or mediation); and the nature of actual criminal activity and the cultures that sustain this (e.g. violence associated with legal availability and use of guns) (see, for example, Nelken 2009).

FIGURE 25.1   INTERNATIONAL IMPRISONMENT RATES, 2008 AND 2013

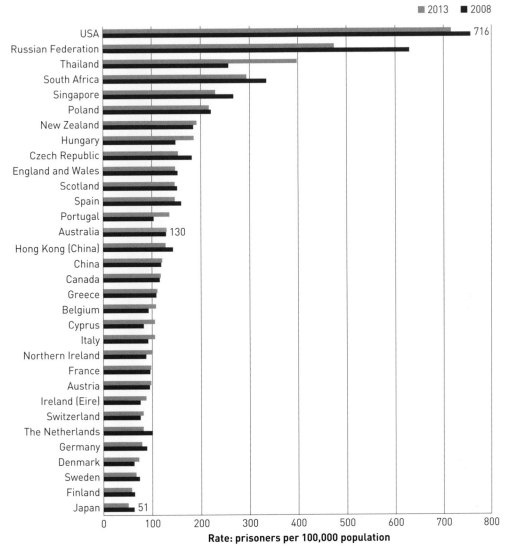

Source: Walmsley (2013)

As mentioned earlier, there are also variations within a national context. Thus, for example, and as indicated in Figure 25.2, the imprisonment rate in the Northern Territory is substantially higher than anywhere else in Australia at 821 per 100,000 adults, compared to 173 in New South Wales, 120 in Victoria and 170 nationally (ABS 2014g). As demonstrated in Table 25.1, the overall rate of imprisonment, nationally and for most states and territories, is growing and there are early indications that this upward trajectory is now being mirrored in the case of juvenile persons held in detention (AIC 2008).

FIGURE 25.2   IMPRISONMENT RATES IN AUSTRALIAN STATES AND TERRITORIES, 2013

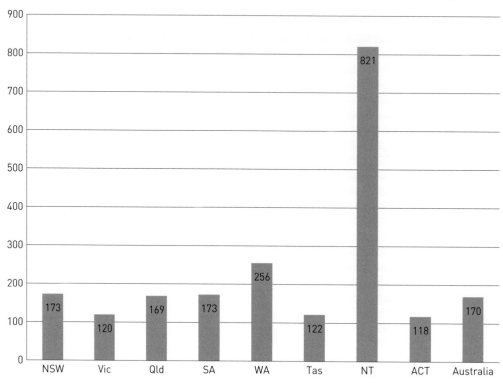

Source: ABS (2014g)

COMPARING JURISDICTIONS

The gathering and presentation of inter-jurisdictional prison data requires the 'counting rules' to be applied uniformly across jurisdictions. Although national standards and classifications are adopted in the compilation of correctional services statistics in Australia, some discrepancies remain between the states and territories based on legislative and procedural differences, and administrative differences in data-recording systems. For example, correctional services data might be based upon the number of people in prison on a particular day (e.g. the night of 30 June, when the National Prisoner Census is undertaken annually, or the first day of each month) or may be averaged out over a particular month (counts are taken on each day of the month and then divided by the number of days in the month) or year (based on counts taken on each day of the month). When making comparisons between jurisdictions it is also important to bear three things in mind:

- the actual number of people who are in prison (prison population totals)
- the rate of imprisonment (measured in relation to overall population size—usually expressed in terms of per 100,000 population or per 100,000 adult population)
- the overall trend in imprisonment (the pattern of movement of prisoner numbers or rates over time, which may trend upwards or downwards or remain reasonably stable). As mentioned previously, trends vary from state to state, and are greatly influence by factors other than crime rates, including local sentencing practices (e.g. mandatory sentencing practices and longer non-parole periods), law enforcement practices (e.g. waging a war on drugs) and legal cultures.

TABLE 25.1 IMPRISONMENT RATES IN AUSTRALIA—PRISONERS PER 100,000 ADULTS BY JURISDICTION, 2003–13

	NSW	VIC	QLD	SA	WA	TAS	NT	ACT	AUST.
2003	171.5	99.6	184.7	122.2	194.7	123.7	507.3	98.5	157.6
2004	182.1	94.6	179.8	125.9	213.0	122.5	505.3	110.9	159.5
2005	190.4	95.0	179.3	123.7	229.7	149.5	566.9	108.5	164.9
2006	188.7	100.5	181.8	130.2	227.8	137.7	536.2	84.7	165.1
2007	195.3	105.7	177.3	145.3	241.9	140.6	599.2	90.2	171.1
2008	196.3	104.4	171.9	157.3	229.3	135.5	610.4	93.3	169.8
2009	205.6	104.9	170.7	156.4	259.5	138.7	652.8	74.0	173.6
2010	199.2	107.2	165.7	154.4	273.4	125.2	660.7	99.9	172.7
2011	180.4	110.2	161.6	157.8	258.9	129.1	756.1	105.5	166.6
2012	171.1	111.6	158.9	160.1	267.1	124.7	825.0	107.3	165.3
2013	173.2	119.8	169.0	172.8	255.8	121.5	821.3	118.3	170.0

Source: Australian Bureau of Statistics (2014g)

Analysis of these three areas generally provides a good indication of the differences and similarities between jurisdictions. In global terms, prison populations have grown significantly in many parts of the world since the 1990s, particularly in the advanced industrialised countries such as the United States and those in Europe (International Centre for Prison Studies 2007; Walmsley 2013). Over the past decade, the Australian prisoner population has increased substantially and, while remaining proportionately small overall, the female prisoner population has increased at a faster rate than the male population. Between June 2000 and June 2013, the total number of prisoners in Australia increased by 42 per cent (from 21,714 to 30,775). While male prisoners increased by 40 per cent over this period (from 20,324 to 28,426), female prisoners increased by 69 per cent (from 1,390 to 2,349), albeit the female increase is from a relatively low base (ABS 2014g).

WHO IS IN PRISON?

Aside from aggregate numbers, examination of prisoner populations offer important comparative insights. With respect to who is actually in prison, the statistical story across Australia varies little. By and large our prisons are filled with people with the following social and demographic characteristics (ABS 2014g; Baldry 2006; Hayes 2005):

- Most prisoners are chronically underemployed or unemployed at the time of arrest or charge.
- Most come from low-income backgrounds.
- Many are homeless at the time of arrest, or living in unsuitable or unstable accommodation.
- Most have not completed higher levels of education (most are undereducated or illiterate).
- Many have an intellectual disability.
- Many are substance dependent (alcohol and/or other drugs).

- Most are men.
- Indigenous people are over-represented in every jurisdiction.

In short, prisoner populations are largely male and drawn from the ranks of the marginalised and disadvantaged (socially, economically, culturally and health-wise) in society.

INDIGENOUS PRISONERS

The specific character of the prison population, however, does vary from jurisdiction to jurisdiction. Examination of age standardised imprisonment rates (see Figure 25.3), in particular, indicates that the situation with respect to Indigenous people warrants special mention. As pointed out by the Royal Commission into Aboriginal Deaths in Custody, Indigenous people have generally been over-represented in the custody statistics across the country (Wootten 1991: 21–2) for many years. This trend continues today. As at 30 June 2013, the age-standardised Indigenous imprisonment rate in Australia (1,959 per 100,000 Indigenous adults in the population) was fifteen times higher than the non-Indigenous rate (131 per 100,000 adults), up from a ratio of 10:1 in 2000. Overall, Indigenous prisoners comprised 27 per cent of the total prisoner population in 2013 compared to 14 per cent in 1992 (ABS 2014g).

The extent of Aboriginal over-representation varies greatly, however, across jurisdictions (ABS 2014g). For instance, in June 2013, the Indigenous population in the Northern Territory comprised 86 per cent of the total prisoner population for that territory. By contrast, Victoria recorded the lowest proportion of Indigenous prisoners relative to its prisoner population (7%). Western Australia and the Australian Capital Territory had the highest ratios of Indigenous to non-Indigenous imprisonment

FIGURE 25.3   AGE-STANDARDISED IMPRISONMENT RATES BY INDIGENOUS STATUS, 2003–13[a]

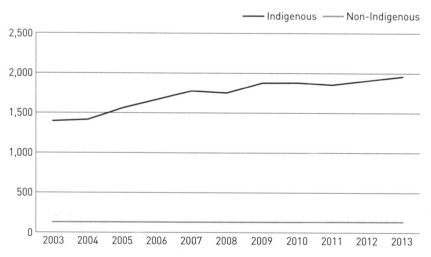

[a]When comparing rates of imprisonment for Indigenous and non-Indigenous prisoners, it is preferable to use age-standardised rates since the Indigenous population has a much younger population profile, based on comparisons conducted in 2001 (54.6% 18 years and over) than the non-Indigenous population (75.8% 18 years and over).

Source: based on ABS (2014g)

(twenty-one and eighteen times respectively). In terms of numbers of people imprisoned, New South Wales, Western Australia, and Queensland recorded the highest numbers of incarcerated Indigenous people in 2013 (n = 2,297, 1,977 and 1,898, respectively). On the other hand, while the ratio of imprisonment of Indigenous people to non-Indigenous people in Tasmania is disproportionately high (3.6 times higher), the total number of Indigenous people in prison is actually quite low (n = 70). Ideally, the level of over-representation in any particular jurisdiction should be calculated by comparing the proportion of the state or territory population that is Indigenous with the proportion of people in adult prisons.

Critical to understanding the disproportionately high levels of Indigenous representation in the prison statistics is the dysfunctional environments and overwhelming poverty faced by many drawn into the criminal justice system. Among the adverse social conditions confronting Indigenous people are inferior housing, poor health (including malnutrition), poor education, alcoholism, substance abuse (illicit drugs as well as sniffing of petrol and solvents), lack of gainful employment, and subjection and/or exposure to high levels of family dislocation and violence from a young age (Anthony 2012; Hunter 2008).

PRISONS AS 'HOLDING TANKS'

Clearly then, the use of imprisonment and the particular characteristics of the prison population do vary in their specific outline, depending upon the jurisdiction. Nevertheless, there are strong continuities across the country's prisons. This is borne out in the broad profile of prisoner characteristics listed above. Prisons are, in effect, holding tanks for the unemployed, the poor and the marginalised— a profile not unique to Australian prisoners (in the United States see, for example, Western & Muller 2013). People without jobs or paid work are the most vulnerable when it comes to spending time in prison or receiving a disposition centred on imprisonment. This is regularly confirmed in Prison Census data from the Australian Bureau of Statistics that show that a minority of prisoners in Australia are employed at the time of conviction.

The issue of who is actually in prison is inseparable from issues of why these people are there. The popular perception is that prisons exist primarily to house the most dangerous and intractable of a society. But are prisoners in prison because of their multiple layers of disadvantage, including unemployment, or because of the nature and seriousness of their offence? Or, is the reason some people are in prison related to the fact that because of their experiences with the criminal justice system they cannot get paid work in the formal spheres of the economy, because imprisonment has added a further layer of disadvantage and marginalisation? These and related questions are linked to the images and realities of modern prison life.

PRISON OBJECTIVES AND POLICY CONTEXTS

The mission statements of most corrective services around the country appear to offer a reasonable and enlightened perspective on the use of prisons. For instance, the mission of the prison service in Tasmania is:

> [T]o contribute to a safer Tasmania by ensuring the safe, secure containment of inmates and providing them with opportunities for rehabilitation and personal development and community engagement. (Tasmania Department of Justice 2011: 5)

In Victoria, the mission is to:

[D]eliver a safe and secure corrections system in which we actively engage offenders and the community to promote positive behaviour change. Our Reducing Re-offending Framework describes how we achieve this mission by assessing, treating and managing offenders in order to reduce their risk of re-offending. (Department of Justice Victoria 2010: 2)

The purpose of the Department of Corrections in Queensland is to:

[B]e the leading provider of corrections in Australia by 2014 ... by breaking the cycle of re-offending, effectively and consistently enforcing the orders of the courts and increasing community safety and confidence in our work. (Corrective Services Queensland 2010: 3)

The Department for Correctional Services in South Australia aims to:

[C]ontribute to public safety through the safe, secure and humane management of offenders and the provision of opportunities for rehabilitation and reintegration. (Department for Correctional Services 2011: 1)

The strategic intent of the Northern Territory Department of Correctional Services for 2013-16 is to:

Meet our commitment to government and the people of the Northern Territory, by achieving a community valued correctional services that makes a positive difference in people's lives. Key focus areas for the department, as we deliver and reform our services and programs, will include:

- Prisoner work readiness
- Indigenous outcomes
- Rising prisoner numbers
- Youth justice reform
- Safe workplaces. (Northern Territory Department of Correctional Services 2013: 6)

In many jurisdictions, these types of mission statements are accompanied by a description of key organisational values (e.g. integrity, accountability and respect for others, and teamwork).

INCOMPATIBLE OBJECTIVES

A close reading of most correctional services documents reveals an uneasy combination of basically incompatible objectives. This reflects the ambiguities of sentencing principles (see Chapter 24) as much as an institutional difficulty in sorting out main priorities. Practical difficulties arise when departments have to weigh up issues such as 'rehabilitative services' with those of 'cost-effectiveness'. Likewise, the public images of prison as being 'too soft' (e.g. sensationalistic news coverage of prisoners enjoying taxpayer-funded 'motel conditions', replete with television sets and swimming pools) or 'too hard' (e.g. ancient prisons with no heating systems) make it difficult to frame a penal response that will satisfy everyone. Objectives relating to rehabilitation, which require intensive and extensive programs and support services for inmates, are seen to contradict the other main current in penal thinking (i.e. the prison experience is often viewed first and foremost as punitive in intent, which means that prisoners ought to suffer some types of deprivation due to the pain they have caused someone else).

OUTSIDE PRESSURES

In addition to perennial problems associated with how to juggle competing objectives, prison authorities also have to deal with 'outside' pressures, such as ensuring that the policies of the government of the day are implemented. This has a direct impact on the specific orientation of a service, and the overall level and type of 'service' it provides to inmates in particular. A South Australian report (South Australian Department for Correctional Services 1995), for example, highlights the main policies of government under which it was compelled to operate in the 1990s. Among these are, for example, prescriptions to:

- abolish the current automatic early release system for prisoners and introduce truth in sentencing
- make good behaviour, abstention from drugs, and participation in productive work and training a condition for parole
- expand education and skills training for prisoners as part of their rehabilitation programs
- allow police to make submissions to the Parole Board on parole applications.

These kinds of policy prescriptions have a major impact on the environment within prisons. In particular, they can restrict or assist prison authorities in terms of their immediate management practices (e.g. through use of earned remission as a social control mechanism) or they can assist in helping to emphasise the rehabilitative potential of the prison. In essence, government policy in areas such as law enforcement and sentencing can have a significant and direct impact on prison administration.

PRISON COSTS

The costs associated with providing a safe, secure and humane institutional setting—and furthermore one that provides a comprehensive treatment and educative offering for inmates—are enormous, averaging approximately $220 per prisoner per day, or $78,840 per annum (see Figure 25.4). These

FIGURE 25.4   CORRECTIVE SERVICES EXPENDITURE PER OFFENDER PER DAY, 2010–11, BY JURISDICTION[a]

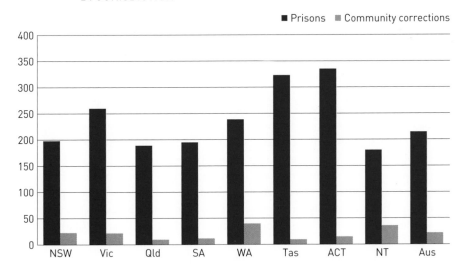

[a]Total net recurrent and capital costs per prisoner per day

Source: AIC (2013a)

costs are compounded by any increases in prison populations, by an increased flow of people into and out of the system, and by longer sentences for offenders generally. Thus, the costs of prison likewise have a major influence on what kind of programs or facilities will be able to be offered in practice.

SPECIAL NEEDS OF FEMALE PRISONERS

A further cost aspect relates to the special needs and unique position of women within the prison system. Despite the fact that women comprise over half the Australian population, they constitute a small percentage of the national prison population: 8 per cent at 30 June 2013 (ABS 2014g). Given the relatively low number of women who are incarcerated, female prisoners tend to be housed together, regardless of official 'security' status (e.g. high, medium or low). Many contemporary programs and services also tend not to cater to the specific needs of women as women, insofar as the system as a whole has a male-centric or masculine bias in its structure and programming; programs are especially not designed for short sentences and remanded prisoners—features of women's incarceration (Alder 1994a,b; Baldry 2010; Silberman 2007). Historically, where there have been women-specific programs, these were more than likely to be built upon conservative and limiting assumptions regarding proper 'women's work' as connected to domesticity (e.g. as domestic servants or housekeepers) and ideal notions of 'femininity' (e.g. to act in more passive and submissive ways, to dress in particular ways and to exhibit moral virtue). Failure to comply with these kinds of behavioural and occupational prescriptions could lead to trouble for the female inmate (see Easteal 1994; Smart 1976).

To cater for the special needs of female offenders once they are in the system will require much more expenditure than is usually provided at present, and the introduction and evaluation of a wide range of programs dealing with issues such as sexual and other forms of abuse, employment, education and personal empowerment (Baldry 2010; Cameron 2001; Dolan & Whitworth 2013). These issues are further compounded in the case of Aboriginal women prisoners, who are particularly disadvantaged, suffering higher rates of mental health disorders, domestic and sexual violence, and homelessness (Baldry 2007; Balfour 2012; Kilroy 2005).

DO PRISONS WORK?

In the end, we might ask, regardless of immediate policy and administrative arrangements and goals, do prisons really work to achieve any of their stated objectives in the long term, beyond that of incapacitation? The short answer to this is no, especially with regards to the deterrent effects of imprisonment (Ritchie 2011; Sarre 2011). The most appropriate analogy to use in this context is that of the prison conveyor belt or revolving door, for in most jurisdictions the recidivism rate for offenders who have spent time in prison is in the order of 60 to 70 per cent. More specifically, re-imprisonment rates amongst ex-prisoners are consistently high. As at 30 June 2013, the majority (58%) of prisoners in custody in Australia had served a sentence in an adult prison prior to the current episode. The proportion of reincarcerated ex-prisoners is substantially higher among the Indigenous population, with 77 per cent of prisoners previously serving a term of imprisonment (ABS 2014g). It is reasonable to ask, then, whether the prison itself is criminogenic (Brown 2010; Goulding et al. 2008). To understand the reason for this persistent reoffending rate, and thus the failure of the prison's mission, it is essential to delve more closely into the actual experiences of prison life.

DANGEROUSNESS AND VIOLENCE

> Almost all the people in Risdon will eventually live in my society. I want to live in a safe society, so I want rehabilitation for people in prison. I am less safe whenever these programs are placed at risk. So I resent attempts to curtail them. I want good people coming out of prison, not angry resentful people. (Flint 2003)

The commonly held view is that offenders must be placed in prison because they have deviated from society's norms. They are misfits and law-breakers. Placing such supposed 'bad fits' into prison, however, is hardly likely to resolve the maladjustment (Morris 1984; Sarre 2011). Simultaneously, the community also demands protection from such individuals because they are perceived to be dangerous. Again, the question is raised as to whether prison is the best place to put dangerous people—especially in the light of the fact that most will eventually return to mainstream society.

IMAGES AND PREDICTIONS OF DANGEROUSNESS

The concept of dangerousness is premised on two interrelated notions:

- *The seriousness and nature of the offence committed*: this involves analysis of actual law-breaking behaviour and its relationship to sentencing guidelines for such behaviour.
- *Making predictions with respect to future dangerous behaviour*: this involves analysis and classifications of individuals on the basis of any of the three predictive methods considered in Chapter 24 (anamnestic, actuarial and clinical).

These aspects of dangerousness pervade the whole criminal justice system, and are manifest at a number of levels, including the courts, prisons and early release:

LEGISLATION AND SENTENCING

A person is perceived to be dangerous depending upon the seriousness of their offence and their past record of criminal activity. Sentences are imposed according to guidelines that reflect concerns about the level of danger and social harm associated with particular acts (see Chapter 23).

CLASSIFICATION OF OFFENDERS

Offenders are sentenced to 'x' number of years and are classified according to high, medium and low security risk. Offenders are shunted into facilities that are designated maximum, high/medium or low/minimum institutional settings, or into community-based programs of various kinds, based on discretionary decisions. Prisoner classification levels vary across jurisdictions and also within particular institutions. Hence, while Queensland, Tasmania and Western Australia have adopted the three-tier system described above, in New South Wales an additional hierarchy of security levels exists (AA, A1, A2, B, C1, C2 and C3), and in Victoria (A1*, A2, B, C1, C2), which further separates the inmates according to the perceived seriousness of the consequences if a prisoner were to escape or be a risk to other inmates' safety.

At one end of the spectrum (AA and A1*) lie those offenders classified as serious offenders on the basis that they represent a special risk to national security, while at the other end (C3, C2) lie those offenders considered at very low risk of escape, who are trusted to remain in open conditions without physical barriers and constant supervision (McWilliam 2007). Factors commonly taken into consideration in the determination of 'dangerousness' include: age, character, length of sentence, nature

* Asterisk denotes different classification levels.

and notoriety of offence, and behaviour while incarcerated (current and previous terms of imprisonment, escape history and other relevant factors) (McWilliam 2007).

DANGEROUSNESS

Measures are generally available to inmates to reduce the length of their sentence, but these depend upon their behaviour while inside prison and on the nature of the offence for which they have been convicted. Mechanisms such as parole, temporary release programs, day work-release programs, and so on are allocated, at least in part, according to the perceived dangerousness of the individual prisoner (see Chapter 26).

The impression held by many, and shaped largely by selective media images of incarceration, is that all prisoners are automatically dangerous (Cecil & Leitner 2009; Wilson & O'Sullivan 2004). However, if we look at a profile of the prison population, this picture does not ring true. For example, the majority of women are in prison for property, driving and drug offences, or victimless crimes such as prostitution. Significantly, a higher proportion of women (53%) than men (41%) in prison in 2013 had no prior imprisonment (ABS 2014g). A number are there for welfare fraud; that is, for attempting to meet the needs of their children and families. Furthermore, many women who are initially placed on community-based orders breach the terms of those orders due to a lack of adequate childcare. The response of the state is generally to step up the penalty tariff in such cases and, as a consequence, many of these women end up in prison.

The majority of women in jail are thus not there for major offences. In 2013, 34 per cent of women were sentenced to prison for violent offences (see Table 25.2). In regards to these relatively few women (n = 579), the violence committed is frequently associated with 'domestic' pressures or abuses of some kind. For example, a New South Wales study found that 80 per cent of women imprisoned had themselves been the victim of incest and/or other forms of violence perpetrated against their person (Women Against Prison Collective 1990; see also Dolan & Whitworth 2013). It is notable, as well, that Aboriginal and Torres Strait Islander women are over-represented in the female prison population. Indigenous women comprised a third (33%) of all female prisoners in 2013 and were imprisoned at a far greater rate than were non-Indigenous women (ABS 2014g). Serious questions need to be asked regarding the link between being a victim of violence and abuse, the nature of the offences engaged in (e.g. drug abuse and property crime), and how the relationship between victimisation and criminal behaviour impacts on the type and length of sentence handed down, and where the female offender will serve her sentence.

In the light of the offence (and offender) profile of female prisoners, the facilities available to them are grossly inappropriate. It has been pointed out, for example, that 'while women are imprisoned for less serious or violent offences than men, they are more likely to spend all or most of their imprisonment in a maximum security institution' (Hampton 1993: 4). The facility itself connotes 'dangerousness'—but the reality is that very few of the women inside are in fact dangerous or a major threat to society.

Having reviewed the basis for women's imprisonment, we turn now to the profile of convicted male prisoners. Just over half of sentenced male prisoners are in prison for violent offences (see Table 25.2). The other half of male prisoners are there for property, drug-related and other offences (including public order offences and driving offences). A significant number of people in prison are there simply for failure to pay fines—in other words, they are in prison not because of the seriousness of the offence, or because they are dangerous people, but because they do not have the financial resources to pay off things like traffic fines. In a similar vein, a significant number of offenders have been imprisoned

TABLE 25.2 MOST SERIOUS OFFENCE OF PRISONERS SENTENCED IN 2013, BY SEX

OFFENCE	MALE		FEMALE	
	NUMBER	%	NUMBER	%
Violent				
Homicide	2,144	10	187	11
Acts intended to cause injury	3,722	17	252	15
Sex offences	2,928	14	34	2
Robbery	2,143	10	106	6
Property				
Unlawful entry with intent	2,671	12	164	10
Theft	793	4	132	8
Other				
Fraud	429	2	178	10
Illicit drug offences	2,290	11	300	18
Offences against justice procedures[a]	2,406	11	193	11
Other[b]	35	9	5	9
Total	**21,628**	**100**	**1,708**	**100**

[a] Includes offences such as breach of court order, breach of parole, escape from custody, offences against justice procedures, treason, sedition and resisting customs officials
[b] Includes other offences against the person and property, public order offences and driving offences

Source: ABS (2014g)

for relatively short sentences of less than a year (approximately 16% in 2013). These individuals are typically imprisoned for relatively minor offences, such as those against justice procedures, vehicle and driving offences, theft (including motor vehicle theft), minor assault, and breaking and entering.

A number of men, in particular young offenders, also have a history of having been subjected to violence and abuse (Anthony 2011). In talking about dangerousness, therefore, we must look at the profiles and the backgrounds of the people who are being put into our prisons. It is notable, as well, that there are high rates of self-harm, among both men and women in custody situations, with suicide estimated to be at least four times higher than in the general community (Camilleri & McArthur 2008). Hence, we have a prison paradox—these people are so dangerous that they are killing themselves.

There are nevertheless some people who do commit violence, and who may do so on a repetitive basis. The question here is should these individuals be placed in prison rather than secure custody of some other kind (e.g. a psychiatric facility)? Secondly, if they are placed in custody, should they be housed with non-dangerous inmates? Should they be housed with other dangerous prisoners?

We might well ask whether the truly dangerous end up in prison anyway. How should the system deal with the truly dangerous?

STIGMA AND EXPERIENCES OF DANGEROUSNESS

The problem with concentrating on notions of dangerousness, and viewing the prison as the institution of the dangerous, is that all convicts acquire the reputation of being dangerous. Television programs and movies, for example, often depict prisoners as smouldering with rage and malice. This image applies also to release—if you have spent time in prison then you must be dangerous. It is important here to recall the generally non-violent profile of most prisoners before they enter into prison life.

It is important here, as well, to make a distinction between those people who have a record of actual serious violent offending, and those who do not. Furthermore, we need to distinguish between a specific criminological understanding of the term 'dangerousness', which speaks to actual violent behaviour, and a general notion of 'dangerousness', which implies being a risk or threat to others or being a problem in some way to institutional authorities, but which does not refer to formally defined serious and repeat violent offending. Dangerousness in the first instance is determined via the courts and the sentencing process. In the latter case, the idea of dangerousness refers more to overall threatening behaviour, rather than specific incidents. It is the perceived threat posed by offenders generally that is at the heart of much of the imagery associated with the prison.

For example, connotations of dangerousness are tied up with the architecture of the prison system itself. The notion of dangerousness is reinforced through the segregation of the 'dangerous' prison population from the rest of the community. High walls and razor wire reinforce the idea that the 'animals' are kept at bay only through intensive security arrangements. And the management practices of prisons are generally tied into notions of control rather than rehabilitation. For example, the prison regime is usually structured around a series of carrots and sticks—ranging from the possibility of early release and sentence remissions for good conduct to solitary confinement and internal segregation for bad conduct.

Conceptually, dangerousness is usually wrapped around certain crimes more than others. In particular, the focus is on predatory crimes of a certain kind, usually street crimes involving robbery, assault causing bodily harm, homicide and rape. Conversely, other crimes that may be more dangerous, from the point of view of number of people affected and number of lives lost, are customarily not perceived to involve dangerous people. This is the case, for instance, with regard to some forms of corporate crime involving preventable workplace death or the sale of unsafe products (Perrone 2000, 1999; see also Chapter 12).

Those classified as dangerous are usually treated as though the 'dangerousness' associated with them is basically a personal problem. That is, there is a general perception that violence resides in the individual, and is therefore related solely to individual pathology. This view is frequently voiced with respect to particular violent men. This is despite the evidence provided by social surveys that a sizeable proportion of men condone domestic violence in certain situations (Women Against Prison Collective 1990). Subscribing to the view that violence is born out of some personal malaise can obscure the fact that such behaviour is widespread and constitutes a social, rather than simply individual, problem (Anthony 2011). The individualising and finely targeted use of the notion of 'dangerousness' does, however, have major implications for how inmates are treated and controlled during their prison sentence period.

The concept of dangerousness, when attached to persons in a prison setting (most of whom have committed 'street' rather than 'suite' crime), serves to dehumanise the inmates and strip away their rights to criticise and make political demands (see Box 25.1). It is hardly likely, for example, that persons who have been classified and defined as dangerous will be listened to when they claim abuse or the infringement of rights. The concept of dangerousness also puts enormous power into the hands of professionals such as psychiatrists, psychologists and prison officers. This has serious implications insofar as it is relatively easy both to ensure that inmates are disempowered and to undercut the accountability of the system. For instance, the threat is always there that those who speak out and protest against prison conditions may be reclassified as 'dangerous'. Thus, the concept can be used as an administrative control strategy to deal with certain types of inmates.

BOX 25.1   SUPERMAX PRISONS AND DEHUMANISATION

In the book *Imprisoning resistance: life and death in an Australian supermax*, Bree Carlton (2007) provides a critical investigation of the conditions and consequences associated with living and working in a high security **supermax** prison, a facility structured to house the 'worst of the worst' inmates; that is, those classified as violent, assaultive and/or a major security or escape threat. The institution itself is linked to dehumanisation of both correctional staff and inmates, due to the nature of the emphasis on total social control. Reference is made to the Pentridge Prison Jika Jika High-Security Unit in Victoria, which, like other supermax prisons, attempted to apply hi-tech security devices and advances, sophisticated architectural design, and complex managerial and disciplinary strategies to maximise control over prisoners. The damage caused to prisoners by measures that involved extended periods of lockdowns (up to 23 hours a day), social isolation, unique sensory deprivation and unaccountable power structures was to eventually result in a form of resistance—in this case the building of a barricade and lighting of a fire—that led to the deaths of five prisoners and Jika's closure as a high-security prison.

> **SUPERMAX**
> An abbreviation of supermaximum prison, which denotes a free-standing 'control unit' prison, or discrete unit within a prison, that provides for the most secure level of custody in the correctional system of some countries.

The key message from this case study is that the more a particular regime becomes unaccountable, restrictive and coercive, the more extreme prisoner actions will become in resisting such. More recently, Carlton (2008) has also examined the implications of using supermax prisons in the 'war on terror', again with major questions being raised as to the negative social consequences and denial of basic human rights implicated in the use of such measures.

In the United States of America, supermax facilities have grown exponentially to number approximately 60 in 1999 (Briggs et al. 2003); a growth attributed not to evidence of effectiveness, but to the decline in the rehabilitative ideal as a guiding correctional philosophy, the concomitant rise in punitive, retributivist and deterrent ideals, and the profit-centred expansionist philosophy of the prison industry (Campbell 2013; Drucker 2011; Mears 2008; Western & Muller 2013). Against this backdrop, a new penology (Feely & Simon 1992) has emerged, in which correctional management is increasingly focused on managing risk and, specifically, the identification, classification and management of groups of prisoners according to levels of perceived dangerousness. Critics of supermax institutions cite the heightened levels of cruelty and violation of human and constitutional rights, as well as the increasing levels of psychological problems among inmates, as costly and unacceptable consequences of this new management style (see further Haney 2008; Pizarro & Narag 2008).

FOSTERING A VIOLENT ATMOSPHERE

Imprisonment itself is a major contributing factor to making some dangerous people even more dangerous. Prisons create and foster violence, and the lack of post-release programs means that angry people will remain that way. The prison infrastructure and prison culture can actively promote violent behaviour, particularly among men. Consider, for example, the consequences of a rapid increase in the male prison population. This can easily occur in the context of tough 'law and order' policies, accompanied by changes in sentencing practices (see Hogg & Brown 1998; Western & Muller 2013). Harsher sentencing laws can produce a rapid increase in the prison population. This is often accompanied by substantial increases in things such as prison overcrowding, prisoners on protection, and assaults (including sexual assault) and deaths within the prison walls (see, for example, Heilpern 2005; Steering Committee for the Review of Government Service Provision 2014). Over time, concern heightens regarding the escalation in expenditure on prisons, and it is not uncommon in this situation to see the removal of mechanisms of accountability and review, and the slashing of educational and rehabilitative programs, insofar as the objective is to rationalise infrastructure costs. The net result of these kinds of trends and strategies is, ultimately, riots and damage to prison property.

Part of the reason for these kinds of explosions in violent behaviour is attributable to changes in sentencing laws and policies. For instance, 'truth in sentencing' means that individuals are expected to serve out their time without remissions. Yet, traditionally, social control in prisons has been based on the concept of remissions and early release as rewards for good conduct. The 'truth in sentencing' approach undermines this concept and thus the dynamic between prison management and prisoner behaviour is subject to fundamental change.

PRISONISATION: A CULTURE OF VIOLENCE

Prison culture, or what can be described as 'prisonisation', also requires examination if we are to understand how prisons produce dangerousness. The process of 'prisonisation' involves the adoption of the norms of inmate subculture based on an adversarial relationship between guards and inmates. Generally speaking, behaviour that the institutional authorities view as conformity is viewed by inmates as deviant, and vice versa. Once an individual enters the prison system, they undergo a symbolic depersonalisation transition—they are stripped, probed, re-dressed and bestowed the status of convict. As part of this process, the individual is required to take on the mores, customs and culture of the prison, all of which are premised upon a basic conflict between inmate and guard. The prison setting and prison resources heavily shape prison culture as well (see Box 25.2).

The kinds of things that influence how an inmate responds to the prison environment include:

- *crowding*: for example, cell size and total prison population in relation to capacity
- *denial of responsibility*: for example, in most prisons the inmates are told when to get up, wash and do everything else, and even their lights are commonly controlled by an officer from outside the cell
- *type of work*: for example, menial and/or uninteresting
- *social isolation*: for example, correspondence and a drop-off in number of outside visitors over time
- *families*: for example, punishing of families on the outside, single parenting and poverty
- *relationships*: for example, little choice in 'new' friends, or escape from them
- *control and intimidation*: for example, strip searches, cell searches and dependence on 'privileges'
- *deterioration*: for example, increased introversion and increased self-directed hostility.

BOX 25.2   FACILITIES AND SERVICES IN PRISON

To gauge the nature of prison life and its potential impact on prison culture, prisoner experiences, behaviour and physical wellbeing, it is important to consider the following kinds of provisions:

- *type of reception*: for example, testing, medical examination, body search, fingerprinting, photographing, information briefings and allocation of clothing
- *living accommodation*: for example, size of cell, toilet facilities, overcrowding, ventilation, heating and cooling, furniture and decoration
- *choice of work*: for example, availability, industry, farming, domestic duties, maintenance, pay, and skilled or unskilled
- *nature of education*: for example, priority within prison, availability of teaching staff, privilege or right, adequate materials, library resources and cultural basis
- *communication channels*: for example, between inmates and authority figures, family access, transportation, censorship of letters and telephone privileges
- *medical and health provision*: for example, availability of doctors, serious cases, medicalisation of prisoners, reporting of incidents, and range of food
- *sport and recreation*: for example, use and availability of TVs, videos and computers, drama groups, sports facilities, camps and gardens
- *treatment programs*: for example, drug and alcohol, sex offender and anger management.

Facilities, services and programs can be evaluated on the basis of quality, availability, content of provision and cultural appropriateness, and how well these match both immediate offender and management requirements, as well as international standards (see for example, United Nations conventions pertaining to prison standards and prisoner rights, European Union standards for the treatment of prisoners, and the Standard Guidelines for Corrections in Australia; for commentary, see Brown & Wilkie 2002; Grant & Memmott 2007–08; Murdoch 2006).

The interface between prison environment and outside community is complicated by the nature of coercive internment in the first place. It is also made worse by procedures—such as strip searches—that reinforce the isolation and abuse of prisoners and their family members (see Box 25.3).

The contours of prison culture may involve both 'internal' and 'external' factors. (See Bondeson 1989; Hartnagel and Gillian 1980; Morash et al. 2010; Slotboom et al. 2011) For example, it is sometimes asked whether prison culture emerges:

- as an adaptation to the deprivations of prison life—a normative mechanism for mitigating the 'pains of imprisonment', such as physical and psychological deprivations and degradations
- because prisoners bring antisocial or antagonistic ideas in with them—the importation or diffusion of personal characteristics and values (especially criminal values) originating outside of the prison context
- due to a combination of the two.

In a similar vein, we might analyse how the rules and regulations themselves structure the relationships of prisoners to the prison authorities.

PRISON INFORMERS

If, for example, we change existing practices and introduce the imposition of fixed terms with no remissions, then this will have an impact on the prison culture. In New South Wales, where such

BOX 25.3   PRISON STRIP SEARCHES

PURPOSES OF SEARCHES

The purpose of a formal search is to detect the presence of drugs, weapons or metal articles. Any visitor to the prison can be subjected to a search. These may be 'targeted' to specific individuals or randomly applied across the visitor population.

STRIP SEARCHES AS ABUSE

Strip searches are personally intrusive and violate the basic bodily integrity of the individual. It is humiliating for most participants. This humiliation is compounded by searches taking place in rooms that are dirty and that look as if they are rarely cleaned.

Strip searches are not generally applied in a random manner, but are targeted at specific individuals and families. Often the reason given for the search is 'information received' regarding the possibility of drugs or other items being smuggled in. In many cases, this involves inmates 'dobbing in' other inmates, often out of malice, and often with the intent of making prisoners suffer by ensuring that their families undergo the indignity and affront of a strip search. In this sense and under these circumstances, strip searches are intended from the very beginning to be a form of harassment and intimidation in respect to specific inmates and their family members.

Strip searches carried out on adults and children can be extremely traumatic and embarrassing. It means literally exposing oneself to the gaze of strangers. For children and adults who have suffered violent and/or sexual abuse in their lives, the pains of such searches are even worse than ordinarily may be the case.

EFFECTS OF STRIP SEARCHES

The main consequence of strip searches is to dissuade family and friends of inmates from visiting them in prison. This is especially the case in regards to young children who are especially vulnerable to intimidation, and to teenagers, particularly young women, who are highly self-conscious and protective of their bodies. Children have been known to have recurring nightmares as they relive the strip search, and to not want to visit their fathers again precisely because of the experience.

Conversely, inmates may sometimes discourage visitors in order to avoid either themselves or their visitors from being strip searched. This can result in the social isolation of the prisoner.

There is considerable evidence that contact visits are of vital importance in maintaining family support and ties, and that such links are crucial to rehabilitation and reducing recidivism. Evidence also demonstrates that strip searches are not an effective way in which to deal with prison drug issues. Visitors are not the main source by which illicit drugs enter the prison.

There are alternative security techniques that are more effective and less intrusive than strip searches. These include, for example, the use of sniffer dogs and the use of x-ray search machines. Sniffer dogs are effective and inoffensive, and they could provide a generally unobtrusive way to regularly check prison employees, as well as periodic visitors. The use of these alternatives is relatively inexpensive, especially if considered in the context of human rights issues and prison rehabilitation objectives. Their use also forgoes possible legal action by those whose rights have been violated or who have suffered discrimination in the application of existing strip search procedures.

STRIP SEARCHES MUST END

Strip searches degrade and demean those individuals subjected to them. They are an abuse of human rights, personal dignity and self-respect. They humiliate and they terrify.

Strip searches can too easily be used as a 'management tool' that meets the control agenda of prison officials, or reflects the malice of particular inmates, rather than being used for bona fide purposes. They can be used to keep prisoners in line, or to intimidate those visitors who demand respect and rights for their loved ones.

Strip searches are unnecessary as a means to deal with drug issues or the bringing in of unwanted items into the prison. There are alternatives that can be used, here and now, to ensure that such things are not brought into the prison.

The practice of stripping anyone—inmate, adult visitor, prison employee or child—is abhorrent, and in the way it is concretely applied is highly unjust and discriminatory. It is time that strip searches were replaced by humane, non-intrusive alternatives. Strip searches must end.

Source: Prison Action & Reform (2002); see also Bogdanic (2009)

---

reforms were introduced, the result was an escalation in the use of prison informers, insofar as this was one of the few ways in which to gain time off a fixed sentence. If there is no hope of early release, then the attitude among some inmates is why not 'dob in' other prisoners—even if this means fabricating allegations. More generally, such a phenomenon is demoralising and soul-destroying in that prisoners live in an environment of constant suspicion and fear. As one commentator put it:

> The promotion of informing as one of the few remaining incentives in the prison system encourages manipulative and dishonest behaviour, brings the criminal justice system into disrepute, and induces cynicism against a system which is seen to have a price for everything, in which even criminality can be turned into a commodity. (Brown 1993: 83)

ROLE OF PRISON GUARDS

If we are to understand prison culture we also must look at prison guards—who they are, what their role is, and what they are attempting to do. Working within prisons has become highly complex in recent years, particularly with the introduction of initiatives such as 'integrated offender management'. Prison officers are being asked to perform a wider range of tasks than merely that of turn-key, and this has implications for their in-service and pre-service training, career structures, levels of work-related stress and general staff relations (O'Toole & Eyland 2005).

There is also the issue of the guards' perceptions of violence. Prison officers have publicly commented that at least once a week they experience fear of violence, hence reproducing for public consumption notions of the dangerousness and violent nature of inmates. 'Survival of the fittest' is a phrase used by some officers to describe the prison situation. They claim that they must act like animals when the prisoners start acting dangerously (see *The Age* September 1993). Such accounts serve to reinforce the image of the prison system as a dangerous place, where there are not only prisoner codes of conduct but also warden codes of 'dos and don'ts'.

TYPES OF PRISON REGIMES

The evidence suggests that the nature of the prison regime itself is a big factor influencing prison culture (see Brown & Wilkie 2002). For example, authoritarian regimes (including supermax facilities) tend to be associated with antagonistic relationships between staff and inmates, high levels of violence (self-harm/suicide and inmate to inmate violence, as well as prison officer to prisoner and prisoner to prison officer violence) and 'codes of behaviour' that are reflected in, and reinforced by, both inmate and custodian institutional practices (see Bierie 2012; Carlton 2007; Goulding 2007; Mears 2008; South & Wood 2006).

These unspoken codes present significant barriers to justice within prisons. In particular, the 'code of silence' serves to suppress prisoner complaints, for to express dissatisfaction with treatment at the hands of the authorities invites further risk of victimisation within the prison, including subjection to violence and threats (both officially sanctioned and hidden), even more restrictive regimes (e.g. being locked in cells for up to 23 hours a day), being charged with prison offences and being denied access to work, education or programs (de Krester 2007). Ultimately, prisoners learn the art of becoming 'con-wise'; that is, sophisticated in the art of pretending to be a model prisoner (Bondeson 1989).

The problems associated with an antagonistic prison environment, and high levels of distrust and dishonesty, make change on either side very difficult. For example, prison officers who individually adopt a 'humane' approach to their tasks, and who wish to establish a closer, more positive relationship with inmates, are invariably exploited by some prisoners. Over time, this can lead to cynicism and disenchantment about the possibilities of reform.

Prisonisation is a process that varies according to basic penal philosophy (e.g. punishment versus rehabilitation), the nature of local prison conditions (e.g. lighting, heating and adequate bed numbers), the historical relationship between the prison philosophy and inmate (e.g. control orientation versus helping hand), use of technology (e.g. level of surveillance), gender relations and the different ways in which men and women identify themselves (e.g. positive or negative association with a criminal subculture and the perceived importance of social status), and operational management (e.g. state versus **private prisons**). What appears to be constant is the fact that most inmates experience prison as a 'total institution', within which their liberties and rights have been essentially taken away.

PRISONERS RE-ENTERING OUTSIDE SOCIETY

Further to this, it is rare indeed to find a prisoner who leaves the institution with the social skills, educational or vocational training, and emotional wellbeing suited to finding accommodation, securing full-time employment and fitting back into conventional society. The prison experience is far removed from the realities of outside life, and this is a central factor in why reintegration can be so difficult. The prison leaves indelible marks on the inmate. The stigma of serving prison time is 'inscribed on their body' (Moran 2012: 564)—both in terms of personal agonies and frustrations relating to the physical legacy of incarceration (tattoos, rotten teeth and feelings of worthlessness) and with respect to the official blot on their record that will dog them the rest of their lives, and severely affect their chances of successfully finding employment and re-entering the mainstream of social life (Graffam et al. 2008; Moran 2012).

This factor is clearly highlighted by the findings of a study of 350 ex-prisoners released from New South Wales and Victorian prisons. The research revealed that 66 per cent of the sample had been previously imprisoned, 75 per cent had not completed secondary education (indeed, most had not completed Year 10) and 20 per cent were homeless. Aboriginal research participants experienced particular difficulties post-release, with 66 per cent returning to the prison environment within 9 months of release. Clear evidence was presented of the deterioration in social and economic conditions experienced by participants as a direct consequence of their incarceration, with approximately 70 to 80 per cent excluded from the formal economy (i.e. legitimate employment). The sample was generally

PRIVATE PRISON
A privately run prison, jail or detention centre in which a third party is contracted by a local, state or federal government agency that commits those prisoners to the facility. Private prison companies are generally paid a per diem or monthly rate for each prisoner confined in the facility.

best typified as socially excluded, lacking basic social skills, poorly educated, poor, homeless or in unstable living environments, and receiving minimal social support (Baldry & Maplestone 2003; Baldry et al. 2003).

Recent empirical evidence emerging from the United States lends support to the proposition that trends in mass incarceration have substantially contributed to increased rates of poverty (several million more people) (DeFina & Hannon 2013). A number of studies also suggest that in the absence of structured drug treatment and other rehabilitative programs, many prisoners returning to the community (especially women) are at high risk of unnatural death from drug overdose and suicide in the immediate post-release period. This is due to the less structured nature of the outside environment, as well as the strong triggers for drug use relapse and experiences of social exclusion (Binswanger et al. 2012; Carlton & Segrave 2011).

THE PAINS OF IMPRISONMENT

The prison environment violates many of the known principles of social and psychological development. It promotes norms and practices that legitimate rather than reduce deviance. The pains of imprisonment can be summarised as follows (see Mathiesen 1990; Sykes 1958):

- *Deprivation of liberty*: this involves massive restrictions on movement, and the cutting off of people from their friends, families and loved ones.
- *Deprivation of goods and services*: this involves a drastic reduction in material possessions.
- *Deprivation of ordinary, loving, sexual relationships*: this involves major physiological and psychological problems that call into question one's sexuality and sexual status.
- *Deprivation of autonomy*: this involves the subjection of the individual to a vast body of rules, regulations and commands that are imposed and total in nature.
- *Deprivation of security*: this involves being thrown together into anxiety-provoking situations of forced and prolonged intimacy with others who in many instances have a history of violent behaviour (including guards).
- *Deprivation of power*: this involves the power that the prison wields in controlling both formal and informal benefits and burdens in the lives of the incarcerated.

ALTERNATIVES TO USE OF PRISONS

Given this portrayal of prison life, what are the alternative options? The concept of *decarceration* refers to the closure of institutions and the abolition of prisons. History has shown that it is in fact possible for major penal systems to be frozen in size, reduced in size, partially abolished or fully abolished. Each of these strategies implies a major reduction in the level of people incarcerated. It is argued by Mathiesen (1990) that, fundamentally, the move toward prison abolition needs to be based upon certain ideological principles. For example, given the social background of most victims and offenders, one such principle is that of solidarity with the politically and socially weak. Secondly, there is the principle of compensation, which in essence can be seen as the mechanism to translate solidarity into practice. Each of these principles precludes the use of imprisonment as the answer to crime.

Instead, it is argued that there should be 'depenalisation' on the one hand, and 'decriminalisation' on the other. The first refers to efforts to expand the range of non-imprisonable offences to make prison truly the last resort of the courts and applicable in only the direst of cases (see Freiberg et al. 1996).

As we have seen, a significant proportion of inmates currently in prison are not 'dangerous' or there for particularly 'serious' offences. A second strategy is to narrow the scope of criminal law, and to allow for civil remedies in many instances of social conflict. Prison closures are essential if such strategies are actually to provide an alternative to, rather than supplementing, the use of prisons. So, too, it is necessary for expanded provision of supportive, community-based alternatives to the closed environment of the prison. This latter point is worth pursuing in greater depth from the point of view of financial costs (see also Chapter 26).

COSTS, SERVICES AND PROGRAMS

How much money is spent on corrections, and where the money is spent within corrections, are vital issues in any consideration of system goals and operational efficacy (see White 2004). From a financial point of view, there are matters of both quantity (i.e. how much to spend on which parts of the corrections system) and quality (i.e. how much to spend in order to ensure adequate 'return' for the money being allocated). To put it differently, assessment of budgets and finances is both a matter of determining system prioritisation and of evaluating service quality.

Chapter 26 demonstrates one major fact; that is, the use of imprisonment is considerably more expensive than community corrections. While broadly supporting this proposition, what the information presented in Figure 25.4 cannot reveal is the way in which the money is actually spent within each type of service provision. Specifically, it does not tell us how much money is allocated to 'security' and how much goes into 'services and programs' for offenders. This is also crucial to know, since the success or otherwise of imprisonment and community corrections depends, at least to some degree, on the services and programs on offer. For instance, sex-offender programs are expensive, but they do have an impact in terms of preventing some offenders from reoffending . However, their expensive nature means that in some jurisdictions they are deemed to be prohibitive (e.g. Tasmania had no sex-offender program at Risdon prison for many years, due to the costs involved). An adequate evaluation of prison costs and the costs of community corrections would need to include specific detailed information about services provided and programs on offer.

Nevertheless, Figure 25.4 highlights that any trend toward greater reliance upon prisons relative to community corrections will cost considerably more. Likewise, net-widening represents a significant increase in expenditure on corrective services (see Chapter 26). Conversely, decreased use of prisons and community corrections either represents a real saving, or the transfer of monies into diversionary areas that, at the least in the case of imprisonment, are much less expensive than incarceration. Fluctuating numbers are also cost ineffective, insofar as systems have to be designed to cater for growth in numbers, as well as accepting lower numbers of participants. Projections and perspectives on capacity, as well as actual use, have cost implications.

In-depth cost analysis would also have to consider the relative growth in expenditure relative to any changes to staff numbers, offender numbers and the number of professional staff. Furthermore, expenditure patterns can be tracked over time in the case of both prisons and community corrections. It could well be argued that:

> much more needs to be spent on the human infrastructure of corrections (rather than bricks and mortar) given the central importance of programmes in opening the door for offenders to achieve futures in which offending becomes less of an option. When security costs out-weigh service and programme outlays then prisons, and community corrections, become places of (temporary) containment and offender management,

not opportunities for rehabilitation or restorative justice. Money is not spent for the purposes of change (on the part of individual offenders, or with respect to community environments). The result inevitably is 'more of the same': the failure of prison and corrections generally as reflected in high recidivism rates. (White 2004: 49)

Although inconclusive, the weight of cost–benefit evidence indicates that, while the prison may be an efficient sentencing option for more serious offenders, it is an inefficient and ineffective mechanism when applied to less serious offenders, with the costs outweighing the intended incapacitation, rehabilitative and specific deterrent benefits. On this basis, Marsh et al. (2009: 155) conclude that from an economic perspective 'using [prisons] for anyone but those convicted of serious offences is a waste of public resources' (see also Ritchie 2011).

A key challenge then for policy-makers is how best to reduce prison populations to the extent that expenditure can be used efficiently and effectively to cater to the small number of hard-core, serious and recalcitrant offenders. The issue of 'what works' in a prison context is dictated by size of prison population in relation to service, program and security budgets. In addition, we need to bear in mind that prisons intrinsically bear with them a series of pains of imprisonment (as discussed above) from which many women and men have difficulty recovering. The trauma associated with incarceration is linked to social and economic cost, which can be avoided in many cases by redirecting people into the community corrections sector (especially for less serious offences, fine defaulters, short-term sentences and so on).

REQUIRED PRISON REFORMS

Just as alternatives to prison must be based upon ways to encourage a positive community response to crime, likewise the prison regime, with its brutalising and punitive character, is seen to be in need of major reform that incorporates the notions of community, caring and conciliation. There is considerable scope to achieve this through the application of restorative and therapeutic justice principles to the prison environment (see Chapters 26 and 27).

The concept of restorative prisons is a relatively recent phenomenon. While applied in a piecemeal fashion within some prisons in England and Wales, and even within some Australian prisons, its practical application as a total philosophy informing all activities and practices has, to date, been confined to the Belgian prison system (Goulding et al. 2009). At the core of restorative prison regimes is a concern to examine the relationship between the prison, the prisoner and the wider community and, more specifically, to explore whether the 'development of a restorative regime inside a prison can contribute to altering human relationships and to changing the perceptions that prisoners, staff, victims and the wider community have of each other' (International Centre for Prison Studies, cited in Goulding et al. 2009).

To operate effectively within a correctional environment, Goulding et al. (2009: 237) argue that **restorative justice** processes should address the following areas of concern:

- providing reparation to victims and communities through meaningful prisoner work and activities that effectively assist individual victims and/or local communities
- restructuring of all grievance procedures within prisons to include and promote alternative dispute resolution processes; this would include prisoner to prisoner disputes, prisoner to staff disputes, and all prisoner and prison staff grievances

RESTORATIVE JUSTICE
Restorative justice promotes non-adversarial processes, which foster dialogue between the offender, the victim and the community. This theory of justice emphasises repairing harm and involving victims, as well as offenders, in the reparation process.

- encouraging prisoners to recognise that their criminal actions have caused harm to victims and their families, and their own families and communities
- encouraging prisoners to engage in counselling and/or therapeutic programs within the prison, with supportive networks of family or peers in order to address the underlying issues that resulted in their offending behaviour patterns
- encouraging prisoners to engage in interactions with victims (not necessarily their own victims) where appropriate within the prison setting
- building positive relationships between prisoners and prison staff
- fostering new relationships between prisoners, the prison and the local community as a first step towards reconciliation and successful prisoner reintegration
- counteracting the negative stereotypical images of prisoners within local communities, thus effectively increasing the opportunity for successful reintegration.

ISSUES FOR CONSIDERATION

PRISONERS AND THEIR FAMILIES

The prison experience affects not only prisoners but whole families—children, partners, parents, siblings and other family members—who are often described as the 'hidden' face of imprisonment, or 'collateral damage' (Drucker 2011). Although not guilty of any crime, they too are punished by the deprivations and degradations of incarceration, including physical and emotional separation, and the consequent stresses on family relationships, economic vulnerability, declining emotional health and the social stigma attached to having a family member incarcerated, which often results in social isolation (Arditti et al. 2003; Manning 2011). Of particular concern is the relationship between parents and children within the context of incarceration and the potential adverse impact on child development and development of intergenerational offending (see Casey-Acevedo et al. 2004; Dawson et al. 2012; Healy et al. 2001; O'Connor 1996; Quilty et al. 2004).

This child–parent issue is especially pertinent to female inmates, in that while most male prisoners can depend on any children they have being cared for by the child's mother, separation from children, for mothers, is especially painful and arranging care for dependent children difficult (Flynn 2013). The reality is that parents in prison will eventually resume their parenting responsibilities upon release and it therefore appears in the interests of families that parents in custodial facilities be exposed to regimes that permit the familial relationship to resume a semblance of normalcy upon the prisoner's release (Cunningham 2001; Healy et. al. 2001; O'Toole 2002).

RISK-TAKING BEHAVIOURS

There are a number of health and safety issues associated with risk-taking behaviour by inmates, three of the foremost of these being drug use, unprotected sexual activity and tattooing, which some argue are normative responses to the deprivations of prison life and the quest for social status. Due to a combination of factors, including the lack of protection, contaminated drug-injecting equipment and confined populations, prisoners are especially vulnerable to blood-borne viruses, such as hepatitis C, hepatitis B and HIV, which are prevalent in prison environments (Butler et al. 2007; Fortuin 1992; Read & Douglas 2011, 2007).

Contrary to the decline in tobacco smoking rates in developed countries, the prevalence of prisoners smoking relative to national population rates is extraordinarily high (estimated to be between 64 and 92%). This represents a major public concern. While some countries have moved to impose total bans on smoking in prisons, others have introduced restricted smoking areas. Key questions remain regarding the appropriateness and effectiveness of these interventions in the light of human rights considerations (of the smoker and those subject to passive smoking) and the broader shifts in public health policy (Ritter et al. 2011).

PRISONERS WITH MENTAL HEALTH ISSUES

Another issue here is how prison authorities and others respond to the special needs of people with mental health issues (psychological and psychiatric illnesses), and those with intellectual and physical disabilities, who are over-represented within the prison system and especially vulnerable to victimisation (Cunneen et al. 2013; Walsh 2006; Wolf & Shi 2009).

For example, Baksheev et al. (2011) recently found that three-quarters of detainees in police facilities in Melbourne met the criteria for mental disorder diagnosis, and the rates of mental illness and acquired brain injury among prisoner populations are significantly higher than for the general population (see Forsythe & Gaffney 2012; Ogloff et al. 2007). Recent figures from New South Wales reflect similar observations, with up to 78 per cent of male, and a staggering 90 per cent of women, prisoners observed with a mental disorder upon reception (ACT Community Coalition on Corrections 2008); this prompted the ACT Human Rights Commission to observe that 'prisons have become substitute accommodation for people with mental health problems' (AHRC 2007: 32, 98; see also Hayes 2005). This issue of over-representation is complicated by the generally high recidivism rates recorded for offenders with an intellectual disability, especially among sex offenders (between 40 and 70%) (Klimecki et al. 1994; Lindsay & Holland 2000).

Against this backdrop, it is worthwhile considering that while tougher penalties are ostensibly promoted in support of the rights of victims of crime, O'Connor (2007) questions the validity of such claims by drawing attention to the dual status of many prisoners as both offenders and victims; victims of psychiatric, as well as drug and alcohol disorders, sexual and physical abuse, and intellectual disability. In the face of sentencing laws that are meant to increase the length of time that people spend in prison, there are also issues associated with prison gerontology; that is, the care of the aged and infirm in a prison setting (see Grant 1999).

HUMAN RIGHTS WITHIN PRISONS

According to the Revised Standards for Corrections in Australia, 'people are sent to prison as punishment not for punishment. Prison systems should ensure that prisoners are not further punished for their crimes over and above the sentence imposed by the Court' (Attorney General's Department 2004: 14). The human rights and fundamental freedoms of prisoners in this regard are clearly outlined in a number of international covenants and conventions, including the International Covenant on Civil and Political Rights (ICCPR) (articles 7, 10 and 25), the Universal Declaration of Human Rights (UDHR) (articles 5 and 8), the Convention on the Rights of the Child (CRC) (article 37) and the Convention Against Torture and other Cruel, Inhuman or Degrading Treatment or Punishment (CAT).

Notwithstanding these standards, some prisoners continue to be denied basic rights. For example, currently in Australia, people who have been sentenced for more than 3 years in prison are denied the right to vote in federal elections (Koch & Hill 2008; Munn 2011). Moreover, the right of all prisoners to challenge their daily conditions (classification, management, discipline and control) through judicial review is non-existent in Australia. It should be noted, however, that in an effort to balance the need for effective prison management and security concerns, and the need to hold authorities accountable for prison management, Victoria and Tasmania have enacted legislation that confers specific rights on prisoners. These rights are expressed in general terms, but broadly reflect the minimum standards of international human rights. The legislation does not, however, specify a remedy for breaches of those rights. The remaining states and territories have developed their own specific procedures and regulations, which outline inmate entitlements and prison management procedures and rules for reviewing prisoner complaints and conditions of custody (Howel 2009; McWilliam 2007).

POST-RELEASE SUPPORT

The issue of post-release support for prisoners is an important and complex issue, especially when considering the complex nature of the intersection between victimisation and criminalisation (see Balfour 2012; Borzycki & Baldry 2003; Graffam et al. 2008; Hunter 2008). Discussion here needs to take place regarding the provision of halfway houses, vocational and social skills training, finding suitable accommodation, provision of drug rehabilitation programs and other efforts designed to assist inmates to make the transition back into mainstream society. Family counselling and financial advice are also important aspects of the transition.

More generally, there are crucial differences in the provision of programs and facilities both in prison and outside of prison when it comes to men and women particularly from an Indigenous background. Because the system is dominated by non-Indigenous male inmates and staff, the resources and planning have tended to reflect Anglo-Australian male priorities and needs. Gender and culturally specific services are therefore important to consider in any reform process (Baldry 2010; Hunter 2008).

PRIVATISATION OF PRISONS

The issue of the privatisation of prisons continues to be a matter of some concern (see Andrew 2010; Harding 1997; Moyle 2000; Schwartz & Nurge 2004; Spivak & Sharp 2008). There are a number of issues that need further discussion and critical evaluation. They include: the role of the state as representative of the 'community' versus that of private corporations, which represent private interests; issues of public accountability in cases involving private contractors; the provision and quality of prison services (including rehabilitation); the outflow of money from Australia to the foreign companies that manage and operate the private prisons; and the built-in expansionary logic of systems that are premised on making profit through the housing of prisoners.

The use of private prisons is premised on neo-liberal ideological principles relating to 'free enterprise' and private provision of public services, and the cost-effectiveness of private industry in relation to public institutions. Any discussion of private prisons, therefore, should reference the competing philosophical rationales behind state-run or privately run prisons and the underlying premise of cost-effectiveness (Lundahl et al. 2009), as well as to the practical difficulties and ethical implications of turning prisons into commodities that are run for commercial benefit (see Andrew 2010).

It is noteworthy that, in Victoria, the damning findings of a coronial inquiry into the state's private jails—which revealed high rates of self-mutilation, assaults and drug abuse; staff inexperience and lack of training; defective emergency procedures; and poor cell design—led to a contraction of privately run prisons, with the state government reclaiming control of the majority of privately run facilities (Department of Justice 2000).

CONCLUSION

This chapter has surveyed a wide range of issues pertaining to the use of imprisonment as a penal sanction. It has reviewed the extent of incarceration in the Australian context, and provided an indication of the mission statements of correctional authorities in this country. It was noted that most inmates come from vulnerable and disadvantaged backgrounds, and that Indigenous people in particular are highly over-represented among the prison population nationally.

The broad effects of incarceration are, in the main, negative. The known effects include:

- *degradation*: for example, lack of care and caring, restrictions, boredom, little contact with meaningful things, and elimination of ordinary sexual relations
- *violence*: for example, suicide, attacks on others and self-mutilation
- *recidivism*: for example, inability to adjust to outside world, no income or employment options, and longer-term effects of incarceration, reputation and stigma.

The effects of incarceration are disproportionately felt by socio-economically disadvantaged prisoners and their families. The experience serves to add an additional layer of disadvantage and social marginalisation.

Regardless of theoretical intention and purpose, it is clear that prisons do little to either deter future offending or to rehabilitate offenders. Instead, they are oppressive and hostile sites where depression, self-mutilation, substance abuse, violence, despair, mistrust, and antisocial behaviour and attitudes are prevalent (Dear 2008; Thompson 2007–08). The negative experiences of prison and the effects of prisonisation are glaringly obvious, as noted by the Women Against Prison Collective (1990: 27, 28), who argue that 'the high rate of suicide among female prisoners is an epitaph to suffering'. They further point out that: 'Prisons are brutal places and they create brutal people. Men released from prison go back to wives, mothers, lovers and sisters who are left to cope with the damage. Women thus become victims of male imprisonment.'

The financial costs and social burdens associated with maintaining and expanding prisons are enormous. Important questions need to be asked, therefore, regarding their continuing popularity as a favoured sanction among politicians and other members of the wider community. As O'Toole (2002: 242) warns: 'More prisons and police inevitably come at a cost and that cost may be school closures, declines in public health care and other basic social services.'

The next chapter continues the theme of the latter part of this discussion. That is, what kinds of alternatives are there to the formal and more punitive aspects of the criminal justice system? To answer this, we need to consider the philosophies and practices of community corrections.

DISCUSSION QUESTIONS

1   Should family-sensitive practices be adopted within the prison context? For example:
  - Should babies and young children be permitted to remain with their incarcerated parents, or should they be separated?
  - Can alternatives be devised that will ensure that the family can be kept together as a unit?
  - Given that a healthy relationship between partners or spouses also includes sexual relations, and that both the offender and the offender's partner suffer from the enforced deferment of sexual liaison, is there a way to overcome this problem?

2   How might prisons be reformed to better cater for the high treatment needs of special populations?

3   Within the context of a discussion on human rights and fundamental freedoms, should prisoners:

- have access to things such as condoms, clean syringes, and bleach for sterilisation purposes?

- have the right to vote?

- be provided with special dietary food for medical, religious or ethical (e.g. practicing vegetarians or vegans) reasons?

4   What are the practical and philosophical challenges to achieving prisoner rehabilitation and ensuring human rights in private prisons? How might regulatory practices be altered to improve accountability and effectiveness (see Wright 2009)? Should prisoner challenges to the conditions of their containment be subject to judicial review?

5   How might we account for the variation in incarceration rates across developed countries?

FURTHER READING

Brown, D. & Wilkie, M (eds) (2002) *Prisoners as citizens: human rights in Australian prisons*, The Federation Press, Sydney.

Carlton, B. & Segrave, M. (2011) 'Women's survival post-imprisonment: connecting imprisonment with pains past and present', *Punishment & Society*, 13(5): 551–79.

Christie, N. (1993) *Crime control as industry: towards gulags, western style?*, Routledge, London.

Mathiesen, T. (1990) *Prison on trial*, Sage, London.

Western, B. & Muller, C. (2013) 'Mass incarceration, macrosociology, and the poor', *The Annals of the American Academy of Political and Social Sciences*, 647: 166–89.

COMMUNITY CORRECTIONS

26

CHAPTER OVERVIEW

- COMMUNITY CORRECTIONS: THE HISTORICAL CONTEXT
- COMMUNITY-BASED SANCTIONS
- THE RATIONALE FOR COMMUNITY CORRECTIONS
- THE IMPACT OF COMMUNITY CORRECTIONS
- PRISONER RELEASE AND POST-PRISON TRANSITIONS
- QUESTIONING COMMUNITY-BASED SOCIAL CONTROL
- ISSUES FOR CONSIDERATION
- CONCLUSION
- DISCUSSION QUESTIONS
- FURTHER READING

INTRODUCTION

If, as suggested in Chapter 25, imprisonment is problematic in terms of overall social consequences and economic costs, then the question arises regarding whether we can collectively deal with criminal justice matters in a more positive, and perhaps less intrusive manner. As indicated in Chapter 22, the establishment of alternative dispute-resolution measures, ranging from mediation centres to family group conferences, has been generally driven by concerns to keep people out of the more formal institutions of criminal justice, and to deal with social or individual problems in a more participatory and conciliatory manner than the adversarial methods of the courts, as outlined in Chapter 19. Similar trends also can be observed with regard to the mode of punishment or treatment deemed to be appropriate for most classes of offender.

In particular, the concepts of deinstitutionalisation and decarceration gained substantial support by the late 1970s in Australia and have had an influence on how offenders are dealt with today, even in the context of rising prison populations. The political rationale in support of these ideas varies considerably, from concerns to cut the economic costs of penal regimes, through to humanitarian concerns to minimise the harm done to offenders in serving their sentences in a correctional environment. Many of the diversionary strategies adopted under the aegis of community corrections in fact, have been components of the formal 'corrections' system for many years. Others, however, are relatively new, as technology (e.g. electronic monitoring through the use of bracelets and anklets) has opened up new possibilities of community-based control, including home detention.

This chapter provides a broad overview of the nature and forms of community corrections. It discusses the main impetuses behind establishment of community corrections, and the various philosophies underpinning this mode of social control. It then provides an examination of the role of community corrections in providing an alternative to prison, and as a form of post-release transition process.

COMMUNITY CORRECTIONS: THE HISTORICAL CONTEXT

The term **community corrections** refers to community-based management of a suite of court-ordered sanctions and post-custodial administrative arrangements that enable offenders to serve their punishment (either wholly or in part) in the community (as opposed to a correctional institution) and/or assist prisoners to reintegrate back into the community under a regime of continuing supervision.

While community corrections are often considered a modern penal reform, Wodahl and Garland (2009) point out that two of its cornerstones, probation and parole, date back to the mid-nineteenth century, originating in America and Europe, respectively. Drawing on historical evidence of the New South Wales penal colonies, Chan (1991) traces the implementation of broad community-based correctional initiatives further back to 1790, when colonial governors were granted powers, through the ticket-of-leave and pardon system, to permit the absolute or conditional remittance of transported prisoners' sentences.

It is only in the past 40 years or so, however, that community corrections have become a substantial component of the correctional services system. To understand the development of community-based corrections, it is necessary to briefly consider their evolution within the context of wider conceptual developments in the field of criminal justice and, in particular, growing disillusionment with the effectiveness of the criminal justice system overall, and prisons in particular. As intimated in Chapters 24 and 25, the sources of disenchantment have been many, including (see also Wodahl & Garland 2009):

- the growing *medicalisation* of correctional discourse (attribution of crime to environmental, biological or psychological forces) and the subsequent realisation that prisons failed to address the individualised, criminogenic needs of offenders
- mounting evidence of the *general failure of the correctional services* system to both stem recidivism (to deter offenders) and realise the rehabilitative ideals and objectives of penal policy espoused by progressive reformists (i.e. to do offenders good)
- concerns expressed by civil libertarians regarding the potential for *abrogation of human rights and legal safeguards* introduced by reformative models of treatment
- humanitarian concerns for the *unintended, negative effects of incarceration* on prisoners, including stigmatisation, physical and/or psychological harm, unremitting exposure to criminal peers and the difficulties of successfully reintegrating ex-prisoners into the community
- *rapidly increasing prison populations*, leading to overcrowding and a consequent intensification of fiscal pressures on the state.

THE MOVEMENT AGAINST PENAL INSTITUTIONS

Concerted movement against the use, and indeed the very existence, of penal institutions, originated in the United States in the 1960s and 1970s, following a series of prison riots that highlighted the abysmal and often inhumane conditions suffered by incarcerated populations (Chan 1991). It is important to emphasise that this movement took place within a broader context of radical shifts in the conceptualisation and reorganisation of social control.

In particular, the destructuralist policies of **decarceration** and **deinstitutionalisation** that emerged at this time were born of a fundamental distrust of the 'professions' (psychiatrist, psychologists and criminologists) and a concern for the harms caused by formal, closed institutions of social control based on the segregation of 'sick', 'dangerous' and 'problematic' populations (e.g. mental asylums, prisons and reformatories). They advocated, instead, the removal or diversion of individuals from institutional facilities and the adoption of community-based measures, and programs of care and control across a variety of disciplines, including criminology (Skull 1984).

Within the justice system specifically, it led to a proliferation of community-based programs and interventions across a number of domains, including the law (through decriminalisation), crime prevention, courts (diversionary practices), victimology (restorative justice practices) and corrections (pre and post). In other words, the movement in support of community corrections is related to general tendencies and processes affecting all parts of the criminal justice system—specifically, the incorporation of 'the community' into the criminal justice field at many different levels and in many different ways (see Cohen 1985). As argued by Cunneen et al. (2013), there are also countervailing forces pushing in the direction of massive, albeit selective, use of incarceration and the imposition of harsher sanctions, including within the community corrections sphere.

COMMUNITY-BASED SANCTIONS

Within criminology, decarceration and deinstitutionalisation are umbrella terms used to describe a variety of government policies and diversionary strategies that seek to reduce the use of imprisonment to punish offenders. The two terms are often used variably, and interchangeably, but in the context of community corrections, they are described as follows:

- *Deinstitutionalisation*: is the use of alternatives to imprisonment that permit the offender to remain within the community, albeit under some kind of conditional control and/or surveillance.
- *Decarceration*: attempts to remove individuals from the prison environment entirely, or to reduce the time they might otherwise have been required to spend there.

Hence, while deinstitutionalisation *diverts* people from prison, decarceration *removes* them from prison.

CLASSIFYING COMMUNITY-BASED ORDERS

This section provides a general overview of community-based **sanctions** that are presently being applied across the Australian jurisdiction. The specific sanctions available in any instance are shaped by legislation and policy within each particular state or territory. In the sentencing hierarchy, community-based orders that meet the criminological definitions of deinstitutionalisation and decarceration, as outlined above, are considered intermediate options, situated as they are between imprisonment (as the most severe sanction), and a range of lower-end diversionary options that do not place the offender within the supervision of community correctional services, such as (Freiberg & Ross 1999):

- *fines*: where the court imposes on the offender a monetary penalty, either as a standalone measure or in conjunction with another sentencing order
- *dismissals*: where a court finds an offender guilty of an offence but dismisses the offender without recording a conviction or any other sentencing option
- *discharges*: where a court finds an offender guilty of an offence and records a conviction, but discharges them without imposing any further sentencing options or conditions
- *adjourned undertakings*: where a court finds an offender guilty and releases them into the community (either with or without conviction) unsupervised for a specified period. Conditions may be attached to the adjournment, most commonly a promise to be of good behaviour (i.e. not commit further offences) for the duration of the undertaking or to demonstrate that rehabilitation has taken place.

DEINSTITU-TIONALISATION
A profound social policy shift prompting the large-scale restructuring of human services delivery. This customarily resulted in the diversion of offenders, patients and clients away from institutions (including prisons and asylums) and towards community-based alternatives.

INTERMEDIATE SANCTIONS
Custodial and non-custodial sentencing orders that sit between immediate imprisonment and lower-level community-based options, such as fines, dismissals, discharges and adjournments. These sanctions serve as substitutes for a term of imprisonment or alternative sanctions.

These options (in some form or other) can be imposed on both adult and juvenile offenders. There is a much wider range of intermediate sentencing options available to judges and magistrates when punishing adult offenders. While these vary across Australian jurisdictions (see Table 26.1), they can broadly be classified as non-custodial, custodial and post-custodial orders.

TABLE 26.1 COMMUNITY CORRECTIONAL DISPOSITIONS IN AUSTRALIA

DISPOSITION TYPE	JURISDICTION	DETAILS
Supervised bail	NSW, WA, SA, TAS, ACT, NT	• NSW—sentence deferred and bail granted to allow offender to participate in an intervention program • SA—granted on condition of supervision by community corrections and/or home detention conditions and/or electronic monitoring • WA—granted on condition of home detention/electronic monitoring on release to a community hostel, curfew conditions, possible participation in program of training, personal development or rehabilitation and possible supervision by community corrections • TAS—supervised bail as part of court-mandated diversion for drug offenders • ACT—may require participation in a program of personal development, training or rehabilitation • NT—may require court-mandated supervision by community corrections, with possible curfew, residence and program participation requirements
Conditionally deferred conviction/ sentence	VIC, NSW, QLD, WA, TAS, NT	• NSW—Drug Court Program • VIC—Drug Treatment Order • QLD—Intensive Drug Rehabilitation Order • WA—Pre-sentence orders issued by a Drug Court • TAS—Drug Treatment Order (court mandated diversion program) • NT—Substance Misuse Assessment and Referral for Treatment Order (SMART)
Fine/ Conversion	VIC, NSW, QLD, WA, TAS, SA, NT	• Fine can be converted to Community Based Order, Community Service Order or Community Work Order
Community Service Order	VIC, NSW, QLD, WA, TAS, SA, ACT, NT	• VIC, SA and QLD—can be without conviction
Probation/ Community Based/ Community Correctional Order (CBO/ CCO)/Good Behaviour Bond (GBB)/Order	VIC, NSW, QLD, WA, TAS, SA, NT, ACT	• ACT—Good Behaviour Order • NSW—GBB • NT—Community Work Order, Release on Bond • QLD—Probation, Non-contact Order • VIC—probation until 1986 and thereafter Community Correctional Order • VIC, TAS and QLD—CBO/CCO probation can be without conviction

DISPOSITION TYPE	JURISDICTION	DETAILS
Drug Treatment Order	VIC	• Drug Court only
Supervised Suspended Sentence	NSW, WA, SA, TAS, NT, ACT	• VIC and QLD—suspended sentence also available without conditions • SA—supervised bond may also have a suspended sentence component
Intensive Correction Order/Intensive Supervision Order	VIC, QLD, NSW, WA	• WA—ISO (similar to a CBO but imposes mandatory supervision and may also include conditions relating to undertaking of programs, community service and adherence to a curfew)
Home detention	NSW, SA, NT	• SA—term of imprisonment required to be served before home detention order can be made • VIC—abolished in January 2012
Compulsory Drug Treatment Detention	NSW	• NSW Drug Court only
Post Prison Order (Parole, release on licence)	VIC, NSW, QLD, WA, TAS, SA, NT, ACT	• Release on licence available only to federal offenders serving a federal sentence of imprisonment/recognisance release order
Post Sentence Supervision Order	NSW, QLD, VIC, WA	• NSW—Extended Supervision Order • VIC—Extended Supervision Order • QLD—Supervision Order • WA—Supervision Order
Periodic detention	ACT	• Abolished in NSW in October 2010
Transition/ Re-entry Release Order	WA	• Parole Board may impose this order where an offender has been in custody for at least 12 months and be eligible for release in 6 months
Continuing Detention Order/Detention Order	NSW, VIC, QLD, WA, TAS	• NSW—Continuing Detention Order • VIC—Detention Order • QLD—Continuing Detention Order • WA—Continuing Detention Order • TAS—A person convicted of a violent offence can be declared a Dangerous Criminal under the *Sentencing Act* 1997, Section 19(1) and be held in prison custody until the declaration is discharged by the court

Source: adapted from Steering Committee for the Review of Government Service Provision (2014); Sentencing Advisory Council (2008b, 2014)

NON-CUSTODIAL ORDERS

In keeping with the philosophy of deinstitutionalisation, these are considered front-end community-based measures in that they specifically divert low-risk offenders from custody. As described by Freiberg and Ross (1999), these stand-alone options serve as 'alternative sanctions' to imprisonment. While they permit the offender to remain within the community for the entire duration of their sentence, they impose some form of supervision by community correctional services, prior to and/or post sentencing (Department of Justice 2008a; Sentencing Advisory Council 2009, 2014; Steering Committee for the Review of Government Service Provision 2014).

(A) UNSENTENCED

- *Supervised bail*: determination of sentence is deferred and the offender is granted bail while they participate in an intervention program (personal development, training or rehabilitation). This disposition generally requires the offender to be under community corrections supervision and may also involve residential conditions (e.g. home detention conditions or placement in a community hostel).
- *Conditionally deferred sentence/conviction*: a court (generally a specialist court such as a drug court) defers passing a sentence, or indeed conviction, pending participation by the offender or accused person in a rehabilitation program. Under this option, the person is placed under the supervision of community corrections.

(B) SENTENCED

- *Fine/conversion order*: A person who has previously been sentenced to a fine may apply to the court to have it converted to a Community Based Order (CBO) (see below). Alternatively, a Community Service or Community Work Order may be imposed in default of payment of a fine (see below).
- *Community Service/Community Work Order*: where a person has been convicted of an offence punishable by imprisonment, the court may elect instead to order that the person perform community work, for a specified number of hours, as reparation to the community for the offence and also make useful contacts that will serve to reconnect the person to mainstream society. This sentencing option does not generally include a rehabilitative component.
- *Probation/Community Based Order/Community Correctional Order (CBO/CCO)/Good Behaviour Bond (GBB (supervised or non-supervised))*: while variously described across jurisdictions, this class of disposition generally equates to a sentence that is served by an offender in the community on a promise or surety (recognisance or bond) to be of good behaviour for a specified period. Aside from GBBs, where supervision is discretionary, offenders are required to attend regular meetings with a community corrections/parole officer to discuss the factors underlying their offending behaviour and develop an individualised case management plan. A variety of conditions may also be attached to this disposition, generally a combination of treatment programs and/or work. Special conditions may also be attached, including submission to urinalysis (alcohol and drug detection), fitting of an alcohol ignition interlock system (for drink-driving offences) and medical, psychological or psychiatric assessment.
- *Supervised suspended sentence*: this is a prison term that is suspended (wholly or partially depending on the severity of the offence), subject to the condition of good behaviour (e.g. not to commit another offence) and supervision, for a specified period (in South Australia, supervised bonds may also have a suspended sentence component).
- *Drug treatment order*: this combines a term of imprisonment with drug treatment, except the term of imprisonment is suspended. If an offender successfully completes the specified treatment program,

they will not serve any time in prison; however, freedom of movement and association is controlled via a process of strict supervision.

- *Intensive Corrections Order/Intensive Supervision Order*: a sentence of imprisonment served in the community under intensive supervised treatment, education and unpaid community work arrangements (up to 12 hours per week). There are a number of core conditions that an offender must comply with, but the courts have the option of imposing special conditions specific to the needs of the offender and may also impose other movement and association restrictions (see non-association and place restriction orders below).

CUSTODIAL/PART-CUSTODIAL ORDERS

In keeping with the philosophy of decarceration, these are considered back-end community-based measures, in that they are 'custodial' in nature (involving some loss of liberty), but serve as 'substitutional sanctions' to imprisonment (Freiberg & Ross 1999). That is, upon imposing a sentence of imprisonment upon an offender, they empower the courts to alter the form and/or duration of that imprisonment. While the offender may serve part of, or their entire, sentence within the community, they are subject to a more stringent regimen of supervision and therapeutic intervention during their period of confinement and/or post release than otherwise available under non-custodial sentencing options (Sentencing Advisory Council 2009, 2014; Steering Committee for the Review of Government Service Provision 2014).

(A) SENTENCED

- *Home Detention Order*: an offender is ordered to serve part of or their entire sentence at home (this is therefore both a front- and back-end option), subject to certain requirements or conditions (see Box 26.1). While offenders may still participate in employment and maintain family and community ties, their freedom of movement is significantly restricted. Offenders are subject to a monitoring system, as well as observing a strict curfew and submitting to random breath and urine tests. The idea here is that the offender is in effect a prisoner in their own home rather than being placed in a secure, mass correctional facility.
- *Compulsory Drug Treatment Detention*: repeat male offenders with long-term illicit drug dependency, crime and imprisonment are ordered to serve their sentence in compulsory drug treatment detention (18 months to 3 years), during which time they receive a therapeutic program of drug treatment and rehabilitation to address offending behaviour. The program progressively moves offenders from closed detention to semi-open detention and, finally, community custody, with active linkages to education and employment, income support, healthcare, housing and other services.
- *Periodic Detention Order (PDO)*: this allows an offender to live within the community most of the time, keeping their job and family contacts, while serving a period of detention (two consecutive days within a one-week period) for a period of up to three years. Offenders may also be required to undertake community service activities as part of a PDO.
- *Post-prison Order (parole, release on licence)*: an offender serving out a sentence in prison is permitted to serve the remaining portion of their sentence in the community, under the supervision of a parole or correctional services officer. A non-association and/or place restriction order may be imposed where the court 'is satisfied that it is reasonably necessary to do so to ensure that the offender does not commit any further offences'. Prison sentences will generally specify a 'non-parole' period; this constitutes the minimum portion of the sentence that must be served in custody before an offender may apply to the Adult Parole Board to be conditionally released.

BOX 26.1   TYPES OF HOME DETENTION PROGRAMS IN AUSTRALIA AND NEW ZEALAND

Types of home detention

Home detention takes a variety of forms and is used for several different purposes. The different types of home detention include:

- *front-end detention*: where home detention is imposed by a court as a direct sentence resulting from an offence
- *back-end detention*: where home detention is imposed by the parole board on selected prisoners (those classified as non-violent and low security), as a period of supervised release following a period of incarceration
- *bail home detention*: where home detention is imposed by a court prior to sentencing as an alternative to remand or as a condition of supervised bail
- *as part of another order*: where home detention is imposed by a court as part of another order served in the community, such as a home curfew order.

Eligibility criteria

Eligibility criteria regarding suitability vary across jurisdictions, but may include:

- *Offence history*: offenders with a history of violence, sex offences, offences involving firearms or prohibited weapons, stalking, or commercial drug trafficking and family violence intervention order breaches are generally considered ineligible regardless of the nature of their current offence.
- *Distance*: offenders may be ineligible if intended residence falls outside of a specified radius of the central business district
- *Evidence of efforts to rehabilitate*: factors regarded favourably may include a clean record of mandatory or voluntary drug tests during supervision, a guarantee of employment and evidence of family or peer support.

Conditions

General conditions on an offender that guide the imposition of home detention:

- Be of good behaviour and must not commit an offence during the period of the order
- Must comply with reasonable directions of an officer.

Specific conditions of home detention that an offender must adhere to:

- The offender must reside only at an approved premise.
- The offender must remain at the approved premise at all times as agreed.
- The offender must submit to searches or things under the immediate control of the offender by an officer.
- The offender must submit to a strict curfew.
- The offender must submit to random breath and urine tests.

Monitoring

Monitoring takes various forms, including:

- offenders wearing a tamper-sensitive electronic bracelet, which interacts with a small monitoring unit attached to the telephone at the offender's residence. Supervising officers use mobile units that interact with the bracelet to check whether the offender is at an approved location
- impromptu phone or in-person checks by appropriate correctional authorities at any time (also a specific condition of home detention).

Source: adapted from Henderson (2006)

(B) PRE-RELEASE

- *Transition permits/Re-entry release order*: aims to facilitate the successful re-entry of prisoners into the community by permitting them to participate in educational, work-related or other personal development, treatment or community service activities while still serving their sentence in custody. These activities can be ordered as a precursor to release on parole or release to freedom. To be eligible, the prisoner must have been in custody under sentence for at least 12 months and be eligible for release within 6 months.

(C) POST-RELEASE

- *Post Sentence Supervision Order (also known as Extended Supervision Order (ESO))*: provides for the continued strict supervision (up to 15 years) of serious sex offenders (those assessed as being at high risk of reoffending) after they have served a custodial sentence and been released into the community. There are a number of core conditions attached to an ESO, including requirements to attend for supervision, monitoring or assessment as directed, a prohibition on changing address without approval, and a requirement to notify the authorities of any change in employment. Moreover, a parole board may impose additional, rigorous conditions, including: the use of electronic monitoring to ensure that the offender observes curfew; refusal of access to the internet; prohibitions on contact with children; random drug and alcohol testing; the requirement to be accompanied by Corrections staff when leaving the registered residence; and the establishment of 'no go' zones that the offender is not permitted to enter.
- *Post Sentence Detention Order (Continuing Detention Order)*: provides for indefinite, post-sentence detention of offenders deemed to be highly likely to reoffend, and therefore classified as 'dangerous', 'since they pose an unacceptable risk to the community' (customarily violent, sexual offenders). The intention here is not punishment of the offender, but prevention of future offending and community protection.

The above sentencing options may be imposed on an offender as stand-alone measures, or as part of a combination sentence, which involves the imposition of an additional penalty, such as the payment of a fine or some type of order, including:

- *Reparation Order*: where the offender is required to pay the victim some amount of compensation for the harm done (compensation order) and/or they are required to return property to the victim (restitution order)
- *Non-association/Non-contact Order*: where the offender is prohibited from associating with a specified person for a specified term. A limited non-association order prohibits personal contact, while an unlimited non-association order extends to all forms of contact and personal association, including post, telephone, facsimile and email
- *Place Restriction Order*: where the offender is prohibited from visiting or frequenting specified places or districts
- *Rehabilitation Program Order*: where a domestic violence offender is required to take part in a structured treatment program designed to reduce the likelihood of reoffending.

The above mentioned orders (excluding Rehabilitation Program Orders) may also be imposed on young offenders in some jurisdictions. Intermediate sentencing options are also available for juvenile offenders. However, in keeping with the philosophy of reserving custodial sentences as a measure of last resort, these are almost unexceptionally 'alternative' (e.g. Community Service Order, good behaviour bond, probation or juvenile conferencing) rather than 'substitutional' sanctions (e.g. the use of home detention as a measure additional to detention in a youth training centre).

Overall, community-based intermediate sentencing options (custodial and non-custodial) can be classified as falling into one or more of the following categories (see Figure 26.1):

- *reparation*: dispositions that require the offender to undertake unpaid work
- *supervision*: dispositions that require some level of formal management and supervision by agents of community correctional services
- *restricted movement*: dispositions that involve restricting an offender's freedom of movement within the community through some form of intensive supervision and/or electronic monitoring (e.g. home detention).

FIGURE 26.1   AVERAGE DAILY COMMUNITY CORRECTIONS POPULATION, 2012 AND 2013, BY TYPE OF ORDER (NUMBER)

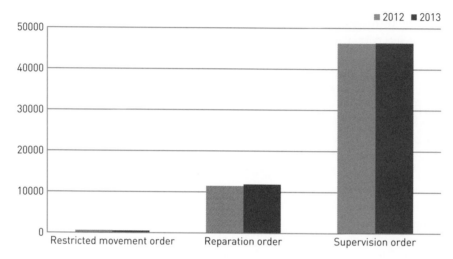

Source: ABS (2014g)

There are differences in both the nature and extent of reparation and supervision attached to community correctional dispositions, as well as the nature of any attached conditions and the degree of restriction imposed on a person's freedom of movement within the community (AIC 2009). These variances exist both across community-based orders generally and within particular sentencing orders across jurisdictions.

THE RATIONALE FOR COMMUNITY CORRECTIONS

The overall mission of community corrections as a specific form of justice intervention is informed by how punishment is viewed and what the intended outcomes of intervention are meant to be (see Worrall 1997; see also Chapter 24). The desired outcomes will vary not only in relation to the relative prioritisation of intended sentencing objectives (e.g. punishment, deterrence (general and specific), denunciation, community protection and rehabilitation), but also in accordance with the broad orientation or philosophical objectives of the community correctional sanction imposed; that is, whether it is intended to divert from imprisonment (alternative sanction) or to alter the form or duration of imprisonment (substitutive sanction).

PHILOSOPHICAL OBJECTIVES

The main philosophies of community corrections have changed considerably over time, but generally include two main orientations (White & Tomkins 2003b: 2):

- *Community incapacitation*: emphasises concepts of community safety and protection through implementation of offender control practices. This involves restricting offender movement and/or association, as well as intensive monitoring and supervision of offenders in community settings. The aim of community corrections, from this perspective, is to keep offenders under close surveillance and to thereby deter them from reoffending.
- *Community-level rehabilitation*: directs efforts to changing offender thoughts and behaviour in positive ways, as well as improving community relationships through the use of supportive participatory measures. The aim of community corrections, from this point of view, is to prevent recidivism through individualised behaviour modification, which promotes personal development and enhanced capabilities. This is generally achieved via some type of therapeutic and/or skills-based intervention and the supported, graduated transition into society of those imprisoned.

Within community supervision, there may be a tension in balancing what appear to be conflicting objectives underlying 'control and contain' strategies (which preference the retributive, deterrent and community protection dimensions of punishment) and 'rehabilitative' strategies (which assist the offender to reform and reintegrate into society). So, too, there may be differences between interventions designed as prison alternatives and those related to post-prison transitions. Nevertheless, how community corrections workers actually carry out their work will largely be dictated by the dominant service philosophy at any point in time. A third service philosophy, restorative justice, is also starting to emerge and has been especially influential in the area of juvenile justice.

- *Restorative justice*: presents as an alternative to retributive justice, in that is focuses on building stronger communal relationships through positive and constructive offender activities: 'Restorative justice involves the offender in activities intended to repair the harm to victims and the wider community. The aim of community corrections, based upon restorative assumptions, is to restore harmony through the offender doing something for and by themselves to make things better in the community. The emphasis is on improving the well-being of offender, victim and community' (White & Tomkins 2003b: 2).

While there are many models of restorative justice (see Box 26.2), they all seek to reintegrate offenders back into the community while empowering those most affected by the harm (victims, families and communities) through their direct involvement in the harm-reparation process (Wing Lo et al. 2006). Restorative justice elevates the role of the victim and the community to a prominent, respectful and equal position in the justice process (alongside offenders) and seeks to engender a sense of shame and responsibility in the offender. It also seeks to achieve effective and practical outcomes for the offender, including enabling positive life outcomes and preventing reoffending (Maxwell et al. 2004).

While there is no solitary set of objectives or characteristics common to community corrections across Australia, in general, corrective services aim to:

> provide a safe, secure and humane custodial environment and an effective community corrections environment in which prisoners and offenders are effectively managed, commensurate with their needs and the risks they pose to the community. Additionally, corrective services aim to reduce the risk of re-offending by providing services and program interventions that address the causes of offending, maximise the chances of successful reintegration into the community and encourage offenders to adopt a law-abiding way of life. (Steering Committee for the Review of Government Service Provision 2014: 8.1)

BOX 26.2 RESTORATIVE JUSTICE

There is a range of specific models and institutional approaches to restorative justice around the world, from family group and community conferencing, through to circle sentencing and victim–offender mediation programs (Bazemore 1997; Braithwaite 1999; Daly & Hayes 2001; Harding & Potter 2003; Wing Lo 2006). Some approaches are based upon moral categories (e.g. reintegrative shaming) where the aim is to shame the offence, while offering offenders forgiveness (Braithwaite 1989). Others are based upon strategic assessment of offenders and events (e.g. balanced restorative approach), where the aim is to design interventions that best address issues of offender accountability, competency development and community safety (Bazemore 1991; Bilchik 1998; Shaw & Wierenga 2002). Some approaches focus almost exclusively on meeting victim needs (usually via some method of restitution or compensation involving the offender); others place emphasis on widespread community engagement in tackling underlying problems and issues, of which offending is but one specific manifestation (see Chapter 27).

The most popular example of the restorative justice approach in Australia is the juvenile conferencing model (see also Chapter 21). This type of intervention is based on the idea of bringing the young offender (once they have made the necessary admissions of guilt), the victim, and their respective families and friends together in a supported environment (a conference), chaired by an appropriate independent adult (juvenile justice worker or police officer). Collectively, the group goes through the reasons for the crime, the harms, losses and emotions suffered, and the best ways to repair the damage caused and prevent future reoffending. Usually some kind of apology is made by the offender to the victim, as well as the payment of some form of restitution to, or the undertaking of work for, the victim or the community, and/or attendance at counselling, education or training programs.

Under the restorative justice umbrella, there are differences between those who see restorative justice as, essentially, a form of diversion from the formal criminal justice system and those who view it as a potential alternative to that system (see Bazemore Erbe 2004; Bazemore & Walgrave 1999). An example of the latter approach is the Restorative Resolutions Program (Maloney & Lloyd 2003). Commencing in Manitoba, Canada, in 1993, the program involves the development of an alternative (community-based) sentencing plan for adult offenders facing a prison term of at least 9 months. The plan, which is submitted to the sentencing judge for consideration, aims to address victim concerns as well as the individual needs of the offender. While not dissimilar to a pre-sentence report prepared by Probation Services, the plan differs with regards to the involvement of the offender, the victim and the community in the development process. Program participants are held accountable in their own communities and are assisted to take responsibility for their actions.

Whatever the specific differences, the central thread underlying restorative justice is the spirit within which 'justice' is undertaken—the intent and outcomes of the process are meant to be primarily oriented toward repairing harm that has been caused by a crime, and this means working to heal victims, offenders and communities that have been directly injured by the crime (Bazemore & Walgrave 1999; Zehr & Mika 1998). While critics claim that restorative justice is a soft option, proponents suggest it is more successful in stemming recidivism vis-à-vis traditional justice approaches (see, for example, Bonta et al. 2002; Fields 2003).

In practice then, the explicit service rationale for any particular community corrections system generally incorporates elements that acknowledge the importance of community safety as well as individualised assessment and treatment to tackle offender needs and risks; and, in doing so, enhance offender transition into the community and prevent recidivism. Different demands on community corrections, reflecting quite different philosophical orientations, can, however, create major tensions within a service.

PRACTICAL IMPERATIVES

Quite aside from the various philosophical orientations against which community correctional outcomes may be discerned and evaluated, there are two discrete, though interrelated, practical drivers of community corrections (Sentencing Advisory Council 2009):

- *Reducing prison overcrowding:* while recognising the greater rehabilitative potential of community-based corrections relative to imprisonment, Western governments began embracing community corrections from the mid-twentieth century, principally as a check against the rapidly expanding prison population and its corollary, prison overcrowding.
- *Punishing more economically:* proponents of community corrections emphasise that it is a lower-cost alternative to traditional incarceration, both in absolute and relative terms.

Much of what occurs within community corrections is influenced by the general political climate. It has been argued that in recent years in many Western jurisdictions the prevailing climate is one based upon a 'culture of severity', with a strong emphasis on punitive law-and-order politics (Cunneen et al. 2013; Hughes et al. 1998; Pratt 2007). This can affect the operation of community corrections in at least two different ways. First, the response of service providers may be to stress 'public safety' and rigorous control of offenders over all other objectives. Secondly, service providers may continue to emphasise restitution, rehabilitation and repairing of harm, but do so through the adoption of more intensive modes of work. The nature and degree of intervention on the part of community corrections will manifest either as intrusive, coercive measures designed to control offender behaviour, or as supportive, participatory measures intended to change offender behaviour in positive ways, as well as improving community relationships.

As indicated earlier, there are numerous ambiguities and contradictions in the area of community corrections and, if anything, these have intensified in recent years. Changes to the overarching political environment, in which 'law and order' has come to the fore in many jurisdictions, have placed greater emphasis on punitive rather than rehabilitative or restorative principles. Yet the latter has become the guiding diversionary philosophy in areas such as juvenile justice (see Cunneen & White 2011). Meanwhile, government concerns with fiscal matters have frequently translated into more work but fewer resources being allocated to the corrections area, a problem not uncommon across the human services (White 2002).

As the American experience seems to indicate, very often there are changes at the level of professional ideology and practice as well, and these, too, are making community corrections ever more complicated. For example, the heightened concern about victim involvement and perspectives in dealing with offenders, new procedures and instruments in risk assessment, and the slowly permeating influence of restorative justice ideals are currently being reworked into the professional lexicon and toolkits of parole and probation officers (see Burke 2001). The challenge is to construe 'good practice' within community corrections in the light of the theoretical and practical impetus of restorative principles. More broadly, where, and how community corrections fits into the overall scheme of punishment is an issue of ongoing concern.

THE IMPACT OF COMMUNITY CORRECTIONS

This section examines the 'success' of community-based sanctions in delivering against the various philosophical and practical objectives outlined earlier.

PRISON ALTERNATIVES: THE DIVERSIONARY IMPACT

An underlying humanitarian principle of 'community' corrections is that a proportion of offenders should be permitted to continue with various aspects of their lives and are therefore best managed in the community, rather than spending a lot of (or indeed any) time in prison. This implies that prison may be inappropriate for less serious classes of offender; that it may actually do more harm than good for specific categories of offenders to be incarcerated; and that such offenders do not pose a significant 'security' threat to other members of the community.

'Just deserts' proponents question the legitimacy of punishing offenders within a community context, principally on the grounds that community-based sanctions are regarded as 'soft options'; that is, they inadequately reflect the severity of the offenders' criminality and fail to command the denunciatory power enjoyed by imprisonment.

The growing popularity of intermediate sanctions in Australia and other Western jurisdictions has, in part, been attributed to their ability to provide an effective response to just deserts concerns, while achieving other key objectives, such as (Sentencing Advisory Council 2008b):

- reducing the demand for prison beds and the costs associated with building, staffing and maintaining prisons
- offering greater rehabilitative potential, thereby reducing recidivism and providing greater overall safety for the public
- providing credible and proportionately scaled punishments that reflect both the nature and intensity of the crime and society's denunciation of it.

The rationale, therefore, is to divert offenders from expensive and overcrowded prisons, while protecting the public from further offending and offering (to some extent) services that may reduce the likelihood of offending when the sentence is completed. Could it be the case, however, that community-based measures, while referred to as 'alternatives to imprisonment', might simply be used as alternatives 'to each other', rather than as measures that genuinely reduce the flow of offenders into prisons or reduce the amount of time they spend inside? In evaluating the use and diversionary impact of such sanctions, we need to investigate three broad areas: distributions of penalty, expansion or contraction of the system, and escalation of penalty.

DISTRIBUTIONS OF PENALTY

As indicated by Figure 26.2, the vast majority (63%) of all offenders managed by correctional services authorities in 2013 were under a community-based order, compared with offenders serving a term of imprisonment (37%). However, in order to determine whether community-based sanctions are really alternatives to the use of imprisonment, we would need to compare, over time, the proportion of sentenced offenders sent to prison relative to those involved in some way with community corrections.

One way in which to do this is to consider the percentage of sentences imposed across the different types of dispositions available to the court. The key questions here are which sanctions are being used by the courts, and how and if the patterns of specific use are changing over time. Specifically, the nature and distribution of orders provide some indication of whether community corrections are being directed mainly at containment, rehabilitation or restorative objectives.

FIGURE 26.2   OFFENDER'S TYPE OF CORRECTIONAL ORDER, 2013[a]

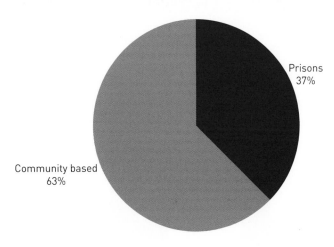

Prisons
37%

Community based
63%

n = 88,950
[a] Figures based on daily population (prisons and community corrections)

Source: ABS (2014g)

Various commentators have suggested that intermediate orders have not had the desired impact on the rate of imprisonment in Australia and, rather than displacing imprisonment, have actually intruded into the terrain previously occupied by lower-level orders; that is, they have become a substitute for fines and bonds (Cunneen et al. 2013; Freiberg 2005; Sentencing Advisory Committee 2008). As indicated by Figure 26.3, there is certainly some evidence for this proposition. Between 2006 and 2008, there was a 4 per cent reduction in the use of fines within community corrections in Australia and a 12 per cent reduction in the use of community service type orders. Within the same timeframe, supervision orders increased by approximately 3 per cent. Examining trends over time, the number of supervision orders increased by a staggering 22 per cent from 2000–01 to 2007–08, while the number of reparation orders (including fine options and community service), decreased by 40 per cent (Australian Institute of Criminology 2009; for an increase in the use of detention orders for juveniles in Tasmania, see Prichard 2010). The practice of subjecting offenders to more punitive sanctions than they may otherwise have received (simply because higher-level options exist), is commonly referred to as **net widening**, while the use of longer sentences and the attachment of conditions to community-based orders is referred to as 'sentence inflation' (Sentencing Advisory Committee 2008).

In relation to total numbers of people in correctional services and the rate of imprisonment specifically, it may well be that incarceration is not used to the same degree as previously as a court disposition relative to other sanctions. Nevertheless, the overall imprisonment rate has continued to grow nationally from 112 per 100,000 adults in 1990 to 170 per 100,000 adults in 2013 (see Chapter 25). This could be due to a number of factors, including:

- increased numbers of people going through the sanctions process as a whole (e.g. number of offenders sentenced)
- serious offenders being imprisoned for longer periods of time (e.g. leading to an overall increase in the number of people in prison)
- increasing levels of sentencing punitiveness disproportionate to levels of actual offence seriousness.

NET WIDENING
The implementation of a more severe sentencing disposition than would otherwise have been required to achieve the intended purposes of sentencing.

FIGURE 26.3   PERSONS IN COMMUNITY CORRECTIONS, 2011–13, BY TYPE OF ORDER
(NUMBER)

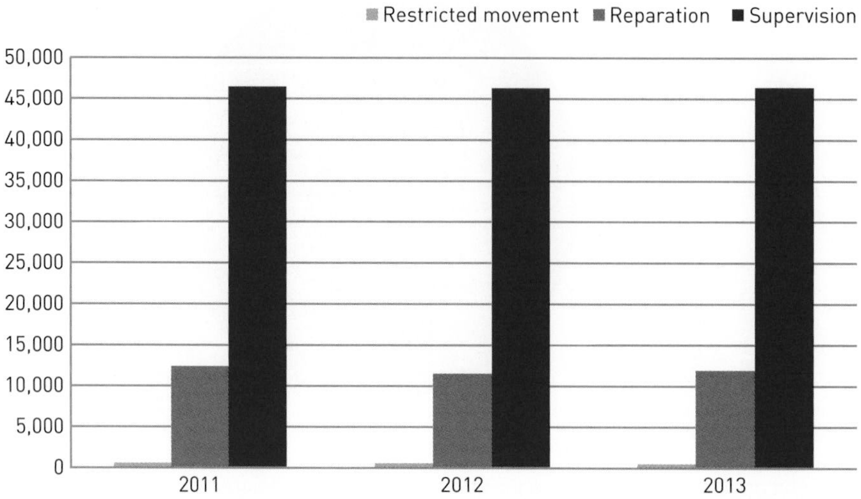

Source: ABS (2014g)

EXPANSION OR CONTRACTION OF SYSTEM AS A WHOLE

Another issue to consider is the patterns of use of community-based sanctions over time, and how these in effect may be increasing the total number of people under some kind of system control. Here we would need to combine total figures of people imprisoned and those on community corrections orders, and track any changes in each category and combined categories over time.

The prison population has grown in the 30-year period from 1984 to 2014, with the overall imprisonment rate per 100,000 of the adult population increasing from eighty-eight to 170. By contrast, both the national imprisonment rate and the average daily numbers of offenders on community correction orders has remained relatively steady over the past few years. The national imprisonment rate was 169 (per 100,000 adult population) in 2008 and 170 in 2013 (ABS 2014g, 2009). The rate of community corrections in 2013 was 306 per 100,000 adults, decreasing from 338 in 2008 (ABS 2014g; Steering Committee for the Review of Government Services 2009).

Although relatively steady in the past five years, the overall trend toward greater rather than reduced rates of incarceration (see Figure 26.4), and the fact that both the number of people in community corrections and the rate of offenders on community corrections orders have remained fairly constant, indicates that the system as a whole is tending towards expansion rather than contraction. While the specific options for alternatives to imprisonment seem to be growing, the use of such options has not translated into a significant expansion of community corrections as such. Conversely, nor has their use led to a reduction in prisoner numbers. As noted by Findlay et al. (2005: 243), '[c]ommunity corrections in most States have evolved not so much as a complete alternative to imprisonment, but rather as an appendage to it'.

Not surprisingly then, as indicated by Figure 26.5, the expansion of community corrections has failed to deliver on the promised cost savings. In fact, real recurrent expenditure on the correctional services system per head of population increased by approximately 15 per cent from 2003–04 to 2007–08 and a further 18 per cent in 2007–08, with national expenditure on correctional services

FIGURE 26.4   COMMUNITY CORRECTIONS RATES[a] AS AT MARCH 2013 AND 2014

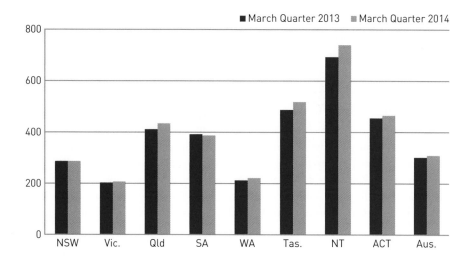

[a] Rate is the number of prisoners per 100,000 adult population, based on average number on the first day of the month

Source: ABS (2014g)

FIGURE 26.5   REAL NET OPERATING EXPENDITURE PER PRISONER PER DAY (2012–13 DOLLARS)[a, b]

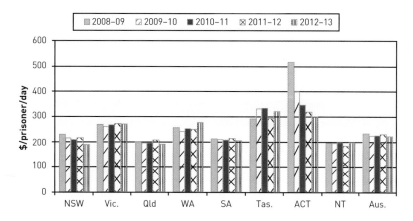

[a] Based on operating expenditure on prisons, net of operating revenues, and excluding payroll tax, capital costs, and transport and escort services expenditure where this is reported separately by jurisdictions.
[b] Data are adjusted to 2012–13 dollars using the General Government Final Consumption Expenditure (GGFCE) chain price deflator (2012–13 = 100)

Source: Productivity Commission Report on Government Services 2014. Volume C: Justice, *Steering Committee for the Review of Government Service Provision*, Melbourne.

totalling over $2.7 billion in 2007–08 and $3.2 billion in 2012–13 (Steering Committee for the Review of Government Services 2014, 2009). The potential cost savings of community-based approaches to offender management are, however, unambiguous, with the total cost per prisoner per day recorded at $297 nationally (or real net cost excluding capital costs and payroll tax of $222 per prisoner) in 2012–13, compared to $23 per community corrections client (Steering Committee for the Review of Government Service Provision 2011).

ESCALATION OF PENALTY

In looking at the relationship between custodial and community-based sanctions, it is also important to consider the potential impact of the latter on the former. As the diversionary potential of intermediate sanctions is directly related to breach rates, with some non-custodial measures towards the upper end of the hierarchy of penalties, there is the danger that the inevitable proportion of failures will actually boost prison numbers. To put it differently, a breach of conditions of a very strict order will almost certainly result in a period of imprisonment. A breach of a less strict order, however, may well result in the offender being given a second or even third chance in the community.

Overall, Australian corrections data support the proposition that offenders sentenced to community-based orders are less likely to return to the correctional services system than offenders sentenced to imprisonment (see, for example, Bartels 2009; Sentencing Advisory Committee 2008; Smith & Jones 2008; Trotter 2012; Weatherburn & Bartels 2008). However, there are two issues, in particular, that need to be addressed regarding the diversionary effectiveness of these kinds of sanctions:

- They are effective if they are used in the way for which they are designed; that is, if they are used only for offenders who would otherwise receive only short sentences of imprisonment.
- They are not effective if, as the evidence suggests, they are used for everyone but the original target group; that is, they tend to draw offenders 'up' from less intrusive sanctions lower down in the hierarchy.

The matter of alternatives to prison, therefore, must be framed in terms of pathways for individuals and in the light of systemic developments across the two major corrections sectors. More options for offenders, in terms of sentencing and sanctions, do not necessarily translate into deinstitutionalisation or decarceration at the wider systems level.

PRISONER RELEASE AND POST-PRISON TRANSITIONS

There are different kinds of release available to inmates, some of which are tied to temporary absence and others that constitute transitions towards reintegration back into the community. Access to different forms of early release varies across state and international jurisdictions, and includes:

- *temporary release*: special purpose leave that is event-specific and generally non-recurrent (e.g. to attend the funeral of a family member, to participate in a sporting event or to undergo medical treatment)
- *remissions*: reductions in sentence length that are either earned (as a reward for good behaviour) or automatic (as an incentive for good behaviour unless exhibited breaches of discipline)
- *day-leave schemes*: structured pre-release programs that seek to enhance a prisoner's prospects of successful reintegration into the community by permitting them to take advantage of educational, counselling or work-related activities outside the prison environment, while still serving their sentence in some type of secure facility

- *parole*: 'conditional early release' of the offender from prison (prisoners are generally eligible once two-thirds of a sentence have been served). The term is derived from the French notion of *parole d'honneur*, which refers to the military practice of releasing prisoners on their word that they would not again raise arms against captors.

The issue of allowing inmates the ability to re-enter the community in controlled conditions, such as day release, has been the subject of considerable debate within the community in Australia and overseas. Much of the argument has been based on the legitimacy and safety of permitting convicted offenders to access the general community before their full sentence has been completed or they are eligible for full parole; these debates are periodically ignited following much publicised escapes of prisoners on day-release or their involvement in serious offending (see, for example, ABC 2003; Martin 2009; Sheppard 2006). While much of the concern centres on the potential threats to community safety, a study by the Correctional Service of Canada (Grant & Gillis 1999) concluded that day release does not substantially increase the risk to the community. Furthermore, the authors argue that since the goal of corrections is to reintegrate the offender into the community, having some of the sentence completed in the community setting is useful. Such programs also have positive implications with regard to generating potential employment connections for offenders in the transition from prison to community.

Most criminologists would agree on the strategic value of such programs in preparing prisoners for life on the outside. By way of contrast, and as recognised in professional literature on parole and pre-release issues (see Nelson & Trone 2000), there is often negative media when, first, certain classes of prisoners are publicly exposed as being on certain leave programs, and, secondly, when particular victims are accorded considerable attention in voicing their objections to the release of 'their' prisoner. The net result of sensationalised media treatment that focuses on these types of issues is the potential de-legitimation of such programs. This is problematic for a number of reasons, ranging from their destructive impact upon socially useful prisoner transition processes through to the undermining of newly created procedures designed to enhance victims' rights in general.

IMPORTANCE OF PRE-RELEASE PROGRAMS

Part of the impetus for pre-release and parole programs, both in Australia and overseas, is the sheer number of people entering and leaving the prison systems. With major increases in prison populations in places such as Australia, the United States and the United Kingdom, increasing concern and attention have been directed at what happens to inmates once they have been released (see Petersilia 2001a,b; Shinkfield & Graffam 2009). In the United States, for example, approximately 600,000 prisoners are released into the community every year (Drucker 2001). It has been observed that 'if even a modest proportion of those returning to the community become involved in new crime, the human costs in terms of victimization and community destabilization—as well as the fiscal costs in terms of incarceration—will be staggering' (Burke 2001: 12). A key issue, therefore, is how best to achieve successful and safe re-entry for offenders, or to prevent them from entering into prison in the first place.

A recent audit of prisoners in Australia has indicated that over half (58% for non-Indigenous prisoners and 77% for Indigenous prisoners) have served a sentence in an adult prison prior to their current incarceration (ABS 2014g; see also Payne 2007), which is comparable to re-imprisonment patterns in other jurisdictions (see, for example, Langin & Levin 2002; Nadesu 2009). Moreover, increasing recidivism among the adult prisoner population has been identified as one of the reasons for the increase in the prisoner population (Productivity Commission 2014). Research indicates that community corrections have a major role to play in diminishing recidivism tendencies. Ellis and

Marshall (2000), for example, demonstrated that the use of supervised release in the United Kingdom has had a positive effect on reducing recidivism. In similar research, Grant and Gillis (1999) studied the Day Parole outcomes of federal inmates in Canada. Day Parole is a program designed to introduce inmates to the outside world prior to their ability to apply for full parole. This program allows an inmate to move into a community housing setting, and to attend educational, vocational or treatment programs, but he or she is required to return at a set time (Grant & Gillis 1999: 1). The study found a significant relationship between the use of the day-release programs and the successful completion of full parole (Grant & Gillis 1999: 45). Indeed, 85 per cent of inmates that successfully completed day parole went on to fulfil the full parole obligations without any intervention from the criminal justice system (Grant & Gillis 1999: 45).

Other research, however, cautions against a wholesale extrapolation of these promising findings to all community-based correctional orders. There is clear evidence that the effectiveness of community-based sanctions in reducing recidivism is more likely to be enhanced where punishment and deterrence-oriented approaches (e.g. supervision and electronic monitoring) are combined with prosocial or rehabilitation-oriented interventions (e.g. substance abuse treatment programs, vocational education and community service) (Aos et al. 2006; Cullen & Gendreau 2000). Furthermore, the effectiveness of individual sanctions is likely to vary according to the type of offender targeted. Hence, while intensive supervision orders with treatment conditions appear useful for reducing recidivism among high-risk offenders, they appear to be counterproductive when applied to low-risk offenders (Lowenkamp & Latessa 2002). The effectiveness of rehabilitation efforts for prisoners transitioning out of custody and onto community-based orders is considerably more complicated (see, for example, Burzycki 2005; Shinkfield & Graffam 2009).

Overall, however, such reviews and studies conclude that having offenders complete at least part of their sentence in a community setting allows them to participate more fully in rehabilitative and restorative types of programs. Cunneen and Luke (2007) also emphasise the importance of looking beyond recidivism as a measure of rehabilitative success, especially where juvenile offenders are concerned. Community-based sanctions, they argue, have a significant role to play in promoting social integration outcomes, including improved life, interpersonal and employment skills. From the point of view of programming, it is increasingly recognised that there should be better provision of an integrated transition from one part of the corrective system to another. For community corrections, in particular, recent developments also raise questions about how best to respond to issues of recidivism, and which strategic focus ought to be favoured at a practitioner level.

Getting prepared for release is essential if community reintegration is to be achieved with the most positive outcome. A significant reason why pre-release is needed is indicated in the following observations:

> When supervision works well it provides some of the ballast people need during their first months in the community, but many newly released inmates find it hard to meet the broadly defined conditions of probation and parole. Accustomed to being told exactly what to do and how to do it, they often expect their supervision officers to forge a path for them—get them a job, find the right drug treatment program. Disappointed when their unrealistic expectations are not met, some people never form trusting relationships with those who supervise them. As for the officers, they begin the process with no information about how the people they have to supervise respond to authority figures and what they want to do with their lives. (Nelson & Trone 2000: 2)

Testing the water, and getting used to forging one's own path, are vital to offender resettlement back into the community.

SCREENING INMATES AHEAD OF TIME

There may be different objectives involved in selecting who is going to be eligible for pre-release programs. Factors to take into account include, for example:

- universal programs designed so that every prisoner gets the opportunity for some type of pre-release experience (e.g. transition classes held outside the prison)
- concentration of resources on certain inmates (by identifying, for instance, only those inmates who would most likely benefit from job training, or whose abilities and learning styles are matched to the methods adopted by any given program, or whose assessed criminogenic needs are amenable to change)
- limiting service provision to people more likely to reoffend (e.g. high-risk groups identified as such on the basis of crime of conviction, criminal history, time served, age and employment history).

From the point of view of recidivism, it is important that some type of pre-release transitional program is put into place, that post-release systems are available to assist former prisoners, and that community corrections are resourced adequately in order to engage in helpful assistance. Moreover, it is essential that the high-risk groups are an integral part of this process. Eventually, we have to live with those we punish, and this includes people with particularly bad records: 'In many jurisdictions, high-risk offenders include people serving time for violent crimes or with a history of such convictions. Serving them involves taking some political risk but makes sense from a public safety perspective' (Nelson & Trone 2000: 6).

If no transitional pathway is allowed for, there is much greater likelihood that these particular offenders will reoffend—and thereby create even more victims than otherwise may be the case. Overall, the institution of parole rests on the assumption that if the state has seen fit to remove a person from society by placing them in prison, it equally has an obligation and interest in aiding their reintegration into society.

PAROLE, ASSESSMENT AND OFFENDER MANAGEMENT

One way in which to gauge the purposes of parole is to examine the reasons for the granting or denial of parole. This involves various kinds of assessment of behaviour and prediction relating to the inmate, as well as consideration of the expectations of the victim, the sentencing authority and the wider community.

PAROLE BOARDS

Offenders released from prison on parole remain under a sentence of imprisonment and, as such, at any time may be recalled to prison to serve the remaining portion of their sentence. It thus represents a variation in the conditions under which a sentence of imprisonment is served. In most jurisdictions, control of the parole process has a twofold character:

1   The executive or judiciary sets out the conditions under which an individual will become eligible for parole. These conditions may either be specified as a 'discretionary' component of the sentencing process, which enables each offender to be treated individually on their own merits (e.g. setting out the parole eligibility period), or they may be 'standardised', via statutory provisions, so that like cases are treated alike (e.g. legislation establishing a minimum parole period of 50 per cent of sentence).
2   Administrators (normally a parole board) have the task of making decisions about whether an individual is suitable for early release.

In many cases there are two parole boards—an Adult Parole Board to deal with cases in the adult jurisdiction, and a Youth Parole Board to deal with children and young people. A parole board has very broad discretionary powers in relation to decisions concerning:

- whether to grant parole or defer consideration to a later date
- the conditions that are imposed on people granted parole
- whether to cancel an offender's parole.

The board mainly sees offenders serving sentences where a non-parole period has been set (e.g. maximum sentence with minimum non-parole period), plus those prisoners who have been released on parole at an earlier point but who are before the board either for a breach matter or because they wish to be re-released.

Factors taken into consideration by a parole board include such things as (Department of Justice Victoria 2008b):

- the nature and circumstances of the offence(s)
- comments made by the judge when imposing the sentence
- the offender's criminal history
- previous history of supervision in the community
- potential risk to the community and/or the individual offender
- release plans
- reports, assessments and recommendations made by a variety of professionals, including medical practitioners, psychiatrists, psychologists, custodial staff and/or community corrections officers
- submissions made by the offender, the offender's family, friends and potential employers, or any other relevant individuals
- representations made by the victim or by persons related to the victim
- representations made by the offender or others with an interest in the case. In Victoria, for example, a Victims' Register was established in 2004 to enable victims to receive information about adult offenders who have been convicted of violent crimes against them. Victims have a statutory right to make submissions to the Adult Parole Board regarding their concerns about an offender prior to parole. When requested, the board may disclose to the victim details about the release of an offender on parole, including any special conditions of the parole (Department of Justice 2008b).

If it is considered necessary, the board will also interview the offender, or others involved in the management of the case, to assist in its deliberations.

The public perception of 'parole' and 'temporary release' is important. While most offenders do not reoffend while on parole in a serious way (although many may breach technical conditions of release such as failing a drug test, failing to report or attend treatment, or failing to obey a non-association order, the few occasions where this does happen unfortunately can influence how and under what conditions prisoners in general will be released 'early' from confinement (see also Chapter 6).

EVALUATION OF READINESS FOR RELEASE

Parole board assessments regarding prisoner readiness for release raise the issue of how best to gauge inmate behaviour. For example, one part of the prisonisation process relates to how prisoners behave themselves while in prison. From a management point of view, the concern is to provide incentives that will encourage positive behaviour while the inmate is in custody. However, in assessing whether a prisoner is 'ready' for release, we also have to be aware that different prisoners react to the prison experience in different ways (see Gosselin 1982):

- *withdrawal*: refusal of all personal participation beyond immediate presence
- *intransigence*: voluntary challenge to institution and refusal to cooperate
- *installation*: institutionalisation, whereby inmate builds up stable and relatively satisfying experience
- *conversion*: prisoner seems to adopt attitudes of administration and tries to play the role of the model inmate.

Therefore, it is important to question whether offenders should be evaluated on the basis of how they relate to the prison as an institution (e.g. a management issue), or on how they may be able to cope with life outside of the prison walls (e.g. general life skills). For example, a 'good' prisoner from prison management point of view may in fact not be in the best position to make the transition back to outside life.

Similarly, while offender-specific risk factors are important insofar as parole board decisions are concerned, it is equally important to consider the composition of the prison population and the conditions of imprisonment, and how these factors also have a number of potential consequences in terms of increasing risk. For example, as prisons come to take on an increasingly serious group of offenders, the risks associated with parole release increase. Similarly, the prison environment itself can contribute to the creation of risk through the prisonisation process (e.g. the production of violent behaviour) (see Chapter 25). There is a need, therefore, for accurate assessment of risk (i.e. appropriate ways to measure risk).

Interestingly, a New South Wales study of reoffending among parolees (Jones et al. 2006) found that while offenders tended to reoffend fairly rapidly after release on parole (approximately 25% within three months of release), Parole-Authority-issued parolees tended to reoffend more slowly than court-issued parolees. Despite recent controversy surrounding the soundness of parole board decisions, it would therefore appear that parole boards are better placed (perhaps by virtue of their access to information pertaining to offender risk factors) to assess risk of reoffending. Secondly, there is a need for high-quality supervision in the community, as well as evidence-based crime prevention programs and interventions that tackle known risk factors for reoffending among parolees, as well as offender needs (Jones et al. 2006).

RISK ASSESSMENT

Not surprisingly, then, a substantial part of community corrections work is based upon close assessment of offender needs and of the risks of the offender committing another crime. Factors that are examined include such things as:

- age at first conviction
- number of prior convictions
- alcohol usage problems
- other drug usage problems
- employment history
- family relationships
- academic and/or vocational skills
- companions and associations
- health
- mental ability
- emotional stability.

These factors are assessed in ways that attempt to provide a general profile of offender risk (see Box 26.3).

BOX 26.3   ASSESSMENT OF OFFENDER RISK

Without adequate and precise risk assessment, it is unlikely that community corrections interventions will be successful in reducing or preventing recidivism. Yet, the concept and use of 'risk' in criminal justice is highly contentious, even though in recent years it has come to dominate correctional discourses and practices. The intersection of public anxieties about offender risk and community protection has heightened concern about risk assessments and the idea that we need to make sure that the 'risky' and the 'dangerous' are identified and responded to adequately. Yet, these same assessments reinforce certain categories of people as being particularly worthy targets for intervention—the 'vulnerable' (see also Chapter 17)—without addressing the structural issues of inequality and colonialism that entrench vulnerability. Moreover, formal assessments provide a platform for highly intrusive methods of dealing with individuals including the development of risk-based post-sentence containment measures (see Cunneen et al. 2013).

One of the issues surrounding risk assessment is: what is actually being assessed? For instance, a criminogenic risk assessment specifically targets those factors directly related to the offending behaviour (e.g. alcohol use and violent behaviour). On the other hand, risk assessment based upon social factors tends to direct attention to wider contexts of health and wellbeing (e.g. poverty and unemployment). From the point of view of program orientation and implementation, the most effective forms of intervention are said to be those directed at criminogenic causes (see Bonta & Andrews 2007). Nevertheless, the social context within which these factors become significant is a critical contributor to the offending behaviour and cannot be ignored (see Ward & Maruna 2007). Research indicates that programs that seek to address offender risks and needs must cut across the full suite of variables known to influence reintegration; these factors can be conceptualised as falling within three domains: intrapersonal conditions (physical, psychological and emotional health, substance abuse and educational levels); subsistence conditions (finance, employment and housing); and support conditions (social support, formal support services and criminal justice support) (Shinkfield 2006).These issues will be discussed at greater length in Chapter 27.

Another issue relating to assessment has to do with different parts of corrective services using different assessment models and criteria. The difficulty may arise as to how to provide an **integrated offender management**; strategy if the diagnostic tools are not the same. Alternatively, the problem may simply be one of communication and articulation of different assessment projects within the overarching systems and philosophical framework.

INTEGRATED OFFENDER MANAGEMENT
A holistic and integrated system of intervention, which uses evidence-based approaches to identify, assess and treat offenders within correctional and community environments.

RESPONDING TO OFFENDERS

An accurate and comprehensive assessment of needs and risks provides the platform for program development and individual offender case management. The kinds of issues that are considered in assessing offender needs are outlined in Box 26.4.

BOX 26.4   ASSESSMENT OF OFFENDER NEEDS

- *Marital and family relationships*: for example, some dysfunction but potential for improvement
- *Academic and vocational skills*: for example, minimal skill level causing serious problems
- *Employment*: for example, unsatisfactory employment or unemployed but has adequate job skills
- *Financial management*: for example, situational or minor difficulties
- *Companions*: for example, associations almost completely negative
- *Health*: for example, disability or illness interferes with functioning but treatment is self-managed
- *Mental ability*: for example, deficiencies severely limit independent functioning; moderate or significant intellectual impairment
- *Emotional stability*: for example, emotional instability or psychiatric disorder significantly reduces adequate functioning (e.g. lashes out or retreats into self)
- *Alcohol usage*: for example, frequent abuse or serious disruption
- *Other drug use*: for example, frequent substance abuse or serious disruption
- *Community correction officer's impression of offender's needs*: for example, minimum through to maximum

Source: White & Tomkins (2003a)

Responses, which are structured, targeted and offence focused may include such things as:
- referrals to appropriate training, counselling, drug and alcohol rehabilitation, and other community-based agencies
- non-therapeutic and non-treatment programs such as the 'Cognitive Skills Program', which is designed to provide skills training to high- and medium-risk offenders.

The level of supervision and the type and intensity of programmatic response/intervention depends upon the assessment of individual risks and needs.

INTEGRATED OFFENDER MANAGEMENT

One way in which to describe service delivery in corrections today is that of 'integrated offender management' (IOM). This refers to an attempt to provide an integrated system of intervention that covers prison inmates and post-release offenders throughout the total course of their sentence. It also includes those who have been sentenced to community-based orders as well as those who have been incarcerated. The status of the offender, therefore, does not change the overall orientation of the intervention strategy.

Integrated offender management is a structured, scientific approach to offender management, which uses psychotherapeutic principles to identify and treat criminogenic motivators of crime and change offending behaviour. It relies heavily on the use of standardised instruments to generate inmate security ratings, assess offenders' criminogenic needs (e.g. living, integration, motivation, reformation and educational) and develop comprehensive offender management profiles. This approach enables the criminal justice system to use consistent and objective induction, assessment and offender (sentence planning and management) processes, and to offer a range of effective and targeted interventions matched to offender status, needs and motivation (Mellor 2002: 3; Newbold 2008: 389–91). Sentence planning is a guide for all interactions with the offender and specifically guides offender reintegration. The sentence plan is developed on the basis of information derived from the assessment processes. In essence, the higher the assessed risk of serious reoffending, the more intensively the offender is managed (Mellor 2002: 4). Essentially, this is a risk-management approach designed to enhance community protection, as well as preventing reoffending.

THROUGHCARE PRINCIPLES

The crux of IOM is that each offender ought to be treated on the basis of 'throughcare principles' (see New South Wales Department of Corrective Services 2008). These principles are premised on the idea that there is a continuous, coordinated and integrated system of offender assessment, program allocation, service provision, evaluation of program impacts, and smooth transition back into community life. Integrated offender management thus describes the total intervention process between and within institutional and community-based settings, which is designed to reduce the impact on a prisoner of the shift from prison to the community (White & Graham 2010). Within this framework, a sentence plan may be devised that basically describes the treatment, educational or vocational options available to an offender once needs and risks have been rigorously assessed. Case management describes the process of implementation of the sentence plan, and includes ongoing evaluation and review (see Merrington & Hine 2001).

For throughcare principles to operate effectively, strong strategic partnerships must be built and maintained between government and non-government agencies engaged in offender management and community reintegration. As such, key issues surrounding integrated offender management include the need for clear-cut policy guidelines regarding agency operating philosophy, staff training and development with respect to understanding the concepts and skills associated with this type of intervention system, and sufficient resources to adequately ensure that the risks and needs of offenders are actually addressed at a program level.

GOOD LIVES MODEL

It should be noted that Victoria's *Offender Management Framework* (Department of Justice Victoria 2010) supplements the risk–need approach by drawing upon the 'good lives model', a broader psychological theory of antisocial behaviour that individualises offender interventions according to determined physical, social and psychological needs see Chapter 27. This approach introduces a self-management dimension to community reintegration, which focuses on enhancing offender skills to prevent reoffending. Offender management is also underpinned by a third theory, therapeutic jurisprudence, which is concern for the wellbeing of individuals within the criminal justice system. It highlights the importance of correctional staff in engaging offenders in prosocial ways.

On a practical level, 'offender management' can refer to two different things. First is how to best target resources to meet particular offender's needs and to address pertinent risk factors. This is primarily a matter of assessment of discrete individuals, and discerning those criminogenic needs most closely associated with the offending behaviour (Roberts 2001). Second, offender management refers to allocation of resources relative to specific groups of offenders. In this case, the key issue is how best to assign particular categories of offender greater attention and resources than others, based upon risk and needs assessment. It is assumed that, on the basis of past experience and offender profiles, that some offenders will require greater care and intervention than others.

From a management perspective, it is necessary to prioritise resource allocation in the most effective manner. This might take the form of a 'casebank' model. This refers to an organisational method of allocating resources in which non-targeted offenders are ranked in order of level of risk and needs, and as individuals move through the system, resources that have been freed up are distributed on the basis of the ranking order (Clawson 2001). Offenders who are deemed to be low risk and low needs may receive very little in the way of direct supervision or intervention by correctional services staff. Conversely, those deemed to be high risk and high need will be allocated supervisory staff and program support as a matter of priority. They collectively constitute targeted cases, and are thus not considered suitable for the casebank model.

Selection of programs for offenders depends upon the quality of the assessment process, the ways in which offender interventions are prioritised and allocated, and the availability of programs. There may be conflicts over whether to put time, energy and resources into 'generic' programs (e.g. employment or education) or 'specialist' programs (e.g. anger management and sex offender). Much hinges upon whether trained professional staff is available to offer various types of programs. So, too, unless community-based programs are evaluated and monitored closely, there is no way of really knowing how a program is assisting an offender or is working to reduce the likelihood of reoffending. One essential question to ask is: does the program address the criminogenic factors giving rise to the original offending behaviour?

Long-established ways of doing things, reliance on the same old community networks, and limited staff development opportunities are all factors that influence how offenders are dealt with at a day-to-day level. Moreover, there is often tension between 'rehabilitation' and 'control' objectives and imperatives at the coalface of corrective services. One consequence of this is that, regardless of 'official' institutional philosophy, there may be resistance among some staff to the adoption of innovative methods of working with offenders. Alternatively, the institution may acquire the new language of corrections for policy document purposes (we do 'case management'), but the actual practices may reflect traditional or conventional corrections agendas (our main task is containment of the offender). The development of appropriate offender services frequently reflects these ambiguities and conflicts over purposes.

QUESTIONING COMMUNITY-BASED SOCIAL CONTROL

The so-called community-based forms of social control are extensive. They relate to a wide scope of activities in the area of criminal justice, and include a wide diversity of agencies, centres, services and programs that sit beyond the formal community correctional system and directly involve the community in some way or other. Concrete examples of community-based interventions include, among other things:

- pre-trial (family group conferencing and community panels)
- releases (weekend, work, study, supervised and unsupervised)
- community residential centres and supported accommodation projects
- homes (foster and group)
- houses (halfway and quarter-way)
- forestry camps, and wilderness and outward bound projects
- centres (attendance, day, training, drop-in and shopfront)
- hostels, shelters and boarding schools
- weekend detention and other forms of partial detention
- community service orders and reparation schemes
- citizen alert programs, hotlines, listening posts and radio-watches
- use of pre-emptive test scales and diagnostic devices
- electronic monitoring.

Thus, when thinking of the justice system, we should not think merely of police, courts and prisons; we must think also of the proliferation of community programs and institutions.

In specific terms, problem areas can be identified in each phase or point of intervention. For example, we might ask whether community corrections actually prevent recidivism, or whether alternatives to formal adjudication actually reduce the number of court cases and/or prison sentences. Regardless of the specific rationale behind the 'destructuring impulse', it has been argued that at a general level much of the swing toward community-based alternatives and strategies has not in fact 'worked' in the way it was supposed to (see Chan 1992; Cohen 1985; Polk 1987). The point of such measures is, at the level of overt rationale or theory, to decrease the impact and intrusions of the formal criminal justice system, while achieving the same or better effects than the traditional structures. Critics argue, however, that the opposite has been the case.

For example, Cohen (1985: 44) argues that such moves, while defended on the basis of being less intrusive and less coercive than formal criminal justice institutions such as prisons, serve as a form of net widening. Specifically, it is argued that we need to be aware of and evaluate the impacts of apparently benign 'community-based' programs such as those described above. Using a net analogy, Cohen (1985) points out that:

- There is an increase in the total number of 'deviants' getting into the system in the first place and many of these are new deviants who would not have been processed previously (wider nets).
- There is an increase in the overall intensity of intervention, with old and new deviants being subject to levels of intervention (including traditional institutionalisation) that they might not have previously received (denser nets).
- New agencies and services are supplementing rather than replacing the original set of control mechanisms (different nets).

In other words, the old institutions have remained (e.g. courts and prisons) while the overall system has expanded to incorporate the community-based institutions of control. What appears to have happened in many cases is that distinctions are being drawn between 'hard' and 'soft' offenders, and traditional criminological measures are still implemented in an effort to deal with the hard offenders, but community options are now available for the soft offenders. This implies that there has been an intensification of control over the soft offenders, and, in essence, an unnecessary drawing-in of more people into the criminal justice net (Sentencing Advisory Council 2008b).

Cohen (1985) argues that only traditional diversion is true diversion in the sense of diverting from the system. The new diversion—for better or worse—diverts into the system. The processes of net-widening occur at a variety of different levels, from preventative programs at the community level (e.g. police truancy patrols) to a greater emphasis on community surveillance and responsibility for itself (e.g. neighbourhood watch) through to the major expansion of juvenile conferencing.

However, rather than treating as suspect every effort to shift some of the activities and functions of the formal justice system to the informal community-based agencies and programs, Chan (1992) cautions us that each development must be evaluated in its own right. That is, not every initiative in fact constitutes a further net widening of social control, nor does every community-based program reflect a strict 'crime control' model of law and order. Chan (1992) argues that each mechanism of decarceration or diversion must be analysed in a way that separates out the actual practice from the rhetoric used to justify it. Furthermore, it is argued that not all state intervention or policy implementation is necessarily oriented to 'negative' social control, and if community-oriented programs are simply criticised in total, then we are left with only the much more harsh and socially un-redeeming measures, such as the prison.

ISSUES FOR CONSIDERATION

OPERATIONAL CONSTRAINTS

While a less-expensive option compared to imprisonment, community corrections face the same resourcing and staffing challenges confronted by correctional services, specifically the quantum of money available for specialist training, development of professional expertise, volume and reten-tion of staff, and types and availability of programs (White 2004). While throughcare is a sound concept, in practice community correctional officers struggle to locate the resources required post-release, and this is often compounded by poor communication practices between prisons and community corrections (Baldry 2007). Community corrections ought not to be seen as the 'poor cousin' of prisons. Rather, to be socially useful and to 'work' in a positive way, community correc-tions needs greater expansion of an already small funding base in order to ensure suitable case-loads, and efficient and effective implementation of integrated offender management practices.

If resources are not forthcoming to ensure an effective community corrections sector, and if intensive supervision and support is not provided in the prisons to those who most need them, then reoffending is guaranteed to stay the same or increase. The net result of this is pressure to build more facilities—to expend capital on physical infrastructure—in order to house those who otherwise could be making a contribution to society, rather than being a drain on the public purse.

COMMUNITY CORRECTIONS: THE HIDDEN PERILS

The use of diversionary schemes has tended to be biased against Indigenous people, who are drawn into the formal system much more quickly and more deeply than their non-Indigenous counterparts (Cunneen 2001; Cunneen & Luke 1995; Gale et al. 1990). Interestingly, Aboriginal young people appear to be under-represented in the use of juvenile diversion schemes (Polk 2003). Some attempts are being made to establish community alternatives to imprisonment that make sense to members of specific Indigenous communities from the point of view of punishment, repa-ration and rehabilitation. The scale and nature of community options designed to meet the specific needs and issues of Indigenous people requires much more analysis and evaluation (see, espe-cially, Cunneen et al. 2013; Blagg 2008a).

More generally, it can be argued that the rhetoric of 'community' can cloud the specific impacts, processes and institutional arrangements impinging upon citizens who may or may not have offended. The term 'community' implies consensus, general social approval and positive out-comes. However, we need to critically evaluate just who the 'community' actually is, which mem-bers of the community are making the crucial decisions concerning law and justice, and whose interests are represented in the general community-based programs. There are major differences, for example, between an approach that sees offender reform as the main goal, and one that sees the goal as being offender reintegration. The first demands that the offender change; the second accepts that, in addition to this, the community itself will need to offer acceptance, support and opportunities for the offender.

The relationship between the state and community-based organisations and agencies also warrants a close examination. For instance, far from being somehow more democratic, or grass-roots-oriented, most community programs are controlled directly, or through financial means, by the formal agents of the criminal justice system. If anything, 'community' often simply refers to low-cost ways to process greater numbers of people through legal processes and punishment measures. How and if this occurs in specific jurisdictions is of critical importance in any evaluation of whether such initiatives constitute an alternative, or whether they are an adjunct, to the existing formal institutions.

The advent of home detention as an alternative to institutional imprisonment is a case in point. The 'electronic ball and chain' (Gibbs & King 2003: 2), which enables homes to be regarded as potential prisons, introduces, for all practical purposes, an almost unlimited capacity for offender control and surveillance (Feiner, cited in George 2006). By implicating offenders' families in the monitoring and enforcement of conditions of the order (curfews and restrictions on gambling, drinking and associating with acquaintances), they are rendered veritable unpaid jailers, shouldering significant responsibility for the prevention of reoffending, often under the guise of free consent. In reality, the prospect that a loved one faces imprisonment, should consent to participate in home detention arrangements be denied, serves to mitigate free 'choice'. Numerous commentators have noted the significant, though unintended, consequences for family members living under home-detention arrangements, including feelings that they too are under surveillance and control, tantamount to serving a sentence alongside the detainee; a sense of burden in ensuring the detainee is not sent back to prison; and reinforcement of traditional gender roles (George 2006; Gibbs & King 2003; Martinovic 2007).

RE-ENTERING THE COMMUNITY: THE BATTLE FOR PUBLIC ACCEPTANCE

Public acceptance remains one of the biggest challenges confronting offenders re-entering the community, especially and increasingly in the case of sex offenders. While there is some recent indication of growing community support for community-based sentences in Australia (Gelb 2008), community-based alternatives do not enjoy widespread acceptance among the general public. This ongoing opposition manifests itself in various ways. In particular, communities are generally hostile to the idea of having halfway houses or residential centres for law violators situated within their neighbourhoods for fear that crime will rise and adjacent property values will decline. This is perhaps one of the reasons why the New South Wales government decided in 2008 to situate virtually all of its Community Offender Support Programs (residential centres for offenders on community-based orders) either in the grounds or adjacent to correctional centres (Weelands 2009).

CONCLUSION

This chapter has provided an overview of trends and processes related to community corrections. Questions can be asked regarding the specific place of community corrections within the overall criminal justice system—both in terms of its role as an alternative to imprisonment, and in regards to post-prison transitions. More work needs to be done, for example, on evaluation of community corrections programs, especially if particular polices, programs or approaches are touted as 'doing good' by reducing offender recidivism and repairing harm to victims and communities.

The appeal of community-based programs is understandable given the limitations and barriers associated with the formal court process, and the failures of the traditional methods of punishment such as the prison. In addition to raising specific questions regarding issues such as net widening and what is meant by the notion of 'community' to begin with, there is another issue that also underlies this chapter; that is, if the 'community' is so positive or therapeutic, and if the point of community intervention is to reintegrate the offender, then how did the offender get where they did in the first place? We might well ask, is the 'community' the source of the problem, as well as its solution?

Further research is needed into the advantages of new alternatives in community corrections; for example, electronic monitoring and attendance centres. With a better educated public, more informed government and an urgent need for changes to the system, community corrections will undoubtedly become an even more significant aspect of the criminal justice system.

The importance of appropriately tailored community supports for offenders re-entering society post incarceration is essential to rehabilitating offenders and preventing recidivism—issues that are examined in greater detail in Chapter 27.

DISCUSSION QUESTIONS

1   Cohen (1985) asks us to think of community-based intervention as part of a large drift net, and poses a number of questions regarding the nature of this net:
    - Are we casting a bigger net than before?
    - When we cast the net are we measuring who is captured and, if so, how?
    - What is the capacity of the net to keep growing?
    - What is its density and intensity? What is the capacity of the net for change?
    - Is the net visible?
    - How does the net operate in terms of its control and management?

2   What are the advantages and disadvantages of shifting control over order/program placements (e.g. back-end transfers from prison to home detention or parole) from judges to correctional officers (probation, prison and parole authorities)?

3   What are the philosophical, ethical and legal challenges to electronic monitoring and confinement of individuals to home detention? (See Aungles 1994; Gibbs & King 2003; Keay 2000.)

4   Can offender rehabilitation and community reintegration programs sited in custodial settings legitimately claim community-based status?

5   What strategies can be adopted to further encourage community and judicial acceptance of intermediate orders as legitimate substitutes for imprisonment?

FURTHER READING

Martinovic, M. (2007) 'Home detention: issues, dilemmas and impacts for detainees' co-residing family members', *Current Issues in Criminal Justice*, 19(1): 90–104.

Prichard, J. (2010) 'Net-widening and the diversion of young people from court: a longitudinal analysis with implications for restorative justice', *Australian & New Zealand Journal of Criminology*, 43(1): 112–29.

Trotter, C. (2012) 'Effective community-based supervision for young offenders', *Trends & Issues in Crime and Criminal Justice*, No. 448, Australian Institute of Criminology, Canberra.

White, R. (2004) 'Community corrections and restorative justice', *Current Issues in Criminal Justice*, 16(1): 42–56.

Worrall, A. (1997) *Punishment in the community: the future of criminal justice*, Longman, London.

27 RECIDIVISM, REHABILITATION AND RESTORATIVE JUSTICE

CHAPTER OVERVIEW

- RECIDIVISM AND DESISTANCE
- REHABILITATION AND REINTEGRATION
- WORKING WITH OFFENDERS
- RESTORATIVE JUSTICE AND GENERATIVITY
- ISSUES FOR CONSIDERATION
- CONCLUSION
- DISCUSSION QUESTIONS
- FURTHER READING

INTRODUCTION

Recent years have seen a major expansion in the use of imprisonment in Australia (see Chapter 25). The number of people coming into prison, combined with the changing composition of prison populations (involving for example greater proportions of individuals with mental health and drug addiction problems), has raised concerns about the impact of incarceration as people leave prison and return to the community. As discussed in Chapter 26, the management of offenders within a community context, either instead of imprisonment or as part of the transition from imprisonment, is informed by different objectives. Among these is the idea of rehabilitation. Generally this involves attempts to transform the life worlds and behaviours of offenders in ways that ensure that they do not offend again. The emphasis is therefore not on punishment but how intervention can be utilised in a positive way to diminish potential criminal behaviour.

The aim of this chapter is to consider contemporary developments regarding rehabilitation, and to discuss the related area of restorative justice as this is presently institutionalised within Australia. The chapter begins by considering relevant key concepts in this area, and then explores the practical manifestation of these within criminal justice. It concludes with a discussion of the possibilities of rehabilitation in the context of coercion and penalisation.

RECIDIVISM AND DESISTANCE

The impetus for criminological and policy development in the areas of rehabilitation and restorative justice stems in part from the sheer volume of people going through contemporary corrections systems, nationally and worldwide, and the effects of this on future offending. Specifically, it is well known that putting someone into prison increases the likelihood of their reoffending. With prison numbers continuing to rise, the question is how crime and victimisation can be reduced if the system itself is simultaneously preparing the ground for yet more of the same into the future. One answer to this is to find better ways to encourage offenders to not come back. For some, this can be achieved by offering alternative pathways out of the system, and incentives to engage in prosocial rather than antisocial behaviour.

Recidivism is the name given to repeat offending. It can involve repeating the same kinds of offences (e.g. drug dealing), an escalation in the kinds of offences (e.g. from graffiti to robbery) and an increase in the number of offences. It is a common phenomenon among those who end up within the more punitive parts of the correctional system (see Chapter 25).

The accompanying tables provide some indication of how entrenched the problem of recidivism actually is. Table 27.1 demonstrates that a sizeable proportion of prisoners return to prison within two years of release. The recidivism figures go up when we consider individuals who may not return to prison but who nevertheless do return to some part of the corrections system, as indicated in Table 27.2. The third table (Table 27.3) is perhaps the most revealing. It shows that the majority of offenders in prison for serious offences have been there before. This is particularly striking in the case of Indigenous people (both male and female prisoners), who have a disproportionately high rate of recidivism.

RECIDIVISM
Repeat offending, which can involve repeating the same offences (e.g. drug dealing), an escalation in the type of offence (say, from graffiti to robbery) and an increase in the number of offences.

TABLE 27.1 PRISONERS RELEASED WHO RETURN TO PRISON UNDER SENTENCE WITHIN TWO YEARS (PERCENTAGE), 2008–09 TO 2012–13

	NSW	VIC	QLD	WA	SA	TAS	ACT	NT	AUST.
2008-09	42.9	34.0	37.9	44.7	32.2	36.4	..	47.3	40.0
2009–10	42.4	33.7	33.5	45.3	30.2	31.7	..	47.9	38.5
2010-11	43.3	37.1	35.2	44.2	29.8	36.2	NA	47.1	39.8
2011–12	42.5	35.1	37.7	36.1	29.1	36.4	40.8	52.4	39.3
2012-13	42.7	36.8	38.3	36.3	29.0	39.1	46.6	57.5	40.3

.. not applicable (NSW houses the majority of full-time prisoners sentenced in the ACT)
NA not available
Source: Report on Government Services (2014)

TABLE 27.2 PRISONERS RELEASED DURING 2010–11 WHO RETURNED TO CORRECTIVE SERVICES WITH A NEW CORRECTIONAL SANCTION WITHIN TWO YEARS (PERCENTAGE)[a]

	NSW	VIC	QLD	WA	SA	TAS	ACT	NT	AUST.
Prisoners returning to:									
prison	42.7	36.8	38.3	36.3	29.0	39.1	46.6	57.5	40.3
corrective services[b]	47.9	45.3	43.5	43.2	41.0	50.6	58.4	58.4	46.4

[a] Refers to all prisoners released following a term of sentenced imprisonment including prisoners subject to correctional supervision following release; that is, offenders released on parole or other community corrections orders. Data include returns to prison resulting from the cancellation of a parole order.
[b] Includes a prison sentence or a community corrections order.
Source: Report on Government Services (2014)

TABLE 27.3 PREVIOUS IMPRISONMENT BY CURRENT OFFENCE AND INDIGENOUS STATUS, 30 JUNE 2013

	INDIGENOUS		NON-INDIGENOUS	
	Number	%	Number	%
Homicide	506	56.7	2,317	32.2
AICI (Acts intended to cause injury)	2,856	78.6	3,378	54.7
Sexual assault	715	61.0	2,791	26.1
Robbery	831	74.1	2,161	60.5
UEWI (Unlawful entry with intent)	1,306	80.0	2,311	76.9
Theft	279	79.2	953	66.9
Illicit drug offences	147	62.6	3,437	32.8

Source: ABS (2014g)

The question, therefore, is not how to get people into prison; it is how to keep them out of prison once they have served their term. The answer lies both in preventing people from being put into prison in the first place (through various diversionary schemes and therapeutic justice measures—see Chapters 20, 22 and 26), and in building platforms for them upon release that enable them to lead crime-free lives. In either case, the emphasis is on 'rehabilitation', since this is about changing the offender and the offender's circumstances in ways that will allow them to desist from offending.

DESISTANCE
A central concept in life course or criminal career criminology. It refers to the social process in which an offender de-escalates and ultimately ceases taking part in further criminal or antisocial behaviour.

The concept of **desistance** is clearly a central goal in the rehabilitation endeavour. Desistance is 'a behavioural term meaning the absence of repeated behaviour among those who had established a pattern of such behaviour' (Maruna 2012: 79), and it refers to ceasing and refraining from crime. Desistance is not an event but a process; one that belongs to the desister themselves (McNeill 2006). Some give up crime for a time, with lapses or relapses along the way, while others give up and never return. How and why people change and ultimately stop offending over the life course is related to how services, structures and social relations within and beyond the criminal justice system can be reconfigured to successfully support change (see, for example, Farrall & Calverley 2012b, 2006; Graham & White 2015; McNeill et al. 2012a; Maruna 2012).

There are three substantive theoretical perspectives that explain how and why people stop offending (Graham & White 2015):

1. *Ontogenic desistance* theories: these highlight the age–crime curve, which demonstrates how crime is disproportionately committed by young people under the age of 30, suggesting most people (even persistent offenders) grow out of crime and desist as part of the maturation process (Kazemian 2007; Maruna 2001; Uggen 2000).

2. *Sociogenic desistance* theories: these suggest desistance is associated with the changing social bonds and informal social controls related to the life course transition to adulthood; for example, joining sporting or social groups, 'securing meaningful employment, developing successful intimate relationships, investing in becoming a parent' (McNeill 2012b).

3. *Identity theories* of desistance: these highlight the subjective dimensions and changes associated with human development and social bonds. For example, Stevens (2012: 527) describes this subjective process as one of 'purposive and agentic reconstruction of identity and narrative reframing, so

that a "new" and "better" person emerges whose attitudes and behaviours cohere with long-term desistance from crime.'

Desistance theories include both psychological and sociological emphases, and are concerned with those processes (and outcomes) whereby people desist or refrain from offending once a career or life course pattern of offending has been established. The concept of desistance as *outcome* is measured predominantly by reconviction data (e.g. repeat offending or recidivism). The concept of desistance as *process* is gauged predominantly by narrative data (e.g. what individuals feel and perceive; how they make meaning of their lives). The desire and propensity to desist or to engage in offending is linked to both structural and personal influences (Barry 2006). In general, there tends to be 'persisters' and 'desisters' when it comes to crime and much of this is age as well as circumstance related. The point of intervention is to break the cycle of reoffending by addressing the factors associated with it. This is the essence of rehabilitation.

REHABILITATION AND REINTEGRATION

The resurgent interest in **rehabilitation** is based upon not only a concern to stop offenders from reoffending, but also to smooth the path of re-entry into the community after time spent in prison. It is thus about institutional transitions as well as personal change. The more able a person is to adjust back into the community, the better are their chances of reintegrating in a manner that is crime-free. The pains of imprisonment can be partially offset by providing support for offenders as they transition back to mainstream society.

Rehabilitation and reintegration is not only about putting the right program elements in place or choosing the right approach. It is also about the philosophy and the politics of intervention generally (see Graham & White 2015). For instance, supporting offenders in making a new life for themselves is not about rewarding them for their misbehaviour; it is an acknowledgement of the causal reasons for the type of offending that most frequently comes to the attention of the state. As this book has demonstrated, it is the most disadvantaged and vulnerable sections of the population who commit certain kinds of crime, and who are most likely to end up within the criminal justice system. How to break this pattern is of great importance, not only at the pragmatic level of preventing future offending, but also in regards to the ideals of social justice.

A suitable intervention strategy might, for example, be premised upon the idea that while offenders are in many cases not *socially responsible* for their actions they nevertheless bear a *moral responsibility* for the harms they cause. This **duality of responsibility** has certain practical implications (White & Graham 2010):

* First, it means that offender support is a societal imperative, given the personal background and social disadvantages of most offenders. As such, rehabilitation demands that significant community resources be put into changing the life circumstances and social opportunities of offenders. Society has to give something to the offender in order for that individual to move beyond offending.
* Secondly, responsibility of a moral kind requires that individual offenders should have an interest in making things right, in repairing the harm, in addressing the wrongs which they have perpetrated. Rehabilitation in this context thus demands something from the offender themselves; the offender has to give something back to society.

REHABILITA-TION
A therapeutic intervention designed to give offenders the opportunity, through appropriate treatment, to rehabilitate and redeem themselves, and to ameliorate their behaviour, so that upon release they can reintegrate into society in a productive and law-abiding fashion.

DUALITY OF RESPONSIBILITY
This refers to the notion that addressing the causes of crime and offending is a societal-level responsibility as well as one that individual offenders have to take responsibility for; each therefore must be included in any discussion of the 'crime problem'.

To appreciate the first point, we can reconsider the social context and backdrop to much offending (see Chapter 7). In summary, there is a complex but demonstrated relationship between low socio-economic status and offending. This relationship is reinforced under contemporary corrective services regimes insofar as prisons and community corrections do not have adequate resources, trained staff, effective programs and variety of services to counter the social disadvantages that weigh so heavily on those who feature the most within the criminal justice system.

WORKING WITH OFFENDERS

RESTORATIVE JUSTICE
An approach to dealing with offenders that emphasises repairing harm, and involving victims and communities as well as offenders in the reparation process. Restorative justice offers hope that opportunities will be enhanced for victims, offenders and their immediate communities.

Once a person has been drawn into the formal processes of the criminal justice system, several institutional approaches might be adopted in regards to their offending behaviour. The usual debate here is over a perceived split between a 'justice' approach and a 'welfare' approach. This divide has now been supplemented by reference to a third path—that of **restorative justice** (see Bazemore 1991; Cunneen & Hoyle 2010). The relationship between these three perspectives is uneasy at best, and often results in various hybrid formations at an organisational level. Nevertheless, they do signal quite different ways of doing justice regardless of the ambiguities associated with their practical implementation (see Chapters 21 and 26).

Generally speaking, the first approach emphasises such things as 'responsibility' for one's actions, punishment, control-oriented objectives and a focus on what the offender has actually done wrong. Justice is thus *something that is done to you*. Often this involves the use of incarceration in a prison or detention centre, or stringent penalties of some other kind. The idea is to get tough on the offender, and to punish them for what they have done. Rehabilitation, as such, is not on the agenda but nonetheless may be an unintended consequence of a punitive regime.

The second approach places the emphasis on the offender, and favours greater use of community-based sanctions, individual treatment services and attempts to re-socialise or address the 'deficits' within the person, which are seen to be associated with the commission of crime. In this case, justice is *something that is done for you*. The point of this intervention is rehabilitation, taking into account the vulnerability and special needs of people who offend. Most justice systems around the country embody elements drawn from the justice and welfare models.

The third approach has gained popularity in recent years and emphasises 'restorative justice'. This approach adopts a paradigm of justice that wishes to maintain a relationship of respect with the offender while making amends for the harm caused. Here, justice is *something that is done by you*. It involves active engagement by the offender in assuming personal accountability and repairing the harm wrought but also developing individual competencies.

There may be a tension between 'control and contain' strategies and 'rehabilitative' strategies. So, too, there may be differences between interventions designed as prison alternatives and those related to post-prison transitions. Nevertheless, how corrections workers actually carry out their work will largely be dictated by the dominant service philosophy—control, welfare or restoration (see Chapter 26). So, too, how justice 'innovation' is understood within the larger correctional enterprise has a bearing on what happens at the ground level (see Box 27.1).

Where resources are not forthcoming to ensure an effective (i.e. rehabilitative) community corrections sector, and where intensive supervision and support is not provided in the prisons to those who most need them, then reoffending is likely to persist or escalate. To address recidivism

BOX 27.1   INNOVATIVE JUSTICE

Dramatic shifts in penal culture in recent times, accompanied by rising incarceration rates, do not bode well for those who see imprisonment as fundamentally a costly and damaging social phenomenon. Yet, in the midst of these trends there are nonetheless examples and exemplars of projects and programs that offer hope and the possibilities for progressive, positive change.

A recent book *Innovative justice* (Graham & White 2015) provides an informed and critical assessment of projects from around the world—Australia to Chile, the United States to Italy, Singapore to Israel, Northern Ireland to Saudi Arabia—demonstrating that good things can still manifest from bad systems, and that offenders and communities can benefit from relevant and appropriate forms of intervention. Examples in the book include: programs that facilitate long-term integration of offenders into communities, including former terrorists; greening justice projects that incorporate scientific activities as well as community gardens; therapy programs that include dogs and prisoners in a mutually reinforcing positive relationship; prison–community interfaces that involve production of goods and provision of real jobs, and concerted attempts to build upon the natural entrepreneurial skills and capacities of offenders in developing legal pathways to employment and income.

It is argued that if social justice is to underpin criminal justice reforms, then questions of 'success' and 'what works' and 'what helps' demand answers from outside the logic of social control and the realm of conventional offender management. From this perspective, creative initiatives and rehabilitative approaches that seek to support desistance are innovative only insofar as they push the boundaries and transcend the corrective mission and the urge to punish. Innovative justice, in this sense, therefore has an *a priori* commitment to human rights, desistance and safety for the benefit of all stakeholders—otherwise it is not innovative and it is not just.

Source: Graham & White (2015)

requires a major commitment to changing the life circumstances of offenders. Simultaneously, this also generally means that the communal relationships and social problems that serve as the launching pad for criminal and antisocial activity must be addressed. There are two models of intervention that presently dominate the rehabilitation landscape in Australia and other jurisdictions across the globe.

RISK–NEED–RESPONSIVITY MODEL (RNR MODEL)

The dominant rehabilitation model is based on assessment and action around **risks, needs and responsivity** (see, for example, Andrews et al. 2011; Bonta & Andrews 2007). This theoretical framework, which offers an explanation for the fundamental causes of persistent offending and broad principles for addressing criminal involvement, is fundamental to rehabilitative approaches adopted in both the adult and juvenile justice correctional systems worldwide. The RNR model is based upon three guiding principles:

1   The *need* principle: the assumption is that the most effective and ethical approach to the treatment of offenders is to target dynamic and static criminogenic risk factors (broadly characterised as antisocial attitudes, antisocial associations, antisocial personality/temperament, history of varied antisocial behaviour, substance abuse and unfavourable family/marital circumstances, social /work circumstances and leisure/recreational circumstances).

RISK–NEED–RESPONSIVITY (RNR) MODEL
The dominant rehabilitation model in use today, the RNR model is based on assessment and action around risk (to society), need (targeting of dynamic risk factors) and responsivity (matching the intervention to the individual).

2　The *risk* principle: this is the assumption that the treatment of offenders ought to be organised according to the level of risk they pose to society—the higher the level of risk, the greater the dosage or intensity of treatment should be; low-risk offenders should receive minimal intervention.

3　The *responsivity* principle: this is the assumption that correctional interventions should be designed and delivered in ways that engage offenders and are matched to certain characteristics of participations, such as motivation, learning preferences and abilities and ethnic identity.

Central to the RNR model is the precept that interventions designed to assist offenders to address their engagement in crime ultimately benefits the community and that effective intervention can only be achieved through the delivery of compassionate, collaborative and dignified interventions that target risk factors for crime.

The RNR model uses psychometric testing as a key diagnostic instrument. These tests are delivered shortly after a person has entered into the corrective services system, whether this is a prison or community corrections order. On the basis of test results, individual management plans are developed that reflect the assessed risks and needs. This provides the template upon which offender profiles are developed, and behaviour is thereafter monitored in relation to progress against the key areas of risk revealed for each individual. The kinds of questions that relate to assessment of risks and needs of offenders were discussed in detail in Chapter 26. Such testing constitutes the basis for integrated offender management around the world.

Based as it is on extensive theoretical and empirical data, the RNR model has explanatory depth, empirical validity and broad practical utility (see Polaschek 2012). However, a number of weaknesses have also been identified with the model, primarily related to its perceived complexity and rigidity.

One initial critique of the RNR model is that concentrating on reducing dynamic risk factors (**criminogenic needs**) is a necessary but not sufficient condition for effective correctional interventions. The model is said, for instance, to be overly deterministic, neglecting the role of self-identity and personal agency. In practice, there are a range of interlinked contextual and ecological factors underlying optimum personal fulfilment, considered essential to treatment success, such as the existence and strength of trusting relationships, enjoyable and rewarding work, and intellectually challenging environments (Polaschek 2012; Ward & Maruna 2007; Ward et al. 2012). Furthermore, due to its highly prescriptive approach (i.e. manualised interventions), the RNR model has often been characterised as being at variance with its own 'responsivity' principle, and that consideration of the 'total person' requires tailoring of interventions in a more holistic manner.

THE GOOD LIVES MODEL (GLM)

In response to the perceived failings of the RNR model, the **Good Lives Model (GLM)** was developed as a strengths-based rehabilitative framework that shifts the focus away from criminogenic needs and other deficits and, instead, focuses on what the individual can contribute to his or her family, community and society. In essence, this perspective aims to equip offenders with the resources (both internal and external) to enable them to live good lives, or better lives; in other words, it promotes strategies that assist in the achievement of useful, purposeful and personally meaningful lives (Ward & Brown 2004; Ward et al. 2012; Wils et al. 2013).

This approach starts from the assumption that offenders are essentially persons with similar needs and aspirations to non-offending members of the community.

All humans are naturally predisposed to seek certain *primary human goods*, albeit these are weighted in accordance with different values and life priorities. These include, for example, life (including

---

CRIMINOGENIC NEEDS
The needs that are directly related to the nature of the original offending; for example, an offender may engage in burglary because of the pressures of an illicit drug habit. The criminogenic need here relates to the need for drug treatment and rehabilitation.

GOOD LIVES MODEL (GLM)
The core goals of the GLM are to promote human goods and to reduce risk. The GLM includes adopting strengths-based approaches that shift the focus away from criminogenic needs and ask what individuals can contribute to their family, community and society.

healthy living and physical functioning), excellence in play and work (including mastery experiences), agency (i.e. autonomy and self-directedness), inner peace and happiness (i.e. freedom from emotional turmoil and stress), friendship (including intimate, romantic and family relationships) and spirituality (in the broader sense of finding meaning and purpose in life). *Secondary goods* are approach goals, which provide the instrumental means of securing the primary goods. The GLM focuses on developing secondary goods as a means of attaining primary goods.

Many offenders come from families with a history of offending, have chaotic lifestyles, have problems associated with drug and alcohol use, have experienced significant personal trauma in their lives, and have little positive experience with schooling and training programs. In the light of this, the considerations that underpin applying the GLM to offender treatment include:

- Prisoners and probationers as whole individuals are more than the sum of their criminal record. They have expertise and a variety of strengths that can benefit society. Interventions should promote and facilitate these contributions whenever possible.
- At the same time, many prisoners and probationers are likely to have experienced adversarial developmental experiences, and have lacked the opportunities and support necessary to achieve a coherent life plan.
- Consequently, such individuals lack many of the essential skills and capabilities necessary to achieve a fulfilling life.
- Criminal actions frequently represent attempts to achieve desired goods where the skills or capabilities necessary to achieve them are not possessed (direct route). Alternatively, offending can arise from an attempt to relieve the sense of incompetence, conflict or dissatisfaction that arises from not achieving valued human goods (indirect route).
- The absence of certain human goods seems to be more strongly associated with offending: self-efficacy/sense of agency, inner peace, personal dignity/social esteem, generative roles and relationships, and social relationships.
- Intervention is therefore seen as an activity that should add to an individual's repertoire of personal functioning, rather than as an activity that simply removes a problem or is devoted to managing problems, as if a lifetime of grossly restricting one's activities is the only way to avoid offending (Mann et al. 2004, cited in Ward & Maruna 2007: 128).

In order to make a more comprehensive assessment of each individual's potential for achieving a good life, workers need to build trust and strong relationships with offenders so that they can better understand their abilities, likely opportunities, deep preferences and values. The importance of getting offenders involved directly in their own rehabilitation also features in other approaches to and understandings of offender behaviour, such as restorative justice.

RESTORATIVE JUSTICE AND GENERATIVITY

Restorative justice refers to a theoretical framework for achieving justice that focuses on reparation of harms flowing from offender actions. It promotes a conciliatory and holistic approach, involving victims and communities as well as offenders in the reparation process. Restorative justice thus emphasises reintegrative and developmental principles, and offers the hope that opportunities will be enhanced for victims, offenders and their immediate communities, with the direct participation of all concerned in this process.

In Australia, the restorative justice approach has primarily been used in relation to young offenders. All states and territories have now implemented some form of juvenile conferencing. The intended outcome of the conferences is that the young offender is expected to complete some kind of agreement or undertaking; thus: 'The sanctions or reparations that are part of agreements include verbal and written apologies, paying some form of monetary compensation, working for the victim or doing other community work, and attending counselling sessions, among others' (Daly & Hayes 2001: 2). The form of the conference is basically the same, although there are jurisdictional differences in terms of the kinds of offences that are conferenced, the volume of activity that is engaged in through conferencing, the upper limit on conference outcomes, the statutory basis for conferencing, and the organisational placement or administration of the conferencing process. Evaluation research that has been carried out to date indicates that 'conferences are perceived as fair and participants are satisfied with the process and outcomes' (Chan 2005; Daly & Hayes 2001: 6; see also Kim & Gerber 2012; Strang 2001).

Restorative justice, with its emphasis on repairing harm, emphasises reintegrative and developmental principles. It offers the hope that opportunities will be enhanced for victims, offenders and their immediate communities, with the direct participation of all concerned in this process. The benefits of restorative justice are its emphasis on 'active agency' (young people doing things for themselves), cost-effectiveness (compared with detention or imprisonment), victim recognition and engagement (often through face-to-face meetings with offenders) and community benefit (through participation and through community service). While it can be argued that juvenile conferencing actually incorporates elements of retributive justice, rehabilitative justice and restorative justice, at least at the experiential level (see Daly 2002), there is nevertheless a distinctiveness in orientation that marks this approach off from others within the field.

The restorative perspective is driven by the idea that the offender deserves respect and dignity (they are persons), and that they already have basic competencies and capacities, which need to be developed further (if they are not to reoffend). In this framework, the emphasis is on what the person *could do*, rather than what they *should do*. What is important is that the offender achieves things at a concrete level, for themselves, including making reparation to their victim. In the end, the point of dealing with offenders in particular ways is to reinforce the notion that they have done something wrong, to repair the damage done as far as possible, and to open the door for the reintegration of the offender back into the mainstream of society.

GENERATIVITY

GENERATIVITY
Generativity involves a process of giving to others with the consequence of positive changes in the self-esteem and social attitudes of those doing the giving.

An important concept allied to that of restorative justice is **generativity**. This refers to the notion that doing something for others (e.g. community service, paying it back or helping others) ultimately translates into personal fulfilment and positive feelings about oneself. Enhancing the scope for generativity within criminal justice is viewed as an important aspect of the rehabilitative project.

For example, Barry (2006) examines youth offending from the point of view of diverse forms of social, cultural, economic and symbolic capital. She argues that it is not just the accumulation of capital that preoccupies young people, but also its expenditure. It is also the expenditure of accumulated capital that brings the rewards of individual gratification and social stability. Examples of this include buying your own clothes, engaging in volunteer work, and generally encouraging and helping others. Barry (2006) talks about the expenditure of capital as including:

- *social capital*: having responsibilities to one's family, partner or children; becoming a parent; giving love, friendship or attention to others; seeking custody of one's child
- *economic capital*: 'buying' clothes and other consumables (as opposed to stealing them); spending money on one's house or children; paying taxes and other state contributions

- *cultural capital*: contributing towards others' development or welfare through employment, teaching or influence, based on one's own skills or experience; setting an example by one's actions or words; encouraging and helping others
- *symbolic capital*: wanting to give of oneself (as mentor, volunteer, worker etc.); wanting to offer restoration or reparation to the community; having responsibilities towards one's house or job.

Social recognition and self-esteem generally are built through expenditure of capital (doing something for oneself and for someone else). If this is so, then it also ought to be an important component in the development of juvenile justice intervention strategies. This means addressing the constraints, as well as acknowledging the importance of spending what the young person has accumulated in their life:

> Although many offenders talk of restitution to society once they have stopped offending, it may be worth examining the extent to which generativity is rehabilitative for the individual as a result of shame or guilt or whether it is more of a pragmatic desire to give of one's own experiences in preventing similar problems for others. Certainly this research suggested the latter. (Barry 2006: 168)

It is not only young people who can benefit by giving something back to the communities and individuals they have harmed. The same can be said about adult offenders. The concept of restorative justice has, for example, been systematically introduced across the correctional services system in Belgium. Each prison has developed its own secular restorative justice regime across all sectors of the prison, with 'earned redemption' through civic community service a core component (Stamatakis & Vandeviver 2013). As illustrated in Box 27.2, even when delivered outside of a structured restorative justice framework, the act of doing something that offers opportunities for positive change has rehabilitative potential.

BOX 27.2   PRISONERS HELPING OTHERS

In an examination of the role that prisoners played in responding to Cyclone Larry, it was found that, in fact, cyclone work works (see Coventry & Westerhuis 2009; White & Coventry 2008). The prisoners who volunteered to participate in the extended clean-up phase following the cyclone worked hard at their tasks, up to 16-hour days, 6–7 days per week. The work included pulling down sheds, removing trees off fence lines, cutting trees, stacking roofing tin and repairing fences.

Many of the prisoners were interviewed about their experiences (Coventry & Westerhuis 2009). Typical of the responses were the following:
- 'We [prisoners] get little praise, like those on the Good Morning Shows [sic] flying them up here ... but we CHOSE to come out and work.' (Prisoner 1)
- '[The farmers] treat us like normal human beings.' (Prisoner 3)
- 'giving them a hand, feeling good' (Prisoner 5)
- 'didn't treat us like prisoners' (Prisoner 4)
- 'By going out we are paying back, not just the taxpayers ... we don't do it shoddy.' (Prisoner 5)
- 'At Innisfail, they had a lot of pride, they bust their guts. You don't need to do that while you are in jail.' (Prisoner 4)
- '[The work program] helps reintegration into the community, and makes jail time easier.' (Prisoner 5)

Sources: Coventry & Westerhuis (2009); White & Coventry (2008)

Coventry and Westerhuis (2009) tap into the emotional side of the rehabilitative process, consistent with notions about the quality of life required by all, not just prisoners re-entering communities. This group was proud of their work, felt strongly that they positively contributed to an area in crisis after a natural disaster, and developed a sense of belonging with the Atherton Tablelands. For dairy farmers, their work thwarted the loss of herds to mastitis and the ensuing financial devastation of such herd losses. For prisoners, the experiences opened the door to the outside world and how they might connect to it. Working in the Cyclone Larry clean-up was about the exertion of labour power, some skill development, and the opportunity to play a constructive and meaningful role in contributing to the community. Such positive responses from prisoners themselves reaffirm the importance of work to the re-entry process. It also confirms that giving freely is a significant source of satisfaction, pride and self-esteem.

The dynamics and forms of restorative justice need not be restricted to settings mainly or exclusively associated with the formal institutions of criminal justice. For example, in some exceptional cases, restorative justice has allowed young people themselves a pivotal role in the justice process as decision makers, as well as participating as offenders or victims (see Box 24.3). That is, individuals can be drawn into the justice process, not solely as protagonists but as adjudicators. In such circumstances, magistrates and police may in fact not be direct participants in the process.

BOX 27.3   YOUNG PEOPLE DOING JUSTICE

It is from the grassroots up that significant change is most likely to occur when it comes to realising the possibilities offered by restorative justice. For example, in Edmonton, Canada, the Youth Restorative Action Project (YRAP) has emerged in counterpoint to the usual adult-dominated, highly controlled and ultimately conservative operationalisation of juvenile conferencing. Starting from the premise that 'community' also includes young people themselves, the YRAP has challenged both the participatory elements of standard restorative justice forums (by engaging youth in the decision-making processes directly) and the purposive elements of standard restorative justice forums (by mobilising discussions and resources around social justice issues).

In their first case, for instance, the YRAP dealt with an incident involving a racially provoked knife attack by an Asian youth. The case was sent to the YRAP for sentencing recommendations, a process that involved participation by a committee of racially diverse young people, some of whom had experienced racism in the past. This particular 'conference' was held in a creative space for young people (a place of art and music activities). While understanding the sense of victimhood on the part of the offender, the YRAP group made it clear that violence was not justified. They then probed the young offender about how he could have more positively handled the situation. In the end, the 'sanction' agreed upon was for the offender to produce a statement on the negative elements of racism, through an audio or visual project using the local recording facilities. The result was a hip-hop song—penned, produced and performed by the young offender. Such creativity in dealing with offending behaviour, and explicit acknowledgement of the social context within which offences are committed, stemmed from the experiences of the young members of YRAP as young people. Furthermore, a commitment to social justice—arising from first-hand experience of marginalisation and social inequality—ensures that they are emboldened to act without the cultural and bureaucratic baggage of conventional justice systems.

Source: adapted from Hogeveen (2006)

ISSUES FOR CONSIDERATION

VICTIMS AND OFFENDERS

One of the great misfortunes accompanying victimisation is that all too often the emotional needs of the victim are forgotten in the criminal justice process (see Chapter 6). To some extent this is a matter of providing adequate counselling and other support services to guide victims through the difficult stages of transition and victim recovery. It is also vital that *offenders* be given the opportunity to be exposed to the victims' plight. Discussion of the preparation of prisoners for release, including via pre-release leave programs, requires that offenders at least begin to understand the impact of their actions on victims. More than this, however, many jurisdictions also now demand some kind of involvement in restitution, reparation or restorative justice activities, both while an offender is in prison and while they are on leave from prison or on parole. Where appropriate, and where suitable human and material resources have been put into place, such mechanisms can be usefully applied in relation to pre-release programs and strategies for a variety of offences, including homicide and sexual offending.

There are two key issues here. One is how best to give victims a forum in which they can best and most positively voice their feelings. The second is how to arrange for offenders to 'hear' the victims' voice, without compromising their own safety, future opportunities and rehabilitation processes. Options can range from face-to-face meetings between individual victims and individual offenders (in the community or in prison confines), family or juvenile group conferences that involve family members and support people, through to 'surrogate victims' in the form of panels of victims telling their stories to offenders and restorative boards of Inquiry, which adjudicate unresolved disputes regarding responsibility of an offence in a non-adversarial manner (see Centre for Innovative Justice 2014; Fulkerson 2001; Mawby 2007; Nicholl 2001; Seymour 2001).

ENTRENCHING SOCIAL INJUSTICE?

Partly due to the diversity of opinion, values, and models that reside under the restorative justice tag, there has been a tendency for specific forms of restorative justice to be implemented in a manner that actively reproduces the dominant forms of social control. For example, juvenile conferencing may be used solely for first-time offenders and/or trivial offences (as a means of diversion at the 'soft' end of the juvenile justice spectrum), and therefore as a filter that reinforces the logic and necessity of the 'hard' end of the system (the 'real justice' of retribution and punishment). The former thus may well help to legitimise the latter, rather than constitute a challenge to it.

Substantial variations in the introduction of restorative justice are apparent across diverse jurisdictions, if we compare legislative, administrative and operational frameworks (Daly & Hayes 2001; see also Chan 2005). In almost all cases, however, restorative justice has been blended into existing institutional patterns, as part of the continuing hybridisation of criminal justice. How this 'blending' occurs is important, of course, as it makes a major difference in terms of overall system orientation. The degree of expansion of restorative justice into the criminal justice system, for example, to include more serious kinds of offences and offenders with extensive criminal records, could provide one indication of potential systemic change.

THE THERAPEUTIC PRISON

The composition of the contemporary prison population, which includes a significant number of persons with mental disorder and/or drug abuse problems, has made some commentators wary of the presumed 'rehabilitation' mission associated with criminal justice. They argue that what is being constructed is a 'therapeutic prison', one into which certain people with complex needs are systematically being funnelled (Cunneen et al. 2013). The object is still predominantly one of control and containment, and the fact that the prison is somehow seen as therapeutic is seen as part of an 'imagined penality' that does not accord with the real-world experiences of actual inmates and prison workers.

Conversely, desistance researchers and practitioners argue that, regardless of its growth and its changing composition, those caught up in the criminal justice system deserve every chance to break the chains of institutional restraint and social disadvantage. In other words, positive developments can still emerge from within bad systems and terrible situations (Graham & White 2015). It is possible, therefore, to critique the overall orientation of the system without necessarily dismissing the importance of progressive change and supportive practices that are also evident, albeit in a circumscribed way. Such developments, as well, provide substantive examples of 'what could be'. As such, they supply an alternative vision for and understanding of rehabilitation, reintegration and redemption.

REHABILITATION AND POST-SENTENCE LAWS: AN INHERENT CONTRADICTION

In 2003, the *Dangerous Prisoners (Sexual Offenders) Act* was enacted in Queensland, in response to the release of Dennis Raymond Ferguson, a convicted child-sex offender who, having served a 14-year prison term, and having failed to participate in treatment programs while incarcerated, openly declared his intention to commit further child-sex offenders. This Act enabled post-sentence detention (or supervised release) of sexual offenders deemed dangerous, for the purposes of community protection and continuing care, control or treatment oriented towards rehabilitation (Doyle & Ogloff 2009). Similar legislation has since been enacted in Western Australia (*Dangerous Sexual Offenders Act 2006*), New South Wales (*Crimes (Serious Sex Offenders) Act 2006*), Victoria (*Serious Sex Offenders Monitoring Act 2005* and the *Serious Sex Offenders (Detention and Supervision) Act 2009*) and South Australia (*Sentencing (Sentencing of Sex Offenders) Act 2005*).

Although serious sex offenders subject to post-sentence management have completed their sentence, they are subject to civil schemes that aim to protect the community. Despite the schemes claiming to be non-punitive in intent or operation (see, for example, Department of Justice Victoria 2012), in practice, the overriding objective of community protection means that rehabilitative purposes are subordinated. In practice, where the nature of the ongoing risk posed to the community is deemed unacceptable, some offenders are subject to significant restrictions, including being 'warehoused' within prison boundaries, being monitored via electronic bracelet, placed on sex offender registers and being compelled to participate in treatment programs. Reconciling the competing aims of post-sentence detention is challenging. While the offender's interests of rehabilitation and safety should be of relevance to the public interest insofar as they are intended to promote desistance, they are often regarded by populist media as antithetical to the public interests of community safety (Rodrick 2011).

The anti-therapeutic effects and ethical and human rights implications of the various post-sentence schemes have been well canvassed; the justifiability of subjecting sexual offenders to such schemes is questionable given the empirical concerns regarding the ability of 'experts' to 'identify high-risk offenders to a level of certainty expected by the legislation' (Doyle & Ogloff 2009: 198; Ward & Salmon 2011).

CONCLUSION

'There are few presumptions in human relations more dangerous than the idea that one knows what another human being needs better than they do themselves.' (Michael Ignatieff, cited in Ward & Maruna 2007: 17)

This chapter has explored the social determinates of offender actions, and recent approaches that attempt to tap into offender potentials and strengths as an avenue toward offender rehabilitation. The primary concepts underpinning the discussions have been those of desistance, restoration and generativity. Importantly, these concepts place the emphasis on active offender engagement and on giving (both to and by the offender). Changing offender circumstances is viewed as vital to changing offender behaviour. This is a collective project with responsibility for transformation to be shared by the offender and the community, from start to finish.

As Chapter 28 highlights, the community context is also critically important in considerations of community efforts to prevent crime.

DISCUSSION QUESTIONS

1   Why do prisoners dislike the idea of 'rehabilitation' in its more conventional sense?

2   Is it possible both to address criminogenic needs and deal with individual offenders in a holistic way?

3   What is being restored in restorative justice?

4   What are the benefits of the philosophy and practice of 'giving' for the offender, the victim and the community?

5   'To prevent recidivism requires the engagement of the whole community, as well as the offender'. Discuss.

FURTHER READING

Andrews, D.A., Bonta, J. & Wormith, J.S. (2011) 'The Risk–Need–Responsivity (RNR) model: does adding the good lives model contribute to effective crime prevention?', *Criminal Justice and Behavior* 38(7): 735–55.

Barry, M. (2006) *Youth offending in transition: the search for social recognition,* Routledge, London.

Cunneen, C. & Hoyle, C. (2010) *Debating restorative justice,* Hart Publishing, Oxford.

Ward, T. & Maruna, S. (2007) *Rehabilitation: beyond the risk paradigm,* Routledge, London.

Ward, T., Yates, P.M. & Willis, G.M. (2011) 'The good lives model and the risk need responsivity model: a critical response to Andrews, Bonta and Wromith (2011)', *Criminal Justice and Behavior,* 39(1): 94–110.

28 CRIME PREVENTION

CHAPTER OVERVIEW
- CONCEPTUALISING COMMUNITY CRIME PREVENTION
- STRATEGIES OF COMMUNITY CRIME PREVENTION
- CRIME PREVENTION THROUGH ENVIRONMENTAL DESIGN
- ISSUES FOR CONSIDERATION
- CONCLUSION
- DISCUSSION QUESTIONS
- FURTHER READING

INTRODUCTION

Chapter 27 examined the advent of community-based corrections in the traditional armoury of state-sanctioned social control and punishment; a development that occurred within the broader decarceration movement. As discussed, while efforts to relocate the correctional system within a community-based context appear to have ameliorated many of the problems encountered in conventional correctional settings, in practice, new problems have emerged. Although these alternative systems are less formal in nature, the conceptual and practical links between formal and informal state and community-run systems require constant and critical consideration. Additionally, at a more fundamental level, the notion of 'community' is highly problematic. Many of the same conceptual uncertainties and practical problems apply to community-based or community-oriented crime prevention schemes.

The aim of this chapter is to provide an overview of the main approaches to, and models of, crime prevention and to survey briefly some of the better-known practical techniques and measures currently being used to prevent crime. These approaches range from situational and environmental prevention (which encompasses crime prevention through environmental design) through to social and communal development.

A specific concern of this chapter is to highlight the diverse political and philosophical assumptions underpinning the various paradigms of crime prevention. This is important because each broad approach has particular implications for policy development and its translation into practical interventions, which in turn have consequences socially, politically and economically. Furthermore, these perspectives may complement each other in some respects, but in many regards they are viewed as competing and opposed approaches to issues of crime control. The chapter concludes by raising a series of issues pertaining to the social consequences (intended and unintended) of implementing various kinds of crime prevention strategies.

CRIME PREVENTION
The creation and implementation of proactive programs and strategies that are intended to prevent crime before it occurs, and to address and diminish the fear of crime.

CONCEPTUALISING COMMUNITY CRIME PREVENTION

The past two decades have witnessed rapid growth in the lexicon of community **crime prevention** and its impact on criminological debates, government policies and practical interventions within both Australia and internationally (Crawford 1998; Sutton 1994a; Sutton et al. 2014). The concept of community crime prevention is, however, ideologically problematic in so far as the definitional boundaries to be drawn around its constituent components of 'community' 'crime' and 'prevention' remain fluid and highly contestable. Moreover, crime-prevention policies and concomitant interventionary approaches are not value-neutral; they embody (either explicitly or explicitly) divergent assumptions regarding human nature, crime causation and social relations (Crawford 1998; see, for example, Box 28.1).

POLITICAL PERSPECTIVES ON COMMUNITY CRIME PREVENTION

One method of classifying crime-prevention approaches is to place them into a framework of political perspectives (conventional, social problem and structural), which can assist us to unpack and evaluate their underlying assumptions and the broad orientation of the concrete programs and strategies they favour (Iadicola 1986; White 1996b). However, in practice, there is usually considerable overlap in approach regardless of the political orientation of the theory informing intervention (see Sutton et al. 2014).

CONVENTIONAL APPROACH

The key idea behind a *conventional approach* to crime prevention is to reduce the situational opportunities for crime. This can be achieved by changing the physical setting of a neighbourhood and/or by encouraging citizens to participate in crime-prevention efforts. Thus, for example, within this model, neighbourhood residents become the eyes and ears of police and, generally, the community is used to supplement or enhance the role of the police. The crime-prevention agenda is defined by the

---

BOX 28.1   AN INCLUSIVE VALUES-BASED APPROACH TO CRIME PREVENTION

One of the key lessons from crime prevention is that it ought to be based largely on a problem-solving, rather than a policy-prescribed, model of intervention. This is one of the messages of the book by Sutton et al. (2014) titled *Crime prevention: principles, perspectives and practices*. Different kinds of places and activities lend themselves to different sorts of harms and different kinds of intervention. A problem-solving approach to crime prevention demands a certain level of specificity. That is, general pronouncements about the nature of harm need to be accompanied by particular site or harm analysis. Responses need to be tailored to local circumstances; they ought to involve a wide range of participants from within the greater community; and they can incorporate many different types of techniques and approaches.

Contrasting crime-prevention policies with law-and-order policies, it is argued that strategies should include both social prevention (e.g. programs addressing the social causes of crime) and environmental prevention (e.g. reducing crime by minimising opportunities). Good crime prevention is thus defined in terms of explicit guiding values, progressive planning principles and extensive social participation. Ultimately, it is always linked to a strategic vision of what kind of society we want to achieve, and how to best achieve this in ways that sustain an exciting, pleasurable, safe and secure environment.

Source: Sutton et al. (2014)

police (in terms of main crime focus and operational priorities), and the role of the community is to assist in its implementation.

From the point of view of crime control, as most crime is considered to be opportunistic in nature, the solution lies in manipulating the situational features that may influence crime, thereby increasing the costs and reducing the opportunities for, and benefits of, crime. The effectiveness of this approach essentially rests on the strength of its deterrence capabilities, enhanced through certainty of detection and apprehension (Clarke 1997; Cornish & Clark 1986). Advocates of this approach argue that it is the immediate circumstances influencing crime that are most amenable to preventative interventions, and that such interventions are relatively easy to implement and offer better prospects of shorter-term, measurable success (Ekblom & Tilley 2000).

There are, however, several limitations or weaknesses pertaining to this approach (see generally Crawford 1998). For example, a climate may be created whereby individuals become increasingly suspicious of neighbours and neighbourhood activities, and individuals deemed problematic (e.g. young people) or activities deemed problematic (e.g. graffiti in urban spaces) are 'designed out' (Currie 1988; White 1993, 1990) or subject to military-style surveillance (Iveson 2010). Related to this, while there may be a strong cost impetus for encouraging the development of community crime control, such programs can actually increase dependence upon police. For instance, whereas previously suspicious-looking individuals might have been dealt with informally, neighbourhood watch networks may now resort to phoning police.

SOCIAL PROBLEM APPROACH

The social problem approach to crime prevention is based upon the concept of enhancing opportunities for lawful behaviour in the pursuit of culturally approved goals (Crawford 1998; Iadicola 1986). This approach favours positive, youth-oriented programs; better recreational, educational and training facilities; and ways to improve overall community life. This can include, for example, a neighbourhood environmental renewal strategy whereby the local neighbourhood is, literally, cleaned up. The building of positive, healthy neighbourhood groups and connections is also emphasised.

At a broader level, neighbourhood regeneration, community capacity-building and social support, mobilisation, and integration strategies may be employed as a means of overcoming phenomena such as youth disconnection and alienation (Crawford 1998).

One of the limitations of this model is that, while premised on the notion of building community capacity to control crime, it rarely makes the link between local conditions and wider socio-economic opportunity structures, both state and federal (e.g. labour policies, unemployment and poverty). Indeed, local communities are often very limited both materially (in terms of resources) and legally (in terms of jurisdictional power and responsibility) in their capacity to address general structural issues such as unemployment. Hope (1995: 24) refers to this central paradox of community crime prevention as, 'the problem of trying to build community institutions that control crime in the face of their powerlessness to withstand the pressures toward crime in the community, whose source, or the forces that sustain them, derive from the wider social structure'.

STRUCTURAL APPROACH

A structural approach to crime prevention presses for community control, and the need for social change to avert crime. The main strategies employed by this approach include calls to redress institutional inequalities by taking action to ensure full employment, to reduce the number of working poor, and to redistribute community resources and reallocate wealth. The approach sees as a central concern the communalisation of social control; that is, a democratisation of all facets of the community so that those at the grassroots have an active say in how their lives are run. Power should be devolved to the local level so that the community has the ability to make decisions about people who form part of that community (e.g. the establishment of neighbourhood courts and Indigenous courts, and justice practices; see Marchetti & Daly 2004).

On the other hand, commentators argue that focusing on the structural imperatives for crime may subdue crime-prevention efforts to ameliorate factors and situations more readily amenable to change (Russell 1999). Structural changes of this type may appear an unachievable task, particularly in the short term. This is especially the case if we view the movement towards radical transformation as a single development. However, according to Iadicola (1986) three stages of community involvement can be envisaged that offer concrete direction to the development of a structural approach to crime prevention:

- *Reactive stage*: the process commences when members of a geographical area share in common a concern about something that is perceived to be an outside threat (e.g. the closing down of a factory or environmental pollution). This perception of fear of crime galvanises the residents into community action.
- *Preactive stage*: attempts are made to decentralise basic services such as schools and policing, the control of which is vested in the hands of people at the local level.
- *Proactive stage*: power is decentralised to the extent that citizens have direct control in relation to the running of the community and the satisfaction of community needs. Community solidarity, class consciousness and equal access to resources are key features at this stage.

However, as critics highlight, it is precisely the divisions between people in the here and now that constitute the principal barriers to the adoption of such a crime prevention approach.

Crime prevention is a political process and the nature of any particular program, strategy or technique is ultimately shaped by the political environment (institutional structures and debates) within which it is developed (see Crawford 1998; Sutton 1994a; Sutton & Hazlehurst 1996; Sutton et al. 2014; White 1996a). This brings us back to the importance of defining what is meant by terms such as 'community'.

THE NOTION OF 'COMMUNITY'

As indicated earlier, a major difficulty in discussions of crime prevention is that too often pivotal terms are imprecisely defined and used rhetorically rather than analytically, resulting in a failure to appreciate the social processes and dynamics involved in shaping the crime prevention agenda. This criticism applies particularly to the use of phrases such as 'community' and 'community participation' (McLaughlin 2002). Although the notion of 'community' is treated unproblematically in much of the crime-prevention literature, it is important to acknowledge the wide range of conceptual variations, which ultimately renders the term 'perennially resistant to ideological categorisation' (Little 2002: 7).

References to 'community', and the more recently coined expressions 'social capital' and 'communalism' (often used interchangeably), commonly assume the existence of social networks built upon a shared set of attitudes and beliefs and the associated norms of 'reciprocity' and 'trust' (Putnam 2002). In simple terms, this translates to communities delineated by territorial boundaries in which residents consider themselves strongly connected to one another through shared identity, interest and informal relationship bonds; namely, 'neighbourliness'. These boundaries may include:

- geography (local, regional or international)—people living in the same area
- power structures (federal, state and local government)—defined by electoral boundaries
- services (transport line or school)—defined by service providers such as local councils.

Community character hence is strongly influenced by a set of collective attitudes able to be reconstructed merely by engendering attitudinal shifts in the mindsets of residents (Currie 1988).

An overriding assumption here is that the 'community' is a homogenous, tightly knit entity founded upon consensual values. However, the reality of modern urban living suggests that this assumption is fundamentally flawed. According to Giddens (1990), contemporary urban living—which is characteristically cosmopolitan (diverse ages, cultures, religions, identities etc.), highly mobile and private (self-interested, consumerist and politically apathetic)—has resulted in relationships that are fragmented, loose and transitory, hence eroding closely bonded, mutually supportive and harmonious communities (see also Carson 2004a).

STRUCTURAL AWARENESS

An alternative approach to community advanced by Currie (1988) is the 'structural awareness' approach. According to this perspective, the bonds of 'community' are more than a set of attitudes that can be imported into, or mobilised within, a geographical community. Instead, they are the product of, and subject to the pressures of, interconnected and deeply embedded institutional influences and interests (e.g. work, religion and communal associations), broader structural contexts (e.g. housing policy and employment opportunities) and social factors (e.g. gender, race and class), such as:

- social profile (income, class, age, ethnicity, gender, religion and public/private housing)—people sharing similar backgrounds
- self-definition (a club or group)—communal associations and networks comprising like-minded people with a common concern
- types of industry or employment (retail outlets, commercial trade or factories)—what people do for a living
- organised interests (resident groups, unions and business groups)—political lobby groups.

To speak of community crime prevention, therefore, we need to have a clear idea of which particular 'community' we are referring to, and how and why this particular community is relevant to the strategy. As indicated by the three political perspectives on crime prevention presented earlier, there is often considerable dispute over which members of the community are to be involved and with what purposes in mind.

ALTERNATIVE IDEAS OF PARTICIPATION

Similar qualifications are necessary with respect to the concept of 'community participation'. Here we can likewise identify a number of different criteria for participation and interpretation regarding what this actually means. Some of the alternative ideas of participation include (see Sandercock 1983):

- market research (polls, telephone interviews and surveys etc.)—what people think about certain issues or social problems
- appointment to decision-making bodies (representatives of the community sit on advisory boards and committees)—what representatives think about certain issues or social problems

- incorporation of opposition groups (inviting diverse community leaders into a central decision-making forum)—making confidential or silencing an opposing view by positioning it as simply one voice among many
- social therapy (neighbourhood clean-up campaigns)—the community actually takes part, but performs work or provides services as determined by someone else
- grassroots activism (street watch or pollution watch committees)—people on the ground do things for themselves, by themselves, and make decisions on how to intervene in the world around them.

In addition to acknowledging the diverse ways in which 'community participation' can be conceived, and the different degrees of control and involvement associated with these, it is also useful to consider the embeddedness of social interests around which particular forms of neighbourhood organise. For instance, a crime-prevention strategy might be seen in at least three different ways when it comes to motivations and intentions:

1 It might simply reflect a concern with professional intervention and service delivery, and thus be driven by the priorities of the police officer, the criminologist, the welfare worker or other 'experts'.
2 It may be related to the material interests of those who would benefit most from neighbourhood improvement and protection of property, such as the affluent, the investor and the homeowner.
3 Organising at the neighbourhood level might involve collective political activism directed at changing existing social structures, and empowering people who have few resources or little say in the dominant political–economic system.

COMMUNITY AND EXCLUSION

As implied by this review of social interest, then, one cannot assume the existence of egalitarian power relations within communities. The empirical evidence indeed suggests that communities are hierarchical structures, divided along many lines, including gender, class, religion and age. Consequently, as Crawford (1998: 159) suggests, the 'moral voice of a community' may actually reflect the interests of a dominant, powerful minority, and may operate oppressively to silence difference and promote exclusion and inequality.

Furthermore, discussion of community bonds and networks in a crime-prevention context are almost invariably cast in a positive light, as a vehicle for preserving or restoring social unity and order. However, as highlighted by Carson (2004a,b), by its very nature the act of defining a community implies exclusion. In particular, geographical constructions of community identity tend to promote an 'us and them' approach to crime prevention, in which the offender is accorded 'outsider' status and viewed as existing beyond the 'community' (e.g. the perennial refrain: he/she/that is 'unAustralian'). Furthermore, the same characteristics of close bonding and supportive network structures regarded as central to community and social capital are equally observable in nefarious enterprises, such as organised crime syndicates.

It is therefore essential, when speaking of 'community' crime control and 'community' participatory organisations, to bear in mind that there are different interests, different groups, different struggles, different agendas, different strategies and different relationships to the state. We need to take account of these when considering specific crime prevention measures.

STRATEGIES OF COMMUNITY CRIME PREVENTION

To this point we have examined community-based crime prevention in an abstract, theoretical fashion, taking particular note of the implicit or underlying political divisions in community crime prevention strategies. Of crucial importance has been the notion of 'community', and how it is subject to variable interpretation by theorists and practitioners. Similarly, we also need to clarify what we mean by 'community participation', because it varies from active participation through to passive support for pre-arranged programs and official agencies.

Too often in criminology the idea is conveyed that nothing works; that is, existing programs are critiqued but alternatives seem to be in short supply (for discussion, see Sutton 1994a,b). This section seeks to redress that imbalance to some extent by moving beyond the theoretical to deal with community crime prevention in a practical fashion. Our intention is briefly to review specific approaches to community crime prevention and the strategies they employ. There are a number of possible areas to be covered in this discussion, including topics as diverse as:

- situational crime prevention
- crime prevention through environmental design
- auxiliary justice
- social crime prevention
- community development
- community policing
- targeted policing operations
- shame and reintegration strategies
- vigilante justice.

Given that some of these strategies are covered elsewhere in the book, our main emphasis will be on situational prevention, crime prevention through environmental design, auxiliary justice, social crime prevention, community development, and vigilante justice.

SITUATIONAL CRIME PREVENTION

Situational crime prevention is based upon the idea that for someone who is capable of, and not averse to offending, the decision to commit a specific crime will be a function of both whether an opportunity presents itself and whether the likely rewards from exploiting that opportunity are sufficient to offset the perceived efforts and risks (Sutton et al. 2014). Situational prevention revolves around identifying modifiable conditions that are susceptible to intervention, and that can reduce or pre-empt perceived opportunities for crime (Clarke 2005, 1980; Clarke & Homel 1997; Tilley 2005). Table 28.1 outlines the broad approaches and specific techniques of situational crime prevention (see also Sutton et al. 2014).

Situational crime prevention is about removing the opportunity to commit crime and increasing the likelihood of apprehension. This approach is particularly useful and effective in that different kinds of harm tend to call forth different kinds of responses.

Situational approaches to crime prevention seek to resolve problems in targeted locations or 'crime hot spots'. This typically involves modifications to the physical environment (buildings, landscapes and products), as well as the promotion of active intervention strategies on the part of shopkeepers,

SITUATIONAL CRIME PREVENTION Offence-focused strategies designed to reduce the opportunities for crime; in this case, through deterrents to crime. Strategies include increasing the degree of difficulty to commit crime, increasing the likelihood of detection and arrest, ensuring the effort to commit crime does not pay off) and inducing shame or guilt).

TABLE 28.1 APPROACHES AND TECHNIQUES OF SITUATIONAL PREVENTION

BROAD APPROACHES	SPECIFIC TECHNIQUES
Increase the effort of crime	• Harden targets • Control access to facilities • Screen entries and exits • Deflect offenders • Control tools/weapons
Increase the risks	• Extend guardianship • Facilitate natural surveillance • Reduce anonymity • Utilise place managers • Strengthen formal surveillance
Reduce the rewards	• Conceal targets • Remove targets • Identify property • Disrupt markets • Deny benefits
Reduce provocations	• Reduce frustration and stress • Avoid disputes • Reduce emotional arousal • Neutralise peer pressure • Discourage imitation
Remove excuses	• Set rules • Post instructions • Alert conscience • Assist compliance • Control access to drugs, alcohol and other facilitators

Source: Clarke & Eck (2003)

law-enforcement officials and other members of the community, usually in the form of surveillance and management of public space. Changes to the physical design and management of the environment are intended to increase the risks associated with offending, and hence to make crime less attractive to offenders (Clarke 1997; Ekblom 1998).

The evolution of this perspective, which focuses primarily on the circumstances of the immediate problem (the offence, rather than the offender), has been heavily influenced by rational choice theory and, in particular, the Routine Activities Theory (Cohen & Felson 1979; Cornish & Clarke 1986; Crow & Bull 1975). According to this view of crime causation, all predatory crimes begin with a motivated offender who logically plans their intended course of action. Whether the offender's proposed actions come to fruition, however, depends upon the opportunity structures for crime, as determined by the behaviour of others. As demonstrated in Figure 28.1, crime is essentially opportunistic—a product of the non-random convergence of three prerequisite elements in time and space: motivated offenders, suitable targets and the absence of capable guardians who exercise surveillance and social control functions.

FIGURE 28.1   ROUTINE ACTIVITIES APPROACH

Motivated offender

Suitable target

Crime risk

Absence of capable guardian

Essentially, then, offenders are highly adaptable agents whose actions are directly influenced by environmental inducements and opportunities, and the key to crime prevention is deterrence, with a focus on certainty of detection rather than severity of sanction. Table 28.1 provides an indication of the methods that may be employed by this strategy. Though situational crime prevention techniques are varied, they can be grouped under five broad strategies relating to effort, risks, rewards, provocations and excuses (for extensive discussion, see Clarke & Eck 2003; Clarke & Homel 1997). Box 28.2 provides concrete examples of situation crime prevention techniques as these relate to efforts, risks and rewards.

Recent application of situational crime-prevention techniques to the illegal wildlife trade indicates the utility of such methods across varied crime domains (see Lemieux 2014) and illustrates the continuing efforts to refine and supplement the diverse range of measures presently adopted in this area of crime prevention. The appeal of such measures is obvious—they offer something achievable, manageable and apparently successful when it comes to basic intervention strategies. They appear to work, and to work well in the specific contexts and situations within which they are applied, thus countering some of the scepticism of the 'nothing works' era in criminology—although one size does not fit all (Exum et al. 2010). While critics argue that situational crime prevention approaches fail to prevent expressive crimes (e.g. sexual assault, arson and murder, which involve a significant element of emotion, such as anger, hostility and excitement), Farrell (2010) offers a series of examples that suggest otherwise (see also Pratt et al. 2010).

BOX 28.2   SITUATIONAL CRIME PREVENTION: EFFORTS, RISKS AND REWARDS

INCREASING THE EFFORT TO COMMIT CRIME

This group of strategies seeks to hinder the commission of crime by increasing the degree of difficulty in reaching the target. Contained within this objective are the following techniques:

- *Target hardening*: here the offender's efforts are obstructed through the use of physical barriers. For example, banks have anti-bandit screens made of toughened plexiglass. In the car industry, target hardening takes the form of steering-column locks, engine immobilisers and other disabling devices fitted as standard equipment on new vehicles. These devices are automatically activated when the ignition key is removed, thus making it more difficult to steal the vehicle.
- *Access control*: this strategy harks back to the medieval era, where a defensible space was secured around a castle by the use of a moat and drawbridge, thus enabling the owner to restrict access. In the modern era, access to one's home can be similarly restricted with a fenced front garden and locked gates. In the case of an apartment, entry phones serve a similar entry restriction function. Another example here is the use of personal identification numbers (PINs) as a means of restricting access to a bank account or computer data files.
- *Deflecting offenders from targets*: this strategy seeks to control offensive behaviour by, among other things, channelling people's energies towards acceptable alternatives. In nineteenth-century Italy, the construction of public urinals was suggested as a solution to the persistent problem of people urinating in the streets. The provision of graffiti boards is an attempt to tackle a modern-day problem, as is the channelling of graffiti artists into approved projects such as the painting of bus shelters or trams or the walls of designated laneways. Street closures seek to stop the practice of 'cruising', where males drive up and down popular entertainment strips seeking excitement or sex workers. On a larger scale, the practice of segregating sporting fans at major events is designed to prevent physical altercations.
- *Controlling crime facilitators*: the idea here is that certain items facilitate crime and their sale or usage should therefore be controlled. The monitoring of sales of spray paint cans, alcohol and knives to young people is one example. Another is the argument that access to guns should be tightly controlled because countries where guns are readily available (e.g. the United States) have higher homicide rates than countries where access is restricted (for a review of this proposition, see McPhedran et al. 2010). Other examples include the use of photographs on credit cards to confirm identity and the adoption of toughened glass bottles in pubs to control any likely damage resulting from their use as weapons.

INCREASING THE RISKS

The next group of techniques is designed to increase the risks, whether real or perceived, associated with illegal or criminal activity. Risks are defined in terms of the likelihood of detection and apprehension. Such measures include:

- *Screen entry and exit points*: at first glance, entry screening appears to be the same as access control, but the objective here is not so much to exclude people from entering as to increase the likelihood of detecting individuals who do not fulfil entry requirements. At airports, Customs acts as a screening point for baggage and persons, which ensures that prohibited goods (e.g. weapons) or substances (e.g. foodstuffs or pests) do not enter the country. The introduction of electronic ticket machines, which permit only those passengers with prepaid fare cards onto the public transport system, is an example of an attempt to tackle the problem of fare evasion. It also provides a financial justification for the retrenchment of employees; this may in fact contradict the crime prevention measure of deterring offending by means of a visible employee presence. By contrast, exit screening serves to deter individuals from illegally removing objects from an area. For example, merchandising tags (beepers or dyes) are used in an effort to dissuade individuals from stealing items from shops.

- *Formal surveillance*: individuals who have a formal surveillance function are used to deter potential offenders. Shop detectives are one example, as are security guards accompanying cash in transit and other forms of large-scale precious goods transfers. Police have an obvious role to play here, and in recent years their surveillance capabilities have been significantly enhanced through technological developments. For instance, lead-foot motorists must now do battle with radar detectors, CB radios, police-radio scanners, and speed and red light detection cameras—measures that are more difficult to circumvent than the chance patrol car. Burglar alarms are another form of formal electronic surveillance device used in both residential and commercial contexts.

- *Surveillance by employees*: in addition to their primary functions, many employees, especially those dealing with the public, are also used in the surveillance effort. For example, parking attendants, customer assistance officers and protective services officers (present on trains and in public places of significance), serve to protect both people and property. Closed circuit television (CCTV) and other forms of video surveillance often are used in conjunction with employee surveillance. For example, the Victorian rail system has witnessed a gradual installation of live cameras (many of which are commuter-activated)—both as a measure against vandalism and also as a personal security measure.

- *Natural surveillance*: this is provided by good street lighting, trimming foliage in front of buildings, installing sensor lighting, and leaving interior lights and other devices (e.g. the TV and radio) operating while the premises are unoccupied. These items can now be activated by timer devices. The idea here is to provide clear lines of sight to the premises, and to give the impression that home, office or factory is constantly in use or occupied.

REDUCING THE REWARDS

This next set of techniques tries to deter offenders by making sure that the effort to commit crime does not pay off. For example:

- *Removing targets*: an example is cash-reduction policies directed at reducing burglaries. For instance, pizza delivery drivers no longer carry more than a specified amount of money (say, $30), and convenience stores do not have certain drugs on the premises and carry a maximum of $100 in the till at any one time. The display of empty cash tills in shop windows is an obvious indicator that the target has been removed. Another example is the use of exact fare or non-cash systems (e.g. Myki in Victoria) on public transport, which ensures that large amounts of money are not held or not held at all. Target removal measures have also been implemented to prevent persistent vandalism of public phone booths: phone cards have increasingly replaced coins, the glass doors have been removed altogether and the side panels have been partly replaced with wire grilles. These measures have been taken in response to studies that revealed that in vandalised phone booths, it was the glass that was traditionally attacked.

- *Identifying property*: there are various levels of sophistication here from the crude method of cattle branding to advanced methods of identification achieved through the use of secret markers. The tactic is to deter potential thieves by providing incontrovertible signs of ownership to prevent resale of the stolen item. Another kind of identification is vehicle licensing and the use of licence plate recognition technology.
- *Removing inducements*: the objective here is to reduce temptation to commit an offence. The 'broken window' theory is also relevant when it comes to removing inducements. If a broken window is left in a state of disrepair, it is most likely that the remaining windows of that building will soon be broken. According to this theory, damaged property should be removed or repaired as quickly as possible in order to deter further vandalism. Other examples include gender-neutral phone listings, and providing off-street parking for residences and businesses.
- *Removing benefits*: closely related to the removal of inducements are efforts geared towards denying the offender the material 'benefits' of crime. For example, a train littered with graffiti is immediately taken out of service, cleaned and put back into operation. Eventually offenders get bored, or realise that graffiti is futile because neither they nor anyone else ever gets a chance to view their handiwork. Other examples here include the removal of compact discs from containers, so that only the packaging is displayed; the use of ink merchandise tags, which, if removed illegally, spoil garments; and the practice of disabling stolen mobile phones, thus rendering them useless.
- *Setting rules*: one way of regulating criminal behaviour is to establish rules or procedures. For example, libraries have rules governing the duration of loans. Were such rules not in existence, we might be tempted to keep the books indefinitely. Similarly, most business organisations have rules for their employees, such as restrictions on the use of telephones and the internet for personal use. Harassment codes in the work-place are another example of rules that are intended to prevent offensive behaviour.

Source: adapted from Clarke (1997)

CRIME PREVENTION THROUGH ENVIRONMENTAL DESIGN

In addition to being influenced by rational choice theory, the development of situational crime prevention is closely related to developments in **Crime Prevention Through Environmental Design** (CPTED) (Jacobs 1961; Jeffery 1971). This approach seeks to transform what appear to be unsafe situations in homes, cities and neighbourhoods into safe ones by enhancing the design of the physical environment in order to enhance surveillance capabilities and therefore diminish the opportunities for crime. These environmental changes are primarily achieved through design, architectural means and planning initiatives.

The notion of designing out crime did not originate within criminological circles. It was instead inspired by planners and urban architects who criticised, in particular, the design of residential environments that made it difficult for residents to secure a 'defensible space'—one that excludes

CRIME PREVENTION THROUGH ENVIRONMEN-TAL DESIGN
Planning and design of the physical environment such that it decreases opportunities for crime and enhances surveillance capabilities in specific places.

predators and thus inhibits crime (see Newman 1972a,b). In particular, the high rate of victimisation experienced by residents of large-scale public housing estates was attributed to poor planning. The scale of such estates, for example, prevents residents from recognising strangers, and the large number of uncontrolled 'indefensible' access points (areas such as underpasses, lifts, corridors and stairwells that belong to no one and consequently remain undefended) enables offenders to enter, commit a crime and exit undetected (Coleman 1989).

As originally conceived of by Newman, the concept of a 'defensible space' comprises four features (see Martin 2000; Mills 1996):

1   *Territoriality*: the desire to protect one's 'own space' from outsiders. This is achieved through the demarcation of public and private space (comprising both real and symbolic barriers), so that the inhabitant's or user's sphere of influence and proprietorship is established.

2   *Natural surveillance*: seeking to keep intruders under observation. This is achieved through strategic design that clears the line of sight and/or the presence of natural guardians (social 'eyes', such as residents, passers-by and workers).

3   *Image*: building design that promotes the appearance of harmonious co-existence with, rather than peculiarity to, the surrounding environment. The idea here is that the architectural design should avoid the stigma of neglect and vulnerability (particularly apparent in public housing estates).

4   *Environment*: the location of developments such as public housing estates in 'safe zones'; that is, away from areas under constant threat.

Newman regarded this model as a vehicle for 'restructuring the residential environments of our cities so they can again become liveable and controlled, controlled not be police but by a community of people sharing a common terrain' (1972: 2). Clearly, then, as originally envisaged, CPTED was primarily concerned with broad issues of planning rather than targeting specific areas or problems. The approach however, has subsequently become legislated in every state and territory of Australia and therefore ingrained into the urban design planning process, with many city councils requiring the siting and design of buildings to be mindful of CPTED principles (Clancy et al. 2012; Fisher & Piracha 2012; Martin 2000).

CRIME PREVENTION AUDIT

Although interpreted in a variety of ways, much of the focus of CPTED has been directed towards the identification of unsafe or potentially unsafe sites (Geason & Wilson 1989). Activities geared towards the identification of unsafe sites initially require an individual or individuals to engage in a crime-mapping exercise. The purpose of this activity is to identify the local conditions and factors that may be contributing to patterns of crime already occurring in the area, or may contribute to the creation of unsafe situations in the future. This crime-prevention audit needs to take into account aspects of the physical environment and the character of the specific site, as well as the social dynamics of public life within this environment (see Planning Collaborative (Vic.) Pty Ltd 1993; White 1999).

First, consultants, such as criminologists, look at different sites or locations and examine the attractors; that is, a profile is established of venues or sites that attract a lot of pedestrian movement, especially outside regular business hours. These include, for instance, hotels and taverns, discos, cafés, takeaway food premises, convenience stores, video hire shops, car parks, public toilets, public telephones and other public places. Second, an examination is made of all the waiting locations; that is, locations where people congregate while waiting for transport. Included here are, for example, tram, bus and train stops, and taxi ranks. Third, movement routes are traced and assessed; for instance, from an entertainment venue to a pub or food outlet, public transport stops and car parks.

Throughout the mapping exercise, the immediate environment of each 'attractor', 'waiting location' and 'movement route' is traced, the objective being to identify, analyse and respond to unsafe situations. In response to perceived unsafe situations, several environmental design strategies could be adopted. For instance, changes may be required in the building design. Safety features could be integrated into planning regulations and construction design. For example, shopfronts that have a recess in the entry point present a potential threat, since an attacker may be hidden from view; big columns with set-back façades also offer hiding places; automatic teller machines in obscure locations offer an opportunity for robbery to occur away from the public view (concerns over the safety of teller machines have increased following a number of brutal attacks); and tiered car parks adjacent to pedestrian routes provide a possibility for the abduction of pedestrians, who may be dragged into a vehicle unobserved.

The solutions to these problems are seen to be fairly simple. For instance, underpasses or lanes whose corners conceal a clear exit can be remedied through the installation of mirrors that enable individuals to view the underpass before entering. Similarly, decked car parks near pedestrian walkways can be made safer by fencing off the bottom level.

A second and related strategy is to examine aspects of civic design (see Planning Collaborative (Vic.) Pty Ltd 1993). Here it is seen that certain things that we do to make inner cities aesthetically pleasing can present potential dangers. For example, dense shrubbery in raised planter beds or situated near public toilets, particularly in parks, may look nice but can conceal attackers. The planting of groundcovers or trees with sparse foliage is suggested in such locations. Another problem relates to essential movement routes, such as through car parks or at transport waiting locations. Often, they are poorly lit, perhaps because the civic authorities do not want to highlight their unattractiveness. These dangerous areas could of course be remedied through increased or improved lighting. In many cases, it is local councils that provide funding for environmental design studies and that build such crime prevention measures into their planning and building processes.

SOCIAL MAPPING

Planning a crime-prevention strategy, however, involves more than a matter of choosing the right technique to remedy an identified problem, for these techniques are never neutral in application and they invariably have certain social and economic consequences. Accordingly, it is extremely important that in addition to mapping the physical layout and design of a development site, crime-prevention audits conducted as part of a planning process should also include a social mapping exercise. This activity should seek to gauge the diversity of groups that use a site or amenity and the range of uses to which a specific public area is put. For instance, among the users of a mall, one is likely to find shop owners, managers, office staff, buskers, police and other authority figures (e.g. private security guards) and a wide range of visitors, including young people, seniors, people from diverse ethnic backgrounds and tourists. Based on this diversity of users, one begins to identify the multiple ways in which the mall is used, including commercial (buying and selling), recreational (congregating, hanging out, strolling, sightseeing and window shopping), movement (transit route to work and/or transport and civic parades) and work purposes.

Social planning audits assist in the identification of a number of issues important to the design and subsequent management of public spaces, including the:

- tensions between various user interests, such as that between commercial interests and recreational interests
- need to cater to the specific needs of diverse user groups, especially the disadvantaged, through the provision of suitable access points for those with physical disabilities and the need for spaces sensitive to cultural and religious differences
- different perceptions and concerns within the community regarding safety and security.

Efforts to uncover site-specific social issues are enhanced through the adoption of an inclusive and ongoing consultation process, which may assist in encouraging dialogue between apparently competing interest groups.

AUXILIARY JUSTICE

Also broadly situated alongside the situational and environmental community crime-prevention models are various forms of auxiliary justice, which have gained currency in Australia since the 1980s. Programs under this banner call upon citizens in one way or another to play a supporting role alongside the existing formal institutions of the criminal justice system, primarily acting as the eyes and ears of police, reporting suspicious movements or behaviour.

Key to the success of auxiliary justice initiatives is the collective and cooperative nature of citizen involvement. The prevailing assumption is that citizens are familiar with one another or have a desire to acquire that familiarity, and that they will work cooperatively to watch out for crime and intervene appropriately. In short, these initiatives depend on reciprocal trust and a preparedness to assume responsibility for the safety of oneself and others. Specific examples of auxiliary justice programs include (Challinger 2003; Charlton & Taylor 2003; Laycock & Tilley 1995; Mukherjee & Wilson 1987; Thomas 1999):

- *Neighbourhood Watch*: this partnership initiative between the local community (suburban residents, schools, traders etc.) and police encourages increased natural surveillance ('watching') of 'strangers' and 'unusual' activity, and the reporting of that activity to relevant authorities and/or the potential victim(s). Potential offenders are theoretically deterred from engaging in crime in the neighbourhood through signposting and publicity alerting the existence of the program.
- *Business Watch*: modelled closely along the lines of Neighbourhood Watch, this scheme seeks to reduce rates of crime against the business community by encouraging surveillance and alerting fellow businesses and/or relevant authorities. Additional complementary activities include the distribution to relevant persons of educational resources on crime prevention, property marking, and use of advertising stickers and posters that serve to deter potential offenders.
- *Safety houses*: residents volunteer to designate their homes 'safe' as a means of providing children with a ready escape route from possible predations from 'strangers' in a neighbourhood. Signage to that effect is installed in a prominent position on the house to alert potential victims and offenders.
- *Phone-in informant programs and operations*: this involves the use of the media to encourage members of the general public to provide information (which may not otherwise be provided) to the police anonymously on unsolved crimes, wanted offenders, and individuals or organisations suspected of involvement in criminal enterprises. Specific initiatives include Crime Stoppers, the annual Operation Noah (which asks citizens to 'dob in' drug dealers) and Operation Paradox (which deals with child sexual abuse).

A number of questions can be asked about such strategies: some relate to objectives, and others to notions of the community's role in crime prevention. For example, one might inquire into the logic of such programs—do they actually control crime, or control the fear of crime at a local level? Though few systematic cost–benefit evaluations have been conducted into the effectiveness of situational crime-prevention strategies (including auxiliary justice), those that do exist point to their cost-effectiveness at both the individual property level and on a citywide scale (Chisholm 2000; Walsh & Farrington 2001). It is suggested by some that the mere existence and publicity of these programs elevates community awareness, and hence fear of the crimes being targeted publicity, at least in the short term. In the longer term, the reliance on community resources (volunteers), supplemented by meagre government financial contributions, means that some of these initiatives cannot be sustained in the longer term. For example, Safety House programs—an Australian initiative replicated internationally—have ceased operation in a number of jurisdictions, including Victoria, the Australian Capital Territory (2013) and Queensland (2014).

With regard to community participation, auxiliary justice initiatives are often heralded as an avenue for making the police service more democratically responsive and responsible (through citizen participation and oversight activities) to the local 'community' and its needs. It is apparent, however, that in most cases the police remain effectively in charge of the program, controlling the local crime-prevention agenda and making key decisions regarding intervention (McNamara 1992).

WHO IS REPRESENTED?

It is important as well to examine the degree to which community participants in the oversight of these initiatives are representative of the community as a whole. The principal organisers of programs such as Neighbourhood Watch tend to already be organisationally active (e.g. Scouts, Rotary, Red Cross, Toastmasters and church groups), are long-term residents and tend towards senior age. While ostensibly promoting 'community partnerships' and 'community spirit', the nature of the specific relationships operating in these programs—among private citizens who are concerned about safety and protection of property; insurance companies, which have a clear commercial interest; and the police and the state—suggests a narrower agenda.

The conjunction of specific social and financial interests means that the emphasis of such programs is circumscribed, and tends to focus on the protection of (insured) private property, rather than on issues such as the reallocation or redistribution of resources at the local community level or crimes of a different nature (e.g. toxic waste or pollution) that affect entire communities.

SOCIAL CRIME PREVENTION

In contrast to situational and environmental approaches, which are offence focused and concerned with reducing the opportunities for crime, **social crime prevention** approaches are offender focused and concerned with criminality prevention; that is, deterring potential offenders and offenders from engaging or re-engaging in crime. Rather than intervening to alter physical environments, this approach involves changes to social environments and the motivational conditions thought to predispose individuals and groups of individuals to crime.

In particular, much of the preventative activity promoted by this perspective is directed at young people and their socialisation processes along the transitional pathways from childhood to adulthood. Social crime-prevention initiatives can either seek to intervene early in the childhood

SOCIAL CRIME PREVENTION
An offender-focused approach concerned with criminality prevention (e.g. deterring potential offenders and offenders from engaging or re-engaging in crime). This approach involves changes to social environments and the motivational conditions that predispose individuals and groups of individuals to crime.

developmental process to prevent the onset of crime (primary intervention) or may target people and groups identified as being 'at risk' of offending (secondary intervention) (Crawford 1998; Tonry & Farrington 1995).

While acknowledging the multifaceted and complex nature of crime causation, social prevention approaches basically view crime as the product of predispositional factors, the two most important being (Gottfredson & Hirschi 1990; Hirschi 1969):

- An insufficient degree of restraint or self-control against offending behaviour—said to be caused by under-socialisation. As the principal institutions responsible for the early socialisation of young people and the inculcation within them of self-control, families and schools are regarded as fundamental agents of crime prevention.
- The lack of a personal stake in conformist behaviour—the absence of incentives to be law-abiding. This state of social marginalisation is caused by a lack of legitimate socio-economic opportunity structures (e.g. education and/or employment) that facilitate the attainment of dominant cultural goals (e.g. income, possessions and status).

Based on the above reasoning, a primary concern is the early identification and elimination of risk factors that undermine self-restraint and conformity, leading to social marginalisation and a propensity toward crime. A concomitant concern is to identify and bolster the protective factors in a young person's life that enhance the opportunities for lawful behaviour by enhancing social connectedness. Risk factors commonly identified include (Catalano & Hawkins 1996; Coventry et al. 1992; Crime Prevention Victoria & Australian Institute of Family Studies 2002a,b; Lincoln & Wilson 1994; National Crime Prevention 1999):

- *personality and behavioural factors*: for example, impulsivity, hyper-activity, restlessness, aggression and poor social skills
- *family contexts*: for example, poverty, family size, poor parental supervision and discipline, family dissolution (separation and/or conflict) and parental neglect and/or physical abuse
- *peer influences*: for example, negative peer associations and activities such as substance abuse
- *living conditions*: for example, poor housing and high residential mobility
- *school influences*: for example, truancy, school exclusion and expulsion, bullying and poor educational attainment
- *employment opportunities*: for example, access to vocational training and employment
- *recreational outlets*: for example, activities and spaces.

Efforts to address these criminogenic factors may occur at the social policy level, through the provision of universal social welfare, education and health strategies, services and programs that build cultural, family and personal resilience. These have the potential to impact positively on crime by enhancing opportunity structures and strengthening the capacity of families, neighbourhoods, schools and the professions to promote social inclusion and hence reduce youth marginalisation, but are not crime-prevention policies per se (see, for example, Fagan et al. 2009). Alternatively, those individuals and families identified as being 'at risk' who have already failed to respond to broad-based ameliorative efforts may be diverted to programs that tailor interventions to the specific underlying problems and facilitate direct linkages to existing opportunity structures.

INSTITUTIONAL REFORM

Social crime prevention, however, does not merely seek to enhance opportunities. It also includes analysis and action to reform existing institutional processes that may be part of the problem. For example, to understand the relationship between school, delinquency and crime, it is necessary to understand the impact of schooling processes on young people. School-related offences and offensive behaviour can occur both within and against the institution. A significant issue today is discipline, as is the widespread truanting behaviour among compulsory school-aged young people. We must examine those who persistently truant, and ask ourselves what is so offensive about school that makes them not want to attend. Factors might include boredom, meaningless curricula, the authority structure of the school and lack of respect on the part of teachers (White 1996c). The school should be a liberating institution, but many find it repressive. This can be seen as an important factor in the creation of deviant, criminal and antisocial behaviour.

The object of social prevention is to move away from the coercive relationships of the state. As alluded to above, some issues of relevance are the role of school, the issue of compulsory education, increasing retention rates, and the alienation of young people from the schooling process. We also need to understand that it is not necessarily the poor who commit crime, but that if you are poor, your behaviour and position in society are increasingly being criminalised. Crime in society is attributed, at least in part, to the removal of adequate income support and paid work opportunities for many individuals.

Accordingly, it is important to consider a variety of youth group formations and the way in which the authorities seek to stigmatise and regulate the behaviour of the marginalised in society, especially among the young (see Cunneen & White 2011; see also Chapters 7 and 8). Specific populations, particularly ethnic minority youth and Indigenous young people, have been denied legitimate participation in the spheres of production, consumption and the utilisation of public space. The alienation of people by the system and the brutalisation of people in the scramble to make ends meet are seen to breed alienated and brutal people.

UNEQUAL AND DISADVANTAGED

The solution, from the point of view of crime prevention, is to consider seriously the unequal or 'disadvantaged' position of a large number of people in the political economy, and to bolster their ability to participate legitimately in the economy. This may take the form of measures such as job creation, education and training programs, and provision of a basic income.

Attention is directed to the means of life, and how these can be improved for those who have been denied them. Second, the existing institutional structures and processes are criticised as contributing to alienated behaviour and marginalised status. Thus, not only are resources to be expended upon enhancing job and school opportunities but also on revamping the present systems to suit the needs of the users better.

In more recent years, the concept of justice reinvestment has emerged, which attempts to redirect public monies away from the expansion of coercive justice institutions (prisons) towards education, housing, healthcare, jobs and social programs designed to address the underlying causes of crime in targeted, high-crime areas, or areas with high populations of returning ex-prisoners (see, for example, Brown et al. 2012; Young & Solonec 2011).

COMMUNITY DEVELOPMENT

From a structural perspective, crime is an inevitable outcome of wider structural forces (economic, political and cultural) and the negative social conditions they create, such as poverty, inequality, marginalisation, oppression and exclusion (Hope 1997; Hughes 1998; Weatherburn 1992; Whitworth 2012b). Accordingly, the key to preventing crime in the long term lies in the adoption of a multi-pronged approach that has at its core a process of social empowerment, particularly of marginalised groups. This process can only be achieved through the democratisation of all facets of community decision-making, including policing and crime prevention.

COMMUNITY DEVELOPMENT
A process that stresses a collective approach to problem-solving and decision-making about needs, goals, priorities and programs. Underpinning this approach are a number of fundamental values, including a commitment to pursuing social justice, participatory democracy and social inclusion.

Community development initiatives provide a vehicle for achieving that end. As described by Henderson et al. (1980: 5), community development is a process that 'stresses a collective approach to problem solving and decision-making about needs, goals, priorities, and programs. In particular it seeks to enable marginal groups to migrate into "the acting community" of decisions and decision-makers'.

Underpinning this approach are a number of fundamental values, including a commitment to pursuing social justice (tackling discrimination and inequalities such as those focusing on gender, race and religion), participatory democracy (which includes diversity) and an inclusive concept of the 'common good' (Lane & Henry 2004). At the wider societal level, energies are directed towards redistribution of community resources and wealth in an effort to remove the economic disparities that give rise to criminal activity. Specific strategies associated with this perspective include citizen participation lobbying and activism, consciousness raising and social planning.

At a state wide level, concepts of community development clearly underpin the Victorian Aboriginal Justice Agreement (Victorian Department of Justice 2013, 2004c). This agreement was adopted as a means of reforming the delivery of justice services to Aboriginal people across Victoria, in an effort to tackle the disproportionately high levels of Indigenous disadvantage and persistent over-representation in the criminal justice system. It establishes a formal partnership between the Aboriginal community and the departments of Justice and Human Services and their respective agencies. Among the objectives outlined in the agreement is the empowerment of local communities to be involved directly in the development and implementation of policy, planning and services (see also Blagg 2008a).

VIGILANTE JUSTICE

VIGILANTE JUSTICE
A form of civic activism—the coming together of select, autonomous individuals who voluntarily band together in a self-help approach to community crime prevention—that can take the form of legal (e.g. the Guardian Angels) or illegal (e.g. lynch mobs) groups.

Vigilante justice is a term often referred to when speaking of 'social empowerment', or 'active citizenship' in the sense of the community taking justice into its own hands (Drum & Baldino 2012; McNamara 1992). The growth of community justice oriented crime prevention follows increasing acknowledgment, and acceptance, that the function of policing is no longer the exclusive preserve of the police. It has often been driven by the demands arising within a particular constituency for policing to be sensitive and responsive to local needs and concerns. In practice, however, practical application of this concept varies considerably (Johnston & Shearing 2003; Rigakos 2003).

For example, vigilantism is often associated with extreme right-wing groups, which argue that the state is 'too soft' on offenders and that they will therefore mete out the punishment to 'known offenders'. Often there is a connection of some kind to political right-wing extremists, such as the Ku-Klux-Klan (to take an American example), which espouse racist ideologies. Such individuals band together to protect sectional interests that are not necessarily crime concerns. A racist agenda might merge with a law-and-order agenda in that the targets of action in both cases may be people of colour or, in the Australian case, Indigenous people.

Vigilante justice, if defined simply as members of the community taking control over the justice and punishment process, may also refer to those instances where a particular community acknowledges traditional methods of law enforcement. For example, the use of Aboriginal customary law (e.g. tribal spearing) may be viewed in this light, although in this instance there is often a level of legitimacy regarding the process that renders the term 'vigilante justice' a misnomer. This is because such action takes place within the context of accepted community norms and values (and tribal law), and thus with the approval of the community generally.

In another sense, vigilante justice can denote civic activism—the coming together of select, autonomous individuals who voluntarily band together in a self-help approach to community crime prevention. This principle is commonly given effect through organised Citizen's Patrols (Leach 2003). Although observable in countries as diverse as South Africa, Peru, Canada and Ghana, the most famous example of this approach is the Guardian Angels in New York—not-for-profit volunteers who are trained in self-defence. Members of the organisation do not have formal police powers, but they ride the trains and through their very presence attempt to deter crime and ensure that commuters are safe. Founded in 1979, the Guardian Angels organisation has chapters in over fifteen countries worldwide (over 144 cities).

Opposition to organic self-policing initiatives such as the Guardian Angels stems mainly from the perception that they interfere with police work and operate without a legal mandate. They also attract criticism on the basis that they tap into conventional notions of crime and that though they regulate other people's behaviour, they themselves are not directly accountable to anyone. Those who support the concept argue that it is a community self-help activity—at least they are doing something, and doing it openly.

INDIGENOUS COMMUNITY JUSTICE ORGANISATIONS

In Australia, Aboriginal communities in remote rural and urban areas are increasingly adopting initiatives of this type. Initially established in the Northern Territory as 'Night Patrols', over 130 Aboriginal community self-policing operations (variously referred to as Street Patrols, Bare Foot Patrols or Mobile Assistance Patrols) have been identified throughout Australia (Barcham 2010; Blagg 2008a; Blagg & Valuri 2003a, b; Drum & Baldino 2012). Increasingly, these initiatives have entered partnerships with government and non-government organisations to form 'security networks'. Though community patrols vary in operation, they commonly involve Indigenous people self-policing localities (on foot and in vehicles) in a culturally sensitive manner, in an effort to prevent crime and antisocial behaviour and/or convey people 'at risk' (e.g. those intoxicated or under the influence of drugs) to a safe destination. The range of locally specific drivers underlying the development of these initiatives, include the perceived need to (Blagg & Valuri 2003a: 8):

* fill a void created by under-policing; for example, the Jalalikari scheme in Northern Territory
* avoid over-policing and divert Indigenous people away from unnecessary contact with the justice system; for example, Kullarri in Broome
* provide complementary crisis response services that act as an adjunct to community justice initiatives and existing outreach services; for example, community justice panels, sobering-up shelters, and youth, domestic violence and medical services
* specifically tackle juvenile crime and antisocial behaviour; for example, Yamatji and Nyoongar Community Patrols in Western Australia and the Street Beat program in New South Wales
* address identified Aboriginal health and safety issues; for example, the Marrala Patrol in Western Australia.

While evaluations of these initiatives point to positive outcomes for the Indigenous community, some caution against the possibility that certain forms of self-policing, progressed under the guise of self-determination, actually operate insidiously to reinforce informal institutions of social control (Grabosky 2001). It is argued that these security networks, when operating alongside more powerful government and business agencies, may actually serve to meet non-Indigenous interests (e.g. eradicating Aboriginal people from public space) rather than the needs of Indigenous people (Blagg & Valuri 2004).

Many diverse approaches and techniques have been canvassed in this section. It is frequently the case, however, that from a problem-solving perspective, a combination of measures will be required (Homel 2009). This is illustrated in Figure 28.2, which looks at the issue of crime prevention and motor vehicle theft.

As indicated in Figure 28.2, motor vehicle theft has been declining over the past decade and a half in Australia. This is due in no small part to the National Motor Vehicle Theft Reduction Strategy, which has involved strategic planning, the bringing together of diverse interest groups, and the adoption of a combination of crime prevention techniques and approaches (see, for example, Brown 2013; CARS 2014; NMVTRC 2006). The council is a joint initiative of Australian governments and the insurance industry. It works actively with police, insurers, the motor trades, vehicle manufacturers, registration authorities and justice agencies, as well as providing information and educational materials to local communities. The NMVTRC employs a wide range of strategies to reduce car theft and as the dynamics of car theft change over time, it remains open to new strategies. These include:

- *situational techniques* that focus on the offence: increasing the risks and efforts (e.g. fitting alarms and tracking devices, engine immobilisers, steering column locks and data dots)
- *CPTED measures* that focus on the physical environment: designing out crime opportunities (e.g. improved lighting, improved design of car parks, installation of entrance barriers and electronic access)
- *social crime prevention* approaches that focus on the offender: addressing motivations and social circumstances (e.g. comic books and other educational materials to help young people become more aware of the risks and social and legal consequences of vehicle crime; and intensive trade-based training for young recidivist car thieves) (Sutton et al. 2014).

The success in reducing the incidence of motor vehicle theft demonstrates the importance of adopting multi-pronged approaches that draw upon social and situational measures, and that involve a wide range of stakeholders in the process.

FIGURE 28.2   CRIME PREVENTION AND CAR THEFT

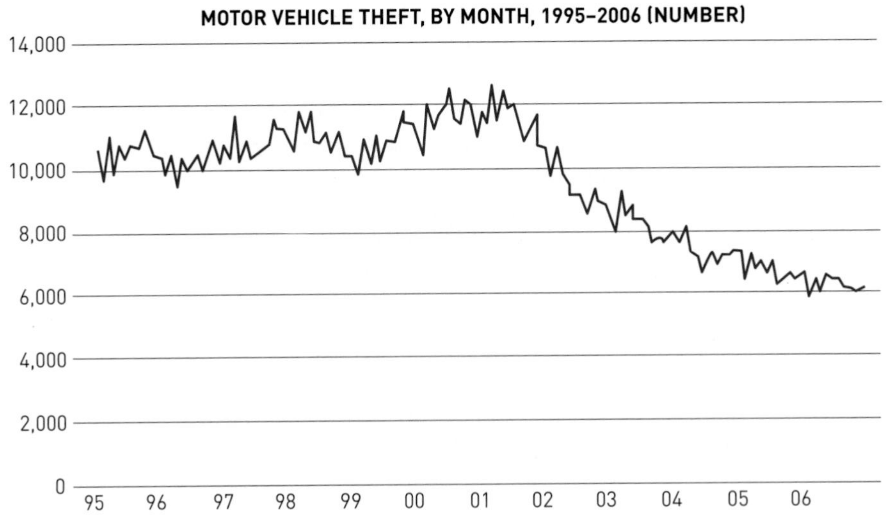

MOTOR VEHICLE THEFT, BY MONTH, 1995–2006 (NUMBER)

Source: AIC (2008)

ISSUES FOR CONSIDERATION

THE IMPORTANCE OF CONTEXT: TAILORING CRIME PREVENTION

Recent criminological work on illegal poaching of elephants and rhinoceros, and on illegal trade in parrots, has exposed the conjunction of many different factors that go into why and how such activity takes place (White & Heckenberg 2014). A key lesson from this research is that tailoring responses to the specific context and the specific crime is essential. For example, a variety of traditional situational crime prevention measures have been suggested or adopted in relation to particular types of wildlife crime:

- *elephant poaching:* (e.g. closure of logging roads, DNA coding of ivory, use of pilot-less drones and banning of international trade in ivory)
- *illegal trade in parrots:* (e.g. protecting the nests of target species during breeding season, use of CCTV surveillance, active focus on geographical area where most species are concentrated (hot spots), identification and shutting-down of key city markets, and road blocks on widely used trafficking roads)
- *rhinoceros poaching:* (e.g. more rangers and military patrols on the ground, dehorning animals and other science-based interventions such as microchipping, investment in community-based eco-tourism projects, and bilateral government agreements to cooperatively curb the illegal trade) (see Ayling 2013; Lemieux & Clarke 2009; Pires & Clarke 2013, 2012, 2011; Pires & Moreto 2011).

One of the key areas of interest throughout this extensive and growing literature is that of disrupting markets. That is, systematic and rigorous analysis of poaching is demonstrating the importance of studying harvesting networks, and the resilience of these networks to environmental law-enforcement efforts (Ayling 2013). The relationship between specific networks of actors—from the local through to intercity through to regional and transnational levels—and specific markets and marketplaces (including eBay and other internet mechanisms) allows identification of weak points in the supply chains as well as diverse participant motivations. This means that crime-prevention responses can be contemplated that take into account factors such as specific communal circumstance (e.g. high levels of poverty and unemployment among local residents) and trade routes (smuggling avenues in remote areas and in cities), among other related criminogenic factors.

CHALLENGES AND UNINTENDED CONSEQUENCES

In terms of practical application, it is customarily the first two approaches to crime prevention—situational crime prevention and crime prevention through environmental design—that are usually talked about when discussions turn to leading-edge crime-prevention strategies. It is important to acknowledge, however, that while these approaches offer practical solutions to the crime problem, they also raise a number of debatable issues.

On one level, there is merit in broader planning initiatives, but, as with any strategy, problems are encountered (see Sutton & Hazlehurst 1996; White & Sutton 1995). Do such programs deal with and address the causes of crime? The answer to this question is a qualified 'no'. But they certainly do make a difference in the nature both of crime commission and of crime control.

Such programs can reduce the opportunity for crime, for example, but this can have other implications, such as *displacement* (see Barlow 1993; Barr & Pease 1990). The suggestion here is that by successfully reducing the opportunities for crime in one area, criminal activity will simply be averted for a while, until another opportunity arises in the same location—this is known as *temporal displacement*. Alternatively, crime may simply be directed towards more vulnerable areas or targets, which is referred to respectively as *spatial displacement* and *target displacement*. For example, the installation of steering locks and engine immobilisers in modern cars simply causes thieves to target older cars not fitted with such devices or to break into homes to access keys (see Chapter 9). There is also the possibility that frustrated offenders may escalate the nature of their activities: instead of seeking to rob a house, for instance, they turn to mugging individuals—this is known as *offence displacement*. If changes occur in the method by which an offender perpetrates a crime, such as from committing an unarmed to an armed robbery, then *tactical displacement* is said to have occurred. Both tactical and offence displacement may result in the additional victimisation of already vulnerable groups in society, such as the elderly and the poor. A final form of displacement is *perpetrator displacement*, where crime prevention strategies and initiatives disable offenders for a period of time through incarceration, but other offenders emerge to fill the vacuum. While not discounting displacement as an unintended consequence of situational crime-prevention initiatives, recent studies suggest the possibility of *benign displacement*, where the net social gains are spread to areas and populations that are not the immediate target of the measures (see Clarke & Weisburd 1994; Ratcliffe & Makkai 2004).

Another related problem is that such measures may *amplify the excitement* of crime: the threat of punishment may actually invite offending. For example, in shopping centres, where there is a high security presence, some may perceive it a challenge or cause for a good chase. The challenge presented by situational crime prevention measures may also result in *creative adaptations*; that is, more innovative ways of pulling off the crime. For example, the use of gates or shutters to protect businesses has seen a rise in the phenomenon of 'ram raids', in which thieves smash through shop-fronts with vehicles. Adaptive measures may at times entail more brutal forms of victimisation. For example, in an effort to combat security barriers in banks, robbers may decide to take hostages.

It is also important to examine which crimes are being targeted over others: property or behavioural crimes? We must assess here the social interests and class impact of some community crime-prevention programs. The commodification of protective and surveillance devices serves to reinforce the crime-control agenda of the right-wing law-and-order lobby, and to orient programs and policing strategies toward containment rather than dealing with the social conditions that generate crime. Commercial and private property crimes tend to be targeted over other social harms, such as white-collar crime or domestic violence.

The rapid proliferation of overt and covert CCTV in Australian public and public/private spaces (e.g. streets, banks, petrol stations, automatic teller machines and entertainment precincts) raises questions regarding the desirability of living in a surveillance state and, in particular, of trading privacy for *potentially* enhanced 'safety and security' (Anderson & McAtamney 2011). Of particular concern is the current absence of legislation governing regulation of CCTV operations in Australia—accountability is generally sought through voluntary Codes of Practice (Wilson 2003; Wilson & Sutton 2003).

A common effect of situational crime-prevention measures is the destruction of accessible public space and the hardening of streetscapes against the homeless (e.g. removal of comfortable seating used as beds, caging bins, and limiting access to toilets through timed sprinkler systems), resulting in the creation of divisive and hostile environments. Security measures are often expensive, and the more sophisticated versions are often only seen in the wealthier sections of the city, not the high-rental, low-income areas. Hence, economic exclusivity forms the basis of crime prevention measures and a clear chasm emerges between the crime prevention 'ghettos' and the privileged enclaves, where applications of the 'defensible space' concept are taken to the extreme. The potential for explosive situations in this protected community context was clearly demonstrated in the Los Angeles riots. The wealthier sections of Los Angeles resemble urban fortresses or gated communities, characterised by private security patrols, extensive spy camera networks, and highly developed and secure shopping centres, where in some instances shoppers are required to produce some form of identification to be permitted entry (Blakely & Snyder 1997; Davis 1990; Vilalta 2011). Such measures are clearly oriented towards excluding those who cannot afford such security-oriented luxuries. Martin (2000) and Kerr (2001) draw our attention to parallel developments in CPTED and public space regulation in Australia that are contributing to community polarisation.

Another related question is who are the targets of designing out crime? The measures appear neutral, but they target the marginalised and vulnerable people in society, such as the poor, unemployed, Aboriginal people and young people. It is argued by some that the objective of environmental modification is not simply technical—that is, to reduce the opportunity for crime—but has social and political consequences. In some cases it has the explicit objective of seeking to reduce the very presence and visibility of such 'undesirable' groups in particular public spaces (Sutton 1997; White & Sutton 1995). For instance, shopping centres are generally constructed around the concept of socially excluding young people (especially the poor) who are deemed 'non-consumers'. Police and private security personnel are regularly called in to move these groups away from commercial premises and affluent suburbs. Issues here relate to where such people can go to claim a space of their own and how we are to include them in our concept of 'community'.

Following on from the above, we need to question the desirability of social and spatial planning processes and place-based management strategies that presuppose a particular cultural usage of urban space, irrespective of the cultural composition of the local population. Such presuppositions may engender a monocultural use of public space, which not only excludes other cultural forms and identity but also ultimately results in the criminalisation of entire cohorts of visibly different individuals. As indicated by Lee and Herborn (2003: 32) this issue 'raises questions about questions of race, ethnicity and subculture and the ability of the dominant culture to prescribe an "authentic" vision of particular social space' (see also Harvey 1994).

Finally, while the underlying objective of crime-prevention programs is to reduce the fear of crime, empirical evidence suggests that such initiatives actually serve to *generate an unwarranted degree of fear and suspicion* (Sutton 1994b). Stopping crime is always a theoretical possibility if we had sufficient resources, tools and power. But, do we really want to create a kind of 'surveillance state' where we are all free from crime, but prisoners of our own security systems; a society where no one is to be trusted?

CONCLUSION

The coercive institutions of the state, such as the police, prisons and the courts, operate through violence or the threat of violence. When speaking of crime prevention, we are, however, not necessarily speaking only of state institutions per se. There is a whole range of other social institutions that we need to consider under the broad umbrella of crime control. These include institutions of both coercion and development.

This chapter has provided an outline of a variety of specific strategies and techniques, usually linked to particular crime-prevention approaches, which are currently in use. In practice, however, such methods are rarely unproblematic from the point of view of criteria such as actual success rates, reductions in the fear of crime, or philosophical desirability. It is vital in fact to 'read' each proposed method or strategy to see how it fits with the models of crime prevention reviewed at the beginning of the chapter, for our methods of tackling crime prevention are ultimately linked to the kind of society we wish to have, and the central interests that should drive political action and policy development.

These concerns also raise issues relating to the role of the criminologist in the crime-prevention process (see Sutton 1994b). In particular, crime prevention should not be conceptualised as simply a matter of choosing the right techniques or strategies. In many cases, appropriate intervention to prevent crime requires an explicitly political, rather than technical, approach; that is, the best strategy or tactic to combat certain types of crimes, in certain areas, may well be to engage in advocacy for structural change. Crime prevention includes reference to ideological vision and political campaigning, as well as specific programs and techniques—they are not mutually exclusive.

DISCUSSION QUESTIONS

1   'The notion of "community" means all things to all people'. Discuss.

2   What are the key differences between situational, environmental and social prevention measures?

3   'Crime prevention is never socially neutral. It always affects different groups of people in different ways'. Discuss.

4   'Integrated crime prevention is the most meaningful way to approach issues relating to crime and social harm'. Examine specific types of crime or harm and apply this principle.

5   'Crime prevention might get rid of crime but could also destroy the basic fabric of a society'. Discuss by comparing Australia with Singapore, the United States and Italy.

FURTHER READING

Clancy, G., Lee, M. & Fisher, D. (2012) 'Crime Prevention through environmental design (CPTED) and the New South Wales crime risk assessment guidelines: A critical review', *Crime Prevention and Community Safety*, 14(1): 1–15.

Clarke, R. (ed.) (1997) *Situational crime prevention: successful case studies*, Harrow and Heston, Albany.

Crawford, A. (1998) *Crime prevention and community safety: politics, policies and practices*, Addison Wesley Longman Limited, United Kingdom.

Lemieux, A. (ed.) (2014) *Situational prevention of poaching*, Routledge, London.

Sutton, A., Cherney, A. & White, R. (2014) *Crime prevention: principles, perspectives and practices*, Cambridge University Press, Melbourne.

ACCESS TO JUSTICE

A concept that refers to the ability of individuals and groups to use the law, including access to lawyers, and having their issues heard and dealt with adequately within the legal system, including the courts.

ACTUS REUS

A Latin term meaning 'guilty act'. An element of criminal responsibility comprising the physical components of a crime. These may be wrongful acts, omissions or a state of affairs that constitute a violation of the law.

ADJUDICATED FINALISATION

Occurs when all charges against a person or organisation have been finalisation by way of a judgment or decision by the court. This involves the court making a determination regarding whether or not the defendant is guilty of the charge(s) laid against them (this may be based on a guilty plea or a finding of guilt be a jury in a contested matter).

ALTERNATIVE DISPUTE RESOLUTION

A set of methods and strategies of dispute resolution that are less formal and less expensive than those provided by formal justice institutions, and which are in many cases directed at positive problem-solving and involve active citizen participation.

ANOMIE

A lack of social regulation in which the unrestricted appetites of the individual conscience are no longer held in check ('anything goes'); that is, a state of normlessness where appropriate norms are not in place to inhibit deviant behaviour.

ASSAULT

The direct infliction of force, injury or violence upon a person, including attempts or threats, providing the attempts or threats are in the form of face-to-face direct confrontation and there is reason to believe that the attempts or threats can be immediately enacted.

BURGLARY

The unlawful entry of a dwelling, house or any other premises, such as a business, school or shop, with or without force, with the intent to steal; in some states, burglary is referred to in the statutes as 'break, enter and steal'.

CHIVALRY THESIS

The theory that one of the reasons for the apparently low female crime rate is that traditional male attitudes to women as weak and in need of protection, together with their role as child-rearers, makes male law enforcers reluctant to apply the full weight of the law.

CIVIL LAW

Civil law generally involves cases dealing with two (or more) parties, be they people, corporations, the state or any combination thereof. One party, who believes its rights have been infringed, brings a civil action or suit against another party, whom it believe has wronged him or her, consequently resulting in injury or loss. The two branches of civil law are the law of torts and the law of contracts.

CLASS

A concept fundamental to understanding how people access societal resources, whether these are economic, social cultural or political. It refers to specific relationships of people to the means of production in a society; that is, the ownership and control of production (e.g. land, rent and labour property). Class situation is linked to specific types of criminality. Where individuals are located in the class structure will influence the kinds of criminal activity they engage in, the propensity to engage in such activity and the intensity of that involvement.

CLASSICAL THEORY

Classical theory locates the source of criminality within the rational, reasoning individual, and sees it as a matter of choice and intent on the part of the offender. The classical school of criminology emphasises choice, responsibility and intent.

COLLECTIVE CONSCIOUSNESS

Shared ideas, beliefs and values that establish society's moral foundations and which operate as a unifying force within society.

COLONIALISM

The process by which Indigenous people have been dispossessed of their lands and culture by the invading culture. Colonialism has had a severe impact on Indigenous cultures and ways of life, as have its continuing effects of discriminatory policies and practices on Indigenous life chances within mainstream social institutions.

COMMON LAW

A type of legal system that has incorporated many of the values, principles, procedures and rules developed initially in England; for example, a range of measures has been developed to safeguard the rights of the accused, such as the presumption that a person is innocent until proved guilty. In contrast, other legal systems are premised on the idea that one is guilty until proven innocent. This term also refers to judge-made law based upon tradition (commonly accepted customs) and judicial precedent, which looks to previous decisions in similar cases as a measure of how to adjudicate in the present.

COMMUNITY CORRECTIONS

Community-based management of a variety of court-ordered sanctions, which serve as either non-custodial sentencing alternatives or post-custodial mechanisms for reintegrating ex-prisoners back into the community. Community-based correctional orders vary greatly with respect to the extent and nature of supervision and conditions.

COMMUNITY DEVELOPMENT

A process that stresses a collective approach to problem-solving and decision-making about needs, goals, priorities and programs. Underpinning this approach are a number of fundamental values, including a commitment to pursuing social justice, participatory democracy and social inclusion.

COMMUNITY LEGAL CENTRES

Legal organisations informed by an ethos of addressing the unmet legal needs of the poor, disadvantaged and vulnerable, and using the law as a mechanism for substantive social reform.

COMMUNITY POLICING

A style of policing that emphasises a conciliatory, rather than coercive, approach to police work. It seeks to move away from the police-centred authoritarian nature of traditional approaches, focusing instead on a co-participatory model of crime prevention that accepts that the community has a legitimate, active role to play in the policing process.

COMORBIDITY

Overlapping problems of homelessness, abuse, family difficulties, mental illness and deteriorating physical health. Commonly used to refer to the combination of drug and alcohol abuse with a medically defined mental illness.

CONCEPTS OF RISK

Concepts of risk underpin contemporary juvenile justice systems and intervention practices, and focus on matters pertaining to the causes and predictions of crime, and the assessment and management of young offenders.

CONCURRENT SENTENCE

A deviation from standard sentencing procedure, whereby a person convicted of multiple offences is permitted to serve each sentence simultaneously.

CONSECUTIVE/CUMULATIVE SENTENCE

A standard sentencing procedure where a person convicted of multiple offences receives a separate penalty for each crime, to be served consecutively.

CORPORATE CRIME

The illegal activities of businesses against members of the public, the environment, creditors, investors or corporate competitors; it includes crimes committed by corporate officials for their corporation, as well as the offences of the corporation itself.

CRIME

Acts that are legally prohibited by the state and deemed to be deserving of punishment and control.

CRIME CONTROL

The ways in which society responds to crime; in particular, how different institutions of criminal justice, including state- and community-based agencies and bodies, prevent or limit the harms associated with crime and offensive behaviour.

CRIME PREVENTION

The creation and implementation of proactive programs and strategies that are intended to prevent crime before it occurs, and to address and diminish the fear of crime.

CRIME PREVENTION THROUGH ENVIRONMENTAL DESIGN

Planning and design of the physical environment such that it decreases opportunities for crime and enhances surveillance capabilities in specific places.

CRIME WAVE

The way in which increased reporting of particular types of crime (especially street crimes such as assault, rape or homicide) increase public awareness of this crime. There need not have been an actual increase in the crime for a crime wave to occur; the increase exists only in public perception. It is closely linked but separate from the concept of *moral panic.*

CRIMINAL DAMAGE

A wide range of offences against property, including vandalism, where the objective is destruction, damage or defacement of the property rather than financial gain.

CRIMINALISATION

The process by which certain acts or particular people or groups are defined as criminal. What is deemed to be 'criminal' and who is defined as an 'offender' involves a social process, by which officials of the state formally intervene and designate certain acts and certain actors as warranting a criminal label. Until an act, or actor, has been processed in particular ways by the state, there is no 'crime' as such.

CRIMINOGENESIS

The origins or causes of crime; situations or factors tending to produce or promote crime or criminality.

CRIMINOGENIC NEEDS

The needs that are directly related to the nature of the original offending; for example, an offender may engage in burglary because of the pressures of an illicit drug habit. The criminogenic need here relates to the need for drug treatment and rehabilitation. A violent offender, by contrast, may have need for anger management training.

CRIMINOLOGICAL THEORY

The frameworks within which the main explanations for criminal behaviour or criminality are located. Perspectives include the individual (sees crime as stemming from individual characteristics of the offender or victim); the situational (sees crime as stemming from the immediate situation or circumstances within which criminal activity or deviant behaviour occurs); and the structural (sees crime in terms of broader social relationships and the major social institutions of society as a whole).

CRIMINOLOGY

The systematic study of crime, criminality and criminal justice systems, focusing on the definitions and causes of crime, the process of criminalisation, crime prevention, systems of social control, and the treatment, rehabilitation and punishment of offenders.

CRITICAL CRIMINOLOGY

Critical criminology builds upon the basic concepts and strategic concerns of the Marxist and feminist perspectives, generally from the point of view of a broadly anti-capitalist position. Critical criminology is basically concerned with structures of power: how power is conceptualised and exercised. Essentially it concerns itself with the critique of domination; that is, unveiling institutionalised power structures that maintain select social interests through oppressive conditions of domination experienced by vulnerable groups within society.

CULTURAL CRIMINOLOGY

Cultural criminology refers to a body of scholarship that views crime and social control agencies as cultural products. A main focus is on the emotions of crime; the varied emotional dynamics and experiential attractions (pleasures, excitement and control) that constitute an essential element of much crime and antisocial behaviour. Since the emotions associated with everyday life and those associated with crime overlap, a common theme is that certain modes of deviance and criminality offer the perpetrator a means of 'self-transcendence' or psychic resolution; that is, a way of overcoming the conventionality and ordinariness of everyday life.

CUSTODY

This involves physically depriving a person of their liberty by confining them to some form of institution (prison, mental asylum, police cell etc.) under lawful process or authority. In the case of a remand prisoner, this involves placement into custody whist awaiting the outcome of legal proceedings. Remandees may be unconvicted (remanded in custody for trial), convicted but awaiting sentence (remanded in custody for sentence) or awaiting deportation.

CYBER-BULLYING

Cyber-bullying refers to repeated and targeted harassment and bullying involving the use of information technologies such as the internet.

CYBER-CRIME

Cyber-crime involves the use of information technology to commit a crime, the destruction or altering of stored information, and the use of computers to store information about an offence.

CYBER SAFETY

Cyber-safety involves concerns about the nature and types of risks and threats associated with the use of information technology.

CYBER-VICTIMISATION

Crimes against the person relating to the use and misuse of computer technologies, such as identity theft, cyber harassment and online sexual exploitation of children.

'DARK FIGURE' OF CRIME

A criminological term used to describe criminal acts and omissions that are not detected and/or reported to the police and therefore are not captured in officially recorded crime statistics.

DEATHS IN CUSTODY

Deaths, wherever occurring, of people who are in prison custody or police custody or detention; whose deaths are caused or contributed to by traumatic injuries sustained, or by lack of proper care, while in custody or detention; who are fatally injured in the process of police or prison officers attempting to detain them; or who are fatally injured in the process of escaping or attempting to escape from prison custody or police custody or juvenile detention.

DECARCERATION

Originating in the mid-twentieth century, this movement advocates removal of individuals from institutions, such as prisons or mental hospitals. This philosophy became a central influence in the reconceptualisation of social control, and greatly influenced the development of programs of community care and community control.

DEINSTITUTIONALISATION

A profound social policy shift prompting the large-scale restructuring of human services delivery. This customarily resulted in the diversion of offenders, patients and clients away from institutions (including prisons) and towards community-based alternatives.

DESISTANCE

A central concept in life course or criminal career criminology. It refers to the social process in which an offender de-escalates and ultimately ceases taking part in further criminal or antisocial behaviour.

DEVIANCE

Behaviour that breaks a rule within a social group and is viewed with disapproval and negatively labelled by the group. Deviance implies deviation from some presumed norm, and the transgression marks the person as an outsider to the mainstream.

DEVIANCY AMPLIFICATION

The public labelling attached to particular groups or activities (e.g. graffiti) that can actually generate further or increased deviant behaviour (because of the public notoriety or fame associated with being, say, a graffiti artist).

DIFFERENTIAL ASSOCIATION

A theory that seeks to explain how criminal behaviour is learnt in interactions between people. This theory argues that people learn to define a situation and their conduct in relation to the law, and that this learning takes place within specific group contexts. A person becomes delinquent in circumstances in which the attitudes of the people with whom they associate tend, on balance, to favour the violation of the law rather than law abidance.

DIFFERENTIAL POLICING

A style of policing that makes decisions based on sexual, racial and class dimensions, and in and of itself represents an abuse of police discretionary power.

DIVERSION

The movement of young offenders away from the more formal and/or harshest aspects of the criminal justice system in the light of their vulnerable social position, based on specific age-related needs and interests.

DOMINION

Within criminological theory, 'dominion' refers to republican notions of liberty. Dominion is a form of freedom or positive liberty that is protected by the law and culture of a community. Crime occurs when the dominion status of an individual is diminished or destroyed, and the community as a whole feels threatened.

DOUBLE VICTIMISATION

The way in which the state's response to victimisation can add further burdens to the victim; for instance, rape victims may be doubly victimised because of the way in which courtroom processes put women 'on trial' by suggesting they invited the incident in some way.

DUALITY OF RESPONSIBILITY

Refers to the notion that addressing the causes of crime and offending is a societal-level responsibility as well as one that individual offenders have to take responsibility for, and each therefore must be included in any discussion of the 'crime problem'.

ECCLESIASTICAL JUSTICE

The creation and administration of law and punishment on the basis of theological (religious) principles drawn from Christian teachings on personal morality.

ECO-GLOBAL CRIMINOLOGY

A criminological approach informed by ecological considerations and a critical analysis that is worldwide in its scale and perspective. It is based upon eco-justice conceptions of harm, which include consideration of transgressions against environments, non-human species and humans. Within ecoglobal criminology, three broad approaches to justice have been identified, each with its specific conceptions of what is harmful: environmental rights and environmental justice; ecological citizenship and ecological justice; and animal rights and species justice.

ECOCIDE

Ecocide describes the extensive damage, destruction to or loss of eco-systems of a given territory; where this occurs as a result of human agency, it is purported that a crime has occurred.

EGOISM

A normative phenomenon in which a value has been placed on the unrestricted pursuit of individual desires ('greed is good'); that is, the presence of norms that actively encourage the development of unregulated aspirations, and thus encourage and sustain deviant behaviour.

ENLIGHTENMENT

An intellectual and philosophical movement away from the Middle Ages and its foundational principles, including the divine right of kings, religious authority, oligarchy and the aristocracy. At the core of enlightenment thinking is the concept of rational, scientific discourse and judgment (as opposed to personal judgment) along with an emphasis on the existence of natural laws (deism), individual rights and freedom for common people.

ENTREPRENEURIAL CRIME

Punishable acts committed by individuals in positions of control within corporations, for personal benefit, by exploiting the resources and power deriving from the corporate form.

ENVIRONMENTAL CRIME

Unauthorised acts or omissions that violate the law, and are therefore subject to criminal prosecution and criminal sanctions; more broadly, those activities that may be legal and 'legitimate', but which nevertheless have a negative impact on people and environments.

ENVIRONMENTAL VICTIMISATION

Specific forms of harm that are caused by acts (e.g. dumping of toxic waste) or omissions (e.g. failure to provide safe drinking water) leading to the presence or absence of environmental agents (e.g. poisons or nutrients) that are associated with human injury. Under certain circumstances, specific eco-systems and non-human animals can be considered victims too.

EPISTEMOLOGY

A branch of philosophy focused on the nature, scope and acquisition of knowledge.

ETHNIC MINORITY

Australians whose cultural background is neither Anglo-Australian nor Indigenous.

ETHNICITY

Cultural attributes within social groups that form the basis of a shared sense of identity both within the group itself and by those outside it. Commonalities may include: physical appearance, religious allegiance, language, custom, attachment to an ancestral homeland or some combination of these.

EUGENICS

A social philosophy advocating the improvement of the genetic quality of the human race via scientific means; that is, controlled human reproduction to promote breeding of individuals with desired heritable traits (positive eugenics) and reduce breeding of individuals with undesirable heritable traits (negative eugenics).

FEAR OF CRIME

Fear of crime is basically about emotions. The basis for such fears may be rational or irrational, depending upon specific types of evidence and specific types of harm. The key point is that such feelings propel people to act, think and behave in particular ways. A universalised fear of crime provides the ground upon which emotive responses to complex social problems can predominate over and above those offered on the basis of criminological evidence or alternative political ideologies.

FEMINIST PERSPECTIVES

Feminist perspectives provide a gendered critique of structural relations within society. Society is regarded as fundamentally androcentric (centred on men); female subjugation and male domination are considered to be an entrenched feature of patriarchal society. Crime (committed against women and by women) is attributable to social oppression and economic dependency. Gender inequality, discrimination and disempowerment are embodied in the law and the criminal justice system, and this is reflected in the state's response to women both as offenders and victims.

FINALISATION
Occurs when all charges against a person or organisation have been formally dealt with by the court.

FORENSIC EVIDENCE
Forensic evidence is the evidence presented in court that is based on specific areas of technical and vocational expertise.

FORENSIC SCIENCE
Specific areas of technical and vocational expertise, including training in chemistry, ballistics, fingerprint analysis, DNA testing and computer forensics. Crime scene investigation (including specific types of crime scene, such as arson and bushfire arson cases) demands the development of particular skills, capacities and expertise.

FORENSIC STUDIES
The study of forensics as a social phenomenon. The question here is less to do with 'how to' (e.g. laboratory science and crime scene techniques) than with the overall implications of forensics for society as a whole. The concern is to learn about how science and technology shape the work of the justice system.

GENDER
Gender refers to the distinction between masculine and feminine. It is a social construct (masculinities and femininities vary from culture to culture), not a biological given (as in the case of male–female). The social construction of gender shapes both the incidence of lawbreaking and the response of the criminal justice system to this.

GENDER RATIO IN POLICING
The number of males relative to females in policing. This has implications with regard to which decisions are made, at which level, by whom and in which areas of police work. The higher the rank, the fewer women there are, both in real numbers and in proportion to the overall gender composition of the police services.

GENERATIVITY
Generativity involves a process of giving to others with the consequence of positive changes in the self-esteem and social attitudes of those doing the giving.

GENOCIDE
What distinguishes genocide from other forms of group violence is not so much the degree of violence but the fact that the action is consciously designed to destroy another group. Genocide can occur without physical killing, it can occur with mixed motives (some of which may be perceived to be beneficial) and it can occur without the complete destruction of the group.

GOOD LIVES MODEL (GLM)
The two core therapeutic goals of the GLM are to promote human goods and to reduce risk. The GLM includes the adoption of strengths-based approaches that shift the focus away from criminogenic needs and other deficits and instead ask what individuals can contribute to their family, community and society. In other words, how can their life become useful and purposeful? This approach starts from the assumption that offenders are essentially human beings with similar needs and aspirations to non-offending members of the community.

GRAFFITI
The unsolicited, unauthorised and deliberate defacement of public or private property by writing, scratching, marking, spraying, stencilling or affixing of materials.

GRAFT
Those instances in which state officials make deals with businesses in return for money or favours.

GREEN OR ENVIRONMENTAL CRIMINOLOGY
The study by criminologists of environmental harms, laws and regulations. Within green criminology, the three broad approaches to the conceptualisation of environmental harm are environmental justice (main focus is on humans), ecological justice (main focus is on the environment) and species justice (main focus is on animals).

HARM
Physical or other kinds of injury, distress or damage to humans, environments and non-human animals resulting from acts or omissions that are either legal or illegal.

HATE CRIME
Violence that is directed at individuals or groups on the basis of their actual or perceived sexuality, disability or membership of a racial, ethnic or religious group.

HETEROSEXISM
The domination of a particular kind of gender order, one that assumes binary categories of sexuality (e.g. gay or straight) and that privileges one over the other (straight over gay). It is linked to the practices of

hegemonic masculinity that assert the dominance of males over females.

HOMICIDE

Unlawful interpersonal assaults and other acts directed against another person that occur outside the context of warfare and prove fatal (includes murder and manslaughter).

HYPOTHESES

Proposed explanations for a phenomenon that require evaluation to establish merit.

IDEAL TYPE

An ideal type is an analytical tool, rather than a moral statement of what ought to be. It comprises a process of choosing different aspects of social phenomena and combining them into a typical model or example.

ILLICIT DRUG OFFENCES

Offences that include the possession, sale, dealing or trafficking, importing or exporting, manufacture or cultivation of drugs or other substances prohibited under legislation (e.g. cannabis or heroin).

IMPRISONMENT

This involves physical confinement of a convicted offender to a penal institution (open or secure prison or jail) as a lawful punishment by the courts (a sentence of imprisonment).

IMPRISONMENT RATE

Provides an indication of the size of the prison population relative to the broader population. These may be expressed as the number of prisoners per 100,000 adults, or the number of prisoners per 100,000 people Imprisonment rates allow for meaningful comparison to be drawn of prison populations across jurisdictions, since they control for differences in population size.

INTEGRATED OFFENDER MANAGEMENT

A holistic and integrated system of intervention, which uses evidence-based approaches to identify, assess and treat offenders within correctional and community environments.

INTELLECTUAL PROPERTY

Property of the mind or intellect that is protected by legal safeguards, including copyright law, patents and trademarks, the aim of which is to ensure that the profits of creative work or intellectual effort are returned to the legal owners.

INTERMEDIATE SANCTIONS

Custodial and non-custodial sentencing orders that sit between immediate imprisonment and lower-level community-based options, such as fines, dismissals, discharges and adjournments. These sanctions serve as substitutes for a term of imprisonment or alternative sanctions, which are not dependent on a term of imprisonment being imposed.

INTERNATIONAL LAW

That body of law pertaining to the global community. It deals with relations between countries, issues relating to human rights, and international conventions and covenants that are intended to shape how each national government deals with political, legal and social issues.

INTERPRETIVE DATA

Data collection concerned with critical analysis, and intended to be a form of reflection on the social meaning of human action. Human action is regarded as both meaningful and historically contingent, therefore actions (laws, official documents, statistical collections, policy statements, media reports etc.) and attitudes cannot be analysed independently of cultural and historical specificity.

JUSTICE REINVESTMENT

Refers to the idea of taking funds and resources from criminal justice institutions such as prisons (which deal with the consequences of crime) and re-investing these in communities where imprisoned offenders originate and/or in individuals needing rehabilitation (addressing the source of the problem).

JUVENILE JUSTICE

Juvenile justice refers to those laws, institutions and programs designed specifically with the needs and interests of young people under the age of 18 in mind.

LABELLING

A labelling approach to the definition of crime argues that crime only really exists when there has been a social response to a particular activity that labels that activity as criminal. If there is no label, there is in effect no crime. The approach sees crime as maintained, perpetuated or amplified by the labelling process. Criminality is thus something that is conferred upon some individuals, and on some types of behaviour, by those people who have the power to do it, and who have the power to make a label stick.

LAW ENFORCEMENT

The police skills involved in crime fighting, including activities such as detection, investigation, apprehension and prosecution of offenders. This function effectively comprises a minor proportion of police time. The bulk of all detections, arrests and prosecutions are conducted by general duties uniformed officers in the course of their routine patrolling activities.

LEGISLATION
Laws made in state and federal parliaments, and referred to as 'Acts' or 'statutes'.

MANSLAUGHTER
Culpable homicide that satisfies the element of murder but involves mitigating circumstances; for example, as a result of provocation or excessive self-defence (voluntary manslaughter) or as a result of negligent acts or omissions, or unlawful or dangerous acts (involuntary manslaughter).

MARXIST PERSPECTIVES
Marxist perspectives focus on individuals' relative position within the economic structure of a society, as defined by their relationship to the means of production; a relationship entered into independently of will. It is the state, as a legal and political superstructure, which sets the conditions of economic relations, thereby defining the social consciousness, which includes concepts of crime. Importantly, individual behaviour is said to be conditioned by social structure, and social control is said to be directed towards the most marginalised in society at the expense of the most powerful.

MENS REA
A Latin term meaning 'guilty mind'. An element of criminal responsibility comprising the mental components of a crime. The focus is on criminal intent; that is, a person's awareness that their actions were wilful and wrongful.

MODUS OPERANDI
Certain actions or procedures an offender engages in to commit a crime successfully. The Modus Operandi (MO) is a behaviour pattern that the offender learns as he or she gains experience in committing the offence.

MORAL PANIC
A moral panic is generated when moral outrage is created by the media labelling certain groups or activities as deviant and a threat to the social and moral order. The media convey a sensationalised image of crime, and a protective view of police and policing practices—and make unusual events usual events in our lives.

MURDER
The intentional killing of another by a person who is sane, and who is old enough to be legally responsible for the act, or a killing resulting from reckless indifference to life or the taking of a life without intention in the course of committing a crime (felony murder).

NEO-LIBERALISM
A political philosophy that supports the enhancement of the private sector in modern society through economic liberalist measures, including freeing up trade, opening markets, privatisation and deregulation.

NET WIDENING
The implementation of a more severe sentencing disposition than would otherwise have been required to achieve the intended purposes of sentencing.

NEUROCRIMINOLOGY
A form of biological positivism that concentrates on studying the (psychopathic) brains of criminals. The objective is to use scientific techniques to identify those with genetic and neurological predispositions for violent behaviour and engineer a treatment or prevention strategy.

OCCUPATIONAL CRIME
Criminal acts committed by employees in the course of their work, for personal gain.

ORDER MAINTENANCE
The restoration of disruptive situations to normalcy, often without arresting individuals; that is, without recourse to the enforcement of the law per se. Such activities include public order surveillance, intervention and monitoring of specific groups in particular locations; for example, major public events such as parades and sporting events, strikes, marches and football matches. The role of police in these situations is to control and circumscribe public behaviour.

OVER-POLICING
The practice whereby certain groups, such as young people, ethnic minorities (e.g. people of Arab background), Indigenous people and known criminals are subject to disproportionate policing; that is, they are regularly targeted by the police for surveillance and intervention.

PANOPTICON
Architectural design for a prison conceived by English philosopher and social theorist, Jeremy Bentham, in 1785. The design is based on the concept that an

observer (opticon) is permitted to watch all (pan) prisoners without the prisoners being able to determine whether they are being watched.

PARALEGAL
Someone who is not trained as a lawyer but who engages in legal-related work; for example, researching the situation of residents affected by toxic environments, in order to assist communities on public interest matters and/or to provide basic legal advice.

PARAMILITARY POLICING
An approach to crime control that emphasises rapid response to activity or behaviour after it has occurred (also described as reactive or demand-driven policing). It also includes crime-prevention strategies based upon armed-response capabilities as a deterrent to possible crime commission. The emphasis is on use of force and military-style engagement.

PARENS PATRIAE
Parens patriae refers to the idea of the state acting in the role of parent on behalf of children and young people, in their best interests.

PEACEMAKING CRIMINOLOGY
Drawing upon various peacemaking traditions, peacemaking criminology criticises models of interaction based upon the idea of winners and losers. It promotes instead mediation, conflict resolution and reconciliation as preferred responses to wrongdoing, violence and human suffering.

PHALLOGENTROCISM
The privileging of males in the construction of social meaning.

PHRENOLOGY
A seventeenth-century pseudoscience that amalgamated primitive neuroanatomy and moral philosophy. Phrenologists believed that human personality and character was determined by skull size. Although discredited, phrenology influenced the development of nineteenth-century psychiatry and modern neuroscience.

PLEA BARGAINING
An agreement in a criminal case whereby the defendant is offered the opportunity to plead guilty by the prosecution, usually in exchange for a sentence discount (lesser charge or fewer charges) or a recommendation of a lighter maximum sentence, subject to court approval.

POSITIVISM
The hallmark of positivism is that behaviour is determined, in the sense that individual behaviour is shaped by factors outside the individual's control, such as physiology, personality and social upbringing. Positivism further asserts that offenders vary, that individual differences exist between offenders, and that these in turn can be acknowledged and classified or measured in some way. The focus is on individuals, who are seen to require treatment, since they are not necessarily responsible for their criminality. Positivists concentrate on the offender and the offender's characteristics. The three main strands of positivism include the biological, the psychological and the biosociological.

POSTMODERNISM
A late-twentieth-century cultural and intellectual movement founded on a radical reappraisal of the global political and social assumptions and innovations introduced by the modernist era. While disparate in their thinking, proponents of postmodernism share a fundamental distrust, or outright rejection of (e.g. Michel Foucault and Julia Kristeva), modern assumptions about culture, identity, history or language.

POST-STRUCTURALISM
A movement closely related to, postmodernism, but heavily influenced by existential phenomenology. Central to post-structuralism is a belief that depictions of the 'self' as separate and singular, and 'identity' as a stable 'self', are fictional constructs. Instead, it is argued that different and competing knowledge claims relating to gender, class, race and profession create tensions in the personal concept of self. Understanding these tensions is critical, for self-perception plays a critical role in an individual's interpretation of meaning. Also rejected is the notion of ascribing a single purpose and meaning to literary text. Instead, each individual reader is thought to imbue any given text with new and individual purpose, meaning and existence.

PRIMARY DEVIATION
Primary deviation occurs when individuals engage, at some stage in their early development, in activities regarded as deviant, usually for a variety of social, cultural and psychological reasons. At this stage, when people engage in deviant activity they do not fundamentally change their self-concept; that is, individual psyches do not undergo a symbolic reorientation or transformation. There is no change in identity, and deviance is seen as nothing more than a passing event.

PRIMARY VICTIMS

Those who are subject to and feel the direct impacts of a crime.

PRINCIPAL OFFENCE

Where an individual or organisation is charged with multiple offences, the principal offence is the most serious offence type proven guilty or the most serious offence acquitted.

PRINCIPAL SENTENCE

Where a defendant is found guilty of multiple offences, the principal sentence relates to the most serious one based on the hierarchy of the Sentence Type Classification.

PRISONISATION

Changes a prisoner undergoes in prison (described as the 'pains of imprisonment'), which socialises them into the culture and social life of prison society. Also known as the 'convict code', this prison sub-culture generally involves a code of silence, distrust of and antagonism towards prison staff, and loyalty to other prisoners.

PRIVATE POLICING

Policing activities carried out by private agencies, usually in the areas of protecting property or personnel. Activities include security at train stations; in shopping malls, banks and office buildings; and in residential communities and quasi-government premises, such as dockyards and schools.

PRIVATE PRISON

A privately run prison, jail or detention centre in which a third party is contracted by a local, state or federal government agency that commits those prisoners to the facility. Private prison companies are generally paid a per diem or monthly rate for each prisoner confined in the facility. Privatisation of prisons refers to the situation in which the management of existing public facilities is taken over by a private operator, or the building and operation of new and additional prisons by for-profit organisations.

PROCESSUAL ACCOUNT

A processual account of crime involves the study of the processes of creating crime and deviancy rather the discrete acts themselves or their aetiology.

PROFILING

The gathering of various kinds of information about a person or persons. Criminal profiling is an attempt to identify demographic variables, geographical location and behavioural patterns of an offender based on characteristics of previous offenders who have committed similar offences.

PROHIBITION STRATEGIES

Programs for controlling drug use that focus on banning the availability of illegal substances.

PROVOCATION

The legal defence in cases of homicide where the behaviour of the victim precipitated his or her death by causing the offender to suddenly and temporarily lose self-control; if this is accepted as a mitigating circumstance, the charge of murder is commuted to manslaughter.

PUBLIC ORDER OFFENCES

Offences involving personal conduct that breaches or may lead to a breach of public order and decency, or that is indicative of criminal intent, or that is otherwise regulated or prohibited on moral or ethical grounds. The 'victim' of these offences is generally the public at large. However, some offences, such as offensive language and offensive behaviour, may be directed towards a single victim.

PUNISHMENT

The practice of imposing a penalty (physical pain, shame or restraint) onto an individual who has acted disobediently and/or defiantly by engaging in behaviour deemed legally and/or morally wrong in accordance with individual, communal, governmental, legal or religious principles.

QUALITATIVE DATA

Data concerned with understanding and describing meaning and experience rather than drawing statistical inferences. It is concerned with exploring human behaviour and interactions within particular settings, as well as people's thoughts, feelings, attitudes and perceptions with respect to particular issues and how they make meaning of their experiences.

QUANTITATIVE DATA

Data that has numerical significance; that is, it can be counted and measured on a numerical scale. This data is used to investigate broad statistical inferences through the use of scientific methods. It focuses on establishing such things as the frequency, incidence, prevalence, rate and statistical trends in phenomenon and the association or correlation between two or more variables associated with the observed phenomena.

RACE

Not a biological given but a social construct, based upon perceived differences between groups on the basis of factors such as physical features, cultural background, language, religion and country of origin.

REASONABLE MAN

A legal principle that determines what an ordinary 'reasonable' person would do in particular circumstances, based on an abstract legal subject that tends to reflect a male, middle-class masculinity.

RECIDIVISM

Repeat offending, which can involve repeating the same offences (e.g. drug dealing), an escalation in the type of offence (say, from graffiti to robbery) and an increase in the number of offences.

REHABILITATION

A therapeutic intervention designed to give offenders the opportunity, through appropriate treatment, to rehabilitate and redeem themselves, and to ameliorate their behaviour, so that upon release they can reintegrate into society in a productive and law-abiding fashion.

REPEAT VICTIMISATION

Victimisation that occurs when a crime occurs in the same location or is perpetrated against the same individual on more than one occasion.

RESPONSIBILISATION

The shift in the burden of responsibility for crime and safety matters from the state to individuals, families and communities.

RESTORATIVE JUSTICE

An approach to dealing with offenders that emphasises repairing harm, and involving victims and communities as well as offenders in the reparation process. Restorative justice offers hope that opportunities will be enhanced for victims, offenders and their immediate communities.

RISK–NEED–RESPONSIVITY (RNR) MODEL

The dominant rehabilitation model in use today, the RNR model is based on assessment and action around risk (to society), need (targeting of dynamic risk factors) and responsivity (matching the intervention to the individual).

ROBBERY

The unlawful taking of property, with intent to permanently deprive the owner of the property, from the immediate possession of a person or an organisation, or control, custody or care of a person, accompanied by the use and/or threatened use of immediate force or violence.

RULE OF LAW

The rule of law within which all people should be treated alike: without fear or favour; rich or poor; male or female; established Australian or migrant. The law is to apply universally to all classes of people. By extension, the state itself is bound by its own laws and principles of law.

SECONDARY DEVIATION

Secondary deviation is said to occur when, because of the social reaction to primary deviation, a person experiences a fundamental reorientation of his or her self-concept, and thus his or her behaviour.

SECONDARY VICTIMS

Individuals other than primary victims who are witnesses to or impacted by a crime, including family members, friends, neighbours, bystanders and whole communities, who may also suffer tangible losses and/or intangible harms, including trauma, as a result of a crime.

SECULARISM

A principle espousing the separation of legal and governmental principles, practices and institutions from religion and/or religious doctrine.

SENTENCE

A penalty or penalties imposed by a court upon a defendant who is proven guilty of a criminal offence. The sentencing process constitutes the final act in the adjudication process and represents the symbolic principal act connected to the judicial function.

SHOPLIFTING

The action of stealing merchandise from a shop or business establishment while pretending to be a customer.

SIGNATURE OR PERSONATION

Behaviour that goes beyond what is necessary to commit the crime. For example, the signature of a serial killer may involve certain items that are left or removed from the scene, or other symbolic patterns, such as writing on a wall.

SITUATIONAL CRIME PREVENTION

Offence-focused strategies designed to reduce the opportunities for crime; in this case, through deterrents to crime. Strategies include increasing the degree of difficulty to commit crime (e.g. target hardening), increasing the likelihood of detection and arrest (e.g. formal surveillance), ensuring the effort to commit crime does not pay off (e.g. identifying property) and inducing shame or guilt (e.g. strengthening moral condemnation).

SOCIAL CAPITAL

Reciprocal relations between people that include valued relations with significant others, generated through relationships, which in turn bring resources from networks and group membership (e.g. peer groups).

SOCIAL CRIME PREVENTION

An offender-focused approach concerned with criminality prevention (e.g. deterring potential offenders and offenders from engaging or re-engaging in crime). This approach involves changes to social environments and the motivational conditions that predispose individuals and groups of individuals to crime.

SOCIAL DEVIANCE

The way in which some groups in society are presented and dealt with via mainstream social institutions that tend to treat their defining social characteristics as liabilities that, in turn, are associated with criminal tendencies or the propensity to engage in activities that are deemed to be socially unacceptable. What makes people 'different' from each other is defined through social processes of typification and acknowledgment: certain groups can be seen as a problem insofar as their actions or appearance seem to disturb the status quo in some way.

SPECIESISM

The practice of discriminating against non-human animals because they are perceived as inferior to the human species, similar to the way sexism and racism involve prejudice and discrimination against women and people of different colour.

STAGING

The intentional alteration of a crime scene before the arrival of the police, and is frequently done by someone who has an association or relationship with the victim. It can involve trying to alter the crime scene in order to divert suspicion such as by wiping fingerprints from a weapon and putting it close to the body in such a way that the death looks like suicide.

STATE CRIME

Crimes involving the state acting against its own citizens, or against the citizens of another state as part of interstate conflict.

STATE-SPONSORED VIOLENCE

A form of crime committed by the state that involves gross violation of human rights. This includes serious crimes against humanity and the systematic deprivation of rights through the use of repressive measures.

STATUS OFFENCES

Offences that apply only to young people, such as 'uncontrollability', 'not allowed to drink alcohol' and 'in need of care and protection'; the assumption is that until they reach a suitable age (as determined by legislators and courts), young people should be subject to particular types of social controls.

STREET CRIME

Highly visible crimes that occur in public spaces and usually involve little skill on the part of perpetrators.

STRUCTURALIST CRIMINOLOGY

Structuralist criminology is concerned with the exercise of power that leads to oppression and domination both in terms of structural relations in society (economic, cultural and political) and in terms of social control systems and practices. The focus of analysis is both the crimes of the powerful (from the point of view of issues relating to ideology, political economy and the rise of the managerial state) and crimes of the less powerful (from the point of view of the specific experiences of particular sections of the population such as Indigenous people, ethnic minorities, women and children).

SUBCULTURES

Small cultural groups that have fragmented from the mainstream and have formed alternative values and meanings about life.

SUBORDINATE STATUS

The unequal positioning of a particular group in society; for example, the historical position of women within male-dominated or patriarchal societies has meant that female criminality has tended to be portrayed and understood in very sex-specific ways.

SUPERMAX

An abbreviation of supermaximum prison, which denotes a free-standing 'control unit' prison, or discrete unit within a prison, that provides for the most secure level of custody in the correctional system of some countries. These facilities are designed to manage and securely control inmates officially classified as the security risk in the prison system; that is, extremely violent, dangerous, difficult to manage or posing a national threat.

TECHNIQUES OF NEUTRALISATION

A term used to describe the ways in which young people use certain techniques of neutralisation as a way of denying the moral bind of law; for example, 'they started it' or 'no one got hurt'. The techniques broadly include denial of responsibility, denial of injury, denial of the victim, condemnation of the condemners and the appeal to higher loyalties.

THEFT

The taking of another person's property with the intention of permanently depriving the owner of the property illegally and without permission, but without force, threat of force, use of coercive measures, deceit or having gained unlawful entry to any structure, even if the intent was to gain theft.

THERAPEUTIC JURISPRUDENCE

A philosophy that recognises the impact that laws, legal practices and procedures, and legal personnel (e.g. magistrates, judges and lawyers) can have on the psychological and emotional wellbeing of court participants. It argues for law reforms that centre on rehabilitating criminal tendencies, mitigating negative effects, and promoting positive behavioural change and the enhancement of individual wellbeing alongside justice principles, such as community protection.

TRANSITIONAL JUSTICE PRACTICE

Various judicial and non-judicial practices adopted by countries around the world, including international prosecutions, truth commissions, reparations programs and various kinds of institutional reforms, that are designed to redress the legacies of massive human rights abuses, such as war crimes and genocide.

TRANSNATIONAL CRIME

Crime that is global in scope and reflects broad socio-economic processes and trends associated with globalisation. It includes, for example, illegal trade in wildlife, the international transfer of toxic waste, terrorism, illegal arms trade and people trafficking.

TWO-TIER/TWO-STAGE APPROACH TO SENTENCING

The establishment of a notional starting point for sentencing by considering the aspects of a case that more easily lend themselves to objective analysis (e.g. the gravity of the crime) and the allowable penalties within the relevant statutory range. This starting point is then adjusted once the more subjective, circumstantial aspects of a case are considered in the light of the individual circumstances of offender (e.g. offender culpability) to arrive at a sentence.

TYPIFICATION

The process of defining situations in ways that allow for mutual communication, as well as defining what is 'normal' and what is 'abnormal'. How people typify one another (e.g. 'mentally ill'), and how people relate to one another on the basis of these typifications, have major social consequences.

UNDERCLASS

People who are not working, whose source of income lies permanently outside the capital–wage relationship, and whose economic conditions are normally at or below relative subsistence level. While linked to the working class, the underclass is separated from it structurally and behaviourally.

UNDER-POLICING

The practice whereby certain offences (e.g. racist or homophobic violence) are subject to less surveillance and intervention than otherwise ought to be the case.

UNIVERSAL SUFFRAGE

The idea that every person in society should be able to have a vote in relation to the selection of their political leaders. Those who make the laws—the legislators and legislature—are thus supposedly in a position to reflect the 'will of the people' if they are voted into government on this principle.

UTILITARIANISM

A principle central to classical theory, which is grounded in normative ethics; that is, an appropriate or ideal standard of behaviour. This principle holds that a normative course of action is the one that results in maximum utility, typically defined as maximising happiness and minimising suffering.

VICTIMISATION

The process by which a person learns to be a victim (how to act in certain ways after being affected by a crime) and/or to the ways in which authority figures determine who is or who is not 'worthy' of being deemed a victim (e.g. police responses to a fistfight outside a pub) and/or the processes that surround becoming a victim (e.g. time delays in the effects of toxic waste disposal on personal health).

VICTIMOLOGY

Victimology is the study of victimisation, including societal conceptualisation of 'victim', victimisation profiles and risk distribution for various categories of crime, the relationship between victims and offenders, and interactions between victims and the criminal justice system.

VICTIMS

Persons who, individually or collectively, have suffered harm, including physical or mental injury, emotional suffering, economic loss or substantial impairment of their fundamental rights. These harms may have arisen through acts or omissions that are in violation of criminal laws operative within a state, including those laws proscribing criminal abuse of power.

VIGILANTE JUSTICE

A form of civic activism—the coming together of select, autonomous individuals who voluntarily band together in a self-help approach to community crime prevention—that can take the form of legal (e.g. the Guardian Angels) or illegal (e.g. lynch mobs) groups.

WELFARE FRAUD

Also referred to as 'benefit fraud' or 'social security fraud', this is the practice of fraudulently claiming Commonwealth benefits when not entitled.

WHITE-COLLAR CRIME

Broadly, crime committed by a person of respectability and high social status in the course of his or her occupation. However, the term is sometimes used to describe all crimes committed by non-manual workers in the course of their occupation.

YOUNG OFFENDER

A young offender is a person under the age of 18 who has been officially designated by the criminal justice system as having committed a crime.

REFERENCES

A

Aaltonen, M., Kivivuori, J. & Martikainen, P. (2011) 'Social determinants of crime in a welfare state: do they still matter?', *Acta Sociologica*, 54(2): 161–81.

Aaltonen, M., Kivivuori, J., Martikainen, P. & Salmi, V. (2012) 'Socio-economic status and criminality as predictors of male violence', *British Journal of Criminology*, 52(6): 1192–211.

Aas, K. (2007) *Globalization & crime*, Sage, Los Angeles.

ABC—see Australian Broadcasting Corporation.

Abrahams, N., Devries, K., Watts, C., Pallitto, C., Petzold, M., Shamu, S. & García-Moreno, C. (2014) 'Worldwide prevalence of non-partner sexual violence: a systematic review', *The Lancet*, 13: 62243–6.

ABS—see Australian Bureau of Statistics.

ABC News (2009) 'Truth in sentencing laws in effect from today', *ABC News*, 14 January, Australian Broadcasting Corporation (ABC).

ACC—see Australian Crime Commission.

Access Economics (2004) *The cost of domestic violence to the Australian economy*, Commonwealth Office of the Status of Women, Australian Government, Canberra.

Access to Justice Advisory Committee (1994) *Access to justice: an action plan*, Australian Government Publishing Service, Canberra.

ACT Community Coalition on Corrections (2008) *Healthy or harmful? Mental health and the operational regime of the new ACT prison*, Canberra.

Adams, L. (2012) 'A glass half empty: perspectives on criminalising homelessness and alcohol dependence', *Parity*, 25(2): 15–17.

Adeola, F. (2000) 'Cross-national environmental injustice and human rights issues', *American Behavioral Scientist*, 43(4): 686–706.

Agnew, R. (2012) 'It's the end of the world as we know it: the advance of climate change from a criminological perspective', in R. White (ed.), *Climate change from a criminological perspective*, Springer, New York.

AIC—see Australian Institute of Criminology.

AIHW—see Australian Institute of Health and Welfare.

Airo-Farulla, G. (1992) 'Community policing and self-determination', *Aboriginal Law Bulletin*, 2(54): 8–9.

Aitkin, D. (2013) 'Academia's harshest lesson: go back to basics', *The Age*, 25 July: 22.

Akella, A. & Cannon, J. (2004) *Strengthening the Weakest Links: Strategies for Improving the Enforcement of Environmental Laws Globally*, Conservation International, Washington DC.

Akers, R.L. (1990) 'Rational choice, deterrence, and social learning theory in criminology: the path not taken', *The Journal of Criminal Law and Criminology*, 81(3): 653–76.

A-Khavari, A. (2003) 'The passage of time in international environmental disputes', *Murdoch University Electronic Journal of Law*, 10(4), <www.murdoch.edu/elaw/issues/v10n4/akhavari104nf. html>.

Alcorn, G. (2013) 'Spies, journalists and inconvenient truths', *The Age*, 22 November: 22.

Al-Damkhi, A., Khuraibet, A., Abdul-Wahab, S., & Al-Attar, F. (2009) 'Toward Defining the Concept of Environmental Crime on the Basis of Sustainability', *Environmental Practice*, 11(2): 115–24.

Alder, C. (1985) 'Theories of female delinquency', in A. Borowski & J. Murray (eds), *Juvenile delinquency in Australia*, Methuen, North Ryde.

Alder, C. (1994a) 'Women and the criminal justice system', in D. Chappell & P. Wilson (eds), *The Australian criminal justice system: the mid-1990s*, Butterworths, Sydney.

Alder, C. (1994b) 'The policing of young women', in R. White & C. Alder (eds), *The police and young people in Australia*, Cambridge University Press, Melbourne.

Alder, C. (1997) 'Young women and juvenile justice: objectives, frameworks and strategies', paper presented at the Australian Institute of Criminology Conference *Towards Juvenile Crime and Juvenile Justice: Towards 2000 and Beyond*, Adelaide.

Alder, C., Chappell, D. & Polk, K. (2011) 'Frauds and fakes in the Australian Aboriginal art market', *Crime, Law and Social Change*, 56(2): 189–207.

All Party Parliamentary Group on Women in the Penal System (2012) *Inquiry on girls: from courts to custody*, The Howard League for Penal Reform, London.

Allard, T., Chrzanowski, A. & Stewart, A. (2013) 'Targeting crime prevention: identifying communities that generate chronic and costly offenders', ACI Reports, *Research and Public Policy Series*, No.123, Australian Institute of Criminology, Canberra.

Allas, R. & James, S. (1997) *Justice gone walkabout: a study of*

Victorian Aboriginal offending 1989–90 to 1993–94, Victorian Aboriginal Legal Service Cooperative, Melbourne.

Allen, K. (2012) 'Off the radar and ubiquitous: text messaging and its relationship to "drama" and cyberbullying in an affluent, academically rigorous US high school', *Journal of Youth Studies*, 15(1): 99–117.

Alleyne, B. (2010) 'Sociology of hackers—revisited', *The Sociological Review*: 1–35.

ALRC—see Australian Law Reform Commission.

Ambagtsheer, F., Zaitch, D. & Weimar, W. (2013) 'The battle for human organs: organ trafficking and transplant tourism in the global context', *Global Crime*, 14(1): 1–26.

Ame, R.K. & Alidu, S.M. (2010) 'Truth and reconciliation commissions, restorative justice, peacemaking criminology and development', *Criminal Justice Studies*, 23(3): 253–68.

Amnesty International (2014) *Death sentences and executions 2013*, Amnesty International Publications, London.

Anderson, J. (2007) 'Groundbreaking initiative to protect underwater habitats', press release, 4 April, New Zealand Government, Auckland.

Anderson, J. & McAtamney, A. (2011) 'Considering local context when evaluating a closed circuit television system in public spaces', *Trends & Issues in Crime and Criminal Justice*, No. 430, Australian Institute of Criminology, Canberra.

Anderson, J. & Renouf, G. (2003) 'Legal services for the public good', *Alternative Law Journal*, 28(1): 13–17.

Anderson, J.F., Reinsmith-Jones, K. & Manels, N.J. (2011) 'Need for triangulated methodologies in criminal justice and criminological research: exploring legal techniques as an additional

method', *Criminal Justice Studies*, 24(1): 83–103.

Anderson, K. (1993a) 'Place narratives and the origins of inner Sydney's Aboriginal settlement 1972–73', *Journal of Historical Geography*, 19(3): 314–35.

Anderson, K. (1993b) 'Constructing geographies: race, place and the making of Sydney's Aboriginal Redfern', in P. Jackson & J. Penrose (eds), *Constructions of race, place and nation*, University College London Press, London.

Anderson, T. (1995) 'Victims' rights or human rights?', *Current Issues in Criminal Justice*, 6(3): 335–45.

Andreas, P. & Nadelmann, E. (2006) *Policing the globe: criminalization and crime control in international relations*, Oxford University Press, New York.

Andrew, J. (2010) 'Prison privatization: the (ir)relevance of accounting', *Accounting and The Public Interest*, 10: 122–37.

Andrews, D.A., Bonta, J. & Wormith, J.S. (2011) 'The risk–need–responsivity (RNR) model: does adding the good lives model contribute to effective crime prevention?', *Criminal Justice and Behavior* 38(7): 735–55.

Anthony, T. (2011) 'Moral Panics and Misgivings over Indigenous Punishment: Sentencing Cultural Crimes in Australia's Northern Territory', *Cambrian Law Review*, 42: 91–112.

Anthony, T. (2012) 'Is There Social Justice In Sentencing Indigenous Offenders?', *UNSW Law Journal*, 35(2): 563–97.

Anthony, T. & Cunneen, C (eds) (2008) *The critical criminology companion*, Federation Press, Sydney.

Aos, S., Miller, M. & Drake, E. (2006) *Evidence-based adult corrections programs: what works and what does not*, Washington State Institute for Public Policy, Olympia, WA.

Aosved, A.C. & Long, P.J (2006) 'Co-occurrence of rape myth

acceptance, sexism, racism, homophobia, ageism, classism, and religious intolerance', *Sex Roles*, 55(7): 481–92.

Arditti, J.A., Lambert-Shute, J. & Joest, K. (2003) 'Saturday morning at the jail: implications for families and children', *Family Relations*, 52(3): 195–204.

Aries, P. (1973) *Centuries of childhood*, Cape, London.

Arnulf, J.K. & Gottschalk, P. (2013) 'Heroic leaders as white-collar criminals: an empirical study', *Journal of Investigative Psychology and Offender Profiling*, 10(1): 96–113.

Arrigo, B. & Bernard, T. (1997) 'Postmodern criminology in relation to radical and conflict criminology', *Critical Criminology*, 8(2): 39–60.

Arthur, L. (2011) 'Does case management undermine the rule of law in pursuit of access to justice?' *Journal of Justice Administration*, 20: 240–7.

Asal, V., Sommer, U. & Harwood, P.G. (2012) 'Original sin: a cross-national study of the legality of homosexual acts', *Comparative Political Studies*, 46(3): 320–51.

Ascione, F. (2001) 'Animal abuse and youth violence', *Juvenile Justice Bulletin*, Office of Juvenile Justice and Delinquency Prevention, US Department of Justice Washington, DC.

Ashworth, A. (1987) 'Criminal justice, rights and sentencing: a review of sentencing policy and problems', in I. Pota (ed.), *Sentencing in Australia: issues, policy and reform*, Australian Institute of Criminology, Canberra.

Ashworth, A. (2002) *Sentencing and penal policy*, Weidenfeld and Nicholson, London.

Ashworth, A. (2010) *Sentencing and criminal justice* (5th edn), Cambridge University Press, New York.

Ashworth, A. & von Hirsh, A. (1993) 'Desert and the three Rs',

Current Issues in Criminal Justice, 5(1): 9–12.

Ashworth, A., Genders, E., Mansfield, G., Peay, J. & Player, E. (1984) *Sentencing in the crown court: report of an exploratory study*, Occasional Paper No. 10, Centre for Criminological Research, University of Oxford, Oxford.

Asquith, N. (2008) 'Race riots on the beach: a case for criminalising hate speech?' Paper presented to the British Society of Criminology Conference 9–11 July: London, England, Conference Proceedings, Vol. 8: 50–64

Atkinson, T., Luttrell, D. & Rosenblum, H. (2013) *How bad was it? The costs and consequences of the 2007–09 financial crisis*, Staff Papers, No. 20, Federal Reserve Bank of Dallas, Dallas.

Attorney General's Department (2004) 'Revised Standard Guidelines for Corrections in Australia', <http://www.nt.gov.au/justice/docs/corrservs/Standard_Guidelines_2004.pdf >.

Aungles, A. (1994) *The prison and the home*, Monograph No. 5, Institute of Criminology, Sydney.

Australian Broadcasting Corporation (2003) 'Prison escape prompts day release review', 9 October, <www.abc.net.au/news/newsitems/200310/s962996.htm>.

Australian Broadcasting Corporation (2009) 'Truth in sentencing laws in effect from today', *ABC News*, 14 January, <http://abc.com.au/news/stories/2009/01/14/2465437.htm?site=news>.

Australian Broadcasting Corporation (2013a) '"Gatecrasher" refused bail over metal bar attack' *ABC News*, 16 January, <www.abc.net.au/news/2013-01-15/teen-arrested-over-gatecrashing-assault/4466486>.

Australian Broadcasting Corporation (2013b) 'New push for sex work decriminalisation', *ABC News*, 19 May, <www.abc.net.au/news/2013-05-19/new-push-for-sex-work-decriminilisation/4698798>.

Australian Broadcasting Corporation (2014a) 'Wedding guests pelted with bricks by gatecrashers', *ABC News*, 6 April, <www.abc.net.au/news/2014-04-06/fight-breaks-out-after-youths-gatecrash-wedding/5370482>.

Australian Broadcasting Corporation (2014b) 'One-punch law in force on NSW streets tonight', *ABC News*, 31 January, <www.abc.net.au/news/2014-01-31/one-punch-law-in-force-on-nsw-streets-tonight/5229716>.

Australian Bureau of Statistics (1993) *Women in Australia*, Australian Government Publishing Service, Canberra.

Australian Bureau of Statistics (2008a) *National survey of mental health and wellbeing: summary of results, 2007*, Cat. No. 4326.0, Australian Government Publishing Service, Canberra.

Australian Bureau of Statistics (2008b) *Personal fraud 2007*, Cat. No. 4528.0, Australian Government Publishing Service, Canberra.

Australian Bureau of Statistics (2008c) *Prisoners in Australia 2008*, Cat. No. 4517.0, Australian Government Publishing Service, Canberra.

Australian Bureau of Statistics (2009a) National Aboriginal and Torres Strait Islander Social Survey, Cat. No. 4714.0, Australian Government Publishing Service, Canberra.

Australian Bureau of Statistics (2009b) *Prisoners in Australia, 2009*, Cat. No. 4517.0, Australian Government Publishing Service, Canberra.

Australian Bureau of Statistics (2010) *Prisoners in Australia, 2010*, Cat. No. 4517.0, Australian Government Publishing Service, Canberra.

Australian Bureau of Statistics (2011a) *Prisoners in Australia, 2011*, Cat. No. 4517.0, Australian Government Publishing Service, Canberra.

Australian Bureau of Statistics (2011b) *Australian and New Zealand Standard Offence Classification (ANZSOC), 2011*, Cat. No.1234.0.

Australian Bureau of Statistics (2011c) *In focus: crime and justice statistics, December 2011: In the eye of the beholder: Perceptions of social disorder in Australia*, Cat. No. 4524.0, Australian Government Publishing Service, Canberra.

Australian Bureau of Statistics (2011d) In focus: *crime and justice statistics, September 2011: Youth victimisation and offending: A Statistical snapshot*, Cat. No. 4524.0, Australian Government Publishing Service, Canberra.

Australian Bureau of Statistics (2012a) *Exploring relationships between crime victimisation and social wellbeing*, Cat. No. 4524.0, Australian Government Publishing Service, Canberra.

Australian Bureau of Statistics (2012b) *Australian social trends, March 2012*, Cat. No. 4102.0, Australian Government Publishing Service, Canberra.

Australian Bureau of Statistics (2012c) *Prisoners in Australia, 2012*, Cat. No. 4517.0, Australian Government Publishing Service, Canberra.

Australian Bureau of Statistics (2012d) *Labour force characteristics of Aboriginal and Torres Strait Islander Australians, estimates from the labour force survey, 2011*, Cat. No. 6287.0, Australian Government Publishing Service, Canberra.

Australian Bureau of Statistics (2012e) *Personal fraud, 2010–2011*, Cat. No. 4528.0, Australian Government Publishing Service, Canberra.

Australian Bureau of Statistics (2013a) *Recorded crime—victims, Australia, 2012*, Cat. No. 4510.0,

Australian Government Publishing Service, Canberra.

Australian Bureau of Statistics (2013b) *Personal safety, Australia, 2012*, Cat. No. 4906.0, Australian Government Publishing Service, Canberra.

Australian Bureau of Statistics (2013c) *Employee earnings and hours, Australia, May 2012*, Cat. No. 6306.0, Australian Government Publishing Service, Canberra.

Australian Bureau of Statistics (2013d) *Census of population and housing: socio-economic indexes for areas (SEIFA), Australia, 2011*, Cat. No. 2033.0.55.001, Australian Government Publishing Service, Canberra.

Australian Bureau of Statistics (2013e) *Prisoners in Australia, 2013*, Cat. No. 4517.0, Australian Government Publishing Service, Canberra.

Australian Bureau of Statistics (2013f) *Migration, Australia, 2011–12 and 2012–13*, Cat. No. 3412.0, Australian Government Publishing Service, Canberra.

Australian Bureau of Statistics (2014a) *Recorded crime— offenders 2012–13*, Cat. No. 4519.0, Australian Government Publishing Service, Canberra.

Australian Bureau of Statistics (2014b) *Crime victimisation, Australia, 2012–13*, Cat. No. 4530.0, Australian Government Publishing Service, Canberra.

Australian Bureau of Statistics (2014c) *Labour force, Australia, March 2014*, Cat. No. 6202.0, Australian Government Publishing Service, Canberra.

Australian Bureau of Statistics (2014d) *Australian social trends, April 2013*, Cat. No. 4102.0, Australian Government Publishing Service, Canberra.

Australian Bureau of Statistics (2014e) *Australian demographic statistics, Sep 2013*, Cat. No. 3101.0, Australian Government Publishing Service, Canberra.

Australian Bureau of Statistics (2014f) *Criminal courts, Australia, 2012–13*, Cat. No. 4513.0, Australian Government Publishing Service, Canberra.

Australian Bureau of Statistics (2014g) *Prisoners in Australia, 2013*, Cat. No. 4517.0, Australian Government Publishing Service, Canberra.

Australian Capital Territory Gay and Lesbian Police Liaison Network (1994) *Harassment and violence survey*, Canberra.

Australian Capital Territory Human Rights Commission (2007) *Human rights audit on the operation of ACT correctional facilities under corrections legislation*, <www.hrc.act.gov.au/assetss/docs/Corrections%20Audit%202007.pdf>.

Australian Competition & Consumer Commission (2013) *Scam Watch* 'Identity theft', ACCC.

Australian Competition & Consumer Commission (2012) *Targeting scams: report of the ACCC on scam activity 2011*, ACCC, Canberra.

Australian Content Industry Group (2011) 'The Impact of Internet Piracy on the Australian Economy', Sphere Analysis.

Australian Council of Social Service (ACOSS) (2012) *Poverty in Australia 2012* (3rd edn), Australian Council of Social Service, Strawberry Hills.

Australian Crime Commission (2011) *Organised crime in Australia 2011*, Australian Crime Commission, Commonwealth of Australia, Canberra.

Australian Crime Commission (2013) *Organised crime in Australia 2013*, Australian Crime Commission, Commonwealth of Australia, Canberra.

Australian Drug Foundation (2010) *Position statement on secondary supply of alcohol to young people on private property*, Australian Drug Foundation, Melbourne.

Australian Human Rights Commission (2007) *Human rights audit on the operation of ACT correctional facilities under corrections legislation*, Australian Human Rights Commission, ACT.

Australian Human Rights Commission (2009) *Social justice report 2009*, Ch.2: Justice reinvestment—a new solution to the problem of Indigenous over-representation in the criminal justice system, Australian Human Rights and Equal Opportunity Commission, Sydney.

Australian Human Rights Commission (2011) 'Cyber-racism and human rights', *Cyber racism fact sheet*, AHRC.

Australian Human Rights Commission (2014) *Equal Before the law: towards disability justice strategies*, Australian Human Rights Commission.

Australian Institute of Criminology (2004b) 'Understanding problem-oriented policing', *AIC Crime Reduction Matters*, No. 17, Australian Institute of Criminology, Canberra.

Australian Institute of Criminology (2005) 'The age of criminal responsibility', *Crime Facts Info*, No. 106, Australian Institute of Criminology, Canberra.

Australian Institute of Criminology (2008) 'Burglary: prevalence in Australia and overseas', *Crime Facts Info*, No. 174, Australian Institute of Criminology, Canberra.

Australian Institute of Criminology (2009) 'Mental disorders and incarceration history', *Crime Facts Info*, No. 184, Australian Institute of Criminology, Canberra.

Australian Institute of Criminology (2010a) 'Covert and cyber bullying', *Research in Practice, Tipsheet No. 9*, February 2010.

Australian Institute of Criminology (2010b) 'Composition of

Australia's police services as at 30 June 2006', Crime and Criminal Justice Statistics, Australian Institute of Criminology, Canberra.

Australian Institute of Criminology (2012) *Australian crime facts and figures 2011*, Australian Institute of Criminology, Canberra.

Australian Institute of Criminology (2013a) *Australian crime facts and figures 2012*, Australian Institute of Criminology, Canberra.

Australian Institute of Criminology (2013b) *Homicide in Australia: 2008–09 to 2009–10 National Homicide Monitoring Program annual report*, Australian Institute of Criminology, Canberra.

Australian Institute of Health and Welfare (2011a) *The health and welfare of Australia's Aboriginal and Torres Strait Islander people: An overview*, AIHW, Canberra.

Australian Institute of Health and Welfare (2011b) *2010 National drug strategy household survey report*. Drug statistics series No. 25. Cat. No. PHE 145, AIHW, Canberra.

Australian Institute of Health and Welfare (2012a) *Juvenile justice in Australia 2010–11*, Juvenile Justice Series No.10, AIHW, Canberra.

Australian Institute of Health and Welfare (2012b) *Girls and young women in the juvenile justice system 2010–11*, Bulletin 107, AIHW, Canberra.

Australian Institute of Health and Welfare (2013a) 'Alcohol and other drug treatment services in Australia 2011–12', *Drug Treatment Series* No. 21. Cat. No. HSE 139. AIHW, Canberra.

Australian Institute of Health and Welfare (2013b) *Youth detention population in Australia*, AIHW, Canberra.

Australian Institute of Health and Welfare (2013c) *Youth justice fact sheet no.18*. Comparisons between Australian and international youth justice systems: 2011–12. Cat. No. JUV30, AIHW, Canberra.

Australian Institute of Health and Welfare (2013d) *Child protection Australia 2011–12*, Australian Institute of Health and Welfare Child Welfare Series No. 55, Canberra.

Australian Institute of Health and Welfare (2013e) *The health of Australia's prisoners 2012*, Cat. No. PHE 170, AIHW, Canberra.

Australian Institute of Health and Welfare (2014a) *Youth justice in Australia 2012–13*, AIHW Bulletin 120, Cat. No. AUS179, AIHW, Canberra.

Australian Institute of Health and Welfare (2014b) *Youth justice legislation*, <www.aihw.gov.au/youth-justice/legislation/>.

Australian Institute of Health and Welfare (2014c) *Youth justice*, <www.aihw.gov.au/youth-justice/>.

Australian Law Reform Commission (1992) *Multiculturalism and the law*, Report No. 57, Australian Government Printing Services, Canberra.

Australian Law Reform Commission (1994a) *Access to justice: an action plan*, Australian Government Publishing Service, Canberra.

Australian Law Reform Commission (1994b) *Equality before the law: justice for women*, Report No. 69, Commonwealth of Australia, Sydney.

Australian Law Reform Commission (2000) *Managing justice*, Report No. 89, Commonwealth of Australia, Sydney.

Australian Law Reform Commission (2006) *Same crime, same time: sentencing of federal offenders*, Report No. 103, Canberra.

Australian Psychological Society (2004) 'Psychological aspects of mobile phone use among adolescents', (Vol. 3), November.

Australian Youth Affairs Coalition (2013) *Insights from the Coalface: The value of justice reinvestment for young Australians*, Surry Hills, AYAC.

AYAC 2013—see Australian Youth Affairs Coalition

Ayling, J. (2013) 'Harnessing third parties for transnational environmental crime prevention', *Transnational Environmental Law*, 2(2): 339–62.

Ayres, D. & Gonzales, S. (1997) 'Simpson faces financial ruin after guilty verdict', *The Age*, 1 February: 6, 8, 11.

B

Badgery-Parker, J. (1995) 'The criminal process in transition: balancing principle and pragmatism: part II', *Journal of Judicial Administration*, 4(4): 193–219.

Bagaric, M. (2000) 'Proportionality in sentencing: its justification, meaning and role', *Current Issues in Criminal Justice*, 12(2): 143–65.

Bagaric, M. & Alexander, T. (2012) 'The capacity of criminal sanctions to shape the behaviour of offenders: specific deterrence doesn't work, rehabilitation might and the implications for sentencing', *Criminal Justice Journal*, 36: 159–72.

Bagaric, M. & Edney, R. (2003) 'What's instinct got to do with it? A blueprint for a coherent approach to punishing criminals', *Criminal Law Journal*, 27(3): 119–41.

Bagaric, M. & Edney, R. (2007) *Australian sentencing: principles and practice*, Cambridge University Press Melbourne.

Baglione, S.L., Diemer, R. & Zimmerer, T. (2010) 'The internet: exacerbating white-collar crime', *International Journal of Business and Public Administration*, 7(2): 91–104.

Baines, P. with Kelly, H. (2005) 'Tsunami: a police perspective',

Australian Police Journal, 59(2): 54–66.

Bakan, J. (2004) *The corporation: the pathological pursuit of profit and power*, Constable, London.

Baker, R. & McKenzie, N. (2013) 'Drug trial plea for addicts', *The Age*, 31 August: 1–2.

Baksheev, G.N., Ogloff, J. & Thomas, S.D.M. (2011) 'Identification of mental illness in police cells: a comparison of police processes, the brief jail mental health screen and the jail screening assessment tool', *Psychology, Crime & Law*, 18(6): 529–42.

Baldry, E. & Maplestone, P. (2003) 'Barriers to social and economic inclusion for those leaving prison', *Human Rights Defender*, 12(1): 24–6.

Baldry, E. (2006) 'Ex-prisoners, homelessness and the state in Australia', *Australian and New Zealand Journal of Criminology*, 39(1): 20–33.

Baldry, E. (2007) 'Recidivism and the role of social factors post-release', *Precedent*, July–August, 81: 4–7.

Baldry, E. (2010) 'Women in transition: from prison to...', *Current Issues in Criminal Justice*, 22(2): 253–67.

Baldry, E., McDonnell, D. & Maplestone, P. (2003) 'Ex-prisoners, housing and social integration', *Parity*, 16(5): 13–15.

Baldry, E., McDonnell, D., Maplestone, P. & Peeters, M. (2002) 'Ex-prisoners and accommodation: what bearing do different forms of housing have on social reintegration or ex-prisoners?', paper presented at the *Housing, Crime and Stronger Communities conference* convened by the Australian Institute of Criminology and the Australian Housing and Urban Research Institute, 6–7 May 2002, Melbourne.

Balfour, G. (2006). 'Re-Imagining a Feminist Criminology', *Canadian Journal of Criminology and Criminal Justice*, 48(5): 741–57.

Balfour, G. (2012) 'Theorizing the intersectionality of victimizatio, criminalization and punishment of women: An introduction to the special issues', *International Review of Victimology*, 19(1): 3–5.

Bangura, Y. (2011) 'Inequality and the politics of redistribution', *European Journal of Development Research*, 23(4): 531–6.

Barash, D.P. (1991) *Introduction to peace studies*, Wadsworth, Belmont.

Barcham, M. (2010) 'Indigenous community policing: building strength from within', in J. Putt (ed.), *Community policing in Australia, Research and public policy Series* No. 111, Australian Institute of Criminology, Canberra.

Barkan, S.E. (2013) *Sociology: exploring and changing the social world*, Flat World Knowledge, Nyack.

Barlass, T. (2013) 'Deadly anaesthetic drip yet to be banned', *The Age*, 1 September: 3.

Barlow, H. (1993) *Introduction to Criminology*, HarperCollins, New York.

Barnes, G. (1999) 'Private violence, gendered violence: are gender constructions integral to understanding lethal violence as an act of self-defence?', *Alternative Law Journal*, 24(2): 67–70.

Barnes, J.C. & Jacobs, B.A. (2012) 'Genetic risk for violent behavior and environmental exposure to disadvantage and violent crime: the case for gene-environment interaction', *Journal of Interpersonal Violence*, 18(1): 92–120.

Barnett, R.E. (1995) *Making O.J. pay*, Liberty Publishing, <www.libertysoft.com.liberty/features/barnett.html>.

Barns, G. (2011) 'Relevance of mental illness in sentencing', *Precedent*, 102 (January/February): 42–3.

Barr, R. & Pease, K. (1990) 'Community placement,

displacement and deflection', in M. Tonry & N. Morris (eds), *Crime and justice: an annual review of research*, University of Chicago Press, Chicago.

Barratt, M.J., Cakic, V. & Lenton, S. (2013) 'Patterns of synthetic cannabinoid use in Australia', *Drug and Alcohol Review*, 32: 141–6.

Barry, M. (2006) *Youth offending in transition: the search for social recognition*, Routledge, London.

Bartel, R. (2005) 'When the heavenly gaze criminalises: satellite surveillance, land clearance regulation and the human–nature relationship', *Current Issues in Criminal Justice*, 16(3): 322–39.

Bartels, L. (2009) 'The weight of the sword of Damocles: a reconviction analysis of suspended sentences in Tasmania', *Australian and New Zealand Journal of Criminology*, 42(1): 72–100.

Bartels, L (2010) 'Indigenous women's offending patterns: a literature review', *Research and Public Policy Series*, No. 107, Australian Institute of Criminology, Canberra.

Bartels, L. (2012a) 'Painting the picture of Indigenous women in custody in Australia', *Queensland University of Technology Law & Justice*, 12(2): 1–17.

Bartels, L. (2012b) 'Sentencing scammers: law and practice', *Trends & Issues in Crime and Criminal Justice*, No.443, Australian Institute of Criminology, Canberra.

Bartholomew, A.A. & Milte, K.L. (1976) 'The reliability and validity of psychiatric diagnoses in the criminal courts', *Australian Law Journal*, 50: 450–8.

Bartkowiak-Theron, I. & Asquith, N. (eds) (2012) Policing vulnerability, Federation Press, Annandale, NSW.

Bartkowiak-Theron, I. & Crehan, A. (2010) 'A new movement in community policing? From community policing to vulnerable people policing', in J. Putt (ed.), *Community policing in Australia*, Australian Institute of Criminology, Canberra.

Bartol, C. & Bartol, A. (2005) *Criminal behaviour: a psychosocial approach*, Pearson, Upper Saddle River.

Bartunek, R. (2014) 'Belgium signs off on child euthanasia', *The Age*, 15 February: 9.

Basel Action Network/Silicon Valley Toxics Coalition (2002) *Exporting Harm: The High-Tech Trashing of Asia*, BAN/SVTC, Seattle & San Jose.

Baskin, D. (1988) 'Community mediation and the public/private problem', *Social Justice*, 15(1): 98–115.

Bastian, B., Costello, K., Loughnan, S. & Hodson, G. (2012) 'When closing the human–animal divide expands moral concern: the importance of framing', *Social Psychological and Personality Science*, 3(4): 421–29.

Bayley, D. (1999a) 'Capacity-building in law enforcement', *Trends and Issues in Crime and Criminal Justice*, No. 123, Australian Institute of Criminology, Canberra.

Bayley, D. (1999b) 'Policing: the world stage', in R.I. Mawby (ed.), *Policing across the world: issues for the twenty-first century*, University College London, London.

Bazemore, G. (1991) 'Beyond punishment, surveillance and traditional treatment: themes for a new mission in US juvenile justice', in J. Hackler (ed.), *Official responses to problem juveniles: some international reflections*, International Institute for the Sociology of Law, Onati.

Bazemore, G. (1997) 'The "community" in community justice: issues, themes, and questions for the new neighbourhood sanctioning models', *Justice System Journal*, 19(2): 193–227.

Bazemore, G. & Erbe, C. (2004) 'Reintegration and restorative justice: towards a theory and practice of informal social control and support', in S. Maruna & R. Immarigeon (eds), *After crime and punishment: pathways to offender reintegration*, Willian Publishing, Portland.

Bazemore, G. & Walgrave, L. (eds) (1999) *Restorative juvenile justice: repairing the harm of youth crime*, Criminal Justice Press: Monsey, NY.

Beaumont, L. (2005) 'Saving teens from the living hell of mental illness', *The Age*, 9 January: 8.

Beaver, K., DeLisi, M., Vaughn, M. & Barnes, J. (2010) 'Monoamine oxidase a genotype is associated with gang membership and weapon use', *Comprehensive Psychiatry*, 51(2): 130–4.

Beccaria, C. (1764) *Dei delitti e delle pene [An essay on crimes and punishments]*, <www.constitution.org/cb/crim_pun.htm>.

Becker, H. (1963) *Outsiders: studies in the sociology of deviance*, Free Press, New York.

Beirne, P. (2004) 'From animal abuse to interhuman violence? A critical review of the progression thesis', *Society & Animals*, 12(1): 39–65.

Beirne, P. (2009) *Confronting animal abuse: law, criminology and human–animal relationships*, Rowman & Littlefield, Lanham.

Beirne, P. & South, N. (eds) (2007) *Issues in green criminology: confronting harms against environments, humanity and other animals*, Willan Publishing, Devon.

Beitzel, T. & Castle, T. (2013) 'Achieving justice through the international criminal court in Northern Uganda: Is Indigenous/restorative justice a better approach?', *International Criminal Justice Review*, 23(1): 41–55.

Belknap, J. (2007) *The invisible woman: gender, crime, and justice*, Wadsworth, Belmont CA.

Belknap, J. (2010) 'Offending women: a double entendre', *Journal of Criminal Law and & Criminology*, 100(3): 1061–97.

Bell, S. & McGillivray, D. (2008) *Environmental Law*, 7th edn, Oxford University Press, Oxford.

Bellamy, A.J. & Hanson, M. (2002) 'Justice beyond borders? Australia and the International Criminal Court', *Australian Journal of International Affairs*, 56(3): 417–33.

Bellanta, M. (2010) 'The larrikin girl', *Journal of Australian Studies*, 34(4): 499–512.

Benson, M.L. & Simpson, S.S. (2009) *White collar crime: an opportunity perspective, criminology and justice series*, Routledge, New York.

Bentham, J. (1789) *An introduction to the principles of morals and legislation*, <http://oll.libertyfund.org/titles/bentham-an-introduction-to-the-principles-of-morals-and-legislation>.

Bentham, J. (1995) 'Preface', in M. Bozovic (ed.), *Panopticon writings*, Verso, London.

Benton, T. (1998) 'Rights and justice on a shared planet: more rights or new relations?', *Theoretical Criminology*, 2(2): 149–175.

Beresford, Q. & Omaji, P. (1996) *Rites of passage: Aboriginal youth, crime and justice*, Fremantle Arts Centre Press, South Fremantle.

Berg, M.T., Slocum, L.A. & Loeber, R. (2013) 'Illegal behavior, neighborhood context, and police reporting by victims of violence', *Journal of Research in Crime and Delinquency*, 50(1): 75–103.

Berger, P. & Luckmann, T. (1971) *The social construction of reality*, Allen Lane, London.

Berkovic, N. (2011) '"Junk forensic science" soiling courtroom evidence', *The Australian*, 15 April 2011.

Bernard, T. (1992) *The Cycle of Juvenile Justice*, Oxford University Press, New York.

Besthorn, F. (2013) 'Speaking Earth: Environmental Restoration and Restorative Justice', in K. Wormer & Walker (eds), *Restorative Justice Today: Practical Applications*, Sage, Los Angeles.

Beston, B. (2010) 'Access to justice for indigenous people', *Precedent*, 6 (January/February): 27–9.

Bevir, M. & Kedar, A (2008) 'Concept formation in political science: an anti-naturalist critique of qualitative methodology', *Perspectives on Politics*, 6(3): 503–517.

Beyer, R. (1993) *Community policing: lessons from Victoria*, Australian Institute of Criminology, Canberra.

Bibby, P. & Harrison, D. (2014) 'Norrie glad to have no delusions of gender', *The Age*, 3 April: 4, 5.

Bierie, D.M. (2012) 'Is tougher better? The impact of physical conditions on inmate violence', *International Journal of Offender Therapy and Comparative Criminology*, 56(3): 338–55.

Bilchik, S. (1998) *Guide for implementing the balanced and restorative justice model*, Office of Juvenile Justice and Delinquency Prevention, Washington, DC.

Biles, D. (1992) 'Aboriginal imprisonment: a statistical analysis', in D. Biles & D. McDonald (eds), *Deaths in custody Australia, 1980–1989*, Australian Institute of Criminology, Canberra: 85–105.

Binswanger, I.A., Nowels, C., Corsi, K.F., Glanz, J., Long, J., Booth, R.E. & Steiner, J.F. (2012) 'Return to drug use and overdose after release from prison: a qualitative study of risk and protective factors', *Addiction Science & Clinical Practice*, 7(3): 1–9.

Biondo, S. (2004) 'Police accountability and the need to establish an independent system of police oversight and review in Victoria', *Just Policy*, 33: 46–52.

Bird, G. (1992) 'Policing multicultural Australia', in P. Moir & H. Eijkman (eds), *Policing Australia: old issues, new perspectives*, Macmillan, Melbourne.

Birgden, A. (2007) '*Serious Sex Offenders Monitoring Act 2005* (Vic): A therapeutic jurisprudence analysis', *Psychiatry, Psychology and Law*, 14(1): 78–94.

Birnbauer, W. (2003) 'The insider and the ghost of Rolah McCabe', *The Age*, 19 July.

Bishop, E.C. (2013) 'Challenging homogenous representations of rural youth through a reconceptualisation of young rural Tasmanian's sexual health strategies', *Health Sociology Review*, 22(2): 124–6.

Black, D. (1983) 'Crime as Social Control', *American Sociological Review*, 48(1): 34–45.

Black, E. (2003). *War against the weak: eugenics and America's campaign to create a master race*, Basic Books, New York.

Black, M. (2003) 'Victim submissions to parole boards: the agenda for research', *Trends and Issues in Criminal Justice*, No. 251, Australian Institute of Criminology, Canberra.

Black, M. & Smith, R.G. (2003) 'Electronic monitoring in the criminal justice system', *Trends and Issues in Crime and Criminal Justice*, No. 254, Australian Institute of Criminology, Canberra.

Blackman, S. (2010) 'Youth subcultures, normalisation and drug prohibition: the politics of contemporary crisis and change?', *British Politics*, 5(3): 337–66.

Blagg, H. (2008a) *Restorative visions: crime, Aboriginality and the decolonisation of justice*, Hawkins Press, Sydney.

Blagg, H. (2008b) 'Colonial critique and critical criminology: issues in Aboriginal law and Aboriginal violence', in T. Anthony & C. Cunneen (eds), *The critical criminology companion*, Hawkins Press, Sydney.

Blagg, H. & Valuri, G. (2003a) *An overview of night patrols in Australia*, National Crime Prevention, Canberra.

Blagg, H. & Valuri, G. (2003b) 'Aboriginal community patrols in Australia: self-policing, self-determination and security', paper presented at *In Search of Security: An International Conference on Policing and Security*, Canada Law Reform Commission conference, 19–22 February, Montreal.

Blagg, H. & Valuri, G. (2004) 'Self-policing and community safety: the work of Aboriginal community patrols in Australia', *Current Issues in Criminal Justice*, 15(3): 205–19.

Blagg, H. & Wilkie, M. (1995) *Young people and police powers*, Australian Youth Foundation, Sydney.

Blakely, E. J. & Snyder, M. G. (1997) *Fortress America: Gated Communities in the United States*, Brookings Lincoln, Cambridge, MA.

Blalock, H.M. (1967) *Towards a Theory of Minority-Group Relations*, Wiley, New York.

Bliuc, A, McGarty, C., Hartley, L. & Muntele, D. (2012) 'Manipulating national identity: the strategic use of rhetoric by supporters and opponents of the "Cronulla riots" in Australia', *Ethnic and Racial Studies*, 35(12): 2174–94.

Block, A. (2002) 'Environmental crime and pollution: wasteful reflections', *Social Justice*, 29(1–2): 61–81.

Bloustien, G & Israel, M. (2003) 'Real Crime and the Media' in A. Goldsmith, M. Israel, M & K. Daly (eds) *Crime and Justice in Australia*, Lawbook Company, Sydney.

Boekhout van Solinge, T. (2008a) 'Crime, conflicts and ecology in Africa', in R. Sullund (ed.), *Global harms: ecological crime and speciesism*, Nova Science Publishers, New York.

Boekhout van Solinge, T. (2008b) 'The land of the orangutan and the bird of paradise under threat', in R. Sullund (ed.), *Global harms: ecological crime and speciesism*, Nova Science Publishers, New York.

Boekhout van Solinge, T. (2010) 'Deforestation crimes and conflicts in the Amazon', *Critical Criminology*, 18: 263–77.

Bogdanic, A. (2009) *Strip searching of female prisoners in Queensland*, <www.wipan.info/publications/AnnaBogdanic2.pdf>.

Bond, C.E.W. & Jeffries, (2010) 'Sentencing Indigenous and non-Indigenous women in Western Australia's higher courts', *Psychiatry, Psychology and Law*, 17(1): 70–8.

Bond, C.E.W. & Jeffries, S. (2012) 'Indigeneity and the likelihood of imprisonment in Queensland's adult and children's courts'. *Psychiatry, Psychology and Law*, 19(2): 169–83.

Bondeson, U. (1989) *Prisoners in prison societies*, Transaction Publishers, New Brunswick.

Boniface, D. (2008) 'Juror misconduct, secret jury business and the exclusionary rule', *Criminal Law Journal*, 32, 18–37.

Bonney, R. (1989) *NSW Summary Offences Act 1988*, NSW Bureau of Crime and Statistics Research, Attorney General's Dept, Sydney.

Bonta, J. & Andrews, D. (2007) *Risk–need–responsivity model for offender assessment and rehabilitation*, Public Safety Canada, Ottawa.

Bonta, J., Wallace-Capretta, S., Rooney, J. & Mcanoy, K. (2002) 'An outcome evaluation of a restorative justice alternative to incarceration', *Contemporary Justice Review*, 5(4): 319–38.

Bookman, Z. (2008) 'Convergences and omissions in reporting

corporate and white collar crime', *DePaul Business and Commercial Law Journal*, 6: 347–92.

Booth, T. (2002) 'Delivering justice to victims of crime', *Law Society Journal* (February): 64–6.

Booth, T. (2012) '"Cooling out" victims of crime: managing victim participation in the sentencing process in a superior sentencing court', *Australian and New Zealand Journal of Criminology*, 45(2): 214–30.

Borzycki, M. & Baldry, E. (2003) 'Promoting integration: the provision of prisoner post-release services', *Trends and Issues in Crime and Criminal Justice*, No. 262, Australian Institute of Criminology, Canberra.

Bottomley, S., Gunningham, N. & Parker, S. (1991) *Law in context*, Federation Press, Sydney.

Bottoms, A. (1995) 'The philosophy and politics of punishment and sentencing', in C. Clarkson & R. Morgan (eds), *The politics of sentencing reform*, Clarendon Press, Oxford.

Bourdieu, P. (1986) 'The forms of capital', in J.G. Richardson (ed.), *Handbook of theory and research for the sociology of education*, Greenwood Press, New York: 241–58.

Bourdieu, P. (1990) *In other words: essays towards a reflexive sociology*, Polity Press, Cambridge.

Bourdieu, P. & Wacquant, L. (1992) *An invitation to reflexive sociology*, Polity Press, Cambridge.

Box, S. (1983) *Power, crime and mystification*, Tavistock, London.

Boyd, D. (2003) *Unnatural law: rethinking Canadian environmental law and policy*, UBC Press, Vancouver.

Boyden, N. (2005) 'Butter knives into swords: section 12 bonds (suspended sentences) and their revocation', *Law Society Journal*, 43(June): 73–5.

Bradbury, B (1988) *Welfare fraud, work incentives and income support for the unemployed*,

Social Welfare Research Centre, University of New South Wales, Sydney.

Bradford, D. & Payne, J. (2012) 'Illicit drug use and property offending among police detainees', *Crime and Justice Bulletin. Contemporary Issues in Crime and Justice*, No. 9: 1–12, NSW Bureau of Crime Statistics and Research.

Bradley, L. (2003) 'The age of criminal responsibility revisited', *Deakin Law Review*, 8(1): 71–90.

Brady, N. (2011a) '"Sexting" youths placed on sex offenders register', *The Age*, 24 July: 11.

Brady, N. (2011b) 'Scourge of the school yard: how one rash moment can ruin a young life', *The Age*, 10 July: 4–5.

Brain, K. (2000) *Youth, alcohol and the emergence of the post-modern alcohol order*, Occasional Paper No. 1, Institute of Alcohol Studies, London.

Braithwaite, J. (1984) *Corporate crime in the pharmaceutical industry*, Routledge & Kegan Paul, London.

Braithwaite, J. (1989) *Crime, shame and reintegration*, Cambridge University Press, Cambridge.

Braithwaite, J. (1992) 'Reducing the crime problem: a not so dismal criminology: the John Barry memorial lecture', *Australian and New Zealand Journal of Criminology*, 25(1): 1–10.

Braithwaite, J. (1999) 'Restorative justice: assessing optimistic and pessimistic accounts', in M. Tonry (ed.), *Crime and Justice: A Review of Research* (Vol. 25), University of Chicago Press, Chicago: 1–127.

Braithwaite, J. (2001) 'Crime in a Convict Republic', *The Modern Law Review*, 64(1): 11–50.

Braithwaite, J. (2009) 'Restorative justice for banks through negative licensing', *British Journal of Criminology*, 49(4): 439–50.

Braithwaite, J. & Pettit, P. (1990) *Not just deserts: a republican theory of criminal justice*, Oxford University Press, Oxford.

Braithwaite, J., Braithwaite, V., Cookson, M. & Dunn, L. (2010) *Anomie, and violence: non-truth and reconciliation in Indonesian peacebuilding*, Australian National University Press EPress, Canberra.

Brantingham, P. & Brantingham, P. (1981) *Environmental criminology*, Sage, Beverly Hills.

Brennan, I.R., Moore, S.C. & Shepherd, J.P. (2010) 'Risk factors for violent victimisation and injury from six years of the British crime survey', *International Journal of Victimology*, 17: 209–29.

Brennan, T., Breitenbach, M., Dieterich, W., Salisbury, E.J. & Van Voorhis, P. (2012) 'Women's pathways to serious and habitual crime: a person-centred analysis incorporating gender responsive factors', *Criminal Justice and Behaviour*, 39(11): 1481–508.

Breyer, S. (1994) 'Televise Executions Solid Pick, Breyer', *Gazette*, 17 May, p. 4.

Brickey, K. (2008) *Environmental Crime: Law, Policy, Prosecution*, Aspen Publishers, New York.

Brickey, S. & Comack, E. (eds) (1986) *The social basis of law: critical readings in the sociology of law*, Garamond Press, Toronto.

Bricknell, S. (2008) 'Trends in violent crime', *Trends and Issues in Crimes and Criminal Justice*, No. 359, Australian Institute of Criminology, Canberra.

Bricknell, S. (2010) *Environmental Crime in Australia*. AIC Reports Research and Public Policy Series 109, Australian Institute of Criminology, Canberra.

Briggs, C.S., Sundt, J.L. & Castellano, T.C. (2003) 'The effect of supermaximum security prisons on aggregate levels of institutional violence, *Criminology* 41(4): 1341–78.

Briggs, D. & Auty, K. (2003) 'Koori Court Victoria: *Magistrates' Court (Koori Court) Act 2002'*,

paper presented at *Controlling Crime: Risks and Responsibilities, Australian and New Zealand Society of Criminology Conference*, 1–3 October, Sydney.

Brightman, H.J. (2009) *Today's white-collar crime: legal, investigative and theoretical perspectives*, Routledge, New York.

Briody, M. (2002) 'The effects of DNA evidence on sexual offence cases in court', *Current Issues in Criminal Justice*, 14(2): 159–181.

Briody, M., (2004) 'The effects of DNA evidence on homicide cases in court', *Australian and New Zealand Journal of Criminology*, 37(2): 231–53.

Briscoe, S. & Donnelly, N. (2001) *Assaults on licensed premises in inner-urban areas*, New South Wales Bureau of Crime Statistics and Research, Sydney.

Briscoe, S. & Donnelly, N. (2003) 'Problematic licensed premises for assaults in inner Sydney, Newcastle and Wollongong', *Australian and New Zealand Journal of Criminology*, 36(1): 23–33.

Brisman, A. (2008). 'Crime-environment relationships and environmental justice', *Seattle Journal for Social Justice*, 6(2): 727–817.

Britz, M. (2009) *Computer forensics and cyber crime: an introduction*, Prentice Hall, Upper Saddle River.

Broadhurst, R. (1994) 'Aborigines, cowboys, "firewater" and jail: the view from the frontier', *Australian and New Zealand Journal of Criminology*, 27(1): 50–6.

Brogden, R. (1999) 'Community policing as cherry pie', in R.I. Mawby (ed.), *Policing across the world: issues for the twenty-first century*, University College, London.

Bronfenbrenner, U. (1977) 'Toward an experimental ecology of human development', *American Psychologist*, 32(7): 513–31.

Bronitt, S. & Hogg, R. (2003) 'The role and future of the jury in the

Australian legal system', *Legaldate*, 15(3): 1–4.

Brook, D. (2000) 'Environmental genocide: native Americans and toxic waste', *American Journal of Economics and Sociology*, 57(1): 105–13.

Brotherhood of St Laurence (2014) *Australian youth unemployment snapshot: my chance, our future youth employment campaign*, Brotherhood of St Laurence, Fitzroy.

Brown, C. (1979) *Understanding society: an introduction to sociological theory*, John Murray, London.

Brown, D. (1993) 'Prison informers: where the grasses are greener', *Alternative Law Journal*, 18(2): 80–5.

Brown, D. (2002a) '"Losing my religion": reflections on critical criminology in Australia', in K. Carrington & R. Hogg (eds), *Critical criminology: issues, debates, challenges*, Willan, Devon.

Brown, D. (2002b) 'The politics of law and order', *Law Society Journal*, 40(9): 64–72.

Brown, D. (2010) 'The limited benefit of prison in controlling crime', *Current Issues in Criminal Justice*, 22(1): 137–48.

Brown, D. & Hogg, R. (1992) 'Essentialism, radical criminology and left realism', *Australian and New Zealand Journal of Criminology*, 25(3): 195–230.

Brown, D. & Wilkie, M. (eds) (2002) *Prisoners as citizens: human rights in Australian prisons*, Federation Press, Sydney.

Brown, D., Farrier, D. & Weisbrot, D. (1996a) *Criminal laws: materials and commentary on criminal law and process in New South Wales* (Vol. 1, 2nd edn), Federation Press, Sydney.

Brown, D., Farrier, D. & Weisbrot, D. (1996b) *Criminal laws: materials and commentary on criminal law and process in New South Wales* (Vol. 2, 2nd edn), Federation Press Sydney.

Brown, D., Farrier, D., Egger, S. & McNamara, L. (2001) *Criminal laws: materials and commentary on criminal law and process in New South Wales*, Federation Press, Sydney.

Brown, D., Schwartz, M. & Boseley, L. (2012) 'The promise of justice reinvestment', *Alternative Law Journal*, 37(2): 96–102.

Brown, R. (2013) 'Regulating crime prevention design into consumer products: Learning the lessons from electronic vehicle immobilisation', *Trends & Issues in Crime and Criminal Justice*, No. 453, Australian Institute of Criminology, Canberra.

Browne, R. (2013) 'Screen violence "hard wires" growing brain', *The Age*, 5 October: 8.

Brownlee, I. (1998) *Community punishment: a critical introduction*, Addison Wesley Longman, London.

Brownmiller, S. (1976) *Against our will*, Penguin, Harmondsworth.

Bryant, C. & Willis, M. (2008) 'Risk factors in Indigenous violent victimisation'. *Technical and Background Paper Series*, No. 79, Australian Institute of Criminology, Canberra.

Bryce, Q. (2013) 'Watching the women', *Boyer lecture*, 10 November.

Bryett, K., Harrison, A. & Shaw, J. (1994) *The role and functions of police in Australia*, Vol. 2, Butterworths, Sydney.

Buchanan, C. & Hartley, P. (1992) *Criminal choice: the economic theory of crime and its implications for crime control*, Centre for Independent Studies, Sydney.

Buckingham, J.I. (2004) '"Newsmaking" criminology or "infotainment" criminology?', *Australian and New Zealand Journal of Criminology*, 37(2): 253–75.

Bullard, R. (1994) *Unequal protection: environmental justice and communities of color*, Sierra Club Books, San Francisco.

Bullard, R. (ed.) (2005) *The quest for environmental justice: human rights and the politics of pollution*. Sierra Club Books, San Francisco.

Bullock, K. & Tilley, N. (2009) 'Police Reform: the Prospects for Evidence Based Policing and Crime Reduction', *Policing: An International Journal of policy and Practice*: 381–7.

Buonanno, P. & Montolio, D. (2008) 'Identifying the socio-economic and demographic determinants of crime across Spanish provinces', *International Review of Law and Economics*, 28(2): 89–97.

Burke, P. (2001) 'Collaboration for successful prisoner re-entry: the role of parole and the courts', *Corrections Management Quarterly*, 5(3): 11–22.

Bursik, R.J. and Grasmick, H.G. (1996) 'The use of contextual analysis in models of criminal behaviour', in J. Hawkins (ed.), *Delinquency and crime: current theories*, Cambridge University Press, New York.

Burzycki, M. (2005) *Interventions for prisoners returning to the community*, Attorney-General's Department, Canberra.

Butcher, S. (2009) 'Repeat sex offender denied release', *The Age*, 19 June.

Bute, J. (1981) 'Practicing from theory: work with youths and reflections on radical criminology', *Crime & Delinquency*, 27(1): 106–21.

Butler, T., Boonwaat, L., Hailstone, S., Falconer, T., Lems, P., Ginley, T., Read, V., Smith, N., Levy, M., Dore, G. & Kaldor, J. (2007) 'The 2004 Australian prison entrants' blood-borne virus and risk behaviour survey', *Australian and New Zealand Journal of Public Health*, 31(1): 44–50.

Butt, C. (2014) 'Keyed-in car thieves upgrading to newer models', *The Age*, 3 January: 4–5.

Buzawa, E. & Buzawa, C. (1993) 'The impact of arrest on domestic violence', *American Behavioural Scientist*, 36(5): 558–74.

Byrne, P. (1988) 'Criminal law and justice: plea bargaining', *Australian Law Journal*, 62(10): 799–803.

C

Cain, M. (1996) *Recidivism of Juvenile Offenders in New South Wales*. NSW Department of Juvenile Justice, Sydney.

Cain, M. & Howe, A. (eds) (2008) *Women, crime and social harm: towards a criminology for the global era*, Hart Publishing, Oxford.

Caita-Zufferey, M. (2013) 'From danger to risk: categorising and valuing recreational heroin and cocaine use', *Health, Risk & Society*, 14(5): 427–43.

Calabresi, M. (2012) 'The street fighter', *Time*, 179(6): 22–7.

Calabria, B., Doran, C.M., Vos, T., Shakeshaft, A.P. & Hall, W. (2010) 'Epidemiology of alcohol related burden of disease among Indigenous Australians', *Australian and New Zealand Journal of Public Health*, 34 (suppl. 1): 47–51.

Callinan, R. (2014) 'Chasing new highs', *The Age*, Insight, 11 January: 13.

Calvert, A.F. (1894) *Western Australia: its history and progress*, Simpkin, Marshall, Hamilton, Kent and Co., London.

Cameron, M. (2001) 'Women prisoners and correctional programs', *Trends and Issues in Crime and Criminal Justice*, No. 194, Australian Institute of Criminology, Canberra.

Camilleri, P. & McArthur, M. (2008) 'Suicidal behaviour in prisons: learning from Australian and international experiences', *International Journal of Law and Psychiatry*, 31(4): 297–307.

Campbell, M.C. (2013) 'The transformation of America's penal order: a historicized political sociology of punishment',

American Journal of Sociology, 118(5): 1375–423.

Canadian Medical Association (2013) 'White coats and white-collar crime', *Canadian Medical Association Journal*, 185(1): 19–20.

Cannon, A. (2008) 'Smoke and mirrors or meaningful change: the way forward for therapeutic jurisprudence', *Journal of Justice Administration*, 17(4): 217–22.

Capper, S. & Crooks, M. (2010) New homicide laws have proved indefensible', *The Age*, 23 May: 21.

Caputo, G.A. & King, A. (2011) 'Shoplifting: work, agency, and gender', *Feminist Criminology*, 6(3): 159–177.

Carey, A. & Dowling, J. (2013) 'Behind the rage behind the wheel', *The Age*, Focus, 20 March: 16–17.

Carlen, P. & Worrall, A. (2004) *Analysing women's imprisonment*, Willan Publishing, Devon.

Carlton, B. (2007) *Imprisoning resistance: life and death in an Australian supermax*, Institute of Criminology, University of Sydney, Sydney.

Carlton, B. (2008) 'Isolation as counter-insurgency: supermax prisons and the war on terror', in C. Cunneen & M. Salter (eds), *Proceedings of the 2nd Australian and New Zealand Critical Criminology Conference*, Crime & Justice Research Network, University of New South Wales, Sydney.

Carlton, B. & Segrave, M. (2011) 'Women's survival post-imprisonment: connecting imprisonment with pains past and present', *Punishment & Society*, 13(5): 551–79.

Carrabine, E., Iganski, P., Lee, M., Plummer, K. & South, N. (2004) *Criminology: a sociological introduction*, Routledge, London.

Carrington, K. (1989) 'Girls and graffiti', *Cultural Studies*, 3(1): 89–100.

Carrington, K. (1993) *Offending girls*, Allen & Unwin, Sydney.

Carrington, K. (2006) 'Does feminism spoil girls? Explanations for the official rises in female delinquency', *Australian and New Zealand Journal of Criminology*, 39(1): 34–53.

Carrington, K. (2013) 'Girls and violence: the case for a feminist theory of female violence', *International Journal for Crime, Justice and Social Democracy*, 2(2): 63–79.

Carrington, K. & Hogg, R. (eds) (2002) *Critical criminology: issues, debates, challenges*, Willan Publishing, Devon.

Carrington, K. & Pereira, M. (2009) *Offending youth: sex, crime and justice*, The Federation Press, Sydney.

Carrington, K., McIntosh, A. & Scott, J. (2010) 'Globalization, frontier masculinities and violence—booze, blokes and brawls', *British Journal of Criminology*, 50(3): 393–413.

CARS (2014) *Motor vehicle theft and socio-economic status in Australia*, CARS, South Australia.

Carson, K. & O'Malley, P. (1989) 'The institutional foundations of contemporary Australian criminology', *Australian and New Zealand Journal of Sociology*, 25(3): 333–55.

Carson, W.G. (1982) *The other price of Britain's oil*, Rutgers University Press, New York.

Carson, W.G. (2004a) 'Is communalism dead? Reflections on the present and future practice of crime prevention: Part 1', *Australian and New Zealand Journal of Criminology*, 37(1): 1–22.

Carson, W.G. (2004b) 'Is communalism dead? Reflections on the present and future practice of crime prevention: Part 2', *Australian and New Zealand Journal of Criminology*, 37(2): 192–210.

Carter, L.E., (2012) 'Torture and the war on terror: the need for consistent definitions and legal remedies', *Journal of National Security Law & Policy*, 6(1): 291–317.

Carvan, J. (2002) *Understanding the Australian legal system*, Law Book Book Co., Sydney.

Case, S. (2007) 'Questioning the "Evidence" of Risk that Underpins Evidence-led Youth Justice Interventions', *Youth Justice: An International Journal*, 7(2): 91–106.

Cuthbert, D. & Quartly, M. (2012) 'Forced Adoption in the national story of apology and regret', *Australian Journal of Politics and History*, 58(1): 82–96.

Casey-Acevedo, K., Bakken, T. & Karle, A. (2004) 'Children visiting mothers in prison: the effects on mothers' behaviour and discipline adjustment', *Australian and New Zealand Journal of Criminology*, 37(1): 418–30.

Cashman, K. & Henning, T. (2012) 'Lawyers and DNA: issues in understanding and challenging the evidence', *Current Issues in Criminal Justice*, 24(1): 69–83.

Castiglione, D., van Deth, J.W. & Wolleb, G. (2008) 'Social capital's fortune: an introduction', in D. Castiglione, J.W. van Deth & B. Wolleb (eds), *The handbook of social capital*, Oxford University Press, Oxford.

Castles, A. (1982) *An Australian legal history*, The Law Book Company, Sydney.

Catalano, R. & Hawkins, J. (1996) 'The social development model: a theory of antisocial behaviour', in J. Hawkins (ed.), *Delinquency and crime: current theories*, Cambridge University Press, New York.

Catalano, S., Smith, E., Snyder, H. & Rand, M. (2009) *Female victims of violence*, Office of Justice Programs, Bureau of Justice Statistics, Washington, DC.

Cavadino, M. & Dinigan, J. (2006) 'Penal policy and political economy', *Criminology and Criminal Justice*, 6(4): 435–56.

Cecil, D.K. & Leitner, J.L. (2009) 'Unlocking the gates: an examination of MSNBC investigates lockup', *Howard Journal*, 48(2): 184–99.

Centre for Innovative Justice (2014) *Innovative Justice Responses to Sexual Offending—Pathways to better outcomes for victims, offenders and the community*, RMIT, Melbourne.

Centre for Retail Research (2009) *Global retail theft barometer 2009—the worldwide shrinkage survey*, Centre for Retail Research, England.

Chakraborti, N. & Garland, J. (2012) 'Reconceptualizing hate crime victimization through the lens of vulnerability and difference', *Theoretical Criminology*, 16(4): 499–514.

Challinger, D. (2003) 'Crime stoppers: evaluating Victoria's program', *Trends and Issues in Crime and Criminal Justice*, No. 272, Australian Institute of Criminology, Canberra.

Chambliss, W. (1975) 'Towards a political economy of crime', *Theory and Society*, 2(2): 150–70.

Chambliss, W. (1994) 'The law of vagrancy', in J.E. Jacoby (ed.), *Classics of criminology* (2nd edn), Wavelength Press, Inc, Prospect Heights.

Chambliss, W., Michalowski, R. & Krammer, R. (2010) (eds) *State crime in the global age*, Willan Publishing, Uffculme.

Chan, A. & Payne, J. (2013) 'Homicide in Australia: 2008–09 to 2009–10. National Homicide Monitoring Program Annual Report', *AIC Monitoring Report*, No. 21, Australian Institute of Criminology, Canberra.

Chan, J. (1991) 'Decarceration and imprisonment in New South Wales: a historical analysis of early release', *UNSW Law Journal*, 13(2): 393–416.

Chan, J. (1992) *Doing less time: penal reform in crisis*, Monograph Series, No. 2, Institute of Criminology, Sydney.

Chan, J. (1995) 'Systematically distorted communication? Criminological knowledge, media representation and public policy', *Australian and New Zealand Journal of Criminology*, special supplementary issue: *Crime, Criminology and Public Policy*, 23–30.

Chan, J. (1996) 'Changing police culture', *British Journal of Criminology*, 36(1): 109–31.

Chan, J. (1997) *Changing police culture: policing in a multicultural society*, Cambridge University Press, Melbourne.

Chan, J. (ed.) (2005) *Reshaping Juvenile Justice: The NSW Young Offenders Act 1997*, Sydney Institute of Criminology, University of Sydney.

Chan, J. (2008) 'Police culture: a brief history of a concept', in T. Anthony & C. Cunneen (eds), *The critical criminology companion*, Hawkins Press, Sydney.

Chan, S. (1999) 'Bubbling acid: Sydney's techno underground', in R. White (ed.), *Australian youth subcultures: on the margins and in the mainstream*, Australian Clearinghouse for Youth Studies, Hobart.

Chapman, B., Freiberg, A., Quiggin, J. & Tait, D. (2003) *Rejuvenating financial penalties: using the tax system to collect fines*, Australian National University, Canberra.

Chapman, B., Weatherburn, D., Kapuscinski, C., Chilvers, M. & Roussel, S. (2002) 'Unemployment duration, schooling and property crime', *Crime and Justice Bulletin*, 74, New South Wales Bureau of Crime Statistics and Research, Sydney.

Charlesworth, S. & Robertson, D. (2012) 'Policing, Gender and Working Time: An Australian case study' *Police Practice and Research: An International Journal*, 13(3): 241–53.

Charlton, K. & Taylor, N. (2003) 'Implementing business watch: problems and solutions', *Trends and Issues in Crime and Criminal Justice*, No. 244, Australian Institute of Criminology, Canberra.

Charlton, R. & Dewdney, M. (2004) *The mediator's handbook: skills and strategies for practitioners*, The Law book Book Co., Sydney.

Chesney-Lind, M. & Sheldon, R. (1992) *Girls, delinquency and juvenile justice*, Brooks/Cole publishing, California.

Chesterman, J. (1993) 'Does alternative dispute resolution provide access to justice?', *Socio-Legal Bulletin*, 10: 21–3.

Chiricos T., Welch, K. & Gertz, M. (2004) 'Racial typification of crime and support for punitive measures', *Criminology*, 42(2): 359–89.

Chisholm, J. (2000) 'Benefit–cost analysis and crime prevention', *Trends and Issues in Crime and Criminal Justice*, No. 147, Australian Institute of Criminology, Canberra.

Chisholm, R. & Nettheim, G. (2002) *Understanding law: an introduction to Australia's legal system* (6th edn), Butterworths, Sydney.

Christensen, T. (2010) 'Presumed guilty: constructing deviance and deviants through techniques of neutralization', *Deviant Behaviour*, 31(6): 552–77.

Christie, N. (1986) 'The ideal victim', in E.A. Fattah (ed.), *From crime policy to victim policy*, Macmillan, London.

Christie, N. (1993) *Crime control as industry: towards gulags western style?*, Routledge, London.

Clancy, G., Lee, M. & Fisher, D. (2012) 'Crime prevention through environmental design (CPTED) and the New South Wales crime risk assessment guidelines: a critical review', *Crime Prevention and Community Safety*, 14(1): 1–15.

Clarke, R. (ed.) (1997) *Situational crime prevention: successful case studies* (2nd edn), Harrow & Heston, New York.

Clarke, R. V. (1980), 'Situational crime prevention: Theory and practice', *British Journal of Criminology*, Vol. 20, No. 2, pp. 136–47.

Clarke, R. V. (2005), 'Seven Misconceptions of Situational Crime Prevention', in N. Tilley (ed.), *Handbook of Crime Prevention and Community Safety*, Willan Publishing, Cullompton, Devon.

Clarke and Eck (2003) Clarke, R. and Eck, J. (2003) *Crime Analysis for Problem Solvers in 60 Small Steps*, Office of Community Oriented Policing Services, Centre for Problem Oriented Policing, U.S. Department of Justice.

Clarke, R. & Homel, R. (1997) 'A revised classification of situational crime prevention techniques', in S. Lab (ed.), *Crime prevention at the crossroads*, Anderson, Cincinnati.

Clarke, R. & Weisburd, D. (1994) 'Diffusion of crime control benefits', in R.V. Clarke (ed.), *Crime prevention studies*, Criminal Justice Press, Monsey.

Clarke, R.V. & Cornish, D.B. (1985) 'Modeling offenders' decisions: a framework for research and policy', *Crime & Justice*, 16: 147–85.

Clarke R.V. & Petrossian (2012) *Shoplifting. Guide No. 11* (2nd edn), Centre for Problem Oriented Policing, <www.popcenter.org/problems/pdfs/Shoplifting.pdf>.

Clawson, E. (2001) *Redesigning community corrections: the Multnomah County experience*, Multnomah County Department of Corrections.

Clement, K.E. & Barbrey, J.W. (2008) 'Criminal laws on the fringe: an analysis of legislated punishments for morality crimes in the 50 states', *Critical Criminology*, 16(2): 105–21.

Clifford, M. (ed.) (1998) *Environmental Crime: Enforcement, Policy, and Social Responsibility*, Aspen Publishers, Gaithersburg, Maryland.

Clinard, B. (1974) *The sociology of deviant behaviour*, Holt, Rinehart & Winston, New York.

Clinard, M.B. (1990) *Corporate corruption: the abuse of power*, Praeger, New York.

Clinard, M.B. & Yeager, P.C. (1980) *Corporate crime*, Free Press, New York.

Clough, J. & Mulhern, C. (2002) *The prosecution of corporations*, Oxford University Press, Melbourne.

Clough, J., Goodman-Delahunty, J., Ogloff, J., Brewer, N., Tait, D. & Horan, J. (2007) *Practices and procedures that affect juror satisfaction in Australia*, Criminology Research Council, Canberra.

Cloward, R. & Ohlin, L. (1960) *Delinquency and opportunity: a theory of delinquent gangs*, Free Press, Chicago.

COAG Reform Council (2013) *Education in Australia 2012: five years of performance*, Sydney.

Cohen, A. (1955) *Delinquent boys: the culture of the gang*, Free Press, Chicago.

Cohen, L.E. & Felson, M. (1979) 'Social change and crime rate trends: a routine activity approach', *American Sociological Review*, 44(4): 588–608.

Cohen, S. (1972) *Folk devils and moral panics: the creation of the mods and rockers*, MacGibbon & Kee, London.

Cohen, S. (1973a) 'Property destruction: motives and meanings', in C. Ward (ed.), *Vandalism*, Architectural Press, London.

Cohen, S. (1973b) *Folk devils and moral panics*, Paladin, London.

Cohen, S. (1981) 'Footprints in the sand: a further report on criminology and the sociology of deviance in Britain', in M. Fitzgerald, G. McLennan & J. Pawson (eds), *Crime and society: readings in history and theory*, Routledge & Kegan Paul in association with Open University Press, London.

Cohen, S. (1985) *Visions of social control crime, punishment and classification*, Polity Press, Cambridge.

Cohen, S. (1989) 'The critical discourse on "social control": notes on the concept as a hammer', *International Journal of the Sociology of Law*, 17(3): 347–58.

Cohen, S. (1993) 'Human rights and crimes of the state: the culture of denial', *Australian and New Zealand Journal of Criminology*, 26(2): 97–115.

Cohen, S. (2001) *States of denial: knowing about atrocities and suffering*, Polity Press, Cambridge.

Coleman, A. (1989) 'Disposition and situation: two sides of the same crime', in D. Evans & D. Herbert (eds), *The geography of crime*, Routledge, London.

Collins, J.H., Noble, G., Poynting, S. & Tabar, P. 2000, *Kebabs, kids, cops and crime*, Pluto Press, Sydney.

Collins, D. & Lapsley H. (2008) 'The costs of tobacco, alcohol and illicit drug abuse to Australian society in 2004–05'. *National Drug Strategy Monograph Series*, No. 66, Australian Government Department of Health and Ageing, Canberra.

Collins, H. (1982) *Marxism and law*, Oxford University Press, Oxford.

Collins, J. (2005) Ethnic minorities and crime in Australia: moral panic or meaningful policy responses, paper presented at a public seminar organised by the Office of Multicultural Interest, 8 November 2005, Perth Western Australia.

Collins, J. (2007) 'The landmark of Cronulla', in J. Jupp & J. Nieuwenhuysen with E. Dawson (eds), *Social cohesion in Australia*, Cambridge University Press, Port Melbourne.

Collins, J. & Reid, C. (2009) 'Minority youth, crime, conflict, and belonging in Australia', *Journal of International Migration & Integration*, 10(4): 377–91.

Collins, J., Noble, G., Poynting, S. & Tabar, P. (2000) *Kebabs, kids, cops and crime: youth, ethnicity and crime*, Pluto Press, Sydney.

Collin, P., Rahilly, K., Richardson, I. & Third, A. (2010) *The benefits of social networking services: literature review*, Cooperative Research Centre for Young People, Technology and Wellbeing, Melbourne.

Commonwealth of Australia (2012) *House of Representatives Practice* (6th edn) Department of the House of Representatives, Commonwealth of Australia, Canberra.

Connell, R. (1983) 'Intellectuals and intellectual work', in R. Connell, *Which way is up? Essays on class, sex and culture*, Allen & Unwin, Sydney.

Connell, R. (2007) *Southern theory: the global dynamics of knowledge in social science*, Allen & Unwin, Sydney.

Conner, T. & Haines, F. (2013) 'Networked regulation as a solution to human rights abuses in global supply chains? The case of trade union rights violations by Indonesian sports shoe manufacturers', *Theoretical Criminology*, 17(2): 197–214.

Connor, X. (2004) 'Acting judges are bad for democracy', *The Age*, 16 November, 15.

Conroy, P. (1996) 'Concern on legal aid rules: judge', *The Age*, 26 March.

Conte, A. (2004) 'Human rights, non-parole periods and preventive detention', *New Zealand Law Journal*, June, 202–4.

Conway-Smith, E. (2013) 'Uganda votes in life terms for gays', *The Age*, 22 December: 8.

Cook, B., David, F. & Grant, A. (1999) 'Victims' needs, victims' rights: policies and programs for victims of crime in Australia', *Research and Public Policy* Series, No. 19, Australian Institute of Criminology, Canberra.

Cook, H. (2013) 'Thousands to be denied legal aid', *The Age*, 3 September: 8.

Cook, H. & Lee, J. (2013) 'Justice fear as Legal Aid cuts bite', *The Age*, 17 January: 5.

Cooke, M. (1987) 'The practical problems of the sentencer', in D.C. Pennington & S. Lloyd-Bostock (eds), *The psychology of sentencing: approaches to consistency and disparity*, Centre for Socio-Legal Studies, Oxford.

Cooper, J.S. (1999) 'State of the nation: therapeutic jurisprudence and the evolution of the right of self-determination in international law', *Behavioural Sciences and the Law*, 17(5): 607–43.

Copes, H. (1999). 'Routine activities and motor vehicle theft: a crime specific approach'. *Journal of Crime and Justice*, 22(2): 125–146.

Corderoy, A. (2013) 'Legally high', *The Age*, 22 June: 16–17.

Cornforth, M. (1976) *Dialectical materialism: an introduction. Vol. 2: Historical materialism*, Lawrence & Wishart, London.

Cornish, D. & Clarke, R. (1986) *The reasoning criminal*, Springer-Verlag, New York.

Corrective Services Queensland (2008) *Queensland Corrective Services: Annual Report 2007–08*, Brisbane.

Cottee, S.Y. (2012) 'Are fish the victims of "speciesism"? A discussion about fear, pain and animal consciousness', *Fish Physiology and Biochemistry*, 38(5): 5–15.

Cottingham, J.G. (1979) 'Varieties of retribution', *Philosophical Quarterly*, July: 238–46.

Coumarelos, C. (1994) *Juvenile Offending: Predicting Persistence and Determining Cost-Effectiveness of Interventions*, NSW Bureau of Crime Statistics and Research, Sydney.

Coupe, R. (2002) *Australia's convict past*, New Holland, Frenchs Forest.

Coventry, G. & Westerhuis, D. (2009) '*Preparation for freedom: Cyclone Larry and prison work*', James Cook University, Townsville.

Coventry, G., Muncie, J. & Walters, R. (1992) *Rethinking social policy for young people and crime prevention*, Discussion Paper No. 1, National Centre for Socio-Legal Studies, La Trobe University, Melbourne.

Covey, H.C., Menard, S. & Franzese, J. (2013) 'Effects of adolescent physical abuse, exposure to neighborhood violence, and witnessing parental violence on adult socioeconomic status', *Child Maltreatment*, 18:(2): 85–97.

Cowdery, N. (2001) *Getting justice wrong*, Allen & Unwin, Sydney.

Cowdery, N. (2006) 'Negotiating with the DPP', paper presented to the *Legal Aid Commission of NSW, Criminal Law Conference*, 3 August.

Cowlishaw, G. (1988) 'Black, white or brindle', *Race in Rural Australia*, Cambridge University Press, Sydney.

Crabbe, M. & Corlett, D. (2010) 'Eroticising inequality: technology, pornography and young people', *Domestic Violence Resource Centre Victoria*, 3(Spring): 1–6.

Cranston, R. (1992) 'Access to justice: courts, tribunals and alternative institutions', *Legal issues resource kit: access to justice*, Legal Service Bulletin Co-operative, Melbourne.

Crawford, A. (1998) *Crime prevention and community safety: politics, policies and practices*, Longman, Harlow.

Crawford, J. & Opeskin, B. (2004) *Australian courts of law* (4th edn), Oxford University Press, Melbourne.

Craze, I. & Moyniban, P. (1994) 'Violence, meaning and the law: responses to Gary David', *Australian and New Zealand Journal of Criminology*, 27(1): 30–45.

Crelinsten, R. (2003) 'The world of torture: a constructed reality', *Theoretical Criminology*, 7(3): 293–318.

Critchter, C. (2011) 'For a political economy of moral panics', *Crime Media Culture*, 7(3): 259–75.

Crime Prevention Victoria & Australian Institute of Family Studies (2002a) *Patterns and precursors of adolescent antisocial behaviour: the first report*, Crime Prevention Victoria, Melbourne.

Crime Prevention Victoria & Australian Institute of Family Studies (2002b) *Patterns and precursors of adolescent antisocial behaviour: the second report*, Crime Prevention Victoria, Melbourne.

Criminal Law Review Division (1998) *Final report of the 'homosexual advance defence' working party*, Criminal Law Review Division, Attorney-General's Department, New South Wales, Sydney.

Crockett, A. (2001) 'What price justice?', *Legalgate*, 13(4): 5–7.

Croft, P., Hubbard, P. & Prior, J. (2013) 'Policing, planning and sex: governing bodies, spatially', *Australian & New Zealand Journal of Criminology*, 46(1): 51–69.

Crofts, T. & Loughnan, A. (2013) 'Provocation: the good, the bad and the ugly', *Criminal Law Journal* 37: 23–37.

Cromwell, P., Olson, J. & Avary, D. (1991) *Breaking and entering: an ethnographic analysis of burglary*, Sage, Los Angeles.

Crooks, M. (2004) 'It's time women had a better deal from the law', *The Age*, 1 November, 17.

Crow, W.J. & Bull, J.L. (1975) *Robbery, deterrence: an applied behavioural science demonstration*, WBSI, La Jolla.

Culhane, S.E., Hosch, H.M. & Weaver, W.G. (2004) 'Crime victims serving as jurors: is there bias present?', *Law and Human Behavior*, 28(6): 649–59.

Cullen, F. & Gendreau, P. (2000) 'Assessing correctional rehabilitation: policy, practice, and prospects', *Criminal Justice*, 3: 109–75.

Cullen, F.T. (2011) 'Beyond adolescence-limited criminology: Choosing our future—the American Society of Criminology 2010 Sutherland address', *Criminology*, 49(2): 287–330.

Cullen, F.T., Hartman, J.L., & Jonson, C.L. (2009) 'Bad guys: why the public supports punishing white-collar offenders', *Crime, Law and Social Change*, 51(1): 31–44.

Cunneen, C. (1985) 'Working class boys and crime: theorising the class/gender mix', in P. Patton & R. Poole (eds), *War/masculinity*, Intervention Publications, Sydney.

Cunneen, C. (1990a) *Aboriginal–police relations in Redfern: with special reference to the police raid of 8 February 1990*, Human Rights and Equal Opportunity Commission, Sydney.

Cunneen, C. (1990b) *A study of Aboriginal juveniles and police violence*, Human Rights and Equal Opportunity Commission, Sydney.

Cunneen, C. (1992a) 'Commentary on the Report of the Aboriginals and the Law Mission, International Commission of Jurists, Australian Section', *Australian and New Zealand Journal of Criminology*, 25(2): 186–91.

Cunneen, C. (ed.) (1992b) *Aboriginal perspectives on criminal justice*, Monograph Series, No. 1, Institute of Criminology, Sydney.

Cunneen, C. (1994) 'Enforcing genocide? Aboriginal young people and the police', in R. White & C. Alder (eds), *The police and young people in Australia*, Cambridge University Press, Melbourne.

Cunneen, C. (1999a) 'Criminology, genocide and the forced removal of Indigenous children from their families', *Australian and New Zealand Journal of Criminology*, 32(2): 124–38.

Cunneen, C. (1999b) 'Zero tolerance policing: implications for Indigenous people', paper prepared for the Law and Justice section of the Aboriginal and Torres Strait Islander Commission, Institute of Criminology, University of Sydney, Sydney.

Cunneen, C. (2001) *Conflict, politics and crime: Aboriginal communities and the police*, Allen & Unwin, Sydney.

Cunneen, C. (2007) 'Riot, resistance and moral panic: demonising the colonial other', in S. Poynting & G. Morgan (eds), *Outrageous! Moral panics in Australia*, ACYS Publishing, Hobart.

Cunneen, C. & Hoyle, C. (2010) *Debating Restorative Justice*, Hart Publishing, Oxford.

Cunneen, C. & Kerley, K. (1995) 'Indigenous women and criminal justice', in K.M. Hazlehurst, (ed.), *Perceptions of justice*, Avebury, Aldershot: 71–90.

Cunneen, C. & Luke, G. (1995) 'Discretionary decisions in juvenile justice and the criminalisation of Indigenous young people: a NSW study', *Youth Studies Australia*, 14(4): 38–46.

Cunneen, C. & Robb, T. (1987) *Criminal justice in north-west*

New South Wales, NSW Bureau of Crime Statistics and Research, Sydney.

Cunneen, C. & White, R. (1995) *Juvenile justice: an Australian perspective*, Oxford University Press, Melbourne.

Cunneen, C. & White, R. (2006) 'Australia: Control, Containment or Empowerment?', in J. Muncie & B. Goldson (eds) *Comparative Juvenile Justice*, Sage, London.

Cunneen, C. & White, R. (2007) *Juvenile justice: youth and crime in Australia* (3rd edn), Oxford University Press, Melbourne.

Cunneen, C. & White, R. (2011) *Juvenile justice: youth and crime in Australia* (4th edn), Oxford University Press, Melbourne.

Cunneen, C., Baldry, E., Brown, D., Brown, M., Schwartz, M. & Steel, A. (2013) *Hyperincarceration and Penal Culture: The Revival of the Prison*, Ashgate, Surry.

Cunneen, C., Findlay, M., Lynch, R. & Tupper, V. (1989) *Dynamics of collective conflict: riots at the Bathurst motorcycle races*, Law Book Company, North Ryde.

Cunneen, C., Fraser, D. & Tomsen, S. (1997) 'Introduction: defining the issues', in C. Cunneen et al. (eds), *Faces of hate: hate crime in Australia*, Hawkins Press, Sydney.

Cunningham, A. (2001) 'Forgotten families: the impacts of imprisonment', *Family Matters*, 59(Winter): 35–8.

Curcio, A.A. (1996) 'Painful publicity: an alternative punitive damages sanction', *De Paul Law Review*, 45, 341–93.

Currie, E. (1988) 'Two visions of community crime prevention', in T. Hope & M. Shaw (eds), *Communities and crime reduction*, HMSO, London.

Curson, P. & Clark, L. (2004) 'Pathological environments', in R. White (ed.), *Controversies in environmental sociology*, Cambridge University Press, Melbourne.

D

Dadds, M., Turner, C. & McAloon, J. (2002) 'Developmental links between cruelty to animals and human violence', *Australian and New Zealand Journal of Criminology*, 35(3): 3633–82.

Dadds, V. & Scheide, T. (2000) 'Police performance and activity measurement', *Trends and Issues in Crime and Criminal Justice*, No. 180, Australian Institute of Criminology, Canberra.

Dagistanli, S. (2007) '"Like a pack of wild animals": moral panics around "ethnic" gang rape in Sydney', in S. Poynting & G. Morgan (eds), *Outrageous! Moral panics in Australia*, Australian Clearning House for Youth Studies, Hobart.

Daily Miner (2004) 'High court rejects Donahue's request to televise execution', *Daily Miner*, 18 May: 2.

Daly, K. (2002) 'Restorative Justice: the Real Story', *Punishment and Society*, 4(1): 55–79.

Daly, K. (2006) 'The limits of restorative justice', in D. Sulivan & L. Tifft (eds), *Handbook of restorative justice: A global perspective*, (pp. 134–45), Routledge, New York.

Daly, K. (1995) 'Celebrated crime cases and the public's imagination: from bad press to bad policy?', *Australian and New Zealand Journal of Criminology*, special supplementary issue, *Crime, Criminology and Public Policy*: 6–22.

Daly, K. & Bordt, R. (1995) 'Sex effects and sentencing: an analysis of the statistical literature', *Justice Quarterly*, 12(1): 143–77.

Daly, K. & Hayes, H. (2001) 'Restorative justice and conferencing in Australia', *Trends and Issues in Crime and Criminal Justice*, No. 186, Australian Institute of Criminology, Canberra.

Daly, M. & Wilson, M. (1988) *Homicide*, Aldine de Gruyter, New York.

Darbyshire, P. (2000) 'The mischief of plea bargaining and sentence rewards', *Criminal Law Review*, 3: 895–919.

Davey, M. (2014) 'Blame the brain', *The Age: Pulse*, 27 January: 28–9.

David, M., Rohloff, A., Petley, J. & Hughes, J. (2011) 'The idea of moral panic—ten dimensions of dispute', *Crime, Media, Culture*, 7(3): 215–28.

Davies, M. (1994) *Asking the law question*, The Law Book Co., Sydney.

Davis, B. & Dossetor, K. (2010) '(Mis)perceptions of crime in Australia', *Trends & Issues in Crime and Criminal Justice*, No. 396, Australian Institute of Criminology, Canberra.

Davis, C. & Abraham, J. (2013) 'Is there a cure for corporate crime in the drug industry?', *British Medical Journal*, 6 February: 346–8.

Davis, M. (1990) *City of Quartz: Excavating the future in Los Angeles*, Verso, London.

Davis, J. (2007) 'Sentencing and the psychology of justice', *Alternative Law Journal*, 32(3): 144–8.

Davis, J. (2009) 'Judicial reasoning and the "just world delusion": using the psychology of justice to evaluate legal judgments', paper presented at the *Judicial Reasoning: Art or Science?* conference, February 2009, National Judicial College of Australia/ANU College of Law/Australian Academy of Forensic Sciences, Canberra.

Davis, M. (1986) 'Why attempts deserve less punishment than complete crimes', *Law and Philosophy*, 5(April): 1–32.

Davis, R. & Williams, G. (2003) 'Reform of the judicial appointments process: gender and the bench of the High Court of Australia', *Melbourne University Law Review*, 27(3): 819–63.

Dawes, J. & Grant, A. (2002) 'Corrections', in P. Grabosky & A. Graycar (eds), *The Cambridge* handbook of Australian criminology, Cambridge University Press, Cambridge.

Dawson, A., Jackson, D. & Nyamathi, A. (2012) 'Children of incarcerated parents: insights to addressing a growing public health concern in Australia', *Children and Youth Services Review*, 34(12): 2433–41.

Day, A., Jones, R., Nakata, M. & McDermott, D. (2012) 'Indigenous family violence: an attempt to understand the problems and inform appropriate and effective responses to criminal justice system interventions', *Psychiatry, Psychology and Law*, 19(1): 104–17.

De Bortoli, L., Coles, J. & Dolan, M. (2013) 'Maternal infanticide in Australia: mental disturbances during the postpartum period', *Psychiatry, Psychology and Law*, 20(2): 301–11.

de Castella, K., Platow, M.J., Wenzel, M., Tyler, O.& Feather, N.T. (2011) 'Retribution or restoration? Anglo–Australian views towards domestic violence involving Muslim and Anglo–Australian victims and offenders', *Psychology, Crime & Law* 17(5): 403–20.

de Frances, C. & Titus, R. (1993) 'The environment and residential burglary outcomes', paper presented to the *International Seminar on Environmental Criminology and Crime Analysis*, Florida Criminal Justice Executive Institute, Coral Gables.

De Haan, W. & Loader, I. (2002) 'On the emotions of crime, punishment and social control', *Theoretical Criminology*, 6(3): 243–54.

de Krester, H. (2007) 'Prison litigation: barriers to justice', *Precedent*, 81(July/August): 28–33.

De Mesmaecker, V. (2012) 'Antidotes to injustice? Victim statements' impact on victims' sense of security', *International Review of Victimology*, 18(2): 133–53.

de Zwart, M., Lindsay, D., Henderson, M. & Phillips, M. (2011) 'Randoms vs weirdos: teen use of social networking sites and perceptions of legal risk', *Alternative Law Journal*, 36(3): 153–7.

Dear, G.E. (2008) 'Ten years of research into self-harm in the Western Australian prison system: where to next?', *Psychiatry Psychology and Law*, 15(3): 469–81.

Deaton, A. (2009) *Instruments of development: randomization in the tropics, and the search for the elusive keys*, NBER Working Paper No. 14690, National Bureau of Economic Research, Cambridge.

Decker, S. & Pyrooz, D. (2011) 'Leaving the Gang: Logging Off and Moving On', paper commissioned by Google Ideas, The Council on Foreign Relations.

DeFina, R. & Hannon, L. (2013) 'The impact of mass incarceration on poverty', *Crime & Delinquency*, 59(4): 562–86.

Dell'Amore, C. (2014) 'Copenhagen Zoo kills 4 lions after controversial giraffe death', *National Geographic*, 26 March.

Della Porta, D. & Reiter, H. (2006) 'The Policing of Global Protest: The G8 at Genoa and its Aftermath', in D. Della Porta, A. Peterson & H. Reiter (eds) *The Policing of Transnational Protest*, Ashgate Publishing, London.

den Heyer, G. & Beckley, A. (2013) 'Police independent oversight in Australia and New Zealand', *Police Practice and Research: An International Journal*, 14(2): 130–43.

Department for Correctional Services (2011) 'DCS Strategic Plan 2011–2014', *Department for Correctional Services*, Government of South Australia.

Department of Justice (2000) *Report of the Independent Investigation into the Management and Operations of Victoria's Private Prisons*, Victorian Office of the Correctional Services Commissioner.

Department of Justice Victoria (2008a) 'Extended supervision'.

Department of Justice Victoria (2008b) 'Parole'.

Department of Justice Victoria (2010) *Corrections Victoria offender management framework— achieving the balance, prisons and community correctional services*, Corrections Victoria, Melbourne.

Department of Justice Victoria 2012 *Correctional Management Standards Post-Sentence Supervision and Detention Scheme for Serious Sex Offenders 2012*, Department of Justice, Victoria.

Desmond, M. & Valdez, N. (2013) 'Unpolicing the Urban Poor: Consequences of Third-Party Policing for Inner-City Women', *American Sociological Review*, 78(1): 117–41.

Developmental Crime Prevention Consortium (1999) *Pathways to prevention: Developmental and early intervention approaches to crime in Australia*, National Crime Prevention, Attorney-General's Department, Canberra.

Devery, C. (1991) *Disadvantage and Crime*, NSW Bureau of Crime Statistics and Research, Sydney.

Deville, A. & Harding, R. (1997) *Applying the Precautionary Principle*, The Federation Press, Sydney.

Devries, K.M., Child, J.C., Bacchus, L.J., Mak, J., Falder, G., Graham, K., Watts, C. & Heise, L. (2013) 'Intimate partner violence victimization and alcohol consumption in women: a systematic review and meta-analysis', *Addiction*, 109(3): 379–91.

Dhillon, A. (2014) 'The women who've had enough', *The Age*, 13 February: 18–19.

Diba, M. (2002) 'Peace or justice? Amnesties and the International Criminal Court', *Melbourne Journal of International Law*, 3(2): 247–79.

Dixon, D. (1998) 'Broken windows, zero tolerance, and the New York miracle', *Current Issues in Criminal Justice*, 10(1): 96–106.

Dixon, M. (ed.) (1985) *On trial: Reagan's war against Nicaragua, testimony of the permanent people's tribunal*, Zed Books, London.

Dodd, A. (2003) 'Giants pair off as net pirates stop the music', *Weekend Australian*, Weekend Money, 8–9 November: 29.

Dolan, M. & Whitworth, H. (2013) 'Childhood sexual abuse, adult psychiatric morbidity, and criminal outcomes in women assessed by medium secure forensic service', *Journal of Child Sexual Abuse*, 22(2): 191–208.

Domestic Violence Benchbook (1995) 'The O.J. Simpson symposium', special issue, *Hastings Women's Law Journal*, 6(2).

Dorling, P. (2013) 'Forget the needle, take the haystack', *The Age*, Focus, 6 December: 16–17.

Douglas, H. & Finnane, M. (2012) *Indigenous crime and settler law: white sovereignty after empire*, Macmillan, Basingstoke, Palgrave.

Douglas, R. (1987) 'Is chivalry dead? Gender and sentencing in the Victorian courts', *Australian and New Zealand Journal of Sociology*, 23: 343–57.

Dovey, K., Wollan, S. & Woodcock, I. (2012) 'Placing graffiti: creating an contesting character in inner-city Melbourne', *Journal of Urban Design*, 17(1): 21–41.

Dow, S. (2013) 'Hopelessly out of tune on same-sex marriage', *The Age*, 19 April: 22.

Dowie, M. (1977) 'Pinto madness', *Mother Jones*, September/October: 18–32.

Downes, D. & Morgan, R. (2007) 'No turning back: the politics of law and order in the millennium', in M. Maguire, R. Morgan & R. Reiner (eds), *The Oxford handbook of criminology* (4th edn), Oxford University Press, Oxford.

Downes, D. (1966) *The delinquent solution*, Routledge & Kegan Paul, London.

Doyle, D.J. & Ogloff, J.R.P. (2009) 'Calling the tune without the music: a psycho-legal analysis of Australia's post-sentence legislation', *Australian & New Zealand Journal of Criminology*, 42(2): 179–203.

Drakulich, K.M. & Rose, K. (2013) 'Being male or living with a female: fear for partners by sex and sexual orientation', *Journal of Interpersonal Violence*, 28(9): 1765–97.

Drucker, E. (2011) A plague of prisons: the epidemiology of mass incarceration in America, The New Press, New York and London.

Drum, M. & Baldino, D. (2012) 'Community-based policing as an alternative to 'stop and search? The example of Northbridge, Western Australia', *Public Policy*, 7(2): 183–98.

Duff, C. (2003) 'Drugs and youth cultures: is Australia experiencing the "normalisation" of adolescent drug use?', *Journal of Youth Studies*, 6(1): 433–46.

Duff, R.A. (1996) 'Penal communications: recent work in the philosophy of punishment', *Crime and Justice: An Annual Review*, Vol. 20, University of Chicago Press, Chicago.

Duff, R.A. & Garland, D. (1995) *A reader on punishment*, Oxford University Press, Oxford.

Duncanson, I. (ed.) (1991) 'Legal education and legal knowledge', *Law in Context*, 9(2), special issue.

Dunn, P. (2012) 'Men as victims: "victim" identities, gay identities, and masculinities', *Journal of Interpersonal Violence*, 27(17): 3442–7.

Dunne, B. (1985) 'Community justice centres: a critical appraisal', *Legal Service Bulletin*, 10(3): 188–91.

Dupont, B. (2006) 'Power struggles in the field of security: implications for democratic

transformation', in J. Wood & B. Dupont (eds) *Democracy, society and the governance of security*, Cambridge University Press, Cambridge.

Durkheim, É. (1951) *Suicide* (trans. G. Simpson), Free Press, New York.

Durkheim, É. (1962) 'The normal and the pathological', in M. Wolfgang, L. Savitz & N. Johnston (eds), *The sociology of crime and delinquency*, John Wiley & Sons, New York.

Durkheim, É. (1982) *The Rules of Sociological Method*, The Free Press, New York.

Durkheim, É. (1997) *The division of labor in society* (trans. W.D. Halls), Free Press, New York.

Durkheim, É. (2004) 'The rules of sociological method', in K. Thompson (ed.), *Readings from Emile Durkheim*, Routledge, New York.

Dusmohamed, S. & Burvill, M. (2003) 'Development of a specialist sentencing court in South Australia', *Canberra Bulletin of Public Administration*, 106: 41–4.

Dwyer, A. (2011a) '"It's not like we're going to jump them": How transgressing heteronormativity shapes police interactions with LGBT young people', *Youth Justice*, 11(3): 203–20.

Dwyer, A. (2011b) 'Policing lesbian, gay, bisexual and transgender young people: a gap in the research literature', *Current Issues in Criminal Justice*, 22(3): 415–433.

E

Easteal, P. (1994) 'Ethnicity and crime', in D. Chappel & P. Wilson (eds), *The Australian criminal justice system: the mid 1990s*, Butterworths, Sydney.

Easteal, P. (2001) *Less than equal: women and the Australian legal system*, Butterworths, Chatswood.

Easteal, P. & Easteal, S. (1990) 'The forensic use of DNA profiling', *Trends and Issues in Crime and Criminal Justice*, No. 26, Australian Institute of Criminology, Canberra.

Easteal, P., Bartels, L. & Bradford, S. (2012) 'Language, gender and "reality": violence against women', *International Journal of Law, Crime and Justice*, 40(4): 324–37.

Edgley, M. (2007) 'Preventing crime or punishing propensities? A purposive examination of the preventative detention of sex offenders in Queensland and Western Australia', *University of Western Australia Law Review*, 33(2): 351–86.

Edmond, G. (2008) 'Specialised knowledge, the exclusionary discretions and reliability: reassessing incriminating expert opinion evidence', *University of New South Wales Law Journal*, 31(1): 1–55.

Edmond, G. (2012) 'Advice for the courts? Sufficiently reliable assistance with forensic science and medicine (Part 2)', *International Journal of Evidence & Proof*, 16(3): 263–97.

Edmond, G. & Roberts, A. (2011) 'The Law Commission's report on expert evidence in criminal proceedings: sufficiently reliable?', *Criminal Law Review*, 11: 844–62.

Edmond, G. & San Roque, M. (2012) 'The cool crucible: forensic science and the frailty of the criminal trial', *Current Issues in Criminal Justice*, 24(1): 51–68.

Edney, R. (2005) 'Just deserts in post-colonial society: problems in the punishment of Indigenous offenders', *Southern Cross University Law Review*, 9: 73–106.

Edney, R. (2006) 'Models of understanding criminal behaviour and the sentencing process: a place for criminological theory?', *Journal of Criminal Law*, 70(3): 247–71.

Edwards, A. & Sheptycki, J. (2009) 'Third wave criminology: guns, crime and social order',

Criminology and Criminal Justice, 9(3): 379–97.

Edwards, I. (2012) 'Sentencing councils and victims', *The Modern Law Review*, 75(3): 324–46.

Edwards, K. (2006) 'Cold hit complacency: the dangers of DNA databases re-examined', *Current Issues in Criminal Justice*, 18(1): 92–124.

Egger, S. (1994) 'Victimisation, moral panics: a reply to Richard Harding', *Current Issues in Criminal Justice*, 6(1): 43–53.

Einstadter, W. & Henry, S. (1995) *Criminological theory: an analysis of its underlying assumptions*, Harcourt Brace, New York.

Ekblom, P. (1998) 'Situational crime prevention: effectiveness of local initiatives', in *Reducing offending: an assessment of research evidence on ways of dealing with offending behaviour*, Home Office Study Report No. 187, Home Office, London.

Ekblom, P. & Tilley, N. (2000) 'Going equipped: criminology, situational crime prevention and the resourceful offender', *British Journal of Criminology*, 40(3): 376–98.

Ekstedt, J. & Griffiths, C. (1984) *Corrections in Canada: policy and practice*, Butterworths, Toronto.

Elgar F.J. & Aitken, N. (2010) 'Income inequality, trust and homicide in 33 countries', *European Journal of Public Health*, 21(2): 241–6.

Ellickson, R. (1989) 'Bringing culture and human frailty to rational actors: a critique of classical law and economics', *Chicago–Kent Law Review*, 65: 23–55.

Elliot, L. (ed.) (2007) *Transnational environmental crime in the Asia–Pacific: a workshop report*, Department of International Relations, Australian National University, Canberra.

Ellis, T. & Marshall, P. (2000) 'Does parole work? A post-release comparison of reconviction rates for paroled and non-paroled

prisoners', *Australian and New Zealand Journal of Criminology*, 33(3): 300–17.

Empey, L. (1982) *American delinquency: its meaning and construction*, Dorsey, Chicago.

Englebrecht, C.M. (2011) 'The struggle for "ownership of conflict": an exploration of victim participation and voice in the criminal justice system', *Criminal Justice Review*, 36(2): 129–51.

Erdogan, S., Yalçin, M. & Dereli, M.A. (2013) 'Exploratory spatial analysis of crimes against property in Turkey', *Crime Law & Social Change*, 59(1): 63–78.

Erez, E. (1994) 'Victim participation in sentencing: And the debate goes on', *International Review of Victimology*, 3(1–2): 17–32.

Erez, E. & Rogers, L. (1999) 'Victim impact Statements and Sentencing outcomes and Processes: The Perspectives of Legal Professionals', *British Journal of Criminology*, 39(2): 216–39

Erez, E., Roeger, L. & Morgan, F. (1994) *Victim impact statements in South Australia: an evaluation*, Office of Crime Statistics, South Australian Attorney-General's Department, Adelaide.

Ericson, R., Baranek, P. & Chan, J. (1991) *Representing order: crime, law and justice in the news media*, Open University Press, Milton Keynes.

European Monitoring Centre for Drugs and Drug Addiction & Europol (2013) *EU drug markets report: a strategic analysis*, The Hague, Lisbon & Europol.

Evans, S. (2002) 'The rule of law, constitutionalism and the MV *Tampa*', *Public Law Review*, 13(2): 94–101.

Exum, M.L., Kuhns, J.B., Koch, B. & Johnson, C. (2010) 'An examination of situational crime prevention strategies across convenience stores and fast-food restaurants', *Criminal Justice Policy Review*, 21(3): 269–95.

Eysenck, H. (1984) 'Crime and personality', in D. Muller, D. Blackmann & A. Chapmann (eds), *Psychology and law*, John Wiley & Sons, New York.

F

Fader, J.J. (2011) 'Conditions of a successful graduation status graduation ceremony: formerly incarcerated urban youth and their tenuous grip on success', *Punishment and Society*: 13(1): 29–46.

Fagan, A.A. & Mazerolle, P. (2011) 'Repeat offending and repeat victimization: assessing similarities and differences in psychosocial risk factors', *Crime & Delinquency*, 57(5): 732–55.

Fagan, A.A., Brooke-Weiss, B. & Cady, R. (2009) 'If at first you don't succeed ... keep trying: strategies to enhance coalition/school-based prevention programming', *Australian and New Zealand Journal of Criminology*, 42(3): 387–405.

Fairchild, P. (1994) 'The emerging police complex: hoogenboom and Australian inter agency cooperation', *Australian and New Zealand Journal of Criminology*, 27(2): 111–32.

Fajnzylber, P., Lederman, D. & Loayza, N. (2002) 'Inequality and violent crime', *Journal of Law and Economics*, 45(1): 1–40.

Family and Community Development Committee (2013) *Betrayal of trust: inquiry into the handling of child abuse by religious and other non-government organisations*, Parliament of Victoria, East Melbourne, <www.parliament.vic.gov.au/fcdc/article/1788>.

Farley, F.H. & Sewell, T. (1976) 'Test of an arousal theory of delinquency', *Criminal Justice and Behaviour*, 31(3): 5–20.

Farrant, D. (2001) 'The riddle of rape', *The Age*, News Extra, 24 November: 1, 5.

Farrell, A. (1992) *Crime, class and corruption: the politics of the police*, Bookmarks, London.

Farrell, G. (2010) 'Situational crime prevention and its discontents: rational choice and harm reduction versus 'cultural criminology', *Social Policy & Administration*, 44(1): 40–66.

Farrall, S., & Calverley, A. (2006) *Understanding Desistance from Crime: Theoretical Directions in Resettlement and Rehabilitation*, Open University Press, Berkshire.

Farrington, D. (1996a) 'The development of offending and antisocial behavior from childhood to adulthood', in P. Cordella & L. Siegel (eds), *Readings in contemporary criminological theory*, Northeastern University Press, Boston.

Farrington, D. (1996b) 'The explanation and prevention of juvenile offending', in J. Hawkins (ed.), *Delinquency and crime: current theories*, Cambridge University Press, Cambridge.

Farrington, D. & Tarling, R. (1983) *Criminological prediction*, Home Office Research and Planning Unit, London.

Fattah, E. (2010) 'The Evolution of a Young, Promising Discipline: Sixty Years of Victimology, a Retrospective and Prospective Look', in S. Shoham, P. Knepper & M. Kett (eds) *International Handbook of Victimology*, CRC Press, Boca Raton, FL.

Feely, M. & Simon, J. (1992) 'The new penology: notes on the emerging strategy of corrections and its implication', *Criminology*, 30(4): 449–74.

Feinberg, J. (1991) 'The justification of punishment: the classic debate', in J. Feinberg & H. Gross (eds), *Philosophy of law* (4th edn), Wadsworth Publishing Company, Belmont.

Feinberg, J. & Gross, H. (eds) (1991) *Philosophy of law* (4th edn),

Wadsworth Publishing Company, Belmont.

Felson, M. (1994) *Crime and everyday life: insights and implications for society*, Pine Forge, London.

Felson, R.B., Savolainen, J., Bjarnason, T., Anderson, A.L. & Zohra, I.T. (2011) 'The cultural context of adolescent drinking and violence in 30 European countries', *Criminology*, 49(3): 699–728.

Feneley, R. (2013) 'Up to 80 men murdered, 30 cases unsolved. Dozens of killers now walking free', *The Age*, Good Weekend, 27 July: 24–30.

Ferrante, A.M. (2013) 'Assessing the influence of "standard" and "culturally specific" risk factors on the prevalence and frequency of offending: the case of Indigenous Australians, *Race and Justice*, 3(1): 58–82.

Ferrari, M. & Costi, A. (2012) 'Learnings from community legal education', *Alternative Law Journal*, 37(1): 52–3.

Ferrell, J. (1996) *Crimes of style: urban graffiti and the politics of criminality*, Northeastern University Press, Boston.

Ferrell, J. (1997) 'Youth, crime and cultural space', *Social Justice*, 24(4): 21–38.

Ferrell, J. & Sanders, C. (1995) *Cultural criminology*, Northeastern University Press, Boston.

Ferrell, J. & Weide, R. (2010) 'Spot theory', *City*, 14(1): 48–62.

Ferrell, J., Hayward, K., Morrison, W. & Presdee, M. (eds) (2004) *Cultural criminology unleashed*, Glasshouse Press, London.

Ferrell, J., Hayward, K. & Young, J. (2008) *Cultural criminology: an invitation*, Sage, Los Angeles.

Field, D. (2002) 'Plead guilty early and convincingly to avoid disappointment', *Bond Law Review* 14(2): 251–84.

Fields, B.A. (2003) 'Restitution and restorative justice', *Youth Studies Australia*, 22(4): 44–51.

Finch, L. (1993) 'On the streets: working class youth culture in the nineteenth century', in R. White (ed.), *Youth subcultures: theory, history and the Australian experience*, National Clearinghouse for Youth Studies, Hobart: 75–9.

Findlay, M. (2004a) *Introducing policing: challenges for police and Australian communities*, Oxford University Press, Melbourne.

Findlay, M. (2004b) 'The demise of corrections fifteen years on: any hope for progressive punishment?', *Contemporary Issues in Criminal Justice*, 16(1): 56–70.

Findlay, M. & Duff, P. (eds) (1988) *The jury under attack*, Butterworths, Sydney.

Findlay, M., Egger, S. & Sutton, J. (eds) (1983) *Issues in criminal justice administration*, Allen & Unwin, Sydney.

Findlay, M., Odgers, S. & Yeo, S. (2005) *Australian criminal justice* (3rd edn), Oxford University Press, Melbourne.

Fine, B. (1984) *Democracy and the rule of law: liberal ideals and Marxist critiques*, Pluto, London.

Finkelstein, R. (2003) 'Decision-making in a vacuum?', *Monash University Law Review*, 29(1): 11–29.

Finn, H. (1998) 'Mandatory and guideline sentencing: recent developments', Briefing Paper No. 18, New South Wales Parliamentary Library Research Service, NSW.

Finnane, M. (ed.) (1987) *Policing in Australia: historical perspectives*, New South Wales University Press, Sydney.

Finnane, M. (1990) 'Police and politics in Australia: the case for historical revision', *Australian and New Zealand Journal of Criminology*, 23: 218–28.

Finnane, M. (1994a) 'Larrikins, delinquents and cops: police and young people in Australian history', in R. White & C. Alder (eds), *The police and young people in Australia*, Cambridge University Press, Melbourne.

Finnane, M. (1994b) *Police and government: histories of policing in Australia*, Oxford University Press, Melbourne.

Finnane, M. (1998) 'Sir John Barry and the Melbourne Department of Criminology: some other foundations of Australian criminology', *Australian and New Zealand Journal of Criminology*, 31(1): 69–81.

Finnane, M. (2000) 'Police unions in Australia: a history of the present', *Current Issues in Criminal Justice*, 12(1): 5–19.

Finnane, M. (2012) '"Irresistible impulse": historicizing a judicial innovation in Australian insanity jurisprudence', *History of Psychiatry*, 23(4): 454–68.

Fishbein, D. (1990) 'Biological perspectives in criminology', *Criminology*, 28(1): 27–72.

Fisher, D.G. & Piracha, A. (2012) 'Crime prevention through environmental design: a case study of multi-agency collaboration Sydney, Australia', *Australian Planner*, 49(1): 79–87.

Fisher, S. (2012) 'From violence to coercive control: renaming men's abuse of women', *Australasian Policing*, 4(1): 35–7.

Fisse, B. & Braithwaite, J. (1993) *Corporations, crime and accountability*, Cambridge University Press, Melbourne.

Fitri, N. (2011) 'Democracy Discourses through the Internet Communication: Understanding the Hacktivism for the Global Changing', *Online Journal of Communication and Media Technologies*, 1(2): 1–24.

Fitzgerald, G. (1989) *Report of the commission of possible illegal activities and associated police misconduct*, Queensland Government Printer, Brisbane.

Fitzgerald, J. (1999) *Women in prison: the criminal court perspective*, Crime and Justice Statistics Bureau Brief, New South Wales Bureau of Crime Statistics and Research, Sydney.

Fitzgerald, J. (2000) *Graffiti in NSW*, Crime and Justice Statistics Bureau Brief, New South Wales Bureau of Crime Statistics and Research, Sydney.

Fitzgerald, J. & Poynton, S. (2011) 'The changing nature of objects stolen in household burglaries', *Crime and Justice Statistics*, Issue paper No. 62, NSW Bureau of Crime Statistics and Research, Sydney.

Fitz-Gibbon, K. & Pickering, S. (2012) 'Homicide law reform in Victoria, Australia', *British Journal of Criminology*, 52(1): 159–80.

Fitz-Gibbon, K. & Stubbs, J. (2012) 'Divergent directions in reforming legal responses to lethal violence', *Australian & New Zealand Journal of Criminology*, 45(3): 318–36.

Fitzroy Legal Service (2013) *The law handbook*, Fitzroy Legal Service, Melbourne.

Fleming, J. (2010) 'Community policing: the Australian connection', in J. Putt (ed.), *Community policing in Australia*, Australian Institute of Criminology, Canberra.

Flynn, A. (2007) 'Carl Williams: secret deals and bargained justice: the underworld of Victoria's plea bargaining system', *Current Issues in Criminal Justice*, 19(1): 120–6.

Flynn, A. (2009) 'Sentence indications for indictable offences: increasing court efficiency at the expense of justice? A response to the Victorian legislation', *Australian & New Zealand Journal of Criminology*, 42(2): 244–68.

Flynn, A. (2011a) '"Fortunately we in Victoria are not in that UK situation'": Australian and United Kingdom legal perspectives on plea bargaining reform', *Deakin Law Review*, 16(2): 361–404.

Flynn, A. (2011b) 'Bargaining with justice: victims plea bargaining and the *Victims' Charter Act 2006* (VIC)', *Monash University Law Review*, 37(3): 73–96.

Flynn, A. & Fitz-Gibbon, K. (2010) 'The honeymoon killer: Plea bargaining and intimate femicide—a response to Watson', *Alternative Law Journal*, 35(4): 203–7.

Flynn, A. & Fitz-Gibbon, K. (2011) 'Bargaining with defensive homicide: examining Victoria's secretive plea bargaining system post–law reform', *Melbourne University Law Review*, 35(3): 905–32.

Flynn, A. & Henry, N. (2012) 'Disputing consent: the role of jury directions in Victoria', *Current Issues in Criminal Justice*, 24(2): 167–84.

Flynn, C. (2013) 'Mothers facing imprisonment: arranging care for their adolescent children', *Women & Criminal Justice*, 23: 43–62.

Foley, T. (2013) 'Are retributive aims achievable in a restorative justice setting?', *Journal of Justice Administration*, 22(3): 130–7.

Fordham, J. (2012) 'Bad press: does the jury deserve it?', *Precedent* (September/October): 36–40.

Forni, O. (2010) 'Mapping Environmental Crimes', *Freedom From Fear Magazine*, March 2010: 34–7. United Nations Interregional Crime and Justice Research Institute, Turin.

Forrester, L. (1993) 'Youth-generated cultures in western Sydney', in R. White (ed.), *Youth subcultures: theory, history and the Australian experience*, National Clearinghouse for Youth Studies, Hobart.

Forsyth, L. (2013) 'Cost of violence against women', paper presented at the *White Ribbon International Conference*, 13–15 May 2013, Sydney.

Forsythe, L. & Gaffney, A. (2012) 'Mental disorder prevalence at the gateway to the criminal justice system', *Trends & Issues in Crime and Criminal Justice*, No. 438, Australian Institute of Criminology, Canberra.

Fortuin, J. (ed.) (1992) *Issues in HIV/AIDS in the Australian prison system*, Australian Institute of Criminology, Canberra.

Foucault, M. (1980) 'Truth and power' in C. Gordon (ed.), *Power/ knowledge: selected interviews and other writings 1972–1977*, Pantheon, New York.

Foucault, M. (1991) *Discipline and punish: the birth of the prison*, Penguin, Harmondsworth.

Fougere, D., Kramarz, F. & Pouget, J. (2006) *Youth unemployment and crime in France*, Centre for Research in Economics and Statistics, Paris.

Fox, R. (1994) 'The meaning of proportionality in sentencing', *Melbourne University Law Review*, 19: 489–511.

Fox, R. (2002) *Victorian criminal procedures: state and federal law* (11th edn), Law Book Co-operative, Clayton.

Fox, R. (2006) 'Sentencing in the Garden of Eden', *Monash University Law Review*, 32(1): 4–27.

Fradella, H., Owen, S. & Burke, T. (2007) 'Building bridges between criminal justice and the forensic sciences to create forensic studies programs', *Journal of Criminal Justice Education*, 18(2): 261–82.

Francis, R., Armstrong, A. & Totikidis, V. (2006) 'Ethnicity and crime: a statewide analysis by local government areas', *Asian and Pacific Migration Journal*, 15(2): 201–18.

Fraser, A. (2013) 'Ethnography at the periphery: redrawing the borders of criminology's world-map', *Theoretical Criminology*, 17(2): 251–60.

Freckelton, I. & Selby, H. (1988) 'Police accountability', in M. Findlay & R. Hogg (eds), *Understanding crime and criminal justice*, The Law Book Co., Sydney.

Freeman, K. (1996) 'Young people and crime', *Crime and Justice Bulletin*, 32, New South Wales Bureau of Crime Statistics and Research, Sydney.

Freiberg, A. (2001) 'Problem-oriented courts: innovative solutions to intractable problems?', *Journal of Judicial Administration'*, 11(1): 8–27.

Freiberg, A. (2003) 'Therapeutic jurisprudence in Australia: paradigm shift or pragmatic incrementalism?', *Law in Context*, 20(2): 6–23.

Freiberg, A. (2005) 'Problem-oriented courts: an update', *Journal of Judicial Administration*, 14(4): 196–219.

Freiberg, A. & Gelb, K. (2008) *Penal populism, sentencing councils and sentencing policy*, Hawkins Press, Sydney.

Freiberg, A. & Krasnostein, S. (2011) 'Statistics, damn statistics and sentencing', *Journal of Justice Administration*, 21: 73–92.

Freiberg, A. & Ross, S. (1995) 'Change and stability in sentencing: a Victorian study', *Law in Context*, special issue, *Sentencing: Some Key Issues*, 13(2): 107–42.

Freiberg, A. & Ross, S. (1999) *Sentencing reform and penal change: the Victorian experience*, The Federation Press, Leichhardt.

Freiberg, A., Fox, R. & Hogan, M. (1988) *Sentencing young offenders*, Australian Law Reform Commission, Sydney.

Freiberg, A., Ross, S. & Tait, D. (1996) *Change and stability in sentencing: a Victorian study*, Department of Criminology, University of Melbourne, Melbourne.

Freilich, J.B. & Howard, G.J (2002) 'Exporting and importing criminality: incarceration of the foreign born', *International Journal of Comparative and Applied Criminal Justice*, 26(2): 143–63.

French, H. (2007) 'Riots in a village in China as pollution protest heats up', *New York Times*, 19 July: 3.

French, V. (2007) 'Juries: a central pillar or an obstacle to a fair and timely criminal justice system? A very personal view', *Reform Issue*, 90: 40–2.

Freund, J. (1969) *The sociology of Max Weber*, Vintage, New York.

Friedrichs, D. (1996) *Trusted criminals: white collar crime in contemporary society*, Wadsworth, Belmont.

Friedrichs, D. (2007) 'Transnational crime and global criminology: definitional, typological, and contextual conundrums', *Social Justice*, 34(2): 4–18.

Friedrichs, D. (2009–10) 'On resisting state crime: conceptual and contextual issues', *Social Justice*, 36(3): 4–27.

Fry, M-L. (2011) 'Seeking the pleasure zone: understanding young adult's intoxication culture', *Australasian Marketing Journal*, 19(1): 65–70.

Fuentes-Nieva, R. & Galasso, N. (2014) *Working for the few: political capture and economic inequality*, Oxfam International, Oxford.

Fulcher, G. (1989) *Disabling policies? A comparative approach to education policy and disability*, Falmer Press, London.

Fulkerson, A. (2001) 'The use of victim impact panels in domestic violence cases: a restorative justice approach', *Contemporary Justice Review*, 4(3–4): 355–68.

Fyfe, J. (1991) 'Why won't crime stop?', *Sunday Star: Bulletin and Advertiser*, 24 March: B1–3.

Fyfe, N. & Reeves, A. (2009) 'The Thin Green Line? Police Perceptions of the Challenges of Policing Wildlife Crime in Scotland', in R. Mawby & R. Yarwood (eds) *Policing, Rurality and Governance*, Ashgate, Aldershot.

G

Gailey, J.A. (2009) 'Starving is the most fun a girl can have: the pro-ana subculture as edgework', *Critical Criminology*, 17(2): 93–108.

Gale, F., Bailey-Harris, R. & Wundersitz, J. (1990) *Aboriginal youth and the criminal justice system: the injustice of justice?*, Cambridge University Press, Melbourne.

Gallagher, R. (2013) 'Snowden's revelations are only the beginning', *The Age*, 30 December: 14.

Galliher, J.F. & Guess, T.J. (2009) 'Two generations of Sutherland's white-collar crime data and beyond', *Crime, Law and Social Change*, 51: 163–74.

Gans, J. & Urbas, G. (2002) 'DNA identification in the criminal justice system', *Trends and Issues in Crime and Criminal Justice*, No. 226, Australian Institute of Criminology, Canberra.

Garcia-Moreno, C. & Watts, C. (2011) 'Violence against women: an urgent public health priority', *Bulletin of the World Health Organization*, 89: 2.

Gardiner, G. (2005) '"Racial profiling": DNA forensic procedures and Indigenous people in Victoria', *Current Issues in Criminal Justice*, 17(1): 47–68.

Garkawe, S. (2002) 'Crime victims and prisoners' rights', in D. Brown & M. Wilkie (eds), *Prisoners as citizens: human rights in Australian prisons*, Federation Press, Sydney.

Garland, D. (1995) *Punishment and modern society: a study in social theory*, Clarendon Press, Oxford.

Garland, D. (2001) *The culture of control: crime and social order in contemporary society*, University of Chicago Press, Chicago.

Garland, D. & Sparks, R. (2000) 'Criminology, social theory and the challenge of our times', *British Journal of Criminology*, 40(2): 189–204.

Garland, J. (2011) 'Difficulties in defining hate crime victimization', *International Journal of Victimology*, 18(1): 25–37.

Gately, N., Fleming, J., Morris, R. & McGregor, C. (2012) 'Amphetamine users and crime in Western Australia, 1999–2009', *Trends & Issues in crime and Criminal Justice*, No. 437, Australian Institute of Criminology, Canberra.

Gatti U., Tremblay, R. & Vitaro, F. (2009) 'Iatrogenic effect of juvenile justice', *Journal of Child Psychology and Psychiatry*, 50(8): 991–8.

Gatto, C. (1999) *European drug policy: analysis and case studies*, Norml Foundation, San Francisco.

Gay Men and Lesbians against Discrimination (1994) *Not a day goes by, report on the GLAD survey into discrimination and violence against lesbians and gay men in Victoria*, Union Publications Department, Sydney.

Geason, S. & Wilson, P. (1989) *Designing out crime: crime prevention through environmental design*, Australian Institute of Criminology, Canberra.

Gelb, K. (2003) 'Women in prison: why the rate of incarceration is increasing', paper presented at the Evaluation in Crime and Justice: Trends and Methods Conference, Australian Institute of Criminology and Australian Bureau of Statistics, Canberra, 24–25 March.

Gelb, K. (2008) *Myths and conceptions: public opinion versus public judgement about sentencing*, Sentencing Advisory Council, Melbourne.

Gelb, K. (2010) *Gender differences in sentencing outcomes*, Sentencing Advisory Council, Melbourne.

Gelsthorpe, L. & Morris, A. (eds) (1990) *Feminist perspectives in criminology*, Open University Press, Milton Keynes.

Gelsthorpe, L. & Worrall, A. (2009). 'Looking for trouble: a recent history of girls, young women and youth justice', *Youth Justice*, 9(3): 209–23.

Genge, N. (2004) *The forensic casebook: the science of crime scene investigation*, Ebury Press, London.

George, A. (2006) 'Women and home detention: home is where the prison is', *Current Issues in Criminal Justice*, 18(1): 79–91.

Gerber, P. (2003) 'When is plea bargaining justified?', *Queensland University of Technology Law and Justice Journal*, 3(1): 210–15.

Gibbons, D. (1977) *Society, crime and criminal careers*, Prentice Hall, Englewood Cliffs.

Gibbs, A. & King, D. (2003) 'The electronic ball and chain? The operation and impact of home detention with electronic monitoring in New Zealand', *Australian and New Zealand Journal of Criminology*, 36(1): 1–17.

Gibbs, C., Gore, M., McGarrell, E. & Rivers III, L. (2010a) 'Introducing conservation criminology: towards interdisciplinary scholarship on environmental crimes and risks', *British Journal of Criminology*, 50: 124–44.

Gibbs, C., McGarrell, E. & Axelrod, M. (2010b) 'Transnational white-collar crime and risk: lessons from the global trade in electronic waste', *Criminology & Public Policy*, 9(3): 543–60.

Giddens, A. (1990) *The consequences of modernity*, Polity Press, Cambridge.

Giddings, J., Hook, B. & Nielsen, J. (2001) 'Legal services in rural communities: issues for clients and lawyers', *Alternative Law Journal*, 26(2): 57–63.

Gilbert, M.J. & Russell, S. (2002) 'Globaliztion of justice in the corporate context', Crime, Law and Social Change, 38(3): 211–38.

Gilchrist, C. (2007) 'This relic of the cities of the plain: penal flogging, convict morality and the colonial imagination', *Australian Journal of Colonial History*, 9(1): 1–28.

Giles, D. (2001) 'Crusader supports televised executions', *Courier Mail*.

Gillham, P.F. & Marx, G.T. (2000) 'Complexity and Irony in Policing and Protesting: The World Trade Organization in Seattle', Social Justice, 27(2): 212–36.

Gilling, D. (1997) *Crime prevention: theory, policies and politics*, UCL Press, London.

GLAD—see Gay Men and Lesbians against Discrimination.

Glanville, L. (1999) 'Community legal centres: can CLCs advocate for themselves?', *Alternative Law Journal*, 24(3): 154–6.

Glasbeek, H. (1998) 'Occupational health and safety law: criminal law as a political tool', *Australian Journal of Labour Law*, 11: 95–119.

Glasbeek, H. (2003) 'The invisible friend: investors are irresponsible, corporations are amoral', *New Internationalist*, 358.

Glasbeek, H. (2004) *Wealth by stealth: corporate crime, corporate law, and the perversion of democracy*, Between the Lines, Toronto.

Gleeson, M. (2003) 'The state of the judicature', paper presented at the 13th Commonwealth law conference, 10 October, Melbourne.

Global Commission on Drug Policy (2011) *War on drugs*, United Nations, <http://issuu.com/gcdp/docs/global_commission_report_english/1?e=0>.

Global Commission on Drug Policy (2012) *The war on drugs and HIV/AIDS: how the criminalization of drug use fuels the global pandemic*, United Nations, <http://issuu.com/gcdp/docs/gcdp_hiv-aids_2012_reference/1?e=0>.

Global Commission on Drug Policy (2013) *The negative impact of the war on drugs on public health: the hidden hepatitis C epidemic*, United Nations.

Glueck, S. & Glueck, E. (1950) *Unraveling juvenile delinquency*, The Commonwealth Fund, New York.

Goddard, R., Csillag, K. & Havecroft, D. (2012) 'Homelessness in Alice Springs and a law and order approach', *Parity*, 25(2): 11–14.

Goderis, B. & Versteeg, M. (2012) 'Human rights violations after 9/11 and the role of constitutional constraints', *Journal of Legal Studies*, 41(1): 131–64.

Godfrey, B. & Cox, D. (2008) '"The last fleet": crime, reformation, and punishment in Western Australia after 1868', *Australian and New Zealand Journal of Criminology*, 41(2): 236–58.

Goffman, E. (1963) *Stigma: notes on the management of spoiled identity*, Prentice-Hall, Englewood Cliffs.

Goffman, E. (1974) *Frame analysis*, Harper & Row, New York.

Golden, C.J., Jackson, M.L. & Crum, T.A. (1999) 'Hate crimes: etiology and intervention', in H.V. Hall & L.C. Whittaker (eds), *Collective Violence: effective strategies for assessing and interviewing in fatal group and institutional aggression*, CRC Press, Boca Raton.

Goldsmith, A. (2001) 'The pursuit of police integrity: leadership and governance dimensions', *Current Issues in Criminal Justice*, 13(1): 185–202.

Goldsmith, A. & Lewis, C. (eds) (2000) *Civilian oversight of policing: governance, democracy and human rights*, Hart Publishing, Oxford.

Goldson, B. (2005) 'Taking liberties: policy and the punitive turn', in H. Hendrick (ed.), *Child welfare and social policy*, Policy Press, Bristol.

Goldson, B. (2010) 'The sleep of (criminological) reason: knowledge-policy rupture and Labour's youth justice legacy', *Criminology and Criminal Justice*, 10(1): 155–78.

Goldson, B. (ed.) (2011) *Youth in crisis? 'Gangs', territoriality and violence*, Routledge, London.

Goldstein, H. (1990) *Problem-Oriented Policing*, McGraw-Hill Inc., New York.

Gonzalez, G.A. (2012) *Energy and empire: the politics of nuclear and solar power in the United States*, State University of New York Press, Albany.

Good Weekend (2013) 'The bad seeds', *The Age*, 9 February: 14–17.

Gooda, M. (2010) National Family Violence Prevention Forum AIATSIS and CDFVR, *Justice reinvestment: a new strategy to address family violence*. Aboriginal and Torres Strait Islander Social Justice Commissioner, Australian Human Rights Commission, Wednesday 19 May 2010.

Goodall, H. (1990) 'Saving the children', *Aboriginal Law Bulletin*, 2(44): 6–9.

Goode, E. & Ben-Yehuda, N. (1994) *Moral panics: the social construction of deviance*, Blackwell, Oxford.

Goodman-Delahunty, J. & Hewson, L. (2010a) 'Enhancing fairness in DNA jury trials', *Trends & Issues in Crime and Criminal Justice*, No. 392, Australian Institute of Criminology, Canberra.

Goodman-Delahunty, J. & Hewson, L. (2010b) *Improving jury understanding and use of expert DNA evidence*, Technical and Background Paper, No. 37, Australian Institute of Criminology, Canberra.

Goodman-Delahunty, J. & Wakabayashi, K. (2012) 'Adversarial forensic science

experts: an empirical study of jury deliberation', *Current Issues in Criminal Justice*, 24(1): 85–103.

Goodwin, C.J. & Goodwin, K.A. (2013). *Research in psychology: methods and design*, (7th edn) Wiley, Hoboken.

Goodwin, V. (2007) *Burglary in Tasmania: the offender's perspective*, Briefing Paper No. 4, Tasmanian Institute of Law Enforcement Studies, University of Tasmania, Hobart.

Goring, C. (1913), *The English convict: a statistical study*, HMSO, London.

Gosselin, L. (1982) *Prisons in Canada*, Black Rose Books, St Laurents.

Gottfredson, M. & Hirschi, T. (1990) *A general theory of crime*, Stanford University Press, Stanford.

Gough, D. (2004) 'Ramage manslaughter verdict under attack', *The Age*, 30 October: 3.

Gough, D. & Arup, T. (2013) 'Out of the blue: street artist's statement cops a spray paint', *The Age*, 27 August: 2–3.

Goulding, D. (2007) *Recapturing Freedom*, Hawkins Press, Sydney.

Goulding, D., Hall, G. & Steels, B. (2008) 'Restorative prisons: towards radical prison reform', *Current Issues in Criminal Justice*, 20(2): 231–42.

Gouldner, A. (1970) *The coming crisis in western sociology*, Heinemann, London.

Grabosky, P. (1977) *Sydney in ferment: crime, dissent and official reaction 1788 to 1973*, Australian National University Press, Canberra.

Grabosky, P. (1989) *Wayward governance: illegality and its control in the public sector*, Australian Institute of Criminology, Canberra.

Grabosky, P. (1995) 'Burglary prevention', *Trends and Issues in Crime and Criminal Justice*, No. 49, Australian Institute of Criminology, Canberra.

Grabosky, P. (2001) 'Crime control in the 21st century', *Australian and New Zealand Journal of Criminology*, 34(3): 221–34.

Grabosky, P. (2007) *Electronic crime*, Master Series in Criminology, Pearson, New Jersey.

Grabosky, P. & Rizzo, C. (1983) 'Dispositional disparities in courts of summary jurisdiction: the conviction and sentencing of shoplifters in SA and NSW, 1980', *Australian and New Zealand Journal of Criminology*, 16: 146–62.

Grabosky, P. & Wilson, P. (1989) *Journalism and justice: how crime is reported*, Pluto, Leichhardt.

Grabosky, P., Smith, R. & Dempsey, G. (2001) *Electronic theft: crimes of acquisition in cyberspace*, Cambridge University Press, Cambridge.

Graffam, J., Shinkfield, A.J. & Hardcastle, L. (2008) 'The perceived employability of ex-prisoners and offenders', *International Journal of Offender Therapy and Comparative Criminology*, 52(6): 673–85.

Graham, K. & Homel, R. (2008) *Raising the bar: preventing aggression in and around bars, pubs and clubs*, Willan Publishing, Devon.

Graham, H. & White, R. (2015) *Innovative Justice*, Routledge, London.

Graham, K., Bernards, S., Wells, S., Osgood, D.W., Abbey, A., Felson, B. & Saltz, R.F. (2011) 'Behavioural indicators of motives for barroom aggression: implications for preventing bar violence', *Drug and Alcohol Review*, 30(5): 554–63.

Grant, A. (1999) 'Elderly inmates: issues for Australia', *Trends and Issues in Crime and Criminal Justice*, No. 115, Australian Institute of Criminology, Canberra.

Grant, A., David, F. & Cook, B. (2002) 'Victims of crime', in A. Graycar & P. Grabosky (eds),

The Cambridge handbook of Australian criminology, Cambridge University Press, Melbourne.

Grant, B. & Gillis, C. (1999) *Day parole outcomes, criminal history and other predictors of successful sentence completion*, Research Branch Corporate Development, Correctional Services of Canada, Ottawa.

Grant, E. & Memmott, P. (2007–08) 'The case for single cells and alternative ways of viewing custodial accommodation for Australian Aboriginal peoples', *Flinders Journal of Law Reform*, 10(3): 631–47.

Grauerhotz, L. (2000) 'An ecological approach to understanding sexual revictimization: linking personal, interpersonal, and sociocultural factors and processes, *Child Maltreatment*, 5(1): 5–17.

Graycar, R. & Morgan, J. (1990) *The hidden gender of law*, Federation Press, Sydney.

Graycar, R. & Morgan, J. (1999) 'A quarter century of feminism in law: back to the future', *Alternative Law Journal*, 24(3): 117–20, 159.

Graycar, R. & Morgan, J. (2002) *The hidden gender of law* (2nd edn), Federation Press, Sydney.

Green, P.J. and Ward, T. (2000) 'State Crime, Human Rights, And the Limits of Criminology', *Social Justice*, 27(1): 101–115.

Green, P. & Ward, T. (2004) *State crime: governments, violence and corruption*, Pluto, London.

Green, P., Ward, T. & McConnachie, K. (2007) 'Logging and legality: environmental crime, civil society, and the state', *Social Justice*, 34(2): 94–110.

Green, R. & Moore, D. (2013) '"Meth circles" and "pipe pirates": crystal methaphetamine smoking and identity management among a social network of young adults', *Substance Use & Misuse*, 48(9): 691–701.

Green, S. (2007) 'Crime, victimisation and vulnerability', in S. Walklate (ed.), *Handbook of victims and victimology*, Willan Publishing, Devon.

Green, S. (2013) 'Out of harm's way', *The Age*, Focus, 11 June: 16–17.

Grenfell, L. & Hewitt, A. (2012) 'Gender regulation: restrictive, facilitative or transformative laws?', *Sydney Law Review*, 34(4): 761–83.

Grewcock, M. (2012) 'Public criminology, victim agency and researching state crime', *State Crime*, 1(1): 109–23.

Gronn, P., Allix, N. & Penna, C. (2004) *'Part of a wheel'? An evaluation of the police schools involvement program*, Faculty of Education, Monash University, Melbourne.

Gros, J.-G. (2008) 'Trouble in paradise: crime and collapsed states in the age of globalization', in N. Larsen & R. Smandych (eds), *Global criminology and criminal justice: current issues and perspectives*, Broadview Press, Peterborough.

Gross, H. (1991) 'Culpability and desert', in J. Feinberg & H. Gross (eds), *Philosophy of law* (4th edn), Wadsworth Publishing Company, Belmont.

Grove, L. (2011) 'Preventing repeat domestic burglary: a meta-evaluation of studies from Australia, the UK and the United States'. *Victims and Offenders*, 6(4): 370–85.

Grubesic, T.H. & Alex-Pridemore, W. (2011) 'Alcohol outlets and clusters of violence', *International Journal of Health Geographics*, 10(1): 30–41.

Gumbert, J. (2008) 'Jurors behaving badly', *Law Society Journal*, 46: 55–9.

Guthridge, S.L., Ryan, P., Condon, J.R., Bromfield, L.M., Moss, J.R. & Lynch, J.W. (2012) 'Trends in reports of child maltreatment in the Northern Territory, 1999–2010', *Medical Journal of Australia*, 3(17): 637–41.

Gutman, J. (2009) 'The reality of non-adversarial justice: principles and practice', *Deakin Law Review*, 14(1): 30–51.

H

Haberfield, I. (1996) 'Poor face jail: lawyers warn', *Ballarat Courier*, 28 March.

Haebich, A. (2011) 'Forgetting Indigenous histories: cases from the history of Australia's stolen generations', *Journal ofSocial History*, 44(4): 1032–46.

Hagan, J. (1987) *Modern criminology: crime, criminal behavior and its control*, McGraw-Hill, Toronto.

Hagan, J. (1996) 'Class and crime controversy', in J. Hagan, A. Gillis & D. Brownfield (eds), *Criminological controversies: a methodological primer*, Westview Press, Boulder.

Hagan, K. (2012) 'Protecting daughters from primitive rites', *The Age*, 15 December, 15.

Hagan, K. (2013) 'Unpredictable ice users put paramedics in fear', *The Age*, 11 October: 2.

Hagedorn, J. (ed.) (2007) *Gangs in the global city: alternatives to traditional criminology*, University of Illinois Press, Urbana and Chicago.

Hagedorn, J. (2008) *A world of gangs: armed young men and gangsta culture*, University of Minnesota Press, Minneapolis.

Haggerty, K. (2004) 'Displaced expertise: three constraints on the policy relevance of criminological thought', *Theoretical Criminology* 8(2): 211–31.

Hague, G. & Sardinha, L. (2010) 'Violence against women: devastating legacy and transforming services', *Psychiatry, Psychology and the Law*, 17(4): 503–22.

Haines, F. (1997) *Corporate regulation: beyond 'punish or persuade'*, Clarendon Press, Oxford.

Hall, B. (2014) 'Too many mouths', *The Age*, 9 February: 17.

Hall, J. (1952) *Theft, law and society* (2nd edn), Bobbs-Merrill, Indianapolis.

Hall, M. (2011) 'Environmental Victims: Challenges for criminology and victimology in the 21st century', *Journal of Criminal Justice and Security*, 4: 371–91.

Hall, M. (2013) *Victims of Environmental Harm: Rights, Recognition and Redress under National and International Law*, Routledge, London.

Hall, S. & Scraton, P. (1981) 'Law, class and control', in M. Fitzgerald, G. McLennan & J. Pawson (eds), *Crime and society: readings in history and theory*, Routledge & Kegan Paul and Open University Press, London.

Hall, W., Hunter, E. & Spargo, R. (1994) 'Alcohol use and incarceration in a police lockup among Aboriginals in the Kimberley region of Western Australia', *Australian and New Zealand Journal of Criminology*, 27(1): 57–73.

Halsey, M. (2005) *Deleuze and environmental damage: the violence of the text*, Ashgate, London.

Halstead, B. (1992) 'Entrepreneurial crime: impact, detection and regulation', *Trends and Issues in Crime and Criminal Justice*, No. 34, Australian Institute of Criminology, Canberra.

Hamilton, J.P. (1999) 'Judicial independence and impartiality: old principles, new developments', paper presented to the 13th South Pacific Judicial Conference, 28 June–2 July, Apia.

Hampel, G. (1990) 'Sentencing and the plea in mitigation', *Law Institute Journal*, 64: 853–4.

Hampstead, L. & Freeman, M. (1985) *Lloyd's introduction to jurisprudence* (5th edn), Stevens & Sons, London.

Hampton, B. (1993) *Prisons and women*, New South Wales University Press, Sydney.

Hands, T. & Williams, V. (2008) 'Court intervention programs: addressing offending behaviour', *Brief*, 35(7): 18–22.

Haney, C. (2008) 'A culture of harm: taming the dynamics of cruelty in supermax prisons', *Criminal Justice and Behavior*, 35: 956–84.

Hannaford, A. (2013) 'One of our dinosaurs is missing', *The Age*, Focus, 5 November: 10–11.

Harding, M. & Potter, S. (2003) 'Reaching meaningful outcomes in family conferencing', paper presented at the *Juvenile Justice: From Lessons of the Past to a Road Map for the Future Conference*, 1–2 December, Sydney, Australian Institute of Criminology in conjunction with the New South Wales Department of Juvenile Justice.

Harding, R. (1994) 'Victimisation, moral panics, and the distortion of criminal justice policy: a review essay of Ezzat Fattah's "Toward a critical victimology"', *Current Issues in Criminal Justice*, 6(1): 27–42.

Harding, R. (1997) *Private prisons and public accountability*, Open University Press, Milton Keynes.

Harding, R. & Maller, R. (1997) 'An Improved Methodology for Analyzing Age-Arrest Profiles: Application to a Western Australian Offender Population', *Journal of Quantitative Criminology*, 13(4): 349–72.

Harris, M. (2004) 'From Australian courts to Aboriginal courts in Australia: bridging the gap', *Current Issues in Criminal Justice*, 16(1): 26–41.

Harrison, L., Kelly, P., Lindsay, J., Advocat, J. & Hickey, C. (2011) '"I don't know anyone that has two drinks a day": Young people, alcohol and the government of pleasure', *Health, Risk & Society*, 13(5): 469–86.

Hart, C., de Vet, R., Moran, P., Hatch, S.L. & Dean, K. (2012) 'A UK population-based study of the relationship between mental disorder and victimisation', *Social Psychiatry and Psychiatric Epidemiology*, 47(10): 1581–90.

Hartnagel, T.F. & Gillian, M.E. (1980) 'Female prisoners and the inmate code', *Pacific Sociological Review*, 23(1): 85–104.

Harvey, D. (1994) 'Flexible accumulation and urbanisation: reflections on "post modernism" in the American city', in A. Amin (ed.), *Post-Fordism: a reader*, Blackwell, Oxford.

Harvey, D. (1996) *Justice, Nature and the Geography of Difference*, Blackwell, Oxford.

Hasinoff, A.A. (2012) 'Sexting as media production: rethinking social media and sexuality', *New Media & Society*, 15(4): 449–65.

Hatty, S. (1989) 'Policing and male violence in Australia', in J. Hanmer, J. Radford & E. Stanko (eds), *Women, policing and male violence*, Routledge, London.

Hatzistergos, J. (2010) 'Reconciling the purposes and principles of criminal punishment', *Law Society Journal*, 48(7): 78–90.

Hawkins, G. (1969) 'Punishment and deterrence: The educative, moralizing, and habituative effects', *Wisconsin Law Review*, 2: 550–65.

Hawthorne, M. (2011) 'McCabe family reaches settlement with tobacco giant over landmark case', *Sydney Morning Herald*, 13 March.

Hayes, R., Barnett, M., Sullivan, D.H., Nielssen, O. & Large, M. (2009) 'Justifications and rationalizations for the civil commitment of sex offenders', *Psychiatry, Psychology and Law*, 16(1): 141–9.

Hayes, R., Johns, T., Scicchitano, M., Downs, D. & Pietrawska, B. (2011) 'Evaluating the effects of protective keeper boxes on "hot product" loss and sales:

A randomized controlled trial'. *Security Journal*, 24(4): 1–13.

Hayes, R.M. & Levett, L.M. (2013) 'Community members' perceptions of the CSI effect', *American Journal of Criminal Justice*, 38(2): 216–35.

Hayes, S. (2005) 'A review of non-custodial interventions with offenders with intellectual disabilities', *Current Issues in Criminal Justice*, 17(1): 69–77.

Hayman, G. & Brack, D. (2002) *International environmental crime: the nature and control of environmental black markets, sustainable development programme*, Royal Institute of International Affairs, London.

Hayward, K.J. (2002) 'The vilification and pleasures of youthful transgression', in J. Muncie, G. Hughes & E. McLaughlin (eds), *Youth justice: critical readings*, Sage, London.

Hayward, K.J. (2004) *City limits: crime, consumer culture and the urban experience*, Glasshouse Press, London.

Hayward, K.J. & Young, J. (2004) 'Cultural criminology: Some notes on script', *Theoretical Criminology*, 8(3): 303–19.

Hazlehurst, K.M. (1987) *Migration, ethnicity and crime in Australian society*, Australian Institute of Criminology, Canberra.

Hazlehurst, K. & Kerley, M. (1989) 'Migrants and the criminal justice system', in J. Jupp (ed.), *The challenge of diversity: policy options for a multicultural Australia*, Office of Multicultural Affairs, AGPS, Canberra.

Head, M. (2002a) '"Counter-terrorism" laws: a threat to political freedom, civil liberties and constitutional rights', *Melbourne University Law Review*, 26(3): 666–89.

Head, M. (2002b) 'Refugees, global inequality and a new concept of global citizenship', *Australian International Law Journal*: 57–79.

Head, M. & Hoffman, R. (2003) 'Unprecedented police state measures passed by Australian Parliament', World Socialist website, <www.wsws.org/en/articles/2003/07/asio-j01.html>.

Healy, K., Foley, D. & Walsh, K. (2001) 'Families affected by the imprisonment of a parent: towards restorative practices', *Children Australia*, 26(1): 12–19.

Hearn, R. (1993) 'Policing or serving? The role of police in the criminalisation of young people with mental health problems', *Youth Studies Australia*, 12(1) 40–4.

Hebenton, B. & Jou, S. (2008) 'Conceptual approaches to the study of "national" traditions in criminology', *International Journal of Law, Crime and Justice*, 36(2): 115–30.

Heckenberg, D. (2010) 'The global transference of toxic harms', in R. White (ed.), *Global environmental harm: criminological perspective*, Willan Publishing, Devon.

Heckenberg, D. & White, R. (2013) 'Innovative approaches to researching environmental crime', in N. South & A. Brisman (eds) *Routledge International Handbook of Green Criminology*, Routledge, New York.

Hedderman, C. & Gelsthorpe, L. (1992) *Understanding the Sentencing of Women*, Home Office Research and Statistics Directorate, London.

Heidensohn, F. (2012) 'The future of feminist criminology', *Crime Media Culture*, 8(2): 123–34.

Heilpern, D. (1999) 'Judgement: *Police v Shannon Thomas DUNN*, Dubbo Local Court', *Alternative Law Journal*, 24(5): 238–42.

Heilpern, D. (2005) 'Sexual assault of prisoners: reflections', *UNSW Law Journal*, 28(1): 286–92.

Henderson, L. (1985) 'The wrongs of victim's rights', *Stanford Law Review*, 37(4): 937–1021.

Henderson, M. (2006) *Benchmarking study of home detention programs in Australia and New Zealand: Report to the National Corrections Advisory Group*. <www.google.com.au/url?url=http://www.correctiveservices.nsw.gov.au>.

Henderson, P. (1988) *Parliament and politics in Australia: political institutions and foreign relations* (5th edn), Heinemann Education Australia, Melbourne.

Henderson, P., Jones D. & Thomas, D.N. (eds) (1980) *The boundaries of change in community work*, Allen & Unwin, London.

Henham, R. (1999) 'Theory, rights and sentencing policy', *International Journal of the Sociology of Law*, 27(2): 167–83.

Henry, S. & Milovanovic, D. (1994) 'The constitution of constitutive criminology: a postmodern approach to criminological theory', in D. Nelken (ed.), *The Futures of Criminology*, Sage, London.

Herald Sun (2008) 'George Williams appeal fails after plea from son Carl', 6 June.

Herbig, F. & Joubert, S. (2006) 'Criminological semantics: conservation criminology—vision or vagary?', *Acta Criminologica*, 19(3): 88–103.

Herbig, J. (2010) 'The illegal reptile trade as a form of conservation crime: a South African criminological investigation', in R. White (ed.), *Global environmental harm: criminological perspectives*, Willan Publishing, Devon.

Herman, S. & Wasserman, C. (2001) 'A role for the victim in offender reentry', *Crime and Delinquency*, 47(3): 428–45.

Herrnstein, R. & Murray, C. (1994) *The bell curve*, Basic Books, New York.

Hewton, T. (2010) 'Instinctive synthesis, structured reasoning, and punishment guidelines: Judicial discretion in the modern sentencing process', *Adelaide Law Review*, 31(1): 79–93.

Higgins, P. (2012) *Earth is Our Business: Changing the Rules of the Game*, Shepheard-Walwyn Publishers, London.

Hil, R. & Fisher, L. (1994) 'Symbolising panic: the construction of a "black juvenile crime problem" in Queensland', *Socio-Legal Bulletin*: 39–46.

Hinds, L. (2005) 'Three strikes and you're out in the west: a study of newspaper coverage of crime control in Western Australia', *Current Issues in Criminal Justice*, 17(2): 239–53.

Hipp, J.R. (2013) 'Assessing crime as a problem: the relationship between residents' perception of crime and official crime rates over 25 years', *Crime & Delinquency*, 59(4): 616–48.

Hirschi, T. (1969) *Causes of delinquency*, University of California Press, Berkeley.

Hocking, B. (1993) *Beyond terrorism: the development of the Australian security state*, Allen & Unwin, Sydney.

Hogeveen, B. (2006) 'Unsettling youth justice and cultural norms: the youth restorative action project', *Journal of Youth Studies*, 9(1): 47–66.

Hogg, R. (1991) 'Disciplinary regimes of punishment', *Journal of Social Justice Studies*, 4: 117–32.

Hogg, R. & Brown, D. (1998) *Rethinking law and order*, Pluto Press, Sydney.

Hogg, R. & Golder, H. (1987) 'Policing Sydney in the late nineteenth century', in M. Finnane (ed.), *Policing in Australia: historical perspectives*, New South Wales University Press, Sydney.

Holfretzer, K., Van Slyke, S., Bratton, J. & Getz, M. (2008) 'Public perceptions of white-collar crime and punishment', *Journal of Criminal Justice*, 36(1): 50–60.

Hollands, R. (1995) *Friday night, Saturday night: youth cultural identification in the post-industrial city*, Department of Social Policy, University of Newcastle, Newcastle Upon Tyne.

Holmgren, J.A. & Fordham, J. (2011) 'The CSI effect and the Canadian and the Australian jury', *Journal of Forensic Science*, 56(1): 63–71.

Holstein, J.A. & Miller, G. (1990) 'Rethinking victimisation: an international approach to victimology', *Symbolic Interactionism* 13(1): 103–22.

Homel, P. (2009) 'Improving crime prevention knowledge and practice', *Trends & Issues in Crime and Criminal Justice*, No. 385, Australian Institute of Criminology, Canberra.

Homel, R., Lincoln, R. & Herd, B. (1999) 'Risk and resilience: crime and violence prevention in Aboriginal communities, *Australian and New Zealand Journal of Criminology*, 32(2): 182–96.

Homelessness Taskforce (2008) *The road home: a national approach to reducing homelessness*, Commonwealth of Australia, Canberra.

Hope, T. (1995) 'Community crime prevention', in M. Tonry & D.P. Farrington (eds), *Building a safer society: crime and justice: a review of research* (Vol. 19), University of Chicago Press, Chicago.

Hope, T. (1997) 'Inequality and the future of community crime prevention', in S. Lab (ed.), *Crime prevention at a crossroads*, Academy of Criminal Justice Sciences and Anderson Publishing, Kentucky.

Hope, T. (2004) 'Pretend it works: evidence and governance in the evaluation of reducing burglary initiative', *Criminal Justice*, 4(3): 287–308.

Hopkins, A. (2012) 'The relevance of Aboriginality in sentencing: 'sentencing a person for who they are', *Australian Indigenous Law Journal*, 16(1): 30–52.

Horan, J. & Tait, D. (2007) 'Do juries adequately represent the community?: A case study of civil juries in Victoria', *Journal of Judicial Administration*, 16(3): 179–99.

Hovenkamp, H. (1990) 'Positivism in law and economics', *California Law Review*, 78(4): 815–52.

Howard, J. & Zibert, E. (1990) 'Curious, bored and wanting to feel good: the drug use of detained young offenders', *Drug and Alcohol Review*, 9: 225–31.

Howe, A. (1994) *Punish and critique: towards a feminist analysis of penalty*, Routledge, London.

Howell, J. (2000) 'Youth gang programs and strategies: summary', US Department of Justice, Office of Justice Programs, Office of Juvenile Justice and Delinquency Prevention, Washington, DC.

Howie, R. (2008) 'Sentencing discounts: are they worth the effort?', *Judicial Review*, 8(4): 473–88.

HREOC—see Human Rights and Equal Opportunity Commission.

Hudson, S. (2011) *'Alcohol restrictions in Indigenous communities and frontier towns*, Policy Monograph No. 116, Centre for Independent Studies (Australia), Sydney.

Hudson, S. (2013) *Panacea to prison? Justice reinvestment in Indigenous communities*, Centre for Independent Studies.

Hughes, G. (1998) *Understanding crime prevention: social control, risk and late modernity*, Open University Press, Buckingham.

Hughes, G. & Lawson, C. (2011) 'RSPCA and the criminology of social control', *Crime, Law and Social Change*, 55(5): 375–89.

Hughes, G. & Robinson, N. (2007) 'Williams deal saved family home', *Australian*, 2 March.

Hughes, G., Pilkenson, A. & Leisten, R. (1998) 'Diversion in a culture of severity', *Howard Journal*, 37(1): 16–33.

Hughes, R. (2003) *The fatal shore: A history of transportation of convicts to Australia 1787–1868*, Vintage, London.

Human Rights and Equal Opportunity Commission (1991a) *Racist violence: report of the national inquiry into racist violence in Australia*, Australian Government Publishing Service, Canberra.

Human Rights and Equal Opportunity Commission (1991b) *State of the nation: report on people of non-English speaking background*, Australian Government Publishing Service, Canberra.

Human Rights and Equal Opportunity Commission (1993) *Report of the National Inquiry into the Human Rights of People With Mental Illness*, Human Rights and Equal Opportunity Commission: NSW.

Human Rights and Equal Opportunity Commission (1997) *Bringing them Home. Report of the National Inquiry into the Separation of Aboriginal and Torres Strait Islander Children from Their Families*, HREOC, NSW.

Human Rights and Equal Opportunity Commission (2004) *Listen: national consultations on eliminating prejudice against Arab and Muslim Australians*, Human Rights and Equal Opportunity Commission, Sydney.

Humber, Y. (2013) 'Radioactive water the latest dilemma for Japan', *The Age*, 31 August: 12.

Humphrey, M. (2003) 'Refugees: an endangered species?', *Journal of Sociology*, 39(1): 31–43.

Humphrey, M. (2007) 'Culturalising the abject: Islam, law and moral panic in the west', *Australian Journal of Social Issues*, 42(1): 9–25.

Hunt, A. (1976) 'Perspectives in the sociology of law', in P. Carlen (ed.), *The sociology of law*, Sociological Review Monograph No. 23.

Hunt, E. (2008) 'Williams' dad bids for freedom', *Herald Sun*, 20 May.

Hunter, D. (2008) 'How the criminal justice system can be best utilised to reduce the increasing rate of offending and imprisonment of Western Australia's Indigenous population', *Murdoch University Electronic Journal of Law*, 15(2): 134–44.

Hunter, R. & McKelvie, H. (1999) 'Gender and legal practice: the relevance of gender to practice as a barrister', *Alternative Law Journal*, 24(2): 57–61.

I

Iacopino, V. & Xenakis, S.N. (2011) 'Neglect of medical evidence of torture in Guantánamo Bay: a case series', *PLoS Med*, 8(4):1–6.

Iadicola, P. (1986) 'Community crime control strategies', *Crime and Social Justice*, 25(Spring/Summer), 140–65.

Ibrahim D.M. (2006) 'The anti-cruelty statute: a study in animal welfare', *Journal of Animal Law & Ethics*, 1(1): 175–203.

Imai, K., Tingley, D. & Yamamoto, T. (2013) 'Experimental designs for identifying causal mechanisms', *Journal of the Royal Statistical Society*, 176(1): 5–51.

IMF—see International Monetary Fund.

Indermaur, D. (1995) *Violent property crime*, Federation Press, Sydney.

Indermaur, D. (1996) 'Violent crime in Australia: interpreting the trends', *Trends and Issues in Crime and Criminal Justice*, No. 61, Australian Institute of Criminology, Canberra.

Indermaur, D. (2000) 'Violent crime in Australia: patterns and politics', *Australian and New Zealand Journal of Criminology*, 33(3): 287–99.

Indermaur, D. & Roberts, L. (2003) 'Drug courts in Australia: the first generation', *Current Issues in Criminal Justice*, 15(2): 136–54.

Ingram, M. (1990) *Church courts, sex and marriage in England, 1570–1640*, Cambridge University Press, Cambridge.

International Centre for Prison Studies (2007) 'World prison brief', *Prison brief: highest to lowest rates: entire world*, Kings College, London.

International Centre for Prison Studies (2013) 'World prison brief', *Prison brief: highest to lowest rates: entire world*, Kings College, London.

International Monetary Fund (2007) *Reaping the benefits of financial globalization*, International Monetary Fund, Washington DC.

International Monetary Fund (2014) *World economic outlook: an uneven global recovery continues*, International Monetary Fund. Washington DC.

Interpol (2009) *Electronic waste and organised crime: assessing the links*, Phase II Report for the Interpol Pollution Crime Working Group, Lyon, Interpol.

Inverarity, J., Lauderdale, P. & Feld, B. (1983) *Law and society: sociological perspectives on criminal law*, Little Brown, Boston.

Internal Revenue Service (2012) *IRS releases the dirty dozen tax scams for 2012*, <www.irs.gov/uac/IRS-Releases-the-Dirty-Dozen-Tax-Scams-for-2012>.

IRS—see Internal Revenue Service.

Israel, M. (2000) 'The commercialisation of university-based criminological research in Australia', *Australian and New Zealand Journal of Criminology*, 33(1): 1–20.

Iverson, G.R. (1991) *Contextual analysis*, Sage Publications, Thousand Oaks.

Iveson, K. (2000) 'Beyond designer diversity: planners, public space and a critical politics of difference', *Urban Policy and Research*, 18(2): 219–38.

Iveson, K. (2010) 'The wars on graffiti and the new military urbanism', *City: Analysis of Urban Trends, Culture, Theory, Policy, Action*, 14(1–2): 115–34.

J

Jackson, N. (2001) 'Understanding population ageing: a background paper', *Australian Social Policy*, Department of Family and Community Services, Canberra.

Jackson, S.L. (2005) *Research methods and statistics: a critical thinking approach*, Cengage Learning, Wadsworth.

Jackson-Jacobs, C. (2004) 'Taking a beating: the narrative gratifications of fighting as an underdog', in J. Ferrell, K. Hayward, W. Morrison & M. Presdee (eds), *Cultural criminology unleashed*, Glasshouse Press, London.

Jacobs, B. & Wright, R. (2010) 'Bounded rationality, retaliation, and the spread of urban violence', *Journal of Interpersonal Violence*, 25(10): 1739–66.

Jacobs, J. (1961) *The death and life of great American cities*, Jonathan Cape, London.

Jaishankar, K. (2008) 'What ails victimology?', *International Journal of Criminal Justice Sciences*, 3(1): 1–7.

Jaishankar, K. (2009) 'Sexting: a new form of victimless crime?', *International Journal of Cyber Criminology*, 3(1): 21–5.

Jakubowicz, A. & Goodall, H. (1994) *Racism, ethnicity and the media*, Allen & Unwin, St Leonards.

James, M. & Carcach, C. (1998) 'Homicide between intimate partners in Australia', *Trends and Issues in Crime and Criminal Justice*, No. 90, Australian Institute of Criminology, Canberra.

James, M. & Murray, B. (2003) *Computer crime and compromised commerce*, research note, Department of the Parliamentary Library (6), 11 August, Commonwealth of Australia.

James, S. (1994a) 'Police in Australia', in D. Das (ed.), *Police practices: an international review*, Scarecrow Press, Metuchen.

James, S. (1994b) 'Contemporary programs with young people: beyond traditional law enforcement', in R. White & C. Alder (eds), *The police and young people in Australia*, Cambridge University Press, Melbourne.

James, S. & Nordby, J. (eds) (2003) *Forensic science: an introduction to scientific and investigative techniques*, CRC Press, Boca Raton.

James, S. & Warren, I. (1995) 'Police culture', in J. Bessant, C. Carrington & S. Cook (eds), *Cultures of crime and violence: the Australian experience*, La Trobe University Press, Bundoora.

Jamieson, R. (1999) 'Genocide and the social production of immorality', *Theoretical Criminology*, 3(2): 131–46.

Jamrozik, A. (2009) *Social policy in the post-welfare state: Australian society in a changing world*, Pearson Education Australia, Frenchs Forest.

Jarrell, M. & Ozymy, J. (2012) 'Real Crime, Real Victims: Environmental crime victims and the Crime Victims' Rights Act (CVRA)', *Crime, Law and Social Change*, 58(4): 373–89.

Jeffery, C.R. (1971) *Crime prevention through environmental design* (2nd edn), Sage, Beverly Hills.

Jefferson, T. (1990) *The case against paramilitary policing*, Open University Press, London.

Jeffreys, E., Matthews, K & Thomas, A. (2010) 'HIV criminalisation and sex work in Australia', *Reproductive Health Matters* 18(35): 129–36.

Jeffreys, S. (1993) 'Consent and the politics of sexuality', *Current Issues in Criminal Justice*, 5(2): 173–83.

Jeffries, S. & Bond, C.E.W. (2010) 'Sex and Sentencing disparity in South Australia's higher courts', *Current Issues in Criminal Justice*, 22(1): 81–97.

Jennings, W.G., Piquero, A.R. & Reingle, J.M. (2012) 'On the overlap between victimization and offending: A review of the literature', *Aggression and Violent Behaviour*, 17(1): 16–26.

Jevons, W.S. (1879) *The theory of political economy*, Macmillan, London.

Jewkes, Y. (2008) *Media and crime*, Sage, London.

Jochelson, R. (1997) 'Aborigines and public order legislation in New South Wales', *Crime and Justice Bulletin*, 34, NSW Bureau of Crime Statistics and Research, Sydney.

John Howard Society of Alberta (1997) *Victim impact statements*, <www.johnhoward.ab.ca/pub/C53.htm>.

Johnson, H., Ollus, N. & Nevada, S. (2008) *Violence against women: an international perspective*, Springer, New York.

Johnson, S.D. (2010) 'A brief history of the analysis of crime concentration', *European Journal of Applied Mathematics*, 21: 349–70.

Johnston, E. (1991) *Report of the Royal Commission into Aboriginal deaths in custody* (5 vols), Australian Government Publishing Service, Canberra.

Johnston, L. & Shearing, C. (2003) *Governing security: explorations in policing and justice*, Routledge, London.

Jones, C. & Weatherburn, D. (2010) 'Public confidence in the NSW criminal justice system: a survey of the NSW public', *Australian & New Zealand Journal of Criminology*, 43(3): 506–25.

Jones, C., Hua, J., Donnelly, N., McHutchison, J. & Heggie, K. (2006) 'Risk of re-offending among parolees', *Crime and Justice Bulletin: Contemporary Issues in Crime and Justice*, 9: 1–12, NSW

Bureau of Crime Statistics and Research.

Jordan, J. (2008) *Serial survivors: women's narrative of surviving rape*, Federation Press, Sydney.

Jordan, T. & Taylor, P. (2004) *Hacktivism and cyberwars: rebels with a cause?* Routledge, New York.

Julian, R. & Kelty, S. (2012) 'Introduction: forensic science and justice: from crime scene to court and beyond', *Current Issues in Criminal Justice*, 24(1): 1–6.

Julian, R., Kelty, S. & Robertson, J. (2012) '"Get it right the first time": critical issues at the crime scene', *Current Issues in Criminal Justice*, 24(1): 25–37.

Junger-Tas, J. (1994) 'Delinquency in thirteen western countries: some preliminary conclusions', in J. Junger-Tas, G.-J. Terlouw & M. Klein (eds), *Delinquency behavior among young people in the western world: first results of the international self-report delinquency study*, Kugler Publications, Amsterdam.

Jupp, V., Davies, P. & Francis, P. (eds) (2011) *Doing criminological research* (2nd edn), Sage, London.

K

Kabir, N.A. (2011) 'A study of Australian Muslim youth identity: the Melbourne case', *Journal of Muslim Minority Affairs*, 31(2): 243–58.

Kahlor, L. & Eastin, M.S. (2011) 'Television's role in the culture of violence towards women: a study of television viewing and the cultivation of rape myth acceptance in the United States', *Journal of Broadcasting and Electronic Media*, 55(2): 215–31.

Kapuscinski, C.A., Braithwaite, J. & Chapman, B. (1998) 'Unemployment and crime: toward resolving the paradox', *Journal of Quantitative Criminology*, 14(3): 215–41.

Karmen, A. (1996) *Crime victims: an introduction to victimology*, Wadsworth, Belmont.

Karmen, A. (2000) 'Poverty, crime, and criminal justice' in W. Heffernan & J. Kleinig (eds), *From social justice to criminal justice*, Oxford University Press, New York.

Katz, J. (1988) *Seductions of crime: moral and sensual attractions of doing evil*, Basic Books, New York.

Kaukinen, C.E., Meyer, S. & Akers, C. (2013) 'Status compatibility and help-seeking behaviors among female inmate partner violence victims', *Journal of Interpersonal Violence*, 28(3): 577–601.

Kauzlarich, D., Mullins, C. & Matthews, R. (2003) 'A complicity continuum of state crime', *Contemporary Justice Review*, 6(3): 241–54.

Kayrooz, C., Kinnear, P. & Preston, P. (2001) *Academic freedom and commercialisation of Australian universities: perceptions and experiences of social scientists*, Discussion Paper No. 37, Australia Institute, Canberra.

Kazemian, L. (2007) 'Desistance from Crime: Theoretical, Empirical, Methodological and Police Considerations', *Journal of Contemporary Criminal Justice*, 23(1): 5–27.

Keay, N. (2000) 'Home detention: an alternative to prison?', *Current Issues in Criminal Justice*, 12(1): 98–105.

Kelley, C.M. (1976) 'Accountants and auditors vs white collar crime', *Internal Auditor*, 33(3): 35–9.

Kelly, L., Lovett, J. & Regan, L. (2005) *A gap or a chasm? Attrition in reported rape cases*, Home Office Research Study No. 293, Home Office Research, Development and Statistics Directorate, London.

Kelly, P. (2011) 'Breath and the truth of youth at risk: allegory and the social scientific imagination',

Journal of Youth Studies, 14(4): 431–47.

Kelty, S. (2012a) 'Professionalism in crime scene examination: the seven key attributes of top crime scene examiners', *Forensic Science Policy & Management: An International Journal*, 2(4): 175–86.

Kelty, S. (2012b) 'Professionalism in crime scene examination: recruitment strategies using the seven key attributes of top crime scene examiners', *Forensic Science Policy & Management: An International Journal*, 2(4): 198–204.

Kelty, S., Julian, R. & Ross, A. (2012) 'Dismantling the justice silos: avoiding the pitfalls and reaping the benefits of information-sharing between forensic science, medicine and law', *Forensic Science International*, 10(230): 8–15.

Kennedy, K.C. (1983) 'A critical appraisal of criminal deterrence theory', *Dickinson Law Review*, 88, 1–13.

Kerr, D. (2001) 'Private policing on the rise', *New South Wales Police News*, 81(9): 43–7.

Kershaw, C., Nicholas, S. & Walker, A. (2008) *Crime in England and Wales 2007/08*, Home Office, London.

Khalil, L. (2011) 'Youthquake in the Middle East', *Australian Literary Review*, 6 April: 3–4, 22.

Kilroy, D. (2005) 'The prison merry go round: no way off', *Indigenous Law Bulletin*, 6(13): 25–7.

Kim, H.J.& Gerber, J. (2012) 'The effectiveness of reintegrative shaming and restorative justice conferences: focusing on juvenile offenders' perceptions in Australian reintegrative shaming experiments', *International Journal of Offender Therapy and Comparative Criminology*, 56(7): 1063–79.

Kimm, J. (2004) *A fatal conjunction: two laws, two cultures*, Federation Press, Melbourne.

King, M.S. (2002) 'Geraldton alternative sentencing regime: applying therapeutic and holistic jurisprudence in the bush', *Criminal Law Journal*, 26(5): 260–71.

King, M.S. (2008a) 'Problem-solving court judging, therapeutic jurisprudence and transformational leadership', *Journal of Judicial Administration*, 17(3): 155–77.

King, M.S. (2008b) 'Restorative justice, 'therapeutic jurisprudence and the rise of emotionally intelligent justice', *Melbourne University law review*, 32(3): 1096–126.

King, M.S. (2012) 'Reflections on ADR, judging and non-adversarial justice: Parallels and future developments', *Journal of Justice Administration*, 22(2): 76–84.

King, M.S. & Guthrie, R. (2008) 'Therapeutic jurisprudence, human rights and the Northern Territory emergency response', *Precedent*, 89: 39–41.

King, M. & Waddington, D. (2004) 'Coping with disorder? The Changing Relationship between Police Public Order Strategy and Practice—A critical analysis of the Burnley Riot', Policing and Society, 14 (2): 118–37.

Kinner, S.A., George, J., Campbell, G. & Dengenhardt, L. (2009) 'Crime, drugs and distress: patterns of drug use and harm among criminally involved injecting drug users in Australia', *Australian and New Zealand Journal of Public Health*, 33(3): 223–7.

Kirby, M. (1998) 'Speaking to the modern jury: new challenges for judges and advocates', paper presented at *Worldwide Advocacy Conference*, London.

Kirby, M. (2001) 'The future of courts: do they have one?', <www.hcourt.gov.au/assets/publications/speeches/former-justices/kirbyj/kirbyj_future1.htm>.

Kirby, M. (2003) 'Talking about death: The High Court of Australia and the death penalty', *Human Rights Defender*, 12(3): 5–7.

Kirby, M. (2006) 'Precedent—Report on Australia', paper presented at the *International Academy of Comparative Law Conference*, 17 July 2006, Utrecht, The Netherlands.

Kirby M. (2007) 'Precedent law, practice and trends in Australia' *Australian Bar Review*, 28(3): 243–53.

Kirby, M. (2010) 'Forensic evidence: instrument of truth or potential for miscarriage?', *Journal of Law, Information and Science*, 20(1): 1–22.

Kirchengast, T. (2009) 'Criminal injuries compensation, victim assistance programs and restoration in Australian sentencing law', *International Journal of Punishment and Sentencing*, 5(3): 96–119.

Kirchengast, T. (2010) 'Proportionality in sentencing and the restorative justice paradigm: 'just deserts' for victims and defendants alike?', *Criminal Law and Philosophy*, 4(2): 197–213.

Kitchen, P. (2006) *Exploring the link between crime and socio-economic status in Ottawa and Saskatoon: a small area geographical analysis*, report prepared for the Department of Justice Canada, Ottawa.

Klein, M., Kerner, H.J., Maxson, C. & Weitekamp, E. (2001) *The Eurogang paradox: street gangs and youth groups in the US and Europe*, Kluwer Academic Publishers, Dordrecht.

Kleinman, R. (2014) 'Out of here in a body bag', *The Age*, 27 March: 16–17.

Klemke, L.W. (1982) 'Exploring juvenile shoplifting', *Sociology and Social Research*, 67, 59–75.

Klimecki, M., Jenkinson, J. & Wilson, L. (1994) 'A Study of recidivism amongst offenders with an intellectual disability', *Australian and New Zealand Journal of Developmental Disabilities Research*, 19(3): 209–19.

Kneebone, S. (ed.) (2004) *The refugee convention 50 years on: globalisation and international law*, Ashgate, Burlington.

Knowles, D. (2004) 'Shocking violence in mall prompts call for tough response from authorities', *Sunday Mail*, 27 June: 4–5.

Koch, C. & Hill, L. (2008) 'The ballot behind bars after Roach. Why disenfranchise prisoners?', *Alternative Law Journal*, 33(4): 220–4.

Koster, F., Goudriaan, H. & van der Schans, C. (2009) 'Shame and punishment: an international comparative study on the effects of religious affiliation and religiosity on attitudes to offending', *European Journal of Criminology*, 6(6): 481–95.

Kraft, E. & Wang, J. (2009) 'Effectiveness of cyber bullying prevention strategies: a study on students' perspectives', *International Journal of Cyber Criminology*, 3(2): 513–35.

Kramer, R.C. (2010) 'From Guernica to Hiroshima to Baghdad: The normalization of the terror bombing of civilian populations', in W. Chambliss, R. Michalowski and R. Krammer (eds), *State crime in the global age*, Willan Publishing, Uffulme, UK.

Kramer, R.C. (2013) 'Carbon in the atmosphere and power in America: climate change as state-corporate crime', *Journal of Crime & Justice*, 36(2): 153–70.

Krasner, S.D. (2001) 'Abiding sovereignty', *International Political Science Review*, 22(3): 229–51.

Krasnovsky, T. & Lane, R. (1998) 'Shoplifting: A review of the literature', *Aggression and Violent Behavior* 3(3): 219–35.

Kraszlan, K. & West, R. (2001) 'Western Australia trials a specialist court', *Alternative Law Journal*, 26(4): 197–8, 210.

Krisberg, B. (2005) *Juvenile justice: redeeming our children*, Sage, Thousand Oaks.

Kruttschnitt, C., Gartner, R. & Hussemann, J. (2008) 'Female violent offenders: moral panics or more serious offenders?', *Australian and New Zealand Journal of Criminology*, 41(1): 9–35.

Kunst, M. & Van Wilsem, J. (2012) 'Trait impulsivity and change in mental health problems after violent crime victimization: a prospective analysis of the Dutch longitudinal internet studies for the social sciences database, *Journal of Interpersonal Violence*, 2(8): 1642–56.

L

La Grange, T. (1996) 'Marking up the city: the problem of urban vandalism', in G. O'Bireck (ed.), *Not a kid anymore: Canadian youth, crime and subcultures*, Nelson, Toronto.

La Vigne, N., Bieler, S., Cramer, L., Ho, H., Kotonias, C., Mayer, D., McClure, D., Pacifici, L., Parks, E., Peterson, B. & Samuels, J. (2014) *Justice reinvestment initiative state assessment report*, The Urban Institute and Bureau of Justice Assistance, US Department of Justice, Washington, DC.

Landry, D. (2013) 'Are we human? Edgework in defiance of the mundane and measurable', *Critical Criminology*, 21(1): 1–14.

Lane, M. & Henry, K. (2004) 'Beyond symptoms: crime prevention and community development', *Australian Journal of Social Issues*, 39(2): 201–13.

Lane, P. (1998) 'Ecofeminism meets criminology', *Theoretical Criminology*, 2(2): 235–48.

Langbein, J.H. (1991) 'Torture and plea bargaining', in J. Feinberg &

H. Gross (eds), *Philosophy of law* (4th edn), Wadsworth, Belmont.

Langdon, M. (2007) *Acquired brain injury and the criminal justice system: Tasmanian issues*, Brain Injury Association of Tasmania, Hobart.

Langton, M. (1988) 'Medicine square', in I. Keen (ed.), *Being black: Aboriginal culture in 'settled' Australia*, Aboriginal Studies Press, Canberra.

Langton, M. (1998) *Burning questions: emerging environmental issues for Indigenous peoples in northern Australia*, Centre for Indigenous Natural and Cultural Resource Management, Darwin.

Larcombe, W. & Heath, M. (2012) 'Developing the common law and rewriting the history of rape in marriage in Australia: *PGA v The Queen*, *Sydney Law Review*, 34(4): 785–807.

Larsen, N. & Smandych, R. (eds) (2008) *Global criminology and criminal justice: current issues and perspectives*, Broadview Press, Peterborough.

Lasslett, K. (2010) 'Crime or social harm? A dialectical perspective', *Crime, Law and Social Change*, 54(1): 1–19.

Lasslett, K. (2012) 'Power, struggle and state crime: researching through resistance', *State Crime*, 1(1):126–48.

Law and Justice Foundation of New South Wales (2003) *Access to justice roundtable: proceedings of a workshop July 2002*, Law and Justice Foundation of New South Wales.

Law Council of Australia (2004) 'Federal election 2004: key issues for the Law Council of Australia', <www.lawcouncil.asn.au/get/media/2403412930>.

Law Society of New South Wales (1998) *Access to justice: final report*, Law Society of New South Wales, Sydney.

Lawrence, J.A. & Homel, R. (1992) 'Sentencer and offender factors

as sources of discrimination in magistrates' penalties for drinking drivers', *Social Justice Research*, 5(4): 355–413.

Lawrence, R. & Freeman, K. (2002) 'Design and implementation of Australia's first drug court', *Australian and New Zealand Journal of Criminology*, 35(1): 63–78.

Lawry, C. (2010) 'Reigniting the access to justice debate', *Alternative Law Journal*, 35(2): 105–6.

Laxminarayan, M. (2012) 'Procedural justice and psychological effects of criminal proceedings: the moderating effect of offence type', *Social Justice Research*, 25(4): 390–405.

Laxminarayan, M. (2013) 'Interactional justice and the legal system: needs of vulnerable victims', *International Review of Victimology*, 19(2): 145–58.

Laxminarayan, M., Porter, R. & Sosa, L. (2013) 'Victim satisfaction with criminal justice: a systematic review', *Victims and Offenders*, 8(2): 119–47.

Laycock, G. & Tilley, N. (1995) *Policing and neighbourhood watch: strategic issues*, Policy and Research Series No. 60, Home Office, London.

Lea, J. (1998) 'Criminology and postmodernity', in P. Walton & J. Young (eds), *The new criminology revisited*, Macmillan, London.

Lea, J. & Young, J. (1984) *What Is To Be Done About Law and Order?* Penguin, London.

Leach, P. (2003) 'Citizen policing as civic activism: an international inquiry', paper presented at *In Search of Security: An International Conference on Policing and Security*, 19–22 February, Canada Law Commission, Montreal.

Leaver, J. (2011) 'Swear like a Victorian: Victoria's swearing laws and similar provisions in NSW and Queensland', *Alternative Law Journal*, 36(3): 163–5.

Lee, J. (2013) 'One in two state prisoners has acquired brain injury', *The Age*, 25 March: 3.

Lee, J. & Dow, A. (2013) Legal Aid triples debt despite cuts', *The Age*, 16 October: 2.

Lee, M. (2005) 'Public dissent and governmental neglect: isolating and excluding Macquarie Fields', *Current Issues in Criminal Justice*, 18(1): 32–50.

Lee, M. (2007) *Inventing fear of crime: criminology and the politics of anxiety*, Willan Publishing, Devon.

Lee, M. & Herborn, P. (2003) 'The role of place management in crime prevention: some reflections on governmentality and government strategies', *Current Issues in Criminal Justice*, 15(1): 26–39.

Lee, E., & Leets, L. (2002) 'Persuasive storytelling by hate groups online: Examining its effects on adolescents', *American Behavioral Scientist*, 45(6): 927–57.

Lee, M., Crofts, T., Salter, M., Milivojevic, S. & McGovern, A. (2013) '"Let's get sexting": risk, power, sex and criminalisation in the moral domain', *International Journal for Crime and Justice*, 2(1): 35–49.

Legal Information Access Centre (2005) *Hot topics 55: Sentencing*.

Leicester, S. (1995) 'Policing in Wiluna', *Alternative Law Journal*, 20(1): 16–19.

Lemert, E. (1969) 'Primary and secondary deviation', in D. Cressy & D. Ward (eds), *Delinquency, crime and social process*, Harper & Row, New York.

Lemieux, A. (ed.) (2014) *Situational Prevention of Poaching*, Routledge, London.

Lemieux, A. & Clarke, R. (2009) 'The international ban on ivory sales and its effects on elephant poaching in Africa', *The British Journal of Criminology*, 49(4): 451–71.

Lemon, S. (2009) 'Obama tells Chinese students information should be free', IDG News Service, *PCWorld*, 15 November, <http://www.pcworld.com/article/182228/article.html>.

Lens, K.M.E, Pemberton, A. & Bogaerts, S. (2013) 'Heterogeneity in victim participation: a new perspective in delivering a victim impact statement', *European Journal of Criminology*, 10(4): 479–95.

Leober, R. & Farrington, D. (eds) (1998) *Serious & Violent Juvenile Offenders: Risk Factors and Successful Intervention*, Sage, Thousand Oaks.

Lester, A. & Pannick, D. (eds) (2004) *Human rights and practice* (2nd edn), LexisNexis, London.

Levi, M. & Horlick-Jones, T. (2013) 'Interpreting the Fukushima Daiichi nuclear incident: some questions for corporate criminology', *Crime, Law and Social Change*, 59(5): 487–500.

Levy, J. & Jakobsson, P. (2014) 'Sweden's abolitionist discourse and law: effects on the dynamics of Swedish sex work and on the lives of Sweden's sex workers', *Criminology & Criminal Justice*, 1–15 published online <http://crj.sagepub.com/content/early/2014/03/31/1748895814528926>.

Lewis, C.S. (1953) 'The humanitarian theory of punishment', *Res Judicatae*, 5: 225–37.

Liazos, A. (1994) 'The poverty of the sociology of deviance: nuts, sluts and "preverts"', in S. Traub & C. Little (eds), *Theories of deviance*, F.E. Peacock, Ithaca.

Liberman, J. (2002) 'The shredding of BAT's defence: *McCabe v British American Tobacco Australia*', *Tobacco Control*, 11: 271–74.

Lincoln, R. & Wilson, P. (1994) 'Aboriginal offending: patterns and causes', in D. Chappell & P. Wilson (eds), *The Australian criminal justice system: the mid-1990s*, Butterworths, Sydney: 61–86.

Lindgren, S. & Lundstrom, R. (2011) 'Pirate culture and hactivist mobilization', *New Media and Society*, 13(6): 999–1018, published online 27 June 2011.

Lindsay, J. (2012) 'The gendered trouble with alcohol: young people managing alcohol related violence', *International Journal of Drug Policy*, 23(3): 236–41.

Lindsay, R. (2009) 'Punishment without finality: one year in the life and death of Alan Egan', *Criminal Law Journal*, 33: 45–54.

Lindsay, W. & Holland, A. (2000) 'Changing services for offenders with intellectual disability, *Journal of Intellectual Disability Research*, 44(3, 4): 367–8.

Linebaugh, P. (2003) *The London hanged: crime and civil society in the eighteenth century*, Verso, London.

Lippke, R.L. (2011) 'Social deprivation as tempting fate', *Law and Philosophy*, 5(3): 277–91.

Lipsey, M.W. & Wilson, D.B. (2001) *Practical meta-analysis*, Sage, Thousand Oaks.

Little, A. (2002) *The politics of community: theory and practice*, Edinburgh University Press, Edinburgh.

Loader, I. & Sparks, R. (2010) *Public criminology?* Routledge, Abingdon.

Lois, J. (2005) 'Gender and emotion management in the stages of Edgework', in S. Lyng (ed.), *Edgework: the sociology of risk-taking*, Routledge, New York.

Longstaff, S. (2003) 'Terrorism & capital punishment', *Living Ethics*, 53(Spring), 1–4.

Lopes, G., Krohn, M.D., Lizotte, A.J., Schmidt, N.M., Vásquez, B.E. & Bernburg, J.G. (2012) 'Labelling and cumulative disadvantage: the impact of formal police intervention on life chances and crime during emerging adulthood, *Crime and Delinquency*, 58(3): 456–88.

Loughnan, A. (2010) 'Drink spiking and rock throwing: the creation and construction of criminal offences in the current era', *Alternative Law Journal*, 35(1): 18–21.

Lovegrove, A. (2004) 'Sentencing the multiple offender: judicial practice and legal principle', *Research and Public Policy Series*, No. 59, Canberra.

Lovegrove, A. (2007) 'Public opinion, sentencing and lenience: an empirical study involving judges consulting the community', *Criminal Law Review*, 769–81.

Lovegrove, A. (2008) 'A decision framework for judicial sentencing: judgement, analysis and the intuitive synthesis', *Criminal Law Journal*, 32(5): 269–86.

Lowe, P. (2011) 'Technology Undermines jury system, as does complexity', *Law Society Journal*, (October): 20–21.

Lowenkamp, C. & Latessa, E. (2002) *Evaluation of Ohio's community-based correctional facilities and halfway house programs University of Cincinnati*, Center for Criminal Justice Research, Cincinnati, OH.

Lucken, K. (2013) 'You say regulation, I say punishment: the semantics and attributes of punitive activity', *Critical Criminology*, 21(2): 193–210.

Luke, G. & Cunneen, C. (1995) *Aboriginal over-representation and discretionary decisions in the NSW juvenile justice system*, Juvenile Justice Advisory Council of New South Wales, Sydney.

Lundahl, B.W., Kunz, C., Brownell, C., Harris, N. & Van Vleet, R. (2009) 'Prison privatization: a meta-analysis of cost and quality of confinement indicators', *Research on Social Work Practice*, 19(4): 383–94.

Lundman, R. (1980) *Police misconduct*, Holt, Rinehart & Winston, New York.

Lurigio, A.J. (2013) 'Forty years after Abramson: beliefs about the criminalization of people with serious mental illness', *International Journal of Offender Therapy and Comparative Criminology*, 57(7): 763–5.

Lusk, J.L. & Norwood, F.B. (2012) 'Speciesism, altruism and the economics of animal welfare', *European Review of Ecological Economics*, 39(2): 189–212.

Lynch, M. (1990) 'The greening of criminology: a perspective on the 1990s', *Critical Criminologist*, 2(3): 1–4, 11–12.

Lynch, M. & Krzycki, L. (1998) 'Popular culture as an ideological mask: mass produced popular culture and the remaking of criminal justice-related imager, *Journal of Criminal Justice*, 26(4): 321–36.

Lynch, M. & Stretesky, P. (2001). 'Toxic crimes: examining corporate victimization of the general public employing medical and epidemiological evidence', *Critical Criminology*, 10(3): 153–72.

Lynch, M. & Stretesky, P. (2003) 'The meaning of green: contrasting criminological perspectives', *Theoretical Criminology*, 7(2): 217–38.

Lynch, M., Stretesky, P. & Hammond, P. (2000) 'Media coverage of chemical crimes, Hillsborough County, Florida, 1987–97', *British Journal of Criminology*, 40(1): 112–26.

Lynch, M., Stretesky, P. & McGurrin, D. (2002) 'Toxic crimes and environmental justice: examining the hidden dangers of hazardous waste', in G. Potter (ed.), *Controversies in white-collar crime*, Anderson Publishing, Cincinnati.

Lynskey, M.T. & Hall, W.D. (1998) *Cannabis use among Australian youth*, National Drug & Alcohol Research Centre, Randwick.

Lyons, E. (1995) 'New clients, old problems: Vietnamese young people's experiences with police', in C. Guerra & R. White (eds), *Ethnic minority youth in Australia*, National Clearinghouse for Youth Studies, Hobart.

M

MacDowell, R. (2005) 'The real CSI', *Sun Herald*, Sydney, 23 January.

MacDonald, R. (2006) 'Social exclusion, youth transitions and criminal careers: five critical reflections on "risk"', *Australian and New Zealand Journal of Criminology*, 39(3): 371–83.

Machin, D. & Mayr, A. (2012) 'Corporate crime and the discursive deletion of responsibility: a case study of the Paddington rail crash', *Crime, Media, Culture*, 9(1): 63–82.

Mack, K. & Anleu, S. (1995) *Pleading guilty: issues and practices*, Australian Institute of Judicial Administration Incorporated, Melbourne.

Mackay, M. & Munro, T. (1996) *Aborigines and good-order offences: the case of Victoria*, Discussion Paper No. 3, Koori Research Centre, Monash University, Melbourne.

Mackenzie, G. (2006) 'Judges' attitudes and perceptions toward the sentencing process', paper presented to the *Sentencing Principles, Perspectives and Possibilities Conference*, 10–12 February, Canberra.

Mackenzie, G. (2007) 'The guilty plea discount: does pragmatism win over proportionality and principle?', *Southern Cross University Law Review*, 11(3): 205–23.

McKenzie, J. (2013) *Insights from the Coalface: The value of justice reinvestment for young Australians*, Surry Hills, Australian Youth Affairs Coalition (AYAC).

Mackenzie, G., Spiranovic, C., Warner, K., Stobbs, N., Gelb, K., Indermaur, D., Roberts, L., Broadhurst, R. & Bouhours, T. (2012) 'Sentencing and public confidence: results from a national survey on public opinion towards sentencing', *Australian*

& *New Zealand Journal of Criminology*, 45(1): 45–65.

Mackenzie, S. (2011) 'Illicit deals in cultural objects as crimes of the powerful', *Crime, Law and Social Change*, 56(2): 133–53.

Mackie, J. L (1991) 'Retributivism: a test case for ethical objectivity', in J. Feinberg & H. Gross (eds), *Philosophy of law* (4th edn), Wadsworth, Belmont.

Macnaghten, P. & Urry, J. (1998) *Contested natures*, Sage, London.

MacNair, R. (2002) *Perpetration-induced traumatic stress: the psychological consequences of killing*, Praeger, London.

MacPherson, C. (ed.) (1978) *Property: mainstream and critical positions*, University of Toronto Press, Toronto.

Madsen, F. (2009) *Transnational organized crime*, Routledge, London.

Magdoff, F. (2013) 'Twenty-first-century land grabs: accumulation by agricultural dispossession', paper presented to the *Rural Sociology Society*, 7 August 2013: New York City.

Maguire, M. (2004) 'The crime reduction programme in England and Wales: reflections on the vision and the reality', *Criminology and Criminal Justice*, 4(3): 213–37.

Mahomad, H. (2011) *Background paper: retail crime*, Attorney-General and Justice, New South Wales Government.

Maier-Katkin, D., Mears, D.P. & Bernard, T.J. (2009) 'Towards a criminology of crimes against humanity', *Theoretical Criminology*, 13(2): 227–55.

Makkai, T. (1998) 'Alcohol & disorder in the Australian community: part II: perpetrators', *Trends and Issues in Crime and Criminal Justice*, No. 77, Australian Institute of Criminology, Canberra.

Malleson, K. (2002) 'Another nail in the coffin', *New Law Journal*, 152: 1573–7.

Maloney, L. & Lloyd, W. (2003) *Restorative resolutions: a community based sentencing alternative*, John Howard Society of Manitoba, Canada.

Mandel, E. (1982) *Introduction to Marxism*, Pluto Press, London.

Manderson, D. (1993) *From Mr Sin to Mr Big: a history of Australian drug laws*, Oxford University Press, Melbourne.

Mann, K. (2009) 'Remembering and rethinking the social division of welfare: 50 years on', *Journal of Social Policy*, 38(1): 1–18.

Manning, M., Smith, C. & Mazerolle, P. (2013) 'The societal costs of alcohol misuse in Australia', *Trends & Issues in Crime and Criminal Justice*, No. 454, Australian Institute of Criminology, Canberra.

Manning, P. (1989) 'The police occupational culture in Anglo–American societies', in Hoover, L. & Dowling, J. (eds), *Encyclopedia of police science*, New York.

Manning, R. (2011) 'Punishing the Innocent: Children of Incarcerated and Detained Parents', *Criminal Justice Ethics*, 30(3): 267–87.

Manz, B. (2008) 'The continuum of violence in post-war Guatemala', *Social Analysis*, 52(2): 151–64.

Marantelli, S.E. (1994) *Legal studies for year 11: the eleventh court*, Rydalmere, Sydney.

Marchetti, E. & Daly, K. (2004) 'Indigenous courts and justice practices in Australia', *Trends and Issues in Crime and Criminal Justice*, No. 277, Australian Institute of Criminology, Canberra.

Marien, M. (2012) '"Cross-over kids"—childhood and adolescent abuse and neglect and juvenile offending', paper presented to the *National Juvenile Justice Summit*, 26–27 March 2012, Melbourne.

Marks, J. (1994) 'Judicial independence', *Australian Law Journal*, 68(3): 173–87.

Marsh, K., Fox, C. & Hedderman, C. (2009) 'Do you get what you pay for? Assessing the use of prison from an economic perspective', *Howard Journal*, 48(2): 144–57.

Marshall, H., Douglas, K. & MacDonnell, D. (2007) *Deviance and social control: who rules?*, Oxford University Press, Oxford.

Marshall, I. (2008) 'The criminological enterprise in Europe and the United States: a contextual exploration', in N. Larsen & R. Smandych (eds), *Global criminology and criminal justice: current issues and perspectives*, Broadview Press, Peterborough, ONT.

Marshall, J. & Marshall, K. (2003) *Gambling and crime in South Australia*, Attorney-General's Department, Office of Crime Statistics and Research, Adelaide.

Marston, G. & Walsh, T. (2008) 'A case of misrepresentation: social security fraud and the criminal justice system in Australia', *Griffith Law Review*, 17(1): 285–300.

Martin, B. (2013) 'Euthanasia tactics: patterns of injustice and outrage', *Martin SpringerPlus*, 2(1): 256–65.

Martin, C. (2000) 'Crime and control in Australian urban space', *Current Issues in Criminal Justice*, 12(1): 79–92.

Martin, G. (2009) 'Subculture, style, chavs and consumer capitalism: towards a critical cultural criminology of youth', *Crime, Media, Culture*, 5(2): 123–45.

Martin, J. (2013) 'Lost on the Silk Road: online drug distribution and the "cryptomarket"', *Criminology and Criminal Justice*, published online 7 October 2013.

Martin, S. (1996) 'Investigating hate crimes: case characteristics and law enforcement responses', *Justice Quarterly*, 13(3): 455–80.

Martin, W. (2008) 'Courts in 2020: should they do things differently?', paper presented to *Australian Justice System in 2020 Conference*, National Judicial College of Australia, 25 October, Sydney.

Martin, W. (2010) 'Popular punitivism—the role of the courts in the development of criminal justice policies', *Australian & New Zealand Journal of Criminology*, 43(1): 1–16.

Martinovic, M. (2007) 'Home detention: issues, dilemmas and impacts for detainees' co-residing family members', *Current Issues in Criminal Justice*, 19(1): 90–104.

Martinson, R. (1974) 'What works? Questions and answers about prison reform', *Public Interest*, 35, 22–54.

Maruna, S. (2001) *Making Good: How Ex-Convicts Reform and Rebuild Their Lives*, American Psychological Association, Washington, DC.

Maruna, S. (2012) 'Elements of Successful Desistance Signaling', Criminology & Public Policy, 11(1): 73–86.

Marx, K. & Engels, F. (1848) *The communist manifesto*, <www.marxists.org/archive/marx/works/1848/communist-manifesto/index.htm>.

Mason, G. (2002) *The spectacle of violence: homophobia, gender and knowledge*, Routledge, London.

Mason, G. (2011a) 'Naming the "R" word in racial victimization: violence against Indian students in Australia', *International Review of Victimology*, 18(1): 39–56.

Mason, G. (2011b) 'Punishing prejudice and hatred', *Precedent*, 101 (January/February): 10–14.

Mason, G. (2012) '"I am tomorrow": violence against Indian students in Australia and political denial', *Australian & New Zealand Journal of Criminology*, 45(1): 4–25.

Massari, M. & Monzini, P. (2004) 'Dirty Business in Italy: A Case-study of Illegal Trafficking in Hazardous Waste', *Global Crime*, 6 (3&4): 285–304.

Mastrocinque, J.M. (2010) 'An overview of the victims' rights movement: historical, legislative, and research developments', *Sociology Compass*, 4(2): 95–110.

Matthews, R. & Young, J. (eds) (2003) *The new politics of crime and punishment*, Willan Publishing, Devon.

Mathiesen, T. (1990) *Prisons on trial: a critical assessment*, Sage, London.

Matthews, R. (2009) 'Beyond 'so what' criminology: rediscovering realism', *Theoretical Criminology*, 13(3): 341–62.

Matza, D. (1964) *Delinquency and drift*, John Wiley & Sons, New York.

Maunders, D. (1984) *Keeping them off the streets: a history of voluntary youth organizations in Australia 1850–1980*, Centre for Youth and Community Studies, Phillip Institute of Technology, Melbourne.

Mawby, R. (2007) 'Public sector services and the victim of crime', in S. Walklate (ed.), *Handbook of victims and victimology*, Willan Publishing, Devon.

Mawby, R. & Walklate, S. (1994) *Critical victimology: international perspectives*, Sage, London.

Maxwell, G.M. & Morris, A. (1994) 'The New Zealand model of family group conferences', in C. Alder & J. Wundersitz (eds), 'Family conferencing and juvenile justice: the way forward or misplaced optimism?', *Australian Studies in Crime and Justice*, Australian Institute of Criminology, Canberra.

Maxwell, G.M., Kingi, V., Morris, A. & Cunningham, C. (2004) *Achieving effective outcomes in youth justice*, Ministry of Social Development, Auckland.

May, D. & Headley, J. (2003) *Identity theft*, Studies in Crime and Punishment No. 13, Peter Lang, New York.

May, L. (2013) 'Targeted killings and proportionality in law', *Journal of International Criminal Justice*, 11: 47–63.

Mazerolle, L. & Ransley, J. (2005) *Third Party Policing*, Cambridge University Press, Cambridge, UK.

Mazerolle, L., White, G., Ransley, J. & Ferguson, P. (2012) 'Violence in and around entertainment districts: a longitudinal analysis of the impact of late-night lockout legislation', *Law & Policy*, 34(1): 55–79.

McAuliffe, C. (2012) 'Graffiti or street art? Negotiating the moral geographies of the creative city', *Journal of Urban Affairs*, 34(2): 189–205.

McAuliffe, C. (2013) 'Legal walls and professional paths: the mobilities of graffiti writers in Sydney', *Urban Studies*, 50(30): 518–37.

McBarnet, D.J. (1981) *Conviction: law, the state and the construction of justice*, Macmillan, London.

McCallum, D. (2009) 'Punishing Welfare: Genealogies of Child Abuse', *Griffith Law Review*, 18(1): 114–28.

McCarthy, T. (1993) 'Victim impact statements: a problematic remedy', position paper prepared by the *Project for Legal Action Against Sexual Assault*, endorsed by Victorian Services Against Sexual Assault, Melbourne.

McCartney, C. (2006a) *Forensic Identification and Criminal Justice*, Willan Publishing, Collumpton.

McCartney, C. (2006b) 'The DNA expansion programme and criminal investigation', *British Journal of Criminology*, 46(2): 175–92.

McCausland, R. & Vivian, A. (2010) 'Why do some Aboriginal communities have lower crime rates than others? A pilot study, *Australian New Zealand Journal of Criminology*, 43(2): 301–32.

McClellan, P. (2011) 'Looking inside the jury room', *Bar News*, (Winter): 64–72.

McClintock, T. (1997) 'Is the jury trial a lottery?', *Journal of Forensic Psychiatry*, 8(1): 118–26.

McCulloch, J. (2001a) *Blue army: paramilitary policing in Australia,*

Melbourne University Press, Melbourne.

McCulloch, J. (2001b) 'Paramilitary surveillance: S11, globalisation, terrorist and counter-terrorists', *Current Issues in Criminal Justice*, 13(1): 23–35.

McCulloch, J. (2002a) '"Either you are with us or you are with the terrorists": The war's home front', in P. Scraton (ed.), *Beyond September 11: an anthology of dissent*, Pluto Press, London: 54–9.

McCulloch, J. (2002b) 'War at home: national security arrangements post 11 September 2001', *Alternative Law Journal*, 27(2): 87–91.

McCulloch, J. (2003) '"Counter-terrorism", human security and globalisation: from welfare to warfare state?', *Current Issues in Criminal Justice*, 14(3): 283–98.

McCulloch, J. (2004) 'National (in)security politics in Australia: fear and the federal election', *Alternative Law Journal*, 29(2): 87–91.

McCulloch, J. (2008) 'Key issues in a critical approach to policing', in T. Anthony & C. Cunneen (eds), *The critical criminology companion*, Hawkins Press, Sydney.

McCulloch, J. & Clayton, M. (1996) 'Victoria on the move! Move! Move!', *Alternative Law Journal*, 21(3): 103–8.

McCulloch, J. & Pickering, S.J. (eds) (2012) *Crime and Borders*, PanMacmillan USA, Scraton.

McDonald, W.F. (eds) (1997) *Crime and Law Enforcement in the Global Village*, Anderson Publishing, Cincinati.

McKenzie, G. (2007) 'The guilty plea discount: does pragmatism win over proportionality and principle?', *Southern Cross University Law Review*, 11: 205–23.

McDonald, K. (2012) 'They can't do nothin' to us today', *Thesis Eleven*, 109(1): 17–23.

McElroy, W. (2004) 'Seeking criminal justice in civil court', <www.ifeminists.net/introduction/editorials/2004/0811.html>.

McEvoy, K. (2003) 'Beyond the metaphor: political violence, human rights and "new" peacemaking criminology', *Theoretical Criminology*, 7(3): 319–46.

McEvoy, K. & McConnachie, K. (2012) 'Victimology in transitional justice: victimhood, innocence and hierarchy', *European Journal of Criminology*, 9(5): 527–38.

McGee, J.A & Byingon, J.R. (2009) 'The threat of global white-collar crime', *Journal of Corporate Accounting & Finance*, September/October: 25–9.

McGillis, D. (1997) *Community mediation programs: developments and challenges, office of justice programs*, US Department of Justice, Washington.

McGilvray, A. (2008) 'Dangerous chemistry', *Australian Doctor*, 10: 17–21.

McGowen, R.M. (1995) 'The well-ordered prison: England, 1780–1865', in N. Morris & D. Rothman (eds), *The Oxford history of the prison: the practice of punishment in western society*, Oxford University Press, New York.

McGrath, A. (2010) 'The subjective impact of contact with the criminal justice system: The role of gender and stigmatization', *Crime & Delinquency*, epub ahead of print 28 November 2010.

McGrow, L. (2013) 'Sex workers are not pitiful victims in need of rescue', *The Age*, 22 December: 13.

McGuffee, K., Garland, T.S. & Eigenberg, H. (2007) 'Is jury selection fair? Perceptions of race and the jury selection process', *Criminal Justice Studies*, 20(4): 445–68.

McGuire, J. & Priestly, P. (1992) 'Some things do work:

psychological interventions with offenders and the effectiveness debate', in F. Losel, D. Bender & T. Bliesener (eds), *Psychology and the law: international perspectives*, Walter de Gruyter Publishers, Berlin.

McHugh, M. (2004) 'Women justices for the High Court', speech delivered at *High Court dinner, Western Australian Law Society*, Western Australia.

McKemmish, R. (1999) 'What is forensic computing?', *Trends and issues in crime and criminal justice*, No. 118, Australian Institute of Criminology, Canberra.

McKenna, M. (2012) 'Transplanted to savage shores: Indigenous Australians and British birthright in the mid nineteenth-century Australian colonies, 13(1), *Special Issue: Indigenous People and Settler Self Government*. E-journal: <http://dx.doi.org/10.1353/cch.2012.0009>.

McKenzie, N. & Baker, R. (2013a) 'Going rogue: claims of corruption' *The Age*, Insight, 5 October: 17–19.

McKenzie, N. & Baker, R. (2013b) 'Directors blamed over graft', *The Age*, 4 October: 1, 4, 5.

McLaren, K (2000) *Tough is Not Enough—Getting Smart About Youth Crime: A Review of Research on What Works to Reduce Offending by Young People*, Ministry of Youth Affairs, Wellington, NZ.

McLaughlin, E. (2002) 'The crisis of the social and political materialization of community safety', in E. Hughes & J. Muncie (eds), *Crime prevention and community safety*, Sage, London.

McLeay, F. (2003) 'Public interest: partners in the same endeavour', *Alternative Law Journal*, 28(1): 38–9.

McLeod-Kilmurray, H. (2012) 'Commoditizing nonhuman animals and their consumers: industrial livestock production, animal welfare, and ecological justice', *Bulletin of Science & Technology*, 32(1): 71–85.

McMahon, N. (2013) 'The rights and wrongs of designer humans', *The Age*, 14 September: 16.

McMullan, J. & Perrier, D. (2002) 'Lobster poaching and the ironies of law enforcement', *Law & Society Review*, 36(4): 679–720.

McNally, M. & Newman, G. (eds) (2008) *Perspectives on Identity Theft*, Criminal Justice Press, New York.

McNamara, L. (1992) 'Retrieving the law and order issue from the right: alternative strategies and community crime prevention', *Law in Context*, 10(1): 91–122.

McNamara, L. (2002) *Regulating racism: racial vilification laws in Australia*, Monograph Series, No. 16, Sydney Institute of Criminology, Sydney.

McNeill, F. (2006) 'A Desistance Paradigm for Offender Management' Criminology and Criminal Justice 6(1): 39–62.

McNeill, F. (2012a) 'Four Forms of 'Offender' Rehabilitation: Towards an Interdisciplinary Perspective', *Legal and Criminological Psychology* 17(1): 18–36.

McNeill, F. (2012b) 'Ex-Offenders' or 'Re-Citz'?', Discovering Desistance Blog and Knowledge Exchange', http://blogs.iriss.org.uk/discoveri ngdesistance/2012/06/29/ex-offenders-or-re-citz/.

McNeill F., Farrall, S., Lightowler, C., & Maruna, S. (2012a) 'Re-Examining Evidence-Based Practice in Community Corrections: Beyond "A Confined View" of What Works', Justice Research and Policy, 14(1), 35–60.

McNeill, F., Farrall, S., Lightowler, C., & Maruna, S. (2012b) *How and Why People Stop Offending: Discovering Desistance* [IRISS Insight #15], Institute for Research and Innovation in Social Services, Glasgow.

McPhedran, S., Baker, J. & Singh, P. (2010) 'Firearm homicide in Australia, Canada, and New Zealand: what can we learn from long-term international comparisons?', *Journal of Interpersonal Violence*, 26(2): 348–359.

McShane, M. & Williams III, F. (1992) 'Radical victimology: a critique of the concept of victim in traditional victimology', *Crime and Delinquency*, 38(2): 258–71.

McSherry, B. (2004) 'Risk assessment by mental health professionals and the prevention of future violent behaviour', *Trends and Issues in Crime and Criminal Justice*, No. 281, Australian Institute of Criminology, Canberra.

McSherry, B. (2008) '"Dangerous" legislation', in K. Fritzon and P. Wilson (eds), *Forensic psychology and criminology: an Australasian perspective*, McGraw-Hill, Sydney.

McWilliam, V. (2007) 'Judicial review of prison conditions', *Precedent*, 81: 14–19.

Mears, D.P. (2008) 'An assessment of supermax prisons using an evaluation research framework', *Prison Journal*, 88(1): 43–68.

Measham, F. (2006) 'The new policy mix: alcohol, harm minimisation and determined drunkenness in contemporary society', *International Journal of Drug Policy*, 17(4): 258–68.

Medew, J. (2013a) 'Call for crackdown on doctors abusing drugs', *The Age*, 21 September: 7.

Medew, J. (2013b) 'Crystal meth probe as addiction grows', *The Age*, 16 September: 2.

Medew, J. (2014) 'He was on the bed gasping in terrible pain and looking for some relief', *The Age*, 8 May: 6.

Meek, M.K. (1999) *Nutshell guides: the Australian legal system* (4th edn), LBC Information Services, Sydney.

Mehta, M. (2009) *In the Public Interest: Landmark Judgement & Orders of the Supreme Court of India on Environment & Human Rights*, Vols. 1–3, Prakriti Publications, New Delhi.

Meisenkothen, C. (1999) 'Chemical castration: breaking the cycle of paraphiliac recidivism', *Social Justice*, Spring: 1–15.

Mellor, T. (2002) 'Integrated offender management: changing the way we work with offenders in New Zealand', paper presented at the *Probation and Community Corrections: Making the Community Safer Conference*, Perth, 23–24 September.

Melvern, L. (2002) *A people betrayed: the role of the west in Rwanda's genocide*, Zed Books, London.

Memmott, P. (2010) 'On regional and cultural approaches to Australian Indigenous violence', *Australian & New Zealand Journal of Criminology*, 43(2): 333–55.

Merchant, C. (2005) *Radical Ecology: The Search for a Livable World*, Routledge, New York.

Merkel, R. (1993) 'Chemical castration of sex offenders', *Arena*, 4: 8–9.

Merrington, S. & Hine, J. (2001) *Probation work with offenders*, Home Office, London.

Merton, R. (1957) *Social theory and social structure*, Free Press, New York.

Meredyth, D., McKernan, H. & Evans, R. (2010) 'Police and Vietnamese-Australian communities in multi-ethnic Melbourne', *Policing*, 4(3): 233–40.

Mesko, G., Dimitrijevic, D. & Fields, C. (eds) (2010) *Understanding and managing threats to the environment in south Eastern Europe*, Springer, Dordrecht.

Messerschmidt, J. (1986) *Capitalism, patriarchy and crime*, Rowman & Littlefield, New Jersey.

Messerschmidt, J. (1997) *Crime as structured action: gender, race,* class, and crime in the making, Sage, London.

Meyer, E. & Post, L.A. (2006) 'Alone at night: a feminist ecological model of community violence', *Feminist Criminology*, 1(3): 207–27.

Michaelsen, C. (2003) 'International human rights on trial: the United Kingdom's and Australia's legal response to 9/11', *Sydney Law Review*, 25(3): 275–303, <www.austlii.edu.au/au/journals/SydLRev/2003/13.html>.

Michalowski, R. (2010) 'Keynote address: critical criminology for a global age', *Western Criminological Review*, 11(1): 3–10.

Michalowski, R. & Carlson, S. (1999) 'Unemployment, imprisonment, and social structures of accumulation: historical contingency in the Rusche-Kirchheimer hypothesis', *Criminology*, 37(2): 217–49.

Michalowski, R. & Kramer, R.C. (2006) *State-corporate crime: wrongdoing at the intersection of business and government* (eds), Rutgers University Press, New Brunswick.

Middendorp, C. (2013) 'When an addict is a star not a junkie', *The Age*, 27 July: 22.

Milgram, S. (1973) 'The perils of obedience', *Harper's*, 247(1483): 62–77.

Miller, P. (2011) 'Torture approval in comparative perspective', *Human Rights Review*, 12: 441–63.

Millett, P. (2006) 'Journeying the punishment: convicts and their punitive journeys to Western Australia 1850–1868', *Studies in Western Australian History*, 24(1): 1–15.

Mills, C.W. (1959) *The sociological imagination*, Oxford University Press, New York.

Mills, K.M. (1996) 'Crime prevention through environmental design: public facilities, applications and strategies', *Security Journal*, 7(2): 109–15.

Mills, M. & Keddie, A. (2010) 'Cultural reductionism and the media: polarising discourse around schools, violence and masculinity in the age of terror', *Oxford Review of Education*, 36(4): 427–44.

Ministry of Justice and the Ministry of Social Development (2002) 'Te Haonga youth offending strategy: preventing and reducing offending and re-offending by children and young people'.

Miralis, D. (2008) 'Tougher sentences for NSW offenders pleading guilty', *Law Society Journal*, August, 69–71.

Mitchell, C. & Vanya, M. (2009) 'Explanatory frameworks of intimate partner violence', in C. Mitchell & D. Anglin (eds) *Intimate partner violence: a health-based perspective*, Oxford University Press, Oxford.

Moffitt, T. (1996) 'The neuropsychology of conduct disorder', in P. Cordella & L. Siegel (eds), *Readings in contemporary criminological theory*, Northeastern University Press, Boston.

Mold, A (2008) *Heroin: the treatment of addiction in twentieth-century Britain*, Northern Illinois University Press, DeKalb.

Moles, R.N. (2004) *A state of injustice*, Lothian, Melbourne.

Moore, L.J. (2013) 'Speciesism', *Contexts*, 12(1): 12–13.

Moore, M.H. (1987) 'The moral worth of retribution', in F. Schoeman (ed.), *Responsibility, character and emotions*, Cambridge University Press, Cambridge.

Moran, D. (2012) 'Prisoner reintegration and the stigma of prison time inscribed on the body', *Punishment & Society*, 14(5): 564–83.

Morash, M., Jeong, S.J. & Zang N. (2010) 'An exploratory study of the characteristics of men known to commit prisoner-on-prisoner sexual violence', *The Prison Journal*, 90(2): 161–78.

Morfesse, L. & Gregory, A. (2004) 'Police demand new powers', *West Australian*, 28 January: 1.

Morgan, A., Boxall, H., Lindeman, K. & Anderson, J. (2012) 'Effective crime prevention interventions for implementation by local government', *Research and Public Policy Series*, No.120, Australian Institute of Criminology, Canberra.

Morgan, G. (2012) 'Urban renewal and the creative underclass: Aboriginal youth subcultures in Sydney's Redfern–Waterloo', *Journal of Urban Affairs*, 34(2): 207–22.

Morgan, G. & Poynting, S. (2012) 'Introduction: the transnational folk devil', in G. Morgan & S. Poynting (eds), *Global Islamophobia: Muslims and moral panic in the west*, Ashgate, Farnham.

Morgan, J. (2002) *Who kills whom and why: looking beyond legal categories*, Victorian Law Reform Commission, Melbourne.

Morgan, J. (2012) 'Homicide law reform and gender: configuring violence', *Australian & New Zealand Journal of Criminology*, 45(3): 351–366.

Morley, K. & Hall, W. (2003) 'Is there a genetic susceptibility to engage in criminal acts?', *Trends and Issues in Crime and Criminal Justice*, No. 263, Australian Institute of Criminology, Canberra.

Morris, A. & Giller, H. (1987) *Understanding juvenile justice*, Croom Helm, London.

Morris, B. (1995) 'States of siege in the far west', in J. Bessant, K. Carrington & S. Cook (eds), *Cultures of crime and violence: the Australian experience*, La Trobe University Press, Melbourne.

Morris, G., Cook, C., Creyke, R. & Geddes, R. (1992) *Laying down the law: the foundations of legal reasoning, research and writing* in Australia and New Zealand, Butterworth, Sydney.

Morris, N. (1995) '"Dangerousness" and incapacitation', in A. Duff & D. Garland (eds), *A reader on punishment*, Oxford University Press, Oxford.

Morris, A. & Maxwell, G. (2003) 'Restorative justice in New Zealand', In A. von Hirsch., J. Roberts., A. Bottoms., K. Roach, & M. Schiff (eds), *Restorative and criminal justice: Competing or reconcilable paradigms?*, Hart: Oxford, UK, (257–72).

Morris, N. & Miller, M. (1985) 'Predictions of dangerousness', in M. Tonry & N. Morris (eds), *Crime and justice: an annual review of research*, Vol. 6, University of Chicago Press, Chicago.

Morris, N. & Rothman, D. (1998) *The Oxford history of the prison: the practice of punishment in western society*, Oxford University Press, New York.

Morris, R. (1984) 'Prison abolition: lunacy or practical goal', *Canadian Dimension*, 18(4): 5–8.

Morrison, B.E. & Vaandering, D. (2012) 'Restorative justice: pedagogy, praxis, and discipline', *Journal of School Violence*, 11(2): 138–55.

Morrison, W. (1994) 'Criminology, modernity and the "truth" of the human condition: reflections on the melancholy of postmodernism', in D. Nelken (ed.), *The futures of criminology*, Sage, London.

Morrissey, M. (2006) 'The Australian state and Indigenous people 1990–2006', *Journal of Sociology*, 42(4): 347–54.

Mosc, M. (2003) 'Chemical castration', *Adelaide Advertiser*, 10 September.

Mostyn, B., Gibbon, H. & Cowdery, N. (2012) 'The criminalisation of drugs and the search for alternative approaches', *Current Issues in Criminal Justice*, 24(2): 261–72.

Moulton, E. (2013) 'Myth and reality: interpreting the dynamics of crime trends: lies, damn lies and (criminal) statistics', *Police Practice and Research*, 14(3): 219–27.

Mouzos, J. (2002) 'Homicide in Australia: 2000–2001', *National Homicide Monitoring Program annual report*, Australian Institute of Criminology, Canberra.

Mouzos, J. & Makkai, T. (2004) 'Women's experiences of male violence: Findings from the Australian component of the international violence against women survey (IVAWS)', *Research and Public Policy Series*, No. 56, Australian Institute of Criminology, Canberra.

Mouzos, J. & Thompson, S. (2000) 'Gay-hate related homicide: an overview of major findings in NSW', *Trends and Issues in Crime and Criminal Justice*, No. 155, Australian Institute of Criminology, Canberra.

Moyer, I. (2001) *Criminological theories: traditional and nontraditional voices and themes*, Sage, Thousand Oaks.

Moyle, P. (2000) *Profiting from punishment private prisons in Australia: reform or regression?*, Pluto Press, Sydney.

Mudge, S. (2008) 'Environmental forensics and the importance of source identification', *Issues in environmental science and technology*, 26: 1–16.

Muftic, L.R., Finn, M.A. & Marsh, E.A. (2012) 'The victim–offender overlap, intimate partner violence, and sex: assessing differences among victims, offenders and victim–offenders', *Crime & Delinquency*, August: 1–28, Published online, <http://metatoc. com/papers/183-the-victim-offender-overlap-intimate-partner-violence-and-sex-assessing-differences-among-victims-offenders-and-victim-offenders>.

Mukherjee, S. (1997) 'The dimensions of juvenile crime' in Borowski, A. & O'Connor, I.

(eds), *Juvenile crime, justice and corrections*, Longman, Sydney.

Mukherjee, S. (1999) 'Ethnicity and crime', *Trends and Issues in Crime and Criminal Justice*, No. 117, Australian Institute of Criminology, Canberra.

Mukherjee, S. & Carcach, C. (1998) 'Repeat victimisation in Australia', *Australian Institute of Criminology Research and Public Policy Series*, No. 15, Canberra.

Mukherjee, S. & Graycar, A. (1997) *Crime & justice in Australia* (2nd edn), Hawkins Press, Sydney.

Mukherjee, S. & Wilson, P. (1987) 'Neighbourhood watch: issues and policy implications', *Trends and Issues in Crime and Criminal Justice*, No. 8, Australian Institute of Criminology, Canberra.

Munch, C. (2012) *Youth correctional statistics in Canada*, Statistics Canada.

Muncie, J. (1996) 'The construction and deconstruction of crime', in in J. Muncie & E. McLaughlin (eds), *The problem of crime*, Sage, London.

Muncie, J. (2004) 'Youth justice: responsibilisation and rights', in J. Roche, S. Tucker, R. Thomson & R. Flynn (eds), *Youth in Society: Contemporary theory, policy and practice*, Sage, in association with The Open University, London.

Muncie, J. (2009) *Youth & crime* (3rd edn), Sage, London.

Muncie, J. (2013) 'International juvenile (in)justice: penal severity and rights compliance', *International Journal for Crime, Justice and Social Democracy*, 2(2): 43–62.

Muncie, J. & Goldson, B. (eds) (2006) *Comparative youth justice*, London, Sage.

Munn, N. (2011) 'The limits of criminal disenfranchisement', *Criminal Justice Ethics*, 30(3): 223–39.

Munro, I. (2004a) 'Call to review murder defence', *The Age*, 10 November: 3.

Munro, I. (2004b) 'Hulls moves to create pool of short-term judges', *The Age*, 14 October: 7.

Munro, I. (2004c) 'Recovery under the Marshall Plan', *The Age*, 26 July: 8.

Munro, L. (2004d) 'Animals, "nature" and human interests', in R. White (ed.), *Controversies in environmental sociology*, Cambridge University Press, Melbourne.

Munro, I. & Butcher, S. (2007) 'Williams guilty', *The Age*, 1 March.

Murdoch, J. (2006) *The treatment of prisoners: European standards*, Council of Europe.

Murer, J.S. (2012) 'Ethnic conflict: an overview of analyzing and framing communal conflicts from comparative perspectives', *Terrorism and Political Violence*, 24(4): 561–80.

Murphy, B. & Morrison, R. (2007) *Introduction to environmental forensics*, Elsevier, Amsterdam.

Murphy, J.G. (1995) 'Retributivism, moral education and the liberal state', *Criminal Justice Ethics*, 4: 3–11.

Murphy, K. & Helmer, I. (2013) 'Testing the importance of forgiveness for reducing repeat offending', *Australian & New Zealand Journal of Criminology*, 46(1): 138–56.

Murphy, T. & Whitty, N. (2013) 'Making history: academic criminology and human rights', *British Journal of Criminology*, 55(3): 568–587.

Murray, J. (1973) *Larrikins: 19th century outrage*, Lansdowne Press, Melbourne.

Murray, S. (2011) 'Violence against homeless women: safety and social policy', *Australian Social Work*, 64(3): 346–60.

N

Nadesu, A. (2009) 'Reconviction patterns of released prisoners: a 60-month follow-up analysis', *Policy, Strategy and Research*, Department of Corrections, Auckland.

Naffine, N. (1987) *Female crime: the construction of women in criminology*, Allen & Unwin, Sydney.

Naffine, N. (1990) *Law and the sexes: explorations in feminist jurisprudence*, Allen & Unwin, Sydney.

Naffine, N. (1997) *Feminism & criminology*, Allen & Unwin, Sydney.

Napier, J. & Spencer, D. (2007) 'A sign of the times', *Reform Issue*, 90: 35–7.

Nasaw, D. (2010) 'FBI using Facebook in fight against crime', *The Guardian*, Tuesday, 16 March 2010.

Natali, L. (2010) 'The big grey elephants in the backyard of Huelva, Spain', in R. White (ed.), *Global environmental harm: criminological perspectives*, Willan Publishing, Devon.

Natarajan, M. (ed.) (2011) *International Crime and Justice*, Cambridge University Press, New York.

National Academy of Sciences (2009) *Strengthening Forensic Science in the United States: A path forward*, National Academy of Sciences, National Academies Press, Washington, DC.

National Alternative Dispute Resolution Advisory Council (2000) *The development of standards for ADR discussion paper*, Government Printer, Canberra.

National Crime Prevention (1999) *Pathways to Prevention: developmental and early intervention approaches to crime in Australia*, Attorney-General's Department, Canberra.

National Inquiry into the Separation of Aboriginal and Torres Strait Islander Children from their Families (Australia) (NISATSIC), Wilson, R.D. (1997) *Bringing them home: report of the national inquiry into the separation of Aboriginal and Torres Strait Islander children from their families*, Human Rights and Equal Opportunity Commission, Sydney.

National Institute of Economic and Industry Research (2009) *The global financial crisis: projections of property crime rates*, report prepared for the Victorian Police Association, National Institute of Economic and Industry Research, Victoria.

National Motor Vehicle Theft Reduction Council (NMVTRC) (2006) *Annual report 2006: The benefits of theft-reform*, NMVTRC, Melbourne.

National Motor Vehicle Theft Reduction Council (NMVTRC) (2013) *Annual report 2013: adapting to new challenges*, NMVTRC, Melbourne, <www.carsafe.com.au>.

Naylor, B. (1992) *Gender and Sentencing in the Victorian Magistrates' Court: A Pilot Project*, Report to the Criminology Research Council, Law Faculty, Monash University, Melbourne.

Neal, D. (1973) 'Free society, penal colony, slave society, prison?', *Historical Studies*, 22(89): 497–524.

Neal, S. (2010) 'Cybercrime, transgression and virtual environments', in J. Muncie, D. Talbot & R. Walters (eds), *Crime: local and global*, Willan Publishing in association with The Open University, Devon.

Needleman, H., McFarland, C., Ness, R.B., Fienberg, S.E. & Tobin, M.J. (2002) 'Bone lead levels in adjudicated delinquents: a case control study', *Neurotoxicology and Teratology*, 24(6): 711–17.

Nelken, D. (1994) *The futures of criminology*, Sage, London.

Nelken, D. (2009) 'Comparative criminal justice: beyond ethnocentrism and relativism', *European Journal of Criminology*, 6(4): 291–311.

Nelson, D. & Perrone, S. (2000) 'Understanding and controlling retail theft', *Trends and Issues in Crime and Criminal Justice*, No. 152, Australian Institute of Criminology, Canberra.

Nelson, M. & Trone, J. (2000) *Why planning for release matters*, State Sentencing and Corrections Program, Vera Institute of Justice, New York.

Nelson, R. (2013) 'Sterilisation first option for the disabled', *The Age*, 2 January: 3.

Nettler, G. (1984) *Explaining crime*, McGraw Hill, New York.

Nevin, R. (2007) 'Understanding international crime trends: the legacy of preschool lead exposure', *Environmental Research*, 104(3): 315–36.

New South Wales Department of Corrective Services (2008) 'Throughcare', <www.203.202.1.170/ Information/Publications/ Throughcare/Throughcare.pdf>.

New South Wales Law Reform Commission (1986) *Criminal procedure: the jury in a criminal trial*, Report No. 48, Sydney.

New South Wales Law Reform Commission (1996) *Sentencing*, Discussion Paper No. 33, Sydney.

New South Wales Law Reform Commission (2005) *Expert Witnesses, Report No 109*, NSW Law Reform Commission, Sydney.

New South Wales Law Reform Commission (2006) *Blind or deaf jurors*, Report No. 114, Sydney.

New South Wales Law Reform Commission (2007a) *Jury selection*, Report No. 117, Sydney.

New South Wales Law Reform Commission (2007b) *Role of juries in sentencing*, Report No. 118, Sydney.

New South Wales Office of Public Prosecutions (October 2003) *Charge negotiations and agreements: agreed statement of facts: form 1*, <www.odpp.nsw.gov. au/guidelines/guidelines.html>.

Newbold, G. (2004) 'The legality of preventive detention', *New Zealand Law Journal*, 205–7.

Newbold, G. (2008) 'Another one bites the dust: recent initiatives in correctional reform in New Zealand', *Australian and New Zealand Journal of Criminology*, 41(3): 384–401.

Newman, G. & McNally, M. (2005) *Identity theft literature review*, United States Department of Justice, Washington, DC.

Newman, O. (1972a) *Defensible space: people and design in the violent city*, Architectural Press, London.

Newman, O. (1972b) *Defensible space: crime prevention through urban design*, Macmillan, New York.

Nicholas, R. (2008) *Understanding and responding to alcohol-related social harms in Australia: options for policing*, National Drug Law Enforcement Research Fund, Commonwealth of Australia, Hobart.

Nicholl, C. (2001) *Implementing restorative justice: a toolbox for the implementation of restorative justice and the advancement of community policing*, Office of Community Oriented Policing Services, US Department of Justice: Washington, DC.

Nicholson, J. (2012) 'Sentencing— good, bad and indifferent', *Criminal Law Journal*, 36: 205–15.

Niemi, J (2010) 'What we talk about when we talk about buying sex', *Violence Against Women*, 16(2): 159–72.

NMVTRC—see National Motor Vehicle Theft Reduction Council.

Noble, G. (ed.) (2009) *Lines in the sand: the Cronulla riots, multiculturalism and national belonging*, Sydney Institute of Criminology, Sydney.

Noble, P. (2012) 'The Future of Community Legal Centres',

Alternative Law Journal, 37(1): 22–5.

Noone, M. (1988) 'Paralegals: a growth area in times of restraint?', *Legal Service Bulletin*, 13(4): 253–5.

Noone, M. & Tomsen, S. (2006) *Lawyers in conflict: Australian lawyers and legal aid*, Federation Press, Sydney.

Norris, N. (1991) *Law, ideology and punishment: retrieval and critique of the liberal ideal of criminal justice*, Kluwer Academic Publishers, Dordrecht.

Northern Territory Department of Correctional Services (2013) 'Annual report 2012–2013', *Northern Territory Department of Correctional Services*, <www. correctionalservices.nt.gov.au/ AboutUs/Publications/Pages/ default.aspx>.

Nossiter, A. (2014) 'Nigeria uses the law and a whip to "sanitise" gays', *The Age*, 20 February: 17.

Nunn, C. (2010) 'Spaces to speak: challenging representations of Sudanese-Australians', *Journal of Intercultural Studies*, 31(2): 183–98.

O

O'Brien, J. (2004) *International law*, Cavendish, London.

O'Brien, P. (1995) 'The prison on the continent: Europe, 1865–1965', in N. Morris & D. Rothman (eds), *The Oxford history of the prison: the practice of punishment in western society*, Oxford University Press, New York.

O'Brien, P.K. (2013) 'Medical marijuana and social control: escaping criminalization and embracing medicalization', *Deviant Behavior*, 34: 423–43.

O'Connor, B. (1996) 'Creating choices: or just softening the blow? The contradictions of reform: inmate mothers and their children', *Current Issues in Criminal Justice*, 8(2): 144–51.

O'Connor, C. (2007) 'Victims or offenders? Mental health issues in women's prisons', *Precedent*, 81: 26–8.

O'Leary, C. & Platt, T. (2001) 'Pledging allegiance: the revival of prescriptive patriotism', *Social Justice*, 28(3): 41–4.

O'Leary, J. (2011) 'Twelve angry peers or one angry judge: an analysis of judge alone trials in Australia', *Criminal Law Journal*, 35(3): 154–69.

O'Malley, N. (2013a) 'Waiting to inhale', *The Age*, 24 February: 15.

O'Malley, N. (2013b) 'The trouble with keeping secrets', *The Age*, 11 June: 13.

O'Malley, P. (1983) *Law, capitalism and democracy*, Allen & Unwin, Sydney.

O'Malley, P. (1996) 'Post-social criminologies: some implications of current political trends for criminological theory and practice', *Current Issues in Criminal Justice*, 8(1): 26–38.

O'Toole, S. (2002) 'The politics of punishment', *Alternative Law Journal*, 27(5): 242–3.

O'Toole, S. & Eyland, S. (eds) (2005) *Corrections criminology*, Hawkins Press, Sydney.

OECD—see Organisation for Economic Co-operation and Development.

Office of the Deputy Prime Minister (2002) *Reducing re-offending by ex-prisoners*, Social Exclusion Unit, ODPM, London.

Ogden, R. (2008) 'Fisheries forensics: the use of DNA tools for improving compliance, traceability and enforcement in the fishing industry', *Fish and Fisheries*, 9(4): 462–72.

Ogilvie, E. & Van Zyl, A. (2001) 'Young Indigenous males, custody and the rites of passage', *Trends and Issues in Crime and Criminal Justice*, No. 204, Australian Institute of Criminology, Canberra.

Ogloff, J., Davis, M., Rivers, G. & Ross, S. (2007) 'The Identification of mental disorders in the criminal justice system', *Trends and Issues in Crime and Criminal Justice* No. 334, Australian Institute of Criminology, Canberra.

Ogwang, T., Cox, L. & Saldanha, J. (2006) 'Paint on their lips: paint-sniffers, good citizens and public space in Brisbane', *Journal of Sociology*, 42(4): 412–28.

Ojelabi, L.A. (2011a) 'Community legal centres' views on ADR as a means of improving access to justice—Part I', *Alternative Dispute Resolution Journal*, 22: 111–17.

Ojelabi, L.A. (2011b) 'Community legal centres' views on ADR as a means of improving access to justice—Part II', *Alternative Dispute Resolution Journal*, 22: 173–9.

Okimoto, T.G., Wenzel, M. & Feather, N.T. (2009) 'Beyond retribution: conceptualizing restorative justice and exploring its determinants', *Social Justice Research*, 22(1): 156–90.

Old Bailey (2009) *Proceedings of the Old Bailey, London's Central Criminal Court, 1674–1913*, <www.oldbaileyonline.org>.

Olsen, A. (2009) 'Consuming e: ecstasy use and contemporary social life', *Contemporary Drug Problems*, 36 (Summer/Spring): 175–91.

Organisation for Economic Co-operation and Development (2013) *OECD Employment Outlook 2013*, OECD Publishing, Paris.

Otusanya, O.J. (2012) 'An investigation of the financial criminal practices of the elite in developing countries', *Journal of Financial Crime*, 19(2): 175–206.

P

Painter, K. (1992) 'Different worlds: the spatial, temporal and social dimensions of female victimization', in D. Evans, N. Fyfe & D. Herbert (eds), *Crime, policing and place: essays in environmental criminology*, Routledge, London.

Pajá, J.A. (2002) 'Some ideas for a new international framework: a replacement for the United Nations', *Australian International Law Journal* 9: 106–25.

Pallo, B. & Barken, M. (2010) 'The Domestic and International Dimensions of Methylmercury Contamination in Tuna: An Analysis of the Efficacy of the Fish Advisory Standards of Two Federal Agencies', in D. Taylor (ed.) *Environmental and Social Justice: An International Perspective*, Research in Social Problems and Public Policy, Vol. 18.

Palmer, D. (1999) 'Talking about the Problems of Young Nyungars', in R. White (ed.) *Australian Youth Subcultures: On the Margins and in the Mainstream*, Australian Clearinghouse for Youth Studies, Hobart.

Palmer, D. & Collard, L. (1993) 'Aboriginal young people and youth subcultures', in R. White (ed.), *Youth subcultures: theory, history and the Australian experience*, National Clearinghouse for Youth Studies, Hobart.

Panahi, R. (2013) 'Let's get serious on animal cruelty', *Herald Sun Melbourne*, 25 November: 22–3.

Pape, R. (2005) *Dying to win: the strategic logic of suicide*, Scribe, New York.

Papps, K. & Winkelmann, R. (2000) 'Unemployment and crime: new evidence for an old question', *New Zealand Economic Papers*, 34(1): 53–72.

Parker, H. (2005) 'Normalization as a barometer: recreational drug use and the consumption of leisure by younger Britons, *Addiction Research and Theory*, 13(3): 205–15.

Parker, H., Aldridge, J. & Measham, F. (1998) *Illegal leisure: the normalization of adolescent drug use*, Routledge, London.

Parliament of Australia (2010) *Joint select committee on cyber-safety*, Parliament House, Canberra.

Parliament of Victoria Law Reform Committee (2013) *Inquiry into sexting: report of the law reform committee for the inquiry into sexting*, Parliamentary Paper No.230, Parliament of Victoria, Melbourne.

Parliamentary Office of Science and Technology (2005) *Science in court*, Postnote No.248, POST, London.

Parole and Community Corrections Officers Association (2003) 'The foundations of corrections based services for victims of crime: A PACCOA Position Paper', *PACCOA Papers* 1(1).

Parthimos, E. (1993) *Plea bargaining: it's like a placebo effect*, unpublished Honours thesis, Department of Criminology, University of Melbourne, Melbourne.

Pasadakis, N., Gidarakos, E., Kanellopoulou, G. & Spanoudakis, N. (2008) 'Identifying sources of oil spills in a refinery by gas chromatography and chemometrics: a case study', *Environmental Forensics*, 9: 33–9.

Pasko, L. (2010) 'Damaged daughters: the history of girls' sexuality and the juvenile justice system', *Journal of Criminal Law & Criminology*, 100(3): 1099–130.

Passant, J. (2013) 'How the poor are shunted into deeper poverty jut for political capital', *The Age*, 4 January: 11.

Patchin, J.W. & Hinduja, S. (edn.) (2012) *Cyberbullying Prevention and Response: Expert Perspectives*, Routledge, New York.

Paternoster, R. (2010) 'How much do we really know about criminal deterrence?', *Journal of Criminal Law & Criminology*, 100(3): 765–823.

Paxinos, S. (1999) 'Driver jailed over truck crash', *The Age*, 23 November: 6.

Payne, J. (2006) *Specialty courts: current issues and future prospects*, Trends and Issues, No. 317, Australian Institute of Technology, Canberra.

Payne, J. (2007) 'Recidivism in Australia: findings and future research', *Research and Public Policy Series*, No. 8. Australian Institute of Criminology, Canberra.

Payne, J. & Gaffney, A. (2012) 'How much crime is drug or alcohol related? Self-reported attributions of police detainees', *Trends & Issues in Crime and Criminal Justice*, No. 1439, Australian Institute of Criminology, Canberra.

Pearce, F. & Tombs, S. (1998) *Toxic capitalism: corporate crime and the chemical industry*, Dartmouth Publishing Co., Aldershot.

Pearson, G. (1983) *Hooligan: a history of respectable fears*, Macmillan, London.

Pellow, D. (2007) *Resisting global toxics: transnational movements for environmental justice*, MIT Press, Cambridge.

Peltier-Rivest, D. (2012) 'Thieves from within: occupational fraud in Canada', *Journal of Financial Crime*, 19(1): 54–64.

Pennay, A. & Room, R. (2012) 'Prohibiting public drinking in urban public spaces: a review of the evidence', *Drugs Education, Prevention and Policy*, 19(2): 91–101.

Pepinsky, H. (1991) 'Peacemaking in criminology and criminal justice', in H. Pepinsky & R. Quinney (eds), *Criminology as peacemaking*, Indiana University Press, Bloomington.

Pepinsky, H.E. & Quinney, R. (eds) (1991) *Criminology as peacemaking*, Indiana University Press, Bloomington.

Pepper, D. (1993) *Eco-socialism: from deep ecology to social justice*, Routledge, New York.

Pepper, D. (2013) 'Expert evidence in the Land and Environment Court' <www.lec.justice.nsw.gov.au/.../expert evidence in the land and environment court>.

Percy, T. (2006) 'Jury vetting in Western Australia', *Brief*, September: 6–8.

Perkins, M. (2014) '"Staggering" rise in Aboriginal child protection in Victoria', *The Age*, 14 April: 6.

Perrone, S. (1999) 'Violence in the workplace', *Australian Institute of Criminology Research and Public Policy Series*, No. 22, Canberra.

Perrone, S. (2000) 'When life is cheap: governmental responses to work-related fatalities in Victoria 1987–1990', unpublished PhD manuscript, University of Melbourne.

Perrone, S. & White, R. (2000) 'Young people and gangs', *Trends and Issues in Crime and Criminal Justice*, No. 167, Australian Institute of Criminology, Canberra.

Perrone, S., Jansons, D. & Morrison, L. (2013) Problem gambling and the criminal justice system, Victorian Responsible Gambling Foundation, Melbourne.

Perry, B. (2009) 'The sociology of hate: theoretical approaches', in B. Levin (ed.), *Hate crimes volume 1: understanding and defining crime*, Praegar, Westport.

Peters, E. (1995) 'Prison before the prison: the ancient and medieval worlds', in N. Morris & D. Rothman (eds), *The Oxford history of the prison: the practice of punishment in western society*, Oxford University Press, New York.

Petersilia, J. (2001a) 'When prisoners return to the community: political, economic, and social consequences', *Correctional Management Quarterly*, 5(3): 1–10.

Petersilia, J. (2001b) 'Prison reentry: public safety and reintegration challenges', *Prison Journal*, 81(3): 360–75.

Petrie, A. (2013a) 'Killers abusing defence law', *The Age*, 16 June: 1–2.

Petrie, A. (2013b) 'Warning to elderly on financial abuse', *The Age*, 1 September: 8.

Petrisor, I. & Westerfield, W. (2008) 'Hot environmental and legal topics: greenhouse gas regulation and global warming', *Environmental Forensics*, 9(1): 1–5.

Pettit, P. & Braithwaite, J. (1993) 'Not Just deserts, even in sentencing', *Current Issues in Criminal Justice*, 4(3): 225–39.

Pettman, J. (1992) *Living in the margins: racism, sexism and feminism in Australia*, Allen & Unwin, Sydney.

Pew Center on the States (2008) *One in 100: behind bars in America 2008*, Pew Charitable Trusts, Washington, DC.

Pew Center on the States (2009) *One in 31: the long reach of American corrections*, Pew Charitable Trusts, Washington, DC.

Phillips, B., Miranti, R., Vidyattama, Y. & Cassells, R. (2013) *Poverty, social exclusion and disadvantage in Australia*, National Centre for Social and Economic Modelling, Canberra.

Pickering, S. (2005) *Refugees and state crime*, Federation Press, Sydney.

Pickering, S. & Lambert, C. (2002) 'Deterrence: Australia's refugee policy', *Current Issues in Criminal Justice*, 14(1): 65–86.

Pickering, S., McCulloch, J. & Wright-Neville, D. (2008) *Counter-terrorism policing: community, cohesion and security*, Springer, New York.

Pilcher, H. (2013) 'The third factor: beyond nature and nurture', *The Age*, 22 September: 10.

Pinderhughes, R. (1996) 'The impact of race on environmental quality: an empirical and theoretical discussion', *Sociological Perspectives*, 39(2): 231–48.

Piper, A. (2010) '"A growing vice": the truth about Brisbane girls and drunkenness in the early twentieth century', *Journal of Australian Studies*, 34(4): 485–97.

Pires, S. & Clarke, R. (2011) 'Sequential Foraging, Itinerant Fences and Parrot Poaching in Bolivia', *The British Journal of Criminology*, 51(2): 314–35.

Pires, S. & Clarke, R. (2012) 'Are Parrots CRAVED? An Analysis of Parrot Poaching in Mexico', *Journal of Research in Crime and Delinquency*, 49(1): 122–46.

Pires, S. & Clarke, R. (2013) 'The Heterogeneity of Illicit Parrot Markets: An Analysis of 7 Neo-Tropical Markets', *European Journal on Criminal Policy and Research*.

Pires, S. & Moreto, W. (2011) 'Preventing Wildlife Crimes: Solutions That Can Overcome the "Tragedy of the Commons"', *European Journal on Criminal Policy and Research*, 17(101–23).

Pizarro, J.M. & Narag, R.E. (2008) 'Supermax prisons: what we know, what we do not know and where we are going', *Prison Journal*, 88(1): 23–42.

Planning Collaborative (Vic.) Pty Ltd (1993) *The role of building design and urban design in the creation of safe public spaces*, prepared for City of Frankston, City of Bendigo and City of Box Hill, PCPL, Melbourne.

Plummer, K. (1979) 'Misunderstanding labelling perspectives', in D. Downes & P. Rock (eds), *Deviant interpretations*, Martin Robertson, Oxford.

Plummer, K. (2011) 'Labelling theory revisited: forty years on', in H. Peters & M. Dellwing (eds), *Langweiliges Verbrechen* (*Boring Crimes*), VS Verlag, Weisbaden <http://kenplummer.com/publications/selected-writings-2/344-2/>.

Polaschek, D.L.L. (2012) 'An appraisal of the risk-need-responsivity (RNR) model of offender rehabilitation and its application in correctional treatment', *Legal and Criminological Psychology*, 17(1): 1–17.

Polk, K. (1987) 'When less means more: an analysis of destructuring in criminal justice', *Crime and Delinquency*, 33(2): 358–78.

Polk, K. (1994a) 'Family conferencing: theoretical and evaluative questions', in C. Alder & J. Wundersitz (eds), *Family conferencing and juvenile justice*, Australian Institute of Criminology, Canberra.

Polk, K. (1994b) *Why men kill: scenarios of masculine violence*, Cambridge University Press, Melbourne.

Polk, K. (2003) 'Juvenile diversion in Australia: a national review', paper presented at the *Juvenile Justice: From Lessons of the Past to a Road Map for the Future Conference*, 1–2 December, Australian Institute of Criminology in conjunction with the NSW Department of Juvenile Justice, Sydney.

Polk, K. & Warren, I. (1996) 'Crimes against the person', in K. Hazlehurst (ed.), *Crime and justice*, The Law Book Co., Sydney: 183–203.

Pollack, O. (1961) *The criminality of women*, University of Pennsylvania Press, Philadelphia.

Potas, I. (2005) 'The sentencing information system', *Reform Issue*, 86 (Winter): 19–23.

Powell, A. (2010) 'Configuring consent: emerging technologies, unauthorised sexual images and sexual assault', *Australian & New Zealand Journal of Criminology*, 43(1): 76–90.

Poynting, S. (1999) 'When "zero tolerance" looks like racial intolerance: "Lebanese youth gangs", discrimination and resistance', *Current Issues in Criminal Justice*, 11(1): 74–8.

Poynting, S. (2002) 'Bin Laden in the suburbs: attacks on Arab and Muslim Australians before and after 11 September', *Current Issues in Criminal Justice*, 14(1): 43–64.

Poynting, S. (2007) '"Thugs" and "grubs" at Cronulla: from media beat-ups to beating up migrants', in S. Poynting & G. Morgan (eds), *Outrageous! Moral panics in Australia*, ACYS Publishing, Hobart.

Poynting, S. & Mason, V. (2008) 'The new integrationism, the state and Islamophobia: retreat from multiculturalism in Australia', *International Journal of Law, Crime and Justice*, 36(4): 230–46.

Poynting, S. & Morgan, G. (eds) (2007) *Outrageous! Moral panics in Australia*, ACYS Publishing, Hobart.

Poynting, S., Noble, G. & Tabar, P. (2001) 'Middle Eastern appearances: "ethnic gangs", moral panic and media framing', *Australian and New Zealand Journal of Criminology*, 34(1): 67–90.

Poynting, S., Noble, G., Tabar, P. & Collins, J. (2004) *Bin Laden in the suburbs: criminalising the Arab other*, Sydney Institute of Criminology Series No. 18, Sydney Institute of Criminology, Sydney.

Pratt, J. (2002a) 'The globalization of punishment', *Corrections Today*, 64(3): 64–6.

Pratt, J. (2002b) *Punishment and civilization*, Sage, London.

Pratt, J. (2007) *Penal populism*, Routledge, London.

Pratt, J. (2008a) 'Scandinavian Exceptionalism in an era of penal excess. Part 1: the nature and roots of Scandinavian exceptionalism', *British Journal of Criminology*, 48(2): 119–37.

Pratt, J. (2008b) 'Scandinavian exceptionalism in an era of penal excess. Part 2: does Scandinavian exceptionalism have a future?', *British Journal of Criminology*, 48(3): 275–92.

Pratt, J. & Priestley, Z. (1999) 'The Australian and New Zealand Journal of Criminology thirty years on', *Australian and New Zealand Journal of Criminology*, 32(3): 315–24.

Pratt, T.C., Holtfreter, K. & Reisig, M.D. (2010) 'Routine online activity and internet fraud targeting: extending the generality of routine activity theory', *Journal of Research in Crime and Delinquency*, 47(3): 267–96.

Prenzler, T. (1995) 'Equal opportunity and policewomen in Australia', *Australian and New Zealand Journal of Criminology*, 28(3): 258–77.

Prenzler, T. (2011) 'Welfare fraud in Australia: dimensions and issues', *Trends and Issues in Crime and Criminal Justice*, No. 98, Australian Institute of Criminology, Canberra.

Prenzler, T. & Fleming, J. (2011) 'Where are we now? The status of women in Australian and New Zealand policing—2003–2008', *Australasian Policing: A Journal of Professional Practice and Research*, 2(2): 28–33.

Prenzler, T. & Sarre, R. (1998) 'Regulating private security in Australia', *Trends and Issues in Crime and Criminal Justice*, No. 421, Australian Institute of Criminology, Canberra.

Prenzler, T., Earle, K. & Sarre, R. (2009) 'Private security in Australia: trends and key characteristics', *Trends and Issues in Crime and Criminal Justice* No. 374, Australian Institute of Criminology, Canberra.

Presdee, M. (2000) *Cultural criminology and the carnival of crime*, Routledge, London.

Presdee, M. & Walters, R. (1998) 'The perils and politics of criminological research and the threat to academic freedom', *Current Issues in Criminal Justice*, 10(2): 156–67.

Preston, B. (2011) 'The use of restorative justice for environmental crime', *Criminal Law Journal*, 35: 136–45.

Price, M. & Dalgleish, J. (2010) 'Cyberbullying: experiences, impacts and coping strategies as described by Australian young people', *Youth Studies Australia*, 29(2): 51–9.

Prichard, J. (2010) 'Net-widening and the diversion of young people from court: a longitudinal analysis with implications for restorative justice', *Australian & New Zealand Journal of Criminology*, 43(1): 112–29.

Priday, E. (2006) 'New directions in juvenile justice: risk and cognitive behaviourism', *Current Issues in Criminal Justice*, 17(3): 343–59.

Prison Action & Reform (2002) 'Strip searches in prison: issues and responses for prison visitors', pamphlet, Prison Action & Reform: Hobart.

Productivity Commission (2014) *Access to justice arrangements: Productivity Commission draft report*, Commonwealth of Australia, Melbourne.

Putnam, R.D. (2002) *Bowling alone: the collapse and revival of American community*, Simon & Schuster, New York.

Putnins, A. (2001) *Substance use by South Australian young offenders*, Office of Crime Statistics Information Bulletin No. 19, Attorney-General's Department, Adelaide.

Putt, J. (2010) 'Community policing in Australia', Research and Public Policy Series No. 111, Australian Institute of Criminology, Canberra.

Pyeritz, R., Schreier, H., Madansky, C., Miller, L. & Beckwith, J. (1977) 'The XYY male: the making of a myth', in A. Arbor (eds), *Science for the people: biology as a social weapon*,

Burgess Pub. Co, Minneapolis: 86–100.

Q

Queensland Corrective Services (2007) *Electronic monitoring*, Fact Sheet No. 1, Queensland Government, <www.correctiveservices.qld.gov.au/About_Us/The_Department/Probation_and_Parole/Electronic_Monitoring/index.shtml>.

Queensland Law Reform Commission (2010) *A review of jury selection*, Discussion Paper WP, No 69, June 2010.

Queensland Police Service (2014) *Out of Control Events: Frequently asked questions Fact Sheet*, Drug & Alcohol Coordination Unit, QLD Police, QLD, <http://www.police.qld.gov.au/programs/drugs/Documents/OOCE_Information%20Sheet.pdf>.

Quilter, J. (2014) 'One-punch laws, mandatory minimums and "alcohol-fuelled" as an aggravating factor: implications for NSW criminal law', *International Journal of Crime, Justice and Social Democracy*, 31: 81–106.

Quilty, S., Levy, M.H., Barratt, K.H.A. & Butler, T. (2004) 'Children of prisoners: a growing public health problem', *Australian and New Zealand Journal of Public Health*, 28(4): 339–43.

Quinault, R. (2009) 'Victorian juries', *History Today*, 59(5): 47–53.

Quinney, R. (1975) 'Crime control in a capitalist society', in I. Taylor, P. Walton & J. Young (eds), *Critical criminology*, Routlege & Kegan Paul, London: 181–202.

Quinney, R. (1991) 'The way of peace: on crime, suffering and deviance', in H.E. Pepinsky & R. Quinney (eds), *Criminology as peacemaking*, Indiana University Press, Bloomington.

R

Radzinowicz, L. (1999) *Adventures in criminology*, Routledge, London.

Rafter, N. (2008) 'Criminology's darkest hour: biocriminology in Nazi Germany', *Australian and New Zealand Journal of Criminology*, 41(2): 287–306.

Raine, A. (2013) *The anatomy of violence: the biological roots of crime*, Pantheon, New York.

Rankin, M. (2011) 'The disappearing crime of abortion and the recognition of a woman's right to abortion: discerning a trend in Australian abortion law', *Flinders Law Journal* 13(2): 1–48.

Ratcliffe, J. (2001) 'Policing urban burglary', *Trends and Issues in Crime and Criminal Justice*, No. 213, Australian Institute of Criminology, Canberra.

Ratcliffe, J. (2003) 'Intelligence-led policing', *Trends and Issues in Crime and Criminal Justice* No. 248, Australian Institute of Criminology, Canberra.

Ratcliffe, J. (2008) *Intelligence-led policing*, Willan Publishing, Devon.

Ratcliffe, J. & Makkai, T. (2004) 'Diffusion of benefits: evaluating a policing operation', *Trends and Issues in Crime and Criminal Justice* No. 278, Australian Institute of Criminology, Canberra.

Rawls, J. (1955) 'The two concepts of rules', *Philosophical Review*, 64(1): 3–32.

Rawls, J. (1971) *A theory of justice*, Belknap Press, Cambridge.

Raz, J. (1986) *The morality of freedom*, Clarendon, London.

Read, P. & Douglas, J. (2011) 'HIV support and treatment in prisons', *HIV Australia*, 9(1): 8–11.

Rebetzke, G. (2009) 'Evidence by Interpreter: be prepared!', *Precedent*, 93(July/August): 23–7.

Reed, C. (1997) 'Race against time', *The Age*, 1 February: 26.

Reeve, K. (2013) 'The morality of the "immoral": the case of homeless, drug-using street prostitutes', *Deviant Behaviour*, 34(10): 824–40.

Regan, F. (1990) 'Access to legal services: paralegals could make a difference to the provision of legal services', *Legal Service Bulletin*, 15(3): 122–5.

Reiff, D. (1995) *Slaughterhouse: Bosnia and the failure of the west*, Vintage, London.

Reiman, J. (1979) *The rich get richer and the poor get prison: ideology, class and criminal justice*, John Wiley & Sons, New York.

Reiman, J. (1998) *The rich get richer and the poor get prison*, Allyn & Bacon, Boston.

Reiner, R. (1985) *The politics of the police*, Wheatsheaf Books, Hemel Hempstead, Sussex.

Reiner, R. (1992) *The politics of the police* (2nd edn), Wheatsheaf Books, Hemel Hempstead, Sussex.

Reist, M.T. (2013) 'Victims suffer all over again in a world where sexual violence sells', *The Age*, 3 November: 11.

Rengert, G.F., Piquero, A.R. & Jones, P.R. (1999) 'Distance decay re-examined', *Criminology*, 37(2): 427–45.

Report on Government Services (2014) *Volume C, Justice*, Steering Committee for the Review of Government Service Provision, Productivity Commission: Canberra.

Reporters Without Borders (2013) *Era of the digital mercenaries*, <http://surveillance.rsf.org/en/>.

Reuters (1997) 'Jury hits OJ for another $33m', *The Australian*, 12 February: 1, 7.

Reynolds, H. (2006) *The other side of the frontier: Aboriginal resistance to the European invasion of Australia*, UNSW Press, Sydney.

Rice, S. (2011) 'Access to a lawyer in rural Australia: thoughts on the evidence we need', *Dean Law Review*, 16(1): 14–46.

Rice, S. (2012) 'Are CLCs finished?', *Alternative Law Journal*, 37(1): 17–21.

Richards, K. (2009) 'Juveniles' contact with the criminal justice system in Australia', *Monitoring*

Report No. 7, Australian Institute of Criminology.

Richards, K. (2011) 'What makes juvenile offenders different from adult offenders?', *Trends & Issues in crime and Criminal Justice*, No. 409, Australian Institute of Criminology, Canberra.

Ricketts, A. & Avolio, H. (2009–10) 'Corporate liability for manslaughter: the need for further reform', *Southern Cross University Law Review*, 13: 57–86.

Rigakos, G. (2003) *The new para-police: risk markets and commodified social control*, University of Toronto Press, Toronto.

Rigby, K. (2003) 'Addressing Bullying in Schools: Theory and Practice', *Trends and Issues in Crime and Criminal Justice*, 259, Australian Institute of Criminology, Canberra.

Ritchie, D. (2011) *Does imprisonment deter? A review of the evidence*, Sentencing Advisory Council, Melbourne.

Ritchie, D. (2012) *How Much Does Imprisonment Protect the Community Through Incapacitation?*, Sentencing Advisory Council, Melbourne.

Ritter, C., Stover, H., Levy, M., Etter, J. & Elger, B. (2011) 'Smoking in prisons: the need for effective and acceptable interventions', *Journal of Public Health Policy*, 32(1): 32–45.

Ritter, R. McLeod, R. & Shanahan M. (2013) *Government drug policy expenditure in Australia—2009/10*, Drug Policy, Modelling Program, Sydney.

Roach Anleu, S.L. (2002) 'Law in Australian society', in J.M. Najman & J.S. Western (eds) *A sociology of Australian society*, Macmillan, Melbourne.

Roach Anleu, S. & Mack, M. (2009) 'Intersections between in-court procedures ad production of guilty pleas', *Australian & New Zealand Journal of Criminology*, 42(1): 1–23.

Roberto, K.A., Brossoie, N., McPherson, M.C., Pulsifer, M.B. & Brown, P.N. (2013) 'Violence against rural older women: promoting community awareness and action', *Australian Journal on Ageing*, 32(1): 2–7.

Roberts, A. (2012) 'Motor vehicle recovery: a multilevel event history analysis of NIBRS data', *Journal of Research in Crime and Delinquency*, 49(3): 444–67.

Roberts, C. (2001) 'Organising effective interventions: prison and probation perspective', paper presented at the *What Works: What Really Does Work? Conference*, Heureka Science Centre, Helsinki, 25 October.

Roberts, G. (2008) 'The bad oil on ethanol: biofuels are losing favour but some governments are still backing them', *The Weekend Australian*, 31 May–1 June, 2008: 20 Inquirer.

Roberts, J.V. (2012) 'Structured sentencing: lessons from England and Wales for common law jurisdictions', *Punishment & Society*, 14(3): 267–82.

Roberts, J.V. & Manikis, M. (2012) 'Victim personal statements in England and Wales: latest (and last) trends from the witness and victim experience survey', *Criminology and Criminal Justice*, 13(3): 245–61.

Roberts, L. (2008) *Cyber-victimisation in Australia: extent, impact on individuals and responses*, Briefing Paper 6, Tasmanian Institute of Law Enforcement Studies, University of Tasmania, Hobart.

Roberts, L.D. & Indermaur, D. (2007) 'Predicting punitive attitudes in Australia', *Psychiatry, Psychology and Law*, 14(1): 56–65.

Roberts, S. (1994) 'Re-exploring the pathways to decision making', in O. Mendelsohn & L. Maher (eds), *Courts tribunals and new approaches to justice*, La Trobe University Press, Bundoora.

Robertson, G. (1988) 'Arrest patterns among mentally disordered offenders', *British Journal of Psychiatry*, 153: 313–16.

Robson, R.A. (2010) 'Crime and punishment: rehabilitating retribution as a justification for organizational criminal liability', *American Business Law Journal*, 47(1): 109–44.

Roche, A., Bywood, P., Borlagdan, J., Lunney, B., Freeman, T., Lawton, L., Toveli, A. & Nicholas, R. (2008) *Young people and alcohol: the role of cultural influences*, Drinkwise Australia Ltd, Melbourne.

Roche, D. (1999) 'Mandatory sentencing', *Trends and Issues in Crime and Criminal Justice*, No. 138, Australian Institute of Criminology, Canberra.

Roche, D. (2003) *Accountability and restorative justice*, Clarendon Press, Oxford.

Rock, P. (2007) 'Theoretical perspectives on victimisation', in S. Walklate (ed.), *Handbook of victims and victimology*, Willan, Cullompton.

Rocque, M., Welsh, C. & Raine, A. (2012) 'Biosocial criminology and modern crime prevention', *Journal of Criminal Justice*, 40(3): 306–12.

Rodrick, S. (2011) 'Open justice, the media and reporting on preventive supervision and detention orders imposed on serious sex offender in Victoria', *Monash University Law Review*, 37(2): 232–76.

Roffey, P., Provan, P., Duffy, M., Wang, A., Blanchard, C. & Angel, L. (2004) 'Pyhlogenetic DNA profiling: a tool for the investigation of poaching', paper presented at *Australian Institute of Criminology Outlook Conference*, Melbourne.

Rogers, J. (2010) 'Trauma and testimony. Sexual assault in the gaze of the law', *Precedent*, 100 (September/October): 30–3.

Ronalds, C., Chapman, M. & Kitchener, K. (1983) 'Policing Aborigines', in M. Findlay, S. Egger & J. Sutton (eds), *Issues in criminal justice administration*, Allen & Unwin, Sydney.

Ronczkowski, M. (2004) *Terrorism and organized hate crime: intelligence gathering, analysis and investigations*, CRC Press, New York.

Ronken, C. & Johnstone, H. (2008) 'Balancing Rights: Arguments for indefinite detention of dangerous sex offenders', Paper presented to the Sentencing 2008 Conference, 8–10 February, National Judicial College of Australia/ ANU College of Law, Canberra. <http://njca. anu.edu.au/Professional%20 Development/programs%20 by%20year/2008/Sentencing%20 Conference%202008/papers/ Ronken%20Johnson.pdf>.

Room, R. & Rossow, I. (2001) 'The share of violence attributable to drinking', *Journal of Substance Use*, 6: 218–28.

Rose, N. (2000) 'Government and control', *British Journal of Criminology*, 40(2): 321–39.

Rosebury, B. (2011) 'The political logic of victim impact statements', *Criminal Justice Ethics*, 30(1): 39–67.

Rosenberg, S., Hickie, I. & Mendoza, J. (2009) 'National mental health reform: less talk, more action', *Medical Journal of Australia*, 190(4): 193–5.

Rosevear, L. (2012) 'The impact of structural ageing on crime trends: a South Australian case study', *Trends and Issues in Crime and Criminal Justice*, No. 431, Australian Institute of Criminology, Canberra.

Rosoff, S., Pontell, H. & Tillman, R. (1998) *Profit without honor: white-collar crime and the looting of America*, Prentice Hall, Upper Saddle River.

Ross, S. & Forster, K. (2000). 'Female prisoners: using imprisonment statistics to understand the place of women in the criminal justice system', paper presented at the *Women in Corrections: Staff and Clients Conference*, Adelaide 31 October – 1 November 2000.

Roth, J. (1994) *Understanding and preventing violence. Research in brief*, National Institute of Justice, US Department of Justice: Washington, DC.

Rothe, D.L. (2010) 'Facilitating corruption and human rights violations: the role of international financial institutions', *Crime, Law and Social Change*, 53(5): 457–76.

Rothe, D.L. & Friedrichs, D.O. (2015) *Crimes of globalization: new directions in critical criminology*, Routledge, New York.

Roux, C., Crispino, F. & Ribaux, O. (2012) 'From forensics to forensic science', *Current Issues in Criminal Justice*, 24(1): 7–24.

Rowe, S., Wiggers, J., Kingsland, M., Nicholas, C. & Wolfenden, L. (2012) 'Alcohol consumption and intoxication among people involved in police-recorded incidents of violence and disorder in non-metropolitan New South Wales', *Australian and New Zealand Journal of Public Health*, 36(1): 33–40.

Rowe, S., Wiggers, J.H., Wolfenden, L. & Francis, J.L. (2010) 'Establishments licensed to serve alcohol and their contribution to police-recorded crime in Australia: further opportunities for harm reduction', *Journal of Studies on Alcohol and Drugs*, November: 909–16.

Rubington, E. & Weinberg, M. (eds) (1978) *Deviance: the interactionist perspective*, Macmillan, New York.

Ruggiero, V. (1996) *Organized and corporate crime in Europe: offers that can't be refused*, Aldershot, Dartmouth.

Rusche, G. & Kirchheimer, O. (2003) *Punishment and social structure*, Transaction Pub, New Brunswick.

Rush, P., McVeigh, S. & Young, A. (1997) *Criminal legal doctrine*, Oxford University Press, Oxford.

Rush, S. (2002) 'Aboriginal resistance to the abuse of their national resources: the struggles for trees and water', in S. Boyd, D. Chunn & R. Menzies (eds), *Toxic criminology: environment, law and the state in Canada*, Fernwood Publishing, Halifax.

Russell, B. (1999) 'Violence in the workplace', unpublished briefing paper, Strategic Operations Group, WorkCover NSW, Sydney.

Russell, S. (1997) 'The failure of postmodern criminology', *Critical Criminologist*, 8(2): 61–90.

Ryder, R.D. (1975) *Victims of science: the use of animals in research*, Davis-Poynter, London.

S

Sachs, A. (1976) 'The myth of judicial neutrality: the male monopoly cases', in P. Carlen (ed.), *The sociology of law*, Sociological Review Monograph No. 23, University of Keele, Staffordshire.

Sackville, R. (2003) Opening address, cited in Law and Justice Foundation of New South Wales (2003) *Access to justice roundtable: proceedings of a workshop July 2003*, Law and Justice Foundation of New South Wales, Sydney.

Sackville, R. (2005) 'Acting judges and judicial independence', paper presented at the *Judicial Conference of Australia* 28 February 2005.

Sackville, R. (2011) 'Access to justice: towards an integrated approach', *The Judicial Review*, 10(2): 221–36.

Safe Work Australia (2014a) 'Worker fatalities', <www.safeworkaustralia. gov.au/sites/swa/statistics/ work-related-fatalities/pages/ worker-fatalities>.

Safe Work Australia (2014b) *Asbestos-related disease indicators*, Safe Work Australia, Canberra.

Saferstein, R. (2007) *Criminalistics: an introduction to forensic science*, Pearson International, New York.

Saha, R. & Mohai, P. (2005) 'Historical context and hazardous waste facility siting: understanding temporal patterns in Michigan', *Social Problems*, 52(4): 618–48.

Sakurai, Y. & Smith, R.G. (2003) 'Gambling as a motivation for the commission of financial crime', *Trends and Issues in Crime and Criminal Justice*, No. 271, Australian Institute of Criminology, Canberra.

Salmelainen, P. (1995) *The correlates of offending frequency: a study of juvenile theft offenders in detention*, NSW Bureau of Crime Statistics and Research, Sydney.

Salter, M., Crofts, T. & Lee, M. (2013) 'Beyond criminalisation and responsibilisation: sexting, gender and young people', *Current Issues in Criminal Justice* 24(3): 301–16.

Sampson, R.J. & Laub, J.H. (1993) *Crime in the making: pathways and turning points through life*, Harvard University Press, Cambridge.

Sampson, R.J. & Laub, J.K. (1997) A Life-Course Theory of Cumulative Disadvantage and the Stability of Delinquency', in T.P Thornberry (edn) *Developmental Theories of Crime and Delinquency*, Transition Publishers, New Brunswick, New Jersey.

Samuels, A.C. (2002) *Review of the New South Wales Director of Public Prosecution's policy and guidelines for charge bargaining and tendering of agreed facts*, <www.google.com.au/url?url=http://www.lawlink.nsw.gov.au>.

Sandercock, L. (1983) 'Who gets what out of public participation', in L. Sandercock & M. Berry, *Urban political economy: the Australian case*, George Allen & Unwin, Sydney.

Sankoff, P. & White, S. (eds) (2009) *Animal law in Australasia: a new dialogue*, The Federation Press, Sydney.

Sarat, A. (1986) 'Access to justice: citizen participation and the American legal order', in L. Lipson & S. Wheeler (eds), *Law and the social sciences*, Russell Sage Foundation.

Saro-Wiwa, K. (1995) *A month and a day: a detention diary*, Penguin, London.

Sarre, R. (1989) 'Towards the notion of policing "by consent" and its implications for police accountability', in D. Chappell & P. Wilson (eds), *Australian policing: contemporary issues*, Butterworths, Sydney.

Sarre, R. (1994) 'Violence: patterns of crime', in D. Chappell & P. Wilson (eds), *The Australian criminal justice system: the mid-1990s*, Butterworths, Sydney.

Sarre, R. (2011) 'We get the crime we deserve: Exploring the political disconnect in crime policy', *James Cook University Law Journal*, 18: 144–61.

Sarre, R. & Prenzler, T. (2012) 'Pluralised policing in Australia: answering the questions', *Australasian Policing*, 4(1): 31–2.

Sarre, R. & Tomaino, J. (eds) (2004) *Key issues in criminal justice*, Australian Humanities Press, Unsley.

Schauss, S. (1980) *Diet, crime and delinquency*, Parker House, Berkeley.

Schetzer, L. (2000) *A review of the law on the age of criminal responsibility of children: Discussion Paper 3*, National Children's and Youth Law Centre, Sydney.

Schinkel, W. (2004) 'The will to violence', *Theoretical Criminology*, 8(1): 5–32.

Schirmann, F. (2013) 'Badness, madness and the brain—the late 19th-century controversy on immoral persons and their malfunctioning brains', *History of the Human Sciences*, 26(2): 33–50.

Schissel, B. (2002) 'Youth crime, youth justice, and the politics of marginalization', in B. Schissel & C. Brooks (eds), *Marginality and condemnation: an introduction to critical criminology*, Fernwood Publishing, Halifax.

Schissel, B. & Brooks, C. (eds) (2002) *Marginality and condemnation: an introduction to critical criminology*, Fernwood Publishing, Halifax.

Schlosberg, D. (2007). *Defining environmental justice: theories, movements, and nature*, Oxford University Press, Oxford.

Schmidt, L. (2013) 'Still breathing the devil's dust', *The Age*, Focus, 19 June: 16–17.

Schneider, J. (2008) "Reducing the illicit trade in endangered wildlife: the market reduction approach", *Journal of Contemporary Criminal Justice*, 24(3): 274–95.

Schneider, J. (2012) *Sold into Extinction: The Global Trade in Endangered Species*, Praeger, New York.

Schneider, R. & Kitchen, T. (2002) *Planning for crime prevention: a transatlantic perspective*, Routledge, London.

Schneiders, B. (2012) 'The right to leave', *The Age*, Insight, 27 October: 15.

Schofield, P., Butler, T., Hollis, S., Smith, N., Lee, S. & Kelso, W. (2006) 'Traumatic brain injury among Australian prisoners: rates, recurrence and sequelae', *Brain Injury*, 20(5): 499–506.

Schur, E. (1965) *Crimes without victims: deviant behavior and public policy: abortion, homosexuality, drug addiction*, Prentice Hall, New York.

Schwartz, M. (2010) 'Building communities, not prisons: justice reinvestment and Indigenous over-imprisonment', *Australian Indigenous Law Review*, 14(1): 1–17.

Schwartz, M.D. & Nurge, D.M. (2004) 'Capitalist punishment: ethics and private prisons', *Critical Criminology*, 12(2): 133–56.

Schwendinger, H. & Schwendinger, J. (1975) 'Defenders of order or guardians of human rights?', in I. Taylor, P. Walton & J. Young (eds), *Critical criminology*, Routledge & Kegan Paul, London: 1134–6.

Scott, C.L. & Holmberg, T. (2003) 'Castration of sex offenders: prisoners' rights versus public safety', *Journal of the American Academy of Psychiatry and the Law*, 31(4): 502–9.

Scottish Government (2005) *Social focus on deprived areas 2005*. Scottish Executive National Statistics Publication, Edinburgh.

Scott-Storey, K. (2011) 'Cumulative abuse: do things add up? An evaluation of the conceptualization, operationalization, and methodological approaches in the study of the phenomenon of cumulative abuse', *Trauma, Violence & Abuse*, 12(3): 135–50.

Scraton, P. (1985) *The state of the police*, Pluto, London.

Scraton, P. (2000) 'A response to Lynch and the Schwendingers', *Critical Criminologist*, 11(2): 1–3.

Scraton, P. & Chadwick, K. (1991) 'The theoretical and political priorities of critical criminology', in K. Stenson & D. Cowell (eds), *The politics of crime control*, Sage, London.

Scutt, J. (1990) *Women and the law: commentary and materials*, The Law Book Co., Sydney.

Scutt, J. (1995) 'Judicial bias or legal bias? Battery, women and the law', in J. Bessant, K. Carrington & S. Cook (eds), *Cultures of crime and violence: the Australian experience*, La Trobe University Press, Bundoora.

Seagrave, M. & Carlton, B. (2011) 'Counting the costs of imprisonment: researching women's post-release deaths

in Victoria', *Australian & New Zealand Journal of Criminology*, 44(1): 41–55.

Seba, L. (2013) 'Is sentencing reform a lost cause? A historical perspective on conceptual problems in sentencing research', *Law & Contemporary Problems*, 76: 237–64.

Segelov, T. (2012) 'Third-wave asbestos cases', *Precedent*, 109: 40–3.

Segrave, M., Milivojevic, S. & Pickering, S. (2009) *Sex trafficking: international context and response*, Willan Publishing, Devon.

Seifman, R. & Freiberg, A. (2001) 'Plea-bargaining in Victoria: the role of counsel', *Criminal Law Journal*, 25(2) 64–74.

Seiter, R, (2005) *Corrections: an introduction*, Pearson Prentice Hall, Upper Saddle River.

Senate Legal and Constitutional Affairs Reference Committee (Cth) (2009) *Access to Justice*, Commonwealth of Australia, Canberra.

Senate Standing Committee on Legal and Constitutional Affairs (1994) *Gender bias and the judiciary*, Parliament of Australia, Canberra.

Senate Standing Committee on Legal and Constitutional Affairs (2004) *Legal aid and access to justice*, Parliament of Australia, Canberra.

Sentencing Advisory Council (2007) *Sentence indication and specified sentence discounts: final report*, <www.sentencingcouncil.vic. gov.au>.

Sentencing Advisory Council (2008a) *Mandatory sentencing information paper*, <www. sentencingcouncil.vic.gov.au>.

Sentencing Advisory Council (2008b) *Suspended Sentences and intermediate sentencing orders suspended sentences final report: part 2*, Melbourne, <www. sentencingcouncil.vic.gov.au>.

Sentencing Advisory Council (2009) *National imprisonment rates*,

<www.sentencingcouncil.vic. gov.au>.

Sentencing Advisory Council (2014) *Sentencing options*, <www.sentencingcouncil.vic. gov.au>.

Sercombe, H. (1995) 'The face of the criminal is Aboriginal', in J. Bessant, K. Carrington & S. Cook (eds), *Cultures of crime and violence: the Australian experience*, La Trobe University Press, Melbourne.

Sewell, J. (2001) '"I just bashed somebody up. Don't worry about it Mum, he's only a poof": The "homosexual advance defence" and discursive constructions of the "gay" victim', *Southern Cross University Law Review*, 5: 47–81.

Seymour, A. (2001) *The victim's role in offender reentry: a community response manual*, Office for Victims of Crime, US Department of Justice, Washington, DC.

Seymour, J. (1988) *Dealing with young offenders*, The Law Book Co., Sydney.

Shaffer, J.N. & Ruback, R.B. (2002) *Violent victimization as a risk factor for violent offending among juveniles*, Office of Juvenile Justice and Delinquency Prevention, Washington, DC.

Shapiro, S. (1990) 'Collaring the crime, not the criminal: reconsidering the concept of white collar crime', *American Sociological Review*, 55(3): 346–65.

Sharkey, P. (2008) 'The intergenerational transmission of context', *American Journal of Sociology*, 113(4): 931–69.

Sharkey, P. (2013) *Stuck in place: urban neighbourhoods and the end of progress towards racial equality*, University of Chicago, Chicago.

Shaw, A. (1977) *Convicts and the colonies*, Melbourne University Press, Melbourne.

Shaw, C.R. & McKay, H.D. (1942) *Juvenile delinquency and urban areas*, University of Chicago Press, Chicago.

Shaw, G. & Wierenga, A. (2002) *Restorative practices/community conferencing pilot*, University of Melbourne.

Shea, C. (2013) 'Science's shock to the system reverberates 50 years on', *The Age*, 24 November: 12.

Shearing, C. (1992) 'The relation between public and private policing', in M. Tonry & N. Morris (eds) *Modern policing*, University of Chicago Press, Chicago.

Shearing, C. (1995) 'Transforming the culture of policing: thoughts from South Africa', *Australian and New Zealand Journal of Criminology*, special supplementary issue, *Crime, Criminology and Public Policy*: 54–61.

Shearing, C. & Ericson, R. (1991) 'Culture as figurative action', *British Journal of Sociology*, 42(4): 481–506.

Shearing, C. & Stenning, P (eds) (1987) *Private policing*, Sage, Newbury Park.

Sheehan, R. & Borowski, A. (eds) (2013) *Australia's children's courts today and tomorrow*, Springer, New York.

Sheehy, E., Stubbs, J. & Tolmie, J. (2012a) 'Defences to homicide for battered women: a comparative analysis of laws in Australia, Canada and New Zealand', *Sydney Law Review*, 34(3): 467–92.

Sheehy, E., Stubbs, J. & Tolmie, J. (2012b) 'Battered women charged with homicide in Australia, Canada and New Zealand: how do they fare?', *Australian & New Zealand Journal of Criminology*, 45(3): 383–99.

Sheldon, W.H. (1940) *The varieties of human physique (an introduction to constitutional psychology)*, Harper & Brothers, New York.

Shepherd, S.M., Luebbers, S. & Dolan M. (2012) 'Gender and ethnicity in juvenile risk assessment', *Criminal Justice and Behavior*, 40(4): 388–408.

Sheppard, B. (2006) 'Pair on day release from jail join jewel shop raid', *Telegraph*.

Sheptycki, J. (2004) 'Relativism, transnationalism and comparative criminology', in J. Sheptycki, A. Wardak & J. Hardie-Bick (eds), *Transnational and comparative criminology*, Routledge, London.

Sherman, L.D., Farrington, C., Brandon, B.W. & Layton, D. (2006) *Evidence-based crime reduction*, Routledge, London.

Shildrick, T. (2002) 'Young people, illicit drug use and the question of normalization', *Journal of Youth Studies*, 5(1): 35–48.

Shiner, M. (2013) 'British drug policy and the modern state: reconsidering the criminalisation thesis', *Journal of Social Policy*, 42(3): 623–43.

Shinkfield, A.J. (2006) 'A three-part ecological model of community reintegration of ex-prisoners', unpublished doctoral dissertation, Deakin University, Melbourne.

Shinkfield, A.J. & Graffam, J. (2009) 'Community reintegration of ex-prisoners: type and degree of change in variables influencing successful reintegration', *International Journal of Offender Therapy and Comparative Criminology*, 53(1): 29–42.

Shiva, V. (2008) *Soil not oil: environmental justice in an age of climate crisis*. South End Press, Brooklyn.

Short, J. & Hughes, L. (eds) (2006) *Studying youth gangs*, AltaMira Press, Walnut Creek.

Short, M. (2013a) 'The problem with porn', *The Age*, 22 May: 16–17.

Short, M. (2013b) 'How to beat addiction', *The Age*, 3 June: 20–21.

Short, M. (2013c) *Saving women and girls*, The Age 28 May: 12–13.

Shover, N. (2012) 'Ethnographic methods in criminological research: rationale, reprise and warning', *American Journal of Justice*, 37(2): 139–45.

Shover, N. & Wright, J. (eds) (2001) *Crimes of privilege: readings in white-collar crime*, Oxford University Press, New York.

Shroyer, T. (1973) *Critiques of domination: the origins and development of critical theory*, G Braziller, New York.

Shtier R. (2011) *The steal: a cultural history of shoplifting*, Penguin Press, New York.

Siegel, N. (2003) '"Court" in the system: the impact of the circuiting bush court upon criminal justice administration and domestic violence prosecution in Aboriginal communities', *Current Issues in Criminal Justice*, 15(1): 56–60.

Silberman, M. (2007) 'The Muncy way: the reformatory idea at the end of the 20th century', *Prison Journal*, 87(3): 271–94.

Silverman, D. (2011) *Interpreting qualitative data*, Sage, London.

Silverman, H. (2011) 'Twins jailed for gatecrashing 18th birthday party and assaulting guests', *Adelaide Now*, 20 May.

Sim, J., Scraton, P. & Gordon, P. (1987) 'Introduction: crime, the state and critical analysis', in P. Scraton (ed.), *Law, order and the authoritarian state*, Open University Press, Milton Keynes.

Simon, D.R. (2012) *Elite deviance* (10th edn), Pearson, New York.

Singer, P. (2002) *Animal liberation*, HarperCollins, New York.

Situ, Y. & Emmons, D. (2000) *Environmental crime: the criminal justice system's role in protecting the environment*, Sage, Thousand Oaks.

Skogan, W.G. (2006) *Police and Community in Chicago: A tale of three cities*, Oxford University Press, New York.

Skolnik, J. (1975) *Justice without trial: law enforcement in democratic society*, John Wiley & Sons, New York.

Skolnik, J. & Fyfe, J. (1993) *Above the law: police and the excessive use of force*, Free Press, New York.

Skull, S. (1984) *Decarceration, Community Treatment and the Deviant: A Radical View*, Rutgers University Press, New Brunswick, New Jersey.

Slapper, G. & Tombs, S. (1999) *Corporate crime*, Pearson Education, London.

Slotboom, A., Kruttschnitt, C., Bijleveld, C. & Menting, B. (2011) 'Psychological well-being of incarcerated women in the Netherlands: importation or deprivation?', *Punishment & Society*, 13(2): 176–97.

Smandych, R. & Larsen, N. (2008) 'Introduction: foundations for a global criminology and criminal justice', in N. Larsen & R. Smandych (eds) *Global criminology and criminal justice: current issues and perspectives*, Broadview Press, Peterborough, ONT.

Smart, C. (1976) *Women, crime, and criminology: a feminist critique*, Routledge & Kegan Paul, London.

Smart, C (1989) *Feminism and the power of law*, Routledge, London.

Smith, J. (2003) *Seeds of deception: exposing industry and government lies about the safety of the genetically engineered foods you're eating*, Yes! Books, Fairfield, Iowa.

Smith, L. & Louis, E. (2010) 'Cash in transit armed robbery in Australia', *Trends & Issues in Crime and Criminal Justice*, No. 397, Australian Institute of Criminology, Canberra.

Smith, N.E. & Jones, C. (2008) 'Monitoring trends in re-offending among adult and juvenile offenders given non-custodial sanctions' *Crime and Justice Bulletin: Contemporary Issues in Crime and Justice*, 110: 1–12.

Smith, R. & Akerman, T. (2008) 'Raising public awareness of consumer fraud in Australia',

Trends & Issues in Crime and Criminal Justice, No. 349, Australian Institute of Criminology, Canberra.

Snell, K. & Tombs, S. (2011) 'How do you get your voice heard when no-one will let you? Victimization at work', *Criminology and Criminal Justice*, 11(3): 207–23.

Snider, L. (2000) 'The sociology of corporate crime: an obituary (or: whose knowledge claims have legs?)', *Theoretical Criminology*, 4(2): 169–206.

Sollund, R. (ed.) (2008) 'Causes for speciesism: difference, distance and denial', in R. Sollund (ed.) *Global harms: ecological crime and speciesism*, Nova Science, New York.

Sollund, R. (2012) 'Speciesism as Doxic Practice Versus Valuing Difference and Plurality', in R. Ellefsen, R. Sollund, and G. Larson (eds), *Eco-global Crimes: Contemporary problems and future challenges*, Ashgate, Farnham.

Sourdin, T. (2012) 'Civil dispute resolution obligations: what is reasonable?', *University of New South Wales Law Journal*, 35(3): 889–913.

South Australian Department for Correctional Services (1995) *Annual Report 1994–1995*, Government of South Australia.

South, C.R. & Wood, J. (2006) 'Bullying in prisons: the importance of perceived social status, prisonization, and moral disengagement', *Aggressive Behaviour*, 32(5): 490–501.

South, N. & Wyatt, T. (2011) 'Comparing illicit trades in wildlife and drugs: an exploratory study', *Deviant Behaviour*, 32: 538–61.

South, N. (1998) 'A green field for criminology? A proposal for a perspective', *Theoretical Criminology*, 2(2): 211–33.

South, N. (2007) 'The "corporate colonisation of nature": bio-prospecting, bio-piracy and the development of green criminology', in P. Beirne &

N. South (eds), *Issues in green criminology: confronting harms against environments, humanity and other animals*, Willan, Devon.

Spalding, L.M. (1998) 'Florida's 1997 chemical castration law: a return to the dark ages' *Florida State University Law Review*, 25(2): 117–39.

Sparks, R. (2000) 'The media and penal politics', *Punishment and Society*, 2(1): 98–105.

Spelman, W. & Eck, E. (1987) *Problem-oriented policing*, U.S. Department of Justice, National Institute of Justice, Washington, D.C.

Spierenberg, P. (1995) 'The body and the state: early modern Europe', in N. Morris & D. Rothman (eds), *The Oxford history of the prison: the practice of punishment in western society*, Oxford University Press, New York.

Spigelman, J.J. (2001) 'Judicial ethics: accountability and education', paper presented at the *Judicial Ethics Training Course*, National Judicial College, Beijing.

Spigelman, J.J. (2008) 'Consistency and sentencing', *Australian Law Journal*, 82(7): 450–60.

Spitzer, S. (1975) 'Toward a Marxian theory of deviance', *Social Problems*, 22(5): 638–51.

Spivak, A.L. & Sharp, S.F. (2008) 'Inmate recidivism as a measure of private prison performance', *Crime and Delinquency*, 54(3): 482–508.

Spooner, R. & Butt, C. (2013) 'Males dominate sex crime, females tend to smuggle', *The Age*, 4 January: 3.

Stadler, W.A. & Benson, M.L. (2012) 'Revisiting the guilty mind: the neutralization of white-collar crime', *Criminal Justice Review*, 3(4): 494–511.

Stamatakis, N. & Vandeviver, C. (2013) 'Restorative justice in Belgian prisons: the results of an empirical research', *Crime, Law, Social Change*, 59(1): 79–111.

Stanko, E. (1995) 'Policing domestic violence: dilemmas and contradictions', *Australian and New Zealand Journal of Criminology*, special supplementary issue, *Crime, Criminology and Public Policy*: 31–44.

Stanley, E. (2008a) *Torture, truth and justice: the case of Timor-Leste*, London, Routledge.

Stanley, E. (2008b) 'Torture and terror', in T. Anthony & C. Cunneen (eds), *The critical criminology companion*, Hawkins Press, Sydney.

Stark, J. (2013) 'A toxic legacy' *The Age*, Extra, 7 July: 9.

Steering Committee for the Review of Government Service Provision (2009) *Report of Government Services 2009*, Productivity Commission, Canberra.

Steering Committee for the Review of Government Service Provision (2011) *Overcoming Indigenous disadvantage: key indicators 2011*, Productivity Commission, Canberra.

Steering Committee for the Review of Government Service Provision (2014) *Report on government services 2014: Indigenous compendium*, Productivity Commission, Canberra.

Steffensmeier, D.J., Schwartz, J. & Roche, M. (2013) 'Gender and twenty-first-century crime: female involvement and the gender gap in Enron-era corporate frauds', *American Sociological Review*, 78(3): 448–76.

Stenning, P. (2000) 'Powers and accountability of private police', *European Journal on Criminal Policy and Research*, 8(3): 325–52.

Stenson, K.M. & Sullivan, R.R. (2001) *Crime, risk and justice: the politics of crime control in liberal democracies*, Willan Press, Cullhompton.

Stephens, A. (2013) 'Unhinged', *The Age*, 23 November: 12–14.

Stevens, A. (2012) 'I Am the Person Now I Was Always Meant to Be': Identity Reconstruction and Narrative Reframing in Therapeutic Community Prisons', *Criminology and Criminal Justice*, 12(5): 527–47.

Stewart, F. & Freiberg, A. (2008) 'Provocation in sentencing: a culpability-based framework', *Current Issues in Criminal Justice*, 19(3): 283–308.

Stigler, G.J. (1990) 'The optimum enforcement of laws', *Journal of Political Economy*, 78: 526–36.

Stone, C. (1972) 'Should Trees Have Standing?: Toward legal rights for natural objects', *Southern California Law Review*, 45: 450–87.

Strang, H. (2001) *Restorative Justice Programs in Australia: A Report to the Criminology Research Council*, Australian Institute of Criminology, Canberra.

Stretesky, P. & Hogan, M. (1998) 'Environmental justice: an analysis of superfund sites in Florida', *Social Problems*, 45(2): 268–87.

Stretesky, P. & Lynch, M. (1999) 'Corporate Environmental Violence and Racism', *Crime, Law & Social Change*, 30:163–84.

Stuart, C. (1997) 'Simpson faces financial ruin', *Australian*, 6 February: 1, 11.

Stubbs, J. (2011) 'Indigenous women in Australian criminal justice: over-represented but rarely acknowledged', *Australian Indigenous Law Review*, 15(1): 47–63.

Stylianou, S. (2010) 'Victimless deviance: toward a classification of opposition justifications', *Western Criminology Review*, 11(2): 43–56.

Sugden, N. (2003) 'Questioning the aptness of police pre-entry physical test', *Current Issues in Criminal Justice*, 15(2): 180–5.

Summers, A. (2013) 'I feel like a million dollars, then sex rears its ugly head', *The Age*, 5 January: 19.

Sumner, C. (1994) 'Durkheim, modernity and doubt: the birth', in *The sociology of deviance: an obituary*, Open University Press, Milton Keynes.

Sunstein, C. & Nussbaum, M. (eds) (2006) *Animal rights: current debates and new directions*, Oxford University Press, Oxford.

Sutherland, E. (1940) 'White collar criminality', *American Sociological Review*, 5, 1–12.

Sutherland, E. (1949) *White collar crime: the uncut version*, Yale University Press, London.

Sutherland, E. & Cressy, D. (1974) *Criminology*, Lippincott, New York.

Sutton, A. (1994a) 'Community crime prevention: a national perspective', in D. Chappell & P. Wilson (eds), *Australian criminal justice: the mid-1990s*, Butterworths, Sydney.

Sutton, A. (1994b) 'Crime prevention: promise or threat?', *Australian and New Zealand Journal of Criminology*, 27(1): 5–20.

Sutton, A. (1997) 'Policy dilemmas: a personal account', in P. O'Malley & A. Sutton (eds), *Crime prevention in Australia: issues in policy and research*, Federation Press, Sydney.

Sutton, A. & Hazlehurst, J. (1996) 'Crime prevention', in K. Hazlehurst (ed.), *Crime and justice*, LBC Information Services, Sydney.

Sutton, A., Cherney, A. & White, R. (2014) *Crime Prevention: Principles, Perspectives and Practices*, Cambridge University Press, Melbourne.

Sutton, A., Cherney, A. & White, R. (2008) *Australian crime prevention: principles, policies and practices*, Cambridge University Press, Melbourne.

Svard, P.-A. (2008) 'Protecting the animals? An abolitionist critique of animal welfarism and green ideology' in R. Sollund (ed.), *Global harms: ecological crime and speciesism*, Nova Science, New York.

Sweeney, J. & Payne, J. (2011) 'Poly drug use among police detainees', *Trends & Issues in Crime and Criminal Justice*, No. 425, Australian Institute of Criminology, Canberra.

Sykes, G. (1958) *The society of captives: a study of a maximum security prison*, Princeton University Press, Princeton.

Sykes, G. & Matza, D. (1957) 'Techniques of neutralization: a theory of delinquency', *American Sociological Review*, 22(6): 664–70.

T

Tabuchi, H. (2013) 'Alarm bells over Fukushima leaks', *The Age*, 25 August: 13.

Tahiri, H. & Grossman, M. (2013) *Community and radicalisation: an examination of perceptions, ideas, beliefs and solutions throughout Australia*, Counter-Terrorism Coordination Unit, Victoria Police, Melbourne.

Tailby, R. & Gant, F. (2002) 'The illegal market in Australian abalone', *Trends & Issues in Crime and Criminal Justice*, No. 225, Australian Institute of Criminology, Canberra.

Talbott, W.J. (2005) *Which rights should be universal?*, Oxford University Press, Oxford.

Talbott, W.J. (2010) *Human rights and human well-being*, Oxford University Press, Oxford.

Tame, C. (1991) 'Freedom, responsibility and justice: the criminology of the "new right"', in K. Stenson & D. Cowell (eds), *The politics of crime control*, Sage, London.

Tannenbaum, F. (1938) *Crime and community*, Columbia University Press, London and New York.

Tarling, R. (1993) *Analysing offending*, HMSO, London.

Task Force Victor (1994) *Police shootings: a question of balance*, Government of Victoria, Melbourne.

Tasmania Department of Justice (2011) 'Breaking the Cycle: A Strategic Plan for Tasmanian Corrections 2011–2020, Incorporating the 2011–2013 Breaking the Cycle Action Plan, *Corrective Services*, Department of Justice: Tasmania <www.justice.tas.gov.au/correctiveservices/breaking_the_cycle>.

Taylor, C. (2004) *Court licensed abuse: patriarchal lore and the legal response to intrafamilial sexual abuse of children*, Peter Lang, New York.

Taylor, D. & Mackenzie, G. (2013) 'Staying focused on the big picture: should Australia legislate for corporate manslaughter based on the United Kingdom model?' *Criminal Law Journal*, 37: 99–113.

Taylor, G. (2002) 'Should addiction to drugs be a mitigating factor in sentencing?', *Criminal Law Journal*, 26(6): 324–48.

Taylor, G. (2004) 'Is addiction to gambling relevant in sentencing?', *Criminal Law Journal*, 28(3): 141–59.

Taylor, I (1995) 'Private homes and public others', *British Journal of Criminology*, 35(2): 263–85.

Taylor, I., Walton, P. & Young, J. (1973) *The new criminology: For a social theory of deviance*, Routledge & Kegan Paul, London.

Taylor, I., Walton, P. & Young, J. (1975) *Critical Criminology*, Routledge & Kegan Paul, London.

Taylor, M. (2013) 'Toward understanding the street code of silence that exists among prolific graffiti offenders', *Victims & Offenders*, 8(2): 185–208.

Taylor, M.F, Marais, I. & Cottman, R. (2012) 'Patterns of graffiti offending: towards recognition that graffiti offending is more than "kids messing around"', *Policing and Society*, 22(2): 152–68.

Taylor, N. (2007) 'Juror attitudes and biases in sexual assault cases', *Trends and Issues in Crime and Criminal Justice*, No. 344, Australian Institute of Criminology, Canberra.

Taylor, N. & Mayhew, P. (2002) 'Patterns of victimisation among small retail businesses', *Trends and Issues in Crime and Criminal Justice*, No. 221, Australian Institute of Criminology, Canberra.

Tedeschi, C. (1994) 'Taking the bias out of the bench', *Good Weekend*, 6 August: 41–6.

Temkin, J. & Krahé, B. (2008) *Sexual assault and the justice gap: a question of attitude*, Hart Publishing, Oxford and Portland.

Teplin, L.A. (1984) 'Criminalizing mental disorder', *American Psychologist*, 39(7): 794–803.

Terblanche, S. (2008) 'Mandatory sentences in South Africa: lessons for Australia?', *Australian and New Zealand Journal of Criminology*, 41(3): 402–20.

Terry, A. & Giungni, D. (2003) *Business, society and the law* (3rd edn), Thomson Learning, Melbourne.

The Age (2006) 'For Australia, freedom from execution is not negotiable', editorial, *The Age*, 26 January: 13.

The Age (2013) 'Confronting the scale of violence in the home', editorial, *The Age*, 22 April: 18.

The Age (2013a) 'Why smacking should be regarded as a crime', editorial, *The Age*, 29 July: 18.

The Age (2013b) 'Compensating terror victims', editorial, *The Age*, 10 October: 10.

The Age (2013c) 'Strong punishment for teen folly', *The Age*, 24 July: 16.

Third, A., Richardson, I., Collin, P., Rahilly, K. & Bolzan, N. (2010) *Intergenerational attitudes towards social networking and cybersafety: a living lab–research report*, Cooperative Research Center for Young People, Technology and Wellbeing, Melbourne.

Thomas, G. (1999) 'Business watch as an effective security management strategy for industrial estates: reality or mythology?', *Security Journal*, 21(1): 53–62.

Thomas, N. K. (2011) 'On Turning a Blind Eye and a Deaf Ear: Society's Response to the Use of Torture', *International Journal of Group Psychotherapy*, 61(1): 7–25.

Thomas, W.I. (1923) *The unadjusted girl*, Little, Brown, New York.

Thompson, A. (1992) 'Foreword: critical approaches to law: who needs legal theory?', in I. Grigg-Spall & P. Ireland (eds), *The critical lawyers' handbook*, Pluto Press, London.

Thompson, A. (2007–08) 'The revolving door of penal institutions: a narrative of lived experience', *Flinders Journal of Law Reform*, 10(3): 591–608.

Thompson, A. & Doherty, E. (2012) 'Teen gatecrashers warned they will be named, shamed online', *Herald Sun*, 24 September.

Thorne, S., Kirkham, S.R. & O'Flynn-Magee, K. (2004) 'The analytical challenge in interpretive description', *International Journal of Qualitative Methods*, 3(1): 1–21.

Thornton, M. (2000) 'Law as business in the corporatised university', *Alternative Law Journal*, 25(6): 269–73.

Tiedt, A. (2010) 'Turning yourself in. What sentencing discounts can be expected for assisting authorities?', *Law Society Journal*, 48(11): 66–8.

Tilley, N. (2005), 'Driving down crime at motorway service areas', in M. J. Smith & N. Tilley (eds), *Crime Science: New Approaches to Preventing and Detecting Crime*, Willan Publishing, Cullompton, Devon, pp. 104–25.

Tillman, R. (2009) 'Making the rules and breaking the rules: the political origins of corporate corruption in the new economy', *Crime, Law and Social Change*, 51(1): 73–86.

Titterington, V.B., Rivolta, P.M. & Schraufnagel, S. (2013) 'Right-to-die legislation: a note on factors associated with its adoption', *Sociological Spectrum*, 33(4): 358–73.

Tomaino, J. & Kapardis, A. (2004) 'Sentencing theory', in R. Sarre & J. Tomaino (eds), *Key issues in criminal justice*, Australian Humanities Press, Unsley.

Tomasic, R. (1994) 'Corporate crime', in D. Chappell & P. Wilson (eds), *The Australian criminal justice system: the mid 1990s*, Butterworths, Sydney.

Tomazin, F. (2013) 'Radical judicial plan offers a voice to sexual assault victims', *The Age*, 15 December: 5.

Tombs, S. (2012) 'State-corporate symbiosis in the production of crime and harm', *State Crime*, 1(2): 170–95.

Tombs, S. & Whyte, D. (2004) *Unmasking the crimes of the powerful: scrutinizing states and corporations*, Peter Lang, New York.

Tomkins, K. (2005) 'Police, law enforcement and the environment', *Current Issues in Criminal Justice*, 16(3): 294–306.

Tomsen, S. (1997a) 'A top night: social protest, masculinity and the culture of drinking violence', *British Journal of Criminology*, 37(1): 90–102.

Tomsen, S. (1997b) 'Youth violence and the limits of moral panic', *Youth Studies Australia*, 16(1): 25–30.

Tomsen, S. (2001) 'Hate crime and masculinity: new crimes, new responses and some familiar patterns', paper presented at the 4th National Outlook Symposium on Crime in Australia, Australian Institute of Criminology, Canberra.

Tomsen, S. (2002) 'Hatred, murder and male honour: anti-homosexual homicides in New South Wales, 1980–2000', *Australian Institute of Criminology Research and Public Policy Series*, No. 43, Australian Institute of Criminology, Canberra.

Tomsen, S. (2009) *Violence, prejudice and sexuality*, Routledge, New York.

Tomsen, S. & Crofts, T. (2012) 'Social and cultural meanings of legal responses to homicide among men: masculine honour, sexual advances and accidents', *Australian & New Zealand Journal of Criminology*, 45(3): 423–37.

Tonry, M. (1996) *Sentencing matters*, Oxford University Press, New York.

Tonry, M. (ed.) (2004) *The future of imprisonment*, Oxford University Press, Oxford.

Tonry, M. & Farrington, D.P. (1995) 'Strategic approaches to crime prevention', in M. Tonry & D.P. Farrington (eds), *Building a safer society: crime and justice: a review of research* (Vol. 19), University of Chicago Press, Chicago.

Toohey, P. (2003) 'Party animals', *Weekend Australian Magazine*, 12–13 July: 16–19.

Toole, K. (2012) 'Self-defence and the reasonable woman: equality before the new Victorian law', *Melbourne University Law Review*, 36(1): 250–86.

Torok, M., Darke, S. & Kaye, S. (2012) 'Predisposed violent drug users versus drug users who commit violence. Does the order of onset translate to differences in the severity of violent offending?', *Drug and Alcohol Review*, 31(4): 558–65.

Torre, A. & Wraith, D. (2013) 'The demand for sentence discounts: some empirical evidence', *Criminal Law Journal*, 37(3): 193–200.

Torres, B. (2007) *Making a killing: the political economy of animal rights*, AK Press, Oakland.

Toumbourou, J.W. (1999) 'Implementing communities that

care in Australia: A community mobilisation approach to crime prevention', *Trends and Issues in Crime and Criminal Justice*, No. 122, Australian Institute of Criminology, Canberra.

Tressider, J., Macaskill, P., Bennett, D. & Nutbeam, D. (1997) 'Health risks and behaviour of out-of-school 16-year-olds in New South Wales', *Australian and New Zealand Journal of Public Health*, 21(2): 168–74.

Trigger, D. (1995) 'Everyone's agreed, the west is all you need', *Media Information Australia*, 75: 102–22.

Trimboli, L. (2008) 'Juror understanding of judicial instructions in criminal trials', *Crime and Justice Bulletin*, No. 119, Bureau of Crime Statistics and Research, Sydney.

Triotv (2004) 'Two thirds of Americans support televised executions', <www.nbcnews.com/id/4353934/ns/us_news-crime_and_courts/t/two-thirds-americans-support-tv-executions/>.

Trotter, C. (1995) *The supervision of offenders: what works? First and second reports to the Australian Criminology Research Council*, Department of Social Work and Human Services, Monash University, Melbourne.

Trotter, C. (2012) 'Effective community-based supervision for young offenders', *Trends & Issues in Crime and Criminal Justice*, No. 448, Australian Institute of Criminology, Canberra.

Tulloch, J., Lupton, D., Blood, W., Tulloch, M., Jennett, C. & Enders, M. (1998) *Fear of Crime, Volume 2*, National Campaign Against Violence and Crime Unit, Attorney-General's Department, Canberra.

Tynan, D. (2001) 'Mandatory sentencing rights and wrongs: do we care for equality?', *Human Rights Defender*, 10(1): 14–15.

U

Uggen, C. (2000) 'Work as a Turning Point in the Lifecourse of Criminals: A Duration Model of Age, Employment and Recidivism', *American Sociological Review* 65(4): 529–46.

Ulmer, J.T., Bader, C. & Gault (2008) 'Do moral communities play a role in criminal sentencing? Evidence from Pennsylvania', *Sociological Quarterly*, 49(4): 737–68.

UNHCR—see United Nations High Commission for Refugees.

UNICEF (2008) 'Child marriage and the law', legislative reform initiative paper series, global policy section, New York.

United Kingdom Attorney General's Department (2009) *Attorney General's guidelines on the acceptance of pleas and the prosecutor's role in the sentencing exercise*, <https://www.gov.uk/the-acceptance-of-pleas-and-the-prosecutors-role-in-the-sentencing-exercise>.

United Nations (2013) *Promotion of activities relating to combating cybercrime, including technical assistance and capacity-building: Report of the Secretary-General*, UN Economic and Social Council, Vienna.

United Nations High Commission for Refugees (UNHCR) (2014) 'War's human cost', *Global Trends 2013*, <http://unhcr.org.au/unhcr/images/Global%20Trends%202013.pdf>.

United States Bureau of Justice Assistance (1998) *Addressing community gang problems: a practical guide*, US Department of Justice, Washington, DC.

United States Department of Health & Human Services (2013) 'Prevent Cyberbullying', http://www.stopbullying.gov/cyberbullying/prevention.

United States Environmental Protection Agency (2001) *Report prepared for 13th Interpol Forensic Science Symposium*, Lyon, France, October 16–19, Office of Criminal Enforcement, Forensics, and Training Environmental Crime, USEPA.

United States Federal Rules of Criminal Procedure (1966) summary available at Cornwell University Law School (2009) *Federal rules of criminal procedure*, <www.law.cornell.edu/rules/frcrmp>.

Urbas, G. (2000) *The age of criminal responsibility*, Trends and Issues in Crime and Criminal Justice No. 181, Australian Institute of Criminology, Canberra.

Urbas, G. & Bronitt, S. (2002) 'Courts, criminal law and procedure', in A. Graycar & P. Grabosky (eds), *The Cambridge handbook of Australian criminology*, Cambridge University Press, Cambridge.

V

Valier, C. (2004) *Crime and punishment in contemporary society*, Routledge, London.

van Caenegem, W. (2003) 'Adversarial systems and adversarial mindsets: do we need either?', *British Law Review*, 15(2): 111–22.

Van der weele, J. (2012) 'Beyond the state of nature: introducing social interactions in the economic model of crime', *Review of Law and Economics*, 8(2): 401–32.

Van Dijk, J. (2008) *The world of crime: breaking the silence on problems of security, justice, and development across the world*, Sage, Los Angeles.

Van Sanningen, R. (1999) 'Reclaiming critical criminology: social justice and the European tradition', *Theoretical Criminology*, 3(1): 5–28.

Van Slyke, S.R. & Bales, W.D. (2013) 'Gender dynamics in the sentencing of white-collar offenders', *Criminal Justice Studies: A Critical Journal of Crime, Law and Society*, 26(2): 168–96.

Vess, J. (2009) 'Fear and loathing in public policy: ethical issues in laws for sex offenders', *Aggression and Violent Behavior*, 14(4): 264–272.

Vess, J. (2011) 'Ethical practice in sex offender assessment: considerations of actuarial and polygraph methods', *Sexual Abuse*, 23(3): 381–96.

VicHealth (2006) *Two steps forward, one step back. Community attitudes to violence against women: progress and challenges in creating safe and healthy environments*, VicHealth, Melbourne.

VicHealth (2011) *Preventing violence against women in Australia, research summary*, VicHealth, Melbourne.

Victoria Police (2004) *About local priority policing*, <www.police.vic.gov.au/showContentPage.cfm?contentPageId=8244>.

Victorian Community Council Against Violence (1994) Victims of crime: inquiry into services, *VCCAV*, Melbourne.

Victorian Department of Justice (2000) *Independent investigation into the management and operation of Victoria's private prisons*, Victorian Government, Melbourne.

Victorian Department of Justice (2004a) *Attorney General's justice statement: new directions for the Victorian justice system 2004–2014*, Victorian Government, Melbourne.

Victorian Department of Justice (2004b) *Magistrates' Court of Victoria: sentencing statistics 1996–97 to 2001–02*, Victorian Government, Melbourne.

Victorian Department of Justice (2004c) *Victorian Aboriginal justice agreement*, Victorian Government, Melbourne.

Victorian Department of Justice (2013) *Victorian Aboriginal Justice Agreement Phase 3 (AJA3): A partnership between the Victorian Government and Koori Community*, Koori Justice Unit, Department of Justice, Melbourne.

Victorian Law Reform Commission (2003) *Defences to homicide options paper*, Victorian Government Printer, Melbourne.

Victorian Law Reform Commission (2004) *Defences to homicide final report*, Victorian Government Printer, Melbourne.

Victorian Law Reform Commission (2008) 'Changing the role of experts', *Civil justice review: report*, VLRC, Melbourne.

Vieraitis, L.M., Piquero, N.L., Piquero, A.R., Tibbetts, S.G. & Blankenship, M. (2012) 'Do women and men differ in their neutralizations of corporate crime?', *Criminal Justice Review*, 37(4): 478–93.

Vilalta, C.J. (2011) 'Fear of crime in gated communities and apartment buildings: a comparison of housing types and a test of theories', *Journal of Housing and the Built Environment*, 26(2): 107–21.

Vinson, T. (2004) *Community adversity and resilience: the distribution of social disadvantage in Victoria and New South Wales and the mediating role of social cohesion*, Ignatius Centre for Social Policy and Research, Sydney.

VLRC—see Victorian Law Reform Commission.

Void, G., Bernard, T. & Snipes, J. (2002) *Theoretical criminology* (5th edn), Oxford University Press, New York.

Vollard, B. (2013) 'Preventing crime through selective incapacitation', *Economic Journal*, 123(567): 262–84.

Von Hentig, H. (1948) *The Criminal and his victim: studies in the sociobiology of crime*, Yale University Press, New Haven.

von Hirsch, A. (1976) *Doing justice: the choice of punishments*, Hill & Wang, New York.

von Hirsch, A. (1985) *Past or future crimes: deservedness and dangerousness in the sentencing of criminals*, Rutgers University Press, New Brunswick.

von Hirsch, A. (1993) *Censure and sanctions*, Clarendon Press, Oxford.

von Hirsch, A. (ed.) (2003) *Restorative justice and criminal justice: contemporary or reconcilable paradigms?*, Hart, Oxford.

von Hirsch, A. & Ashworth, A.J. (eds) (1992) *Principled sentencing*, Northeastern University Press, Boston.

von Hirsch, A. & Jareborg, N. (2005) 'Gauging Crime Seriousness: "A Living Standards" Conception of Criminal Harm,', in A. von Hirsch & A. Ashworth, Proportionate Sentencing: *Exploring the Principles, Oxford Monographs on Criminal Law and Justice*, Oxford University Press, Oxford.

W

Wacquant, L. (2008) *Urban outcasts: a comparative sociology of advanced marginality*, Polity Press, Cambridge.

Wacquant, L. (2012) 'A Janus-faced institution of ethnoracial closure: a sociological specification of the ghetto', in R. Hutchinson & B. Haynes (eds), *The ghetto: contemporary global issues and controversies*, Westview Press, Boulder.

Waddington, P. (1991) *The strong arm of the law: armed and public order policing*, Clarendon Press, Oxford.

Walby, K. & Carrier, N. (2010) 'The rise of biocriminology: capturing observable bodily economies of criminal man', *Criminology and Criminal Justice*, 10(3): 261–310.

Waldron, J. (2005) 'Legislation', in M. Golding & W. Edmundson (eds), *Philosophy of law and legal theory*, Blackwood Publishing, Australia.

Walgrave, L. (1999) 'Community service as a cornerstone of a systemic restorative response to (juvenile) crime', in G. Bazemore

& L. Walgrave (eds), *Restorative juvenile justice: repairing the harm of youth crime*, Criminal Justice Press, Monsey, New York.

Walker, J. & McDonald, D. (1995) 'The over-representation of indigenous people in custody in Australia', *Trends & Issues in Criminal Justice*, No. 47, Australian Institute of Criminology, Canberra.

Walker, L. (1999) 'Hydraulic sexuality and hegemonic masculinity: young working-class men and car culture', in R. White (ed.), *Australian youth subcultures: on the margins and in the mainstream*, Australian Clearinghouse for Youth Studies, Hobart.

Walker, N. (1991) *Why punish?*, Oxford University Press, New York.

Walker, N. & Hough, M. (eds) (1988) *Public attitudes to sentencing: surveys from five countries*, Gower, Aldershot.

Walker, S., Sanci, L. & Temple-Smith, M. (2011) 'Sexting and young people', *Youth Studies Australia*, 30(4): 8–16.

Walklate, S. (1990) 'Researching victims of crime: radical victimology', *Social Justice*, 17(3): 25–42.

Walklate, S. (2007) (ed.) *Handbook of victims and victimology*, Willan Publishing, Devon.

Walklate, S. (2011) 'Reframing criminal victimization: finding a place for vulnerability and resilience', *Theoretical Criminology*, 15(2): 179–94.

Walklate, S. (2012) 'Who is the victim of crime? Paying homage to the work of Richard Quinney', *Crime Media Culture*, 8(2): 173–84.

Wall, D. (2007) *Cybercrimes: The Transformation of Crime in the Information Age*, Polity Press, Cambridge.

Waller, I. (2011) *Rights for victims of crime: rebalancing justice*, Rowman & Littlefield, Plymouth.

Walmsley, R. (2013) *World prison population list* (10th edn), International Centre for Prison Studies, London.

Walsh, A. & Ellis, L. (2004) 'Ideology: criminology's Achilles' heel', *Quarterly Journal of Ideology*, 27: 1–25.

Walsh, B.C. & Farrington, D.P. (2001) 'A review of research on the monetary value of preventing crime', in B.C. Walsh, D.P Farrington & L.W. Sherman (eds), *Costs and benefits of preventing crime*, Westview, Boulder.

Walsh, J. & Taylor, R. (2007). 'Community structural predictors of spatially aggregated motor vehicle theft rates: Do they replicate?', *Journal of Criminal Justice*, 35(3): 297–310.

Walsh, T. (2005) 'Won't pay or can't pay? Exploring the use of fines as a sentencing alternative for public nuisance type offences in Queensland', *Current Issues in Criminal Justice*, 17(20): 217–36.

Walsh, T. (2006) 'Is corrections correcting? An examination of prisoner rehabilitation policy and practice in Queensland', *Australian and New Zealand Journal of Criminology*, 39(1): 109–33.

Walters, R. (2003) 'New modes of governance and the commodification of criminological knowledge', *Social and Legal Studies*, 12(1): 5–26.

Walters, R. (2004) 'Criminology and genetically modified food', *British Journal of Criminology*, 44(1): 151–67.

Walters, R. (2005) 'Crime, bio-agriculture and the exploitation of hunger', *British Journal of Criminology*, 46(1): 26–45.

Walters, R. (2011) *Eco crime and genetically modified food*, Routledge, New York.

Walton, M. (2003) 'Australia changes its position on the death penalty', *Human Rights Defender*, 12(1): 13–14.

Ward, T. & Brown, M. (2004) 'The good lives model and conceptual issues in offender rehabilitation', *Psychology, Crime & Law*, 10(3): 243–57.

Ward, T. & Durrant, R. (2011) 'Evolutionary behavioural science and crime: aetiological and intervention implications', *Legal and Criminological Psychology*, 16(2): 193–210.

Ward, T. & Green, P. (2000) 'Legitimacy, civil society, and state crime', *Social Justice*, 27(4): 76–93.

Ward, T. & Maruna, S. (2007) *Rehabilitation: beyond the risk paradigm*, Routledge, London.

Ward, T. & Salmon, K. (2011) 'The ethics of care and treatment of sex offenders', *Sexual Abuse*, 23(3): 397–413.

Ward, T., Yates, P.M. & Willis, G.M. (2012) 'The Good Lives Model and the Risk Need Responsivity Model, A Critical Response to Andrews, Bonta and Wormwith (2011)', *Criminal Justice and Behavior*, 39(1): 94–110.

Warner, K. (1994) 'The rights of the offender in family conferences', in C. Alder & J. Wundersitz (eds), *Family conferencing and juvenile justice*, Australian Institute of Criminology, Canberra.

Warner, K. (2003a) 'The role of guideline judgements in the law and order debate in Australia', *Criminal Law Journal*, 27(1): 8–22.

Warner, K. (2003b) 'Sentencing review 2002–03', *Criminal Law Journal*, 27(6): 325–40.

Warner, K. (2004) 'Gang rape in Sydney: crime, the media, politics, race and sentencing', *Australian and New Zealand Journal of Criminology*, 37(3): 344–61.

Warner, K. (2007) 'Sentencing scholarship in Australia', *Current Issues in Criminal Justice*, 18(2): 241–65.

Warner, K. (2010) 'Sentencing review 2008–2009', *Criminal Law Journal*, 34(1): 16–32.

Warner, K., Davis, J., Walter, M., Bradfield, R. & Vermey, R. (2009) 'Gauging public opinion on sentencing: can asking jurors help?', *Trends and Issues in Crime and Criminal Justice*, No. 371, Australia Institute of Criminology, Canberra.

Warner, K., Davis, J., Walter, M., Bradfield, R. & Vermey, R. (2011) 'Public judgement on sentencing: final results from the Tasmanian jury sentencing study', *Trends & Issues in Crime and Criminal Justice*, No. 407, Australian Institute of Criminology, Canberra.

Warr, M. (1991) 'America's perceptions of crime and punishment', in Sheldey, J. (ed.), *Criminology*, Wadsworth, Belmont.

Watts, R. (1996) 'John Braithwaite and crime, shame and reintegration: some reflections on theory and criminology', *Australian and New Zealand Journal of Criminology*, 29(2): 121–41.

Waugh, J. (2008) 'Two steps forward, one step back: reform of jury exemption provisions in NSW', paper presented to the *5th annual Jury Research and Practice Conference*, 11 December 2007, Parliament House, Sydney.

Weatherburn, D. (1996) 'Property crime: linking theory to policy', in K. Hazlehurst (ed.), *Australian crime & justice*, Law Book Company, Sydney: 205–32.

Weatherburn, D. (2006) 'Riots, Policing and Social Disadvantage: Learning from the Riots in Macquarie Fields and Redfern', *Current Issues in Criminal Justice*, 18(1): 20–31.

Weatherburn, D. (2011) 'Uses and abuses of crime statistics', *Crime and Justice Bulletin*, 153, Bureau of Crime Statistics and Research, Sydney.

Weatherburn, D. & Bartels, L. (2008) 'The recidivism of offenders given supsended suspended sentences in New South Wales, Australia', *British Journal of Criminology*, 48(5): 667–83.

Weatherburn, D. & Lind, B. (2001) *Delinquent-prone communities*, Cambridge University Press, Cambridge.

Weatherburn, D., Lind, B. & Ku, S. (2001) 'The short-run effects of economic adversity on property crime', *Australian and New Zealand Journal of Criminology*, 34: 134–47.

Weatherburn, D., Matka, E. & Lind, B. (1996) 'Crime perception and reality: public perception of the risk of criminal victimisation in Australia', *Crime and Justice Bulletin*, No. 28, Bureau of Crime Statistics and Research, Sydney.

Weatherburn, D., Snowball, L. & Hunter, B. (2006) 'The economic and social factors underpinning indigenous contact with the justice system: results from the NATSISS survey', *Crime and Justice Bulletin*, 104, NSW Bureau of Crime Statistics and Research, Sydney.

Webber. A (2010) *Literature review: cost of crime*, Attorney General & Justice Department, NSW Government.

Weber, L. (2002) 'The detention of asylum seekers: 20 reasons why criminologists should care', *Current Issues in Criminal Justice*, 14(1): 9–30.

Weber, M. (1954) in M. Rheinstein (ed.), *On law in economy and society*, Simon & Schuster, New York.

Weber, M. (1957) in T. Parsons (ed.), *The theory of social and economic organisation* (trans. A.M. Henderson & T. Parsons), Free Press, New York.

Weber, L. & Pickering, S. (2011) *Globalization and borders: death at the global frontier*, Palgrave Macmillan, Hampshire.

Webster, A. (2011) 'Expanding the role of victims and the community in sentencing', *Criminal Law Journal*, 35(1): 21–33.

Weelands, D. (2009) 'Residential centre or day prison? The case of COSP', *Current Issues in Criminal Justice*, 20(3): 485–9.

Weinberg, M. (2008) 'The Australian justice system: what is right and what is wrong with it?', paper presented to the *Australian Justice System in 2020 Conference*, 25 October, National Judicial College of Australia, Sydney.

Weisbrot, D. (1990) *Australian lawyers*, Longman Cheshire, Melbourne.

Weitekamp, E.G.M. (1999) 'The history of restorative justice', in G. Bazemore & L. Walgrave (eds), *Restorative juvenile justice: repairing the harm of youth crime*, Monsey, New York.

Wellsmith, M. (2010) 'The applicability of crime prevention to problems of environmental harm: a consideration of illicit trade in endangered species', in R. White (ed.), *Global environmental harm: criminological perspectives*, Willan Publishing, Devon.

West, A., Lewis, J. & Currie, P. (2009) 'Students' Facebook "friends": public and private spheres', *Journal of Youth Studies*, 12(6): 615–27.

Western Australia Office of Youth Affairs (2000) *Youth facts WA: young people and legal issues*, Office of Youth Affairs, Perth.

Western, B. & Muller, C. (2013) 'Mass incarceration, macrosociology, and the poor', *Annals of the American Academy of Political and Social Sciences*, 647: 166–89.

Wexler, M.N. (2010) 'Financial edgework and the persistence of rouge traders', *Business and Society Review*, 115(1): 1–25.

Wheate, R. (2010) 'The importance of DNA evidence to juries in criminal trials', *International*

Journal of Evidence and Proof, 14: 129–45.

White, R. (1990) *No space of their own: young people and social control in Australia*, Cambridge University Press, Melbourne.

White, R. (1993) 'Young people and the policing of community space', *Australian and New Zealand Journal of Criminology*, 26: 207–18.

White, R. (1996a) 'Racism, policing and ethnic youth gangs', *Current Issues in Criminal Justice*, 7(3): 302–13.

White, R. (1996b) 'Situating crime prevention: models, methods and political perspective', *Crime Prevention Studies*, 5: 97–113.

White, R. (1996c) The Poverty of the Welfare State: Managing an Underclass, in P. James (ed.) *The State in Question: Transformations of the Australian State*, Allen and Unwin, Sydney, 109–37.

White, R. (1997) 'Young people, waged work and exploitation', *Journal of Australian Political Economy*, 40: 61–79.

White, R. (1999) *Hanging out: negotiating young people's use of public space*, National Crime Prevention, Attorney General's Department, Canberra.

White, R. (2001) 'Graffiti, crime prevention & cultural space', *Current Issues in Criminal Justice*, 12(3): 253–68.

White, R. (2002) 'Indigenous young Australians, criminal justice and offensive language', *Journal of Youth Studies*, 5(1): 21–34.

White, R. (2004) 'Community corrections and restorative justice', *Current Issues in Criminal Justice*, 16(1): 42–56.

White, R. (2005) 'Environmental crime in global context: exploring the theoretical and empirical complexities', *Current Issues in Criminal Justice*, 16(3): 271–85.

White, R. (2006a) 'Doing evaluation research', in M. Walter (ed.), *Social research methods: an Australian perspective*, Oxford University Press, Melbourne.

White, R. (2006b) 'Youth gang research in Australia', in J. Short & L. Hughes (eds), *Studying youth gangs*, AltaMira Press, New York, 161–79.

White, R. (2008a) 'Class analysis and the crime problem', in T. Anthony & C. Cunneen (eds), *The critical criminology companion*, Federation Press, Sydney.

White, R. (2008b) *Crimes against nature: environmental criminology and ecological justice*, Willan Publishing, Devon.

White, R. (2008c) 'Disputed Definitions and Fluid Identities: The Limitations of Social Profiling in Relation to Ethnic Youth Gangs', *Youth Justice: an International Journal*, 8(2): 149–61.

White, R. (2009a) 'Researching transnational environmental harm', *International Journal of Comparative and Applied Criminal Justice*.

White, R. (ed.) (2009b) *Environmental crime: a reader*, Willan Publishing, Devon.

White, R. (2009c) 'Toxic, cities: globalising the problem of waste', *Social Justice*, 35(3): 107–19.

White, R. (2009d) 'Ethnic diversity and differential policing in Australia: the good, the bad and the ugly', *International Migration & Integration*, 10: 359–75.

White, R. (2011) *Transnational environmental crime: toward an eco-global criminology*, Routledge, London.

White, R. (2013a) *Youth gangs, violence and social respect: Exploring the nature of provocations and punch-ups*, Palgrave Macmillan, Basingstoke.

White, R. (2013b) *Environmental harm: an eco-justice perspective*, Policy Press, Bristol.

White, R. & Alder, C. (eds) (1994) *The police and young people in Australia*, Cambridge University Press, Melbourne.

White, R. & Coventry, G. (2000) *Evaluating community safety: a guide*, Department of Justice, Melbourne.

White, R. & Coventry, G. (2008) 'Prisoners, work and reciprocal reintegration', in C. Cunneen & M. Salter (eds), *Proceedings of the 2nd Australian & New Zealand Critical Criminology Conference*, Crime and Justice Research Network, University of New South Wales, Sydney.

White, R. & Graham, H. (2010) *Working with Offenders: A Guide to Concepts and Practices*, Cullumpton, Willan Publishing.

White, R. & Habibis, D. (2005) *Crime and society*, Oxford University Press, Melbourne.

White, R. & Heckenberg, D. (2014) *Green criminology: an introduction to the study of environmental harm*. London: Routledge.

White, R. & Mason, R. (2006) 'Youth gangs and youth violence: charting the key dimensions', *Australian and New Zealand Journal of Criminology*, 39(1): 54–70.

White, R. & Perrone, S. (1997) *Crime and social control*, Oxford University Press, Melbourne.

White, R. & Perrone, S. (2001) 'Racism, ethnicity and hate crime', *Communal/Plural*, 9(2): 161–81.

White, R. & Richards, C. (1992) 'Police unions and police powers', *Current Issues in Criminal Justice*, 4(2): 157–74.

White, R. & Sutton, A. (1995) 'Crime prevention, urban space and social exclusion', *Australian and New Zealand Journal of Sociology*, 31(1): 82–99.

White, R. & Tomkins, K. (2003a) *Community corrections service Tasmania*, Briefing Paper No. 1, Criminology Research Unit, School of Sociology and Social Work, University of Tasmania, Hobart.

White, R. & Tomkins, K. (2003b) *Issues in community corrections*, Briefing Paper No. 2, Criminology Research Unit, School of Sociology & Social Work, University of Tasmania, Hobart.

White, R. & van der Velden, J. (1995) 'Class and criminality', *Social Justice*, 22(1): 51–74.

White, R. & Wyn, J. (2013) *Youth and society: exploring the social dynamics of youth experience* (3rd edn), Oxford University Press, Melbourne.

White, R., Aumair, M., Harris, A. & McDonnell, L. (1997) *Any which way you can: youth livelihoods, community resources and crime*, Australian Youth Foundation, Sydney.

White, R., Haines, F. & Asquith, N. (2012) *Crime and criminology: an introduction* (5th edn), Oxford University Press, Melbourne.

White, R., Perrone, S., Guerra, C. & Lampugnani, R. (1999) *Ethnic youth gangs in Australia: do they exist? Overview report*, Australian Multicultural Foundation, Melbourne.

Whitworth, A. (2012a) 'Inequality and crime across England: a multilevel modelling approach', *Social Policy and Society*, 11(1): 27–40.

Whitworth, A. (2012b) 'Local inequality and crime: exploring how variation in the scale of inequality measures affects relationships between inequality and crime', *Urban Studies*, 50(4): 725–41.

Wikileaks (2011) *What is Wikileaks?*, <www.wikileaks.org>

Wilkinson, G. (2007) 'Killer could tell more', *Herald Sun*, 6 March: 27.

Wilkinson, I (2009) *Risk, vulnerability and everyday life*, Routledge, London.

Wilkinson, V. & Froyland, I. (1996) 'Women in policing', *Trends and Issues in Crime and Criminal Justice*, No. 58, Australian

Institute of Criminology, Canberra.

Williams, C. (1996) 'An environmental victimology', *Social Justice*, 23(4): 16–40.

Williams, F. (1989) *Social policy: an introduction: issues of race, gender and class*, Polity Press, Cambridge.

Williams, C. (1996) 'An Environmental Victimology', *Social Justice*, 23(4): 16–40.

Williams, R. & Johnson, P. (2008) *Genetic policing: the use of DNA in criminal investigations*, Willan Publishing, Devon.

Willis, C.L., Evans, T.D. & LaGrange, R.L. (1999) '"Down home" criminology: the place of indigenous theories of crime', *Journal of Criminal Justice*, 27(3): 227–38.

Willis, M. (2004) 'Bushfire arson: a review of the literature', *Research and Public Policy Series*, No. 61, Australian Institute of Criminology, Canberra.

Willis, M. (2010) 'Aboriginal liaison officers in community policing', in J. Putt (ed.), *Community policing in Australia*, Australian Institute of Criminology, Canberra.

Willis, M. (2011) 'Non-disclosure of violence in Australian Indigenous communities', *Trends & Issues in Crime and Criminal Justice*, No. 405, Australian Institute of Criminology, Canberra.

Wilmott, J. & Dowse, J. (2002) *Process and participation: politics and law in Australia*, Politics Law, Perth.

Wils, G.M., Yates, P.M., Gannon, T.A. & Ward, T. (2013) 'How to Integrate the Good Lives Model Into Treatment Programs for Sexual Offending: An Introduction and Overview', *Sex Abuse*, 25(2): 123–42.

Wilson, D. & O'Sullivan, S. (2004) *Images of incarceration: representations of prisons in film and on television drama*, Waterside Press, Winchester.

Wilson, D. & Sutton, A. (2003) 'Open-street CCTV in Australia',

Trends and Issues in Crime and Criminal Justice No. 271, Australian Institute of Criminology, Canberra.

Wilson, D. (2003) 'Smile! You're on mandated camera', *Arena*, 63: 33–4.

Wilson, J. & Herrnstein, R. (1985) *Crime and human nature*, Simon & Schuster, New York.

Wilson, P. (1987) 'Corporate crime in Australia', *Trends and Issues in Crime and Criminal Justice*, No. 5, Australian Institute of Criminology, Canberra.

Wilson, P., Keogh, D. & Lincoln, R. (1994) 'Private policing: the major issues', in P. Moyle (ed.), *Private prisons and police: recent Australian trends*, Pluto Press, Sydney.

Wilson, W.J. (1996) *When work disappears: the world of the new urban poor*, Knopf, New York.

Windshuttle, K. (1978) 'Granny versus the hooligans', in P. Wilson & J. Braithwaite (eds), *Two faces of deviance*, University of Queensland Press, St Lucia.

Wing Lo, T., Maxwell, G.M. & Wong, D.S.W. (2006) 'Diversion from youth courts in five Asia–Pacific jurisdictions: welfare or restorative solutions', *International Journal of Offender Therapy and Comparative Criminology*, 50(1): 5–20.

Winick, B.J. & Wexler, D.B. (2003) *Judging in a therapeutic key: therapeutic jurisprudence and the courts*, Carolina Academic Press, NC.

Wise, J. (2010) Providing the CSI treatment: criminal justice practitioners and the CSI effect', *Current Issues in Criminal Justice*, 21(3): 383–99.

Wise, S. (2001) *Rattling the cage: toward legal rights for animals*, Perseus Books, Cambridge.

Wise, S. (2004) 'Animal rights, one step at a time', in C. Sunstein & M. Nussbaum (eds), *Animal rights: current debates and new directions*, Oxford University Press, New York.

Wodahl, E.J. & Garland, E. (2009) 'The evolution of community corrections: the enduring influence of the prison', *Prison Journal*, 89(1): supplement: 81S–104S.

Wodtke, G.T., Harding, D.J. & Felix, E. (2011) 'Neighbourhood effects in temporal perspective: the impact of long-term exposure to concentrated disadvantage on high school graduation' *America Sociological Review*, 76(5): 713–36.

Wolf, N. & Shi, J. (2009) 'Victimisation and feelings of safety among male and female inmates with behavioural problems', *Journal of Forensic Psychiatry & Psychology*, 20(S1): 56–77.

Women Against Prison Collective (1990) 'Women, prison and law and order', *Legal Service Bulletin*, 15(1): 26–9.

Wong, J. (2013) 'Dangerous minds: mental illness and future danger', *Law Society Journal*, 51(2): 80–2.

Wood, J. (1996) *Royal Commission into the New South Wales Police Service: Interim Report*, New South Wales Government Printer, Sydney.

Wood, J. (1997) *Royal Commission into the New South Wales Police Service* <www.pic.nsw.gov.au/Report.aspx?ReportId=100 1>.

Wood, J. (2007a) 'Summing up in criminal trials: a new direction?', paper delivered to the *5th annual Jury Research and Practice Conference*, 11 December, Parliament House, Sydney.

Wood, J. (2007b) 'The trial under siege: towards making criminal trials simpler', paper delivered to *District and County Court Judges Conference*, 27 June–1 July 2007, Fremantle.

Woodley, M. (2013) 'Bargaining over corporate manslaughter—what price a life?', *Journal of Criminal Law*, 77: 33–40.

Wootten, H. (1991) '99 reasons: the royal commission into black deaths in custody', *Polemic*, 2(3): 124–8.

Worrall, A. (1997) *Punishment in the community: the future of criminal justice*, Longman, London.

Wozniak, J.F. (2009) 'C. Wright Mills and higher immorality: implications for corporate crime, ethics, and peacemaking criminology', *Crime, Law and Social Change*, 51: 189–203.

Wozniak, J.F., Braswell, M.C., Vogel, R.E. & Belvins, K.R. (edn) (2008) *Transformative justice: critical and peacemaking themes influenced by Richard Quinney*, Lexington Books, Lanham.

Wright Mills, C. (1959) *The sociological imagination*, Oxford University Press, New York.

Wright, J.P. & Cullen, F.T. (2012) 'The future of biosocial criminology: beyond scholars' professional ideology', *Journal of Contemporary Criminal Justice*, 28(3): 237–53.

Wright, K.A. (2009) 'Strange bedfellows? Reaffirming rehabilitation and prison privatization', *Journal of Offender Rehabilitation*, 49(1): 74–90.

Wright, M. (1991) *Justice for victims and offenders*, Open University Press, Milton Keynes.

Wundersitz, J. (2007) *Criminal justice responses to drug and drug-related offending: are they working?*, Technical and Background Paper No. 25, Australian Institute of Criminology, Canberra.

Wundersitz, J. (2010) 'Indigenous perpetrators of violence: prevalence and risk factors for offending', *Research and Public Policy Series*, No. 105, Australian Institute of Criminology, Canberra.

Wyatt, T. (2013) *Wildlife Trafficking: A deconstruction of the crime, the victims, and the offenders*, Palgrave Macmillan, Basingstoke.

Wyn, J. and Cuervo, (2005) *Young People, Wellbeing and Communication Technologies*, Victorian Health Promotion Foundation (VicHealth), Melbourne.

Wyn, J. & White, R. (1997) *Rethinking youth*, Allen & Unwin, Sydney.

Y

Yannoulidis, S.T. (2003) 'Mental illness, rationality, and criminal responsibility', *Sydney Law Review*, 25(2): 189–222.

Yavuz, N. & Welch, W. (2010) 'Addressing fear of crime in public space: gender differences in reaction to safety measures in train transit', *Urban Studies*, 47(12): 2491–515.

Ybarra, M. & Mitchell, K. (2004) 'Youth Engaging in Online Harassment: Associations with Caregiver–Child Relationships, Internet Use, and Personal Characteristics', *Journal of Adolescence*, 27: 319–36.

Yeager, M.G. (1996). *Immigrants and criminality: a meta survey*, Ministry of Citizenship and Immigration, Government of Canada, Ottawa.

Yochelson, S. & Samenow, S. (1976). *The criminal personality. Vol. I: a profile for change*, Jason Aronson, Inc., New York.

Yoon, L. (2012) 'Total global losses from financial crisis: $15 trillion', *Wall Street Journal*, 1 October, <http://blogs.wsj.com/economics/2012/10/01/total-global-losses-from-financial-crisis-15-trillion/tab/comments/>.

Young, A. (2012) 'Criminal images: the affective judgement of graffiti and street art', *Crime, Media, Culture*, 8(3): 297–314.

Young, J. (1971) 'The role of the police as amplifiers of deviancy, negotiators of reality and translators of fantasy: some consequences of our present system of drug control as seen in

Notting Hill', in S. Cohen (ed.), *Images of Deviance*, Penguin, London.

Young, J. (1981) 'Thinking seriously about crime: some models of criminology', in M. Fitzgerald, G. McLennon & J. Pawson (eds), *Crime and society: readings in history and theory*, Routledge & Kegan Paul, London.

Young, J. (2004) 'Voodoo criminology and the numbers game', in J. Farrell, K. Hayward, W. Morrison & M. Presdee (eds), *Cultural criminology unleashed*, The Glasshouse Press, London.

Young, J. (2011) *Criminological imagination*, Polity Press, Cambridge.

Young, W. & Solonec, T. (2011) 'Epidemic incarceration and justice reinvestment: it's time for change', *Indigenous Law Bulletin*, 7(26): 15–21.

Youth Justice Coalition (1990) *Kids in justice: a blueprint for the 90s*, Youth Justice Coalition, Sydney.

Youth Support and Advocacy Service (2013) *YSAS snapshot: young women in youth alcohol and other drug services*, YSAS, Melbourne.

YSAS—see Youth Support and Advocacy Service.

Z

Zehr, H. & Mika, H. (1998) 'Fundamental concepts of restorative justice', *Contemporary Justice Review*, 1(1): 47–56.

Zehr, H. (1990) *Changing lens: a new focus for crime and justice*, Herald Press, Scottsdale.

Zimring, A. (1983) 'Sentencing reform in the states: lessons from the 1970s', in M. Tonry & A. Zimring (eds), *Reform and punishment*, University of Chicago Press, Chicago.

INDEX